ALL-NEW COMPLETE
Cooking Light®
COOKBOOK

Grilled Tuna Niçoise,
page 421

ALL-NEW COMPLETE

Cooking Light®

COOKBOOK

compiled and edited by
Anne C. Cain

Oxmoor House®

©2006 by Oxmoor House, Inc.
Book Division of Southern Progress Corporation,
P.O. Box 2262, Birmingham, Alabama 35201-2262

ISBN-13: 978-0-8487-3023-9
ISBN-10: 0-8487-3023-2
Library of Congress Control Number: 2006929981
Printed in the United States of America
First printing 2006

Oxmoor House, Inc.

Editor in Chief: Nancy Fitzpatrick Wyatt
Executive Editor: Katherine M. Eakin
Copy Chief: Allison Long Lowery

All-New Complete Cooking Light® Cookbook

Editor: Anne C. Cain, M.P.H., M.S., R.D.
Copy Editor: Jacqueline Giovanelli
Editorial Assistants: Julie Boston, Brigette Gaucher,
Rachel Quinlivan, R.D.
Senior Designer: Emily Albright Parrish
Photography Director: Jim Bathie
Senior Photographer: John O'Hagan
Senior Photo Stylist: Kay E. Clarke
Photo Stylist: Katherine Eckert
Director, Test Kitchens: Elizabeth Tyler Austin
Assistant Director, Test Kitchens: Julie Christopher
Food Stylist: Kelley Self Wilton
Test Kitchens Professionals: Nicole Lee Faber,
Kathleen Royal Phillips
Director of Production: Laura Lockhart
Senior Production Manager: Greg A. Amason
Production Assistant: Faye Porter Bonner

Contributors:
Assistant Editor: Susan M. McIntosh, M.S., R.D.
Copy Editor: Dolores Hydock
Interns: Jill Baughman, Mary Katherine Pappas,
Lucas Whittington
Proofreader and Indexer: Mary Ann Laurens
Photographer: Lee Harrelson
Photo Stylist: Lydia DeGaris-Pursell

Cooking Light®

Editor in Chief: Mary Kay Culpepper
Executive Editor: Billy R. Sims
Art Director: Susan Waldrip Dendy
Managing Editor: Maelynn Chung
Senior Food Editor: Alison Mann Ashton
Features Editor: Phillip Rhodes
Projects Editor: Mary Simpson Creel, M.S., R.D.
Food Editor: Ann Taylor Pittman
Associate Food Editors: Julianna Grimes Bottcher,
Timothy Q. Cebula
Assistant Food Editor: Kathy C. Kitchens, R.D.
Assistant Editors: Cindy Hatcher, Brandy Rushing
Test Kitchens Director: Vanessa Taylor Johnson
Senior Food Stylist: Kellie Gerber Kelley
Food Stylist: M. Kathleen Kanen
Test Kitchens Professionals: Sam Brannock, Kathryn Conrad,
Mary H. Drennan, Jan Jacks Moon, Tiffany Vickers, Mike Wilson
Assistant Art Director: Maya Metz Logue
Senior Designers: Fernande Bondarenko, J. Shay McNamee
Designer: Brigette Mayer
Senior Photographer: Randy Mayor
Senior Photo Stylist: Cindy Barr
Photo Stylists: Melanie J. Clarke, Jan Gautro
Studio Assistant: Celine Chenoweth
Copy Chief: Maria Parker Hopkins
Senior Copy Editor: Susan Roberts
Copy Editor: Johannah Paiva
Production Manager: Liz Rhoades
Production Editors: Joanne McCrary Brasseal, Hazel R. Eddins
CookingLight.com Editor: Jennifer Middleton Richards
Online Producer: Abigail Masters
Administrative Coordinator: Carol D. Johnson
Office Manager: Rita K. Jackson
Editorial Assistant: Melissa Hoover
Correspondence Editor: Michelle Gibson Daniels

Contributors: David Bonom, Maureen Callahan, Lorrie Holston
Corvin, Lia Huber, Karen MacNeil, Gin Miller, Marge Perry,
Becky Luigart-Stayner, Billy Strynkowski, Joanne Weir

Shown on Cover: Chocolate Cheesecake (page 137)
page 1: Lasagna Rolls with Roasted Red Pepper Sauce (page 279)

Fontina and Red Pepper-Stuffed Garlic Focaccia, page 100

Spiced Chicken Thighs, page 375

Savannah-Style Crab Soup, page 496

contents

welcome to the *All-New Complete* Cooking Light® *Cookbook*

In my family, we quip that our mother's chief advice has always been to "look it up." Whatever "it" was—a word, a historical reference, a spot on the map—Mom would direct us to the proper source and set us to it. So when I expressed interest in learning how to cook when I was about seven or so, she was true to form.

"If you can read, you can cook," she said, pointing to the stash of cookbooks on the kitchen counter. So I started reading. A lifetime later, I'm still at it, and I have a well-developed sense for just how right she is.

The freshest example is in your hands. Just leaf through the pages of the *All-New Complete* Cooking Light *Cookbook,* and you're bound to learn something new to help you in the course of making healthy, delicious meals for yourself, your family, and your friends.

It's hard to believe it's been six years since we published this book's best-selling predecessor, *The Complete* Cooking Light *Cookbook.* In the ensuing years, we've run thousands of new recipes in the magazine; this volume reprises the very best of them. They're the recipes we at the magazine find ourselves using over and over again, and we hope you will, too.

There are some terrific new features in this book that will make healthful cooking faster, simpler, and more pleasurable. We've added prep and cook times for every recipe. You'll find colored tags in the recipe index to help you easily locate recipes that are quick and easy, make-ahead, and freezable,

just as we have in the magazine. And since you expect them in the regular issues of *Cooking Light,* we've featured complete menus—including a special entertaining section perfect for holidays, special days, and *Cooking Light* Supper Clubs. There are also helpful suggestions for pairing well-chosen wines with our menus, and even some lovely table-setting ideas.

And, to be sure, there's a brilliant selection of tips and techniques—the very things Mom would instruct me to read up on. Want to know the six foolproof steps for making a layer cake? Check out page 115. Need to trim a soft-shell crab? Four steps come to the rescue on page 247. Want to know the secret for incredibly flavorful, all-natural chicken stock? Turn to page 471.

Knowledge is power, and this powerful book will expand your talents while you indulge your passion for healthful cooking. We hope it becomes your favorite source for information to help you eat smart, be fit, and live well—indeed, your first place to "look it up."

Mary Kay Culpepper
Editor in Chief

healthy
cooking

5 keys to healthy cooking

Diet trends come and go, but *Cooking Light* strives to use guidelines that you can follow for a lifetime. We consider the following five elements essential for healthy cooking: necessary nutrients, the right tools, safety savvy, quality ingredients, and the right technique.

1 Necessary Nutrients Pay attention to the nutrients you need to live well and stay fit.

The Facts on Fat

Not all fats are created equal. For a healthy heart, it's important to limit foods high in saturated fats and trans fats and to include a moderate amount of monounsaturated and polyunsaturated fats. It appears that monounsaturated fats and some polyunsaturated fats actually have the potential to boost your health. But total fat still counts because all fats—polys, monos, and saturated—are concentrated sources of calories. In the United States, where over half the population is overweight and childhood obesity is increasing, concentrated sources of calories are a concern.

Saturated fat is found in animal products, such as meat, poultry, and dairy products, so it's a good idea to limit high-fat meats and full-fat milk, cheese, and yogurt. Saturated fat can raise harmful cholesterol levels and increase the risk of heart disease.

Trans fats are found in margarines, fried foods, fast-food items cooked in hydrogenated shortening, and many commercial snack foods, such as crackers, cookies, pastries, candy bars, boxed cakes, and frozen dinners. Any packaged food that has the words "hydrogenated oil" or "partially hydrogenated oil" on the ingredient list is a source of trans fat. Because trans fats are now believed to behave similarly to saturated fats (raising harmful cholesterol levels and increasing the risk of heart disease), trans fat values are now listed on the nutrition label of packaged foods.

Monounsaturated and polyunsaturated fats (particularly omega-3 fats) appear to have health benefits. Monounsaturated fats are the fats of choice when it comes to heart health, as they help lower total cholesterol and "bad" cholesterol. (See facing page for the best sources of monounsaturated fats.) Polyunsaturated fats also help lower total cholesterol. Vegetables oils such as corn, safflower, and soybean oil are rich in polyunsaturated fats. Fatty fish such as salmon, flaxseed, and walnuts are the best sources of heart-healthy omega-3 fatty acids, another type of polyunsaturated fat.

So how does *Cooking Light* cut down on saturated fat while incorporating "good" fats, and still keep from adding too many calories? **We use the good fats judiciously, using just enough to enliven flavor without piling on the calories.** For instance, in our salmon dishes, most of the fat comes from the salmon itself. The rest of the flavoring comes primarily from herbs, spices, and other low-fat flavoring ingredients. We think it's the perfect solution.

good fats Here are some of the top sources of good fats.

Best sources of monounsaturated fat:
- avocado
- nuts: almonds and peanuts
- oils: canola, olive, and safflower
- olives
- natural peanut butter

Best sources of omega-3s:
- flaxseed
- salmon
- walnuts

Playing Percentages

The healthfulness of a food can't be judged by its fat percentage (the percentage of calories from fat) alone. Vegetables and fruits have few calories, so even the smallest addition of fat, such as a teaspoon of oil, can push the percentage of calories from fat above 35. (The recommendation is for 20 to 35 percent or less of calories per day to come from fat.)

Pay attention, instead, to the number of fat grams per serving—it's a truer indicator of how much fat you're eating. Percentages can be deceiving. Some of our cream pies, for example, have about

9 grams of fat per serving, while some of our vegetable recipes may range from 2 to 5 grams per serving. However, the recipes have almost exactly the same fat percentage. But *Cooking Light's* philosophy is that both types of food can be enjoyed as part of a diet that stays within the bounds of daily recommendations. We use both parameters—fat grams and percentage of calories from fat—when we consider the fat content of our recipes.

Bring Back the Carbs

There are two basic types of carbohydrates: simple and complex. Sugar is an example of a simple carb; rice, potatoes, fruits, and vegetables provide complex carbs. **When we recommend eating more carbs, we mean the complex ones that are high in fiber such as whole grains, vegetables, and fruits.**

Although sugar is a simple carb, it's never been proven to be the underlying cause of disease (although it's an important consideration in diabetes management). However, the simple carbs found in ice cream, cake, candy, cookies, and dough-

nuts generally are accompanied by fat, while complex carbs are generally accompanied by fiber, disease-fighting phytochemicals, vitamins, and minerals.

The Fiber Factor

There are two types of fiber in the foods we eat: soluble and insoluble. Soluble fiber, found in some fruits, grains, and cereals, is absorbed by your digestive system; insoluble fiber doesn't dissolve but passes through your system largely intact. Both types help maintain digestive regularity, but soluble fiber goes a step further to reduce harmful cholesterol and reduce the risk of heart disease. It also aids in controlling blood sugar in people with diabetes. Both types of fiber contribute to weight loss because high-fiber foods are digested slowly, resulting in a feeling of satiety.

You should eat 20 to 35 grams of fiber each day, 5 to 10 grams of which should come from soluble fiber. The best sources of fiber, both soluble and insoluble, are fresh fruits and vegetables, and whole wheat and whole grain breads and cereals.

oil change We now call for canola oil instead of vegetable oil as a mild-flavored oil that can handle high temperatures before burning or smoking. Canola oil has the lowest saturated fat of all common cooking oils, is second only to olive oil in the amount of monounsaturated fat, and offers the additional benefit of providing omega-3 fatty acids, which may protect against heart attack and stroke. Vegetable oils are most often made from corn or soybeans and, although they contain mostly polyunsaturated fat, they have more than twice the saturated fat, less than half the monounsaturated fat, and about a third fewer omega-3 fatty acids than canola oil.

Take It with a Grain of Salt

Nine out of ten Americans consume almost twice as much sodium as they should. We're advised in the 2005 U.S. Dietary Guidelines to eat less than 2,300 milligrams of sodium (approximately 1 teaspoon of salt) per day. Cutting sodium intake may help reduce high blood pressure as well as lower the risk of heart disease, strokes, and kidney disease.

We pay close attention to the amount of sodium in recipes. Rather than reaching for the salt shaker, we'll often opt for a squeeze of fresh lemon or a sprinkling of fresh herbs to balance the flavors in a dish. It's true that *Cooking Light* occasionally runs recipes for high-sodium meats or recipes that use high-sodium procedures such as brining. (See page 395.) **To fit these higher-sodium foods into your diet, follow the advice we always give: Incorporate balance and moderation. For example, if you're having a higher-sodium dish for dinner, round out the meal with low-sodium vegetables and fruits.**

Most of the sodium we eat comes from processed foods, not necessarily from the salt shaker.

Counting on Calcium

Preventing osteoporosis used to be the key health reason for consuming calcium, but now research indicates that increased calcium intake can help promote weight loss. Calcium can also help reduce the risk of hypertension, certain cancers, kidney stones, and possibly even premenstrual syndrome. If you're getting enough calcium for bone health, you're probably getting enough to reduce the risk of the other disorders as well.

We think the most pleasurable way to get your calcium is from foods. The top healthful food sources are low-fat yogurt, part-skim ricotta cheese, fat-free milk, vanilla frozen yogurt, buttermilk, black-eyed peas, Cheddar cheese, canned salmon (with bones), Parmesan cheese, low-fat cottage cheese, cooked spinach, and molasses.

Daily Nutritional Guide

Here's a helpful guide to put our nutrition analysis numbers into perspective. Remember, one size doesn't fit all, so take your lifestyle, age, and circumstances into consideration when determining your nutrition needs. For example, pregnant or breast-feeding women need more protein, calories, and calcium. And men over 50 need 1,200mg of calcium daily, 200mg more than the amount recommended for younger men.

In our nutritional analysis, we use these abbreviations:

sat	saturated fat	**CHOL**	cholesterol
mono	monounsaturated fat	**CALC**	calcium
poly	polyunsaturated fat	**g**	gram
CARB	carbohydrates	**mg**	milligram

Your Daily Nutrition Guide

	women ages 25 to 50	women over 50	men over 24
Calories	2,000	2,000 or less	2,700
Protein	50g	50g or less	63g
Fat	65g or less	65g or less	88g or less
Saturated Fat	20g or less	20g or less	27g or less
Carbohydrates	304g	304g	410g
Fiber	25g to 35g	25g to 35g	25g to 35g
Cholesterol	300mg or less	300mg or less	300mg or less
Iron	18mg	8mg	8mg
Sodium	2,300mg or less	1,500mg or less	2,300mg or less
Calcium	1,000mg	1,200mg	1,000mg

The nutritional values used in our calculations either come from The Food Processor, Version 7.5 (ESHA Research) or are provided by food manufacturers.

The Right Tools

Whether stocking your kitchen from scratch or paring down to the basics, here are the tools and equipment we recommend. You'll discover that light cooking, like any type of cooking, is easier when you have the proper equipment.

Top 12 Tools

Chef's Knife The chef's knife (along with a cutting board) is the workhorse of the *Cooking Light* Test Kitchens. It's ideal for chopping herbs, onions, garlic, fruits, and vegetables and for cutting boneless meats (it even cuts through small bones, such as those of chicken and fish), slicing and dicing, and general cutting tasks.

Colanders/Strainers We use both metal and plastic colanders in varying sizes. A large colander works well for draining pasta and salad greens and rinsing vegetables. A small strainer is great for separating fruit juice or pulp from seeds. Mesh strainers are the most versatile because nothing can get through the holes except liquid.

Cutting Boards We use both wood and plastic cutting boards. Whichever you choose, wash the board thoroughly to avoid food contamination. Wipe wooden boards with diluted bleach, and wash thoroughly; sanitize plastic ones in the dishwasher.

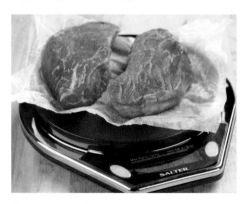

Food Scales To measure the correct amount of cheese or to make sure that pieces of meat, poultry, and fish are the specified size, use a scale. The Salter digital scale is small, lightweight, and accurate. The food service balance scales by Pelouze also work well.

Instant-Read Thermometer Use an instant-read thermometer to check meringues, meat, and poultry to be sure they're cooked to the correct temperature. Don't leave the thermometer in the oven while the food is cooking; remove it from the food after you read the temperature.

Kitchen Shears Keep kitchen shears handy to mince small amounts of herbs, chop canned tomatoes, trim fat from meat and skin from poultry, and make slits in bread dough.

Having at least two sets of dry measuring cups and spoons and a variety of sizes of liquid measuring cups is a great time-saver that will keep you from having to rinse in the middle of a recipe.

Measuring Cups Dry measuring cups, available in metal or plastic, are flat across the rim and are used for ingredients like flour, grains, and cereals. We use a 1, ½, ⅓, and ¼ nest of cups. Liquid measuring cups, sized from 1 cup to 4 cups, are available in clear glass or plastic so that you can see the level of liquid through the cup.

Measuring Spoons Sometimes a "pinch of this" and a "dash of that" results in less-than-desired flavor. Measuring spoons ensure that your recipes come out just right.

Peeler A peeler removes the skin from both vegetables and fruits. Select one with a comfortable grip and an eyer to remove potato eyes and other blemishes on vegetables and fruits. It's also handy for making Parmesan cheese shavings or chocolate curls.

Pepper Mill Give your food a bit of pungent flavor with a sprinkle of cracked or freshly ground pepper from a pepper mill. A variety of pepper mills are now readily available in the spice section of supermarkets or in the kitchen wares department of discount stores.

Stainless-Steel Box Grater A box-style grater gives you a choice of hole sizes. Use the smaller holes for grating hard cheese or chocolate and the largest holes for shredding foods like Cheddar cheese or carrots.

Whisks Whisks in assorted sizes are ideal for beating eggs and egg whites, blending salad dressings, and dissolving solids in liquids. We consider them essential when making creamy sauces. Whisks are available both in stainless steel and nylon; the nylon ones won't scratch nonstick surfaces.

Essential Cookware

In addition to the top 12 kitchen tools we recommend, here are the basic pieces of cookware you should keep on hand.

Baking Pans	Pots	Other Bakeware

Baking Pans

Springform pan

- Baking sheet
- Bundt pan
- Jelly-roll pan
- Loaf pan
- Muffin pan: miniature, regular
- Round cake pan
- Springform pan
- Square cake pan
- Tart pan (round, removable-bottom)
- Tube pan

Pots

Dutch oven

- Dutch oven (3- to 6-quart)
- Grill pan
- Heavy saucepans (1½-, 2-, and 3-quart)
- Nonstick skillets (10-inch, 12-inch)
- Pasta pot
- Roasting pan
- Vegetable steamer

Other Bakeware

Glass baking dishes

- Glass baking dishes (11 x 7–inch, 13 x 9–inch)
- Glass casseroles (1-, 1½-, 2-quart)
- Glass pie plate
- Custard cups (6-ounce, 8-ounce)
- Ramekins (4-, 6-, 8-ounce)

Nonstick or Stainless Steel?

Nonstick skillets: For healthy cooking, a nonstick skillet is essential because it requires little added fat. We recommend heavy nonstick skillets for (1) quick sautéing and stir-frying meats, seafood, and vegetables; (2) cooking with little or no fat; (3) sautéing delicate foods such as fish; and (4) cooking scrambled eggs, pancakes, and crepes. In *Cooking Light* recipes, we preheat the nonstick skillet over medium heat or medium-high heat, remove the skillet from the heat, and coat it lightly with cooking spray. (Some manufacturers recommend that you don't use cooking spray on their nonstick pans because an invisible buildup will affect the nonstick coating.) Nonstick skillets don't brown foods as well as other pans, nor do they conduct heat as well. You shouldn't place nonstick skillets over high heat, and many have plastic handles that can't go in the oven.

Stainless steel and cast-iron skillets: If you want to leave browned bits in the skillet for deglazing or achieve a dark brown surface on meats, a heavy stainless steel or cast-iron skillet works better than a nonstick skillet. Use a stainless steel or cast-iron skillet for (1) searing, sautéing, and stir-frying meats, seafood, and vegetables; (2) browning and creating "crusts" on foods; and (3) deglazing (see page 19). You'll need to use some type of fat when cooking in stainless steel pans, and delicate foods tend to stick.

Is there one perfect type of skillet for everything? Not exactly—it depends on what you want to achieve. While there are a number of other choices for skillets (anodized aluminum, copper, enamel-coated carbon steel), we use either heavy nonstick skillets, stainless steel, or cast iron in our Test Kitchens.

3 Safety Savvy
Use these food preparation tips, cooking temperature guidelines, and storage times to make sure your food is safe to eat.

Keep It Clean

Here are some tips for preventing food-borne illness.

• **Wash your hands** in soapy water before you prepare food and between tasks.

• **Keep work surfaces clean** using a multi-purpose cleaner for everyday spills and a disinfectant to kill bacteria.

• **Sanitize cutting boards** after each use to avoid cross-contamination.

• **Clean utensils between use** to avoid cross-contamination. For example, don't use the same knife to slice raw meat and then chop vegetables without cleaning it in between.

• **Don't taste food** with the stirring spoon.

• **Wash dish towels** and dishcloths often.

• **Discard dirty sponges**, or wash them in a bleach-water solution.

• **Wash all fresh fruits and vegetables** with clean running water.

• **Marinate meat, poultry, and seafood** in covered, nonmetallic containers in the refrigerator. (The acid in a marinade can react with the metal in a dish, giving the food a metallic off flavor, then that metal can leach into the food.) Don't marinate at room temperature. If the marinade has been in contact with the raw meat, don't use it for basting unless you boil the marinade first.

• **Avoid eating raw** seafood, meat, poultry, and eggs.

• **Avoid stuffing poultry** because the center of the stuffing often can't reach a safe temperature before the bird is done.

Safe Temperatures

For food safety, as well as for the best flavor, cook meat and poultry to the correct internal temperature. Insert a meat or instant-read thermometer into the center of the item, making sure you don't touch the bone.

Meat, Fish, or Poultry	Internal Cooked Temperature (°F)
Fresh beef, veal, lamb	
Ground	160° or until no longer pink and juices run clear
Roasts and Steaks	
Medium-rare	145°
Medium	160°
Well done	170°
Fresh pork	
All cuts	
Medium	160°
Well done	165° to 170°
Ham	
Fresh, raw	160°
Fully cooked, to reheat	140°
Fish	145°
Poultry	
Ground	165°
Breasts	170°
Thighs, wings	180°
Whole chicken, turkey	180°
Duck, goose	180°

Cold Storage

To keep perishable food safe, it's important to wrap it and store it in the refrigerator properly. Here are our top ten storage tips.

1. Store all foods in covered containers or wrapped in heavy-duty plastic wrap or foil.

2. Don't store food in ceramic dishes or leaded crystal. Lead can leach out when acidic foods and beverages come in contact with ceramic containers or leaded crystal.

3. Store cooked food in small portions and in shallow containers for faster cooling. Large portions can take a long time to drop to the safe storage temperature of 40°F.

4. Keep raw meat, poultry, and fish in separate plastic bags, in a bowl or pan, on the lowest refrigerator shelf to keep the juices from dripping onto other foods.

5. Store food quickly when you get home from the grocery store.

6. Don't overload your refrigerator. Cold air needs room to circulate.

7. Keep your refrigerator cold, between 34° and 40° F. Use an inexpensive refrigerator thermometer to check.

8. Don't leave the refrigerator door open too long.

9. Don't leave leftovers out on the counter for more than two hours.

10. Discard foods that have passed the expiration date printed on the food package. These foods could contain spoilage bacteria and may not be safe to eat.

Freezer Fare

To get a jump-start on meal preparation, cook several dishes, and freeze for later use. When seasonal items are available, stock up and store them in the freezer so you'll have them when you need them. To keep foods safe and get the best results when freezing, check out the following tips.

Don't overcook food items that are for the freezer; be particularly careful to slightly undercook pasta, rice, and vegetables.

Cool foods completely by placing them in the refrigerator for an hour before freezing.

Label (with a permanent ink marker) with reheating instructions before freezing to streamline your preparation. Include the name of the meal, date frozen, number of servings, temperature and length of time it bakes, and any other necessary information.

Use airtight containers or plastic zip-top bags made for the freezer. The two biggest enemies of frozen food are air and moisture because they can cause freezer burn.

Never store food in plastic sandwich bags or in plastic produce or bread bags. They're fine for the refrigerator, but won't keep frozen foods fresh.

Don't reuse plastic containers that food items were originally purchased in, such as tubs for butter or margarine; containers for ricotta cheese, cottage cheese or yogurt; or jugs for milk or juice. They're not airtight or moistureproof and may not keep frozen foods fresh. Likewise, most glass jars are not airtight. To be safely used for freezing foods, glass containers must have the label "Ball" or "Kerr" on them and they must have wide mouths.

Thaw uncooked casseroles in the refrigerator (unless directed otherwise in the recipe) before baking. In most cases, taking frozen unbaked dishes straight from the freezer to the oven causes uneven baking. The outer edges tend to overcook, while the middle is uncooked.

Allow time for frozen cooked foods to thaw before reheating. About 24 to 48 hours in the refrigerator will allow most food items to completely thaw.

shelf-life lingo Here's what the dates stamped on food products mean.

Pack Date: When a product was packaged. It's not necessarily an indicator of freshness.

Sell-by Date: The last day a retailer can display the product for sale; the food should remain safe to eat for as many as 10 days afterward if refrigerated properly.

Use-by Date: A food is safe to eat until this date. However, mishandling at home or the store, which can impact quality, isn't considered.

Best-if-used-by Date: This is the most reliable one to follow, because it takes possible mishandling into account.

Storage Times

Proper storage in the refrigerator or freezer is essential for food quality and safety. Use this storage guide to see how long you can store a variety of foods. (For dairy products, the times are for both full-fat and low-fat versions.)

Food	Refrigerator	Freezer
Eggs		
Fresh, in shell	3 to 5 weeks	don't freeze
Raw egg yolks, whites	2 to 4 days	1 year
Hard-cooked	1 week	don't freeze
Egg substitutes, opened	3 days	don't freeze
Egg substitutes, unopened	10 days	1 year
Dairy		
Butter	1 to 3 months	6 to 9 months
Buttermilk	7 to 14 days	3 months
Cheese, hard, unopened	6 months	6 months
Cheese, hard, opened	3 to 4 weeks	6 months
Cheese, soft	1 week	6 months
Cottage cheese, ricotta	1 week	don't freeze
Cream cheese	2 weeks	don't freeze
Cream, aerosol can, real whipped cream	3 to 4 weeks	don't freeze
Cream, aerosol can, nondairy topping	3 months	don't freeze
Cream, half-and-half	3 to 4 days	4 months
Milk	7 days	3 months
Sour Cream	7 to 21 days	don't freeze
Yogurt	7 to 14 days	1 to 2 months
Fish and Shellfish		
Fish, lean	1 to 2 days	6 months
Fish, fatty	1 to 2 days	2 to 3 months
Fish, cooked	3 to 4 days	4 to 6 months
Fish, smoked (vacuum packaged)	14 days or date on package	2 months in package
Shrimp, scallops, crayfish, squid, shucked clams, mussels, and oysters	1 to 2 days	3 to 6 months
Live clams, crab, lobster, mussels, and oysters	2 to 3 days	2 to 3 months
Shellfish, cooked	3 to 4 days	3 months

Food	Refrigerator	Freezer
Meats		
Luncheon meats, opened	3 to 5 days	1 to 2 months
Luncheon meats, unopened	2 weeks	1 to 2 months
Bacon	7 days	1 month
Sausage, raw	1 to 2 days	1 to 2 months
Smoked breakfast links, patties	7 days	1 to 2 months
Hard sausage/pepperoni	2 to 3 weeks	1 to 2 months
Ham, fully cooked, whole	7 days	1 to 2 months
Ham, fully cooked, half	3 to 5 days	1 to 2 months
Ham, fully cooked, slices	3 to 4 days	1 to 2 months
Ground beef, veal, lamb, pork	1 to 2 days	3 to 4 months
Steaks	3 to 5 days	6 to 12 months
Chops	3 to 5 days	4 to 6 months
Roasts	3 to 5 days	4 to 12 months
Cooked meat, casseroles	3 to 4 days	2 to 3 months
Cooked soups/stews	3 to 4 days	2 to 3 months
Poultry		
Ground chicken, turkey	1 to 2 days	3 to 4 months
Chicken or turkey, whole	1 to 2 days	1 year
Chicken or turkey, pieces	1 to 2 days	9 months
Cooked poultry, casseroles	3 to 4 days	4 to 6 months
Cooked, plain	3 to 4 days	4 months
Cooked, covered with broth, gravy	1 to 2 days	6 months
Dough		
Tube cans of biscuits, pizza dough, rolls, etc.	Use-by date	don't freeze
Ready-to-bake pie crust	Use-by date	2 months
Fats		
Margarine	4 to 5 months	12 months
Mayonnaise	2 months	don't freeze
Juices		
Unopened	3 weeks	8 to 12 months
Opened	7 to 10 days	don't freeze

Quality Ingredients

Ingredients that deliver big, bold flavor elevate recipes from simply good to truly extraordinary.

When it comes to selecting fruits, vegetables, herbs, seafood, and meats, the fresher the better. Buy seasonal produce whenever possible, especially fresh local products. For nonperishable items, keep your pantry stocked with a variety of high-quality basic ingredients. (See the Pantry Checklist, page 18.)

Herbs

We almost always prefer to use fresh herbs because the flavor is generally much better than that of dried. However, herbs such as rosemary, dill, and thyme dry well and maintain good flavor. Sometimes fresh herbs aren't available or handy; that's why quality dried herbs are an important part of a basic pantry, especially when it comes to convenience and last-minute meal preparation.

dried herb substitution Fresh herbs aren't as concentrated as their dried counterparts. The standard substitution is 1 teaspoon dried to 1 tablespoon fresh. (For rosemary, sometimes equal amounts of dried and fresh are used.)

Spices

Derived from the bark, buds, fruit, roots, seeds, or stems of plants and trees, spices are a key flavor component of *Cooking Light* recipes. For the most subtle effect, use spices whole. For more flavor, bruise or crush them lightly. The finer you crush, grind, or mill spices, the more powerful and pervasive their effect on the finished product. Here are some tips for buying and storing spices.

Shelf Life Ground spices have a shelf life of about one year. A good rule of thumb is the smell test: If ground spices don't emit an aroma when the jar is opened, they'll be lackluster in the recipe, too.

Jar Size Buy the smallest size possible so they don't lose flavor before you use them.

Storage Store spices in a cool, dark place instead of in a decorative wall spice rack near the oven or dishwasher because heat and sunlight hasten flavor loss.

Premium Oils

High-quality oils are like good wines: No two are alike, and each has a distinct character. The use of premium oils is often one of the features that makes the food you eat in fine restaurants memorable.

The oils we keep in our Test Kitchens and use most frequently are canola, olive, and dark sesame. When cooking with olive oil, it's fine to use a mid-range priced oil instead of a premium extravirgin olive oil because when it's heated, it loses some of the flavor anyway. But when you're using olive oil for its flavor—tossing with vegetables or drizzling on bread—we recommend a higher-priced extravirgin oil.

Vinegars

We use vinegars a lot because a few drops is all you need to add depth and brightness to a dish—and vinegar is fat free. When buying vinegar, read the label to see how long the vinegar has aged; the longer the aging, the more complex the flavor. Some are aged for as long as 30 years. One of our favorites is balsamic vinegar. We also like to keep on hand the following vinegars: cider, red wine, rice, sherry, and white wine.

Pantry Checklist

A well-stocked pantry of top-notch ingredients is the key to creating quick and healthy meals. With these ingredients on hand, you'll always be able to get a tasty, healthy meal on the table, and you won't have to settle for just "so-so" dishes. Here's a list of items we recommend keeping in your kitchen. (See the chart on page 543 if you wish to make low-fat substitutions for any of these items.)

Pantry Basics

- ❑ **Broth**
  - ❑ beef
  - ❑ chicken
  - ❑ vegetable
- ❑ **Canned beans**
  - ❑ black
  - ❑ cannellini
  - ❑ garbanzo
  - ❑ Great Northern
  - ❑ pinto
- ❑ **Canned salmon**
- ❑ **Canned or packaged tuna**
- ❑ **Cornmeal**
- ❑ **Grains**
  - ❑ barley
  - ❑ bulgar
  - ❑ millet
  - ❑ quinoa
- ❑ **Grits or polenta**
- ❑ **Pastas**
  - ❑ couscous
  - ❑ penne
  - ❑ spaghetti
- ❑ **Pasta sauce**
- ❑ **Rice**
  - ❑ Arborio
  - ❑ basmati
  - ❑ jasmine
  - ❑ white
  - ❑ wild
- ❑ **Tomato products, canned**

Condiments

- ❑ **Anchovy paste**
- ❑ **Bottled roasted red bell peppers**
- ❑ **Capers**
- ❑ **Chili paste**
- ❑ **Chipotle chiles in adobo sauce**
- ❑ **Chutneys**
- ❑ **Curry paste**
- ❑ **Dried herbs and spices**
- ❑ **Fresh garlic**
- ❑ **Jams**
- ❑ **Jellies**
- ❑ **Mustards**
  - ❑ Dijon
  - ❑ honey
  - ❑ stone-ground
- ❑ **Oil**
  - ❑ canola
  - ❑ dark sesame
  - ❑ olive
- ❑ **Peanut butter**
- ❑ **Raisins**
- ❑ **Salsa**
- ❑ **Sauces**
  - ❑ fish
  - ❑ hoisin
  - ❑ low-sodium soy
  - ❑ oyster sauce

- ❑ **Seasoning blends**
- ❑ **Sun-dried tomatoes**
- ❑ **Vinegars**
  - ❑ balsamic
  - ❑ cider
  - ❑ red wine
  - ❑ rice
  - ❑ sherry
  - ❑ white wine
- ❑ **Wines**
  - ❑ red
  - ❑ sherry
  - ❑ white

Refrigerator/Freezer

- ❑ **Beef**
  - ❑ ground
  - ❑ roasts
  - ❑ steaks
  - ❑ tenderloin
- ❑ **Butter**
- ❑ **Cheeses**
  - ❑ blue
  - ❑ feta
  - ❑ mozzarella
  - ❑ Parmesan
  - ❑ Romano
- ❑ **Chicken**
  - ❑ rotisserie
  - ❑ skinless, breast halves
  - ❑ thighs
- ❑ **Eggs**
- ❑ **Egg substitute**
- ❑ **Fresh chiles**
  - ❑ jalapeño
  - ❑ serrano
- ❑ **Fresh or frozen fish/shellfish**
  - ❑ salmon
  - ❑ shrimp
- ❑ **Fresh herbs**
- ❑ **Lemons**
- ❑ **Limes**
- ❑ **Oranges**

- ❑ **Nuts**
  - ❑ almonds
  - ❑ hazelnuts
  - ❑ pecans
  - ❑ pine nuts
  - ❑ walnuts
- ❑ **Olives**
  - ❑ black
  - ❑ green
  - ❑ kalamata
  - ❑ niçoise
- ❑ **Pork tenderloin**
- ❑ **Salad dressings**
- ❑ **Tofu**
  - ❑ firm
  - ❑ soft
- ❑ **Tubes of polenta**
- ❑ **Vegetables, frozen**

Sweets

- ❑ **Cocoa**
- ❑ **Honey**
- ❑ **Maple syrup**
- ❑ **Molasses**
- ❑ **Semisweet chocolate**
- ❑ **Sugars**
  - ❑ brown
  - ❑ granulated
  - ❑ powdered
  - ❑ turbinado

5 The Right Technique
Often, flavor comes as much from how food is cooked as from the food itself. Here are some of our favorite high-flavor, low-fat cooking techniques.

Braising

Cooking with a small amount of liquid in a tightly covered container (such as a Dutch oven) over low heat creates intensely flavored meats and sauces. Preparation is quick—brown the meat, add the vegetables and liquids, such as tomatoes and wine, then let everything simmer or bake, checking in only every 20 minutes or so.

Some of the most flavorful cuts of meat are tough when cooked by dry-heat methods. But when you braise them (cook them steeped in moist heat), their very nature transforms. They become remarkably tender and succulent as the tough parts literally melt away to produce rich, delicious sauces. Some of the best cuts of meat to use for braising are:

Beef: Bottom round, chuck, eye of round, round steak, rump roast

Lamb: Leg of lamb, neck, shanks, shoulder, sirloin

Pork: Blade end of loin, Boston butt, leg, picnic shoulder, shank

Veal: Breast, shank, shoulder

Deglazing

You might think that those browned, crunchy bits left behind in the pan after cooking your favorite meat or poultry should be scoured out and thrown away. But that's not the case. Deglazing turns these crunchy bits into powerful nuggets of flavor.

While the pan is still hot, pour in a little broth, wine, water, sherry, apple juice, tea, cider, or other compatible liquid. Keep the heat turned up and scrape the browned bits in the pan loose. The liquid you've added will help to dissolve the browned bits, creating a rich broth. As the liquid begins to cook away, the flavors intensify.

We recommend using a stainless steel or cast-iron skillet for recipes that call for deglazing. Both skillets can be heated to a temperature that is hot enough to quickly sear the meat. During this process, any meat juices quickly evaporate, leaving crunchy brown bits stuck to the bottom of the pan. Deglazing dissolves these flavor nuggets.

Grilling

Because it's a dry, high-heat cooking method, grilling accentuates the natural flavor of food. No amount of seasoning will change the essential quality of the ingredients you use, so start with the best cuts of meat and the freshest vegetables.

Charcoal or gas? Our staff doesn't really have a preference. Some people claim to detect a taste advantage with charcoal, but we really haven't found that to be the case as long as the two fuels provide a similar temperature range.

There are two basic types of grilling: direct and indirect. Direct grilling involves putting the food on the grill rack directly over the coals. For indirect grilling, both sides of the grill are fired up, then one side is turned off (or the coals are pushed to one side). A drip pan is placed directly over the coals on the side of the grill where the heat has been turned off or where the charcoal has been moved. The food is then placed on the grill rack over the pan.

Lamb Shanks on Cannellini Beans, page 340

Chicken with Pancetta and Figs, page 376

Grilled Mahimahi with Peach and Pink Grapefruit Relish, page 239

19

Marinating

You can add flavor to (and sometimes tenderize) a food by letting it soak in a seasoned liquid called a marinade. The key ingredients in a marinade are an acid such as wine, citrus juice, or vinegar, oil, and seasonings. Generally speaking, the longer you marinate a food, the more pronounced the flavor will be. Remember, however, that some foods, such as delicate fish, shouldn't marinate longer than two to four hours. Meats and poultry can generally marinate in a low-acid marinade for up to 48 hours, but meat or poultry in a high-acid liquid shouldn't marinate for more than one or two hours.

As a rule, ⅔ to 1 cup of marinade will flavor 1 to 1½ pounds of food. Marinate food in nonmetal containers such as glass dishes, plastic bowls, or zip-top plastic bags that won't react with acidic ingredients. Always marinate raw meats in the refrigerator.

Marinated foods lend themselves well to grilling because you can baste the food with the remaining marinade. If you plan to baste with the liquid that was in contact with the raw food, put the marinade in a saucepan and bring it to a boil before basting to avoid any cross-contamination.

Roasting

When you turn the oven dial up to the max, a scorching 475° to 500°, the heat intensifies the natural flavors of foods. Thanks to caramelization, roasting concentrates flavors of fruits, vegetables, and meats with little or no added fat, giving the foods a crispy exterior, tender interior, and rich, dark color.

You need only a few essentials for roasting: an oven; a heavy, shallow roasting pan; and a meat thermometer to determine doneness. (See page 14 for the end temperatures at which meats and poultry will be succulent as well as safe.) Position the oven rack in the center—usually the second level from the bottom—so hot air can evenly surround the food.

Roasting generally requires tender cuts of meat, which are usually higher in fat. We recommend using beef tenderloin, pork loin, or whole chicken, which are all moderately lean. Some fruits and vegetables that are suitable for roasting include peaches and plums, bell peppers, asparagus, green beans, onions, potatoes, and squash. When you're roasting vegetables, it's important to spread the pieces out in a single layer in the pan. If they're piled up, not all of the vegetables will get roasted.

Stir-Frying

Stir-frying is to quickly cook small pieces of food over high heat while stirring constantly. (Stir-frying and sautéing are essentially the same thing.) It requires very little fat, and because the food cooks quickly, it retains its great natural flavor. Lean meats, poultry, and fresh vegetables are ideal for stir-frying.

Vegetables should be sliced, chopped, or diced in roughly the same size. This ensures they'll cook quickly and evenly. Slice vegetables on the diagonal so more of their surface area comes in contact with the pan. Slice lean cuts of meat thinly across the grain, or cut them into cubes.

A stir-fry pan or skillet with a nonreactive stainless-steel or anodized-aluminum surface is a terrific alternative to a wok, and is what we prefer. Unlike the round-bottom woks, which require a ring on which the vessel sits, a stir-fry pan has a wide, flat bottom that rests evenly on a smooth-top cooking surface. Most stir-fry pans have a long stay-cool handle and a small helper handle on the opposite end.

For stirring and tossing ingredients, use a long-handled stir-fry spatula, a long-handled wooden spoon, or a heat-resistant rubber spatula.

Wasabi-Miso Marinated Flank Steak, page 322

Cider-Roasted Chicken, page 379

Brussels Sprouts with Pecans, page 516

entertaining

entertaining guide

Our philosophy of entertaining at *Cooking Light* is one that emphasizes the joy of good friends and good food in a relaxed setting. Let these planning and time-saving tips and simple decorating ideas inspire you to create your own special style the next time you have a few people over.

Getting Started

Whether it's a month or a week ahead, you'll need to make some decisions about the type of event, the date and time, the food, and the number of guests.

Before you get into the details of your party, decide on the style. Think about your space and the type of entertaining that's most suitable, either formal or informal. Then start selecting beverages, food, and decorations.

Planning the Menu

The occasion and your serving style will help determine your menu. One rule of thumb is that the more guests you invite, the simpler the menu should be. We suggest that you use this "mental checklist" as you select the recipes:

- How many guests will there be?
- Will there be guests with special dietary needs?
- How many dishes are needed?
- What dishes are realistic in terms of time and money?
- Is there a balance of flavors, colors, shapes, and temperatures?
- Is there enough variety?
- What is the season or theme?

For some of our favorite menus, see our Top 10 Quick & Easy Menus on page 27 and the Special Occasions menus on pages 29-30.

Serving Styles

Although every event can take on a life of its own in terms of theme, season, and occasion, there are some basic styles of serving that we use in a variety of ways. No matter which style works best for your party, you can create a formal or informal style by the tableware and decorations that you choose.

Buffet-style: This style of serving works for both large and small groups. Arrange the food on a sideboard or additional table, and let guests serve themselves. Buffets work whether you're serving a meal or only desserts or appetizers. Instead of placing all the food in one place, you can vary the buffet style by placing dishes in a couple of locations.

Family-style: Usually informal, this style can work for a more formal holiday gathering as well. Here, you place the food on large platters or in serving dishes, arrange those serving pieces on the table, and let guests pass the food around the table. Family-style serving doesn't usually work well for large groups.

Restaurant-style: If you have a small table without a lot of room for platters, you can plate the food in the kitchen and bring the individual plates to the table.

setting up a buffet
Having a sideboard isn't required to be able to serve a buffet. Set the buffet on a dining room table, a kitchen counter, or a chest—anything that will allow room for a stack of plates, utensils, and some dishes of food. Since your guests will be serving themselves, arrange the buffet in a way that allows for easy circulation and traffic flow.

Saving Time

When you have friends and family over, you want everything to be enjoyable for them—and manageable for you. Here are some ideas to help simplify your next gathering and secure your reputation as a gracious host.

There is a way to entertain both stylishly and simply, and you can do it with these time-saving tips from the *Cooking Light* food stylists and editors.

Stick with what you know. Prepare dishes that are equal to your capabilities. Making the recipes will take less time if you aren't trying to figure out new procedures and unfamiliar ingredients.

Less is more. Often, one or two well-prepared dishes are just as impressive and enjoyable as a huge buffet of food. Concentrate on a couple of special things, and make them the best they can be.

Use convenience products. Give up your need to make everything you serve from scratch. With the abundance of quality items in the market today, you can round out the meal with the best store-bought items you can find. For example, instead of preparing an appetizer recipe, serve an assortment of imported cheeses and some seasonal fresh fruit. Don't spend your time baking bread—buy an artisan loaf from a local bakery. Also consider using bagged salad greens, pre-cut fresh fruit, store-bought relishes, salsas, and chutneys, ice creams and sorbets, and frozen vegetables.

Simplify the stuff. When planning your menu, think about the tools and equipment you'll need to use, and try to select recipes that won't require you to get out every cooking utensil, pot, and pan you own. Using less equipment will also save clean-up time.

Jump-start your meal. As you look over potential recipes, select a few that are make-aheads, specifically those that don't require any additional preparation other than heating up or taking out of the freezer. When you've got dishes already prepared, you'll be more relaxed on the day of your party and able to enjoy your guests. (See the Index beginning on page 548 for a guide to the recipes in this book that are make ahead.) Even if a complete dish can't be prepared ahead, you might be able to do some pre-prep by chopping vegetables, making breadcrumbs, or pureeing sauces a day or two ahead.

Put your guests to work. Cooking together is a lot of fun, so consider moving the party to the kitchen and letting your guests pitch in with the preparations. You might want to have the ingredients for the different dishes pre-assembled at different stations.

Making It Festive

Adding a few unique touches can transform an ordinary meal into an extraordinary event and make it a memorable occasion for your guests.

When you entertain, let your individual style shine in the table setting and decorations. Here at *Cooking Light*, we tend to shy away from formal dinners with intimidating place settings and lean toward a simpler style of dining. These days, unless you're having a formal dinner, you can relax and color outside the box when it comes to tableware and decorating. Let your imagination soar as you think of new ways to enhance the beauty of your table.

We've gone back over the pages of the magazine for our favorite entertaining features and gathered some of our favorite table-top ideas. These ideas come from our food editors, stylists, and photographers, and sometimes come about by happy accident rather than advance planning! They reflect what we like to call "the *Cooking Light* look," but that look is ever-evolving as our tastes and preferences change. We hope these ideas will give you a place to start and inspire you to find a style and look that is all you.

Table Coverings

• For a casual gathering, don't worry about adding a tablecloth; show off your table, and add interest with colorful napkins. Or, make a runner with a remnant piece of fabric. You don't even need to stitch it—just use a hot glue gun to fold under and seal the ragged edges.
• For a more formal look, go ahead and get out the white linen tablecloth that your grandmother gave you.

Flowers

• You don't need a dozen roses to make an impact. Sometime just a few perfect ones, artfully arranged in a small vase, can be quite dramatic.
• Rather than depositing a store-bought bouquet of mixed blossoms in a large vase, divide it into smaller bunches, bundling the blossoms you like best.
• Buy a bouquet of just one type of flower. The repetition offers a sophisticated look.

• Experiment with any type of container that appeals to you. Use wine glasses, water goblets, and salt shakers as vases for single flowers.

Candles

• Cluster a collection of candles in the center of the table for dramatic impact. Tuck in sprigs of greenery, fresh herbs, or berries among the candles.
• To add height, light, and dimension to the table, place pillar candles in clear glass vases; fill in around the bottom of the candles with glass beads, cranberries, or nuts.
• To add a warm holiday glow, use votive candleholders throughout the dining room and the house.
• Use candles of a uniform color or varying shades of one color in a variety of shapes and sizes. Arrange them in unique combinations of candleholders.
• Fill a crystal bowl with water; add a few floating candles for a romantic centerpiece.

Or, for a smaller decoration, put one floating candle in a water-filled wine glass.
• If you'll be lighting the candles on the dining table, it's best to use unscented candles so that the aroma doesn't interfere with the taste of the food.

Flatware

• Mix and match silver patterns for a charming, vintage look. Flea markets, tag sales, and estate sales are great places to find old silver. Whether your look is classic or contemporary, you can find flatware to match your style.
• When serving buffet-style, place the utensils in interesting containers such as terra cotta pots, baskets, glass vases, or ceramic bowls.
• Wrap utensils in colorful napkins, and tie with ribbon or raffia.

Glasses

• Clear glassware with simple, traditional shapes is adaptable enough to go formal or informal.
• If you don't have enough wineglasses, serve wine in juice glasses or an assortment of antique glasses.

• It's fine to mix and match wineglasses, and it's not absolutely necessary to have different glasses for red and white. If you want to have an all-purpose wineglass, go with one that has a generous-sized bowl (12 to 20 ounces); it will work for both reds and whites.
• Use glassware for something other than beverages. For example, a pudding, custard, or fruit dessert can make a stunning presentation when served in a stemmed glass.

Plates and Platters

• We love simple white plates because you can create both formal and informal moods simply by switching out the linens, flatware, and serving pieces. Plus, we think food always looks good on white plates.
• Don't be afraid to mix and match your plates and serving pieces. Vintage china patterns lend themselves to mixing and matching, so if you've inherited several place settings, combine them for a charming, eclectic look.
• Don't limit yourself to conventional serving dishes or the pieces that match your china: Use pieces of pottery, glass bowls, or baskets lined with colorful cloths.

plate pizzazz Here are some food presentation pointers from the *Cooking Light* food stylists.

• Heavily patterned china distracts your guests' focus from the food. In general, the more complex and colorful the finished dish is, the more it needs a simple plate. Plain white or off-white dishes really showcase the food.
• Stacking or overlapping portions gives the illusion of a bigger serving and highlights colors and textures. If the bottom layer is rice, polenta, or mashed potatoes, so much the better: Pale foods, like white dishes, act as a neutral backdrop for your entrée.
• Garnish your finished dish with some of the fresh herbs you used to prepare it. And remember, citrus zest, grated or julienned, is also a fine garnish.
• Soups and stews benefit from a scattering of chopped herbs, rather than sprigs.
• Use your vegetable peeler to shave Parmesan cheese into thin shards for entrées or to shave chocolate for desserts. Ribbons of vegetables, made in the same way, are terrific to accent soups.
• Dust sweets with powdered sugar, cocoa, or cinnamon; use paprika on savory dishes. The key is to sift the sugar or spice through a small sieve.
• Whatever your dessert, berries make it better. Berries add color and the idea of freshness. If you put fresh berries on a store-bought dessert, it looks homemade. Herbs can garnish desserts, too. Mint will go on almost anything.
• Pooling dessert sauces on plates provides a canvas for dazzling desserts. Put a thicker sauce in a squeeze bottle to make squiggles or dots.

Serving Spirits
Here's how to be savvy about serving and tasting wine, plus a guide for a well-stocked bar.

Wine Wisdom

Trust your instincts when pairing wine and food. Matching wine and food is an exploration more than an exact science. Don't limit yourself to serving white wines with fish and poultry and red wine with meats. Instead, consider offering light-bodied wines with delicately flavored foods and full-bodied wines with hearty, strongly flavored dishes. Use the wine tips sprinkled throughout the recipe chapters for additional suggestions.

Focus on one country's wines at a time. When you go to the wine shop, the choices can be overwhelming, so it's easier if you narrow your choices. For example, you might spend a few months drinking only a variety of Australian wines, then switch to American.

Another option is to focus on only one variety of white wine and one variety of red. For a set time of six months, for example, stick with just two kinds of wine such as sauvignon blanc and shiraz. Try lots of different producers. When you feel as though you've mastered those, move on to two other types.

Don't worry about accessories. While expensive gadgets, glassware, and corkscrews are nice, they aren't necessary. Glasses don't need to match. You don't need an ice bucket for chilling white or sparkling wines—almost any large round container or planter can double as an ice bucket. A glass pitcher will work as a decanter, and just about any corkscrew will get the job done.

Be an efficient buyer. Get a mixed case of different wines instead of buying one bottle at a time. You'll get a bit of a discount this way, and you won't have to go by the wine shop quite as often.

Create a permanent wine spot in your refrigerator and always keep a bottle of white wine there. Have a red on hand, too.

Share wine tastings with friends. You need not be totally responsible for wine choices. Tasting with friends is fun and allows you to explore some new wines and get opinions from others.

Write it down. To build knowledge that will make wine decisions easier, begin developing a personal catalog of wines. The easiest way is to keep a journal—a spiral-bound notebook will do—handy on the kitchen counter.

Appoint a wine captain when you're entertaining. It's impossible to keep an eye on the food in the oven and serve the wine at the same time.

Invest in a good wine book. The more you know about wine, the simpler and more enjoyable it is. (We recommend *Wine, Food & Friends* and *The Wine Bible* by Karen MacNeil.)

The Well-Stocked Bar

If you're serving cocktails in addition to wine, here's what we recommend for a well-stocked bar.

Beer

Hard Liquor
- Bitters
- French vermouth (dry white)
- Kentucky bourbon
- Liqueurs
- Rum (dark and medium)
- Rye whiskey
- Single-malt scotch
- Tequila
- Vodka

Nonalcoholic beverages
- Club soda and tonic
- Fruit juices
- Soft drinks
- Water

Wine
- Red
- White
- Desserts wines
  (Ice wine, madeira, port, sherry)

Other
- Assorted glasses (highball, martini, old-fashioned, wine)
- Cocktail shaker
- Corkscrew
- Ice, bucket and tongs
- Jigger
- Lemons
- Limes
- Olives

Top 10 Quick & Easy Menus

When you have last-minute guests, or are simply having friends over for a casual meal, turn to these speedy menus.

1

Quick Pizza Margherita
(page 302)

- Mixed green salad with balsamic vinaigrette
- Fruit sorbet

2

Thai Beef Salad
(page 423)

- Steamed rice
- Fresh pineapple slices

3

Veal Marsala
(page 335)

- Egg noodles
- Minted green peas
- French bread

4

Chicken with Black Bean Salsa
(page 366)

- Yellow rice

5

Citrus-Roasted Salmon
(page 241)

- Sautéed zucchini
- Whole wheat rolls

6

Vegetarian Pad Thai
(page 288)

- Steamed asparagus

7

Red Bell Pepper Frittata
(page 307)

- English muffins
- Fresh cantaloupe wedges

8

Flank Steak with Cilantro-Almond Pesto
(page 322)

- Grilled corn
- Spinach salad with citrus vinaigrette

9

Simple Seared Scallops
(page 253)

- Orzo tossed with chopped tomato, feta, and basil

10

Twenty-Minute Chili
(page 492)

- Raw vegetables with low-fat dressing
- Corn bread sticks

Special Occasions
Holidays, birthdays, anniversaries, promotions, and graduations are all reasons to celebrate with family and friends. Or maybe your supper club needs new innovative menu ideas. Here are some of our favorite entertaining menus—start here and create your own memorable meals.

Holiday Dinner Party: Basic Mashed Potatoes (page 527), sautéed zucchini, Roast Beef with Horseradish-Mushroom Sauce (page 332)

Mediterranean Spinach
Strata, page 311

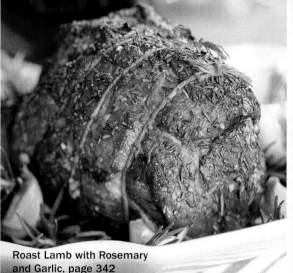

Roast Lamb with Rosemary
and Garlic, page 342

Lemon-Buttermilk Ice
Cream, page 191

New Year's Day Brunch Buffet

Serves 10

Bloody Marys (page 69)

Apricot-Almond Muffins (page 78)

Mediterranean Spinach Strata (page 311)

Cheese Grits (page 262)

Poppy Seed Fruit Salad (page 398)

Sour Cream Coffee Cake (page 86)

Superbowl Party

Serves 8

Crisp and Spicy Snack Mix (page 40)

Tomatillo Salsa (page 455)

Baked tortilla chips

All-American Chili (page 493)

Quick Buttermilk Corn Bread (page 76)

Butter Pecan-Toffee Brownies (page 161)

Valentine's Dinner

Serves 2

Beet, Jícama, and Watercress
Salad (page 403)

Deviled Crab Boules with
Beurre Blanc (page 248)

Chocolate Chunk
Bread Puddings (page 177)

Spring Celebration

Serves 8

Strawberry-Champagne Soup (page 474)

Roast Lamb with Rosemary
and Garlic (page 342)

Roasted Asparagus with Balsamic
Browned Butter (page 514)

Steamed new potatoes

Lemonade Layer Cake (page 118)

Mother's Day Brunch

Serves 6

Raspberry-Orange Sunrises (page 67)

Lemon-Blueberry Muffins (page 77)

Spicy-Sweet Melon Salad (page 398)

Tomato-Basil Tart (page 312)

Bridal Shower Luncheon

Serves 8

A Cool Drink (page 64)

Curried Chicken Salad (page 424)

Sliced tomatoes

Lemon-Glazed Zucchini
Quick Bread (page 80)

Strawberry-Blueberry Compote in Red
Wine Syrup (page 197)

Patio Dinner Party

Serves 8

Teo's Punch (page 64)

Bruschetta Gorgonzola
and Apples (page 42)

Hoisin and Bourbon-Glazed
Pork (page 349)

Three-Fruit Salsa (page 39)

Grilled Asparagus (page 517)

Strawberry-Swirl Frozen Pie (page 210)

4th of July Barbecue

Serves 8

White Bean and Bacon Dip (page 34)

Rosemary Pita Chips (page 41)

Grilled chicken

White Barbecue Sauce (page 451)

Tomato, Basil, and Fresh Mozzarella
Salad (page 409)

Farm Stand Potato Salad (page 412)

Lemon-Buttermilk Ice Cream
(page 191)

**Note: Some recipes may need to be doubled
if prepared to go with a specific menu.**

Teo's Punch, page 64

Lemon-Sage Turkey with Wild-Mushroom Gravy, page 394

Savory Yogurt Cheesecake, page 47

Summer Supper Club

Serves 8

Tomato-Basil Soup (page 483)

Grilled Vegetable Antipasto (page 525)

Rosemary-Scented Flatbread with Black Grapes (page 101)

Basil Dipping Oil (page 468)

Mediterranean Shrimp-and-Pasta Salad (page 419)

Tiramisu Anacapri (page 186)

Cocktail Supper

Serves 12

Mini Black Bean Cakes with Green Onion Cream and Avocado Salsa (page 54)

Chipotle Shrimp Cups (page 56)

Pork Tenderloin Studded with Rosemary and Garlic (page 351)

Whole wheat dinner rolls

Gazpacho Salad with Tomato Vinaigrette (page 410)

Cocoa Fudge Cookies (page 144)

Coconut Meringues (page 147)

Mango Martini (page 69)

Mojito (page 69)

Autumn Harvest Celebration

Serves 6

Apple Bisque with Chestnuts (page 478)

Butternut Squash and Parmesan Bread Pudding (page 311)

Bitter Greens with Tarragon Vinaigrette and Pine Nuts (page 402)

Walnut-and-Rosemary Loaves (page 95)

Vanilla-Scented Harvest Crisp with Pistachios (page 225)

Classic Thanksgiving

Serves 12

Baby Spinach Salad with Candied Hazelnuts (page 404)

Curried Butternut Soup (page 486)

Lemon-Sage Turkey with Wild-Mushroom Gravy (page 394)

Corn Bread Dressing (page 537)

Spiced Sweet Potato Casserole (page 531)

Brussels Sprouts with Pecans (page 516)

Whole wheat rolls

Gingered Pumpkin Pie (page 215)

Appetizer Open House

Serves 20

Red Pepper-Cheese Dip (page 32)

Smoked Trout Spread (page 38)

Assorted crackers and breadsticks

Savory Yogurt Cheesecake with Caramelized Onions (page 47)

Stuffed Mushrooms (page 52)

Curried Crab Cakes (page 57)

Bourbon Fudge Brownies (page 161)

Pecan Tassies in Cream Cheese Pastry (page 219)

Holiday Dinner Party

Serves 12

Cream of Mushroom Soup with Sherry (page 477)

Roast Beef with Horseradish-Mustard Sauce (page 332)

Basic Mashed Potatoes (page 527)

Sautéed zucchini

Whole wheat rolls

Chocolate Cheesecake (page 137)

appetizers & beverages

Fresh Herbed Heirloom Tomatoes
and Goat Cheese Crostini, page 44

Dips, Spreads & Salsas

From smooth, cool dips and sassy salsas to hot and creamy veggie dips, these appetizers are welcome at any party.

Red Pepper-Cheese Dip

Make this flavorful dip a day ahead. Serve it with crisp breadsticks.

Prep: 15 minutes • Cook: 60 minutes
Other: 20 minutes

- 1 large red bell pepper
- 1 small onion, peeled and halved
- Cooking spray
- 1 whole garlic head
- 1 cup plain fat-free yogurt
- ½ cup (4 ounces) block-style fat-free cream cheese
- ¼ teaspoon ground cumin
- ⅛ teaspoon ground red pepper
- ¼ cup chopped fresh flat-leaf parsley

1. Preheat broiler.
2. Cut bell pepper in half lengthwise; discard seeds and membranes. Place pepper halves, skin sides up, on a foil-lined baking sheet; flatten. Broil 15 minutes or until blackened. Place in a zip-top plastic bag; seal. Let stand 10 minutes. Remove and discard peel. Set roasted pepper aside.
3. Reduce oven temperature to 400°.
4. Place onion halves, cut sides down, on a baking sheet coated with cooking spray. Remove white papery skin from garlic (do not peel or separate cloves). Wrap garlic in foil, and place on baking sheet with onion. Bake at 400° for 15 minutes; turn over onion halves. Bake 15 minutes or until onions are soft and begin to brown. Place onion on a plate. Return garlic to oven, and bake an additional 15 minutes. Cool 10 minutes. Separate cloves; squeeze to extract garlic pulp. Discard skins.
5. Place pepper, onion, and garlic in a food processor; process until smooth. Add yogurt, cheese, cumin, and ground red pepper; process until smooth. Spoon dip into a bowl, and stir in parsley. Cover and chill. Serve with breadsticks or fresh vegetables. Yield: 2 cups (serving size: 2 tablespoons).

CALORIES 20 (9% from fat); FAT 0.2g (sat 0.1g, mono 0g, poly 0g); PROTEIN 1.9g; CARB 3.1g; FIBER 0.3g; CHOL 1mg; IRON 0.2mg; SODIUM 85mg; CALC 37mg

how to roast red peppers

1. Cut the peppers in half lengthwise; discard the seeds and membranes. Place the halves, skin sides up, on a foil-lined baking sheet; use the palm of your hand to slightly flatten the peppers.

2. Broil 15 minutes. Place the peppers in a zip-top bag until the skins are loose. Peel; discard the skins.

Asian Peanut Dip

You can also use this dip as a spread for "grown-up" peanut butter sandwiches.

Prep: 4 minutes

- ½ cup natural-style peanut butter
- ⅓ cup reduced-fat firm silken tofu
- 3 tablespoons light brown sugar
- 2 tablespoons fresh lime juice
- 2 tablespoons low-sodium soy sauce
- ½ to ¾ teaspoon crushed red pepper
- 2 garlic cloves, crushed

1. Place ingredients in a blender; process until smooth. Store in refrigerator up to two days. Serve with crudités. Yield: 1 cup (serving size: 2 tablespoons).

CALORIES 122 (57% from fat); FAT 7.7g (sat 1.5g, mono 3.8g, poly 2.5g); PROTEIN 5.4g; CARB 7.4g; FIBER 0.5g; CHOL 0mg; IRON 0.4mg; SODIUM 131mg; CALC 19mg

Pumpkin Dip

Serve this appetizer version of pumpkin pie with apple slices or gingersnaps.

Prep: 10 minutes

- ¾ cup (6 ounces) block-style ⅓-less-fat cream cheese
- ½ cup packed brown sugar
- ½ cup canned pumpkin
- 2 teaspoons maple syrup
- ½ teaspoon ground cinnamon

1. Place first 3 ingredients in a bowl; beat with a mixer at medium speed until blended. Add syrup and cinnamon; beat until smooth. Cover and chill. Yield: 1½ cups (serving size: 2 tablespoons).

CALORIES 77 (36% from fat); FAT 3.1g (sat 2g, mono 0g, poly 0g); PROTEIN 1.6g; CARB 11.1g; FIBER 0.4g; CHOL 10mg; IRON 0.4mg; SODIUM 68mg; CALC 23mg

Creamy Hummus

Red Pepper-Walnut Dip

Sweet raisins and toasted nuts enhance the flavor and texture of this dip.

Prep: 6 minutes

- ¾ cup walnuts, toasted
- ½ cup raisins
- ½ cup plain low-fat yogurt
- ¼ teaspoon salt
- ⅛ teaspoon ground red pepper
- 1 (12-ounce) bottle roasted red bell peppers, drained

1. Place all ingredients in a food processor; process until smooth. Serve with toasted pita wedges or sourdough baguette slices. Yield: 1¾ cups (serving size: about 2½ tablespoons).

CALORIES 75 (53% from fat); FAT 4.4g (sat 0.5g, mono 0.6g, poly 3.1g); PROTEIN 2.1g; CARB 7.9g; FIBER 0.9g; CHOL 1mg; IRON 0.5mg; SODIUM 160mg; CALC 31mg

Test Kitchen Tip: To toast walnuts, place them in a dry skillet over medium heat; stir for 1 to 2 minutes or until they're toasted.

Creamy Hummus

Hummus, a dip or sauce made from mashed chickpeas, is for garlic lovers. The signature ingredients are garlic, lemon juice, and sometimes tahini.

Prep: 9 minutes

- ¾ cup water
- ½ cup tahini (sesame-seed paste)
- 6 garlic cloves, peeled
- 6 tablespoons fresh lemon juice
- 1 tablespoon extravirgin olive oil
- 1 teaspoon ground cumin
- ½ teaspoon salt
- ¼ teaspoon pepper
- 2 (19-ounce) cans chickpeas (garbanzo beans), rinsed and drained

1. Place first 3 ingredients in a food processor; process until smooth. Add juice and remaining ingredients; process until smooth, scraping sides of bowl occasionally. Serve with pita wedges. Yield: 4 cups (serving size: 1 tablespoon).

CALORIES 34 (40% from fat); FAT 1.5g (sat 0.2g, mono 0.6g, poly 0.6g); PROTEIN 1.2g; CARB 4.3g; FIBER 0.9g; CHOL 0mg; IRON 0.3mg; SODIUM 69mg; CALC 8mg

Field Pea Dip

A take on Middle Eastern hummus, this dip contains field peas instead of chickpeas.

Prep: 7 minutes • Cook: 35 minutes

    2 cups fresh pink-eyed peas
    2 (14-ounce) cans fat-free, less-sodium
       chicken broth
    6 tablespoons low-fat mayonnaise
    2 tablespoons tahini (sesame-seed
       paste)
    2 tablespoons hot pepper vinegar
       (such as Crystal)
    1 tablespoon fresh lemon juice
    2 teaspoons paprika
    2 garlic cloves, minced
    2 tablespoons chopped fresh chives
       (optional)

1. Combine peas and broth in a large saucepan; bring to a boil. Reduce heat; simmer, partially covered, 30 minutes or until tender. Drain peas. Place peas in a food processor; pulse 10 times or until coarsely chopped.
2. Combine peas, mayonnaise, and next 5 ingredients in a bowl, stirring until blended. Garnish with chives, if desired. Serve with pita chips. Yield: 2 cups (serving size: 2 tablespoons).

CALORIES 109 (27% from fat); FAT 3.3g (sat 0.5g, mono 1.6g, poly 1g); PROTEIN 5.5g; CARB 15.2g; FIBER 2.5g; CHOL 2mg; IRON 1.9mg; SODIUM 53mg; CALC 28mg

Test Kitchen Tip: Although there are subtle flavor differences in field peas, most can be interchangeable in recipes. Some common varieties are pink-eyed, black-eyed, lady, crowder, and zipper.

White Bean and Bacon Dip

Serve this garlicky bean dip with Rosemary Pita Chips (page 41) or store-bought pitas or bagel chips.

Prep: 10 minutes • Cook: 21 minutes

    2 applewood-smoked bacon slices,
       chopped (such as Nueske's)
    4 garlic cloves, minced
 ⅓ cup fat-free, less-sodium chicken broth
    1 (19-ounce) can cannellini beans,
       rinsed and drained
 ¼ cup chopped green onions
    1 tablespoon fresh lemon juice
 ½ teaspoon hot sauce
 ⅛ teaspoon salt
 ⅛ teaspoon paprika
  Rosemary Pita Chips (page 41)

1. Cook bacon in a small saucepan over medium heat until crisp. Remove bacon from pan with a slotted spoon; set aside. Add garlic to drippings in pan; cook 1 minute, stirring frequently. Add broth and beans; bring to a boil. Reduce heat, and simmer, uncovered, 10 minutes.
2. Place bean mixture, onions, and next 4 ingredients in a food processor, and process until smooth. Spoon mixture into a bowl; stir in 1 tablespoon reserved bacon. Sprinkle dip with remaining bacon just before serving. Serve with Rosemary Pita Chips. Yield: 8 servings (serving size: 3 tablespoons dip and 3 pita chips).

(Totals include Rosemary Pita Chips) CALORIES 137 (25% from fat); FAT 3.8g (sat 1.3g, mono 1.5g, poly 0.7g); PROTEIN 4.7g; CARB 20.5g; FIBER 2.6g; CHOL 3.8mg; IRON 1.4mg; SODIUM 397mg; CALC 39mg

Test Kitchen Tip: Rinsing canned beans under cold running water improves the appearance of the beans and reduces the sodium by 40 percent.

Spiced Red Lentil Dip

The striking red color of this dip makes it an impressive holiday party dish.

Prep: 10 minutes • Cook: 21 minutes

    1 cup dried small red lentils
    1 bay leaf
    1 tablespoon olive oil
    1 cup finely chopped onion
    2 tablespoons pine nuts
    1 tablespoon tomato paste
    1 teaspoon fine sea salt
    1 teaspoon ground coriander seeds
 ½ teaspoon ground cumin
 ½ teaspoon ground caraway seeds
 ⅛ teaspoon ground red pepper
    3 garlic cloves, minced
    3 tablespoons fresh lemon juice
  Pita Crisps (page 41)

1. Place lentils and bay leaf in a saucepan; cover with water to 2 inches above lentils. Bring to a boil. Cover, reduce heat, and simmer 8 minutes or until tender. Drain well. Discard bay leaf.
2. Heat oil in a small nonstick skillet over medium-high heat. Add onion and nuts; sauté 5 minutes or until nuts are lightly browned. Stir in tomato paste and next 6 ingredients; cook 5 minutes, stirring occasionally. Stir in juice. Place lentils and onion mixture in a food processor; process until smooth. Serve with Pita Crisps. Yield: 10 servings (serving size: about ¼ cup dip and 2 crisps).

(Totals include Pita Crisps) CALORIES 159 (15% from fat); FAT 2.6g (sat 0.4g, mono 1.4g, poly 0.6g); PROTEIN 7.4g; CARB 27g; FIBER 3.9g; CHOL 0mg; IRON 2mg; SODIUM 395mg; CALC 46mg

Test Kitchen Tip: Because pine nuts are expensive, we toast them—it provides more flavor with fewer nuts.

Classic Makeover: Spinach Dip

This ever-popular party pleaser, seemingly nutritious because of the vegetables and the cheese, is very high in fat. But with a few small changes, we were able to reduce the fat by 67 percent. First, we got rid of the marinated artichoke hearts and switched to canned, which cut the fat by 15 percent. Then we substituted lower-fat sour cream and cheese for the full-fat versions. Once the fat in the dip was reduced, we didn't forget about the dippers: Instead of high-fat corn chips, we serve this hot and bubbly dip with baked tortilla chips.

Before	After
• 196 calories	• 99 calories
• 16.8g fat	• 5.5g fat
• 9.7g saturated fat	• 1.8g saturated fat
• 330mg sodium	• 204mg sodium

Spinach and Artichoke Dip

To make this hearty dip ahead, assemble it the night before, cover and refrigerate, and bake it just before serving.

Prep: 11 minutes • Cook: 30 minutes

 2 cups (8 ounces) shredded part-skim
    mozzarella cheese, divided
 ½ cup fat-free sour cream
 ¼ cup (1 ounce) grated fresh Parmesan
    cheese, divided
 ¼ teaspoon pepper
 3 garlic cloves, crushed
 1 (14-ounce) can artichoke hearts,
    drained and chopped
 1 (8-ounce) block ⅓-less-fat cream
    cheese, softened
 1 (8-ounce) block fat-free cream
    cheese, softened
 1 (10-ounce) package frozen chopped
    spinach, thawed, drained, and
    squeezed dry

1. Preheat oven to 350°.
2. Combine 1½ cups mozzarella, sour cream, 2 tablespoons Parmesan, pepper, and next 5 ingredients in a large bowl, and stir until well blended. Spoon mixture into a 1½-quart baking dish. Sprinkle with ½ cup mozzarella and 2 tablespoons Parmesan. Bake at 350° for 30 minutes or until bubbly and golden brown. Serve with baked tortilla chips or crackers. Yield: 4½ cups (serving size: ¼ cup).

CALORIES 99 (50% from fat); FAT 5.5g (sat 1.8g, mono 0.8g, poly 0.1g); PROTEIN 8.1g; CARB 4.3g; FIBER 0.5g; CHOL 19mg; IRON 0.6mg; SODIUM 204mg; CALC 169mg

Spinach-Parmesan Dip

This creamy dip features fresh spinach and basil with a little punch from garlic and fresh Parmesan. At first, the spinach will seem to overflow in the skillet, but keep stirring—as it begins to wilt, it reduces in volume.

Prep: 8 minutes • Cook: 5 minutes

  1 teaspoon olive oil
  3 garlic cloves, chopped
  ¼ teaspoon salt
  1 (10-ounce) package fresh spinach
  ½ cup fresh basil leaves, loosely packed
  ⅓ cup (about 3 ounces) block-style
      ⅓-less-fat cream cheese, softened
  ⅛ teaspoon pepper
  ⅓ cup plain fat-free yogurt
  ¼ cup (1 ounce) grated fresh Parmesan
      cheese

1. Heat oil in a large skillet over medium-high heat. Add garlic; sauté 1 minute. Add salt and spinach; sauté 3 minutes or until spinach wilts. Place spinach mixture in a colander; press until drained.

2. Place spinach mixture, basil, cream cheese, and pepper in a food processor; process until smooth. Spoon spinach mixture into a medium bowl. Stir in yogurt and Parmesan. Cover and chill. Serve with crudités or hearty wheat crackers. Yield: 2 cups (serving size: ¼ cup).

CALORIES 63 (60% from fat); FAT 4.2g (sat 2.3g, mono 1.4g, poly 0.2g); PROTEIN 4.1g; CARB 3g; FIBER 0.9g; CHOL 11mg; IRON 1.1mg; SODIUM 209mg; CALC 112mg

Wild Mushroom and Artichoke Dip

Brimming with meaty portobello mushrooms and chopped artichoke hearts, this hot dip can hold its own alongside meat appetizers on a holiday appetizer buffet.

Prep: 14 minutes • Cook: 36 minutes

  1 teaspoon olive oil
  2 cups sliced shiitake mushroom caps
      (about 4 ounces)
  1 (6-ounce) package presliced
      portobello mushrooms, chopped
  ½ cup low-fat mayonnaise
  ¼ cup (1 ounce) grated fresh
      Parmesan cheese
  ¼ cup finely chopped celery
  ¼ cup finely chopped onion
  ¼ cup thinly sliced green onions
  2 tablespoons chopped fresh parsley
  1 teaspoon garlic powder
  1 teaspoon black pepper
  ¾ teaspoon salt
  ¼ teaspoon ground red pepper
  1 (14-ounce) can artichoke hearts,
      drained and coarsely chopped
  1 (8-ounce) block ⅓-less-fat cream
      cheese
  1 (8-ounce) block fat-free cream
      cheese
Cooking spray

1. Preheat oven to 350°.

2. Heat oil in a large nonstick skillet over medium-high heat. Add mushrooms; sauté 5 minutes or until tender. Combine mushrooms, mayonnaise, and remaining ingredients except cooking spray in a large bowl, stirring until well blended.

3. Spoon mixture into a 2-quart casserole coated with cooking spray. Bake at 350° for 30 minutes or until thoroughly heated. Serve with pita chips or toasted

baguette slices. Yield: 5 cups (serving size: ¼ cup).

CALORIES 66 (30% from fat); FAT 2.2g (sat 1g, mono 0.3g, poly 0.1g); PROTEIN 4.5g; CARB 7.6g; FIBER 1.2g; CHOL 6mg; IRON 0.2mg; SODIUM 377mg; CALC 50mg

Cool and Crunchy Crab Dip

While fresh crabmeat makes this dip extraspecial, canned lump crabmeat is a good substitute and can be kept in the pantry to use at a moment's notice.

Prep: 10 minutes

¾ cup fat-free sour cream
½ cup (4 ounces) block-style ⅓-less-fat cream cheese, softened
1 cup finely chopped celery
¼ cup minced fresh chives
¼ cup fat-free Thousand Island dressing
¾ teaspoon salt
1 (8-ounce) container lump crabmeat, drained and shell pieces removed
Chopped fresh chives (optional)

1. Combine sour cream and cream cheese in a large bowl; stir with a whisk until smooth. Stir in celery, minced chives, dressing, and salt. Gently fold in crabmeat. Garnish with chopped chives, if desired. Serve with crackers and raw vegetables. Yield: 3 cups (serving size: ¼ cup).

CALORIES 67 (38% from fat); FAT 2.8g (sat 1.6g, mono 0.7g, poly 0.2g); PROTEIN 5.6g; CARB 4.5g; FIBER 0.4g; CHOL 28mg; IRON 0.2mg; SODIUM 304mg; CALC 54mg

Test Kitchen Tip: The most desirable type of fresh crabmeat is called lump, jumbo, or backfin; the second-best grade consists of smaller pieces of body meat and is called flake crabmeat.

Tapenade

Spread this versatile, thick olive paste from Provence on toasted baguette slices, stir it into pasta, or use it as a sandwich spread or a pizza topping.

Prep: 9 minutes

2 garlic cloves, peeled
2 cups pitted kalamata olives
¼ cup capers
2 canned anchovy fillets
¼ cup finely chopped fresh parsley

1. With food processor on, drop garlic through food chute; process until minced. Add olives, capers, and anchovies; process until finely chopped. Add parsley; pulse to combine. Yield: 1¼ cups (serving size: 2 tablespoons).

CALORIES 56 (80% from fat); FAT 5g (sat 0.6g, mono 3.8g, poly 0.6g); PROTEIN 0.7g; CARB 2.2g; FIBER 0.3g; CHOL 1mg; IRON 0.3mg; SODIUM 433mg; CALC 13mg

Test Kitchen Tip: To quickly dislodge the pits from olives, place olives on a cutting surface. Lay the wide, flat side of a heavy chef's knife on top of the olive, and give a good sharp whack to the dull side of the blade with the heel of your hand. The olives will pop open, exposing the pits for easy removal.

To pit a large volume of olives, wrap them in a cloth towel; smack them with a rolling pin or the bottom of a skillet.

Black Bean Spread with Lime and Cilantro

Fresh lime juice and cilantro dress up canned black beans for an easy, delicious appetizer. Serve the spread with baked tortilla chips, and use any remaining spread in quesadillas or burritos.

Prep: 7 minutes

3 garlic cloves, peeled
½ cup chopped fresh cilantro
2 tablespoons fresh lime juice
1½ tablespoons extravirgin olive oil
½ teaspoon salt
1 (15-ounce) can black beans, rinsed and drained
1 (15-ounce) can black beans, undrained
Cilantro sprig (optional)

1. With food processor on, drop garlic through food chute; process until minced. Add chopped cilantro and next 5 ingredients, and process until smooth. Garnish with cilantro sprig, if desired. Serve with baked tortilla chips. Yield: 2½ cups (serving size: ¼ cup).

CALORIES 64 (28% from fat); FAT 2g (sat 0.3g, mono 1.5g, poly 0.2g); PROTEIN 3.2g; CARB 11.2g; FIBER 3.8g; CHOL 0mg; IRON 1.2mg; SODIUM 325mg; CALC 28mg

Test Kitchen Tip: Rinse and drain only one can of beans; leave the other one undrained. The liquid from one can helps to thin the spread to a nice consistency.

Smoked Trout Spread

Thanks to the richness of the smoked trout, there's no need to add a lot of seasoning. Look for smoked trout in the same section of the grocery store that has fresh fish.

Prep: 9 minutes

1   (8-ounce) package smoked trout
½   cup fat-free sour cream
⅓   cup low-fat mayonnaise
⅓   cup finely chopped red onion
⅓   cup shredded carrot
⅓   cup finely chopped green bell
    pepper

1. Remove and discard skin from fish; finely chop fish.

2. Place fish, sour cream, and mayonnaise in a medium bowl, and mash with a fork. Stir in onion, carrot, and bell pepper. Serve with bagel chips, Melba toasts, or toasted baguette slices. Yield: 2 cups (serving size: ¼ cup).

CALORIES 77 (29% from fat); FAT 2.5g (sat 0.7g, mono 0.6g, poly 0.9g); PROTEIN 6.9g; CARB 6.5g; FIBER 0.3g; CHOL 18mg; IRON 0.1mg; SODIUM 534mg; CALC 26mg

Country Chicken Pâté

We kept the smooth texture of this lightened classic by using low-fat sour cream and fat-free cream cheese instead of a lot of butter and heavy cream. Serve this rich appetizer with a French bread baguette, coarse-grained mustard, and gherkins.

**Prep: 14 minutes • Cook: 1 hour, 10 minutes
Other: 8 hours**

1   teaspoon butter
½   cup finely chopped onion
2   garlic cloves, chopped
4   ounces chicken livers
2   tablespoons port or other sweet red
    wine
½   teaspoon salt
½   teaspoon pepper
¼   teaspoon dried thyme
¼   teaspoon ground nutmeg
Dash of ground cinnamon
Dash of ground allspice
1   tablespoon low-fat sour cream
1   pound skinless, boneless chicken
    breast, cut into ½-inch pieces
1   (8-ounce) block fat-free cream cheese,
    cubed and softened
Cooking spray

1. Preheat oven to 325°.
2. Melt butter in a small nonstick skillet over medium heat. Add onion and garlic, and sauté 4 minutes. Add chicken livers; cook 2 minutes or until livers lose their pink color. Add port, and cook 3 minutes or until most of liquid evaporates. Cool.
3. Place chicken liver mixture, salt, and next 5 ingredients in a food processor or blender; process until smooth, scraping sides of bowl occasionally. Add sour cream, chicken breast, and cream cheese; process until smooth, scraping sides of bowl occasionally. Spread chicken mixture into an

8 x 4–inch loaf pan coated with cooking spray. Bake at 325° for 1 hour or until a thermometer registers 170°. Cool; cover and chill 8 hours. Serve at room temperature. Yield: 10 servings (serving size: 1 slice).

CALORIES 95 (16% from fat); FAT 1.7g (sat 0.7g, mono 0.4g, poly 0.3g); PROTEIN 15.9g; CARB 2.4g; FIBER 0.2g; CHOL 82mg; IRON 1.4mg; SODIUM 297mg; CALC 76mg

Grilled Corn and Vidalia Onion Salsa

The sweetness of summer abounds in this fresh salsa.

Prep: 13 minutes • Cook: 30 minutes

    4 ears shucked corn
    1 Vidalia or other sweet onion, cut
       into ½-inch-thick slices
       Cooking spray
    ¼ cup finely chopped fresh cilantro
 1 ¼ cups chopped seeded yellow tomato
    3 tablespoons rice vinegar
    ½ teaspoon kosher salt
    ½ teaspoon crushed red pepper
    ½ teaspoon freshly ground black pepper

1. Prepare grill or preheat broiler.
2. Place corn on grill rack or on a broiler pan; cook 20 minutes or until corn is lightly browned, turning every 5 minutes. Cool. Cut kernels from corn to measure 3 cups. Place onion on grill rack or on a broiler pan coated with cooking spray; cook 5 minutes on each side. Cool onion; chop.
3. Combine corn, onion, and remaining ingredients in a large bowl, and toss well to combine. Serve with baked tortilla chips. Yield: 4 cups (serving size: 1 cup).

CALORIES 102 (12% from fat); FAT 1.4g (sat 0.2g, mono 0.4g, poly 0.6g); PROTEIN 3.8g; CARB 22.5g; FIBER 3.8g; CHOL 0mg; IRON 0.9mg; SODIUM 255mg; CALC 13mg

Three-Fruit Salsa

Tropical ingredients and Thai flavorings blend to create a unique salsa.

Prep: 14 minutes

    1 cup finely chopped peeled
       cantaloupe
    1 cup finely chopped peeled mango
    1 cup sliced small strawberries
    ½ cup finely chopped seeded peeled
       cucumber
    ½ cup finely chopped green bell pepper
    ½ cup finely chopped red onion
    2 tablespoons finely chopped seeded
       jalapeño pepper
 1 ½ tablespoons chopped fresh mint
    1 tablespoon chopped fresh basil
    2 tablespoons fresh lime juice
    1 tablespoon honey
    ¼ teaspoon salt

1. Combine all ingredients in a bowl. Serve salsa with a slotted spoon. Serve with chips or over grilled fish or pork. Yield: 4½ cups (serving size: about ¾ cup).

CALORIES 59 (6% from fat); FAT 0.4g (sat 0.1g, mono 0.1g, poly 0.1g); PROTEIN 1g; CARB 14.7g; FIBER 2.1g; CHOL 0mg; IRON 0.5mg; SODIUM 103mg; CALC 19mg

Avocado Salsa

You can store an uncut ripe avocado in the refrigerator for two to three days.

Prep: 7 minutes

    ½ cup finely chopped peeled avocado
    ⅓ cup chopped seeded tomato
    2 tablespoons finely chopped onion
    1 tablespoon finely chopped seeded
       jalapeño pepper
    1 tablespoon chopped fresh cilantro
    1 tablespoon fresh lime juice
    ⅛ teaspoon salt

1. Combine all ingredients, and toss mixture gently. Serve immediately with baked tortilla chips. Yield: 1 cup (serving size: about 2½ tablespoons).

CALORIES 59 (79% from fat); FAT 5.2g (sat 0.8g, mono 3.2g, poly 0.7g); PROTEIN 0.8g; CARB 3.7g; FIBER 1.9g; CHOL 0mg; IRON 0.5mg; SODIUM 54mg; CALC 6mg

Granny Smith-Green Chile Salsa

In New Mexico, apples are often paired with green chiles to create a tart and spicy-hot flavor combination.

Prep: 12 minutes • Cook: 13 minutes

    2 large tomatillos (about 4 ounces)
    1 cup chopped Granny Smith apple
    ½ cup chopped onion
    ½ cup chopped Roasted Anaheim
       Chiles (page 465)
    3 tablespoons chopped fresh cilantro
    3 tablespoons fresh lime juice
    ¼ teaspoon salt
    ¼ teaspoon white pepper

1. Discard husks and stems of tomatillos. Cook tomatillos in boiling water 10 minutes or until tender. Drain.
2. Place tomatillos in a blender; process until smooth. Combine tomatillo puree, apple, and remaining ingredients. Serve with baked tortilla chips. Yield: 2 cups (serving size: ⅓ cup).

(Totals include Roasted Anaheim Chiles) CALORIES 42 (11% from fat); FAT 0.5g (sat 0.1g, mono 0.1g, poly 0.3g); PROTEIN 1.6g; CARB 9.5g; FIBER 3.4g; CHOL 0mg; IRON 0.5mg; SODIUM 108mg; CALC 16mg

For additional salsa recipes, see pages 455-456 in the Sauces & Condiments chapter.

Snacks & Chips

When you need a crispy dipper or a crunchy snack, these recipes are sure to satisfy. And they boast the benefit of being low in fat.

Crisp and Spicy Snack Mix

If you haven't gobbled up all this savory snack mix before dinner, use what's left as a crunchy salad topping.

Prep: 17 minutes • Cook: 30 minutes

  2 cups crisscross of corn and rice cereal (such as Crispix)
  1 cup tiny pretzel twists
  ½ cup reduced-fat wheat crackers (such as Wheat Thins)
  ½ cup reduced-fat Cheddar crackers (such as Cheez-It)
1½ tablespoons butter, melted
  1 tablespoon ginger stir-fry sauce (such as Lawry's)
  1 teaspoon chili powder
  1 teaspoon ground cumin
  ¼ teaspoon salt
Cooking spray

1. Preheat oven to 250°.
2. Combine first 4 ingredients in a bowl. Combine butter, stir-fry sauce, chili powder, cumin, and salt; drizzle over cereal mixture, tossing to coat. Spread mixture into a jelly-roll pan coated with cooking spray. Bake at 250° for 30 minutes or until crisp, stirring twice. Yield: 4 cups (serving size: ½ cup).

CALORIES 117 (30% from fat); FAT 3.9g (sat 1.7g, mono 0.7g, poly 0.5g); PROTEIN 2.2g; CARB 18.5g; FIBER 0.8g; CHOL 6mg; IRON 2.6mg; SODIUM 368mg; CALC 17mg

Asian Party Mix

Sesame rice crackers and wasabi peas add crunch and fire to this old favorite. Look for dried green peas coated with wasabi in Asian markets or gourmet markets that have bins of nuts and snack foods.

Prep: 10 minutes • Cook: 47 minutes

2 cups crispy corn cereal squares (such as Corn Chex)
2 cups crispy rice cereal squares (such as Rice Chex)
2 cups sesame rice crackers, broken
1 cup tiny pretzel twists
¾ cup wasabi peas
¼ cup lightly salted dry-roasted peanuts
3 tablespoons unsalted butter
1 tablespoon sugar
1 tablespoon curry powder
1 tablespoon low-sodium soy sauce
1 teaspoon Worcestershire sauce
½ teaspoon garlic powder
½ teaspoon ground cumin
¼ teaspoon salt
¼ teaspoon ground red pepper
Cooking spray

1. Preheat oven to 200°.
2. Combine first 6 ingredients in a large bowl; set aside.
3. Melt butter in a small saucepan over medium heat. Add sugar and next 7 ingredients, stirring with a whisk. Pour butter mixture over cereal mixture, tossing gently to coat. Spread mixture on a jelly-roll pan coated with cooking spray. Bake at 200° for 45 minutes. Cool completely before serving. Yield: 8 cups (serving size: ½ cup).

CALORIES 116 (29% from fat); FAT 3.7g (sat 1.6g, mono 1.3g, poly 0.6g); PROTEIN 2.9g; CARB 18.6g; FIBER 1.2g; CHOL 6mg; IRON 2.8mg; SODIUM 269mg; CALC 38mg

Pita Crisps

Pita bread chips are an ideal accompaniment for dips and salads. Try these with Spiced Red Lentil Dip (page 34).

Prep: 5 minutes • Cook: 20 minutes

4 (6-inch) pitas, each cut into 5 wedges
Cooking spray
⅛ teaspoon fine sea salt
⅛ teaspoon freshly ground black pepper

1. Preheat oven to 350°.
2. Coat 1 side of each pita wedge with cooking spray; sprinkle wedges evenly with ⅛ teaspoon salt and pepper. Arrange in a single layer on a baking sheet. Bake at 350° for 20 minutes or until golden. Yield: 10 servings (serving size: 2 pita crisps).

CALORIES 66 (4% from fat); FAT 0.3g (sat 0g, mono 0g, poly 0.1g); PROTEIN 2.2g; CARB 13.4g; FIBER 0.5g; CHOL 0mg; IRON 0.6mg; SODIUM 186mg; CALC 21mg

Spiced Parmesan Cheese Crisps

Transform basic egg roll wrappers into crispy cheese-flavored snacks. Serve these sturdy chips with hearty Wild Mushroom and Artichoke Dip (page 36).

Prep: 10 minutes • Cook: 5 minutes

10 egg roll wrappers
Cooking spray
2 large egg whites, lightly beaten
1 cup (4 ounces) grated fresh Parmesan cheese
1 teaspoon dried oregano
1 teaspoon dried basil
½ teaspoon ground red pepper

1. Preheat oven to 425°.

2. Place egg roll wrappers in a single layer on baking sheets coated with cooking spray. Lightly brush with egg whites; cut each wrapper into 8 wedges. Combine cheese and remaining 3 ingredients; sprinkle evenly over wedges. Bake at 425° for 5 minutes or until lightly browned. Yield: 20 servings (serving size: 4 crisps).

CALORIES 75 (24% from fat); FAT 2g (sat 1.1g, mono 0.5g, poly 0.1g); PROTEIN 4.3g; CARB 9.6g; FIBER 0.4g; CHOL 6mg; IRON 0.7mg; SODIUM 203mg; CALC 88mg

Rosemary Pita Chips

Take plain pita chips up a notch by adding rosemary and garlic powder. Serve these chips with White Bean and Bacon Dip (page 34).

Prep: 5 minutes • Cook: 20 minutes

½ teaspoon dried crushed rosemary
¼ teaspoon salt
¼ teaspoon garlic powder
⅛ teaspoon freshly ground black pepper
3 (6-inch) pitas, each cut into 8 wedges
Cooking spray

1. Preheat oven to 350°.
2. Combine first 4 ingredients. Arrange pita wedges in a single layer on a baking sheet. Coat wedges with cooking spray; sprinkle with rosemary mixture. Lightly recoat wedges with cooking spray. Bake at 350° for 20 minutes or until golden. Yield: 12 servings (serving size: 2 chips).

CALORIES 42 (4% from fat); FAT 0.2g (sat 0g, mono 0g, poly 0.1g); PROTEIN 1.4g; CARB 8.4g; FIBER 0.4g; CHOL 0mg; IRON 0.4mg; SODIUM 130mg; CALC 14mg

Test Kitchen Tip: Store remaining pita chips in a zip-top plastic bag or other airtight container.

Bruschetta & Crostini

Whether thick or thin, these "tiny toasts" are usually brushed with olive oil, rubbed with garlic, and sprinkled with toppings such as cheese, tomato, and herbs.

Bruschetta Gorgonzola and Apples

We used Gorgonzola for its creaminess, but any quality blue cheese will do.

Prep: 15 minutes • Cook: 4 minutes

- ⅓ cup (about 1½ ounces) crumbled Gorgonzola cheese
- 2 tablespoons butter, softened
- 1 tablespoon brandy or cognac
- ⅛ teaspoon pepper
- 12 (1-ounce) slices diagonally cut French bread (about 1 inch thick)
- Cooking spray
- 6 garlic cloves, halved
- 3 Granny Smith apples, each cut into 8 wedges (about 18 ounces)

1. Prepare grill.

2. Combine first 4 ingredients in a small bowl, stirring until blended.

3. Place bread on grill rack coated with cooking spray; cook 2 minutes on each side or until lightly browned. Remove from grill. Rub cut sides of garlic over one side of each bread slice. Spread 2 teaspoons cheese mixture over each bread slice. Serve with apple wedges. Yield: 12 servings (serving size: 1 bruschetta and 2 apple wedges).

CALORIES 148 (30% from fat); FAT 5g (sat 2.7g, mono 0.9g, poly 0.3g); PROTEIN 4.1g; CARB 21.4g; FIBER 1.7g; CHOL 13mg; IRON 0.9mg; SODIUM 263mg; CALC 68mg

Caponata with Garlic Crostini

This Sicilian-style appetizer will keep in the refrigerator up to two days. Serve at room temperature to bring out the flavor of the eggplant, sweet peppers, and garlic.

Prep: 30 minutes • Cook: 16 minutes

Caponata:
- 1 tablespoon olive oil
- 4 cups diced eggplant (about 1 pound)
- 1 cup coarsely chopped Vidalia or other sweet onion
- ½ cup diced red bell pepper
- ½ cup diced yellow bell pepper
- 1 garlic clove, minced
- 1 tablespoon brown sugar
- 2 tablespoons fresh lemon juice
- ½ teaspoon salt
- ¼ cup golden raisins
- 2 tablespoons capers, drained
- 1 tablespoon pine nuts, toasted
- 2 tablespoons chopped fresh or 2 teaspoons dried basil

Crostini:
- 24 (½-inch-thick) slices diagonally cut French bread baguette (about 10 ounces)
- 1 garlic clove, halved
- Olive oil-flavored cooking spray

1. Preheat oven to 375°.

2. To prepare caponata, heat oil in a large nonstick skillet over medium-high heat. Add eggplant, onion, bell peppers, and minced garlic; sauté 5 minutes. Stir in sugar, lemon juice, and salt; cook 1 minute. Stir in raisins, capers, and pine nuts. Place eggplant mixture in a large bowl; stir in basil.

3. To prepare crostini, place bread slices on a baking sheet. Bake at 375° for 7 minutes or until toasted. Rub cut sides of garlic clove over one side of each bread slice. Coat bread slices with cooking spray, and bake an additional 2 minutes. Serve caponata with crostini. Yield: 8 servings (serving size: ⅓ cup caponata and 3 crostini).

CALORIES 174 (20% from fat); FAT 3.8g (sat 0.6g, mono 2g, poly 0.8g); PROTEIN 4.9g; CARB 31.4g; FIBER 3.2g; CHOL 0mg; IRON 1.6mg; SODIUM 552mg; CALC 44mg

Caponata with Garlic Crostini

Goat Cheese, Roasted Garlic, and Tomato Croutes

When you roast garlic, its flavor becomes unbelievably mellow and buttery.
For a more authentic approach, rub the cut side of a raw garlic clove on the toasted
bread slices. Serve cheese and tomatoes on the side.

Prep: 11 minutes • Cook: 45 minutes • Other: 10 minutes

1 whole garlic head
Cooking spray
3 plum tomatoes, each cut into 4 wedges
½ cup (2 ounces) crumbled goat cheese
12 (½-inch-thick) slices diagonally cut French bread
   baguette, toasted

1. Preheat oven to 425°.
2. Remove white papery skin from garlic head (do not peel or separate cloves). Wrap garlic head in foil. Line a baking sheet with foil; coat foil with cooking spray. Arrange tomato wedges in a single layer on foil. Bake garlic and tomatoes at 425° for 40 minutes, turning tomatoes after 20 minutes. Remove tomatoes from oven; bake garlic an additional 5 minutes. Remove garlic from oven; cool 10 minutes. Separate cloves; squeeze to extract garlic pulp. Discard skins. Mash garlic pulp and goat cheese with a fork until blended.
3. Spread 2 teaspoons goat cheese mixture over each bread slice. Top each with 1 tomato wedge. Yield: 6 servings (serving size: 2 croutes).

CALORIES 135 (23% from fat); FAT 3.4g (sat 1.7g, mono 0.9g, poly 0.5g); PROTEIN 5g; CARB 21.4g; FIBER 1.5g; CHOL 8mg; IRON 1.2mg; SODIUM 298mg; CALC 90mg

high-flavor cheeses

high-flavor cheeses Here's a rundown of some of our favorite high-flavor cheeses.

Blue Cheese can be made from goat's, cow's, or sheep's milk, but its potent punch and distinctive flavor drives people to love or hate it.

Brie has an earthy and slightly musty or mushroomy flavor. Its buttery taste pairs nicely with sharp, tangy foods.

Feta is best known for its pungent, salty flavor and versatility. Greek feta is more textured and crumbly than French feta, but we use both.

Goat cheese has a mild, salty, acidic flavor and ranges from soft and spreadable to dry and crumbly. It can be found in cones, discs, or logs, which are sometimes rolled in herbs. There are milder goat cheeses similar in flavor and texture to Parmesan and Cheddar; there is also a ricotta-like fromage blanc, and a surface-ripened goat cheese similar to Brie.

Gruyère is a nutty Swiss cheese that pairs well with both sweet and savory dishes.

Parmesan is a hard, dry Italian cheese that has a sharp taste. Using a small amount of Parmesan will boost the flavor and aroma of any dish and will even become more enticing as the cheese melts. For the very best flavor, look for the real thing: Parmesan-Reggiano. It has a sharper flavor and more crumbly texture than domestic Parmesan. For authentic Parmesan-Reggiano, the words should be stamped on the rind of the cheese.

Beet and Goat Cheese Crostini

The sweet earthiness of roasted beets complements the sharpness of goat cheese.

Prep: 20 minutes • Cook: 45 minutes

Beets:

- ¾ pound beets (about 2 medium)
- 1 cup water
- 1 tablespoon balsamic vinegar
- 1 teaspoon grated lemon rind
- 1 teaspoon fresh lemon juice
- ¼ teaspoon sea salt
- ¼ teaspoon freshly ground black pepper

Cheese spread:

- 1 (5-ounce) package goat cheese
- 1 tablespoon light mayonnaise
- 2 teaspoons minced fresh tarragon
- ⅛ teaspoon freshly ground black pepper
- 1 garlic clove, minced
- 24 (½-inch-thick) slices diagonally cut French bread baguette, toasted

1. Preheat oven to 375°.
2. To prepare beets, leave root and 1 inch of stem on beets; scrub with a brush. Place beets in an 11 x 7–inch baking dish; add 1 cup water to dish. Cover and bake at 375° for 45 minutes or until tender. Drain and cool. Trim off beet roots; rub off skins. Cut beets lengthwise into quarters, and cut each quarter crosswise into 9 (⅛-inch) slices.
3. Combine vinegar, rind, juice, salt, and ¼ teaspoon pepper in a medium bowl. Add beets; toss gently to coat.
4. To prepare cheese spread, combine goat cheese and next 4 ingredients. Spread 1 teaspoon cheese mixture over each baguette; top with 3 beet slices. Yield: 12 servings (serving size: 2 crostini).

CALORIES 127 (27% from fat); FAT 3.8g (sat 2g, mono 0.9g, poly 0.3g); PROTEIN 5.2g; CARB 18g; FIBER 1.4g; CHOL 6mg; IRON 1.2mg; SODIUM 297mg; CALC 44mg

Fresh Herbed Heirloom Tomatoes and Goat Cheese Crostini
(pictured on page 31)

Fresh basil and parsley pureed with lemon juice and oil make a lively drizzle for ripe tomatoes. Use a combination of red, green, and yellow tomatoes for a colorful presentation.

Prep: 15 minutes • Cook: 7 minutes

- ¼ cup chopped fresh basil
- ¼ cup chopped fresh parsley
- 2 tablespoons water
- 2 tablespoons fresh lemon juice
- 1 teaspoon extravirgin olive oil
- 8 (¼-inch-thick) slices diagonally cut French bread baguette
- 4 teaspoons goat cheese
- 20 (¼-inch-thick) slices tomato
- ½ teaspoon kosher salt
- ½ teaspoon freshly ground black pepper

1. Preheat oven to 350°.
2. Place first 5 ingredients in a blender; process until smooth.
3. Place baguette slices in a single layer on a baking sheet. Bake at 350° for 7 minutes. Spread ½ teaspoon cheese over each slice.
4. Place 5 tomato slices on each of 4 plates. Drizzle each serving with 1 tablespoon herbed oil. Sprinkle each with ⅛ teaspoon salt and ⅛ teaspoon pepper. Garnish with crostini. Yield: 4 servings (serving size: 5 slices tomato and 2 crostini).

CALORIES 110 (34% from fat); FAT 4.1g (sat 1.2g, mono 1.6g, poly 1g); PROTEIN 3.3g; CARB 16.5g; FIBER 2.3g; CHOL 2mg; IRON 1.2mg; SODIUM 350mg; CALC 25mg

Cold Appetizers

Make-ahead appetizers simplify party preparations. Dishes such as marinated olives, stuffed endive, and savory cheesecake are ready when you are.

Lemon-Macerated Okra and Olives

Offer these zesty morsels in place of peanuts or pretzels at your next party. Or combine with bread, cheese, artichokes, and cold shrimp for an antipasto platter.

Prep: 10 minutes • Other: 48 hours

   3   cups small okra pods
   ½   cup kalamata olives
   1   tablespoon grated lemon rind
   ¼   cup fresh lemon juice
   2   tablespoons extravirgin olive oil
   ½   teaspoon kosher salt
   ½   teaspoon crushed red pepper
   2   garlic cloves, thinly sliced
   2   bay leaves
   2   thyme sprigs

1. Combine all ingredients in a large zip-top plastic bag, and seal. Marinate in refrigerator 48 to 72 hours, turning bag occasionally. Strain okra mixture through a sieve over a bowl; discard marinade, bay leaves, and thyme sprigs. Yield: 14 servings (serving size: ¼ cup).

CALORIES 29 (65% from fat); FAT 2.1g (sat 0.3g, mono 1.6g, poly 0.2g); PROTEIN 0.5g; CARB 2.4g; FIBER 0.8g; CHOL 0mg; IRON 0.2mg; SODIUM 105mg; CALC 20mg

Test Kitchen Tip: One medium lemon usually yields 2 to 3 tablespoons of juice. To get more juice, microwave the lemons for about 30 to 40 seconds or until warm to the touch. Another method is to let the lemons sit on the countertop to bring them to room temperature. Then gently roll the lemons on the countertop to soften them.

Curried Chickpea Canapés with Ginger-Carrot Butter

Look for chickpea flour in supermarkets along with other types of flour or in health food stores. You can also use the same amount of dry polenta or grits.

**Prep: 30 minutes • Cook: 1 hour, 8 minutes
Other: 1 hour**

Canapés:
    1   cup chickpea flour
2⅔   cups cold water
    ¾   teaspoon fine sea salt
    Cooking spray
    1   tablespoon curry powder

Butter:
2⅓   cups thinly sliced carrot
    2   cups water
    1   tablespoon butter
    1   tablespoon honey
    2   teaspoons minced peeled fresh ginger
    1   tablespoon fresh lemon juice
    ¼   teaspoon fine sea salt
    ⅛   teaspoon white pepper
Remaining ingredients:
    2   tablespoons sliced almonds, toasted
    2   tablespoons chopped fresh cilantro

1. To prepare canapés, lightly spoon flour into a dry measuring cup; level with a knife. Combine flour, 2⅔ cups water, and ¾ teaspoon salt in a medium saucepan; stir. Bring to a boil, stirring constantly. Cover, reduce heat, and simmer 20 minutes. Uncover; stir until smooth. Pour into an 11 x 7–inch baking dish coated with cooking spray; sprinkle evenly with curry powder. Chill 1 hour or until firm.
2. Preheat oven to 375°.
3. Cut chickpea mixture into 40 (1-inch) squares; place on a jelly-roll pan coated with cooking spray. Bake at 375° for 20 minutes or until golden. Cool.

4. To prepare butter, combine carrot and next 4 ingredients in a saucepan. Bring to a boil. Cover, reduce heat, and simmer 7 minutes or until carrot is tender. Increase heat to medium-high; uncover and cook 12 minutes or until liquid evaporates.
5. Place carrot mixture, lemon juice, ¼ teaspoon salt, and pepper in a food processor; process until smooth. Place carrot butter in a zip-top plastic bag; seal. Snip a small hole in 1 corner of bag; pipe about 1 teaspoon carrot butter onto each canapé. Sprinkle canapés evenly with almonds and cilantro. Yield: 20 servings (serving size: 2 canapés).

CALORIES 36 (30% from fat); FAT 1.2g (sat 0.4g, mono 0.4g, poly 0.1g); PROTEIN 1.2g; CARB 5.5g; FIBER 0.8g; CHOL 2mg; IRON 0.5mg; SODIUM 127mg; CALC 13mg

Marinated Spanish Olives

You can make and refrigerate these piquant olives up to one week ahead.

Prep: 7 minutes • Other: 8 hours

24   large unpitted Spanish olives
    2   tablespoons sherry vinegar
    1   tablespoon extravirgin olive oil
    2   teaspoons coriander seeds, crushed
    1   teaspoon dried thyme
    1   teaspoon dried rosemary, crushed
    ½   teaspoon crushed red pepper
    2   garlic cloves, thinly sliced

1. Combine all ingredients in a bowl. Cover and marinate in refrigerator at least 8 hours. Serve at room temperature. Yield: 6 servings (serving size: 4 olives).

CALORIES 49 (66% from fat); FAT 3.6g (sat 0.1g, mono 2g, poly 1.4g); PROTEIN 0.2g; CARB 3.1g; FIBER 0.2g; CHOL 0mg; IRON 0.4mg; SODIUM 322mg; CALC 13mg

Endive Stuffed with Goat Cheese and Walnuts

Present stuffed endive as a first course appetizer instead of a salad. The sweetness of oranges and honey balances the tartness of the cheese.

Prep: 20 minutes • Cook: 16 minutes

    ⅓   cup coarsely chopped walnuts
    2   tablespoons honey, divided
    Cooking spray
    ¼   cup balsamic vinegar
    3   tablespoons orange juice
16   Belgian endive leaves (about 2 heads)
16   small orange sections (about 2 navel oranges)
    ⅓   cup (1½ ounces) crumbled goat cheese or blue cheese
    1   tablespoon minced fresh chives
    ¼   teaspoon cracked black pepper

1. Preheat oven to 350°.
2. Combine walnuts and 1 tablespoon honey; spread on a baking sheet coated with cooking spray. Bake at 350° for 10 minutes, stirring after 5 minutes.
3. Combine 1 tablespoon honey, vinegar, and orange juice in a small saucepan. Bring to a boil over high heat, and cook until reduced to 3 tablespoons (about 5 minutes).
4. Fill each endive leaf with 1 orange section. Top each section with 1 teaspoon cheese and 1 teaspoon walnuts. Arrange on a plate. Drizzle vinegar mixture evenly over leaves, and sprinkle evenly with chives and pepper. Yield: 8 servings (serving size: 2 stuffed leaves).

CALORIES 92 (44% from fat); FAT 4.5g (sat 1.1g, mono 0.7g, poly 2.4g); PROTEIN 2.5g; CARB 11.9g; FIBER 2g; CHOL 3mg; IRON 0.6mg; SODIUM 29mg; CALC 43mg

Savory Yogurt Cheesecake with Caramelized Onions

You can serve a slice of this cheesecake as a first-course appetizer, or on an appetizer buffet with crackers or toasted baguette slices. A bonus for this recipe is that one serving provides about one-fourth of the recommended daily amount of calcium for adults up to age 50.

Prep: 25 minutes • Cook: 1 hour, 30 minutes • Other: 12 hours

Filling:

- 1 (32-ounce) carton plain low-fat yogurt
- ½ cup (4 ounces) block-style fat-free cream cheese, softened
- 1 cup part-skim ricotta cheese
- ½ teaspoon salt
- ¼ teaspoon freshly ground black pepper
- 1 large egg yolk

Crust:

- ½ cup all-purpose flour
- ½ cup yellow cornmeal
- 1 teaspoon sugar
- ½ teaspoon salt
- Dash of freshly ground black pepper
- 2½ tablespoons butter, chilled and cut into small pieces
- ¼ cup ice water
- Cooking spray

Onions:

- 1 teaspoon butter
- 8 cups sliced onion (about 1½ pounds)
- 1 tablespoon sugar
- ½ teaspoon salt
- ¼ teaspoon freshly ground black pepper
- 1 teaspoon dried thyme

1. To prepare filling, place colander in a 2-quart glass measure or medium bowl. Line colander with 4 layers of cheesecloth, allowing cheesecloth to extend over outside edges. Spoon yogurt into colander. Cover loosely with plastic wrap; refrigerate 12 hours.

2. Spoon 1¾ cups yogurt cheese into a bowl; discard liquid. Place cream cheese in a bowl; beat with a mixer at medium speed until smooth. Add yogurt cheese, ricotta cheese, ½ teaspoon salt, ¼ teaspoon pepper, and egg yolk. Beat at low speed just until blended.

3. Preheat oven to 350°.

4. To prepare crust, lightly spoon flour into a dry measuring cup; level with a knife. Place flour, cornmeal, 1 teaspoon sugar, ½ teaspoon salt, and dash of pepper in a food processor; pulse 3 times or until combined. Add 2½ tablespoons butter; pulse 4 times or until mixture resembles coarse meal. With processor on, add ice water through food chute, processing just until moist (do not form a ball). Press cornmeal mixture into bottom of an 8-inch springform pan coated with cooking spray. Bake at 350° for 15 minutes or until lightly browned. Cool on a wire rack.

5. To prepare onions, while crust bakes and cools, melt 1 teaspoon butter in a large nonstick skillet over medium heat. Add onion; cook 15 minutes, stirring occasionally. Stir in 1 tablespoon sugar, ½ teaspoon salt, and ¼ teaspoon pepper. Cover and cook 25 minutes or until browned and tender, stirring occasionally. Stir in thyme.

6. Spread yogurt mixture into prepared crust. Bake at 350° for 35 minutes or until almost set. Cool on a wire rack. (Cheesecake will continue to set as it cools.) Serve at room temperature. Cut cheesecake into wedges, and serve with onions. Yield: 10 servings (serving size: 1 cheesecake wedge and about 2 tablespoons onions).

CALORIES 198 (30% from fat); FAT 6.5g (sat 3.7g, mono 1.9g, poly 0.4g); PROTEIN 10.2g; CARB 25.6g; FIBER 2.5g; CHOL 37mg; IRON 1.1mg; SODIUM 454mg; CALC 240mg

Tuna Summer Rolls

Seasoned sushi rice replaces rice noodles in these summer rolls. For a dramatic presentation, we suggest slicing the rolls diagonally to give a preview of the ingredients inside.

Prep: 25 minutes • Cook: 25 minutes • Other: 19 minutes

Rolls:

- 1 cup uncooked sushi rice or short-grain rice
- 1¼ cups water
- 2 tablespoons minced peeled fresh ginger
- 2 tablespoons mirin (sweet rice wine)
- 2 teaspoons minced jalapeño pepper
- 2 teaspoons minced shallots
- 1 teaspoon sugar
- 1 teaspoon fish sauce
- ¼ teaspoon salt
- 1 tablespoon low-sodium soy sauce
- 1 teaspoon sugar
- 1 (½-pound) tuna steak
- 8 (8-inch) round sheets rice paper
- 2 cups trimmed watercress

Sauce:

- ¼ cup white vinegar
- 1 tablespoon sugar
- 1 tablespoon fish sauce
- 1½ teaspoons minced shallots
- 1 teaspoon minced jalapeño pepper

1. To prepare rolls, rinse rice thoroughly in a sieve. Drain well. Bring 1¼ cups water to a boil in a medium saucepan; add rice. Cover, reduce heat, and simmer 20 minutes or until liquid is absorbed. Remove from heat, and let stand 5 minutes. Stir in ginger and next 6 ingredients.

2. Combine soy sauce and 1 teaspoon sugar; brush over tuna. Marinate in refrigerator 10 minutes. Heat a nonstick skillet over medium-high heat. Add tuna to pan, and cook 1½ minutes on each side or until desired degree of doneness. Cut tuna into 8 (¼-inch-thick) slices.

3. Add hot water to a large, shallow dish to a depth of 1 inch. Place 1 rice paper sheet in dish. Let stand 30 seconds or just until soft.

4. Place softened sheet on a flat surface. Arrange ¼ cup watercress to cover half of sheet, leaving a ½-inch border. Top with ⅓ cup rice mixture; spread evenly. Arrange 1 tuna slice over rice. Fold sides of sheet over filling; starting with filled side, roll up jelly-roll fashion. Repeat procedure with remaining rice paper sheets, watercress, rice mixture, and tuna. Cut each roll in half diagonally.

5. To prepare sauce, combine vinegar and remaining 4 ingredients. Serve rolls with sauce. Yield: 8 servings (serving size: 2 roll halves and 2¼ teaspoons sauce).

CALORIES 149 (3% from fat); FAT 0.5g (sat 0.1g, mono 0.1g, poly 0.1g); PROTEIN 9.1g; CARB 25.6g; FIBER 0.7g; CHOL 13mg; IRON 1.1mg; SODIUM 388mg; CALC 24mg

Cambodian Summer Rolls

The rolling takes a little time, but the results are worth it. If you're entertaining, you might want to have all the ingredients ready, then prepare the rolls while your guests gather in the kitchen.

Prep: 35 minutes • Cook: 8 minutes
Other: 14 minutes

Rolls:

  6 cups water
  1 pound medium shrimp
  6 ounces uncooked rice noodles
 12 (8-inch) round sheets rice paper
 ¼ cup hoisin sauce
  3 cups shredded red leaf lettuce
 ¼ cup thinly sliced fresh basil
 ¼ cup thinly sliced fresh mint

Dipping sauce:

 ⅓ cup low-sodium soy sauce
 ¼ cup water
  2 tablespoons sugar
  2 tablespoons chopped fresh cilantro
  2 tablespoons fresh lime juice
  1 teaspoon minced peeled fresh ginger
  1 teaspoon chile paste with garlic
  1 garlic clove, minced

1. To prepare rolls, bring 6 cups water to a boil in a large saucepan. Add shrimp; cook 3 minutes or until done. Drain and rinse with cold water. Peel shrimp; chill.
2. Place noodles in a large bowl; cover with boiling water. Let stand 8 minutes, and drain.
3. Add hot water to a large, shallow dish to a depth of 1 inch. Place 1 rice paper sheet in water. Let stand 30 seconds or until soft. Place rice paper sheet on a flat surface. Spread 1 teaspoon hoisin sauce in center of sheet; top with 2 to 3 shrimp, ¼ cup lettuce, ¼ cup rice noodles, 1 teaspoon basil, and 1 teaspoon mint. Fold

sides of sheet over filling, roll up jelly-roll fashion, and press seam to seal. Place roll, seam side down, on a serving platter; cover to keep from drying. Repeat procedure with remaining rice paper, hoisin sauce, shrimp, lettuce, rice noodles, basil, and mint.
4. To prepare dipping sauce, combine soy sauce and remaining ingredients; stir. Yield: 12 servings (serving size: 1 roll and about 1½ tablespoons sauce).

CALORIES 140 (5% from fat); FAT 0.8g (sat 0.1g, mono 0.1g, poly 0.3g); PROTEIN 9g; CARB 23.5g; FIBER 0.7g; CHOL 47mg; IRON 1.3mg; SODIUM 385mg; CALC 32mg

Test Kitchen Tip: Don't let the sheet of rice paper stand in the water much longer than two minutes or it will get too wet and start to disintegrate.

rice paper Similar to phyllo dough in texture, rice paper is an edible, translucent paper used to wrap Asian-style ingredients. It can be eaten as is or baked. Look for rice paper in large supermarkets on the shelves of the ethnic foods section or in Asian markets. Sometimes you'll see it labeled as "dried pastry flake." Rice paper comes in sealed packets and will keep indefinitely in the dried state. However, as the papers age they become more brittle and may shatter if dropped. To make them into flexible wrappers for spring or summer rolls, you have to moisten them with water.

Shrimp Ceviche Cocktail

While classic ceviche is usually raw fish marinated in fresh lime juice long enough to give it a cooked texture, these ceviche "cocktails" combine cooked seafood with fresh vegetables, hot sauce, lime juice, and ketchup.

Prep: 30 minutes • Cook: 6 minutes
Other: 1 hour

 ½ cup chopped onion
  6 cups water
 ¾ cup fresh lime juice, divided
  1 pound medium shrimp
  1 cup chopped peeled cucumber
 ½ cup ketchup
 ⅓ cup chopped fresh cilantro
  2 tablespoons Mexican hot sauce
  1 tablespoon olive oil
 ¼ teaspoon salt

1. Place chopped onion in a colander, and rinse with cold water. Drain.
2. Bring 6 cups water and ¼ cup lime juice to a boil in a Dutch oven. Add shrimp; cook 3 minutes or until done. Drain. Rinse with cold water; peel shrimp. Combine shrimp and ½ cup juice in a large bowl. Cover; chill 1 hour. Stir in onion and remaining ingredients. Serve immediately, or cover and chill. Yield: 6 servings (serving size: ½ cup).

CALORIES 138 (25% from fat); FAT 3.8g (sat 0.6g, mono 1.9g, poly 0.8g); PROTEIN 16.2g; CARB 10.8g; FIBER 0.8g; CHOL 115mg; IRON 2.1mg; SODIUM 483mg; CALC 53mg

Hot Appetizers

Our steamy first-course favorites include cheesy stuffed mushrooms, spicy crab cakes, and tender dumplings with dipping sauce.

Jack Quesadillas with Cranberry Salsa

Jack Quesadillas with Cranberry Salsa

For meatless quesadillas, use sautéed vegetables in place of the turkey.

Prep: 20 minutes • Cook: 19 minutes

Cranberry Salsa:

- 1 cup whole-berry cranberry sauce
- ¼ cup chopped fresh cilantro
- 2 tablespoons chopped green onions
- 1 tablespoon fresh lime juice
- ½ teaspoon ground cumin
- 1 Anjou pear, cored and finely diced
- 1 jalapeño pepper, seeded and minced

Quesadillas:

- Cooking spray
- ¼ cup (2-inch) slices green onions
- 1 cup (4 ounces) shredded Monterey Jack cheese with jalapeño peppers
- 8 (8-inch) flour tortillas
- 2 cups chopped cooked turkey
- ½ cup fat-free sour cream

1. To prepare salsa, combine first 7 ingredients. Cover and chill.

2. To prepare quesadillas, heat a large nonstick skillet over medium-high heat. Coat pan with cooking spray. Add onions to pan; sauté 3 minutes or until tender. Remove from pan. Remove pan from heat; reduce heat to medium. Sprinkle 2 tablespoons cheese over each of 4 tortillas. Top each cheese-covered tortilla with one-fourth of onions, ½ cup turkey, 2 tablespoons cheese, and 1 tortilla.

3. Place pan over medium heat. Recoat pan with cooking spray. Add 1 quesadilla to pan; cook 2 minutes on each side or until lightly browned and cheese is melted. Remove quesadilla from pan, and keep warm. Repeat with remaining quesadillas. Cut each quesadilla into 6 wedges. Serve with cranberry salsa and sour cream. Yield:

8 servings (serving size: 3 wedges, about ¼ cup salsa, and 1 tablespoon sour cream).

CALORIES 356 (25% from fat); FAT 9.7g (sat 4.2g, mono 3.5g, poly 1.2g); PROTEIN 19.4g; CARB 47.8g; FIBER 3g; CHOL 42mg; IRON 2.7mg; SODIUM 372mg; CALC 218mg

---

All-Time Favorite

Baked Feta with Marinara

Sweet tomatoes and salty cheese is a hard combination to beat, especially when it's spread warm over crusty bread.

Prep: 8 minutes • Cook: 20 minutes

- 1 teaspoon fresh lemon juice
- ¼ teaspoon crushed red pepper
- 2 garlic cloves, minced
- 1 (14.5-ounce) can diced tomatoes with basil, garlic, and oregano, drained
- 1 (4-ounce) package crumbled feta cheese
- Cooking spray
- 32 (½-inch-thick) slices diagonally cut French bread baguette (about 1 pound), toasted

1. Preheat oven to 350°.

2. Combine first 4 ingredients in a bowl. Sprinkle feta evenly into a 6-inch gratin dish or small shallow baking dish coated with cooking spray. Top with tomato mixture. Bake at 350° for 20 minutes. Serve with bread slices. Yield: 16 servings (serving size: 2 bread slices and 2 tablespoons spread).

CALORIES 107 (20% from fat); FAT 2.4g (sat 1.3g, mono 0.3g, poly 0.2g); PROTEIN 4.1g; CARB 16.9g; FIBER 1g; CHOL 6mg; IRON 1mg; SODIUM 352mg; CALC 72mg

holiday open house When you're selecting dishes for an open house or cocktail party, go for foods that are easy for your guests to eat while standing and aren't too messy. Offer an assortment of hot and cold appetizers, as well as a variety of sweet and savory items. Choose a few make-ahead recipes to simplify your party preparations. If you're serving wine and cocktails, be sure to offer a couple of non-alcoholic beverages as well.

Baked Feta with Marinara

mushrooms

We use mushrooms a lot in our Test Kitchens. Here are some tips for buying and storing.

Choose mushrooms that are firm and unblemished. They should have an earthy, fresh smell, and a firm, moist flesh. When selecting portobellos, look for those with a tight underside and lighter-color gills. If the gill area appears very black and spread out, that's a sign the mushroom has aged beyond its best flavor and texture.

Store fresh mushrooms for three to seven days. Avoid the vegetable bin as well as plastic—high humidity is death for mushrooms. The best storage method is to line a wicker basket with a paper towel, then cover the mushrooms with a slightly damp paper towel and store in the refrigerator.

Clean mushrooms in this way: Remove the stems, discarding or saving stems for a later use. Use a damp paper towel or a soft brush to wipe both sides of the cap. If there are little holes, check to be sure insects have not embedded themselves in the cap. If so, discard those mushrooms.

Dried mushrooms shrivel and their flavor concentrates. Select ones that haven't crumbled and don't look too "dusty." Usually dried mushrooms need to be soaked about 30 minutes in a hot liquid such as water or chicken broth. Drain into a fine sieve lined with paper towels or cheesecloth.

Stuffed Mushrooms

These mushroom bites are packed with breadcrumbs and cheese and baked until tender. When you pop one into your mouth, you'll see why they're irresistible!

Prep: 13 minutes • Cook: 26 minutes

  1 tablespoon butter
 ½ cup finely chopped onion
 ½ cup finely chopped green bell
     pepper
  2 garlic cloves, minced
 ⅔ cup fat-free cottage cheese
  2 teaspoons Worcestershire sauce
 ⅓ cup Italian-seasoned breadcrumbs
 24 button mushroom caps
Cooking spray
 ½ teaspoon paprika
  3 tablespoons grated fresh Parmesan
     cheese

1. Preheat oven to 350°.
2. Melt butter in a nonstick skillet over medium-high heat. Add onion, bell pepper, and garlic; sauté 5 minutes or until tender. Stir in cottage cheese and Worcestershire sauce, stirring until cheese melts. Remove from heat; stir in breadcrumbs. (Mixture will be thick.) Spoon mixture evenly into mushroom caps.
3. Place mushroom caps in an 11 x 7–inch baking dish coated with cooking spray. Sprinkle caps evenly with paprika. Bake at 350° for 20 minutes or until tender. Sprinkle with Parmesan cheese. Yield: 6 servings (serving size: 4 mushrooms).

CALORIES 104 (29% from fat); FAT 3.4g (sat 1.9g, mono 0.9g, poly 0.3g); PROTEIN 8.2g; CARB 11.4g; FIBER 1.7g; CHOL 10mg; IRON 1.3mg; SODIUM 358mg; CALC 75mg

Cumin-Roasted Cauliflower and Pepper Skewers

Roasting the cauliflower amplifies its flavor, while the cumin, crushed red pepper, and cilantro contribute spicy heat to these vegetable skewers.

Prep: 20 minutes • Cook: 25 minutes

  3 tablespoons fresh lemon juice
  1 tablespoon extravirgin olive oil
  1 teaspoon fine sea salt
  1 teaspoon ground cumin
  1 teaspoon ground coriander seeds
 ½ teaspoon cumin seeds
 ½ teaspoon crushed red pepper
 30 cauliflower florets (about 1
     medium head)
  1 large yellow bell pepper, cut into
     15 (1-inch) squares
  1 large red bell pepper, cut into 15
     (1-inch) squares
 ½ cup chopped fresh cilantro

1. Preheat oven to 450°.
2. Combine first 7 ingredients in a large bowl, stirring with a whisk. Add cauliflower and bell pepper squares; toss gently to coat.
3. Spoon vegetables into a single layer on a jelly-roll pan. Bake at 450° for 25 minutes or until lightly browned and crisp-tender, stirring after 15 minutes. Cool completely; stir in cilantro.
4. Thread 1 cauliflower floret and 1 bell pepper square onto each of 30 (6-inch) skewers. Yield: 15 servings (serving size: 2 skewers).

CALORIES 25 (40% from fat); FAT 1.1g (sat 0.1g, mono 0.7g, poly 0.1g); PROTEIN 1g; CARB 3.6g; FIBER 1.5g; CHOL 0mg; IRON 0.4mg; SODIUM 167mg; CALC 15mg

Brown Rice-Stuffed Grape Leaves in Tomato Sauce

This appetizer is a version of Greek *dolmades*. You can stuff the grape leaves ahead, and reheat them in tomato sauce just before serving.

Prep: 30 minutes • Cook: 1 hour, 28 minutes

    4 cups water
    1 cup uncooked long-grain brown rice
   ½ teaspoon salt
    2 teaspoons canola oil
    1 cup thinly sliced leek (about 1 large)
    1 garlic clove, minced
    2 tablespoons chopped fresh flat-leaf
       parsley
    2 tablespoons chopped toasted pine
       nuts
    2 tablespoons dried currants
    1 tablespoon chopped fresh dill
    1 tablespoon fresh lemon juice
   ½ teaspoon grated lemon rind
   ½ teaspoon dried savory
   ⅛ teaspoon salt
   ¼ teaspoon pepper, divided
    1 (14.5-ounce) can crushed
       tomatoes, undrained
   24 bottled large grape leaves

1. Bring water to a boil in a medium saucepan; add rice and ½ teaspoon salt. Cover, reduce heat, and simmer 40 minutes or until liquid is absorbed. Remove from heat; uncover and cool rice to room temperature.
2. Heat oil in a large nonstick skillet over medium-low heat. Add leek; cook 10 minutes or until tender, stirring frequently (do not brown). Add garlic; cook 1 minute. Reserve ¼ cup leek mixture; stir remaining leek mixture into rice. Stir parsley and next 7 ingredients into rice mixture. Add ⅛ teaspoon pepper.

3. Combine reserved ¼ cup leek mixture, tomatoes, and ⅛ teaspoon black pepper in pan; bring to a boil. Reduce heat; simmer 10 minutes. Remove from heat; set aside.
4. Rinse grape leaves with cold water; drain well. Pat dry with paper towels. Remove stems; discard. Spoon 1 rounded tablespoon rice mixture onto center of each grape leaf. Bring 2 opposite points of leaf to center; fold over filling. Beginning at one short side, roll up leaf tightly, jelly-roll fashion.
5. Nestle stuffed grape leaves, seam sides down, in tomato sauce. Cover; cook over medium-low heat 20 minutes or until heated. Yield: 8 servings (serving size: 3 stuffed leaves and about ¼ cup sauce).

CALORIES 150 (23% from fat); FAT 3.8g (sat 0.4g, mono 1.4g, poly 1.5g); PROTEIN 4g; CARB 26.9g; FIBER 2.9g; CHOL 0mg; IRON 1.9mg; SODIUM 601mg; CALC 73mg

Test Kitchen Tip: Look for bottled grape leaves in Greek or Italian markets, or with the Mediterranean foods or olives in supermarkets.

how to assemble the leaves

To assemble the grape leaves, mound 1 rounded tablespoon of the rice filling onto the center of each leaf. Fold the sides over the filling, then roll up from the bottom of the leaf.

Green Onion Pancakes with Tomato-Avocado Salsa

Serve these fluffy pancakes and their lively salsa as a first course or as a side dish.

Prep: 20 minutes • Cook: 6 minutes
Other: 10 minutes

Tomato-Avocado Salsa:

1⅔ cups chopped seeded plum tomato
½ cup finely chopped red onion
½ cup diced peeled avocado
2 tablespoons finely chopped seeded jalapeño pepper
2 tablespoons red wine vinegar
1 teaspoon minced fresh oregano
⅛ teaspoon salt
⅛ teaspoon freshly ground black pepper
Dash of sugar

Pancakes:

1½ cups all-purpose flour
2 teaspoons sugar
1 teaspoon baking powder
1 teaspoon baking soda
½ teaspoon salt
⅛ teaspoon freshly ground black pepper
1½ cups low-fat buttermilk
1 large egg, lightly beaten
1 cup chopped green onions
6 tablespoons (1½ ounces) shredded sharp provolone cheese
Cooking spray

1. To prepare salsa, combine first 9 ingredients in a bowl. Cover and chill.
2. To prepare pancakes, lightly spoon flour into dry measuring cups; level with a knife. Combine flour and next 5 ingredients in a bowl; make a well in center of mixture. Combine buttermilk and egg; add to flour mixture. Stir just until moist. Let stand 10 minutes. Fold in green onions and shredded cheese.

3. For each pancake, spoon ¼ cup batter onto a hot nonstick griddle or skillet coated with cooking spray. Turn pancakes when tops are covered with bubbles and edges look cooked (about 3 minutes). Serve salsa over warm pancakes. Yield: 12 servings (serving size: 1 pancake and 3 tablespoons salsa).

CALORIES 128 (23% from fat); FAT 3.2g (sat 1.1g, mono 0.9g, poly 0.3g); PROTEIN 4.8g; CARB 20.5g; FIBER 2g; CHOL 23mg; IRON 1.2mg; SODIUM 352mg; CALC 99mg

---

All-Time Favorite

Mini Black Bean Cakes with Green Onion Cream and Avocado Salsa

Seasoned black beans kick up the southwestern flavor of these cakes while the sour cream topping tempers the heat.

Prep: 15 minutes • Cook: 14 minutes

Cakes:

½ cup bottled salsa
2 teaspoons ground cumin
2 (19-ounce) cans seasoned black beans, rinsed and drained
1 cup dry breadcrumbs, divided
¼ cup thinly sliced green onions
½ teaspoon salt
Cooking spray

Toppings:

½ cup reduced-fat sour cream
¼ cup thinly sliced green onions
¼ cup diced peeled avocado
¼ cup chopped plum tomato
1 teaspoon fresh lime juice

1. Preheat oven to 375°.
2. To prepare cakes, place first 3 ingredients in a food processor; process until smooth. Stir in ½ cup breadcrumbs, ¼ cup green onions, and salt.

3. Divide mixture into 24 equal portions, shaping each into a ½-inch-thick patty. Place ½ cup breadcrumbs in a shallow dish. Dredge patties in breadcrumbs. Place patties on a baking sheet coated with cooking spray. Bake at 375° for 14 minutes, turning after 7 minutes.
4. To prepare toppings, combine sour cream and ¼ cup green onions. Combine avocado, tomato, and juice. Top each patty with 1 teaspoon green onion cream and 1 teaspoon avocado salsa. Yield: 12 servings (serving size: 2 cakes).

CALORIES 99 (25% from fat); FAT 2.8g (sat 1g, mono 0.5g, poly 0.2g); PROTEIN 3.8g; CARB 16.3g; FIBER 0.7g; CHOL 5mg; IRON 1.6mg; SODIUM 421mg; CALC 61mg

---

how to seed an avocado

1. Cut into the avocado all the way around using a sharp knife.

2. Remove the knife, and twist the two sides away from each other to separate.

3. Using the knife, whack the seed; pull the seed out, which will be stuck on the knife.

New Year's Dumpling Delight

Traditionally, the steamer basket is coated with oil to keep the dumplings from sticking. In this recipe, each dumpling is placed on a thinly sliced carrot "disk." When the dumplings come out of the steamer, each has its own serving tray. You can make these dumplings ahead and freeze them.

Prep: 35 minutes • Cook: 20 minutes

Chili-garlic dipping sauce:
- ½ cup low-sodium soy sauce
- 2 tablespoons rice vinegar
- 2 tablespoons lemon juice
- 1 teaspoon sesame oil
- 2 garlic cloves, minced
- 2 tablespoons green onions, minced
- 1 hot red chile, minced

Dumplings:
- 10 ounces ground pork
- 3½ cups shredded napa (Chinese) cabbage
- 1¼ cups thinly sliced leek (about 1 large)
- ¾ cup minced green onions
- 1 cup thinly sliced shiitake mushroom caps (about 3 ounces)
- 1 tablespoon minced peeled fresh ginger
- 1 tablespoon low-sodium soy sauce
- 1 tablespoon sake (rice wine) or sherry
- 1 teaspoon sesame oil
- ¼ teaspoon salt
- ¼ teaspoon black pepper
- 40 wonton wrappers
- 2 large carrots, thinly sliced

1. To prepare dipping sauce, combine first 7 ingredients. Cover and chill.

2. To prepare dumplings, combine pork and next 10 ingredients in a large bowl.

3. Working with 1 wonton wrapper at a time (cover remaining wrappers with a damp towel to keep from drying), spoon 2 teaspoons pork mixture into center of each wrapper. Moisten edges with water; bring 2 opposite corners to center, pinching points to seal. Bring remaining 2 corners to center, pinching points to seal. Pinch 4 edges together to seal. Place dumplings, seam sides up, on carrot slices (cover loosely with a damp towel to keep them from drying).

4. Arrange half of dumplings in a single layer in a bamboo or vegetable steamer. Steam dumplings, covered, 10 minutes. Remove from steamer; place on a platter. Keep warm. Repeat procedure with remaining dumplings. Serve dumplings with dipping sauce. Yield: 8 servings (serving size: 5 dumplings and about 2 tablespoons dipping sauce).

CALORIES 284 (30% from fat); FAT 9.5g (sat 3.1g, mono 3.9g, poly 1.5g); PROTEIN 12.6g; CARB 35.6g; FIBER 2.7g; CHOL 30mg; IRON 2.9mg; SODIUM 973mg; CALC 70mg

Test Kitchen Tip: If you don't have a steamer, use a heat-proof plate. Set it on top of a heat-proof bowl placed in the bottom of a pot filled with two inches of water. Cover and steam.

Chipotle Shrimp Cups

A quick appetizer that gets its smoky heat from commercial salsa, these cups are made even easier with wonton wrappers. You can make all the components the night before (store filling in the refrigerator and cups at room temperature), then heat the assembled cups in the oven just before serving.

Prep: 15 minutes • Cook: 13 minutes

36 wonton wrappers
Cooking spray
1½ cups (6 ounces) shredded reduced-fat sharp Cheddar cheese
1 cup chopped cooked shrimp
1 cup chopped bottled roasted red bell peppers
1 cup bottled chipotle salsa
½ cup chopped green onions

1. Preheat oven to 350°.
2. Fit 1 wonton wrapper into each of 36 mini muffin cups coated with cooking spray, pressing wrappers into sides of cups. Bake at 350° for 7 minutes or until lightly browned. Keep wontons in muffin cups.
3. Combine cheese and remaining 4 ingredients; spoon 1 tablespoon cheese mixture into each wonton cup. Bake at 350° for 6 minutes or until cheese melts. Remove from muffin cups. Serve immediately. Yield: 3 dozen (serving size: 2 filled wonton cups).

CALORIES 98 (24% from fat); FAT 2.6g (sat 1.6g, mono 0.6g, poly 0.4g); PROTEIN 7.6g; CARB 11.8g; FIBER 1.4g; CHOL 28mg; IRON 1mg; SODIUM 202mg; CALC 96mg

Thai-Style Broiled Shrimp

This dish is typically served with the shells on the shrimp. But since it's tricky to devein jumbo shrimp and leave the shells intact, we removed them.

Prep: 20 minutes • Cook: 13 minutes
Other: 30 minutes

1 tablespoon white peppercorns
1 tablespoon minced fresh cilantro stems
1 tablespoon Thai fish sauce
1 teaspoon sugar
1 teaspoon minced serrano chile
¼ teaspoon kosher or sea salt
12 peeled and deveined jumbo shrimp (about 1 pound)
12 garlic cloves, minced
Cooking spray
3 tablespoons canola oil

1. Place peppercorns in a small skillet over medium-high heat; cook 1 minute or until toasted. Place peppercorns in a spice or coffee grinder; process until finely ground.
2. Combine ground pepper, cilantro stems, and next 6 ingredients in a large zip-top plastic bag. Seal; marinate in refrigerator 30 minutes.
3. Preheat broiler.
4. Remove shrimp from bag, shaking off excess marinade; reserve marinade. Place shrimp on a broiler pan coated with cooking spray; broil 5 minutes on each side or until shrimp are done. Keep warm.
5. Heat oil in a large nonstick skillet over medium-high heat. Add marinade; sauté 1 minute or until garlic is golden. Remove from heat; stir in shrimp. Yield: 6 servings (serving size: 2 shrimp).

CALORIES 159 (48% from fat); FAT 8.4g (sat 0.8g, mono 4.3g, poly 2.6g); PROTEIN 16g; CARB 4.4g; FIBER 0.3g; CHOL 115mg; IRON 2mg; SODIUM 423mg; CALC 54mg

Stellar Sesame Shrimp with Miso Dipping Sauce

Combine the shrimp, oil, and seasonings early on the day you're serving them, and refrigerate up to eight hours.

Prep: 20 minutes • Cook: 7 minutes

¼ cup orange-pineapple juice concentrate, thawed and undiluted
1 tablespoon water
1 tablespoon red miso (soybean paste)
2 teaspoons finely chopped peeled fresh ginger
2 teaspoons dark sesame oil
1 garlic clove, minced
24 unpeeled large shrimp (about 1 pound)
2 teaspoons canola oil
¼ teaspoon kosher salt
⅛ teaspoon freshly ground black pepper
1 tablespoon sesame seeds, toasted

1. Combine first 6 ingredients in a bowl; stir well with a whisk. Cover and chill.
2. Preheat oven to 450°.
3. Peel and devein shrimp, leaving tails intact. Combine shrimp, canola oil, salt, and pepper in a bowl; toss gently. Place shrimp on a foil-lined baking sheet; sprinkle with sesame seeds. Bake at 450° for 7 minutes or until shrimp are done. Serve with sauce. Yield: 12 servings (serving size: 2 shrimp and 2 teaspoons sauce).

CALORIES 61 (37% from fat); FAT 2.5g (sat 0.3g, mono 0.7g, poly 0.6g); PROTEIN 6.2g; CARB 5.1g; FIBER 0.1g; CHOL 43mg; IRON 1mg; SODIUM 159mg; CALC 26mg

Curried Crab Cakes

Curry adds a new hot and spicy flavor level to traditional crab cakes.

Prep: 25 minutes • Cook: 30 minutes

2 teaspoons curry powder
½ teaspoon salt
¼ teaspoon dry mustard
¼ teaspoon black pepper
⅛ teaspoon ground red pepper
Cooking spray
1 cup minced fresh onion
1 cup chopped red bell pepper
½ cup chopped celery
2 teaspoons minced peeled fresh ginger
1 garlic clove, minced
1¼ cups dry breadcrumbs, divided
¼ cup light mayonnaise
1 teaspoon grated lemon rind
1 pound lump crabmeat, shell pieces removed
1 large egg, lightly beaten
2 tablespoons butter, divided

1. Combine first 5 ingredients in a small bowl; stir well.
2. Heat a large nonstick skillet over medium-high heat. Coat pan with cooking spray. Add onion, bell pepper, and celery; cover, reduce heat to medium-low, and cook 10 minutes, stirring occasionally. Add curry powder mixture, ginger, and garlic; cook, uncovered, 5 minutes, stirring frequently. Spoon mixture into a large bowl; cool. Wipe pan clean with a paper towel.
3. Add ¾ cup breadcrumbs, mayonnaise, rind, crabmeat, and egg to onion mixture; stir well. Divide mixture into 24 portions; shape each into a ½-inch-thick patty. Place ½ cup breadcrumbs in a shallow dish; dredge crab cakes in breadcrumbs.
4. Melt 2 teaspoons butter in pan over medium heat. Add 8 patties; cook 2 minutes on each side or until browned. Remove from pan; keep warm. Repeat procedure with remaining butter and patties. Yield: 12 servings (serving size: 2 crab cakes).

CALORIES 124 (30% from fat); FAT 4.2g (sat 1.8g, mono 1g, poly 0.3g); PROTEIN 10.4g; CARB 11.2g; FIBER 1g; CHOL 51mg; IRON 1.2mg; SODIUM 377mg; CALC 65mg

Mussels with Fennel

Here's an easy make-ahead tip: Clean the mussels and prepare the broth ahead. Just before serving, add the mussels, and cook until the shells open.

Prep: 20 minutes • Cook: 24 minutes

2 teaspoons olive oil
1½ cups chopped fennel bulb (about 2 small bulbs)
1 teaspoon fennel seeds
2 garlic cloves, minced
¾ cup dry white wine
½ cup water
2 tablespoons fresh lemon juice
½ teaspoon salt
2 (14.5-ounce) cans no-salt-added diced tomatoes, undrained
42 mussels (about 2 pounds), scrubbed and debearded

1. Heat oil in a large skillet over medium-high heat. Add fennel, fennel seeds, and garlic; sauté 3 minutes. Stir in wine, water, juice, salt, and tomatoes; bring to a boil. Reduce heat, and simmer 10 minutes. Add mussels; cover and cook 6 minutes or until shells open. Remove from heat; discard any unopened shells. Yield: 6 servings (serving size: 7 mussels and about ¾ cup broth).

CALORIES 101 (26% from fat); FAT 2.9g (sat 0.5g, mono 1.4g, poly 0.5g); PROTEIN 8.7g; CARB 10.8g; FIBER 0.2g; CHOL 16mg; IRON 3.6mg; SODIUM 383mg; CALC 91mg

Warm Beverages

Treat yourself to a cup of comfort with freshly brewed espresso, spiced tea, or creamy hot cocoa.

Tahitian Coffee

Melted ice cream forms a sweet, foamy top layer for this luscious drink.

Prep: 4 minutes

2¾ cups hot strong brewed coffee
¼ cup dark rum
1 tablespoon sugar
½ cup vanilla low-fat ice cream
4 (3-inch) cinnamon sticks (optional)

1. Combine first 3 ingredients in a pitcher, stirring until sugar dissolves. Pour into mugs, and top with ice cream. Garnish with cinnamon sticks, if desired. Yield: 4 servings (serving size: ¾ cup coffee and 2 tablespoons ice cream).

CALORIES 75 (6% from fat); FAT 0.5g (sat 0.3g, mono 0g, poly 0g); PROTEIN 0.9g; CARB 8.5g; FIBER 0.3g; CHOL 1.3mg; IRON 0.1mg; SODIUM 15mg; CALC 28mg

Espresso au Lait

If you love espresso, but don't have a machine, make yourself a cup using instant espresso.

Prep: 3 minutes • Cook: 1½ minutes

1 tablespoon packed brown sugar
1 tablespoon instant espresso granules
6 tablespoons water
6 tablespoons 2% reduced-fat milk
Orange rind strip (optional)

1. Combine brown sugar and espresso granules in a 1-cup glass measure. Stir in water and milk. Microwave, uncovered, at HIGH 1½ minutes or until heated, stirring after 45 seconds. Garnish with orange rind, if desired. Yield: 1 serving (serving size: 1 cup).

CALORIES 111 (9% from fat); FAT 1.8g (sat 1.1g, mono 0.5g, poly 0.1g); PROTEIN 3.7g; CARB 20g; FIBER 0.1g; CHOL 7mg; IRON 0.5mg; SODIUM 53mg; CALC 131mg

Almond Cappuccino

To heighten your almond experience, serve this with Apple Streusel Cake with Almonds (page 86).

Prep: 5 minutes • Cook: 5 minutes

2 cups fat-free milk
1 vanilla bean, split
2 tablespoons instant espresso granules
⅛ teaspoon almond extract
¼ teaspoon unsweetened cocoa

1. Combine milk and vanilla bean in a medium saucepan; cook over low heat until bubbly. Stir in espresso granules, and remove from heat. Discard vanilla bean; stir in almond extract.
2. Pour 1 cup milk mixture into a blender; process until frothy. Pour into a cup, and sprinkle with ⅛ teaspoon cocoa. Repeat with remaining milk mixture and cocoa. Yield: 2 servings (serving size: 1 cup).

CALORIES 96 (5% from fat); FAT 0.5g (sat 0.3g, mono 0.1g, poly 0g); PROTEIN 8.8g; CARB 13.4g; FIBER 0.1g; CHOL 5mg; IRON 0.3mg; SODIUM 129mg; CALC 307mg

types of coffeemakers

Select the particular grind of coffee that your coffeemaker requires. For a single cup of coffee, use ¾ cup water and 1 tablespoon coffee.

Drip: Assemble drip coffeemaker according to manufacturer's directions. Place ground coffee in the coffee filter or filter basket. Add water, and brew.

Percolator: Pour water into percolator; assemble stem and basket in pot. Add coffee. Place lid on pot. Plug in coffeepot if using an electric percolator, and brew until perking stops. If using a nonelectric model, bring to a boil over high heat; reduce heat, and perk gently five to seven minutes.

Vacuum: Bring water to a boil in lower bowl of vacuum pot. Place a filter in the upper bowl, and fill with ground coffee. Reduce heat. The pressure will force the water up through the coffee grounds. Brew one to three minutes. Remove from heat, and allow coffee to return to lower bowl.

French press: Using fresh, coarse-ground coffee, spoon 1 tablespoon per cup of coffee into the glass or stainless steel carafe. Pour hot (201°) water over the grounds, and put the lid with plunger filter on the pot. Steep and press plunger to filter coffee.

Café Brûlot

Brûlot in French means "spicy" or "burned" with sugar. This beverage is a blend of dark roast coffee and brandy, spiced with cinnamon and orange peel.

Prep: 5 minutes • Cook: 5 minutes

    1   orange
    1   lemon
    6   whole cloves
 1 ¼   cups Triple Sec
    2   tablespoons brandy
    2   (3-inch) cinnamon sticks
    5   cups hot strong brewed coffee
    2   tablespoons fresh orange juice
    1   teaspoon fresh lemon juice

1. Remove rind from orange and lemon in continuous strips using a vegetable peeler, making sure to avoid white pithy part of rind. Stud orange rind piece with 3 cloves. Stud lemon rind piece with 3 cloves.

2. Combine Triple Sec, brandy, and cinnamon sticks in a medium saucepan over medium-low heat. Bring to a simmer. Ignite Triple Sec mixture with a long match. Carefully hold orange and lemon rinds with tongs over flames, turning frequently. Let flames die down; add orange and lemon rinds to Triple Sec mixture.

3. Pour coffee into one side of saucepan. Stir in juices. Discard rinds. Serve in demitasse cups. Yield: 10 servings (serving size: about ½ cup).

CALORIES 98 (1% from fat); FAT 0.1g (sat 0g, mono 0g, poly 0.1g); PROTEIN 0.2g; CARB 12.1g; FIBER 0g; CHOL 0mg; IRON 0.1mg; SODIUM 4mg; CALC 3mg

coffee class The coffee experts offer these tips for brewing a great cup.

Buying: For the freshest coffee with the best flavor, buy whole beans.

Storing: Keep whole bean coffee in the bag and stored in an airtight container. It will stay fresh up to six weeks once opened. Close the bag tightly to allow the coffee to blanket itself with its natural carbon dioxide, which protects it from exposure to oxygen. Coffee—either ground or whole beans—shouldn't be stored in the freezer or refrigerator once opened. Coffee absorbs food odors, and any condensation that may form on the inside of the container can cause the coffee to get stale or develop an "off" flavor. Store coffee in an airtight container at room temperature.

Brewing Tips: Grind only as much as you need for each use. Use 1 tablespoon of ground coffee per 6-ounce cup (the size of a standard coffee cup). Adjust if you prefer your coffee stronger or lighter.

• Use either purified water or fresh, cold tap water. Do not use spring water or hot water from the tap because they can both add strange flavors to the coffee.

• Be sure your maker and pot are as clean as possible. If you use an automatic-drip machine, clean it with a weak vinegar solution followed by a fresh water rinse.

• Use an unbleached paper filter (bleached filters have chlorine, which may change the flavor of your coffee). Once brewed, remove coffee from the heat. Coffee sitting on a burner can start to degrade within 20 minutes. Instead, keep your brewed coffee fresh in a thermal container.

• Never reheat or microwave coffee; this can leave a burnt, bitter taste.

Hot Mocha

Sip on a steaming cup of mocha after dinner or as you warm yourself by the fire.

Prep: 4 minutes • Cook: 4 minutes

    6   cups hot strong brewed coffee
    ½   cup sugar
    ½   cup unsweetened cocoa
    6   tablespoons Kahlúa (coffee-
        flavored liqueur)

1. Combine coffee, sugar, and cocoa in a medium saucepan. Cook coffee mixture over medium heat until hot, stirring frequently (do not boil). Remove coffee mixture from heat; stir in Kahlúa. Yield: 13 servings (serving size: ½ cup).

CALORIES 69 (6% from fat); FAT 0.5g (sat 0.3g, mono 0.2g, poly 0g); PROTEIN 1.1g; CARB 11.8g; FIBER 0g; CHOL 0mg; IRON 1mg; SODIUM 4mg; CALC 7mg

New Mexican Hot Chocolate

A spiced chocolate beverage is a warming treat on a brisk morning and a soothing comfort on a cold evening.

Prep: 4 minutes • Cook: 16 minutes

    ½   cup water
    ⅓   cup honey
    5   tablespoons unsweetened cocoa
    ½   teaspoon ground cinnamon
    ⅛   teaspoon ground nutmeg
    ¼   teaspoon salt
    4   cups 2% reduced-fat milk
    1   teaspoon vanilla extract

1. Combine first 6 ingredients in a large, heavy saucepan. Bring to a boil over medium-high heat, stirring constantly. Reduce heat to medium-low. Stir in milk and extract; cook 13 minutes or until thoroughly heated, stirring frequently. (Do not

boil.) Yield: 8 servings (serving size: about ⅔ cup).

CALORIES 117 (23% from fat); FAT 3g (sat 1.8g, mono 0.2g, poly 0g); PROTEIN 4.8g; CARB 19.9g; FIBER 1.2g; CHOL 10mg; IRON 0.6mg; SODIUM 137mg; CALC 132mg

Hot Chocolate with Ginger

Spice up a snowy-night favorite with ginger. Serve with marshmallows and a dusting of cocoa powder.

Prep: 5 minutes • Cook: 14 minutes

    ⅓   cup chopped peeled fresh ginger
    2   tablespoons sugar
    2   tablespoons water
    4   cups 1% reduced-fat milk
    ½   cup fat-free chocolate syrup

1. Combine first 3 ingredients in a medium saucepan; cook over medium-high heat until sugar dissolves and is golden (about 1 to 2 minutes), stirring frequently. Remove from heat; cool slightly.
2. Stir in milk and chocolate syrup; cook over medium-low heat 13 minutes or until thoroughly heated, stirring frequently (do not boil). Strain milk mixture through a sieve; discard solids. Yield: 4 servings (serving size: ¾ cup).

CALORIES 190 (13% from fat); FAT 2.7g (sat 1.6g, mono 0.6g, poly 0g); PROTEIN 9.8g; CARB 32g; FIBER 0.9g; CHOL 15mg; IRON 0mg; SODIUM 179mg; CALC 275mg

Test Kitchen Tip: Store fresh ginger tightly wrapped in plastic wrap in the vegetable crisper section of the refrigerator up to three weeks.

Hot White Chocolate

Enjoy white chocolate instead of cocoa in this festive drink.

Prep: 3 minutes • Cook: 25 minutes

    ½   cup sugar
    ¼   cup water
    8   cups fat-free milk
    1   cup (about 5 ounces) chopped
        premium white baking chocolate
        Chopped peppermint candies (optional)

1. Combine sugar and water in a large saucepan; cook over medium-high heat until sugar dissolves and mixture is golden (about 2 minutes), stirring frequently. Remove from heat, and cool slightly.
2. Add milk and chocolate, stirring with a whisk. Heat over medium-low heat 23 minutes or until thoroughly heated, stirring frequently (do not boil). Sprinkle with chopped peppermint candies, if desired. Yield: 8 servings (serving size: 1 cup).

CALORIES 210 (21% from fat); FAT 5g (sat 3g, mono 1.4g, poly 0.2g); PROTEIN 9.2g; CARB 32.8g; FIBER 0g; CHOL 7mg; IRON 0.1mg; SODIUM 139mg; CALC 331mg

white chocolate White chocolate isn't really chocolate since it contains no chocolate liquor from the cocoa beans. It may contain cocoa butter, however, which is derived from chocolate liquor. For the best-quality white chocolate, look for cocoa butter on the ingredient list. To be labeled white chocolate, the product must include cocoa butter, milk solids, milk fat, and sugar or high-fructose corn syrup. If it contains palm kernel oil, then it's just white confectionery coating and can't be labeled "white chocolate."

Mulled Cranberry-Orange Cider

Winter holiday spices infuse cider with an irresistible aroma and flavor.

Prep: 6 minutes • Cook: 15 minutes
Other: 30 minutes

- 4   whole cloves
- 4   whole allspice
- 2   star anise
- 1   (3-inch) cinnamon stick, broken in half
- 5   cups apple cider
- 3   cups cranberry juice cocktail
- ¼   cup packed brown sugar
- 4   orange slices
- 8   star anise (optional)
- 8   small orange slices (optional)

1. Place first 4 ingredients on a cheesecloth square. Gather edges of cheesecloth together; tie securely. Combine spice bag, cider, cranberry juice, sugar, and 4 orange slices in a Dutch oven. Bring to a boil. Reduce heat; simmer, partially covered, 10 minutes. Remove from heat; let stand 30 minutes. Discard spice bag and orange slices. Serve with additional anise and orange slices, if desired. Yield: 8 servings (serving size: 1 cup).

CALORIES 155 (1% from fat); FAT 0.1g (sat 0g, mono 0g, poly 0.1g); PROTEIN 0.6g; CARB 38.5g; FIBER 0.1g; CHOL 0mg; IRON 0.3mg; SODIUM 20mg; CALC 21mg

Test Kitchen Tip: It's safer to use only pasteurized cider or apple juice rather than homemade cider or apple juice from a roadside stand or farmers' market. Also, keep ciders and juices refrigerated. Apples are sometimes exposed to a strain of E. coli bacteria that can cause illness. The apple industry is working on a solution to this problem.

Mulled Cranberry-Guava Toddies

Guava nectar has a sweet, strawberry-banana-pineapple flavor and is available in the ethnic foods section of most supermarkets.

Prep: 4 minutes • Cook: 15 minutes

- 3   quarts cranberry juice cocktail
- ¼   cup sliced peeled fresh ginger
- 2   teaspoons whole cloves
- 16   (¼-inch-thick) slices orange (about 4 oranges)
- 1   (12-ounce) can guava nectar
- 2   cups dark rum

1. Combine first 5 ingredients in a large saucepan; bring to a boil. Cover, reduce heat, and simmer 10 minutes. Discard ginger and cloves. Stir in rum. Yield: 16 servings (serving size: about ¾ cup).

CALORIES 185 (1% from fat); FAT 0.2g (sat 0g, mono 0g, poly 0.1g); PROTEIN 0g; CARB 30.4g; FIBER 0.2g; CHOL 0mg; IRON 0.3mg; SODIUM 5mg; CALC 15mg

Russian Tea

Orange juice and spices perk up a cup of tea—and your morning.

Prep: 9 minutes

¾   cup boiling water
1   regular-size English breakfast tea bag
¼   cup orange juice
¼   teaspoon ground cinnamon
⅛   teaspoon ground cloves
Sugar (optional)

1. Combine boiling water and tea bag in a large mug; cover and steep 5 minutes. Discard tea bag. Stir orange juice, cinnamon, and cloves into mug. Serve with sugar, if desired. Yield: 1 serving (serving size: 1 cup).

CALORIES 31 (3% from fat); FAT 0.1g (sat 0g, mono 0g, poly 0g); PROTEIN 0.5g; CARB 7.4g; FIBER 0.3g; CHOL 0mg; IRON 0.3mg; SODIUM 1mg; CALC 14mg

Test Kitchen Tip: We use tea bags for some tea recipes and loose tea for others. Tea bags are convenient and easy to use, while loose tea results in a stronger brew, which is sometimes preferable. If you don't have loose tea, cut tea bags open and measure out the amount specified. We usually test with supermarket brands instead of teas from specialty shops.

Hot Spiced Cheer

Serve this citrusy cider in a decorative punch bowl alongside a small pitcher of rum for those who want to add a splash of spirits.

Prep: 7 minutes • Cook: 28 minutes

10   whole cloves
4   (3-inch) cinnamon sticks
4   pieces crystallized ginger, chopped
1   gallon apple cider
4   cups pineapple juice
2   cups orange juice
¼   cup fresh lemon juice
⅓   cup sugar
¼   teaspoon salt
White rum (optional)

1. Place first 3 ingredients on a double layer of cheesecloth. Gather edges of cheesecloth together; tie securely.
2. Combine cheesecloth bag, cider, and next 5 ingredients in a large stockpot; bring to a boil. Reduce heat, and simmer 20 minutes. Discard cheesecloth bag. Serve with rum, if desired. Yield: 22 cups (serving size: 1 cup).

CALORIES 133 (1% from fat); FAT 0.2g (sat 0g, mono 0g, poly 0.1g); PROTEIN 0.4g; CARB 33g; FIBER 0.5g; CHOL 0mg; IRON 0.8mg; SODIUM 33mg; CALC 23mg

Test Kitchen Tip: If you don't have cheesecloth, remove tea leaves from an ordinary tea bag, fill the empty bag with the cloves and ginger, and tie it securely with the tea bag string; let the cinnamon sticks float separately while simmering.

how to make mulled cider

1. Place the cloves and cinnamon sticks on a cheesecloth square.

2. Bring the ends together, and tie securely at the top.

3. Simmer the cider and spice bag as directed. Discard the spice bag before serving.

Cold Beverages

Chill out with with a refreshing glass of iced tea or old-fashioned lemonade, or relax with a wine cooler or a cup of rum punch.

Iced Mint Tea

Mint tea, made with spearmint, is the traditional drink of Morocco and North Africa. A few leaves of fresh or dried lemon verbena add a lovely citrus tang. For a lighter minty flavor, remove the mint sprigs before chilling. This tea is traditionally very sweet, but you can use less sugar, if desired. In the southern part of the United States, sweet mint tea is also very popular, but Southerners typically use a black tea such as orange pekoe.

Prep: 13 minutes

  8 cups boiling water
  1 tablespoon loose Chinese green tea
 25 fresh mint sprigs (about 1½ ounces)
  ½ cup sugar

1. Combine water and tea in a medium bowl; cover and steep 2½ minutes. Strain tea mixture through a fine sieve into a bowl, and discard tea leaves. Add mint; steep 5 minutes. Add sugar; stir until sugar dissolves. Cover and chill. Serve over ice. Yield: 8 cups (serving size: 1 cup).

CALORIES 52 (2% from fat); FAT 0.1g (sat 0g, mono 0g, poly 0.1g); PROTEIN 0.2g; CARB 13.3g; FIBER 0.4g; CHOL 0mg; IRON 0.3mg; SODIUM 9mg; CALC 18mg

Test Kitchen Tip: For the best flavor, use Chinese green tea, such as Gunpowder Green, Young Hyson, or Formosa Oolong. Once it's opened, store green tea in a sealed container in a cool, dark place for no more than six months.

Fresh-Squeezed Lemonade

To get the most juice out of lemons, bring them to room temperature before juicing. Or microwave them about 30 seconds before squeezing.

Prep: 20 minutes

    3   cups fresh lemon juice (about
        20 lemons)
  2¼   cups sugar
   12   cups chilled water
        Lemon slices (optional)

1. Combine juice and sugar in a 1-gallon container; stir until sugar dissolves. Stir in water. Serve over ice. Garnish with lemon slices, if desired. Yield: 16 servings (serving size: 1 cup).

CALORIES 120 (0% from fat); FAT 0g; PROTEIN 0.2g; CARB 32.1g; FIBER 0.2g; CHOL 0mg; IRON 0.1mg; SODIUM 6mg; CALC 7mg

Ginger-Zapped Lemonade

Because of the fresh grated ginger, this refreshing beverage has a bit more bite than traditional lemonade.

**Prep: 13 minutes • Cook: 5 minutes
Other: 2 hours**

    6   cups water, divided
    1   cup sugar
   ¼   cup grated peeled fresh ginger
  1½   cups fresh lemon juice (about 8
        lemons)

1. Combine 1 cup water and sugar in a small saucepan over medium-high heat; cook 5 minutes or until sugar dissolves, stirring with a whisk.
2. Place ginger on a double layer of cheesecloth. Gather edges of cheesecloth together; tie securely. Place cheesecloth bag in a large pitcher, and add lemon juice. Add sugar mixture and 5 cups water to pitcher, and stir well. Refrigerate lemonade 2 hours or until chilled. Discard cheesecloth bag. Yield: 8 servings (serving size: 1 cup).

CALORIES 109 (0% from fat); FAT 0g; PROTEIN 0.2g; CARB 29.1g; FIBER 0.2g; CHOL 0mg; IRON 0mg; SODIUM 1mg; CALC 4mg

A Cool Drink

Serve this colorful beverage in clear pitchers at a patio or poolside party. Orange-flower water is a flavoring distilled from bitter orange blossoms. It's used in baked goods, sweet and savory dishes, and beverages. Look for it in liquor stores, gourmet markets, or Middle Eastern and Mediterranean grocery stores.

Prep: 20 minutes

    6   cups cold water
    4   cups fresh orange juice (about 10
        oranges)
    1   cup fresh lime juice (about 6 limes)
   ⅔   cup sugar
   ¼   cup grenadine
    4   teaspoons orange-flower water
        (optional)
   20   lime slices (optional)

1. Combine first 6 ingredients in a pitcher; stir until sugar dissolves. Chill. Serve over ice; garnish with lime slices, if desired. Yield: 10 servings (serving size: 1 cup).

CALORIES 124 (1% from fat); FAT 0.2g (sat 0g, mono 0.1g, poly 0.1g); PROTEIN 0.8g; CARB 31.5g; FIBER 0.3g; CHOL 0mg; IRON 0.2mg; SODIUM 5mg; CALC 14mg

Test Kitchen Tip: Sometimes grenadine contains alcohol and sometimes it doesn't, so check the label. In most recipes, either type will work.

Teo's Punch

Add some rum to this simple punch for a decidedly adult enhancement.

Prep: 3 minutes

    2   cups apple juice
    2   (6-ounce) cans pineapple juice
    1   (12-ounce) can thawed cranberry
        juice concentrate, undiluted
    1   (6-ounce) can thawed orange juice
        concentrate, undiluted
    4   cups club soda, chilled

1. Combine first 4 ingredients; stir until blended. Add soda just before serving. Serve over ice. Yield: 10 servings (serving size: about 1 cup).

CALORIES 134 (1% from fat); FAT 0.1g (sat 0g, mono 0g, poly 0.1g); PROTEIN 0.6g; CARB 33.4g; FIBER 0.3g; CHOL 0mg; IRON 0.4mg; SODIUM 23mg; CALC 23mg

Citrus Slush

To create a jazzy presentation, drizzle a teaspoon of a flavored, colored syrup over the top of the slush just before serving.

Prep: 7 minutes

    2   cups frozen lemon sorbet
    1   cup fresh orange juice (about 3
        oranges)
   ½   cup fresh grapefruit juice
   ¼   cup honey
    8   ice cubes

1. Place first 4 ingredients in a blender; process until smooth. With blender on, add ice cubes, 1 at a time, and process mixture until smooth. Yield: 4 servings (serving size: 1 cup).

CALORIES 244 (0% from fat); FAT 0.1g (sat 0g, mono 0g, poly 0.1g); PROTEIN 0.6g; CARB 60.9g; FIBER 0.2g; CHOL 0mg; IRON 0.2mg; SODIUM 17mg; CALC 9mg

Fresh Banana-Berry Shake

Fresh Banana-Berry Shake

If the shake is too thick to process, add an extra tablespoon or two of juice.

Prep: 8 minutes

- 2 cups sliced banana
- 1 cup quartered strawberries
- ¼ cup fresh orange juice
- 3 cups vanilla low-fat ice cream

1. Place first 3 ingredients in a blender; process until smooth. Add ice cream; process until smooth. Serve immediately. Yield: 4 cups (serving size: 1 cup).

CALORIES 226 (20% from fat); FAT 4.8g (sat 2.8g, mono 1.3g, poly 0.3g); PROTEIN 4.9g; CARB 44.6g; FIBER 2.8g; CHOL 14mg; IRON 0.5mg; SODIUM 85mg; CALC 150mg

Tropical Tofu Smoothie

Start the day with this power beverage; it contains soy protein, calcium, and vitamin C.

Prep: 7 minutes

- ⅔ cup soft tofu, drained (about 3 ounces)
- 1 cup cubed pineapple, chilled
- 1 cup sliced strawberries, chilled
- ½ cup vanilla low-fat frozen yogurt
- ⅓ cup orange juice
- 1 teaspoon sugar
- Dash of ground nutmeg (optional)

1. Place tofu in a blender; process until smooth. Add pineapple and next 4 ingredients; process until smooth. Sprinkle with nutmeg, if desired. Serve immediately. Yield: 2 servings (serving size: 1 cup).

CALORIES 147 (15% from fat); FAT 2.5g (sat 0.6g, mono 0.1g, poly 0.5g); PROTEIN 4.8g; CARB 28.9g; FIBER 2.8g; CHOL 4mg; IRON 1.2mg; SODIUM 17mg; CALC 94mg

Strawberry-Kiwi Smoothie

You can use frozen blueberries, raspberries, or blackberries in place of the strawberries.

Prep: 7 minutes

- 1 cup frozen unsweetened whole strawberries
- 1 cup low-fat vanilla soy milk
- 2 teaspoons honey
- ½ teaspoon vanilla extract
- 3 peeled kiwifruit, halved
- 3 firm bananas, peeled and halved

blender basics Look for these features when you're choosing a blender.

Multiple speeds: If you're only going to make milk shakes or frozen drinks, a blender with one or two speeds will work fine. But for more versatility, choose a blender with several speeds (a pulse option is great, too). If you'll be making lots of frozen beverages, look for an ice-crushing mode.

Clear glass jar: Stainless steel jars look sleek and retro, but they don't allow you to see what you're blending. And although plastic jars won't break, they hold odors; blending a slushy drink after whipping up a garlicky sauce in one may not yield appetizing results.

Not-too-deep-base: It makes cleanup easier, food won't get caught beneath the blades during blending, and when you make a small amount, the food is mixed by the blades instead of being whirled to the side.

1. Place all ingredients in a blender; process until smooth. Chill thoroughly. Yield: 4 servings (serving size: 1 cup).

CALORIES 176 (7% from fat); FAT 1.4g (sat 0.2g, mono 0.2g, poly 0.4g); PROTEIN 2.9g; CARB 42.2g; FIBER 3.9g; CHOL 0mg; IRON 1mg; SODIUM 26mg; CALC 57mg

Chocolate-Peanut Butter Smoothie

This smoothie is nutrient-packed—perfect for a breakfast-on-the-run or an afternoon snack.

Prep: 5 minutes

- ½ cup 1% low-fat milk
- 2 tablespoons chocolate syrup
- 2 tablespoons creamy peanut butter
- 1 frozen sliced ripe banana
- 1 (8-ounce) carton vanilla low-fat yogurt

1. Place all ingredients in a blender; process until smooth. Yield: 2 servings (serving size: about 1 cup).

CALORIES 332 (29% from fat); FAT 10.8g (sat 3.2g, mono 4.5g, poly 2.3g); PROTEIN 12.7g; CARB 49.8g; FIBER 3.1g; CHOL 8mg; IRON 1mg; SODIUM 194mg; CALC 282mg

Banana-Berry Smoothie

Frozen berries ensure a thick, creamy consistency, but you can also use fresh ones. Other frozen fruits, such as peaches or mangoes, work well, too.

Prep: 5 minutes

- 1¼ cups calcium-fortified orange juice
- 1¼ cups frozen mixed berries
- 1 cup sliced ripe banana
- ½ cup vanilla fat-free yogurt
- ⅓ cup nonfat dry milk
- 1 tablespoon sugar

1. Place all ingredients in a blender; process until smooth. Yield: 3 servings (serving size: 1 cup).

CALORIES 204 (3% from fat); FAT 0.6g (sat 0.2g, mono 0.1g, poly 0.2g); PROTEIN 6.6g; CARB 45.6g; FIBER 3.3g; CHOL 2mg; IRON 0.6mg; SODIUM 71mg; CALC 327mg

Raspberry Sparkler

You can use club soda or sparkling water in place of the Champagne.

Prep: 4 minutes

- 3 cups cran-raspberry juice (such as Ocean Spray), chilled
- 1 tablespoon fresh lime juice
- 1 (750-milliliter) bottle brut Champagne or sparkling wine, chilled
- 6 thin slices lime

1. Combine cran-raspberry juice and lime juice in a pitcher, and stir well. Pour ½ cup juice mixture into each of 6 Champagne glasses; top with chilled Champagne. Garnish with lime slices. Serve immediately. Yield: 6 servings (serving size: 1 cup).

CALORIES 172 (0% from fat); FAT 0g (sat 0g, mono 0g; poly 0g); PROTEIN 0.5g; CARB 23.6g; FIBER 0.3g; CHOL 0mg; IRON 0.6mg; SODIUM 13mg; CALC 21mg

Champagne Champagne, by definition, comes from the Champagne region of France. Wines made in other regions by the same method are called sparkling wines. The term "Brut" on a label of sparkling wine signifies a very dry wine with less than 1.5 percent sugar. The term "extra-dry," oddly, refers to a sparkling wine that's slightly sweeter than Brut. "Sec" indicates a lightly sweet wine, and "Demi-Sec" is sweet, with 3.3 to 5 percent sugar.

Raspberry-Orange
Sunrises

Easy Sangría

Serve this traditional Spanish beverage chilled in glass pitchers with the sliced fruit floating on top. After the last of the sangría has been poured, enjoy the wine-infused orange wedges as a special treat.

Prep: 10 minutes • Other: 2 hours

- 1 (1.5-liter) bottle dry red wine, divided
- 2 tablespoons brandy
- 2 tablespoons Triple Sec (orange-flavored liqueur)
- ⅓ cup sugar
- ⅔ cup fresh orange juice
- 2 tablespoons fresh lime juice
- 2 tablespoons fresh lemon juice
- 5 whole cloves
- 3 whole allspice
- 1 (3-inch) cinnamon stick
- 2 cups sparkling water, chilled
- 8 orange wedges
- 5 lemon slices
- 5 lime slices

1. Combine 1 cup wine, brandy, Triple Sec, and sugar, stirring well to dissolve sugar. Stir in remaining wine, juices, cloves, allspice, and cinnamon. Chill at least 2 hours.

2. Strain mixture into a pitcher; discard solids. Just before serving, stir in sparkling water and remaining ingredients. Yield: 8 servings (serving size: about ¾ cup).

CALORIES 199 (0% from fat); FAT 0.1g (sat 0g, mono 0g, poly 0.1g); PROTEIN 0.6g; CARB 15.8g; FIBER 0.1g; CHOL 0mg; IRON 0.9mg; SODIUM 10mg; CALC 18mg

Raspberry-Orange Sunrises

Offer a sparkling beverage with a hint of red at your next holiday brunch.

Prep: 10 minutes

- 4 cups fresh orange juice (about 8 oranges)
- 1 cup frozen unsweetened raspberries
- 1½ cups semisweet sparkling wine
- 3 orange slices, halved (optional)

1. Place orange juice and raspberries in a blender; process until smooth. Pour mixture into a pitcher; stir in wine. Serve over ice. Garnish with orange slices, if desired. Yield: 6 servings (serving size: 1 cup).

CALORIES 178 (1% from fat); FAT 0.2g (sat 0g, mono 0g, poly 0.1g); PROTEIN 1.6g; CARB 33.2g; FIBER 2.5g; CHOL 0mg; IRON 0.8mg; SODIUM 10mg; CALC 33mg

Kir Champagne Cocktail

The next time you entertain, make a toast with this elegant cocktail.

Prep: 3 minutes

- 6 sugar cubes
- 6 tablespoons crème de cassis (black currant-flavored liqueur)
- 3 cups Champagne or sparkling wine, chilled

1. Place 1 sugar cube in the bottom of each of 6 Champagne glasses. Add 1 tablespoon crème de cassis and ½ cup Champagne to each glass. Yield: 6 servings (serving size: ½ cup wine plus 1 tablespoon liqueur).

CALORIES 118 (0% from fat); FAT 0g (sat 0g, mono 0g; poly 0g); PROTEIN 0.4g; CARB 4.8g; FIBER 0g; CHOL 0mg; IRON 0.6mg; SODIUM 6mg; CALC 7mg

Wine Coolers

Combine equal parts of cranberry juice, orange juice, and red wine for the base of this refreshing summertime drink.

Prep: 4 minutes

- ½ cup cranberry-mango juice
- ½ cup orange juice
- ½ cup merlot or other dry red wine
- ⅔ cup seltzer water
- 2 lime slices
- 2 orange slices

1. Combine first 4 ingredients in a pitcher. Serve over ice. Garnish with lime and orange slices. Yield: 2 servings (serving size: 1 cup).

CALORIES 101 (0% from fat); FAT 0g (sat 0g, mono 0g, poly 0g); PROTEIN 0.5g; CARB 16g; FIBER 0.1g; CHOL 0mg; IRON 0.3mg; SODIUM 46mg; CALC 18mg

Bul

Bul (BOOL) is a popular Cuban drink. It's best made with a pale ale or light-colored beer.

Prep: 4 minutes

- ⅓ cup fresh lime juice
- 1 (12-ounce) bottle beer, chilled
- 1 (12-ounce) bottle ginger ale, chilled
- 4 lime slices (optional)

1. Combine first 3 ingredients in a pitcher. Serve over ice. Garnish with lime slices, if desired. Yield: 4 servings (serving size: about ¾ cup).

CALORIES 69 (0% from fat); FAT 0g (sat 0g, mono 0g, poly 0g); PROTEIN 0.4g; CARB 12.4g; FIBER 0.3g; CHOL 0mg; IRON 0.2mg; SODIUM 10mg; CALC 9mg

Mango-Mint-Rum Slush

Fresh mint brightens the flavor of this icy cooler.

Prep: 9 minutes • Other: 1 hour

- 3 cups coarsely chopped peeled mango
- 1 cup ice cubes
- 1 cup mango nectar
- ¾ cup white rum
- ¼ cup fresh lime juice
- 2 tablespoons sugar
- 1 tablespoon chopped fresh mint

1. Place mango in freezer 1 hour.
2. Place mango, ice cubes, and remaining ingredients in a blender; process until smooth. Serve immediately. Yield: 4 servings (serving size: about 1 cup).

CALORIES 242 (2% from fat); FAT 0.4g (sat 0.1g, mono 0.1g, poly 0.1g); PROTEIN 0.8g; CARB 34.8g; FIBER 2.4g; CHOL 0mg; IRON 0.3mg; SODIUM 5mg; CALC 17mg

Mango Martini

Here's a fun twist on a classic martini.

Prep: 3 minutes

Crushed ice
- ¼ cup white rum
- 2 tablespoons Triple Sec
- 2 tablespoons mango juice
- 2 teaspoons fresh lime juice

1. Place crushed ice in a martini shaker. Add rum, liqueur, and juices; shake to combine. Strain mixture into a martini glass. Yield: 1 serving (serving size: about ½ cup).

CALORIES 247 (1% from fat); FAT 0.2g (sat 0g, mono 0g, poly 0.1g); PROTEIN 0.3g; CARB 16.4g; FIBER 0.1g; CHOL 0mg; IRON 0.2mg; SODIUM 3mg; CALC 2mg

Spicy Rum Punch

Add the ginger beer and rum just before serving so the punch will be fizzy. Ginger beer, which actually contains no alcohol, tastes like a spicy ginger ale.

**Prep: 5 minutes • Cook: 5 minutes
Other: 30 minutes**

- ¼ cup chopped crystallized ginger
- 2 tablespoons black peppercorns
- 6 star anise
- 4 (3-inch) cinnamon sticks
- 2 (64-ounce) bottles cranberry-pineapple juice drink
- 2 cups dark rum
- 4 (12-ounce) bottles ginger beer

1. Combine first 5 ingredients in a large Dutch oven; bring to a boil. Remove from heat; let stand 30 minutes.
2. Strain cranberry mixture through a fine sieve into a bowl; discard solids. Chill thoroughly. Stir in rum and ginger beer

just before serving. Yield: 20 servings (serving size: about ¾ cup).

CALORIES 205 (0% from fat); FAT 0g (sat 0g, mono 0g, poly 0g); PROTEIN 0.2g; CARB 38.2g; FIBER 0.2g; CHOL 0mg; IRON 0.1mg; SODIUM 4mg; CALC 13mg

Mojito

A mojito is a popular Cuban beverage. This one mirrors the traditional version but with slightly less sugar.

Prep: 4 minutes

- 2 teaspoons sugar
- 10 small mint leaves
- ¼ cup white rum
- 2 tablespoons fresh lime juice
- 1 (6-ounce) bottle club soda, chilled

1. Place sugar and mint leaves in a tall glass; crush with back of a long spoon. Fill glass with crushed ice. Add rum, juice, and club soda. Yield: 1 serving (serving size: about 1 cup).

CALORIES 169 (0% from fat); FAT 0g (sat 0g, mono 0g, poly 0g); PROTEIN 0.2g; CARB 11.2g; FIBER 0.2g; CHOL 0mg; IRON 0.1mg; SODIUM 37mg; CALC 13mg

Peach Cooler

You'll get the best flavor using fresh peaches, but if they're not in season, use frozen.

**Prep: 10 minutes • Cook: 2 minutes
Other: 7 hours, 30 minutes**

- 3 cups chopped peeled peaches
- 1½ cups water, divided
- ¾ cup sugar
- 2 tablespoons fresh lemon juice
- 2 tablespoons white rum

1. Place chopped peaches and ½ cup water in a blender or food processor;

process until smooth. Press mixture through a fine sieve into a bowl; discard solids.
2. Combine 1 cup water and sugar in a medium saucepan; bring to a boil. Remove from heat. Stir in peach mixture, juice, and rum. Pour into an 8-inch square baking dish. Cover; freeze 4 hours or until firm.
3. Place mixture in a food processor; process until slushy. Freeze 3 hours. Soften in refrigerator 30 minutes before serving. Yield: 8 servings (serving size: ⅔ cup).

CALORIES 109 (0% from fat); FAT 0.1g (sat 0g, mono 0g, poly 0.1g); PROTEIN 0.5g; CARB 26.1g; FIBER 0.8g; CHOL 0mg; IRON 0.1mg; SODIUM 0mg; CALC 4mg

Test Kitchen Tip: Let firm peaches stand on the kitchen counter for a few days or until they're soft to the touch.

Bloody Marys

A splash of lime juice contributes tartness to this brunch beverage.

Prep: 6 minutes

- 7 cups low-sodium tomato juice
- ¾ cup vodka
- 3 tablespoons fresh lime juice
- 2 tablespoons prepared horseradish
- 2 tablespoons Worcestershire sauce
- 1½ teaspoons hot sauce
- 1 teaspoon garlic salt
- 1 teaspoon ground celery seed
- 1 teaspoon black pepper

1. Combine all ingredients in a pitcher, stirring well. Chill. Serve over ice. Yield: 8 servings (serving size: 1 cup).

CALORIES 97 (2% from fat); FAT 0.2g (sat 0g, mono 0g, poly 0.1g); PROTEIN 1.8g; CARB 10.5g; FIBER 2g; CHOL 0mg; IRON 1.5mg; SODIUM 231mg; CALC 28mg

Wasabi Bloody Marys

Wasabi paste is the green Japanese version of horseradish.

Prep: 8 minutes

½	cup fresh lime juice
1½	tablespoons wasabi paste
6	cups low-sodium vegetable juice
3	tablespoons Worcestershire sauce
1¼	teaspoons hot pepper sauce
¾	teaspoon salt
1½	cups vodka

1. Combine juice and wasabi; stir with a whisk until wasabi dissolves. Combine wasabi mixture, vegetable juice, Worcestershire, pepper sauce, and salt. Chill.

2. Stir in vodka. Serve over ice. Yield: 8 servings (serving size: about 1 cup).

CALORIES 166 (0% from fat); FAT 0g (sat 0g, mono 0g, poly 0g); PROTEIN 1.6g; CARB 11.3g; FIBER 1.8g; CHOL 0mg; IRON 1.2mg; SODIUM 395mg; CALC 43mg

Frosty Cappuccino

A frosty coffee drink is the coolest way to chill out on a sultry summer day.

Prep: 10 minutes • Other: 4 hours

2¼	cups hot strong brewed coffee
⅓	cup packed brown sugar
1	cup 2% reduced-fat milk
¼	teaspoon ground cinnamon
2	tablespoons bourbon

Mocha Mudslides

1. Combine brewed coffee, sugar, milk, and cinnamon in a large bowl. Cool to room temperature. Pour 2 tablespoons coffee mixture into each of 28 ice cube tray compartments; freeze 4 hours or until firm.

2. Place coffee ice cubes and bourbon in a food processor. Process 4 minutes or until smooth, scraping sides of bowl twice. Serve immediately. Yield: 4 servings (serving size: 1 cup).

CALORIES 120 (10% from fat); FAT 1.2g (sat 0.7g, mono 0.3g, poly 0g); PROTEIN 2.2g; CARB 21.4g; FIBER 0g; CHOL 5mg; IRON 1mg; SODIUM 40mg; CALC 94mg

Mocha Mudslides

To keep it thick, use a whisk to stir this milk shake cocktail.

Prep: 5 minutes

2	cups chocolate low-fat ice cream, softened
½	cup 1% chocolate low-fat milk
¼	cup Kahlúa (coffee-flavored liqueur)
1	tablespoon grated semisweet or bittersweet chocolate (about ½ ounce)
½	teaspoon instant coffee granules
½	teaspoon vanilla extract

1. Combine all ingredients in a medium bowl; stir with a whisk just until blended. Serve immediately. Yield: 4 servings (serving size: ½ cup).

CALORIES 181 (15% from fat); FAT 3.1g (sat 1.9g, mono 0.2g, poly 0g); PROTEIN 3.3g; CARB 27.7g; FIBER 0.9g; CHOL 6mg; IRON 0.5mg; SODIUM 70mg; CALC 96mg

breads

Rustic White Bread,
page 90

Quick Breads

Leavened with baking powder and baking soda instead of yeast, these biscuits, scones, muffins, pancakes, and waffles are homey additions to your plate.

Drop Biscuits

The batter for these biscuits is spooned into muffin tins instead of onto a baking sheet. The result is still a free-form shape like that of traditional drop biscuits, but it's easier to keep the size consistent when you spoon into muffin cups.

Prep: 9 minutes • Cook: 12 minutes

    2 cups all-purpose flour
    1 tablespoon baking powder
    1 teaspoon sugar
    ½ teaspoon salt
    ¼ cup chilled butter, cut into small
       pieces
    1 cup fat-free milk
    Cooking spray

1. Preheat oven to 450°.
2. Lightly spoon flour into dry measuring cups; level with a knife. Combine flour, baking powder, sugar, and salt in a bowl; cut in butter with a pastry blender or 2 knives until mixture resembles coarse meal. Add milk; stir just until moist.
3. Spoon batter evenly into 12 muffin cups coated with cooking spray. Bake at 450° for 12 minutes or until golden. Remove from pan immediately; place on a wire rack. Yield: 1 dozen (serving size: 1 biscuit).

CALORIES 119 (31% from fat); FAT 4.1g (sat 2.5g, mono 1.1g, poly 0.2g); PROTEIN 2.9g; CARB 17.6g; FIBER 0.6g; CHOL 11mg; IRON 1.1mg; SODIUM 270mg; CALC 97mg

Sun-Dried Tomato Semolina Biscuits

This recipe calls for semolina flour, which has the consistency of fine cornmeal. The dough is sticky, but don't add more flour; it'll make the biscuits tough.

Prep: 15 minutes • Cook: 15 minutes
Other: 15 minutes

     2 cups boiling water
    10 sun-dried tomatoes, without oil
     2 cups all-purpose flour
    ¼   cup semolina flour or yellow cornmeal
     1 tablespoon sugar
    1½ teaspoons baking powder
    ¾   teaspoon salt
    ½   teaspoon baking soda
     1 teaspoon dried basil
    ¼   teaspoon ground red pepper
    ¼   cup chilled butter, cut into small pieces
     1 cup low-fat buttermilk
     Cooking spray

1. Combine boiling water and sun-dried tomatoes in a bowl; let stand 15 minutes. Drain and chop.
2. Preheat oven to 425°.
3. Lightly spoon flours into dry measuring cups; level with a knife. Combine all-purpose flour, semolina flour, and next 6 ingredients in a bowl; cut in butter with a pastry blender or 2 knives until mixture resembles coarse meal. (Flour mixture and butter can also be combined in a food processor; pulse until mixture resembles coarse meal.) Add tomatoes and buttermilk; stir just until moist.

4. Turn dough out onto a heavily floured surface; knead 5 times. Roll to a ½-inch thickness; cut with a 2½-inch biscuit cutter. Place on a baking sheet coated with cooking spray. Bake at 425° for 15 minutes or until golden. Yield: 1 dozen (serving size: 1 biscuit).

CALORIES 140 (29% from fat); FAT 4.5g (sat 2.6g, mono 1.3g, poly 0.3g); PROTEIN 3.4g; CARB 21.3g; FIBER 0.9g; CHOL 10mg; IRON 1.4mg; SODIUM 345mg; CALC 67mg

how to cut butter into flour

Cut the chilled butter into the flour using a pastry blender until the mixture resembles coarse meal.

If you don't have a pastry blender, use two knives, or you can pulse the mixture in your food processor.

Buttermilk Biscuits

The buttermilk adds flavor and tenderness so you don't have to use as much butter in these flaky, "melt-in-your-mouth" biscuits. For the best biscuits, it's important to measure the flour correctly. See page 116 for the correct way to measure.

Prep: 12 minutes • Cook: 12 minutes

2 cups all-purpose flour
2 teaspoons baking powder
¼ teaspoon baking soda
¼ teaspoon salt
3 tablespoons plus 1 teaspoon chilled butter, cut into small pieces
¾ cup low-fat or fat-free buttermilk
Honey (optional)

1. Preheat oven to 450°.
2. Lightly spoon flour into dry measuring cups; level with a knife. Combine flour and next 3 ingredients in a bowl. Cut in butter with a pastry blender or 2 knives until mixture resembles coarse meal. Add buttermilk; stir just until dry ingredients are moist.
3. Turn dough out onto a lightly floured surface; knead 4 or 5 times. Roll dough to a ½-inch thickness; cut with a 2½-inch biscuit cutter. Place on a baking sheet. Bake at 450° for 12 minutes or until biscuits are golden. Drizzle biscuits with honey, if desired. Yield: 1 dozen (serving size: 1 biscuit).

CALORIES 102 (23% from fat); FAT 2.6g (sat 1.2g, mono 1g, poly 0.2g); PROTEIN 2.7g; CARB 16.9g; FIBER 0.6g; CHOL 6mg; IRON 1.1mg; SODIUM 189mg; CALC 67mg

Test Kitchen Tip: Cut the dough with a biscuit cutter dipped in flour. Don't twist the cutter; this could seal the edges and hinder the biscuits from rising.

Dried Pear and Cardamom Scones

Dried pears lend sweetness and cardamom adds spice. Traditional scone recipes often have both butter and cream; we've used less butter and replaced the cream with low-fat buttermilk.

Prep: 17 minutes • Cook: 25 minutes

1½   cups all-purpose flour
½   cup whole wheat flour
¼   cup sugar
2   teaspoons baking powder
½   teaspoon salt
⅛   teaspoon ground cardamom
3   tablespoons chilled butter, cut into small pieces
10   tablespoons low-fat buttermilk
1   teaspoon grated lemon rind
1   teaspoon vanilla extract
1   large egg, lightly beaten
1   cup chopped dried pears
2   teaspoons all-purpose flour
Cooking spray
1   large egg white, lightly beaten

1. Preheat oven to 350°.
2. Lightly spoon 1½ cups all-purpose flour and whole wheat flour into dry measuring cups; level with a knife. Combine flours, sugar, baking powder, salt, and cardamom in a large bowl; cut in butter with a pastry blender or 2 knives until mixture resembles coarse meal.
3. Combine buttermilk, rind, vanilla, and 1 egg in a medium bowl; stir in dried pears. Add buttermilk mixture to flour mixture, stirring just until moist (dough will be sticky).
4. Turn dough out onto a lightly floured surface; knead lightly 4 or 5 times with floured hands. Dust top of dough with 2 teaspoons all-purpose flour, and pat into

an 8-inch circle on a baking sheet coated with cooking spray. Cut dough into 8 wedges, cutting into but not through dough. Brush egg white over wedges. Bake at 350° for 25 minutes or until golden. Serve warm. Yield: 8 servings (serving size: 1 wedge).

CALORIES 228 (23% from fat); FAT 5.7g (sat 3.1g, mono 1.6g, poly 0.4g); PROTEIN 5.7g; CARB 39.5g; FIBER 2.6g; CHOL 39mg; IRON 1.8mg; SODIUM 349mg; CALC 105mg

Test Kitchen Tip: The less scones are handled, the better. Stir just until moist, and use a soft touch when patting the dough.

how to knead the dough

Once you add the milk mixture, turn the dough out onto a floured surface, and knead four or five times. The dough will be sticky, but don't add more flour.

Dried Pear and Cardamom Scones (left) and Curried Butternut Soup (page 486)

Ham and Cheese Scones

Pair these savory scones with salad or soup for a light meal.

Prep: 16 minutes • Cook: 20 minutes

- 2 cups all-purpose flour
- 1 tablespoon baking powder
- 2 teaspoons sugar
- ¼ teaspoon salt
- ¼ teaspoon ground red pepper
- 3 tablespoons chilled butter, cut into small pieces
- ¾ cup (3 ounces) reduced-fat shredded extrasharp Cheddar cheese
- ¾ cup finely chopped 33%-less-sodium ham (about 3 ounces)
- ¾ cup fat-free buttermilk
- 2 large egg whites
- Cooking spray

1. Preheat oven to 400°.

2. Lightly spoon flour into dry measuring cups; level with a knife. Combine flour, baking powder, sugar, salt, and pepper in a large bowl; cut in butter with a pastry blender or 2 knives until mixture resembles coarse meal. Stir in cheese and ham. Combine buttermilk and egg whites, stirring with a whisk. Add to flour mixture, stirring just until moist.

3. Turn dough out onto a lightly floured surface; knead lightly 4 or 5 times with floured hands. Pat dough into an 8-inch circle on a baking sheet coated with cooking spray. Cut dough into 8 wedges, cutting into but not through dough. Bake at 400° for 20 minutes or until lightly browned. Yield: 8 servings (serving size: 1 wedge).

CALORIES 217 (30% from fat); FAT 7.2g (sat 4.1g, mono 1.6g, poly 0.4g); PROTEIN 10.4g; CARB 27.1g; FIBER 0.9g; CHOL 26mg; IRON 1.8mg; SODIUM 519mg; CALC 235mg

how to make scones

Pat the dough into an 8-inch circle on a baking sheet coated with cooking spray. Cut it into wedges; do not separate the pieces unless specified in the recipe.

Swedish Limpa Soda Bread

Soda bread is a quick bread that's leavened when baking soda is activated by an acidic ingredient—usually buttermilk. This recipe is similar to Irish Soda Bread, but is flavored with aniseed and orange rind.

Prep: 20 minutes • Cook: 55 minutes

- 3 cups all-purpose flour
- ½ cup whole wheat flour
- ½ cup rye flour
- 1½ teaspoons baking powder
- 1¼ teaspoons salt
- 1 teaspoon baking soda
- 1 teaspoon aniseed
- 5 tablespoons chilled butter, cut into small pieces
- ¾ cup low-fat buttermilk
- ¾ cup Guinness Stout or dark beer
- ¼ cup honey
- 1 tablespoon grated orange rind
- 2 tablespoons molasses
- 1 tablespoon canola oil
- Cooking spray
- 2 teaspoons cornmeal
- 2 teaspoons 1% low-fat milk

1. Preheat oven to 375°.

2. Lightly spoon flours into dry measuring cups; level with a knife. Combine flours and next 4 ingredients in a large bowl; cut in butter with a pastry blender or 2 knives until mixture resembles coarse meal. (Flour mixture and butter can also be combined in a food processor; pulse until mixture resembles coarse meal.) Make a well in center of mixture. Combine buttermilk and next 5 ingredients in a bowl; add to flour mixture. Stir just until moist (dough will be sticky).

3. Turn dough out onto a lightly floured surface; knead lightly 1 minute with floured hands. Divide dough in half; shape each half into a 6 x 4–inch oval loaf. Place loaves on a baking sheet coated with cooking spray and sprinkled with cornmeal. Make 1 lengthwise cut ¾ inch deep across top of each loaf using a sharp knife. Brush loaves with 2 teaspoons milk. Bake at 375° for 30 minutes. Reduce oven temperature to 350° (do not remove bread from oven); bake an additional 25 minutes or until loaves are browned on bottom and sound hollow when tapped. Remove loaves from pan; cool completely on a wire rack. Yield: 2 loaves, 10 servings per loaf (serving size: 1 slice).

CALORIES 139 (26% from fat); FAT 4g (sat 2g, mono 1.2g, poly 0.4g); PROTEIN 2.9g; CARB 23.2g; FIBER 1.2g; CHOL 8mg; IRON 1.2mg; SODIUM 248mg; CALC 36mg

Test Kitchen Tip: If your quick breads aren't rising properly, check the expiration dates on your baking powder and baking soda. These products start to weaken after six months.

Quick Buttermilk Corn Bread

For down-home bread that's crispy on the outside, moist and tender on the inside, bake corn bread in a cast-iron skillet.

Prep: 8 minutes • Cook: 15 minutes
Other: 15 minutes

  2 tablespoons canola oil
  2 cups yellow cornmeal
  1 teaspoon salt
  ½ teaspoon baking powder
  ½ teaspoon baking soda
1¾ cups fat-free buttermilk
  ⅛ teaspoon pepper
  1 large egg, lightly beaten

1. Preheat oven to 450°.
2. Pour oil into a 9-inch cast-iron skillet. Place skillet in a 450° oven for 10 minutes.
3. Combine cornmeal, salt, baking powder, and baking soda in a large bowl. Combine buttermilk, pepper, and egg, stirring with a whisk. Add egg mixture to cornmeal mixture, stirring just until moist.
4. Remove pan from oven. Tip pan to coat bottom and sides with oil; carefully pour excess oil into batter, stirring to combine. Pour batter into pan, spreading evenly. Bake at 450° for 15 minutes or until a wooden pick inserted in center comes out clean. Let stand 5 minutes before serving. Yield: 8 servings (serving size: 1 wedge).

CALORIES 170 (27% from fat); FAT 5.1g (sat 0.8g, mono 1.3g, poly 2.6g); PROTEIN 5.2g; CARB 26.5g; FIBER 2.2g; CHOL 28mg; IRON 1.2mg; SODIUM 473mg; CALC 88mg

Jalapeño Corn Bread

Cut a wedge of this corn bread to serve with a bowl of chili. Adding whole-kernel corn to the batter creates a corn bread that is extramoist and tender.

Prep: 13 minutes • Cook: 25 minutes
Other: 12 minutes

  1 teaspoon canola oil
Cooking spray
1¼ cups all-purpose flour
1¼ cups yellow cornmeal
  2 tablespoons sugar
  1 tablespoon baking powder
  1 teaspoon salt
  1 teaspoon ground cumin
  1 cup fat-free milk
  ½ cup chopped red bell pepper
  ¼ cup minced seeded jalapeño pepper
     (about 2)
  3 tablespoons butter, melted
  2 tablespoons minced fresh cilantro
  2 large eggs, lightly beaten
  1 (7-ounce) can whole-kernel corn, drained

1. Preheat oven to 425°.
2. Coat a 10-inch cast-iron or heavy ovenproof skillet with oil and cooking spray. Place pan in a 425° oven for 7 minutes.
3. Lightly spoon flour into dry measuring cups; level with a knife. Combine flour and next 5 ingredients. Combine milk and remaining ingredients; add to cornmeal mixture. Stir just until moist. Pour into prepared pan. Bake at 425° for 25 minutes or until a wooden pick inserted in center comes out clean. Let stand 5 minutes before serving. Yield: 12 servings (serving size: 1 wedge).

CALORIES 171 (25% from fat); FAT 4.7g (sat 2.2g, mono 1.4g, poly 0.6g); PROTEIN 4.8g; CARB 28.9g; FIBER 1.8g; CHOL 43mg; IRON 1.7mg; SODIUM 396mg; CALC 104mg

Corn Bread Muffins

You can also use this basic recipe for corn sticks or a pan of corn bread.

Prep: 7 minutes • Cook: 20 minutes

  1 cup yellow cornmeal
  ¾ cup all-purpose flour
1½ teaspoons baking powder
  ¼ teaspoon baking soda
  ¼ teaspoon salt
  1 cup low-fat buttermilk
  2 tablespoons butter, melted
  1 large egg, lightly beaten
Cooking spray

1. Preheat oven to 400°.
2. Lightly spoon cornmeal and flour into measuring cups; level with a knife. Combine cornmeal, flour, baking powder, baking soda, and salt in a large bowl, stirring with a whisk. Make a well in center of mixture. Combine buttermilk, butter, and egg. Pour buttermilk mixture into cornmeal mixture; stir just until moist.
3. Spoon batter evenly into 6 muffin cups coated with cooking spray. Bake at 400° for 20 minutes or until a wooden pick inserted in center comes out clean. Remove from pan immediately; cool on a wire rack. Yield: 6 muffins (serving size: 1 muffin).

CALORIES 205 (25% from fat); FAT 5.6g (sat 2.9g, mono 1.5g, poly 0.5g); PROTEIN 6.1g; CARB 32.1g; FIBER 2.1g; CHOL 48mg; IRON 1.1mg; SODIUM 345mg; CALC 111mg

cornmeal To make cornmeal, dried corn kernels are ground into a fine, medium, or coarse texture. The stone-ground method of grinding retains some of the hull and the germ of the corn, so it's more nutritious than cornmeal ground by steel rollers that remove the hull and germ completely.

Lemon-Blueberry Muffins

You can make these muffins up to two days ahead, and glaze them just before serving.

Prep: 20 minutes • Cook: 20 minutes

2 cups all-purpose flour
½ cup sugar
1 teaspoon baking powder
½ teaspoon baking soda
½ teaspoon salt
⅛ teaspoon ground nutmeg
¼ cup chilled butter, cut into small pieces
1¼ cups low-fat buttermilk
1 tablespoon grated lemon rind
1 large egg, lightly beaten
1 cup fresh blueberries
Cooking spray
1 tablespoon fresh lemon juice
½ cup powdered sugar

1. Preheat oven to 400°.

2. Lightly spoon flour into dry measuring cups; level with a knife. Combine flour and next 5 ingredients in a medium bowl; cut in butter with a pastry blender or 2 knives until mixture resembles coarse meal. Make a well in center of mixture.

3. Combine buttermilk, rind, and egg; stir well with a whisk. Add to flour mixture; stir just until moist. Gently fold in blueberries.

4. Spoon batter into 12 muffin cups coated with cooking spray. Bake at 400° for 20 minutes or until muffins spring back when lightly touched. Remove muffins from pans immediately, and place on a wire rack to cool.

5. Combine lemon juice and powdered sugar in a small bowl. Drizzle glaze evenly over cooled muffins. Yield: 1 dozen (serving size: 1 muffin).

CALORIES 187 (23% from fat); FAT 4.8g (sat 2.7g, mono 1.4g, poly 0.3g); PROTEIN 3.7g; CARB 32.6g; FIBER 1g; CHOL 30mg; IRON 1.1mg; SODIUM 264mg; CALC 59mg

Apricot-Almond Muffins

Almonds provide more vitamin E—which protects your heart against disease—than any other single food.

Prep: 15 minutes • Cook: 20 minutes

½	cup apricot preserves
¼	teaspoon almond extract
1	cup all-purpose flour
1	cup whole wheat flour
1½	teaspoons baking powder
½	teaspoon baking soda
½	teaspoon salt
½	cup packed brown sugar
1	large egg
1	large egg white
1	cup low-fat buttermilk
3	tablespoons canola oil
2	teaspoons grated orange rind
1	teaspoon vanilla extract
	Cooking spray
2	teaspoons granulated sugar
¼	cup sliced almonds

1. Preheat oven to 400°.

2. Combine preserves and almond extract in a small bowl.

3. Lightly spoon flours into dry measuring cups, and level with a knife. Combine flours, baking powder, baking soda, and salt in a large bowl; make a well in center of mixture.

4. Combine brown sugar, egg, and egg white in a medium bowl, and stir well with a whisk. Stir in buttermilk, canola oil, orange rind, and vanilla. Add to flour mixture, stirring just until moist.

5. Spoon 2 tablespoons batter into each of 12 muffin cups coated with cooking spray. Spoon apricot mixture evenly into centers of muffin cups (do not spread over batter), and top with remaining batter. (Muffin cups will be full.) Sprinkle batter evenly with 2 teaspoons granulated sugar and almonds.

6. Bake at 400° for 20 minutes or until muffins spring back when touched lightly in center. Run a knife or spatula around outer edge of each muffin cup. Carefully remove muffins immediately, and place on a wire rack. Yield: 1 dozen (serving size: 1 muffin).

CALORIES 209 (26% from fat); FAT 6.1g (sat 0.8g, mono 3.3g, poly 1.6g); PROTEIN 4.7g; CARB 35.3g; FIBER 2g; CHOL 18mg; IRON 1.3mg; SODIUM 242mg; CALC 85mg

Blueberry Muffins with Almond Streusel

These muffins are loaded with B vitamins from whole wheat flour, calcium from milk and yogurt, antioxidants from blueberries, and heart-friendly monounsaturated fat from almonds and canola oil.

Prep: 15 minutes • Cook: 15 minutes
Other: 10 minutes

Muffins:

1½	cups all-purpose flour
1	cup whole wheat flour
1	cup quick-cooking oats
1	cup granulated sugar
1	tablespoon baking powder
1	teaspoon baking soda
¼	teaspoon salt
2	cups vanilla low-fat yogurt
½	cup 2% reduced-fat milk
3	tablespoons canola oil
2	teaspoons vanilla extract
1	large egg, lightly beaten
1½	cups fresh blueberries
	Cooking spray

Streusel:

¼	cup all-purpose flour
¼	cup slivered almonds, chopped
1	tablespoon brown sugar
1	tablespoon butter, melted

1. Preheat oven to 400°.

2. To prepare muffins, lightly spoon flours into dry measuring cups; level with a knife. Combine flours, oats, granulated sugar, baking powder, baking soda, and salt in a large bowl, stirring with a whisk. Make a well in center of mixture. Combine yogurt, milk, oil, vanilla, and egg, stirring with a whisk. Add yogurt mixture to flour mixture; stir just until moist. Fold in blueberries. Spoon 2 rounded tablespoons batter into each of 30 muffin cups coated with cooking spray.

3. To prepare streusel, combine ¼ cup all-purpose flour, almonds, brown sugar, and butter. Sprinkle evenly over batter. Bake at 400° for 15 minutes or until muffins spring back when touched lightly in center. Cool in pans 10 minutes on a wire rack; remove from pans. Serve warm or at room temperature. Yield: 2½ dozen (serving size: 1 muffin).

CALORIES 123 (23% from fat); FAT 3.2g (sat 0.6g, mono 1.6g, poly 0.7g); PROTEIN 3.1g; CARB 21.1g; FIBER 1.2g; CHOL 9mg; IRON 0.8mg; SODIUM 129mg; CALC 68mg

muffin musts

- Overstirring the batter results in muffins that are tough. Another common cause for tough muffins is too much flour, generally caused by "scooping" instead of "spooning." To measure flour accurately, stir it with a fork to aerate; lightly spoon it into a dry measuring cup, leveling the top with a knife (see page 116).
- If all the cups aren't used when filling the muffin pan with batter, pour water into the empty cups to keep the pan from buckling.
- Muffins are best eaten the day they're made, but they also freeze well. Cover tightly; freeze up to one month.

Oat Bran Muffins

Featuring triple-grain goodness, these muffins contain high-fiber oat bran, flaxseed, and whole wheat flour. Plus they're packed with high-power nutrients from raisins, carrot, apple, and orange—a great way to start your day.

Prep: 20 minutes • Cook: 20 minutes

  1   cup all-purpose flour
  1   cup whole wheat flour
  1¾ cups oat bran
  ¾   cup packed brown sugar
  ⅓   cup nonfat dry milk
  ¼   cup flaxseed
  4   teaspoons ground cinnamon
  2   teaspoons baking soda
  2   teaspoons baking powder
  ½   teaspoon salt
  2   cups shredded carrot
  2   cups chopped Granny Smith apple
  1   cup raisins
  1   cup fat-free milk
  ¼   cup canola oil
  2   teaspoons vanilla extract
  3   large egg whites
  1   thin-skinned orange, unpeeled and quartered
  Cooking spray

1. Preheat oven to 375°.
2. Lightly spoon flours into dry measuring cups; level with a knife. Combine flours and next 8 ingredients in a large bowl, stirring well with a whisk. Stir in carrot, apple, and raisins. Make a well in center of flour mixture.
3. Place milk, oil, vanilla, egg whites, and orange in a blender or food processor; process until smooth. Add milk mixture to flour mixture; stir just until moist.
4. Spoon 3 tablespoons batter into each of 28 muffin cups coated with cooking spray.

Bake at 375° for 20 minutes or until muffins are browned and spring back when touched lightly in center. Remove muffins from pans immediately, and place on a wire rack. Yield: 28 muffins (serving size: 1 muffin).

CALORIES 114 (22% from fat); FAT 2.8g (sat 0.3g, mono 1.3g, poly 0.8g); PROTEIN 3.5g; CARB 22.6g; FIBER 3g; CHOL 0mg; IRON 1.1mg; SODIUM 188mg; CALC 61mg

Pumpkin Muffins

A combination of brown sugar and granulated sugar creates a crunchy topping that contrasts with the cakelike texture of the muffins.

Prep: 15 minutes • Cook: 25 minutes

  2¾ cups all-purpose flour
  1   cup granulated sugar
  1   tablespoon baking powder
  1   teaspoon baking soda
  1   teaspoon ground cinnamon
  ½   teaspoon salt
  1   cup canned pumpkin
  ¾   cup fat-free sour cream
  ⅓   cup fat-free milk
  ¼   cup canola oil
  1   teaspoon vanilla extract
  1   large egg, lightly beaten
  1   large egg white, lightly beaten
  Cooking spray
  1   tablespoon granulated sugar
  1½ teaspoons brown sugar

1. Preheat oven to 375°.
2. Lightly spoon flour into dry measuring cups; level with a knife. Combine flour and next 5 ingredients in a medium bowl, stirring with a whisk. Make a well in center of mixture.
3. Combine pumpkin and next 6 ingredients in a medium bowl; add to flour

mixture, stirring just until moist. Spoon batter into 18 muffin cups coated with cooking spray.
4. Combine 1 tablespoon granulated sugar and brown sugar; sprinkle over muffins.
5. Bake at 375° for 23 to 25 minutes or until muffins spring back when touched lightly in center. Remove muffins from pans immediately, and cool on a wire rack. Yield: 1½ dozen (serving size: 1 muffin).

CALORIES 164 (19% from fat); FAT 3.5g (sat 0.6g, mono 0.8g, poly 1.9g); PROTEIN 3.5g; CARB 29.7g; FIBER 1g; CHOL 12mg; IRON 1.2mg; SODIUM 269mg; CALC 78mg

how to mix muffins

1. Combine the dry ingredients; stir well. Make a well in the center of the mixture; pour the liquid ingredients into the well.

2. Stir the batter just until the dry ingredients are moistened. Overmixing at this point will make the muffins tough.

Cranberry Quick Bread with Raisins and Hazelnuts

The batter is a pale tan, but the finished bread is a rich golden brown. You can use chopped walnuts in place of the hazelnuts.

**Prep: 12 minutes • Cook: 50 minutes
Other: 10 minutes**

1⅓ cups all-purpose flour
 ⅔ cup whole wheat flour
  1 cup sugar
  1 teaspoon baking powder
 ½ teaspoon baking soda
 ¼ teaspoon salt
 ¾ cup apple juice
  3 tablespoons canola oil
  1 teaspoon grated orange rind
  1 large egg, lightly beaten
1⅓ cups chopped fresh cranberries
 ⅓ cup golden raisins
 ¼ cup chopped hazelnuts
  Cooking spray

1. Preheat oven to 350°.
2. Lightly spoon flours into dry measuring cups; level with a knife. Combine flours and next 4 ingredients in a large bowl; make a well in center of mixture. Combine juice, oil, rind, and egg; add to flour mixture, stirring just until moist. Fold in cranberries, raisins, and hazelnuts.
3. Spoon batter into a 9 x 5–inch loaf pan coated with cooking spray. Bake at 350° for 50 minutes or until a wooden pick inserted in center comes out clean. Cool 10 minutes in pan on a wire rack; remove from pan. Cool completely on wire rack. Yield: 16 servings (serving size: 1 slice).

CALORIES 162 (23% from fat); FAT 4.2g (sat 0.4g, mono 2.5g, poly 1.1g); PROTEIN 2.6g; CARB 29.6g; FIBER 1.6g; CHOL 13mg; IRON 1mg; SODIUM 112mg; CALC 27mg

Lemon-Glazed Zucchini Quick Bread

Garden-fresh zucchini contributes to the irresistibly moist texture of this sweet loaf, and the citrusy glaze makes it special enough for dessert.

Prep: 20 minutes • Cook: 55 minutes • Other: 10 minutes

2⅓ cups all-purpose flour
 ¾ cup granulated sugar
  2 teaspoons baking powder
  1 teaspoon ground cinnamon
 ½ teaspoon baking soda
 ½ teaspoon salt
 ¼ teaspoon ground nutmeg
  1 cup finely shredded zucchini
 ½ cup 1% low-fat milk
 ¼ cup canola oil
  2 tablespoons grated lemon rind
  1 large egg
  Cooking spray
  1 cup sifted powdered sugar
  2 tablespoons fresh lemon juice

1. Preheat oven to 350°.
2. Lightly spoon flour into dry measuring cups; level with a knife. Combine flour and next 6 ingredients in a large bowl; make a well in center of mixture. Combine zucchini, milk, oil, rind, and egg in a bowl; add to flour mixture. Stir just until moist.
3. Spoon batter into an 8 x 4–inch loaf pan coated with cooking spray. Bake at 350° for 55 minutes or until a wooden pick inserted in center comes out clean. Cool loaf 10 minutes in pan on a wire rack; remove loaf from pan. Cool completely on wire rack.
4. Combine powdered sugar and lemon juice; stir with a whisk. Drizzle over loaf. Yield: 14 servings (serving size: 1 slice).

CALORIES 192 (22% from fat); FAT 4.7g (sat 0.5g, mono 2.5g, poly 1.3g); PROTEIN 3g; CARB 34.9g; FIBER 0.9g; CHOL 15mg; IRON 1.2mg; SODIUM 210mg; CALC 59mg

Classic Banana Bread

As it bakes, banana bread should form a crack down the center—a sign that the baking soda is doing its job.

Prep: 15 minutes • Cook: 1 hour
Other: 10 minutes

  2   cups all-purpose flour
  ¾   teaspoon baking soda
  ½   teaspoon salt
  1   cup sugar
  ¼   cup butter, softened
  2   large eggs
1½   cups mashed ripe banana (about
       3 bananas)
  ⅓   cup plain low-fat yogurt
  1   teaspoon vanilla extract
Cooking spray

1. Preheat oven to 350°.
2. Lightly spoon flour into dry measuring cups; level with a knife. Combine flour, baking soda, and salt, stirring with a whisk.
3. Place sugar and butter in a large bowl, and beat with a mixer at medium speed until well blended (about 1 minute). Add eggs, 1 at a time, beating well after each addition. Add banana, yogurt, and vanilla; beat until blended. Add flour mixture; beat at low speed just until moist.
4. Spoon batter into an 8 x 4–inch loaf pan coated with cooking spray. Bake at 350° for 1 hour or until a wooden pick inserted in center comes out clean. Cool 10 minutes in pan on a wire rack; remove from pan. Cool completely on wire rack. Yield: 14 servings (serving size: 1 slice).

CALORIES 187 (21% from fat); FAT 4.3g (sat 2.4g, mono 1.2g, poly 0.3g); PROTEIN 3.3g; CARB 34.4g; FIBER 1.1g; CHOL 40mg; IRON 1mg; SODIUM 198mg; CALC 20mg

---

All-Time Favorite

Jamaican Banana Bread

Don't stop with the bananas: Really go tropical by adding coconut, lime, and rum. After one bite of the coconut-pecan topping, you'll be in paradise.

Prep: 25 minutes • Cook: 1 hour, 2 minutes
Other: 10 minutes

Bread:
  2   tablespoons butter, softened
  2   tablespoons (1 ounce) block-style
       ⅓-less-fat cream cheese, softened
  1   cup granulated sugar
  1   large egg
  2   cups all-purpose flour
  2   teaspoons baking powder
  ½   teaspoon baking soda
  ⅛   teaspoon salt
  1   cup mashed ripe banana (about 2
       bananas)
  ½   cup fat-free milk
  2   tablespoons dark rum or
       ¼ teaspoon imitation rum extract
  ½   teaspoon grated lime rind
  2   teaspoons lime juice
  1   teaspoon vanilla extract
  ¼   cup chopped pecans, toasted
  ¼   cup flaked sweetened coconut
Cooking spray

Topping:
  ¼   cup packed brown sugar
  2   teaspoons butter
  2   teaspoons lime juice
  2   teaspoons dark rum or ⅛ teaspoon
       imitation rum extract
  2   tablespoons chopped pecans,
       toasted
  2   tablespoons flaked sweetened
       coconut

1. Preheat oven to 375°.
2. To prepare bread, beat 2 tablespoons butter and cheese with a mixer at medium speed; add granulated sugar, beating well. Add egg; beat well.
3. Lightly spoon flour into dry measuring cups; level with a knife. Combine flour, baking powder, baking soda, and salt. Combine banana and next 5 ingredients. Add flour mixture to creamed mixture alternately with banana mixture, beginning and ending with flour mixture; mix after each addition. Stir in ¼ cup pecans and ¼ cup coconut.
4. Pour batter into an 8 x 4–inch loaf pan coated with cooking spray. Bake at 375° for 1 hour. Cool in pan 10 minutes, and remove from pan. Cool loaf slightly on a wire rack.
5. To prepare topping, combine brown sugar and 2 teaspoons each butter, lime juice, and rum in a saucepan; bring to a simmer. Cook 1 minute, stirring constantly. Remove from heat. Stir in 2 tablespoons each pecans and coconut; spoon over loaf. Yield: 16 servings (serving size: 1 slice).

CALORIES 193 (26% from fat); FAT 5.5g (sat 2.4g, mono 1.9g, poly 0.7g); PROTEIN 2.9g; CARB 32.3g; FIBER 1.1g; CHOL 20mg; IRON 1mg; SODIUM 163mg; CALC 55mg

Test Kitchen Tip: We routinely test quick-bread recipes in shiny metal pans, but glass or dark metal pans are OK, too. Glass conducts heat better, though, so you'll need to decrease the oven temperature by 25°, and bake about 10 minutes less than our recipes indicate. Also, when using dark metal pans, decrease the cooking time by 10 minutes.

Classic Makeover: Popovers

Because they're typically flavored with butter, 50 percent of the calories comes from fat in a traditional popover recipe. With a few simple substitutions, we reduced the fat by more than half.

We used 1% low-fat milk instead of whole milk, which saved almost 50 calories and 5.5 grams of fat. We cut the number of eggs in half and decreased the fat by another 5.5 grams. But we got the most significant cut in fat—22.5 grams—from cutting out two-thirds of the butter. These changes more than halved the fat without changing the popovers' shape, golden crust, and flavor.

Before	After
• 198 calories	• 96 calories
• 10.9g fat	• 3.3g fat
• percentage of calories from fat 50%	• percentage of calories from fat 31%

Popovers

Although it's tempting, don't open the oven door to peek at the popovers—use the oven light and view through the glass to see if they're golden brown. Opening the oven door before the popovers are done may cause them to deflate.

Prep: 9 minutes • Cook: 40 minutes
Other: 35 minutes

  1 cup all-purpose flour
 ½ teaspoon salt
  1 cup 1% low-fat milk
  2 large eggs, lightly beaten
  1 tablespoon butter, melted
Cooking spray
  1 teaspoon canola oil

1. Lightly spoon flour into a dry measuring cup; level with a knife. Combine flour and salt, stirring with a whisk. Combine milk and eggs in a medium bowl, stirring with a whisk until blended; let stand 30 minutes. Gradually add flour mixture, stirring well with a whisk. Stir in butter.
2. Preheat oven to 375°.
3. Coat 9 popover cups with cooking spray; brush oil evenly in cups to coat. Place popover cups in a 375° oven for 5 minutes. Divide batter evenly among prepared popover cups. Bake at 375° for 40 minutes or until golden. Serve immediately. Yield: 9 servings (serving size: 1 popover).

CALORIES 96 (31% from fat); FAT 3.3g (sat 1.4g, mono 1.2g, poly 0.8g); PROTEIN 3.9g; CARB 12.2g; FIBER 0.4g; CHOL 51mg; IRON 0.9mg; SODIUM 172mg; CALC 47mg

Test Kitchen Tip: Muffin pan cups are smaller than popover pan cups, so if you're using muffin pans, the popovers will need 5 minutes less baking time.

Waffles with Two-Berry Syrup

Wheat germ and flaxseed are the ingredients that give these waffles a wonderful nuttiness. But it's the syrup, laced with maple and two kinds of berries, that elevates this breakfast bread to the sublime.

Prep: 12 minutes • Cook: 5 minutes per batch

Waffles:

- 2 tablespoons flaxseed
- 1 cup all-purpose flour
- ½ cup whole wheat flour
- ¼ cup toasted wheat germ
- 2 tablespoons sugar
- 1½ teaspoons baking powder
- ½ teaspoon salt
- 1½ cups fat-free milk
- ¾ cup egg substitute
- 1½ tablespoons canola oil
- 1 teaspoon vanilla extract
  Cooking spray

Two-Berry Syrup:

- 1½ cups fresh or frozen blueberries
- 1½ cups fresh or frozen unsweetened raspberries
- ½ cup maple syrup
- ¼ teaspoon ground cinnamon

1. To prepare waffles, place flaxseed in a clean coffee grinder or blender; process until ground to measure ¼ cup flaxseed meal. Lightly spoon flours into dry measuring cups; level with a knife. Combine flaxseed meal, flours, wheat germ, sugar, baking powder, and salt in a large bowl; make a well in center of mixture. Combine milk, egg substitute, oil, and vanilla; add to flour mixture, stirring just until moist.
2. Preheat waffle iron. Coat iron with cooking spray. Spoon ¼ cup batter for each 4-inch waffle onto hot waffle iron, spreading batter to edges. Cook 5 to 6 minutes or until steaming stops.
3. To prepare syrup, combine berries, maple syrup, and ground cinnamon in a saucepan. Cook over medium heat until thoroughly heated. Serve warm over waffles. Yield: 12 servings (serving size: 1 waffle and about 2 tablespoons syrup).

CALORIES 166 (18% from fat); FAT 3.3g (sat 0.4g, mono 1.2g, poly 1.4g); PROTEIN 5.4g; CARB 30.2g; FIBER 3.2g; CHOL 1mg; IRON 1.6mg; SODIUM 200mg; CALC 100mg

Test Kitchen Tip: Look for flaxseed, a grain rich in heart-healthy omega-3 fats, in health-food stores or large supermarkets.

waffle tips

- Spray the waffle iron with cooking spray before spreading the batter.
- Pour the batter in the middle of the waffle iron, and spread close to the edge using a rubber spatula.
- After spreading the batter, close the lid and cook until steaming stops. It's important to keep the waffle iron lid closed for a couple of minutes to prevent separating the top and bottom of the waffle.
- Let the waffle iron cool completely before cleaning it. Wipe with a damp paper towel to pick up any remaining crumbs—no soap is needed.
- Waffles freeze well. Cool them to room temperature; freeze in a single layer on a baking sheet. Store in a freezer-safe zip-top plastic bag up to three months. To reheat, place frozen waffles on a baking sheet in a 350° oven for 10 minutes. You can also heat sturdier waffles in a toaster oven.

Buttermilk Pancakes

To freeze any leftovers, place wax paper between the pancakes, and wrap them tightly in foil.

Prep: 8 minutes • Cook: about 4 minutes per batch

- 1 cup all-purpose flour
- 2 tablespoons sugar
- 1 teaspoon baking powder
- ½ teaspoon baking soda
- ¼ teaspoon salt
- 1 cup low-fat buttermilk
- 1 tablespoon canola oil
- 1 large egg, lightly beaten
  Cooking spray

1. Lightly spoon flour into a dry measuring cup; level with a knife. Combine flour and next 4 ingredients in a large bowl; make a well in center of mixture. Combine buttermilk, oil, and egg; add to flour mixture, stirring until smooth.
2. Spoon about ¼ cup batter for each pancake onto a hot nonstick griddle or nonstick skillet coated with cooking spray. Turn pancakes when tops are covered with bubbles and edges look cooked. Yield: 9 (4-inch) pancakes (serving size: 1 pancake).

CALORIES 94 (24% from fat); FAT 2.5g (sat 0.5g, mono 1.2g, poly 0.6g); PROTEIN 3g; CARB 14.9g; FIBER 0.4g; CHOL 25mg; IRON 0.8mg; SODIUM 226mg; CALC 67mg

Test Kitchen Tip: Once the edges of the pancake turn golden and bubbles surface, slide a wide nylon spatula beneath the pancake. The width will help you grab more, and the nylon won't scratch the pan. Quickly flip over and cook two more minutes.

Blueberry Buttermilk Pancakes

Blueberries, either fresh or frozen, give ordinary pancakes a big flavor boost, not to mention a healthy dose of antioxidants. Rather than stirring the blueberries into the batter, heaping tablespoons of berries are sprinkled over the pancakes as they cook, ensuring that the last pancakes cooked have just as many berries as the first.

Prep: 10 minutes • Cook: about 4 minutes per batch

    2   cups all-purpose flour
    1   tablespoon sugar
    1   teaspoon baking powder
    1   teaspoon salt
    ½   teaspoon baking soda
  1½   cups low-fat buttermilk
    ½   cup 1% low-fat milk
    1   tablespoon canola oil
    1   large egg, lightly beaten
  Cooking spray
    2   cups blueberries

1. Lightly spoon flour into dry measuring cups, and level with a knife. Combine flour, sugar, baking powder, salt, and baking soda in a large bowl; make a well in center of mixture. Combine buttermilk, milk, oil, and egg in a bowl, and add to flour mixture, stirring until smooth.
2. Spoon ¼ cup pancake batter for each pancake onto a hot nonstick griddle or large nonstick skillet coated with cooking spray, and sprinkle with 2 heaping table-spoons blueberries. Turn pancakes when tops are covered with bubbles and edges look cooked. Yield: 12 (5-inch) pancakes (serving size: 1 pancake).

CALORIES 114 (16% from fat); FAT 2g (sat 0.3g, mono 0.9g, poly 0.5g); PROTEIN 3.2g; CARB 21.1g; FIBER 1.1g; CHOL 18mg; IRON 1.1mg; SODIUM 307mg; CALC 41mg

Chocolate Chip Dutch Baby

A Dutch baby is a baked pancake. The batter is poured into a preheated cast-iron skillet. When it emerges from the oven, it's puffed and golden.

Prep: 13 minutes • Cook: 17 minutes • Other: 15 minutes

    ¾   cup 2% reduced-fat milk
    ½   cup all-purpose flour
    2   tablespoons sugar
    ¼   teaspoon salt
    2   large eggs
    2   tablespoons butter, divided
    ⅓   cup semisweet chocolate chips
    3   large firm bananas, halved crosswise then lengthwise
    ½   cup Kahlúa (coffee-flavored liqueur)
    ½   cup frozen reduced-calorie whipped topping, thawed

1. Preheat oven to 450°.
2. Place a 9-inch cast-iron skillet in a 450° oven for 15 minutes. Combine first 5 ingredients; stir with a whisk until smooth.

Melt 1 tablespoon butter in preheated pan until browned, swirling to evenly coat pan. Add batter; sprinkle evenly with chocolate chips. Bake at 450° for 10 minutes or until puffed and browned.
3. While Dutch baby bakes, melt 1 tablespoon butter in a large skillet over medium-high heat. Add bananas; cook 2 minutes on each side or until browned. Add liqueur, and simmer 1 minute; serve with Dutch baby. Top Dutch baby with whipped topping. Yield: 6 servings (serving size: 1 Dutch baby wedge, 2 banana pieces, and about 1½ tablespoons whipped topping).

CALORIES 326 (28% from fat); FAT 10g (sat 5.7g, mono 2.9g, poly 0.6g); PROTEIN 5.3g; CARB 47.8g; FIBER 2.5g; CHOL 83mg; IRON 1.3mg; SODIUM 175mg; CALC 55mg

Coffee Cakes

These sweet, cakelike breads are delicious for breakfast or brunch. Sometimes they're made with yeast, but these recipes use baking powder and/or baking soda for leavening.

Pear Cake with Pine Nuts

When you pair a savory ingredient such as pine nuts with a sweet one such as pear, one flavor helps bring out the best of the other.

Prep: 20 minutes • Cook: 45 minutes

1¼ cups all-purpose flour
¾ cup sugar
⅛ teaspoon salt
¼ cup chilled butter, cut into pieces
2 tablespoons pine nuts, toasted
¼ teaspoon ground cinnamon
⅓ cup fat-free sour cream
¼ cup 1% low-fat milk
1 teaspoon grated lemon rind
1 teaspoon vanilla extract
½ teaspoon baking powder
¼ teaspoon baking soda
1 large egg
Cooking spray
2 cups thinly sliced peeled pear

1. Preheat oven to 350°.
2. Lightly spoon flour into dry measuring cups, and level with a knife. Combine flour, sugar, and salt in a large bowl; stir well with a whisk. Cut in butter with a pastry blender or 2 knives until mixture resembles coarse meal. Remove ⅓ cup flour mixture; place in a small bowl. Stir in pine nuts and cinnamon; set aside.
3. Combine remaining flour mixture, sour cream, and next 6 ingredients in a large bowl. Beat with a mixer at medium speed until well blended. Pour batter into a 9-inch round cake pan coated with cooking spray. Arrange pear slices evenly over batter, then sprinkle with pine nut mixture. Bake at 350° for 45 minutes or until a wooden pick inserted in center comes out clean; cool completely on a wire rack. Cut into wedges. Yield: 8 servings (serving size: 1 wedge).

CALORIES 252 (28% from fat); FAT 7.9g (sat 4g, mono 2.4g, poly 0.9g); PROTEIN 4.2g; CARB 41.9g; FIBER 1.7g; CHOL 43mg; IRON 1.4mg; SODIUM 191mg; CALC 53mg

Most coffee cakes can be made a day ahead and taste just as good at room temperature as they do warm.

Apple Streusel Cake with Almonds

A splash of amaretto complements the sweet tartness of the apples.

Prep: 25 minutes • Cook: 45 minutes Other: 10 minutes

Streusel:

- 2 tablespoons all-purpose flour
- 2 tablespoons brown sugar
- ⅛ teaspoon ground cinnamon
- 1 tablespoon butter
- 2 tablespoons sliced almonds

Cake:

- ¾ cup granulated sugar
- ¼ cup (2 ounces) block-style ⅓-less-fat cream cheese, softened
- ¼ cup butter, softened
- 2 tablespoons amaretto (almond-flavored liqueur)
- 1 teaspoon vanilla extract
- ¼ teaspoon almond extract
- 1 large egg
- 1¼ cups all-purpose flour
- ½ teaspoon baking powder
- ¼ teaspoon baking soda
- ¼ teaspoon salt
- ¾ cup low-fat buttermilk
  Cooking spray
- 1½ cups thinly sliced peeled Braeburn apple (about ¾ pound)

1. Preheat oven to 350°.
2. To prepare streusel, combine first 3 ingredients in a medium bowl; cut in 1 tablespoon butter with a pastry blender or 2 knives until mixture resembles coarse meal. Stir in almonds.
3. To prepare cake, beat granulated sugar, cream cheese, and ¼ cup butter in a large bowl with a mixer at medium speed until smooth. Add amaretto, extracts, and egg, beating well.
4. Lightly spoon flour into dry measuring cups; level with a knife. Combine flour, baking powder, baking soda, and salt in a medium bowl, stirring well with a whisk. Add flour mixture and buttermilk alternately to egg mixture, beginning and ending with flour mixture.
5. Pour batter into a 9-inch round cake pan coated with cooking spray; sharply tap pan once on counter to remove air bubbles. Arrange apple slices over batter; sprinkle with streusel.
6. Bake at 350° for 45 minutes or until a wooden pick inserted in center comes out clean. Cool in pan 10 minutes on a wire rack; remove from pan. Cool completely on wire rack. Cut into wedges. Yield: 9 servings (serving size: 1 wedge).

CALORIES 277 (31% from fat); FAT 9.5g (sat 5.3g, mono 3g, poly 0.6g); PROTEIN 4.4g; CARB 43.8g; FIBER 1.9g; CHOL 47mg; IRON 1.3mg; SODIUM 249mg; CALC 56mg

Test Kitchen Tip: If you don't want to use amaretto, you can just use an additional ¼ teaspoon almond extract.

Sour Cream Coffee Cake

We've reduced the fat by decreasing the butter, using reduced-fat sour cream, and adding egg whites instead of whole eggs.

Prep: 20 minutes • Cook: 45 minutes

- ½ cup packed brown sugar
- ¼ cup chopped walnuts
- 2 teaspoons ground cinnamon
- 1 cup granulated sugar
- ¼ cup butter, softened
- 2 large egg whites
- 1 cup reduced-fat sour cream
- 1 teaspoon vanilla extract
- 1¾ cups all-purpose flour
- 1 teaspoon baking powder
- 1 teaspoon baking soda
- ½ teaspoon salt
  Cooking spray

1. Preheat oven to 350°.
2. Combine first 3 ingredients; set aside.
3. Place granulated sugar and butter in a large bowl; beat with a mixer at medium speed until well blended. Add egg whites, 1 at a time, beating well after each addition. Beat in sour cream and vanilla. Lightly spoon flour into dry measuring cups; level with a knife. Combine flour, baking powder, baking soda, and salt; stir well. Gradually add flour mixture to sugar mixture; beat well. Spread half of batter into an 8-inch square baking pan coated with cooking spray. Sprinkle half of streusel over batter. Spread remaining batter over streusel. Top with remaining streusel.
4. Bake at 350° for 45 minutes or until a wooden pick inserted in center comes out clean. Cool on a wire rack. Cut into wedges. Yield: 12 servings (serving size: 1 wedge).

CALORIES 243 (30% from fat); FAT 8.1g (sat 4g, mono 2.2g, poly 1.4g); PROTEIN 3.6g; CARB 40g; FIBER 0.7g; CHOL 18mg; IRON 1.2mg; SODIUM 253mg; CALC 54mg

Yeast Breads
Whether shaped into rolls, rounds, or loaves, these breads develop their unique flavors through the fermentation of yeast and the rising of the dough.

Homemade White Bread

If you're not an experienced bread maker, this basic white bread is a great place to start. All you need to begin are a few simple ingredients, a large bowl, and your hands.

**Prep: 30 minutes • Cook: 45 minutes
Other: 2 hours, 10 minutes**

- 1 package dry yeast (about 2¼ teaspoons)
- 1 tablespoon sugar
- 1⅔ cups warm fat-free milk (100° to 110°)
- 2 tablespoons butter, melted
- 4¾ cups all-purpose flour, divided
- 1½ teaspoons salt
- Cooking spray

1. Dissolve yeast and sugar in warm milk in a large bowl; let stand 5 minutes. Stir in butter.

2. Lightly spoon flour into dry measuring cups; level with a knife. Add 4¼ cups flour and salt to yeast mixture; stir until blended. Turn dough out onto a floured surface. Knead until smooth and elastic (about 10 minutes); add enough of remaining flour, 1 tablespoon at a time, to prevent dough from sticking to hands (dough will feel tacky).

3. Place dough in a large bowl coated with cooking spray, turning to coat top. Cover and let rise in a warm place (85°), free from drafts, 1 hour or until doubled in size. (Gently press two fingers into dough.

If indention remains, dough has risen enough.)

4. Punch dough down; let rest 5 minutes. Roll into a 14 x 7–inch rectangle on a floured surface. Roll up rectangle tightly, starting with a short edge, pressing firmly to eliminate air pockets; pinch seam and ends to seal. Place roll, seam side down, in a 9 x 5–inch loaf pan coated with cooking spray. Cover and let rise 1 hour or until doubled in size.

5. Preheat oven to 350°.

6. Uncover dough. Bake at 350° for 45 minutes or until loaf is browned on bottom and sounds hollow when tapped. Remove loaf from pan, and cool on a wire rack. Yield: 16 servings (serving size: 1 slice).

CALORIES 162 (11% from fat); FAT 1.9g (sat 0.4g, mono 0.7g, poly 0.6g); PROTEIN 4.9g; CARB 30.5g; FIBER 1.1g; CHOL 1mg; IRON 1.8mg; SODIUM 219mg; CALC 38mg

Variations

Cheese Bread: Add 1 cup (4 ounces) shredded reduced-fat extrasharp Cheddar cheese to 4¼ cups flour and salt. Proceed with recipe.

CALORIES 176 (17% from fat); FAT 3.3g (sat 1.2g, mono 1.1g, poly 0.6g); PROTEIN 6.8g; CARB 29.3g; FIBER 1.1g; CHOL 5mg; IRON 1.7mg; SODIUM 301mg; CALC 100mg

Herb Bread: Add ½ cup grated Parmesan cheese, 1 teaspoon each of onion flakes, dried oregano, and dried basil, and ½ teaspoon each of garlic powder and coarsely ground black pepper to 4¼ cups flour and salt. Proceed with recipe.

CALORIES 175 (14% from fat); FAT 2.7g (sat 0.9g, mono 0.9g, poly 0.6g); PROTEIN 6g; CARB 30.9g; FIBER 1.2g; CHOL 2mg; IRON 2mg; SODIUM 297mg; CALC 76mg

choosing flour There isn't much difference between a yeast bread made with bread flour and one made with all-purpose flour. Bread flour is a little higher in protein and can, for the most part, be used instead of all-purpose. Some of our recipes call for bread flour, but we also like using all-purpose because that's what most people have on hand. What's really important is how you measure the flour—spoon it into the measuring cup instead of scooping and packing. (See the technique photos on page 116.)

1. Proofing the Yeast Making sure that your yeast is alive, a process known as proofing, is the most crucial step in baking bread. That's because if the yeast is dead, it can't leaven your bread. Live yeast will swell and foam (or activate) a few minutes after it's stirred into the warm liquid.

2. Making the Dough To make the initial bread dough, add most of the flour to the liquid ingredients all at once, and stir just until the mixture is combined. (Be sure to save some of the flour for kneading.) Then dump the dough onto a floured surface, and you're ready to knead.

3. Kneading the Dough Knead the dough with authority—push it out with the heels of your hands, fold it over, give it a quarter-turn, and repeat. You may not use all the remaining flour—in fact, try to use as little of it as possible. After about 10 minutes of kneading, the dough should be smooth and elastic but still feel tacky.

5. Punching it Down Punch the dough down to deflate it. Then turn the dough out onto a floured surface for rolling.

6. Rolling it Out To shape the bread, begin by rolling it out. Lift the rolling pin up slightly as you near each end of the rectangular shape.

7. Rolling it Up You're almost there, but remember: Rolling up the dough, or shaping, is just as important as rolling it out. The purpose is to eliminate air bubbles, giving a better crumb—or texture—to the bread. To accomplish this, roll the dough tightly, pressing firmly as you go.

4. The First Rising Place the dough in a large bowl because during this rising, the dough will double in size. During the rising, cover the bowl with a slightly damp lightweight dish towel. **The Touch Test** To tell when the dough has risen enough, simply press two fingers into it. If an impression remains, the dough is ready. If the dough springs back, it needs more rising time.

8. The Second Rising Once you roll up the dough and place it in a loaf pan, let it rise a second time. Watch carefully. If the dough rises too much and starts to fall, the bread will be dense. To avoid this problem, check the dough to be sure it has not begun to deflate. Once it's doubled in size, the dough is ready to bake.

French Bread Baguette

French bread tastes best when you eat it the same day it's baked. If you have any left over, do as the French do: Use it to make French toast or a bread pudding.

Prep: 20 minutes • Cook: 20 minutes
Other: 1 hour, 20 minutes

  1 package dry yeast (about 2¼
      teaspoons)
  1 cup warm water (100° to 110°)
  3 cups bread flour
  1 teaspoon salt
Cooking spray
  1 tablespoon water
  1 large egg white, lightly beaten

1. Dissolve yeast in warm water in a small bowl; let stand 5 minutes.
2. Lightly spoon flour into dry measuring cups; level with a knife. Place flour and salt in a food processor; pulse 2 times or until blended. With processor on, slowly add yeast mixture through food chute; process until dough forms a ball. Process 1 additional minute. Turn dough out onto a lightly floured surface; knead lightly 4 or 5 times.
3. Place dough in a large bowl coated with cooking spray, turning to coat top. Cover dough; let rise in a warm place (85°), free from drafts, 45 minutes or until doubled in size. (Gently press two fingers into dough. If indentation remains, dough has risen enough.)
4. Punch dough down, and shape into an 9 x 8–inch rectangle. Roll up dough, starting at long side, pressing firmly to eliminate air pockets. Pinch seam ends to seal. Cover dough, and let rise 30 minutes or until doubled in size.
5. Preheat oven to 450°.

6. Uncover dough, and make 3 (¼-inch-deep) diagonal cuts across top of loaf, using a sharp knife. Combine 1 tablespoon water and egg white, and brush mixture over top of loaf.
7. Bake at 450° for 20 minutes or until loaf sounds hollow when tapped. Yield: 12 servings (serving size: 1 slice).

CALORIES 127 (5% from fat); FAT 0.7g (sat 0.1g, mono 0.1g, poly 0.3g); PROTEIN 4.6g; CARB 25.1g; FIBER 0.2g; CHOL 0mg; IRON 1.6mg; SODIUM 200mg; CALC 6mg

Test Kitchen Tip: If you want a crusty crust, you need to create some steam in the oven. Use an inexpensive plastic bottle such as a plant sprayer, and spritz the inside of the oven several times during baking. Be careful not to spray water directly on the oven light. Also, to get a crust that is as close to the thick-crusted loaves you see at bakeries, bake the bread on a pizza stone placed on the lower shelf of the oven. Preheat the pizza stone on the lower shelf before you place the loaf on the stone.

Rustic White Bread

This is basically the same recipe as the French Bread Baguette (page 89), but the flour and yeast are not combined in the food processor, and the dough is shaped into a free-form round instead of a traditional loaf.

Prep: 20 minutes • Cook: 20 minutes • Other: 1 hour, 40 minutes

1 package dry yeast (about 2¼ teaspoons)
1 cup warm water (100° to 110°)
3 cups bread flour, divided
1 teaspoon salt
Cooking spray
1 teaspoon cornmeal
1 teaspoon water
1 large egg white, lightly beaten

1. Dissolve yeast in 1 cup warm water in a large bowl, and let stand 5 minutes.

2. Lightly spoon flour into dry measuring cups; level with a knife. Add 2¾ cups flour and salt to yeast mixture; stir until a soft dough forms. Turn dough out onto a floured surface. Knead until smooth and elastic (about 8 minutes); add enough of remaining flour, 1 tablespoon at a time, to prevent dough from sticking to hands (dough will feel tacky).

3. Place dough in a large bowl coated with cooking spray, turning to coat top. Cover and let rise in a warm place (85°), free from drafts, 45 minutes or until doubled in size. (Gently press two fingers into dough. If indentation remains, dough has risen enough.)

4. Punch dough down. Cover and let rest 5 minutes. Shape dough into a 6-inch round; place on a baking sheet sprinkled with cornmeal. Lightly coat surface of dough with cooking spray. Cover and let rise 45 minutes or until doubled in size.

5. Preheat oven to 450°.

6. Uncover dough. Combine 1 teaspoon water and egg white, stirring with a whisk; brush over dough. Make 3 (4-inch) cuts ¼-inch-deep across top of dough using a sharp knife.

7. Bake at 450° for 20 minutes or until bread is browned on bottom and sounds hollow when tapped. Remove from pan; cool on a wire rack. Yield: 12 servings (serving size: 1 slice).

CALORIES 128 (4% from fat); FAT 0.6g (sat 0.1g, mono 0.1g, poly 0.3g); PROTEIN 4.6g; CARB 25.3g; FIBER 1g; CHOL 0mg; IRON 1.6mg; SODIUM 201mg; CALC 6mg

Sunflower-Wheat Loaf

We used dried blueberries, but you can use chopped dried apples or apricots or omit the fruit for a straightforward multigrain bread.

Prep: 25 minutes • Cook: 45 minutes
Other: 2 hours, 55 minutes

  1 package dry yeast (about 2¼ teaspoons)
  1 cup warm water (100° to 110°)
  2 cups whole wheat flour
  ¼ cup honey
  2 tablespoons canola oil
  1 tablespoon dark molasses
  1 teaspoon salt
  ¼ cup wheat germ
  2 tablespoons cornmeal
1¼ cups bread flour, divided
  ⅓ cup raw unsalted sunflower seeds
  ¼ cup dried blueberries
     Cooking spray

1. Dissolve yeast in warm water in a large bowl; let stand 5 minutes.

2. Lightly spoon whole wheat flour into dry measuring cups; level with a knife. Add whole wheat flour, honey, oil, molasses, and salt to yeast mixture, stirring well. Cover; let stand at room temperature 1 hour.

3. Add wheat germ and cornmeal to sponge. Spoon bread flour into dry measuring cups; level with a knife. Add 1 cup flour to sponge; stir until a soft dough forms. Turn out onto a floured surface. Knead until smooth and elastic (about 8 minutes); add enough of remaining flour, 1 tablespoon at a time, to prevent dough from sticking to hands (dough will feel tacky). Knead in seeds and blueberries. Place in a bowl coated with cooking spray; turn to coat top. Cover; let rise in a warm place (85°), free from drafts, 1 hour or until doubled in size.

(Gently press two fingers into dough. If indentation remains, dough has risen enough.) Punch dough down. Cover; let rest 5 minutes. Roll into a 14 x 7–inch rectangle on a floured surface. Roll up tightly, starting with a short edge, pressing firmly to eliminate air pockets; pinch seam and ends to seal. Place, seam side down, in an 8 x 4–inch loaf pan coated with cooking spray. Coat with cooking spray. Cover; let rise 45 minutes or until doubled in size.

4. Preheat oven to 375°.

5. Uncover dough; bake at 375° for 45 minutes or until loaf is browned on bottom and sounds hollow when tapped. Remove from pan; cool on a wire rack. Yield: 16 servings (serving size: 1 slice).

CALORIES 151 (20% from fat); FAT 3.4g (sat 0.3g, mono 1.3g, poly 1.5g); PROTEIN 4.5g; CARB 27.6g; FIBER 3g; CHOL 0mg; IRON 1.6mg; SODIUM 149mg; CALC 16mg

Crusty Rye Loaf

The sponge can be made ahead and refrigerated up to 24 hours, but bring it back to room temperature before making the bread.

Prep: 30 minutes • Cook: 30 minutes
Other: 3 hours, 55 minutes

Sponge:
    1   package dry yeast (about 2¼ teaspoons)
    ⅔   cup warm water (100° to 110°)
    ½   cup rye flour—medium
    ¼   cup bread flour

Dough:
    2   cups bread flour
    ½   cup rye flour—medium
    ½   cup water
    2   teaspoons caraway seeds
    1¼ teaspoons salt
    2   tablespoons bread flour
    Cooking spray

1. To prepare sponge, dissolve yeast in warm water in a large bowl; let stand 5 minutes.

2. Lightly spoon ½ cup rye flour and ¼ cup bread flour into dry measuring cups; level with a knife. Add ½ cup rye flour and ¼ cup bread flour to yeast mixture, stirring with a whisk. Cover and let stand in a warm place (85°), free from drafts, 2 hours.

3. To prepare dough, lightly spoon 2 cups bread flour and ½ cup rye flour into dry measuring cups; level with a knife. Add 2 cups bread flour, ½ cup rye flour, ½ cup water, caraway seeds, and salt to sponge; beat with a mixer at medium speed until smooth. Turn dough out onto a lightly floured surface. Knead until smooth and elastic (about 10 minutes); add 2 tablespoons bread flour, 1 tablespoon at a time, to prevent dough from sticking to hands. Shape dough into a round loaf; place loaf on a baking sheet coated with cooking spray. Cover and let rise 1½ hours or until doubled in size. (Gently press two fingers into dough. If indentation remains, dough has risen enough.)

4. Preheat oven to 425°.

5. Uncover and pierce loaf 1 inch deep in several places with a wooden pick. Bake at 425° for 30 minutes or until loaf is browned on bottom and sounds hollow when tapped. Let stand 20 minutes before slicing. Yield: 12 servings (serving size: 1 slice).

CALORIES 131 (5% from fat); FAT 0.7g (sat 0.1g, mono 0.1g, poly 0.3g); PROTEIN 4.3g; CARB 26.7g; FIBER 2.2g; CHOL 0mg; IRON 1.5mg; SODIUM 246mg; CALC 9mg

Thirded Bread

In the late 1860s, bread was often made with readily available rye flour and cornmeal. Sometimes wheat flour was added, which accounts for the name.

Prep: 25 minutes • Cook: 45 minutes
Other: 2 hours, 50 minutes

    1   cup stone-ground yellow cornmeal
    1½ cups water
    1½ cups 1% low-fat milk
    ¼   cup unsalted butter, cut into pieces
    ½   cup molasses
    3½ cups all-purpose flour, divided
    1½ cups whole wheat flour
    1   cup stone-ground rye flour
    1   tablespoon salt
    2   packages quick-rise yeast (about 2¼ teaspoons)
    Cooking spray

1. Combine first 3 ingredients in a large, heavy saucepan; bring to a boil over medium heat, stirring occasionally. Cook 2 minutes, stirring frequently with a whisk. Remove from heat; add butter, stirring until melted. Stir in molasses. Let stand 15 minutes or until warm (100° to 110°).

2. Lightly spoon flours into dry measuring cups; level with a knife. Combine 3 cups all-purpose flour, whole wheat flour, rye flour, salt, and yeast in a large bowl. Add warm cornmeal mixture to flour mixture, stirring with a wooden spoon until mixture is combined. Turn dough out onto a floured surface. Knead until smooth and elastic (about 8 minutes); add enough of remaining flour, 1 tablespoon at a time, to prevent dough from sticking to hands (dough will feel tacky). Place dough in a large bowl coated with cooking spray, turning to coat top. Cover dough, and let rise in a warm place (85°), free from drafts, 1½ hours or until doubled in size. (Gently press two fingers into dough. If indentation remains, dough has risen enough.) Punch dough down. Cover and let rest 5 minutes.

3. Divide dough in half. Working with one portion at a time (cover remaining dough to keep from drying), roll dough into a 14 x 7–inch rectangle on a lightly floured surface. Roll up rectangle tightly, starting with a short edge, pressing firmly to eliminate air pockets; pinch seam and ends to seal. Place roll, seam side down, in an 8 x 4–inch loaf pan coated with cooking spray. Coat loaves with cooking spray; cover and let rise 1 hour or until doubled in size.

4. Preheat oven to 375°.

5. Uncover and bake at 375° for 40 minutes or until loaves are lightly browned and sound hollow when tapped. Remove loaves from pans, and cool completely on wire racks. Yield: 2 loaves, 12 slices per loaf (serving size: 1 slice).

CALORIES 169 (14% from fat); FAT 2.7g (sat 1.4g, mono 0.7g, poly 0.3g); PROTEIN 4.5g; CARB 32.3g; FIBER 2.5g; CHOL 6mg; IRON 1.8mg; SODIUM 324mg; CALC 39mg

Irish Oatmeal Bread

The dough for this hearty bread is dense because of the oats, so we recommend using a stand mixer for mixing.

Prep: 30 minutes • Cook: 45 minutes
Other: 1 hour, 55 minutes

2¼ cups boiling water
1¾ cups steel-cut oats
1 tablespoon salt
3 tablespoons butter
3 tablespoons light brown sugar
Dash of granulated sugar
2 packages dry yeast (about
    2¼ teaspoons each)
½ cup warm water (100° to 110°)
3¼ cups all-purpose flour, divided
3 cups whole wheat flour
Cooking spray
1 large egg, lightly beaten

1. Combine first 5 ingredients in bowl of a stand mixer, and let stand 25 minutes.

2. Dissolve granulated sugar and yeast in warm water; let stand 5 minutes or until foamy. Add to oat mixture. Lightly spoon flours into dry measuring cups; level with a knife. Gradually add 2¾ cups all-purpose flour and 3 cups whole wheat flour to oat mixture. Beat at medium speed until well blended. Turn dough out onto a floured surface. Knead until smooth and elastic (about 8 minutes); add enough of remaining all-purpose flour, 1 tablespoon at a time, to prevent dough from sticking to hands (dough will feel sticky).

3. Place dough in a large bowl coated with cooking spray, turning to coat top. Cover and let rise in a warm place (85°), free from drafts, 1 hour or until doubled in size. (Gently press two fingers into dough. If indentation remains, dough has risen enough.) Punch dough down; cover and let rest 5 minutes. Divide dough in half. Working with one portion at a time (cover remaining dough to prevent drying), roll

dough into a 14 x 8–inch rectangle on a floured surface. Roll up rectangle tightly, starting with a short edge, pressing firmly to eliminate air pockets; pinch seam and ends to seal. Place loaf, seam side down, in a 9-inch loaf pan coated with cooking spray. Cover and let rise 20 minutes or until doubled in size.

4. Preheat oven to 350°.

5. Uncover dough, and brush egg evenly over loaves. Bake at 350° for 45 minutes or until loaves are browned on bottom and sound hollow when tapped. Remove from pans, and cool on wire racks. Yield: 2 loaves, 14 servings per loaf (serving size: 1 slice).

CALORIES 154 (15% from fat); FAT 2.5g (sat 1g, mono 0.7g, poly 0.4g); PROTEIN 5.1g; CARB 28.9g; FIBER 3g; CHOL 11mg; IRON 1.8mg; SODIUM 267mg; CALC 15mg

Test Kitchen Tip: Make sure the oatmeal mixture is cool before combining it with the yeast mixture.

Rice Bread

Adding cooked basmati rice to the flour mixture yields a slightly chewy texture.

**Prep: 30 minutes • Cook: 1 hour, 7 minutes
Other: 2 hours**

1½	cups water
½	cup basmati rice
1¼	cups warm water (100° to 110°)
6	cups all-purpose flour, divided
1	package quick-rise yeast (about 2¼ teaspoons)
2	teaspoons salt

Cooking spray

1. Combine 1½ cups water and rice in a medium saucepan over medium-high heat; bring to a boil. Cover, reduce heat, and simmer 20 minutes or until liquid is absorbed. Spoon rice into a large bowl; cool to room temperature. Stir in 1¼ cups warm water.

2. Lightly spoon flour into dry measuring cups; level with a knife. Add 2 cups flour and yeast to rice mixture; stir well to combine. Cover with plastic wrap; let stand 1 hour (batter should become very bubbly and almost double in size).

3. Add 2 cups flour and salt to batter; stir with a wooden spoon 1 minute or until well combined.

4. Scrape dough onto a heavily floured surface; sprinkle dough with 1 cup flour. Knead until smooth and elastic (about 8 minutes); add enough of remaining flour, 1 tablespoon at a time, to prevent dough from sticking to hands (dough will feel tacky).

5. Divide dough in half. Working with one portion at a time (cover remaining dough to keep from drying), roll dough into a 14 x 7–inch rectangle on a lightly floured surface. Roll up rectangle tightly, starting with a short edge, pressing firmly to eliminate air pockets; pinch seam and ends to seal. Place roll, seam side down, in an 8 x 4–inch loaf pan coated with cooking spray.

6. Lightly coat loaves with cooking spray. Cover; let rise in a warm place (85°), free from drafts, 1 hour or until doubled in size.

7. Preheat oven to 375°.

8. Uncover loaves. Bake at 375° for 45 minutes or until loaves are lightly browned and sound hollow when tapped. Cool in pans on wire racks. Yield: 2 loaves, 12 slices per loaf (serving size: 1 slice).

CALORIES 129 (3% from fat); FAT 0.5g (sat 0.1g, mono 0.1g, poly 0.2g); PROTEIN 3.7g; CARB 27g; FIBER 1.1g; CHOL 0mg; IRON 1.6mg; SODIUM 196mg; CALC 6mg

Rich Tomato Bread

Because the water used to rehydrate the tomatoes is used in the bread, the tomatoes' flavor and color permeate the loaf.

Prep: 30 minutes • Cook: 42 minutes
Other: 1 hour, 55 minutes

- 1 cup boiling water
- 20 sun-dried tomato halves, packed without oil
- 1 package dry yeast (about 2¼ teaspoons)
- 3½ cups bread flour, divided
- 2 tablespoons extravirgin olive oil
- 1 teaspoon salt
- 1 large egg, lightly beaten
- Cooking spray
- 1 tablespoon butter, melted

1. Combine boiling water and tomatoes in a small bowl. Cover; let stand 30 minutes.
2. Drain tomato mixture through a sieve over a bowl, reserving liquid. Finely chop tomatoes. Heat reserved liquid to 100° to 110°. Place liquid in a large bowl, and stir in yeast. Let stand 5 minutes.
3. Lightly spoon flour into dry measuring cups; level with a knife. Add 3 cups flour, chopped tomatoes, oil, salt, and egg to yeast mixture; stir until a soft dough forms.
4. Turn dough out onto a floured surface. Knead until smooth and elastic (about 8 minutes); add enough of remaining flour, 1 tablespoon at a time, to prevent dough from sticking to hands (dough will feel tacky).
5. Place dough in a large bowl coated with cooking spray, turning to coat top. Cover; let rise in a warm place (85°), free from drafts, 45 minutes or until doubled in size. (Gently press two fingers into dough. If indentation remains, dough has risen enough.)
6. Punch dough down; cover and let rest 5 minutes. Roll dough into a 14 x 7–inch rectangle on a lightly floured surface. Roll up rectangle tightly, starting with a short edge, pressing firmly to eliminate air pockets; pinch seam and ends to seal. Place roll, seam side down, in an 8 x 4–inch loaf pan coated with cooking spray. Coat dough with cooking spray. Cover and let rise 30 minutes or until doubled in size.
7. Preheat oven to 350°.
8. Uncover dough; bake at 350° for 40 minutes or until loaf is browned on bottom and sounds hollow when tapped. Remove from pan; place on a wire rack. Brush with melted butter. Yield: 16 servings (serving size: 1 slice).

CALORIES 145 (20% from fat); FAT 3.3g (sat 0.9g, mono 1.7g, poly 0.5g); PROTEIN 4.7g; CARB 23.9g; FIBER 1.3g; CHOL 15mg; IRON 1.8mg; SODIUM 233mg; CALC 11mg

Walnut and Rosemary Loaves

Walnuts give this herbed rustic bread a bit of crunch.

Prep: 30 minutes • Cook: 40 minutes
Other: 2 hours, 10 minutes

- 2 cups warm 1% low-fat milk (100° to 110°)
- ¼ cup warm water (100° to 110°)
- 3 tablespoons sugar
- 2 tablespoons butter, melted
- 2 teaspoons salt
- 2 packages dry yeast (about 4½ teaspoons)
- 5½ cups all-purpose flour, divided
- 1 cup chopped walnuts
- 3 tablespoons chopped fresh rosemary
- 1 large egg, lightly beaten
- Cooking spray
- 1 tablespoon yellow cornmeal
- 1 tablespoon 1% low-fat milk
- 1 large egg, lightly beaten

1. Combine first 5 ingredients in a large bowl, stirring with a whisk. Add yeast, stirring with a whisk; let stand 5 minutes.
2. Lightly spoon flour into dry measuring cups; level with a knife. Add 2 cups flour to yeast mixture, stirring with a whisk. Cover and let rise in a warm place (85°), free from drafts, 15 minutes.
3. Add 2½ cups flour, walnuts, rosemary, and 1 egg, stirring with a whisk. Turn dough out onto a lightly floured surface. Knead until smooth and elastic (about 10 minutes), adding enough of remaining flour, ¼ cup at a time, to prevent dough from sticking to hands.
4. Place dough in a large bowl coated with cooking spray, turning to coat top. Cover; let rise in a warm place (85°), free from drafts, 1 hour or until doubled in size. (Gently press two fingers into dough. If indentation remains, dough has risen enough.)
5. Punch dough down; turn out onto a lightly floured surface. Divide dough in half, shaping each portion into a round. Place on a baking sheet dusted with cornmeal. Cover and let rise 30 minutes or until doubled in size.
6. Preheat oven to 400°.
7. Uncover dough. Combine 1 tablespoon milk and 1 egg, and brush over loaves. Make 3 diagonal cuts ¼ inch deep across top of each loaf using a sharp knife.
8. Place loaves in oven; reduce oven temperature to 375°, and bake 40 minutes or until bottom of each loaf sounds hollow when tapped. Let loaves stand 20 minutes before slicing. Yield: 2 loaves, 12 servings per loaf (serving size: 1 piece).

CALORIES 170 (28% from fat); FAT 5.2g (sat 1.2g, mono 1g, poly 2.6g); PROTEIN 5.2g; CARB 25.7g; FIBER 1.3g; CHOL 21mg; IRON 1.7mg; SODIUM 222mg; CALC 39mg

Stout-Chocolate-Cherry Bread

An overnight sponge made with stout creates a rich, bittersweet bread. Pearl sugar (available at gourmet stores and large supermarkets) adds texture.

Prep: 35 minutes • Cook: 30 minutes
Other: 11 hours, 5 minutes

4¼   cups bread flour, divided
  1   (12-ounce) bottle Guinness Stout
  1   package dry yeast (about 2¼
       teaspoons)
  1   tablespoon granulated sugar
  1   teaspoon salt
  ½   cup dried tart cherries
  4   ounces bittersweet chocolate,
       coarsely chopped
Cooking spray
  1   teaspoon water
  1   large egg white, lightly beaten
  1   teaspoon pearl sugar (optional)

1. Lightly spoon flour into dry measuring cups; level with a knife. Combine 2 cups flour, beer, and yeast in a large bowl, stirring with a whisk. Cover and refrigerate 8 hours or overnight.
2. Remove from refrigerator; let dough stand 1 hour.
3. Add 2 cups flour, granulated sugar, and salt to yeast mixture; stir until a soft dough forms. Turn dough out onto a floured surface. Knead until smooth and elastic (about 8 minutes); add enough of remaining flour, 1 tablespoon at a time, to prevent dough from sticking to hands (dough will feel sticky). Knead in cherries and chocolate.
4. Place dough in a large bowl coated with cooking spray, turning to coat top. Cover and let rise in a warm place (85°), free from drafts, 1 hour or until doubled in size. (Gently press two fingers into dough. If indentation remains, dough has risen enough.)

5. Punch dough down; cover and let rest 5 minutes. Shape dough into a 9-inch round; place on a baking sheet lined with parchment paper. Lightly coat dough with cooking spray. Cover and let rise 1 hour or until doubled in size.
6. Preheat oven to 350°.
7. Uncover dough. Combine water and egg white, stirring with a whisk; brush over dough. Sprinkle dough with pearl sugar, if desired. Make a ¼-inch-deep cut down center of dough using a sharp knife.
8. Bake at 350° for 30 minutes or until bread is browned on bottom and sounds hollow when tapped. Remove from pan; cool on a wire rack. Yield: 20 servings (serving size: 1 slice).

CALORIES 156 (14% from fat); FAT 2.4g (sat 1.3g, mono 0.2g, poly 0.2g); PROTEIN 4.3g; CARB 28.1g; FIBER 1.3g; CHOL 0mg; IRON 1.4mg; SODIUM 121mg; CALC 5mg

Three-Seed Épi

Traditionally known in France as *pain d'épi* (épi is the central flower in a wheat stalk), this beautiful bread gets its name from the wheat stalk it resembles. It works as an edible centerpiece.

Prep: 25 minutes • Cook: 20 minutes • Other: 1 hour, 25 minutes

1 package dry yeast (about 2¼ teaspoons)
1 cup warm water (100° to 110°)
3 cups bread flour, divided
1 tablespoon extravirgin olive oil
1¼ teaspoons salt
Cooking spray
1 teaspoon cornmeal
1 teaspoon water
1 large egg white, lightly beaten
1 teaspoon poppy seeds
1 teaspoon sesame seeds
½ teaspoon mustard seeds

1. Dissolve yeast in 1 cup warm water in a large bowl; let stand 5 minutes.

2. Lightly spoon flour into dry measuring cups; level with a knife. Add 2¾ cups flour, oil, and salt to yeast mixture; stir until a soft dough forms. Turn dough out onto a floured surface. Knead until smooth and elastic (about 8 minutes); add enough flour, 1 tablespoon at a time, to prevent dough from sticking to hands (dough will feel tacky).

3. Place dough in a large bowl coated with cooking spray, turning to coat top. Cover; let rise in a warm place (85°), free from drafts, 45 minutes or until doubled in size. (Gently press two fingers into dough. If indentation remains, dough has risen enough.)

4. Punch dough down. Cover and let rest 5 minutes. Shape dough into a 21-inch rope; place on a baking sheet sprinkled with cornmeal. (If your pan isn't long enough, form rope into a slight semicircle until it fits.)

5. Starting at one end, make hard diagonal cuts on 1 side of loaf 1½ to 2 inches apart, cutting three-fourths of the way through dough to other side of loaf. Carefully flip every other section to the opposite side of loaf to form a leaflike shape. (Loaf should resemble a branch with leaves.)

6. Combine 1 teaspoon water and egg white; stir with a whisk. Combine poppy, sesame, and mustard seeds. Brush dough evenly with egg white mixture, and sprinkle evenly with seeds. Cover and let rise 30 minutes or until doubled in size.

7. Preheat oven to 400°.

8. Uncover dough, and bake at 400° for 20 minutes or until bread is browned on bottom and sounds hollow when tapped. Remove from pan, and cool on a wire rack. Yield: 14 servings (serving size: 1 slice).

CALORIES 121 (13% from fat); FAT 1.7g (sat 0.2g, mono 0.9g, poly 0.4g); PROTEIN 4.1g; CARB 21.8g; FIBER 0.9g; CHOL 0mg; IRON 1.5mg; SODIUM 214mg; CALC 11mg

Test Kitchen Tip: For rolls, divide the dough into 14 equal portions; shape each into a ball, and proceed as the recipe directs in Step 6.

Fig-Swirl Coffee Cake

Figs and other dried fruits are excellent sources of fiber. The whole wheat flour in the dough also boosts the fiber content. This high-nutrition recipe proves that "good for you" and "great to eat" do go together.

**Prep: 40 minutes • Cook: 30 minutes
Other: 2 hours, 10 minutes**

  1   package dry yeast (about 2¼ teaspoons)
 ½   teaspoon granulated sugar
 ¼   cup warm water (100° to 110°)
 ⅓   cup fat-free milk
  2   teaspoons vanilla extract, divided
  1   large egg
1½   cups all-purpose flour
1¼   cups whole wheat flour
 ⅓   cup granulated sugar
  3   tablespoons chilled butter, cut into small pieces
 ¾   teaspoon salt
Cooking spray
1½   cups dried Calimyrna or Black Mission figs (about 12 ounces)
 ½   cup fresh orange juice (about 1 orange)
  1   cup powdered sugar
  2   tablespoons fresh lemon juice

1. Dissolve yeast and ½ teaspoon granulated sugar in warm water in a small bowl; let stand 5 minutes. Stir in milk, 1 teaspoon vanilla, and egg.

2. Lightly spoon flours into dry measuring cups; level with a knife. Place flours, ⅓ cup granulated sugar, butter, and salt in a food processor; pulse 5 times or until blended. With processor on, slowly add yeast mixture through food chute; process until dough forms a ball. Process 1 additional minute. Turn dough out onto a floured surface; knead lightly 4 or 5 times (dough will feel sticky).

3. Place dough in a large bowl coated with cooking spray, turning to coat top. Cover and let rise in a warm place (85°), free from drafts, 1 hour or until dough is almost doubled in size. (Gently press two fingers into dough. If indentation remains, dough has risen enough.)

4. Trim stems off figs. Place 1 teaspoon vanilla, figs, and orange juice in food processor, and process until finely chopped. Set aside.

5. Punch dough down; cover and let rest 5 minutes. Roll dough into a 15 x 10–inch rectangle on a floured surface. Spread fig mixture evenly over the dough, leaving a 1-inch margin along one long edge. Roll up rectangle tightly, starting with opposite long edge, pressing firmly to eliminate air pockets; pinch seam to seal. Place roll, seam side down, on floured surface; split roll in half lengthwise using a serrated knife. Working on a 12-inch pizza pan coated with cooking spray, coil one half of dough, cut side up, around itself in a spiral pattern. Place other half of dough, cut side up, at end of the first strip, pinching ends together to seal; continue coiling dough to form a circle. Cover and let rise 1 hour or until doubled in size.

6. Preheat oven to 350°.

7. Uncover and bake at 350° for 30 minutes or until golden. Place cake on a plate. Combine powdered sugar and lemon juice in a small bowl; drizzle over hot cake. Serve warm or at room temperature. Yield: 16 servings (serving size: 1 wedge).

CALORIES 208 (13% from fat); FAT 3.1g (sat 1.6g, mono 0.9g, poly 0.4g); PROTEIN 4g; CARB 43g; FIBER 4.2g; CHOL 20mg; IRON 1.5mg; SODIUM 142mg; CALC 45mg

Test Kitchen Tip: The coffee cake dough can be made ahead. Follow the recipe as directed through Step 2. Punch the dough down, and return it to the bowl. Cover the dough with plastic wrap, and chill eight hours. When ready to use, shape and bake according to recipe instructions.

how to roll fig-swirl coffee cake

Coil the dough, cut side up, around itself in a spiral pattern.

Challah

This traditional Jewish bread is rich, light, and airy. It can be formed into many shapes, but a braid is the most classic.

Prep: 30 minutes • Cook: 35 minutes
Other: 3 hours, 20 minutes

- ½ teaspoon sugar
- 1 package dry yeast (about 2¼ teaspoons)
- ¾ cup warm water (100° to 110°)
- ¼ cup canola oil
- 1 large egg, lightly beaten
- 3⅓ cups all-purpose flour
- 1¼ teaspoons salt
- Cooking spray
- 2 teaspoons water
- 1 large egg yolk, lightly beaten

1. Dissolve sugar and yeast in warm water in a large bowl; let stand 5 minutes. Add oil and 1 egg, stirring with a whisk.
2. Lightly spoon flour into dry measuring cups; level with a knife. Add flour and salt to yeast mixture; beat with a mixer at medium speed until smooth.
3. Turn dough out onto a lightly floured surface. Knead until smooth and elastic (about 10 minutes). Place dough in a large bowl coated with cooking spray, turning to coat top. Cover; let rise in a warm place (85°), free from drafts, 1 hour or until doubled in size. (Gently press two fingers into dough. If indentation remains, dough has risen enough.)
4. Punch dough down; shape into a ball. Return dough to bowl; cover and let rise 1 hour or until doubled in size.
5. Punch dough down; turn dough out onto a lightly floured surface. Cover and let rest 15 minutes.
6. Divide dough into 3 equal portions. Working with one portion at a time (cover remaining dough to keep from drying), shape portion into a 15-inch rope. Place ropes lengthwise on a baking sheet coated with cooking spray (do not stretch); pinch ends together at one end to seal. Braid ropes, and pinch loose ends together to seal. Cover; let rise 1 hour or until doubled in size.
7. Preheat oven to 375°.
8. Uncover dough. Combine 2 teaspoons water and egg yolk; brush over braid. Bake at 375° for 35 minutes or until loaf is browned on bottom and sounds hollow when tapped. Remove from pan; cool on a wire rack. Yield: 16 servings (serving size: 1 slice).

CALORIES 135 (29% from fat); FAT 4.4g (sat 0.5g, mono 2.3g, poly 1.2g); PROTEIN 3.4g; CARB 20.2g; FIBER 0.8g; CHOL 26mg; IRON 1.4mg; SODIUM 190mg; CALC 7mg

Red Onion Focaccia

Resist the urge to add more flour to this dough. A slightly wet dough makes a crisp focaccia with a light texture.

Prep: 40 minutes • Cook: 41 minutes
Other: 10 hours, 15 minutes

Sponge:
- 1 package dry yeast (about 2¼ teaspoons)
- 1 teaspoon honey
- 2 cups warm water (100° to 110°)
- 2 cups all-purpose flour

Dough:
- 1 cup bread flour
- 1 cup whole wheat flour
- 4 teaspoons olive oil, divided
- 2 teaspoons sea salt

Topping:
- 1 teaspoon olive oil
- 5 cups thinly sliced red onion
- 1 tablespoon chopped fresh rosemary
- ¼ teaspoon sea salt
- ¼ teaspoon crushed red pepper

1. To prepare sponge, dissolve yeast and honey in warm water in a large bowl; let stand 5 minutes. Lightly spoon all-purpose flour into dry measuring cups; level with a knife. Stir all-purpose flour into yeast mixture. Cover; chill overnight.
2. To prepare dough, stir yeast mixture with a spoon; let stand 30 minutes or until it begins to bubble. Lightly spoon bread flour and whole wheat flour into dry measuring cups; level with a knife. Combine yeast mixture, bread flour, whole wheat flour, 1 tablespoon oil, and 2 teaspoons sea salt in a large bowl. Beat with a mixer at medium speed 15 minutes or until dough pulls away from sides of bowl. Cover; let rise in a warm place (85°), free from drafts, 1 hour or until doubled in size (dough will be wet).
3. Spread 1 teaspoon oil evenly over bottom of a 15 x 10–inch jelly-roll pan. Pour dough into pan; let stand 5 minutes. Gently press dough to fill pan; let stand 30 minutes.
4. Preheat oven to 425°.
5. To prepare topping, heat 1 teaspoon oil in a large nonstick skillet over medium heat. Add onion and rosemary; cook 15 minutes or until browned. Arrange onion over top of dough. Sprinkle with ¼ teaspoon sea salt and crushed red pepper. Bake at 425° for 25 minutes or until golden brown. Cool 5 minutes. Cut into wedges. Yield: 12 servings (serving size: 1 wedge).

CALORIES 197 (12% from fat); FAT 2.6g (sat 0.4g, mono 1.5g, poly 0.5g); PROTEIN 5.9g; CARB 38g; FIBER 3.4g; CHOL 0mg; IRON 2.1mg; SODIUM 426mg; CALC 23mg

Test Kitchen Tip: Starting with a sponge and an overnight rising in the refrigerator helps the yeast develop slowly, so its flavor will be more pronounced. But you can skip the overnight rise, if desired.

Fontina and Red Pepper-Stuffed Garlic Focaccia

Roasted garlic is mashed into a paste and added to the dough so that every bite is infused with a distinct mellow note.

**Prep: 45 minutes • Cook: 1 hour, 30 minutes
Other: 9 hours, 50 minutes**

  1 package dry yeast (about 2¼ teaspoons)
  1 cup warm water (100° to 110°)
3¼ cups bread flour, divided
  1 whole garlic head
1½ tablespoons extravirgin olive oil, divided
1¼ teaspoons salt, divided
  Cooking spray
  1 teaspoon cornmeal
  ¼ cup chopped fresh basil
  ¾ cup chopped bottled roasted red bell peppers
  ½ cup (2 ounces) shredded fontina cheese

1. Dissolve yeast in 1 cup warm water in a large bowl; let stand 5 minutes.
2. Lightly spoon flour into dry measuring cups; level with a knife. Add 1 cup flour to yeast mixture, stirring well. Cover; let stand at room temperature 8 hours or overnight to create a sponge (mixture will become very bubbly).
3. Preheat oven to 350°.
4. Remove papery skin from garlic head (do not peel or separate cloves). Wrap in foil. Bake at 350° for 1 hour; cool 10 minutes.
5. Separate cloves; squeeze to extract garlic pulp. Discard skins. Place garlic pulp, 1 tablespoon oil, and 1 teaspoon salt in a small bowl, and mash with a fork until smooth. Stir into sponge.
6. Add 2 cups flour to sponge; stir until a soft dough forms. Turn dough out onto a floured surface. Knead until smooth and elastic (about 8 minutes); add enough of remaining flour, 1 tablespoon at a time, to prevent dough from sticking to hands (dough will feel tacky).
7. Place dough in a large bowl coated with cooking spray, turning to coat top. Cover; let rise in a warm place (85°), free from drafts, 45 minutes or until doubled in size. (Gently press two fingers into dough. If indentation remains, dough has risen enough.)
8. Punch dough down. Cover and let rest 5 minutes. Divide dough in half; roll each half into a 10-inch round.
9. Place 1 dough round on a baking sheet sprinkled with cornmeal. Arrange basil over dough, leaving a ¼-inch border; top with bell peppers. Sprinkle evenly with cheese. Top with other dough round; pinch edges to seal. Lightly coat with cooking spray. Cover and let rise 45 minutes or until dough is doubled in size.
10. Preheat oven to 400°.
11. Uncover dough. Make indentations in top of dough with a knife. Gently brush dough with 1½ teaspoons oil, and sprinkle with ¼ teaspoon salt. Bake at 400° for 30 minutes or until focaccia is browned on bottom and sounds hollow when tapped. Remove from pan; cool on a wire rack. Yield: 14 servings (serving size: 1 wedge).

CALORIES 150 (20% from fat); FAT 3.3g (sat 1.1g, mono 1.5g, poly 0.5g); PROTEIN 5.3g; CARB 24.4g; FIBER 1g; CHOL 5mg; IRON 1.6mg; SODIUM 265mg; CALC 33mg

how to assemble stuffed focaccia

With a rolling pin, roll top dough evenly over the filling; pinch edges to seal.

Flatbread with Oven-Dried Tomatoes, Rosemary, and Fontina

It takes about four hours to make the Oven-Dried Tomatoes, but they can be made ahead and refrigerated until you need them.

Prep: 30 minutes • Cook: 10 minutes
Other: 1 hour, 40 minutes

  2   tablespoons olive oil
  4   rosemary sprigs
2¾   cups all-purpose flour
  1   package dry yeast (about 2¼ teaspoons)
  1   cup plus 2 tablespoons very warm water (120° to 130°)
  2   teaspoons chopped fresh or ½ teaspoon dried rosemary
  1   teaspoon salt, divided
Cooking spray
  ¾   cup Oven-Dried Tomatoes (page 465), halved lengthwise
  1   cup (4 ounces) fontina cheese, diced

1. Place oil and rosemary sprigs in a small bowl; microwave at HIGH 30 seconds. Let stand 15 minutes. Gently squeeze oil from rosemary; discard sprigs.
2. Lightly spoon flour into dry measuring cups; level with a knife. Combine ½ cup flour and yeast in a large bowl, stirring with a whisk. Add ½ cup warm water; let stand 20 minutes. Add rosemary oil, 2 cups flour, ½ cup plus 2 tablespoons warm water, chopped rosemary, and ¾ teaspoon salt; stir until a soft dough forms. Turn dough out onto a lightly floured surface. Knead until smooth and elastic (about 8 minutes); add enough of remaining flour, 1 teaspoon at a time, to prevent dough from sticking to hands (dough will feel tacky).
3. Place dough in a large bowl coated with cooking spray, turning to coat top. Cover; let rise in a warm place (85°), free from drafts, 1 hour or until doubled in size. (Gently press two fingers into dough. If indentation remains, dough has risen enough.) Punch dough down; form into a ball. Place on a baking sheet coated with cooking spray. Let rest 5 minutes.
4. Preheat oven to 500°.
5. Roll dough into a 12-inch circle. Arrange tomatoes on top of dough, leaving a ½-inch border. Sprinkle with cheese; gently press toppings into dough. Sprinkle with ¼ teaspoon salt. Bake at 500° for 10 minutes or until golden brown. Yield: 12 servings (serving size: 1 wedge).

(Totals include Oven-Dried Tomatoes) CALORIES 162 (25% from fat); FAT 4.5g (sat 2g, mono 1.7g, poly 0.4g); PROTEIN 6g; CARB 24.2g; FIBER 1.4g; CHOL 11mg; IRON 1.7mg; SODIUM 335mg; CALC 59mg

Rosemary-Scented Flatbread with Black Grapes

Blue or red grapes also work well in this recipe as long as they're fresh and firm.

Prep: 35 minutes • Cook: 20 minutes
Other: 2 hours, 5 minutes

3¼   cups all-purpose flour, divided
  1   teaspoon sugar
  1   package dry yeast (about 2¼ teaspoons)
1¼   cups warm water (100° to 110°)
  ½   cup white cornmeal
1¼   teaspoons salt, divided
1½   teaspoons chopped fresh rosemary
2½   teaspoons olive oil, divided
Cooking spray
  1   cup seedless black grapes, quartered and divided

1. Lightly spoon flour into dry measuring cups; level with a knife. Dissolve sugar and yeast in 1¼ cups warm water in a large bowl. Stir in 1 cup flour. Cover loosely with plastic wrap; let stand 30 minutes.
2. Add 2 cups flour, cornmeal, 1 teaspoon salt, rosemary, and 1½ teaspoons oil to yeast mixture; stir until a soft dough forms. Turn dough out onto a floured surface. Knead until smooth and elastic (about 8 minutes); add enough of remaining flour, 1 tablespoon at a time, to prevent dough from sticking to hands (dough will feel tacky).
3. Place dough in a large bowl coated with cooking spray, turning to coat top. Cover; let rise in a warm place (85°), free from drafts, 1 hour or until doubled in size. (Gently press two fingers into dough. If indentation remains, dough has risen enough.)
4. Punch dough down, and turn out onto a lightly floured surface. Arrange ⅔ cup grapes over dough, and knead gently 4 or 5 times or just until grapes are incorporated into dough. Let rest 5 minutes.
5. Press dough into a 15 x 10–inch rectangle. Place on a large baking sheet coated with cooking spray. Brush surface of dough with 1 teaspoon oil. Cover and let rise 30 minutes or until doubled in size.
6. Preheat oven to 475°.
7. Uncover dough. Make indentations in top of dough using handle of a wooden spoon or your fingertips. Sprinkle surface of dough with ⅓ cup grapes; gently press grapes into dough. Sprinkle with ¼ teaspoon salt. Bake at 475° for 20 minutes or until golden. Yield: 12 servings (serving size: ¹⁄₁₂ of loaf).

CALORIES 164 (8% from fat); FAT 1.4g (sat 0.2g, mono 0.8g, poly 0.3g); PROTEIN 4.4g; CARB 33g; FIBER 1.6g; CHOL 0mg; IRON 2mg; SODIUM 246mg; CALC 8mg

If your dough rises too much, punch it back down and let it rise again.
The texture may be a little more dense, but the flavor won't be affected.

Dinner Rolls, Five Ways

One dough yields five dinner roll variations. To freeze rolls, bake, cool completely, wrap in heavy-duty foil, and freeze. Thaw, and reheat (still wrapped) at 350° for 12 minutes or until warm.

Prep: 30 minutes • Cook: 20 minutes
Other: 1 hour, 25 minutes

2	teaspoons sugar
1	package dry yeast (about 2¼ teaspoons)
1	(12-ounce) can evaporated fat-free milk, warmed (100° to 110°)
4	cups all-purpose flour, divided
1	large egg, lightly beaten
1	teaspoon salt

Cooking spray

1	teaspoon cornmeal
2	tablespoons butter, melted and cooled to room temperature

Poppy seeds (optional)

1. Dissolve sugar and yeast in warm milk in a large bowl; let stand 5 minutes.
2. Lightly spoon flour into dry measuring cups; level with a knife. Add 3 cups flour and egg to milk mixture, stirring until smooth; cover and let stand 15 minutes.
3. Add ¾ cup flour and salt; stir until a soft dough forms. Turn dough out onto a floured surface. Knead until smooth and elastic (about 8 minutes); add enough of remaining flour, 1 tablespoon at a time, to prevent dough from sticking to hands (dough will feel tacky). Place dough in a large bowl coated with cooking spray,

turning to coat top. Cover and let rise in a warm place (85°), free from drafts, 40 minutes or until doubled in size. (Gently press two fingers into dough. If indentation remains, dough has risen enough.) Punch dough down; cover and let rest 5 minutes.
4. Divide dough into 16 equal portions. Working with one portion at a time (cover remaining dough to prevent drying), shape portion into desired form. Place shaped dough portions on 2 baking sheets, each lightly sprinkled with ½ teaspoon cornmeal. Lightly coat shaped dough portions with cooking spray; cover with plastic wrap. Let rise in a warm place (85°), free from drafts, 20 minutes or until doubled in size.
5. Preheat oven to 400°.
6. Brush dough portions with butter; sprinkle with poppy seeds, if desired. Place one baking sheet on bottom oven rack and one baking sheet on middle oven rack. Bake at 400° for 10 minutes; rotate baking sheets. Bake 10 minutes or until rolls are lightly browned on top and sound hollow when tapped on bottom. Place on wire racks. Serve warm, or cool on wire racks. Yield: 16 servings (serving size: 1 roll).

CALORIES 151 (13% from fat); FAT 2.1g (sat 1.1g, mono 0.5g, poly 0.2g); PROTEIN 5.4g; CARB 27g; FIBER 0.9g; CHOL 18mg; IRON 1.7mg; SODIUM 187mg; CALC 69mg

Test Kitchen Tip: Heat milk just until barely warm, no more than 110°. If it's too warm, it will kill the yeast and the dough won't rise.

five ways to shape rolls

Divide the dough into 16 equal portions.

Roll: Shape each portion into a ball.

Knot: Shape each portion into an 8-inch rope. Tie each rope into a single knot; tuck top end of rope under bottom edge of roll.

Snail: Shape each portion into a 20-inch rope. Coil each rope around itself in a spiral; pinch tail of coil to seal.

Twist: Shape each portion into an 18-inch rope. Fold each rope in half so both ends meet; hold one end of rope in each hand, and twist.

Cloverleaf: Divide each portion into three balls. Press balls together to form a cloverleaf roll.

Dinner Rolls,
Five Ways

Parmesan and Cracked Pepper Grissini

Grissini are thin, crisp breadsticks. This recipe builds on the recipe for Rustic White Bread (page 90). Use a sharp knife, pastry wheel, or pizza cutter to quickly cut the dough, and use a ruler as a guide to make dividing the dough easier.

Prep: 40 minutes • Cook: 12 minutes
Other: 1 hour, 15 minutes

- 1 package dry yeast (about 2¼ teaspoons)
- 1 cup warm water (100° to 110°)
- 3 cups bread flour, divided
- 1¼ teaspoons salt
- Cooking spray
- 1 teaspoon water
- 1 large egg white, lightly beaten
- ½ cup (2 ounces) grated fresh Parmesan cheese
- 1 tablespoon cracked black pepper
- 2 teaspoons cornmeal

1. Dissolve yeast in 1 cup warm water in a large bowl; let stand 5 minutes.
2. Lightly spoon flour into dry measuring cups; level with a knife. Add 2¾ cups flour and salt to yeast mixture; stir until a soft dough forms. Turn dough out onto a floured surface. Knead until smooth and elastic (about 8 minutes); add enough of remaining flour, 1 tablespoon at a time, to prevent dough from sticking to hands (dough will feel tacky).
3. Place dough in a large bowl coated with cooking spray, turning to coat top. Cover and let rise in a warm place (85°), free from drafts, 45 minutes or until doubled in size. (Gently press two fingers into dough. If indentation remains, dough has risen enough.)
4. Punch dough down. Cover and let rest 5 minutes. Turn dough out onto a lightly floured surface; roll into a 12 x 8–inch rectangle.
5. Combine 1 teaspoon water and egg white, stirring with a whisk; brush evenly over dough. Sprinkle dough with cheese and pepper. Lightly coat dough with cooking spray; cover with plastic wrap. Gently press toppings into dough; remove plastic wrap.
6. Sprinkle each of 2 baking sheets with 1 teaspoon cornmeal. Cut dough in half lengthwise to form 2 (12 x 4–inch) rectangles. Cut each rectangle crosswise into 12 (1-inch-wide) strips.
7. Working with one strip at a time (cover remaining strips to prevent drying), gently roll strip into a log. Holding ends of log between forefinger and thumb of each hand, gently pull log into a 14-inch rope, slightly shaking it up and down while pulling. (You can also roll each strip into a 14-inch rope on a lightly floured surface.) Place rope on a prepared pan, curving into a series of shapes so that rope fits on pan. (There should be 12 ropes on each pan.)
8. Lightly coat ropes with cooking spray. Cover and let rise 20 minutes or until doubled in size.
9. Preheat oven to 450°.
10. Uncover dough; bake at 450° for 6 minutes with one pan on bottom rack and one pan on second rack from top. Rotate pans; bake an additional 6 minutes or until golden brown. Remove breadsticks from pans; cool completely on wire racks. Yield: 12 servings (serving size: 2 breadsticks).

CALORIES 148 (12% from fat); FAT 1.9g (sat 0.9g, mono 0.4g, poly 0.3g); PROTEIN 6.4g; CARB 25.9g; FIBER 1.1g; CHOL 3mg; IRON 1.8mg; SODIUM 326mg; CALC 64mg

Buttered Sweet Potato Knot Rolls

Not only do the sweet potatoes add a touch of sweetness to these buttery rolls, they also add antioxidants, which can help prevent heart disease and certain cancers.

Prep: 45 minutes • Cook: 15 minutes
Other: 1 hour, 25 minutes

1   package dry yeast (about 2¼ teaspoons)
1   cup warm 2% reduced-fat milk (100° to 110°)
¾   cup canned mashed sweet potatoes
3   tablespoons butter, melted and divided
1¼ teaspoons salt
2   large egg yolks, lightly beaten
5   cups bread flour, divided
Cooking spray

1. Dissolve yeast in warm milk in a large bowl; let stand 5 minutes.
2. Add sweet potatoes, 1 tablespoon butter, salt, and egg yolks to yeast mixture, stirring with a whisk.
3. Lightly spoon flour into dry measuring cups, and level with a knife. Add 4½ cups flour to sweet potato mixture; stir until a soft dough forms. Turn dough out onto a floured surface. Knead until smooth and elastic (about 8 minutes); add enough of remaining flour, 1 tablespoon at a time, to prevent dough from sticking to hands (dough will feel soft and sticky). Place dough in a large bowl coated with cooking spray, turning to coat top. Cover and let rise in a warm place (85°), free from drafts, 45 minutes or until dough has doubled in size. (Gently press two fingers into dough. If indentation remains, dough has risen enough.) Punch dough down. Cover and let rest 5 minutes.

4. Line 2 baking sheets with parchment paper. Divide dough into 24 equal portions. Working with one portion at a time (cover remaining dough to prevent drying), shape portion into a 9-inch rope. Shape rope into a knot; tuck top end of knot under roll. Place 12 rolls on each pan. Lightly coat rolls with cooking spray; cover and let rise 30 minutes or until doubled in size.
5. Preheat oven to 400°.
6. Uncover rolls. Bake at 400° for 8 minutes with one pan on bottom rack and one pan on second rack from top. Rotate pans; bake an additional 7 minutes or until rolls are golden brown and sound hollow when tapped. Remove from pans; place on wire racks. Brush with 2 tablespoons butter. Yield: 2 dozen (serving size: 1 roll).

CALORIES 134 (17% from fat); FAT 2.6g (sat 1.2g, mono 0.7g, poly 0.3g); PROTEIN 4.3g; CARB 23g; FIBER 0.9g; CHOL 22mg; IRON 1.4mg; SODIUM 147mg; CALC 21mg

Citrus-Cream Cheese Pull-Aparts

Place a piece of foil under the pan in case the cream cheese mixture runs over.

Prep: 20 minutes • Cook: 25 minutes
Other: 2 hours, 15 minutes

1   (25-ounce) package frozen roll dough
Cooking spray
¼   cup butter, melted
½   cup sweetened dried cranberries
1   cup granulated sugar, divided
⅔   cup (6 ounces) block-style ⅓-less-fat cream cheese, softened
2   tablespoons fresh orange juice
1   large egg
1   tablespoon grated lemon rind
1   tablespoon grated orange rind
1   cup powdered sugar
5   teaspoons fresh lemon juice

1. Thaw roll dough at room temperature 30 minutes.
2. Cut rolls in half. Place 24 halves, cut sides down, in bottom of each of 2 (9–inch) round cake pans coated with cooking spray. Brush butter evenly over rolls. Cover and let rise in a warm place (85°), free from drafts, 30 minutes.
3. Sprinkle with dried cranberries. Combine ¼ cup granulated sugar, cream cheese, orange juice, and egg in a bowl; beat with a mixer at medium speed until well blended. Pour cream cheese mixture evenly over rolls. Combine ¾ cup granulated sugar and rinds. Sprinkle evenly over rolls. Cover and let rise 1 hour or until doubled in size.
4. Preheat oven to 350°.
5. Uncover rolls. Bake at 350° for 20 minutes. Cover with foil. Bake an additional 5 minutes or until the rolls in the center are done. Remove from oven; cool 15 minutes.
6. Combine powdered sugar and lemon juice. Drizzle over rolls. Yield: 4 dozen (serving size: 2 rolls).

CALORIES 174 (29% from fat); FAT 5.6g (sat 2.8g, mono 1.9g, poly 0.6g); PROTEIN 3.6g; CARB 27.7g; FIBER 0.6g; CHOL 20mg; IRON 0.3mg; SODIUM 203mg; CALC 10mg

Variation

Overnight Pull-Aparts: After pouring cream cheese mixture over rolls, cover with plastic wrap and refrigerate 12 hours. Gently remove plastic wrap from rolls; sprinkle with rind mixture. Let stand at room temperature 30 minutes or until dough has doubled in size. Proceed with recipe as directed.

Triple-Play Cinnamon Rolls

Three sugars go into these rolls to make them extraspecial: Granulated sweetens the dough, brown adds a light molasses flavor to the filling, and powdered sweetens the glaze.

Prep: 45 minutes • Cook: 20 minutes
Other: 2 hours, 40 minutes

Dough:
  1 package dry yeast (about 2¼ teaspoons)
  ¼ cup warm water (100° to 110°)
  ½ cup warm 1% low-fat milk (100° to 110°)
  ⅓ cup granulated sugar
  ¼ cup butter, softened
  1 teaspoon vanilla extract
  ¾ teaspoon salt
  1 large egg, lightly beaten
  3½ cups all-purpose flour, divided
  Cooking spray

Filling:
  ¾ cup raisins
  ⅔ cup packed brown sugar
  1 tablespoon ground cinnamon
  2 tablespoons butter, melted

Glaze:
  1 cup powdered sugar
  2 tablespoons 1% low-fat milk
  ½ teaspoon vanilla extract

1. To prepare dough, dissolve yeast in warm water in a large bowl; let stand 5 minutes.
2. Add ½ cup warm milk and next 5 ingredients; stir with a wooden spoon until combined (batter will not be completely smooth).
3. Lightly spoon flour into dry measuring cups; level with a knife. Add 3 cups flour to yeast mixture; stir until a soft dough forms. Turn dough out onto a lightly floured surface. Knead until smooth and elastic (about 8 minutes); add enough of remaining flour, 1 tablespoon at a time, to prevent dough from sticking to hands (dough will feel slightly tacky).
4. Place dough in a large bowl coated with cooking spray; turn to coat top. Cover and let rise in a warm place (85°), free from drafts, 1 hour or until doubled in size. (Gently press two fingers into dough. If indentation remains, dough has risen enough.)
5. To prepare filling, combine raisins, brown sugar, and cinnamon. Roll dough into a 15 x 10–inch rectangle; brush with 2 tablespoons melted butter. Sprinkle filling over dough, leaving a ½-inch border. Beginning with a long side, roll up dough, jelly-roll fashion; pinch seam to seal (do not seal ends of roll). Wrap roll in plastic wrap; chill 20 minutes.
6. Unwrap roll, and cut into 20 (¾-inch) slices. Arrange slices, cut sides up, 1 inch apart on a jelly-roll pan coated with cooking spray. Cover and let rise in a warm place (85°), free from drafts, 1 hour and 15 minutes or until doubled in size.
7. Preheat oven to 350°.

8. Uncover dough. Bake at 350° for 20 minutes or until rolls are golden brown. Remove from pan; place on wire racks.
9. To prepare glaze, combine powdered sugar, 2 tablespoons milk, and ½ teaspoon vanilla, stirring well with a whisk. Drizzle glaze over warm rolls. Yield: 20 servings (serving size: 1 roll).

CALORIES 200 (18% from fat); FAT 4g (sat 2.3g, mono 1.1g, poly 0.3g); PROTEIN 3.2g; CARB 38.3g; FIBER 1.1g; CHOL 20mg; IRON 1.5mg; SODIUM 134mg; CALC 28mg

how to cut the dough

Use dental floss to make cutting the dough easier.

Orange Rolls

Keep any remaining rolls in the baking pan. Cover the pan with foil, and store it in the refrigerator. To reheat, place the foil-covered pan in a 300° oven for 15 minutes or until the rolls are warm.

Prep: 55 minutes • Cook: 25 minutes
Other: 2 hours, 10 minutes

Dough:

- 1 package dry yeast (about 2¼ teaspoons)
- ½ cup warm water (100° to 110°)
- 1 cup sugar, divided
- ½ cup reduced-fat sour cream
- 2 tablespoons butter, softened
- 1 teaspoon salt
- 1 large egg, lightly beaten
- 3½ cups all-purpose flour, divided
- Cooking spray
- 2 tablespoons butter, melted
- 2 tablespoons grated orange rind

Glaze:

- ¾ cup sugar
- ¼ cup butter
- 2 tablespoons fresh orange juice
- ½ cup reduced-fat sour cream

1. To prepare dough, dissolve yeast in warm water in a large bowl; let stand 5 minutes.
2. Add ¼ cup sugar, ½ cup sour cream, softened butter, salt, and egg to yeast mixture, and beat with a mixer at medium speed until smooth. Lightly spoon flour into dry measuring cups; level with a knife. Add 2 cups flour to yeast mixture; beat until smooth. Add 1 cup flour to yeast mixture, stirring until a soft dough forms. Turn dough out onto a floured surface. Knead until smooth and elastic (about 10 minutes); add enough of remaining flour, 1 tablespoon at a time, to prevent dough from sticking to hands (dough will feel sticky).

3. Place dough in a large bowl coated with cooking spray, turning to coat top. Cover and let rise in a warm place (85°), free from drafts, 1 hour and 15 minutes or until doubled in size. (Gently press two fingers into dough. If indentation remains, dough has risen enough.)
4. Punch dough down; cover and let rest 5 minutes. Divide dough in half. Working with one portion at a time (cover remaining dough to prevent drying), roll dough into a 12-inch circle on a floured surface. Brush surface of circle with 1 tablespoon melted butter. Combine ¾ cup sugar and orange rind. Sprinkle half of sugar mixture over each circle. Cut each circle into 12 wedges. Roll up wedges tightly, beginning at wide end. Place rolls, point sides down,

in a 13 x 9–inch baking pan coated with cooking spray. Cover and let rise 25 minutes or until doubled in size.
5. Preheat oven to 350°.
6. Uncover dough. Bake at 350° for 25 minutes or until golden brown.
7. While rolls bake, prepare glaze. Combine ¾ cup sugar, ¼ cup butter, and orange juice in a small saucepan; bring to a boil over medium-high heat. Cook 3 minutes or until sugar dissolves, stirring occasionally. Remove from heat; cool slightly. Stir in ½ cup sour cream. Drizzle glaze over warm rolls; let stand 20 minutes before serving. Yield: 2 dozen (serving size: 1 roll).

CALORIES 178 (28% from fat); FAT 5.6g (sat 3.2g, mono 1.3g, poly 0.3g); PROTEIN 2.8g; CARB 30g; FIBER 0.6g; CHOL 24mg; IRON 1mg; SODIUM 146mg; CALC 23mg

Pumpkin-Cinnamon Streusel Buns

To make these buns when pumpkins aren't in season, substitute canned pumpkin puree, and add an extra cup of all-purpose flour.

Prep: 50 minutes • Cook: 30 minutes
Other: 1 hour, 35 minutes

Buns:

    1   package dry yeast (about
        2¼ teaspoons)
    ¼   cup warm water (100° to 110°)
    2¾ cups all-purpose flour, divided
    ½   cup Pumpkin Puree
    ½   cup 1% low-fat milk
    ¼   cup butter, melted
    1   tablespoon granulated sugar
    1¼ teaspoons salt
    ¼   teaspoon ground nutmeg
        Cooking spray
    3   tablespoons granulated sugar
    3   tablespoons brown sugar
    2   tablespoons all-purpose flour
    1½ teaspoons ground cinnamon
    2   tablespoons chilled butter, cut into
        small pieces

Glaze:

    ¾   cup sifted powdered sugar
    1   tablespoon hot water
    ¼   teaspoon vanilla extract

1. To prepare buns, dissolve yeast in warm water in a large bowl; let stand 5 minutes.
2. Lightly spoon 2¾ cups flour into dry measuring cups, and level with a knife. Add 2 cups flour, pumpkin puree, and next 5 ingredients to yeast mixture; beat with a mixer at medium speed until smooth. Turn dough out onto a floured surface. Knead until smooth and elastic (about 10 minutes); add enough of remaining ¾ cup flour, 1 tablespoon at a time, to prevent dough from sticking to hands (dough will feel tacky).

3. Place dough in a large bowl coated with cooking spray, turning to coat top. Cover and let rise in a warm place (85°), free from drafts, 45 minutes or until doubled in size. (Gently press two fingers into dough. If indentation remains, dough has risen enough.)
4. Combine 3 tablespoons granulated sugar, brown sugar, 2 tablespoons flour, and cinnamon in a small bowl. Cut in chilled butter with a pastry blender or 2 knives until mixture resembles coarse meal.
5. Punch dough down; cover and let rest 5 minutes. Roll dough into a 12 x 10–inch rectangle on a floured surface. Sprinkle with brown sugar mixture. Roll up rectangle tightly, starting with a long edge, pressing firmly to eliminate air pockets; pinch seam and ends to seal. Cut roll into 12 (1-inch) slices. Place slices in a 9-inch square baking pan coated with cooking spray. Cover and let rise 25 minutes or until doubled in size.
6. Preheat oven to 375°.
7. Uncover rolls. Bake rolls at 375° for 20 minutes or until golden brown. Cool 15 minutes in pan on a wire rack.

8. To prepare glaze, combine powdered sugar, 1 tablespoon water, and vanilla extract in a small bowl, stirring with a whisk until smooth. Drizzle glaze over buns. Serve warm. Yield: 12 servings (serving size: 1 bun).

(Totals include Pumpkin Puree) CALORIES 219 (25% from fat); FAT 6.2g (sat 3.7g, mono 1.8g, poly 0.3g); PROTEIN 3.8g; CARB 36.9g; FIBER 1.2g; CHOL 16mg; IRON 1.6mg; SODIUM 311mg; CALC 24mg

Pumpkin Puree

    1   (2-pound) pumpkin

1. Cut pumpkin in half lengthwise, discarding membranes and saving seeds for another use. Place pumpkin halves, cut sides down, in a baking dish; add ¼ cup water to dish. Cover with heavy-duty plastic wrap, and vent. Microwave at HIGH 10 minutes (or about 5 minutes per pound) until pumpkin is tender when pierced with a fork. Cool slightly, and scoop out filling. Yield: about 2½ cups.

CALORIES 165 (3% from fat); FAT 0.6g (sat 0.3g, mono 0.1g, poly 0g); PROTEIN 6.4g; CARB 41.3g; FIBER 3.2g; CHOL 0mg; IRON 5.1mg; SODIUM 6mg; CALC 133mg

Ethnic Breads
Almost every culture has a distinctive type of bread. Here are some of our favorites to enjoy by themselves or with other fillings and toppings.

Pitas

A pizza stone yields puffier bread. If you don't have one, bake the dough on the back of a heavy jelly-roll pan. After the dough has risen, you can keep it refrigerated for three days.

Prep: 35 minutes • **Cook:** 7 minutes per batch • **Other:** 15 hours, 5 minutes

- ½ teaspoon dry yeast
- 1¼ cups warm water (100° to 110°)
- 1¼ cups whole wheat flour, divided
- 1½ teaspoons fine sea salt
- ½ teaspoon olive oil
- 1¾ cups bread flour
- Cooking spray

1. Dissolve yeast in warm water in a large bowl; let stand 5 minutes. Lightly spoon whole wheat flour into dry measuring cups; level with a knife. Add 1 cup whole wheat flour to yeast mixture, stirring with a whisk. Cover; let rise in a warm place (85°), free from drafts, 2 hours (batter will be bubbly).
2. Stir in salt and oil. Lightly spoon bread flour into dry measuring cups; level with a knife. Add bread flour, stirring with a spoon. Turn dough out onto a lightly floured surface. Knead until smooth and elastic (about 10 minutes); add enough of remaining whole wheat flour, 1 tablespoon at a time, to prevent dough from sticking to hands (dough will feel tacky). Coat inside of a large zip-top plastic bag with cooking spray; add dough. Seal and refrigerate 12 hours or overnight.
3. Turn dough out onto lightly floured surface; shape into a 12-inch log. Divide dough into 6 equal portions. Working with one portion at a time (cover remaining dough to keep from drying), shape portion into a ball. Cover; let rest 1 hour.
4. Place pizza stone on bottom rack in oven. Preheat oven to 500°.
5. Roll each ball into a 6-inch circle. Place 3 circles on pizza stone. Bake at 500° for 5 minutes. Transfer pitas to top rack; bake an additional 2 minutes. Cool on a wire rack. Repeat with remaining dough circles. Yield: 6 servings (serving size: 1 pita).

CALORIES 233 (6% from fat); FAT 1.5g (sat 0.2g, mono 0.4g, poly 0.5g); PROTEIN 8.3g; CARB 47.3g; FIBER 4.1g; CHOL 0mg; IRON 2.8mg; SODIUM 578mg; CALC 15mg

salt
If all salt is sea salt, what's the difference? The three salts we use most are kosher, sea, and table salt.

Kosher salt is a larger grain that is dry, moderately salty, and is either hollow or a flattened cube. It's especially useful in brining and preserving foods.

Sea salt is often the same as table salt. The difference may be how it was manufactured. If it costs more, it was probably processed naturally—by time, sun, and wind.

Table salt consists of small, hard, dry cubes that dissolve slowly. The taste ranges from mild to sharp depending on the part of the taste palate it touches.

Chapatis

A *chapati* is an unleavened pancakelike bread from India. Pieces of chapati are torn off and used as a scoop or pusher for many East Indian dishes.

Prep: 20 minutes • **Cook:** 4 minutes per portion • **Other:** 1 hour, 3 minutes

- 1 cup whole wheat flour
- ¾ cup bread flour
- 1 teaspoon fine sea salt
- ¾ cup warm water (100° to 110°)
- 2 tablespoons olive oil

1. Lightly spoon flours into dry measuring cups; level with a knife. Combine flours and salt in a large bowl. Stir in water and oil to form a thick dough; mix well.
2. Turn dough out onto a lightly floured surface. Knead until smooth and elastic (about 10 minutes). Cover and let rest at room temperature 1 hour.
3. Divide dough into 8 equal portions. Working with one portion at a time (cover remaining dough to keep from drying), shape portion into a ball. Roll ball into a 6-inch circle on a lightly floured surface; let rest 3 minutes.
4. Heat a large cast-iron skillet over medium-high heat. Cook circle 1 to 2 minutes on each side or until lightly browned with dark spots. Yield: 8 servings (serving size: 1 chapati).

CALORIES 127 (26% from fat); FAT 3.6g (sat 0.5g, mono 2.5g, poly 0.3g); PROTEIN 4g; CARB 20.3g; FIBER 2.3g; CHOL 0mg; IRON 1.3mg; SODIUM 288mg; CALC 0mg

Corn Tortillas

Tortilla presses are available at kitchen stores, but you can also use a rolling pin.

Prep: 10 minutes
Cook: 2 minutes, 15 seconds per tortilla
Other: 15 minutes

1½ cups masa harina
1 cup plus 1 tablespoon water
½ teaspoon salt

1. Lightly spoon masa harina into dry measuring cups; level with a knife. Combine masa harina, water, and salt in a large bowl, stirring with a whisk. Knead 30 seconds on a lightly floured surface. Cover; let stand 15 minutes.
2. Divide dough into 8 equal portions; shape each portion into a ball. Place one ball between two sheets of heavy-duty plastic wrap (cover remaining balls to prevent drying). Place ball, still covered, on a tortilla press. Close press to flatten dough, moving handle from side to side. Open press; turn dough one-half turn. Close press to flatten. Remove dough. Carefully remove plastic wrap from flattened dough. Repeat with remaining balls; stack flattened dough between sheets of wax paper.
3. Heat a large nonstick skillet over medium-high heat. Place 1 tortilla in pan; cook 1 minute or until it begins to brown. Turn tortilla over; cook 1 minute. Turn tortilla once more; cook 15 seconds. Repeat. Yield: 8 servings (serving size: 1 tortilla).

CALORIES 83 (11% from fat); FAT 1g (sat 0.2g, mono 0.2g, poly 0.6g); PROTEIN 2.1g; CARB 17.8g; FIBER 1.9g; CHOL 0mg; IRON 0.7mg; SODIUM 148mg; CALC 43mg

Naan

Naan, a bread of India, is dense and chewy, like focaccia but thinner. If you don't have a pizza peel, use the back of a baking sheet to transfer the dough to a hot pizza stone.

Prep: 30 minutes • Cook: 6 minutes per portion • Other: 4 hours, 35 minutes

1 teaspoon dry yeast
¾ cup warm water (100° to 110°)
½ cup plain low-fat yogurt
2¼ cups bread flour, divided
1 cup whole wheat flour
1¼ teaspoons sea salt
1 tablespoon olive oil
Cooking spray
4 tablespoons cornmeal, divided

1. Dissolve yeast in warm water in a large bowl; let stand 5 minutes. Stir in yogurt. Lightly spoon flours into dry measuring cups; level with a knife. Add ½ cup bread flour and whole wheat flour to yeast mixture; stir with a whisk until smooth. Cover; let rise in a warm place (85°), free from drafts, 2 hours (batter will be bubbly and lacy).
2. Stir in salt and oil. Add 1½ cups bread flour (½ cup at a time); stir with a wooden spoon (dough will become difficult to stir).
3. Turn dough out onto a lightly floured surface. Knead until smooth and elastic (about 10 minutes); add enough of remaining bread flour, 1 tablespoon at a time, to prevent dough from sticking to hands (dough will feel tacky). Place in a large bowl coated with cooking spray, turning to coat top. Cover and let rise in a warm place (85°), free from drafts, 2 hours or until doubled in size. (Press two fingers into dough. If indentation remains, dough has risen enough.) Punch dough down; turn onto a lightly floured surface. Cover; let rest 5 minutes.
4. Divide dough into 8 equal portions. Working with one portion at a time, (cover remaining dough to keep from drying), stretch portion into a 6-inch oval. Cover and let rest 5 minutes.
5. Place pizza stone on bottom rack in oven. Preheat oven to 500°.
6. Make indentations in top of dough portions using handle of a wooden spoon or your fingertips. Cover; let rise 20 minutes.
7. Place two dough portions on the back of a pizza peel dusted with 1 tablespoon cornmeal. Slide onto preheated pizza stone or a baking sheet lined with parchment paper. Bake at 500° for 6 minutes or until lightly browned. Repeat with remaining portions and cornmeal. Cut or tear into pieces. Yield: 8 servings (serving size: 1 piece).

CALORIES 216 (12% from fat); FAT 2.9g (sat 0.5g, mono 1.4g, poly 0.6g); PROTEIN 7.5g; CARB 40.4g; FIBER 3.1g; CHOL 1mg; IRON 2.4mg; SODIUM 371mg; CALC 39mg

Corn Tortillas

Pizza Dough

Double this recipe, and freeze half after kneading the dough so you can have fresh pizza for another night. Place frozen dough in the refrigerator overnight or until completely thawed.

Prep: 15 minutes
Other: 1 hour, 20 minutes

- ½ teaspoon sugar
- 1 package dry yeast (about 2¼ teaspoons)
- ⅔ cup warm water (100° to 110°)
- 1½ cups bread flour
- 2½ tablespoons cornmeal, divided
- 2 teaspoons extravirgin olive oil
- ½ teaspoon salt
- 2 tablespoons bread flour
- Cooking spray

1. Dissolve sugar and yeast in warm water in a large bowl; let stand 5 minutes. Lightly spoon flour into dry measuring cups; level with a knife. Add flour, 1½ tablespoons cornmeal, oil, and salt to yeast mixture; stir until a soft dough forms. Turn dough out onto a floured surface. Knead 5 minutes. Add 2 tablespoons bread flour, as needed, to prevent dough from sticking to hands (dough will feel tacky).

2. Place dough in a large bowl coated with cooking spray, turning to coat top. Cover and let rise in a warm place (85°), free from drafts, 45 minutes or until doubled in size. (Gently press two fingers into dough. If indentation remains, dough has risen enough.) Punch dough down; shape into a ball. Lightly respray bowl with cooking spray; place dough in bowl, turning to coat top. Cover; let rise in a warm place (85°), free from drafts, 30 minutes.

3. Roll into a 12-inch circle on a lightly floured surface. Place on a 12-inch pizza pan or baking sheet coated with cooking spray and sprinkled with 1 tablespoon cornmeal. Top and bake according to recipe directions. Yield: 1 (12-inch) pizza crust.

(Totals are for 1 {12-inch} crust) CALORIES 828 (12% from fat); FAT 11.4g (sat 1.2g, mono 7.8g, poly 1.8g); PROTEIN 29.4g; CARB 162g; FIBER 7.8g; CHOL 0mg; IRON 10.2mg; SODIUM 119mg; CALC 6mg

Whole Wheat Pizza Dough

When kneading, don't overwork the dough or it will absorb too much flour, producing a dense, dry, tough crust. Usually 10 minutes of kneading makes a tender, crispy crust.

Prep: 20 minutes • Other: 55 minutes

- 1 package dry yeast (about 2¼ teaspoons)
- ¼ teaspoon sugar
- 1½ cups warm water (100° to 110°)
- 2½ to 2¾ cups all-purpose flour, divided
- 1 cup whole wheat flour
- 1 tablespoon olive oil
- 1½ teaspoons salt
- Cooking spray
- 1 tablespoon yellow cornmeal

1. Dissolve yeast and sugar in warm water in a large bowl; let stand 5 minutes. Lightly spoon flour into dry measuring cups; level with a knife. Add 2¼ cups all-purpose flour, whole wheat flour, oil, and salt to yeast mixture, stirring until well blended. Turn dough out onto a floured surface. Knead until smooth and elastic (about 10 minutes); add enough of remaining flour, 1 tablespoon at a time, to prevent dough from sticking to hands (dough will feel tacky).

2. Place dough in a large bowl coated with cooking spray, turning to coat top. Cover and let rise in a warm place (85°), free from drafts, 45 minutes or until doubled in size. (Gently press two fingers into dough. If indentation remains, dough has risen enough.) Punch dough down; cover and let rest 5 minutes. Divide dough in half; roll each half into a 12-inch circle on a floured surface. Place on a 12-inch pizza pan or baking sheet coated with cooking spray and sprinkled with cornmeal. Top and bake according to recipe directions. Yield: 2 (12-inch) pizza crusts.

(Totals are for 1 [12-inch] crust) CALORIES 871 (10% from fat); FAT 9.4g (sat 1.3g, mono 5.3g, poly 1.7g); PROTEIN 23.9g; CARB 188.8g; FIBER 6.9g; CHOL 0mg; IRON 10.8mg; SODIUM 1,762mg; CALC 36mg

how to shape pizza dough

To shape the dough, pat it with floured hands, or stretch it with a rolling pin, starting at the center of the dough and moving toward the edge. To get an even crust, roll the dough into a 12-inch circle. For a free-form shape with bumps and blisters, try stretching the dough with your fists, as they do in pizzerias. Don't worry if the dough tears slightly, just pinch it back together.

Basic Crepes

Our crepes are low in fat because there's no butter, fat-free milk instead of whole, and fewer eggs. Crepes will keep up to five days in the refrigerator. To freeze, stack in wax paper or plastic wrap, place in a zip-top bag, and freeze up to two months.

Prep: 5 minutes • Cook: 1½ minutes per crepe • Other: 15 minutes

     1   cup all-purpose flour
     1   tablespoon sugar
    ¼   teaspoon salt
  1½   cups fat-free milk
     2   large eggs, lightly beaten
  Cooking spray

1. Lightly spoon flour into a dry measuring cup; level with a knife. Combine flour, sugar, and salt in a bowl; stir with a whisk. Combine milk and eggs in a bowl; stir well with a whisk. Add milk mixture to flour mixture, stirring with a whisk until smooth. Cover batter; chill 15 minutes.
2. Heat an 8-inch crepe pan or nonstick skillet over medium-high heat. Pour a scant ¼ cup batter into pan; quickly tilt pan in all directions so batter covers pan with a thin film. Cook about 1 minute.
3. Carefully lift edge of crepe with a spatula. Crepe is ready to turn when it can be shaken loose from pan and underside is lightly browned. Turn crepe over; cook 30 seconds.
4. Place crepe on a towel; keep warm. Repeat procedure until all of batter is used, stirring batter between cooking crepes. Stack crepes between single layers of wax paper or paper towels to prevent sticking. Yield: 8 servings (serving size: 1 crepe).

CALORIES 100 (14% from fat); FAT 1.5g (sat 0.5g, mono 0.5g, poly 0.2g); PROTEIN 5g; CARB 16.2g; FIBER 0.4g; CHOL 54mg; IRON 1mg; SODIUM 119mg; CALC 75mg

These basic crepes can be used for a variety of fillings, both sweet and savory. If you're making savory recipes, you might want to omit the sugar.

how to make crepes

1. Add the liquids to the flour mixture; whisk just until combined. Don't over-stir—this will make the crepes tough.

2. The ideal crepe batter should be smooth, not lumpy, and about the consistency of heavy cream.

3. Heat the skillet, and then pour in the batter, tilting the pan to cover the bottom. It doesn't matter if the crepes are perfectly round, but you do want to cover most of the skillet or they'll be too small for the fillings.

4. Crepes cook quickly. Check the bottom after about 1 minute. If the crepe is a speckled light brown, that side is ready. Flip it over with a spatula, and cook only about 30 seconds on the other side. Remove to a towel or plate to cool.

cakes

Lemonade Layer Cake,
page 118

Layer Cakes, Sheet Cakes & Cupcakes
These cakes contain shortening or butter, flour, eggs, a liquid, and a leavening agent such as baking powder or baking soda. Their flavorings, frostings, shapes, and sizes set them apart from each other.

Old-Fashioned Caramel Layer Cake

With tender, sweet layers of white cake and thick caramel frosting, this is one of our best-tasting cakes.

**Prep: 40 minutes • Cook: 38 minutes
Other: 12 minutes**

Cake:
Cooking spray
1 tablespoon all-purpose flour
1½ cups granulated sugar
½ cup butter, softened
2 large eggs
1 large egg white
2¼ cups all-purpose flour
2½ teaspoons baking powder
½ teaspoon salt
1¼ cups fat-free milk
2 teaspoons vanilla extract

Frosting:
1 cup packed dark brown sugar
½ cup evaporated fat-free milk
2½ tablespoons butter
2 teaspoons light-colored corn syrup
Dash of salt
2 cups powdered sugar
2½ teaspoons vanilla extract

1. Preheat oven to 350°.

2. To prepare cake, coat 2 (9-inch) round cake pans with cooking spray; line bottoms with wax paper. Coat wax paper with cooking spray; dust with 1 tablespoon flour.

3. Beat granulated sugar and ½ cup butter with a mixer at medium speed until well blended (about 5 minutes). Add eggs and egg white, 1 at a time, beating well after each addition. Lightly spoon 2¼ cups flour into dry measuring cups; level with a knife. Combine 2¼ cups flour, baking powder, and salt; stir well with a whisk. Add flour mixture to sugar mixture alternately with 1¼ cups milk, beginning and ending with flour mixture. Stir in 2 teaspoons vanilla.

4. Pour batter into prepared pans; sharply tap pans once on counter to remove air bubbles. Bake at 350° for 25 minutes or until a wooden pick inserted in center comes out clean. Cool in pans 10 minutes on a wire rack; remove from pans. Peel off wax paper; cool completely on wire rack.

5. To prepare frosting, combine brown sugar and next 4 ingredients in a saucepan. Bring to a boil over medium-high heat; stir constantly. Reduce heat; simmer 5 minutes, stirring occasionally. Remove from heat. Add powdered sugar and 2½ teaspoons vanilla; beat at medium speed until smooth and slightly warm. Cool 2 to 3 minutes (frosting will be thin but thickens as it cools).

6. Place 1 cake layer on a plate; spread with ½ cup frosting. Top with remaining cake layer. Frost top and sides of cake. Store loosely covered in refrigerator. Yield: 18 servings (serving size: 1 slice).

CALORIES 307 (22% from fat); FAT 7.5g (sat 4.4g, mono 2.2g, poly 0.4g); PROTEIN 3.8g; CARB 56.7g; FIBER 0.4g; CHOL 43mg; IRON 1.2mg; SODIUM 251mg; CALC 97mg

how to make a layer cake

1. Since we don't heavily grease the pans, sometimes we call for lining the cake pans with wax paper to ensure that the cake will not stick to the pan. Coat the inside bottoms of the pans with cooking spray, and then line them with wax paper. Coat the wax paper with cooking spray, and dust with flour.

2. Although we don't call for sifting all-purpose flour, it's still a good idea to stir it to make sure there aren't any lumps. To measure the flour accurately, lightly spoon it into a dry measuring cup, and level it with a knife. Don't scoop or pack the flour into the cup—you'll likely get too much, and the cake will be dry.

3. When you beat the shortening (or butter) and sugar together (a technique called creaming) for a low-fat cake, the mixture will not look creamy and fluffy as in a traditional cake recipe. Instead, the consistency will be more like damp sand—fine-textured, but not cohesive. This is because less fat is used.

4. We usually opt for whole eggs (as opposed to whites or substitutes) because the fat from the yolks makes the cake moist and tender. Add the eggs, one at a time, to the batter, beating each one thoroughly before adding the next.

5. Add the flour mixture alternately with the liquid, as you would with any cake. Beat just until each component is incorporated. Overbeating at this stage can produce a tough cake.

6. When frosting the cake, first brush away any loose crumbs with a pastry brush or your hands. Then tear off four strips of wax paper, each 3 inches wide. Place them in a square on the cake plate. Place the cake layers on top of the strips. Frost the cake (a metal spatula is best), and remove the wax paper strips—you'll be left with a clean cake plate.

Double-Caramel Turtle Cake

It's hard to believe this decadent cake, which plays off the popular Turtle candies, is light.

Prep: 30 minutes • **Cook: 32 minutes**
Other: 10 minutes

Cake:

Cooking spray
1 tablespoon all-purpose flour
1½ cups boiling water
¾ cup unsweetened cocoa
1½ cups granulated sugar
6 tablespoons butter, softened
1 teaspoon vanilla extract
2 large eggs
1⅔ cups all-purpose flour
1 teaspoon baking soda
¾ teaspoon baking powder
¼ teaspoon salt

Frosting:

2 tablespoons butter
¼ cup packed dark brown sugar
2 to 3 tablespoons fat-free milk, divided
2 teaspoons vanilla extract
2 cups sifted powdered sugar

Topping:

⅔ cup fat-free caramel apple dip
¼ cup finely chopped pecans, toasted

1. Preheat oven to 350°.

2. To prepare cake, coat bottoms of 2 (8-inch) round cake pans with cooking spray (do not coat sides). Line bottoms with wax paper; coat with cooking spray. Dust with 1 tablespoon flour.

3. Combine boiling water and cocoa, stirring well with a whisk. Cool completely.

4. Place granulated sugar, 6 tablespoons butter, and vanilla in a large bowl; beat with a mixer at medium speed until well blended (about 5 minutes). Add eggs, 1 at a time, beating well after each addition. Lightly spoon 1⅔ cups flour into dry measuring cups; level with a knife. Combine 1⅔ cups flour, baking soda, baking powder, and salt, stirring well with a whisk. Add flour mixture and cocoa mixture alternately to sugar mixture, beginning and ending with flour mixture.

5. Pour batter into prepared pans; sharply tap pans once on counter to remove air bubbles. Bake at 350° for 30 minutes or until a wooden pick inserted in center comes out clean. Cool in pans 10 minutes on a wire rack; remove from pans. Peel off wax paper; cool completely on wire rack.

6. To prepare frosting, melt 2 tablespoons butter in a saucepan over medium heat. Add brown sugar and 2 tablespoons milk; cook 1 minute or until sugar melts. Remove from heat; cool slightly. Combine butter mixture and 2 teaspoons vanilla in a large bowl. Gradually add powdered sugar; beat with a mixer at medium speed until smooth. Add additional milk, 1 teaspoon at a time, beating until spreading consistency.

7. Place 1 cake layer on a plate; spread top with half of frosting. Place caramel dip in a small zip-top plastic bag. Snip a small hole in 1 corner of bag; drizzle half of caramel dip over frosting. Top with other cake layer. Spread remaining frosting over top of cake; drizzle with remaining caramel dip. Sprinkle with pecans. Yield: 16 servings (serving size: 1 slice).

CALORIES 309 (24% from fat); FAT 8.4g (sat 4.3g, mono 2.9g, poly 0.8g); PROTEIN 3.7g; CARB 56.7g; FIBER 1.9g; CHOL 42mg; IRON 1.5mg; SODIUM 249mg; CALC 41mg

how to measure flour

1. Lightly spoon the flour into a dry measuring cup, without compacting it.

2. Level the top of the flour with a knife to get an even cup.

Overbaking is more of a problem with low-fat cakes than traditional ones. Check for doneness 5 to 10 minutes before the stated time in the recipe.

Blackberry Jam Cake

This classic butter cake is infused with spices and topped with blackberry jam.
Let the cake stand at room temperature for 1 to 2 hours before you top it with the jam. The jam will
be easier to spread and the cake easier to slice when the cake is completely cool.

Prep: 25 minutes • Cook: 25 minutes • Other: 1 hour

Cooking spray
1 tablespoon all-purpose flour
1 cup granulated sugar
½ cup butter, softened
1 tablespoon vanilla extract
3 large eggs
2¼ cups all-purpose flour
2½ teaspoons baking powder
½ teaspoon salt
½ teaspoon ground cinnamon
⅛ teaspoon ground nutmeg
1¼ cups fat-free milk
1 cup seedless blackberry jam
1 tablespoon powdered sugar

1. Preheat oven to 350°.
2. Coat bottoms of 2 (9-inch) round cake pans with cooking spray (do not coat sides). Line bottoms with wax paper; coat with cooking spray. Dust with 1 tablespoon flour.
3. Place granulated sugar, butter, and vanilla in a large bowl; beat with a mixer at medium speed until well blended (about 5 minutes). Add eggs, 1 at a time, beating well after each addition. Lightly spoon 2¼ cups flour into dry measuring cups; level with a knife. Combine 2¼ cups flour, baking powder, and next 3 ingredients, stirring well with a whisk. Add flour mixture and milk alternately to sugar mixture, beginning and ending with flour mixture.

4. Pour batter into prepared pans; sharply tap pans once on counter to remove air bubbles. Bake at 350° for 18 to 19 minutes or until a wooden pick inserted in center comes out clean. Cool in pans 10 minutes on a wire rack; remove from pans. Peel off wax paper; cool completely on wire rack.
5. Place jam in a small bowl, and stir with a whisk until smooth. Place 1 cake layer on a plate; spread with ½ cup jam. Top with other cake layer; spread ½ cup jam over top of cake. Sprinkle with powdered sugar. Yield: 16 servings (serving size: 1 slice).

CALORIES 240 (26% from fat); FAT 6.9g (sat 3.9g, mono 2.1g, poly 0.4g); PROTEIN 3.8g; CARB 41.1g; FIBER 0.5g; CHOL 56mg; IRON 1.1mg; SODIUM 240mg; CALC 76mg

Lemonade Layer Cake
(pictured on page 113)

The combination of bright, citrusy frosting and delicate, white cake makes this a real crowd pleaser. When making the frosting, be sure the cream cheese is cold. When warm, it's softer, which makes the frosting too thin. We loved this cake chilled, but it's also good at room temperature.

Prep: 30 minutes • Cook: 20 minutes
Other: 1 hour, 10 minutes

Cake:
  Cooking spray
1⅓ cups granulated sugar
  6 tablespoons butter, softened
  1 tablespoon grated lemon rind
  3 tablespoons thawed lemonade
     concentrate
  2 teaspoons vanilla extract
  2 large eggs
  2 large egg whites
  2 cups all-purpose flour
  1 teaspoon baking powder
  ½ teaspoon salt
  ½ teaspoon baking soda
1¼ cups fat-free buttermilk

Frosting:
  2 tablespoons butter, softened
  2 teaspoons grated lemon rind
  2 teaspoons thawed lemonade
     concentrate
  ½ teaspoon vanilla extract
  1 (8-ounce) block ⅓-less-fat cream
     cheese
3½ cups powdered sugar

1. Preheat oven to 350°.
2. To prepare cake, coat 2 (9-inch) round cake pans with cooking spray; set cake pans aside.

3. Combine granulated sugar and next 4 ingredients in a large bowl; beat with a mixer at medium speed until well blended (about 5 minutes). Add eggs and egg whites, 1 at a time, beating well after each addition. Lightly spoon flour into dry measuring cups; level with a knife. Combine flour, baking powder, salt, and baking soda; stir well with a whisk. Add flour mixture to sugar mixture alternately with buttermilk, beginning and ending with flour mixture; beat well after each addition.
4. Pour batter into prepared pans; sharply tap pans once on counter to remove air bubbles. Bake at 350° for 20 minutes or until a wooden pick inserted in center comes out clean. Cool in pans 10 minutes on a wire rack; remove from pans. Cool completely on wire rack.
5. To prepare frosting, place 2 tablespoons butter and next 4 ingredients in a large bowl; beat with a mixer at high speed until fluffy. Add powdered sugar, and beat at low speed just until blended (do not overbeat). Chill 1 hour.
6. Place 1 cake layer on a plate; spread with ½ cup frosting. Top with remaining cake layer. Spread remaining frosting over top and sides of cake. Store cake loosely covered in refrigerator. Yield: 16 servings (serving size: 1 slice).

CALORIES 322 (28% from fat); FAT 9.9g (sat 5.9g, mono 2.9g, poly 0.5g); PROTEIN 5g; CARB 54.1g; FIBER 0.5g; CHOL 53mg; IRON 1mg; SODIUM 293mg; CALC 60mg

Test Kitchen Tip: Make a pitcher of lemonade with the remaining concentrate, or transfer to an airtight container and refreeze.

Double-Coconut Cake

This cake has everything you expect in a traditional coconut cake: moist cake layers, fluffy white frosting, and a generous amount of coconut. The surprise is that it has about half the fat of the traditional version.

Prep: 35 minutes • Cook: 38 minutes
Other: 10 minutes

Cake:
  Cooking spray
  1 tablespoon cake flour
2¼ cups sifted cake flour
2¼ teaspoons baking powder
  ½ teaspoon salt
1⅔ cups sugar
  ⅓ cup butter, softened
  2 large eggs
  1 (14-ounce) can light coconut milk
  1 tablespoon vanilla extract

Frosting:
  4 large egg whites
  ½ teaspoon cream of tartar
Dash of salt
  1 cup sugar
  ¼ cup water
  ½ teaspoon vanilla extract
  ¼ teaspoon coconut extract

Remaining ingredient:
  ⅔ cup flaked sweetened coconut

1. Preheat oven to 350°.
2. To prepare cake, coat 2 (9-inch) round cake pans with cooking spray; dust with 1 tablespoon flour.
3. Combine 2¼ cups flour, baking powder, and salt, stirring with a whisk. Place sugar and butter in a large bowl; beat with a mixer at medium speed until well blended (about 5 minutes). Add eggs, 1 at a time, beating well after each addition. Add flour mixture and milk alternately to sugar

mixture, beginning and ending with flour mixture. Stir in vanilla.

4. Pour batter into prepared pans. Sharply tap pans once on countertop to remove air bubbles. Bake at 350° for 30 minutes or until a wooden pick inserted in center comes out clean. Cool in pans 10 minutes on a wire rack, and remove from pans. Cool completely on wire rack.

5. To prepare frosting, place egg whites, cream of tartar, and salt in a large bowl; beat with a mixer at high speed until stiff peaks form. Combine sugar and water in a saucepan; bring to a boil. Cook, without stirring, until candy thermometer registers 250°. Pour hot sugar syrup in a thin stream over egg whites, beating at high speed. Stir in extracts.

6. Place 1 cake layer on a plate; spread with 1 cup frosting. Sprinkle with ⅓ cup coconut. Top with remaining cake layer; spread remaining frosting over top and sides of cake. Sprinkle ⅓ cup coconut over top of cake. Store cake loosely covered in refrigerator. Yield: 14 servings (serving size: 1 slice).

CALORIES 298 (24% from fat); FAT 7.9g (sat 5g, mono 1.7g, poly 0.3g); PROTEIN 3.4g; CARB 53.8g; FIBER 0.4g; CHOL 42mg; IRON 1.6mg; SODIUM 273mg; CALC 52mg

Test Kitchen Tip: Cake flour is a fine-textured wheat flour that usually makes cakes more tender. It must be sifted before measuring. If you don't have cake flour, you can substitute ¾ cup plus 2 tablespoons of all-purpose flour for 1 cup of cake flour.

Fudgy Sheet Cake

It's hard to beat a sheet cake for simplicity and ease.
And who can resist a chocolate cake with chocolate icing?

Prep: 20 minutes • Cook: 30 minutes • Other: 10 minutes

Cake:
- ½ cup unsweetened cocoa
- ½ cup boiling water
- 2 cups sifted cake flour
- 1 teaspoon baking soda
- ½ teaspoon salt
- 1½ cups granulated sugar
- ⅓ cup vegetable shortening
- 2 teaspoons vanilla extract
- 2 large eggs
- 1 cup low-fat buttermilk
- Cooking spray

Frosting:
- 3 cups sifted powdered sugar
- ⅓ cup unsweetened cocoa
- ¼ cup 1% low-fat milk
- 2 teaspoons butter, softened
- 1 teaspoon vanilla extract

1. Preheat oven to 350°.

2. To prepare cake, combine ½ cup cocoa and water in a small bowl; cool. Combine flour, baking soda, and salt, stirring well with a whisk. Place granulated sugar, shortening, and 2 teaspoons vanilla in a large bowl; beat with a mixer at medium speed until well blended. Add eggs, 1 at a time, beating well after each addition. Beat in cocoa mixture. Add flour mixture and buttermilk alternately to sugar mixture, beginning and ending with flour mixture and beating well after each addition.

3. Pour batter into a 13 x 9–inch baking pan coated with cooking spray. Bake at 350° for 28 minutes or until cake springs back when lightly touched. Cool in pan 10 minutes on a wire rack.

4. To prepare frosting, combine powdered sugar and ⅓ cup cocoa in a medium bowl, stirring well with a whisk. Add milk, butter, and 1 teaspoon vanilla; stir with a whisk until smooth. Spread frosting over cake. Yield: 16 servings (serving size: 1 piece).

CALORIES 260 (21% from fat); FAT 6g (sat 2g, mono 2g, poly 1.2g); PROTEIN 3.3g; CARB 50.3g; FIBER 1.7g; CHOL 28mg; IRON 1.6mg; SODIUM 184mg; CALC 35mg

Devil's Food Cake

Espresso makes each bite of this dark, dense cake sinfully rich and flavorful.

Prep: 14 minutes • Cook: 26 minutes
Other: 10 minutes

  Cooking spray
   2 teaspoons all-purpose flour
   5 tablespoons butter
  ½ cup Dutch process cocoa
   1 cup packed dark brown sugar
   2 large eggs
  ½ teaspoon baking soda
  1½ teaspoons vanilla extract
  ¼ teaspoon salt
  ¾ cup all-purpose flour
  ½ cup hot water
   1 teaspoon instant espresso granules
   1 tablespoon powdered sugar

1. Preheat oven to 350°.
2. Coat an 8-inch square baking pan with cooking spray; dust with 2 teaspoons flour.
3. Place butter in a large microwave-safe bowl. Cover and microwave at HIGH 1 minute. Add cocoa; stir well with a whisk. Add brown sugar; stir until mixture pulls away from sides of bowl. Add eggs, 1 at a time, stirring with a whisk until smooth. Stir in baking soda, vanilla, and salt. Spoon flour into a dry measuring cup; level with a knife. Add ¾ cup flour, stirring just until blended. Combine hot water and espresso. Add to flour mixture; stir just until blended.
4. Pour batter into pan. Bake at 350° for 25 minutes or until a wooden pick inserted in center comes out clean. Cool 10 minutes on a wire rack. Sprinkle with powdered sugar. Serve warm or at room temperature. Yield: 9 servings (serving size: 1 square).

CALORIES 221 (33% from fat); FAT 8.2g (sat 4.7g, mono 2.5g, poly 0.5g); PROTEIN 3.5g; CARB 36g; FIBER 1.7g; CHOL 65mg; IRON 1.9mg; SODIUM 225mg; CALC 36mg

Lemon-Glazed Gingerbread

The tangy lemon syrup balances the sweet molasses in this old-fashioned favorite.

Prep: 15 minutes • Cook: 30 minutes

  ⅓ cup butter, cut into small pieces
  ⅔ cup hot water
   1 cup light or dark molasses
   1 large egg
  2¾ cups all-purpose flour
  1½ teaspoons baking soda
  1½ teaspoons ground ginger
   1 teaspoon ground cinnamon
  ½ teaspoon salt
  ¼ teaspoon ground cloves
  Cooking spray
  1½ cups powdered sugar
   6 tablespoons fresh lemon juice
   1 cup frozen reduced-fat whipped topping, thawed

1. Preheat oven to 350°.
2. Combine butter and hot water in a bowl; stir with a whisk until butter melts. Add molasses and egg; stir with a whisk until blended. Lightly spoon flour into dry measuring cups, and level with a knife. Combine flour, baking soda, ginger, 1 teaspoon ground cinnamon, salt, and cloves. Add flour mixture to molasses mixture, stirring just until moist. Spoon into a 9-inch square cake pan coated with cooking spray. Bake at 350° for 30 minutes or until a wooden pick inserted in center comes out clean.
3. Combine sugar and lemon juice, stirring until well blended. Pierce top of ginger-bread liberally with a wooden skewer. Pour glaze over gingerbread. Top with whipped topping. Yield: 12 servings (serving size: 1 square and 1½ tablespoons topping).

CALORIES 296 (20% from fat); FAT 6.5g (sat 3.7g, mono 1.7g, poly 0.4g); PROTEIN 3.6g; CARB 57.3g; FIBER 1g; CHOL 35mg; IRON 2.8mg; SODIUM 322mg; CALC 68mg

Triple-Lemon Génoise with Buttercream and Raspberries

This versatile cake has always been a key element in a French pastry chef's repertoire. It's often the basis for layer cakes, tortes, ice cream cakes, jelly-rolls, and petits fours.

Prep: 40 minutes • Cook: 24 minutes

Génoise:
  Cooking spray
   1 tablespoon cake flour
   2 tablespoons butter
   1 cup unsifted cake flour
  ⅛ teaspoon salt
  ½ cup sugar
   1 teaspoon vanilla extract
   4 large eggs
   1 teaspoon grated lemon rind
Buttercream frosting:
   2 tablespoons butter, softened
   1 tablespoon fresh lemon juice
   1 teaspoon vanilla extract
   1 (8-ounce) block ⅓-less-fat cream cheese, chilled
   2 cups powdered sugar
Lemon syrup:
  ⅓ cup boiling water
  ¼ cup granulated sugar
   2 tablespoons fresh lemon juice
Remaining ingredient:
  1½ cups fresh raspberries

1. Preheat oven to 375°.
2. Coat a 9-inch springform pan with cooking spray; line with wax paper. Coat paper with cooking spray; dust with 1 tablespoon flour. Set aside.
3. Cook butter in a small saucepan over medium heat until lightly browned (about 4 minutes). Pour into a bowl; let cool.
4. Lightly spoon 1 cup flour into a dry measuring cup; level with a knife. Combine

1 cup flour and salt in a sifter. Sift flour and salt once. Beat sugar, vanilla, and eggs with a mixer at high speed until egg mixture falls in ribbons from beaters and holds its shape (about 10 to 15 minutes). Stir in lemon rind. Lightly spoon one-third of flour mixture onto egg mixture; quickly fold. Repeat procedure twice with remaining flour mixture.

5. Stir 1 cup batter into cooled browned butter. Gently fold butter mixture into remaining batter. Spoon batter into prepared pan; spread evenly. Bake at 375° for 20 minutes or until a wooden pick inserted in center comes out clean or cake springs back when touched lightly in center. Loosen from sides of pan; turn out onto a wire rack. Carefully peel off wax paper. Cool completely.

6. Beat butter and next 3 ingredients with a mixer at medium speed until smooth. Spoon powdered sugar into dry measuring cups; level with a knife. Gradually add powdered sugar to butter mixture; beat at low speed just until blended (do not overbeat). Cover and chill.

7. Combine water and granulated sugar; stir until sugar dissolves. Stir in 2 tablespoons lemon juice; cool to room temperature.

8. Split génoise in half horizontally using a serrated knife. Place bottom layer, cut side up, on a serving platter; brush with half of lemon syrup. Spread with ¾ cup frosting. Arrange ¾ cup raspberries on top of frosting. Top with remaining cake layer, cut side down; brush with remaining syrup. Spread remaining frosting over top and sides of cake. Top with ¾ cup raspberries. Store cake loosely covered in refrigerator. Yield: 12 servings (serving size: 1 slice).

CALORIES 278 (33% from fat); FAT 10.2g (sat 5.7g, mono 3.1g, poly 0.6g); PROTEIN 5g; CARB 42.3g; FIBER 1.1g; CHOL 98mg; IRON 1.1mg; SODIUM 161mg; CALC 29mg

how to make a génoise

1. Coat the pan with cooking spray, line the bottom with wax paper, then recoat with cooking spray and dust with flour.

2. Cook the butter over medium heat until lightly browned. Be sure to use butter; margarine will not brown.

3. Sift flour and salt together. This "lightens" the flour, which minimizes lumps.

4. Combine sugar, vanilla, and eggs; beat until mixture falls in ribbons.

5. Using a rubber spatula, fold one-third flour mixture into the egg mixture.

6. Stir about 1 cup batter into the cooled butter; fold into remaining batter.

Coffee Cupcakes

With espresso in the batter and in the syrup, these cupcakes are grown-up treats. If you'd prefer a single-layer cake to cupcakes, use a 9-inch square baking pan or round cake pan. Bake the cake at 350° for 25 minutes or until a wooden pick inserted in the center comes out clean.

**Prep: 20 minutes • Cook: 25 minutes
Other: 10 minutes**

Cupcakes:

    2 tablespoons boiling water
    4 teaspoons instant espresso granules
       or 8 teaspoons instant coffee granules
    ⅓ cup low-fat buttermilk
  1¼ cups all-purpose flour
    ½ teaspoon baking soda
    ¼ teaspoon salt
    ¾ cup granulated sugar
    5 tablespoons butter, softened
    2 teaspoons vanilla extract
    2 large eggs

Espresso syrup:

    ¼ cup granulated sugar
    ¼ cup water
    2 tablespoons instant espresso granules
       or ¼ cup instant coffee granules
    2 tablespoons light-colored corn syrup
    ¼ teaspoon vanilla extract
    2 tablespoons powdered sugar

1. Preheat oven to 350°.

2. To prepare cupcakes, combine 2 tablespoons boiling water and 4 teaspoons espresso, stirring until espresso dissolves. Stir in buttermilk.

3. Lightly spoon flour into dry measuring cups; level with a knife. Combine flour, baking soda, and salt, stirring well with a whisk.

4. Place ¾ cup granulated sugar, butter, and 2 teaspoons vanilla in a large bowl; beat with a mixer at medium speed until

well blended (about 5 minutes). Add eggs, 1 at a time, beating well after each addition. Add flour mixture and buttermilk mixture alternately to sugar mixture, beginning and ending with flour mixture.

5. Spoon batter into 12 muffin cups lined with paper liners. Bake at 350° for 18 to 19 minutes or until a wooden pick inserted in center comes out clean. Cool in pan 10 minutes on a wire rack; remove from pan.

6. To prepare syrup, combine ¼ cup granulated sugar, ¼ cup water, 2 tablespoons

espresso, and corn syrup in a small saucepan; bring mixture to a boil. Reduce heat; simmer 3 minutes. Stir in ¼ teaspoon vanilla. Pierce cupcake tops several times with a wooden skewer. Brush espresso syrup evenly over cupcakes. Cool completely on wire rack. Sprinkle cupcakes lightly with powdered sugar. Yield: 1 dozen (serving size: 1 cupcake).

CALORIES 192 (27% from fat); FAT 5.8g (sat 3.3g, mono 1.8g, poly 0.4g); PROTEIN 3g; CARB 31.8g; FIBER 0.4g; CHOL 49mg; IRON 0.9mg; SODIUM 173mg; CALC 19mg

Individual Chocolate Mousse Cakes

When you bake the ramekins in a baking pan filled with hot water, the cakes cook with a gentle heat that keeps the chocolate mousse from curdling.

Prep: 20 minutes • Cook: 30 minutes

1¼ cups sugar, divided
½ cup unsweetened cocoa
2 tablespoons all-purpose flour
⅛ teaspoon salt
¾ cup water
5 ounces bittersweet chocolate, finely chopped
1 tablespoon dark rum
1 teaspoon vanilla extract
2 large eggs
1 large egg white
Cooking spray

1. Preheat oven to 350°.
2. Combine ¾ cup sugar, cocoa, flour, and salt in a small saucepan. Add water; stir well with a whisk. Bring to a simmer over medium heat; cook 2 minutes, stirring constantly. Place chopped chocolate in a large bowl. Pour hot cocoa mixture over chocolate; stir until chocolate melts. Stir in rum and vanilla.
3. Place ½ cup sugar, eggs, and egg white in a bowl; beat with a mixer at high speed 6 minutes. Gently fold egg mixture into chocolate mixture.
4. Divide chocolate mixture evenly among 10 (4-ounce) ramekins coated with cooking spray. Place ramekins in a 13 x 9–inch baking pan; add hot water to pan to a depth of 1 inch. Bake cakes at 350° for 25 minutes or until puffy and set. Serve warm. Yield: 10 servings (serving size: 1 cake).

CALORIES 213 (27% from fat); FAT 6.4g (sat 3.6g, mono 1g, poly 0.2g); PROTEIN 3.6g; CARB 36.8g; FIBER 2.6g; CHOL 43mg; IRON 0.9mg; SODIUM 49mg; CALC 12mg

Chocolate Lava Cakes with Pistachio Cream

These flourless chocolate cakes are as decadent as a restaurant dessert, but they don't have any butter and only a fraction of the fat. When they bake, the gooey filling causes the center to sink in.

Prep: 25 minutes • Cook: 19 minutes
Other: 2 hours, 5 minutes

1 cup shelled dry-roasted pistachios
1¾ cups sugar, divided
¼ cup unsweetened cocoa
2 large eggs
5 large egg whites
2 ounces bittersweet chocolate, coarsely chopped
½ teaspoon baking powder
½ teaspoon vanilla extract
Cooking spray
1 cup 2% reduced-fat milk
Dash of salt
Powdered sugar (optional)

1. Place pistachios in a food processor, and process until a crumbly paste forms (about 3½ minutes), scraping sides of bowl once.
2. Place ¼ cup pistachio butter, 1¼ cups sugar, cocoa, eggs, and egg whites in top of a double boiler; stir well with a whisk. Add chocolate; cook over simmering water until chocolate melts and sugar dissolves (about 3 minutes). Remove from heat; add baking powder and vanilla. Stir with a whisk until smooth. Spoon batter into 12 muffin cups coated with cooking spray. Chill 2 hours.
3. Place remaining ¼ cup pistachio butter and ½ cup sugar in food processor; pulse 4 times or until combined. Add milk and salt; process until smooth. Strain mixture through a sieve into a small saucepan;

discard solids. Bring to a boil. Reduce heat, and simmer 4 minutes or until thick. Remove from heat; pour into a bowl. Cover and chill.
4. Preheat oven to 450°.
5. Bake cakes at 450° for 9 minutes or until almost set (centers will not be firm). Let cool in pan 5 minutes.
6. Using a small metal spatula, loosen cakes from muffin cups. Invert muffin pan onto a baking sheet. Using a wide spatula, carefully transfer cakes to individual dessert plates. Drizzle about 2 teaspoons sauce over each serving. Garnish with powdered sugar, if desired. Yield: 12 servings (serving size: 1 cake).

CALORIES 232 (30% from fat); FAT 7.7g (sat 2.2g, mono 3.1g, poly 1.5g); PROTEIN 6.1g; CARB 37.2g; FIBER 2g; CHOL 37mg; IRON 0.9mg; SODIUM 73mg; CALC 51mg

storing chocolate Semisweet and bittersweet chocolate keep remarkably well for at least a year. Because chocolate absorbs flavors and odors, wrap it securely in plastic and store in a cool, dry place. Milk and white chocolates lose freshness more quickly, so if you purchase more than you will use within a couple of months, freeze the extra chocolate. Wrap it securely in plastic and enclose in a zip-top plastic bag. Before using, thaw the chocolate completely at room temperature without removing it from the bag. Leaving it in the bag will prevent damaging condensation from forming.

Pound Cakes, Shortcakes & Upside-Down Cakes

They're traditional favorites, but there's nothing old-fashioned about these lightened cake recipes.

Double-Banana Pound Cake

This cake packs a double punch of banana from the fruit and liqueur. The banana liqueur gives the cake a pleasing banana flavor. Dusting the pan with dry breadcrumbs after coating it with cooking spray keeps the cake from sticking.

Prep: 25 minutes • Cook: 1 hour
Other: 10 minutes

  Cooking spray
  3 tablespoons dry breadcrumbs
  3 cups all-purpose flour
  1 teaspoon baking powder
  ¼ teaspoon salt
  ¼ teaspoon ground mace
  1 cup mashed ripe banana
  ½ cup fat-free milk
  ½ cup banana liqueur or ½ cup fat-free milk and 1 tablespoon banana extract
  ¾ cup butter, softened
  2 cups granulated sugar
1½ teaspoons vanilla extract
  3 large eggs
  1 tablespoon powdered sugar

1. Preheat oven to 350°.
2. Coat a 10-inch tube pan with cooking spray; dust with breadcrumbs.
3. Lightly spoon flour into dry measuring cups; level with a knife. Combine flour, baking powder, salt, and mace; stir well with a whisk. Combine mashed banana, milk, and banana liqueur in a bowl. Beat butter in a large bowl with a mixer at medium speed until light and fluffy. Gradually add granulated sugar and vanilla, and beat mixture until well blended. Add eggs, 1 at a time, beating well after each addition. Add flour mixture to sugar mixture alternately with banana mixture, beating at low speed, beginning and ending with flour mixture.
4. Spoon batter into prepared pan. Bake at 350° for 1 hour or until a wooden pick inserted in center comes out clean. Cool in pan 10 minutes on a wire rack; remove from pan. Cool completely on wire rack. Sift powdered sugar over top of cake. Yield: 18 servings (serving size: 1 slice).

CALORIES 286 (28% from fat); FAT 8.9g (sat 5.1g, mono 2.6g, poly 0.5g); PROTEIN 3.8g; CARB 44.8g; FIBER 0.9g; CHOL 58mg; IRON 1.3mg; SODIUM 163mg; CALC 37mg

Lemon-Poppy Seed Pound Cake

Ideal for afternoon tea, this loaf-style pound cake has poppy seeds in the batter and is brushed with a tangy powdered sugar glaze.

Prep: 25 minutes • Cook: 1 hour
Other: 10 minutes

　 Cooking spray
　 1　teaspoon all-purpose flour
　 1　cup granulated sugar
　⅓　cup butter, softened
　 2　large egg whites
　 1　large egg
　 1　tablespoon grated lemon rind
　 1　teaspoon vanilla extract
1⅔　cups all-purpose flour
　 2　tablespoons poppy seeds
　 1　teaspoon baking powder
　¼　teaspoon baking soda
　⅛　teaspoon salt
　¾　cup low-fat buttermilk
　⅔　cup powdered sugar
　 4　teaspoons fresh lemon juice

1. Preheat oven to 350°.
2. Coat an 8 x 4–inch loaf pan with cooking spray; dust with 1 teaspoon flour.
3. Beat granulated sugar and butter with a mixer at medium speed until well blended (about 4 minutes). Add egg whites and egg, 1 at a time, beating well after each addition. Beat in lemon rind and vanilla. Lightly spoon 1⅔ cups flour into dry measuring cups; level with a knife. Combine 1⅔ cups flour and next 4 ingredients in a large bowl, stirring well with a whisk. Add flour mixture to sugar mixture alternately with buttermilk, beginning and ending with flour mixture.
4. Pour batter into prepared pan; bake at 350° for 1 hour or until a wooden pick

inserted in center comes out clean. Cool in pan 10 minutes on a wire rack; remove from pan. Poke holes in top of cake using a wooden skewer. Combine powdered sugar and lemon juice in a small bowl; brush over warm cake. Cool completely. Yield: 12 servings (serving size: 1 slice).

CALORIES 226 (27% from fat); FAT 6.7g (sat 3.6g, mono 1.8g, poly 0.8g); PROTEIN 3.8g; CARB 38.2g; FIBER 0.6g; CHOL 32mg; IRON 1.1mg; SODIUM 166mg; CALC 70mg

lemon lessons

- The colored portion of the lemon (not the white pith) is called the zest. Because the zest contains aromatic oils, zest or grated rind can add great flavor to food.
- To remove the lemon zest (rind), use a special zester, handheld grater, or our favorite—the Microplane Food Grater, which peels several strips at a time.
- You can also peel the lemon, being careful to remove as little of the white pith as possible (it's very bitter), place in a food processor, and pulse until you have a fine zest.
- Once you've removed the zest or peel from a lemon (or any other citrus fruit), you can refrigerate the fruit for up to one week.
- It's important not to use too much zest, which can add bitterness rather than tartness.
- In general, fresh lemons convert to these standard measurements:
　 1 medium lemon = 2 to 3 tablespoons juice
　 1 medium lemon = 1 teaspoon grated rind (zest)
　 5 to 6 lemons = 1 cup juice

Sour Cream Pound Cake

For entertaining, you just can't go wrong with a traditional sour cream pound cake. This version has remained one of our most popular recipes for more than 10 years.

Prep: 20 minutes • Cook: 1 hour, 35 minutes
Other: 10 minutes

　 3　cups sugar
　¾　cup butter, softened
1⅓　cups egg substitute
1½　cups low-fat sour cream
　 1　teaspoon baking soda
4½　cups sifted cake flour
　¼　teaspoon salt
　 2　teaspoons vanilla extract
　 Cooking spray
　 Fresh blackberries (optional)
　 Mint sprigs (optional)

1. Preheat oven to 325°.
2. Place sugar and butter in a large bowl; beat with a mixer at medium speed until well blended (about 5 minutes). Gradually add egg substitute, beating well.
3. Combine sour cream and baking soda. Stir well. Combine flour and salt. Add flour mixture to sugar mixture alternately with sour cream mixture, beginning and ending with flour mixture. Stir in vanilla.
4. Pour batter into a 10-inch tube pan coated with cooking spray. Bake at 325° for 1 hour and 35 minutes or until a wooden pick inserted in center comes out clean. Cool in pan 10 minutes on a wire rack; remove from pan. Cool completely on wire rack. Garnish with blackberries and mint, if desired. Yield: 18 servings (serving size: 1 slice).

CALORIES 333 (28% from fat); FAT 10.3g (sat 3.1g, mono 4.1g, poly 2.5g); PROTEIN 4.7g; CARB 55.9g; FIBER 0g; CHOL 8mg; IRON 2.4mg; SODIUM 227mg; CALC 33mg

Cornmeal Pound Cake

With the flavor of sweet corn bread and the richness of an old-fashioned pound cake, this cake is delicious with strawberries and peaches. The unexpected crunch comes from grits.

**Prep: 25 minutes • Cook: 50 minutes
Other: 15 minutes**

Cooking spray
1   tablespoon stone-ground white cornmeal
2   cups sugar, divided
⅔   cup butter, softened
1   teaspoon grated lemon rind
1   teaspoon vanilla extract
5   large egg yolks
1   cup low-fat sour cream
2   cups all-purpose flour
½   cup stone-ground white cornmeal
½   cup stone-ground white grits
½   teaspoon salt
½   teaspoon baking soda
5   large egg whites

1. Preheat oven to 325°.
2. Coat a 10-inch tube pan with cooking spray; dust with 1 tablespoon cornmeal.
3. Place 1¾ cups sugar, butter, rind, and vanilla in a large bowl; beat with a mixer at medium speed until light and fluffy. Add egg yolks, 1 at a time, beating well after each addition. Beat in sour cream.
4. Lightly spoon flour into dry measuring cups; level with a knife. Combine flour, ½ cup cornmeal, grits, salt, and baking soda in a medium bowl; stir well with a whisk. Add flour mixture to sugar mixture, stirring to combine.
5. Beat egg whites with a mixer at high speed until foamy, using clean, dry beaters. Gradually add ¼ cup sugar, 1 tablespoon at a time, beating until stiff peaks form. Gently stir one-fourth of egg white mixture into batter; fold in remaining egg white mixture. Spoon batter into prepared tube pan.
6. Bake at 325° for 50 minutes or until a wooden pick inserted in cake comes out clean. Cool in pan 15 minutes on a wire rack; remove from pan. Cool cake completely on wire rack. Yield: 18 servings (serving size: 1 slice).

CALORIES 261 (30% from fat); FAT 8.8g (sat 5.9g, mono 0.5g, poly 0.2g); PROTEIN 4.2g; CARB 41.8g; FIBER 0.5g; CHOL 81mg; IRON 1.1mg; SODIUM 180mg; CALC 25mg

pleasing pounds Here's what we've learned over the years about baking and storing light pound cakes.

Be precise when measuring flour. If you use too much, you'll end up with a cake that's dry and heavy. (See page 115 or 116 for the proper techniques for measuring flour.)

We prefer to bake pound cakes in 10-inch tube pans, but you can use a 12-cup Bundt pan. Just reduce the oven temperature to 325°.

Dust the tube pan with dry bread-crumbs after coating it with cooking spray to keep the cake from sticking.

To freeze pound cake, let it cool completely on a wire rack. Place unglazed cake in a heavy-duty zip-top plastic bag. Remove excess air from bag; seal and place bag in the freezer up to four months. To thaw, let bag stand at room temperature.

Brown Sugar Pound Cake

The brown sugar gives this pound cake its caramel-like flavor.

Prep: 20 minutes • Cook: 1 hour, 5 minutes
Other: 10 minutes

Cooking spray
3 tablespoons dry breadcrumbs
3 cups all-purpose flour
1 teaspoon baking powder
¼ teaspoon salt
¾ cup butter, softened
2 cups packed light brown sugar
1 tablespoon vanilla extract
3 large eggs
1 cup fat-free milk
1 tablespoon powdered sugar

1. Preheat oven to 350°.
2. Coat a 10-inch tube pan with cooking spray, and dust with breadcrumbs.
3. Lightly spoon flour into dry measuring cups; level with a knife. Combine flour, baking powder, and salt in a bowl; stir mixture well with a whisk. Beat butter in a large bowl with a mixer at medium speed until butter is light and fluffy. Gradually add brown sugar and vanilla, beating until well blended. Add eggs, 1 at a time, beating well after each addition. Add flour mixture to sugar mixture alternately with milk, beating at low speed, beginning and ending with flour mixture.
4. Spoon batter into prepared pan. Bake at 350° for 1 hour and 5 minutes or until a wooden pick inserted in center of cake comes out clean. Cool cake in pan 10 minutes on a wire rack. Remove from pan; cool completely on wire rack. Sift powdered sugar over top of cake. Yield: 18 servings (serving size: 1 slice).

CALORIES 265 (30% from fat); FAT 8.9g (sat 5.1g, mono 2.6g, poly 0.5g); PROTEIN 3.9g; CARB 42.6g; FIBER 0.6g; CHOL 58mg; IRON 1.7mg; SODIUM 176mg; CALC 65mg

Chocolate Bundt Cake

This cake is slightly smaller than one made in a standard Bundt pan or tube pan. Look for 6-cup Bundt pans at specialty kitchen shops or order online. You can use a 9-inch round cake pan; reduce the bake time to 20 minutes.

Prep: 13 minutes • Cook: 35 minutes • Other: 10 minutes

1 cup all-purpose flour
1 cup sugar
½ cup unsweetened cocoa
½ teaspoon baking soda
¼ teaspoon salt
¼ cup butter, softened
2 large egg whites
1 large egg
½ cup 1% low-fat milk
2 teaspoons instant espresso granules
1½ teaspoons vanilla extract
Cooking spray
Rich Chocolate Sauce, page 457 (optional)

1. Preheat oven to 350°.
2. Lightly spoon flour into a dry measuring cup; level with a knife. Combine flour and next 4 ingredients in a large bowl, and stir well with a whisk. Add butter, egg whites, and egg to flour mixture; beat with a mixer at low speed 1 minute. Beat mixture at high speed 1 minute. Add milk, espresso granules, and vanilla; beat 1 minute. Pour batter into a 6-cup Bundt pan coated with cooking spray.
3. Bake at 350° for 35 to 40 minutes or until a wooden pick inserted near center comes out clean. Cool in pan 10 minutes. Remove from pan; cool completely on a wire rack. Drizzle with Rich Chocolate Sauce, if desired. Yield: 10 servings (serving size: 1 slice).

CALORIES 192 (28% from fat); FAT 6g (sat 3.5g, mono 1.8g, poly 0.3g); PROTEIN 4g; CARB 32.8g; FIBER 1.8g; CHOL 34mg; IRON 1.3mg; SODIUM 225mg; CALC 27mg

Classic Makeover: Shortcake

Strawberry shortcake probably originated with American colonists' appreciation of a Native American dish of wild strawberries pounded into corn bread. The colonists created their own version by splitting the common biscuit in half, generously buttering it, and filling it with berries and whipped cream. We followed their lead but reduced the amount of butter and switched from whipping cream to fat-free whipped topping. While our dessert has one-third fewer calories and two-thirds less fat than the original, it still has a tender, moist shortcake and plenty of creamy topping.

Before	After
• 384 calories	• 246 calories
• 26g fat	• 7.4g fat
• percentage of calories from fat 61%	• percentage of calories from fat 27%

Strawberry Shortcake

Due to its lower fat content, this shortcake can overcook and crumble quickly, so watch it carefully while it's in the oven—don't allow it to get too brown.

**Prep: 30 minutes • Cook: 15 minutes
Other: 1 hour, 10 minutes**

Strawberries:
    4 cups sliced strawberries
    ¼ cup sugar

Shortcake:
    2 cups all-purpose flour
    ¼ cup sugar
    2 teaspoons baking powder
    1 teaspoon grated lemon rind
    ½ teaspoon salt
    ¼ teaspoon baking soda
    6 tablespoons chilled butter, cut into small pieces
    ⅔ cup fat-free buttermilk
    ½ teaspoon vanilla extract
       Cooking spray
    1 large egg white, lightly beaten
 1½ teaspoons turbinado sugar or granulated sugar

Remaining ingredients:
    2 cups frozen fat-free whipped topping, thawed
       Whipped topping (optional)
       Whole strawberry (optional)

1. To prepare strawberries, combine sliced strawberries and ¼ cup sugar; cover and chill 1 hour.

2. Preheat oven to 400°.

3. To prepare shortcake, lightly spoon flour into dry measuring cups; level with a knife. Combine flour and next 5 ingredients in a large bowl, stirring with a whisk. Cut in butter with a pastry blender or 2 knives until mixture resembles coarse meal. Combine buttermilk and vanilla; add to flour mixture, stirring just until moist (dough will be sticky).

4. Turn dough out onto a lightly floured surface; knead lightly 4 times with floured hands. Pat dough into an 8-inch circle on a baking sheet coated with cooking spray. Brush top with egg white; sprinkle with 1½ teaspoons sugar.

5. Bake at 400° for 15 minutes or until a wooden pick inserted in center comes out clean. Cool 10 minutes on a wire rack. Carefully split shortcake in half horizontally using a serrated knife; cool layers separately on wire racks.

6. Place bottom half of shortcake, cut side up, on a serving plate. Drain strawberries, reserving juice; drizzle juice over bottom half of shortcake. Spread 2 cups whipped topping over shortcake layer; arrange drained strawberries over whipped topping. Top with remaining shortcake layer, cut side down. Garnish with additional whipped topping and whole strawberry, if desired. Yield: 10 servings (serving size: 1 wedge).

CALORIES 246 (27% from fat); FAT 7.4g (sat 4.4g, mono 2.1g, poly 0.5g); PROTEIN 4g; CARB 40.3g; FIBER 2.2g; CHOL 19mg; IRON 1.6mg; SODIUM 348mg; CALC 90mg

Test Kitchen Tip: To shorten the preparation and cleanup time, place all the dry ingredients and the lemon rind in a food processor; pulse to mix. Add butter, pulsing until it resembles coarse meal. Add the buttermilk and vanilla; pulse just until it's moist. Dust a large zip-top plastic bag with flour, add the dough, and knead. Turn it out onto a Silpat-lined cookie sheet, and keep your hands in the bag to shape the dough. (See page 149 for more information on Silpat mats.)

Triple-Fruit Shortcakes

Blueberries and orange sections are welcome additions to the more traditional strawberries-only version. Sugar tenderizes these biscuitlike shortcakes and allows for caramelization, which creates a sugary crust.

Prep: 30 minutes • Cook: 25 minutes • Other: 2 hours, 5 minutes

Filling:
- 4 cups sliced strawberries
- 2 cups blueberries
- ½ cup orange sections
- ⅓ cup sugar
- ¼ cup fresh orange juice

Shortcakes:
- 2 cups all-purpose flour
- ½ cup sugar
- 2 teaspoons baking powder
- ½ teaspoon salt
- ½ cup chilled butter, cut into small pieces
- ¾ cup fat-free buttermilk
- Cooking spray
- 2 teaspoons water
- 1 large egg white
- 2 teaspoons sugar

1. To prepare filling, combine first 5 ingredients in a bowl. Cover and chill 2 hours.

2. Preheat oven to 400°.

3. To prepare shortcakes, lightly spoon flour into dry measuring cups; level with a knife. Combine flour, ½ cup sugar, baking powder, and salt in a large bowl; stir well with a whisk. Cut in butter with a pastry blender or 2 knives until mixture resembles coarse meal. Add buttermilk; stir just until moist.

4. Turn dough out onto a lightly floured surface; knead lightly 4 or 5 times. Pat dough into a 9-inch round cake pan coated with cooking spray. Cut dough into 10 wedges, cutting into but not through dough. Combine water and egg white; brush egg white mixture over dough. Sprinkle 2 teaspoons sugar over dough.

5. Bake at 400° for 25 minutes or until golden. Cool in pan 5 minutes on a wire rack; remove from pan. Cool completely on wire rack. Cut shortcake into 10 wedges. Split each wedge in half horizontally. Fill each wedge with ½ cup filling. Yield: 10 servings (serving size: 1 wedge).

CALORIES 292 (30% from fat); FAT 9.8g (sat 5.8g, mono 2.8g, poly 0.6g); PROTEIN 4.4g; CARB 48.3g; FIBER 3.2g; CHOL 25mg; IRON 1.6mg; SODIUM 335mg; CALC 99mg

Cranberry Upside-Down Cake with Cognac Cream

Cranberry-studded upside-down cake is an easy treat to make for the holidays. The cognac-flavored cream topping elevates this simple dessert to simply spectacular.

Prep: 30 minutes • Cook: 47 minutes
Other: 5 minutes

  2 tablespoons butter, melted
Cooking spray
  ½ cup packed brown sugar
  ¼ cup chopped pecans, toasted
  1 (12-ounce) package fresh cranberries
1⅓ cups all-purpose flour
1½ teaspoons baking powder
  ⅛ teaspoon salt
  ¾ cup granulated sugar
  3 tablespoons butter, softened
  2 large egg yolks
  1 teaspoon vanilla extract
  ½ cup fat-free milk
  2 large egg whites
  1 cup frozen fat-free whipped topping, thawed
  1 tablespoon cognac

1. Preheat oven to 350°.
2. Pour melted butter into an 8-inch square baking pan coated with cooking spray; sprinkle with brown sugar. Bake sugar mixture at 350° for 2 minutes. Remove from oven, and top with pecans and cranberries.
3. Lightly spoon flour into dry measuring cups; level with a knife. Combine flour, baking powder, and salt in a bowl; stir with a whisk.
4. Place sugar and softened butter in a large bowl; beat with a mixer at medium speed until well blended. Add egg yolks, 1 at a time, beating well after each addition. Stir in vanilla.

5. Add flour mixture and milk alternately to butter mixture, beginning and ending with flour mixture; mix after each addition. Beat egg whites with a mixer at high speed until stiff peaks form, using clean, dry beaters; fold into batter.
6. Spread batter evenly over cranberries in prepared pan. Bake at 350° for 45 minutes. Cool in pan 5 minutes on a wire rack. Loosen edges of cake with a sharp knife. Place a plate upside down on top of cake pan; invert onto plate.
7. Combine whipped topping and cognac, and serve with warm cake. Yield: 9 servings (serving size: 1 cake piece and about 2 tablespoons cognac cream).

CALORIES 316 (29% from fat); FAT 10.2g (sat 4.6g, mono 3.7g, poly 1.2g); PROTEIN 4.3g; CARB 51.7g; FIBER 2.4g; CHOL 65mg; IRON 1.5mg; SODIUM 210mg; CALC 88mg

Maple-Pear Upside-Down Cake

Maple syrup, cooked down to a glaze with fresh pears, is the topping for this upside-down cake.

Prep: 20 minutes • Cook: 38 minutes
Other: 5 minutes

  ⅓ cup maple syrup
  3 peeled Bartlett or Anjou pears, each cored and cut into 8 wedges
  1 cup all-purpose flour
  ¾ teaspoon baking powder
  ¼ teaspoon baking soda
  ¼ teaspoon ground ginger
  ¼ teaspoon salt
  ⅔ cup sugar
  ⅓ cup butter, softened
  1 teaspoon vanilla extract
  2 large eggs
  ½ cup low-fat buttermilk

1. Preheat oven to 350°.
2. Bring syrup to a boil in an ovenproof skillet over medium-high heat; cook 2 minutes. Remove from heat; arrange pears in pan in a spokelike fashion. Place pan over medium-high heat, and cook until syrup thickens (about 4 minutes), gently shaking pan frequently.
3. Lightly spoon flour into a dry measuring cup; level with a knife. Combine flour and next 4 ingredients, stirring well with a whisk. Place sugar, butter, and vanilla in a large bowl; beat with a mixer at medium speed until well blended (about 2 minutes). Add eggs, 1 at a time, beating well after each addition. Stir in flour mixture alternately with buttermilk, beginning and ending with flour mixture.
4. Pour batter evenly over pear mixture in prepared pan. Bake at 350° for 30 minutes or until cake springs back when touched lightly in center. Loosen cake from sides of pan using a narrow metal spatula. Cool in pan 5 minutes. Place a plate upside down on top of cake; invert onto plate. Serve warm. Yield: 8 servings (serving size: 1 wedge).

CALORIES 288 (30% from fat); FAT 9.6g (sat 5.3g, mono 2.8g, poly 0.6g); PROTEIN 4.1g; CARB 47.9g; FIBER 1.9g; CHOL 76mg; IRON 1.3mg; SODIUM 262mg; CALC 71mg

Test Kitchen Tip: Maple syrup comes in different grades, ranging in color from light golden to dark brown. The lighter the color, the milder the syrup. We like to use a dark maple syrup for baking because it adds an intense maple flavor.

Angel Food Cakes, Jelly-Roll Cakes & Sponge Cakes

These cakes depend on beaten eggs or egg whites for lightness.

Classic Angel Food Cake

This master recipe is good as is, but it's also easy to modify to suit any craving. See the flavor variations below. (See the technique photos for making angel food cake on the next page.)

Prep: 20 minutes • Cook: 55 minutes

    1   cup sifted cake flour
 1½   cups sugar, divided
   12   large egg whites
    1   teaspoon cream of tartar
   ¼   teaspoon salt
 1½   teaspoons vanilla extract
 1½   teaspoons fresh lemon juice
   ½   teaspoon almond extract

1. Preheat oven to 325°.
2. Combine flour and ¾ cup sugar, stirring with a whisk.
3. Place egg whites in a large bowl; beat with a mixer at high speed until foamy. Add cream of tartar and salt; beat until soft peaks form. Add ¾ cup sugar, 2 tablespoons at a time, beating until stiff peaks form. Beat in vanilla, juice, and almond extract.
4. Sift ¼ cup flour mixture over egg white mixture; fold in. Repeat with remaining flour mixture, ¼ cup at a time.
5. Spoon batter into an ungreased 10-inch tube pan, spreading evenly. Break air pockets by cutting through batter with a knife. Bake at 325° for 55 minutes or until cake springs back when lightly touched. Invert pan; cool completely. Loosen cake from sides of pan using a narrow metal spatula.

Invert cake onto a plate. Yield: 12 servings (serving size: 1 slice).

CALORIES 146 (0% from fat); FAT 0.1g (sat 0g, mono 0g, poly 0.1g); PROTEIN 4.2g; CARB 31.8g; FIBER 0.1g; CHOL 0mg; IRON 0.6mg; SODIUM 104mg; CALC 4mg

Variations

Chocolate: Add ¼ cup sifted unsweetened cocoa to the flour mixture.

Orange: Fold 2 tablespoons grated orange peel and 1 teaspoon orange extract into batter.

Peppermint: Add ¼ teaspoon red food coloring to the batter; fold in ¼ cup finely crushed hard peppermint candies.

Spiced: Add 1½ teaspoons pumpkin pie spice to the flour mixture.

Test Kitchen Tip: Store angel food cake, tightly covered, at room temperature up to two days, or freeze up to four weeks.

how to make a great angel food cake

1. Separate eggs while they're still cold—the yolks and whites will be more firm and separate more easily. Don't allow any pieces of yolk to mix with the whites, or the whites won't beat to maximum volume. To make sure that the whites stay free of any yolks, separate each egg over a small bowl, then pour the whites into a clean, large glass or metal bowl (free of even the faintest trace of grease).

2. Make sure the beaters are clean and dry. When stiff peaks form, the whites will look shiny, moist, and snowy, and the peaks will hold high when you lift the beaters. Be careful not to overbeat the whites—lightly underbeaten egg whites will work, but overbeaten whites will make a tough cake.

3. Sprinkle the flour a little at a time over the beaten egg whites. Then, with a large spatula, use large sweeping motions to fold the flour into the whites. The goal is to work in the dry ingredients without deflating the whites. Gently scrape the batter into an ungreased pan—preferably an angel food tube pan with a removable bottom. Smooth the top of the batter evenly.

4. Run a knife through the batter to break up any air pockets that may have formed when the batter was poured into the pan. Place the cake in the center of the oven for even baking. Don't open the oven door until the baking time is up (or very nearly so); the fragile egg whites may begin to deflate as cool air rushes into the oven.

5. Cool the cake upside down so that the cake doesn't deflate while it's still warm. If your pan doesn't have "feet," invert it by placing the center hole on the neck of a wine bottle.

6. To remove the cooled cake from the pan, run a narrow metal spatula or thin knife around the edges, including the center tube; take care to dislodge as little crust as possible. If your pan has a removable bottom, push it up to dislodge the cake, then use the same spatula method to loosen the cake.

Five-Spice Toasted-Coconut Cake Roll with Tropical Fruit Compote

Freeze the rolled cake up to two days before serving it with the compote. To soften the sorbet for spreading on the cake, let it stand at room temperature for 30 to 45 minutes.

Prep: 30 minutes • Cook: 20 minutes
Other: 1 hour, 23 minutes

Cake:
- ½ cup sifted cake flour
- ¾ cup granulated sugar, divided
- ¾ teaspoon five-spice powder
- 6 large egg whites
- ½ teaspoon cream of tartar
- Dash of salt
- 1 teaspoon fresh lemon juice
- 1 teaspoon vanilla extract
- ½ teaspoon coconut extract
- ⅓ cup flaked sweetened coconut
- 2 tablespoons powdered sugar
- 1 pint mandarin orange with passion-fruit sorbet, softened

Tropical Fruit Compote:
- 1 cup (½-inch) cubed peeled ripe mango
- 1 cup (½-inch) cubed fresh pineapple
- 1 cup (½-inch) cubed peeled kiwifruit
- 2 tablespoons brown sugar
- 2 tablespoons dark rum or ½ teaspoon rum extract

Remaining ingredient:
- ¼ cup flaked sweetened coconut, toasted

1. Preheat oven to 325°.
2. Line bottom of a 15 x 10–inch jelly-roll pan with wax paper; set aside.
3. To prepare cake, combine flour, 6 tablespoons granulated sugar, and five-spice powder, stirring with a whisk.
4. Place egg whites in a large bowl; beat with a mixer at high speed until foamy.

Add cream of tartar and salt; beat until soft peaks form. Add 6 tablespoons granulated sugar, 2 tablespoons at a time, beating until stiff peaks form. Beat in juice and extracts.
5. Sift ¼ cup flour mixture over egg white mixture; fold in. Repeat with remaining flour mixture, ¼ cup at a time. Spread batter into prepared pan. Sprinkle with ⅓ cup coconut. Bake at 325° for 20 minutes or until cake springs back when touched.
6. Place a clean dish towel over a large wire rack; dust with powdered sugar. Loosen cake from sides of pan; turn out onto towel. Carefully peel off wax paper; cool 3 minutes. Starting at narrow end, roll up cake and towel together. Place,

seam side down, on wire rack; cool cake completely. Unroll cake, and remove towel. Spread sorbet over cake, leaving a ½-inch border around outside edges. Reroll cake. Wrap cake in plastic wrap; freeze 1 hour or until firm.
7. To prepare compote, combine mango and next 4 ingredients; let stand 20 minutes.
8. To serve, cut cake into 16 slices, and place 2 slices on each of 8 plates. Top with compote and toasted coconut. Yield: 8 servings (serving size: 2 slices cake, about ¼ cup compote, and 1½ teaspoons coconut).

CALORIES 245 (8% from fat); FAT 2.1g (sat 1.6g, mono 0.1g, poly 0.1g); PROTEIN 4g; CARB 51.6g; FIBER 1.7g; CHOL 0mg; IRON 1.2mg; SODIUM 80mg; CALC 22mg

Tres Leches Cake

Tres leches ("three milks") is a cake drenched in sweet, milky syrup and topped with meringue.

Prep: 30 minutes • Cook: 28 minutes
Other: 5 minutes

Cake:
 Cooking spray
  1 tablespoon all-purpose flour
 ¼ teaspoon salt
  4 large egg whites
 ⅔ cup sugar
  1 teaspoon vanilla extract
  3 large eggs
 ⅔ cup all-purpose flour

Milk mixture:
  1 cup half-and-half
  1 (14-ounce) can fat-free sweetened condensed milk
  1 (12-ounce) can fat-free evaporated milk

Meringue:
  3 large egg whites
  1 cup sugar
 ⅓ cup water
  1 teaspoon lemon rind
  1 teaspoon vanilla extract

1. Preheat oven to 350°.
2. To prepare cake, coat a 13 x 9–inch baking dish with cooking spray; dust with 1 tablespoon flour.

3. Place salt and 4 egg whites in a large bowl; beat with a mixer at high speed until soft peaks form. Add ⅔ cup sugar, 1 tablespoon at a time, beating until stiff peaks form. Place 1 teaspoon vanilla and 3 eggs in a large bowl; beat until thick and pale (about 3 minutes). Fold egg white mixture into egg mixture. Lightly spoon ⅔ cup flour into dry measuring cups; level with a knife. Fold flour into egg mixture. Spoon batter into prepared dish. Bake at 350° for 20 minutes or until cake springs back when touched lightly in center. Cool 5 minutes in pan on a wire rack.
4. Combine half-and-half, condensed milk, and evaporated milk. Pierce entire top of cake with a fork, and pour milk mixture over cake.
5. To prepare meringue, beat 3 egg whites with a mixer at high speed until foamy, using clean, dry beaters. Combine 1 cup sugar and ⅓ cup water in a saucepan; bring to a boil. Cook, without stirring, until candy thermometer registers 250°. Pour hot sugar syrup in a thin stream over egg whites, beating at high speed. Stir in rind and 1 teaspoon vanilla. Spread over cake. Store cake loosely covered in refrigerator. Yield: 12 servings (serving size: 1 piece).

CALORIES 309 (11% from fat); FAT 3.9g (sat 1.9g, mono 1.2g, poly 0.4g); PROTEIN 9.7g; CARB 58.5g; FIBER 0.2g; CHOL 68mg; IRON 0.7mg; SODIUM 171mg; CALC 197mg

Raspberry Jelly-Roll with Apricot Coulis

To make a jelly-roll, you spread jams, jellies, frosting, or whipped cream onto a thin, flat cake, and roll it into a log. You can try many varieties of fillings, flavors, and sauces in this versatile jelly-roll cake. Try peach jam and strawberry sauce, lemon curd and orange sauce, or any of your favorite fruit combinations. While the cake is still warm and flexible, roll it up in a towel, and let it cool so it won't resist being rolled a second time.

Prep: 30 minutes • Cook: 10 minutes
Other: 1 hour, 1 minute

Cake:
 Cooking spray
 ⅔ cup all-purpose flour
  1 teaspoon baking powder
 ⅛ teaspoon salt
  4 large eggs
 ¾ cup granulated sugar
 1½ teaspoons vanilla extract
 ½ teaspoon grated lemon rind
 ¼ teaspoon almond extract
 ¼ cup powdered sugar, divided
  1 (10-ounce) bottle seedless raspberry jam

Apricot Coulis:
  1 (15-ounce) can apricot halves in light syrup, undrained
  1 tablespoon honey
  1 tablespoon amaretto (almond-flavored liqueur) or ¼ teaspoon almond extract
  2 cups fresh raspberries

1. Preheat oven to 400°.
2. To prepare cake, coat a 15 x 10–inch jelly-roll pan with cooking spray, and line with wax paper. Coat paper with cooking spray; set aside.

Tres Leches
Cake

3. Lightly spoon flour into a dry measuring cup, and level with a knife. Combine flour, baking powder, and salt, stirring with a whisk. Beat eggs in a large bowl with a mixer at high speed until pale and fluffy (about 4 minutes). Gradually add granulated sugar, vanilla, rind, and almond extract, beating until thick (about 4 minutes). Sift half of flour mixture over egg mixture; fold in. Repeat procedure with remaining flour mixture. Spoon batter into prepared pan; spread evenly.

4. Bake at 400° for 8 to 10 minutes or until cake springs back when touched lightly in center. Loosen cake from sides of pan; turn out onto a dish towel dusted with 2 tablespoons powdered sugar. Carefully peel off wax paper; cool 1 minute. Starting at narrow end, roll up cake and towel together. Place, seam side down, on a wire rack; cool completely (about 1 hour). Unroll carefully; remove towel. Spread jam over cake, leaving a ½-inch border. Reroll cake, and place, seam side down, on a platter. Sprinkle with 2 tablespoons powdered sugar. Cut into 8 slices.

5. To prepare coulis, drain apricots in a colander over a bowl, reserving 1 tablespoon juice. Place apricots, 1 tablespoon reserved juice, honey, and amaretto in a blender; process until smooth. Serve with cake. Garnish with berries. Yield: 8 servings (serving size: 1 cake slice, about 2 tablespoons coulis, and ¼ cup raspberries).

CALORIES 320 (8% from fat); FAT 2.8g (sat 0.8g, mono 1g, poly 0.5g); PROTEIN 4.6g; CARB 68.9g; FIBER 3.2g; CHOL 106mg; IRON 1.4mg; SODIUM 146mg; CALC 62mg

how to make a jelly-roll cake

1. First, spray the pan with cooking spray, line with a sheet of wax paper, then coat the wax paper with cooking spray. Spraying both the pan and wax paper will prevent the cake from sticking. Next, pour the batter, and bake.

2. While the cake is baking, lay a dry kitchen towel slightly larger than the pan on a flat surface, and dust the towel with a thin layer of powdered sugar. The sugar prevents the cake from sticking.

3. Remove the cake from the oven, and turn the pan over onto the towel, releasing the cake and wax paper. Slowly peel the wax paper from the cake. It's OK if a thin layer of cake remains on the paper.

4. Roll the towel and the cake together, pressing gently. Be sure to move slowly and carefully throughout the entire rolling process. The towel will end up coiled inside the cake.

5. Cool the cake on a wire rack, seam side down. After 1 hour, unroll and remove the towel. The cake will be slightly wavy. Carefully spread the filling as directed, and reroll the cake.

Cheesecakes
All cheesecakes start with cheese—usually cream cheese—and most have some type of crumb crust. Beyond those basic elements, the variations are many, all rich and luxurious. Here are some of our favorites: chocolate, vanilla with cherries, Black Forest, lemon-swirled, and orange-glazed.

German Chocolate Cheesecake

We took the components of a German chocolate layer cake—cocoa, coconut, pecans—and put them in a rich, creamy cheesecake.

**Prep: 25 minutes • Cook: 1 hour, 13 minutes
Other: 8 hours**

Crust:
- ⅔ cup all-purpose flour
- 2 tablespoons sugar
- 2 tablespoons chilled butter, cut into small pieces
- 1 tablespoon ice water

Cooking spray

Filling:
- ½ cup Dutch process cocoa
- ½ cup fat-free hot fudge topping
- ¼ cup 2% reduced-fat milk
- 2 (8-ounce) blocks fat-free cream cheese, softened
- 1½ cups (12 ounces) ⅓-less-fat cream cheese, softened
- 1½ cups sugar
- 3 tablespoons all-purpose flour
- 2 teaspoons vanilla extract
- ¼ teaspoon coconut extract
- 2 large eggs
- 2 large egg whites

Topping:
- ⅔ cup fat-free caramel sundae topping
- ⅓ cup chopped pecans, toasted
- ⅓ cup flaked sweetened coconut, toasted

1. Preheat oven to 400°.

2. To prepare crust, lightly spoon ⅔ cup flour into dry measuring cups; level with a knife. Place ⅔ cup flour and 2 tablespoons sugar in a food processor; pulse until combined. Add butter; pulse 3 times or until mixture resembles coarse meal. With processor on, pour ice water through chute, processing just until blended (do not form a ball). Press into bottom of a 9-inch springform pan coated with cooking spray. Bake at 400° for 8 minutes or until lightly browned. Cool on a wire rack. Reduce oven temperature to 325°.

3. To prepare filling, combine cocoa, fudge topping, and milk in a small bowl. Beat cheeses with a mixer at high speed until smooth. Add 1½ cups sugar, 3 tablespoons flour, and extracts. Add eggs and egg whites, 1 at a time, beating until blended. Add cocoa mixture; beat well.

4. Pour cheese mixture into prepared crust. Bake at 325° for 1 hour or until almost set. Cheesecake is done when center barely moves when pan is touched. Remove cheesecake from oven; run a knife around outside edge. Cool to room temperature. Cover cheesecake, and chill at least 8 hours. Top each serving with caramel sundae topping, chopped pecans, and toasted coconut. Yield: 16 servings (serving size: 1 wedge, about 2 teaspoons caramel topping, 1 teaspoon pecans, and 1 teaspoon coconut).

CALORIES 314 (29% from fat); FAT 10g (sat 5.3g, mono 3.2g, poly 0.8g); PROTEIN 9.7g; CARB 46.1g; FIBER 1.1g; CHOL 53mg; IRON 1.2mg; SODIUM 352mg; CALC 128mg

Chocolate Cheesecake
(pictured on cover)

The thick chocolate cookie crust is one of
the best things about this rich chocolate
cheesecake.

Prep: 20 minutes • Cook: 1 hour, 5 minutes
Other: 8 hours

Crust:
- 1 cup chocolate sandwich cookie
  crumbs (such as Oreo) (about 10
  cookies)
- 2 tablespoons sugar
- 1 tablespoon butter, melted
- Cooking spray

Filling:
- ¼ cup 1% low-fat milk
- 3 ounces semisweet chocolate
- ½ cup Dutch process cocoa
- 4 (8-ounce) blocks fat-free cream
  cheese, softened
- 1 (8-ounce) block ⅓-less-fat cream
  cheese, softened
- 1½ cups sugar
- 2 teaspoons vanilla extract
- 3 tablespoons all-purpose flour
- 4 large eggs

Toppings:
- 1 cup frozen fat-free whipped topping
  (optional)
- 2 tablespoons sliced almonds, toasted
  (optional)
- 1 cup fat-free chocolate sundae syrup
  (optional)

1. Preheat oven to 325°.
2. To prepare crust, combine first 3 ingredients in a bowl; toss with a fork until moist.
Press mixture into bottom of a 9-inch
springform pan coated with cooking spray.
3. To prepare filling, combine milk and
chocolate in a small bowl. Microwave at
HIGH 1 minute. Stir until smooth. Whisk

in cocoa. Combine cheeses in a large bowl,
stirring well. Beat cheeses with a mixer at
high speed until smooth. Add 1½ cups
sugar and vanilla; beat well. Add chocolate
mixture; beat well. Add flour; beat well.
Add eggs, 1 at a time, beating until blended.
4. Pour mixture into prepared crust; bake
at 325° for 1 hour or until almost set.
Remove from oven; run a knife around
outside edge. Cool to room temperature.
Cover and chill at least 8 hours. Garnish
with whipped topping, almonds, and
chocolate syrup, if desired. Yield: 16 servings (serving size: 1 wedge).

CALORIES 241 (30% from fat); FAT 8g (sat 3.9g, mono 2.4g,
poly 1.1g); PROTEIN 10.3g; CARB 30.8g; FIBER 0.3g; CHOL 51mg;
IRON 1.2mg; SODIUM 386mg; CALC 147mg

Test Kitchen Tip: When you're stirring the cream cheeses, make sure you stir
well enough to get rid of the large clumps,
then beat with a mixer until smooth. Fat-free cream cheese tends to form little
clumps, and if these aren't smoothed out,
you'll end up with white specks in the
cheesecake.

Topping Variations

Caramel-Chocolate Cheesecake: Top
each wedge with 1 tablespoon fat-free
whipped topping and 1 tablespoon fat-free
caramel sundae topping.

Raspberry-Chocolate Cheesecake: Top
each wedge with 1 tablespoon Raspberry
Sauce (page 182) and garnish with fresh
raspberries.

Triple-Chocolate Cheesecake: Top each
wedge with 1 tablespoon Warm Chocolate
Sauce (page 457) and sprinkle with grated
semisweet chocolate.

cheesecake tips Making luscious,
light cheesecakes is easier than you may
think. Here are some tips from our Test
Kitchens.

Doneness: Your cheesecake is done if
the center will jiggle slightly and is about
3 inches in diameter. Place the pan on
a wire rack, and run a knife around the
outside edge; cool completely to room
temperature.

Cracking: Don't worry if your cheesecake
cracks. Some cracking is normal and can
even make it look prettier. The most
common cause of cracking is a drastic
change in temperature when cooking or
cooling. Generally, the slower the
cheesecake is cooked, the less chance
of cracking. To bake slowly and evenly,
use an oven thermometer to see if your
oven is staying the correct temperature.
You can also prevent cracking if you run
a knife or small metal spatula around
the edge of the cheesecake immediately
after removing it from the oven. This
allows the loosened sides to contract.

Springform pans: To make a cheesecake,
you'll need a springform pan: a round
metal pan with high, straight sides encircled by a metal belt, or spring, that
clamps tight, molding the shape of the
cake. When the cheesecake is done,
unclamp the spring and remove the sides.
The pan bottom holds the finished
cheesecake and can be used for serving.
There are two basic types of springform
pans: shiny aluminum and those with a
dark, almost black surface. If you use a
dark pan, decrease the baking time by 10
minutes. Springform pans come in 8-, 9-,
and 10-inch sizes.

Vanilla Cheesecake with Cherry Topping

You can make the cheesecake topping up to three days ahead and store separately in the refrigerator. Or make the cheesecake up to two months ahead and freeze. Before freezing, chill the cooled cheesecake in the pan for two hours; then wrap the pan in heavy-duty plastic wrap. Thaw in the refrigerator.

Prep: 30 minutes • Cook: 1 hour, 33 minutes
Other: 8 hours

Crust:
- ¾ cup graham cracker crumbs (about 4½ full cracker sheets)
- ¼ cup sugar
- 2 tablespoons butter, melted
- 2 teaspoons water
- Cooking spray

Filling:
- 3 (8-ounce) blocks fat-free cream cheese, softened
- 2 (8-ounce) blocks ⅓-less-fat cream cheese, softened
- 1 cup sugar
- 3 tablespoons all-purpose flour
- ¼ teaspoon salt
- 1 (8-ounce) carton fat-free sour cream
- 4 large eggs
- 2 teaspoons vanilla extract
- 1 vanilla bean, split lengthwise

Topping:
- ⅔ cup port or other sweet red wine
- ½ cup sugar
- 2 (10-ounce) bags frozen pitted dark sweet cherries
- 2 tablespoons fresh lemon juice
- 4 teaspoons cornstarch
- 4 teaspoons water

1. Preheat oven to 400°.
2. To prepare crust, combine first 3 ingredients, tossing with a fork. Add 2 teaspoons water; toss with a fork until moist and crumbly. Gently press mixture into bottom and 1½ inches up sides of a 9-inch springform pan coated with cooking spray. Bake at 400° for 5 minutes; cool on a wire rack.
3. Reduce oven temperature to 325°.
4. To prepare filling, beat cheeses with a mixer at high speed until smooth. Combine 1 cup sugar, flour, and salt, stirring with a whisk. Add to cheese mixture; beat well. Add sour cream; beat well. Add eggs, 1 at a time, beating well after each addition. Stir in vanilla extract. Scrape seeds from vanilla bean; stir seeds into cheese mixture, reserving bean halves.
5. Pour cheese mixture into prepared crust; bake at 325° for 1 hour and 15 minutes or until cheesecake center barely moves when pan is touched. Remove cheesecake from oven, and run a knife around outside edge. Cool to room temperature. Cover and chill at least 8 hours.
6. To prepare topping, combine port, ½ cup sugar, cherries, and reserved vanilla bean halves in a large saucepan; bring to a boil. Cook 5 minutes or until cherries are thawed and mixture is syrupy. Remove vanilla bean halves; discard.
7. Combine juice, cornstarch, and 4 teaspoons water, stirring with a whisk until well blended. Stir cornstarch mixture into cherry mixture; bring to a boil. Reduce heat; simmer 3 minutes or until mixture is slightly thickened and shiny. Remove from heat; cool to room temperature. Cover and chill. Serve over cheesecake. Yield: 16 servings (serving size: 1 wedge cheesecake and about 2 tablespoons topping).

CALORIES 324 (30% from fat); FAT 10.7g (sat 6.1g, mono 3.2g, poly 0.7g); PROTEIN 12.2g; CARB 42.8g; FIBER 1g; CHOL 83mg; IRON 0.8mg; SODIUM 458mg; CALC 134mg

Black Forest Cherry Cheesecake

A topping including dark, sweet cherries offsets the filling and crust for a dramatic look and the best cherry flavor.

Prep: 30 minutes • Cook: 1 hour, 4 minutes
Other: 8 hours, 40 minutes

Topping:
- 2 cups pitted dark sweet cherries
- ¼ cup sugar
- 1 tablespoon fresh lemon juice
- 2 teaspoons cornstarch

Crust:
- 1⅓ cups chocolate graham cracker crumbs (about 8 full cracker sheets)
- ¼ cup sugar
- 1 tablespoon butter, melted
- 1 large egg white
- Cooking spray

Filling:
- 1 cup fat-free sour cream
- ½ cup fat-free sweetened condensed milk
- 1 (8-ounce) block ⅓-less-fat cream cheese, softened
- 1 (8-ounce) block fat-free cream cheese, softened
- 1¼ cups sugar
- 3 tablespoons unsweetened cocoa
- 2 teaspoons vanilla extract
- 2 large eggs
- ½ cup semisweet chocolate minichips
- 36 dark sweet cherries, pitted and halved

1. To prepare topping, place 2 cups cherries in a blender or food processor; process until smooth. Combine pureed cherries, ¼ cup sugar, lemon juice, and cornstarch in a small saucepan. Bring to a boil; cook 1 minute, stirring constantly.

Pour cherry topping into a bowl; cover and chill.

2. Preheat oven to 350°.

3. To prepare crust, combine crumbs, ¼ cup sugar, butter, and egg white in a bowl; toss with a fork until well blended. Press crumb mixture into bottom of a 10-inch springform pan coated with cooking spray. Bake at 350° for 10 minutes; cool on a wire rack. Reduce oven temperature to 300°.

4. To prepare filling, combine sour cream, milk, and cheeses in a large bowl. Beat with a mixer at medium speed until well blended. Add 1¼ cups sugar, cocoa, vanilla, and eggs; beat well. Stir in minichips. Pour cheese mixture into prepared crust. Bake at 300° for 50 minutes or until almost set (center will not be firm, but will set up as it chills). Turn oven off; cool cheesecake in closed oven 40 minutes.

5. Remove cheesecake from oven; cool on a wire rack. Spread cherry topping over cheesecake. Top with cherry halves. Cover and chill 8 hours. Yield: 16 servings (serving size: 1 wedge).

CALORIES 292 (25% from fat); FAT 8.1g (sat 4.3g, mono 2.5g, poly 0.7g); PROTEIN 7.6g; CARB 47.5g; FIBER 1.1g; CHOL 43mg; IRON 0.8mg; SODIUM 233mg; CALC 106mg

Test Kitchen Tip: If you don't want to get out your food processor to make the graham cracker crumbs, place crackers in a large zip-top plastic bag, and roll with a heavy rolling pin or bottle to make crumbs.

Lemon-Swirled Cheesecake

Try adding 1 tablespoon finely chopped fresh rosemary to the crust. It lends a subtle savory note to complement the sweetness of the crust and the filling.

Prep: 27 minutes • Cook: 1 hour, 33 minutes
Other: 8 hours

Crust:
  ⅔ cup all-purpose flour
  2 tablespoons sugar
  2 tablespoons chilled butter, cut into small pieces
  1 tablespoon ice water
     Cooking spray
Filling:
  3 (8-ounce) blocks fat-free cream cheese, softened
  2 (8-ounce) blocks ⅓-less-fat cream cheese, softened
1¾ cups sugar
  3 tablespoons all-purpose flour
2½ teaspoons grated lemon rind
  2 teaspoons vanilla extract
  ¼ teaspoon salt
  5 large eggs
  1 cup Lemon Curd (page 460)

1. Preheat oven to 400°.

2. To prepare crust, lightly spoon ⅔ cup flour into dry measuring cups; level with a knife. Place ⅔ cup flour and 2 tablespoons sugar in a food processor; pulse 2 times or until combined. Add chilled butter; pulse 6 times or until mixture resembles coarse meal. With processor on, slowly pour ice water through food chute, processing just until blended (do not allow dough to form a ball). Firmly press mixture into bottom of a 9-inch springform pan coated with cooking spray. Bake at 400° for 10 minutes; cool on a wire rack.

3. Reduce oven temperature to 325°.

4. To prepare filling, beat cheeses with a mixer at high speed until smooth. Add 1¾ cups sugar and next 4 ingredients; beat well. Add eggs, 1 at a time, beating well after each addition.

5. Pour cheese mixture into prepared crust. Spoon mounds of Lemon Curd over filling, and swirl together using tip of a knife. Bake at 325° for 1 hour and 15 minutes or until cheesecake is almost set. Remove cheesecake from oven, and cool to room temperature. Cover and chill at least 8 hours. Yield: 16 servings (serving size: 1 wedge).

CALORIES 310 (33% from fat); FAT 11.4g (sat 6.4g, mono 3.5g, poly 0.6g); PROTEIN 12.2g; CARB 39g; FIBER 0.2g; CHOL 126mg; IRON 0.7mg; SODIUM 458mg; CALC 155mg

Lemon-Swirled Cheesecake

Orange-Glazed Cheesecake with Gingersnap Crust

The gingersnap crust provides a hint of spice for this sweet citrus cheesecake.

**Prep: 25 minutes • Cook: 1 hour, 15 minutes
Other: 8 hours**

Crust:
- 1 cup gingersnap crumbs (about 20 cookies, finely crushed)
- 2 tablespoons sugar
- 1 tablespoon butter, melted
- Cooking spray

Filling:
- 2 (8-ounce) blocks fat-free cream cheese, softened
- 2 (8-ounce) blocks ⅓-less-fat cream cheese, softened
- 1 (8-ounce) carton reduced-fat sour cream
- ¼ cup all-purpose flour
- 1½ cups sugar
- ¼ cup thawed orange juice concentrate, undiluted
- 1 tablespoon Grand Marnier (orange-flavored liqueur) or orange juice
- 2 teaspoons vanilla extract
- 3 large eggs
- 2 large egg whites

Topping:
- ½ cup orange marmalade
- 1 tablespoon Grand Marnier (orange-flavored liqueur) or orange juice
- 1 orange, peeled and sliced

1. Preheat oven to 325°.

2. To prepare crust, combine first 3 ingredients; toss with a fork until moist. Press into bottom of a 9-inch springform pan coated with cooking spray. Bake at 325° for 5 minutes.

3. To prepare filling, beat cheeses and sour cream in a large bowl with a mixer at high speed until smooth. Lightly spoon flour into a dry measuring cup; level with a knife. Add flour, 1½ cups sugar, and next 3 ingredients to cheese mixture, and beat well. Add eggs and egg whites, 1 at a time, beating well after each addition.

4. Pour cheese mixture into prepared crust; bake at 325° for 1 hour and 10 minutes or until almost set. Cheesecake is done when center barely moves when pan is touched. Remove cheesecake from oven, and run a knife around outside edge. Cool to room temperature. Remove sides.

5. To prepare topping, combine marmalade and 1 tablespoon liqueur. Spread half of mixture over top of cheesecake. Cut orange slices in half, and arrange over cheesecake. Spread with remaining marmalade mixture. Cover and chill at least 8 hours. Yield: 16 servings (serving size: 1 wedge).

CALORIES 310 (33% from fat); FAT 11.3g (sat 6.5g, mono 3.1g, poly 0.5g); PROTEIN 10.1g; CARB 42.4g; FIBER 0.6g; CHOL 73mg; IRON 1mg; SODIUM 365mg; CALC 119mg

cookies

Oatmeal-Walnut
Cookies, page 142

Drop Cookies
Whether you're making oatmeal, chocolate chip, or meringue cookies, drop the same amount of dough for each onto the baking sheet for even cooking.

Oatmeal-Walnut Cookies
(pictured on page 141)

Sweet golden raisins and crunchy walnuts give these cookies extra sweetness and a pleasing crunch.

**Prep: 14 minutes • Cook: 12 minutes
Other: 2 minutes**

½ cup granulated sugar
⅓ cup packed dark brown sugar
¼ cup butter, softened
1 teaspoon vanilla extract
1 large egg
¾ cup all-purpose flour
1 cup regular oats
¼ teaspoon salt
⅔ cup golden raisins
¼ cup chopped toasted walnuts
Cooking spray

1. Preheat oven to 350°.
2. Place first 5 ingredients in a large bowl. Beat with a mixer at medium speed until well blended. Lightly spoon flour into dry measuring cups; level with a knife. Add flour, oats, and salt to egg mixture; beat well. Stir in raisins and walnuts.
3. Drop by level tablespoons 1½ inches apart onto a large baking sheet coated with cooking spray. Bake at 350° for 12 minutes or until lightly browned. Remove from oven, and let stand 2 minutes. Remove cookies from pan; cool on a wire rack. Yield: 2 dozen (serving size: 1 cookie).

CALORIES 109 (28% from fat); FAT 3.4g (sat 1.4g, mono 0.9g, poly 0.9g); PROTEIN 2.1g; CARB 18.3g; FIBER 1.1g; CHOL 14mg; IRON 0.7mg; SODIUM 24mg; CALC 12mg

Oatmeal Cookies with A-Peel

Take the flavor of a basic oatmeal cookie up a notch by adding sweetened dried cranberries soaked in orange juice instead of raisins and stirring in orange rind.

Prep: 20 minutes • Cook: 8 minutes per batch • Other: 10 minutes

1 cup sweetened dried cranberries (such as Craisins) or raisins
½ cup orange juice
½ cup granulated sugar
½ cup packed brown sugar
¼ cup butter, softened
2 tablespoons light-colored corn syrup
1 large egg
1½ cups all-purpose flour
1 teaspoon baking soda
½ teaspoon baking powder
½ teaspoon salt
3 cups regular oats
⅓ cup coarsely chopped walnuts
1 tablespoon grated orange rind
Cooking spray

1. Preheat oven to 375°.
2. Combine cranberries and orange juice in a bowl; cover and let stand 10 minutes.
3. Beat sugars and butter with a mixer at medium speed until light and fluffy. Add corn syrup and egg; beat well. Stir in cranberry mixture.
4. Lightly spoon flour into dry measuring cups, and level with a knife. Combine flour, baking soda, baking powder, and salt in a bowl, stirring well with a whisk.

Add oats, walnuts, and orange rind; stir well. Add to sugar mixture; stir until well blended.
5. Drop by level tablespoons 2 inches apart onto baking sheets coated with cooking spray. Bake at 375° for 8 minutes or until almost set. Remove from pans; cool on a wire rack. Yield: 4 dozen (serving size: 1 cookie).

CALORIES 78 (22% from fat); FAT 1.9g (sat 0.7g, mono 0.5g, poly 0.5g); PROTEIN 1.6g; CARB 13.8g; FIBER 0.8g; CHOL 7mg; IRON 0.5mg; SODIUM 69mg; CALC 10mg

---

holiday cookie swap
serves 10 to 12

Cream Cheese Brownies (page 160)

Cranberry-Chocolate Chip Biscotti (page 164)

Oatmeal-Walnut Cookies (left)

Coconut Meringues (page 147)

Christmas Sugar Wafers with Vanilla Icing (page 150)

Ginger Shortbread (page 151)

Russian Tea (page 62)

New Mexican Hot Chocolate (page 60)

Lemon-Honey Drop Cookies

You can make these citrusy cookies with orange rind and orange juice instead of lemon.

Prep: 15 minutes • Cook: 12 minutes per batch

- ½ cup granulated sugar
- 7 tablespoons butter, softened
- 2 teaspoons grated lemon rind
- ⅓ cup honey
- ½ teaspoon lemon extract
- 1 large egg
- 1¾ cups all-purpose flour
- 1 teaspoon baking powder
- ½ teaspoon salt
- ¼ cup plain fat-free yogurt
- Cooking spray
- 1 cup powdered sugar
- 2 teaspoons grated lemon rind
- 2 tablespoons fresh lemon juice

1. Preheat oven to 350°.

2. Beat first 3 ingredients with a mixer at medium speed until light and fluffy. Add honey, extract, and egg; beat until well blended. Lightly spoon flour into dry measuring cups; level with a knife. Combine flour, baking powder, and salt, stirring well with a whisk. Add flour mixture to sugar mixture alternately with yogurt, beginning and ending with flour mixture. Drop by level tablespoons 2 inches apart onto baking sheets coated with cooking spray. Bake at 350° for 12 minutes or until lightly browned.

3. Combine powdered sugar and juice in a small bowl; stir with a whisk. Brush powdered sugar mixture evenly over warm cookies. Sprinkle evenly with 2 teaspoons rind. Remove cookies from pans; cool on wire racks. Yield: 32 cookies (serving size: 1 cookie).

CALORIES 89 (28% from fat); FAT 2.8g (sat 1.6g, mono 0.8g, poly 0.2g); PROTEIN 1.1g; CARB 15.3g; FIBER 0.2g; CHOL 14mg; IRON 0.4mg; SODIUM 81mg; CALC 15mg

cookie class Here are some tips from our Test Kitchens on how to make great cookies every time.

Pans For even baking, use a heavy baking or cookie sheet (which has a lip on one or both ends). A larger baking sheet (17 x 14 inches) allows you to bake more cookies at a time than a standard 15 x 12–inch pan. The air-cushioned pans work fine, but they're not necessarily better than a good-quality heavy baking sheet. And you can't put the air-cushioned pans in the dishwasher.

Ingredients Don't replace butter with diet margarine or tub-style spread. These have too much water and too little fat to produce the right results. Measure flour correctly; too much flour will make the cookies tough. (See page 116 for how to measure flour.)

Dropping Dough When the recipe says to "drop by level tablespoons," use a measuring spoon, not a tableware spoon.

Baking Bake cookies in an oven that has been preheated for 15 minutes, and place the rack in the second position from the bottom of the oven. Cookies bake more evenly when they're about the same size. And don't forget that they need plenty of space between them to allow for spreading. Check for doneness at the earliest suggested time. Opening and closing the oven door too often can change the baking time. Be sure there is room left for air to circulate on all sides after the baking sheet is placed on the rack.

Cocoa Fudge Cookies

You can mix these incredibly easy cookies right in the saucepan. When freshly baked, these thin cookies have crisp edges and chewy centers.

Prep: 13 minutes • Cook: 8 to 10 minutes per batch • Other: 2 minutes

1	cup all-purpose flour
¼	teaspoon baking soda
⅛	teaspoon salt
5	tablespoons butter
7	tablespoons unsweetened cocoa
⅔	cup granulated sugar
⅓	cup packed brown sugar
⅓	cup plain low-fat yogurt
1	teaspoon vanilla extract

Cooking spray

1. Preheat oven to 350°.

2. Lightly spoon flour into a dry measuring cup; level with a knife. Combine flour, soda, and salt; set aside. Melt butter in a saucepan over medium heat. Remove from heat; stir in cocoa and sugars. Stir in yogurt and vanilla. Add flour mixture, stirring until moist. Drop by level tablespoons 2 inches apart onto baking sheets coated with cooking spray.

3. Bake at 350° for 8 to 10 minutes or until almost set. Cool on pans 2 to 3 minutes or until firm. Remove cookies from pans; cool on wire racks. Yield: 2 dozen (serving size: 1 cookie).

CALORIES 78 (31% from fat); FAT 2.7g (sat 1.6g, mono 0.8g, poly 0.1g); PROTEIN 1g; CARB 13.4g; FIBER 0.5g; CHOL 7mg; IRON 0.5mg; SODIUM 54mg; CALC 12mg

Black-and-White Cake Cookies

Cocoa Fudge Cookies

Double-Chocolate Cookies

Double-Chocolate Cookies
(pictured at left)

Freezing the dough before baking helps the cookies hold their shape in the oven.

Prep: 15 minutes • Cook: 10 minutes per batch • Other: 2 minutes

1¼ cups all-purpose flour
½ teaspoon baking powder
¼ teaspoon salt
5 tablespoons butter, softened
½ cup granulated sugar
½ cup packed brown sugar
1½ teaspoons vanilla extract
1 large egg white
⅓ cup dried tart cherries
¼ cup semisweet chocolate chunks
2½ tablespoons premium white chocolate chips
   Cooking spray

1. Preheat oven to 350°.
2. Lightly spoon flour into dry measuring cups; level with a knife. Combine flour, baking powder, and salt, stirring well with a whisk.
3. Combine butter and sugars in a large bowl; beat with a mixer at medium speed until well blended. Add vanilla and egg white; beat 1 minute. Stir in flour mixture, cherries, chocolate chunks, and chocolate chips.
4. Drop by level tablespoons 2 inches apart onto baking sheets coated with cooking spray. Place pans in freezer 5 minutes. Bake at 350° for 10 minutes or until lightly browned. Cool on pans 2 minutes. Remove from pans; cool completely on wire racks. Yield: 2 dozen (serving size: 1 cookie).

CALORIES 98 (30% from fat); FAT 3.3g (sat 2g, mono 1g, poly 0.1g); PROTEIN 1g; CARB 16.6g; FIBER 0.4g; CHOL 7mg; IRON 0.5mg; SODIUM 63mg; CALC 12mg

Black-and-White Cake Cookies
(pictured at left)

These cakelike cookies are covered half in chocolate frosting and half in white frosting.

Prep: 30 minutes • Cook: 10 minutes per batch • Other: 37 minutes

Cookies:
1½ cups all-purpose flour
1½ teaspoons baking powder
½ teaspoon salt
⅔ cup applesauce
1 cup granulated sugar
¼ cup butter, softened
1½ teaspoons vanilla extract
2 large egg whites
Frosting:
1½ cups powdered sugar, divided
3 tablespoons 2% reduced-fat milk, divided
¼ teaspoon almond extract
2 tablespoons unsweetened cocoa

1. Preheat oven to 375°.
2. To prepare cookies, lightly spoon flour into dry measuring cups; level with a knife. Combine flour, baking powder, and salt, stirring with a whisk.
3. Spoon applesauce into a fine sieve over a bowl; let stand 15 minutes. Discard liquid.
4. Combine drained applesauce, granulated sugar, and butter in a large bowl; beat with a mixer at medium speed 2 minutes or until well blended. Beat in vanilla and egg whites. Add flour mixture; beat at low speed until blended.
5. Drop dough by level tablespoons 2 inches apart onto parchment-lined baking sheets. Bake at 375° for 10 minutes or until set (not browned). Cool on pans 2 minutes or until firm. Remove from pans; cool completely on wire racks.

6. To prepare frosting, combine ¾ cup powdered sugar, 1 tablespoon milk, and almond extract in a bowl, stirring well with a whisk until smooth. Working with one cookie at a time, hold cookie over bowl, and spread about 1 teaspoon white frosting over half of cookie (scrape excess frosting from edges). Let stand 10 minutes or until frosting is set.
7. Combine ¾ cup powdered sugar and cocoa in a bowl. Gradually add 2 tablespoons milk, stirring with a whisk until smooth. Working with one cookie at a time, hold cookie over bowl, and spread about 1 teaspoon chocolate frosting over other half of cookie (scrape excess frosting from edges). Let stand 10 minutes or until frosting is set. Yield: 2 dozen (serving size: 1 cookie).

CALORIES 106 (17% from fat); FAT 2g (sat 1.2g, mono 0.6g, poly 0.1g); PROTEIN 1.3g; CARB 21.4g; FIBER 0.4g; CHOL 5mg; IRON 0.4mg; SODIUM 100mg; CALC 14mg

baking on parchment

Several of our cookie recipes call for baking on parchment-lined baking sheets. Using parchment paper can help decrease the time between batches because you can be dropping the dough onto a second sheet of parchment while the first batch is in the oven. When the first batch is done, slide the parchment (with the baked cookies) off the baking sheet and slide on the next sheet. Baking with parchment paper helps deliver even results, plus your pan stays clean. Don't use wax paper in place of parchment because the wax can't take the heat of the oven and will smoke. Trim parchment paper to fit your baking sheet; don't let it hang over the edges or touch the oven rack or oven wall.

All-Time Favorite
Chocolate Chip Cookies

This is one of the best chocolate-chip cookies you'll ever make—and it doesn't scrimp on chocolate. Applesauce is the secret to its moist texture.

Prep: 20 minutes • Cook: 10 minutes per batch • Other: 17 minutes

1¼   cups all-purpose flour
1½   teaspoons baking powder
¾   teaspoon salt
½   cup applesauce
1   cup packed brown sugar
¼   cup butter, softened
1   tablespoon vanilla extract
1   large egg
1   cup semisweet chocolate chips
Cooking spray

1. Preheat oven to 375°.

2. Lightly spoon flour into dry measuring cups; level with a knife. Combine flour, baking powder, and salt in a small bowl; stir well with a whisk.

3. Spoon applesauce into a fine sieve over a bowl; let stand 15 minutes. Discard liquid. Scrape drained applesauce into a large bowl. Add sugar and butter; beat with a mixer at medium speed until light and fluffy (about 2 minutes). Beat in vanilla and egg. Add flour mixture; beat at low speed until well blended. Fold in chips.

4. Drop by level tablespoons 2 inches apart onto baking sheets coated with cooking spray. Bake at 375° for 10 minutes or until almost set. Cool on pans 2 to 3 minutes or until firm. Remove cookies from pans; cool on wire racks. Yield: 3 dozen (serving size: 1 cookie).

CALORIES 78 (33% from fat); FAT 2.9g (sat 1.7g, mono 0.9g, poly 0.2g); PROTEIN 0.8g; CARB 12.8g; FIBER 0.2g; CHOL 10mg; IRON 0.5mg; SODIUM 87mg; CALC 20mg

how to drain applesauce

We don't normally replace all the fat in baked goods with applesauce or fruit purees because, in our opinion, products made with applesauce have an inferior texture and flavor. However, there are a few recipes (such as the cookies at left and Black-and-White Cake Cookies, page 145) in which using applesauce to replace part of the fat works quite well. The trick is to drain the applesauce, either by sieve or paper towel.

Sieve Method

1. Place a fine sieve into a bowl large enough so that the sieve doesn't touch the bottom of the bowl.
2. Spoon applesauce into sieve. Let stand 15 minutes.
3. Discard liquid; scrape applesauce into a bowl using a rubber spatula.

Paper-Towel Method

1. Spoon applesauce onto several layers of heavy-duty paper towels; spread to ½-inch thickness.
2. Cover with additional paper towels; let stand 5 minutes.
3. Scrape applesauce into a bowl using a rubber spatula.

Coconut Meringues
(pictured on page 148)

Look for unsweetened, shredded coconut in the produce section of your grocery store.

Prep: 17 minutes • Cook: 1 hour, 30 minutes
Other: 2 hours

  4 large egg whites
  ¼ teaspoon cream of tartar
  ½ cup granulated sugar
  ¾ cup powdered sugar
  1 cup unsweetened shredded coconut,
     divided

1. Preheat oven to 225°.
2. Cover 2 large baking sheets with parchment paper; secure paper with masking tape.
3. Place egg whites and cream of tartar in a large bowl; beat with a mixer at medium speed until soft peaks form. Increase speed to high, and gradually add granulated sugar and then powdered sugar, 1 tablespoon at a time, beating until stiff peaks form. Gently fold in ¾ cup coconut.
4. Drop by tablespoonfuls into 36 mounds onto prepared baking sheets. Sprinkle ¼ cup coconut evenly over meringues. Bake at 225° for 1½ hours. Turn oven off, and cool in closed oven 2 hours or until crisp. Carefully remove from paper. Store in an airtight container. Yield: 3 dozen (serving size: 1 cookie).

CALORIES 30 (18% from fat); FAT 0.6g (sat 0.6g, mono 0g, poly 0g); PROTEIN 0.4g; CARB 6g; FIBER 0.1g; CHOL 0mg; IRON 0mg; SODIUM 11mg; CALC 1mg

Test Kitchen Tip: When baked slowly for a long time, stiffly beaten egg whites turn crisp, as they do in these cookies. Bake them 10 minutes less for a cookie that's slightly chewy on the inside.

Ginger Meringue Cookies

Leaving the cookies in the turned-off oven at least two hours makes them very dry and crisp. If you prefer a chewier cookie, you can remove them from the oven after they're done baking. You can also freeze them in a heavy-duty zip-top plastic bag up to six weeks.

Prep: 15 minutes • Cook: 40 minutes
Other: 2 hours

  2 large egg whites
  ⅛ teaspoon cream of tartar
  ⅓ cup sugar
  1 tablespoon finely chopped
     crystallized ginger
  ¼ teaspoon almond extract

1. Preheat oven to 300°.
2. Cover a baking sheet with parchment paper, and secure paper with masking tape.
3. Place egg whites and cream of tartar in a large bowl; beat with a mixer until soft peaks form. Fold in crystallized ginger and almond extract.
4. Drop batter by 2 tablespoonfuls onto prepared baking sheet. Bake at 300° for 40 minutes or until dry and crisp. Turn oven off, and cool in closed oven at least 2 hours or until crisp. Carefully remove from parchment paper. Store in an airtight container. Yield: 1 dozen (serving size: 1 cookie).

CALORIES 27 (0% from fat); FAT 0g (sat 0g, mono 0g, poly 0g); PROTEIN 0.6g; CARB 6.2g; FIBER 0g; CHOL 0mg; IRON 0.2mg; SODIUM 9mg; CALC 2mg

how to separate eggs

Start with eggs straight from the refrigerator since cool eggs are easier to separate without breaking the yolk than room temperature eggs. Fat, which is found in yolks, is the enemy of light, airy, stiffly beaten whites.

Use the 4-bowl method for the most foolproof way to separate eggs:
- Crack the egg on a flat surface, and break it in half. Hold your hand over bowl 1 (practice bowl).
- Pour the egg into your hand; let the white run through your fingers. Place the egg yolk in bowl 2 (egg yolk bowl).
- If it was a clean break, transfer the white to bowl 3 (egg white bowl). If a small amount of yolk got into the white, use a cotton-tipped swab to absorb it before placing the white in bowl 3.
- If the yolk is broken and can't be cleaned up, transfer the broken yolk and white to bowl 4 (mistake bowl). Cover and refrigerate up to two days, and use for another purpose that calls for whole eggs.
- Before you separate another egg over bowl 1, thoroughly clean the bowl; wipe with a paper towel moistened with vinegar to remove any trace of fat.

Coconut Meringues,
page 147

Thumbprint
Meringues

Thumbprint Meringues

To keep the meringues light and crisp, add the jam mixture just before serving.

Prep: 20 minutes • Cook: 1 hour, 30 minutes
Other: 2 hours

    2 large egg whites
  1/8 teaspoon cream of tartar
  1/2 cup granulated sugar
  1/4 cup powdered sugar
  1/2 teaspoon vanilla extract
  1/4 cup seedless raspberry jam
    2 teaspoons raspberry liqueur

1. Preheat oven to 225°.
2. Cover two large baking sheets with parchment paper; secure paper with masking tape.
3. Place egg whites and cream of tartar in a medium bowl; beat with a mixer at medium speed until soft peaks form. Increase speed to high, and gradually add granulated sugar and then powdered sugar, 1 tablespoon at a time, beating until stiff peaks form. Add vanilla; beat just until combined.
4. Spoon batter into a large zip-top plastic bag. Seal bag; snip off 1 bottom corner of bag. Pipe 24 mounds onto prepared baking sheets. Moisten thumb or a spoon with water; press thumb or spoon into center of each mound to form an indentation.
5. Bake at 225° for 1 1/2 hours. Turn oven off; cool in closed oven 2 hours or until crisp. Carefully remove from paper.
6. Combine jam and liqueur, stirring with a whisk. Place mixture in a zip-top plastic bag. Seal bag; snip off one bottom corner of bag. Pipe about 1/2 teaspoon jam mixture into indention in each cookie. Yield: 2 dozen (serving size: 1 cookie).

CALORIES 37 (0% from fat); FAT 0g (sat 0g, mono 0g, poly 0g); PROTEIN 0.3g; CARB 8.4g; FIBER 0g; CHOL 0mg; IRON 0mg; SODIUM 5mg; CALC 0mg

how to beat egg whites

While eggs straight from the refrigerator are easier to separate, egg whites beat to maximum volume at room temperature (70°). Your best bet is to separate the eggs as your first step before you begin the recipe. The whites should be ready to use by the time you need them. If not, place the bowl of whites in a large bowl filled with very warm water, and stir them gently for a minute or two.

Make sure your bowl and beaters are clean, with no traces of fat. Beat the egg whites and cream of tartar (to stabilize eggs) until soft peaks form before adding sugar. To determine peaks, turn off the mixer, and lift the beaters. The egg whites will fall to one side for soft peaks (A) and stand upright for stiff peaks (B). Add sugar 1 tablespoon at a time to make sure it dissolves completely for a smooth meringue.

Double-Vanilla Meringue Cookies

Add the vanilla bean seeds at the end of the beating process; their natural oils can prevent the egg whites from beating to stiff peaks. If you don't have a vanilla bean, use 2 teaspoons vanilla extract instead of 1.

Prep: 15 minutes • Cook: 35 minutes per batch

1 cup sugar, divided
1 vanilla bean
3 large egg whites
¼ teaspoon cream of tartar
¼ teaspoon salt
1 teaspoon vanilla extract

1. Preheat oven to 325°.
2. Cover two large baking sheets with parchment paper; secure paper with masking tape.
3. Place ¼ cup sugar in a small bowl. Scrape seeds from vanilla bean, and add seeds to sugar; discard bean. Stir well with a whisk.
4. Place egg whites, cream of tartar, and salt in a large bowl; beat with a mixer at high speed until foamy. Gradually add ¾ cup sugar, 1 tablespoon at a time, beating mixture until stiff peaks form. Gradually add vanilla bean mixture and extract; beat until just combined. (Stiff peaks will take on consistency of marshmallow creme.)
5. Drop batter by level tablespoons onto prepared baking sheets. Bake at 325° for 35 minutes or until crisp. Cool on pan on a wire rack. Carefully remove from parchment paper. Store in an airtight container. Yield: 2½ dozen (serving size: 1 cookie).

CALORIES 28 (0% from fat); FAT 0g (sat 0g, mono 0g, poly 0g); PROTEIN 0.3g; CARB 6.7g; FIBER 0g; CHOL 0mg; IRON 0mg; SODIUM 25mg; CALC 0mg

how to shape meringue cookies

Use a spoon to scoop batter, and use your finger to scrape even-sized mounds onto prepared baking sheets lined with parchment paper.

Or place a silpat mat on a baking sheet and pipe the batter out of a pastry bag or a zip-top plastic bag with a corner cut out. Silpat mats are made of a flexible fiberglass and silicone weave and are ideal for light baking because there's no need to grease the mat. There's no sticking, scorching, or burning. For more information, check www.demarleusa.com or call 888-353-9726.

Rolled Cookies
Make new memories in the kitchen—even the youngest cook will enjoy rolling out the dough, cutting it into shapes, and decorating these cookies.

Christmas Sugar Wafers with Vanilla Icing

All good bakers need one basic Christmas cookie recipe in their repertoire, and this one is it. The cookies are crisp, rich-tasting, and perfect for decorating.

Prep: 35 minutes • Cook: 6 minutes per batch • Other: 20 minutes

Cookies:
  6 tablespoons sugar
  ¼ cup butter
  2 tablespoons dark brown sugar
  1½ teaspoons vanilla extract
  2 large egg whites
  1½ cups all-purpose flour
  3 tablespoons cornstarch
  ½ teaspoon baking powder
  ¼ teaspoon baking soda
  ¼ teaspoon salt
  Cooking spray

Vanilla Icing:
  1 cup powdered sugar
  1 tablespoon warm water
  1 teaspoon light-colored corn syrup
  ¼ teaspoon vanilla extract
  Dash of salt

1. To prepare cookies, place first 3 ingredients in a large bowl; beat with a mixer at medium speed until well blended (about 5 minutes). Beat in 1½ teaspoons vanilla. Add egg whites, 1 at a time, beating well after each addition.
2. Lightly spoon flour into dry measuring cups; level with a knife. Combine flour and next 4 ingredients, stirring well with a whisk. Add to butter mixture; beat well. Turn dough out onto a lightly floured surface (dough will be soft). Divide dough into four equal portions. Roll each portion into an 8-inch circle between two sheets of plastic wrap. Freeze dough 20 minutes or until plastic wrap can be easily removed.
3. Preheat oven to 375°.
4. Working with one portion of dough at a time (keep remaining dough in freezer), remove top sheet of plastic wrap. Cut dough with a 3-inch cookie cutter, dipping cutter in flour before each use. Place cookies on baking sheets coated with cooking spray. Discard bottom sheet of plastic wrap; reserve remaining dough scraps. Form ball with reserved dough; repeat rolling, freezing, and cutting procedure.
5. Bake at 375° for 6 minutes or until cookies are lightly browned. Remove from baking sheet; cool on a wire rack.
6. To prepare icing, combine powdered sugar and remaining 4 ingredients in a bowl; stir with a fork until combined. Add additional water, ½ teaspoon at a time, if needed. Spoon icing into a zip-top plastic bag; cut a tiny hole in one corner, and pipe designs onto cookies. Yield: 2 dozen (serving size: 1 cookie).

CALORIES 94 (22% from fat); FAT 2.3g (sat 1.4g, mono 0.6g, poly 0.3g); PROTEIN 0.1g; CARB 17.9g; FIBER 0.3g; CHOL 5mg; IRON 0.4mg; SODIUM 75mg; CALC 5mg

Test Kitchen Tip: Freezing the dough before cutting it is the only way to get it firm enough for cutting out shapes.

Cinnamon Cookies

Not overly sweet, these cookies are a tasty accompaniment to tea.

Prep: 25 minutes • Cook: 8 minutes per batch • Other 20 minutes

    6 tablespoons granulated sugar
    ⅓ cup butter, softened
    2 tablespoons light brown sugar
    2 teaspoons vanilla extract
    2 large egg whites
 1½ cups all-purpose flour
    ¼ cup cornstarch
    ½ teaspoon baking powder
    ¼ teaspoon baking soda
    ¼ teaspoon salt
    ¼ teaspoon ground cinnamon
    ⅔ cup powdered sugar
    2 teaspoons fat-free milk
    ⅛ teaspoon ground cinnamon
    2 tablespoons sliced almonds

1. Place first 4 ingredients in a large bowl; beat with a mixer at medium speed until well blended (about 5 minutes). Add egg whites, 1 at a time, beating well after each addition.

2. Lightly spoon flour into dry measuring cups; level with a knife. Combine flour and next 5 ingredients, stirring well with a whisk. Add to butter mixture; beat well. Divide dough into four equal portions. Roll each portion to ⅛-inch thickness between two sheets of plastic wrap. Freeze dough 20 minutes or until plastic wrap can be easily removed.

3. Preheat oven to 375°.

4. Working with one portion of dough at a time (keep remaining dough in freezer), remove top sheet of plastic wrap. Cut dough with a 2-inch round cookie cutter; place cookies on baking sheets. Discard bottom sheet of plastic wrap.

5. Bake at 375° for 8 minutes or until lightly browned. Remove from baking sheet; cool on a wire rack. Combine powdered sugar, milk, and ⅛ teaspoon cinnamon; drizzle mixture over cookies. Sprinkle with almonds. Yield: 4 dozen (serving size: 1 cookie).

CALORIES 45 (28% from fat); FAT 1.4g (sat 0.8g, mono 0.4g, poly 0.1g); PROTEIN 0.6g; CARB 17.5g; FIBER 0.2g; CHOL 3mg; IRON 0.2mg; SODIUM 39mg; CALC 6mg

Test Kitchen Tip: Adding cornstarch to the dough helps produce a crisp cookie when the amount of butter has been reduced.

Ginger Shortbread

Though it's a lighter version, this traditional-style shortbread has all of the buttery flavor and tender flaky texture of the original. In this recipe, the dough is cut into wedges— a classic shortbread shape. To keep the texture of the bread pleasantly light, handle the dough as little as possible.

**Prep: 15 minutes • Cook: 25 minutes
Other: 25 minutes**

    ¾ cup plus 3 tablespoons cake flour
    ¼ cup granulated sugar
    1 teaspoon ground ginger
 Dash of salt
    5 tablespoons unsalted butter, softened
    1 tablespoon ice water
 Cooking spray
    1 tablespoon turbinado or other
        coarse sugar
    ¼ ounce crystallized ginger, cut into
        16 thin slices

1. Lightly spoon flour into dry measuring cups; level with a knife. Combine flour, ¼ cup sugar, ground ginger, and salt, stirring with a whisk.

2. Place butter in a medium bowl; beat with a mixer at medium speed until smooth (about 1 minute). Add flour mixture; beat at low speed just until combined. Add ice water, and stir just until combined. Press mixture gently into a 4-inch circle on plastic wrap; cover with additional plastic wrap. Chill 20 minutes.

3. Preheat oven to 350°.

4. Slightly overlap two sheets of plastic wrap on a slightly damp surface. Unwrap and place chilled dough on plastic wrap. Cover dough with two additional sheets of overlapping plastic wrap. Roll dough, still covered, into an 8-inch circle (edges of circle will crack slightly). Remove top sheets of plastic wrap, and fit dough, plastic wrap side up, onto a baking sheet coated with cooking spray. Remove remaining plastic wrap.

5. Sprinkle dough with 1 tablespoon turbinado sugar; press gently to help sugar adhere to dough. Lightly score dough into 16 wedges, cutting into, but not through, dough. Place 1 piece of crystallized ginger in each wedge; press gently to adhere.

6. Bake at 350° for 25 minutes or until light gold in color. Remove from oven; cool 5 minutes. Cut through score lines to make 16 wedges. Place on a wire rack; cool completely. Yield: 16 wedges (serving size: 1 wedge).

CALORIES 77 (42% from fat); FAT 3.6g (sat 2.3g, mono 0.9g, poly 0.2g); PROTEIN 0.7g; CARB 10.7g; FIBER 0.2g; CHOL 9mg; IRON 0.6mg; SODIUM 10mg; CALC 3mg

Test Kitchen Tip: For more pronounced ginger flavor, increase the ground ginger by ½ teaspoon. Leave out the ginger for a plain version.

Shaped Cookies Although there are a variety of flavors, the dough is shaped into balls of uniform size.

Molasses Cookies

With just the right blend of sugar and spice, these chewy cookies hit the sweet spot. Drained applesauce replaces some, but not all, the fat. (See page 146 for more information on how to use applesauce as a fat replacement.)

Prep: 20 minutes • Cook: 8 to 10 minutes per batch • Other: 35 minutes

- ½ cup applesauce
- 1¼ cups sugar, divided
- 6 tablespoons butter, softened
- ¼ cup dark molasses
- 1 large egg
- 1 cup all-purpose flour
- 1 cup whole wheat pastry flour
- 2 teaspoons baking soda
- 1 teaspoon ground cinnamon
- ½ teaspoon salt
- ½ teaspoon ground ginger
- ½ teaspoon ground cloves
- Cooking spray

1. Spoon applesauce onto several layers of heavy-duty paper towels; spread to ½-inch thickness. Cover with additional paper towels; let stand 5 minutes. Scrape into a bowl using a rubber spatula.

2. Combine applesauce, 1 cup sugar, and butter; beat with a mixer at medium speed until well blended (about 3 minutes). Add molasses and egg; beat well.

3. Lightly spoon flours into dry measuring cups; level with a knife. Combine flours and next 5 ingredients, stirring well with a whisk. Add flour mixture to sugar mixture, beating until blended. Cover and freeze 30 minutes or until firm.

4. Preheat oven to 375°.

5. With moist hands, shape dough into 32 (1-inch) balls. Roll balls in ¼ cup sugar. Place 3 inches apart on baking sheets coated with cooking spray. Bake at 375° for 8 to 10 minutes. Cool on pans 5 minutes. Remove from pans; cool completely on wire racks. Yield: 32 cookies (serving size: 1 cookie).

CALORIES 88 (25% from fat); FAT 2.4g (sat 1.4g, mono 0.7g, poly 0.1g); PROTEIN 1.2g; CARB 16g; FIBER 0.7g; CHOL 12mg; IRON 0.7mg; SODIUM 141mg; CALC 16mg

Test Kitchen Tip: You can substitute ¾ cup all-purpose flour and ¼ cup whole wheat flour or 1 cup minus 2 tablespoons whole wheat flour for 1 cup whole wheat pastry flour.

Cinnamon-Spiced Date Cookies

To save prep time, use prechopped dates that are lightly coated with sugar. The applesauce adds sweetness instead of functioning as a fat replacement.

Prep: 20 minutes • Cook: 15 minutes per batch • Other: 1 hour, 1 minute

- 1½ cups all-purpose flour
- 1 cup whole wheat flour
- ¾ cup chopped pitted dates
- 1 teaspoon baking powder
- ½ teaspoon baking soda
- ½ teaspoon salt
- ⅛ teaspoon ground ginger
- ⅛ teaspoon ground cinnamon
- 1¼ cups sugar, divided
- ½ cup canola oil
- ½ cup applesauce
- 1 tablespoon water
- ¼ teaspoon vanilla extract
- Cooking spray

Molasses Cookies

1. Lightly spoon all-purpose flour and wheat flour into dry measuring cups, and level with a knife. Combine flours and next 6 ingredients in a large bowl; make a well in center of mixture. Combine 1 cup sugar, oil, applesauce, water, and vanilla in a bowl; add to flour mixture, stirring just until moist. Cover and chill 1 hour or until firm.

2. Preheat oven to 350°.

3. Divide chilled dough into 36 equal portions, and roll each portion into a ball. Place ¼ cup granulated sugar in a small bowl, and gently roll each ball in sugar. Place balls 2 inches apart on baking sheets coated with cooking spray. Bake at 350° for 15 minutes or until cookies are lightly browned. Cool on pans 1 minute. Remove cookies from pans, and cool on a wire rack. Yield: 3 dozen (serving size: 1 cookie).

CALORIES 96 (30% from fat); FAT 3.2g (sat 0.2g, mono 1.9g, poly 1g); PROTEIN 1.1g; CARB 16.5g; FIBER 0.9g; CHOL 0mg; IRON 0.4mg; SODIUM 64mg; CALC 11mg

Test Kitchen Tip: Several things can cause your cookies to burn on the bottom—dark cookie sheets, for one. If your pans are dark, decrease your oven temperature by 25°. Make sure the oven rack is in the second position from the bottom of the oven, and cook only one sheet of cookies at a time to ensure proper air circulation. Finally, check your oven temperature periodically with an oven thermometer. Many ovens have hot spots or heat to a temperature higher than they are set for. If the temperature is inaccurate, adjust the dial accordingly.

Almond-Apricot Macaroons

This lightened version of traditional Greek Passover almond macaroons uses matzo cake meal, a ground form of unleavened matzo bread. You'll find it in Jewish markets and most supermarkets.

Prep: 13 minutes • Cook: 20 minutes

    2 tablespoons matzo cake meal
    ¾ cup whole blanched almonds
    ¾ cup matzo cake meal
    ¾ cup sugar
    ½ cup chopped dried apricots
    1 teaspoon grated orange rind
    ¼ teaspoon almond extract
    3 large egg whites

1. Preheat oven to 325°.

2. Line a baking sheet with parchment paper and sprinkle with 2 tablespoons matzo cake meal.

3. Place almonds in a food processor; pulse 3 to 4 times or until coarsely chopped.

4. Lightly spoon ¾ cup matzo cake meal into a dry measuring cup; level with a knife. Add ¾ cup matzo cake meal, sugar, and remaining 4 ingredients to almonds; pulse 3 to 4 times or just until combined (mixture will be sticky).

5. Using hands dusted with matzo cake meal, divide dough into 16 portions. Roll each portion into a ball; pinch tops to form a pear shape. Place on prepared baking sheet. Bake at 325° for 20 minutes or until lightly browned. Cool on a wire rack. Yield: 16 cookies (serving size: 1 cookie).

CALORIES 117 (27% from fat); FAT 3.5g (sat 0.3g, mono 2.2g, poly 0.8g); PROTEIN 3g; CARB 19.8g; FIBER 1.4g; CHOL 0mg; IRON 0.6mg; SODIUM 13mg; CALC 18mg

how to shape macaroons

Gently pinch each macaroon top to form a rounded tip.

Crisp Pecan Cookies

These cookies are reminiscent of pecan sandies, but significantly lower in fat because we reduced the amount of butter and pecans. To toast pecans, place them in a dry skillet and cook over medium heat 1 to 2 minutes, stirring frequently.

Prep: 25 minutes • Cook: 12 minutes per batch • Other: 42 minutes

  1   cup all-purpose flour
  ½   teaspoon baking powder
  ¼   teaspoon salt
  1   cup packed brown sugar
  5   tablespoons butter, softened
  1   teaspoon vanilla extract
  1   large egg white
  3   tablespoons pecans, toasted and
       finely chopped
  ⅓   cup powdered sugar, divided
Cooking spray

1. Lightly spoon flour into a dry measuring cup; level with a knife. Combine flour, baking powder, and salt, stirring well with a whisk.
2. Combine brown sugar and butter in a bowl, and beat with a mixer at high speed until light and fluffy. Add vanilla and egg white, and beat 1 minute. Stir in flour mixture and chopped pecans. Refrigerate dough 30 minutes.
3. Preheat oven to 350°.
4. Place ¼ cup powdered sugar in a small bowl. Divide dough into 30 equal portions. With moist hands, shape each portion into a ½-inch ball. Roll balls in ¼ cup powdered sugar. Place 2 inches apart on baking sheets coated with cooking spray. Place pans in freezer 10 minutes.
5. Bake at 350° for 12 minutes or until cookies are golden. Cool on pans 2 minutes. Remove from pans; cool completely on wire racks. Using a fine sieve, sprinkle 4 teaspoons powdered sugar over cookies. Yield: 30 cookies (serving size: 1 cookie).

CALORIES 69 (33% from fat); FAT 2.5g (sat 1.2g, mono 0.9g, poly 0.2g); PROTEIN 0.6g; CARB 11.6g; FIBER 0.2g; CHOL 5mg; IRON 0.4mg; SODIUM 50mg; CALC 10mg

---

All-Time Favorite

Macadamia Butter Cookies with Dried Cranberries

These cookies are as humble as peanut butter cookies but not as crumbly. The dough is somewhat sticky; chilling it briefly makes handling easier.

Prep: 25 minutes • Cook: 9 minutes per batch • Other: 10 minutes

  ⅔   cup macadamia nuts
  ½   cup granulated sugar
  ½   cup packed light brown sugar
  1   teaspoon vanilla extract
  1   large egg
  1¼ cups all-purpose flour
  ½   teaspoon baking soda
  ¼   teaspoon salt
  ⅛   teaspoon ground nutmeg
  ½   cup sweetened dried cranberries,
       chopped
  1   tablespoon granulated sugar

1. Preheat oven to 375°.
2. Line two baking sheets with parchment paper.
3. Place nuts in a food processor; process until smooth (about 2 minutes), scraping sides of bowl once. Combine macadamia butter, ½ cup granulated sugar, and brown sugar in a large bowl; beat with a mixer at medium speed. Add vanilla and egg, and beat well.
4. Lightly spoon flour into dry measuring cups; level with a knife. Combine flour, baking soda, salt, and nutmeg, stirring with a whisk. Add flour mixture to sugar mixture; beat at low speed just until combined (mixture will be very thick). Stir in cranberries. Chill 10 minutes.
5. Divide chilled dough into 30 equal portions; roll each portion into a ball. Place 1 tablespoon granulated sugar in a small bowl. Lightly press each ball into sugar. Place balls, sugar sides up, on prepared baking sheets.
6. Gently press top of each cookie with a fork. Dip fork in water; gently press top of each cookie again to form a crisscross pattern.
7. Bake cookies, one baking sheet at a time, at 375° for 9 minutes or until golden. Remove cookies from pans; cool on wire racks. Yield: 30 cookies (serving size: 1 cookie).

CALORIES 76 (30% from fat); FAT 2.5g (sat 0.4g, mono 1.8g, poly 0.1g); PROTEIN 1g; CARB 13.2g; FIBER 0.6g; CHOL 7mg; IRON 0.5mg; SODIUM 44mg; CALC 7mg

Test Kitchen Tip: Mix the dough in a large mixing bowl, not the food processor, or the cookies will be too crumbly. Also, make sure you lightly spoon flour into the measuring cup, never pack it, and level the top of the measuring cup with a straight edge. In light baked products, even a small amount of additional flour can make a difference.

Slice-&-Bake Cookies
These cookies are also called refrigerator cookies because you shape the dough into a log and refrigerate or freeze it until you're ready to slice and bake.

Chocolate Spiderweb Cookies

Let the kids help make the spiderweb design on these Halloween cookies. The chocolaty crunch and white glaze make them a delicious treat for all sorts of ghouls and goblins.

Prep: 20 minutes • Cook: 10 minutes per batch • Other: 2 hours

    1   cup all-purpose flour
    ⅓   cup unsweetened cocoa
    ½   teaspoon baking soda
    ⅛   teaspoon salt
    ⅓   cup vegetable shortening
    ⅔   cup granulated sugar
    1   teaspoon vanilla extract
    1   large egg white
  Cooking spray
    2   cups powdered sugar, sifted
    3   tablespoons 2% reduced-fat milk

1. Lightly spoon flour into a dry measuring cup; level with a knife. Combine flour, cocoa, baking soda, and salt, stirring well with a whisk. Place shortening in a large mixing bowl; beat with a heavy-duty mixer at medium speed until light and fluffy. Gradually add granulated sugar, 1 tablespoon at a time, beating until well blended. Add vanilla and egg white; beat well. Add flour mixture; beat until well blended.

2. Turn dough out onto wax paper; shape into a 6-inch log. Wrap log in wax paper. Freeze 2 hours or until very firm.
3. Preheat oven to 350°.
4. Cut log into 24 (¼-inch) slices, and place slices 1 inch apart on baking sheets coated with cooking spray. Bake at 350° for 10 minutes or until set. Remove from pans; cool completely on wire racks.
5. Combine powdered sugar and milk in a medium bowl; stir with a whisk until smooth. Spoon into a small zip-top plastic bag; seal. Snip a tiny hole in one corner of bag. Working with one cookie at a time, pipe three concentric circles on cookie. Starting at center circle, pull a wooden pick through other circles at regular intervals to create a "web." Yield: 2 dozen (serving size: 1 cookie).

CALORIES 102 (26% from fat); FAT 2.9g (sat 0.8g, mono 1g, poly 0.7g); PROTEIN 1g; CARB 19g; FIBER 1g; CHOL 0mg; IRON 0mg; SODIUM 42mg; CALC 5mg

1. Turn the cookie dough out onto a sheet of wax paper. Working quickly, shape the dough into a 6-inch log.

2. Wrap the dough log in wax paper, and form a compact roll; twist ends of wax paper securely. Freeze the log until very firm (about three hours).

3. Immediately after taking the cookie dough from the freezer, unwrap it and cut into ¼-inch slices with dental floss or a very sharp knife.

Basic Icebox Sugar Cookies

Rich, tender, and buttery, this basic sugar cookie is guaranteed to please. It's delicious unadorned, but it's also an ideal base for frosting, sprinkles, or other decorations.

Prep: 15 minutes • Cook: 8 to 10 minutes per batch • Other: 3 hours

    1   cup all-purpose flour
    ¼   teaspoon baking soda
    ⅛   teaspoon salt
    4   tablespoons butter, softened
    ⅔   cup sugar
    1   teaspoon vanilla extract
    1   large egg white
  Cooking spray

1. Lightly spoon flour into a dry measuring cup, and level with a knife. Combine flour, baking soda, and salt in a bowl. Beat butter with a mixer at medium speed until light and fluffy. Gradually add sugar, beating at medium speed until well blended. Add vanilla and egg white, and beat well. Add flour mixture, and stir until well blended.

2. Turn dough out onto wax paper, and shape into a 6-inch log. Wrap log in wax paper, and freeze 3 hours or until very firm.

3. Preheat oven to 350°.

4. Cut log into 24 (¼-inch) slices; place slices 1 inch apart on a baking sheet coated with cooking spray. Bake at 350° for 8 to 10 minutes. Remove cookies from pan; cool on wire racks. Yield: 2 dozen (serving size: 1 cookie).

CALORIES 58 (31% from fat); FAT 2g (sat 1g, mono 0.8g, poly 0.1g); PROTEIN 0.7g; CARB 9.6g; FIBER 0.1g; CHOL 5mg; IRON 0.2mg; SODIUM 41mg; CALC 2mg

Gingersnap Cookies

This old-fashioned favorite features sweet crystallized ginger and a splash of strong, brewed coffee for another level of rich flavor.

Prep: 20 minutes • Cook: 10 minutes per batch • Other: 8 hours, 15 minutes

1¼   cups all-purpose flour
½   teaspoon baking soda
⅛   teaspoon salt
2   tablespoons dark molasses
1   tablespoon cold strong brewed coffee
½   cup sugar
6   tablespoons butter, softened
2   tablespoons finely chopped crystallized ginger
½   teaspoon ground cinnamon
¼   teaspoon ground cloves
2   tablespoons sugar

1. Lightly spoon flour into dry measuring cups; level with a knife. Combine flour, baking soda, and salt in a bowl; set aside. Combine molasses and coffee in a small bowl; set aside.
2. Beat ½ cup sugar and butter with a mixer at medium speed until light and fluffy. Add ginger, cinnamon, and cloves; beat well. Add flour mixture and molasses mixture; beat at low speed until well blended.
3. Gently press dough into a ball; wrap in plastic wrap, and freeze 15 minutes. Shape dough into a 7-inch roll; flatten to 1-inch thickness. Wrap in plastic wrap; freeze 8 hours or overnight.
4. Preheat oven to 350°.
5. Cover two baking sheets with parchment paper; secure paper with masking tape. Cut dough into 40 (⅛-inch-thick) slices; place ½ inch apart on prepared baking sheets. Sprinkle with 2 tablespoons sugar. Bake at 350° for 10 minutes (cookies will be slightly soft in center, but will harden as they cool). Remove from pans; cool completely on wire racks. Yield: 40 cookies (serving size: 1 cookie).

CALORIES 45 (36% from fat); FAT 1.8g (sat 1.1g, mono 0.6g, poly 0.1g); PROTEIN 0.4g; CARB 7g; FIBER 0.1g; CHOL 5mg; IRON 0.4mg; SODIUM 42mg; CALC 11mg

Chocolate-Mint Cookies

These taste just like mint Girl Scout cookies, but they're low-fat. If you don't have time to roll and slice the dough, the recipe works just as well if you drop spoonfuls directly onto the baking sheet.

Prep: 15 minutes • Cook: 10 minutes per batch • Other: 1 hour

1   cup all-purpose flour
½   cup unsweetened cocoa
¼   teaspoon baking soda
½   cup packed brown sugar
½   cup granulated sugar
3   tablespoons butter, softened
3   tablespoons applesauce
1   teaspoon vanilla extract
¼   teaspoon peppermint extract
1   large egg white, lightly beaten
Cooking spray

1. Lightly spoon flour into a dry measuring cup; level with a knife. Combine flour, cocoa, and baking soda in a small bowl; stirring well with a whisk.
2. Combine brown sugar and next 5 ingredients in a medium bowl; beat with a mixer at high speed 2 minutes. Beat in egg white. Add flour mixture; beat at low speed until well blended.
3. Coat hands lightly with cooking spray. Shape dough into a 6-inch log. Wrap log in plastic wrap; freeze 1 hour or until firm.
4. Preheat oven to 350°.
5. Cut log into 24 (¼-inch) slices, and place 1 inch apart on baking sheets lightly coated with cooking spray. Bake at 350° for 10 minutes. Remove from pans; cool on wire racks. Yield: 2 dozen (serving size: 1 cookie).

CALORIES 76 (22% from fat); FAT 1.8g (sat 1.1g, mono 0.5g, poly 0.1g); PROTEIN 1.2g; CARB 13.7g; FIBER 0.2g; CHOL 4mg; IRON 0.7mg; SODIUM 33mg; CALC 8mg

slice-and-bake cookies

Here are some tips from our Test Kitchens for making slice-and-bake cookies successfully.

- To make dough easier to handle, freeze it for about one hour before slicing the cookies.
- You can freeze logs of dough up to one month, but be sure to double wrap for extra protection.
- Each time you slice a cookie from the log (using dental floss or a very sharp knife), turn the log a quarter turn to prevent flattening on one side.

Raspberry Strippers

Think of these as a variation of thumbprint cookies. Vanilla butter cookies
are filled with fruit preserves and drizzled with a powdered sugar glaze.
To keep the icing intact, store these cookies in a single layer.

Prep: 20 minutes • Cook: 20 minutes • Other: 10 minutes

⅓ cup granulated sugar
5 tablespoons butter, softened
1½ teaspoons vanilla extract
1 large egg white
1 cup all-purpose flour
2 tablespoons cornstarch
¼ teaspoon baking powder
¼ teaspoon salt
Cooking spray
⅓ cup raspberry or apricot preserves
½ cup powdered sugar
2 teaspoons fresh lemon juice
¼ teaspoon almond or vanilla extract

1. Preheat oven to 375°.
2. Beat granulated sugar and butter with a mixer at medium speed until well blended (about 5 minutes). Add 1½ teaspoons vanilla and egg white; beat well. Lightly spoon flour into a dry measuring cup; level with a knife. Combine flour, cornstarch, baking powder, and salt, stirring well with a whisk. Add flour mixture to sugar mixture, stirring until well blended (dough will be stiff).
3. Turn dough out onto a lightly floured surface. Divide dough in half. Roll each portion into a 12-inch log. Place logs 3 inches apart on a baking sheet coated with cooking spray. Form a ½-inch-deep indentation down length of each log using an index finger or end of a wooden spoon. Spoon preserves into indentation. Bake at 375° for 20 minutes or until lightly browned. Remove to a cutting board.
4. Combine powdered sugar, lemon juice, and almond extract; stir well with a whisk. Drizzle sugar mixture over warm logs. Immediately cut each log diagonally into 12 slices (do not separate slices). Cool 10 minutes; separate slices. Transfer slices to wire racks. Cool completely. Yield: 2 dozen (serving size: 1 cookie).

CALORIES 75 (30% from fat); FAT 2.5g (sat 1.5g, mono 0.7g, poly 0.2g); PROTEIN 0.7g; CARB 12.4g; FIBER 0.2g; CHOL 6mg; IRON 0.3mg; SODIUM 56mg; CALC 4mg

how to make raspberry strippers

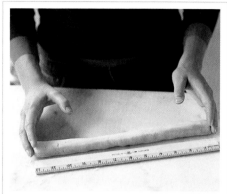

1. Shape each portion of dough into a 12-inch log.

2. Make a trough about ½ inch deep down the center of each log using your index finger or end of a wooden spoon. Spoon preserves into the center, and bake.

3. Drizzle glaze over warm logs; immediately cut diagonally into 12 slices. After letting the cookies cool 10 minutes, transfer to wire racks.

Bar Cookies
There's no rolling, shaping, or slicing involved when you make bar cookies such as brownies and bars.

Peanut Butter-Crispy Rice Bars

Pump up the flavor and the protein in this popular cereal treat by stirring in peanut butter and drizzling with melted peanut butter chips.

Prep: 9 minutes • Cook: 2 minutes, 45 seconds

⅓ cup creamy peanut butter
1 tablespoon butter
1 (10½-ounce) bag miniature marshmallows
6 cups oven-toasted rice cereal (such as Rice Krispies)
Cooking spray
¾ cup peanut butter chips

1. Combine peanut butter and butter in a large microwave-safe bowl. Microwave at HIGH 30 to 45 seconds or until mixture melts. Add marshmallows; microwave at HIGH 1 minute or until smooth, stirring every 30 seconds. Add cereal to peanut butter mixture; toss until well combined. Press cereal mixture into a 13 x 9–inch baking pan coated with cooking spray.
2. Place peanut butter chips in a small microwave-safe bowl. Microwave at HIGH 20 to 30 seconds or until chips melt. Spoon melted chips into a small heavy-duty zip-top plastic bag; seal. Snip a tiny hole in one corner of bag; drizzle melted chips over cereal mixture. Cool slightly; cut into 24 bars. Yield: 2 dozen (serving size: 1 bar).

CALORIES 118 (30% from fat); FAT 3.9g (sat 1.3g, mono 1.5g, poly 0.8g); PROTEIN 2.6g; CARB 19g; FIBER 0.7g; CHOL 1mg; IRON 0.4mg; SODIUM 93mg; CALC 9mg

Test Kitchen Tip: The cereal mixture is very sticky, so coat your hands with cooking spray before pressing it into the pan.

Apricot-Oat Squares

A nutty-tasting oat crust is the base and the topping for the sweet fruit filling. Substitute your favorite fruit preserves in place of the apricot.

Prep: 9 minutes • Cook: 35 minutes

½ cup all-purpose flour
½ cup whole wheat flour
1½ cups regular oats
⅓ cup packed brown sugar
6 tablespoons chilled butter, cut into small pieces
¼ teaspoon ground nutmeg
Cooking spray
¾ cup apricot preserves

1. Preheat oven to 350°.
2. Lightly spoon flours into dry measuring cups, and level with a knife. Place flours, oats, sugar, butter, and nutmeg in a food processor, and pulse 5 times or until oat mixture resembles coarse meal.
3. Press two-thirds of oat mixture into bottom of an 8-inch square baking pan coated with cooking spray. Bake at 350° for 10 minutes. Spread preserves over warm crust. Sprinkle with remaining oat mixture, and press gently. Bake an additional 25 minutes or until lightly browned and bubbly. Cool completely in pan on a wire rack; cut into squares. Yield: 16 squares (serving size: 1 square).

CALORIES 148 (30% from fat); FAT 5g (sat 2.8g, mono 1.4g, poly 0.4g); PROTEIN 2.3g; CARB 24.9g; FIBER 1.5g; CHOL 12mg; IRON 0.8mg; SODIUM 52mg; CALC 14mg

Peanut Butter-Crispy Rice Bars

Classic Makeover: Brownies

Brownies, an All-American favorite, are typically loaded with fat and calories, especially if they're cream cheese brownies. But there's no reason not to enjoy brownie delight—we've figured out a way to reduce the fat significantly yet keep the rich fudginess. You may be surprised to note that we've kept butter in the recipe. We've used less butter than the amount in a traditional cream cheese brownie, but used enough to get a fudgy, dense texture. To further reduce fat, we've used unsweetened cocoa instead of baking chocolate, ⅓-less-fat cream cheese, fat-free sweetened condensed milk, and fat-free milk, and replaced some of the whole eggs with egg whites.

Before	After
• 169 calories	• 131 calories
• 9.7g fat	• 4.2g fat
• percentage of calories from fat 52%	• percentage of calories from fat 29%

Cream Cheese Brownies

Butter gives these brownies a fudgy, dense texture; they're topped with a cheesecake-like layer. Although we reduced the fat in this classic recipe, when you bite into one, we don't think you'll miss the fat one bit.

Prep: 25 minutes • Cook: 35 minutes

Brownies:
  Cooking spray
  ½ cup butter, softened
  1½ cups sugar
  1 teaspoon vanilla extract
  2 large egg whites
  1 large egg
  ⅔ cup unsweetened cocoa
  ½ cup fat-free milk
  1½ cups all-purpose flour
  ½ teaspoon baking powder
  ¼ teaspoon salt

Topping:
  1 (8-ounce) block ⅓-less-fat cream cheese
  1 tablespoon cornstarch
  1 teaspoon vanilla extract
  1 (14-ounce) can fat-free sweetened condensed milk
  1 large egg

1. Preheat oven to 350°.
2. Coat bottom of a 13 x 9–inch baking pan with cooking spray (do not coat sides).
3. To prepare brownies, place butter in a large bowl; beat with a mixer at medium speed until fluffy. Add sugar and 1 teaspoon vanilla; beat until well blended (about 5 minutes). Add egg whites and 1 egg, 1 at a time, beating well after each addition. Add cocoa and ½ cup milk; beat well (mixture will appear curdled). Lightly spoon flour into dry measuring cups; level with a knife. Combine flour,

baking powder, and salt; stir with a whisk. Add to cocoa mixture; beat at low speed just until blended. Spoon batter into prepared pan.

4. To prepare topping, place cream cheese in a large bowl, and beat with a mixer at medium speed until smooth. Gradually add cornstarch and remaining 3 ingredients; beat until smooth. Spread evenly over batter. Bake at 350° for 35 minutes or until set. Cool in pan on a wire rack. Cut into bars. Yield: 3 dozen (serving size: 1 brownie).

CALORIES 131 (29% from fat); FAT 4.2g (sat 2.5g, mono 1.3g, poly 0.2g); PROTEIN 3.2g; CARB 20.7g; FIBER 0.7g; CHOL 23mg; IRON 0.6mg; SODIUM 88mg; CALC 51mg

cocoa **Unsweetened cocoa, or cocoa powder, is made from roasted, ground cacao seeds that have much of their fat removed. There are two types of cocoa: natural (nonalkalized) and Dutch process (alkalized). Both are unsweetened, but their flavors differ subtly. Natural cocoa tastes fruity, tart, and acidic, and is simply untreated cocoa. It's rarely labeled "natural," so you'll just see "cocoa" on the label. Dutch process cocoa is treated with an alkali to reduce its harshness and acidity. This type of cocoa has a rich, dark color and a mellow, toasted flavor.**

If a recipe calls for cocoa and is leavened with baking soda, use the natural variety. Because Dutch process is more alkaline, it may react with the baking soda and alter the texture and flavor of the recipe. In recipes with no baking soda, use either type.

Butter Pecan-Toffee Brownies

This chewy brownie's sweetness comes from a buttery brown sugar batter and a crunchy chocolate-brickle chip topping.

Prep: 13 minutes • Cook: 22 minutes

Cooking spray
- 1 cup packed brown sugar
- 3 tablespoons butter, melted
- 1 teaspoon vanilla extract
- 1 large egg
- ¾ cup all-purpose flour
- 2 tablespoons chopped pecans
- ½ teaspoon baking powder
- ⅛ teaspoon salt
- ⅔ cup powdered sugar
- 2 tablespoons semisweet chocolate minichips, melted
- 1 tablespoon hot water
- 2 tablespoons almond brickle chips (such as Heath)

1. Preheat oven to 350°.
2. Coat bottom of an 8-inch square baking pan with cooking spray (do not coat sides).
3. Combine brown sugar and next 3 ingredients; stir well with a whisk. Lightly spoon flour into a dry measuring cup; level with a knife. Combine flour, pecans, baking powder, and salt; stir into brown sugar mixture. Spread into bottom of prepared pan. Bake at 350° for 22 minutes or until a wooden pick inserted in center comes out almost clean. Cool on a wire rack.
4. Combine powdered sugar, minichips, and hot water; stir until smooth. Spread over brownies; sprinkle with brickle chips. Chill until topping is set. Yield: 16 brownies (serving size: 1 brownie).

CALORIES 141 (27% from fat); FAT 4.3g (sat 2g, mono 1.4g, poly 0.4g); PROTEIN 1.2g; CARB 25g; FIBER 0.2g; CHOL 20mg; IRON 0.7mg; SODIUM 75mg; CALC 24mg

Bourbon Fudge Brownies

These brownies get a subtle kick from a splash of bourbon. Use ¼ cup hot low-fat milk in place of bourbon, if you prefer.

Prep: 15 minutes • Cook: 26 minutes

- ¼ cup bourbon
- ¼ cup semisweet chocolate chips
- 1½ cups all-purpose flour
- ½ cup unsweetened cocoa
- 1 teaspoon baking powder
- ½ teaspoon salt
- 1⅓ cups sugar
- 6 tablespoons butter, softened
- ½ teaspoon vanilla extract
- 2 large eggs
Cooking spray

1. Preheat oven to 350°.
2. Bring bourbon to a boil in a small saucepan; remove from heat. Add chocolate chips, stirring until smooth.
3. Lightly spoon flour into dry measuring cups, and level with a knife. Combine flour, cocoa, baking powder, and salt, stirring with a whisk.
4. Combine sugar and butter in a large bowl; beat with a mixer at medium speed until well combined. Add vanilla and eggs; beat well. Add flour mixture and bourbon mixture to sugar mixture, beating at low speed just until combined.
5. Coat bottom of a 9-inch square baking pan with cooking spray (do not coat sides). Spread batter into pan. Bake at 350° for 25 minutes or until a wooden pick inserted in center comes out clean. Cool in pan on a wire rack. Yield: 20 brownies (serving size: 1 brownie).

CALORIES 148 (30% from fat); FAT 5g (sat 2.9g, mono 1.5g, poly 0.2g); PROTEIN 2.2g; CARB 23.2g; FIBER 1g; CHOL 31mg; IRON 1.5mg; SODIUM 121mg; CALC 20mg

Raspberry-Cream Cheese Brownies

Raspberry and chocolate are a hard-to-beat flavor combination, so when you add a rich cream cheese filling, you get brownies that are irresistible.

Prep: 20 minutes • Cook: 30 minutes

Filling:
- 1/3 cup sugar
- 1/3 cup (3 ounces) 1/3-less-fat cream cheese, softened
- 2 teaspoons all-purpose flour
- 1/2 teaspoon vanilla extract
- 1 large egg white

Brownies:
- Cooking spray
- 3/4 cup all-purpose flour
- 1/4 teaspoon baking powder
- 1/4 teaspoon baking soda
- 1/8 teaspoon salt
- 1 cup sugar
- 2/3 cup unsweetened cocoa
- 1/4 cup butter, melted
- 1 tablespoon water
- 1 teaspoon vanilla extract
- 1 large egg
- 2 large egg whites
- 3 tablespoons raspberry preserves

1. Preheat oven to 350°.

2. Beat first 5 ingredients with a mixer at medium speed until well blended.

3. To prepare brownies, coat bottom of an 8-inch square baking pan with cooking spray (do not coat sides of pan). Lightly spoon 3/4 cup flour into a dry measuring cup; level with a knife. Combine flour, baking powder, baking soda, and salt in a medium bowl. Combine 1 cup sugar and next 6 ingredients, stirring well with a whisk. Add to flour mixture, stirring just until moist. Spread two-thirds of batter in bottom of prepared pan. Pour filling over batter, spreading evenly. Carefully drop remaining batter and preserves by spoonfuls over filling; swirl together using tip of a knife to marble. Bake at 350° for 30 minutes or until a wooden pick inserted in center comes out almost clean. Cool on a wire rack. Yield: 16 brownies (serving size: 1 brownie).

CALORIES 161 (28% from fat); FAT 5g (sat 3g, mono 1.4g, poly 0.2g); PROTEIN 3.3g; CARB 25.9g; FIBER 0.2g; CHOL 26mg; IRON 1mg; SODIUM 113mg; CALC 18mg

Test Kitchen Tip: For fudgy, moist brownies, bake until the wooden pick comes out almost clean. If it's completely clean, the brownies may be slightly overdone.

Chewy Coconut-Butterscotch Bars

Bite into a chewy brown sugar bar topped with sweet coconut, rich chocolate, and butterscotch.

Prep: 12 minutes • Cook: 25 minutes

- Cooking spray
- 1 1/4 cups all-purpose flour
- 1 1/4 teaspoons baking powder
- 1/8 teaspoon salt
- 1 cup packed dark brown sugar
- 3 tablespoons canola oil
- 1 teaspoon vanilla extract
- 1 large egg
- 1 large egg white
- 1/3 cup chopped pitted dates
- 1/4 cup flaked sweetened coconut
- 2 tablespoons semisweet chocolate minichips
- 2 tablespoons butterscotch morsels

1. Preheat oven to 350°.

2. Coat bottom of an 8-inch square baking pan with cooking spray (do not coat sides).

3. Lightly spoon flour into dry measuring cups, and level with a knife. Combine flour, baking powder, and salt in a bowl. Combine sugar, oil, vanilla, egg, and egg white in a bowl; stir with a whisk until well blended. Add flour mixture and dates; stir just until blended. Spread in bottom of pan. Bake at 350° for 15 minutes; remove from oven. Combine coconut, minichips, and butterscotch morsels; sprinkle over brownies. Bake 10 minutes or until a wooden pick inserted in center comes out almost clean; cool on a wire rack. Yield: 16 bars (serving size: 1 bar).

CALORIES 131 (30% from fat); FAT 4.3g (sat 1.3g, mono 1.8g, poly 0.9g); PROTEIN 1.8g; CARB 21.5g; FIBER 0.6g; CHOL 14mg; IRON 0.8mg; SODIUM 73mg; CALC 36mg

Raspberry-Cream Cheese Brownies

Biscotti

Because of their crunchy texture, these twice-baked Italian-style cookies are perfect for dipping into a cup of coffee or a glass of milk.

White Chocolate-Lemon Biscotti

For a variation on this crisp Italian cookie recipe, substitute orange for lemon and semisweet chocolate chips for the chopped white chocolate.

Prep: 20 minutes • Cook: 55 minutes
Other: 10 minutes

- ¾   cup sugar
- 2   teaspoons grated lemon rind
- 1   teaspoon vanilla extract
- ¼   teaspoon lemon extract
- 2   large eggs
- 1⅔ cups all-purpose flour
- ½   teaspoon baking soda
- ¼   teaspoon salt
- 1   (6-ounce) bar premium white chocolate, chopped (about 1¼ cups)

Cooking spray

1. Preheat oven to 300°.
2. Place first 5 ingredients in a large bowl; beat with a mixer at medium speed until well blended. Lightly spoon flour into dry measuring cups; level with a knife. Combine flour, baking soda, and salt; gradually add to sugar mixture, beating until well blended. Stir in chocolate.
3. Turn dough out onto a lightly floured surface. Knead lightly 7 or 8 times. Shape dough into 2 (9-inch-long) rolls. Place rolls on a large baking sheet coated with cooking spray, and pat to 1-inch thickness.

4. Bake at 300° for 35 minutes. Remove rolls from baking sheet; cool 10 minutes on a wire rack.
5. Cut each roll diagonally into 12 (½-inch) slices. Place, cut sides down, on baking sheet. Bake at 300° for 10 minutes. Turn cookies over; bake an additional 10 minutes (cookies will be slightly soft in center but will harden as they cool). Remove from baking sheet; cool completely on wire rack. Yield: 2 dozen (serving size: 1 biscotto).

CALORIES 103 (26% from fat); FAT 3g (sat 1.6g, mono 0.2g, poly 0.1g); PROTEIN 1.9g; CARB 16.9g; FIBER 0.3g; CHOL 19mg; IRON 0.5mg; SODIUM 64mg; CALC 24mg

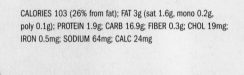

Cranberry-Chocolate Chip Biscotti

These cookies make a great ending to a holiday dinner. But you can enjoy them in any season because they contain dried cranberries instead of fresh.

Prep: 15 minutes • Cook: 55 minutes
Other: 10 minutes

2¾ cups all-purpose flour
1 cup sugar
½ cup dried cranberries
⅓ cup semisweet chocolate chips
2 teaspoons baking powder
⅛ teaspoon salt
1 tablespoon canola oil
1 teaspoon almond extract
1 teaspoon vanilla extract
3 large eggs
Cooking spray

1. Preheat oven to 350°.
2. Lightly spoon flour into dry measuring cups, and level with a knife. Combine flour and next 5 ingredients in a large bowl. Combine oil, extracts, and eggs; add to flour mixture, stirring until well blended (dough will be dry and crumbly). Turn dough out onto a lightly floured surface; knead lightly 7 or 8 times. Divide dough in half. Shape each portion into an 8-inch-long roll. Place rolls 6 inches apart on a large baking sheet coated with cooking spray; pat to 1-inch thickness.
3. Bake at 350° for 35 minutes. Remove rolls from baking sheet; cool 10 minutes on a wire rack. Cut each roll diagonally into 15 (½-inch) slices. Place slices, cut sides down, on baking sheet. Reduce oven temperature to 325°, and bake 10 minutes. Turn cookies over; bake an additional 10 minutes (cookies will be slightly soft in center but will harden as they cool).

Remove from baking sheet; cool completely on wire rack. Yield: 2½ dozen (serving size: 1 biscotto).

CALORIES 95 (15% from fat); FAT 1.6g (sat 0.5g, mono 0.7g, poly 0.3g); PROTEIN 2g; CARB 18.4g; FIBER 0.5g; CHOL 21mg; IRON 0.7mg; SODIUM 50mg; CALC 23mg

how to make biscotti

1. Use your hands to gently shape the dough into rolls.

2. Carefully flatten each roll to 1-inch thickness.

3. After the first baking, cut each roll diagonally into slices of equal width using a serrated or electric knife.

Cashew-and-Golden Raisin Biscotti

Golden raisins add an extra note of sweetness and cashews add crunchy saltiness.

Prep: 22 minutes • Cook: 1 hour, 5 minutes
Other: 10 minutes

1⅔ cups all-purpose flour
¾ teaspoon baking powder
½ teaspoon grated whole nutmeg
¼ teaspoon baking soda
¼ teaspoon ground mace
¾ cup sugar
2 teaspoons vanilla extract
2 large eggs
¾ cup dry-roasted cashews
¾ cup golden raisins
Cooking spray

1. Preheat oven to 300°.
2. Lightly spoon flour into dry measuring cups, and level with a knife. Combine flour and next 4 ingredients in a large bowl. Beat sugar, vanilla, and eggs in a large bowl with a mixer at medium speed until thick. Stir in flour mixture, cashews, and raisins. Turn dough out onto a floured surface, and knead lightly 7 or 8 times. Shape dough into a 12-inch roll. Place roll on a baking sheet coated with cooking spray, and pat to 1-inch thickness. Bake at 300° for 45 minutes. Cool 10 minutes on a wire rack.
3. Cut roll diagonally into 24 (½-inch) slices; stand slices upright on baking sheet. Bake 20 minutes (cookies will be slightly soft in center but will harden as they cool). Remove from baking sheet; cool completely on wire rack. Yield: 2 dozen (serving size: 1 biscotto).

CALORIES 102 (23% from fat); FAT 2.6g (sat 0.6g, mono 1.4g, poly 0.5g); PROTEIN 2.2g; CARB 18g; FIBER 0.7g; CHOL 18mg; IRON 0.8mg; SODIUM 52mg; CALC 14mg

desserts

Brown Sugar Pavlovas
with Fruit, page 200

Custards
We've reduced the fat in creamy egg-based desserts such as crème caramel, flan, and crème brûlée by using fewer yolks and reduced-fat dairy products.

Classic Crème Caramel

Who can resist a decadent custard? (See the technique photos on facing page.)

Prep: 8 minutes • Cook: 51 minutes
Other: 4 hours

⅓ cup sugar
3 tablespoons water
Cooking spray
3 large eggs
1 large egg white
2 cups 2% reduced-fat milk
1 tablespoon vanilla extract
⅔ cup sugar
⅛ teaspoon salt
Raspberries (optional)

1. Preheat oven to 325°.
2. Combine ⅓ cup sugar and 3 table-spoons water in a small, heavy saucepan over medium-high heat; cook until sugar dissolves, stirring frequently. Continue cooking 4 minutes or until golden.

Immediately pour into 6 (6-ounce) ramekins or custard cups coated with cooking spray, tilting each cup quickly until sugar coats bottom of cup.
3. Beat eggs and egg white in a bowl with a whisk. Stir in milk, vanilla, ⅔ cup sugar, and salt. Divide mixture evenly among custard cups. Place cups in a 13 x 9–inch baking pan; add hot water to pan to a depth of 1 inch. Bake at 325° for 45 min-utes or until a knife inserted in center comes out clean. Remove cups from pan. Cover and chill at least 4 hours.
4. Loosen edges of custards with a thin, sharp knife. Place a dessert plate, upside down, on top of each cup; invert onto plates. Drizzle remaining syrup over custards. Garnish with raspberries, if desired. Yield: 6 servings (serving size: 1 custard).

CALORIES 212 (18% from fat); FAT 4.3g (sat 1.8g, mono 1.5g, poly 0.4g); PROTEIN 6.5g; CARB 37.6g; FIBER 0g; CHOL 117mg; IRON 0.4mg; SODIUM 131mg; CALC 113mg

crème caramel troubleshooting

To keep the sugar from crystallizing, stir it as little as possible after it has melted. If some caramel crystallizes on the side of the pan, wash the crys-tals down with a wet pastry brush. Never touch or taste hot caramel.

If the caramel has a blackish-brown color, it's probably burned. To start over, allow the caramel to cool, add some water to the pan, and heat over low heat until the caramel dissolves. Discard the liquid, rinse the pan out, and add more sugar and water.

For neater pouring, mix the custard ingredients in a bowl with a spout, or mix them in a regular bowl, then trans-fer to a 4-cup glass measuring cup before pouring into the custard cups.

Check the custards for doneness 5 minutes before the end of the rec-ommended baking time because oven temperatures can vary. Remember, custard continues to cook as it cools.

Chill the crème caramel thoroughly (we recommend at least 4 hours), so that none of the caramel sticks to the bottom of the cup. If it does, scrape out the remaining syrup with a rubber spatula.

how to make crème caramel

1. Combine the sugar and water in a heavy saucepan over medium-high heat; stir until the sugar dissolves.

2. Continue to cook without stirring. In about 2 minutes, the mixture will start to caramelize and turn light brown. Cook 1 to 2 more minutes until it's a deep golden brown.

3. Immediately pour just enough caramel into a ramekin or custard cup to cover the bottom of the cup.

4. Tilt the cup so that its bottom is completely covered with caramel. Repeat for remaining cups.

5. Divide the custard mixture (eggs, milk, and flavorings) evenly among prepared cups.

6. Place the cups in a 13 x 9–inch baking pan. Carefully add hot tap water to the pan to a depth of 1 inch. Bake at 325° for recommended baking time.

7. After the custards have cooled and chilled, run a thin knife along the edge of each to loosen it from its cup.

8. Place a dessert plate, upside down, on top of each cup. Invert the cup and plate. Lift the cup; the custard should slip out easily with the caramel syrup on top. Scrape out any remaining syrup with a rubber spatula.

*You can't use egg substitutes to make custards
because the substitutes don't have yolks. Without yolks,
custards wouldn't be smooth and creamy.*

Coconut Crème Caramel with Pineapple Concassé

A water bath (see page 172) insulates the delicate egg custard to ensure a velvety texture. The cream of coconut replaces some of the milk and sugar that is used in the Classic Crème Caramel on page 166. This is a great make-ahead dessert because both the crème caramel and the concassé (a coarsely chopped mixture) need to chill for at least four hours. Basil adds an interesting, fresh flavor to the concassé.

**Prep: 13 minutes • Cook: 56 minutes
Other: 4 hours**

  ⅓ cup sugar
  3 tablespoons water
Cooking spray
  3 large eggs
  1 large egg white
1⅔ cups 2% reduced-fat milk
  ½ cup sugar
  ⅓ cup cream of coconut
  2 teaspoons vanilla extract
  ⅛ teaspoon salt
Pineapple Concassé

1. Preheat oven to 325°.
2. Combine ⅓ cup sugar and water in a small, heavy saucepan over medium-high heat; cook until sugar dissolves, stirring frequently. Continue cooking 4 minutes or until golden. Immediately pour into 6 (6-ounce) ramekins or custard cups coated with cooking spray, tilting each ramekin quickly until caramelized sugar coats bottom of cup.
3. Place eggs and egg white in a medium bowl; stir well with a whisk. Add milk and next 4 ingredients, stirring until well blended. Divide egg mixture evenly among prepared ramekins. Place ramekins in a 13 x 9–inch baking pan; add hot water to pan to a depth of 1 inch. Bake at 325° for 50 minutes or until a knife inserted in center comes out clean. Remove ramekins from pan. Cover and chill at least 4 hours.
4. Loosen edges of custards with a knife or rubber spatula. Place a dessert plate, upside down, on top of each ramekin; invert onto plate. Serve with Pineapple Concassé. Yield: 6 servings (serving size: 1 custard and ¼ cup Pineapple Concassé).

(Totals include Pineapple Concassé) CALORIES 239 (26% from fat); FAT 6.9g (sat 4.2g, mono 1.5g, poly 0.5g); PROTEIN 6.6g; CARB 38.5g; FIBER 0.9g; CHOL 111mg; IRON 0.7mg; SODIUM 132mg; CALC 99mg

Pineapple Concassé

1½ cups finely chopped pineapple
  1 tablespoon thinly sliced fresh basil
  1 teaspoon sugar
  1 teaspoon fresh lime juice

1. Combine all ingredients in a small bowl. Cover and chill at least 4 hours. Yield: 6 servings (serving size: ¼ cup).

CALORIES 22 (8% from fat); FAT 0.2g (sat 0g, mono 0g, poly 0.1g); PROTEIN 0.2g; CARB 5.6g; FIBER 0.5g; CHOL 0mg; IRON 0.2mg; SODIUM 0mg; CALC 3mg

Pumpkin-Praline Custards

Substituting soy milk for dairy milk in custards and puddings is a tasty way to increase beneficial soy protein in your diet. A crunchy topping of crumbled praline candy adds a festive touch to this homey dessert.

**Prep: 12 minutes • Cook: 54 minutes
Other: 3 hours**

Custards:
1½ cups vanilla soy milk
  ¾ cup canned pumpkin
  ⅔ cup sugar
1½ teaspoons ground cinnamon
  ½ teaspoon ground nutmeg
  ½ teaspoon vanilla extract
  ¼ teaspoon salt
  2 large eggs
  2 large egg whites
Cooking spray
Praline:
  ¼ cup sugar
  2 tablespoons water
  ¼ cup chopped pecans

1. Preheat oven to 325°.
2. To prepare custards, combine first 9 ingredients in a bowl; stir well with a whisk. Divide pumpkin mixture evenly among 6 (6-ounce) custard cups coated with cooking spray. Place cups in a 13 x 9–inch baking pan; add hot water to pan to a depth of 1 inch. Bake at 325° for 50 minutes or until a knife inserted in center

comes out clean. Remove cups from pan, and cool completely on a wire rack. Cover and chill at least 3 hours.

3. To prepare praline, combine ¼ cup sugar and water in a small skillet. Cook over medium-high heat 4 minutes or until golden, stirring occasionally. Remove from heat; stir in pecans. Immediately scrape pecan mixture onto a baking sheet coated with cooking spray, spreading evenly; cool completely. Break praline into small pieces. Sprinkle praline over custards. Yield: 6 servings (serving size: 1 custard and about 1 tablespoon praline).

CALORIES 220 (25% from fat); FAT 6.2g (sat 0.9g, mono 2.9g, poly 1.7g); PROTEIN 5.7g; CARB 37g; FIBER 1.7g; CHOL 71mg; IRON 1mg; SODIUM 235mg; CALC 101mg

Test Kitchen Tip: When you (carefully) tap the side of the ramekin, the custard should jiggle. If it ripples like water, it's not done; if it doesn't jiggle at all, has shrunk, or is beginning to crack, it's overcooked.

Angela's Flan

Flan is the Spanish version of crème caramel. We've reduced the fat by substituting low-fat milks for whole. And we've used a blender rather than a whisk to combine the egg and milk mixture.

**Prep: 11 minutes • Cook: 1 hour
Other: 8 hours**

    ½ cup sugar
    1 tablespoon water
    Cooking spray
    2 cups 2% reduced-fat milk
    1 tablespoon white rum
    ½ teaspoon vanilla extract
    ½ teaspoon almond extract
    ⅛ teaspoon ground cinnamon
    4 large eggs
    1 (14-ounce) can low-fat sweetened
       condensed milk

1. Preheat oven to 350°.
2. Combine sugar and water in a small, heavy saucepan, and cook over medium-high heat until sugar dissolves, stirring frequently. Continue cooking mixture 3 to 4 minutes or until golden. Immediately pour into 8 (6-ounce) custard cups coated with cooking spray, tilting each cup quickly until caramelized sugar coats bottom of cup.

3. Place 2% reduced-fat milk and remaining 6 ingredients in a blender; process until smooth. Divide mixture evenly among prepared custard cups. Place cups in bottom of a broiler pan; add hot water to pan to a depth of 1 inch. Bake at 350° for 55 minutes or until a knife inserted in center comes out clean. Remove cups from pan; cool completely on a wire rack. Cover and chill at least 8 hours.

4. Loosen edges of custards with a knife or rubber spatula. Place a dessert plate, upside down, on top of each cup, and invert custards onto plates. Drizzle any remaining caramelized syrup over each custard. Yield: 8 servings (serving size: 1 custard).

CALORIES 269 (19% from fat); FAT 5.6g (sat 2.7g, mono 1.7g, poly 0.4g); PROTEIN 9.1g; CARB 44.6g; FIBER 0g; CHOL 118mg; IRON 0.6mg; SODIUM 115mg; CALC 224mg

Angela's Flan

Dulce de Leche Flan

Dulce de leche is sweetened milk that's cooked down to a thick paste. Cooling the flan in a water bath helps it reach room temperature gradually, which reduces the chances of shrinking and cracking.

**Prep: 10 minutes • Cook: 1 hour, 33 minutes
Other: 3 hours**

>   1   (14-ounce) can fat-free sweetened
>   condensed milk
>   ½   cup sugar
>   ¼   cup water
>   Cooking spray
>   2   cups 2% reduced-fat milk
>   3   large eggs, lightly beaten
>   2   large egg whites, lightly beaten
>   ½   teaspoon vanilla extract

1. Preheat oven to 425°.
2. Pour condensed milk into a 1-quart baking dish; cover and place in bottom of a broiler pan. Add hot water to pan to a depth of 1 inch. Bake at 425° for 45 minutes or until milk is thick and caramel colored. Remove dish from pan; uncover and cool to room temperature.
3. Reduce oven temperature to 325°.
4. Combine sugar and ¼ cup water in a small, heavy saucepan, and cook over medium-high heat until sugar dissolves, stirring frequently. Continue cooking 5 minutes or until golden. Immediately pour into a 9-inch round cake pan coated with cooking spray, tipping quickly until caramelized sugar coats bottom of pan.
5. Spoon condensed milk into a large bowl. Add 2% milk, eggs, egg whites, and vanilla extract; stir with a whisk until well blended. Strain milk mixture through a fine sieve into prepared pan; discard solids.
6. Place cake pan in bottom of broiler pan; add hot water to broiler pan to a depth of 1 inch. Bake at 325° for 40 minutes or until a knife inserted in center comes out clean. Remove from oven, and cool flan to room temperature in water bath. Remove cake pan from water bath; cover and chill at least 3 hours or overnight.
7. Loosen edges of flan with a knife or rubber spatula. Place a plate, upside down, on top of cake pan; invert flan onto plate. Drizzle any remaining caramelized syrup over flan. Yield: 8 servings (serving size: 1 wedge).

CALORIES 250 (12% from fat); FAT 3.2g (sat 1.3g, mono 1.1g, poly 0.3g); PROTEIN 9.6g; CARB 45.7g; FIBER 0g; CHOL 88mg; IRON 0.3mg; SODIUM 120mg; CALC 223mg

---

All-Time Favorite
Espresso Crème Brûlée

Crème brûlée, French for "burned cream," is a custard with a sugar topping that's melted and caramelized. You can use either a small kitchen torch or the stovetop method (see techniques on facing page) to brown the sugar on top of the custards. Cold custards stand up well to the heat of the torch, so it's best to make the custards one to two days ahead, then top with sugar just before serving.

**Prep: 12 minutes • Cook: 25 minutes
Other: 4 hours, 30 minutes**

>   2   cups 2% reduced-fat milk
>   1   cup whole espresso coffee beans
>   ¾   cup nonfat dry milk
>   3   tablespoons sugar, divided
>   1   teaspoon vanilla extract
>   Dash of salt
>   4   large egg yolks, lightly beaten
>   ¼   cup sugar

1. Combine 2% milk, espresso beans, dry milk, and 2 tablespoons sugar in a medium saucepan. Heat over medium heat to 180° or until tiny bubbles form around edge (do not boil), stirring occasionally. Remove from heat. Cover and steep 30 minutes.
2. Preheat oven to 300°.
3. Strain milk mixture through a sieve into a bowl; discard solids. Stir in vanilla.
4. Combine 1 tablespoon sugar, salt, and egg yolks in a medium bowl, stirring well with a whisk.
5. Gradually add milk mixture to egg mixture, stirring constantly with a whisk. Divide mixture evenly among 4 (4-ounce) ramekins, custard cups, or shallow baking dishes. Place ramekins in a 13 x 9–inch baking pan, and add hot water to pan to a depth of 1 inch.
6. Bake at 300° for 25 minutes or until center barely moves when ramekin is touched. Remove ramekins from pan; cool completely on a wire rack. Cover and chill at least 4 hours or overnight.
7. Sift 1 tablespoon sugar evenly over each custard. Holding a kitchen blow torch about 2 inches from top of each custard, heat sugar, moving torch back and forth, until sugar is completely melted and caramelized (about 1 minute). Serve immediately or within 1 hour. Yield: 4 servings (serving size: 1 custard).

CALORIES 262 (26% from fat); FAT 7.7g (sat 3.2g, mono 2.7g, poly 0.7g); PROTEIN 11.3g; CARB 36g; FIBER 0g; CHOL 225mg; IRON 0.6mg; SODIUM 215mg; CALC 315mg

Test Kitchen Tip: If your supermarket doesn't have whole espresso beans, you can get them at a coffee shop.

Serve crème brûlée within an hour of caramelizing the sugar or the hard sugar shells will start to melt into the custards.

how to brûlée

using a kitchen torch

1. Carefully sift the sugar, using a small sieve, over each custard. This disperses the sugar evenly.

2. Torch the sugar immediately after it's sifted onto custards or it will start to dissolve. Hold the torch about 2 inches away and work from side to side until all the sugar is melted and caramelized.

using the stovetop

1. In a small saucepan or skillet, cook the sugar over medium heat until golden (about 5 to 8 minutes). Resist the urge to stir because doing so will allow the sugar to crystallize.

2. Working quickly, evenly pour sugar topping over cold custards. Using a rubber spatula coated with cooking spray, spread caramel evenly to form a thin layer. Work quickly because the caramel hardens quickly.

kitchen blow torch

Some recipes are worth the investment in special equipment. Case in point: brûlées. For caramelizing the custard's delicate sugar crust, a torch is an indispensable tool. There are two types— industrial propane torches and smaller butane-powered torches—and both come with simple, safe, single-click lighting mechanisms. "If you already have a propane torch, there's no need to consider a kitchen torch," says *Cooking Light* Test Kitchens Staffer Kathryn Conrad. But if you don't, she recommends the kitchen variety. "It's lighter and has a smaller flame." In addition to finishing crème brûlée, use your torch to brown meringues, toast marshmallows, and blister peppers.

Vanilla Bean Crème Brûlée

Melt the sugar topping in the microwave oven, and pour it evenly over each chilled custard. Vanilla beans, found in the spice section at the supermarket, are worth the extra expense. Nonfat dry milk thickens the custard.

Prep: 11 minutes • Cook: 1 hour, 5 minutes Other: 4 hours

    4   large egg yolks
    1   teaspoon granulated sugar
  ⅛   teaspoon salt
    2   cups 2% reduced-fat milk
    1   (3-inch) piece vanilla bean, split
        lengthwise, or 1 teaspoon vanilla
        extract
    3   tablespoons granulated sugar
  ¾   cup nonfat dry milk
  ¼   cup packed light brown sugar
1½   teaspoons water

1. Preheat oven to 300°.
2. Combine first 3 ingredients in a medium bowl; stir well with a whisk. Set aside.
3. Pour 2% milk into a medium saucepan. Scrape seeds from vanilla bean; add seeds, bean, 3 tablespoons granulated sugar, and dry milk to pan. Heat over medium heat to 180° or until tiny bubbles form around edge (do not boil), stirring occasionally with a whisk. Discard bean.
4. Gradually add hot milk mixture to egg mixture, stirring constantly with a whisk. Divide milk mixture evenly among 6 (4-ounce) ramekins or custard cups. Place ramekins in a 13 x 9–inch baking pan; add hot water to pan to a depth of 1 inch. Bake at 300° for 1 hour or until center barely moves when ramekin is touched. Remove ramekins from pan; cool completely on a wire rack. Cover and chill at least 4 hours or overnight.

5. Combine brown sugar and water in a 1-cup glass measure. Microwave at HIGH 30 seconds; stir until sugar dissolves. Microwave at HIGH 20 seconds or until golden; pour evenly over each dessert, quickly tipping ramekins to coat tops of brûlées (there will be a thin layer of melted sugar). Let sugar mixture harden. Yield: 6 servings (serving size: 1 custard).

CALORIES 185 (25% from fat); FAT 5.2g (sat 2.1g, mono 1.8g, poly 0.5g); PROTEIN 10g; CARB 24.7g; FIBER 0g; CHOL 155mg; IRON 0.6mg; SODIUM 177mg; CALC 309mg

Test Kitchen Tip: Since you use only the yolks of the four eggs in the brûlée, save the whites to use in the Brown Sugar Pavlovas with Fruit on page 200. To store individual egg whites, drop one white in each section of an ice cube tray and freeze. Remove egg white cubes and store in a heavy-duty zip-top bag.

Rum Crème Brûlée

This brûlée may remind you of traditional eggnog—the kind with a splash of whiskey.

Prep: 12 minutes • Cook: 56 minutes Other: 4 hours

    1   cup evaporated fat-free milk
    1   cup 2% reduced-fat milk
  ⅔   cup nonfat dry milk
  ¼   cup sugar
    1   teaspoon sugar
  ⅛   teaspoon salt
    5   large egg yolks
1½   tablespoons dark rum
    3   tablespoons sugar

1. Preheat oven to 300°.
2. Combine first 4 ingredients in a medium, heavy saucepan. Heat mixture

over medium heat to 180° or until tiny bubbles form around edge (do not boil), stirring occasionally. Remove from heat.
3. Combine 1 teaspoon sugar, salt, and egg yolks in a medium bowl, stirring well with a whisk. Gradually add hot milk mixture to egg mixture, stirring constantly with a whisk. Stir in rum.
4. Divide milk mixture evenly among 6 (4-ounce) ramekins or custard cups. Place ramekins in a 13 x 9–inch baking pan; add hot water to pan to a depth of 1 inch. Bake at 300° for 50 minutes or until center barely moves when ramekin is touched. Remove ramekins from pan; cool completely on a wire rack. Cover and chill 4 hours or overnight.
5. Sift 1½ teaspoons sugar evenly over each custard. Holding a kitchen blow torch about 2 inches from the top of each custard, heat sugar, moving back and forth, until sugar is completely caramelized (about 1 minute). Serve immediately or within 1 hour. Yield: 6 servings (serving size: 1 custard).

CALORIES 197 (24% from fat); FAT 5.2g (sat 1.9g, mono 1.9g, poly 0.6g); PROTEIN 9.6g; CARB 26.3g; FIBER 0g; CHOL 183mg; IRON 0.7mg; SODIUM 166mg; CALC 285mg

Test Kitchen Tip: A water bath (or *bain marie*) is the process of cooking delicate foods, such as custards, in a shallow pan of hot water. It insulates and protects custards from the oven heat so they cook slowly and evenly. The depth of the water should be half the height of the custard container. If you're baking multiple custards, the pan must be large enough so that the individual containers don't touch. A 13 x 9–inch baking pan is a good size.

Puddings, Soufflés & Chilled Desserts
From flavorful puddings to elegant soufflés, you'll find a dessert to suit every occasion.

Chocolate Espresso Pudding

Packed with decadent chocolate richness, this dessert is also high in health-promoting isoflavones because of the soy milk.

Prep: 7 minutes • Cook: 5 minutes
Other: 4 hours

- ½ cup packed brown sugar
- ¼ cup cornstarch
- 3 tablespoons unsweetened cocoa
- 1 tablespoon instant coffee granules
- ⅛ teaspoon salt
- 2 cups fat-free soy milk
- 2 ounces bittersweet chocolate, chopped
- 1 teaspoon vanilla extract

1. Combine first 5 ingredients in a medium, heavy saucepan, and stir well with a whisk. Gradually stir in milk, and bring to a boil over medium heat. Reduce heat, and simmer 1 minute or until thick.
2. Remove from heat, and add chocolate, stirring until melted. Stir in vanilla. Pour about ½ cup pudding into each of 4 dessert dishes; cover surface of pudding with plastic wrap. Chill at least 4 hours. Remove plastic wrap to serve. Yield: 4 servings (serving size: 1 pudding).

CALORIES 281 (15% from fat); FAT 4.8g (sat 2.8g, mono 1.6g, poly 0.1g); PROTEIN 5.5g; CARB 56.2g; FIBER 0.6g; CHOL 0mg; IRON 2mg; SODIUM 134mg; CALC 237mg

Test Kitchen Tip: Look for soy milk in the organic or soy product section of your supermarket. It's usually sold in non-refrigerated quart and 8-ounce cartons, but you can also find it refrigerated in plastic containers near other refrigerated dairy products. Store unopened soy milk at room temperature for several months; once opened, store in the refrigerator for five days.

Bittersweet Chocolate Pudding

Adding cornstarch to this pudding lessens the possibility of its curdling. To prevent the custard from tipping and taking on ice water, make sure the bowl you use for the ice bath is only slightly larger than the custard bowl.

Prep: 8 minutes • Cook: 13 minutes
Other: 15 minutes

½ cup granulated sugar
⅓ cup unsweetened cocoa
3 tablespoons cornstarch
3 tablespoons dark brown sugar
⅛ teaspoon salt
4 cups 2% reduced-fat milk
3 large egg yolks, lightly beaten
2 ounces bittersweet chocolate, chopped
1 teaspoon vanilla extract

1. Combine first 5 ingredients in a large saucepan. Gradually add milk, stirring with a whisk. Bring to a boil over medium heat, stirring constantly. Cook 1 minute, stirring constantly.
2. Place egg yolks in a bowl. Gradually add hot milk mixture to egg yolks, stirring constantly. Return milk mixture to pan. Cook over medium heat 5 minutes or until thick, stirring constantly. Remove from heat, and add chopped chocolate and vanilla extract, stirring until chocolate melts. Spoon pudding into a small bowl. Place bowl in a large ice-filled bowl for 15 minutes or until pudding is cool, stirring occasionally. Remove bowl from ice; cover surface of pudding with plastic wrap and chill. Yield: 6 servings (serving size: ¾ cup).

CALORIES 282 (30% from fat); FAT 9.5g (sat 5.1g, mono 2.4g, poly 0.5g); PROTEIN 8.4g; CARB 43g; FIBER 2.4g; CHOL 119mg; IRON 1.2mg; SODIUM 138mg; CALC 222mg

Rich Butterscotch Pudding

With three egg yolks, butter, and a generous amount of brown sugar, this is the Rolls-Royce of butterscotch puddings.

Prep: 7 minutes • Cook: 10 minutes
Other: 3 hours

2 tablespoons butter
1 cup evaporated fat-free milk, divided
¾ cup packed dark brown sugar
2 cups 1% low-fat milk
3 tablespoons cornstarch
⅛ teaspoon salt
3 large egg yolks
1½ teaspoons vanilla extract

1. Melt butter in a 3-quart heavy saucepan over medium heat. Add ¼ cup evaporated milk and brown sugar, stirring constantly; cook 2 minutes. Bring mixture to a boil, and cook 30 seconds. Remove pan from heat.
2. Heat 1% milk over medium-high heat in a heavy saucepan to 180° or until tiny bubbles form around edge (do not boil). Remove from heat.
3. Combine ¾ cup evaporated milk, cornstarch, salt, and egg yolks in a medium bowl; stir well with a whisk. Gradually add hot milk, stirring constantly. Stir hot milk mixture into brown sugar mixture. Cook over medium heat until mixture comes to a boil, stirring constantly; cook 1 minute. Remove from heat; stir in vanilla.
4. Spoon ½ cup pudding into each of 6 (6-ounce) ramekins. Cover surface of pudding with plastic wrap; chill 3 hours or until pudding is set. Yield: 6 servings (serving size: 1 pudding).

CALORIES 254 (26% from fat); FAT 7.4g (sat 3.8g, mono 2.4g, poly 0.5g); PROTEIN 7.4g; CARB 39.4g; FIBER 0g; CHOL 124mg; IRON 1mg; SODIUM 192mg; CALC 260mg

Rice Pudding with Pomegranate Syrup

See the technique shots for seeding a pomegranate on page 467.

Prep: 11 minutes • Cook: 65 minutes

3½ cups 2% reduced-fat milk, divided
½ cup uncooked Arborio rice or other short-grain rice
⅓ cup sugar
1 tablespoon butter
1 large egg
1 teaspoon vanilla extract
2 large pomegranates, halved crosswise
¼ cup sugar
6 tablespoons pomegranate seeds

1. Combine 3 cups milk, rice, ⅓ cup sugar, and butter in a medium saucepan; bring to a boil. Reduce heat, and simmer, uncovered, 10 minutes, stirring occasionally. Remove from heat.
2. Combine ½ cup milk and egg; stir with a whisk. Stir about one-fourth of warm rice mixture into egg mixture; add to pan, stirring constantly. Simmer, uncovered, 30 minutes or until rice is tender, stirring occasionally. Remove from heat; stir in vanilla.
3. Reserving 6 tablespoons seeds, squeeze juice from pomegranate halves using a juicer to measure 1 cup. Combine juice and ¼ cup sugar in a small saucepan, and bring to a boil. Reduce heat; simmer mixture until reduced to ⅓ cup (about 20 minutes), stirring frequently.
4. Drizzle syrup over pudding; sprinkle with seeds. Yield: 6 servings (serving size: ½ cup pudding, about 1 tablespoon syrup, and 1 tablespoon seeds).

CALORIES 296 (18% from fat); FAT 5.9g (sat 3.2g, mono 1.8g, poly 0.2g); PROTEIN 7.7g; CARB 53.1g; FIBER 0.7g; CHOL 52mg; IRON 0.5mg; SODIUM 131mg; CALC 171mg

Classic Makeover: Banana Pudding

We reduced the fat in a traditional banana pudding by 66 percent by making a few simple changes. First, we replaced the whole milk with 2% reduced-fat milk. Using 2% milk instead of fat-free keeps the pudding luscious and creamy. Then we replaced some of the whole eggs with egg whites because most of the fat in eggs is in the yolks. Although using a vanilla bean instead of extract doesn't affect the fat or calories, we think it contributes to the superb rich flavor of the pudding.

Before	After
• 559 calories	• 289 calories
• 15g fat	• 5.1g fat
• percentage of calories from fat 24%	• percentage of calories from fat 16%
• 92mg cholesterol	• 33mg cholesterol

Banana Pudding

We've lightened the ultimate comfort food.

Prep: 20 minutes • Cook: 34 minutes

⅔ cup all-purpose flour
2 cups sugar, divided
½ teaspoon salt
4 cups 2% reduced-fat milk
1 (4-inch) vanilla bean, split lengthwise
2 large eggs, lightly beaten
4 large egg whites
80 vanilla wafers (about 1 box)
5 cups sliced banana (about 6 bananas)

1. Preheat oven to 325°.
2. Lightly spoon flour into dry measuring cups; level with a knife. Combine flour, 1¼ cups sugar, and salt in a large saucepan, stirring with a whisk. Gradually add milk, stirring until smooth. Scrape seeds from vanilla bean; add to milk mixture. Cook over medium heat 12 minutes or until thick and bubbly, stirring constantly.
3. Place eggs in a large bowl; gradually add hot milk mixture, stirring constantly. Pour mixture in pan; cook over medium heat 2 minutes or until thick and bubbly, stirring constantly. Discard vanilla bean.
4. Place egg whites in a large bowl; beat with a mixer at high speed until egg whites are foamy. Add ¾ cup sugar, 1 tablespoon at a time, beating until stiff peaks form.
5. Arrange 33 vanilla wafers in bottom of a 3-quart round baking dish. Arrange half of banana over wafers. Pour half of custard over banana. Repeat with 33 vanilla wafers, banana, and custard. Top with meringue. Arrange remaining vanilla wafers around edge of meringue.
6. Bake at 325° for 20 minutes or until lightly browned. Serve pudding warm or chilled. Yield: 16 servings (serving size: ¾ cup).

CALORIES 289 (16% from fat); FAT 5.1g (sat 1.6g, mono 1.5g, poly 0.2g); PROTEIN 6.1g; CARB 57.1g; FIBER 1.2g; CHOL 33mg; IRON 1.2mg; SODIUM 202mg; CALC 94mg

Creamy Apple-Amaretto Rice Pudding

Apples are cooked down to a sauce that's then stirred into the rice pudding. Arborio rice, used for risotto, contributes to the creaminess.

**Prep: 10 minutes • Cook: 1 hour, 12 minutes
Other: 8 hours**

  3 McIntosh, Jonathan, or Winesap apples, peeled and cut into quarters (about 1 pound)
  ¼ cup apple cider
  5 cups 2% reduced-fat milk
  ¾ cup sugar
  ⅛ teaspoon salt
  ¾ cup uncooked Arborio rice or other short-grain rice
  ⅛ teaspoon ground nutmeg
  2 tablespoons amaretto
  1 teaspoon vanilla extract
  2 large eggs

1. Combine apple and cider in a medium, heavy saucepan. Bring to a boil, stirring frequently. Cover, reduce heat to medium, and cook 20 minutes or until apple is very soft. Spoon apple mixture into a small bowl; cool.
2. Combine milk, sugar, and salt in pan; bring to a simmer. Add rice and nutmeg; stir well. Reduce heat; simmer 40 minutes or until rice is tender, stirring occasionally. Place apple mixture, amaretto, vanilla, and eggs in a blender or food processor; process until smooth. Stir egg mixture into rice mixture; cook until thick (about 5 minutes), stirring constantly (do not boil). Spoon rice mixture into a large bowl. Cover; chill 8 hours. Yield: 8 servings (serving size: ¾ cup).

CALORIES 276 (15% from fat); FAT 4.5g (sat 2.1g, mono 1.3g, poly 0.4g); PROTEIN 8g; CARB 51.3g; FIBER 1.2g; CHOL 68mg; IRON 1.1mg; SODIUM 129mg; CALC 196mg

Baked Spelt Pudding

This dish is a rustic take on baked rice pudding. The long stint in the oven (3½ hours) gives the pudding a rich, creamy texture.

**Prep: 10 minutes • Cook: 3 hours, 35 minutes
Other: 1 hour, 5 minutes**

  ½ cup uncooked spelt (farro), rinsed and drained
  4 cups 2% reduced-fat milk
  ½ cup sugar
  ¼ teaspoon salt
  ⅛ teaspoon ground cardamom
  1 vanilla bean, split lengthwise
     Cooking spray
     Dash of ground cinnamon

1. Place spelt in a medium saucepan. Cover with water to 2 inches above spelt; bring to a boil. Cook 2 minutes; remove from heat. Cover; let stand 1 hour. Drain. Place spelt in a food processor; process 45 seconds or until spelt resembles coarse meal.
2. Preheat oven to 275°.
3. Combine spelt, milk, sugar, salt, cardamom, and vanilla bean in a 2-quart casserole coated with cooking spray. Bake at 275° for 3½ hours, stirring every hour to prevent a skin from forming. Remove vanilla bean. Let stand 5 minutes. Sprinkle with cinnamon. Serve warm or chilled. Yield: 6 servings (serving size: ⅔ cup).

CALORIES 211 (17% from fat); FAT 3.9g (sat 2g, mono 1g, poly 0g); PROTEIN 7.4g; CARB 39g; FIBER 2.6g; CHOL 13mg; IRON 0.8mg; SODIUM 185mg; CALC 185mg

spelt Also known as farro, spelt is an ancient grain that's making a comeback because of its nutty flavor and health benefits. Look for spelt at health food stores or in either the grains or organic section of the supermarket.

Toasted-Coconut Tapioca Pudding

Traditional tapioca pudding employs starchy tapioca pearls for thickening. In this old-fashioned dessert, the pearls partially dissolve, but leave tiny bubbles surrounded by creamy pudding. The somewhat flavorless tapioca provides a background for the sweet coconut flavor.

**Prep: 7 minutes • Cook: 3 minutes
Other: 5 minutes**

  ¾ cup light coconut milk
  ¾ cup fat-free milk
  3 tablespoons sugar
  4 teaspoons uncooked quick-cooking tapioca
  2 tablespoons egg substitute
     Dash of salt
  ¼ teaspoon vanilla extract
  2 tablespoons flaked sweetened coconut, toasted

1. Combine first 6 ingredients in a medium saucepan, and let stand 5 minutes.
2. Bring mixture to a boil over medium-high heat, stirring constantly. Remove from heat, and stir in vanilla. Divide mixture evenly between 2 dessert bowls. Cover and chill until thick.
3. Sprinkle pudding with toasted coconut. Yield: 2 servings (serving size: 1 pudding and 1 tablespoon coconut).

CALORIES 222 (28% from fat); FAT 6.9g (sat 6g, mono 0.3g, poly 0.1g); PROTEIN 4.8g; CARB 35g; FIBER 0.3g; CHOL 2mg; IRON 1mg; SODIUM 194mg; CALC 120mg

Test Kitchen Tip: A 14-ounce can of light coconut milk contains about 2 cups. Transfer the remaining coconut milk into an airtight container, and store in the refrigerator up to three days.

Chocolate Chunk Bread Puddings

Hawaiian bread is a soft, sweet bread found in the bakery section of most grocery stores. This recipe is easily doubled if you want to serve more than two.

Prep: 8 minutes • Cook: 40 minutes • Other: 30 minutes

1¾ cups (½-inch) cubed Hawaiian
     sweet bread
⅔ cup 2% reduced-fat milk
2 tablespoons sugar
1½ tablespoons unsweetened cocoa
1 tablespoon Kahlúa (coffee-flavored
     liqueur)
½ teaspoon vanilla extract
1 large egg, lightly beaten
Cooking spray
1 ounce semisweet chocolate, chopped
2 tablespoons frozen fat-free whipped
     topping, thawed

1. Preheat oven to 350°.
2. Arrange bread cubes in a single layer on a baking sheet. Bake at 350° for 5 minutes or until toasted.
3. Combine milk and next 5 ingredients in a bowl; stir well with a whisk. Add bread, tossing gently to coat. Cover; chill 30 minutes or up to 4 hours.
4. Preheat oven to 325°.
5. Divide half of bread mixture evenly between 2 (6-ounce) ramekins or custard cups coated with cooking spray; sprinkle evenly with half of chocolate. Divide remaining bread mixture between ramekins; top with remaining chocolate.
6. Place ramekins in an 8-inch square baking pan; add hot water to pan to a depth of 1 inch. Bake at 325° for 35 minutes or until set. Serve warm with whipped topping. Yield: 2 servings (serving size: 1 pudding and 1 tablespoon whipped topping).

CALORIES 319 (30% from fat); FAT 10.6g (sat 5.2g, mono 3.6g, poly 0.8g); PROTEIN 9.8g; CARB 45.3g; FIBER 2.1g; CHOL 121mg; IRON 1.8mg; SODIUM 141mg; CALC 125mg

Test Kitchen Tip: Instead of Kahlúa, you can use 1 tablespoon of strong brewed coffee and ½ teaspoon sugar.

Mexican Bread Pudding

Unlike bread puddings with custard bases, a Mexican bread pudding typically features layers of nuts, cheese, dried fruit, and bread drizzled with cinnamon-infused sugar syrup. And because there's no custard, there's no need for a water bath.

**Prep: 10 minutes • Cook: 48 minutes
Other: 30 minutes**

1¼ cups packed dark brown sugar
1¼ cups water
2 (3-inch) cinnamon sticks
4½ cups (½-inch) cubed French bread
     (about 8 ounces)
¼ cup golden raisins
¼ cup slivered almonds, toasted
2 tablespoons butter, cut into small
     pieces
Cooking spray
¾ cup (3 ounces) shredded Monterey
     Jack cheese

1. Combine first 3 ingredients in a medium saucepan; bring to a boil. Reduce heat; simmer 10 minutes. Discard cinnamon sticks.
2. Combine bread, raisins, almonds, and butter in a large bowl. Drizzle with warm sugar syrup, tossing gently to coat. Spoon mixture into an 8-inch square baking dish coated with cooking spray. Top with cheese. Cover with foil; chill 30 minutes or up to 4 hours.
3. Preheat oven to 350°.
4. Bake at 350° for 20 minutes. Uncover and bake an additional 15 minutes or until cheese is golden brown. Serve warm. Yield: 8 servings (serving size: 1 square).

CALORIES 313 (27% from fat); FAT 9.3g (sat 4.4g, mono 3.6g, poly 0.9g); PROTEIN 5.8g; CARB 52.6g; FIBER 1.4g; CHOL 19mg; IRON 1.6mg; SODIUM 289mg; CALC 140mg

Irish Bread Pudding with Caramel-Whiskey Sauce

We couldn't imagine a more fitting nod to St. Patrick's Day than Irish Bread Pudding with Caramel-Whiskey Sauce. Its whiskey-soaked raisins, hint of cinnamon, and decadent caramel sauce make it one of our favorites.

Prep: 12 minutes • Cook: 1 hour, 5 minutes • Other: 15 minutes

¼ cup light butter, melted
1 (10-ounce) French bread baguette, cut into 1-inch-thick slices
½ cup raisins
¼ cup Irish whiskey
1¾ cups 1% low-fat milk
1 cup sugar
1 tablespoon vanilla extract
1 (12-ounce) can evaporated fat-free milk
2 large eggs, lightly beaten
Cooking spray
1 tablespoon sugar
1 teaspoon ground cinnamon
Caramel-Whiskey Sauce

1. Preheat oven to 350°.
2. Brush melted butter on one side of French bread slices; place bread, buttered sides up, on a baking sheet. Bake at 350° for 10 minutes or until lightly toasted. Cut bread into ½-inch cubes; set aside.
3. While bread is toasting, combine raisins and whiskey in a small bowl; cover and let stand 10 minutes or until soft (do not drain).

4. Combine 1% milk and next 4 ingredients in a large bowl; stir well with a whisk. Add bread cubes and raisin mixture, pressing gently to moisten; let stand 15 minutes. Spoon bread mixture into a 13 x 9–inch baking dish coated with cooking spray. Combine 1 tablespoon sugar and cinnamon, and sprinkle over pudding. Bake at 350° for 35 minutes or until pudding is set. Serve warm with Caramel-Whiskey Sauce. Yield: 12 servings (serving size: 1 [3-inch] square and 2 tablespoons sauce).

(Totals include Caramel-Whiskey Sauce) CALORIES 360 (18% from fat); FAT 7.3g (sat 3.2g, mono 1.9g, poly 0.5g); PROTEIN 7.3g; CARB 65.9g; FIBER 1g; CHOL 57mg; IRON 1.1mg; SODIUM 275mg; CALC 164mg

Test Kitchen Tip: Instead of Irish whiskey, you can substitute ¼ cup apple juice for the Irish whiskey in the pudding and 1 tablespoon imitation rum extract and 3 tablespoons water for the whiskey in the sauce.

Caramel-Whiskey Sauce

1½ cups sugar
⅔ cup water
¼ cup light butter
¼ cup (2 ounces) ⅓-less-fat cream cheese
¼ cup Irish whiskey
¼ cup 1% low-fat milk

1. Combine sugar and water in a small, heavy saucepan over medium-high heat; cook until sugar dissolves, stirring constantly. Cook 15 minutes or until golden (do not stir). Remove from heat. Carefully add butter and cream cheese, stirring constantly with a whisk (mixture will be hot and bubble vigorously). Cool slightly, and stir in whiskey and milk. Yield: 1½ cups (serving size: 2 tablespoons).

CALORIES 138 (22% from fat); FAT 3.3g (sat 1.3g, mono 0.6g, poly 0.1g); PROTEIN 0.6g; CARB 25.9g; FIBER 0g; CHOL 11mg; IRON 0mg; SODIUM 45mg; CALC 11mg

Mincemeat Charlottes

A charlotte is a classic molded dessert lined with spongecake, ladyfingers, or buttered bread and filled with fruit or custard. Instead of one large mold, this one features individual servings. You can substitute apple juice for cognac.

Prep: 20 minutes • Cook: 30 minutes
Other: 5 minutes

  1 (9-ounce) package condensed
      mincemeat (such as Borden's)
Cooking spray
  1 tablespoon sugar
24 slices very thin white bread, divided
  1 cup chopped peeled apple
¼ cup butter, melted
¼ cup cognac

1. Preheat oven to 350°.
2. Reconstitute mincemeat according to package directions to yield 2 cups. Lightly coat 8 (6-ounce) ramekins with cooking spray; evenly dust ramekins with sugar.
3. Place 16 bread slices on a cutting board or work surface. Cut 16 bread circles with a 2-inch round cutter; discard bread trimmings. Place 1 circle in bottom of each ramekin; reserve remaining circles.
4. Trim crusts from 8 bread slices. Cut each slice into 3 (3 x 1–inch) rectangles; cut each in half to produce 6 (1½ x 1–inch) rectangles. Line sides of each ramekin with 6 rectangles, arranged vertically, side by side. Press rectangles gently to fit.
5. Combine mincemeat, apple, butter, and cognac. Place ⅓ cup mincemeat mixture in each ramekin; top each with 1 remaining bread circle, pressing circles gently onto mincemeat filling. Place ramekins on a baking sheet. Bake at 350° for 30 minutes or until golden. Remove from oven; cool on baking sheet 5 minutes. Place a dessert plate, upside down, on top of each ramekin; invert onto plates. Serve warm. Yield: 8 servings (serving size: 1 charlotte).

CALORIES 303 (23% from fat); FAT 7.7g (sat 3.6g, mono 2.2g, poly 1.2g); PROTEIN 4.1g; CARB 53.6g; FIBER 2.3g; CHOL 16mg; IRON 1.4mg; SODIUM 499mg; CALC 57mg

cooking with liqueurs The liqueur in a recipe should complement the flavors with which it's being combined and not overwhelm the dish. We recommend using a less expensive brand of liqueur when the alcohol will be cooked and premium brands when the liqueur is added after cooking. If you don't want to use liqueurs, see the alcohol substitution chart on page 546.

Double-Lemon Soufflés

The double dose of tangy lemon comes from fresh lemon (the rind and the juice) and lemon curd—a creamy cooked mixture of lemon juice, sugar, butter, and egg yolks.

Prep: 30 minutes • Cook: 38 minutes
Other: 25 minutes

Cooking spray
  2 tablespoons granulated sugar
¼ cup all-purpose flour
1½ cups 2% reduced-fat milk
1½ teaspoons grated lemon rind
⅓ cup fresh lemon juice
¼ cup granulated sugar
  3 large egg yolks
  5 large egg whites
¼ teaspoon cream of tartar
Dash of salt
⅓ cup granulated sugar
½ cup Lemon Curd (page 460)
⅓ cup powdered sugar

1. Coat 8 (6-ounce) ramekins or custard cups with cooking spray; sprinkle with 2 tablespoons granulated sugar. Place prepared ramekins on a baking sheet.
2. Lightly spoon flour into a dry measuring cup, and level with a knife. Place flour in a small saucepan. Gradually add milk, stirring with a whisk until well blended. Stir in lemon rind, lemon juice, and ¼ cup granulated sugar. Cook lemon mixture over medium heat until thick and bubbly (about 5 minutes), stirring constantly. Gradually add hot lemon mixture to egg yolks, stirring constantly with a whisk. Return milk mixture to pan, and cook over medium heat until thick (about 3 minutes), stirring constantly. Remove from heat. Place pan in a large ice-filled bowl 25 minutes or until custard comes to room temperature, stirring occasionally.
3. Preheat oven to 400°.
4. Beat egg whites, cream of tartar, and salt with a mixer at high speed until soft peaks form. Gradually add ⅓ cup granulated sugar, 1 tablespoon at a time, beating egg white mixture until stiff peaks form. Gently fold one-fourth of egg white mixture into lemon mixture; gently fold in remaining egg white mixture. Spoon mixture into prepared ramekins.
5. Bake at 400° for 20 minutes or until soufflés are puffy and set. Heat Lemon Curd in a small saucepan over low heat until warm. Spoon Lemon Curd over soufflés, and sprinkle with powdered sugar. Serve immediately. Yield: 8 servings (serving size: 1 soufflé, 1 tablespoon Lemon Curd, and 2 teaspoons powdered sugar).

(Totals include Lemon Curd) CALORIES 209 (20% from fat); FAT 4.6g (sat 2g, mono 1.5g, poly 0.5g); PROTEIN 5.8g; CARB 37.1g; FIBER 0.1g; CHOL 109mg; IRON 0.6mg; SODIUM 101mg; CALC 72mg

Grand Marnier Soufflé with Vanilla Sauce

Top this ethereally light soufflé, which is delicately flavored with orange liqueur, with a silky vanilla custard sauce. Using whole milk in the sauce adds extra body and richness, but for the soufflé, reduced-fat is fine.

Prep: 25 minutes • Cook: 45 minutes

Vanilla Sauce:
- 2   large egg yolks, lightly beaten
- 1   cup whole milk
- 2½   tablespoons sugar
- 1   teaspoon vanilla extract
- Dash of salt

Soufflé:
- Cooking spray
- 1   tablespoon sugar
- 3   large egg yolks, lightly beaten
- 3   tablespoons all-purpose flour
- ⅔   cup 2% reduced-fat milk
- ¼   cup sugar
- 1   tablespoon butter
- 3   tablespoons Grand Marnier (orange-flavored liqueur)
- 2   teaspoons vanilla extract
- 5   large egg whites
- ½   teaspoon cream of tartar
- ⅛   teaspoon salt
- 2   tablespoons sugar

1. Place 2 egg yolks in a bowl. Combine whole milk and 2½ tablespoons sugar in a small, heavy saucepan over medium heat; cook to 180° or until tiny bubbles form around edge (do not boil). Gradually add hot milk mixture to 2 egg yolks, stirring constantly with a whisk. Return mixture to pan; cook over medium heat until thick and bubbly (about 3 minutes), stirring constantly. Remove from heat. Stir in 1 teaspoon vanilla and dash of salt. Pour into a glass bowl; cover and chill.

2. Preheat oven to 375°.

3. Coat a 1½-quart soufflé dish with cooking spray; sprinkle with 1 tablespoon sugar.

4. Place 3 egg yolks in a bowl; set aside. Place flour in a small, heavy saucepan; gradually add 2% milk, stirring with a whisk. Stir in ¼ cup sugar; add butter. Cook over medium heat until thick (about 5 minutes), stirring constantly. Gradually add hot milk mixture to 3 egg yolks, stirring constantly with a whisk. Return mixture to pan; cook over medium heat until thick and bubbly (about 3 minutes), stirring constantly. Stir in liqueur and 2 teaspoons vanilla; cook 1 minute, stirring constantly. Remove from heat.

5. Place egg whites, cream of tartar, and ⅛ teaspoon salt in a large bowl; beat with a mixer at high speed until soft peaks form. Add 2 tablespoons sugar, 1 tablespoon at a time, beating until stiff peaks form. Gently stir one-fourth of egg white mixture into warm milk mixture; fold in remaining egg white mixture.

6. Spoon into soufflé dish. Place soufflé dish in a 9-inch square baking pan; add hot water to pan to a depth of 1 inch. Bake at 375° for 30 minutes or until puffy and set. Serve immediately with sauce. Yield: 6 servings (serving size: ⅙ of soufflé and 3 tablespoons sauce).

CALORIES 242 (30% from fat); FAT 8.1g (sat 3.7g, mono 2.7g, poly 0.8g); PROTEIN 7.9g; CARB 30g; FIBER 0.1g; CHOL 190mg; IRON 0.7mg; SODIUM 179mg; CALC 104mg

how to beat and fold in egg whites

1. When you beat egg whites to form soft peaks, they will maintain a glossy appearance. The texture of the egg whites is only slightly stiff. Next, you gradually add sugar and beat until stiff peaks form. (See page 149.)

2. Using a wide rubber spatula, gently fold egg whites into the milk mixture by making a scooping motion from the bottom of the bowl to the top. This prevents the egg whites from deflating.

Bittersweet Chocolate Soufflés

These chocolaty soufflés garnered our Test Kitchens' highest rating.

Prep: 20 minutes • Cook: 20 minutes • Other: 3 minutes

Cooking spray
- 2 tablespoons granulated sugar
- ¾ cup granulated sugar, divided
- ½ cup Dutch process cocoa
- 2 tablespoons all-purpose flour
- ⅛ teaspoon salt
- ½ cup 1% low-fat milk
- 1 teaspoon vanilla extract
- 2 large egg yolks
- 4 large egg whites
- ⅛ teaspoon cream of tartar
- 3 ounces bittersweet chocolate, finely chopped
- 1 tablespoon powdered sugar

1. Preheat oven to 350°.

2. Coat 8 (4-ounce) ramekins with cooking spray, and sprinkle evenly with 2 tablespoons granulated sugar. Place ramekins on a baking sheet.

3. Combine ½ cup granulated sugar, cocoa, flour, and salt in a small saucepan. Gradually add milk, stirring with a whisk until blended. Bring to a boil over medium heat; cook until thick (about 3 minutes), stirring constantly. Remove from heat; let stand 3 minutes. Gradually stir in vanilla and egg yolks. Spoon chocolate mixture into a large bowl; cool.

4. Place egg whites in a large bowl; beat with a mixer at high speed until foamy. Gradually add ¼ cup granulated sugar and cream of tartar, beating until stiff peaks form. Gently stir one-fourth of egg white mixture into chocolate mixture; gently fold in remaining egg white mixture and chopped chocolate. Spoon into prepared ramekins.

5. Bake at 350° for 15 minutes or until puffy and set. Sprinkle with powdered sugar. Serve immediately. Yield: 8 servings (serving size: 1 soufflé).

CALORIES 206 (24% from fat); FAT 5.5g (sat 3g, mono 1g, poly 0.3g); PROTEIN 5.2g; CARB 34.1g; FIBER 2.3g; CHOL 55mg; IRON 1mg; SODIUM 75mg; CALC 33mg

Test Kitchen Tip: Because chocolate absorbs flavors and odors, wrap it securely in plastic, and store in a cool, dry place. If your chocolate has a grayish-white coating, don't worry. This is called "bloom" and develops when chocolate is stored in warm or humid conditions. Bloom doesn't affect flavor or cooking quality, and will go away when the chocolate is heated.

Double-Chocolate Soufflé Torte with Raspberry Sauce

Instead of being baked in a soufflé dish or ramekins, this soufflé is baked in a springform pan, cut into wedges, and topped with sauce. Raspberry sauce is the perfect partner for the deep, rich chocolate.

Prep: 25 minutes • Cook: 55 minutes • Other: 1 hour

Raspberry Sauce:

- 1 cup water
- ½ cup sugar
- 1 tablespoon cornstarch
- ⅛ teaspoon salt
- 1 (10-ounce) package frozen raspberries in light syrup, thawed and undrained
- 1 tablespoon Grand Marnier (orange-flavored liqueur)

Torte:

- 3 ounces semisweet chocolate, chopped
- 2 tablespoons Grand Marnier (orange-flavored liqueur)
- 3 tablespoons butter, softened
- ¾ cup sugar, divided
- 1 large egg
- ¼ cup fat-free milk
- ¼ cup Dutch process cocoa or unsweetened cocoa
- 2 tablespoons cornstarch
- 4 large egg whites
- ¼ teaspoon cream of tartar
- ⅛ teaspoon salt
- Cooking spray
- Mint sprigs (optional)

1. To prepare raspberry sauce, combine first 4 ingredients in a medium, heavy saucepan; stir well with a whisk. Bring to a boil over medium heat, stirring frequently. Cook 2 minutes. Stir in raspberries; cook 4 minutes, stirring gently. Remove from heat. Stir in 1 tablespoon liqueur. Pour sauce into a bowl; cover and chill 1 hour.

2. Preheat oven to 300°.

3. To prepare torte, combine chocolate and 2 tablespoons liqueur in a small, heavy saucepan; cook over low heat until chocolate melts and mixture is smooth, stirring occasionally with a whisk. Place butter and ½ cup sugar in a medium bowl; beat with a mixer at medium speed 1 minute or until fluffy. Add 1 egg; beat 1 minute. Gradually add milk; beat at low speed (mixture will look curdled). Add chocolate mixture, cocoa, and 2 tablespoons cornstarch; beat at low speed until combined.

4. Place egg whites, cream of tartar, and ⅛ teaspoon salt in a medium bowl; beat with a mixer at high speed until soft peaks form using clean, dry beaters. Gradually add ¼ cup sugar, 1 tablespoon at a time, beating until stiff peaks form. Gently fold one-fourth of egg white mixture into chocolate mixture; gently fold in remaining egg white mixture. Spoon chocolate mixture into an 8-inch springform pan coated with cooking spray. Bake at 300° for 45 minutes or until a wooden pick inserted in center comes out almost clean; loosen torte from sides of pan using a narrow metal spatula. (Torte falls as it cools.) Cool on a wire rack. Serve with raspberry sauce. Garnish with mint, if desired. Yield: 8 servings (serving size: 1 wedge and ¼ cup sauce).

CALORIES 298 (26% from fat); FAT 8.7g (sat 5.2g, mono 2.6g, poly 0.4g); PROTEIN 4.1g; CARB 53g; FIBER 1.7g; CHOL 34mg; IRON 1.2mg; SODIUM 155mg; CALC 28mg

Test Kitchen Tip: Grand Marnier adds a wonderful depth of flavor to this indulgent-tasting dessert. But if you want to go alcohol-free, substitute water or orange juice.

Blancmange

Blancmange (blawnh-MAHNZH), a French favorite, is a cooked pudding that's poured into individual ramekins and chilled. Unmolded puddings are often served with a fruit sauce or compote.

Prep: 13 minutes • Cook: 5 minutes
Other: 4 hours, 30 minutes

  2   envelopes unflavored gelatin
4½   cups 1% low-fat milk, divided
1⅓   cups sliced almonds, toasted
  ½   cup sugar
  ¼   teaspoon salt
  ¼   teaspoon almond extract
  8   ounces frozen fat-free whipped
      topping, thawed
      Cooking spray

1. Sprinkle gelatin over ½ cup milk in a small bowl; set aside.
2. Place 4 cups milk and almonds in a blender, and process until smooth. Strain through a sieve into a medium saucepan; discard solids. Stir in sugar, salt, and extract; bring to a boil. Add gelatin mixture, stirring until gelatin dissolves; remove from heat.
3. Place pan in a large ice-filled bowl 30 minutes or until milk mixture comes to room temperature; stir occasionally. Gently stir one-fourth of whipped topping into milk mixture; fold in remaining topping.
4. Spoon ⅔ cup milk mixture into each of 9 (6-ounce) custard cups coated with cooking spray. Cover and chill at least 4 hours or overnight. Loosen edges of pudding with a knife or rubber spatula. Place a dessert plate upside down on top of each cup, and invert onto plates. Yield: 9 servings (serving size: 1 pudding).

CALORIES 150 (12% from fat); FAT 2g (sat 0.9g, mono 0.7g, poly 0.2g); PROTEIN 5.6g; CARB 25.5g; FIBER 0.1g; CHOL 5mg; IRON 0.1mg; SODIUM 267mg; CALC 153mg

Panna Cotta with Vermont Blue Cheese and Roasted Stone Fruit

Panna Cotta with Vermont Blue Cheese and Roasted Stone Fruit

Panna cotta is a light, silky Italian cream dessert. Its delicate sweetness is a blank slate that showcases the bold flavors of roasted stone fruit and blue cheese.

Prep: 20 minutes • Cook: 24 minutes
Other: 2 hours

  2   cups pear nectar
  3   envelopes unflavored gelatin
  2   cups whole milk
      Cooking spray
  1   cup pitted sweet cherries
  ¼   cup tawny port or other sweet
      red wine
  3   tablespoons honey
  4   plums, each cut into 4 wedges
      (about 1 pound)
  3   peaches, each peeled and cut into
      6 wedges (about 1 pound)
  1   cup (4 ounces) crumbled Vermont
      or other blue cheese

1. Strain pear nectar through a fine sieve over a small bowl, and discard solids.

Sprinkle gelatin over strained pear nectar, and let stand 1 minute.
2. Place milk in a medium saucepan; stir in gelatin mixture. Cook mixture over medium-low heat until gelatin dissolves, stirring constantly. Pour evenly into 8 (4-ounce) ramekins or muffin cups coated with cooking spray. Chill 2 hours or until gelatin is set.
3. Preheat oven to 400°.
4. Combine cherries and next 4 ingredients in a 13 x 9–inch baking dish coated with cooking spray, tossing to coat. Bake at 400° for 20 minutes or until tender, stirring once. Cool.
5. Loosen edges of panna cottas with a knife or rubber spatula. Place a dessert plate, upside down, on top of each ramekin; invert onto plates. Spoon roasted fruit around each panna cotta. Sprinkle with cheese. Yield: 8 servings (serving size: 1 custard, ½ cup fruit, and 2 tablespoons cheese).

CALORIES 213 (28% from fat); FAT 6.7g (sat 4.1g, mono 1.9g, poly 0.3g); PROTEIN 8g; CARB 30.6g; FIBER 2g; CHOL 19mg; IRON 0.4mg; SODIUM 236mg; CALC 158mg

Chocolate Mousse

Make sure to process the tofu for a full two minutes to get a smooth consistency.

Prep: 14 minutes • Cook: 6 minutes
Other: 4 hours

- ¾ cup semisweet chocolate chips, melted
- 1 (12.3-ounce) package reduced-fat extrafirm silken tofu (such as Mori-Nu)
- ¼ teaspoon salt
- 3 large egg whites
- ½ cup sugar
- ¼ cup water
- Frozen fat-free whipped topping, thawed (optional)
- Grated chocolate (optional)

1. Place melted chocolate chips and tofu in a food processor or blender, and process 2 minutes or until smooth.
2. Place salt and egg whites in a medium bowl, and beat with a mixer at high speed until stiff peaks form.
3. Combine sugar and water in a small saucepan; bring to a boil. Cook, without stirring, until candy thermometer registers 250°. Pour hot sugar syrup in a thin stream over egg whites, beating at high speed. Gently stir one-fourth of meringue into tofu mixture; gently fold in remaining meringue. Spoon ½ cup mousse into each of 8 (6-ounce) custard cups. Cover and chill at least 4 hours. If desired, garnish with whipped topping and grated chocolate. Yield: 8 servings (serving size: ½ cup).

CALORIES 147 (34% from fat); FAT 5.6g (sat 3.3g, mono 1.8g, poly 0.5g); PROTEIN 5.2g; CARB 22.5g; FIBER 0.2g; CHOL 0mg; IRON 0.9mg; SODIUM 134mg; CALC 26mg

Chocolate Mousse

Zuppa Inglese

This dessert, pronounced ZOO-puh in-GLAY-zay, literally translates as "English soup." It's an Italian trifle made with custard and chocolate layered with liqueur-soaked cake.

Prep: 25 minutes • Cook: 10 minutes
Other: 4 hours

- 1 cup powdered sugar
- 6 large egg yolks
- 6 tablespoons all-purpose flour
- 3 cups 2% reduced-fat milk
- 2 teaspoons grated lemon rind
- 1 (10-ounce) loaf angel food cake, cut into ¼-inch-thick slices
- ¼ cup grenadine or raspberry syrup
- 2 tablespoons Drambuie or cognac
- 2 tablespoons cognac
- 1 tablespoon white rum
- 2 ounces semisweet chocolate, melted
- ¼ cup coarsely chopped almonds

1. Place sugar and yolks in a bowl; beat with a mixer at high speed until pale yellow. Gradually add flour, beating until smooth.
2. Heat milk over medium-high heat in a heavy saucepan to 180° or until tiny bubbles form around edge (do not boil). Gradually add hot milk to sugar mixture, stirring constantly with a whisk. Return milk mixture to pan. Cook mixture over medium heat until thick (about 8 minutes), stirring constantly. Remove from heat. Stir in rind.
3. Spoon ¼ cup custard into bottom of a 2-quart soufflé dish or compote. Arrange one-third of cake slices in a single layer over custard. Combine grenadine, Drambuie, cognac, and rum. Brush grenadine mixture over cake slices until wet. Spread 1¼ cups custard over cake slices. Arrange one-third of cake slices in a single layer over custard. Brush grenadine mixture over cake slices until wet. Combine 1¼ cups custard and chocolate, and spread over cake slices. Arrange remaining cake slices over custard. Brush with remaining grenadine mixture. Spread remaining custard over cake slices. Sprinkle with almonds. Cover and chill at least 4 hours. Yield: 9 servings (serving size: ⅔ cup).

CALORIES 306 (26% from fat); FAT 8.8g (sat 3.5g, mono 3.4g, poly 1g); PROTEIN 7.9g; CARB 45.1g; FIBER 1g; CHOL 152mg; IRON 1.2mg; SODIUM 283mg; CALC 170mg

White Russian Tiramisu

Tiramisu is a popular Italian dessert with ladyfingers soaked in a liqueur mixture
and layered with mascarpone cheese and grated chocolate. In this heavenly version,
we've incorporated the flavors of a White Russian Cocktail—Kahlúa and cream.

Prep: 20 minutes • Other: 2 hours

½ cup ground coffee beans
1¾ cups cold water
¼ cup Kahlúa (coffee-flavored liqueur), divided
½ cup (3½ ounces) mascarpone cheese or ½ cup (3½ ounces) cream cheese
1 (8-ounce) block fat-free cream cheese, softened
⅓ cup packed brown sugar
¼ cup granulated sugar
24 ladyfingers (2 [3-ounce] packages)
3 teaspoons unsweetened cocoa, divided

1. Assemble drip coffee maker according to manufacturer's directions. Place ground coffee in coffee filter or filter basket. Add 1¾ cups cold water to coffee maker, and brew to make 1½ cups. Combine brewed coffee and 2 tablespoons Kahlúa in a shallow dish, and cool.

2. Combine cheeses in a large bowl. Beat with a mixer at high speed until smooth. Add sugars and 2 tablespoons Kahlúa, and beat until well blended.

3. Split ladyfingers in half lengthwise.

4. Quickly dip 24 ladyfinger halves, flat sides down, into coffee mixture; place dipped sides down in bottom of an 8-inch square baking dish, slightly overlapping ladyfinger halves. Spread half of cheese mixture over ladyfingers, and sprinkle with 1 teaspoon cocoa. Repeat with remaining ladyfinger halves, coffee mixture, and cheese mixture.

5. Place one wooden pick in each corner and one in the center of tiramisu (to prevent plastic wrap from sticking to cheese mixture); cover with plastic wrap. Chill 2 hours. Sprinkle evenly with 2 teaspoons cocoa before serving. Yield: 12 servings (serving size: about ⅔ cup).

CALORIES 134 (30% from fat); FAT 4.5g (sat 2.2g, mono 1.5g, poly 0.4g); PROTEIN 3.3g; CARB 21.7g; FIBER 0g; CHOL 31mg; IRON 0.3mg; SODIUM 139mg; CALC 77mg

All-Time Favorite
Tiramisu Anacapri

Instant pudding mix, frozen whipped topping, and packaged ladyfingers help make this impressive dessert easy to prepare. Look for ladyfingers in the bakery or the frozen-food section of the supermarket. We used soft ladyfingers, which are made to be split.

Prep: 10 minutes
Other: 8 hours, 30 minutes

    1   cup cold water
    1   (14-ounce) can fat-free sweetened
        condensed milk
    1   (1-ounce) package sugar-free
        vanilla instant pudding mix
    1   (8-ounce) block ⅓-less-fat cream
        cheese, softened
    1   (8-ounce) tub frozen reduced-
        calorie whipped topping, thawed
    1   cup hot water
    ½   cup Kahlúa (coffee-flavored liqueur)
    1   tablespoon instant espresso or
        2 tablespoons instant coffee granules
   24   ladyfingers (2 [3-ounce] packages)
    3   tablespoons unsweetened cocoa

1. Combine first 3 ingredients in a large bowl, and stir well with a whisk. Cover with plastic wrap; chill 30 minutes or until firm.
2. Remove plastic wrap, and add cream cheese. Beat mixture with a mixer at medium speed until well blended. Gently fold in whipped topping.
3. Combine hot water, Kahlúa, and espresso in a medium bowl. Split ladyfingers in half lengthwise. Arrange 16 ladyfinger halves, flat sides down, in a trifle bowl or large glass bowl. Drizzle with ½ cup Kahlúa mixture. Spread one-third of pudding mixture evenly over ladyfingers, and sprinkle with 1 tablespoon cocoa. Repeat layers, ending with cocoa. Cover; chill at least 8

hours. Yield: 12 servings (serving size: about ⅔ cup).

CALORIES 310 (26% from fat); FAT 9.1g (sat 6g, mono 2.1g, poly 0.3g); PROTEIN 7.8g; CARB 44g; FIBER 0.2g; CHOL 95mg; IRON 1.1mg; SODIUM 265mg; CALC 124mg

Test Kitchen Tip: If you don't want to use Kahlúa, use ½ cup strong brewed coffee plus 4 teaspoons sugar.

Frozen Desserts

Chill out with our collection of sorbets, granitas, and home-made ice creams. There's nothing better between courses or as a light ending to a meal.

Chambord Granita

This refreshing frozen treat received our Test Kitchens' highest rating. Even if you don't normally keep liqueurs on hand, it's worth the effort for this dessert.

Prep: 10 minutes • Cook: 2 minutes
Other: 8 hours, 10 minutes

- 3 cups water, divided
- 1 cup sugar
- 4 cups fresh raspberries
- 1 cup Chambord (raspberry-flavored liqueur)

1. Combine 1 cup water and sugar in a saucepan; bring to a boil, stirring until sugar dissolves. Remove from heat; cool completely.

2. Place raspberries in a blender; process until smooth. Press raspberry puree through a sieve into a medium bowl, and discard seeds. Stir in sugar syrup, 2 cups water, and liqueur. Pour mixture into an 11 x 7–inch baking dish. Cover and freeze 8 hours or until firm.

3. Remove mixture from freezer; let stand 10 minutes. Scrape with a fork until fluffy. Yield: 16 servings (serving size: ½ cup).

CALORIES 105 (2% from fat); FAT 0.2g (sat 0g, mono 0g, poly 0.1g); PROTEIN 0.3g; CARB 21.3g; FIBER 0g; CHOL 0mg; IRON 0.2mg; SODIUM 0mg; CALC 7mg

Green Tea Granita

Any type of tea will work in this recipe. Brew it stronger or weaker according to your preference. Garnish this delicate dessert with wafer-thin slices of lemon.

Prep: 10 minutes • Other: 8 hours, 15 minutes

- 3 cups boiling water
- 4 regular-sized green tea bags
- 1 (2-inch) piece peeled fresh ginger, quartered
- ½ cup honey
- 3 tablespoons fresh lemon juice

1. Pour boiling water over tea bags and ginger in a medium bowl. Cover; let stand 5 minutes. Add honey and lemon juice; stir to combine. Strain mixture through a sieve into a bowl; discard solids. Cool completely. Pour mixture into an 8-inch square baking dish. Cover; freeze 8 hours or until firm.

2. Remove tea mixture from freezer; let stand 10 minutes. Scrape entire mixture with a fork until fluffy. Yield: 6 servings (serving size: about ½ cup).

CALORIES 88 (0% from fat); FAT 0g (sat 0g, mono 0g, poly 0g); PROTEIN 0.1g; CARB 23.9g; FIBER 0.1g; CHOL 0mg; IRON 0.1mg; SODIUM 1.2mg; CALC 2.2mg

Strawberry Granita

This frozen dessert requires no ice-cream maker—just freeze the mixture in a pan and scrape with a fork. To spruce up the granita, top with chopped or halved fresh strawberries and grated lemon zest.

Prep: 10 minutes
Other: 8 hours, 10 minutes

- ½ cup sugar
- ½ cup warm water
- 3 cups sliced strawberries
- 2 tablespoons fresh lemon juice

1. Place sugar and water in a blender; process until sugar dissolves. Add strawberries and juice; process until smooth. Pour mixture into an 8-inch square baking dish. Cover and freeze 3 hours; stir well. Cover and freeze 5 hours or overnight.

2. Remove mixture from freezer; let stand 10 minutes. Scrape entire mixture with a fork until fluffy. Yield: 4 servings (serving size: 1 cup).

CALORIES 136 (3% from fat); FAT 0.5g (sat 0g, mono 0.1g, poly 0.2g); PROTEIN 0.8g; CARB 34.4g; FIBER 2.9g; CHOL 0mg; IRON 0.5mg; SODIUM 2mg; CALC 18mg

Test Kitchen Tip: When selecting fresh strawberries, choose brightly colored berries that still have their green caps attached. Don't wash strawberries until you're ready to use them. Store them (in a single layer, if possible) in a moisture-proof container in the refrigerator for two to three days.

Pineapple
Sorbet

Meyer Lemon Sorbet

This tangy, sweet sorbet is the perfect ending to a spicy meal.

Prep: 10 minutes • Other: 1 hour, 25 minutes

   2   cups water
1 ⅓   cups sugar
   2   tablespoons grated lemon rind
   ⅔   cup fresh Meyer lemon juice (about
       3 lemons)
   ½   cup fresh lime juice (about 2 limes)
Mint sprigs (optional)
Lemon rind strips (optional)

1. Combine first 5 ingredients in a medium bowl, stirring until sugar dissolves.
2. Pour mixture into freezer can of an ice-cream freezer, and freeze according to manufacturer's instructions. Spoon sorbet into a freezer-safe container; cover and freeze 1 hour or until firm. Garnish with mint sprigs and lemon rind strips, if desired. Yield: 8 servings (serving size: ½ cup).

CALORIES 138 (0% from fat); FAT 0g (sat 0 g, mono 0g, poly 0g); PROTEIN 0.2g; CARB 36.6g; FIBER 0.1g; CHOL 0mg; IRON 0mg; SODIUM 1mg; CALC 5mg

Test Kitchen Tip: Because Meyer lemons are sometimes hard to find, we also tested the sorbet with regular lemons, and it still tasted great.

Lemon-Ginger Sorbetto

Sorbetto is the Italian word for sorbet. Fresh lemon juice and ginger give this honey-sweet sorbet a hit of intense flavor.

Prep: 15 minutes • Cook: 3 minutes
Other: 1 hour, 25 minutes

   3   cups water
   1   cup sugar
   6   tablespoons honey
   1   (2-inch) piece peeled fresh ginger
   1   cup fresh lemon juice (about 8 lemons)

1. Combine water and sugar in a saucepan; bring to a boil, stirring until sugar dissolves. Remove from heat; stir in honey. Cool completely.
2. Grate ginger; place on several layers of damp cheesecloth. Gather edges of cheesecloth together; squeeze cheesecloth bag over a bowl to measure 1 tablespoon ginger juice. Combine sugar mixture, ginger juice, and lemon juice in a large bowl.
3. Pour into freezer can of an ice-cream freezer; freeze according to manufacturer's instructions. Spoon into a freezer-safe container; cover and freeze 1 hour or until firm. Yield: 8 servings (serving size: ½ cup).

CALORIES 153 (0% from fat); FAT 0g (sat 0 g, mono 0g, poly 0g); PROTEIN 0.2g; CARB 40.7g; FIBER 0.1g; CHOL 0mg; IRON 0.1mg; SODIUM 1mg; CALC 4mg

Pineapple Sorbet

If you don't have an ice-cream freezer, use a covered metal bowl. Freeze the mixture three hours or until it's hard on the outside but slushy in the middle. Remove it from the freezer, beat with a whisk until smooth, cover it, and freeze for four hours or until sorbet is firm.

Prep: 10 minutes • Other: 1 hour, 25 minutes

   1   small pineapple, peeled and cored
   2   tablespoons fresh lemon juice
   1   cup plus 2 tablespoons sugar
Mint sprigs (optional)

1. Cut pineapple into 2-inch pieces. Place pineapple and lemon juice in a food processor; process until smooth. Add sugar; process 1 minute or until sugar dissolves.
2. Pour mixture into freezer can of an ice-cream freezer; freeze according to manufacturer's instructions. Spoon sorbet into a freezer-safe container. Cover and freeze 1 hour or until firm. Garnish with mint sprigs, if desired. Yield: 9 servings (serving size: ½ cup).

CALORIES 116 (2% from fat); FAT 0.2g (sat 0g, mono 0.1g, poly 0.1g); PROTEIN 0.2g; CARB 30g; FIBER 0.5g; CHOL 0mg; IRON 0.2mg; SODIUM 1mg; CALC 3mg

Bittersweet Chocolate Sorbet

The deep chocolate lusciousness belies this dessert's low-fat status. Freeze the sorbet up to two days in advance; let it stand at room temperature 15 minutes to soften before scooping.

Prep: 5 minutes • Cook: 7 minutes
Other: 1 hour, 25 minutes

2½ cups water
1¼ cups sugar
 ½ cup unsweetened cocoa
  3 ounces bittersweet chocolate, finely chopped
  2 teaspoons vanilla extract

1. Bring water to a boil in a medium saucepan. Stir in sugar and cocoa; reduce heat, and simmer 5 minutes, stirring frequently. Remove from heat; add chocolate and vanilla, stirring until chocolate melts. Cover and chill completely.

2. Pour chocolate mixture into freezer can of an ice-cream freezer; freeze according to manufacturer's instructions. Spoon sorbet into a freezer-safe container; cover and freeze 1 hour or until firm. Yield: 6 servings (serving size: about ⅔ cup).

CALORIES 190 (25% from fat); FAT 5.3g (sat 3.2g, mono 0.9g, poly 0.1g); PROTEIN 1.8g; CARB 39.6g; FIBER 2.6g; CHOL 0mg; IRON 1.1mg; SODIUM 2mg; CALC 8mg

White Chocolate Sorbet with Warm Clementine Sauce

Clementine juice flavors the sorbet, and sections are added to the sauce. Clementines are small, loose-skinned oranges with a thin peel and tangy-sweet reddish-orange flesh that's usually seedless. Juice the clementines just as you would oranges. You can substitute fresh orange or tangerine juice.

Prep: 20 minutes • Cook: 22 minutes
Other: 1 hour, 30 minutes

Sorbet:
 ½ cup clementine juice (about 5 clementines)
  5 ounces premium white chocolate, chopped
2½ cups water
 ¾ cup sugar
 ½ cup fresh lemon juice
 ¼ teaspoon vanilla extract

Warm Clementine Sauce:
  1 tablespoon water
  1 teaspoon cornstarch
 ½ cup clementine juice (about 5 clementines)
 ¼ cup water
  2 teaspoons sugar
  1 teaspoon fresh lemon juice
  3 cups clementine sections (about 3 clementines)

1. To prepare sorbet, bring ½ cup clementine juice to a boil in a small saucepan. Reduce heat; simmer until reduced to ¼ cup (about 12 minutes).

2. Place chocolate in a large bowl. Combine 2½ cups water and ¾ cup sugar in a small saucepan; bring to a boil. Cook 1 minute; remove from heat. Pour over chocolate; let stand 2 minutes. Stir gently with a whisk until smooth. Add reduced clementine juice, ½ cup lemon juice, and vanilla to chocolate mixture, stirring well. Cool completely.

3. Pour mixture into freezer can of ice-cream freezer; freeze according to manufacturer's instructions. Spoon sorbet into a freezer-safe container; cover and freeze 1 hour or until firm.

4. To prepare sauce, combine 1 tablespoon water and cornstarch in a small bowl, stirring well with a whisk. Combine ½ cup clementine juice, ¼ cup water, 2 teaspoons sugar, and 1 teaspoon lemon juice in a small saucepan; bring to a simmer. Add cornstarch mixture to juice mixture, and bring to a boil. Cook 1 minute or until thickened, stirring constantly.

5. Remove from heat, and gently stir in clementine sections. Cover and let stand 2 minutes. Serve sauce warm with sorbet. Yield: 5 servings (serving size: about ⅓ cup sorbet and about ½ cup sauce).

CALORIES 320 (26% from fat); FAT 9.2g (sat 5.5g, mono 2.6g, poly 0.3g); PROTEIN 2.4g; CARB 59.6g; FIBER 0.2g; CHOL 6mg; IRON 0.2mg; SODIUM 27mg; CALC 75mg

Test Kitchen Tip: We recommend using a premium white chocolate such as Ghiradelli instead of vanilla bark coating for this sorbet. The premium white chocolate results in a richer-tasting product.

Bittersweet Chocolate Sorbet

Strawberry-Buttermilk Gelato

Gelato is American ice cream's distant Italian cousin. This one's flavored with seasonal fresh strawberries and is low in fat.

Prep: 10 minutes • Cook: 2 minutes
Other: 1 hour, 25 minutes

- 2 cups sugar
- 2 cups water
- 5 cups quartered strawberries (about 4 pints)
- 2 cups low-fat buttermilk

1. Combine sugar and water in a large saucepan; bring to a boil, stirring until sugar dissolves. Pour into a large bowl; cool completely.
2. Place strawberries in a blender; process until smooth. Add strawberry puree and buttermilk to sugar syrup; stir to combine.
3. Pour strawberry mixture into freezer can of an ice-cream freezer, and freeze according to manufacturer's instructions. Spoon gelato into a freezer-safe container; cover and freeze 1 hour or until firm. Yield: 16 servings (serving size: ½ cup).

CALORIES 134 (5% from fat); FAT 0.8g (sat 0.3g, mono 0.2g, poly 0.1g); PROTEIN 1.6g; CARB 31.7g; FIBER 1.7g; CHOL 1mg; IRON 0.3mg; SODIUM 17mg; CALC 48mg

Peach Ice Cream

Ripe peaches at peak season are key to this summertime ice cream.

Prep: 10 minutes • Other: 2 hours, 25 minutes

- 3 cups sliced peeled peaches (about 1½ pounds)
- 1 cup half-and-half
- ½ cup sugar
- ½ cup whole milk
- 1 teaspoon vanilla extract

1. Place peaches in a blender or food processor; process until finely chopped. Combine peaches and remaining ingredients in a large bowl.
2. Pour peach mixture into freezer can of an ice-cream freezer; freeze according to manufacturer's instructions. Spoon ice cream into a freezer-safe container; cover and freeze 2 hours or until firm. Yield: 8 servings (serving size: ½ cup).

CALORIES 125 (29% from fat); FAT 4g (sat 2.5g, mono 1.2g, poly 0.2g); PROTEIN 1.8g; CARB 21.3g; FIBER 1.2g; CHOL 13mg; IRON 0.1mg; SODIUM 20mg; CALC 53mg

All-Time Favorite
Lemon-Buttermilk Ice Cream

Three different kinds of milk provide a rich, creamy consistency.

Prep: 10 minutes • Other: 1 hour, 25 minutes

- 1½ cups sugar
- 1 cup fresh lemon juice (about 10 lemons)
- 2 cups half-and-half
- 2 cups whole milk
- 2 cups fat-free buttermilk

1. Combine sugar and lemon juice in a large bowl, stirring with a whisk until sugar dissolves. Add half-and-half, whole milk, and buttermilk.
2. Pour mixture into freezer can of an ice-cream freezer, and freeze according to manufacturer's instructions. Spoon into a freezer-safe container. Cover and freeze 1 hour or until firm. Yield: 18 servings (serving size: ½ cup).

CALORIES 130 (25% from fat); FAT 3.6g (sat 2.3g, mono 1.2g, poly 0g); PROTEIN 2.8g; CARB 21.4g; FIBER 0.1g; CHOL 18mg; IRON 0mg; SODIUM 54mg; CALC 93mg

all in the gelato family

Gelato (jeh-LAH-toh)—which comes from *gelare*, the Italian word for "to freeze"—is the umbrella term for any frozen Italian dessert.

Gelato—in addition to its more general definition, it also refers to a milk-based concoction with a dense, buttery consistency similar to that of American ice cream. You can serve it in an ice-cream cone.

Sorbetto (sor-BAY-toh)—a fruit-based gelato that doesn't contain any dairy products. You may know it better as sorbet.

Granita (GRAH-nee-tah)—another fruit-based gelato, it has a decidedly different texture from that of sorbetto or gelato. Because it's frozen and then scraped to form coarse ice granules, granita is slushy.

Peppercorn Ice Cream with Rum-Glazed Pineapple

Sometimes matching unlikely flavors creates surprisingly perfect unions, and that's the case with peppercorns and sweet pineapple.

Prep: 20 minutes • Cook: 11 minutes
Other: 1 hour, 35 minutes

 2 cups 1% low-fat milk, divided
 1 teaspoon black peppercorns, coarsely crushed
 2 large egg yolks
 2 tablespoons granulated sugar
 1 tablespoon vanilla extract
 ¼ teaspoon grated lime rind
 1 tablespoon fresh lime juice
 1 (14-ounce) can fat-free sweetened condensed milk
 ¼ cup packed brown sugar
 ¼ cup dark rum or 1 teaspoon rum extract plus ¼ cup water
 7 (½-inch-thick) slices pineapple
Cooking spray

1. Combine 1¼ cups low-fat milk and peppercorns in a medium, heavy saucepan; bring to a simmer. Remove from heat. Let stand, covered, 10 minutes. Strain milk through a cheesecloth-lined sieve into a bowl; discard solids.
2. Place egg yolks in a bowl. Gradually add hot milk to egg yolks, stirring constantly with a whisk. Return milk mixture to pan. Add granulated sugar; cook over medium heat until milk mixture coats a metal spoon (about 3 minutes), stirring constantly. Combine ¾ cup low-fat milk, vanilla, lime rind, lime juice, and condensed milk in a medium bowl. Gradually add custard, stirring with a whisk. Cover; chill completely.
3. Pour mixture into freezer can of an ice-cream freezer; freeze according to manufacturer's instructions. Spoon ice cream into a freezer-safe container; cover and freeze 1 hour or until firm.
4. Combine brown sugar and rum in a small microwave-safe bowl; microwave at HIGH 1 minute or until sugar dissolves, stirring after 45 seconds.
5. Prepare grill.
6. Place pineapple on grill rack coated with cooking spray; cook 2 minutes on each side or until lightly browned, basting occasionally with rum mixture. Place pineapple on dessert plates; top with ice cream. Yield: 7 servings (serving size: 1 pineapple slice and ½ cup ice cream).

CALORIES 266 (8% from fat); FAT 2.4g (sat 0.9g, mono 0.8g, poly 0.2g); PROTEIN 7.6g; CARB 52.5g; FIBER 0.2g; CHOL 71mg; IRON 0.6mg; SODIUM 98mg; CALC 249mg

Peppermint Ice Cream

If the ice cream is frozen solid, remove it from the freezer 30 minutes before serving to soften.

Prep: 5 minutes • Cook: 4 minutes
Other: 1 hour, 25 minutes

2½ cups 2% reduced-fat milk, divided
 2 large egg yolks
 2 teaspoons vanilla extract
 1 (14-ounce) can fat-free sweetened condensed milk
 ⅔ cup crushed peppermint candies (about 25 candies)

1. Combine 1¼ cups 2% milk and yolks in a heavy saucepan over medium heat. Cook until mixture is slightly thick and coats the back of a spoon; stir constantly (do not boil). Cool slightly.
2. Combine egg mixture, 1¼ cups 2% milk, vanilla, and condensed milk in a bowl. Cover and chill. Stir in candies.
3. Pour mixture into freezer can of an ice-cream freezer; freeze according to manufacturer's instructions. Spoon ice cream into a freezer-safe container; cover and freeze 1 hour or until firm. Yield: 8 servings (serving size: ½ cup).

CALORIES 268 (10% from fat); FAT 2.9g (sat 1.3g, mono 0.9g, poly 0.2g); PROTEIN 7.6g; CARB 52.2g; FIBER 0g; CHOL 62mg; IRON 0.3mg; SODIUM 99mg; CALC 238mg

Cookies-and-Cream Ice Cream

What better way to increase your intake of soy than with cookies and ice cream?

Prep: 10 minutes • Other: 1 hour, 25 minutes

 1 (12.3-ounce) package reduced-fat firm tofu, drained
 ½ cup sugar
 ½ cup half-and-half
 1 teaspoon vanilla extract
 ¼ teaspoon salt
 2 cups frozen fat-free whipped topping, thawed
 10 cream-filled chocolate sandwich cookies (such as Oreos), crushed

1. Place first 5 ingredients in a food processor; process until smooth. Place mixture in a bowl. Fold in whipped topping. Pour into freezer can of an ice-cream freezer; freeze according to manufacturer's instructions. Stir in crushed cookies during last 5 minutes of freezing. Spoon into a freezer-safe container; cover and freeze 1 hour or until firm. Yield: 8 servings (serving size: ½ cup).

CALORIES 184 (25% from fat); FAT 5.2g (sat 1.8g, mono 1.9g, poly 0.6g); PROTEIN 3.8g; CARB 29.3g; FIBER 0.4g; CHOL 6mg; IRON 0.7mg; SODIUM 307mg; CALC 31mg

Peanut Butter-Banana Ice Cream

Chunky peanut butter adds pleasing crunch to plain vanilla ice cream; banana adds fruity sweetness.

Prep: 6 minutes • Other: 45 minutes

  4 cups vanilla low-fat ice cream
  1 cup mashed ripe banana (about 2 small bananas)
  ¼ cup chunky peanut butter

1. Place a large bowl in freezer. Let ice cream stand at room temperature 45 minutes or until softened.
2. Combine banana and peanut butter in a small bowl; mash with a fork until well blended. With a rubber spatula or stand mixer, combine softened ice cream and banana mixture in chilled bowl. Cover and freeze to desired consistency. Yield: 8 servings (serving size: ½ cup).

CALORIES 183 (30% from fat); FAT 6.1g (sat 1.8g, mono 1.9g, poly 1.2g); PROTEIN 5.2g; CARB 27.3g; FIBER 2.2g; CHOL 5mg; IRON 0.2mg; SODIUM 84mg; CALC 105mg

Mocha Ice Cream

Start with a commercial low-fat ice cream to make a dessert that appeals to those who don't like excessively sweet desserts.

Prep: 5 minutes • Cook: 30 seconds • Other: 45 minutes

  4 cups chocolate low-fat ice cream
  ¼ cup Kahlúa (coffee-flavored liqueur)
  1 tablespoon instant coffee granules
  2 ounces bittersweet chocolate, finely chopped

1. Place a large bowl in freezer. Let ice cream stand at room temperature 45 minutes or until softened.
2. Combine liqueur and coffee granules in a small bowl. Microwave at HIGH 30 seconds; stir until coffee dissolves. Cool.
3. With a rubber spatula or stand mixer, combine softened ice cream, coffee mixture, and chopped chocolate in chilled bowl. Cover, and freeze to desired consistency. Yield: 8 servings (serving size: ½ cup).

CALORIES 206 (30% from fat); FAT 6.9g (sat 4.5g, mono 1.5g, poly 0.2g); PROTEIN 3.6g; CARB 30.5g; FIBER 0.6g; CHOL 15mg; IRON 0.4mg; SODIUM 101mg; CALC 101mg

Mocha Ice Cream

Peanut Butter-Banana Ice Cream

Dulce de Leche Ice Cream

Many older recipes for *dulce de leche* (Spanish for "sweet milk") call for cooking a can of sweetened condensed milk in boiling water, but this procedure is no longer recommended. Our oven method is simpler and safer. The milk caramelizes as it's baking, creating a thick, rich caramel sauce.

Prep: 5 minutes • Cook: 1 hour, 30 minutes
Other: 45 minutes

    1   (14-ounce) can fat-free sweetened
          condensed milk
    4   cups vanilla low-fat ice cream

1. Preheat oven to 400°.
2. Pour milk into a 9-inch pie plate; cover with foil. Place pie plate in a shallow roasting pan. Add hot water to pan to a depth of halfway up the sides of pie plate. Bake milk at 400° for 1½ hours, adding additional water as needed. Remove pie plate from water. Uncover; stir milk with a whisk until smooth. Cool.
3. Place a large bowl in freezer. Let ice cream stand at room temperature 45 minutes or until softened.
4. With a rubber spatula or stand mixer, combine softened ice cream and caramelized milk in chilled bowl. Cover and freeze to desired consistency. Yield: 8 servings (serving size: ½ cup).

CALORIES 248 (8% from fat); FAT 2.1g (sat 1g, mono 0.6g, poly 0.1g); PROTEIN 7.4g; CARB 48.9g; FIBER 1g; CHOL 8mg; IRON 0mg; SODIUM 97mg; CALC 239mg

Pineapple-Brown Sugar Frozen Yogurt

This recipe makes 9 cups, but you can easily halve it if you have a small ice-cream freezer.

Prep: 5 minutes • Cook: 3 minutes
Other: 1 hour, 25 minutes

    1½ cups packed light brown sugar
    2   (15¼-ounce) cans crushed
          pineapple in juice, undrained
    4   cups vanilla low-fat yogurt
    2   teaspoons vanilla extract

1. Combine sugar and pineapple in a medium saucepan over medium heat, and cook until sugar dissolves, stirring occasionally. Remove from heat, and cool slightly. Chill.
2. Combine pineapple mixture, yogurt, and vanilla in a large bowl. Pour mixture into freezer can of an ice-cream freezer; freeze according to manufacturer's instructions. Spoon yogurt into a freezer-safe container; cover and freeze 1 hour or until firm. Yield: 18 servings (serving size: ½ cup).

CALORIES 142 (4% from fat); FAT 0.7g (sat 0.4g, mono 0.2g, poly 0.1g); PROTEIN 2.7g; CARB 32.4g; FIBER 0.4g; CHOL 3mg; IRON 0.5mg; SODIUM 41mg; CALC 109mg

For additional quick and easy dessert ideas, see "Deadline Desserts" on page 220.

Banana Split Ice Cream Sandwiches

The vanilla cookies are very thin and are made from a batter that requires chilling before shaping. They'll be soft when warm but crisp after they cool. Gooey toppings make this a good knife-and-fork dessert. Assemble just before serving.

Prep: 20 minutes • Cook: 12 minutes
Other: 2 hours

Cookies:
    7   tablespoons powdered sugar
    6   tablespoons all-purpose flour
    ¼   teaspoon vanilla extract
    1   large egg
Filling:
    2   cups vanilla low-fat ice cream,
          softened
    ¾   cup ripe mashed banana (about 1½
          bananas)
    ¼   cup coarsely chopped dry-roasted
          peanuts
Remaining ingredients:
    6   tablespoons frozen fat-free whipped
          topping, thawed
    6   tablespoons chocolate syrup
    2   tablespoons coarsely chopped
          dry-roasted peanuts
    6   maraschino cherries, drained

1. To prepare cookies, combine sugar and flour, stirring with a whisk. Add vanilla and egg; beat with a mixer at medium speed 2 minutes. Cover; refrigerate 2 hours.
2. Preheat oven to 350°.
3. Cover a large baking sheet with parchment paper. Draw 6 (3-inch) circles on paper. Turn paper over; secure with masking tape. Spoon 1 tablespoon batter into center of each circle; spread batter to edge. Bake at 350° for 6 minutes or until edges begin to brown. Carefully remove cookies

from paper, and cool completely on wire racks. Repeat procedure with remaining batter, reusing parchment paper.

4. To prepare filling, combine ice cream, banana, and ¼ cup peanuts, stirring well.

5. Place 1 cookie, flat side up, on each of 6 plates. Carefully spread about ⅓ cup ice cream mixture over each cookie. Top with remaining cookies, flat sides down, pressing gently. Top each sandwich with 1 tablespoon whipped topping, 1 tablespoon chocolate syrup, 1 teaspoon peanuts, and 1 cherry. Serve immediately. Yield: 6 servings (serving size: 1 sandwich).

CALORIES 310 (20% from fat); FAT 7g (sat 1.6g, mono 2.3g, poly 1.6g); PROTEIN 6.9g; CARB 55.9g; FIBER 2.3g; CHOL 39mg; IRON 0.8mg; SODIUM 54mg; CALC 79mg

Banana Split Ice Cream Sandwiches

Frozen White Chocolate and Hazelnut Mousse

Place a freezer-safe container in the freezer before you start the recipe; a chilled container helps preserve a light, fluffy texture.

Prep: 20 minutes • Cook: 13 minutes
Other: 8 hours

  2 large egg yolks, lightly beaten
  3 tablespoons water
  1 teaspoon butter
  2 ounces premium white baking chocolate, finely chopped
  ¼ cup Frangelico (hazelnut-flavored liqueur)
  ½ teaspoon cream of tartar
 Dash of salt
  6 large egg whites
  ¾ cup sugar
  ⅔ cup water
 1½ cups frozen fat-free whipped topping, thawed
  3 tablespoons chopped hazelnuts, toasted

1. Place egg yolks in a medium bowl. Combine 3 tablespoons water, butter, and chocolate in a large, heavy saucepan. Cook over medium heat, stirring constantly, until chocolate melts. Gradually add chocolate mixture to egg yolks, stirring constantly with a whisk. Return chocolate mixture to pan; cook over medium heat until thick (about 3 minutes), stirring constantly. Remove from heat; stir in liqueur. Cool slightly.

2. Place cream of tartar, salt, and egg whites in a large bowl; beat with a mixer at high speed until foamy. Combine ¾ cup sugar and ⅔ cup water in a saucepan; bring to a boil. Cook, without stirring, until candy thermometer registers 250°. Gradually pour hot sugar syrup in a thin stream into egg white mixture, beating at high speed until stiff peaks form (5 to 7 minutes).

3. Gently stir one-fourth of egg white mixture into chocolate mixture; gently fold in remaining egg white mixture. Fold in whipped topping and hazelnuts. Spoon mixture into a chilled freezer-safe container; freeze 8 hours or overnight. Yield: 8 servings (serving size: about ¾ cup).

CALORIES 207 (25% from fat); FAT 5.7g (sat 2.2g, mono 2.5g, poly 0.5g); PROTEIN 4.2g; CARB 30g; FIBER 0.3g; CHOL 56mg; IRON 0.3mg; SODIUM 81mg; CALC 25mg

Peppermint Patties

Coarsely crush the peppermint candies in a large zip-top plastic bag by lightly tapping with a rolling pin or heavy skillet (a food processor would just pulverize them).

Prep: 25 minutes • Cook: 11 minutes per batch • Other: 5 hours

Cookies:

1½ cups all-purpose flour
⅓ cup Dutch process cocoa
½ teaspoon baking soda
¼ teaspoon salt
½ cup granulated sugar
½ cup packed brown sugar
½ cup butter, softened
1 teaspoon vanilla extract
1 large egg
Cooking spray

Filling:

30 hard peppermint candies, crushed (about 1 cup)
3 cups vanilla low-fat ice cream, softened

1. To prepare cookies, lightly spoon flour into dry measuring cups; level with a knife. Combine flour, cocoa, baking soda, and salt, stirring with a whisk. Combine sugars and butter in a large bowl; beat with a mixer at medium speed until well blended. Add vanilla and egg; beat well. Add flour mixture to sugar mixture; beat at low speed until well blended.

2. Lightly coat hands with cooking spray. Divide dough in half. Shape each half into a 6-inch log. Wrap logs individually in plastic wrap; freeze 1 hour or until firm.

3. Preheat oven to 350°.

4. Cut each dough log into 24 (¼-inch) slices; place cookies 1 inch apart on baking sheets coated with cooking spray. Bake at 350° for 11 minutes or until set. Cool completely on wire racks.

5. To prepare filling, place candies in a shallow bowl. Spread 2 tablespoons ice cream onto flat side of each of 24 cookies. Top with remaining cookies, flat sides down, pressing gently. Lightly roll sides of each sandwich in candy. Wrap each sandwich tightly in plastic wrap; freeze 4 hours or until firm. Yield: 12 servings (serving size: 2 sandwiches).

CALORIES 321 (30% from fat); FAT 10.6g (sat 6.2g, mono 2.4g, poly 0.4g); PROTEIN 4.3g; CARB 51.6g; FIBER 1.1g; CHOL 56mg; IRON 1.3mg; SODIUM 216mg; CALC 69mg

Test Kitchen Tip: Substitute regular unsweetened cocoa powder in the cookies if you don't have Dutch process.

Fruit Desserts

Capitalize on the natural sweetness of fresh fruits by featuring them in compotes, crepes, and meringues, or topping them with a creamy sauce.

Strawberry-Blueberry Compote in Red Wine Syrup

Simmering red wine with spices and herbs creates a fragrant syrup for the distinctive ruby-hued compote. Serve over ice cream or pound cake or with almond biscotti, and garnish with mint.

Prep: 9 minutes • Cook: 23 minutes

1 cup dry red wine
¼ cup sugar
½ teaspoon whole black peppercorns
2 (2½-inch) orange rind strips
1 cinnamon stick
1 bay leaf
4 cups sliced strawberries
1 cup blueberries

1. Combine first 6 ingredients in a small, nonaluminum saucepan; bring to a boil. Reduce heat; simmer, uncovered, 20 minutes or until liquid is reduced to ½ cup.
2. Strain wine mixture through a colander into a large bowl; discard solids. Add berries; toss to coat. Serve warm, or chill up to 2 hours. Yield: 8 servings (serving size: ½ cup).

CALORIES 61 (6% from fat); FAT 0.4g (sat 0g, mono 0.1g, poly 0.2g); PROTEIN 0.7g; CARB 15g; FIBER 2.4g; CHOL 0mg; IRON 0.5mg; SODIUM 4mg; CALC 15mg

Sauternes-Poached Apricots with Fresh Berries and Vanilla Crème Fraîche

Crème fraîche is a thickened cream with a slightly tangy, nutty flavor and a smooth, rich texture. You can use sour cream in place of crème fraîche, if desired, but the flavor will not be exactly the same.

**Prep: 12 minutes • Cook: 27 minutes
Other: 8 hours**

Apricots:
2 cups sugar
1¾ cups Sauternes or other sweet white wine
1¼ cups water
⅛ teaspoon salt
2 (6-inch) vanilla beans, split lengthwise
12 apricots

Vanilla Crème Fraîche:
½ cup commercial crème fraîche
1 tablespoon sugar
½ teaspoon vanilla extract
Dash of salt

Remaining ingredients:
1½ cups fresh blueberries
1½ cups fresh raspberries

1. To prepare apricots, combine first 4 ingredients in a saucepan. Scrape seeds from vanilla beans; add seeds and beans to wine mixture. Bring to a boil; add apricots. Reduce heat; simmer 2 minutes. Remove apricots with a slotted spoon. Bring wine mixture to a boil; cook until reduced to 2¼ cups (about 20 minutes). Cool to room temperature. Cut apricots in half, and remove pits. Combine wine mixture and apricot halves in a shallow dish; discard vanilla beans. Cover and chill 8 hours.

2. To prepare crème fraîche, combine commercial crème fraîche, 1 tablespoon sugar, vanilla, and dash of salt.

3. Arrange fruit on dessert plates. Drizzle with wine mixture; top with crème fraîche. Yield: 8 servings (serving size: 3 apricot halves, 3 tablespoons blueberries, 3 tablespoons raspberries, 2 tablespoons wine mixture, and 1 tablespoon crème fraîche).

CALORIES 288 (11% from fat); FAT 3.5g (sat 1.9g, mono 1g, poly 0.3g); PROTEIN 1.8g; CARB 65.7g; FIBER 3.7g; CHOL 6mg; IRON 0.7mg; SODIUM 69mg; CALC 36mg

Fresh Peaches with Sabayon

Sabayon is the French version of *zabaglione*, which is a foamy Italian custard made by whisking together egg yolks, wine, and sugar over simmering water.

Prep: 11 minutes • Cook: 7 minutes

¼ cup sugar
3 large egg yolks
¼ cup Marsala wine
2 tablespoons water
8 cups sliced peeled peaches (about 4 pounds)
Mint sprigs (optional)

1. Combine sugar and yolks in top of a double boiler, beating with a mixer at medium speed until foamy. Add wine and water. Cook over simmering water until mixture reaches 160° (about 7 minutes), beating with a mixer at medium speed. Serve immediately over peaches. Garnish with fresh mint sprigs, if desired. Yield: 8 servings (serving size: 1 cup peaches and ½ cup sabayon).

CALORIES 125 (15% from fat); FAT 2.1g (sat 0.6g, mono 0.8g, poly 0.3g); PROTEIN 2.2g; CARB 25.7g; FIBER 3.4g; CHOL 80mg; IRON 0.4mg; SODIUM 3mg; CALC 17mg

Mixed Marinated Fruit

Letting the fruit stand in the marinade infuses it with the flavor of the orange juice and brandy. You can use any combination of fruit in this versatile dessert.

Prep: 10 minutes • Other: 2 hours

2 cups chopped cantaloupe
1 cup chopped peeled peaches
1 cup chopped strawberries
1 cup blueberries
⅔ cup chopped peeled nectarines
2 peeled kiwifruit, halved lengthwise and thinly sliced
½ cup fresh orange juice (about 1 orange)
¼ cup sugar
2 tablespoons grappa (Italian brandy) or brandy
1½ teaspoons grated lemon rind

1. Place all ingredients in a large bowl, and toss gently to combine. Cover mixture, and chill 2 hours. Yield: 5 servings (serving size: 1 cup).

CALORIES 154 (4% from fat); FAT 0.7g (sat 0.1g, mono 0.1g, poly 0.3g); PROTEIN 1.8g; CARB 34.8g; FIBER 4.2g; CHOL 0mg; IRON 0.5mg; SODIUM 10mg; CALC 27mg

ripening peaches Leave unripe peaches at room temperature for a few days to allow them to develop their full, sweet potential. Refrigeration retards ripening, resulting in flat-tasting, mealy fruit.

Honey-Roasted Pears with Sweet Yogurt Cream

Pears for roasting are best if they're a little on the firm side. Because the skins take on a beautiful deep-amber glaze when roasted, we left them on.

Prep: 10 minutes • Cook: 52 minutes
Other: 24 hours, 10 minutes

  8 firm Bosc pears, cored and quartered
Cooking spray
  3 tablespoons chilled butter, cut into small pieces
  ¾ cup apple cider
  ½ cup honey
  1 tablespoon fresh lemon juice
  2 teaspoons vanilla extract
Sweet Yogurt Cream

1. Preheat oven to 400°.
2. Place pears in a 13 x 9–inch baking dish coated with cooking spray; dot with butter.
3. Combine cider, honey, juice, and vanilla in a saucepan. Bring to a boil; pour over pears. Cover; bake at 400° for 20 minutes. Uncover; bake 30 minutes or until tender, basting occasionally. Remove from oven; let stand 10 minutes. Serve warm with Sweet Yogurt Cream. Yield: 8 servings (serving size: 4 pear quarters, 2 tablespoons liquid, and 2 tablespoons cream).

(Totals include Sweet Yogurt Cream) CALORIES 263 (20% from fat); FAT 5.9g (sat 3.3g, mono 1.7g, poly 0.4g); PROTEIN 3.8g; CARB 52.8g; FIBER 4.1g; CHOL 15mg; IRON 0.7mg; SODIUM 86mg; CALC 127mg

Sweet Yogurt Cream

  1 (16-ounce) container plain low-fat yogurt
  4½ teaspoons honey
  ¼ teaspoon vanilla extract

1. Place a colander in a 2-quart glass measure or medium bowl. Line colander with 4 layers of cheesecloth, allowing cheesecloth to extend over edges. Spoon yogurt into colander. Cover yogurt with plastic wrap; refrigerate 24 hours. Spoon yogurt cheese into a bowl, and discard liquid. Stir in honey and vanilla. Yield: 1 cup (serving size: 2 tablespoons).

CALORIES 48 (17% from fat); FAT 0.9g (sat 0.6g, mono 0.2g, poly 0g); PROTEIN 3g; CARB 7.3g; FIBER 0g; CHOL 4mg; IRON 0.1mg; SODIUM 40mg; CALC 104mg

Crepes with Bananas and Hazelnut-Chocolate Sauce

Spreading sauce on the plate prevents it from discoloring the delicate crepes. A dusting of powdered sugar finishes the dish.

Prep: 15 minutes • Cook: 30 minutes
Other: 15 minutes

    Basic Crepes (page 112)
  ¼ cup hazelnut-chocolate spread (such as Nutella)
  2 tablespoons fat-free milk
  ¼ teaspoon vanilla extract
  2 large firm unpeeled bananas (about 1¾ pounds)
Cooking spray
Powdered sugar (optional)

1. Prepare crepes.
2. To prepare sauce, combine hazelnut-chocolate spread, 2 tablespoons milk, and vanilla in a small saucepan over medium heat, stirring with a whisk until smooth. Keep warm.
3. Peel bananas, and cut in half lengthwise; cut each half crosswise into 2 pieces.
4. Heat a large nonstick skillet coated with cooking spray over medium-high heat. Arrange 4 banana pieces in a single layer in pan. Cook 1 minute or until lightly browned. Turn pieces over; cook 1 minute. Remove banana pieces from pan; keep warm. Repeat procedure with remaining banana pieces.
5. Place 1 banana piece in center of each crepe; fold sides and ends over, and place seam sides down on clean surface.
6. Spoon about 1 tablespoon sauce onto each of 4 plates, spreading to cover center of plates. Arrange 2 crepes on each plate; sprinkle with powdered sugar, if desired. Serve immediately. Yield: 4 servings (serving size: 2 crepes).

(Totals include Basic Crepes) CALORIES 312 (22% from fat); FAT 7.6g (sat 1.8g, mono 4.3g, poly 0.9g); PROTEIN 9.6g; CARB 51.6g; FIBER 3.3g; CHOL 81mg; IRON 2mg; SODIUM 148mg; CALC 141mg

Crepes with Bananas and Hazelnut-Chocolate Sauce

Meringues with Fresh Strawberries and Chocolate Mascarpone

Crisp meringues are topped with a chocolate-cheese mixture and juicy fresh strawberries. Mascarpone cheese is a buttery cream cheese with a texture similar to that of clotted cream.

Prep: 20 minutes • Cook: 1 hour, 30 minutes
Other: 45 minutes

Meringues:
> 2 large egg whites
> ¼ teaspoon cream of tartar
> ½ cup sugar

Chocolate Mascarpone:
> 1½ tablespoons sugar
> 1 tablespoon unsweetened cocoa
> 6 tablespoons (3 ounces) mascarpone cheese, softened
> 1 teaspoon fat-free milk
> ¼ teaspoon vanilla extract

Strawberries:
> 3½ cups quartered small strawberries (about 1½ quarts)
> ¼ cup sugar
> Mint sprigs (optional)

1. Preheat oven to 225°.
2. Cover a baking sheet with parchment paper. Draw 6 (4-inch) circles on paper. Turn paper over; secure with masking tape. Place egg whites and cream of tartar in a large bowl; beat with a mixer at high speed until foamy. Add ½ cup sugar, 1 tablespoon at a time, beating until stiff peaks form (do not underbeat). Divide mixture evenly among 6 circles on baking sheet; spread to fill circles using back of a spoon.
3. Bake at 225° for 1½ hours. Turn oven off; cool meringues in closed oven 30 minutes. Carefully remove meringues from paper. Cool completely. (Meringues can be stored in an airtight container up to one week.)
4. Sift together 1½ tablespoons sugar and cocoa. Combine mascarpone, milk, and vanilla; stir just until combined. Stir in cocoa mixture.
5. Toss berries with ¼ cup sugar; let stand 15 minutes.
6. Place meringues on plates; spread mascarpone mixture on top of meringues. Top with strawberry mixture. Garnish with mint, if desired. Yield: 6 servings (serving size: 1 meringue, 1½ tablespoons mascarpone mixture, and ½ cup strawberry mixture).

CALORIES 211 (30% from fat); FAT 7g (sat 3.6g, mono 1.5g, poly 0.4g); PROTEIN 3g; CARB 35.9g; FIBER 2.5g; CHOL 18mg; IRON 0.5mg; SODIUM 28mg; CALC 32mg

Brown Sugar Pavlovas with Fruit
(pictured on page 165)

A *pavlova* is a crisp meringue shell piled high with whipped cream and fresh berries.

Prep: 25 minutes • Cook: 1 hour
Other: 4 hours

> 4 large egg whites
> 2 teaspoons cornstarch
> ¼ teaspoon salt
> ¾ cup granulated sugar
> ¼ cup packed brown sugar
> 1 teaspoon vanilla extract
> ¾ cup whipping cream
> 2 tablespoons powdered sugar
> ¼ teaspoon ground cinnamon
> 3 cups chopped fresh pineapple
> ¾ cup chopped peeled kiwi
> ¾ cup fresh blackberries or raspberries
> 3 tablespoons fat-free caramel sundae syrup

1. Preheat oven to 350°.
2. Cover a large baking sheet with parchment paper. Draw 6 (4-inch) circles on paper. Turn paper over; secure with masking tape.
3. Beat egg whites, cornstarch, and salt with a mixer at high speed until foamy. Add granulated sugar and brown sugar, 1 tablespoon at a time, beating until thick and glossy. Add vanilla, beating well. Divide egg white mixture evenly among 6 drawn circles. Shape meringues into nests with 1-inch sides using back of a spoon. Place meringues in oven. Immediately reduce oven temperature to 300°; bake for 1 hour. Turn oven off, and cool meringues in closed oven at least 4 hours or until completely dry. (Meringues are done when surface is dry and meringues can be removed from paper without sticking to fingers.) Carefully remove meringue nests from paper.
4. Beat whipping cream, powdered sugar, and cinnamon with a mixer at high speed until stiff peaks form. Dollop whipped cream into each meringue nest. Top with pineapple, kiwi, and blackberries. Drizzle caramel syrup over fruit. Serve immediately. Yield: 6 servings (serving size: 1 meringue nest, ¼ cup whipped cream, ½ cup pineapple, 2 tablespoons kiwi, 2 tablespoons blackberries, and 1½ teaspoons syrup).

CALORIES 356 (29% from fat); FAT 11.5g (sat 6.9g, mono 3.2g, poly 0.6g); PROTEIN 3.5g; CARB 61.9g; FIBER 2.8g; CHOL 41mg; IRON 0.7mg; SODIUM 178mg; CALC 53mg

Test Kitchen Tip: Whipping cream whips better when the bowl and beaters are chilled.

pies &
pastries

Chocolate Silk Pie,
page 207

Crusts   We've come up with three basic crusts that are easy to make and adaptable enough for a variety of fillings.

Graham Cracker Crust

This crust is lower in fat than many commercial graham cracker crusts. The egg white acts as a binder for the cracker crumbs and allows you to use less butter and sugar.

Prep: 5 minutes • Cook: 9 minutes
Other: 15 minutes

- 40   graham crackers (10 full cracker sheets)
- 2   tablespoons sugar
- 2   tablespoons butter, melted
- 1   large egg white
- Cooking spray

1. Preheat oven to 350°.
2. Place crackers in a food processor; process until crumbly. Add sugar, butter, and egg white; pulse 6 times or just until moist. Press crumb mixture into a 9-inch pie plate coated with cooking spray. Bake at 350° for 8 minutes; cool on a wire rack 15 minutes. Yield: 1 piecrust (⅛ of crust).

CALORIES 114 (36% from fat); FAT 4.6g (sat 1.7g, mono 1.8g, poly 0.2g); PROTEIN 1.7g; CARB 16.5g; FIBER 0.6g; CHOL 8mg; IRON 0.7mg; SODIUM 194mg; CALC 142mg

---

graham cracker crumbs
Pulsing cookies in a food processor will give you the best cookie crumbs, but here are some other options.
- Buy boxed graham cracker crumbs; the calories and fat are the same as if you'd made your own crumbs.
- Use a blender instead of a food processor, but make crumbs in smaller batches and pulse; don't pulverize.
- Place the graham crackers in a zip-top plastic bag, and roll with a heavy rolling pin or bottle to make crumbs.

Double-Crust Piecrust

For this double-crust piecrust, you first make a slurry—flour and water whisked together. Vinegar helps "relax" the gluten in the flour and produce a more tender crust. If you're making a savory double-crust pie, omit the powdered sugar.

Prep: 15 minutes • Other: 10 minutes

- 2   cups all-purpose flour, divided
- 6   tablespoons ice water
- 1   teaspoon cider vinegar
- 2   tablespoons powdered sugar
- ½   teaspoon salt
- 7   tablespoons vegetable shortening

1. Lightly spoon 2 cups flour into dry measuring cups; level with a knife. Combine ½ cup flour, ice water, and vinegar, stirring with a whisk until well blended to form a slurry. Combine 1½ cups flour, powdered sugar, and ½ teaspoon salt in a large bowl; cut in shortening with a pastry blender or 2 knives until mixture resembles coarse meal. Add slurry; toss with a fork until flour mixture is moist.
2. Divide dough in half. Press each half into a 4-inch circle on two sheets of overlapping plastic wrap; cover with two additional sheets of overlapping plastic wrap. Roll one dough half, still covered, into a 12-inch circle. Roll other dough half, still covered, into an 11-inch circle. Chill dough 10 minutes or until plastic wrap can be easily removed. Yield: 1 piecrust (serving size: ¹⁄₁₀ of crust).

CALORIES 174 (46% from fat); FAT 8.7g (sat 2.1g, mono 2.8g, poly 2.2g); PROTEIN 2.6g; CARB 20.6g; FIBER 0.7g; CHOL 0mg; IRON 1.2mg; SODIUM 119mg; CALC 4mg

how to make a slurry

1. Make a slurry with ½ cup flour, ice water, and vinegar, stirring with a whisk until well blended.

2. Add the slurry, and toss with a fork until the flour mixture is moist and crumbly (do not form a ball).

Baked Piecrust

Use this recipe for any recipe that calls for baking a refrigerated pie dough.

**Prep: 15 minutes • Cook: 15 minutes
Other: 20 minutes**

1½   cups all-purpose flour
  2   tablespoons sugar
  ¼   teaspoon salt
  3   tablespoons butter
  2   tablespoons vegetable shortening
  4   tablespoons ice water
  Cooking spray

1. Preheat oven to 400°.
2. Lightly spoon flour into dry measuring cups; level with a knife. Combine flour, sugar, and salt; cut in butter and shortening with a pastry blender or 2 knives until mixture resembles coarse meal. Sprinkle surface with ice water, 1 tablespoon at a time; toss with a fork until moist and crumbly (do not form a ball).
3. Press into a 4-inch circle on plastic wrap; cover. Chill 15 minutes. Slightly overlap two sheets of plastic wrap on a slightly damp surface. Unwrap and place chilled dough on plastic. Cover dough with two additional sheets of overlapping plastic wrap. Roll dough, still covered, into a 13-inch circle. Place in freezer 5 minutes or until plastic can be easily removed.
4. Remove top sheets of plastic wrap; fit dough, plastic wrap side up, into a 9- or 10-inch pie plate coated with cooking spray. Remove remaining plastic wrap. Fold edges under; flute. Pierce bottom and sides of dough with a fork; bake at 400° for 15 minutes. Cool on a wire rack. Yield: 1 piecrust (serving size: ¹⁄₁₀ of crust).

CALORIES 113 (48% from fat); FAT 6g (sat 2.7g, mono 2.1g, poly 0.8g); PROTEIN 1.8g; CARB 13g; FIBER 0.5g; CHOL 9mg; IRON 0.8mg; SODIUM 65mg; CALC 1mg

how to make a piecrust

1. Combine flour and salt in a bowl; cut in butter and shortening with a pastry blender or 2 knives until mixture resembles coarse meal. Sprinkle with water, 1 tablespoon at a time; toss with a fork.

2. Press the mixture gently into a 4-inch circle on plastic wrap; cover with additional plastic wrap. Chill 15 minutes.

3. Roll the dough, still covered, into a 13-inch circle; place the dough in the freezer 5 minutes or until the plastic wrap can be easily removed.

4. Remove the top sheet of plastic wrap; fit the dough, plastic wrap side up, into a pie plate coated with cooking spray. Remove the plastic wrap.

5. Press the dough against the bottom and up the sides of the plate. Fold the edges under and flute.

6. Some recipes call for pre-baking the crust using pie weights. Line the bottom of dough with foil; arrange pie weights on foil. Bake as directed. Remove the pie weights and foil; cool on a wire rack.

Pies & Tarts
Master the art of low-fat pies with our collection of cream pies, frosty frozen pies, fruit-packed pies and tarts, and tender turnovers.

Double-Chocolate Cream Pie

Get twice the hit of chocolate with cocoa and semisweet chocolate.

**Prep: 14 minutes • Cook: 18 minutes
Other: 2 hours**

Crust:
- ½ (15-ounce) package refrigerated pie dough (such as Pillsbury) or Baked Piecrust (page 203)

Filling:
- ¾ cup sugar
- ¼ cup unsweetened cocoa
- 3 tablespoons cornstarch
- ⅛ teaspoon salt
- 2 cups 1% low-fat milk
- 1 large egg, lightly beaten
- 1½ ounces semisweet chocolate, grated
- 1 teaspoon vanilla extract
- 1½ cups frozen fat-free whipped topping, thawed

1. Preheat oven to 350°.
2. Prepare and bake piecrust in a 9-inch pie plate. Cool crust completely on a wire rack.
3. To prepare filling, combine sugar, cocoa, cornstarch, salt, and milk in a medium saucepan; stir well with a whisk. Bring to a boil over medium heat, stirring constantly; cook 1 minute. Gradually add ⅓ cup hot milk mixture to egg, stirring constantly with a whisk. Return egg mixture to pan. Cook 2 minutes or until egg mixture thickens, stirring constantly. Remove from heat; add grated chocolate, stirring until chocolate melts and mixture is smooth. Stir in vanilla. Spoon mixture into prepared crust. Cover surface of filling with plastic wrap. Chill until set (about 2 hours). Remove plastic wrap; spread whipped topping evenly over filling. Yield: 10 servings (serving size: 1 wedge).

CALORIES 271 (28% from fat); FAT 8.4g (sat 4g, mono 2.2g, poly 1.4g); PROTEIN 4.9g; CARB 43.9g; FIBER 1.1g; CHOL 32mg; IRON 1.1mg; SODIUM 151mg; CALC 66mg

how to grate chocolate

Grate the chocolate with a handheld grater or zester, or use the smallest holes on a box grater.

Lemon Meringue Pie

The glossy, billowy topping is prepared by beating cooked sugar syrup into slightly beaten egg whites, producing what is known as an Italian meringue. The sugar syrup must reach 250° so that it's hot enough to "cook" the egg whites to the recommended safe temperature of 160°. You'll need a candy thermometer to check the temperature of the sugar syrup.

Prep: 20 minutes • Cook: 20 minutes

Filling:

- ¾ cup sugar
- 2 tablespoons cornstarch
- 2 tablespoons all-purpose flour
- 2 teaspoons grated lemon rind
- Dash of salt
- 1 cup water
- 2 tablespoons butter
- ⅓ cup fresh lemon juice
- 2 large egg yolks
- 1 (6-ounce) reduced-fat graham cracker crust or Graham Cracker Crust (page 202)

Italian Meringue:

- 3 large egg whites
- ¼ teaspoon cream of tartar
- ⅔ cup sugar
- ¼ cup water

1. To prepare filling, combine first 5 ingredients in a saucepan. Add 1 cup water, stirring constantly with a whisk. Bring to a simmer over medium heat, and cook 5 minutes, stirring frequently. Stir in butter; remove from heat. Stir in lemon juice. Add egg yolks, 1 at a time, beating well with a mixer at medium speed after each addition. Place pan over low heat; cook 3 minutes, stirring constantly. Spoon filling into crust. Cool to room temperature.

2. To prepare meringue, place egg whites and cream of tartar in a large bowl; beat with a mixer at high speed until foamy, using clean, dry beaters. Combine ⅔ cup sugar and ¼ cup water in a small saucepan; bring to boil. Cook mixture, without stirring, until candy thermometer registers 250°. Pour hot sugar syrup in a thin stream over egg white mixture, beating at high speed until stiff peaks form. Spread meringue evenly over filling, and seal meringue to edge of crust.

3. Preheat broiler.

4. Broil meringue 1 minute or until lightly browned; cool pie on a wire rack. Chill until set. Yield: 8 servings (serving size: 1 wedge).

CALORIES 292 (24% from fat); FAT 7.7g (sat 2.9g, mono 2.9g, poly 1.6g); PROTEIN 3.3g; CARB 54g; FIBER 0.1g; CHOL 62mg; IRON 0.6mg; SODIUM 172mg; CALC 10mg

Make sure your bowl is dry and clean when you beat the egg whites or they won't beat properly. Glass, ceramic, or metal bowls are best.

how to make an italian meringue

1. Beat the egg whites until soft peaks form (A). Overbeating—incorporating too much air—will cause them to separate (B).

2. Bring the sugar and water to a boil; cook until 250°. Do not stir. Slowly pour the sugar syrup into the egg whites, beating with a mixer at high speed until the syrup is thoroughly incorporated. The meringue should look smooth and glossy.

Classic Makeover: Coconut Pie

A traditional coconut cream pie is loaded with fat from the crust to the topping. We reduced the fat by starting with our lower-fat crust that has slightly less shortening than a traditional crust. For the filling, we decreased the number of eggs, used 1% low-fat milk instead of whole, and omitted the butter. We were able to use less milk and fewer eggs in the filling because we added crushed pineapple. Instead of adding flaked coconut to both the filling and the topping, we stirred a small amount of cream of coconut and coconut extract into the filling, and just sprinkled a small amount of coconut on top of the pie. We reduced the fat even more by topping it with fat-free whipped topping instead of whipped cream.

Before	After
• 525 calories	• 319 calories
• 31.4g fat	• 10g fat
• percentage of calories from fat 54%	• percentage of calories from fat 28%

Coconut Cream Pie with Pineapple

The cream of coconut enhances the flavor of the filling, and the pineapple helps make it even more tropical.

Prep: 30 minutes • Cook: 27 minutes
Other: 2 hours, 10 minutes

Crust:
- 1 cup all-purpose flour, divided
- 3 tablespoons ice water
- 2 tablespoons sugar
- ⅛ teaspoon salt
- ¼ cup vegetable shortening
- Cooking spray

Filling:
- 1 (8¼-ounce) can crushed pineapple in heavy syrup, drained
- ¾ cup sugar
- ¼ cup cornstarch
- ¼ teaspoon salt
- 1½ cups 1% low-fat milk
- 2 large eggs, lightly beaten
- 2 tablespoons cream of coconut
- ¼ teaspoon coconut extract
- ¼ teaspoon vanilla extract
- 1½ cups frozen fat-free whipped topping, thawed
- ¼ cup flaked sweetened coconut, toasted

1. Preheat oven to 425°.

2. To prepare crust, lightly spoon flour into dry measuring cups; level with a knife. Combine ¼ cup flour and water; stir with a whisk until slurry is blended.

3. Combine ¾ cup flour, 2 tablespoons sugar, and ⅛ teaspoon salt in a bowl; cut in shortening with a pastry blender or 2 knives until mixture resembles coarse meal. Add slurry; mix with a fork until flour mixture is moist.

4. Press mixture gently into a 4-inch circle on heavy-duty plastic wrap, and cover with additional plastic wrap. Roll dough, still covered, into a 12-inch circle. Freeze 10 minutes.

5. Remove one sheet of plastic wrap, and fit dough into a 9-inch pie plate coated with cooking spray. Remove top sheet of plastic wrap. Fold edges under, and flute. Line dough with a piece of foil, and arrange pie weights or dried beans on foil. Bake at 425° for 20 minutes or until edge is lightly browned. Remove pie weights and foil from crust; cool crust on a wire rack.

6. To prepare filling, spoon pineapple into prepared crust. Combine ¾ cup sugar, cornstarch, and ¼ teaspoon salt in a saucepan, and stir in milk. Bring to a boil; cook 1 minute, stirring with a whisk. Gradually add about ⅓ cup hot custard to beaten eggs, stirring constantly with a whisk. Return egg mixture to pan. Cook 2 minutes or until thick, stirring constantly. Remove mixture from heat; stir in cream of coconut and extracts. Spoon mixture into prepared crust. Cover surface of filling with plastic wrap; chill until set (about 2 hours).

7. Remove plastic wrap, and spread whipped topping evenly over filling. Sprinkle with coconut. Yield: 8 servings (serving size: 1 wedge).

CALORIES 319 (28% from fat); FAT 10g (sat 6.4g, mono 2.4g, poly 0.5g); PROTEIN 5g; CARB 51.9g; FIBER 0.9g; CHOL 73mg; IRON 1.2mg; SODIUM 226mg; CALC 68mg

Test Kitchen Tip: When you prebake a crust, use pie weights (or uncooked dried beans) to weigh the pastry down and prevent it from puffing up as it bakes. (See page 203.)

Chocolate Silk Pie
(pictured on page 201)

Part of the Italian meringue is folded into the rich chocolate custard to give the pie its silky texture.

Prep: 25 minutes • Cook: 25 minutes
Other: 8 hours, 10 minutes

Crust:
 ½ (15-ounce) package refrigerated pie dough (such as Pillsbury) or Baked Piecrust (page 203)
Filling:
 ⅓ cup all-purpose flour
 ½ cup sugar
 ½ cup unsweetened cocoa
 ¼ teaspoon salt
1¾ cups 2% reduced-fat milk
 4 ounces semisweet chocolate, chopped
Italian Meringue:
 5 large egg whites
 ¼ teaspoon salt
1¼ cups sugar
 ⅔ cup water
 Grated chocolate (optional)

1. Prepare and bake piecrust in a 10-inch deep-dish pie plate. Cool completely on a wire rack.

2. To prepare filling, lightly spoon flour into a dry measuring cup; level with a knife. Combine flour, ½ cup sugar, cocoa, and ¼ teaspoon salt in a medium saucepan; stir with a whisk. Gradually stir in milk. Bring to a boil over medium heat, stirring constantly. Reduce heat; cook 2 minutes or until thick and bubbly, stirring constantly.

3. Remove from heat; add chopped chocolate, stirring until chocolate melts. Spoon chocolate mixture into a bowl; place bowl in a larger ice-filled bowl 10 minutes or until chocolate mixture comes to room temperature, stirring occasionally. Remove bowl from ice.

4. To prepare meringue, place egg whites and ¼ teaspoon salt in a large bowl; beat with a mixer at high speed until soft peaks form. Combine 1¼ cups sugar and water in a saucepan; bring to a boil. Cook, without stirring, until candy thermometer registers 250°. Pour hot sugar syrup in a thin stream over egg whites, beating at high speed until stiff peaks form. Fold 2 cups meringue into chocolate mixture.

5. Spread chocolate mixture into prepared crust. Spread remaining meringue over chocolate mixture. Loosely cover; chill 8 hours. Garnish with grated chocolate, if desired. Yield: 10 servings (serving size: 1 wedge).

CALORIES 314 (26% from fat); FAT 9.1g (sat 3.4g, mono 2.1g, poly 1.6g); PROTEIN 6g; CARB 55.8g; FIBER 2.2g; CHOL 4mg; IRON 1.4mg; SODIUM 257mg; CALC 58mg

Test Kitchen Tip: To make a piecrust flakier, chill flour in the freezer for one hour prior to using. This keeps the butter being cut into the flour from melting, which can result in a tough crust.

Buttered Rum-Raisin Pie

It's important that the filling not cook any longer after it's thickened, so transfer the mixture to a bowl, and place that bowl in a larger ice-filled bowl to stop the cooking process. Cool the pie filling completely before adding the whipped topping.

Prep: 15 minutes • Cook: 25 minutes
Other: 8 hours, 10 minutes

Crust:
- ½ (15-ounce) package refrigerated pie dough (such as Pillsbury) or Baked Piecrust (page 203)

Filling:
- 2 cups golden raisins
- ¼ to ⅓ cup dark rum
- ½ cup sugar
- 3 tablespoons cornstarch
- ¼ teaspoon salt
- 2 large eggs
- 1½ cups 2% reduced-fat milk
- 3½ tablespoons butter
- 1 teaspoon vanilla extract
- 1½ cups frozen fat-free whipped topping, thawed

1. Prepare and bake piecrust in a 9-inch pie plate. Cool completely on a wire rack.
2. To prepare filling, combine raisins and rum in a small microwave-safe bowl; microwave at HIGH 1 minute or until raisins are plump. Set aside.
3. Combine sugar, cornstarch, salt, and eggs in a large bowl, and stir well with a whisk.
4. Heat milk over medium-high heat in a small, heavy saucepan to 180° or until tiny bubbles form around edge (do not boil). Gradually add hot milk to sugar mixture, stirring constantly with a whisk. Return mixture to pan; bring to a boil over medium heat, stirring constantly. Reduce heat;

cook 8 to 10 minutes or until thick and bubbly, stirring constantly. Remove from heat; stir in butter.
5. Spoon custard into a bowl; place bowl in a larger ice-filled bowl 10 minutes or until custard comes to room temperature, stirring occasionally. Remove bowl from ice. Stir in raisins and vanilla; spoon mixture into prepared crust. Cover surface of filling with plastic wrap. Chill 8 hours or until firm. Remove plastic wrap; spread whipped topping evenly over filling. Yield: 10 servings (serving size: 1 wedge).

CALORIES 309 (29% from fat); FAT 10g (sat 3.9g, mono 3.5g, poly 1.9g); PROTEIN 4.2g; CARB 50.4g; FIBER 2.4g; CHOL 56mg; IRON 0.8mg; SODIUM 223mg; CALC 67mg

Fresh Strawberry Pie

Make this recipe when you have a bucket of freshly picked berries. The berries used to make the glaze can be any size, as they're macerated and pureed. But the berries piled in the pie itself should be small—the smaller the better.

Prep: 30 minutes • Cook: 30 minutes
Other: 3 hours

Crust:
- 50 reduced-calorie vanilla wafers
- ¼ cup butter, melted
- 2 tablespoons sugar
- 1 teaspoon grated orange rind
- Cooking spray

Filling:
- 2 cups hulled ripe strawberries
- ½ cup water
- ⅔ cup sugar
- 2 tablespoons cornstarch
- 1 tablespoon fresh lemon juice
- 6 cups hulled small ripe strawberries
- ½ cup frozen reduced-calorie whipped topping, thawed

1. Preheat oven to 350°.
2. To prepare crust, place wafers in a food processor, and process until finely ground. Add butter, 2 tablespoons sugar, and orange rind, and pulse 10 times or just until wafers are moist. Press mixture into bottom and up sides of a 9-inch pie plate coated with cooking spray. Bake crust at 350° for 15 minutes, and cool on a wire rack.
3. To prepare filling, mash 2 cups strawberries with a potato masher. Combine mashed strawberries and water in a small saucepan; bring to a boil, and cook 5 minutes, stirring occasionally. Press strawberry mixture through a sieve into a bowl; reserve 1 cup strawberry liquid (add enough water to measure 1 cup, if necessary). Discard pulp.
4. Combine ⅔ cup sugar and cornstarch in a small saucepan; add strawberry liquid, stirring well with a whisk. Bring to a boil; cook 1 minute, stirring constantly. Reduce heat; cook 2 minutes. Remove from heat; stir in lemon juice.
5. Arrange a layer of small strawberries, stem sides down, in crust. Spoon about one-third of sauce over strawberries. Arrange remaining small strawberries on top, and spoon remaining sauce over strawberries. Chill pie at least 3 hours. Serve pie with whipped topping. Yield: 8 servings (serving size: 1 wedge and 1 tablespoon whipped topping).

CALORIES 285 (27% from fat); FAT 8.5g (sat 4.6g, mono 2.5g, poly 0.9g); PROTEIN 1.9g; CARB 52.2g; FIBER 3.5g; CHOL 16mg; IRON 1.2mg; SODIUM 146mg; CALC 42mg

Test Kitchen Tip: Enjoy strawberries all year long by freezing peak-season berries. Freeze berries in a single layer on a large plastic wrap-lined pan, then transfer into zip-top plastic bags. You can measure out small amounts any time you need them.

Frozen Peanut Butter-Banana Cream Pie

This make-ahead frozen cream pie has a sweet cream cheese and peanut butter
filling that is spread over sliced banana and drizzled with chocolate syrup.

Prep: 10 minutes • Cook: 9 minutes   Other: 8 hours, 30 minutes

Crust:
Graham Cracker Crust (page 202)

Filling:
- ¾ cup packed brown sugar
- ½ cup (4 ounces) ⅓-less-fat cream cheese
- ½ cup reduced-fat peanut butter
- ½ teaspoon vanilla extract
- 1 (8-ounce) container frozen fat-free whipped topping, thawed
- 1 cup sliced banana (about 2 small bananas)
- ¼ cup fat-free chocolate sundae syrup

1. Prepare Graham Cracker Crust.

2. To prepare filling, place ¾ cup brown sugar, cream cheese, peanut butter, and vanilla in a bowl; beat with a mixer at medium speed until smooth. Fold in whipped topping. Arrange banana in bottom of prepared crust. Spread peanut butter mixture over banana; drizzle with syrup. Cover and freeze 8 hours; let stand at room temperature 15 minutes before serving. Yield: 10 servings (serving size: 1 wedge).

(Totals include Graham Cracker Crust) CALORIES 331 (30% from fat); FAT 11g (sat 4.3g, mono 1.2g, poly 0.6g); PROTEIN 5.7g; CARB 52g; FIBER 1.8g; CHOL 14mg; IRON 1mg; SODIUM 256mg; CALC 27mg

Frozen Lemonade Pie with Blueberry Sauce

Enjoy summertime favorites like cold lemonade and fresh blueberries in this frozen pie.

Prep: 9 minutes • Cook: 15 minutes
Other: 7 hours, 45 minutes

Crust:
  Graham Cracker Crust (page 202)
Filling:
  4   cups vanilla low-fat frozen yogurt
  ½   cup thawed lemonade concentrate, undiluted
  Blueberry Sauce (page 460)

1. Prepare Graham Cracker Crust.
2. Freeze piecrust 30 minutes.
3. To prepare filling, place an extralarge bowl in freezer. Remove yogurt from freezer; let stand at room temperature while crust is cooling.
4. Spoon yogurt into chilled extralarge bowl. Fold lemonade concentrate into yogurt; freeze 30 minutes or just until set but not solid.
5. Spoon yogurt mixture into prepared crust; freeze until set. Cover with plastic wrap; freeze 6 hours or until firm.
6. Place pie in refrigerator 30 minutes before serving to soften. Serve pie with Blueberry Sauce. Yield: 8 servings (serving size: 1 wedge and 3 tablespoons sauce).

(Totals include Graham Cracker Crust and Blueberry Sauce)
CALORIES 291 (19% from fat); FAT 6g (sat 2.9g, mono 1.8g, poly 0.9g); PROTEIN 6.4g; CARB 54.5g; FIBER 1.2g; CHOL 13mg; IRON 0.9mg; SODIUM 193mg; CALC 162mg

Strawberry-Swirl Frozen Pie

Double your berry delight with this make-ahead pie featuring sliced fresh strawberries and strawberry frozen yogurt.

Prep: 20 minutes • Cook: 9 minutes
Other: 8 hours, 5 minutes

Crust:
  40   reduced-fat vanilla wafers
  2   tablespoons sugar
  2   tablespoons butter, melted
  1   large egg white
  Cooking spray
Filling:
  3   cups strawberry low-fat frozen yogurt
  1½   cups sliced strawberries
  3   tablespoons sugar
  1   cup frozen reduced-calorie whipped topping, thawed

1. Preheat oven to 350°.
2. To prepare crust, place cookies in a food processor; process until crumbly. Add 2 tablespoons sugar, butter, and egg white; pulse 5 times or just until moist. Press crumb mixture evenly into a 9-inch pie plate coated with cooking spray. Bake at 350° for 8 minutes; cool on a wire rack 15 minutes. Freeze pie-crust 30 minutes.
3. To prepare filling, place an extralarge bowl in freezer. Remove yogurt from freezer; let stand at room temperature while crust is cooling.
4. Combine strawberries and 3 table-spoons sugar in a large bowl; stir well. Let stand 20 minutes. Wipe out food processor bowl with a paper towel. Add sugared strawberries; process until finely chopped.
5. Spoon yogurt into chilled extralarge bowl; fold in strawberry mixture until well blended. Freeze 30 minutes or just until set but not solid.
6. Spoon yogurt mixture into prepared crust; freeze until set. Cover with plastic wrap; freeze 6 hours or until firm.
7. Place pie in refrigerator 30 minutes before serving to soften. Serve with whipped topping. Yield: 8 servings (serving size: 1 wedge and 2 tablespoons topping).

CALORIES 239 (23% from fat); FAT 6.2g (sat 3.4g, mono 1g, poly 0.2g); PROTEIN 4.6g; CARB 41.1g; FIBER 0.6g; CHOL 11mg; IRON 0.6mg; SODIUM 140mg; CALC 121mg

frozen pie tips

- While the piecrust is cooling, take the frozen yogurt or ice cream out of the freezer and let it soften. This makes it easier to fold in the other ingredients for the filling.
- Freeze the piecrust 30 minutes. The ice cream or yogurt mixture won't melt as it would if you put it into a piecrust at room temperature.
- It's best to partially refreeze the filling before spooning it into the pie shell. Combine the slightly softened frozen yogurt or ice cream and other ingredients specified in the recipe in a chilled extralarge bowl. Put the bowl back in the freezer for about 30 to 45 minutes to let it set back up. Don't let the mixture freeze solid, or the consistency will be too hard to spoon into the piecrust.
- Place the filled piecrust in the freezer until set; then cover with plastic wrap.
- Remove pie from freezer; let it stand in the refrigerator about 30 minutes before serving. This step will make it easier to cut the pie into wedges.

Frozen Strawberry Daiquiri Pie with Strawberry-Rum Sauce

Think of a frozen daiquiri in a graham cracker crust, and that's what you have with this pie. For a non-alcoholic version, use white grape juice in place of the rum.

**Prep: 20 minutes • Cook: 9 minutes
Other: 8 hours, 20 minutes**

Crust:
  Graham Cracker Crust (page 202)
Filling:
  4 cups vanilla low-fat frozen yogurt
  ⅓ cup frozen strawberry daiquiri
     concentrate, undiluted
  3 tablespoons white rum
  Strawberry-Rum Sauce (page 460)

1. Prepare Graham Cracker Crust.
2. Freeze piecrust 30 minutes.
3. To prepare filling, place an extralarge bowl in freezer. Remove frozen yogurt and daiquiri concentrate from freezer; let stand at room temperature while crust is cooling.
4. Spoon yogurt into chilled extralarge bowl. Fold concentrate and rum into yogurt. Freeze 45 minutes or until set but not solid.
5. Spoon yogurt mixture into prepared crust; freeze until set. Cover with plastic wrap; freeze 6 hours or until firm.
6. Place pie in refrigerator 30 minutes before serving to soften. Serve pie with Strawberry-Rum Sauce. Yield: 8 servings (serving size: 1 wedge and 3 tablespoons sauce).

(Totals include Graham Cracker Crust and Strawberry-Rum Sauce) CALORIES 293 (19% from fat); FAT 6.1g (sat 2.9g, mono 1.8g, poly 0.9g); PROTEIN 6.5g; CARB 48.8g; FIBER 1.7g; CHOL 13mg; IRON 1mg; SODIUM 224mg; CALC 168mg

Apple Pie

Celebrate the bounty of autumn apple season with a homestyle apple pie. Use the Double-Crust Piecrust recipe on page 202.

Prep: 35 minutes • Cook: 55 minutes • Other: 10 minutes

Crust:
  Double-Crust Piecrust (page 202)
Filling:
  8 cups thinly sliced peeled Braeburn
     apple (about 8 medium)
  1 tablespoon fresh lemon juice
  ⅔ cup sugar
  3 tablespoons all-purpose
     flour
  ½ teaspoon ground cinnamon
  ½ teaspoon ground nutmeg
  ⅛ teaspoon salt
Remaining ingredients:
  Cooking spray
  1 large egg white, lightly beaten
  1 tablespoon sugar

1. Preheat oven to 450°.
2. Prepare Double-Crust Pastry.
3. To prepare filling, combine apple and lemon juice in a large bowl. Combine ⅔ cup sugar and next 4 ingredients in a small bowl. Sprinkle sugar mixture over apple; toss well to coat.

4. Remove top two sheets of plastic wrap from 12-inch dough circle; fit dough, plastic side up, into a 9-inch deep-dish pie plate coated with cooking spray, allowing dough to extend over edge. Remove remaining plastic wrap. Spoon filling into dough; brush edges of dough lightly with water.
5. Remove top two sheets of plastic wrap from 11-inch dough circle, and place dough, plastic wrap side up, over filling. Remove plastic wrap. Press edges of dough together. Fold edges under; flute. Cut 4 (1-inch) slits into top of pastry using a sharp knife. Brush top and edges of pie with egg white; sprinkle with 1 tablespoon sugar.
6. Place pie on a baking sheet; bake at 450° for 15 minutes. Reduce oven temperature to 350° (do not remove pie from oven), and bake an additional 40 minutes or until golden. Cool on a wire rack. Yield: 10 servings (serving size: 1 wedge).

(Totals include Double-Crust Pastry) CALORIES 293 (29% from fat); FAT 9.6g (sat 2.4g, mono 4g, poly 2.5g); PROTEIN 3.3g; CARB 50.1g; FIBER 2.5g; CHOL 0mg; IRON 1.4mg; SODIUM 153mg; CALC 10mg

Warm Apple-Buttermilk Custard Pie

The ultimate in comfort food, this pie features a creamy custard filling and a sweet, crumbly topping.

Prep: 20 minutes • Cook: 1 hour, 20 minutes
Other: 1 hour

Crust:
 ½ (15-ounce) package refrigerated pie dough (such as Pillsbury)
  Cooking spray

Streusel:
 ⅓ cup all-purpose flour
 ⅓ cup packed brown sugar
 ½ teaspoon ground cinnamon
 2½ tablespoons chilled butter, cut into small pieces

Filling:
 5 cups sliced peeled Granny Smith apple (about 2 pounds)
 1 cup granulated sugar, divided
 ½ teaspoon ground cinnamon
 2 tablespoons all-purpose flour
 ¼ teaspoon salt
 3 large eggs
 1¾ cups fat-free buttermilk
 1 teaspoon vanilla extract

1. Preheat oven to 325°.
2. Roll dough into a 14-inch circle; fit into a 9-inch deep-dish pie plate coated with cooking spray. Fold edges under, and flute. Place in refrigerator until ready to use.
3. To prepare streusel, lightly spoon ⅓ cup flour into a dry measuring cup; level with a knife. Combine ⅓ cup flour, brown sugar, and ½ teaspoon ground cinnamon in a medium bowl; cut in butter with a pastry blender or 2 knives until mixture resembles coarse meal. Place streusel in refrigerator.
4. To prepare filling, heat a large nonstick skillet over medium heat; coat pan with cooking spray. Add sliced apple, ¼ cup granulated sugar, and ½ teaspoon cinnamon; cook 10 minutes or until apple is tender, stirring occasionally. Spoon apple mixture into prepared crust.
5. Combine remaining ¾ cup granulated sugar, 2 tablespoons flour, salt, and eggs, stirring with a whisk. Stir in buttermilk and vanilla. Pour over apple mixture. Bake at 325° for 30 minutes. Reduce oven temperature to 300° (do not remove pie from oven); sprinkle streusel over pie. Bake at 300° for 40 minutes or until set. Let stand 1 hour before serving. Yield: 10 servings (serving size: 1 wedge).

CALORIES 317 (29% from fat); FAT 10.1g (sat 4.6g, mono 3g, poly 1.2g); PROTEIN 5g; CARB 52.6g; FIBER 1.3g; CHOL 76mg; IRON 0.8mg; SODIUM 230mg; CALC 73mg

Brown Sugar-Peach Pie with Coconut Streusel

The streusel topping for this juicy peach pie is extracrispy and brown because of the toasted coconut and hearty oats. Quick-cooking tapioca is used to thicken the filling rather than flour or cornstarch.

Prep: 20 minutes • Cook: 1 hour, 13 minutes
Other: 15 minutes

 ½ (15-ounce) package refrigerated pie dough (such as Pillsbury)
 ⅔ cup packed brown sugar, divided
 ¼ cup uncooked quick-cooking tapioca
 ½ teaspoon ground cinnamon
 6 cups sliced peeled ripe peaches (about 3 pounds), divided
 ⅓ cup regular oats
 ¼ cup flaked sweetened coconut
 1½ tablespoons butter, melted

1. Preheat oven to 425°.
2. Fit dough into a 9-inch pie plate. Fold edges under; flute. Line dough with a piece of foil, and arrange pie weights or dried beans on foil. Bake at 425° for 12 minutes. Remove pie weights and foil. Cool crust on a wire rack.
3. Combine ⅓ cup sugar, tapioca, and cinnamon in a bowl; sprinkle over 4½ cups peaches. Toss gently; let stand 15 minutes. Spoon into prepared crust. Top with 1½ cups peaches. Place pie in 425° oven. Immediately reduce oven temperature to 350°; bake 30 minutes. Combine ⅓ cup sugar, oats, coconut, and butter; sprinkle over peach mixture. Shield edges of crust with foil. Bake 30 minutes or until golden. Cool on a wire rack. Yield: 8 servings (serving size: 1 wedge).

CALORIES 307 (31% from fat); FAT 10.5g (sat 5g, mono 3.9g, poly 1g); PROTEIN 2.1g; CARB 52.7g; FIBER 3.1g; CHOL 11mg; IRON 0.8mg; SODIUM 137mg; CALC 27mg

Test Kitchen Tip: Peel peaches with a potato peeler if they're not too ripe. If they're ripe, plunge them in boiling water for about 30 seconds; that makes the skin a cinch to remove with a paring knife.

how to make streusel

To make the streusel, combine the sugar, oats, coconut, and butter with a fork until crumbly and all the dry ingredients are moist, about 2 to 3 minutes.

Lattice-Topped Blueberry Pie

The ingredients for the crust are the same as in our Baked Piecrust (page 203), but you divide the dough so you can make a lattice, and you don't prebake the crust.

**Prep: 30 minutes • Cook: 1 hour, 16 minutes
Other: 10 minutes**

Crust:

1½ cups all-purpose flour
 2 tablespoons sugar
 ¼ teaspoon salt
 3 tablespoons butter
 2 tablespoons vegetable shortening
 4 tablespoons ice water
 Cooking spray

Filling:

 1 cup sugar, divided
3½ tablespoons cornstarch
 ⅛ teaspoon salt
 6 cups fresh blueberries
1½ tablespoons butter, melted
 ¾ teaspoon vanilla extract

1. To prepare crust, lightly spoon flour into dry measuring cups; level with a knife. Combine flour, 2 tablespoons sugar, and ¼ teaspoon salt in a bowl; cut in 3 tablespoons butter and shortening with a pastry blender or 2 knives until mixture resembles coarse meal. Sprinkle surface with ice water, 1 tablespoon at a time; toss with a fork until mixture is moist and crumbly (do not form a ball).

2. Gently press two-thirds of dough into a 4-inch circle on heavy-duty plastic wrap; cover with additional plastic wrap. Roll dough into a 12-inch circle. Press remaining dough into a 4-inch circle on plastic wrap; cover with additional plastic wrap. Roll dough into a 9-inch circle. Freeze both portions of dough 10 minutes.

3. Working with large portion of dough, remove one sheet of plastic wrap; fit dough into a 9-inch pie plate coated with cooking spray. Remove top sheet of plastic wrap.

4. To prepare filling, combine ¾ cup plus 3 tablespoons sugar, cornstarch, and ⅛ teaspoon salt in a bowl, and sprinkle over blueberries. Toss gently. Stir in melted butter and vanilla. Spoon blueberry mixture into crust.

5. Preheat oven to 375°.

6. Remove top sheet of plastic wrap from remaining dough. Cut dough into 6 (1½-inch) strips. Gently remove dough strips from bottom sheet of plastic wrap; arrange in a lattice design over blueberry mixture (technique below). Seal dough strips to edge of crust. Place pie on a baking sheet covered with foil. Sprinkle lattice with 1 tablespoon sugar.

7. Bake at 375° for 1 hour and 15 minutes or until crust is browned and filling is bubbly. Cool on a wire rack. Yield: 8 servings (serving size: 1 wedge).

CALORIES 354 (25% from fat); FAT 10g (sat 4.8g, mono 2.9g, poly 1.2g); PROTEIN 3.2g; CARB 64.6g; FIBER 3.6g; CHOL 17mg; IRON 1.3mg; SODIUM 183mg; CALC 12mg

how to make the lattice

Cut the dough into 6 large (1½-inch) strips. Large strips are easier to work with because you can hold the whole strip with two fingers without tearing it. To form the lattice top, alternate the horizontal and vertical strips of dough.

Pecan and Date Pie

Adding dates to the pecan filling mixture creates a whole new level
of sweetness for this traditional holiday pie.

Prep: 25 minutes • Cook: 55 minutes • Other: 10 minutes

Crust:

- 1   cup all-purpose flour, divided
- 3   tablespoons ice water
- 1   teaspoon fresh lemon juice
- 2   tablespoons powdered sugar
- ¼   teaspoon salt
- ¼   cup vegetable shortening

Cooking spray

Filling:

- ½   cup whole pitted dates, chopped
- ⅓   cup chopped pecans
- 1   cup dark corn syrup
- ½   cup packed brown sugar
- 3   tablespoons all-purpose flour
- 1   teaspoon vanilla extract
- ¼   teaspoon salt
- 4   large eggs

Reduced-calorie whipped topping,
     thawed (optional)

1. Preheat oven to 325°.

2. To prepare crust, lightly spoon 1 cup
flour into a dry measuring cup, and level
with a knife. Combine ¼ cup flour, water,
and juice, stirring with a whisk until well
blended to form a slurry.

3. Combine ¾ cup flour, powdered sugar,
and ¼ teaspoon salt; cut in shortening
with a pastry blender or 2 knives until
mixture resembles coarse meal. Add slurry;
toss with a fork until mixture is moist.
Press mixture into a 4-inch circle on two
sheets of heavy-duty plastic wrap that
overlap; cover with two additional sheets

of overlapping plastic wrap. Roll dough,
still covered, into a 12-inch circle; freeze
10 minutes.

4. Remove top two sheets of plastic wrap,
and let dough stand 1 minute or until
pliable. Fit dough, plastic wrap side up,
into a 9-inch pie plate coated with cooking spray. Remove remaining plastic wrap.
Press dough into bottom and up sides of
pan. Fold edges under; flute.

5. To prepare filling, sprinkle dates and
pecans over crust. Combine corn syrup and
next 5 ingredients in a bowl; beat with a
mixer at medium speed until well blended.
Pour into prepared crust. Bake at 325° for
55 minutes or until a knife inserted 1 inch
from edge comes out clean. Cool on a wire
rack. Serve each slice with whipped topping, if desired. Yield: 10 servings (serving
size: 1 wedge).

CALORIES 321 (29% from fat); FAT 10.2g (sat 2.2g, mono 4.7g,
poly 2.5g); PROTEIN 4.6g; CARB 55.8g; FIBER 1.5g; CHOL 85mg;
IRON 1.5mg; SODIUM 198mg; CALC 33mg

Gingered Pumpkin Pie

A gingersnap streusel topping adds a spiced crunch to classic pumpkin pie.

Prep: 13 minutes • Cook: 55 minutes
Other: 30 minutes

½ (15-ounce) package refrigerated pie
    dough (such as Pillsbury)
10 gingersnaps
2 tablespoons sugar
1 tablespoon all-purpose flour
2 tablespoons chilled butter, cut into
    small pieces
¾ cup sugar
1½ teaspoons ground cinnamon
½ teaspoon ground ginger
¼ teaspoon salt
¼ teaspoon ground nutmeg
1 (15-ounce) can pumpkin
1 (12-ounce) can evaporated fat-free milk
1 large egg
3 large egg whites

1. Roll dough into a 12-inch circle, and fit into a 10-inch deep-dish pie plate. Fold edges under; flute. Freeze 30 minutes.
2. Preheat oven to 350°.
3. Place cookies, 2 tablespoons sugar, and flour in a food processor; process until cookies are ground. Add butter; pulse until crumbly.
4. Combine ¾ cup sugar and remaining ingredients; pour into prepared crust. Bake at 350° for 35 minutes. Sprinkle crumb mixture over pie; bake an additional 20 minutes or until center is set. Cool to room temperature on a wire rack. Yield: 8 servings (serving size: 1 wedge).

CALORIES 338 (31% from fat); FAT 11.5g (sat 5.1g, mono 4.7g, poly 1.1g); PROTEIN 7.2g; CARB 51.7g; FIBER 2.6g; CHOL 41mg; IRON 1.2mg; SODIUM 340mg; CALC 157mg

canned pumpkin While fresh pumpkin is available only in the fall and winter, canned pumpkin is almost always available. You can almost always use canned pumpkin in recipes that call for fresh, mashed pumpkin. Canned pumpkin is just as nutritious as fresh—both are good sources of beta-carotene (an antioxidant that may help prevent certain types of cancer and heart disease), fiber, and potassium.

If you don't need to use the whole can, place the unused portion in an airtight container, and refrigerate up to one week, or freeze up to three months.

Apple Marzipan Galette

Think of a galette as a "free-form" pie in which the pie dough is rolled out into a circle but is not pressed into a pie plate. Before baking, the edges of the dough are folded over to partially cover a juicy fruit filling.

Prep: 20 minutes • Cook: 35 minutes

Cooking spray
½ (15-ounce) package refrigerated pie
    dough (such as Pillsbury)
½ cup marzipan, softened
4 cups sliced peeled Granny Smith
    apple (about 2 pounds)
¾ cup sugar, divided
1 tablespoon all-purpose flour
2 teaspoons lemon juice
1 teaspoon almond extract, divided
Dash of salt

1. Preheat oven to 425°.
2. Line a jelly-roll pan with foil; coat foil with cooking spray. Roll dough to a 14-inch circle on a lightly floured surface. Place on prepared pan. Roll marzipan to a 9-inch circle on a lightly floured surface. Place marzipan on top of dough.
3. Combine apple, ½ cup sugar, flour, juice, ¾ teaspoon extract, and salt in a large bowl; toss well. Spoon apple mixture over marzipan. Fold 2-inch dough border over apple mixture, pressing gently to seal (dough will only partially cover apple mixture). Bake at 425° for 30 minutes or until lightly browned (filling may leak slightly during cooking).
4. Place ¼ cup sugar in a small, heavy saucepan over medium-high heat; cook until sugar dissolves, stirring as needed to dissolve sugar evenly (about 4 minutes). Cook 1 minute or until golden. Remove from heat; carefully stir in ¼ teaspoon almond extract. Drizzle over galette. Cut into 8 wedges. Yield: 8 servings (serving size: 1 wedge).

CALORIES 291 (29% from fat); FAT 9.4g (sat 3g, mono 4.5g, poly 1.4g); PROTEIN 1.7g; CARB 50.8g; FIBER 1.1g; CHOL 5mg; IRON 0.1mg; SODIUM 119mg; CALC 13mg

Test Kitchen Tip: Marzipan (sweetened almond paste) can be found with other baking ingredients in the supermarket. Look for it packaged in a small box or can.

Easy Caramel-Banana Galette

Slice the bananas immediately before arranging on the tart so they don't discolor.

Prep: 14 minutes • **Cook: 38 minutes**
Other: 30 minutes

- ¼ cup golden raisins
- 2 tablespoons dark rum
- ½ (15-ounce) package refrigerated pie dough (such as Pillsbury)
- Cooking spray
- 3 cups (¼-inch-thick) diagonally sliced ripe banana (about 1½ pounds)
- ½ cup sugar
- 2 tablespoons water

1. Combine raisins and rum in a small bowl. Let stand 30 minutes.

2. Preheat oven to 425°.

3. Roll dough into a 10½-inch circle, and place on a foil-lined baking sheet coated with cooking spray. Arrange banana slices in concentric circles on crust, leaving a 1-inch border. Fold dough in over banana slices, forming a 2-inch border of dough that partially covers banana slices. Press gently to seal. Bake at 425° for 30 minutes.

4. Combine sugar and water in a small saucepan; cook over medium heat, without stirring, until golden (about 8 minutes). Remove from heat, and carefully stir in raisin mixture until combined. Cool slightly. Pour over banana slices. Cut into 6 wedges. Yield: 6 servings (serving size: 1 wedge).

CALORIES 318 (27% from fat); FAT 9.7g (sat 2.4g, mono 4g, poly 2.5g); PROTEIN 3.3g; CARB 57.3g; FIBER 2.5g; CHOL 0mg; IRON 0.9mg; SODIUM 160mg; CALC 35mg

Test Kitchen Tip: The trick to making the caramel for this simple dessert is leaving it unstirred for eight minutes; stirring can cause it to harden. It's even easier when you substitute bottled fat-free caramel sauce for the sugar and water. Heat the sauce in the microwave for one minute, then stir in the raisin mixture.

Peach Crème Brûlée Tart

This simple but impressive-looking dessert can be made up to one hour before serving.

Prep: 20 minutes • Cook: 20 minutes
Other: 20 minutes

- ½ (15-ounce) package refrigerated pie dough (such as Pillsbury)
- ¼ cup sugar
- 3½ tablespoons all-purpose flour
- ⅛ teaspoon salt
- 2 cups 2% reduced-fat milk
- 1 (4-inch) piece vanilla bean, split lengthwise
- 1 large egg, lightly beaten
- 2 cups sliced peeled ripe peaches
- ⅓ cup sugar

1. Preheat oven to 450°.
2. Fit dough into a 9-inch round removable-bottom tart pan, and pierce dough with a fork; bake at 450° for 10 minutes or until lightly browned. Cool completely on a wire rack.
3. Place ¼ cup sugar, flour, and salt in a heavy saucepan. Gradually add milk, stirring with a whisk. Scrape seeds from vanilla bean; add seeds and bean to milk mixture. Cook over medium heat until thick and bubbly (about 5 minutes), stirring constantly.
4. Place egg in a large bowl. Gradually stir hot milk mixture into egg. Return milk mixture to pan. Cook 2 minutes or until thick and bubbly, stirring constantly. Spoon custard into a small bowl. Place bowl in a larger bowl filled with ice. Cool 20 minutes or until thoroughly chilled, stirring occasionally. Discard vanilla bean.
5. Spread chilled custard into bottom of prepared crust. Arrange peach slices spoke-like on top of chilled custard. Sprinkle ⅓ cup sugar evenly over peach slices.

Holding a kitchen blowtorch about 2 inches from top of peach slices, heat sugar, moving torch back and forth, until sugar is melted and caramelized (about 3 minutes). Yield: 8 servings (serving size: 1 wedge).

CALORIES 247 (32% from fat); FAT 8.8g (sat 3.7g, mono 3.7g, poly 1g); PROTEIN 4.5g; CARB 37.9g; FIBER 0.9g; CHOL 36mg; IRON 0.3mg; SODIUM 175mg; CALC 80mg

Test Kitchen Tip: You can use either a small kitchen blowtorch or a propane torch to melt the sugar. A large propane torch is more powerful and melts the sugar faster, but the kitchen torch works equally well. You can buy a kitchen torch at most cookware stores; propane torches are usually available at hardware stores.

Apple and Walnut Cream Tart

Instead of pastry dough, the sweet apple filling of this tart is surrounded by crispy thin layers of phyllo pastry.

Prep: 25 minutes • Cook: 1 hour, 3 minutes
Other: 15 minutes

- ⅔ cup coarsely chopped walnuts
- ½ cup sugar
- ¼ cup 2% reduced-fat milk
- ⅛ teaspoon salt
- 1 large egg, lightly beaten
- 2 tablespoons sugar
- ½ teaspoon ground cinnamon
-    Cooking spray
- 6 sheets frozen phyllo dough, thawed
- 1 tablespoon butter
- 5 cups sliced peeled Granny Smith apple (about 2 pounds)
- ⅓ cup raisins
- 3 tablespoons sugar

1. Preheat oven to 400°.
2. Place walnuts in a single layer on a jelly-roll pan. Bake at 400° for 5 minutes or until toasted; cool. Reduce oven temperature to 350°.
3. Place walnuts in a food processor; process until smooth (about 1 minute), scraping sides of bowl once.
4. Combine walnut butter, ½ cup sugar, milk, salt, and egg; stir well with a whisk.
5. Combine 2 tablespoons sugar and cinnamon. Coat a 9-inch pie plate with cooking spray. Working with 1 phyllo sheet at a time, coat sheet with cooking spray; sprinkle with 1 teaspoon cinnamon mixture.
6. Fold phyllo sheet in half lengthwise to form a 13 x 8½–inch rectangle. Gently press folded phyllo sheet into prepared pan, allowing ends to extend over edges; coat phyllo with cooking spray. Repeat procedure with remaining phyllo sheets and cinnamon mixture, arranging folded phyllo sheets in a crisscross pattern. Fold edges of phyllo under.
7. Melt butter in a large nonstick skillet over medium-high heat. Add apple; sauté 5 minutes or until lightly browned. Add raisins and 3 tablespoons sugar; cook 2 minutes, stirring occasionally.
8. Cool apple mixture slightly; arrange in pan on phyllo crust. Pour egg mixture over apples. Bake at 350° for 50 minutes or until center is set. Cool 15 minutes before serving. Yield: 10 servings (serving size: 1 wedge).

CALORIES 209 (30% from fat); FAT 7g (sat 1.6g, mono 1g, poly 3.7g); PROTEIN 2.9g; CARB 36g; FIBER 1.7g; CHOL 25mg; IRON 0.8mg; SODIUM 103mg; CALC 23mg

Test Kitchen Tip: Toast the nuts to deepen the color of the slightly gray walnut butter.

Cranberry-Orange Tart

Impress your holiday guests with this dazzling fruit dessert. You'll need a tart pan with a removable bottom for the most attractive results.

Prep: 20 minutes • Cook: 56 minutes
Other: 20 minutes

Crust:

1½   cups all-purpose flour
2   tablespoons sugar
⅛   teaspoon salt
6   tablespoons chilled butter, cut into small pieces
⅓   cup ice water
  Cooking spray

Filling:

⅓   cup orange juice
2½   tablespoons cornstarch
1   cup sugar
¼   cup orange marmalade
2   tablespoons chopped walnuts, toasted
1   tablespoon grated orange rind
1   (12-ounce) package fresh cranberries

1. Preheat oven to 425°.

2. To prepare crust, lightly spoon flour into dry measuring cups; level with a knife. Combine flour, 2 tablespoons sugar, and salt in a bowl; cut in butter with a pastry blender or 2 knives until mixture resembles coarse meal.

3. Sprinkle surface with ice water, 1 tablespoon at a time; toss with a fork until moist and crumbly (do not form a ball). Press mixture into a 4-inch circle on plastic wrap. Cover dough; chill 15 minutes.

4. Slightly overlap two sheets of plastic wrap on a slightly damp surface. Unwrap and place chilled dough on plastic wrap. Cover dough with two additional sheets

of overlapping plastic wrap. Roll dough, still covered, into a 14-inch circle. Place dough in freezer 5 minutes or until plastic wrap can be easily removed.

5. Remove plastic wrap; fit dough into a 10-inch round removable-bottom tart pan coated with cooking spray. Fold edges under, or flute decoratively.

6. To prepare filling, combine juice and cornstarch in a large bowl, and stir well with a whisk. Stir in 1 cup sugar and

remaining 4 ingredients. Pour mixture into prepared pan.

7. Bake at 425° for 20 minutes. Reduce oven temperature to 350° (do not remove tart from oven); bake an additional 35 minutes or until crust is lightly browned. Cool completely on a wire rack. Yield: 10 servings (serving size: 1 wedge).

CALORIES 274 (27% from fat); FAT 8.2g (sat 4.4g, mono 2.2g, poly 1.1g); PROTEIN 2.5g; CARB 49.4g; FIBER 2.2g; CHOL 19mg; IRON 1.1mg; SODIUM 105mg; CALC 14mg

Pecan Tassies in Cream Cheese Pastry

Cream cheese and a small amount of butter make the pastry for these bite-sized pecan pies exceptionally tender and flaky.

**Prep: 30 minutes • Cook: 20 minutes
Other: 10 minutes**

Pastry:
  1 cup all-purpose flour
  1 tablespoon granulated sugar
  Dash of salt
  ¼ cup (2 ounces) ⅓-less-fat cream cheese, softened
  2 tablespoons butter, softened
  2 tablespoons fat-free milk
  Cooking spray

Filling:
  ⅓ cup finely chopped pecans
  ½ cup packed brown sugar
  ⅓ cup light-colored corn syrup
  1 teaspoon vanilla extract
  ⅛ teaspoon salt
  1 large egg
  1 large egg white

1. Preheat oven to 350°.
2. To prepare pastry, lightly spoon flour into a dry measuring cup, and level with a knife. Combine flour, granulated sugar, and dash of salt in a small bowl. Combine cream cheese, butter, and milk in a large bowl, and beat with a mixer at medium speed until mixture is well blended. Add flour mixture to cheese mixture, and beat at low speed just until blended (mixture will be crumbly). Press flour mixture into a ball.
3. Turn dough out onto a lightly floured surface, and knead lightly 3 to 4 times. Divide dough into 24 portions. Place one dough portion into each of 24 miniature muffin cups coated with cooking spray.

Press dough into bottom and up sides of cups, using lightly floured fingers.
4. To prepare filling, divide pecans evenly among muffin cups. Combine brown sugar and remaining ingredients; spoon 2 teaspoons filling over pecans in each cup.
5. Bake at 350° for 20 minutes or until pastry is lightly browned and filling is puffy. Cool in cups 10 minutes on a wire rack. Run a knife around outside edge of each tassie; remove from pan. Cool completely on a wire rack. Yield: 2 dozen (serving size: 1 tassie).

CALORIES 77 (35% from fat); FAT 3g (sat 1.1g, mono 1.2g, poly 0.4g); PROTEIN 1.4g; CARB 11.3g; FIBER 0.2g; CHOL 14mg; IRON 0.4mg; SODIUM 50mg; CALC 9mg

Test Kitchen Tip: Tassies may be frozen up to one month in an airtight container.

Linzertorte

Named for Linz, Austria, the town where it originated, this lattice-topped tart features a rich almond pastry and a wonderfully gooey blackberry-jam filling.

**Prep: 35 minutes • Cook: 50 minutes
Other: 1 hour, 10 minutes**

  1½ cups all-purpose flour
  ½ cup ground blanched almonds
  ½ teaspoon ground cinnamon
  ¼ teaspoon salt
  ¼ teaspoon baking powder
  ½ cup granulated sugar
  ¼ cup tub-style light cream cheese
  ½ teaspoon vanilla extract
  1 large egg
  Cooking spray
  1¼ cups seedless blackberry jam
  1 teaspoon sifted powdered sugar

1. Spoon flour into dry measuring cups, and level with a knife. Combine flour, almonds, cinnamon, salt, and baking powder.
2. Place granulated sugar and cream cheese in a food processor; pulse 4 times. Add vanilla and egg; pulse 3 times. Add flour mixture; pulse 10 times or until combined. Press two-thirds of dough into a 4-inch circle on heavy-duty plastic wrap; cover with additional plastic wrap. Chill 30 minutes. Press remaining one-third of dough into a 4-inch circle on heavy-duty plastic wrap; cover with additional plastic wrap. Roll into a 9-inch circle. Chill 30 minutes. Roll larger portion of dough, still covered, into an 11-inch circle. Chill 10 minutes or until plastic wrap can be easily removed.
3. Preheat oven to 325°.
4. Working with larger portion of dough, remove one sheet of plastic wrap; fit dough into a 9-inch round removable-bottom tart pan coated with cooking spray. Remove top sheet of plastic wrap; fold edges under. Spoon blackberry jam into prepared crust.
5. Working with smaller portion of dough, remove one sheet of plastic wrap. Cut dough into ½-inch strips. Gently remove dough strips from bottom sheet of plastic wrap; arrange in a lattice design over jam. Seal dough strips to edge of crust. Place tart on a baking sheet.
6. Bake at 325° for 50 minutes or until crust is browned and filling is bubbly. Cool on a wire rack. Sprinkle with powdered sugar. Yield: 9 servings (serving size: 1 wedge).

CALORIES 236 (20% from fat); FAT 5.2g (sat 1.2g, mono 2.4g, poly 0.9g); PROTEIN 5.1g; CARB 44.4g; FIBER 3.7g; CHOL 28mg; IRON 1.3mg; SODIUM 106mg; CALC 39mg

Sweet Plantain and Chocolate Empanaditas

Empanaditas—sweet or savory turnovers—are popular throughout Spain and Latin America. These handheld pies are filled with a smooth mixture of mashed plantains and drizzled with melted chocolate.

Prep: 40 minutes • Cook: 28 minutes Other: 10 minutes

    1   cup (1-inch-thick) sliced soft black
        plantain (about ½ pound)
    2   tablespoons fat-free sweetened
        condensed milk
    2   cups all-purpose flour, divided
    6   tablespoons ice water
    1   teaspoon cider vinegar
    2   tablespoons powdered sugar
    ½   teaspoon salt
    ½   cup vegetable shortening
        Cooking spray
    5   teaspoons 2% reduced-fat milk,
        divided
    ¼   cup granulated sugar
    ¼   cup semisweet chocolate minichips

1. Cook plantain in boiling water 10 minutes or until tender; drain. Combine plantain and condensed milk in a bowl, and mash with a potato masher. Set aside.
2. Lightly spoon flour into dry measuring cups; level with a knife. Combine ½ cup flour, ice water, and vinegar, stirring with a whisk until well blended to form a slurry. Combine 1½ cups flour, powdered sugar, and salt in a bowl; cut in shortening with a pastry blender or 2 knives until mixture resembles coarse meal. Add slurry, tossing with a fork until moist.
3. Slightly overlap two sheets of plastic wrap on a damp surface. Place dough on plastic wrap. Gently press dough into a 4-inch circle; cover with two additional sheets of overlapping plastic wrap. Roll covered dough into an 18 x 12–inch rectangle; freeze 10 minutes or until plastic wrap can be easily removed.
4. Preheat oven to 400°.
5. Remove plastic wrap; place dough on a lightly floured surface. Cut dough into 24 circles using a 3-inch round cutter. Place circles on a baking sheet coated with cooking spray, and lightly moisten edges of dough with water. Spoon 2 teaspoons plantain mixture into each circle. Fold dough over filling; pinch edges together to seal. Brush tops of dough evenly with 1 tablespoon 2% milk; sprinkle evenly with granulated sugar.
6. Bake at 400° for 17 minutes or until lightly browned.
7. Combine chips and 2 teaspoons 2% milk in a small bowl, and microwave at HIGH 30 seconds; stir until smooth. Drizzle melted chocolate over empanaditas. Serve warm. Yield: 2 dozen (serving size: 1 empanadita).

CALORIES 111 (41% from fat); FAT 5g (sat 1.4g, mono 2.1g, poly 1.2g); PROTEIN 1.5g; CARB 15.8g; FIBER 0.6g; CHOL 0mg; IRON 0.6mg; SODIUM 52mg; CALC 9mg

plantains A plantain is a large firm variety of banana that is popular in Latin American cuisine. Plantains are sometimes referred to as "cooking bananas"; they have a mild squashlike flavor and are used much like potatoes in cooking.

deadline desserts When you need a last-minute dessert for unexpected company or a simple treat for a weeknight dinner, here are a few of our favorite no-fuss desserts.

- Angel food cake with lemon curd
- Blueberries with low-fat vanilla yogurt
- Caramel praline crunch frozen yogurt
- Chocolate sorbet
- Chocolate low-fat ice cream with graham crackers
- Flavored coffees with biscotti
- Fortune cookies
- Iced grapes
- Ice wine, sherry, or port
- Lemon sorbet with almond biscotti
- Lemon sorbet with mixed berries
- Low-fat coffee ice cream with amaretti
- Low-fat coffee ice cream with fat-free fudge topping
- Low-fat dulce de leche ice cream
- Low-fat vanilla ice cream with sliced peaches
- Mango slices drizzled with fresh lime juice
- Melon slices
- Oatmeal-raisin cookies
- Roasted plums topped with low-fat vanilla ice cream
- Strawberry sorbet with vanilla wafer cookies
- Strawberries tossed with brown sugar and low-fat sour cream
- Strawberries with a splash of balsamic vinegar
- Vanilla yogurt with honey and roasted walnuts
- Vanilla yogurt with honey and ginger-snap cookies

Unfried Apple Pies

Instead of being fried in oil, these tender fruit turnovers are brushed with an egg white wash, sprinkled with sugar, and baked.

Prep: 40 minutes • Cook: 26 minutes
Other: 2 hours

Crust:
- 1 cup all-purpose flour
- ½ teaspoon salt
- ¼ teaspoon baking powder
- ⅓ cup hot fat-free milk
- ¼ cup vegetable shortening

Filling:
- 1 cup dried apples, chopped
- ½ cup dried cranberries
- ½ cup water
- ½ cup apple cider
- ¼ cup packed brown sugar

Remaining ingredients:
- Cooking spray
- 1 large egg white
- 1 tablespoon water
- 1½ teaspoons turbinado sugar or granulated sugar

1. To prepare crust, lightly spoon flour into a dry measuring cup; level with a knife. Combine flour, salt, and baking powder, stirring with a whisk. Combine milk and shortening in a large bowl, stirring until shortening dissolves. Gradually add flour mixture to milk mixture, tossing with a fork just until blended. Turn dough out onto a piece of plastic wrap. Knead into a ball (dough will feel sticky). Cover and chill at least 2 hours.

2. To prepare filling, combine dried apples, dried cranberries, ½ cup water, and apple cider in a small saucepan. Bring to a boil over medium-high heat. Cover; reduce heat, and simmer 10 minutes or until fruit is tender, stirring occasionally. Stir in brown sugar, and cool to room temperature.

3. Preheat oven to 450°.

4. Divide dough into 8 equal portions. Working with one dough portion at a time (cover remaining portions to prevent drying), roll into a 6-inch circle on a lightly floured surface. Spoon about 2 tablespoons filling onto half of circle; moisten edges of dough with water. Fold dough over filling; press edges together with a fork to seal. Place pies on a baking sheet coated with cooking spray. Combine egg white and 1 tablespoon water, stirring with a whisk; brush over pies. Sprinkle with turbinado sugar. Bake at 450° for 12 minutes or until golden. Place on a wire rack. Serve warm or at room temperature. Yield: 8 servings (serving size: 1 pie).

CALORIES 203 (27% from fat); FAT 6.2g (sat 1.5g, mono 2g, poly 1.6g); PROTEIN 2.5g; CARB 34.2g; FIBER 1.9g; CHOL 0mg; IRON 1mg; SODIUM 188mg; CALC 32mg

Test Kitchen Tip: Hot milk dissolves the shortening in the pastry, creating a soft, easy-to-work dough.

Cobblers, Crisps & Crumbles

Instead of being baked in a pastry crust, these fruit desserts are topped with either a thick biscuit crust or a crumbly pastry or crumb mixture.

Blueberry
Cobbler

Blueberry Cobbler

A traditional cobbler is a baked, deep-dish fruit dessert that's topped with a biscuit crust sprinkled with sugar.

Prep: 15 minutes • Cook: 50 minutes

Filling:

- 6 cups fresh blueberries
- ⅓ cup sugar
- 2 tablespoons cornstarch
- 1 teaspoon grated lemon rind

Topping:

- 1⅓ cups all-purpose flour
- 2 tablespoons sugar
- ¾ teaspoon baking powder
- ¼ teaspoon salt
- ¼ teaspoon baking soda
- 5 tablespoons chilled butter, cut into small pieces
- 1 cup fat-free sour cream
- 3 tablespoons 2% reduced-fat milk
- 1 teaspoon sugar

1. Preheat oven to 350°.

2. To prepare filling, combine first 4 ingredients in an 11 x 7–inch baking dish.

3. To prepare topping, lightly spoon flour into dry measuring cups; level with a knife. Combine flour and next 4 ingredients in a large bowl, stirring with a whisk. Cut in butter with a pastry blender or 2 knives until mixture resembles coarse meal. Stir in sour cream to form a soft dough.

4. Drop dough by spoonfuls onto blueberry filling to form 8 dumplings. Brush dumplings with milk; sprinkle with 1 teaspoon sugar. Place baking dish on a jelly-roll pan. Bake at 350° for 50 minutes or until filling is bubbly and dumplings are lightly browned. Yield: 8 servings (serving size: about 1 cup).

CALORIES 288 (26% from fat); FAT 8.3g (sat 4.9g, mono 2.2g, poly 0.5g); PROTEIN 4.7g; CARB 50.8g; FIBER 3.5g; CHOL 23mg; IRON 1.3mg; SODIUM 265mg; CALC 90mg

Fresh Cherry Cobbler

Fresh cherries are crisp and explode with rich, sweet flavor. The combination of luscious cherries and a sugar-dusted crust is the essence of this old-fashioned dessert.

Prep: 20 minutes • Cook: 55 minutes
Other: 25 minutes

- ½ (15-ounce) package refrigerated pie dough (such as Pillsbury)
- Cooking spray
- 1 large egg white, lightly beaten
- 1 tablespoon sugar
- 4 cups pitted sweet cherries (about 1¾ pounds)
- 1 cup sugar
- 3 tablespoons uncooked quick-cooking tapioca
- 1 tablespoon fresh lemon juice
- ⅛ teaspoon salt
- 2 tablespoons chilled butter, cut into small pieces

1. Preheat oven to 375°.

2. Cut dough into 8 (9 x 1–inch) strips. Arrange dough strips in a lattice design on a baking sheet coated with cooking spray. Brush dough with egg white, and sprinkle evenly with 1 tablespoon sugar. Bake at 375° for 15 minutes or until crust is golden brown. Place pan on a wire rack and cool 10 minutes. Carefully lift crust using 2 spatulas; cool completely on wire rack.

3. Combine cherries, 1 cup sugar, tapioca, juice, and salt. Let stand 15 minutes. Spoon cherry mixture into an 8-inch baking dish coated with cooking spray. Top with butter. Bake at 375° for 40 minutes or until hot and bubbly. Place crust on top of cherry mixture. Yield: 8 servings (serving size: about 1 cup).

CALORIES 312 (30% from fat); FAT 10.4g (sat 4.9g, mono 1g, poly 0.3g); PROTEIN 2.3g; CARB 54g; FIBER 1.7g; CHOL 13mg; IRON 0.3mg; SODIUM 171mg; CALC 12mg

Test Kitchen Tip: The secret to having a cobbler with a juicy filling and a flaky, crisp crust is an easy, old-fashioned method: Bake the crust separately, and then gently slide it onto the hot, baked filling.

Fresh Cherry Cobbler

Peach Cobbler

Brown sugar and almonds are great flavor partners for fresh peaches. Rather than placing the dough on top, just fold it over the filling.

Prep: 30 minutes • Cook: 45 minutes • Other: 35 minutes

2 cups all-purpose flour
1 tablespoon granulated sugar
¼ teaspoon salt
6 tablespoons chilled butter, cut into 6 pieces
6 tablespoons ice water
Cooking spray
6 cups sliced peeled peaches (about 3¾ pounds)
¾ cup packed brown sugar, divided
2½ tablespoons all-purpose flour
1 tablespoon vanilla extract
1 teaspoon ground cinnamon
¼ cup slivered almonds
1 large egg
1 teaspoon water
1 tablespoon granulated sugar

1. Preheat oven to 375°.

2. Lightly spoon 2 cups flour into dry measuring cups; level with a knife. Place flour, 1 tablespoon granulated sugar, and salt in a food processor; pulse 2 or 3 times. Add butter pieces; pulse 10 times or until mixture resembles coarse meal. With processor on, slowly add ice water through food chute, processing just until combined (do not form a ball).

3. Gently press dough into a 4-inch circle. Slightly overlap two sheets of plastic wrap on a slightly damp surface. Place dough on plastic wrap; cover with two additional sheets of overlapping plastic wrap. Roll dough, still covered, into a 15 x 13–inch rectangle. Place in freezer 5 minutes or until plastic wrap can be easily removed; remove top sheets. Fit dough, uncovered side down, into a 2-quart baking dish coated with cooking spray, allowing dough to extend over edges; remove remaining plastic wrap.

4. Combine sliced peaches, ½ cup brown sugar, 2½ tablespoons flour, vanilla, and cinnamon in a large bowl; toss gently. Spoon into prepared dish; fold edges of dough over peach mixture. Sprinkle ¼ cup brown sugar over mixture; sprinkle with almonds.

5. Combine egg and water in a small bowl. Brush egg mixture over dough; sprinkle with 1 tablespoon granulated sugar. Bake at 375° for 45 minutes or until filling is bubbly and crust is lightly browned. Let stand 30 minutes before serving. Yield: 10 servings (serving size: about ¾ cup).

CALORIES 302 (27% from fat); FAT 9.2g (sat 1.6g, mono 4.3g, poly 2.7g); PROTEIN 4.5g; CARB 51.5g; FIBER 2.8g; CHOL 11mg; IRON 1.9mg; SODIUM 149mg; CALC 39mg

Vanilla-Scented Harvest Crisp with Pistachios

Dried fruits and tart apples under a crunchy oatmeal-pistachio topping make an ideal ending to a fall evening.

Prep: 25 minutes • Cook: 40 minutes

Filling:

- 1 tablespoon butter
- 1 cup dried apricots, chopped
- 1 cup apricot nectar
- ½ cup dried figs, chopped
- ¼ cup dried currants or dried cranberries
- 2 tablespoons honey
- 1 tablespoon brown sugar
- 1 tablespoon vanilla extract
- 1½ pounds Granny Smith apples, peeled and chopped (about 4 apples)
- 1 (2-inch) cinnamon stick
  Cooking spray

Topping:

- ½ cup regular oats
- ½ cup all-purpose flour
- ¼ cup packed brown sugar
- ¼ teaspoon salt
- ¼ teaspoon ground cinnamon
- 3 tablespoons chilled butter, cut into small pieces
- 1 cup chopped pistachios

1. Preheat oven to 375°.

2. To prepare filling, melt 1 tablespoon butter in a large saucepan over medium-high heat. Add apricots and next 8 ingredients; bring to a boil. Reduce heat; simmer 10 minutes or until fruit is tender, stirring occasionally. Discard cinnamon stick.

3. Place filling in an 8-inch square baking dish coated with cooking spray.

4. To prepare topping, place oats in a food processor; pulse until coarsely chopped. Place oats in a large bowl. Lightly spoon flour into a dry measuring cup; level with a

Cranberry and Apple Crumble

knife. Add flour, ¼ cup brown sugar, salt, and ground cinnamon to oats; stir to combine. Cut in chilled butter with a pastry blender or 2 knives until mixture resembles coarse meal. Add pistachios; toss well. Sprinkle topping over filling. Bake at 375° for 25 minutes or until golden. Yield: 12 servings (serving size: ⅔ cup).

CALORIES 272 (30% from fat); FAT 9g (sat 3g, mono 3.6g, poly 1.6g); PROTEIN 4.4g; CARB 45.5g; FIBER 5.6g; CHOL 10mg; IRON 2.1mg; SODIUM 92mg; CALC 40mg

Cranberry and Apple Crumble

Serve this dessert with vanilla ice cream. We used Braeburn apples, but any tart variety will do.

Prep: 15 minutes • Cook: 40 minutes

- ½ cup all-purpose flour
- ¼ cup granulated sugar
- ¼ cup packed brown sugar
- ¼ cup chilled butter, cut into small pieces
- 6 cups sliced peeled Braeburn apple
- 1 cup fresh cranberries
- ⅓ cup fresh orange juice
- 2 tablespoons granulated sugar
- 1 tablespoon cornstarch

1. Preheat oven to 375°.

2. Lightly spoon flour into a dry measuring cup; level with a knife. Place flour, ¼ cup granulated sugar, brown sugar, and butter in a food processor; pulse 10 times or until mixture resembles coarse meal.

3. Combine apple and cranberries in a large bowl. Combine juice, 2 tablespoons sugar, and cornstarch; pour over apple mixture. Toss well. Spoon apple mixture into a 2-quart baking dish. Sprinkle with flour mixture. Bake at 375° for 40 minutes or until bubbly and golden brown. Serve warm. Yield: 8 servings (serving size: ⅔ cup).

CALORIES 211 (26% from fat); FAT 6.1g (sat 3.6g, mono 1.7g, poly 0.4g); PROTEIN 1.2g; CARB 40.1g; FIBER 3.4g; CHOL 15mg; IRON 0.7mg; SODIUM 61mg; CALC 17mg

Test Kitchen Tip: It's important to use chilled butter in order to get a tender, flaky crust. Butter that is too soft will surround the flour particles rather than form spaces, and you'll end up with a flat, greasy crust.

Triple-Berry Crisps with Meringue Streusel

In an unusual twist, baked, crumbled meringue enhances the streusel. Because the meringue needs to sit in the oven at least 12 hours, make it a day before serving. Crystallized ginger and orange rind impart a decidedly tart flavor that contrasts with the sweet topping. If you're in a hurry, try the simpler, traditional streusel topping in the variation on the next page.

Prep: 25 minutes
Cook: 2 hours, 40 minutes
Other: 12 hours

Streusel:
    3   large egg whites
    6   tablespoons granulated sugar
  ¼   cup sliced almonds
  ¼   cup flaked sweetened coconut
  ¼   teaspoon ground cinnamon
  ⅓   cup all-purpose flour
  ¼   cup packed brown sugar
    1   tablespoon grated lemon rind
  ½   teaspoon ground nutmeg
  ¼   teaspoon ground cinnamon
 1½ tablespoons chilled butter, cut into small pieces

Filling:
    4   cups blueberries
    2   cups blackberries
    2   cups raspberries
  ½   cup orange juice
  ¼   cup cornstarch
  ¼   cup packed brown sugar
    3   tablespoons chopped crystallized ginger
    2   tablespoons finely grated orange rind
Cooking spray
Low-fat ice cream (optional)

1. Preheat oven to 200°.

2. To prepare meringue, place egg whites in a large bowl; beat with a mixer at high speed until foamy (about 30 seconds). Gradually add granulated sugar, 1 tablespoon at a time, beating until stiff peaks form (about 2 minutes). Fold in almonds, coconut, and ¼ teaspoon cinnamon. Spread evenly onto a parchment-lined 15 x 10–inch jelly-roll pan.

3. Bake at 200° for 2½ hours. Turn oven off, and cool meringue in closed oven 12 hours or until completely dry. Remove meringue from paper. Crumble meringue into ¼-inch pieces.

4. To prepare streusel, lightly spoon flour into a dry measuring cup; level with a knife. Combine flour and next 4 ingredients in a bowl; cut in butter with a pastry blender or 2 knives until mixture resembles coarse meal. Stir in meringue pieces.

5. Preheat oven to 350°.

6. To prepare filling, combine blueberries and next 7 ingredients in a bowl; toss well.

Spoon ½ cup filling into each of 12 (6-ounce) ramekins or custard cups coated with cooking spray. Top each with ⅓ cup meringue streusel mixture. Place ramekins on a baking sheet; bake at 350° for 10 minutes or until bubbly. Serve warm or at room temperature. Top with ice cream, if desired. Yield: 12 servings (serving size: 1 crisp).

CALORIES 175 (17% from fat); FAT 3.4g (sat 1.5g, mono 1.1g, poly 0.4g); PROTEIN 2.6g; CARB 35.6g; FIBER 4.2g; CHOL 4mg; IRON 1.2mg; SODIUM 40mg; CALC 37mg

Variation

Triple-Berry Crisps with Almond Streusel: To prepare streusel, lightly spoon ¾ cup all-purpose flour into a dry measuring cup; level with a knife. Place flour, ½ cup packed brown sugar, and ½ teaspoon salt in a food processor; pulse 2 times or until combined. Add 4½ tablespoons chilled butter, cut into small pieces; pulse 6 times or until mixture resembles coarse meal. Add ¾ cup regular oats and ⅓ cup sliced almonds; pulse 2 times. Sprinkle over berry filling; bake according to recipe directions.

CALORIES 247 (28% from fat); FAT 7.6g (sat 3g, mono 2.7g, poly 0.9g); PROTEIN 4g; CARB 43.7g; FIBER 3.8g; CHOL 12mg; IRON 2mg; SODIUM 151mg; CALC 49mg

Test Kitchen Tip: You can also use a 13 x 9–inch baking dish. Bake 30 minutes or until bubbly.

Pear Dried Cherry Crumble with Almond Streusel

The traditional pairing of almonds and cherries gets a triple dose with almond oil, almond paste, and chopped almonds.

Prep: 25 minutes • Cook: 40 minutes
Other: 10 minutes

Filling:
- ¾ cup dried cherries
- ½ cup apple cider
- 2½ pounds ripe pears, peeled and chopped (about 7 pears)
- 2 tablespoons sugar
- 2 tablespoons all-purpose flour
- Cooking spray

Topping:
- ¾ cup all-purpose flour
- ½ cup whole wheat pastry flour
- ¼ cup sugar
- ¼ cup toasted almonds, finely chopped
- ½ teaspoon salt
- 2 tablespoons almond paste
- 3 tablespoons honey
- 2 tablespoons almond oil
- 1 large egg yolk, lightly beaten

1. Preheat oven to 375°.
2. To prepare filling, combine cherries and cider in a small saucepan; bring to a boil. Remove from heat. Cover; let stand 10 minutes or until cherries are soft. Drain. Combine cherries and pears in a bowl. Sprinkle with 2 tablespoons sugar and 2 tablespoons flour; toss gently to coat. Spoon filling into an 11 x 7–inch baking dish coated with cooking spray.
3. To prepare topping, lightly spoon ¾ cup all-purpose flour and pastry flour into dry measuring cups; level with a knife. Combine flours, ¼ cup sugar, almonds, and salt in a large bowl, stirring with a whisk. Cut in almond paste with a pastry blender or 2 knives until mixture resembles coarse meal. Combine honey, oil, and egg yolk, stirring with a whisk. Add to flour mixture; stir just until moistened. Squeeze handfuls of topping to form large pieces. Crumble over filling. Bake at 375° for 35 minutes or until golden and bubbly. Yield: 10 servings (serving size: about ¾ cup).

CALORIES 270 (21% from fat); FAT 6.2g (sat 0.6g, mono 3.4g, poly 1.1g); PROTEIN 4g; CARB 53.3g; FIBER 2.6g; CHOL 21mg; IRON 1.1mg; SODIUM 121mg; CALC 35mg

Variation

Apple-Cranberry Crumble with Almond Streusel: Substitute dried cranberries for the cherries and chopped peeled apple for the pear. Proceed with recipe as directed.

whole wheat pastry flour
This flour is a low-gluten flour made from soft wheat with the bran included. It has a fine texture and a high starch content. In recipes with less fat, it can help produce a more tender pastry. You can substitute 1 cup minus 2 tablespoons of regular whole wheat flour for 1 cup whole wheat pastry flour, or use ¾ cup all-purpose flour plus ¼ cup whole wheat flour.

Pastries

Our pastries are lower in fat than traditional pastries because we use less butter and sugar in the dough for cream puffs and strudels, or we use phyllo dough.

Espresso Cream
Puffs

Espresso Cream Puffs

We perked up the flavor of cream puffs by adding espresso. To lighten them, we decreased the butter and used fat-free milk. We also added gelatin and whipped topping to the pastry cream for an incredibly light and creamy filling that holds up well.

Prep: 40 minutes • Cook: 55 minutes
Other: 4 hours, 35 minutes

Cream puffs:

- 1   cup all-purpose flour
- 2   teaspoons sugar
- ¼   teaspoon salt
- 1   cup fat-free milk
- 2   tablespoons butter
- 1   tablespoon instant espresso granules or 2 tablespoons instant coffee granules
- 2   large eggs
- 1   large egg white
- Cooking spray

Pastry cream:

- ½   teaspoon unflavored gelatin
- 1   tablespoon water
- ¾   cup fat-free milk
- 6   tablespoons sugar
- 2   tablespoons cornstarch
- ½   teaspoon vanilla extract
- ⅛   teaspoon salt
- 2   large egg yolks
- ¾   cup frozen fat-free whipped topping, thawed
- Powdered sugar (optional)

1. Preheat oven to 400°.

2. To prepare cream puffs, lightly spoon flour into a dry measuring cup; level with a knife. Combine flour, 2 teaspoons sugar, and ¼ teaspoon salt. Combine 1 cup milk, butter, and espresso granules in a large saucepan; bring to a boil. Reduce heat to low; add flour mixture, stirring well until mixture is smooth and pulls away from sides of pan. Remove mixture from heat. Add eggs and egg white, 1 at a time, beating well with a wooden spoon until smooth.

3. Drop dough by level tablespoons, 2 inches apart, onto baking sheets coated with cooking spray. Bake at 400° for 10 minutes. Reduce oven temperature to 350°; bake an additional 10 minutes or until browned and crisp. Remove from oven; pierce side of each cream puff with tip of a sharp knife to allow steam to escape. Turn oven off; let cream puffs stand in partially closed oven 20 minutes. Remove cream puffs from baking sheet; cool completely on a wire rack.

4. To prepare pastry cream, sprinkle gelatin over water in a small bowl. Combine ¾ cup milk and next 5 ingredients in a medium saucepan. Place over low heat; cook until warm, stirring constantly. Stir in gelatin mixture; cook over medium heat until thick (about 8 minutes), stirring constantly. Remove from heat. Place pan in a large ice-filled bowl; let stand 15 minutes or until room temperature (do not allow mixture to set). Remove pan from ice. Gently whisk in whipped topping. Cover; chill 4 hours or until thick.

5. Cut tops off cream puffs; fill each cream puff with 1 tablespoon filling. Replace tops. Sprinkle with powdered sugar, if desired. Yield: 2 dozen (serving size: 1 cream puff).

CALORIES 67 (27% from fat); FAT 2g (sat 0.9g, mono 0.6g, poly 0.2g); PROTEIN 2.2g; CARB 9.9g; FIBER 0.2g; CHOL 40mg; IRON 0.4mg; SODIUM 77mg; CALC 28mg

how to make cream puffs

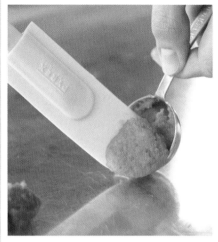

1. Drop the dough by level tablespoonfuls onto baking sheets coated with cooking spray.

2. Cut the tops off the cream puffs; using a measuring spoon, fill each cream puff with 1 tablespoon of filling.

Apple and Cream Cheese Roll-Ups

Resembling small strudels (pastries made of many layers of thin dough, spread with a filling, and rolled), these "pick-up pastries" are convenient for parties and dessert buffets—no forks required.

Prep: 45 minutes • Cook: 18 minutes

Filling:
- 1 cup dried apples, chopped
- ⅓ cup thawed apple juice concentrate, undiluted
- ¼ teaspoon ground cinnamon
- Dash of ground nutmeg
- ¼ cup sugar
- ¼ cup (2 ounces) ⅓-less-fat cream cheese
- 1 large egg

Pastry:
- 12 (18 x 14–inch) sheets frozen phyllo dough, thawed
- Cooking spray
- ½ cup graham cracker crumbs, divided
- ¼ cup sugar, divided

Topping:
- 1½ teaspoons sugar
- ½ teaspoon ground cinnamon

1. To prepare filling, combine first 4 ingredients in a small saucepan over medium-high heat. Bring apple mixture to a boil; cover, reduce heat, and simmer 5 minutes or until most of liquid is absorbed. Cool to room temperature. Combine ¼ cup sugar and cream cheese; beat with a mixer at low speed until blended. Add egg; beat until blended. Fold in apple mixture; cover and set aside.

2. Preheat oven to 350°.

3. To prepare pastry, place 1 phyllo sheet on a large cutting board or work surface (cover remaining dough to keep from drying), and lightly coat with cooking spray. Sprinkle phyllo with 2 teaspoons graham cracker crumbs and 1 teaspoon sugar. Repeat layers twice, ending with crumbs and sugar. Cut phyllo stack lengthwise into 6 (3-inch-wide) strips using a sharp knife. Spoon 1 rounded teaspoon apple mixture ½ inch from end of each phyllo strip. Roll up each strip, beginning with apple mixture end; place strips, seam sides down, on a baking sheet coated with cooking spray, and lightly coat each roll with cooking spray. Repeat procedure three times.

4. To prepare topping, combine 1½ teaspoons sugar and ½ teaspoon cinnamon; sprinkle evenly over phyllo rolls. Bake at 350° for 10 minutes, and cool on a wire rack. Yield: 24 servings (serving size: 1 roll-up).

CALORIES 81 (18% from fat); FAT 1.6g (sat 0.6g, mono 0.6g, poly 0.2g); PROTEIN 1.4g; CARB 15.4g; FIBER 0.6g; CHOL 11mg; IRON 0.5mg; SODIUM 77mg; CALC 6mg

phyllo Greek for "leaf," phyllo (paper-thin sheets of pastry) lends a distinctive layered effect to such specialties as spanakopita and baklava. Working with it is easy once you know one crucial trick: Cover your supply with a piece of plastic wrap, and remove sheets only as you need them to keep them from drying out. Fresh and frozen phyllo dough are sold in supermarkets. Thaw frozen phyllo in the refrigerator; unopened dough will keep in the fridge up to one month.

Rolled Baklava

This baklava is rolled jelly-roll fashion and cut into rolls instead of being assembled in flat layers and cut into triangles. Let the rolls stand for 11 hours; they'll soak up more flavor. Find shredded phyllo called *kataifi* (ka-ta-EE-fee) in Middle Eastern markets.

Prep: 40 minutes • Cook: 41 minutes
Other: 11 hours

Rolls:
- 2 tablespoons olive oil
- 2 tablespoons canola oil
- 2 lemon wedges
- ¾ cup whole almonds (5 ounces), toasted
- 1½ tablespoons sugar
- ½ teaspoon ground cinnamon
- ¼ teaspoon ground nutmeg
- 12 (14 x 9–inch) sheets frozen phyllo dough, thawed
- 8 ounces frozen shredded phyllo dough (*kataifi*), thawed
- Cooking spray

Syrup:
- 1⅓ cups sugar
- 1⅓ cups water
- 1⅓ cups honey
- 4 lemon wedges
- 1 (3-inch) cinnamon stick

1. Preheat oven to 350°.

2. To prepare rolls, combine first 3 ingredients in a small saucepan. Cook over medium-low heat 5 minutes. Cool; discard lemon. Place almonds, 1½ tablespoons sugar, ground cinnamon, and nutmeg in a food processor; process until coarsely chopped.

3. Place 2 phyllo sheets on a large cutting board (cover remaining dough to keep from drying); lightly brush with 1½ teaspoons oil mixture. Top with 2 phyllo sheets, and brush with 1½ teaspoons oil mixture.

Sprinkle 2½ tablespoons almond mixture over phyllo stack, leaving a 1½-inch border on one short edge. Crumble one-third of shredded phyllo over almond mixture; top with 2½ tablespoons almond mixture.

4. Starting at short edge without border, tightly roll up phyllo stack jelly-roll fashion. Brush border and outside of roll with 1½ teaspoons oil mixture. Cut roll into 10 equal pieces. Repeat twice with remaining phyllo sheets, oil mixture, almond mixture, and shredded phyllo. Place rolls on a jelly-roll pan or baking sheet coated with cooking spray. Bake at 350° for 30 minutes.

5. Combine 1⅓ cups sugar and remaining 4 ingredients in a saucepan. Cook over medium heat 5 minutes or until sugar dissolves; discard lemon and cinnamon.

6. Place rolls, cut sides up, in a 13 x 9–inch baking pan coated with cooking spray (rolls will fit snugly). Pour syrup over rolls; let stand at room temperature 3 hours. Carefully turn rolls; cover and let stand 8 hours. Yield: 15 servings (serving size: 2 rolls).

CALORIES 339 (27% from fat); FAT 10.3g (sat 1.2g, mono 6.4g, poly 2.2g); PROTEIN 4.3g; CARB 60.7g; FIBER 1.8g; CHOL 0mg; IRON 1.5mg; SODIUM 148mg; CALC 29mg

how to make rolled baklava

1. After you brush the phyllo with lemon oil and almonds, sprinkle kataifi over the phyllo.

2. Tightly roll up the phyllo, jelly-roll fashion.

3. Slice the roll with a serrated bread knife into 1½-inch pieces.

Rolled Baklava

Apple-Cream Cheese Strudel

A strudel is a pastry made up of many layers of thin dough spread with a filling, then rolled and baked. Part apple pie, part cheesecake, this strudel features a combination of Rome and Granny Smith apples for a sweet-tart flavor.

Prep: 30 minutes • Cook: 27 minutes
Other: 10 minutes

  1 teaspoon butter
1¼ cups thinly sliced peeled Rome apple
1¼ cups thinly sliced peeled Granny
       Smith apple
  2 tablespoons brown sugar
  3 tablespoons thawed apple juice
       concentrate
  ⅛ teaspoon ground cinnamon
  ⅛ teaspoon ground nutmeg
1½ tablespoons finely chopped walnuts
  ½ cup (4 ounces) ⅓-less-fat cream
       cheese, softened
  2 tablespoons granulated sugar
  2 tablespoons fat-free sour cream
  1 teaspoon all-purpose flour
  1 teaspoon vanilla extract
Dash of salt
  1 large egg white
  6 (18 x 14–inch) sheets frozen phyllo
       dough, thawed
Cooking spray
Dash of nutmeg
  1 tablespoon powdered sugar (optional)

1. Preheat oven to 375°.

2. Melt butter in a large nonstick skillet over medium-high heat. Add apple; sauté 3 minutes or until lightly browned. Reduce heat to medium; cook 5 minutes or until tender, stirring frequently. Stir in brown sugar, apple juice concentrate, cinnamon, and ⅛ teaspoon nutmeg. Cook 3 minutes or until sugar melts and mixture is slightly syrupy. Remove from heat; stir in walnuts. Cool.

3. Place cream cheese, granulated sugar, sour cream, and flour in a bowl; beat with a mixer at medium speed until smooth. Beat in vanilla, salt, and egg white.

4. Place 1 phyllo sheet on a large cutting board or work surface (cover remaining dough to prevent drying); lightly coat with cooking spray. Repeat layers with remaining phyllo and cooking spray, ending with phyllo. Gently press phyllo layers together. Lightly coat top phyllo sheet with cooking spray. Spoon apple mixture along one short edge of phyllo, leaving a 2-inch border. Drizzle cream cheese mixture over apple mixture. Fold long edges of phyllo over filling (phyllo will not completely cover filling). Starting at short edge with 2-inch border, roll up jelly-roll fashion. (Do not roll too tightly or strudel may split.) Place strudel, seam side down, on a baking sheet coated with cooking spray. Sprinkle with a dash of nutmeg.

5. Bake at 375° for 15 minutes or until golden brown. Remove from oven; cool 10 minutes on baking sheet on a wire rack. Sprinkle with powdered sugar, if desired. Cut with a serrated knife. Yield: 6 servings (serving size: 1 slice).

CALORIES 217 (29% from fat); FAT 7.1g (sat 3.5g, mono 2.2g, poly 1.2g); PROTEIN 4.6g; CARB 34.6g; FIBER 3g; CHOL 16mg; IRON 1mg; SODIUM 219mg; CALC 32mg

how to roll strudel

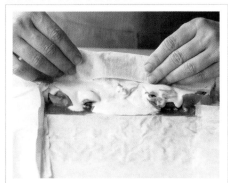

Fold the phyllo edges over the filling and roll up.

fish & shellfish

Shrimp Scampi,
page 254

Fish

Fish is the ultimate "fast food"—with cook times often less than 15 minutes and flavor that's hard to beat. Plus a number of varieties are high in heart-healthy fats.

Grilled Apple-Smoked Striped Bass

Cooking over wood chips infuses the fish with a smokiness that's close to what you'd get if you were grilling over a wood fire.

**Prep: 12 minutes • Cook: 20 minutes
Other: 1 hour**

- ¼ cup apple wood chips
- 2 dried habanero peppers
- 1 tablespoon peanut or canola oil
- 1 teaspoon salt
- ½ teaspoon freshly ground black pepper
- 1 (3-pound) striped bass fillet (about 1 inch thick)
- Cooking spray
- 1 lemon, thinly sliced
- Fresh habanero peppers (optional)

1. Cover apple wood chips with water, and soak 1 hour. Drain well.
2. While wood chips soak, place peppers in a spice or coffee grinder; process until finely ground. Place ⅛ teaspoon ground pepper in a small bowl (reserve remaining ground pepper for another use). Add oil, salt, and pepper, stirring to combine. Rub spice mixture over fish; cover and refrigerate 30 minutes.
3. Prepare grill.
4. Place wood chips on hot coals. Coat a large piece of heavy-duty foil with cooking spray; pierce foil several times with a fork. Place foil on grill rack coated with cooking spray. Place fish on foil; arrange lemon slices over fish. Grill 20 minutes or until fish flakes easily when tested with a

fork. Garnish with habanero peppers, if desired. Serve immediately. Yield: 8 servings (serving size: about 5 ounces).

CALORIES 229 (24% from fat); FAT 6.1g (sat 1.4g, mono 1.7g, poly 2.2g); PROTEIN 40.3g; CARB 0.8g; FIBER 0.1g; CHOL 90mg; IRON 0.7mg; SODIUM 442mg; CALC 30mg

Test Kitchen Tip: A fish basket works great, but a perforated sheet of aluminum foil will also let you easily remove the fish from the grill. The smoke from the wood chips rises through the holes in the foil to flavor the fish.

Creole Catfish with Vidalia-Olive Relish

The tangy olives and sweet onions in the relish make this dish intriguing.

Prep: 14 minutes • Cook: 16 minutes
Other: 2 hours

    2 teaspoons olive oil, divided
    1 cup chopped Vidalia or other sweet
       onion
  1/3 cup chopped red bell pepper
    2 tablespoons chopped pitted green
       olives
    2 tablespoons chopped pitted
       kalamata olives
    2 tablespoons water
    1 tablespoon dried thyme, divided
    1 tablespoon paprika
  1/4 teaspoon salt
  1/4 teaspoon garlic powder
  1/8 teaspoon ground red pepper
    4 (6-ounce) farm-raised catfish fillets
       Cooking spray

1. Heat 1 teaspoon oil in a nonstick skillet over medium-high heat. Add onion; sauté 5 minutes. Spoon onion into a bowl. Stir in bell pepper, olives, water, and 1 teaspoon thyme. Cover; refrigerate at least 2 hours.
2. Prepare grill.
3. Combine 1 teaspoon olive oil, 2 teaspoons dried thyme, paprika, salt, garlic powder, and ground red pepper. Rub paprika mixture over both sides of fish. Place fish on a grill rack coated with cooking spray; grill 5 minutes on each side or until fish flakes easily when tested with a fork. Serve with relish. Yield: 4 servings (serving size: 1 fillet and about 1/3 cup relish).

CALORIES 211 (39% from fat); FAT 9.2g (sat 1.8g, mono 4.4g, poly 1.8g); PROTEIN 25.2g; CARB 6.6g; FIBER 1.8g; CHOL 77mg; IRON 3.5mg; SODIUM 308mg; CALC 93mg

---

All-Time Favorite

Crisp-Crusted Catfish

Hands down, this is the best catfish we've ever eaten. It's baked in the oven rather than deep-fat fried, and it has a double dose of flavor from the ranch dressing and Parmesan-cornmeal coating.

Prep: 9 minutes • Cook: 24 minutes

    2 tablespoons light ranch dressing
    2 large egg whites
    6 tablespoons yellow cornmeal
  1/4 cup (1 ounce) grated fresh
       Parmesan cheese
    2 tablespoons all-purpose flour
  1/4 teaspoon ground red pepper
  1/8 teaspoon salt
    4 (6-ounce) farm-raised catfish fillets
       Cooking spray
    4 lemon wedges

1. Preheat oven to 425°.
2. Combine dressing and egg whites in a small bowl, and stir well with a whisk. Combine cornmeal, cheese, flour, pepper, and salt in a shallow dish. Dip fish in egg white mixture; dredge in cornmeal mixture.
3. Place fish on a baking sheet coated with cooking spray; bake at 425° for 12 minutes on each side or until lightly browned and fish flakes easily when tested with a fork. Serve with lemon wedges. Yield: 4 servings (serving size: 1 fillet and 1 lemon wedge).

CALORIES 313 (26% from fat); FAT 9.1g (sat 2.8g, mono 3.6g, poly 3.3g); PROTEIN 32.9g; CARB 14.3g; FIBER 1.1g; CHOL 87mg; IRON 1.2mg; SODIUM 348mg; CALC 101mg

portion size Our standard serving size for fish and shellfish is 4 to 5 ounces of cooked fish (6 ounces uncooked) per serving.

Cajun Catfish Kebabs

The creamy mayonnaise-horseradish sauce works wonderfully with the spicy catfish.

Prep: 20 minutes • Cook: 11 minutes
Other: 20 minutes

    2 teaspoons paprika
    1 teaspoon garlic powder
    1 teaspoon dried oregano
    1 teaspoon dried thyme
  1/2 teaspoon salt
  1/2 teaspoon ground red pepper
    4 (6-ounce) farm-raised catfish fillets,
       cut into 24 (1-inch) pieces
  1/2 cup fat-free mayonnaise
    1 tablespoon fresh lemon juice
    2 teaspoons capers, chopped
    2 teaspoons prepared horseradish
    2 ears corn, each cut crosswise into
       8 pieces
    3 green bell peppers, each cut into
       8 wedges
       Cooking spray

1. Combine first 6 ingredients in a bowl; add fish, tossing to coat. Cover and refrigerate 20 minutes. Combine mayonnaise, juice, capers, and horseradish; stir with a whisk. Cover and refrigerate.
2. Prepare grill.
3. Cook corn in boiling water 3 minutes, and drain.
4. Thread 3 fish pieces, 2 corn pieces, and 3 pepper pieces alternately onto each of 8 (12-inch) skewers. Place kebabs on grill rack coated with cooking spray; grill 4 minutes on each side or until fish flakes easily when tested with a fork. Serve with sauce. Yield: 4 servings (serving size: 2 kebabs and 2 1/2 tablespoons sauce).

CALORIES 290 (26% from fat); FAT 8.3g (sat 1.8g, mono 2.9g, poly 2.3g); PROTEIN 33.2g; CARB 21.3g; FIBER 2.8g; CHOL 99mg; IRON 3.2mg; SODIUM 645mg; CALC 85mg

Pan-Seared Cod over Vegetable Ragoût

This easy-to-prepare skillet dinner elevates plain white fish to the height of good taste. Cod is incorporated into a Mediterranean-style ragoût chock-full of savory ingredients such as prosciutto and shiitake mushrooms.

Prep: 20 minutes • Cook: 27 minutes

2½ teaspoons olive oil, divided
½ cup diced prosciutto (about 2 ounces)
3 garlic cloves, minced
4 cups thinly sliced shiitake mushroom caps (about 10 ounces)
1½ cups chopped leek
3 cups diced plum tomato (about 1 pound)
¼ teaspoon salt
¼ teaspoon freshly ground black pepper
1 (10-ounce) package fresh spinach, coarsely chopped
1 cup torn fresh basil leaves
4 (6-ounce) cod or other firm white fish fillets (1 inch thick)
1 tablespoon all-purpose flour

1. Heat ½ teaspoon olive oil in a large nonstick skillet over low heat. Add prosciutto; sauté 5 minutes. Stir in garlic; remove from pan. Set aside.

2. Heat 1 teaspoon olive oil in pan over medium-high heat. Add mushrooms and leek; sauté 8 minutes. Stir in tomato, salt, and pepper. Gradually add spinach to pan, and stir until spinach is wilted (about 3 minutes). Stir in prosciutto mixture and basil. Remove from pan; cover and keep warm.

3. Heat 1 teaspoon olive oil in pan over medium-high heat. Dredge fish in flour. Add fish to pan; sauté 3 minutes on each side. Cover and cook 2 minutes or until fish flakes easily when tested with a fork. Place spinach mixture on plates; top with fillets. Yield: 4 servings (serving size: 1 fillet and about 1 cup ragoût).

CALORIES 287 (20% from fat); FAT 6.4g (sat 1.2g, mono 3g, poly 1.4g); PROTEIN 39.1g; CARB 20g; FIBER 5.9g; CHOL 82mg; IRON 5.3mg; SODIUM 525mg; CALC 146mg

Test Kitchen Tip: Fish is fully cooked when the color turns from translucent to opaque (usually white). If just a thin, translucent line remains when the fish is cut or flaked, remove it from the heat; the residual heat from the pan will finish cooking the fish.

Baked Flounder with Fresh Lemon Pepper

Using fresh lemon rind and crushed peppercorns produces better flavor than that of commercial lemon pepper.

Prep: 7 minutes • Cook: 8 minutes

  2 tablespoons grated lemon rind
  1 tablespoon extravirgin olive oil
1¼ teaspoons black peppercorns, crushed
 ½ teaspoon salt
  2 garlic cloves, minced
  4 (6-ounce) flounder fillets
Cooking spray
Lemon wedges (optional)

1. Preheat oven to 425°.
2. Combine first 5 ingredients. Place fish on a jelly-roll pan coated with cooking spray. Rub lemon pepper mixture evenly over fish. Bake at 425° for 8 minutes or until fish flakes easily when tested with a fork. Serve with lemon wedges, if desired. Yield: 4 servings (serving size: 1 fillet).

CALORIES 189 (26% from fat); FAT 5.4g (sat 0.9g, mono 2.9g, poly 0.9g); PROTEIN 32.2g; CARB 1.2g; FIBER 0.4g; CHOL 82mg; IRON 0.8mg; SODIUM 432mg; CALC 39mg

---

menu

serves 4

Baked Flounder with Fresh Lemon Pepper

Sesame-Scented Snow Peas and Carrots (page 524)

Fresh melon slices

Asian Flounder

Since flounder fillets are quite thin, they often end up overcooked and dry when baked or sautéed. Steaming the fish in the microwave cooks it quickly so that it stays moist. The unusual method of folding and arranging the fish is necessary because the food toward the edge of the dish cooks more rapidly than the food in the center.

Prep: 11 minutes • Cook: 4 minutes

  8 green onions
 ¼ cup minced fresh cilantro
  1 tablespoon minced peeled fresh ginger
  2 teaspoons dark sesame oil, divided
  4 (6-ounce) flounder fillets, skinned
  2 teaspoons rice vinegar
  2 teaspoons low-sodium soy sauce
 ⅛ teaspoon salt
  4 lemon slices

1. Remove green tops from onions, and slice onion tops into 1-inch pieces to measure ¼ cup; set aside. Reserve remaining onion tops for another use. Cut white portions of onions into 2-inch pieces.
2. Combine cilantro, ginger, and 1 teaspoon oil in a 9-inch pie plate. Fold each fillet in half crosswise. Arrange fillets over ginger mixture spokelike, with thinnest portions pointing toward center of dish. Arrange white onion pieces between fillets. Combine ¼ cup green onion tops, 1 teaspoon oil, vinegar, soy sauce, and salt; pour over fillets. Cover with heavy-duty plastic wrap. Microwave at HIGH 4 minutes or until fish flakes easily when tested with a fork. Garnish each fillet with a lemon slice. Yield: 4 servings (serving size: 1 fillet).

CALORIES 188 (21% from fat); FAT 4.4g (sat 0.8g, mono 1.3g, poly 1.5g); PROTEIN 32.8g; CARB 2.7g; FIBER 0.9g; CHOL 82mg; IRON 1.3mg; SODIUM 299mg; CALC 57mg

---

Grilled Grouper with Plantains and Salsa Verde

Choose a yellow, underripe plantain for this recipe. If your grill pan is large enough, cook the plantain and fish at the same time.

Prep: 7 minutes • Cook: 16 minutes

Olive oil-flavored cooking spray
  1 underripe plantain
 ¼ teaspoon salt, divided
  2 (6-ounce) grouper fillets (about ½ inch thick)
  1 tablespoon fresh lime juice
  1 tablespoon minced fresh cilantro
 ½ cup bottled green salsa
  2 tablespoons reduced-fat sour cream
Chopped fresh cilantro (optional)

1. Heat a large grill pan coated with cooking spray over medium-high heat.
2. Cut plantain in half lengthwise; cut each half crosswise into 2 pieces. Spray plantain pieces with cooking spray; grill 4 minutes on each side or until golden and slightly soft. Sprinkle with ⅛ teaspoon salt.
3. Drizzle fish with juice; sprinkle with ⅛ teaspoon salt and minced cilantro. Grill 4 minutes on each side or until fish flakes easily when tested with a fork. Top fish with salsa and sour cream, and serve with plantain pieces. Garnish with chopped cilantro, if desired. Yield: 2 servings (serving size: 1 fillet, ¼ cup salsa, 1 tablespoon sour cream, and 2 plantain pieces).

CALORIES 307 (12% from fat); FAT 4g (sat 1.4g, mono 0.4g, poly 0.6g); PROTEIN 35.7g; CARB 33.1g; FIBER 2.7g; CHOL 68mg; IRON 2.3mg; SODIUM 702mg; CALC 80mg

Test Kitchen Tip: To peel a plantain, cut off the top and bottom, make a lengthwise cut through the skin, and peel.

Hoisin Halibut

Update your pantry with a few Asian ingredients such as rice sticks, hoisin sauce, rice vinegar, and chile paste with garlic. They'll come in handy in many other dishes, too.

Prep: 10 minutes • Cook: 12 minutes

    8 ounces uncooked rice sticks
       (rice-flour noodles) or ¾ pound
       vermicelli
    ¼ cup hoisin sauce, divided
    1 cup sliced green onions
    ½ cup fat-free, less-sodium chicken
       broth
    3 tablespoons rice vinegar
    3 tablespoons low-sodium soy sauce
    1 tablespoon canola oil
    1 tablespoon grated peeled fresh
       ginger
    1 teaspoon chile paste with garlic
    ⅛ teaspoon freshly ground black pepper
    8 (6-ounce) halibut steaks (about
       1 inch thick)
       Cooking spray

1. Preheat broiler.
2. Cook noodles according to package directions, omitting salt and fat. Combine noodles, 2 tablespoons hoisin sauce, and next 8 ingredients in a large bowl, and keep warm.
3. Rub fish with 2 tablespoons hoisin sauce. Place fish on a broiler pan coated with cooking spray; broil 4 minutes on each side or until fish flakes easily when tested with a fork. Serve over noodles. Yield: 8 servings (serving size: 1 steak and ¾ cup noodles).

CALORIES 323 (17% from fat); FAT 6.3g (sat 0.7g, mono 2.4g, poly 1.9g); PROTEIN 37.5g; CARB 27.6g; FIBER 0.5g; CHOL 53mg; IRON 1.9mg; SODIUM 455mg; CALC 109mg

Halibut with Charmoula

Charmoula is a traditional Moroccan herb sauce used to season or marinate fish.

Prep: 14 minutes • Cook: 15 minutes

Charmoula:
    1 tablespoon olive oil
    1 teaspoon paprika
    ½ teaspoon salt
    ½ teaspoon ground cumin
    ½ teaspoon pepper
    2 garlic cloves
    1 cup fresh flat-leaf parsley leaves
    1 cup fresh cilantro leaves
    2 tablespoons capers
    2 teaspoons grated lemon rind
    ¼ cup fresh lemon juice
Fish:
    4 (6-ounce) halibut fillets (about
       1 inch thick)
    ¼ teaspoon salt
    ¼ teaspoon pepper
       Cooking spray

1. Preheat oven to 350°.
2. To prepare sauce, place first 6 ingredients in a food processor; process until garlic is finely chopped. Add parsley, cilantro, capers, rind, and juice; pulse until herbs are coarsely chopped.
3. To prepare fish, sprinkle fish with ¼ teaspoon salt and ¼ teaspoon pepper. Place fish on a baking sheet coated with cooking spray.
4. Bake at 350° for 15 minutes or until fish flakes easily when tested with a fork. Serve fish with sauce. Yield: 4 servings (serving size: 1 fillet and 1 tablespoon sauce).

CALORIES 234 (29% from fat); FAT 7.6g (sat 1.1g, mono 3.8g, poly 1.6g); PROTEIN 36.6g; CARB 3.8g; FIBER 1.3g; CHOL 54mg; IRON 2.9mg; SODIUM 701mg; CALC 118mg

Grilled Halibut and Fresh Mango Salsa

Not only does the zesty fruit salsa complement mild fish, it makes an attractively colorful presentation. It's also delicious on grilled chicken and with baked tortilla chips.

Prep: 20 minutes • Cook: 6 minutes

Fresh Mango Salsa:
    2 cups chopped seeded plum
       tomato
    1½ cups diced peeled ripe mango
    ½ cup chopped onion
    ½ cup chopped fresh cilantro
    2 tablespoons fresh lime juice
    1 tablespoon cider vinegar
    1 teaspoon sugar
    1 teaspoon salt, divided
    1 teaspoon pepper, divided
    2 garlic cloves, minced
Fish:
    4 (6-ounce) halibut fillets
    1 tablespoon olive oil

1. Prepare grill.
2. To prepare salsa, combine first 7 ingredients. Stir in ½ teaspoon salt, ½ teaspoon pepper, and garlic.
3. To prepare fish, rub fish with oil; sprinkle with ½ teaspoon salt and ½ teaspoon pepper. Place fish on grill rack; grill 3 minutes on each side or until fish flakes easily when tested with a fork. Serve with mango salsa. Yield: 4 servings (serving size: 1 fillet and ¾ cup salsa).

CALORIES 295 (24% from fat); FAT 7.8g (sat 1.1g, mono 3.9g, poly 1.7g); PROTEIN 37g; CARB 19.5g; FIBER 2.8g; CHOL 54mg; IRON 2.3mg; SODIUM 687mg; CALC 105mg

Grilled Mahimahi with Peach and Pink Grapefruit Relish

Onions, peaches, mint, and grapefruit make a citrusy, sweet relish that pairs well with the flavorful fish.

Prep: 20 minutes • Cook: 11 minutes

⅓ cup rice vinegar
2 tablespoons brown sugar
½ cup finely chopped red onion
2½ cups chopped peeled ripe peaches (about 1½ pounds)
1½ cups pink grapefruit sections (about 2 large grapefruit)
½ cup small mint leaves
6 (6-ounce) mahimahi or other firm white fish fillets (about ¾ inch thick)
¾ teaspoon salt, divided
½ teaspoon pepper, divided
Cooking spray

1. Prepare grill.
2. Place vinegar and sugar in a small saucepan; bring to a boil. Remove from heat. Place onion in a large bowl. Pour vinegar mixture over onion, tossing to coat; cool. Add peaches, grapefruit, mint, ¼ teaspoon salt, and ¼ teaspoon pepper to onion; toss gently.
3. Sprinkle fish with ½ teaspoon salt and ¼ teaspoon pepper. Place fish on grill rack coated with cooking spray, and grill 5 minutes on each side or until fish flakes easily when tested with a fork. Yield: 6 servings (serving size: 1 fillet and about ⅔ cup relish).

CALORIES 226 (5% from fat); FAT 1.4g (sat 0.4g, mono 0.3g, poly 0.4g); PROTEIN 32.8g; CARB 19.3g; FIBER 3.1g; CHOL 124mg; IRON 3.2mg; SODIUM 448mg; CALC 63mg

WINE NOTE: Mint and grapefruit give this dish a cool, tangy quality tailor-made for a crisp sauvignon blanc.

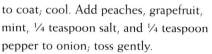

Maple-Glazed Salmon

Briefly marinating the salmon in this tangy-sweet glaze enhances its richness. Look for hoisin sauce and five-spice powder in the Asian food sections of large supermarkets.

Prep: 7 minutes • Cook: 12 minutes
Other: 15 minutes

2 tablespoons maple syrup
1½ tablespoons apple juice
1½ tablespoons fresh lemon juice
2 teaspoons hoisin sauce
1½ teaspoons grated peeled fresh ginger
1½ teaspoons country-style Dijon mustard
¼ teaspoon five-spice powder
4 (6-ounce) salmon fillets (about 1 inch thick)
Cooking spray

1. Combine first 7 ingredients in a large zip-top plastic bag. Add fish to bag; seal. Marinate in refrigerator 15 minutes.
2. Preheat broiler.
3. Remove fish from bag, reserving marinade. Place fish fillets, skin sides down, on a broiler rack coated with cooking spray. Broil 12 minutes or until fish flakes easily when tested with a fork, basting salmon with reserved marinade. Yield: 4 servings (serving size: 1 fillet).

CALORIES 316 (41% from fat); FAT 14.4g (sat 2.5g, mono 6.9g, poly 3.2g); PROTEIN 35g; CARB 9.3g; FIBER 0.1g; CHOL 111mg; IRON 0.9mg; SODIUM 184mg; CALC 18mg

Test Kitchen Tip: If you don't want to use salmon, the maple glaze is good over swordfish or yellowtail tuna.

Alder-Planked Asian Salmon

Wood planks made for cooking are available from gourmet kitchen stores, seafood markets, and other stores where grills and grilling equipment are sold.

**Prep: 15 minutes • Cook: 20 minutes
Other: 1 hour**

1   (15 x 6½ x ⅜-inch) alder grilling
    plank
½   cup rice vinegar
½   cup low-sodium soy sauce
2   tablespoons honey
1   teaspoon ground ginger
½   teaspoon freshly ground black
    pepper
3   garlic cloves, minced
1   lemon, thinly sliced
1   (3½-pound) salmon fillet
¼   cup chopped green onions
1   tablespoon sesame seeds, toasted

1. Immerse and soak plank in water 1 hour; drain.
2. Combine vinegar and next 6 ingredients in a large zip-top plastic bag; seal. Shake to combine. Add fish; seal. Marinate in refrigerator 30 minutes; turn once.
3. To prepare grill for indirect grilling, heat one side of grill to high heat.
4. Place plank on grill rack over high heat; grill 5 minutes or until lightly charred. Carefully turn plank over; move to cool side of grill. Remove fish from bag; discard marinade. Place fish, skin side down, on charred side of plank. Cover and grill 15 minutes or until fish flakes easily when tested with a fork. Sprinkle with onions and sesame seeds. Yield: 9 servings (serving size: 5 ounces).

CALORIES 306 (41% from fat); FAT 14.1g (sat 3.3g, mono 6.1g, poly 3.5g); PROTEIN 38.3g; CARB 4.6g; FIBER 0.5g; CHOL 90mg; IRON 0.9mg; SODIUM 353mg; CALC 36mg

using a plank to grill

Cooking on wood planks is an ancient method that originated with Native Americans. The smoldering plank keeps the food moist and lends a subtle smokiness to the food. Here are some tips for grilling on a plank.

- Submerge the plank in water at least 1 hour before using. Use a can to weight it down. A water-soaked plank produces maximum smoke and is less likely to burn on the grill.
- Grill the water-soaked plank over high heat for at least 5 minutes or until it begins to char and smoke. The moist smoke keeps food from drying as it cooks.
- Turn the plank over so that the charred side faces up.
- Place food on the charred surface of the plank. Food touching the wood takes on more flavor, so arrange it in a single layer on the plank.
- Grill fish and large cuts of meat on planks over indirect heat (food isn't placed directly over hot coals) so they cook evenly; use direct heat for smaller pieces of food such as small fillets, steaks, pork chops, and vegetables.
- Cook with the grill lid closed so that smoke surrounds the food and infuses it with flavor.
- Keep a spray bottle filled with water handy to douse flare-ups.
- Serve the food on the wood plank for an impressive restaurant-style presentation.

Grilled Salmon with Mango-Coconut Salsa

You can prepare the poblano mixture for this salsa up to a day ahead, but add the mango just before serving.

**Prep: 15 minutes • Cook: 20 minutes
Other: 45 minutes**

1   poblano chile
½   cup thinly sliced radishes
¼   cup flaked, sweetened coconut
2   tablespoons fresh lime juice
1   tablespoon olive oil
2   teaspoons minced fresh cilantro
1   garlic clove, minced
2   cups cubed peeled ripe mango
    (about 2 large)
5   (6-ounce) salmon fillets
Cooking spray
Cilantro sprigs (optional)

1. Preheat broiler.
2. Place chile on a foil-lined baking sheet, and broil 10 minutes or until blackened, turning occasionally. Place blackened chile in a zip-top plastic bag, and seal. Let stand 15 minutes. Peel and cut chile in half lengthwise. Discard seeds and membrane. Finely chop chile.
3. Combine chile, radishes, and next 5 ingredients in a medium bowl. Cover and marinate in refrigerator 30 minutes or overnight. Stir in mango.
4. Prepare grill.
5. Place fish, skin sides down, on grill rack coated with cooking spray. Grill 10 minutes or until fish flakes easily when tested with a fork. Serve with salsa; garnish with cilantro sprigs, if desired. Yield: 5 servings (serving size: 1 fillet and 6 tablespoons salsa).

CALORIES 328 (35% from fat); FAT 12.6g (sat 3.5g, mono 5.2g, poly 3.3g); PROTEIN 37g; CARB 19g; FIBER 2.5g; CHOL 89mg; IRON 2.1mg; SODIUM 207mg; CALC 94mg

Smoked Salmon

This recipe gives you moist smoked salmon—not the drier, thinly sliced type called lox that you purchase at a deli. Start soaking the wood chips while the salmon brines. Because kosher salt has big crystals with large surface areas and absorbs more moisture than other types of salt, it's ideal for brining and curing meats.

Prep: 11 minutes • Cook: 25 minutes • Other: 2 hours

3½ cups water
½ cup kosher salt
¼ cup sugar
2 tablespoons dried dill
2 tablespoons low-sodium soy sauce
1 cup ice cubes
1 (1½-pound) salmon fillet (about 1 inch thick)
4 cups hickory wood chips
Cooking spray
Cracked black pepper (optional)
Dill sprigs (optional)

1. Combine first 5 ingredients in a large bowl; stir until salt and sugar dissolve. Pour salt mixture into a large zip-top plastic bag. Add ice and fish; seal. Refrigerate 2 hours, turning bag occasionally.
2. Soak wood chips in water 1 hour. Drain chips well.
3. To prepare grill for indirect grilling, heat one side of grill to medium.

4. Place half of the wood chips on hot coals. Remove fish from bag; discard brine. Pat fish dry with paper towels. Place fish on grill rack coated with cooking spray over unheated side. Close lid; grill 10 minutes. Place remaining wood chips on hot coals; close lid, and grill 15 minutes or until fish flakes easily when tested with a fork. Sprinkle with black pepper, and garnish with dill sprigs, if desired. Yield: 4 servings (serving size: about 4 ounces).

CALORIES 279 (42% from fat); FAT 13.1g (sat 3.1g, mono 5.7g, poly 3.2g); PROTEIN 36.3g; CARB 1.7g; FIBER 0g; CHOL 87mg; IRON 0.7mg; SODIUM 958mg; CALC 28mg

Test Kitchen Tip: Wood chips add smoky flavor to brined meats. Simply toss water-soaked wood chips over hot coals, as called for in this recipe. If you're using a gas grill, wrap soaked chips in aluminum foil, punch holes in the top, and set the package over direct heat.

Citrus-Roasted Salmon

Although we typically associate roasting with meats and poultry, it's also an ideal cooking method for firm-fleshed fish. Roasting concentrates flavors without adding fat and gives the fish a crispy exterior and tender interior.

Prep: 10 minutes • Cook: 19 minutes

1 teaspoon grated lemon rind
2 tablespoons fresh lemon juice
2 tablespoons honey
4 teaspoons chili powder
1 teaspoon ground cumin
½ teaspoon salt
½ teaspoon ground coriander seeds
¼ teaspoon ground red pepper
1 (6-ounce) can thawed orange juice concentrate
4 (6-ounce) salmon fillets, skinned (1 inch thick)
Cooking spray
Orange wedges (optional)
Flat-leaf parsley sprigs (optional)

1. Preheat oven to 400°.
2. Combine first 9 ingredients in a bowl; brush both sides of fish with orange mixture. Reserve remaining orange mixture. Place fish on a broiler pan coated with cooking spray. Bake at 400° for 15 minutes or until fish flakes easily when tested with a fork.
3. Place remaining orange mixture in a small saucepan; bring to a boil, and cook until reduced to ½ cup (about 2 minutes). Serve with fish, and garnish with orange wedges and parsley, if desired. Yield: 4 servings (serving size: 1 fillet and 2 tablespoons orange sauce).

CALORIES 366 (33% from fat); FAT 13.5g (sat 2.3g, mono 6.3g, poly 3g); PROTEIN 33.5g; CARB 27g; FIBER 1.6g; CHOL 102mg; IRON 1.4mg; SODIUM 399mg; CALC 37mg

Steamed Bali-Style Sea Bass

Chili paste and bottled minced ginger are convenient ways to transform basic steamed fish into an amazing Thai-style dinner.

Prep: 15 minutes • Cook: 21 minutes

- 2   teaspoons canola oil
- 1⅔ cups diced shallots (about 4 large shallots)
- 1   tablespoon bottled minced fresh ginger
- ½   teaspoon Thai chili paste (such as Dynasty)
- ¼   teaspoon salt
- 10 macadamia nuts (about ¾ ounce)
- 1   plum tomato, quartered
- 1   garlic clove, peeled
- 2   cups trimmed watercress, coarsely chopped
- 4   (6-ounce) sea bass fillets (about 1 inch thick)

1. Heat oil in a medium nonstick skillet over medium-high heat. Add shallots; sauté 3 minutes. Remove from heat.
2. Place shallot mixture, ginger, and next 5 ingredients in a food processor; pulse until coarsely blended. Set aside.
3. Arrange watercress on a large sheet of foil. Arrange fish on top of watercress; spread shallot mixture over fish. Fold foil over fish to form a packet; loosely seal. Place packet in bottom of a bamboo steamer. Cover with steamer lid. Add water to a large skillet to a depth of 1 inch; bring to a boil. Place steamer in pan; steam fish 15 minutes or until fish flakes easily when tested with a fork. Yield: 4 servings (serving size: 1 fillet).

CALORIES 286 (31% from fat); FAT 9.8g (sat 1.4g, mono 5.6g, poly 2.1g); PROTEIN 35.6g; CARB 13.3g; FIBER 1.2g; CHOL 74mg; IRON 1.5mg; SODIUM 300mg; CALC 68mg

Oven-Roasted Sea Bass with Couscous and Warm Tomato Vinaigrette

The warm tomato topping provides a pleasing contrast to the tender, sweet fish. While the fish is roasting, prepare the couscous so you can serve it as soon as the fish comes out of the oven.

Prep: 15 minutes • Cook: 26 minutes • Other: 5 minutes

- 1   green onion
- 2   tablespoons olive oil
- 2   garlic cloves, minced
- 1   cup chopped tomato
- 3   tablespoons fresh lemon juice, divided
- 1   tablespoon sherry vinegar
- 1   teaspoon kosher salt, divided
- 1¼   cups fat-free, less-sodium chicken broth
- ⅔   cup uncooked couscous
- ¼   cup chopped fresh chives
- 4   (6-ounce) sea bass or halibut fillets (about 1½ inches thick)
- ¼   teaspoon freshly ground black pepper
- Cooking spray
- 8   (¼-inch-thick) slices lemon, halved (about 1 lemon)

1. Preheat oven to 350°.
2. Cut onion into 3-inch pieces; cut pieces into julienne strips.
3. Heat oil in a large nonstick skillet over medium-high heat. Add garlic; sauté 30 seconds or until garlic begins to brown. Add tomato and onion; reduce heat to medium, and cook 1 minute. Remove from heat; stir in 2 tablespoons juice, vinegar, and ½ teaspoon salt. Keep warm.
4. Combine 1 tablespoon juice, ¼ teaspoon salt, and broth in a saucepan, and bring to a boil. Gradually stir in couscous and chopped chives. Remove from heat; cover and let stand 5 minutes. Fluff with a fork. Cover and keep warm.
5. Sprinkle fish with ¼ teaspoon salt and pepper. Place fish in an 11 x 7–inch baking dish coated with cooking spray. Place 4 halved lemon slices on each fillet. Bake at 350° for 20 minutes or until fish flakes easily when tested with a fork. Serve over couscous; top with vinaigrette. Yield: 4 servings (serving size: 1 fillet, ½ cup couscous, and ¼ cup vinaigrette).

CALORIES 346 (29% from fat); FAT 11.2g (sat 1.9g, mono 5.8g, poly 2.2g); PROTEIN 36.5g; CARB 25.2g; FIBER 1.9g; CHOL 70mg; IRON 1.6mg; SODIUM 777mg; CALC 49mg

Snapper Tacos with Chipotle Cream

The fish cooks on top of the vegetables in the same skillet. Break the fish into chunks to finish the taco filling.

Prep: 20 minutes • Cook: 14 minutes

½ cup fat-free sour cream
⅛ teaspoon salt
1 canned chipotle chile in adobo sauce, seeded and minced
1½ cups chopped onion, divided
1½ cups chopped tomato, divided
2 tablespoons butter
1 teaspoon ground cumin
½ teaspoon salt
½ teaspoon ground cinnamon
4 garlic cloves, minced
3 tablespoons chopped fresh cilantro
1 pound red snapper fillets, skinned
1 teaspoon grated lime rind
2 tablespoons fresh lime juice
4 (8-inch) fat-free flour tortillas

1. Combine sour cream, ⅛ teaspoon salt, and chipotle chile, and set aside. Combine ½ cup onion and ½ cup tomato, and set aside.
2. Melt butter in a large nonstick skillet over medium heat. Add 1 cup onion, 1 cup tomato, cumin, ½ teaspoon salt, cinnamon, and garlic; cook 5 minutes, stirring frequently. Stir in cilantro. Arrange fish over onion mixture in pan. Cover; cook 3 minutes. Turn fish. Cover; cook 2 minutes. Break fish into chunks. Stir in rind and juice; cook 2 minutes. Remove from heat.
3. Warm tortillas according to package directions. Fill each tortilla with ½ cup fish mixture and ¼ cup reserved onion mixture; top each serving with 2 tablespoons reserved chipotle cream. Fold in half or roll up. Yield: 4 servings (serving size: 1 taco).

CALORIES 340 (21% from fat); FAT 7.8g (sat 4g, mono 2g, poly 0.9g); PROTEIN 28.1g; CARB 38.1g; FIBER 3.3g; CHOL 56mg; IRON 2mg; SODIUM 896mg; CALC 108mg

Ginger-Lime Swordfish

Serve this fish with broiled pineapple slices. Place the pineapple on the broiler pan at the same time you broil the fish.

Prep: 12 minutes • Cook: 10 minutes

2 teaspoons grated lime rind
½ cup fresh lime juice (about 2 limes)
¼ cup honey
2 tablespoons bottled ground fresh ginger
2 tablespoons minced green onions
1 tablespoon low-sodium soy sauce
2 teaspoons bottled minced garlic
4 (6-ounce) swordfish steaks (about ¾ inch thick)
Cooking spray
¼ teaspoon salt
¼ teaspoon pepper

1. Preheat broiler.
2. Combine first 7 ingredients in a small saucepan. Dip each steak into lime mixture to coat.
3. Place fish on a broiler pan coated with cooking spray. Sprinkle with salt and pepper. Broil 10 minutes or until fish flakes easily when tested with a fork.
4. While fish cooks, place lime juice mixture over medium heat; cook until reduced by half (about 8 minutes). Serve sauce with fish. Yield: 4 servings (serving size: 1 steak and 2 tablespoons sauce).

CALORIES 235 (20% from fat); FAT 5.2g (sat 1.4g, mono 2g, poly 1.2g); PROTEIN 25.8g; CARB 22g; FIBER 0.6g; CHOL 50mg; IRON 1.3mg; SODIUM 397mg; CALC 15mg

Malaysian Lime-Coconut Swordfish

Lemongrass lends a characteristic hint of citrus to many Asian dishes. You'll find this herb with long, thin, gray-green leaves in the produce section of many supermarkets. You can substitute grated lemon peel, but cut the amount you use by half.

Prep: 12 minutes • Cook: 15 minutes

⅓ cup light coconut milk
¼ cup chopped fresh cilantro
2 tablespoons thinly sliced peeled fresh lemongrass (about 1 stalk) or 1 tablespoon grated lemon peel
2 tablespoons fish sauce
1 tablespoon brown sugar
1 teaspoon lime juice
½ teaspoon Thai chili paste (such as Dynasty)
2 shallots, peeled
1 garlic clove, peeled
1 (1½-pound) swordfish steak (about 1 inch thick)
Cooking spray
Cilantro sprigs (optional)
Lemon wedges (optional)

1. Preheat broiler.
2. Place first 9 ingredients in a food processor; pulse 3 times or until coarsely chopped. Place fish on a broiler pan coated with cooking spray; spread ½ cup shallot mixture evenly over fish. Broil 15 minutes or until fish flakes easily when tested with a fork. Serve fish with remaining shallot mixture, and garnish with cilantro sprigs and lemon wedges, if desired. Yield: 4 servings (serving size: 5 ounces fish and 2 tablespoons sauce).

CALORIES 255 (30% from fat); FAT 8.5g (sat 2.7g, mono 2.9g, poly 1.8g); PROTEIN 36.8g; CARB 5.4g; FIBER 0.2g; CHOL 71mg; IRON 2mg; SODIUM 840mg; CALC 18mg

Tilapia with Coconut, Mint, and Chive Relish

Jalapeño and coconut give the refreshing relish some heat and sweetness.

Prep: 25 minutes • Cook: 9 minutes • Other: 30 minutes

Coconut, Mint, and Chive Relish:

- 1 cup chopped seeded peeled cucumber
- ¾ teaspoon salt, divided
- ¾ cup chopped fresh chives
- ½ cup sweetened flaked coconut
- 2 tablespoons finely chopped fresh mint
- 2 tablespoons finely chopped fresh cilantro
- 2 jalapeño peppers, seeded and minced
- 2 tablespoons fresh lime juice
- ½ teaspoon ground cumin
- 1 teaspoon peanut oil
- 1 teaspoon mustard seeds

Fish:

- 2 teaspoons grated lime rind
- 1½ tablespoons fresh lime juice
- 1 teaspoon peanut oil
- ½ teaspoon ground cumin
- ½ teaspoon crushed red pepper
- 6 (6-ounce) tilapia or red snapper fillets
- ¼ teaspoon salt
- ¼ teaspoon freshly ground black pepper
- Cooking spray
- 6 lime wedges

1. To prepare relish, place cucumber in a colander; sprinkle with ½ teaspoon salt. Toss well. Drain 30 minutes. Rinse and drain; pat dry.

2. Preheat broiler.

3. Combine cucumber, chives, coconut, mint, cilantro, and jalapeño. Stir in ¼ teaspoon salt, 2 tablespoons juice, and ½ teaspoon cumin. Heat 1 teaspoon oil in a skillet over medium-high heat. Add mustard seeds; sauté 30 seconds or until seeds begin to pop. Add to cucumber mixture.

4. To prepare fish, combine rind and next 4 ingredients; rub evenly over fillets. Sprinkle fish with ¼ teaspoon salt and black pepper.

5. Place fish, skin sides down, on a broiler pan coated with cooking spray; cook 7 minutes or until fish flakes easily when tested with a fork. Serve with relish and lime wedges. Yield: 6 servings (serving size: 1 fillet, ⅓ cup relish, and 1 lime wedge).

CALORIES 238 (26% from fat); FAT 7g (sat 3.2g, mono 1.4g, poly 1.4g); PROTEIN 35.8g; CARB 6.7g; FIBER 1.1g; CHOL 63mg; IRON 0.8mg; SODIUM 523mg; CALC 72mg

Trout Topped with Cucumber Salsa

Sweet-hot cucumber salsa provides an extra kick to pan-fried trout.

Prep: 12 minutes • Cook: 7 minutes
Other: 2 hours

Cucumber Salsa:

- 2 cups finely chopped seeded peeled cucumber
- ⅓ cup rice wine vinegar
- 2 tablespoons finely chopped shallots
- 1½ tablespoons sugar
- 1 tablespoon minced seeded jalapeño pepper
- 1½ teaspoons minced fresh cilantro

Fish:

- 2 teaspoons butter
- 1 tablespoon minced fresh cilantro
- 1 teaspoon bottled minced garlic
- ¼ teaspoon salt
- ⅛ teaspoon freshly ground black pepper
- 4 (6-ounce) trout fillets

1. To prepare salsa, combine first 6 ingredients. Cover and chill 2 hours.

2. To prepare fish, melt butter in a large nonstick skillet over medium-high heat. Sprinkle 1 tablespoon cilantro, garlic, salt, and black pepper evenly over one side of fish. Add fish, cilantro side down, to pan; cook 3 minutes. Turn and cook 3 minutes or until fish flakes easily when tested with a fork. Serve with salsa. Yield: 4 servings (serving size: 1 fillet and ½ cup salsa).

CALORIES 284 (35% from fat); FAT 11.2g (sat 3.9g, mono 3.2g, poly 3.2g); PROTEIN 36.2g; CARB 7.8g; FIBER 0.6g; CHOL 106mg; IRON 0.7mg; SODIUM 376mg; CALC 130mg

Grilled Tuna with Rain Forest Glaze

Tuna is one of the best fish to grill. Here it works to unite the tart tropical fruit juice with the heat of the habanero pepper.

Prep: 15 minutes • Cook: 26 minutes

    1 cup pineapple juice
    1 cup cranberry juice cocktail
    1 cup mango or apricot nectar
    1 tablespoon sugar
    2 tablespoons lime juice
    1 tablespoon grated peeled fresh ginger
    1 teaspoon chopped seeded habanero
       pepper
  ½ teaspoon salt
  ½ teaspoon grated lemon rind
  ½ teaspoon grated orange rind
    1 tablespoon cornstarch
    1 tablespoon water
    1 cup thinly sliced green onions
    6 (6-ounce) tuna steaks (about ¾ inch
       thick)
       Cooking spray

1. Combine first 10 ingredients in a large saucepan. Bring to a boil, and cook until reduced to 1½ cups (about 15 minutes); remove from heat. Combine cornstarch and water in a small bowl; stir well with a whisk. Add to pan. Bring to a boil; cook 1 minute, stirring constantly. Remove from heat; stir in onions.
2. Prepare grill.
3. Place fish on grill rack coated with cooking spray; grill 3 minutes on each side or until desired degree of doneness, basting frequently with glaze. Yield: 6 servings (serving size: 1 steak).

CALORIES 328 (23% from fat); FAT 8.3g (sat 2.1g, mono 2.7g, poly 2.4g); PROTEIN 38.8g; CARB 23.4g; FIBER 0.7g; CHOL 63mg; IRON 2.3mg; SODIUM 266mg; CALC 25mg

Grilled Tuna with Basil Butter and Fresh Tomato Sauce

Herbed butter and savory tomato sauce are ideal partners for succulent tuna steaks.

Prep: 25 minutes • Cook: 22 minutes

Basil Butter:
  ¾ cup fresh basil leaves
    2 tablespoons butter, softened
    1 tablespoon fresh lemon juice
  ¼ teaspoon salt
    2 garlic cloves, minced
Fresh Tomato Sauce:
    2 teaspoons olive oil
  ½ cup finely chopped red onion
    2 garlic cloves, minced
    3 cups grape or cherry tomatoes, halved
  ½ cup dry white wine
    3 tablespoons capers
    2 tablespoons balsamic vinegar
  ¼ teaspoon sugar
  ¼ cup chopped fresh flat-leaf parsley
Fish:
    4 (6-ounce) tuna steaks (about 1 inch
       thick)
  ½ teaspoon salt
  ¼ teaspoon pepper
       Cooking spray

1. Prepare grill.
2. Place first 5 ingredients in a food processor; process until smooth, scraping sides as needed.
3. Heat oil in a saucepan over medium-high heat. Add onion and 2 garlic cloves; sauté 3 minutes. Add tomatoes; sauté 2 minutes. Stir in wine, capers, vinegar, and sugar; bring to a boil. Reduce heat; simmer 5 minutes, stirring occasionally. Stir in parsley.
4. Sprinkle tuna with ½ teaspoon salt and pepper. Place on grill rack coated with cooking spray; grill 5 minutes on each side or until desired degree of doneness. Serve with butter and sauce. Yield: 4 servings (serving size: 1 steak, ¾ cup sauce, and 1 tablespoon butter).

CALORIES 323 (28% from fat); FAT 10.2g (sat 4.4g, mono 3.7g, poly 1.1g); PROTEIN 41.8g; CARB 10.9g; FIBER 2.4g; CHOL 92mg; IRON 2.7mg; SODIUM 770mg; CALC 72mg

Tuna Puttanesca

Often served with pasta, a puttanesca sauce is a spicy mixture of tomatoes, onions, capers, olives, anchovies, and garlic.

Prep: 10 minutes • Cook: 7 minutes

  ¼ cup chopped pimiento-stuffed olives
    1 tablespoon capers
    2 teaspoons bottled minced garlic
    1 teaspoon fresh lemon juice
    1 teaspoon anchovy paste
  ⅛ teaspoon crushed red pepper
    1 (14.5-ounce) can diced tomatoes,
       drained
    1 tablespoon olive oil
    4 (6-ounce) tuna steaks
  ½ teaspoon salt
  ¼ teaspoon black pepper
  ¼ cup chopped fresh parsley

1. Combine first 7 ingredients.
2. Heat oil in a large nonstick skillet over medium-high heat. Sprinkle tuna with salt and pepper. Add fish to pan; cook 2 minutes on each side or until desired degree of doneness. Remove fish from pan; keep warm.
3. Add tomato mixture to pan; cook 2 minutes or until thoroughly heated. Stir in parsley. Pour sauce over fish. Yield: 4 servings (serving size: 1 steak and ¼ cup sauce).

CALORIES 236 (23% from fat); FAT 6.1g (sat 1.2g, mono 3.5g, poly 0.9g); PROTEIN 38.6g; CARB 5.1g; FIBER 1.7g; CHOL 81mg; IRON 3.1mg; SODIUM 801mg; CALC 85mg

Shellfish
Crabs, shrimp, lobsters, clams, oysters, and mussels all have some type of shell—either jointed, crustlike, and soft, or hard and hinged.

Linguine with Clam Sauce

When you have canned minced clams dispersed throughout the pasta mixture as well as the fresh clams in their shells, you get some clam in every bite. You're also using the clam juice from the canned clams. Store live clams in your refrigerator up to two days.

Prep: 20 minutes • Cook: 29 minutes

1   (12-ounce) package linguine
3   tablespoons butter
5   garlic cloves, minced
½   cup dry white wine or low-sodium chicken broth
½   teaspoon salt
1   (8-ounce) bottle clam juice
2   (6½-ounce) cans minced clams, undrained
24   littleneck clams, scrubbed
1   cup finely chopped fresh parsley
2   tablespoons fresh lemon juice
⅛   teaspoon freshly ground black pepper
Lemon wedges (optional)

1. Cook linguine according to package directions, omitting salt and fat.

2. Melt butter in a large skillet over medium heat. Add garlic to pan; cook 3 minutes or until golden.

3. Stir in wine, salt, and clam juice. Drain minced clams; add juice to pan. Reserve minced clams. Simmer 5 minutes. Add littleneck clams. Cover; cook 3 to 4 minutes or until shells open. Remove from heat; discard any unopened shells. Add reserved minced clams, parsley, lemon juice, and pepper.

4. Place pasta in a large bowl. Add clam mixture to pasta, and toss well. Serve with lemon wedges, if desired. Yield: 6 servings (serving size: about 1 cup pasta mixture and 4 littleneck clams).

CALORIES 332 (19% from fat); FAT 7g (sat 3.8g, mono 1.7g, poly 0.3g); PROTEIN 17.1g; CARB 47.5g; FIBER 2.2g; CHOL 39mg; IRON 8.5mg; SODIUM 627mg; CALC 54mg

Sautéed Soft-Shell Crabs

Here's a basic recipe for soft-shell crabs. You can vary it by adding cayenne pepper, garlic powder, or other seasonings to the flour.

Prep: 20 minutes • Cook: 6 minutes

 4 (5-6–ounce) soft-shell crabs, cleaned
 ½ teaspoon salt
 ¼ teaspoon freshly ground black pepper
 ¼ cup all-purpose flour
 1 tablespoon butter

1. Sprinkle crabs with salt and pepper. Place flour in a shallow bowl. Dredge each crab in flour, turning to coat; shake off excess flour.

2. Melt butter in a large nonstick skillet over medium-high heat. Add crabs to pan, top sides down; cook 3 minutes. Turn crabs over; cook 2 minutes. Yield: 4 servings (serving size: 1 crab).

CALORIES 170 (23% from fat); FAT 4.4g (sat 2.1g, mono 1g, poly 0.7g); PROTEIN 26.3g; CARB 4.6g; FIBER 0.2g; CHOL 118mg; IRON 1.4mg; SODIUM 731mg; CALC 128mg

Soft-Shell Crabs with Fresh Thai Green Curry

The heat of this dish depends on the number of chiles that you use.

Prep: 45 minutes • Cook: 51 minutes

Curry:
 2 cups fresh cilantro sprigs
 ½ cup coarsely chopped shallots
 1 tablespoon grated lime rind
 8 to 12 serrano chiles, seeded
 3 garlic cloves, peeled
 1 (3-inch) piece peeled fresh ginger
 1 teaspoon canola oil
 2 cups sliced red bell pepper
 1½ cups (1-inch) cubed Japanese eggplant
 1½ cups water
 ½ cup diagonally cut carrot
 2 tablespoons brown sugar
 1 (13.5-ounce) can light coconut milk
 2 tablespoons fresh lime juice
 1 teaspoon salt

Crabs:
 ¼ cup cornstarch
 ¼ teaspoon salt
 6 (5-6–ounce) soft-shell crabs, cleaned
 4 teaspoons canola oil, divided
 3 cups hot cooked jasmine rice

1. To prepare curry, place first 6 ingredients in a food processor; process 3 minutes.

2. Heat 1 teaspoon oil in a large Dutch oven over medium-high heat. Add chile mixture; sauté 3 minutes. Add bell pepper and next 5 ingredients; bring to a boil. Cover, reduce heat, and simmer 10 minutes. Uncover; simmer 10 minutes. Stir in lime juice and 1 teaspoon salt; keep warm.

3. To prepare crabs, combine cornstarch and ¼ teaspoon salt in a shallow dish. Dredge crabs in cornstarch mixture.

4. Heat 2 teaspoons oil in a large nonstick skillet over medium-high heat. Place 3 crabs in pan, top sides down; cook 3 minutes, gently pressing body and legs against pan. Turn crabs; cook 2 minutes. Remove from pan. Repeat procedure with remaining oil and crabs. To serve, spoon curry mixture over rice, and top with crab. Yield: 6 servings (serving size: ½ cup rice, ¾ cup curry mixture, 1 crab).

CALORIES 389 (22% from fat); FAT 9.3g (sat 3.9g, mono 2.6g, poly 1.9g); PROTEIN 29.8g; CARB 40.1g; FIBER 2.3g; CHOL 111mg; IRON 2.9mg; SODIUM 941mg; CALC 159mg

how to clean soft-shell crabs

1. Using kitchen shears, cut off the front of the crab, about ½ inch behind the eyes and mouth. Squeeze out the contents of the sack located directly behind cut.

2. Lift one pointed end of the crab's outer shell.

3. Remove and discard the gills. Repeat steps two and three on the other side of the crab.

4. Turn the crab over; snip off the small flap known as the apron. Rinse the entire crab; pat dry. Once cleaned, crabs should be cooked or stored immediately.

Deviled Crab Boules with Beurre Blanc

Crusty individual bread rounds are stuffed with succulent crab and topped with a buttery wine sauce (beurre blanc). You can prepare the bread shells and crab filling up to a day ahead. Store the shells at room temperature in a zip-top plastic bag, and refrigerate the crab filling.

Prep: 25 minutes • Cook: 35 minutes

Boules:

2 (3-ounce) Kaiser rolls

Deviled crab:

¼ cup finely chopped green onions, divided

¼ cup dry white wine

2 garlic cloves, minced

2 tablespoons light mayonnaise

1 tablespoon stone-ground mustard

⅛ teaspoon ground red pepper

⅛ teaspoon paprika

½ pound lump crabmeat, shell pieces removed

Beurre Blanc:

⅓ cup fat-free, less-sodium chicken broth, divided

¼ cup finely chopped shallots

¼ cup dry white wine

2 tablespoons white wine vinegar

1 bay leaf

1 teaspoon cornstarch

1 tablespoon butter

½ teaspoon lemon juice

⅛ teaspoon black pepper

Julienne-cut green onions (optional)

1. Preheat oven to 375°.

2. To prepare boules, hollow out each roll, leaving about ¼-inch-thick shells; reserve torn bread for another use. Place shells on a baking sheet. Bake at 375° for 5 minutes. Remove from oven; set aside.

3. To prepare crab, combine 2 tablespoons chopped onions, ¼ cup wine, and garlic in a saucepan; bring to a boil. Reduce heat; simmer 2 minutes or until reduced to 2 tablespoons. Remove from heat; stir in mayonnaise, mustard, red pepper, and paprika. Add 2 tablespoons chopped onions and crab; toss to combine. Spoon mixture evenly into bread shells. Bake at 375° for 15 minutes or until thoroughly heated.

4. Combine 2 tablespoons broth, shallots, ¼ cup wine, vinegar, and bay leaf in a saucepan; bring to a boil. Reduce heat, and simmer 3 minutes or until reduced to ¼ cup. Strain through a fine sieve into a bowl, reserving liquid; discard solids.

5. Return wine mixture to pan. Combine remaining broth and cornstarch, stirring well with a whisk; stir into wine mixture. Bring to a boil; cook 1 minute, stirring constantly. Remove from heat; add butter, stirring until butter melts. Stir in juice and black pepper. Spoon beurre blanc immediately over warm boules. Garnish with green onions, if desired. Yield: 2 servings (serving size: 1 boule and about ¼ cup sauce).

CALORIES 415 (29% from fat); FAT 13.4g (sat 4.6g, mono 4.4g, poly 1.7g); PROTEIN 34.5g; CARB 34.3g; FIBER 3.4g; CHOL 142mg; IRON 3.2mg; SODIUM 1049mg; CALC 135mg

Classic Makeover: Crab Cakes

Even though crabmeat is low in fat, when you form it into patties and fry the patties in oil, both fat and calories increase significantly. In a traditional crab cake recipe, the crabmeat is combined with egg, onion, breadcrumbs, and sometimes mayonnaise, then pan-fried in butter. We cut the amount of fat in each crab cake by 50 percent by using 2 egg whites instead of 3 whole eggs as the binding agent in the mixture and by cooking the cakes in a small amount of olive oil in a nonstick skillet rather than frying them in butter. We also replaced some of the breadcrumbs with cooked wild rice. The rice adds a nutty flavor as well as fiber, plus it's lower in sodium than the breadcrumbs. Crab cakes are typically served with tartar sauce, which has about 5 grams of fat per tablespoon. We recommend serving with a wedge of lemon instead, which adds a fresh, tangy note to the cakes and brings out the flavor of the crabmeat.

Before	After
• 254 calories	• 186 calories
• 12.3g fat	• 6.4g fat
• 5.9g saturated fat	• 1g saturated fat
• percentage of calories from fat 44%	• percentage of calories from fat 31%
• 849mg sodium	• 524mg sodium

Wild Rice Crab Cakes

The addition of cumin to these hearty crab cakes enhances the nuttiness of the wild rice. If you want to top them with a sauce, combine light mayonnaise with lemon juice and a pinch of curry powder.

Prep: 20 minutes • Cook: 1 hour, 20 minutes

1 ½ cups water
½ cup uncooked wild rice
1 pound lump crabmeat, drained and shell pieces removed
¾ cup dry breadcrumbs
½ cup finely chopped red bell pepper
¼ cup minced shallots
¼ cup light mayonnaise
2 tablespoons Dijon mustard
1 ½ tablespoons fresh lemon juice
½ teaspoon salt
½ teaspoon ground cumin
⅛ teaspoon ground red pepper
⅛ teaspoon black pepper
2 large egg whites, lightly beaten
4 teaspoons olive oil, divided

1. Bring water to a boil in a medium saucepan. Add wild rice; cover. Reduce heat; simmer 1 hour or until tender. Combine cooked wild rice, crab, and next 11 ingredients in a large bowl. Divide mixture into 8 equal portions; shape each into a 1-inch-thick patty.
2. Heat 2 teaspoons oil in a large nonstick skillet over medium heat. Add 4 patties; cook 4 minutes. Carefully turn patties over, and cook 4 minutes or until golden. Repeat procedure with remaining oil and patties. Yield: 8 servings (serving size: 1 crab cake).

CALORIES 186 (31% from fat); FAT 6.4g (sat 1g, mono 2.9g, poly 2g); PROTEIN 15.1g; CARB 16.4g; FIBER 1g; CHOL 59mg; IRON 1.6mg; SODIUM 524mg; CALC 87mg

Boiled Lobster

We think boiling is the best way to cook lobster, but be careful not to overcook or it will be tough.

Prep: 2 minutes • Cook: 27 minutes

　3　gallons water
　¾　cup salt
　4　(1½-pound) live Maine lobsters

1. Bring water and salt to a boil in a 5-gallon stockpot; add lobsters. Cover; cook 12 minutes or until shells are bright orange-red and tails are curled. Yield: 4 servings (serving size: 1 lobster).

CALORIES 111 (6% from fat); FAT 0.7g (sat 0.1g, mono 0.2g, poly 0.1g); PROTEIN 23.2g; CARB 1.5g; FIBER 0g; CHOL 82mg; IRON 0.5mg; SODIUM 2189mg; CALC 70mg

Stuffed Lobster

Instead of fresh lobsters, you can also use 6 frozen lobster tails. Follow the cooking directions on the package of frozen lobster tails, and use the meat from all 6 tails, reserving just 4 of the tails to stuff.

Prep: 30 minutes • Cook: 8 minutes

　4　(1¼-pound) lobsters, cooked
　2　cups crushed reduced-fat round buttery crackers
　¼　cup chopped fresh parsley
　3　tablespoons grated fresh Parmesan cheese
2½　tablespoons butter, melted
　2　tablespoons fresh lemon juice
　2　tablespoons Worcestershire sauce
　4　lemon wedges

1. Preheat broiler.
2. Remove meat from cooked lobster tail and claws; chop meat. Set lobster tail shells aside.

how to remove meat from lobster claws

1. Snap the claws away from the body of the lobster. Gently move the pincer side to side until you feel it snap; gently pull it away.

2. Place the claw on a cutting board with the thorny bottom facing up. Hack straight down into the shell with the dull edge of a heavy-duty chef's knife or cleaver. As soon as you make contact with the shell, pull up the knife to avoid going through the claw.

3. Cut through the shells with kitchen shears.

4. Once you've cut through most of the shell, break the pieces apart, and remove the claw meat.

3. Combine lobster, crackers, and next 5 ingredients in a large bowl. Divide lobster mixture evenly among tail shells. Broil stuffed lobster tails 8 minutes or until golden brown. Serve with lemon wedges. Yield: 4 servings (serving size: 1 stuffed lobster tail and 1 lemon wedge).

CALORIES 379 (37% from fat); FAT 15.5g (sat 7.6g, mono 5.5g, poly 1.7g); PROTEIN 25.9g; CARB 30.7g; FIBER 0.1g; CHOL 95mg; IRON 2.1mg; SODIUM 990mg; CALC 243mg

lobster meat Here's how to get meat from a cooked lobster.
- Twist the tail from the body, then cut the tail lengthwise on top with scissors to split it open; remove the meat.
- Twist off the claws. Pull the pincers apart, and remove the lower pincer. Use a lobster cracker to break the claw shell. Break the legs in half with your hands, and push the meat out with a cocktail or shellfish fork.

Mussels with Tomato-Wine Broth

Serve with a chunk of French bread to soak up the flavorful broth.

Prep: 25 minutes • Cook: 10 minutes

    1   tablespoon olive oil
 1½   teaspoons bottled minced garlic
    ¼   teaspoon crushed red pepper
    1   cup pinot noir or other spicy dry red
        wine
    3   cups chopped seeded peeled tomato
    ½   teaspoon salt
    ¼   teaspoon black pepper
    2   pounds small mussels, scrubbed and
        debearded
    2   cups trimmed arugula or spinach

1. Heat oil in a large skillet over medium heat. Add garlic and red pepper, and cook 1 minute, stirring constantly. Add wine; simmer 3 minutes. Add tomato, salt, and black pepper; cook 1 minute.
2. Add mussels; cover and cook 4 minutes or until shells open. Remove from heat; discard any unopened shells. Stir in arugula; serve immediately. Yield: 2 servings (serving size: about 20 mussels and about 1½ cups sauce).

CALORIES 379 (29% from fat); FAT 12.1g (sat 1.9g, mono 6.1g, poly 2.2g); PROTEIN 26g; CARB 24.1g; FIBER 2g; CHOL 53mg; IRON 9.7mg; SODIUM 873mg; CALC 114mg

Mussels in Red Curry Broth

The Indonesian-style preparation of this dish is a pleasant surprise, since mussels often receive an Italian or French treatment.

Prep: 30 minutes • Cook: 15 minutes

    2   teaspoons olive oil
    ⅓   cup chopped shallots
 1½   teaspoons red curry powder
    1   cup clam juice
    ½   cup dry white wine
    ½   cup light coconut milk
    2   tablespoons finely chopped peeled
        fresh lemongrass
    ¼   teaspoon crushed red pepper
    3   pounds mussels, scrubbed and
        debearded
    2   tablespoons chopped fresh cilantro

1. Heat oil in a large Dutch oven over medium heat. Add shallots; sauté 1 minute. Add curry powder; sauté 30 seconds. Stir in clam juice and next 4 ingredients; bring to a simmer. Add mussels; bring to a boil. Cover, reduce heat, and simmer 5 minutes or until shells open; sprinkle with cilantro. Discard any unopened shells. Yield: 6 servings (serving size: about 12 mussels and about ⅓ cup sauce).

CALORIES 191 (30% from fat); FAT 6.3g (sat 1.6g, mono 2g, poly 1.1g); PROTEIN 20.1g; CARB 9.3g; FIBER 0.2g; CHOL 47mg; IRON 6.2mg; SODIUM 400mg; CALC 41mg

mussels Most mussels on the market come already scrubbed, purged with fresh water, and debearded. Mussels should be alive before they're cooked, so discard any with broken shells or shells that won't close; open mussels are dead. After cooking, discard any mussels that didn't open.

Mussels in Red Curry Broth

Oysters over Angel Hair

It may seem like an unusual combination, but the green onions, garlic, and Parmesan cheese go beautifully with the oysters in this delicate pasta dish. It received raves in our Test Kitchens.

Prep: 15 minutes • Cook: 26 minutes

- 3 tablespoons olive oil
- 1 cup sliced green onions
- ½ cup chopped fresh parsley
- 3 garlic cloves, minced
- 4 cups standard oysters (about 3 [12-ounce] containers), drained
- 2 tablespoons fresh lemon juice
- ¼ teaspoon salt
- ⅛ teaspoon ground red pepper
- ⅛ teaspoon black pepper
- 6 cups hot cooked angel hair (about 14 ounces uncooked pasta)
- ½ cup (2 ounces) grated fresh Parmesan cheese

1. Heat oil in a large nonstick skillet over medium heat. Add onions, parsley, and garlic; cook 8 minutes or until tender, stirring frequently. Add oysters; reduce heat, and cook 5 minutes or until edges of oysters curl. Stir in lemon juice, salt, and peppers. Add pasta and cheese, tossing well to coat. Yield: 6 servings (serving size: 1⅓ cups).

CALORIES 470 (28% from fat); FAT 14.5g (sat 3.7g, mono 6.3g, poly 2.3g); PROTEIN 24.4g; CARB 58.9g; FIBER 2.3g; CHOL 100mg; IRON 14.7mg; SODIUM 450mg; CALC 223mg

Oyster Frittata

If you've never considered oysters as breakfast or brunch fare, this hearty frittata may make you change your mind. Of course, it's great for lunch or a light dinner, too.

Prep: 25 minutes • Cook: 15 minutes

- 12 shucked oysters
- ¼ teaspoon hot sauce
- 3 (8-ounce) cartons egg substitute
- ¼ cup 1% low-fat milk
- ¼ teaspoon salt
- ¼ teaspoon black pepper
- 2 teaspoons olive oil
- 1 cup fresh or frozen corn kernels (about 2 ears)
- ½ cup finely chopped onion
- ¼ cup chopped yellow bell pepper
- ¼ cup chopped green bell pepper
- ¼ cup chopped red bell pepper
- ¼ cup chopped fennel bulb, divided
- 2 tablespoons chopped seeded jalapeño pepper
- ¼ cup (1 ounce) grated fresh Parmesan cheese

1. Preheat broiler.
2. Add water to a small saucepan, filling two-thirds full. Bring to a boil; reduce heat, and simmer. Add oysters, and cook 1 minute or until edges of oysters curl. Drain. Place oysters in a small bowl; sprinkle with hot sauce.
3. Combine egg substitute, milk, salt, and black pepper; stir well with a whisk.
4. Heat oil in a large nonstick skillet over medium heat. Add corn, onion, bell peppers, 2 tablespoons fennel, and jalapeño; cook 3 minutes, stirring frequently. Add oysters, and sauté 1 minute. Add egg mixture; cook 4 minutes or until almost set.
5. Combine 2 tablespoons fennel and cheese. Wrap handle of skillet with foil;

broil egg mixture 1 minute. Top with cheese mixture, and broil 1 minute or until cheese melts. Cut into 4 wedges, and serve warm. Yield: 4 servings (serving size: 1 wedge).

CALORIES 236 (23% from fat); FAT 6g (sat 1.9g, mono 2.5g, poly 0.9g); PROTEIN 26.1g; CARB 20g; FIBER 2.5g; CHOL 29mg; IRON 7mg; SODIUM 596mg; CALC 195mg

how to shuck an oyster

1. With the flat shell on top and the hinged point of the oyster shell toward you, work the knife into the hinge. Using lots of pressure, pry the top and bottom shell apart until you hear the hinge pop.

2. Carefully slide the knife horizontally across the roof of the oyster to release it from the top shell. Then run the knife under the oyster to release it from the bottom shell. Be careful not to spill the translucent liquid; it's flavorful and an ingredient on its own in oyster stew.

Citrus-Glazed Scallops with Avocado Salsa

The fresh ginger glaze pairs nicely with the avocado salsa. The salsa is great hot or cold.

Prep: 25 minutes • Cook: 11 minutes

Scallops:

1½ pounds large sea scallops, cut in half horizontally
¼ teaspoon salt
¼ teaspoon black pepper

Glaze:

¼ cup fresh lime juice
¼ cup fresh orange juice
2 tablespoons fresh lemon juice
1 tablespoon grated peeled fresh ginger
2 tablespoons honey
1 teaspoon olive oil
¼ teaspoon ground red pepper
1 garlic clove, crushed
½ cup chopped green onions
¼ cup finely chopped fresh cilantro

Avocado Salsa:

½ cup chopped seeded plum tomato
½ cup diced peeled avocado
¼ cup finely chopped red onion
1 tablespoon chopped fresh cilantro
1 tablespoon chopped jalapeño pepper
1 tablespoon fresh lime juice
½ teaspoon olive oil
⅛ teaspoon salt
⅛ teaspoon black pepper
1 garlic clove, crushed

1. Heat a large nonstick skillet over medium-high heat. Combine first 3 ingredients in a bowl; toss. Add scallops to pan; cook 2 minutes on each side or until browned. Remove from pan; keep warm.
2. Combine ¼ cup lime juice and next 7 ingredients; stir with a whisk. Add juice mixture to pan. Cook 7 minutes or until glaze becomes shiny and begins to thicken.

Drizzle citrus glaze over scallops; add green onions and ¼ cup cilantro. Toss.
3. Combine chopped tomato and next 9 ingredients; toss. Yield: 4 servings (serving size: ⅔ cup scallops and ¼ cup salsa).

CALORIES 262 (21% from fat); FAT 6.1g (sat 0.9g, mono 3.1g, poly 1g); PROTEIN 29.8g; CARB 22.5g; FIBER 2.2g; CHOL 56mg; IRON 1mg; SODIUM 503mg; CALC 56mg

Grilled Sea Scallops with Pine Nut-Raisin Compote

You can use dry sherry instead of cream sherry, but the dish won't be as sweet.

Prep: 15 minutes • Cook: 16 minutes
Other: 20 minutes

2¼ pounds sea scallops
¼ cup fresh lemon juice
1½ teaspoons olive oil
⅛ teaspoon salt
⅛ teaspoon pepper
¼ cup pine nuts
1½ cups cream sherry
1 cup raisins
Cooking spray

1. Combine first 5 ingredients in a large shallow dish; cover and marinate in refrigerator 20 minutes.
2. Cook pine nuts in a large skillet over medium-high heat 1 minute or until lightly browned, stirring frequently. Remove pine nuts from pan. Add sherry and raisins to pan. Bring to a boil; cook 8 minutes or until raisins are plump and sherry is slightly syrupy. Remove from heat; stir in pine nuts.
3. Prepare grill.
4. Remove scallops from dish; discard marinade. Thread scallops onto 6 (12-inch) skewers. Place skewers on grill rack coated with cooking spray. Grill 2

minutes on each side or until done. Serve with raisin compote. Yield: 6 servings (serving size: 1 kebab and about 2 tablespoons raisin compote).

CALORIES 291 (26% from fat); FAT 8.3g (sat 1.2g, mono 3.1g, poly 3g); PROTEIN 30.5g; CARB 26.2g; FIBER 1.4g; CHOL 56mg; IRON 1.5mg; SODIUM 313mg; CALC 58mg

Simple Seared Scallops

These scallops are crisp and glazed outside, tender and moist inside.

Prep: 6 minutes • Cook: 10 minutes

3 tablespoons all-purpose flour
½ teaspoon salt
½ teaspoon dried marjoram
1½ pounds sea scallops
2 teaspoons olive oil
½ cup dry white wine
1 tablespoon balsamic vinegar

1. Combine first 3 ingredients in a large zip-top plastic bag, and add scallops. Seal bag, and shake to coat scallops.
2. Heat oil in a large skillet over medium-high heat. Add scallops; cook 3 minutes on each side or until done. Remove from pan; keep warm.
3. Add wine and vinegar to pan; cook 3 minutes or until slightly thick, stirring with a whisk. Stir in scallops; remove from heat. Yield: 4 servings (serving size: about 5 ounces scallops).

CALORIES 211 (15% from fat); FAT 3.6g (sat 0.4g, mono 1.7g, poly 0.6g); PROTEIN 29.2g; CARB 9.2g; FIBER 0.2g; CHOL 56mg; IRON 1mg; SODIUM 567mg; CALC 46mg

Test Kitchen Tip: Although you can sear foods in a nonstick skillet, you often get better browning using a heavy stainless steel skillet.

Shrimp Scampi
(pictured on page 233)

Scampi is a Venetian dialect word for a local prawn, rarely found in American markets. So Italian-American cooks use shrimp instead, cooking it with a little garlic.

Prep: 20 minutes • Cook: 6 minutes

 2 teaspoons olive oil
28 jumbo shrimp, peeled and deveined
    (about 1½ pounds)
 3 garlic cloves, minced
⅓ cup dry white wine
½ teaspoon salt
¼ teaspoon freshly ground black pepper
¼ cup chopped fresh flat-leaf parsley
 1 tablespoon fresh lemon juice

1. Heat oil in a large skillet over medium-high heat. Add shrimp; sauté 1 minute. Add garlic; sauté 1 minute. Stir in wine, salt, and pepper; bring mixture to a boil. Reduce heat to medium; cook 30 seconds. Add parsley and juice; toss well to coat. Cook 1 minute or until shrimp are done. Yield: 4 servings (serving size: 7 shrimp).

CALORIES 220 (21% from fat); FAT 5.2g (sat 0.9g, mono 2.1g, poly 1.3g); PROTEIN 34.9g; CARB 3.1g; FIBER 0.2g; CHOL 259mg; IRON 4.5mg; SODIUM 546mg; CALC 100mg

menu

serves 6

Shrimp Scampi

Angel hair pasta

Romaine Lettuce with Red Peppers and Olives (page 401)

Spicy Peanut Noodles with Shrimp

If you don't like spicy food, start with only 1 teaspoon chile paste. If the sauce is too thick, thin it with a little water—it should be the consistency of unwhipped cream.

Prep: 15 minutes • Cook: 21 minutes

Peanut sauce:
⅓ cup creamy peanut butter
¼ to ⅓ cup water
 2 tablespoons low-sodium soy sauce
1½ tablespoons rice vinegar
 1 to 2 teaspoons chile paste with garlic
½ teaspoon sugar
¼ teaspoon salt
Shrimp:
 1 pound medium shrimp, peeled and deveined
¼ teaspoon salt
Cooking spray
Pasta:
 8 ounces uncooked thick udon noodles or linguine
 1 red bell pepper, cut into julienne strips
¾ cup chopped seeded cucumber
¼ cup diagonally cut green onions
 3 tablespoons chopped roasted peanuts
 2 tablespoons cilantro leaves
 4 lime wedges (optional)

1. To prepare sauce, combine first 7 ingredients; stir with a whisk.
2. To prepare shrimp, toss shrimp with ¼ teaspoon salt. Sauté in a nonstick skillet coated with cooking spray over medium-high heat 3 minutes on each side or until done.
3. To prepare pasta, cook noodles according to package directions, omitting salt and fat.
4. Combine peanut sauce, shrimp, noodles, bell pepper, cucumber, and onions in a large bowl; toss well. Sprinkle with peanuts and cilantro. Serve with lime wedges, if desired. Yield: 4 servings (serving size: 1½ cups).

CALORIES 424 (28% from fat); FAT 13.2g (sat 2.6g, mono 5.6g, poly 3.8g); PROTEIN 25g; CARB 51.1g; FIBER 3.5g; CHOL 129mg; IRON 3mg; SODIUM 765mg; CALC 66mg

Orange-Ginger Shrimp Skewers

Use a grill pan to enjoy grilled food when the weather outside is not ideal.

Prep: 30 minutes • Cook: 8 minutes
Other: 15 minutes

- ½ cup fresh orange juice (about 2 oranges)
- 2 tablespoons minced green onions
- 1 tablespoon minced peeled fresh ginger
- 1 tablespoon minced fresh cilantro
- 2 tablespoons rice vinegar
- 2 tablespoons low-sodium soy sauce
- 1 tablespoon canola oil
- 2 teaspoons grated orange rind
- 1½ pounds large shrimp, peeled and deveined
- 2 oranges, peeled, cut in half, and quartered
- Cooking spray

1. Combine first 8 ingredients in a bowl. Add shrimp; toss to coat. Cover and marinate in refrigerator 15 minutes.
2. Remove shrimp from dish, reserving marinade. Thread shrimp and orange quarters alternately onto 8 skewers.
3. Heat a large grill pan coated with cooking spray over medium-high heat. Cook skewers 4 minutes on each side or until done, basting with reserved marinade. Yield: 4 servings (serving size: 2 skewers).

CALORIES 257 (20% from fat); FAT 5.6g (sat 0.8g, mono 2.4g, poly 1.8g); PROTEIN 36.7g; CARB 13.8g; FIBER 2.1g; CHOL 332mg; IRON 5.6mg; SODIUM 649mg; CALC 104mg

Test Kitchen Tip: Ask someone in the seafood department at your supermarket to peel and devein the shrimp. It might cost a little extra, but it's worth it if you're in a hurry.

Coconut Shrimp with Pineapple Salsa

Instead of being deep-fried in oil, this shrimp is dredged in coconut and baked.

Prep: 45 minutes • Cook: 20 minutes

Shrimp:
- 28 large shrimp (about 1½ pounds)
- ⅓ cup cornstarch
- ¾ teaspoon salt
- ½ to ¾ teaspoon ground red pepper
- 3 large egg whites
- 1½ cups flaked sweetened coconut
- Cooking spray

Pineapple Salsa:
- 1 cup finely chopped fresh pineapple
- ⅓ cup finely chopped red onion
- ¼ cup finely chopped fresh cilantro
- ¼ cup pineapple preserves
- 1½ tablespoons fresh lime juice
- 1 tablespoon finely chopped seeded jalapeño pepper
- ¼ teaspoon black pepper

1. Preheat oven to 400°.
2. To prepare shrimp, peel and devein shrimp, leaving tails intact. Rinse shrimp in cold water; drain on paper towels until dry.
3. Combine cornstarch, salt, and red pepper in a shallow dish; stir with a whisk. Place egg whites in a medium bowl; beat with a mixer at medium-high speed until frothy (about 2 minutes). Place coconut in a shallow dish.
4. Working with 1 shrimp at a time, dredge in cornstarch mixture. Dip in egg white, and dredge in coconut, pressing gently with fingers. Place shrimp on a baking sheet coated with cooking spray. Lightly coat shrimp with cooking spray. Bake at 400° for 20 minutes or until shrimp are done, turning after 10 minutes.
5. To prepare salsa, combine chopped pineapple and remaining ingredients in a medium bowl; stir to combine. Yield: 4 servings (serving size: 7 shrimp and about ¼ cup salsa).

CALORIES 397 (26% from fat); FAT 11.4g (sat 8.4g, mono 0.7g, poly 1g); PROTEIN 29.9g; CARB 45g; FIBER 2.2g; CHOL 194mg; IRON 3.9mg; SODIUM 753mg; CALC 80mg

All-Time Favorite
Barbecue Shrimp

The peels are left on the shrimp so they can add flavor to the lush, buttery-peppery sauce.

Prep: 9 minutes • Cook: 11 minutes

- ½ cup fat-free Caesar dressing
- ⅓ cup Worcestershire sauce
- 2 tablespoons butter
- 1 tablespoon dried oregano
- 1 tablespoon paprika
- 1 tablespoon dried rosemary
- 1 tablespoon dried thyme
- 1½ teaspoons black pepper
- 1 teaspoon hot pepper sauce
- 5 bay leaves
- 3 garlic cloves, minced
- 2 pounds large shrimp
- ⅓ cup dry white wine
- 10 (1-ounce) slices French bread baguette
- 10 lemon wedges

1. Combine first 11 ingredients in a large nonstick skillet, and bring to a boil. Add shrimp, and cook 7 minutes, stirring occasionally. Add wine, and cook 1 minute or until shrimp are done. Serve with bread and lemon wedges. Yield: 5 servings (serving size: 5 ounces shrimp with sauce, 2 bread slices, and 2 lemon wedges).

CALORIES 403 (20% from fat); FAT 9.1g (sat 3.8g, mono 2.4g, poly 1.7g); PROTEIN 34.4g; CARB 41.7g; FIBER 2.8g; CHOL 219mg; IRON 7mg; SODIUM 1021mg; CALC 211mg

All-Time Favorite
Prosciutto-Wrapped Shrimp with Lemon Couscous

When you think of maple syrup, you may not envision seafood and chili powder as suitable companions. Yet they're exactly what make this dish one of our favorites. The prosciutto adds saltiness to balance the syrup in the sauce. If you haven't tried prosciutto, this is a worthy application; a little goes a long way, and it's a great accompaniment to shrimp.

Prep: 30 minutes • Cook: 9 minutes
Other: 5 minutes

   3 tablespoons maple syrup
   2 tablespoons bourbon
   1 tablespoon teriyaki sauce
   2 teaspoons Dijon mustard
  ½ teaspoon chili powder
 24 jumbo shrimp (about 1½ pounds)
   6 very thin slices prosciutto or ham (about 3½ ounces)
     Cooking spray
     Lemon Couscous (page 272)

1. Preheat broiler.
2. Combine first 5 ingredients in a bowl, stirring with a whisk. Peel shrimp, leaving tails intact. Add shrimp to maple syrup mixture, tossing to coat. Remove shrimp from bowl; discard marinade.
3. Cut each prosciutto slice lengthwise into 4 strips. Wrap 1 strip around each shrimp. Thread 6 shrimp onto each of 4 (8-inch) skewers. Place skewers on a broiler pan coated with cooking spray; broil 3 minutes on each side or until done. Serve over Lemon Couscous.
Yield: 4 servings (serving size: 6 shrimp and ½ cup couscous).

(Totals include Lemon Couscous) CALORIES 305 (12% from fat); FAT 4.2g (sat 1.2g, mono 1.4g, poly 0.9g); PROTEIN 36.1g; CARB 27.2g; FIBER 1.4g; CHOL 263mg; IRON 5.2mg; SODIUM 927mg; CALC 67mg

Southern Shrimp and Grits

This shellfish specialty of the Carolina Low Country, sometimes called "breakfast shrimp," tastes great anytime. To minimize prep time, start with frozen bell pepper and onion, as well as peeled and deveined shrimp.

Prep: 12 minutes • Cook: 27 minutes

   3 tablespoons fresh lemon juice
  ½ teaspoon hot sauce (such as Tabasco)
 1½ pounds peeled and deveined large shrimp
   2 bacon slices, chopped
   1 cup frozen chopped onion
  ¼ cup frozen chopped green bell pepper
 1½ teaspoons bottled minced garlic
   1 cup fat-free, less-sodium chicken broth
  ½ cup chopped green onions, divided
   5 cups water
 1½ cups uncooked quick-cooking grits
   1 tablespoon butter
   1 teaspoon salt
  ¾ cup (3 ounces) shredded sharp Cheddar cheese

1. Combine first 3 ingredients; set aside.
2. Cook bacon in a large nonstick skillet over medium heat until crisp. Add onion, bell pepper, and garlic to drippings in pan; cook 5 minutes or until tender, stirring occasionally. Stir in shrimp mixture, broth, and ¼ cup green onions; cook 5 minutes or until shrimp are done, stirring frequently.
3. Bring water to a boil in a medium saucepan; gradually add grits, stirring constantly. Reduce heat to low; simmer, covered, 5 minutes or until thick, stirring occasionally. Stir in butter and salt. Serve shrimp mixture over grits; sprinkle with cheese and green onions. Yield: 6 servings (serving size: ⅔ cup shrimp mixture, ⅔ cup grits, 2 tablespoons cheese, and 2 teaspoons green onions).

CALORIES 408 (28% from fat); FAT 12.5g (sat 5.6g, mono 4.1g, poly 1.3g); PROTEIN 32.8g; CARB 39.9g; FIBER 2g; CHOL 246mg; IRON 5.1mg; SODIUM 890mg; CALC 154mg

Test Kitchen Tip: Quick-cooking grits are an alternative to stone-ground grits, which can take 45 minutes to cook.

Spice-Crusted Shrimp with Rémoulade Sauce

A lime-scented rémoulade sauce balances the spiciness of the skillet shrimp.

Prep: 30 minutes • Cook: 14 minutes

Rémoulade Sauce:

¼ cup low-fat mayonnaise
¼ cup plain fat-free yogurt
1½ tablespoons fresh lime juice
1 teaspoon grated lime rind
1 teaspoon capers, chopped
Dash of ground red pepper

Shrimp:

2 teaspoons ground cumin
2 teaspoons paprika
1 teaspoon ground coriander
½ teaspoon garlic powder
¼ teaspoon salt
⅛ teaspoon black pepper
48 large shrimp, peeled and deveined (about 1½ pounds)
1 tablespoon olive oil, divided
Cilantro sprigs (optional)

1. To prepare sauce, combine first 6 ingredients in a bowl; stir with a whisk.
2. To prepare shrimp, combine cumin and next 5 ingredients. Add shrimp; toss well. Heat 1½ teaspoons oil in a large nonstick skillet over medium-high heat; add half of shrimp. Cook 3 minutes on each side or until done. Remove shrimp; keep warm. Repeat procedure with remaining oil and shrimp. Serve shrimp with sauce. Garnish with cilantro, if desired. Yield: 4 servings (serving size: 12 shrimp and about 2 tablespoon sauce).

CALORIES 200 (28% from fat); FAT 6.2g (sat 0.8g, mono 2.8g, poly 1g); PROTEIN 27.4g; CARB 7.4g; FIBER 1g; CHOL 242mg; IRON 4.6mg; SODIUM 600mg; CALC 96mg

Traditional Spanish Paella

Paella has held a place of honor in Spanish homes for centuries. Simplify the recipe by preparing the ingredients the day before serving; this makes the final dish come together much quicker. To round out the meal, choose a good red wine from Spain's Rioja region, a crusty baguette, and a light salad.

Prep: 35 minutes • Cook: 58 minutes
Other: 10 minutes

Herb blend:

1 cup chopped fresh parsley
¼ cup fresh lemon juice
1 tablespoon olive oil
2 large garlic cloves, minced

Paella:

1 cup water
1 teaspoon saffron threads
6 cups fat-free, less-sodium chicken broth
8 unpeeled jumbo shrimp (about ½ pound)
1 tablespoon olive oil
4 skinless, boneless chicken thighs, cut in half
2 links Spanish chorizo sausage (about 6½ ounces) or turkey kielbasa, cut into ½-inch-thick slices
1 (4-ounce) slice prosciutto or 33%-less-sodium ham, cut into 1-inch pieces
2 cups finely chopped onion
1 cup finely chopped red bell pepper
1 cup canned diced tomatoes, undrained
1 teaspoon sweet paprika
3 large garlic cloves, minced
3 cups uncooked Arborio rice or other short-grain rice
1 cup frozen green peas
8 mussels, scrubbed and debearded
¼ cup fresh lemon juice

1. To prepare herb blend, combine first 4 ingredients; set aside.
2. To prepare paella, combine water, saffron, and broth in a large saucepan. Bring to a simmer (do not boil). Keep warm over low heat. Peel and devein shrimp, leaving tails intact; set aside.
3. Heat 1 tablespoon oil in a large paella pan or very large skillet over medium-high heat. Add chicken; sauté 2 minutes on each side. Remove from pan. Add sausage and prosciutto; sauté 2 minutes. Remove from pan. Add reserved shrimp, and sauté 2 minutes. Remove from pan. Reduce heat to medium-low. Add onion and bell pepper; sauté 15 minutes, stirring occasionally.
4. Add tomatoes, paprika, and 3 garlic cloves to pan; cook 5 minutes.
5. Add rice; cook 1 minute, stirring constantly. Stir in herb blend, broth mixture, chicken, sausage mixture, and peas. Bring to a low boil; cook 10 minutes, stirring frequently. Add mussels to pan, nestling them into rice mixture. Cook 5 minutes or until shells open; discard any unopened shells. Arrange shrimp, heads down, in rice mixture, and cook 5 minutes or until shrimp are done. Sprinkle with ¼ cup lemon juice. Remove from heat; cover with a towel, and let stand 10 minutes. Yield: 8 servings (serving size: 1½ cups paella, 1 shrimp, and 1 mussel).

CALORIES 521 (23% from fat); FAT 13.3g (sat 3.7g, mono 6.8g, poly 2g); PROTEIN 25.5g; CARB 72.1g; FIBER 3.6g; CHOL 80mg; IRON 6mg; SODIUM 871mg; CALC 60mg

Sushi

Although the general term *sushi* refers to the rice, the most popular sushi features some type of seafood enclosed in the rice and wrapped in thin sheets of seaweed.

Bagel Roll

This is the sushi version of a bagel with smoked salmon and cream cheese. Use the remaining nori to make the nori strips for Tuna Nigiri (page 260). Nori is toasted seaweed sheets used to hold sushi rolls together.

Prep: 20 minutes • Cook: 25 minutes
Other: 45 minutes

- 3 tablespoons chopped green onions
- 9 tablespoons (4½ ounces) block-style ⅓-less-fat cream cheese
- 1½ teaspoons prepared wasabi
- 6 nori (seaweed) sheets
- 4½ cups cooked Sushi Rice (page 265)
- 2 cups thinly sliced smoked salmon (about 12 ounces)

1. Combine first 3 ingredients. Cut off top quarter of nori sheets along short end; reserve for another use. Place 1 nori sheet, shiny side down, on a sushi mat covered with plastic wrap, with long end toward you. Pat ¾ cup rice over nori with moist hands, leaving a 1-inch border on one long end of nori.

2. Gently flip nori sheet. Spread 1½ tablespoons cream cheese mixture along top third of shiny side of nori; top with ⅓ cup salmon.

3. Lift edge of nori closest to you; fold over filling. Lift bottom edge of sushi mat; roll toward top edge, pressing firmly on sushi roll. Continue rolling to top edge; press mat to seal sushi roll. Repeat with remaining ingredients. Slice each roll into 8 pieces. Yield: 6 servings (serving size: 8 pieces).

CALORIES 341 (23% from fat); FAT 7.7g (sat 3.9g, mono 3.8g, poly 0.8g); PROTEIN 17.1g; CARB 48g; FIBER 2.8g; CHOL 29mg; IRON 3.1mg; SODIUM 769mg; CALC 43mg

A sushi mat is a bamboo mat necessary for making sushi rolls. The mats (as well as nori sheets) are usually available in Asian food markets or in specialty kitchen stores.

how to roll sushi

1. The rice is sticky, so moisten your hands in a bowl of equal parts water and rice vinegar before pressing the rice into the nori.

2. If you prefer rice on the outside (as shown here in making the Bagel Roll), gently flip nori sheet. Position the sheet slightly past the mat edge closest to you. Fold the nori edge closest to you over the filling.

3. Pick up the sushi mat edge closest to you and roll the rice-covered nori tightly over the filling.

4. Gently squeeze the sushi roll to form a tight, round roll.

Shrimp Maki

Maki is the term for the type of sushi that is rolled in nori (seaweed) sheets.

**Prep: 20 minutes • Cook: 25 minutes
Other: 50 minutes**

  6 nori (seaweed) sheets
  4½ cups cooked Sushi Rice (page 265)
  1½ cups cooked medium shrimp, peeled, deveined, and halved (about ¾ pound)
  12 strips julienne-cut carrot
  12 (¼-inch-thick) slices peeled avocado (about 1½ medium)
  6 green onion tops (about 7-inch length)
  1 cucumber, peeled, halved lengthwise, seeded, and cut into 12 (7-inch) julienne-cut strips

1. Cut off top quarter of nori sheets along short end; reserve for another use. Place 1 nori sheet, shiny side down, on a sushi mat covered with plastic wrap, with long end toward you. Pat ¾ cup rice over nori with moist hands, leaving a 1-inch border on one long end of nori. Arrange ¼ cup shrimp, 2 carrot strips, 2 slices avocado, 1 green onion top, and 2 cucumber strips along top third of rice-covered nori.
2. Lift edge of nori closest to you; fold over filling. Lift bottom edge of mat; roll toward top edge, pressing firmly on sushi roll. Continue rolling to top edge; press mat to seal roll. Let rest, seam side down, 5 minutes. Repeat with remaining ingredients. Slice each roll into 8 pieces with a sharp knife. Yield: 6 servings (serving size: 8 pieces).

CALORIES 367 (21% from fat); FAT 8.7g (sat 1.5g, mono 5g, poly 1.3g); PROTEIN 17.8g; CARB 53.6g; FIBER 6.1g; CHOL 111mg; IRON 5mg; SODIUM 377mg; CALC 54mg

Tuna Nigiri

Nigiri are slices of raw or cooked seafood served on a layer of rice.

**Prep: 17 minutes • Cook: 27 minutes
Other: 45 minutes**

  1 (8-ounce) ahi tuna fillet
  ¼ teaspoon salt
  ⅛ teaspoon freshly ground black pepper
  2 cups cooked Sushi Rice (page 265)
  1 teaspoon prepared wasabi
  8 (1 x ½–inch) strips nori (seaweed)

1. Heat a medium nonstick skillet over medium-high heat. Sprinkle fish with salt and pepper. Add fish to pan; cook 1 minute on each side or until desired degree of doneness. Cut fish into 8 strips; cool.
2. Shape ¼ cup rice into a rectangle the size of 1 fish strip. Place 1 fish strip across middle joints of fingers, palm side up. Spread ⅛ teaspoon wasabi over fish; top with shaped rice. Close hand, and gently press rice and fish together.
3. Wrap 1 nori strip around center of nigiri, ending underneath rice. Repeat with remaining ingredients. Yield: 8 servings (serving size: 1 nigiri).

CALORIES 100 (4% from fat); FAT 0.4g (sat 0.1g, mono 0.1g, poly 0.1g); PROTEIN 7.8g; CARB 15.4g; FIBER 0.5g; CHOL 13mg; IRON 1mg; SODIUM 159mg; CALC 6mg

Test Kitchen Tip: Because there is an increased food safety risk associated with eating raw fish, our sushi recipes use cooked seafood. If you choose to use raw, buy only commercially frozen fish because the freezing process helps eliminate the risk of contamination. Look for the words "sushi grade" to indicate that the fish has been commercially frozen.

how to form nigiri

1. Shape the rice into a rectangle.

2. Place the topping and rice across the middle joints of fingers, palm turned up; close your hand to gently press the topping and rice together.

3. After pressing the topping and rice together, you may need to use your other hand to finish shaping the rice to fit snugly against the topping.

grains & pastas

Spaghettini with Oil
and Garlic, page 286

Grains

Grains such as barley, corn, oats, rice, and wheat are packed with nutrients, good sources of fiber, low in fat, and extremely versatile in side dishes as well as entrées.

Wild Mushroom-Barley "Risotto" with Sage

This dish is easier to make than risotto because you don't have to stir constantly. Note that the prep and cook times do not include time for making stock.

**Prep: 10 minutes • Cook: 45 minutes
Other: 2 hours**

- 1 cup uncooked pearl barley
- 2 cups water
- 4 cups Rich Porcini Stock (page 472)
- 1 tablespoon olive oil
- 1 cup finely chopped onion
- 8 cups thinly sliced shiitake mushroom caps (about 1 pound)
- 1½ teaspoons sea salt
- 2 teaspoons chopped fresh sage
- ⅓ cup (about 1½ ounces) grated fresh Parmesan cheese
- 1 tablespoon butter
- ⅛ teaspoon freshly ground black pepper

1. Combine barley and water in a bowl. Let stand 2 hours; drain.

2. Bring stock to a simmer in a saucepan. Heat oil in a Dutch oven over medium heat. Add onion; cook 5 minutes. Add mushrooms and salt; cook 3 minutes. Add barley, stock, and sage to onion mixture. Bring to a boil over medium heat; reduce heat, and simmer 30 minutes. Remove from heat; stir in cheese, butter, and pepper. Yield: 8 servings (serving size: ⅔ cup).

CALORIES 191 (22% from fat); FAT 4.7g (sat 2g, mono 2.1g, poly 0.4g); PROTEIN 6.1g; CARB 26g; FIBER 5.1g; CHOL 7mg; IRON 2mg; SODIUM 448mg; CALC 75mg

Cheese Grits

Simple to make and incredibly flavorful, cheese grits are a quick alternative to mashed potatoes or rice. Try them with the Honey and Thyme-Brined Turkey Breast on page 395 or Shrimp Scampi on page 254.

Prep: 5 minutes • Cook: 10 minutes

- 4 cups water
- 1 cup uncooked quick-cooking grits
- 1 cup (4 ounces) shredded reduced-fat sharp Cheddar cheese
- 1 tablespoon butter
- 1½ teaspoons garlic powder
- ½ teaspoon dried thyme
- ½ teaspoon salt

1. Bring water to a boil in a medium saucepan, and gradually add grits, stirring constantly. Cover, reduce heat to low, and simmer 5 minutes or until thick, stirring occasionally. Remove grits from heat, and stir in shredded cheese and remaining ingredients. Yield: 12 servings (serving size: about ½ cup).

CALORIES 58 (43% from fat); FAT 2.8g (sat 1.7g, mono 0.8g, poly 0.1g); PROTEIN 3.4g; CARB 5.1g; FIBER 0.3g; CHOL 9mg; IRON 2.5mg; SODIUM 286mg; CALC 87mg

Test Kitchen Tip: If you want to add a little kick to your cheese grits, use Monterey Jack cheese with jalapeño peppers instead of Cheddar.

Creamy Grits with Sweet Corn

Create layers of flavor by combining ground corn grits with fresh corn. Serve with wild game meats, smoked fish, or country ham as an alternative to mashed potatoes.

Prep: 10 minutes • Cook: 39 minutes

- 5 cups water
- 1 teaspoon kosher salt
- 1 cup uncooked stone-ground yellow grits
- ½ cup (2 ounces) grated fresh Parmesan cheese
- ¼ cup (1 ounce) shredded white Cheddar cheese
- ¼ teaspoon hot pepper sauce
- ⅛ teaspoon ground white pepper
- 1½ teaspoons butter
- 1 cup fresh corn kernels (about 2 ears)
- ¼ cup sliced green onions

1. Bring water and salt to a boil in a large saucepan; gradually stir in grits. Reduce heat; simmer 30 minutes or until thick and tender, stirring frequently.

2. Remove from heat; stir in cheeses, pepper sauce, and white pepper. Cover.

3. Melt butter in a large nonstick skillet over medium-high heat. Add corn, and sauté 4 minutes or until lightly browned. Add corn and onions to grits mixture, stirring well. Yield: 8 servings (serving size: ½ cup).

CALORIES 141 (25% from fat); FAT 3.9g (sat 2.3g, mono 0.8g, poly 0.2g); PROTEIN 5.7g; CARB 20.8g; FIBER 1.2g; CHOL 10mg; IRON 0.4mg; SODIUM 386mg; CALC 112mg

Grilled Bacon-and-Herb Grit Cakes

Chilling the grits helps them hold their shape when they're cut and grilled.

Prep: 11 minutes • Cook: 25 minutes • Other: 1 hour

4   cups water
1   cup quick-cooking grits
½   cup (2 ounces) shredded white
    Cheddar cheese
1   tablespoon minced fresh or
    1 teaspoon dried thyme
2   teaspoons chopped fresh parsley
½   teaspoon garlic powder
½   teaspoon pepper
3   bacon slices, cooked and crumbled
Cooking spray

1. Bring water to a boil in a large saucepan; gradually stir in grits. Reduce heat; simmer 5 to 7 minutes or until thick.

2. Combine cooked grits, cheese, and next 5 ingredients in a large bowl; stir well. Pour grits into a 10-inch square baking dish coated with cooking spray, spreading evenly. Cover and chill 1 hour or until completely cool.

3. Prepare grill.

4. Invert chilled grits onto a cutting board; cut into 4 squares. Cut each square diagonally into 2 triangles.

5. Place grits triangles on grill rack coated with cooking spray; grill 5 minutes on each side or until lightly browned and thoroughly heated. Yield: 4 servings (serving size: 2 triangles).

CALORIES 255 (30% from fat); FAT 8.5g (sat 4g, mono 2.7g, poly 0.5g); PROTEIN 9.3g; CARB 38.8g; FIBER 2.4g; CHOL 20mg; IRON 15.2mg; SODIUM 695mg; CALC 123mg

Soft Polenta

Similar to cheese grits but slightly creamier, this polenta is made with equal parts cornmeal and semolina, a coarse flour made from hard durum wheat. The polenta can be made ahead and reheated. Add ¼ to ½ cup water or broth to the polenta, then cover and microwave until thoroughly heated. Whisk before serving to break up any lumps.

Prep: 8 minutes • Cook: 25 minutes

1½ cups fat-free, less-sodium chicken
    broth
1½ cups 2% reduced-fat milk
5   tablespoons yellow cornmeal
5   tablespoons semolina
½   teaspoon grated whole nutmeg
¼   teaspoon salt
¼   cup (1 ounce) shredded fontina
    cheese
¼   cup (1 ounce) grated fresh Parmesan
    cheese

1. Combine broth and milk in a large saucepan; bring to a boil, stirring frequently with a whisk. Add cornmeal, semolina, nutmeg, and salt, stirring constantly with a whisk until cornmeal and semolina begin to absorb liquid (about 2 minutes). Reduce heat to low, and cook 20 minutes, stirring frequently. Stir in cheeses. Yield: 4 servings (serving size: ½ cup).

CALORIES 206 (27% from fat); FAT 6.2g (sat 3.7g, mono 1.7g, poly 0.2g); PROTEIN 11g; CARB 25.2g; FIBER 0.9g; CHOL 21mg; IRON 0.7mg; SODIUM 532mg; CALC 227mg

Test Kitchen Tip: To prevent the mixture from bubbling over the edge of the pan, stir the broth and milk as it comes to a boil.

guide to grits and polenta

There's not a lot of difference between grits (also called hominy grits) and polenta—both are made from the milling of corn kernels into cornmeal.

Grits: coarsely ground corn kernels in which the large granules from the corn kernel endosperm are left intact. This type of grits is usually labeled "Old-Fashioned Grits."

Quick-cooking grits: The large granules are passed over smooth rollers, which fracture the granules into smaller ones, allowing the grits to cook faster than regular or stone-ground grits.

Instant grits: precooked and then dried again for packaging. They're usually packaged in single-serving envelopes and prepared by adding boiling water.

Stone-ground grits: have a chunkier texture and a more hearty corn flavor than quick grits because some of the hull and the germ of the corn kernel are kept when the corn kernels are milled.

Yellow grits: include the entire corn kernel.

White grits: include only hulled kernels.

Dry polenta: similar to grits, but with a slightly finer grind of cornmeal. (Grits are made from coarsely ground corn, hull and all—and are usually made from corn that has been processed into hominy, giving grits a grittier texture than polenta.) Many recipes for polenta will call for cornmeal, either whole-grain or regular.

Precooked polenta: precooked and shaped into tubes, often available in a variety of flavors, and found in the produce section of the supermarket. The precooked polenta works well in recipes in which the polenta is cut into slices or cubes and sautéed or grilled.

Creamy Polenta with Warm Tomato Compote

Serve this filling side dish with a simple roasted chicken or pork loin.

Prep: 15 minutes • Cook: 1 hour, 27 minutes Other: 15 minutes

  6 cups cherry tomatoes (about 2 pounds)
Cooking spray
  1 tablespoon olive oil
  ¼ cup sliced shallots (about 3 medium)
1½ tablespoons sugar
  ¾ cup dry white wine or water
1½ teaspoons salt, divided
  ¼ teaspoon pepper
  2 cups 1% low-fat milk
  2 cups water
  1 cup dry polenta
  ½ cup (2 ounces) shaved fresh Parmesan cheese

1. Preheat oven to 425°.
2. Cut several slits in bottom of each tomato; place, stem sides down, in a shallow roasting pan coated with cooking spray. Bake at 425° for 20 minutes. Reduce oven temperature to 375° (do not remove tomatoes from oven); bake 45 minutes or until browned. Cover and let stand 10 minutes.
3. Heat oil in a large nonstick skillet over medium-high heat. Add shallots; sauté 5 minutes or until browned. Add sugar; sauté 5 minutes. Add wine; reduce heat, and simmer 5 minutes. Add ½ teaspoon salt and pepper. Remove from heat; stir in tomatoes. Cover; set aside.
4. Combine milk and water in a large saucepan; bring to a boil, stirring frequently with a whisk. Remove from heat, and gradually add polenta, stirring constantly with a whisk. Cover and cook over medium-low heat 2 minutes. Add 1 teaspoon salt; cover and let stand 5 minutes or until thick, stirring occasionally. Top polenta with tomato compote and Parmesan cheese. Yield: 8 servings (serving size: ½ cup polenta, ⅓ cup tomato compote, and 1 tablespoon Parmesan cheese).

CALORIES 153 (28% from fat); FAT 4.8g (sat 1.9g, mono 2g, poly 0.4g); PROTEIN 6.8g; CARB 21.6g; FIBER 1.7g; CHOL 7mg; IRON 0.9mg; SODIUM 597mg; CALC 169mg

Wholesome Morning Granola

Fruit juices, coconut, and honey contribute extra sweetness to this cereal.

Prep: 10 minutes • Cook: 56 minutes

  4 cups regular oats
  2 cups puffed rice cereal
  ½ cup flaked sweetened coconut
  ½ cup oat bran
  ¼ cup sliced almonds, toasted
  3 tablespoons turbinado sugar
  ¾ cup pineapple juice
  ½ cup apple juice
  ¼ cup honey
Cooking spray
  ¼ cup dried blueberries

1. Preheat oven to 325°.
2. Combine first 6 ingredients.
3. Combine juices in a small saucepan. Bring to a boil; cook until reduced to ⅔ cup (about 10 minutes). Remove from heat; stir in honey. Slowly pour juice mixture over oat mixture, tossing to coat. Spread oat mixture evenly onto a jelly-roll pan coated with cooking spray. Bake at 325° for 40 minutes or until golden, stirring occasionally. Cool slightly; stir in blueberries, and cool completely. Store in an airtight container. Yield: 7½ cups (serving size: ½ cup).

CALORIES 252 (19% from fat); FAT 5.2g (sat 1.6g, mono 1.6g, poly 1.4g); PROTEIN 8.4g; CARB 46.2g; FIBER 5.6g; CHOL 0mg; IRON 2.6mg; SODIUM 10mg; CALC 36mg

Sushi Rice

The rice sticks together better when it's not chilled, so don't make it a day ahead and store in refrigerator. Use Sushi Rice in the recipes for Bagel Roll, Shrimp Maki, and Tuna Nigiri (pages 259 - 260).

Prep: 2 minutes • Cook: 25 minutes
Other: 45 minutes

- 4   cups uncooked short-grain rice
- 4   cups water
- ½   cup seasoned rice vinegar

1. Bring rice and water to a boil in a medium saucepan. Cover, reduce heat, and simmer 15 minutes. Remove from heat; let stand, covered, 15 minutes.
2. Place rice in a large bowl; gently stir in rice vinegar with a spoon until combined. Cover rice mixture; let rest 30 minutes. Yield: 20 servings (serving size: ½ cup).

CALORIES 137 (1% from fat); FAT 0.2g (sat 0g, mono 0.1g, poly 0.1g); PROTEIN 2.4g; CARB 30.5g; FIBER 1g; CHOL 0mg; IRON 1.5mg; SODIUM 158mg; CALC 1mg

Spiced Basmati Pilaf with Garden Peas

This flavorful pilaf features an aromatic broth laced with sautéed onion, cardamom pods, cinnamon, and whole cloves.

Prep: 8 minutes • Cook: 20 minutes
Other: 35 minutes

- 1   tablespoon canola oil
- ⅓   cup chopped onion
- 1   cup uncooked basmati rice
- 2   cups cold water
- 8   cardamom pods
- 6   whole cloves
- 1   (3-inch) cinnamon stick
- ¾   teaspoon salt
- ½   cup frozen green peas

1. Heat oil in a large saucepan over medium-high heat. Add onion; sauté 3 minutes or until lightly browned. Add rice, water, cardamom, cloves, cinnamon, and salt, and bring to a boil. Reduce heat to medium, and cook 5 minutes or until liquid is nearly absorbed. Fold in peas. Cover, reduce heat to low, and cook 8 minutes.
2. Remove from heat; let stand 5 minutes. Remove and discard cardamom, cloves, and cinnamon before eating. Yield: 7 servings (serving size: ½ cup).

CALORIES 126 (16% from fat); FAT 2.2g (sat 0.3g, mono 1.3g, poly 0.8g); PROTEIN 2.6g; CARB 23.4g; FIBER 1.1g; CHOL 0mg; IRON 1.3mg; SODIUM 263mg; CALC 12mg

Test Kitchen Tip: Some packages of basmati rice call for soaking the rice for 30 minutes prior to cooking, then cooking the rice in the soaking liquid. The result is a slightly stickier rice, which is desirable in some dishes. We prepared this recipe both ways—soaking and not soaking—and got a desirable product both times.

Spiced Basmati Pilaf with Garden Peas

types of rice

types of rice There are thousands of rice varieties grown throughout the world, but they generally fall into one of three categories: short-, medium-, and long-grain. Cooking properties, taste, and texture vary, depending on the length of the grain. Long-grain varieties are four to five times longer than wide. Medium-grain rices are two to three times longer than wide and absorb flavors readily. Short-grain rice is plump—almost round—and cooks into soft grains that cling together.

Arborio This popular Italian rice is used to make risotto. Each medium or short grain has a white "eye" that remains firm to the bite, while the rest of the grain softens and lends creaminess. Once grown exclusively in Italy, Arborio is now also grown in California and Texas. Other Italian rices used to make risotto are carnaroli and vialone nano.

Basmati Sometimes called "popcorn rice," this long-grain variety is highly regarded for its fragrance, taste, and slender shape. True basmati is grown in India and Pakistan, although many hybrids are grown elsewhere, including the United States. Texmati, for example, is grown in Texas.

Black Both medium- and short-grain, this rice is grown mostly in Southeast Asia and in limited quantity in California. It gets its color from the black bran that surrounds the endosperm, or kernel. When cooked, the rice might turn purple or lavender—the bran dyes the white kernel inside. Look for Black Japonica or Forbidden Rice.

Brown This is rice that has been hulled with the bran intact. The bran lends chewy texture and nutty flavor, and contains vitamins, minerals, and fiber. It requires a longer cooking time because the bran is a barrier to water.

Glutinous Also called sticky rice, this grain is steamed dry after soaking to yield a sticky, chewy texture. It's a staple food in northern and northeastern Thailand where it's often rolled into a ball and dipped in a spicy sauce.

Instant Also called precooked, this rice has been partially or completely cooked and dried; it takes only a few minutes to prepare.

Jasmine Thailand's favorite, this aromatic rice has more amylopectin, or sticky starch, than other long-grain rice, so it's moist and tender. It's grown in Asia and the United States.

Parboiled or Converted Steam-pressure treatment before milling produces this tan grain that is firm and stays separate when cooked. Don't confuse it with instant rice—parboiled rice takes longer to cook.

Red This aromatic rice with reddish-brown bran has a nutty flavor and a chewy consistency. Look for Wehani (American grown), Bhutanese Red Rice (imported), and Camargue (imported from France's Provence region) in specialty markets. Red rice is great with hearty foods like pork or butternut squash.

Sushi This short-grain sticky rice is glassy and smooth. It grows throughout Asia and in California.

Wild The only rice native to North America, wild rice is actually an aquatic grass. It's often sold mixed with long-grain white rice.

how to cook basic white rice

Cooking flawless long-grain white rice isn't difficult, if you follow these directions:

1. Select a saucepan, deep skillet, or sauté pan with a snug-fitting lid.
2. Heat water to boiling.
   • For soft, tender rice, use 2 cups water per 1 cup rice.
   • For dry, separate grains, use 1¾ cups water per 1 cup rice. (It's not really necessary to rinse rice before cooking, although that method is routine in China. Rinsing removes the white powder caused by polishing and allows the grains to separate during cooking, creating a fluffier rice.)
3. Add the rice and salt; stir once.
4. Return to boiling; stir once.
5. Cover and reduce heat to low.
6. Cook for 15 minutes or until all the water is absorbed. Don't lift the lid or stir. Lifting the lid allows steam to escape, and stirring the rice will release more starch, causing the grains to stick together in lumps.
7. Remove the lid carefully (try not to let the condensation on the lid drip onto the rice).

Brown-and-Wild Rice Pilaf with Date Chutney

Basmati is a delicate, aromatic rice that lends a softer texture than the chewy wild rice. To streamline preparation, cook the onions while the rice is simmering.

Prep: 20 minutes • Cook: 51 minutes
Other: 5 minutes

    3   cups water
    ¾   cup uncooked wild rice
    ½   teaspoon salt
    ¼   teaspoon ground turmeric
    1¼ cups uncooked brown basmati rice
    ¾   cup frozen green peas, thawed
    1   tablespoon olive oil
    1½ cups vertically sliced onion
        Date Chutney (page 463)
    6   tablespoons slivered almonds,
        toasted

1. Combine first 4 ingredients in a large saucepan; bring to a boil. Cover, reduce heat, and simmer 15 minutes. Add basmati rice. Return to a boil; cover, reduce heat, and simmer 25 minutes. Stir in green peas; cook 5 minutes. Remove from heat; let stand, covered, 5 minutes.
2. While rice simmers, heat oil in a large nonstick skillet over medium-high heat. Add onion; sauté 20 minutes or until golden brown, stirring frequently.
3. Place rice mixture on each of 6 plates; top each serving with caramelized onions, chutney, and almonds. Yield: 6 servings (serving size: about ¾ cup rice, about 1½ tablespoons onion, about 2½ tablespoons chutney, and 1 tablespoon almonds).

(Totals include Date Chutney) CALORIES 383 (16% from fat); FAT 6.9g (sat 0.9g, mono 4.2g, poly 1.4g); PROTEIN 9.2g; CARB 74.7g; FIBER 6.5g; CHOL 0mg; IRON 2mg; SODIUM 419mg; CALC 52mg

Baked Mushroom Rice

Rice cooks beautifully in the oven—and you avoid the temptation to lift a saucepan lid and peek.

Prep: 4 minutes • Cook: 29 minutes
Other: 3 minutes

    1   tablespoon olive oil
    1   cup sliced cremini mushrooms
    1½ cups fat-free, less-sodium chicken broth
    1   cup uncooked medium-grain rice
    ¼   teaspoon salt

1. Preheat oven to 400°.
2. Heat oil in a medium oven-proof skillet over medium-high heat. Add mushrooms; sauté 5 minutes. Stir in broth, rice, and salt; bring to a boil. Cover and bake at 400° for 20 minutes. Remove from oven, uncover, and let stand 3 minutes. Yield: 4 servings (serving size: about ¾ cup).

CALORIES 212 (16% from fat); FAT 3.7g (sat 0.5g, mono 2.6g, poly 0.4g); PROTEIN 5.1g; CARB 38.5g; FIBER 0.8g; CHOL 0mg; IRON 2.1mg; SODIUM 319mg; CALC 18mg

Wild Rice with Walnut Oil and Green Onions

Walnut oil adds a distinctive nutty flavor to the rice, but you can substitute olive oil if you prefer.

Prep: 9 minutes • Cook: 1 hour, 15 minutes

    6   cups water
    2   cups uncooked wild rice
    1   teaspoon salt
    ½   cup dried currants
    2   tablespoons walnut oil or olive oil,
        divided
    1   cup chopped green onions, divided
    1   teaspoon grated lemon rind, divided

1. Bring water to a boil in a large saucepan. Add wild rice and salt; cover, reduce heat, and simmer 50 minutes. Stir in currants; cover and cook an additional 10 minutes or until rice is tender and liquid is absorbed. Drain if necessary. Spoon into a large bowl.
2. Heat 1½ tablespoons oil in a nonstick skillet over medium-low heat. Add ¾ cup onions; cook 10 minutes or until soft. Stir 1½ teaspoons oil, cooked onion, and ½ teaspoon rind into rice mixture. Sprinkle with ¼ cup green onions and ½ teaspoon grated lemon rind. Yield: 8 servings (serving size: ¾ cup).

CALORIES 202 (18% from fat); FAT 4.1g (sat 0.4g, mono 2.5g, poly 0.9g); PROTEIN 6.4g; CARB 37g; FIBER 2.5g; CHOL 0mg; IRON 1.2mg; SODIUM 301mg; CALC 26mg

menu

serves 8

Hearts of Romaine Salad with
Creamy Soy Dressing (page 401)

Maple and Calvados-Glazed Pork
Crown Roast with Apple-Chestnut
Puree (page 354)

Green Beans with Crushed Walnuts
(page 515)

Wild Rice with Walnut Oil and
Green Onions

Whole wheat rolls

Orange-Glazed Cheesecake with
Gingersnap Crust (page 140)

Rapid Risotto

When you prepare risotto in a pressure cooker, you only have to stir constantly for 3 minutes. The cooker does the rest of the work. If you prefer not to use wine, add an additional ½ cup chicken broth.

Prep: 6 minutes • Cook: 12 minutes
Other: 5 minutes

- 1 tablespoon olive oil
- 1 cup uncooked Arborio rice or other short-grain rice
- ½ cup frozen chopped onion
- ½ cup dry white wine
- 2 cups fat-free, less-sodium chicken broth
- 1 cup finely chopped plum tomatoes (about ¼ pound)
- 2 tablespoons dried parsley
- ½ teaspoon freshly ground black pepper
- 3 ounces chopped prosciutto (about ¾ cup)
- ¼ cup (1 ounce) shredded fresh Parmesan cheese

1. Heat oil in a 6-quart pressure cooker over medium heat until hot. Add rice and onion, and sauté 1 minute. Stir in wine and broth. Close lid securely, and bring to high pressure over high heat (about 4 minutes). Adjust heat to medium or level needed to maintain high pressure, and cook 3 minutes. Remove from heat, and let stand 5 minutes. Place pressure cooker under cold running water. Remove lid, and stir in tomatoes, dried parsley, pepper, and prosciutto. Cook, uncovered, over medium-high heat 3 minutes, stirring constantly. Stir in cheese. Yield: 4 servings (serving size: 1 cup).

CALORIES 306 (22% from fat); FAT 7.6g (sat 2.4g, mono 4.1g, poly 0.8g); PROTEIN 13g; CARB 45.1g; FIBER 1.7g; CHOL 17mg; IRON 3.3mg; SODIUM 683mg; CALC 98mg

Butternut Squash Risotto

Here's an example of a traditional Italian dish and cooking technique adapted with an American ingredient. The original Italian recipe uses the Italian pumpkin, zucca barucca. We've used butternut squash.

Prep: 12 minutes • Cook: 1 hour

- 2 cups water, divided
- 2 (14-ounce) cans less-sodium beef broth
- 2 teaspoons olive oil
- ½ cup finely chopped yellow onion
- 3 cups (¾-inch) cubed peeled butternut squash (about 1 pound)
- ½ teaspoon salt
- ¼ teaspoon freshly ground black pepper
- 1½ cups Arborio rice or other short-grain rice
- 2 ounces shaved Parmigiano-Reggiano cheese
- 3 tablespoons unsalted butter
- 2 tablespoons finely chopped fresh parsley

1. Bring 1½ cups water and broth to a simmer in a large saucepan (do not boil). Keep warm over low heat.

2. Heat oil in a Dutch oven over medium heat. Add onion; cook 8 minutes or until golden, stirring frequently. Add ½ cup water, squash, salt, and pepper; cook 10 minutes or until squash is tender and water has almost evaporated. Add rice; stir until combined. Stir in ½ cup broth mixture; cook until liquid is nearly absorbed, stirring constantly. Add remaining broth mixture, ½ cup at a time, stirring constantly until each portion of broth is absorbed before adding next (about 30 minutes total). Stir in cheese, butter, and parsley. Serve immediately. Yield: 8 servings (serving size: ⅔ cup).

CALORIES 272 (25% from fat); FAT 7.6g (sat 4g, mono 2.8g, poly 0.5g); PROTEIN 7.9g; CARB 41.4g; FIBER 2.8g; CHOL 15mg; IRON 1mg; SODIUM 275mg; CALC 119mg

Monterey Jack, Corn, and Roasted Red Pepper Risotto

We never seem to run out of ways to make risotto. Here, the creamy rice dish takes on a Southwestern flavor with corn, Monterey Jack cheese, and cumin.

Prep: 11 minutes • Cook: 31 minutes

1¾ cups water
2 (14-ounce) cans vegetable broth
2 teaspoons olive oil
1 cup uncooked Arborio or other short-grain rice
1 teaspoon ground cumin
1 teaspoon ground coriander (optional)
4 garlic cloves, minced
1 cup thinly sliced green onions
¾ cup (3 ounces) shredded Monterey Jack cheese with jalapeño peppers
¼ to ½ teaspoon hot sauce
2 cups frozen whole-kernel corn
¾ cup chopped bottled roasted red bell peppers

1. Combine water and broth in a medium saucepan; bring to a simmer (do not boil). Keep broth mixture warm over low heat.
2. Heat olive oil in a large saucepan over medium-high heat. Add rice, cumin, coriander, if desired, and garlic; sauté 1 minute. Stir in ½ cup broth mixture; cook 2 minutes or until liquid is nearly absorbed, stirring constantly. Add remaining broth mixture, ½ cup at a time, stirring constantly until each portion of liquid is absorbed before adding the next portion (about 20 minutes total). Stir in green onions, cheese, hot sauce, corn, and roasted red bell peppers; cook 3 minutes or until thoroughly heated. Yield: 4 servings (serving size: 1 cup).

CALORIES 383 (24% from fat); FAT 10.4g (sat 4.6g, mono 3.9g, poly 0.9g); PROTEIN 12g; CARB 63.3g; FIBER 3.8g; CHOL 17mg; IRON 3.6mg; SODIUM 583mg; CALC 198mg

Monterey Jack, Corn, and Roasted Red Pepper Risotto

Three-Grain Risotto with Asparagus Spears

Rice, barley, and quinoa give this risotto contrasting textures—creaminess from the rice, chewiness from the barley, and crunch from the quinoa.

Prep: 10 minutes • Cook: 46 minutes

⅛ teaspoon saffron threads, crushed
1 (14-ounce) can fat-free, less-sodium chicken broth
1 tablespoon olive oil
¼ cup finely chopped shallots (about 2 medium)
½ cup uncooked Arborio or other short-grain rice
½ cup uncooked quick-cooking barley
¼ cup uncooked quinoa
½ cup dry white wine or water
1 cup water
1 cup (4 ounces) shredded part-skim mozzarella cheese
⅔ cup 1% low-fat milk
2 teaspoons fresh lemon juice
½ teaspoon salt
½ teaspoon freshly ground black pepper
12 asparagus spears, steamed
1 tablespoon pine nuts, toasted

1. Bring saffron and broth to a simmer in a small saucepan (do not boil). Keep warm over low heat.
2. Heat oil in a large saucepan over medium-high heat. Add shallots; sauté 3 minutes. Add rice, barley, and quinoa; sauté 2 minutes. Add wine; cook 2 minutes or until liquid is nearly absorbed. Stir in 1 cup water; cook 5 minutes or until liquid is nearly absorbed, stirring constantly. Add broth mixture, ½ cup at a time, stirring constantly until each portion is absorbed before adding next (about 25 minutes total).
3. Remove from heat; stir in cheese and next 4 ingredients. Top with asparagus; sprinkle with pine nuts. Yield: 4 servings (serving size: about 1 cup risotto, 3 asparagus spears, and about 1 teaspoon nuts).

CALORIES 393 (24% from fat); FAT 10.5g (sat 3.9g, mono 4.5g, poly 1.4g); PROTEIN 17.3g; CARB 57.3g; FIBER 6.3g; CHOL 18mg; IRON 2.9mg; SODIUM 638mg; CALC 275mg

quinoa This ancient grain is making a big comeback. The tiny beige-colored seeds are about the size of couscous grains, and are an excellent source of protein and fiber.

Wild Rice-Squash Risotto

This main dish features the creaminess you expect in risotto, but has added texture from wild rice and sweetness from squash.

Prep: 9 minutes • Cook: 1 hour, 30 minutes
Other: 30 minutes

- ⅔ cup water
- ⅓ cup uncooked wild rice
- ½ cup uncooked Arborio or other short-grain rice
- 1 cup water
- 1¼ cups diced peeled acorn squash or butternut squash
- 2 poblano chiles (about ¼ pound)
- 1 cup fat-free, less-sodium chicken broth
- ½ cup (2 ounces) grated fresh Romano cheese
- 2 tablespoons butter
- 1 tablespoon chopped fresh or 1 teaspoon dried thyme
- ¼ teaspoon salt
- ¼ teaspoon black pepper

1. Bring ⅔ cup water to a boil in a medium saucepan. Add wild rice; cover, reduce heat, and simmer 1 hour or until tender. Drain, if necessary, and set aside. Bring Arborio rice and 1 cup water to a boil in a medium saucepan. Cover, reduce heat, and simmer 18 minutes. Remove from heat; let stand, covered, 15 minutes.

2. Cook squash in boiling water 4 minutes or until tender. Rinse squash with cold water; drain.

3. Preheat broiler.

4. Cut poblanos in half lengthwise; discard seeds and membranes. Place pepper halves, skin sides up, on a foil-lined baking sheet; flatten with hand. Broil 10 minutes or until blackened, turning occasionally. Place in a zip-top plastic bag; seal. Let stand 15 minutes. Peel and chop poblanos. Set aside.

Vegetable Donburi over Seasoned Rice

5. Bring broth to a boil in a large saucepan. Add cooked wild rice and Arborio rice; cook 2 minutes, stirring constantly. Reduce heat to medium, and add cheese and butter, stirring until cheese melts. Add squash, poblanos, thyme, salt, and pepper; cook 2 minutes or until thoroughly heated. Yield: 4 servings (serving size: 1 cup).

CALORIES 322 (28% from fat); FAT 10g (sat 6.1g, mono 2.9g, poly 0.5g); PROTEIN 10.7g; CARB 47.8g; FIBER 2.4g; CHOL 30mg; IRON 2.6mg; SODIUM 500mg; CALC 179mg

Vegetable Donburi over Seasoned Rice

Donburi (dohn-boo-REE) is "fast food" in Japan—boiled rice topped with broth and either vegetables, meat, fish, or eggs.

Prep: 15 minutes • Cook: 23 minutes

- 5 cups water, divided
- 2½ cups uncooked sushi rice or other short-grain rice
- 1 (14-ounce) can vegetable broth
- 2½ tablespoons miso (soybean paste)
- 2½ tablespoons low-sodium soy sauce
- 1½ tablespoons sugar
- 6 cups thinly sliced shiitake mushroom caps (about 1 pound mushrooms)
- 1 tablespoon minced peeled fresh ginger
- 2 garlic cloves, minced
- 1 cup shredded carrot
- ¾ cup (1-inch) sliced green onions
- 2 large egg whites
- 1 large egg

1. Bring 3 cups water to a boil in a medium saucepan; add rice. Cover, reduce heat, and simmer 12 minutes. Remove from heat, and let stand.

2. Bring 2 cups water and broth to a boil in a large saucepan. Stir in miso, soy sauce, and sugar. Add mushrooms, ginger, and garlic; reduce heat, and simmer 2 minutes. Stir in carrot and onions; cook 2 minutes.

3. Combine egg whites and egg in a small bowl; stir with a whisk. Gently pour egg mixture into broth mixture (do not stir); cook 1 minute. Remove from heat; gently stir.

4. Spoon rice into large soup bowls. Ladle broth mixture evenly over rice. Yield: 6 servings (serving size: 1 cup rice and 1 cup broth).

CALORIES 315 (6% from fat); FAT 2.2g (sat 0.5g, mono 0.5g, poly 0.5g); PROTEIN 8.8g; CARB 64.4g; FIBER 2.8g; CHOL 44mg; IRON 4.4mg; SODIUM 869mg; CALC 33mg

Test Kitchen Tip: Sushi rice, a sticky rice that's available in many large supermarkets, holds together well when topped with vegetables and broth. But any rice will work in this dish. Find miso, a slightly sweet paste made from ground soybeans, in large supermarkets, Asian markets, or health-food stores.

Shrimp Fried Rice

Perfect fried rice relies on chilled cooked rice, so make this great dish when you have leftover rice in the fridge. If you need to prepare some rice, add 20 minutes to the cook time and about 30 minutes for chilling. (See page 266 for instructions on cooking long-grain rice.)

Prep: 30 minutes • Cook: 11 minutes

- 3 tablespoons low-sodium soy sauce
- 2 tablespoons water
- 2 tablespoons rice vinegar
- 1 teaspoon sesame oil
- ¼ teaspoon salt
- ¼ teaspoon crushed red pepper
- 3 tablespoons canola oil, divided
- 1½ pounds medium shrimp, peeled and deveined
- 3 large eggs, lightly beaten
- 2 cups finely chopped green onions
- 1 tablespoon minced peeled fresh ginger
- 4 cups cooked long-grain rice, chilled
- 1½ cups frozen green peas, thawed

1. Combine first 6 ingredients in a small bowl; set aside.

2. Heat 1 tablespoon canola oil in a large nonstick skillet over medium-high heat. Add shrimp; cook 4 minutes or until done. Remove shrimp from pan; keep warm. Heat 2 tablespoons canola oil in pan. Add eggs; stir-fry 30 seconds or until soft-scrambled. Stir in green onions and ginger; stir-fry 1 minute. Stir in soy sauce mixture, shrimp, rice, and peas; cook 3 minutes or until thoroughly heated. Yield: 6 servings (serving size: 1⅓ cups).

CALORIES 376 (28% from fat); FAT 11.7g (sat 1.7g, mono 5.7g, poly 3g); PROTEIN 26.4g; CARB 38.7g; FIBER 3.7g; CHOL 274mg; IRON 5.1mg; SODIUM 610mg; CALC 95mg

---

Cilantro Rice with Chicken

A sauce of fresh cilantro, green onions, ginger, and garlic gives the rice intense fragrance and flavor. Shiitake mushrooms add an earthy smokiness to this one-dish meal.

Prep: 20 minutes • Cook: 38 minutes • Other: 10 minutes

Rice:
- 1 tablespoon olive oil
- 2 cups quartered shiitake mushroom caps (about 6 ounces)
- ¼ cup chopped green onion bottoms
- 1 (½-inch) piece peeled fresh ginger
- 1 garlic clove, crushed
- 2 cups uncooked long-grain rice
- 2 teaspoons ground cumin
- 6 skinless, boneless chicken thighs (about 1¾ pounds), cut into bite-sized pieces
- 3 cups fat-free, less-sodium chicken broth

Sauce:
- 2 cups loosely packed cilantro leaves
- ½ cup fat-free, less-sodium chicken broth
- 2 tablespoons chopped green onion tops
- 1 teaspoon chopped peeled fresh ginger
- ½ teaspoon kosher salt
- 1 garlic clove, peeled

Topping:
- 1 teaspoon olive oil
- 2 cups grape or cherry tomatoes, halved
- 2 tablespoons chopped green onion tops
- Cilantro sprigs (optional)

1. Preheat oven to 350°.

2. To prepare rice, heat 1 tablespoon oil in a Dutch oven over medium heat. Add mushrooms and next 3 ingredients; cook 5 minutes, stirring frequently. Stir in rice, cumin, and chicken; cook 1 minute. Stir in 3 cups broth; bring to a boil. Cover and bake at 350° for 25 minutes. Remove from oven; let stand, covered, 10 minutes.

3. To prepare sauce, place cilantro leaves and next 5 ingredients in a food processor or blender; process until smooth. Stir into rice mixture. Discard ginger piece.

4. To prepare topping, heat 1 teaspoon oil in a medium skillet over medium-low heat. Add tomatoes; cook 2 minutes. Stir in 2 tablespoons green onion tops. Place rice mixture in a large bowl; spoon tomato topping over rice. Garnish with cilantro sprigs, if desired. Yield: 8 servings (serving size: about 1 cup rice mixture and about ¼ cup tomato topping).

CALORIES 339 (18% from fat); FAT 6.8g (sat 1.4g, mono 3g, poly 1.3g); PROTEIN 25.3g; CARB 41.5g; FIBER 1.8g; CHOL 82mg; IRON 3.9mg; SODIUM 416mg; CALC 44mg

Pastas
Versatility may be pasta's most useful quality. In side dishes such as creamy mac and cheese or in main-dish lasagnas, pasta is always a pleaser.

Lemon Couscous

Citrus juices perk up basic couscous. This recipe is part of the Prosciutto-Wrapped Shrimp with Lemon Couscous on page 256, but is also a good stand-alone couscous side dish.

Prep: 6 minutes • Cook: 3 minutes
Other: 5 minutes

1¼ cups water
¾ cup uncooked couscous
¼ cup sliced green onions
2 tablespoons finely chopped fresh parsley
2 tablespoons orange juice
1 teaspoon grated lemon rind
1 tablespoon fresh lemon juice
¼ teaspoon salt
⅛ teaspoon pepper

1. Bring water to a boil in a saucepan; gradually stir in couscous. Remove from heat; cover and let stand 5 minutes. Fluff. Stir in onions and remaining ingredients. Yield: 4 servings (serving size: ½ cup).

CALORIES 102 (3% from fat); FAT 0.3g (sat 0g, mono 0g, poly 0g); PROTEIN 3.7g; CARB 21.8g; FIBER 1.3g; CHOL 0mg; IRON 0.8mg; SODIUM 151mg; CALC 9mg

Creamy Gorgonzola Fettuccine

Two types of cheese intensify the richness of this pasta dish; asparagus and toasted walnuts add a crisp crunch.

Prep: 10 minutes • Cook: 16 minutes

8 ounces uncooked fettuccine
3 cups (1-inch) diagonally sliced asparagus (about 10 ounces)
2 teaspoons butter
4 garlic cloves, minced
1 tablespoon all-purpose flour
1¼ cups fat-free milk
¼ cup (2 ounces) ⅓-less-fat cream cheese
¼ teaspoon salt
½ cup (2 ounces) Gorgonzola or other blue cheese, crumbled
2 tablespoons chopped walnuts, toasted
Freshly ground black pepper (optional)

1. Cook pasta in boiling water 6 minutes. Add asparagus, and cook 2 minutes or until tender.
2. While pasta cooks, melt butter in a medium saucepan over medium-high heat. Add garlic, and cook 3 minutes. Add flour; cook 30 seconds, stirring constantly. Gradually add milk, stirring well with a whisk. Stir in cream cheese and salt; cook 3 minutes or until thick, stirring constantly.

3. Drain pasta and asparagus; place in a large bowl. Add sauce, tossing to coat. Serve with Gorgonzola and walnuts, and sprinkle with pepper, if desired. Yield: 4 servings (serving size: 1¼ cups pasta, 2 tablespoons Gorgonzola, and 1½ teaspoons walnuts).

CALORIES 399 (29% from fat); FAT 12.8g (sat 6.4g, mono 3.3g, poly 2.2g); PROTEIN 18g; CARB 54.3g; FIBER 3.8g; CHOL 28mg; IRON 3.4mg; SODIUM 467mg; CALC 220mg

Fettuccine Alfredo

Use our lightened version of Alfredo Sauce to make this classic pasta dish.

Prep: 5 minutes • Cook: 10 minutes

16 ounces uncooked fettuccine
Alfredo Sauce (page 448)
Freshly ground black pepper (optional)

1. Cook pasta according to package directions, omitting salt and fat. Drain.
2. While pasta cooks, prepare Alfredo Sauce.
3. Combine pasta and sauce in a large bowl, and toss. Sprinkle with freshly ground pepper, if desired. Yield: 6 servings (serving size: 1⅓ cups).

CALORIES 401 (29% from fat); FAT 12.8g (sat 7.4g, mono 3.5g, poly 0.9g); PROTEIN 15.7g; CARB 55g; FIBER 3.2g; CHOL 34mg; IRON 2.8mg; SODIUM 473mg; CALC 244mg

global pasta Although we typically think of Italian pasta (made from durum wheat flour and water), there are pastas from other culinary traditions.

China Translucent **cellophane noodles** are known by a variety of names, including bean threads, Chinese vermicelli, glass noodles, and *bai fun*. Unlike most "pastas," cellophane noodles are made from the starch of mung beans rather than wheat. Instead of boiling, soak them briefly in hot water before serving.

Germany Like dumplings, **spaetzle** is made with eggs, salt, flour, either milk or water, and nutmeg. To create their plump shape, the dough is forced through a colander or rolled and cut. It's typically served as a side, but with your favorite sauce, these noodles make a hearty main course.

Italy Like spaghetti, lasagna, and other dried Italian pastas, **fettuccine** is made from water and semolina. Translated as "small ribbons," fettuccine can also be bought fresh, and made with eggs rather than water.

Japan A blend of buckwheat and wheat flours, water, and eggs, Japanese **soba noodles** are a popular addition to soups in pan-Asian noodle houses. Soba can also be stir-fried or substituted for fettuccine or linguine.

Morocco Actually, **couscous** does qualify as pasta. To create the fine pellets, coarse semolina flour is mixed with water to create a paste, then sieved. Common in North African and Middle Eastern cuisines, couscous can be steamed or soaked in hot water, and served cold as a salad component or warm beneath a saucy stew.

cellophane noodles

spaetzle

fettuccine

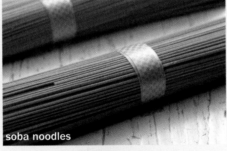
soba noodles

couscous

how to cook pasta

1. Use a large pot as full of water as possible. For 16 ounces of dried pasta, place 6 quarts of water in an 8-quart stockpot.

2. Cover pot, and bring water to a full rolling boil over high heat before adding pasta.

3. Add pasta, and stir with a pasta fork or large tongs to separate strands.

4. Start timing cooking when water returns to a boil. If you use fresh pasta, remember that it cooks more quickly than dried.

5. Always cook pasta uncovered (or only partially covered) over high heat.

6. Start testing for doneness a few minutes before indicated cooking time. Pasta that offers resistance to the bite but has no trace of brittleness is *al dente*. This is how you want it. If an undercooked piece of pasta is cut in half, a white dot or line is clearly visible in the center. Al dente pasta has only a speck of white remaining, meaning the pasta has absorbed just enough water to hydrate it.

7. Set a large colander in the sink so water drains quickly. Do not rinse.

8. Return pasta to the warm cooking pot or add to the skillet with sauce, and toss immediately with large tongs or a pasta fork.

Fusilli with Creamy Pancetta-and-Pea Sauce

Pancetta is a type of Italian bacon cured with salt and spices but not smoked. Substitute American-style bacon if you can't find pancetta.

Prep: 15 minutes • Cook: 20 minutes

  4 cups uncooked fusilli (short twisted spaghetti)
    Cooking spray
  ¼ cup chopped pancetta or bacon (about 1 ounce)
  1 teaspoon olive oil
  1 cup diced onion
  1 garlic clove, minced
  2 tablespoons all-purpose flour
  2 cups 1% low-fat milk
  ¼ cup (2 ounces) ⅓-less-fat cream cheese
  2½ cups frozen green peas, thawed
  1¼ cups (5 ounces) grated fresh Parmesan cheese, divided
  ⅓ cup chopped fresh basil
  ¼ teaspoon salt
  ¼ teaspoon pepper

1. Cook pasta according to package directions, omitting salt and fat. Drain.

2. While pasta cooks, heat a nonstick skillet over medium heat. Coat pan with cooking spray. Add pancetta; cook 1 minute or until browned. Place pancetta in a large bowl. Heat oil in pan. Add onion and garlic; sauté 7 minutes. Add onion mixture to pancetta. Place flour in pan. Gradually add milk; stir with a whisk until blended. Cook over medium heat until thick (about 5 minutes); stir constantly. Add cream cheese; stir until cheese melts. Stir in peas, 1 cup Parmesan, basil, salt, and pepper. Add cheese sauce and pasta to pancetta mixture; toss well. Sprinkle with ¼ cup Parmesan. Yield: 6 servings (serving size: 1⅓ cups).

CALORIES 410 (30% from fat); FAT 13.7g (sat 7.1g, mono 4.6g, poly 1g); PROTEIN 21.6g; CARB 49.5g; FIBER 5.1g; CHOL 30mg; IRON 3mg; SODIUM 656mg; CALC 419mg

Test Kitchen Tip: Prepare the sauce while the pasta is cooking so that everything will be warm when you toss the mixture.

menu

serves 6

Fusilli with Creamy
Pancetta-and-Pea Sauce

*Baby arugula salad with balsamic vinaigrette**

Melon slices

*Combine 3 tablespoons extravirgin olive oil, 1 tablespoon balsamic vinegar, 1½ teaspoons sugar, ½ teaspoon Dijon mustard, ¼ teaspoon salt, and ¼ teaspoon freshly ground black pepper in a small bowl, stirring with a whisk. Combine ⅓ cup thinly sliced red onion, ⅓ cup toasted sliced almonds, and 1 (8-ounce) package prewashed baby arugula in a serving bowl. Pour vinaigrette over arugula mixture, and toss to coat.

Classic Makeover: Seafood Fettuccine

Our traditional seafood fettuccine recipe had, in addition to the seafood and pasta, a pint of heavy cream, ¼ cup butter, and a mountain of grated cheese. To reduce the fat and calories, we started by reducing the butter used to sauté the seafood. A little butter goes a long way when you sauté in a nonstick skillet. That one change shaved off 29 grams of fat. Because Parmesan cheese has such intense flavor, we were able to reduce the cheese by three-fourths and save another 66 grams of fat. Finally, we trimmed an additional 120 fat grams by switching from whipping cream to half-and-half. The dish is still rich and creamy, but with only about a third of the fat as the original. Plus, by reducing the amounts of Parmesan cheese and butter, we decreased the sodium by about a third.

Before	After
• 721 calories	• 438 calories
• 41.7g fat	• 14.9g fat
• percentage of calories from fat 52%	• percentage of calories from fat 30%
• 1145mg sodium	• 747mg sodium

Seafood Fettuccine

Don't worry if the sauce looks thin. It's the perfect consistency for coating the pasta. Pat the shrimp and scallops dry with paper towels before cooking so they don't dilute the sauce.

Prep: 30 minutes • Cook: 31 minutes

- 1 pound uncooked fettuccine
- 1½ tablespoons butter
- 1 cup chopped green onions
- 4 garlic cloves, minced
- 1 pound medium shrimp, peeled
- 1 pound sea scallops
- 2 cups half-and-half
- ½ teaspoon salt
- ¼ teaspoon pepper
- ½ pound lump crabmeat, shell pieces removed
- ¾ cup (3 ounces) shredded fresh Parmesan cheese, divided
- ¼ cup chopped fresh parsley

1. Cook pasta according to package directions, omitting salt and fat. Drain.
2. While pasta cooks, melt butter in a 12-inch nonstick skillet over medium-high heat. Add onions and garlic; sauté 1 minute or until tender. Add shrimp and scallops; sauté 3 minutes or until done. Reduce heat to medium-low. Add half-and-half, salt, pepper, and crabmeat; cook 3 minutes or until thoroughly heated, stirring constantly (do not boil). Sprinkle ½ cup cheese over seafood mixture, stirring constantly; cook 1 minute, stirring constantly. Remove from heat. Combine pasta and seafood mixture in a large bowl. Top with ¼ cup cheese and parsley. Yield: 8 servings (serving size: 1½ cups).

CALORIES 438 (30% from fat); FAT 14.8g (sat 7.7g, mono 3.6g, poly 0.9g); PROTEIN 38.5g; CARB 38g; FIBER 2.2g; CHOL 160mg; IRON 3.4mg; SODIUM 747mg; CALC 257mg

Eggplant Parmesan Lasagna

When you can't decide between lasagna and eggplant parmesan, have both! Here you get seasoned eggplant slices in a savory tomato sauce as well as layers of noodles and cheese.

Prep: 25 minutes • Cook: 1 hour, 34 minutes
Other: 5 minutes

 12 uncooked lasagna noodles
  2 large egg whites
  1 large egg
  1 (1-pound) eggplant, cut crosswise into ¼-inch-thick slices
  3 tablespoons all-purpose flour
  1 cup Italian-seasoned breadcrumbs
 Cooking spray
  2 cups (8 ounces) shredded part-skim mozzarella cheese, divided
  5 tablespoons (1¼ ounces) grated fresh Parmesan cheese, divided
  1 teaspoon dried oregano
  1 teaspoon dried basil
  1 (15-ounce) carton part-skim ricotta cheese
  1 (12-ounce) carton 1% low-fat cottage cheese
  1 large egg white
  1 (26-ounce) bottle fat-free tomato-basil pasta sauce

1. Cook pasta according to package directions, omitting salt and fat. Drain.
2. Preheat oven to 450°.
3. Combine 2 egg whites and egg in a small bowl, stirring with a whisk. Dredge each eggplant slice in flour. Dip each in egg mixture, and dredge in breadcrumbs. Place slices in a single layer on a baking sheet coated with cooking spray. Coat tops of slices with cooking spray. Bake at 450° for 20 minutes, turning eggplant after 10 minutes. Remove from pan; cool. Reduce oven temperature to 375°.
4. Combine 1 cup shredded mozzarella, 3 tablespoons Parmesan, oregano, basil, ricotta, cottage cheese, and 1 egg white in a large bowl.
5. Spread ¼ cup pasta sauce in bottom of a 13 x 9–inch baking dish coated with cooking spray. Arrange 4 lasagna noodles, slightly overlapping, over pasta sauce; top with half of cheese mixture, half of eggplant slices, and ¾ cup pasta sauce. Repeat layers, ending with noodles. Spread remaining pasta sauce over noodles. Sprinkle with 1 cup mozzarella cheese and 2 tablespoons Parmesan cheese. Cover and bake at 375° for 15 minutes. Uncover and bake an additional 35 minutes or until cheese melts. Let stand 5 minutes before serving. Yield: 9 servings (serving size: 1 [3 x 4–inch] rectangle).

CALORIES 432 (23% from fat); FAT 11g (sat 6.2g, mono 3.1g, poly 0.9g); PROTEIN 28.3g; CARB 53.8g; FIBER 3.7g; CHOL 58mg; IRON 3.2mg; SODIUM 976mg; CALC 460mg

Roasted-Vegetable Lasagna

Use a sharp, potent cheese such as provolone, Parmesan, Romano, Asiago, or sharp Cheddar in the filling. Stick to mozzarella for the top, however, because it melts and browns the best.

Prep: 40 minutes • Cook: 1 hour, 37 minutes
Other: 15 minutes

  9 uncooked lasagna noodles
Vegetables:
  4 red bell peppers
  1 teaspoon olive oil
  ½ teaspoon salt
  ½ teaspoon black pepper
  6 yellow squash, halved lengthwise and cut into 1-inch pieces (about 1½ pounds)
  1 large onion, cut into 16 wedges
  4 garlic cloves, minced
Cheese mixture:
  2 cups 2% low-fat cottage cheese
  1½ cups (6 ounces) grated sharp provolone cheese
  ¼ cup chopped fresh basil
  1 teaspoon dried oregano
White sauce:
  3 tablespoons all-purpose flour
  1½ cups 2% reduced-fat milk
  2 tablespoons chopped fresh basil
  ¼ teaspoon black pepper
  Cooking spray
  2 cups spinach leaves
  ½ cup (2 ounces) shredded part-skim mozzarella cheese
  Basil sprigs (optional)

1. Cook pasta according to package directions, omitting salt and fat. Drain.
2. Preheat broiler.
3. To prepare vegetables, cut bell peppers in half lengthwise; discard seeds and membranes. Place pepper halves, skin sides up, on a foil-lined baking sheet; flatten with hand. Broil 15 minutes or until blackened. Place in a zip-top plastic bag; seal. Let stand 15 minutes. Peel; set aside.
4. Preheat oven to 450°.
5. Combine oil, salt, ½ teaspoon black pepper, squash, and onion on a baking sheet; toss well. Bake at 450° for 20 minutes. Remove from oven; combine squash mixture and garlic in a bowl.
6. Decrease oven temperature to 375°.
7. To prepare cheese mixture, combine cottage cheese and next 3 ingredients in a bowl.
8. To prepare white sauce, place flour in a medium saucepan. Gradually add milk; stir with a whisk. Place over medium heat. Cook until thick; stir constantly. Remove from heat; stir in 2 tablespoons chopped basil and ¼ teaspoon black pepper.
9. Spread ¼ cup white sauce in a 13 x 9–inch baking dish coated with cooking spray. Arrange 3 noodles over sauce; top with 1¼ cups cheese mixture, 1 cup spinach, 4 bell pepper halves, 2 cups vegetable mixture, and ¼ cup white sauce. Repeat layers, ending with noodles. Spread remaining white sauce over noodles. Cover and bake at 375° for 15 minutes. Uncover; sprinkle with mozzarella cheese. Bake an additional 20 minutes. Garnish with basil sprigs, if desired. Yield: 9 servings (serving size: 1 [3 x 4–inch] rectangle).

CALORIES 275 (30% from fat); FAT 9.1g (sat 5.2g, mono 2.6g, poly 0.6g); PROTEIN 19.3g; CARB 29.3g; FIBER 2.9g; CHOL 24mg; IRON 2.3mg; SODIUM 564mg; CALC 308mg

Test Kitchen Tip: While layering lasagna isn't an exact science, it helps to follow a few rules. Always spread a little sauce on the bottom of your lasagna dish so the pasta doesn't stick. And always end with sauce on top; if the noodles are exposed at the top while lasagna bakes, they'll turn dry and hard.

Tex-Mex Lasagna

This easy-to-make vegetarian lasagna features precooked noodles and pantry staples such as canned tomatoes, frozen corn, canned beans, and salsa.

Prep: 13 minutes • Cook: 30 minutes
Other: 15 minutes

    ¾   cup bottled salsa
    1½ teaspoons ground cumin
    1   (14.5-ounce) can no-salt-added
        diced tomatoes, undrained
    1   (8-ounce) can no-salt-added tomato
        sauce
        Cooking spray
    6   precooked lasagna noodles (such as
        Barilla or Vigo)
    1   cup frozen whole-kernel corn, thawed
    1   (15-ounce) can black beans, rinsed
        and drained
    2   cups (8 ounces) preshredded
        reduced-fat 4-cheese Mexican blend
        cheese
    ¼   cup chopped green onions

1. Preheat oven to 450°.
2. Combine first 4 ingredients; spread ⅔ cup sauce in bottom of an 8-inch square baking dish coated with cooking spray. Arrange 2 noodles over sauce; top with ½ cup corn and half of beans. Sprinkle with ½ cup cheese; top with ⅔ cup sauce. Repeat layers once; top with 2 noodles. Spread remaining sauce over noodles. Sprinkle with 1 cup cheese. Cover and bake at 450° for 30 minutes or until noodles are tender and sauce is bubbly. Let stand 15 minutes. Sprinkle with onions. Yield: 4 servings (serving size: 1 square).

CALORIES 415 (29% from fat); FAT 13.3g (sat 6.1g, mono 3.8g, poly 0.9g); PROTEIN 27.2g; CARB 55.2g; FIBER 10.4g; CHOL 41mg; IRON 3.9mg; SODIUM 970mg; CALC 518mg

Amounts of Dry and Cooked Pasta

Use this guide to help you determine either how much pasta you'll need or how much you'll get. Approximate cooking times are also included.

Type of Pasta	Dry Weight (8 ounces)	Cooked Volume	Cooking Time
Acini de pepe (small balls similar to orzo)	1¼ cups	3 cups	5 minutes
Alphabets	2 cups	4 cups	5 minutes
Capellini or angel hair	8 ounces	3½ cups	5 minutes
Cavatappi	3 cups	5 cups	8 minutes
Conchiglie rigate (seashell pasta)	3 cups	4 cups	14 minutes
Egg noodles, medium	4 cups	5 cups	5 minutes
Egg noodles, wide	4½ cups	5 cups	5 minutes
Elbow macaroni	2 cups	4 cups	5 minutes
Farfalle (bow tie pasta)	3 cups	4 cups	11 minutes
Fettuccine	8 ounces	4 cups	10 minutes
Fusilli (short twisted spaghetti)	3 cups	4 cups	10 minutes
Gemelli	2 cups	4 cups	10 minutes
Linguine	8 ounces	4 cups	10 minutes
Orecchiette ("little ears" pasta)	2½ cups	4 cups	11 minutes
Orzo (rice-shaped pasta)	1¼ cups	2½ cups	6 minutes
Penne or mostaccioli (tube-shaped pasta)	2 cups	4 cups	10 minutes
Penne rigate	2 cups	4 cups	10 minutes
Perciatelli	8 ounces	4 cups	11 minutes
Radiatore (short coiled pasta)	3 cups	4½ cups	10 minutes
Rigatoni	2½ cups	4 cups	10 minutes
Rotini (corkscrew pasta)	4 cups	4 cups	10 minutes
Small seashell pasta	2 cups	4 cups	8 minutes
Spaghetti	8 ounces	3½ cups	10 minutes
Vermicelli	8 ounces	4 cups	5 minutes
Ziti (short tube-shaped pasta)	3 cups	4 cups	10 minutes

Lasagna Rolls with Roasted Red Pepper Sauce

These rolls require some assembly time but are a nice change of pace from layered pasta. Use baby spinach to eliminate the task of trimming stems.

Prep: 25 minutes • Cook: 33 minutes

Lasagna:

    8   uncooked lasagna noodles
    4   teaspoons olive oil
    ½   cup finely chopped onion
    1   (8-ounce) package sliced mushrooms
    1   (6-ounce) package fresh baby spinach
    3   garlic cloves, minced
    ½   cup (2 ounces) shredded mozzarella cheese
    ½   cup part-skim ricotta cheese
    2   tablespoons minced fresh basil
    ½   teaspoon salt
    ¼   teaspoon crushed red pepper

Roasted Red Pepper Sauce:

    1   tablespoon red wine vinegar
    ¼   teaspoon salt
    ¼   teaspoon freshly ground black pepper
    2   garlic cloves, minced
    1   (14.5-ounce) can diced tomatoes, undrained
    1   (7-ounce) bottle roasted red bell peppers, undrained
    ⅛   teaspoon crushed red pepper

Remaining ingredient:

    2   tablespoons minced fresh basil

1. To prepare lasagna, cook noodles according to package directions, omitting salt and fat. Drain and rinse with cold water. Drain.

2. Heat oil in a large nonstick skillet over medium-high heat. Add onion, mushrooms, spinach, and 3 garlic cloves; sauté 5 minutes. Remove from heat, and stir in cheeses and next 3 ingredients.

3. To prepare sauce, place vinegar and next 6 ingredients in a blender; process until smooth.

4. Place cooked noodles on a flat surface; spread ¼ cup cheese mixture over each noodle. Roll up noodles, jelly-roll fashion, starting with short side. Place rolls, seam sides down, in a shallow 2-quart microwave-safe dish. Pour ¼ cup sauce over each roll, and cover with heavy-duty plastic wrap. Microwave at HIGH 5 minutes or until thoroughly heated. Sprinkle with 2 tablespoons basil. Yield: 4 servings (serving size: 2 rolls).

CALORIES 393 (27% from fat); FAT 11.7g (sat 4.3g, mono 3.6g, poly 1.5g); PROTEIN 19.3g; CARB 58.3g; FIBER 5.9g; CHOL 20mg; IRON 3.8mg; SODIUM 924mg; CALC 253mg

how to fill a lasagna roll

Spoon ¼ cup cheese mixture, by spoonfuls, down the center of each noodle.

menu

serves 4

Lasagna Rolls with Roasted Red Pepper Sauce

Sugar snap peas

Amaretto pears*

**Cut 2 pears into thin slices. Combine pear slices, 2 tablespoons toasted sliced almonds, 1 tablespoon brown sugar, and 1 tablespoon amaretto.*

Peanutty Noodles

This dish comes together quickly when one person prepares the sauce while another sautés the vegetables. Break the pasta in half before cooking to make serving easier. These noodles also become their own main dish when you add cooked shrimp or chicken.

Prep: 20 minutes • Cook: 35 minutes

- 1 pound uncooked linguine
- 2 carrots, peeled
- 1 tablespoon canola oil, divided
- 2 teaspoons grated peeled fresh ginger
- 3 garlic cloves, minced
- 1 cup fat-free, less-sodium chicken broth
- ½ cup natural-style peanut butter (such as Smucker's)
- ¼ cup low-sodium soy sauce
- 3 tablespoons rice or white wine vinegar
- 1 teaspoon chili garlic sauce (such as Lee Kum Kee)
- ¼ teaspoon salt
- Cooking spray
- 2 cups red bell pepper strips
- 1 pound snow peas, trimmed
- ½ cup chopped fresh cilantro (optional)

1. Cook pasta according to package directions, omitting salt and fat. Drain.
2. Shave carrots lengthwise into thin strips using a vegetable peeler, and set aside.
3. Heat 1 teaspoon oil in a small saucepan over medium heat. Add ginger and minced garlic; sauté 30 seconds. Add chicken broth and next 5 ingredients; stir until well blended. Reduce heat, and simmer 7 minutes, stirring occasionally. Remove from heat, and keep warm.
4. Heat 2 teaspoons oil in a large non-stick skillet coated with cooking spray over medium-high heat. Add bell pepper and snow peas; sauté 5 minutes or until tender. Remove from heat. Combine carrot, peanut butter mixture, bell pepper mixture, and linguine in a large bowl and toss well. Serve warm or at room temperature. Sprinkle with cilantro, if desired. Yield: 10 servings (serving size: 1 cup).

CALORIES 296 (27% from fat); FAT 8.8g (sat 1.7g, mono 3.8g, poly 2.7g); PROTEIN 11.7g; CARB 43.1g; FIBER 3.4g; CHOL 1mg; IRON 3.6mg; SODIUM 400mg; CALC 44mg

pasta pronto When you need to get dinner on the table in a hurry, here are three quick and easy pasta-tomato dishes that are sure to satisfy.

Garlicky Pasta with Fresh Tomatoes and Basil: Heat 3 tablespoons olive oil in a Dutch oven over medium-high heat. Add 3 minced garlic cloves; sauté 30 seconds. Add 5 cups chopped plum tomatoes; cook 2 minutes, stirring occasionally. Add 6 cups hot cooked campanella, ⅓ cup chopped fresh basil, ¼ cup grated fresh Parmesan cheese, 1½ teaspoons salt, and ¼ teaspoon pepper. Yield: 6 servings (serving size: 1⅓ cups).

Pasta with Pomodoro (Tomato) Sauce: Heat 2 tablespoons olive oil in a nonstick skillet over medium heat. Add 4 minced garlic cloves; sauté 2 minutes. Stir in ½ teaspoon pepper, ¼ teaspoon salt, and 1 (28-ounce) can diced tomatoes, undrained. Bring to a boil, reduce heat, and simmer 7 minutes or until slightly thick, stirring occasionally. Remove from heat; stir in ¼ cup sliced basil. Serve over 8 cups hot cooked penne. Yield: 6 servings (serving size: ⅔ cups sauce and 1⅓ cups pasta).

Pasta with Watercress, Tomatoes, and Goat Cheese: Cook 3 cups (12 ounces) tubetti according to package directions, omitting salt and fat. Drain. Add 4 cups halved cherry tomatoes, 4 cups chopped trimmed watercress, 4 ounces crumbled goat cheese, ¾ teaspoon salt, and ½ teaspoon pepper. Toss. Yield: 6 servings (serving size: 2 cups).

Linguine with White Clam and Broccoli Sauce

When you combine the clam sauce and linguine, there should be a little extra broth, making the dish extrasaucy.

Prep: 35 minutes • Cook: 29 minutes

¾ cup water

36 littleneck clams in shells, scrubbed (about 2½ pounds)

6 quarts water

2½ teaspoons salt, divided

3 cups broccoli florets

1 pound uncooked linguine

3 tablespoons extravirgin olive oil, divided

6 garlic cloves, sliced

½ teaspoon crushed red pepper

¼ cup chopped fresh flat-leaf parsley

1. Bring ¾ cup water to a boil in a large stockpot. Add clams; cover and cook 4 minutes or until shells open. Remove from pan; reserve cooking liquid. Discard any unopened shells. Cool clams. Remove meat from shells; chop. Discard shells.

2. Bring 6 quarts water and 2 teaspoons salt to a boil in stockpot. Add broccoli, and cook 2 minutes or until broccoli is bright green. Remove broccoli with a slotted spoon (do not drain water from stockpot). Place broccoli in a colander, and rinse with cold water. Drain broccoli; coarsely chop.

3. Return water to a boil in stockpot. Stir in pasta and return to a boil, stirring frequently. Cook 6 minutes or until pasta is al dente, stirring occasionally. Drain.

4. While pasta cooks, heat 2 tablespoons oil in a large nonstick skillet over medium heat. Add garlic, and cook 1 minute or until fragrant and beginning to turn golden, stirring constantly. Add broccoli and pepper, and cook 2 minutes or until broccoli sizzles. Stir in clams and reserved cooking liquid, and bring to a boil. Reduce heat,

and simmer 2 minutes or until broccoli is tender.

5. Add pasta to pan, stirring well to coat. Bring mixture to a boil. Stir in ½ teaspoon salt and chopped parsley; cook 1 minute, stirring constantly. Place pasta mixture in each of 6 bowls; drizzle each serving with ½ teaspoon oil. Serve immediately. Yield: 6 servings (serving size: about 1 cup).

CALORIES 420 (19% from fat); FAT 9g (sat 1.2g, mono 5.2g, poly 1.5g); PROTEIN 22.1g; CARB 61.8g; FIBER 3g; CHOL 30mg; IRON 15.7mg; SODIUM 484mg; CALC 80mg

Test Kitchen Tip: Pasta can be tricky to serve because it has a tendency to slip and slide. The best serving utensil, especially for longer pasta, is a metal or wooden pasta fork or tongs. For short pasta, a large spoon works fine.

Creamy Four-Cheese Macaroni

A true classic, this mac and cheese has become one of our favorites because of its creaminess and blend of cheeses.

Prep: 25 minutes • Cook: 54 minutes

  3 cups uncooked elbow macaroni
  ⅓ cup all-purpose flour
2⅔ cups 1% low-fat milk
  ¾ cup (3 ounces) shredded Swiss cheese
  ½ cup (2 ounces) grated fresh
      Parmesan cheese
  ½ cup (2 ounces) shredded extrasharp
      Cheddar cheese
  3 ounces light processed cheese
  ¼ teaspoon salt
Cooking spray
  ⅓ cup crushed onion melba toasts
  1 tablespoon butter, softened

1. Cook macaroni according to package directions, omitting salt and fat. Drain.
2. Preheat oven to 375°.
3. Lightly spoon flour into a dry measuring cup; level with a knife. Place flour in a large saucepan. Gradually add milk, stirring with a whisk until blended. Cook over medium heat until thick (about 8 minutes), stirring constantly. Add cheeses; cook 3 minutes or until cheese melts, stirring frequently. Remove cheese mixture from heat; stir in cooked macaroni and salt.
4. Spoon mixture into a 2-quart casserole coated with cooking spray. Combine crushed toasts and butter; stir until well blended. Sprinkle over macaroni mixture. Bake at 375° for 30 minutes or until bubbly. Yield: 8 servings (serving size: 1 cup).

CALORIES 350 (29% from fat); FAT 11.2g (sat 6.3g, mono 2.9g, poly 0.9g); PROTEIN 18g; CARB 42.4g; FIBER 2.1g; CHOL 32mg; IRON 1.9mg; SODIUM 497mg; CALC 306mg

Creamy Four-Cheese Macaroni

Vegetable Stir-Fry over Crisp Noodles

It's easy to make the crisp noodle nests. When topped with this colorful vegetable mixture, they make an impressive party presentation.

Prep: 30 minutes • Cook: 54 minutes

Crisp noodles:
  1 (12-ounce) package fine egg noodles
1½ teaspoons dark sesame oil
  1 teaspoon canola oil
Sauce:
1½ cups fat-free, less-sodium chicken
      broth
  6 tablespoons oyster sauce
  ¼ cup sake (rice wine)
1½ tablespoons cornstarch
  1 teaspoon dark sesame oil
  1 teaspoon low-sodium soy sauce
Vegetables:
  2 teaspoons canola oil
1½ tablespoons minced peeled fresh ginger
  4 large garlic cloves, minced
  4 cups julienne-cut leek (about 4 small)
  3 cups shredded carrot (about 6 small)
  2 cups sliced shiitake mushroom caps
      (about 3 ounces)
  4 cups fresh bean sprouts

1. Preheat broiler.
2. To prepare crisp noodles, cook noodles according to package directions, omitting salt and fat. Rinse with cold water; drain well. Combine noodles, 1½ teaspoons sesame oil, and 1 teaspoon canola oil in a large bowl; toss well to coat. Divide noodle mixture evenly into 6 portions on 2 baking sheets. Using the back of a spoon, shape each portion into a 1-inch-thick nest. Place one baking sheet in oven; broil 10 minutes. Carefully turn nests over, and broil 6 minutes or until golden brown. Set aside. Repeat procedure with remaining nests.
3. To prepare sauce, combine broth and next 5 ingredients; stir well with a whisk.
4. To prepare vegetables, heat 2 teaspoons canola oil in a large nonstick skillet over medium-high heat. Add ginger and garlic; stir-fry 10 seconds. Add leek, carrot, and mushrooms; stir-fry 2 minutes. Add sauce; bring to a boil, and cook 2 minutes or until thick. Stir in sprouts; cook until thoroughly heated. Spoon vegetables over nests. Yield: 6 servings (serving size: 1⅓ cups vegetables and 1 nest).

CALORIES 368 (17% from fat); FAT 7.1g (sat 1.2g, mono 2.2g, poly 1.8g); PROTEIN 13.1g; CARB 65.2g; FIBER 5.2g; CHOL 54mg; IRON 5.2mg; SODIUM 586mg; CALC 92mg

Creamy Parmesan Orzo

Unlike traditional pasta, this orzo isn't cooked in a pot of boiling water. Instead, it's cooked slowly in a flavorful broth that captures its starch.

Prep: 6 minutes • Cook: 23 minutes

- 1 tablespoon butter
- 1 cup uncooked orzo (rice-shaped pasta)
- 1¼ cups fat-free, less-sodium chicken broth
- 1¼ cups water
- ¼ cup (1 ounce) grated fresh Parmesan cheese
- 2 tablespoons chopped fresh basil
- ¼ teaspoon salt
- ¼ teaspoon freshly ground black pepper
- 4 teaspoons pine nuts, toasted

1. Heat butter in a medium saucepan over medium heat. Add orzo, and cook 3 minutes, stirring constantly. Stir in broth and water; bring to a boil. Reduce heat; simmer until liquid is absorbed and orzo is done (about 15 minutes).
2. Remove orzo from heat; stir in cheese, basil, salt, and pepper. Sprinkle with pine nuts. Serve immediately. Yield: 4 servings (serving size: ½ cup).

CALORIES 236 (24% from fat); FAT 6.4g (sat 3.2g, mono 1.8g, poly 0.8g); PROTEIN 9.9g; CARB 34.8g; FIBER 1.7g; CHOL 12mg; IRON 1.8mg; SODIUM 412mg; CALC 82mg

Test Kitchen Tip: Orzo, which means "barley" in Italian, is a rice-shaped pasta. It's available in short, plump "grains" and longer, thinner "grains." Either will work in this recipe.

Polpette and Orzo in Broth

Instead of having meatballs (*polpette*) and tomato sauce with spaghetti, offer different Italian fare: meatballs in broth with orzo.

Prep: 15 minutes • Cook: 29 minutes
Other: 5 minutes

- 1 cup uncooked orzo (rice-shaped pasta)
- 1 (1-ounce) slice Italian bread
- ½ cup 1% low-fat milk
- 1 pound ground sirloin
- ½ cup minced fresh onion
- ½ cup (2 ounces) grated fresh Parmesan cheese, divided
- ¼ cup chopped fresh parsley
- ¼ teaspoon salt
- ¼ teaspoon pepper
- 6 cups fat-free, less-sodium chicken broth
- 1 cup shredded carrot
- ¼ cup plus 2 tablespoons chopped fresh parsley

1. Cook pasta according to package directions, omitting salt and fat. Drain.
2. Soak bread in milk 5 minutes, and squeeze moisture from bread. Discard milk. Combine bread, beef, minced onion, ¼ cup cheese, ¼ cup parsley, salt, and pepper in a bowl. Shape mixture into 24 (1½-inch) meatballs.
3. Bring broth to a simmer in a Dutch oven. Keep warm over low heat. Add meatballs and carrot to broth, and bring to a boil. Reduce heat, and simmer 8 minutes. Stir in cooked orzo, and cook 2 minutes. Sprinkle with ¼ cup cheese and ¼ cup plus 2 tablespoons parsley. Yield: 6 servings (serving size: 4 meatballs, 1 cup broth, 2 teaspoons cheese, and 1 tablespoon parsley).

CALORIES 337 (19% from fat); FAT 7.2g (sat 3.2g, mono 2.5g, poly 0.5g); PROTEIN 28.9g; CARB 36.6g; FIBER 2.1g; CHOL 53mg; IRON 4.1mg; SODIUM 823mg; CALC 165mg

Whole Wheat Pasta with Sausage, Leeks, and Fontina

Whole wheat pasta makes this dish especially hearty.

Prep: 15 minutes • Cook: 26 minutes

- 6 quarts water
- 2½ teaspoons salt, divided
- 1 pound uncooked whole wheat penne or rigatoni
- 1 tablespoon olive oil
- 1 (4-ounce) link sweet Italian sausage
- 2 cups chopped leek
- 4 cups shredded Savoy cabbage (about 10 ounces)
- 1 cup fat-free, less-sodium chicken broth
- ¼ teaspoon freshly ground black pepper
- ½ cup (2 ounces) shredded fontina cheese

1. Bring 6 quarts water and 2 teaspoons salt to a boil in a large stockpot. Stir in pasta, and return to a boil, stirring frequently. Cook 8 minutes or until pasta is almost al dente, stirring occasionally. Drain.
2. While pasta cooks, heat olive oil in a Dutch oven over medium-high heat. Remove casing from sausage. Add sausage to Dutch oven; cook 2 minutes, stirring to crumble. Add leek; sauté 2 minutes. Add cabbage; sauté 2 minutes. Add ½ teaspoon salt, broth, and pepper; bring to a boil. Reduce heat; simmer 15 minutes.
3. Add pasta to pan, tossing well to coat; bring to a boil. Reduce heat, and cook 1 minute or until pasta is al dente, stirring constantly. Remove from heat; stir in cheese. Serve immediately. Yield: 6 servings (serving size: 1⅔ cups).

CALORIES 385 (21% from fat); FAT 8.9g (sat 3.2g, mono 3.8g, poly 1.2g); PROTEIN 17.3g; CARB 64.3g; FIBER 8.3g; CHOL 18mg; IRON 3.8mg; SODIUM 658mg; CALC 119mg

Mushroom Rigatoni Bake

A full cup of Italian Asiago cheese gives body and flavor to the velvety sauce, which is laced with sherry. If you don't have Asiago cheese, you can use grated fresh Parmesan. While the sherry does add an extra touch of richness to the sauce, if you prefer not to use it, just leave it out.

Prep: 20 minutes • Cook: 1 hour, 9 minutes

8   ounces uncooked rigatoni or radiatore pasta
2   teaspoons butter
¼   cup sliced shallots
8   ounces sliced shiitake mushroom caps
4   ounces sliced cremini mushrooms
1   tablespoon chopped fresh thyme
½   teaspoon salt
¼   teaspoon freshly ground black pepper
3   garlic cloves, minced
1   tablespoon dry sherry
¼   cup all-purpose flour
2   cups 2% reduced-fat milk
1   cup (4 ounces) grated Asiago cheese, divided
Cooking spray
Thyme sprigs (optional)

1. Preheat oven to 375°.

2. Cook pasta according to package directions, omitting salt and fat. Drain well; set aside.

3. Melt butter in a large nonstick skillet over medium-high heat. Add shallots; sauté 3 minutes. Add mushrooms, thyme, salt, pepper, and garlic; sauté 8 minutes or until mushrooms are tender. Add sherry; cook 1 minute, stirring frequently. Remove from heat.

4. Place flour in a Dutch oven over medium-high heat; gradually add milk, stirring constantly with a whisk. Bring to a boil; cook 1 minute or until slightly thick, stirring constantly with a whisk. Remove from heat; add ½ cup cheese, stirring until melted. Add pasta and mushroom mixture to cheese mixture, tossing well to combine. Spoon pasta mixture into an 8-inch square baking dish lightly coated with cooking spray; sprinkle evenly with ½ cup cheese. Bake at 375° for 30 minutes or until cheese melts and begins to brown. Garnish with thyme sprigs, if desired. Yield: 4 servings (serving size: about 1½ cups).

CALORIES 474 (30% from fat); FAT 16g (sat 8g, mono 4.6g, poly 2.2g); PROTEIN 21.8g; CARB 61.4g; FIBER 3.3g; CHOL 40mg; IRON 3.9mg; SODIUM 745mg; CALC 386mg

Test Kitchen Tip: We prefer to use dry sherry rather than cooking sherry in recipes. Dry sherry has better flavor and is lower in sodium than cooking sherry.

Easy Ravioli Bake

This recipe pairs the convenience of store-bought pasta with a quick, easy homemade sauce. Chop the tomatoes right in the can, snipping them with kitchen scissors. We enjoyed chicken ravioli in this dish, although any variety will work.

Prep: 15 minutes • Cook: 40 minutes

 2 (9-ounce) packages refrigerated chicken ravioli (such as Monterey Pasta Company)
  Cooking spray
 1 cup chopped onion
 ½ cup chopped green bell pepper
 ½ teaspoon dried oregano
 4 garlic cloves, minced
 6 tablespoons tomato paste
 ¼ cup dry white wine or water
 ¾ teaspoon salt
 ½ teaspoon dried basil
 ¼ teaspoon crushed red pepper
 ⅛ teaspoon black pepper
 4 (14.5-ounce) cans no-salt-added whole tomatoes, undrained and chopped
 ½ cup (2 ounces) shredded part-skim mozzarella cheese

1. Cook pasta according to package directions, omitting salt and fat. Drain well.
2. Preheat oven to 400°.
3. Heat a Dutch oven over medium-high heat. Coat pan with cooking spray. Add onion, bell pepper, oregano, and garlic; sauté 5 minutes or until vegetables are tender. Add tomato paste and next 6 ingredients, stirring well to combine; bring to a boil. Reduce heat, and simmer 20 minutes, stirring frequently. Remove from heat. Add pasta to tomato mixture, tossing well to combine. Spoon pasta mixture into an 8-inch square baking dish lightly coated with cooking spray, and sprinkle evenly with cheese. Bake at 400° for 30 minutes or until cheese melts and begins to brown. Yield: 4 servings (serving size: about 1½ cups).

CALORIES 444 (27% from fat); FAT 13.3g (sat 7.8g, mono 3.3g, poly 1.1g); PROTEIN 21.9g; CARB 60.4g; FIBER 8g; CHOL 76mg; IRON 4.5mg; SODIUM 855mg; CALC 361mg

Spaghetti and Meatballs

We often think of spaghetti and meatballs as the quintessential authentic Italian dish. It's actually Italian-American—a cuisine born out of the early Italian immigrants adapting to the New World.

Prep: 25 minutes • Cook: 1 hour, 30 minutes

Sauce:
 5 (14.5-ounce) cans no-salt-added whole tomatoes, undrained
 1 tablespoon olive oil
 1 cup chopped onion
 1 teaspoon crushed red pepper
 ¾ teaspoon salt
 ¼ teaspoon freshly ground black pepper
 2 bay leaves
Meatballs:
 1 (1-ounce) slice white bread
 ⅓ cup (about 1½ ounces) grated Parmigiano-Reggiano cheese
 ¼ cup fat-free milk
 ¼ cup chopped fresh flat-leaf parsley
 ½ teaspoon salt
 ¼ teaspoon freshly ground black pepper
 1 pound ground sirloin
 2 garlic cloves, peeled and minced
 1 large egg white
  Cooking spray
Remaining ingredients:
 1 pound uncooked spaghetti
 ⅓ cup (about 1½ ounces) grated Parmigiano-Reggiano cheese

1. To prepare sauce, place half of tomatoes in a food processor, and process until smooth. Pour pureed tomatoes into a large bowl. Repeat procedure with remaining tomatoes.
2. Heat olive oil in a Dutch oven over medium heat. Add onion; sauté 4 minutes. Stir in pureed tomatoes, red pepper, salt, black pepper, and bay leaves; bring to a boil. Reduce heat, and simmer 30 minutes, stirring occasionally. Remove from heat. Discard bay leaves. Keep warm.
3. To prepare meatballs, preheat oven to 400°. Place bread in food processor; pulse 10 times or until coarse crumbs measure ½ cup. Combine breadcrumbs, ⅓ cup cheese, and next 7 ingredients. Shape mixture into 24 (1-inch) meatballs, and place on a broiler pan coated with cooking spray. Bake at 400° for 15 minutes or until done. Add meatballs to sauce; cook over low heat 15 minutes or until thoroughly heated.
4. Cook pasta according to package directions, omitting salt and fat. Drain pasta; return to pot. Spoon about 2 cups tomato sauce (leaving meatballs in pan) into pasta, and toss well to coat. Transfer pasta mixture to a platter; top with remaining sauce and meatballs. Sprinkle with ⅓ cup cheese. Yield: 8 servings (serving size: about ¾ cup pasta mixture, ½ cup sauce, and 3 meatballs).

CALORIES 394 (26% from fat); FAT 11.5g (sat 4.5g, mono 4.7g, poly 1g); PROTEIN 24.2g; CARB 47.9g; FIBER 3.8g; CHOL 44mg; IRON 4.2mg; SODIUM 612mg; CALC 193mg

Test Kitchen Tip: After adding the pasta to the water, put the lid on the pot, but prop it open slightly with a wooden spoon; the water won't boil over.

Baked Sesame Chicken Noodles

Asian vegetables, fresh ginger, and soy sauce imitate the taste of *lo mein*. Break the spaghetti in half before cooking to make it easier to prepare and serve.

Prep: 25 minutes • Cook: 46 minutes

8 ounces uncooked spaghetti or linguine, broken in half
1 tablespoon dark sesame oil
1 cup red bell pepper strips
8 ounces shiitake mushroom caps, sliced
2 (6-ounce) skinless, boneless chicken breast halves, cut into ½-inch pieces
1 teaspoon minced peeled fresh ginger
3 garlic cloves, minced
¼ cup low-sodium soy sauce
1 cup fat-free, less-sodium chicken broth
1 tablespoon cornstarch
2 tablespoons cream sherry
1 tablespoon rice vinegar
½ teaspoon crushed red pepper
2 cups thinly sliced bok choy
¾ cup sliced green onions
1 tablespoon sesame seeds, divided
Cooking spray
1 cup panko (Japanese) breadcrumbs
2 tablespoons butter, melted

1. Preheat oven to 400°.
2. Cook pasta according to package directions, omitting salt and fat. Drain well.

3. While pasta cooks, heat oil in a Dutch oven over medium-high heat. Add bell pepper and mushrooms; sauté 2 minutes. Add chicken, ginger, and garlic; sauté 3 minutes. Stir in soy sauce; cook 2 minutes, stirring frequently.
4. Combine broth and cornstarch, stirring well with a whisk. Add broth mixture to pan, and cook 2 minutes or until slightly thick, stirring constantly. Remove from heat; stir in sherry, vinegar, and crushed red pepper. Add pasta, bok choy, onions, and 2 teaspoons sesame seeds to pan, tossing well to combine. Spoon pasta mixture into an 8-inch square baking dish lightly coated with cooking spray.
5. Combine breadcrumbs, butter, and 1 teaspoon sesame seeds; sprinkle evenly over pasta mixture. Bake at 400° for 20 minutes or until breadcrumbs begin to brown. Yield: 4 servings (serving size: about 1½ cups).

CALORIES 505 (23% from fat); FAT 12.7g (sat 4.5g, mono 3.4g, poly 2.6g); PROTEIN 32.6g; CARB 60.5g; FIBER 4g; CHOL 65mg; IRON 8.1mg; SODIUM 936mg; CALC 92mg

Spaghettini with Oil and Garlic
(pictured on page 261)

In Italian, simple garlic and olive oil sauce is known as *aglio e olio*. Spaghettini is in between the sizes of vermicelli and spaghetti, so either of those is a good substitute.

Prep: 9 minutes • Cook: 20 minutes

6 quarts water
2¾ teaspoons salt, divided
1 pound uncooked spaghettini
2 tablespoons extravirgin olive oil
10 garlic cloves, sliced
½ cup chopped fresh flat-leaf parsley
½ teaspoon crushed red pepper
1 cup (4 ounces) grated Parmigiano-Reggiano cheese

1. Bring 6 quarts water and 2 teaspoons salt to a boil in a large stockpot. Stir in pasta, and return to a boil, stirring frequently. Cook 6 minutes or until pasta is almost al dente, stirring occasionally. Drain pasta in a colander over a bowl, reserving 1 cup cooking liquid.
2. While pasta cooks, heat oil in a large nonstick skillet over medium heat. Add garlic; cook 2 minutes or until fragrant and beginning to turn golden, stirring constantly. Remove from heat; stir in ¾ teaspoon salt, reserved 1 cup cooking liquid, parsley, and pepper.
3. Add pasta to pan; stir to coat. Return pan to medium heat; cook 1 minute or until pasta is al dente, tossing to coat. Sprinkle with cheese. Yield: 8 servings (serving size: 1 cup pasta and 2 tablespoons cheese).

CALORIES 303 (24% from fat); FAT 8g (sat 2.9g, mono 3.7g, poly 0.8g); PROTEIN 12.7g; CARB 44.4g; FIBER 1.6g; CHOL 10mg; IRON 2.6mg; SODIUM 603mg; CALC 190mg

Pasta Primavera

To keep the prosciutto from sticking together in the pasta, lay it out on a plate to dry after you chop it.

Prep: 25 minutes • Cook: 28 minutes

  12 ounces uncooked vermicelli
2½ cups (3-inch) diagonally sliced
       asparagus (about 1 pound)
1½ cups shelled green peas (about
       1½ pounds unshelled)
   1 tablespoon olive oil, divided
   2 cups diced zucchini
   ½ cup sliced green onions
   1 cup fat-free, less-sodium chicken broth
   ⅓ cup dry white wine
   2 tablespoons minced fresh basil
   2 tablespoons minced fresh oregano
   ½ teaspoon kosher salt
   ¼ teaspoon pepper
   2 ounces thinly sliced prosciutto or
       ham, chopped
   ¾ cup (3 ounces) grated Asiago cheese

1. Bring water to a boil in a large Dutch oven, and add pasta. Cook pasta 5 minutes. Add asparagus, and cook 2 minutes. Add peas, and cook 1 minute. Drain well.
2. Heat 2 teaspoons oil in a large nonstick skillet over medium-high heat. Add zucchini; sauté 5 minutes. Add onions; sauté 1 minute. Add broth and wine; bring to a boil. Stir in pasta mixture, basil, and oregano; cook 1 minute. Remove from heat; stir in 1 teaspoon oil, salt, pepper, and prosciutto. Spoon pasta mixture into 8 shallow bowls; top each serving with cheese. Yield: 8 servings (serving size: 1¼ cups pasta mixture and 1½ tablespoons cheese).

CALORIES 269 (21% from fat); FAT 6.2g (sat 2.4g, mono 2.5g, poly 0.7g); PROTEIN 13.8g; CARB 40g; FIBER 3.2g; CHOL 15mg; IRON 3.1mg; SODIUM 448mg; CALC 154mg

Ziti with Sausage, Onions, and Fennel

Keep more than 3 cups of the pasta cooking water to adjust the sauce. If the pasta appears dry, ladle in more cooking water.

Prep: 20 minutes • Cook: 32 minutes

   1 (1¼-pound) fennel bulb with stalks
   6 quarts water
2¼ teaspoons salt, divided
   1 pound uncooked ziti (short, tube-
       shaped pasta)
   1 tablespoon olive oil
   1 pound sweet Italian sausage
   2 cups (¼-inch-thick) onion wedges
       (about 2 medium)
   ½ teaspoon crushed red pepper
   ¼ cup tomato paste
   ¼ cup (1 ounce) grated fresh pecorino
       Romano cheese

1. Trim fennel, reserving fronds and bulb. Cut bulb in half lengthwise; cut each bulb half lengthwise into (¼-inch-thick) slices. Cut bulb slices into 2-inch-long pieces. Chop fennel fronds to measure ⅓ cup.
2. Bring 6 quarts water and 2 teaspoons salt to a boil in a large stockpot. Stir in pasta, and return to a boil, stirring frequently. Cook 8 minutes or until pasta is almost al dente, stirring occasionally. Drain pasta in a colander over a bowl, reserving 3 cups cooking liquid.
3. While pasta cooks, heat oil in a large Dutch oven over medium-high heat. Remove sausage from casings. Add sausage to Dutch oven; cook 2 minutes or until lightly browned, stirring to crumble. Push sausage to one side of pan. Add onion to open space in pan; cook 1 minute or until onion begins to soften. Stir onion into sausage. Push onion mixture to one side of pan. Add fennel bulb to open space in pan; cook 1 minute or until fennel begins to soften. Stir fennel into onion mixture. Stir in pepper and ¼ teaspoon salt; cook 1 minute. Move sausage and fennel mixture to outside edges of pan, leaving an open space in center. Add tomato paste to open space in pan; cook 1 minute, stirring constantly. Stir tomato paste into fennel mixture.
4. Add 3 cups reserved cooking liquid to pan; bring to a boil. Reduce heat, and simmer 6 minutes or until fennel is tender. Add fennel fronds and pasta; cook 2 minutes or until pasta is al dente, tossing to combine. Remove from heat; stir in cheese. Serve immediately. Yield: 8 servings (serving size: about 1¾ cups).

CALORIES 352 (21% from fat); FAT 8.3g (sat 2.9g, mono 3.6g, poly 0.5g); PROTEIN 19g; CARB 51.7g; FIBER 3.8g; CHOL 20mg; IRON 3.2mg; SODIUM 669mg; CALC 88mg

how to sauté multiple ingredients

By moving ingredients to one side and adding a new ingredient in the open space, each can be sautéed in direct contact with the pan to achieve the right browning, instead of steaming in the mass of ingredients.

Vegetarian Pad Thai

We love this meatless version of Thailand's popular noodle dish.

Prep: 20 minutes • Cook: 25 minutes

- ⅔ cup chili sauce (such as Heinz)
- ¼ cup packed brown sugar
- 2 tablespoons water
- 2 tablespoons fish sauce
- 1½ teaspoons grated peeled fresh ginger
- 1 teaspoon chopped seeded serrano chile
- ½ pound uncooked wide rice stick noodles (*bánh pho*)
- 4 teaspoons canola oil, divided
- 1 (12.3-ounce) package extrafirm tofu, drained and cut into ½-inch cubes
- 2 large egg whites
- 1 large egg
- 3 garlic cloves, minced
- 2 cups fresh bean sprouts
- ¾ cup diagonally cut green onions
- ½ cup minced fresh cilantro, divided
- ⅓ cup coarsely chopped dry-roasted peanuts
- 6 lime wedges

1. Combine first 6 ingredients; set aside.
2. Cook noodles in boiling water 5 minutes or until done. Drain and rinse with cold water; drain well.
3. Heat 2 teaspoons oil in a large nonstick skillet over medium heat. Add tofu; cook 7 minutes or until browned, stirring occasionally. Remove from pan.
4. Combine egg whites and egg, stirring well with a whisk.
5. Heat 2 teaspoons oil in pan over medium-high heat. Add garlic, and sauté 10 seconds. Add egg mixture, and cook 30 seconds or until soft-scrambled, stirring constantly. Stir in chili sauce mixture and noodles; cook 2 minutes. Stir in tofu, bean sprouts, onions, and ¼ cup cilantro, and cook 3 minutes or until thoroughly heated.
6. Sprinkle ¼ cup cilantro and peanuts over noodle mixture. Serve with lime wedges. Yield: 6 servings (serving size: 1⅓ cups noodle mixture, 2 teaspoons cilantro, about 1 teaspoon peanuts, and 1 lime wedge).

CALORIES 347 (25% from fat); FAT 9.6g (sat 1.6g, mono 3.5g, poly 3.5g); PROTEIN 10.9g; CARB 56.7g; FIBER 2.5g; CHOL 37mg; IRON 2.4mg; SODIUM 935mg; CALC 80mg

Soba with Sesame and Tofu

Soba are Japanese noodles made from buckwheat and wheat flour. Because of their dark brownish-gray color and slightly nutty flavor, there isn't a suitable substitute for them.

Prep: 20 minutes • Cook: 13 minutes

- 8 ounces uncooked soba
- ⅓ cup low-sodium soy sauce
- 2 tablespoons rice vinegar
- 1 tablespoon minced peeled fresh ginger
- 1 teaspoon sugar
- 1½ teaspoons dark sesame oil
- ½ teaspoon chili oil or canola oil
- 1½ tablespoons sesame seeds
- 2 cups sliced peeled cucumber
- 1 cup thinly sliced green onions
- 2 cups cubed firm tofu (about 12 ounces)

1. Cook noodles according to package directions, omitting salt and fat. Drain.
2. Combine soy sauce and next 5 ingredients in a small bowl; set aside.
3. Cook sesame seeds in a small saucepan over medium heat 1 minute or until toasted.
4. Combine sesame seeds, noodles, cucumber, and onions in a large bowl; toss gently. Place mixture in bowls; top with tofu and sauce. Yield: 4 servings (serving size: 1 cup noodles, ½ cup tofu, and 2 tablespoons sauce).

CALORIES 310 (24% from fat); FAT 8.4g (sat 1.2g, mono 2.4g, poly 4.2g); PROTEIN 18.3g; CARB 46.3g; FIBER 2.2g; CHOL 0mg; IRON 6.8mg; SODIUM 844mg; CALC 159mg

Vegetarian Pad Thai

meatless
main dishes

Rustic Grilled Pizza,
page 305

Legumes & Vegetables

Beans, peas, lentils, and a variety of garden-fresh vegetables are the stars of these protein-packed meals.

Vegetable and Chickpea Curry

Aromatic Indian spices mingle with chickpeas, green beans, and potatoes. Coconut milk provides a creamy finish. Serve the hearty mixture over couscous.

Prep: 20 minutes • Cook: 6 hours, 7 minutes

    1   tablespoon olive oil
 1½   cups chopped onion
    1   cup (¼-inch-thick) slices carrot
    1   tablespoon curry powder
    1   teaspoon brown sugar
    1   teaspoon grated peeled fresh ginger
    2   garlic cloves, minced
    1   serrano chile, seeded and minced
    2   (15-ounce) cans chickpeas (garbanzo
        beans), rinsed and drained
 1½   cups cubed peeled baking potato
    1   cup diced green bell pepper
    1   cup (1-inch) cut green beans
   ¼   teaspoon black pepper
   ⅛   teaspoon ground red pepper
    1   (14.5-ounce) can diced tomatoes,
        undrained
    1   (14-ounce) can vegetable broth
    3   cups fresh baby spinach
    1   cup light coconut milk
    4   lemon wedges

1. Heat oil in a large nonstick skillet over medium heat. Add onion and carrot; cover and cook 5 minutes or until tender. Add curry powder, sugar, ginger, garlic, and chile; cook 1 minute, stirring constantly.
2. Place onion mixture in a 5-quart electric slow cooker. Stir in chickpeas and next

7 ingredients. Cover and cook on HIGH 6 hours or until vegetables are tender. Add spinach and coconut milk; stir until spinach wilts. Serve with lemon wedges. Yield: 4 servings (serving size: 2 cups vegetable mixture and 1 lemon wedge).

CALORIES 338 (26% from fat); FAT 9.8g (sat 3.5g, mono 3.7g, poly 2.3g); PROTEIN 10.7g; CARB 57g; FIBER 12.5g; CHOL 0mg; IRON 4.7mg; SODIUM 847mg; CALC 139mg

Thyme-Scented White Bean Cassoulet

Buttery breadcrumbs stirred in at the end give this dish a stewlike consistency.

Prep: 20 minutes • Cook: 8 hours, 7 minutes

    1   tablespoon olive oil
 1½   cups chopped onion
 1½   cups (½-inch-thick) slices carrot
    1   cup (½-inch-thick) slices parsnip
    2   garlic cloves, minced
    2   (15-ounce) cans Great Northern
        beans, rinsed and drained
   ¾   cup vegetable broth
   ½   teaspoon dried thyme
   ¼   teaspoon pepper
    1   (28-ounce) can diced tomatoes,
        undrained
    1   bay leaf
   ¼   cup dry breadcrumbs
   ¼   cup (1 ounce) grated fresh Parmesan
        cheese
    2   tablespoons butter, melted
    2   links meatless Italian sausage (such
        as Boca), thawed and chopped
    2   tablespoons chopped fresh parsley

1. Heat oil in a large nonstick skillet over medium heat. Add onion, carrot, parsnip, and garlic; cover and cook 5 minutes or until tender.
2. Place vegetable mixture in a 5-quart electric slow cooker. Stir in beans and next 5 ingredients. Cover and cook on LOW 8 hours or until vegetables are tender.
3. Combine breadcrumbs, cheese, and butter in a small bowl; toss with a fork until moist. Stir breadcrumb mixture and sausage into bean mixture; sprinkle with parsley. Yield: 6 servings (serving size: 1⅓ cups).

CALORIES 314 (29% from fat); FAT 10.2g (sat 3.7g, mono 3.7g, poly 1.7g); PROTEIN 16.4g; CARB 41.9g; FIBER 11.6g; CHOL 13mg; IRON 3.6mg; SODIUM 777mg; CALC 177mg

slow cooker tips

- Be sure your cooker is between half and three-fourths full before starting.
- Many recipes benefit when you sauté some of the ingredients (such as onions) for a few minutes before adding them to the slow cooker. Doing so enhances the flavors and ensures that all the components of the dish will be done at the same time.
- Add delicate ingredients, such as fresh herbs, at the end of cooking.
- Prepare starchy ingredients such as pasta and rice separately; they can become gummy when cooked in the slow cooker.
- Don't peek. When you lift the lid, you lose heat (about 20 minutes), and that will slow down your cooking time.

White Bean, Artichoke, and Chard Ragoût with Fennel Relish

A crisp topping of raw fennel and bell peppers complements the mellowness of this slow-simmered stew.

**Prep: 35 minutes • Cook: 8 hours, 8 minutes
Other: 45 minutes**

Ragoût:

  1 tablespoon olive oil
  3 cups thinly sliced leek (about 2 large)
  1 cup (½-inch-thick) slices carrot
  3 garlic cloves, minced
  2 (15-ounce) cans cannellini beans, rinsed and drained
2½ cups chopped fennel bulb (about 1 large)
  2 cups (½-inch) cubed red potatoes
  1 cup chopped red bell pepper
 ¾ cup water
  1 teaspoon dried basil
 ¼ teaspoon dried oregano
 ¼ teaspoon black pepper
  1 (14.5-ounce) can diced tomatoes with basil, garlic, and oregano, drained
  1 (14-ounce) can vegetable broth
  1 (9-ounce) package frozen artichoke hearts, thawed
  2 cups chopped Swiss chard

Fennel Relish:

  1 cup boiling water
  6 sun-dried tomatoes, packed without oil
  3 cups shredded fennel bulb (about 1 large)
  1 cup diced yellow bell pepper
 ¼ cup chopped fresh parsley
  1 tablespoon fresh lemon juice
  2 teaspoons olive oil
 ½ teaspoon sugar
 ¼ teaspoon salt
 ⅛ teaspoon black pepper

1. To prepare ragoût, heat 1 tablespoon oil in a large nonstick skillet over medium heat. Add leek, carrot, and garlic; cover and cook 5 minutes or until tender.
2. Place leek mixture in a 5-quart electric slow cooker. Stir in beans and next 10 ingredients. Cover and cook on HIGH 8 hours or until vegetables are tender. Add chard; stir until chard wilts.
3. To prepare relish, combine boiling water and sun-dried tomatoes; let stand 15 minutes or until soft. Drain; chop.

Combine sun-dried tomatoes and remaining ingredients; let stand 30 minutes. Yield: 6 servings (serving size: 2 cups ragoût and about ½ cup relish).

CALORIES 290 (16% from fat); FAT 5.3g (sat 0.8g, mono 2.8g, poly 0.7g); PROTEIN 13.6g; CARB 52.4g; FIBER 15.6g; CHOL 0mg; IRON 5.5mg; SODIUM 796mg; CALC 191mg

Test Kitchen Tip: You can make and refrigerate the relish up to a day ahead.

Potato-Black Bean Cakes with Tropical Dressing over Greens

A cross between skillet potato cakes and black bean patties, these little cakes are served over salad greens and topped with a sweet rum dressing.

Prep: 35 minutes • Cook: 39 minutes

Potato cakes:

 1   tablespoon olive oil
 ¼   cup chopped onion
 1   tablespoon minced seeded serrano chile or jalapeño pepper
 1   garlic clove, minced
 ⅓   cup 2% reduced-fat milk
 ½   teaspoon salt
 1   (15-ounce) can black beans, rinsed and drained
 1   large egg white
 2   cups shredded peeled baking potato (about 2 potatoes)
     Cooking spray

Tropical Dressing over Greens:

 1   cup pineapple juice
 ½   cup finely chopped onion
 3   tablespoons brown sugar
 2   tablespoons white rum or water
 1   tablespoon fresh lime juice
 1   tablespoon chopped pecans, toasted
 2   bacon slices, cooked and crumbled
 6   cups gourmet salad greens

1. To prepare potato cakes, heat oil in a large nonstick skillet over medium-high heat. Add ¼ cup onion, chile, and garlic; sauté 3 minutes. Place onion mixture, milk, salt, beans, and egg white in a food processor; process until smooth, scraping sides of bowl once. Stir in potato.

2. Heat pan over medium-high heat. Coat pan with cooking spray. Spoon 1 tablespoon potato mixture per cake into pan, spreading each to form a 2-inch circle; cook 2 minutes or until lightly browned. Carefully turn cakes over; cook 2 minutes on other side. Keep cakes warm.

3. To prepare dressing, combine pineapple juice and next 4 ingredients in a saucepan; bring to a boil. Reduce heat; simmer 5 minutes. Stir in pecans and bacon.

4. Arrange salad greens on plates. Arrange potato cakes around greens. Drizzle warm dressing over each serving. Yield: 6 servings (serving size: 1 cup greens, 4 potato cakes, and ¼ cup dressing).

CALORIES 213 (20% from fat); FAT 4.8g (sat 0.9g, mono 2.8g, poly 0.8g); PROTEIN 7.3g; CARB 35.5g; FIBER 5.9g; CHOL 3mg; IRON 2.2mg; SODIUM 394mg; CALC 85mg

Black Bean Burrito Bake

This dish can be made up to eight hours in advance and chilled; just bring it back to room temperature before baking.

Prep: 13 minutes • Cook: 20 minutes
Other: 10 minutes

 1   (7-ounce) can chipotle chiles in adobo sauce
 ½   cup reduced-fat sour cream
 1   (15-ounce) can black beans, rinsed, drained, and divided
 1   cup frozen whole-kernel corn, thawed
 4   (8-inch) flour tortillas
     Cooking spray
 1   cup bottled salsa
 ½   cup (2 ounces) shredded Monterey Jack cheese

1. Preheat oven to 350°.

2. Remove one chile from can; chop chile. (Reserve remaining adobo sauce and chiles for another use.) Combine sour cream and chopped chile in a medium bowl; let stand 10 minutes.

3. Place half of beans in a food processor; process until finely chopped. Add chopped beans, remaining beans, and corn to sour cream mixture.

4. Spoon ½ cup bean mixture down center of each tortilla. Roll up tortillas; place, seam sides down, in an 11 x 7–inch baking dish coated with cooking spray. Spread salsa over tortillas; sprinkle with cheese. Cover and bake at 350° for 20 minutes or until thoroughly heated. Yield: 4 servings (serving size: 1 burrito).

CALORIES 365 (29% from fat); FAT 11.7g (sat 5.8g, mono 2.8g, poly 0.8g); PROTEIN 15.7g; CARB 55.3g; FIBER 7.2g; CHOL 28mg; IRON 3.5mg; SODIUM 893mg; CALC 311mg

canned beans Canned beans are versatile, adaptable, and a great source of nonmeat protein. They're high in fiber and essentially fat-free. In many recipes, the beans are interchangeable, so you can use any type you choose: black, kidney, navy, Northern, or pinto.

We like the convenience of canned beans, but you can substitute dried if you prefer. (One pound of dried beans yields about 5½ to 6½ cups cooked beans.) If you're limiting the sodium in your diet, you can use no-salt and low-sodium canned beans. Also, rinsing regular canned beans reduces the sodium by 40 percent.

Black Bean Tacos with Avocado Salsa

Seitan, sometimes called "wheat meat," is a protein-rich food made from wheat gluten. It has a firm, chewy, almost "meatlike" texture and a neutral flavor. Look for it in foil- or plastic-wrapped cakes or plastic tubs in the refrigerated sections of health-food stores or Asian markets.

Prep: 27 minutes • Cook: 24 minutes

2   teaspoons olive oil
¾   cup chopped onion
½   teaspoon dried oregano
2   garlic cloves, minced
1   jalapeño pepper, seeded and minced
1   tablespoon dry sherry
1   tablespoon low-sodium soy sauce
1   (15-ounce) can black beans, undrained
1   (8-ounce) package seitan (wheat gluten), finely chopped
½   teaspoon black pepper
12 taco shells
2   cups shredded romaine lettuce
Avocado Salsa (page 456)

1. Heat oil in a large nonstick skillet over medium heat. Add onion, oregano, garlic, and jalapeño; cook 8 minutes, stirring frequently. Stir in sherry, soy sauce, beans, and seitan; bring to a boil. Cook 7 minutes or until almost all liquid is evaporated. Sprinkle with black pepper.
2. Prepare taco shells according to package directions.
3. Spoon about ⅓ cup bean mixture into each shell; top each taco with about 2½ tablespoons lettuce and about 2½ tablespoons Avocado Salsa. Yield: 6 servings (serving size: 2 tacos).

(Totals include Avocado Salsa) CALORIES 283 (30% from fat); FAT 9.3g (sat 1.2g, mono 5.7g, poly 1.6g); PROTEIN 20.4g; CARB 30.0g; FIBER 7.6g; CHOL 0mg; IRON 2.8mg; SODIUM 792mg; CALC 58mg

Curried Kidney Bean Burritos

A hint of curry distinguishes these burritos from the usual Tex-Mex fare.

Prep: 12 minutes • Cook: 21 minutes

1   tablespoon olive oil
1½ cups finely chopped onion
1   tablespoon chopped jalapeño pepper
1   teaspoon sugar
½   teaspoon curry powder
2   (14.5-ounce) cans diced tomatoes, drained
2   (15-ounce) cans kidney beans, rinsed and drained
1   tablespoon minced fresh cilantro
4   (8-inch) flour tortillas

1. Heat oil in a large nonstick skillet over medium-high heat. Add onion; sauté 6 minutes or until lightly browned. Add jalapeño, sugar, curry, and tomatoes; cover, reduce heat, and simmer 10 minutes. Add beans; cover and cook 3 minutes or until thoroughly heated, stirring occasionally. Remove from heat; stir in cilantro.
2. Warm tortillas according to package directions. Spoon 1¼ cups bean mixture down center of each tortilla, and roll up. Yield: 4 servings (serving size: 1 burrito).

CALORIES 414 (17% from fat); FAT 8.0g (sat 1.6g, mono 3.1g, poly 2.7g); PROTEIN 18.4g; CARB 70.3g; FIBER 9.2g; CHOL 0mg; IRON 6.4mg; SODIUM 710mg; CALC 182mg

Lentils with Eggplant and Garam Masala

Garam masala is a combination of ten or more spices that are dry roasted and ground into this blend used to add "heat" to Indian-style dishes. Cook the basmati rice while the lentil mixture simmers.

Prep: 15 minutes • Cook: 1 hour

  2 teaspoons olive oil
  1 cup chopped onion
1½ teaspoons garam masala
  1 cup chopped tomato
  1 teaspoon ground turmeric
  1 teaspoon grated peeled fresh ginger
  2 garlic cloves, minced
  1 (1-pound) eggplant, peeled and chopped
  1 cup dried lentils
  4 cups water
1½ teaspoons salt
  2 bay leaves
  2 cups chopped zucchini
4½ cups hot cooked basmati rice

1. Heat olive oil in a Dutch oven over medium-high heat. Add onion and garam masala; sauté 3 minutes or until onion is tender. Stir in tomato, turmeric, ginger, garlic, and eggplant; sauté 7 minutes or until eggplant is tender.
2. Add lentils, water, salt, and bay leaves to pan; bring to a boil. Cover, reduce heat, and simmer 15 minutes. Stir in zucchini; bring to a boil. Reduce heat, and simmer 10 minutes or until zucchini is tender. Discard bay leaves. Serve over rice. Yield: 6 servings (serving size: 1¼ cups lentil mixture and ¾ cup rice).

CALORIES 447 (7% from fat); FAT 3.3g (sat 0.6g, mono 1.5g, poly 0.8g); PROTEIN 17g; CARB 90.6g; FIBER 12.4g; CHOL 0mg; IRON 4.5mg; SODIUM 587mg; CALC 56mg

Greek-Style Stuffed Eggplant

Leave about ¼ inch eggplant pulp in the shells when you hollow them out. If you're not an eggplant fan, substitute zucchini and reduce the microwave cooking time to three minutes.

Prep: 22 minutes • Cook: 19 minutes

  2 eggplants, cut in half lengthwise
  ¼ cup water
     Cooking spray
  1 cup chopped onion
  1 cup chopped plum tomato
  ¼ cup white wine
  3 garlic cloves, minced
  1 cup (4 ounces) crumbled feta cheese
  ½ cup chopped fresh parsley, divided
  ¾ teaspoon salt, divided
  ¼ teaspoon freshly ground black pepper
  2 (1-ounce) slices French bread
  2 tablespoons grated fresh Parmesan cheese

1. Carefully remove pulp from each eggplant, reserving shells. Coarsely chop pulp to measure 6 cups. Place eggplant shells, cut sides down, in a 10-inch square baking dish. Add ¼ cup water to dish. Cover and microwave at HIGH 5 minutes or until shells are tender. Keep warm.
2. Preheat broiler.
3. Heat a large nonstick skillet over medium-high heat. Coat pan with cooking spray. Add eggplant pulp; sauté 7 minutes. Add onion; sauté 2 minutes. Stir in tomato, wine, and garlic; cook 3 minutes or until liquid almost evaporates, stirring occasionally. Remove from heat; add feta, ¼ cup parsley, ½ teaspoon salt, and pepper, stirring to combine. Spoon ¾ cup eggplant mixture into each eggplant shell.

4. Place bread slices in food processor; pulse 10 times or until coarse crumbs measure 1 cup. Combine breadcrumbs, ¼ cup parsley, ¼ teaspoon salt, and Parmesan, stirring well. Sprinkle ¼ cup breadcrumb mixture over each stuffed shell. Arrange shells on a baking sheet coated with cooking spray; broil 2 minutes or until lightly browned. Yield: 4 servings (serving size: 1 stuffed eggplant half).

CALORIES 250 (30% from fat); FAT 8.4g (sat 5.1g, mono 1.6g, poly 0.6g); PROTEIN 11.3g; CARB 35.3g; FIBER 10.3g; CHOL 29mg; IRON 2.3mg; SODIUM 906mg; CALC 246mg

about eggplant With its colorful, tough skin and meaty, spongy flesh, eggplant is more versatile than you might think. It can be sliced, grilled, mashed, pureed, or sautéed. Because it has a mild flavor, it can take on the flavors of more assertive ingredients such as garlic, tomato, and sharp cheeses.

The eggplant season ranges from summer to early fall. Out-of-season eggplants can be bitter. A fresh eggplant has a sparkling, jewel-like complexion with shiny, smooth, tight skin and a bright green stem. No matter the size, it should feel heavy in your hand (this indicates fully developed flesh and small, underdeveloped seeds). Spongy, dull-skinned eggplants are old. Eggplants come in a variety of sizes and colors, the most common being the large, dark-purple American eggplant. Store eggplants in a cool place, and use them within two days.

Mushroom-Crepe Cannelloni

Instead of stuffing a pasta tube, we've spooned the mushroom filling into crepes, rolled them up, and topped them with tomatoes and a cheesy sauce. The prep and cook time include the time for making 8 Basic Crepes. If you've made the crepes ahead of time, the prep time will be 22 minutes and the cook time will be 30 minutes.

Prep: 27 minutes • Cook: 46 minutes

Mushroom filling:

- 1 teaspoon olive oil
- 2 (8-ounce) packages mushrooms, coarsely chopped
- 1 teaspoon dried oregano
- 1 garlic clove, minced
- ¼ cup dry white wine
- 1 tablespoon tomato paste
- 1 teaspoon all-purpose flour
- ½ cup (2 ounces) part-skim ricotta cheese
- 1 tablespoon (¼ ounce) grated fresh Parmesan cheese
- ½ teaspoon salt
- Dash of black pepper

Parmesan sauce:

- 3 tablespoons all-purpose flour
- 1¼ cups 1% low-fat milk
- ¼ teaspoon salt
- ⅛ teaspoon ground nutmeg
- 2 tablespoons (½ ounce) grated fresh Parmesan cheese

Cannelloni:

- 8 Basic Crepes (page 112)
- Cooking spray
- 1 (14.5-ounce) can no-salt-added diced tomatoes, drained
- 1 tablespoon (¼ ounce) grated fresh Parmesan cheese
- Chopped parsley (optional)

1. To prepare mushroom filling, heat oil in a large nonstick skillet over medium-high heat. Add mushrooms; cook 5 minutes, stirring occasionally. Add oregano and garlic; sauté 1 minute. Add wine, and cook 3 minutes or until liquid evaporates. Stir in tomato paste and 1 teaspoon flour. Remove from heat, and cool. Stir in ricotta cheese, 1 tablespoon Parmesan, ½ teaspoon salt, and black pepper.

2. To prepare Parmesan sauce, place 3 tablespoons flour in a small saucepan. Gradually add milk, stirring with a whisk until blended. Stir in ¼ teaspoon salt and nutmeg. Place over medium heat; cook until thick (about 3 minutes), stirring constantly. Remove from heat; stir in 2 tablespoons Parmesan. Keep warm.

3. Preheat oven to 425°.

4. To prepare cannelloni, spoon ¼ cup mushroom mixture in center of each crepe; roll up. Place, seam sides down, in each of 4 gratin dishes or in a 13 x 9–inch baking dish coated with cooking spray. Spoon half of tomatoes over crepes, and top with Parmesan sauce and remaining tomatoes. Sprinkle with 1 tablespoon Parmesan. Bake at 425° for 15 minutes. Preheat broiler (do not remove dish from oven). Broil 3 minutes or until cheese is lightly browned. Garnish with parsley, if desired. Yield: 4 servings (serving size: 2 cannelloni).

(Totals include Basic Crepes) CALORIES 266 (28% from fat); FAT 8.3g (sat 4.9g, mono 3.3g,poly 0.7g); PROTEIN 17.6g; CARB 31.8g; FIBER 2.3g; CHOL 63mg; IRON 3.4mg; SODIUM 832mg; CALC 353mg

Stuffed Portobello Mushrooms with Olives and Caramelized Onions

Bake the mushrooms on a rack over a pan to catch breadcrumbs that may fall.

Prep: 25 minutes • Cook: 1 hour, 15 minutes

  2 teaspoons olive oil
  4 cups finely chopped sweet onion
  ½ cup dry red wine
  1 tablespoon balsamic vinegar
  2 teaspoons finely chopped fresh
    thyme, divided
  ¼ teaspoon sea salt
  ¾ cup chopped pitted kalamata olives
  1 teaspoon grated lemon rind
  ¼ teaspoon pepper
  4 (4-inch) portobello mushroom caps
Cooking spray
  2 (1-ounce) slices white bread
  ⅓ cup (about 1½ ounces) grated fresh
    Parmesan cheese
  ¼ cup finely chopped fresh parsley

1. Heat oil in a large nonstick skillet over medium-high heat. Add onion; sauté 12 minutes. Stir in wine, vinegar, 1 teaspoon thyme, and salt; bring to a boil. Cover, reduce heat, and simmer 25 minutes. Uncover and increase heat to medium-high; cook 5 minutes or until liquid evaporates. Stir in olives, rind, and pepper.
2. Preheat oven to 350°.
3. Remove stem and brown gills from undersides of mushrooms using a spoon; discard gills. Place mushrooms, stem sides down, on a baking sheet coated with cooking spray. Bake at 350° for 10 minutes; cool mushrooms on a wire rack.
4. Place bread in a food processor; pulse 10 times or until coarse crumbs measure 1 cup. Combine 1 teaspoon thyme, crumbs, cheese, and parsley. Spoon ½ cup onion

mixture into each mushroom, and top with about ¼ cup breadcrumb mixture. Bake at 350° for 20 to 25 minutes or until golden brown. Yield: 4 servings (serving size: 1 stuffed mushroom).

CALORIES 202 (32% from fat); FAT 7.3g (sat 2g, mono 4.3g, poly 0.8g); PROTEIN 5.9g; CARB 27.6g; FIBER 4.1g; CHOL 5mg; IRON 1.9mg; SODIUM 573mg; CALC 169mg

Mushroom Tamales

Making tamales is a holiday ritual in many Latino cultures, and it's more fun with friends and family. Prepare the filling and dough a day ahead to simplify preparation.

Prep: 1 hour • Cook: 2 hours, 28 minutes
Other: 1 hour, 5 minutes

Filling:
  4 garlic cloves, unpeeled
  3 pasilla chiles, stemmed and seeded
  ¼ cup dried porcini mushrooms
    (about ¼ ounce)
  3 sun-dried tomatoes, packed without
    oil
  2 cups boiling water
  1 large ripe tomato
Cooking spray
  ½ cup finely chopped onion
  2 cups chopped portobello mushroom
    caps (about 4 ounces)
  ½ teaspoon dried oregano
  1½ tablespoons chopped fresh cilantro
  1 tablespoon fresh lime juice
  ½ teaspoon salt
  20 large dried cornhusks
Dough:
  ⅔ cup fresh corn kernels
  2½ cups coarse-ground masa harina
  1 teaspoon baking powder
  ½ teaspoon salt
  2¼ cups warm vegetable broth, divided
  3 tablespoons vegetable shortening

1. To prepare filling, heat a large cast-iron skillet over medium heat. Add garlic; cook 15 minutes or until blackened, turning occasionally. Remove garlic from pan. Cool and peel.
2. Add chiles to pan; flatten with spatula. Cook 20 seconds on each side or until blackened.
3. Place chiles, porcini, and sun-dried tomatoes in a large bowl. Pour boiling water over chile mixture. Cover and let stand 30 minutes or until tender. Drain in a colander over a bowl, reserving 2½ tablespoons soaking liquid. Place garlic, chile mixture, and reserved liquid in a food processor; process 1 minute or until smooth. Set aside.
4. Heat pan over medium heat. Add large tomato, and cook 15 minutes or until blackened, turning frequently. Remove tomato from pan, and cool slightly. Peel, core, and chop tomato. Wipe pan clean with paper towels; heat pan over medium-high heat. Coat pan with cooking spray. Add onion, and sauté 4 minutes or until tender. Stir in chile mixture, chopped tomato, portobello mushrooms, and oregano; cook over medium heat 15 minutes or until thick. Stir in cilantro, lime juice, and ½ teaspoon salt; set aside.
5. Place cornhusks in a large bowl of hot water; weigh down husks with another bowl. Soak at least 30 minutes. Drain husks; rinse with cold water. Drain and pat dry. Tear 4 cornhusks lengthwise into 16 (½-inch-wide) strips.
6. To prepare dough, place corn in a food processor; process until smooth. Combine masa, baking powder, and ½ teaspoon salt. Add 2 cups broth; stir until well blended. Place shortening in a large bowl, and beat with a mixer at medium speed 1 minute or until fluffy. Add pureed corn

Mushroom
Tamales

1. Spread 3 tablespoons dough in the center of the cornhusk, leaving a small border.

2. Make sure the dough seals around the filling as you roll.

3. Fold up the tapered end, and tie with a cornhusk strip.

and ¼ cup broth; beat at medium speed until well blended. Add masa mixture; beat 2 minutes or until well blended.

7. Open 1 cornhusk, curved side up. Place 3 tablespoons dough in center of husk, and spread evenly into a 4 x 2–inch rectangle. Arrange about 1½ tablespoons filling down center of dough. Take one long side of husk, and roll dough around filling, making sure dough seals around filling. Fold empty tapered end of husk over bundle. Tie 1 husk strip around tamale and over folded end to secure (top of tamale will be open). Repeat procedure with remaining husks, dough, filling, and husk strips.

8. Stand tamales upright (open end up) in a vegetable steamer in a large Dutch oven. Add water to pan to a depth of 1 inch;

bring water to a boil. Cover and steam tamales 1½ hours or until husks pull away cleanly; add additional water to bottom of pan as necessary. Remove tamales from steamer, and let stand 5 minutes. Remove tamales from cornhusks. Yield: 8 servings (serving size: 2 tamales).

CALORIES 242 (29% from fat); FAT 7.7g (sat 1.5g, mono 2.6g, poly 2.4g); PROTEIN 6.9g; CARB 40.4g; FIBER 5.5g; CHOL 0mg; IRON 2.7mg; SODIUM 648mg; CALC 119mg

Test Kitchen Tip: Coarse-ground masa harina, available at Latin markets and in some large supermarkets, gives the best texture to the tamales. Dried pasilla chiles are medium-hot and contribute some heat to the dish.

Barley-Stuffed Cabbage Rolls with Pine Nuts and Currants

Assemble this dish the night before for a start on the next day's dinner. You can also cook the rolls on LOW for six to eight hours.

**Prep: 25 minutes • Cook: 2 hours, 28 minutes
Other: 5 minutes**

   1   cup uncooked quick-cooking barley
   2   cups water
   1   large head green cabbage, cored
   1   tablespoon olive oil
1½   cups finely chopped onion
 ¾   cup (3 ounces) crumbled feta cheese
 ½   cup dried currants
   2   tablespoons pine nuts, toasted
   2   tablespoons chopped fresh parsley
 ½   teaspoon salt, divided
 ¼   teaspoon pepper, divided
 ½   cup apple juice
   1   tablespoon cider vinegar
   1   (14.5-ounce) can crushed tomatoes, undrained

1. Prepare barley with 2 cups water according to package directions, omitting salt.
2. Steam cabbage head 8 minutes, then cool slightly. Remove 16 leaves from cabbage head, and reserve remaining cabbage for another use. Cut off raised portion of the center vein of each cabbage leaf (do not cut out vein). Set trimmed cabbage leaves aside.
3. Heat oil in a large nonstick skillet over medium heat. Add onion; cover and cook 6 minutes or until tender. Remove from heat; stir in barley, feta cheese, and next 3 ingredients. Stir in ¼ teaspoon salt and ⅛ teaspoon pepper.
4. Place cabbage leaves on a flat surface; spoon about ⅓ cup barley mixture into center of each cabbage leaf. Fold in edges of leaves over barley mixture; roll up. Arrange cabbage rolls in bottom of a 5-quart electric slow cooker.
5. Combine ¼ teaspoon salt, ⅛ teaspoon pepper, apple juice, vinegar, and tomatoes; pour evenly over cabbage rolls. Cover and cook on HIGH 2 hours. Yield: 4 servings (serving size: 4 cabbage rolls and 2 tablespoons sauce).

CALORIES 402 (25% from fat); FAT 11.3g (sat 4.2g, mono 4.4g, poly 1.9g); PROTEIN 11.3g; CARB 70.1g; FIBER 11.3g; CHOL 19mg; IRON 5.0mg; SODIUM 693mg; CALC 234mg

Variation

"Meaty" Barley-Stuffed Cabbage Rolls: Stir in 1 cup thawed frozen meatless crumbles in place of the feta cheese. Proceed with recipe as directed.

CALORIES 399 (18% from fat); FAT 8.2g (sat 1g, mono 3.6g, poly 2.8g); PROTEIN 12.1g; CARB 76.3g; FIBER 12.6g; CHOL 0mg; IRON 5.8mg; SODIUM 546mg; CALC 158mg

Test Kitchen Tip: Trimming away part of the thick center vein from the cabbage leaves makes them more pliable and easier to roll up.

Southwestern Succotash Pot Pie

Ancho chile powder gives this casserole a mild, slightly fruity chile accent. Most supermarkets now carry ancho chile powder, but if you can't find it, substitute regular chili powder. You can make and refrigerate the succotash up to a day ahead.

Prep: 40 minutes • Cook: 46 minutes

Succotash:

  Cooking spray

  3 cups chopped onion

  4 garlic cloves, minced

  2 jalapeño peppers, seeded and finely chopped

  7 cups chopped zucchini (about 2 pounds)

  3 cups fresh corn kernels (about 5 ears)

  1 tablespoon ancho chile powder (such as McCormick's)

  1 teaspoon salt

  ½ teaspoon freshly ground black pepper

  1 cup (4 ounces) crumbled feta cheese

  2 (15-ounce) cans black beans, rinsed and drained

Topping:

  1 cup whole wheat flour

  1 cup all-purpose flour

  2 teaspoons baking powder

  1 teaspoon dried oregano

  ½ teaspoon baking soda

  ¼ teaspoon salt

  ¼ cup chilled butter, cut into small pieces

  ½ cup 1% low-fat milk

  ½ cup plain fat-free yogurt

  1 large egg, lightly beaten

1. To prepare succotash, heat a large nonstick skillet over medium-high heat. Coat pan with cooking spray. Add onion; sauté 5 minutes or until tender. Add garlic and jalapeño; sauté 30 seconds. Add zucchini; sauté 5 minutes or until zucchini is crisp-tender. Stir in corn; sauté 5 minutes or until corn is crisp-tender. Remove from heat; stir in chile powder, 1 teaspoon salt, and black pepper. Combine zucchini mixture, cheese, and beans in a 13 x 9–inch baking dish coated with cooking spray.

2. Preheat oven to 375°.

3. To prepare topping, lightly spoon flours into dry measuring cups; level with a knife. Combine flours, baking powder, oregano, baking soda, and ¼ teaspoon salt in a medium bowl, stirring with a whisk. Cut in butter with a pastry blender or 2 knives until mixture resembles coarse meal. Combine milk and yogurt; add milk mixture to flour mixture, stirring just until moist. Drop dough by tablespoonfuls onto zucchini mixture. Brush beaten egg over topping. Bake at 375° for 30 minutes or until golden. Yield: 9 servings (serving size: about 1½ cups).

CALORIES 322 (28% from fat); FAT 10.1g (sat 5.6g, mono 2.6g, poly 1.1g); PROTEIN 14.6g; CARB 50.4g; FIBER 8.9g; CHOL 49mg; IRON 3.8mg; SODIUM 913mg; CALC 227mg

types of chile peppers

The distinguishing feature of many southwestern or Tex-Mex recipes is the presence of chile peppers. Here are some photos and descriptions of the more common ones.

ancho: The dried version of the poblano chile, the ancho is a deep reddish-brown color and about 4 inches long. It's the sweetest of the dried chiles.

chipotle: This hot chile is really just a dried, smoked jalapeño with wrinkled skin and a smoky, sweet flavor. Chipotles are often pickled and canned in adobo sauce.

habanero: This pepper is one of the hottest chile peppers. A ripe one is about 1 to 2½ inches long and is usually either orange or red.

jalapeño: These smooth, dark-green chiles, which are bright red when ripe, can be very hot. They have a rounded tip and are about 2 inches long.

poblano: A dark-green chile used in chile rellenos, the poblano is usually mild. It's about 3 inches wide and 4 to 5 inches long, tapering from top to bottom in a triangular shape.

serrano: A small, pointed chile (about 1½ inches long), the serrano is very hot. As it matures, it turns from bright green to scarlet red, then yellow.

Greek Greens and Sweet Onion Pie

Fresh dill and feta cheese flavor this double phyllo-crusted pie. Serve it with vegetable soup and crusty bread.

Prep: 20 minutes • Cook: 46 minutes

    2   quarts water
   12   cups torn Swiss chard (about ¾ pound)
    8   cups torn spinach (about ½ pound)
        Cooking spray
    2   cups chopped Vidalia or other sweet onion
    2   garlic cloves, minced
   ¼   cup chopped fresh dill
   ¼   cup chopped fresh flat-leaf parsley
   ¾   cup (3 ounces) crumbled feta cheese
    2   large eggs, lightly beaten
    2   large egg whites, lightly beaten
   ½   teaspoon freshly ground black pepper
   ¼   teaspoon salt
   10   (14 x 9–inch) sheets frozen phyllo dough, thawed

1. Bring 2 quarts water to a boil in a large Dutch oven. Add chard and spinach; cook 2 minutes or until tender. Drain well. Place chard mixture on several layers of paper towels; squeeze until barely moist.

2. Preheat oven to 375°.

3. Heat a large nonstick skillet over medium-high heat. Coat pan with cooking spray. Add onion; sauté 5 minutes or until tender. Add garlic; sauté 1 minute. Add chard mixture, dill, and parsley, stirring well to combine. Cook 1 minute or until thoroughly heated. Remove from heat. Combine chard mixture, cheese, eggs, and egg whites, tossing well to combine. Stir in pepper and salt.

4. Place 1 phyllo sheet on a large cutting board or work surface (cover remaining dough to prevent drying); lightly coat phyllo sheet with cooking spray. Place phyllo sheet in a 9-inch pie plate coated with cooking spray, allowing edges to overlap plate rim. Repeat procedure with 6 phyllo sheets, placing sheets in a criss-cross design. Spoon spinach mixture over phyllo sheets. Lightly coat each of remaining 3 phyllo sheets with cooking spray; place sheets over spinach mixture in a crisscross design. Roll excess phyllo into dish to create a decorative edge; press lightly to hold. Cut 4 (2-inch) slits in top of pie; cover with foil. Bake at 375° for 10 minutes. Uncover and bake an additional 25 minutes or until crust is crisp and golden. Cut pie into 8 wedges. Yield: 4 servings (serving size: 2 wedges).

CALORIES 312 (30% from fat); FAT 10.5g (sat 4.8g, mono 3.5g, poly 1.1g); PROTEIN 16.1g; CARB 40.3g; FIBER 5.9g; CHOL 129mg; IRON 6.1mg; SODIUM 955mg; CALC 264mg

Test Kitchen Tip: Cutting slits into the top phyllo layer allows steam to escape so the crust will be crisp.

Shepherdless Pie

A shepherd's pie is traditionally a dish of cooked ground lamb or beef mixed with gravy and topped with mashed potatoes. We've taken out the meat and replaced it with hearty root vegetables.

Prep: 45 minutes • Cook: 1 hour, 15 minutes

1½ cups diced peeled celeriac (celery root)
2 large peeled baking potatoes, chopped (about 1½ pounds)
½ cup 1% low-fat milk
1⅓ cups chopped peeled Granny Smith apple
1½ tablespoons butter, divided
1 teaspoon salt
1½ cups finely chopped onion
1 cup finely chopped carrot
½ cup finely chopped celery
1 cup finely chopped peeled turnip (about ½ pound)
3½ cups sliced mushrooms
3 tablespoons chopped fresh parsley
1 teaspoon ground savory
1 teaspoon chopped fresh or ¼ teaspoon dried thyme
1 tablespoon all-purpose flour
½ cup apple juice
¾ cup (about 3 ounces) grated Gruyère cheese
1 (10-ounce) bag fresh spinach
Cooking spray
2 tablespoons dry breadcrumbs

1. Place celeriac and potatoes in a saucepan; cover with water, and bring to a boil. Reduce heat; simmer 12 minutes or until potatoes are tender. Drain.

2. Bring milk to a boil in a saucepan over medium heat; add apple, reduce heat, and simmer, uncovered, 7 minutes.

3. Preheat oven to 350°.

4. Place potato mixture, apple mixture, 1½ teaspoons butter, and salt in a food processor; process until smooth. Set aside.

5. Melt 1 tablespoon butter in a large non-stick skillet over medium-high heat. Add onion, carrot, and celery; sauté 5 minutes. Add turnip; cook 3 minutes. Add mushrooms, parsley, savory, and thyme; cook 2 minutes or until vegetables are tender and liquid almost evaporates. Sprinkle with flour; stir well, and cook 2 minutes. Stir in apple juice; cook 2 minutes. Cool to room temperature. Stir in cheese.

6. Steam spinach, covered, 5 minutes or until done. Drain and coarsely chop.

7. Coat 6 (12-ounce) soufflé dishes with cooking spray. Spoon ½ cup potato mixture into each dish. Top each with ⅓ cup spinach; top spinach with ⅔ cup onion mixture. Spoon remaining potato mixture evenly into each dish. Sprinkle evenly with breadcrumbs. Bake at 350° for 30 minutes. Yield: 6 servings (serving size: 1 pie).

CALORIES 259 (30% from fat); FAT 8.7g (sat 4.8g, mono 2.4g, poly 0.7g); PROTEIN 10.7g; CARB 37.8g; FIBER 7.0g; CHOL 24mg; IRON 3.5mg; SODIUM 612mg; CALC 280mg

Test Kitchen Tip: Instead of baking the mixture in individual soufflé dishes, you can bake it in an 11 x 7–inch baking dish.

how to peel celeriac

Celeriac (seh-LER-ay-ak), or celery root, is a knobby, brown vegetable that is actually the root of a special celery cultivated specifically for its root. It can be eaten raw or cooked. Ranging in size from that of an apple to a small cantaloupe, this vegetable's flavor is a cross between strong celery and parsley; its leaves are inedible, though. You'll need to peel celeriac before adding it to recipes. After peeling, either chop, dice, or grate it, depending what form is called for in the recipe.

Cut off the top and bottom, squaring off the bottom so the celeriac will sit securely on the cutting board. Using a sharp knife, cut around the sides to remove the outer layer. Then either chop, dice, grate, or shred.

Pizzas
Whether you prefer your crust thin and crispy or thick and chewy, these cheesy, veggie-topped pizzas are made to order.

Quick Pizza Margherita

Be sure to use fresh mozzarella, which comes packed in water and can be found with other gourmet cheeses.

Prep: 12 minutes • Cook: 20 minutes

- 1 (10-ounce) can refrigerated pizza crust dough
- Cooking spray
- 1 teaspoon extravirgin olive oil, divided
- 1 garlic clove, halved
- 5 plum tomatoes, thinly sliced (about ¾ pound)
- 1 cup (4 ounces) shredded fresh mozzarella cheese
- 1 teaspoon balsamic vinegar
- ½ cup thinly sliced fresh basil
- ⅛ teaspoon salt
- ⅛ teaspoon pepper

1. Preheat oven to 400°.

2. Unroll dough onto a baking sheet coated with cooking spray; pat into a 13 x 11–inch rectangle. Bake at 400° for 8 minutes. Remove crust from oven, and brush with ½ teaspoon oil. Rub crust with cut sides of garlic.

3. Arrange tomato slices on crust, leaving a ½-inch border; sprinkle evenly with cheese. Bake at 400° for 12 minutes or until cheese melts and crust is golden.

4. Combine ½ teaspoon oil and vinegar, stirring with a whisk. Sprinkle pizza evenly with sliced basil, salt, and pepper. Drizzle vinegar mixture evenly over pizza. Cut pizza into 8 rectangles. Yield: 4 servings (serving size: 2 rectangles).

CALORIES 298 (30% from fat); FAT 10.0g (sat 4.6g, mono 3.5g, poly 1.4g); PROTEIN 12.2g; CARB 38.6g; FIBER 2.1g; CHOL 22mg; IRON 2.6mg; SODIUM 595mg; CALC 175mg

Test Kitchen Tip: Baking the dough before topping it with tomato keeps the crust crisp.

Corn and Smoked Mozzarella Pizza

Grilling intensifies the sweetness of just-picked corn, which is delicious with smoked mozzarella.

Prep: 35 minutes • Cook: 19 minutes
Other: 65 minutes

    2 ears shucked corn
  Cooking spray
    2 tablespoons olive oil, divided
   ¼ teaspoon crushed red pepper
    1 garlic clove, minced
    1 package dry yeast (about 2¼
       teaspoons)
   ¾ cup warm water (100° to 110°),
       divided
 2¼ cups all-purpose flour, divided
    2 tablespoons 1% low-fat milk
 1¼ teaspoons salt, divided
    2 tablespoons cornmeal
    1 cup (4 ounces) shredded smoked
       mozzarella cheese
    1 cup very thinly sliced red onion
    2 tablespoons chopped chives
 1½ teaspoons grated lime rind

1. Prepare grill or broiler.
2. Place corn on grill rack or broiler pan coated with cooking spray; cook 10 minutes, turning occasionally. Cool. Cut kernels from corn to measure 1 cup; set aside.
3. Place 1 tablespoon oil and red pepper in a small bowl; microwave at HIGH 30 seconds. Stir in garlic; set aside.
4. Dissolve yeast in ¼ cup warm water in a large bowl; let stand 20 minutes. Lightly spoon flour into dry measuring cups; level with a knife. Add ½ cup warm water, 2 cups flour, milk, 1 tablespoon oil, and ¾ teaspoon salt to yeast mixture; mix well.
5. Turn dough out onto a floured surface. Knead until smooth and elastic (about 10 minutes); add enough of remaining flour, 1 tablespoon at a time, to prevent dough from sticking to hands (dough will feel tacky).
6. Place dough in a large bowl coated with cooking spray, turning to coat top. Cover and let rise in a warm place (85°), free from drafts, 40 minutes or until doubled in size. (Gently press two fingers into dough. If indentation remains, dough has risen enough.) Punch dough down; cover and let rest 5 minutes.
7. Preheat oven to 500°.
8. Divide dough in half; roll each half into a 9-inch circle on a lightly floured surface. Working with one portion at a time, place dough on a pizza pan or baking sheet coated with cooking spray and sprinkled with 1 tablespoon cornmeal. Crimp edges of dough with fingers to form a rim.
9. Brush each dough circle with half of oil mixture; sprinkle with ½ cup cheese. Top with ½ cup corn and ½ cup onion. Sprinkle with ¼ teaspoon salt. Bake at 500° for 8 minutes or until golden. Sprinkle each pizza with 1 tablespoon chives and ¾ teaspoon lime rind. Cut each pizza into 4 wedges. Yield: 4 servings (serving size: 2 wedges).

CALORIES 473 (27% from fat); FAT 14.4g (sat 5.2g, mono 5.3g, poly 1.2g); PROTEIN 15.5g; CARB 70.2g; FIBER 4.5g; CHOL 23mg; IRON 4.3mg; SODIUM 788mg; CALC 194mg

Caramelized Onion Pizza with Gorgonzola and Arugula

The sweetness of the onions and the sharpness of the cheese provide a perfect balance of flavors in this gourmet-style pizza.

Prep: 41 minutes • Cook: 39 minutes
Other: 55 minutes

- ½ recipe Whole Wheat Pizza Dough (page 111)
- 2 teaspoons olive oil
- 12 cups thinly sliced onion (about 3 pounds)
- 2 teaspoons chopped fresh or ½ teaspoon dried rosemary, divided
- ½ teaspoon salt
- ¼ teaspoon pepper
- ½ cup (2 ounces) crumbled Gorgonzola, blue cheese, or feta
- 2 tablespoons coarsely chopped walnuts
- 1 cup trimmed arugula

1. Prepare Whole Wheat Pizza Dough.
2. Heat oil in a large cast-iron or nonstick skillet over medium-high heat. Add onion; sauté 5 minutes, stirring frequently. Stir in 1 teaspoon rosemary, salt, and pepper. Cook 20 to 25 minutes or until onion is a deep golden brown, stirring frequently.
3. Preheat oven to 500°.
4. Crimp edges of pizza dough with fingers to form a rim. Top with onion. Bake at 500° for 10 minutes. Sprinkle with cheese and walnuts; bake an additional 3 minutes or until cheese melts. Remove from oven; sprinkle with 1 teaspoon rosemary and arugula. Cut pizza into 4 wedges. Yield: 4 servings (serving size: 1 wedge).

(Totals include Whole Wheat Pizza Dough) CALORIES 449 (24% from fat); FAT 11.8g (sat 3.6g, mono 4.7g, poly 2.6g); PROTEIN 14.8g; CARB 73.8g; FIBER 10.1g; CHOL 11mg; IRON 3.7mg; SODIUM 944mg; CALC 172mg

Mushroom Pizza with Thyme

Cremini mushrooms offer the juiciness and texture of button mushrooms, but have a slightly richer flavor.

Prep: 40 minutes • Cook: 18 minutes
Other: 55 minutes

- ½ recipe Whole Wheat Pizza Dough (page 111)
- ¼ cup chopped fresh parsley
- 2 teaspoons chopped fresh thyme
- 2 garlic cloves, minced
- 2 teaspoons olive oil
- 4 cups sliced cremini mushrooms
- 3 tablespoons fresh lemon juice
- ½ teaspoon salt
- ¼ teaspoon pepper
- ¼ cup (1 ounce) grated fresh Parmesan cheese

1. Prepare Whole Wheat Pizza Dough.
2. Preheat oven to 500°.
3. Combine parsley, thyme, and garlic in a small bowl. Set aside.
4. Heat oil in a large nonstick skillet over medium-high heat. Add mushrooms and juice, and sauté 5 minutes. Stir in 2 tablespoons parsley mixture, salt, and pepper.
5. Crimp edges of dough with fingers to form a rim. Top with mushroom mixture. Bake at 500° for 12 minutes or until browned. Remove from oven; top with 2 tablespoons parsley mixture and cheese. Cut into 4 wedges. Yield: 4 servings (serving size: 1 wedge).

(Totals include Whole Wheat Pizza Dough) CALORIES 294 (22% from fat); FAT 7.1g (sat 1.9g, mono 3.6g, poly 1.0g); PROTEIN 10.9g; CARB 48.2g; FIBER 4.5g; CHOL 5mg; IRON 4.0mg; SODIUM 853mg; CALC 110mg

Tomato Pizza with Capers, Basil, and Garlic

Use a mixture of tomatoes for this pizza—red, plum, or yellow. A plain pizza crust tastes best with this simply seasoned pizza. (Use the recipe on page 111 or use a refrigerated crust.)

Prep: 30 minutes • Cook: 15 minutes
Other: 1 hour, 20 minutes

- Pizza Dough (page 111)
- ½ cup (2 ounces) shredded part-skim mozzarella cheese
- 4 tomatoes, cut into ½-inch-thick slices (about 1 pound)
- 2 tablespoons capers
- ¼ cup chopped fresh basil
- ½ teaspoon pepper
- ¼ teaspoon salt
- 2 garlic cloves, minced
- 1 teaspoon extravirgin olive oil

1. Prepare Pizza Dough.
2. Preheat oven to 500°.
3. Crimp edges of dough with fingers to form a rim. Sprinkle cheese on crust. Arrange tomato on cheese; sprinkle with capers. Bake at 500° for 15 minutes or until crust is golden. Remove from oven; sprinkle with basil, pepper, salt, and garlic. Drizzle with oil. Cool slightly (tomatoes will be hot). Cut pizza into 4 wedges. Yield: 4 servings (serving size: 1 wedge).

(Totals include Pizza Dough) CALORIES 303 (19% from fat); FAT 6.4g (sat 2g, mono 2.9g, poly 0.9g); PROTEIN 10.9g; CARB 50.8g; FIBER 3.4g; CHOL 8mg; IRON 3.6mg; SODIUM 775mg; CALC 115mg

Rustic Grilled Pizza
(pictured on page 289)

Grilling a refrigerated pizza crust gives it a crisp outside, chewy inside, and the smoky flavor of a brick-oven pizza. Browning both sides of the crust helps to prevent the vegetables from making it soggy. (See pages 32 and 450 for step-by-step photo techniques for roasting peppers.)

Prep: 30 minutes • Cook: 46 minutes
Other: 15 minutes

    3 large red bell peppers
    1 tablespoon minced fresh oregano
    1 tablespoon olive oil, divided
    ¾ teaspoon salt, divided
    3 cups thinly sliced onion
    ¼ teaspoon sugar
    7 ounces shiitake mushrooms, stems
       removed
    1 (10-ounce) can refrigerated pizza
       crust dough
    1 tablespoon cornmeal
    Cooking spray
    ⅔ cup (about 2½ ounces) crumbled
       goat cheese
    1 tablespoon chopped fresh parsley
    ¼ teaspoon freshly ground black pepper

1. Preheat broiler.
2. Cut bell peppers in half lengthwise, and discard seeds and membranes. Place pepper halves, skin sides up, on a foil-lined baking sheet; flatten with hand. Broil 15 minutes or until blackened. Place in a zip-top plastic bag, and seal. Let stand 15 minutes. Peel and cut into ½-inch strips. Combine bell pepper, oregano, 1 teaspoon oil, and ¼ teaspoon salt.
3. Heat 1 teaspoon oil in a large nonstick skillet over medium heat. Add onion and ¼ teaspoon salt; cook 15 minutes, stirring frequently. Increase heat to medium-high.

Sprinkle onion with sugar; sauté 5 minutes or until lightly browned. Remove from pan.
4. Heat 1 teaspoon oil in pan over medium-high heat. Add mushrooms; cover and cook 2 minutes. Uncover and cook 1 minute or until tender, stirring constantly. Combine onion, mushrooms, and ¼ teaspoon salt.
5. Prepare grill.
6. Roll dough into a 12-inch circle on a baking sheet sprinkled with cornmeal. Place dough on grill rack coated with cooking spray; grill 3 minutes or until browned. Turn crust. Arrange onion mixture and bell pepper mixture on crust. Top with cheese. Cover; grill 3 minutes. Sprinkle with parsley and black pepper. Cut into 8 wedges. Yield: 4 servings (serving size: 2 wedges).

CALORIES 338 (27% from fat); FAT 10g (sat 3.2g, mono 3.4g, poly 0.6g); PROTEIN 12.4g; CARB 49.4g; FIBER 5.5g; CHOL 9mg; IRON 3.6mg; SODIUM 955mg; CALC 62mg

menu

serves 4

Rustic Grilled Pizza

Mediterranean green salad*

Bittersweet Chocolate Sorbet
(page 190)

*Combine 1 (5-ounce) package mixed salad greens with 1 red pear, chopped; 2 tablespoons chopped walnuts; and 3 tablespoons fat-free balsamic vinaigrette.

how to grill a pizza

1. Roll each crust into a 12-inch circle.

2. Gently lift the crust from the baking sheet to the grill.

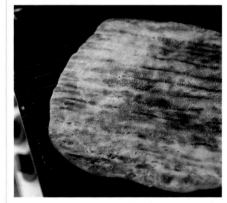

3. Turn the crust, grill-mark side up, after about 3 minutes.

Eggs & Cheese

Veggie-packed frittatas, cheesy omelets, and savory stratas aren't just for breakfast or brunch.

Huevos Rancheros

The New Mexican Red Chile Sauce offers an authentic spicy, slightly bitter flavor to the dish. Substitute a commercial salsa, if you prefer.

Prep: 16 minutes • Cook: 42 minutes

     4   (6-inch) corn tortillas
         Cooking spray
     1   cup chopped onion
    ½   cup chopped green bell pepper
     3   garlic cloves, minced
    ¼   cup canned chopped green chiles
     2   teaspoons New Mexico chile
         powder
     1   teaspoon ground cumin
     1   teaspoon dried oregano
    ½   teaspoon hot sauce
     1   (14.5-ounce) can diced tomatoes,
         undrained
     4   large eggs
    ¼   cup New Mexican Red Chile
         Sauce (page 454)
    ¼   cup (1 ounce) shredded
         Monterey Jack cheese
     2   teaspoons chopped fresh
         cilantro

1. Preheat oven to 350°.

2. Coat tortillas with cooking spray; place on a baking sheet. Bake at 350° for 12 minutes or until crisp.

3. Heat a large nonstick skillet over medium-high heat. Coat pan with cooking spray. Add onion, bell pepper, and garlic; sauté 3 minutes. Add green chiles and next 5 ingredients. Bring to a boil; cook 3 minutes or until thick.

4. Heat a large nonstick skillet over medium-low heat. Coat pan with cooking spray. Add eggs to pan; cook 3 minutes or until done.

5. Place 1 tortilla on each of 4 plates. Top each tortilla with tomato mixture and egg. Spoon New Mexican Red Chile Sauce over each serving; sprinkle with cheese and cilantro. Yield: 4 servings (serving size: 1 tortilla, ½ cup tomato mixture, 1 egg, 1 tablespoon sauce, 1 tablespoon cheese, ½ teaspoon cilantro).

(Totals include New Mexican Red Chile Sauce) CALORIES 222 (35% from fat); FAT 8.6g (sat 3.1g, mono 2.8g, poly 1.3g); PROTEIN 11.7g; CARB 26.7g; FIBER 5.5g; CHOL 219mg; IRON 2.5mg; SODIUM 376mg; CALC 174mg

Mediterranean-Style Poached Eggs

Eggs gently cook atop a mixture of onion, bell pepper, tomatoes, and artichoke hearts and are served over toasted bread.

Prep: 15 minutes • Cook: 21 minutes

   2   teaspoons olive oil
1½   cups chopped onion
   1   cup green bell pepper strips
   1   garlic clove, minced
   ½   teaspoon ground cumin
   ½   teaspoon paprika
2½   cups canned crushed tomatoes
   ¼   teaspoon black pepper
   1   (14-ounce) can artichoke hearts, drained and cut in half
   4   large eggs
   ¼   cup chopped fresh parsley
   ¼   cup chopped pitted kalamata olives
   ¼   cup (1 ounce) grated fresh Parmesan cheese
   4   (1½-ounce) slices French bread, toasted

1. Heat oil in a large nonstick skillet over medium-high heat. Add onion, bell pepper, and garlic; sauté 5 minutes. Add cumin and paprika; sauté 1 minute. Reduce heat to medium; stir in tomatoes, black pepper, and artichokes. Cook 5 minutes, stirring occasionally.
2. Form 4 (3-inch) indentations in vegetable mixture using the back of a spoon. Break 1 egg into each indentation. Cover and cook 8 minutes or until eggs are done. Sprinkle with parsley, olives, and cheese. Serve over bread. Yield: 4 servings (serving size: 1 bread slice, ¾ cup vegetable mixture, and 1 egg).

CALORIES 355 (30% from fat); FAT 11.9g (sat 3.5g, mono 5.4g, poly 1.5g); PROTEIN 17.8g; CARB 46.2g; FIBER 7.5g; CHOL 217mg; IRON 3.8mg; SODIUM 1050mg; CALC 197mg

Red Bell Pepper Frittata

Stirring cooked couscous into a frittata adds texture and makes it more filling. Substitute 1 cup leftover cooked orzo, spaghetti, or vermicelli, if you prefer.

Prep: 12 minutes • Cook: 21 minutes
Other: 10 minutes

   ½   cup water
   ⅓   cup uncooked couscous
   1   tablespoon water
   ¾   teaspoon salt
   ¼   teaspoon black pepper
   4   large egg whites
   3   large eggs
       Cooking spray
   2   cups red bell pepper strips
   1   cup thinly vertically sliced onion
   2   garlic cloves, minced
   ⅓   cup (1½ ounces) shredded Manchego or Monterey Jack cheese

1. Preheat oven to 350°.
2. Bring ½ cup water to a boil in a small saucepan; gradually stir in couscous. Remove from heat; cover and let stand 5 minutes. Fluff with a fork.
3. Combine 1 tablespoon water, salt, black pepper, egg whites, and eggs in a medium bowl, stirring with a whisk.
4. Heat a 10-inch ovenproof nonstick skillet over medium-high heat. Coat pan with cooking spray. Add bell pepper, onion, and garlic; sauté 5 minutes. Stir in couscous and egg mixture; cook over medium heat 5 minutes or until almost set. Sprinkle with cheese. Bake at 350° for 10 minutes or until set. Let stand 5 minutes before serving. Cut into wedges. Yield: 4 servings (serving size: 1 wedge).

CALORIES 204 (30% from fat); FAT 6.8g (sat 3.0g, mono 2.3g, poly 0.7g); PROTEIN 15.0g; CARB 20.6g; FIBER 2.9g; CHOL 167mg; IRON 1.3mg; SODIUM 716mg; CALC 169mg

Fresh Corn Frittata with Smoked Mozzarella

Easy to double and simple to prepare, this frittata is a good light main course. The smoked cheese and the fresh corn provide a pleasing balance of flavors.

Prep: 12 minutes • Cook: 15 minutes

       Cooking spray
1½   cups fresh corn kernels (about 3 ears)
   ¼   cup (1 ounce) shredded smoked mozzarella cheese, divided
   1   tablespoon chopped fresh basil
   ¼   teaspoon salt
   ¼   teaspoon freshly ground black pepper
   5   large egg whites, lightly beaten
   2   large eggs, lightly beaten

1. Preheat broiler.
2. Heat a medium ovenproof skillet over medium-high heat. Coat pan with cooking spray. Add corn, and sauté 5 minutes. Combine corn, 2 tablespoons cheese, basil, and remaining ingredients in a large bowl, stirring with a whisk.
3. Heat pan over medium heat. Coat pan with cooking spray; add corn mixture. Cover and cook 5 minutes or until almost set. Sprinkle with 2 tablespoons cheese. Broil 5 minutes or until set and browned. Cut into wedges. Yield: 4 servings (serving size: 1 wedge).

CALORIES 129 (33% from fat); FAT 4.7g (sat 1.9g, mono 1.7g, poly 0.7g); PROTEIN 10.7g; CARB 12g; FIBER 1.6g; CHOL 112mg; IRON 0.8mg; SODIUM 263mg; CALC 58mg

Test Kitchen Tip: We recommend using a cast-iron or heavy stainless steel skillet for this recipe. Many nonstick skillets have plastic handles that can't withstand temperatures higher than 375°, even if you wrap the handle in foil.

Mushroom and Bell Pepper Omelet with Fontina

If the vegetables leave liquid in the pan, wipe it dry before adding the egg mixture.

Prep: 20 minutes • Cook: 17 minutes

1   teaspoon olive oil, divided
Cooking spray
¼   cup chopped green onions
½   medium-size green bell pepper,
      thinly sliced
2   cups sliced shiitake mushrooms
      (about 6 ounces)
½   cup chopped seeded plum tomato
½   teaspoon salt, divided
⅛   teaspoon black pepper
2   teaspoons chopped fresh parsley
8   large eggs
2   large egg whites
½   teaspoon butter
½   cup (2 ounces) shredded fontina cheese
¼   cup reduced-fat sour cream
Chopped fresh parsley (optional)

1. Heat ½ teaspoon oil in a large nonstick skillet coated with cooking spray over medium-high heat. Add green onions; sauté 1 minute. Add bell pepper; sauté 1 minute. Add mushrooms; cook 3 minutes, stirring frequently. Stir in tomato, ¼ teaspoon salt, and black pepper; cook 30 seconds. Remove mixture from pan. Cover; keep warm.

2. Place ¼ teaspoon salt, parsley, eggs, and egg whites in a bowl; stir well with a whisk to combine.
3. Place ½ teaspoon oil and butter in pan over medium-high heat until butter melts. Add egg mixture to pan; cook until edges begin to set (about 2 minutes). Slide front edge of a spatula between edge of omelet and pan. Gently lift edge of omelet, tilting pan to allow some uncooked egg mixture to come in contact with pan. Repeat procedure on opposite edge of omelet. Continue cooking until center is just set (about 7 minutes).
4. Spoon vegetable mixture evenly over ½ of omelet; top vegetable mixture with cheese. Loosen omelet with a spatula; fold in half. Carefully slide omelet onto a serving platter. Cut omelet into 4 wedges; top with sour cream. Garnish with fresh parsley, if desired. Serve immediately. Yield: 4 servings (serving size: 1 wedge and 1 tablespoon sour cream).

CALORIES 272 (59% from fat); FAT 17.7g (sat 7.3g, mono 6.5g, poly 1.8g); PROTEIN 19.4g; CARB 7.1g; FIBER 1.3g; CHOL 448mg; IRON 2.4mg; SODIUM 576mg; CALC 145mg

Potato, Mushroom, and Pesto Omelet

We packed this omelet so full that it's too thick to fold in half. Serve it open-faced with fresh fruit and muffins. If you want to make your own pesto, see the recipe for Classic Pesto on page 452.

Prep: 13 minutes • Cook: 17 minutes

4   large egg whites
1   large egg
⅛   teaspoon salt
⅛   teaspoon black pepper
Cooking spray
1   cup thinly sliced mushrooms
¼   cup finely chopped red bell pepper
½   cup diced peeled baking potato,
      cooked
1   tablespoon commercial pesto

1. Combine first 4 ingredients in a medium bowl, stirring with a whisk.
2. Heat a small nonstick skillet over medium-high heat. Coat pan with cooking spray. Add mushrooms and bell pepper; sauté 5 minutes. Pour egg mixture into pan; top with potato (do not stir). Cover, reduce heat to medium-low, and cook 8 minutes or until center is set.
3. Spread pesto over omelet. Loosen omelet with a spatula, and cut in half. Slide omelet halves onto plates. Yield: 2 servings (serving size: ½ of omelet).

CALORIES 146 (36% from fat); FAT 5.9g (sat 1.5g, mono 2.6g, poly 1g); PROTEIN 12.7g; CARB 10.8g; FIBER 1.7g; CHOL 112mg; IRON 1.7mg; SODIUM 345mg; CALC 56mg

Feta Omelet with Breadcrumbs

Feta adds a distinctive sharpness to this Mediterranean-style omelet that you don't get with milder cheeses.

Prep: 9 minutes • Cook: 17 minutes

   5 tablespoons water
   ¼ teaspoon salt
   4 large eggs
   4 large egg whites
   1 tablespoon olive oil
   ¾ cup dry breadcrumbs
   ½ cup (2 ounces) crumbled feta cheese
   ¼ cup thinly sliced green onions
   2 tablespoons chopped fresh parsley
   1 tablespoon chopped fresh or
      1 teaspoon dried oregano

1. Preheat broiler.
2. Combine first 4 ingredients in a bowl; stir well with a whisk. Heat oil in a 9-inch cast-iron skillet over medium heat. Add breadcrumbs; cook 1 minute or until lightly browned. Spread egg mixture evenly in pan; top with cheese. Broil 15 minutes or until omelet is firm. Sprinkle with onions, parsley, and oregano. Cut into wedges. Yield: 6 servings (serving size: 1 wedge).

CALORIES 163 (47% from fat); FAT 8.5g (sat 3g, mono 3.8g, poly 0.9g); PROTEIN 9.7g; CARB 11.4g; FIBER 0.5g; CHOL 156mg; IRON 1.6mg; SODIUM 400mg; CALC 104mg

Test Kitchen Tip: Use your hands to separate an egg instead of pouring the egg yolk back and forth from one half of the eggshell to the other (which increases the likelihood of the shell breaking the yolk and the chance of transferring bacteria). Just crack the egg and let the white run through your fingers into a bowl. Wash your hands before and after.

Spanish Potato Omelet

Although its ingredients couldn't be more basic—potatoes, eggs, onions, and oil—they're combined and cooked in a way that makes this dish irresistible and versatile. The potatoes are normally fried, but we've roasted them with excellent results. Unlike American omelets, this one's best made several hours ahead, then served at room temperature.

Prep: 15 minutes • Cook: 1 hour, 11 minutes
Other: 10 minutes

   Cooking spray
   6 cups thinly sliced peeled baking
      potato (about 3 pounds)
   2 cups thinly sliced sweet onion
   2 tablespoons olive oil, divided
   ¾ teaspoon kosher salt, divided
   4 large eggs
   Oregano sprigs (optional)

1. Preheat oven to 350°.
2. Coat a roasting pan with cooking spray. Place potato and onion in a roasting pan.

Drizzle with 1 tablespoon plus 2 teaspoons oil, and sprinkle with ½ teaspoon salt. Toss well. Bake at 350° for 1 hour or until potato is tender, stirring occasionally with a metal spatula to prevent sticking. Remove from oven, and let cool slightly.
3. Combine eggs and ¼ teaspoon salt in a large bowl. Stir in potato mixture; let stand 10 minutes. Heat 1 teaspoon oil in an 8-inch nonstick skillet over medium heat. Pour potato mixture into pan (pan will be very full). Cook 7 minutes or until almost set, gently shaking pan frequently. Place a plate upside down on top of omelet, and invert onto plate. Carefully slide omelet cooked side up into pan; cook 3 minutes or until set, gently shaking pan occasionally. Carefully loosen omelet with a spatula; gently slide omelet onto a plate. Cool. Cut into wedges. Garnish with oregano, if desired. Yield: 6 servings (serving size: 1 wedge).

CALORIES 315 (23% from fat); FAT 8g (sat 1.7g, mono 4.6g, poly 1g); PROTEIN 9g; CARB 52.6g; FIBER 4g; CHOL 142mg; IRON 1.4mg; SODIUM 345mg; CALC 36mg

how to make a potato omelet

1. Roast the potatoes before adding them to the eggs for the omelet. After roasting the potatoes, let them cool while you separate the eggs.

2. Combine the cooled potatoes and eggs; let stand 10 minutes. Pour the mixture into a nonstick pan. Cook. When almost set, invert onto a plate, sliding the omelet back into the pan to cook the other side.

Mushroom, Roasted Red Pepper, and Goat Cheese Bread Pudding

This main-dish bread pudding features distinctive Mediterranean flavors. Crumbled feta cheese makes a fine substitute for goat cheese.

Prep: 25 minutes • Cook: 57 minutes
Other: 10 minutes

¼ cup chopped fresh parsley
1 teaspoon chopped fresh thyme
1 teaspoon chopped fresh rosemary
2 garlic cloves, minced
2 teaspoons olive oil
3 cups sliced cremini mushrooms (about 6 ounces)
3 cups sliced button mushrooms (about 6 ounces)
2 cups sliced shiitake mushroom caps (about 4 ounces)
1 cup thinly sliced leek
½ teaspoon salt, divided
¼ teaspoon black pepper, divided
1 (12-ounce) bottle roasted red bell peppers, drained and chopped
1½ cups 1% low-fat milk
1 cup egg substitute
1¼ cups (5 ounces) crumbled goat cheese, divided
8 ounces (1-inch) cubed day-old sourdough bread (about 9 cups)
Cooking spray

1. Preheat oven to 350°.
2. Combine parsley, thyme, rosemary, and garlic. Set aside.
3. Heat oil in a large nonstick skillet over medium-high heat. Add mushrooms, leek, ¼ teaspoon salt, and ⅛ teaspoon black pepper; sauté 10 minutes or until liquid evaporates and mushrooms are lightly browned. Add half of parsley mixture, and cook 1 minute, stirring constantly. Stir in bell peppers. Remove from heat, and cool slightly.
4. Combine ¼ teaspoon salt, ⅛ teaspoon black pepper, remaining parsley mixture, milk, egg substitute, and ¾ cup cheese in a large bowl, stirring with a whisk. Stir in mushroom mixture. Add bread; stir gently to combine. Let stand 10 minutes. Spoon into a 2-quart baking dish coated with cooking spray. Sprinkle with remaining ½ cup cheese. Bake at 350° for 45 minutes or until pudding is set and lightly browned. Yield: 6 servings (serving size: about 1⅓ cups).

CALORIES 273 (29% from fat); FAT 8.9g (sat 4.4g, mono 2.9g, poly 0.8g); PROTEIN 17.3g; CARB 31.9g; FIBER 2.9g; CHOL 13mg; IRON 3.9mg; SODIUM 766mg; CALC 174mg

perfect bread pudding Savory bread puddings are among the most flexible of recipes. Assemble and bake them immediately, or cover and refrigerate them overnight before baking. Follow these tips for consistent success.

- Use day-old (very dry) bread for the best texture. Very fresh bread will yield a slightly spongy texture.
- Use the bread's ounce/weight measurement as a more accurate guide than the cup measurement.
- If you don't have a kitchen scale and are measuring the bread by cup amounts, be sure not to tightly pack the bread cubes into the measuring cup, or you'll end up with too much bread.
- Leave the crusts on for more texture.
- Whole-grain breads give these puddings a nutty taste and a slightly drier texture. But be sure to taste the bread before using it for a bread pudding. They can be strong in flavor, which might overpower delicate ingredients.

Butternut Squash and Parmesan Bread Pudding

Serve with a side of sautéed kale or mustard greens to provide a counterpoint to the sweet butternut squash.

**Prep: 20 minutes • Cook: 1 hour, 4 minutes
Other: 10 minutes**

- 3 cups (½-inch) cubed peeled butternut squash
- Cooking spray
- ½ teaspoon salt, divided
- 1 teaspoon olive oil
- 1 cup chopped onion
- 1 garlic clove, minced
- 2 cups 1% low-fat milk
- 1 cup (4 ounces) grated fresh Parmigiano-Reggiano cheese, divided
- ¼ teaspoon pepper
- ⅛ teaspoon ground nutmeg
- 3 large eggs
- 2 large egg whites
- 8 ounces (1-inch) cubed day-old French bread (about 9 cups)

1. Preheat oven to 400°.
2. Arrange squash in a single layer on a jelly-roll pan coated with cooking spray. Sprinkle with ¼ teaspoon salt. Bake at 400° for 12 minutes or until tender. Remove from oven; reduce oven temperature to 350°.
3. Heat oil in a medium nonstick skillet over medium-high heat. Add onion; sauté 5 minutes or until tender. Add garlic; sauté 1 minute. Remove from heat; cool slightly.
4. Combine remaining ¼ teaspoon salt, milk, ½ cup cheese, pepper, nutmeg, eggs, and egg whites in a large bowl, stirring with a whisk. Stir in squash and onion mixture. Add bread, and stir gently to combine. Let stand 10 minutes. Spoon into a 2-quart baking dish coated with cooking spray. Sprinkle with remaining ½ cup cheese. Bake at 350° for 45 minutes or until pudding is set and lightly browned. Yield: 6 servings (serving size: about 1⅓ cups).

CALORIES 304 (30% from fat); FAT 10.3g (sat 4.8g, mono 3.7g, poly 0.9g); PROTEIN 18.1g; CARB 35.3g; FIBER 4g; CHOL 122mg; IRON 2.1mg; SODIUM 823mg; CALC 406mg

Mediterranean Spinach Strata

Fresh tomatoes and spinach pair well with Asiago and feta cheese in this make-ahead dish. Substitute Parmesan, Romano, or sharp provolone cheese for the Asiago, if you prefer.

**Prep: 25 minutes • Cook: 1 hour, 4 minutes
Other: 8 hours**

- 2 (8-ounce) loaves French bread baguette, cut into ¾-inch-thick slices
- Cooking spray
- 1 cup chopped onion
- 4 garlic cloves, minced
- 1 (8-ounce) package sliced mushrooms
- 1 tablespoon all-purpose flour
- 2 (7-ounce) bags baby spinach
- ½ teaspoon salt, divided
- ½ teaspoon pepper, divided
- 3 cups thinly sliced plum tomato (about 1 pound)
- 1 (4-ounce) package crumbled feta cheese
- ¾ cup (3 ounces) grated Asiago cheese, divided
- 3 cups fat-free milk
- 2 tablespoons Dijon mustard
- 1½ teaspoons dried oregano
- 5 large eggs, lightly beaten
- 4 large egg whites, lightly beaten

1. Preheat oven to 350°.
2. Place bread slices in a single layer on a baking sheet. Bake at 350° for 12 minutes or until lightly browned.
3. Heat a large nonstick skillet over medium-high heat. Coat pan with cooking spray. Add onion, garlic, and mushrooms; sauté 5 minutes or until tender. Sprinkle flour over mushroom mixture; cook 1 minute, stirring constantly. Add 1 bag of spinach; cook 3 minutes or until spinach wilts. Add remaining spinach; cook 3 minutes or until spinach wilts. Stir in ¼ teaspoon salt and ¼ teaspoon pepper.
4. Place half of bread slices in bottom of a 13 x 9–inch baking dish coated with cooking spray. Spread spinach mixture over bread. Top with tomato slices; sprinkle evenly with feta and half of Asiago cheese. Arrange remaining bread slices over cheese. Combine ¼ teaspoon salt, ¼ teaspoon pepper, milk, and remaining 4 ingredients, stirring well with a whisk. Pour over bread; sprinkle with remaining Asiago cheese. Cover; chill 8 hours or overnight.
5. Preheat oven to 350°.
6. Uncover strata; bake at 350° for 40 to 45 minutes or until lightly browned and set. Serve warm. Yield: 10 servings (serving size: about 1½ cups).

CALORIES 297 (29% from fat); FAT 9.5g (sat 4.4g, mono 2.8g, poly 1g); PROTEIN 17.9g; CARB 36g; FIBER 3.1g; CHOL 125mg; IRON 3.5mg; SODIUM 720mg; CALC 332mg

bread puddings and stratas Although the ingredients may be similar, a strata usually has bread slices that are layered with other ingredients while bread pudding usually contains bread cubes that are stirred into an egg-and-cheese mixture.

Tomato-Basil Tart

This quichelike tart is a great make-ahead main dish because it's good served cold, at room temperature, or hot.

Prep: 25 minutes • Cook: 1 hour
Other: 30 minutes

1   (11-ounce) can refrigerated soft
    breadstick dough
Cooking spray
3   large plum tomatoes
¾   teaspoon salt
1   cup loosely packed basil leaves
¾   cup (3 ounces) shredded part-skim
    mozzarella cheese
⅔   cup fat-free ricotta cheese
½   cup (2 ounces) grated fresh
    Parmesan cheese
¼   teaspoon pepper
2   large egg whites
2   teaspoons olive oil

1. Preheat oven to 425°.
2. Unroll dough, separating into strips. Working on a flat surface, coil 1 strip of dough around itself in a spiral pattern. Add second strip of dough to end of first strip, pinching ends to seal; continue coiling remaining dough. Let rest 10 minutes.
3. Roll dough into a 12-inch circle; fit into bottom and up sides of a 9-inch round removable-bottom tart pan coated with cooking spray. Cover dough with foil; arrange pie weights or dried beans on foil. Bake at 425° for 15 minutes; remove weights and foil. Bake an additional 5 minutes or until edges are lightly browned.
4. Reduce oven temperature to 350°.
5. Cut tomatoes into ¼-inch-thick slices. Sprinkle with salt; place, salt sides down, on several layers of paper towels. Cover with additional paper towels. Let stand 10 minutes, pressing down occasionally.

6. Place basil, cheeses, pepper, and egg whites in a food processor; process until smooth. Spread cheese mixture over crust. Arrange tomato slices over cheese mixture; brush with olive oil. Bake at 350° for 40 minutes or until cheese mixture is set. Let stand 10 minutes before serving. Cut into 6 wedges. Yield: 6 servings (serving size: 1 wedge).

CALORIES 270 (31% from fat); FAT 9.3g (sat 3.2g, mono 1.8g, poly 0.3g); PROTEIN 15.8g; CARB 29.8g; FIBER 1.4g; CHOL 19mg; IRON 1.9mg; SODIUM 938mg; CALC 296mg

Test Kitchen Tip: Salting the tomato slices extracts excess water so the tart won't get soggy. If your tomatoes are watery after cooking, blot them with a paper towel.

Soy Products

Tofu and tempeh offer abundant health benefits, so don't wait any longer to try some of these tempting dishes.

Vietnamese Lettuce Rolls with Spicy Grilled Tofu

This dish contrasts warm and cold sensations, along with firm, soft, and crunchy textures. The tofu is pressed before grilling so that it becomes firmer. Because they're more flexible, the top halves of lettuce leaves make better wrappers than the bottom halves.

Prep: 35 minutes • Cook: 9 minutes
Other: 1 hour, 30 minutes

- 1 (16-ounce) package water-packed firm tofu, drained
- ½ cup fresh lime juice
- ½ cup honey
- ¼ cup thinly sliced peeled fresh lemongrass
- 2 tablespoons low-sodium soy sauce
- ¾ teaspoon chile paste with garlic
- ¼ teaspoon freshly ground black pepper
- 3 garlic cloves, minced
- Cooking spray
- 1 head romaine lettuce
- ½ cup cilantro leaves
- 3 tablespoons chopped dry-roasted peanuts
- 36 small mint leaves
- 36 (2-inch) strips julienne-cut carrot
- 12 basil leaves

1. Cut tofu crosswise into 12 (½-inch) slices. Place tofu slices on several layers of heavy-duty paper towels. Cover tofu with additional paper towels. Place a cutting board on top of tofu; place a cast-iron skillet on top of cutting board. Let stand 30 minutes to 1 hour. (Tofu is ready when a slice bends easily without tearing or crumbling.) Arrange tofu in a single layer in a 13 x 9–inch baking dish.

2. Combine juice and next 6 ingredients in a small saucepan, and bring to a boil. Cook 1 minute, stirring until honey dissolves. Pour over tofu. Cover and let stand at room temperature 1 hour.

3. Prepare grill.

4. Remove tofu from dish; reserve marinade. Coat tofu with cooking spray. Place tofu on grill rack coated with cooking spray. Grill 3 minutes on each side or until browned.

5. Remove 12 large outer leaves from lettuce head; reserve remaining lettuce for another use. Remove bottom half of each lettuce leaf; reserve for another use. Place 1 tofu slice on each lettuce leaf top. Top each leaf top with 2 teaspoons cilantro, ¾ teaspoon peanuts, 3 mint leaves, 3 carrot strips, and 1 basil leaf. Wrap leaf around toppings. Serve with reserved marinade. Yield: 4 servings (serving size: 3 lettuce rolls and about ¼ cup sauce).

CALORIES 294 (29% from fat); FAT 9.5g (sat 1.5g, mono 2.5g, poly 4.9g); PROTEIN 14.8g; CARB 44.9g; FIBER 2.8g; CHOL 0mg; IRON 3.5mg; SODIUM 334mg; CALC 157mg

Tofu Steaks with Red Wine-Mushroom Sauce and Mashed Grilled Potatoes

While the potatoes cook, bake the tofu to get it firm, and begin preparing the sauce. Oven-firming the tofu gives it the springy texture of an uncooked chicken breast.

Prep: 35 minutes • Cook: 57 minutes

Mashed Grilled Potatoes:
Cooking spray
  2 pounds peeled baking potatoes, cut into 1-inch pieces
  6 garlic cloves
  ½ cup 2% reduced-fat milk
  ¼ cup fat-free sour cream
  1 tablespoon butter
  ¾ teaspoon salt
  ½ teaspoon freshly ground black pepper
Tofu:
  1 (16-ounce) package water-packed firm tofu, drained
  ½ teaspoon chopped fresh thyme
  ¼ teaspoon freshly ground black pepper
Red Wine-Mushroom Sauce:
  ⅓ cup finely chopped shallots
  3 cups sliced cremini mushrooms (about 8 ounces)
  3 cups sliced shiitake mushroom caps (about 6 ounces)
  1 (5-inch) portobello mushroom cap, cut into 1-inch pieces (about 4 ounces)
1½ cups dry red wine
  1 cup water, divided
  1 tablespoon red miso (soybean paste)
  ¼ teaspoon salt
  ¼ teaspoon freshly ground black pepper
  2 tablespoons chopped fresh parsley

1. Prepare grill.

2. To prepare potatoes, cut an 18 x 12–inch sheet of heavy-duty foil; lightly coat foil with cooking spray. Place potatoes and garlic in center of foil. Gather edges of foil to form a pouch; tightly seal edges. Pierce foil several times with a fork. Place pouch on grill rack; grill 30 minutes or until potatoes are tender, turning pouch occasionally.

3. Preheat oven to 375°.

4. Place potatoes and garlic in a large bowl; add milk, sour cream, butter, ¾ teaspoon salt, and ½ teaspoon pepper. Mash with a potato masher to desired consistency; keep warm.

5. To prepare tofu, cut tofu lengthwise into 4 slices. Arrange tofu in a single layer on a foil-lined baking sheet coated with cooking spray. Lightly coat tofu with cooking spray. Bake at 375° for 25 minutes or until tofu releases 3 or more tablespoons liquid. Cool slightly.

6. Lightly coat tofu with cooking spray; sprinkle with thyme and ¼ teaspoon pepper. Place tofu on grill rack coated with cooking spray; grill 3 minutes on each side or until browned. Keep warm.

7. To prepare sauce, heat a large nonstick skillet over medium-high heat. Coat pan with cooking spray. Add shallots; sauté 1 minute. Add mushrooms; sauté 6 minutes or until moisture evaporates. Remove mushroom mixture from pan. Add wine to pan. Bring to a boil, and cook until reduced to ¾ cup (about 4 minutes).

8. Combine 1 tablespoon water and miso, stirring with a whisk. Add miso mixture, remaining water, mushroom mixture, ¼ teaspoon salt, and ¼ teaspoon pepper to pan. Bring to a boil; cook until liquid is reduced to about 1 cup (about 4 minutes). Stir in parsley. Serve sauce with tofu and potatoes. Yield: 4 servings (serving size: 1 tofu steak, 1 cup potatoes, and ½ cup mushroom sauce).

CALORIES 457 (28% from fat); FAT 14.0g (sat 3.8g, mono 3.3g, poly 6.0g); PROTEIN 28.2g; CARB 57.8g; FIBER 7.8g; CHOL 11mg; IRON 4.9mg; SODIUM 895mg; CALC 220mg

Tofu with Red Curry Paste, Peas, and Yellow Tomatoes

Look for red curry paste in the ethnic foods or gourmet sections of the supermarket. The paste is a blend of clarified butter (ghee), curry powder, vinegar, and other seasonings. Use either Indian or Asian curry paste; it comes in mild and hot versions, so adjust the heat to suit your preference.

Prep: 20 minutes • Cook: 41 minutes

  1 (14-ounce) package firm tofu, drained and cut into 1-inch cubes
  2 tablespoons fresh lime juice
  1 teaspoon ground turmeric
  ¼ teaspoon salt
  ⅛ teaspoon pepper
  2 teaspoons olive oil
  2 cups thinly sliced onion
  1 cup light coconut milk
  1 to 2 tablespoons red curry paste
  1 cup shelled green peas (about 1 pound unshelled) or frozen green peas, thawed
  ½ cup chopped yellow tomato
  4 cups hot cooked long-grain rice

1. Place a large nonstick skillet over medium-high heat. Add tofu; cook until liquid from tofu is evaporated (about 3 minutes). Remove tofu from pan; sprinkle with lime juice, turmeric, salt, and pepper.

2. Heat oil in pan over medium-high heat. Add onion; sauté 5 minutes. Add tofu, and cook 7 minutes or until golden. Combine milk and curry paste; add to pan. Reduce heat, and simmer 3 minutes. Add peas and tomato; cook 2 minutes. Serve over rice. Yield: 4 servings (serving size: 1 cup tofu mixture and 1 cup rice).

CALORIES 421 (23% from fat); FAT 10.6g (sat 3.1g, mono 2.9g, poly 3.1g); PROTEIN 15.5g; CARB 66.9g; FIBER 5.3g; CHOL 0mg; IRON 8.7mg; SODIUM 344mg; CALC 154mg

Sesame-Crusted Tofu Sticks with Vegetable Sauté

Double-breading the tofu sticks gives them a crisp exterior. Look for Japanese sweet and sour sauce in Asian markets.

Prep: 30 minutes • Cook: 22 minutes

Tofu:
- ½ teaspoon salt
- ¼ teaspoon pepper
- 1 large egg
- 1 large egg white
- 1 cup dry breadcrumbs
- ¼ cup all-purpose flour
- 2 tablespoons sesame seeds
- 1 (15-ounce) package extrafirm tofu, drained and cut into 18 sticks
- 2 tablespoons dark sesame oil, divided

Vegetable Sauté:
- 1 (6-ounce) can pineapple juice
- Cooking spray
- ½ cup chopped shallots
- 1 garlic clove, minced
- ½ pound shiitake mushroom caps (about 10 mushrooms)
- 2 cups (2-inch) sliced green onions
- 1 cup cherry tomatoes, halved
- 1 tablespoon chopped fresh thyme
- 2 tablespoons balsamic vinegar
- 1 tablespoon Japanese sweet and sour sauce (such as ABC sauce; optional)

1. To prepare tofu, combine first 4 ingredients in a shallow dish. Combine breadcrumbs, flour, and sesame seeds in a shallow dish.

2. Working with 1 tofu stick at a time, dip in egg mixture; dredge in breadcrumb mixture. Return tofu to egg mixture; dredge in breadcrumb mixture.

3. Heat 1 tablespoon oil in a large nonstick skillet over medium-high heat. Add half of tofu; cook 4 minutes, turning to brown all sides. Remove from pan. Repeat procedure with remaining oil and tofu. Keep warm.

4. To prepare vegetable sauté, pour pineapple juice into pan. Bring to a boil; cook until juice is reduced to ¼ cup (about 5 minutes). Remove from pan.

5. Heat pan over medium-high heat. Coat pan with cooking spray. Add shallots, minced garlic, and mushrooms; sauté 4 minutes, stirring occasionally. Add green onions, tomatoes, and thyme, and cook 1 minute. Stir in pineapple juice and balsamic vinegar, and cook 30 seconds.

6. Arrange vegetable mixture on each of 6 plates; top each serving with tofu sticks. Drizzle with sweet and sour sauce, if desired. Serve immediately. Yield: 6 servings (serving size: about ½ cup vegetable mixture and 3 tofu sticks).

CALORIES 253 (29% from fat); FAT 8.1g (sat 1.4g, mono 3g, poly 3.1g); PROTEIN 12.5g; CARB 32.9g; FIBER 3g; CHOL 36mg; IRON 3.5mg; SODIUM 846mg; CALC 119mg

tofu tips The labels "soft," "firm," and "extrafirm" on tofu refer to the texture and density. Soft tofu is best for recipes where the tofu is handled as little as possible—added to a soup, simmered in a stew, or in dips and salad dressings. Use firm tofu for marinating, sautéing, or pan-frying. Note that the tofu packed in asceptic packages tends to be more delicate than water-packed tofu, even if it's labeled firm or extrafirm.

You can make tofu firmer by heating it in simmering water, pan-frying, or baking. This toughens the proteins and pulls out the excess water while browning the tofu. (This works best with water-packed tofu.)

Another way to get rid of excess moisture is to press the water-packed tofu, once removed from its liquid, with a heavy weight for about 30 minutes.

Stir-Fried Tofu, Shiitake Mushrooms, and Chinese Peas

Let fresh ginger sit in salt for five minutes to draw out some of the ginger juice, making it drier and better for stir-frying. The process also decreases the ginger's pungency. Bird, or chiltepín, chiles are small, red or green, and very hot. They're often used in Thai-style dishes.

Prep: 12 minutes • Cook: 8 minutes
Other: 5 minutes

- 1 tablespoon julienne-cut peeled fresh ginger
- ½ teaspoon kosher or sea salt
- 1 teaspoon cornstarch
- 1 tablespoon canola oil
- 2 cups thinly sliced shiitake mushroom caps
- 1 cup snow peas, trimmed
- ½ teaspoon minced bird chile or
  1 teaspoon minced serrano chile
- 1 (12.3-ounce) package reduced-fat firm tofu, drained and cubed
- ½ cup (1-inch) sliced green onions
- 3 tablespoons low-sodium soy sauce

1. Combine ginger and ½ teaspoon salt in a small bowl; let stand 5 minutes. Rinse ginger with cold water, and pat dry. Combine ginger and cornstarch in bowl.
2. Heat oil in a wok or large nonstick skillet over medium-high heat. Add mushrooms, and stir-fry 2 minutes or until tender. Add ginger mixture, snow peas, and chile, and stir-fry 2 minutes. Add tofu; stir-fry 1 minute. Add onions and soy sauce; stir-fry 2 minutes. Yield: 2 servings (serving size: 1¾ cups).

CALORIES 208 (41% from fat); FAT 9.4g (sat 0.8g, mono 4.8g, poly 3.1g); PROTEIN 15.4g; CARB 16.2g; FIBER 3.4g; CHOL 0mg; IRON 4.7mg; SODIUM 775mg; CALC 120mg

Vegetable Tagine with Baked Tempeh

Don't let the long ingredient list intimidate you—the deliciously spicy blend of seasonings makes this dish a standout.

Prep: 40 minutes • Cook: 1 hour, 43 minutes

Tagine:

- 1 teaspoon cumin seeds
- 1 teaspoon caraway seeds
- 1 teaspoon coriander seeds
- ½ teaspoon paprika
- ½ teaspoon black peppercorns
- 1 (1-inch) piece cinnamon stick
- 2 teaspoons extravirgin olive oil
- 2 cups finely chopped onion
- ¾ cup finely chopped carrot
- ½ cup finely chopped celery
- ½ teaspoon sea salt
- 2 garlic cloves, peeled
- 2 cups (½-inch) cubed peeled sweet potato
- 2 cups chopped green cabbage
- 1½ cups water
- 1 cup finely chopped yellow squash
- 1 cup finely chopped zucchini
- 1 cup finely chopped peeled tomato
- 1 tablespoon fresh lemon juice

Baked Tempeh:

- ⅔ cup water
- 6 tablespoons fresh lemon juice
- ⅓ cup finely chopped fresh flat-leaf parsley
- 2 teaspoons ground cumin
- 2 teaspoons paprika
- ½ teaspoon sea salt
- ½ teaspoon ground red pepper
- 4 garlic cloves, minced
- 1 pound tempeh, cut into ½-inch cubes

Remaining ingredients:

- 2 cups hot cooked couscous
- 4 teaspoons minced fresh cilantro (optional)

1. To prepare tagine, combine first 6 ingredients in a spice or coffee grinder; process until finely ground.
2. Heat oil in a large Dutch oven over medium heat. Add onion, carrot, celery, ½ teaspoon salt, and 2 peeled garlic cloves; cook 5 minutes, stirring occasionally. Cover, reduce heat to low, and cook 20 minutes.
3. Stir in cumin mixture, sweet potato, and next 5 ingredients; bring to a boil. Reduce heat; simmer, uncovered, 30 minutes or until thick. Stir in lemon juice.
4. To prepare tempeh, preheat oven to 350°.
5. Combine ⅔ cup water and next 7 ingredients in a large bowl. Add tempeh, and toss well to coat. Arrange tempeh mixture in a single layer in an 11 x 7–inch baking dish. Cover with foil.
6. Bake at 350° for 35 minutes. Uncover and bake an additional 5 minutes or until liquid is absorbed. Serve tempeh over tagine and couscous; sprinkle with cilantro, if desired. Yield: 4 servings (serving size: 4 ounces tempeh, ¾ cup tagine, and ½ cup couscous).

CALORIES 507 (29% from fat); FAT 16.1g (sat 3g, mono 5.3g, poly 5.1g); PROTEIN 29.5g; CARB 69.3g; FIBER 16.3g; CHOL 0mg; IRON 6.4mg; SODIUM 642mg; CALC 262mg

tempeh Tempeh is basically a soybean cake. It's made from partially cooked soybeans inoculated with spores of a friendly mold in a process that's similar to cheesemaking. Tempeh is blanched or frozen to slow fermentation and preserve active enzymes. It has a yeasty flavor and a firm texture. Although it can be made from soybeans alone, it's often combined with a grain such as rice or barley.

meats

Jamaican Jerk Beef
Kebabs, page 325

Beef
From ground round to tenderloin, we show you how to braise, broil, grill, and roast your way to magnificent meals.

Picadillo

This classic Cuban dish remains popular because it's so easy to make and because of its appealing sweet and savory nature. Other renditions of picadillo include cinnamon and cloves, but this is the standard version. Typical accompaniments are white rice and ripe plantains. Cook the rice while the meat mixture simmers.

Prep: 8 minutes • Cook: 38 minutes

1 teaspoon olive oil
1 cup finely chopped onion
1 pound ground round
3 garlic cloves, minced
1 cup less-sodium beef broth
⅓ cup raisins
⅓ cup coarsely chopped pimiento-stuffed olives
3 tablespoons capers
1 tablespoon tomato paste
¼ teaspoon freshly ground black pepper
3 cups hot cooked rice
Parsley sprigs (optional)

1. Heat oil in a large nonstick skillet over medium-high heat. Add onion; sauté 5 minutes. Add beef and garlic; cook 5 minutes or until browned, stirring to crumble. Add broth and next 5 ingredients; stir well. Bring to a boil. Cover, reduce heat, and simmer 25 minutes.

Serve with rice. Garnish with parsley sprigs, if desired. Yield: 4 servings (serving size: 1 cup picadillo and ¾ cup rice).

CALORIES 372 (22% from fat); FAT 8.9g (sat 2.9g, mono 4.1g, poly 0.6g); PROTEIN 30.2g; CARB 41.9g; FIBER 2.3g; CHOL 65mg; IRON 3.8mg; SODIUM 457mg; CALC 38mg

Chipotle-Sweet Potato Shepherd's Pie

Smoky, spicy chipotle chiles in adobo sauce balance the sweetness of the potato topping. If you prefer, you can use Yukon gold potatoes or regular baking potatoes.

Prep: 25 minutes • Cook: 1 hour, 10 minutes

Topping:
- 1 (7-ounce) can chipotle chiles in adobo sauce
- 2¼ pounds peeled sweet potatoes, cut into 1-inch pieces
- 1 cup 2% reduced-fat milk
- 1 teaspoon kosher salt
- ¼ teaspoon cracked black pepper

Filling:
- 2 pounds ground sirloin
- Cooking spray
- 2 cups chopped onion
- 1 cup chopped carrot
- 3 garlic cloves, minced
- 1 cup frozen green peas, thawed
- ½ cup crushed tomatoes
- ¼ cup chopped fresh parsley
- 3 tablespoons steak sauce (such as A.1.)
- 2 tablespoons tomato paste
- ½ teaspoon cracked black pepper

1. Preheat oven to 400°.

2. To prepare topping, remove 1 chile and 2 teaspoons sauce from can; reserve remaining chiles and sauce for another use. Coarsely chop 1 chile.

3. Place potatoes in a saucepan; cover with water. Bring to a boil; cook 15 minutes or until very tender. Drain. Place potatoes, chopped chile, 2 teaspoons adobo sauce, milk, salt, and ¼ teaspoon pepper in a large bowl. Beat with a mixer at medium speed until smooth.

4. To prepare filling, cook beef in a large nonstick skillet over medium-high heat until browned, stirring to crumble. Remove from pan; drain.

5. Heat pan over medium-high heat. Coat with cooking spray. Add onion, carrot, and garlic; sauté 8 minutes or until tender. Return beef to pan; stir in peas and remaining 5 ingredients. Cook 2 minutes.

6. Spoon beef mixture into a 3-quart casserole; top with sweet potato mixture, spreading evenly. Bake at 400° for 30 minutes or until thoroughly heated. Yield: 8 servings (serving size: 1½ cups).

CALORIES 408 (29% from fat); FAT 13.2g (sat 5.2g, mono 5.6g, poly 0.7g); PROTEIN 28.3g; CARB 43.4g; FIBER 6.3g; CHOL 84mg; IRON 3.7mg; SODIUM 480mg; CALC 105mg

"Barbecued" Meat Loaf

For a true comfort-food supper, serve the meat loaf with Basic Mashed Potatoes (page 527).

Prep: 20 minutes • Cook: 1 hour, 15 minutes
Other: 10 minutes

- 1 cup ketchup
- 1 tablespoon Worcestershire sauce
- 2 teaspoons chili powder
- 1 tablespoon red wine vinegar
- 1 (½-ounce) slice white bread
- ½ cup 1% low-fat milk
- 1 cup minced fresh onion
- ½ cup (2 ounces) grated fresh Parmesan cheese
- ½ cup finely diced carrot
- ¼ cup minced fresh parsley
- 1 teaspoon chopped fresh or ¼ teaspoon dried rubbed sage
- ½ teaspoon pepper
- 2 garlic cloves, minced
- 1½ pounds ground sirloin
- ½ pound lean ground pork
- 1 large egg, lightly beaten
- Cooking spray

1. Preheat oven to 350°.

2. Combine first 4 ingredients in a bowl.

3. Place bread in a food processor; process until finely ground. Combine bread and milk in a large bowl. Add ½ cup ketchup mixture, onion, and next 9 ingredients; stir until well blended. Place beef mixture in an 8 x 4–inch loaf pan coated with cooking spray. Bake at 350° for 1 hour. Brush remaining ketchup mixture over top. Bake an additional 15 minutes. Let stand 10 minutes. Remove meat loaf from pan. Cut into 8 slices. Yield: 8 servings (serving size: 1 slice).

CALORIES 257 (33% from fat); FAT 9.5g (sat 3.8g, mono 3.7g, poly 0.7g); PROTEIN 28.9g; CARB 13.8g; FIBER 1.4g; CHOL 102mg; IRON 3.3mg; SODIUM 591mg; CALC 135mg

buying ground beef

Ground beef labels can be quite confusing. Some ground beef is labeled by cut (chuck, sirloin, or round), while some is labeled by percent fat to percent lean. By law, the maximum fat content in any ground beef is 30% (70% lean). The leanness of ground beef can be determined from the cut of meat or by the amount of fat that's trimmed before grinding. Ground chuck is usually the highest in fat content (around 20%), round is generally the lowest (about 11%). Sirloin falls between the two (about 15%). The cut on the label isn't necessarily an indication of leanness. All ground beef may have fat added to it; the label must say how much. A package labeled "80% lean ground sirloin" is 20% fat—5% more than a piece of ground sirloin naturally contains. Look for labels that tell the amount of percent fat to percent lean—then there'll be no guessing.

Italian Meat Loaf

Upgrade basic meat loaf to an Italian-flavored entrée by adding sun-dried tomatoes, basil, and provolone cheese.

Prep: 20 minutes • Cook: 1 hour, 2 minutes
Other: 40 minutes

    1   cup boiling water
    ½   cup sun-dried tomatoes, packed
        without oil
    ½   cup ketchup
    1   cup seasoned breadcrumbs
    ¾   cup finely chopped onion
    ¾   cup chopped fresh basil
    ½   cup (2 ounces) shredded sharp
        provolone cheese
    2   large egg whites
    2   garlic cloves, minced
    1   pound ground round
        Cooking spray
    ⅓   cup ketchup

1. Combine boiling water and tomatoes in a bowl; let stand 30 minutes or until soft. Drain tomatoes; finely chop.
2. Preheat oven to 350°.
3. Combine ½ cup ketchup, breadcrumbs, and next 6 ingredients in a large bowl. Add tomatoes to meat mixture. Shape meat mixture into a 9 x 5–inch loaf on a broiler pan coated with cooking spray. Spread ⅓ cup ketchup over meat loaf. Bake at 350° for 1 hour. Let stand 10 minutes before slicing. Cut into 12 slices. Yield: 6 servings (serving size: 2 slices).

CALORIES 294 (27% from fat); FAT 8.7g (sat 3.6g, mono 3.2g, poly 0.7g); PROTEIN 24.3g; CARB 30.8g; FIBER 2.5g; CHOL 53mg; IRON 3.9mg; SODIUM 893mg; CALC 149mg

For additional ground beef recipes, see pages 445-446 in the Sandwiches chapter and pages 493 and 502 in the Soups & Stews chapter.

Grillades and Gravy over Grits

Grillades (gree-YAHDS) is a Creole dish of pounded, seared meat, simmered in gravy. It's typically served over grits but is also good with mashed potatoes. Prepare the grits (or potatoes) while the meat mixture simmers.

Prep: 25 minutes • Cook: 1 hour, 14 minutes

    4   teaspoons canola oil, divided
    2   pounds thin beef or breakfast steaks
    ½   teaspoon salt
    2   teaspoons black pepper, divided
    1   cup diced white onion
    ½   cup chopped celery
    ½   cup chopped green bell pepper
    ¼   cup minced fresh garlic (about 8
        cloves)
    2   tablespoons all-purpose flour
    1   (14.5-ounce) can diced tomatoes,
        undrained
    1   (8-ounce) can tomato sauce
    1   (2¼-ounce) can sliced ripe olives
    1   (14-ounce) can less-sodium beef broth
    2   tablespoons minced fresh basil
    1   teaspoon chopped fresh thyme
    1   teaspoon hot pepper sauce
    ½   cup sliced green onions
    ¼   cup minced fresh parsley
    4   cups hot cooked grits

1. Heat 2 teaspoons oil in a large cast-iron skillet over medium-high heat. Sprinkle steak with salt and 1 teaspoon black pepper. Add one-third of steak to pan; cook 45 seconds on each side. Remove from pan; keep warm. Repeat cooking procedure with remaining steak.
2. Add remaining 2 teaspoons oil to pan. Add onion, celery, bell pepper, and garlic, and sauté 3 minutes or until tender. Sprinkle flour over vegetables; stir well to combine. Add diced tomatoes, tomato sauce, and olives; stir well to combine. Add broth; stir until blended. Add remaining 1 teaspoon black pepper, basil, thyme, and hot pepper sauce.
3. Return steak to pan; bring to a boil. Reduce heat, and simmer 1 hour or until steak is tender. Stir in green onions and parsley. Serve over grits. Yield: 8 servings (serving size: about 3 ounces beef, about ⅓ cup gravy, and ½ cup grits).

CALORIES 325 (30% from fat); FAT 10.7g (sat 3g, mono 5g, poly 1.2g); PROTEIN 29.4g; CARB 27.2g; FIBER 3g; CHOL 71mg; IRON 4.3mg; SODIUM 589mg; CALC 55mg

Cinnamon-Beef Noodles

A hint of cinnamon is what sets this Asian-style beef dish apart. Cook the pasta during the last 15 minutes of simmering time for the meat.

Prep: 20 minutes
Cook: 2 hours, 18 minutes

- 5 cups water
- 1½ cups rice wine or sake
- ¾ cup low-sodium soy sauce
- ¼ cup sugar
- 2 teaspoons canola oil
- 2 pounds beef stew meat, cut into 1½-inch cubes
- 8 green onions, cut into 1-inch pieces
- 6 garlic cloves, crushed
- 2 cinnamon sticks
- 1 (1-inch) piece peeled fresh ginger, thinly sliced
- 1 (10-ounce) package fresh spinach, chopped
- 4 cups hot cooked wide lo mein noodles or vermicelli (about 8 ounces uncooked pasta)

1. Combine first 4 ingredients in a large bowl; stir with a whisk. Set aside.
2. Heat 1 teaspoon oil in a Dutch oven over medium-high heat; add half of beef, browning on all sides. Remove from pan. Repeat with remaining 1 teaspoon oil and beef. Return beef to pan; add water mixture, onions, garlic, cinnamon, and ginger. Bring to a boil; cover, reduce heat, and simmer 2 hours or until beef is tender. Discard ginger and cinnamon. Stir in spinach; cook 3 minutes. Serve over noodles. Yield: 8 servings (serving size: 1 cup beef mixture and ½ cup noodles).

CALORIES 386 (22% from fat); FAT 9.6g (sat 3.1g, mono 4.2g, poly 0.9g); PROTEIN 28g; CARB 33g; FIBER 2.4g; CHOL 71mg; IRON 4.8mg; SODIUM 657mg; CALC 65mg

London Broil with Texas Toast and Red Onion Jam

The round, or upper part of the leg, includes three muscles: top round, eye round, and bottom round. Only top round is tender enough to cook as steak. Often labeled London broil, it's a somewhat chewy cut with great flavor, best served cut into thin slices. You can also use flank steak or sirloin for this recipe.

Prep: 35 minutes • **Cook: 52 minutes**
Other: 2 hours, 10 minutes

Steak:
- ½ cup balsamic vinegar
- 2 tablespoons brown sugar
- 1 tablespoon Dijon mustard
- 3 garlic cloves, crushed
- 1 (2-pound) top round steak, trimmed (about 1½ inches thick)
- ½ teaspoon kosher salt
- ½ teaspoon cracked black pepper
- Cooking spray

Red Onion Jam:
- 1 tablespoon olive oil
- 8 cups sliced red onion (about 1½ pounds)
- ¼ cup balsamic vinegar
- 2 tablespoons brown sugar
- 2 tablespoons minced peeled fresh ginger
- 6 garlic cloves, minced
- 1 tablespoon thinly sliced fresh basil
- ½ teaspoon kosher salt
- ½ teaspoon cracked black pepper

Texas Toast:
- 8 (1½-ounce) slices sourdough bread
- 2 tablespoons butter, melted
- 1 garlic clove, crushed

1. To prepare steak, place first 4 ingredients in a large zip-top plastic bag; add steak. Seal and marinate in refrigerator 2 hours, turning occasionally.
2. Preheat broiler.
3. Remove steak from bag; discard marinade. Sprinkle steak with ½ teaspoon salt and ½ teaspoon pepper. Place steak on a broiler pan coated with cooking spray. Broil 10 minutes on each side (medium-rare) or until desired degree of doneness. Place steak on a cutting board; cover loosely with foil. Let stand 10 minutes. Cut steak against grain into thin slices.
4. To prepare jam, heat oil in a Dutch oven over medium-high heat. Add onion; cook 20 to 25 minutes or until deep golden brown, stirring frequently. Add ¼ cup vinegar, 2 tablespoons sugar, ginger, and 6 minced garlic cloves; cook 2 minutes or until liquid almost evaporates. Stir in basil, ½ teaspoon salt, and ½ teaspoon pepper.
5. Preheat oven to 350°.
6. To prepare toast, place bread slices on a large baking sheet. Bake at 350° for 8 minutes or until lightly browned. Combine butter and 1 crushed garlic clove; brush over toast. Serve steak with toast and jam. Yield: 8 servings (serving size: 3 ounces beef, 1 slice toast, and ¼ cup jam).

CALORIES 398 (25% from fat); FAT 11g (sat 3.8g, mono 4.6g, poly 0.8g); PROTEIN 35.8g; CARB 40.1g; FIBER 4.5g; CHOL 84mg; IRON 4.3mg; SODIUM 549mg; CALC 68mg

Test Kitchen Tip: Tightly wrapped and refrigerated, raw beef will last three to four days (ground beef, one to two days). At that point, it should be cooked or frozen. Use frozen beef within two months.

Wasabi-Miso Marinated Flank Steak

A few simple ingredients converge for bold flavor in this quick and easy dish. Although you may need to make a trip to the Asian market to pick up miso (soybean paste) and mirin (sweet rice wine), look for wasabi powder in your supermarket's spice aisle; it's much milder than the kind found in Japanese markets.

Prep: 8 minutes • Cook: 12 minutes • Other: 2 hours

¼ cup yellow miso
¼ cup mirin
¼ cup dry white wine
1 tablespoon wasabi powder
1 tablespoon rice vinegar
1 (1-pound) flank steak, trimmed
Cooking spray

1. Combine first 5 ingredients in a small bowl; stir well with a whisk. Combine miso mixture and steak in a large zip-top plastic bag. Seal; marinate in refrigerator 2 hours.

2. Prepare grill or broiler.

3. Remove steak from bag, reserving marinade. Place steak on grill rack or broiler pan coated with cooking spray. Grill or broil 6 minutes on each side or until desired degree of doneness, basting occasionally with reserved marinade. Yield: 4 servings (serving size: 3 ounces).

CALORIES 252 (34% from fat); FAT 9.5g (sat 3.7g, mono 3.7g, poly 1g); PROTEIN 25.2g; CARB 9g; FIBER 0.9g; CHOL 57mg; IRON 2.4mg; SODIUM 817mg; CALC 20mg

Test Kitchen Tip: Store miso in a glass jar in the refrigerator; it will keep indefinitely.

Flank Steak with Cilantro-Almond Pesto

Ground almonds and cilantro, rather than pine nuts and basil, flavor this pesto. It's also good as a spread for burgers and sandwiches.

Prep: 13 minutes • Cook: 13 minutes

¾ cup fresh cilantro
2 tablespoons slivered almonds, toasted
1 tablespoon chopped seeded jalapeño pepper
⅛ teaspoon salt
⅛ teaspoon black pepper
1 garlic clove, chopped
3 tablespoons plain fat-free yogurt
1½ teaspoons fresh lime juice
1 (1-pound) flank steak, trimmed
Cooking spray

1. Prepare grill.

2. Place first 6 ingredients in a blender; process until finely chopped (about 15 seconds). Add yogurt and juice; process until smooth.

3. Place flank steak on grill rack coated with cooking spray, and grill 6 minutes on each side or until desired degree of doneness. Cut steak diagonally across grain into thin slices. Serve steak with pesto. Yield: 4 servings (serving size: 3 ounces beef and about 1 tablespoon pesto).

CALORIES 209 (47% from fat); FAT 10.8g (sat 3.9g, mono 4.9g, poly 0.8g); PROTEIN 24.6g; CARB 2.4g; FIBER 0.6g; CHOL 57mg; IRON 2.5mg; SODIUM 152mg; CALC 36mg

WINE NOTE: The tangy herbal flavors in the pesto are well suited for cabernet franc, which has a light, herbal, mintlike underpinning and is sleeker than cabernet sauvignon.

Adobo Flank Steak with Summer Corn-and-Tomato Relish

Sherry vinegar is a crucial ingredient in the relish, so choose a good one. We recommend either Columela Reserva Solera or Gran Capirete.

Prep: 30 minutes • Cook: 18 minutes
Other: 24 hours

Steak:
- 1 teaspoon black peppercorns
- 1 teaspoon cumin seeds
- 2 whole cloves
- 1 (7-ounce) can chipotle chiles in adobo sauce
- 2 tablespoons sherry vinegar
- 1 tablespoon fresh thyme leaves
- 2 teaspoons brown sugar
- ¾ teaspoon kosher salt
- 1 garlic clove, peeled
- 1 (1¼-pound) flank steak, trimmed
- Cooking spray

Summer Corn-and-Tomato Relish:
- 2 cups fresh corn kernels (about 4 ears)
- 1 cup chopped seeded tomato
- ¼ cup chopped bottled roasted red bell peppers
- 2 tablespoons sherry vinegar
- 1 tablespoon extravirgin olive oil
- ¾ teaspoon kosher salt
- Thyme leaves (optional)

1. To prepare steak, cook first 3 ingredients in a small nonstick skillet over medium heat 45 seconds or until toasted. Place peppercorn mixture in a spice or coffee grinder; process until finely ground.
2. Remove 1 chile from can; reserve remaining chiles and sauce for another use. Place peppercorn mixture, chile, 2 tablespoons vinegar, and next 4 ingredients in a blender; process until smooth, scraping sides occasionally. Combine vinegar mixture and steak in a large zip-top plastic bag; seal and marinate in refrigerator 24 hours. Remove steak from bag; discard marinade.
3. Prepare grill.
4. Place steak on grill rack coated with cooking spray; cook 6 minutes on each side or until desired degree of doneness. Cut steak diagonally across grain into thin slices.
5. To prepare relish, heat a large nonstick skillet over medium-high heat. Coat pan with cooking spray. Add corn; sauté 5 minutes or until lightly browned. Remove from heat; stir in tomato and next 4 ingredients. Serve with steak. Garnish with thyme, if desired. Yield: 5 servings (serving size: 3 ounces beef and ½ cup relish).

CALORIES 303 (44% from fat); FAT 14.9g (sat 5.2g, mono 6.7g, poly 1.3g); PROTEIN 25.2g; CARB 16.5g; FIBER 2.7g; CHOL 57mg; IRON 3.2mg; SODIUM 634mg; CALC 20mg

how to check for doneness

It's important to know when meat has reached the desired degree of doneness. For large cuts of meat, use an instant-read thermometer. For steaks, even though a thermometer is the only way to get an actual temperature, you can use the "nick, peek, and cheat" method. Nick the meat with a sharp knife and take a peek inside to check its doneness. Don't worry about juices escaping when you cut into the meat; the small amount you lose is preferable to under- or overcooking your steak.

Grilled Sirloin Skewers with Peaches and Peppers

The sweetness of peaches and red bell peppers contrasts nicely with the cumin-scented steak and parsley-garlic sauce.

Prep: 35 minutes • Cook: 6 minutes • Other: 5 minutes

Kebabs:

- 1½ tablespoons ground cumin
- 1½ tablespoons cracked black pepper
- 2¾ teaspoons kosher salt
- 2 pounds boneless sirloin steak, cut into 48 (1-inch) pieces
- 4 peaches, each cut into 8 wedges
- 2 small red onions, each cut into 8 wedges
- 2 large red bell peppers, each cut into 8 (1-inch) pieces
- Cooking spray

Sauce:

- ½ cup chopped fresh parsley
- ¼ cup red wine vinegar
- 1 teaspoon olive oil
- ¼ teaspoon kosher salt
- ¼ teaspoon cracked black pepper
- 3 garlic cloves, minced
- Parsley sprigs (optional)

1. Prepare grill.

2. To prepare kebabs, combine first 7 ingredients, and toss well. Thread 3 steak pieces, 2 peach wedges, 1 onion wedge, and 1 bell pepper piece alternately onto each of 16 (12-inch) skewers. Place on grill rack coated with cooking spray, and grill 6 minutes or until tender, turning occasionally. Place on a platter and cover loosely with foil. Let stand 5 minutes.

3. To prepare sauce, combine chopped parsley and next 5 ingredients, stirring with a whisk. Spoon over kebabs. Garnish with parsley sprigs, if desired. Yield: 8 servings (serving size: 2 kebabs).

CALORIES 217 (30% from fat); FAT 7.2g (sat 2.4g, mono 3g, poly 0.4g); PROTEIN 25.5g; CARB 12.4g; FIBER 3.2g; CHOL 69mg; IRON 3.8mg; SODIUM 768mg; CALC 38mg

Peruvian Beef Kebabs with Roasted Yellow Pepper Sauce

You'll enjoy the aroma of cumin, onions, roasted peppers, garlic, and grilled beef as you prepare this Peruvian-style dish of grill-charred kebabs with a sunny yellow sauce. Look for aji amarillo, a fiery yellow chile, in Latin food markets.

Prep: 35 minutes • Cook: 21 minutes
Other: 3 hours, 15 minutes

Beef:

- 1½ pounds boneless sirloin steak, trimmed and cut into 1-inch pieces
- 3 tablespoons red wine vinegar
- 2 teaspoons ground aji amarillo or hot paprika
- 1 teaspoon salt
- 1 teaspoon freshly ground black pepper
- ½ teaspoon ground cumin
- ½ teaspoon ground turmeric

Fiery rub:

- 3 tablespoons chopped fresh flat-leaf parsley
- 1 teaspoon salt
- 1 teaspoon ground aji amarillo or hot paprika
- ½ teaspoon freshly ground black pepper
- ¼ teaspoon ground turmeric
- Cooking spray
- Roasted Yellow Pepper Sauce

1. To prepare beef, combine first 7 ingredients in a large bowl; toss well. Cover and chill 3 hours.

2. To prepare fiery rub, combine parsley, 1 teaspoon salt, 1 teaspoon aji amarillo, ½ teaspoon pepper, and ¼ teaspoon turmeric.

3. Prepare grill.

4. Remove beef from bowl; thread beef onto each of 6 (10-inch) skewers. Press fiery rub onto beef. Place kebabs on grill rack coated with cooking spray; grill 6 minutes or until desired degree of doneness, turning once. Serve with Roasted Yellow Pepper Sauce. Yield: 6 servings (serving size: 1 kebab and about 2½ tablespoons sauce).

(Totals include Roasted Yellow Pepper Sauce) CALORIES 188 (34% from fat); FAT 7g (sat 2.7g, mono 3g, poly 0.3g); PROTEIN 26.3g; CARB 3.4g; FIBER 0.8g; CHOL 76mg; IRON 3.6mg; SODIUM 809mg; CALC 23mg

Roasted Yellow Pepper Sauce

1   large yellow bell pepper
¼   cup finely chopped green onions
2   tablespoons white vinegar
1   tablespoon water
1   tablespoon olive oil
1   tablespoon fresh lemon juice
1   teaspoon ground cumin
1   teaspoon ground aji amarillo or
     hot paprika
½   teaspoon ground turmeric
¼   teaspoon salt
¼   teaspoon black pepper
1   garlic clove, minced

1. Preheat broiler.
2. Cut bell pepper in half lengthwise; discard seeds and membranes. Place pepper halves, skin sides up, on a foil-lined baking sheet; flatten pepper with hand. Broil 15 minutes or until blackened. Place in a zip-top plastic bag; seal. Let stand 15 minutes. Peel and coarsely chop. Place bell pepper and remaining 11 ingredients in a blender; process until smooth. Yield: about 1 cup (serving size: 2½ tablespoons).

CALORIES 55 (39% from fat); FAT 2.4g (sat 0.3g, mono 1.7g, poly 0.3g); PROTEIN 0.7g; CARB 8.1g; FIBER 0.8g; CHOL 0mg; IRON 0.5mg; SODIUM 203mg; CALC 12mg

Jamaican Jerk Beef Kebabs
(pictured on page 317)

Jerk is a Jamaican seasoning blend used on beef, pork, chicken, lamb, and fish. Usually, jerk is a dry rub, but you can mix it with liquid to form a paste or marinade. Choose plantains that are black to ensure that they're ripe.

Prep: 30 minutes • Cook: 10 minutes
Other: 20 minutes

½   cup chopped green onions
1   tablespoon ground allspice
2   tablespoons red wine vinegar
1   teaspoon salt
1   teaspoon chopped fresh or
¼   teaspoon dried thyme
2   teaspoons low-sodium soy sauce
½   teaspoon ground cinnamon
⅛   teaspoon ground nutmeg
2   habanero or serrano peppers, seeded
1½ pounds boneless sirloin steak,
     trimmed and cut into 30 cubes
1   red bell pepper, cut into 18 pieces
2   black plantains, peeled and each cut
     into 9 pieces
Cooking spray
Diagonally cut green onions (optional)
Lime wedges (optional)

1. Prepare grill.
2. Place first 9 ingredients in a food processor or blender; process until smooth. Place onion mixture, beef, and bell pepper pieces in a large zip-top plastic bag; seal. Marinate in refrigerator 20 minutes.
3. Remove beef and bell pepper pieces from bag; discard marinade. Place beef, bell pepper pieces, and plantain pieces in a large bowl; toss well to coat.
4. Thread 5 beef cubes, 3 red pepper pieces, and 3 plantain pieces alternately onto each of 6 (12-inch) skewers. Lightly coat with cooking spray. Place kebabs on grill rack coated with cooking spray. Grill 5 to 6 minutes on each side or until desired degree of doneness. Garnish with green onion pieces, and serve with lime wedges, if desired. Yield: 6 servings (serving size: 1 kebab).

CALORIES 260 (25% from fat); FAT 7.1g (sat 2.7g, mono 2.9g, poly 0.3g); PROTEIN 26.9g; CARB 21.3g; FIBER 2.4g; CHOL 76mg; IRON 3.4mg; SODIUM 358mg; CALC 20mg

Test Kitchen Tip: To broil the kebabs, place the skewers on a broiler pan coated with cooking spray, and broil 5 to 6 minutes on each side or to desired degree of doneness.

skewer savvy
- Soak wooden skewers in water for 15 to 30 minutes so they won't burn.
- Shrimp, scallops, and other "wobbly" pieces of food benefit from the double-skewer technique: Thread the pieces on a skewer, then run another one through the pieces parallel to the first, about a half-inch away.
- Expecting vegetarians? Cook the meat and vegetables on separate skewers, so guests who don't want to eat meat can pick up a stick of vegetables. If your guests assemble their own skewers, place the meat and vegetables in separate bowls.

Dry-Rub Steak with Fresh Fruit Salsa

The tangy fruit salsa is best if you prepare it just before you grill the sirloin.

Prep: 25 minutes • Cook: 12 minutes
Other: 2 hours, 35 minutes

Steak:

   1   tablespoon fresh lime juice
1½   teaspoons salt
1½   teaspoons minced garlic
   1   teaspoon chili powder
   1   teaspoon finely chopped fresh or
       ¼ teaspoon dried oregano
   1   teaspoon freshly ground black pepper
   ½   teaspoon ground cumin
   1   (2-pound) boneless sirloin steak,
       trimmed

Fresh Fruit Salsa:

   ½   cup finely chopped red onion
   2   tablespoons fresh lime juice
   ½   teaspoon kosher salt
1½   cups finely chopped peeled mango
   1   cup finely chopped peeled kiwifruit
   ½   cup quartered cherry tomatoes
   ¼   cup chopped green onions
   2   tablespoons minced fresh cilantro
   1   tablespoon chopped fresh mint
   1   teaspoon sugar
   1   jalapeño pepper, seeded and minced
       Cooking spray

1. To prepare steak, combine first 7 ingredients; rub evenly over steak. Cover and refrigerate 2 hours or overnight.
2. Prepare grill or broiler.
3. To prepare salsa, combine red onion, 2 tablespoons juice, and ½ teaspoon salt, tossing to coat. Let stand 30 minutes. Combine mango and next 7 ingredients in a medium bowl. Add onion mixture; toss.
4. Place steak on grill rack or broiler pan coated with cooking spray; grill 6 minutes

on each side or until desired degree of doneness. Place steak on a platter; let stand 5 minutes. Cut diagonally across grain into ¼-inch-thick slices. Serve with salsa. Yield: 8 servings (serving size: 3 ounces beef and about ⅓ cup salsa).

CALORIES 229 (36% from fat); FAT 9.1g (sat 3.4g, mono 3.6g, poly 0.4g); PROTEIN 24.7g; CARB 12.1g; FIBER 2.1g; CHOL 66mg; IRON 2.7mg; SODIUM 535mg; CALC 29mg

---

All-Time Favorite
Churrasco with Chimichurri Sauce

Chimichurri, the Argentinian version of pesto, is made with parsley, garlic, and olive oil. Our sauce is much lower in fat than traditional versions, which contain more than 1 cup of oil.

Prep: 25 minutes • Cook: 16 minutes
Other: 3 hours, 3 minutes

1½   cups cilantro sprigs
   1   cup white vinegar
   ¾   cup chopped onion
   2   teaspoons ground cumin
   2   teaspoons dried oregano
   2   teaspoons dried thyme
   2   teaspoons pepper
   1   teaspoon salt
   6   garlic cloves, chopped (about ¼ cup)
   3   bay leaves
   1   (1½-pound) boneless sirloin steak,
       trimmed
       Cooking spray
       Chimichurri Sauce

1. Combine first 10 ingredients in a large zip-top plastic bag. Add steak to bag, and seal. Marinate in refrigerator 3 hours, turning occasionally. Remove steak from bag; discard marinade.
2. Prepare grill.

3. Place steak on grill rack coated with cooking spray; grill steak 8 minutes on each side or until desired degree of doneness. Let stand 3 minutes. Cut steak diagonally across grain into thin slices. Serve with Chimichurri Sauce. Yield: 6 servings (serving size: 3 ounces beef and about 2½ tablespoons sauce).

(Totals include Chimichurri Sauce) CALORIES 239 (43% from fat); FAT 11.5g (sat 3.3g, mono 6.2g, poly 0.8g); PROTEIN 26.6g; CARB 7.5g; FIBER 1.7g; CHOL 76mg; IRON 5.4mg; SODIUM 459mg; CALC 79mg

Chimichurri Sauce

   ¼   cup white vinegar
   2   tablespoons extravirgin olive oil
   ½   teaspoon salt
   6   garlic cloves
   3   bay leaves
   2   jalapeño peppers, stems removed
   1   cup minced fresh parsley
   ¼   cup minced fresh oregano

1. Place first 6 ingredients in a blender; process until smooth. Add parsley and oregano, and stir well. Yield: 1 cup (serving size: about 2½ tablespoons).

CALORIES 55 (77% from fat); FAT 4.7g (sat 0.7g, mono 3.4g, poly 0.5g); PROTEIN 0.7g; CARB 3.5g; FIBER 0.8g; CHOL 0mg; IRON 1.4mg; SODIUM 202mg; CALC 40mg

menu
serves 6
Churrasco with Chimichurri Sauce
Steamed rice
Zesty Black Bean and Corn Salad
(page 411)

Simply Great Steak with Grilled Fries

A superior steak for grilling needs to be an inch or more thick to provide the right combination of seared surface and juicy interior. Keep the smaller, more tender tip of the steak angled away from the hottest part of the fire to prevent it from cooking too quickly. If you have a large enough grill, start grilling the potatoes with the steak so everything will be done at the same time. Otherwise, tent the beef with foil to keep it warm.

**Prep: 20 minutes • Cook: 36 minutes
Other: 55 minutes**

Steak:
- 1 (2-pound) porterhouse steak (about 1½ inches thick)
- 2 tablespoons Worcestershire sauce
- 1 teaspoon sea or kosher salt
- 1 teaspoon coarsely ground black pepper
- Cooking spray
- 1 teaspoon unsalted butter, softened

Grilled Fries:
- 1 teaspoon sea or kosher salt
- 2 teaspoons paprika
- 1 teaspoon coarsely ground black pepper
- ½ teaspoon garlic powder
- ½ teaspoon onion powder
- ½ teaspoon chili powder
- 1 teaspoon olive oil
- 2 medium baking potatoes, each cut into 12 wedges (about 1½ pounds)
- 2 medium sweet potatoes, each cut into 12 wedges (about 1½ pounds)

1. To prepare steak, coat porterhouse steak with Worcestershire sauce. Cover and marinate steak in refrigerator 30 minutes, turning occasionally.

2. Prepare grill with one side on medium heat and one side on high heat.

3. Remove steak from Worcestershire; discard Worcestershire. Sprinkle steak with 1 teaspoon salt and 1 teaspoon pepper; let stand at room temperature 15 minutes.

4. Place steak on grill rack coated with cooking spray over high heat; grill 3 minutes on each side. Turn steak, and place over medium heat; grill 3 minutes on each side or until desired degree of doneness. Place steak on a platter. Rub butter over top of steak; let stand 10 minutes. Tent with foil to keep warm.

5. To prepare fries, combine 1 teaspoon salt, paprika, 1 teaspoon pepper, garlic powder, onion powder, and chili powder. Combine oil and potatoes in a large bowl, tossing to coat. Sprinkle potatoes with paprika mixture; toss gently to coat.

6. Place potatoes on grill rack coated with cooking spray over medium heat; grill 18 minutes or until sweet potatoes are tender, turning occasionally. Remove sweet potatoes; keep warm. Grill baking potatoes an additional 6 minutes or until tender. Serve fries with steak. Yield: 6 servings (serving size: 3 ounces beef and 8 fries).

CALORIES 446 (29% from fat); FAT 14.6g (sat 5.1g, mono 6.6g, poly 0.7g); PROTEIN 33.1g; CARB 45g; FIBER 5.5g; CHOL 79mg; IRON 6.6mg; SODIUM 898mg; CALC 47mg

WINE NOTE: Steak and cabernet sauvignon make a classic American combo. The char and meatiness of the steak are beautifully offset by the structure of the wine. Try Sebastini cabernet sauvignon (Sonoma County, California).

how hot? The best way to measure the temperature of an open fire is the time-honored hand test. Simply hold your hand about 3 inches above the grate, then time how long you can keep your hand there before you're forced to withdraw it:

- 1 to 2 seconds—the fire is hot and perfect for searing a steak or grilling shrimp.
- 3 seconds—indicates medium-high heat, great for most fish.
- 4 to 5 seconds—signifies a medium range, ideal for most chicken and vegetables.
- 7 to 8 seconds—indicates the temperature is low and perfect for grilling delicate vegetables and fruit.

Thermometers that come with most grills measure only oven temperatures inside the grill when the cover is closed. If you cook with direct heat with the cover down, you get a measurement of the reflected heat that contributes to the cooking process but not the actual grilling temperature on the grate where the food sits. The top side of the food is cooked at the oven temperature indicated, while the bottom side directly above the fire is grilled at a higher temperature.

Peppercorn-Crusted Filet Mignon with Port Jus

Whisking in a small amount of chilled butter to finish the sauce adds just the right touch of richness.
Serve the steaks with Creamy Parmesan Orzo (page 283) and Chive Green Beans (page 515).

Prep: 7 minutes • Cook: 11 minutes

2   teaspoons cracked black pepper
4   (4-ounce) beef tenderloin steaks, trimmed (1 inch thick)
¼   teaspoon salt
½   cup port or other sweet red wine
½   cup fat-free, less-sodium beef broth
1   tablespoon chilled butter, cut into small pieces

1. Heat a cast-iron skillet over medium-high heat. Rub pepper evenly over steaks. Sprinkle salt over bottom of pan. Add steaks to pan; cook 2 minutes on each side or until browned. Remove steaks from pan; set aside.

2. Stir in port and broth, scraping pan to loosen browned bits. Reduce heat to medium. Return steaks to pan; cook 2 minutes on each side or until desired degree of doneness. Remove steaks from pan. Cook until liquid is reduced to ¼ cup. Remove pan from heat. Add butter to pan; stir with a whisk until melted. Drizzle sauce over steaks. Yield: 4 servings (serving size: 1 steak and 1 tablespoon jus).

CALORIES 257 (42% from fat); FAT 12g (sat 5.2g, mono 4.3g, poly 0.5g); PROTEIN 24g; CARB 4.3g; FIBER 0.3g; CHOL 78mg; IRON 3.6mg; SODIUM 313mg; CALC 15mg

Pepper-Crusted Beef Tenderloin with Kumquat Marmalade

Kumquats, carrot juice, mustard, and vinegar create a piquant topping for the tenderloin.

Prep: 15 minutes • Cook: 25 minutes

Kumquat Marmalade:

1½ cups vertically sliced onion
½ cup halved, seeded, and vertically sliced kumquats
½ cup carrot or orange juice
1 tablespoon Dijon mustard
¼ teaspoon salt
2 thyme sprigs
1 bay leaf
2 teaspoons rice vinegar

Steak:

2 teaspoons olive oil
2 tablespoons freshly ground black peppercorns
4 (4-ounce) beef tenderloin steaks, trimmed (about ¾ inch thick)
½ teaspoon salt

1. To prepare marmalade, combine first 7 ingredients in a saucepan; bring to a boil. Reduce heat; simmer 15 minutes or until almost all liquid evaporates, stirring occasionally. Remove from heat. Discard thyme and bay leaf. Stir in vinegar; cool.
2. To prepare steak, heat oil in a large nonstick skillet over medium-high heat. Place pepper in a shallow dish. Dredge steaks in pepper; sprinkle evenly with ½ teaspoon salt. Add beef to pan; cook 3 minutes on each side or until desired degree of doneness. Serve with marmalade. Yield: 4 servings (serving size: 1 steak and about ¼ cup marmalade).

CALORIES 211 (29% from fat); FAT 6.9g (sat 1.9g, mono 3.3g, poly 0.4g); PROTEIN 23.8g; CARB 17.1g; FIBER 3.4g; CHOL 60mg; IRON 4.1mg; SODIUM 611mg; CALC 62mg

Roasted Beef Tenderloin with Merlot Shallot Sauce

The center cut of the tenderloin, also called chateaubriand, may be a bit pricey, but the meltingly tender results are worth it.

Prep: 13 minutes • Cook: 47 minutes
Other: 15 minutes

Tenderloin:

Cooking spray
⅓ cup finely chopped fresh sage
1 tablespoon cracked black pepper
3 tablespoons minced garlic
2 teaspoons kosher salt
1 (2½-pound) center-cut beef tenderloin

Merlot Shallot Sauce:

⅓ cup finely chopped shallots
1½ cups merlot or other dry red wine
1½ cups less-sodium beef broth
1 teaspoon butter
3 tablespoons chopped fresh parsley
¼ teaspoon kosher salt

1. Preheat oven to 350°.
2. To prepare tenderloin, heat an oven-proof skillet over medium-high heat. Coat pan with cooking spray. Combine sage, pepper, garlic, and salt; rub over tenderloin. Add tenderloin to pan; cook 6 minutes, lightly browning all sides.
3. Insert a meat thermometer into thickest portion of tenderloin. Bake at 350° for 25 minutes or until thermometer registers 140° (medium-rare) or desired degree of doneness. Place tenderloin on a cutting board; cover loosely with foil. Let stand 15 minutes (temperature of tenderloin will increase 5° upon standing).
4. To prepare sauce, heat pan over medium-high heat. Coat pan with cooking spray. Add shallots; sauté 3 minutes or until tender. Stir in wine. Bring to a boil; cook until reduced to ¾ cup (about 4 minutes). Stir in broth; cook until reduced to 1¼ cups (about 6 minutes). Add butter, stirring until melted. Stir in parsley and ¼ teaspoon salt. Serve with tenderloin. Yield: 10 servings (serving size: 3 ounces beef and 2 tablespoons sauce).

CALORIES 216 (34% from fat); FAT 8.2g (sat 3.1g, mono 3.1g, poly 0.4g); PROTEIN 25.3g; CARB 3.1g; FIBER 0.3g; CHOL 72mg; IRON 3.6mg; SODIUM 495mg; CALC 28mg

Beef Comparison

Here's how cuts of beef compare in calories and fat.

Cut*	Calories	Fat
Bottom round	164	6.6g
Brisket	207	11.7g
Chuck arm pot roast	186	7.4g
Eye of round	149	4.8g
Flank steak	176	8.6g
Ground beef (regular)	248	16.5g
Ground beef (20% fat)	228	15.0g
Ground beef (15% fat)	204	12.0g
Ground beef (10% fat)	169	9.0g
Porterhouse steak	190	10.9g
Prime rib	215	12.8g
Short ribs	196	11.6g
Sirloin tip roast	170	7.6g
T-bone steak	217	14.4g
Tenderloin	180	8.6g
Top round	176	4.9g
Top sirloin	170	6.6g

*Figures are for 3 ounces of choice-grade cooked meat, trimmed of all visible fat.

Grilled Beef Tenderloin with Chilean Cilantro Sauce

These mouth-watering tenderloin steaks are seasoned with spices that are typical of Salvadoran-style cuisine. After broiling, the steaks are accented with a Chilean herb sauce called *pebre*.

Prep: 25 minutes • Cook: 14 minutes

Cooking spray
 4 cups sliced onion
 ½ teaspoon sugar
 1 (1½-pound) center-cut beef tenderloin
 ½ teaspoon salt
 ½ teaspoon garlic powder
 ½ teaspoon dried oregano
 ½ teaspoon pepper
 ¼ teaspoon ground cumin
 Chilean Cilantro Sauce

1. Place a large skillet over medium heat until hot. Coat pan with cooking spray.

Add sliced onion and sugar; cover and cook 10 minutes or until onion is golden brown, stirring frequently. Set aside, and keep warm.

2. Preheat broiler.

3. Cut beef tenderloin lengthwise with the grain into 6 even steaks. Working with 1 steak at a time, place steak between two sheets of heavy-duty plastic wrap; flatten each steak to an even thickness using a meat mallet or rolling pin. Combine salt and next 4 ingredients in a small bowl. Rub salt mixture over both sides of steaks.

4. Place steaks on a broiler pan coated with cooking spray. Broil steaks 2 minutes on each side or until desired degree of doneness. Top each steak with onion mixture, and drizzle with Chilean Cilantro Sauce. Yield: 6 servings (serving size: 1 steak, ½ cup onion mixture, and 1 tablespoon sauce).

(Totals include Chilean Cilantro Sauce) CALORIES 167 (39% from fat); FAT 7.3g (sat 2.3g, mono 3.4g, poly 0.5g); PROTEIN 17.1g; CARB 8.2g; FIBER 1.7g; CHOL 48mg; IRON 2.5mg; SODIUM 329mg; CALC 27mg

Chilean Cilantro Sauce

 ⅔ cup canned vegetable broth
 ½ cup minced fresh cilantro or parsley
 ½ cup minced fresh onion
 ½ cup minced red bell pepper
 ¼ cup white vinegar
 ¼ cup extravirgin olive oil
 1 teaspoon salt
 1 teaspoon dried oregano
 1 teaspoon crushed red pepper
 ½ teaspoon black pepper
 4 garlic cloves, minced

1. Combine all ingredients, stirring with a whisk until well blended. Yield: 2 cups (serving size: 1 tablespoon).

CALORIES 18 (90% from fat); FAT 1.8g (sat 0.2g, mono 1.3g, poly 0.2g); PROTEIN 0.1g; CARB 0.8g; FIBER 0.2g; CHOL 0mg; IRON 0.1mg; SODIUM 95mg; CALC 4mg

Test Kitchen Tip: Store the remaining sauce in an airtight container in the refrigerator up to two weeks.

Beef Cooked with Carrots, Onions, and Dried Plums

A favorite in the annals of French cooking, this homey dish is served to family or in a café or bistro. For a wonderful supper, serve with mashed potatoes.

Prep: 25 minutes • Cook: 3 hours, 13 minutes
Other: 2 minutes

    1 (2½-pound) boneless chuck roast, trimmed
    2 teaspoons sea salt
    1 teaspoon freshly ground black pepper
    2 teaspoons extravirgin olive oil
    3 cups thinly sliced onion
    4 cups warm water
    2 rosemary sprigs
   20 thyme sprigs
    1 sage sprig
    3 bay leaves
    1 pound baby carrots
    2 cups pitted dried plums
   Sage leaves (optional)

1. Preheat oven to 350°.

2. Tie roast at 2-inch intervals with twine; rub with salt and pepper. Heat oil in Dutch oven over medium-high heat. Add roast; cook 12 minutes, browning on all sides. Remove roast from pan. Add onion and water to pan, scraping pan to loosen browned bits. Return roast to pan.

3. Place rosemary, thyme, sage, and bay leaves on a double layer of cheesecloth. Gather edges of cheesecloth together; tie securely, and add cheesecloth to pan. Bake, covered, at 350° for 1½ hours. Turn roast; bake, covered, an additional 45 minutes. Add carrots and dried plums; bake, covered, an additional 45 minutes or until carrots are tender.

4. Place roast, carrots, and dried plums on a platter; keep warm. Reserve cooking liquid. Discard bag.

5. Place a zip-top plastic bag inside a 2-cup glass measure. Pour reserved cooking liquid into bag; let stand 2 minutes (fat will rise to the top). Seal bag; carefully snip off 1 bottom corner of bag. Drain drippings into measuring cup, stopping before fat layer reaches opening; discard fat. Remove twine, and slice roast; garnish with sage leaves, if desired. Serve with carrot mixture and sauce. Yield: 8 servings (serving size: about 3 ounces beef, ½ cup carrot mixture, and about 1½ tablespoons sauce).

CALORIES 316 (27% from fat); FAT 9.4g (sat 3.2g, mono 4.4g, poly 0.5g); PROTEIN 30.5g; CARB 28g; FIBER 4.6g; CHOL 76mg; IRON 3.7mg; SODIUM 716mg; CALC 59mg

Test Kitchen Tip: Tying the roast with twine helps hold the roast together as it cooks. Once you remove the twine, the meat is fall-apart tender.

how to brown meat and deglaze pan

1. Browning the beef creates a brown crust and adds a deep, rich flavor to the sauce.

2. Deglazing the pan with water and onions captures all the flavorful browned bits from the beef.

Traditional Yankee Pot Roast

Use any roast from the chuck (shoulder section) for pot roast. Shoulder cuts have a lot of fibrous tissue that melts during slow cooking—keeping the meat moist and flavorful.

Prep: 15 minutes • Cook: 3 hours, 20 minutes

  2 teaspoons olive oil
  1 (4-pound) boneless chuck roast, trimmed
  1 tablespoon kosher salt
  1 tablespoon cracked black pepper
  2 cups coarsely chopped onion
  2 cups less-sodium beef broth
 ¼ cup ketchup
  2 tablespoons Worcestershire sauce
  1 cup chopped plum tomato
1¼ pounds small red potatoes
  1 pound carrots, peeled and cut into 1-inch pieces
  2 tablespoons fresh lemon juice

1. Preheat oven to 300°.
2. Heat olive oil in a large Dutch oven over medium-high heat. Sprinkle roast with salt and pepper. Add roast to pan, browning on all sides (about 8 minutes). Remove from pan. Add onion to pan; sauté 8 minutes or until browned. Return roast to pan. Combine broth, ketchup, and Worcestershire; pour over roast. Add tomato; bring to a simmer.
3. Cover and bake at 300° for 2½ hours or until tender. Add potatoes and carrots; cover and bake 30 minutes or until vegetables are tender. Stir in lemon juice. Yield: 10 servings (serving size: 3 ounces beef and about ½ cup vegetables).

CALORIES 290 (26% from fat); FAT 8.4g (sat 2.8g, mono 3.7g, poly 0.5g); PROTEIN 32.9g; CARB 20g; FIBER 3g; CHOL 92mg; IRON 4.3mg; SODIUM 756mg; CALC 36mg

Roast Beef with Horseradish-Mustard Sauce

A dry rub of coriander, pepper, salt, and garlic encrusts the roast. Layer leftover roast and sauce with Swiss cheese on toasted sourdough bread to make great sandwiches.

Prep: 11 minutes • Cook: 1 hour
Other: 15 minutes

Roast:
  2 tablespoons ground coriander seeds
  1 tablespoon cracked black pepper
  2 teaspoons kosher salt
  5 garlic cloves, crushed
  1 (3-pound) sirloin tip roast, trimmed
Cooking spray

Horseradish-Mustard Sauce:
 ¾ cup prepared horseradish
 ½ cup stone-ground mustard
 ¼ cup white vinegar

1. Preheat oven to 450°.
2. To prepare roast, combine first 4 ingredients; rub over roast. Place on a broiler pan coated with cooking spray. Insert a meat thermometer into thickest portion of roast. Bake at 450° for 20 minutes. Reduce oven temperature to 300° (do not remove roast from oven); bake 40 minutes or until thermometer registers 140° (medium-rare) or desired degree of doneness. Place roast on a cutting board; cover loosely with foil. Let stand 15 minutes (temperature will increase 5° upon standing). Cut against grain into thin slices.
3. To prepare sauce, combine horseradish, mustard, and vinegar. Serve with roast beef. Yield: 12 servings (serving size: 3 ounces beef and 2 tablespoons sauce).

CALORIES 203 (36% from fat); FAT 8.1g (sat 2.8g, mono 3.1g, poly 0.4g); PROTEIN 24.9g; CARB 5.3g; FIBER 2.4g; CHOL 70mg; IRON 2.9mg; SODIUM 575mg; CALC 37mg

Lemongrass Beef

Lemongrass, an important seasoning in Thai cooking, contributes a fresh lemon accent to this Asian-style beef. (See page 494 for information on preparing lemongrass.)

Prep: 20 minutes • Cook: 2 minutes
Other: 2 hours, 30 minutes

  1 (2-pound) sirloin tip roast
 ½ cup chopped peeled fresh lemongrass
 ⅓ cup chopped shallots
  3 tablespoons fish sauce
1½ tablespoons sugar
  1 teaspoon dark sesame oil
  1 teaspoon peanut oil
 ¼ teaspoon salt
  6 garlic cloves, crushed
  2 serrano chiles, seeded and chopped
Cooking spray

1. Cover roast with plastic wrap; freeze 30 minutes. Remove beef from freezer, and cut beef horizontally into ⅛-inch-thick slices.
2. Place lemongrass and next 8 ingredients in a food processor; process until smooth (about 1 minute). Combine beef and lemongrass mixture in a large zip-top plastic bag. Seal and marinate in refrigerator 2 to 4 hours.
3. Prepare grill.
4. Remove beef from bag; discard marinade. Place beef on grill rack coated with cooking spray; grill 1 minute on each side or until desired degree of doneness. Yield: 8 servings (serving size: 3 ounces).

CALORIES 158 (29% from fat); FAT 5.1g (sat 1.7g, mono 2g, poly 0.4g); PROTEIN 24.8g; CARB 2g; FIBER 0.1g; CHOL 69mg; IRON 2.8mg; SODIUM 353mg; CALC 10mg

Balsamic-Braised Short Ribs with Horseradish Mashed Potatoes

Short ribs are the meaty ends of the rib bones. Choose cuts from the chuck,
which are the most flavorful, or from the rib, which are a bit leaner. Packages labeled
"short ribs" in the supermarket are likely to come from the chuck.

Prep: 35 minutes • Cook: 2 hours, 56 minutes • Other: 8 hours

Ribs:

Cooking spray

4 pounds beef short ribs, trimmed

1 teaspoon kosher salt, divided

1 teaspoon freshly ground black
   pepper, divided

2 cups finely chopped red onion

¼ cup minced garlic (about 12 cloves)

2 cups less-sodium beef broth

1 cup dry red wine

¾ cup balsamic vinegar

⅓ cup packed brown sugar

2 cups chopped plum tomato

Horseradish Mashed Potatoes:

2½ pounds baking potatoes, peeled and
    cut into quarters

¾ cup warm 1% low-fat milk

2 tablespoons fat-free sour cream

1½ tablespoons prepared horseradish

1 teaspoon kosher salt

½ teaspoon freshly ground black
   pepper

1. Preheat oven to 300°.

2. To prepare ribs, heat a large Dutch oven over medium-high heat. Coat pan with cooking spray. Sprinkle ribs with ½ teaspoon salt and ½ teaspoon pepper. Add half of ribs to pan; cook 8 minutes or until browned, turning occasionally. Remove from pan. Repeat procedure with remaining ribs; remove from pan. Add onion to pan; sauté 8 minutes or until lightly browned. Add garlic; sauté 1 minute. Return ribs to pan. Add broth, wine, vinegar, sugar, and tomato; bring to a simmer.

3. Cover and bake at 300° for 1½ hours or until tender. Cool slightly. Refrigerate 8 hours or overnight.

4. Skim fat from surface of broth mixture; discard fat. Cook broth mixture and ribs over medium heat 30 minutes or until thoroughly heated. Stir in ½ teaspoon salt and ½ teaspoon pepper.

5. To prepare mashed potatoes, place potatoes in a large saucepan, and cover with water. Bring to a boil; cook 20 minutes or until very tender. Drain. Combine potatoes, milk, and remaining 4 ingredients in a large bowl. Mash potato mixture with a potato masher. Serve with ribs and cooking liquid. Yield: 7 servings (serving size: 3 ounces beef, about ¾ cup mashed potatoes, and ⅓ cup cooking liquid).

CALORIES 463 (26% from fat); FAT 13.4g (sat 5.6g, mono 5.7g, poly 0.7g); PROTEIN 27.2g; CARB 53.5g; FIBER 4.2g; CHOL 64mg; IRON 4mg; SODIUM 649mg; CALC 100mg

Test Kitchen Tip: Start this recipe a day ahead. It will taste much better, and chilling the ribs in the cooking liquid will make the solidified fat easy to remove.

Standing Rib Roast with Madeira Sauce and Herbed Yorkshire Puddings

Yorkshire pudding, a holiday classic for generations, derives its name from the Yorkshire region of northern England. Let the roast rest while you finish the sauce and make the puddings; it will be easier to carve.

Prep: 30 minutes • Cook: 2 hours, 30 minutes

Roast:

- 1 (5-pound) French-cut rib-eye roast, trimmed
- 1 garlic clove, halved
- ½ teaspoon salt
- ½ teaspoon freshly ground black pepper
- Cooking spray

Madeira Sauce:

- 1 cup water
- 2 tablespoons all-purpose flour
- ½ cup Madeira wine
- ½ cup beef broth
- ½ teaspoon black pepper

Herbed Yorkshire Puddings:

- 1½ cups all-purpose flour
- 1 teaspoon salt
- ¾ teaspoon freshly ground black pepper
- 1½ cups 1% low-fat milk
- 1 tablespoon chopped fresh or 1 teaspoon dried thyme
- 1 tablespoon chopped fresh parsley
- 1 teaspoon grated lemon rind
- 5 large egg whites
- 2 large eggs

1. Preheat oven to 450°.

2. To prepare roast, rub roast on all sides with garlic. Sprinkle with ½ teaspoon salt and ½ teaspoon pepper. Place roast, fat side up, on a broiler pan coated with cooking spray. Insert a meat thermometer into thickest portion of roast. Bake at 450° for 25 minutes. Reduce oven temperature to 300° (do not remove roast from oven); bake an additional 1½ hours or until thermometer registers 145° (medium) or desired degree of doneness. Place roast on a platter; let stand while finishing sauce and Yorkshire puddings. Reserve 1½ tablespoons drippings from pan for puddings; set aside.

3. To prepare sauce, wipe remaining drippings from pan with paper towels, leaving browned bits on bottom of pan. Combine water and 2 tablespoons flour in a small bowl. Add Madeira to pan, and bring to a boil over medium-high heat, scraping bottom of pan with a wooden spoon to loosen browned bits. Add flour mixture; cook 1 minute or until slightly thick. Stir in broth and ½ teaspoon pepper; cook 2 minutes. Keep warm.

4. Preheat oven to 450°.

5. To prepare puddings, coat 12 muffin cups with reserved pan drippings. Lightly spoon 1½ cups flour into dry measuring cups, and level with a knife. Combine 1½ cups flour, 1 teaspoon salt, and ¾ teaspoon pepper in a medium bowl. Gradually add milk, stirring with a whisk until smooth. Add thyme and remaining 4 ingredients to bowl, stirring with a whisk until smooth. Spoon batter into prepared cups. Bake at 450° for 15 minutes. Reduce oven temperature to 375° (do not remove puddings from oven); bake an additional 15 minutes or until golden. Yield: 12 servings (serving size: 3 ounces beef, 2 tablespoons sauce, and 1 pudding).

CALORIES 304 (38% from fat); FAT 12.8g (sat 5g, mono 5.2g, poly 0.6g); PROTEIN 29g; CARB 16.1g; FIBER 0.6g; CHOL 106mg; IRON 3.5mg; SODIUM 410mg; CALC 58mg

WINE NOTE: For centuries, the British have enjoyed red Bordeaux wines (also called "claret") with hearty, warming fare such as this classic roast. A luscious, sophisticated Bordeaux to consider is Château Lynch-Bages. For a more modest price, try the Château Greysac Cru Bourgeois.

Veal Lean, mild-flavored veal lends itself to recipes with robust sauces, vibrant seasonings, and spicy coatings.

Veal Marsala

Veal scaloppine is a superthin veal cutlet. Here, it's dredged in flour, then pan-fried. Serve over egg noodles or a blend of white and wild rice.

Prep: 11 minutes • Cook: 10 minutes

- 1 pound veal scaloppine
- ¼ cup all-purpose flour, divided
- ⅔ cup beef consommé
- 1 tablespoon butter
- ½ cup dry Marsala
- 1 cup sliced mushrooms
- ¼ teaspoon salt
- 1 tablespoon chopped fresh parsley

1. Dredge veal in 3 tablespoons flour. Combine remaining 1 tablespoon flour and consommé, stirring with a whisk; set aside.

2. Melt butter in a large nonstick skillet over medium-high heat. Add veal; cook 1½ minutes. Turn veal over; cook 1 minute. Remove veal from pan.

3. Add wine to pan, scraping pan to loosen browned bits. Add consommé mixture, mushrooms, and salt; bring to a boil. Reduce heat; simmer 3 minutes or until thick. Return veal to pan; sprinkle with parsley. Yield: 4 servings (serving size: 3 ounces veal and about 2 tablespoons sauce).

CALORIES 193 (28% from fat); FAT 6.1g (sat 3.0g, mono 1.1g, poly 0.4g); PROTEIN 26g; CARB 7.5g; FIBER 0.4g; CHOL 102mg; IRON 1.9mg; SODIUM 481mg; CALC 24mg

Veal Parmesan

Created by Italian-American restaurateurs, this dish takes its name from the cheese used to coat the veal. The breaded veal is baked in tomato sauce and topped with melted mozzarella cheese.

Prep: 18 minutes • Cook: 38 minutes

- 4 (4-ounce) veal cutlets (about ½ inch thick)
- ¼ cup all-purpose flour
- ⅛ teaspoon pepper
- 2 large egg whites, lightly beaten
- ½ cup Italian-seasoned breadcrumbs
- ¼ cup (1 ounce) grated fresh Parmesan cheese
- 2 teaspoons olive oil
- 2 cups Tomato Sauce (page 450)
- Cooking spray
- ¾ cup (3 ounces) shredded part-skim mozzarella cheese

1. Preheat oven to 350°.

2. Place each cutlet between 2 sheets of heavy-duty plastic wrap; flatten to ¼-inch thickness using a meat mallet or rolling pin.

3. Lightly spoon flour into a dry measuring cup; level with a knife. Combine flour and pepper in a large bowl. Place egg whites in a shallow dish. Combine breadcrumbs and Parmesan cheese in a shallow dish.

4. Dredge veal in flour mixture. Dip each cutlet in egg whites; dredge in breadcrumb mixture.

5. Heat oil in a large nonstick skillet over medium-high heat. Add veal, and sauté 1 minute on each side or until browned. Remove from heat.

6. Spread 1 cup Tomato Sauce in an 11 x 7–inch baking dish coated with cooking spray. Arrange cutlets in a single layer on top of sauce; spoon remaining Tomato Sauce over veal. Sprinkle veal with mozzarella. Bake at 350° for 10 minutes. Yield: 4 servings (serving size: 1 veal cutlet and about ½ cup sauce).

(Totals include Tomato Sauce) CALORIES 362 (30% from fat); FAT 12.2g (sat 5.6g, mono 5.2g, poly 1.1g); PROTEIN 36.6g; CARB 25.4g; FIBER 1.7g; CHOL 111mg; IRON 3mg; SODIUM 812mg; CALC 301mg

types of veal Veal is the meat of a calf up to three months of age. Here are the three types of veal available in markets:

Milk-fed veal is the most tender and flavorful. It has a creamy pink color and fine-grained texture.

Formula-fed veal is also tender and pale, but it doesn't have as much flavor as the milk-fed variety.

Free-range veal is from a calf that has been weaned and fed on grass and grains. This veal has a redder color and meatier flavor.

Veal Medallions with Apple-Thyme Sauce

To prevent the apple from turning brown, chop it while the sauce is cooking.

Prep: 10 minutes • Cook: 32 minutes

Apple-Thyme Sauce:

1 cup dry sherry

1¾ cups fat-free, less-sodium chicken broth

¼ cup thawed apple juice concentrate, undiluted

1 tablespoon water

1½ teaspoons cornstarch

½ cup chopped Granny Smith apple

½ teaspoon fresh or ⅛ teaspoon dried thyme

Veal:

4 (2-ounce) veal medallions

⅛ teaspoon salt

⅛ teaspoon pepper

2 teaspoons canola oil

1. To prepare sauce, bring sherry to a boil in a medium saucepan over medium-high heat; cook until reduced to 2 tablespoons (about 8 minutes). Add broth and juice concentrate; cook until reduced to 1 cup (about 12 minutes). Combine water and cornstarch. Add cornstarch mixture; bring to a boil. Cook 1 minute, stirring constantly. Remove from heat; stir in apple and thyme. Cover and keep warm.

2. To prepare veal, sprinkle veal with salt and pepper. Heat oil in a medium non-stick skillet over medium-high heat. Add veal; cook 3 minutes on each side or until lightly browned. Serve veal with sauce. Yield: 2 servings (serving size: 2 medallions and ½ cup sauce).

CALORIES 224 (27% from fat); FAT 6.8g (sat 1g, mono 3.4g, poly 1.6g); PROTEIN 26.9g; CARB 10.8g; FIBER 0.9g; CHOL 88mg; IRON 1.2mg; SODIUM 723mg; CALC 12mg

Osso Buco with Balsamic Onions

A classic rustic Italian dish, *osso buco* is traditionally garnished with gremolata (a mixture of minced parsley, lemon zest, and garlic). In this version, the veal shanks are served with a balsamic onion mixture and garnished with sliced basil and lemon zest.

Prep: 20 minutes • Cook: 2 hours, 38 minutes

4 cups vertically sliced onion (about 2 onions)

1½ cups dry white wine, divided

1 tablespoon sugar

2 teaspoons dried thyme, divided

½ teaspoon black pepper, divided

3 tablespoons balsamic vinegar

4 (10-ounce) veal shanks (1½ inches thick)

3 cups fat-free, less-sodium chicken broth

½ teaspoon crushed red pepper

1 (14.5-ounce) can diced tomatoes with basil, garlic, and oregano

4 garlic cloves, minced

½ cup tubetti (small, tube-shaped pasta)

1 (19-ounce) can cannellini or other white beans, rinsed and drained

¼ cup sliced fresh basil

2 teaspoons lemon zest

1. Combine onion, ½ cup wine, sugar, 1 teaspoon thyme, and ¼ teaspoon black pepper in a large Dutch oven. Cover; cook over medium heat 20 minutes or until onion is soft, stirring occasionally. Add vinegar; cook, uncovered, 15 minutes or until liquid almost evaporates and onions are caramelized. Remove ¾ cup onion mixture; set aside.

2. Sprinkle veal with ¼ teaspoon black pepper. Add 1 cup wine, 1 teaspoon thyme, veal, broth, red pepper, tomatoes, and garlic to pan; bring to a boil. Cover, reduce heat, and simmer 1 hour and 15 minutes, turning veal occasionally. Uncover; cook 30 minutes. Stir in pasta and beans; simmer 15 minutes or until pasta is tender. Serve with reserved onion mixture, basil, and lemon zest. Yield: 4 servings (serving size: 1 veal shank, 1⅔ cups bean mixture, and 3 tablespoons onion mixture).

CALORIES 653 (19% from fat); FAT 14g (sat 4.5g, mono 5g, poly 1.7g); PROTEIN 77.7g; CARB 49.2g; FIBER 7.3g; CHOL 264mg; IRON 7.2mg; SODIUM 1196mg; CALC 216mg

Lamb

Today's lamb cuts are leaner than ever and just as flavorful. Braise, grill, or roast a variety of cuts to create classic dishes.

Lamb Moussaka

This lamb-and-eggplant casserole is a popular Greek dish of layered ground lamb, eggplant, and tomatoes with a béchamel sauce topping. (See page 449 for techniques for preparing béchamel sauce.)

**Prep: 40 minutes • Cook: 2 hours, 6 minutes
Other: 15 minutes**

Lamb mixture:

1½ pounds lean ground lamb or beef
    Cooking spray
  2 cups chopped onion
  ½ cup dried currants or raisins
  1 teaspoon salt
  ½ teaspoon dried oregano
  ½ teaspoon ground cinnamon
  ¼ teaspoon ground nutmeg
  ¼ teaspoon pepper
  4 (14.5-ounce) cans diced tomatoes, undrained
  1 large garlic clove, minced

Sauce:

  2 cups 1% low-fat milk, divided
  1 tablespoon butter
  3 large egg whites
  ¼ cup all-purpose flour
  ½ teaspoon salt

Remaining ingredients:

  2 (1¼-pound) eggplants, cut lengthwise into ¼-inch-thick slices
  1 tablespoon olive oil
  1 pound peeled baking potatoes, cut into ¼-inch-thick slices
  ¼ cup (1 ounce) grated fresh Parmesan cheese, divided
    Oregano sprigs (optional)

1. To prepare lamb mixture, cook lamb in a large Dutch oven over medium-high heat until browned; stir to crumble. Remove from pan; drain. Set aside. Wipe pan with paper towels.

2. Coat pan with cooking spray. Add onion to pan; sauté 5 minutes. Add lamb, currants, and next 7 ingredients; bring to a boil. Cook until thick (about 30 minutes).

3. Preheat broiler.

4. To prepare sauce, cook 1½ cups milk and butter in a heavy saucepan over medium-high heat to 180° or until tiny bubbles form around edge (do not boil). Remove from heat. Combine ½ cup milk, egg whites, flour, and ½ teaspoon salt in a large bowl; gradually add hot milk mixture to egg white mixture, stirring constantly with a whisk. Return milk mixture to pan, and cook until thick (about 15 minutes), stirring constantly. Remove from heat.

5. Place half of eggplant slices on a baking sheet coated with cooking spray, and brush with 1½ teaspoons oil. Broil 4 minutes on each side or until browned. Repeat procedure with remaining eggplant and 1½ teaspoons oil.

6. Preheat oven to 375°.

7. Cook potato slices in boiling water 5 minutes or until crisp-tender; drain. Rinse with cold water; drain well.

8. Arrange potatoes in bottom of a 13 x 9–inch baking dish coated with cooking spray. Arrange half of eggplant slices over potatoes. Pour 4 cups lamb mixture over eggplant, and sprinkle with 1 tablespoon cheese. Arrange remaining eggplant over cheese, and top with remaining lamb mixture. Sprinkle with 1 tablespoon cheese. Spread sauce over cheese, and sprinkle with 2 tablespoons cheese. Bake at 375° for 45 minutes or until top is golden brown. Let stand 15 minutes. Garnish with oregano sprigs, if desired. Yield: 8 servings (serving size: about 1½ cups).

CALORIES 374 (28% from fat); FAT 11.7g (sat 4.3g, mono 4.9g, poly 1g); PROTEIN 28.1g; CARB 40.4g; FIBER 4.7g; CHOL 69mg; IRON 3.5mg; SODIUM 933mg; CALC 200mg

Greek Lamb Chops

Serve these simply-flavored chops with couscous tossed with chopped tomato, cucumber, and feta cheese.

Prep: 9 minutes • Cook: 8 minutes

  1 tablespoon dried oregano
  2 tablespoons lemon juice
  1 tablespoon bottled minced garlic
  ½ teaspoon salt
  ¼ teaspoon pepper
  8 (4-ounce) lamb loin chops, trimmed
    Cooking spray

1. Preheat broiler.

2. Combine first 5 ingredients; rub over both sides of chops. Place chops on a broiler pan coated with cooking spray; broil 4 minutes on each side or until desired degree of doneness. Yield: 4 servings (serving size: 2 chops).

CALORIES 192 (39% from fat); FAT 8.4g (sat 3g, mono 3.6g, poly 0.6g); PROTEIN 25.8g; CARB 1.7g; FIBER 0.1g; CHOL 81mg; IRON 1.8mg; SODIUM 367mg; CALC 36mg

Lamb with Garam Masala Crumbs and Curried Mint Sauce

Adding red curry powder to the mint sauce and seasoning the breadcrumbs with garam masala give this dish an Indian flair.

Prep: 20 minutes • Cook: 19 minutes
Other: 30 minutes

Curried Mint Sauce:
- ½ teaspoon cornstarch
- 1 tablespoon water
- ⅔ cup white wine vinegar
- 3 tablespoons sugar
- ¼ cup chopped fresh mint
- ½ teaspoon red curry powder

Lamb:
- 2 (1-ounce) slices day-old white bread
- 2 teaspoons garam masala
- ½ teaspoon salt
- ½ teaspoon freshly ground black pepper
- 12 (4-ounce) French-cut lamb rib chops, trimmed

1. To prepare sauce, combine cornstarch and water in a small bowl, stirring with a whisk to form a slurry. Bring vinegar and sugar to a simmer in a small saucepan, stirring until sugar dissolves. Add slurry mixture; simmer 2 minutes or until slightly thickened, stirring constantly with a whisk. Remove from heat. Stir in mint and curry powder; cover and let stand 30 minutes. Strain; set aside.

2. Preheat oven to 450°.

3. To prepare lamb, place bread in a food processor; pulse 10 times or until coarse crumbs measure 1 cup. Combine breadcrumbs, garam masala, salt, and pepper in a small bowl. Place lamb on a shallow baking sheet. Press breadcrumb mixture onto lamb. Bake at 450° for 15 minutes or until desired degree of doneness. Serve with sauce. Yield: 6 servings (serving size: 2 chops and about 1½ tablespoons sauce).

CALORIES 381 (33% from fat); FAT 14g (sat 4.9g, mono 5.5g, poly 1.2g); PROTEIN 48.3g; CARB 13.7g; FIBER 0.4g; CHOL 150mg; IRON 4.8mg; SODIUM 405mg; CALC 43mg

frenching To "French" means to trim about 1½ inches of fat and meat from the bone end of the ribs, revealing the bones and getting rid of excess fat. Ask the butcher to French the racks of lamb if it hasn't already been done. You'll still want to trim away some of the outside fat on the rack.

Lamb with Garam Masala Crumbs and Curried Mint Sauce

Lamb Osso Buco over Parmesan Polenta

This version of osso buco uses lamb shoulder chops instead of veal shanks.

Prep: 45 minutes
Cook: 2 hours, 30 minutes
Other: 10 minutes

Osso buco:
- Cooking spray
- 2 cups chopped onion
- 1 cup chopped carrot
- 6 garlic cloves, minced
- ⅓ cup all-purpose flour
- 9 (6-ounce) lamb shoulder chops (about 1 inch thick), trimmed
- 1¼ teaspoons salt, divided
- ½ teaspoon freshly ground black pepper, divided
- 1 tablespoon butter
- 1 cup dry white wine
- 3 thyme sprigs
- 1 (14½-ounce) can diced tomatoes, drained
- 1 (14-ounce) can less-sodium beef broth

Parmesan Polenta:
- 3 cups water
- 3 cups fat-free milk
- 1½ cups yellow cornmeal
- ¾ cup (3 ounces) grated fresh Parmesan cheese
- 1 teaspoon salt

Gremolata:
- ½ cup chopped fresh flat-leaf parsley
- 1 tablespoon grated lemon rind
- ¼ teaspoon kosher salt
- 3 garlic cloves, minced

1. To prepare osso buco, heat a large Dutch oven over medium-high heat. Coat pan with cooking spray. Add onion, carrot, and 6 garlic cloves; sauté 7 minutes. Remove onion mixture from pan.

2. Place flour in a shallow dish. Sprinkle lamb with ½ teaspoon salt and ¼ teaspoon pepper; dredge lamb in flour. Melt 1 teaspoon butter in pan over medium-high heat. Add 3 chops; cook 3 minutes on each side. Remove from pan. Repeat twice with remaining butter and lamb.

3. Return onion mixture to pan. Add wine; cook 4 minutes or until most of liquid evaporates. Add ¾ teaspoon salt, ¼ teaspoon pepper, thyme, tomatoes, and broth. Return lamb to pan; bring to a boil. Cover, reduce heat, and simmer 1 hour. Uncover; simmer 45 minutes. Remove from pan; cover and keep warm. Discard thyme.

4. Strain cooking liquid through a sieve into a bowl, reserving vegetable mixture. Place a zip-top plastic bag inside a 2-cup glass measure. Pour cooking liquid into bag; let stand 10 minutes (fat will rise to top of bag). Seal bag; snip off 1 bottom corner of bag. Drain liquid into bowl, stopping before fat layer reaches opening; discard fat. Add reserved vegetable mixture to liquid.

5. To prepare polenta, combine water and milk in a large saucepan; bring to a boil, stirring occasionally. Add cornmeal, stirring constantly with a whisk. Cover; cook over medium heat 10 minutes or until thick, stirring frequently. Add cheese and 1 teaspoon salt, stirring until cheese melts.

6. To prepare gremolata, combine parsley, rind, ¼ teaspoon kosher salt, and 3 garlic cloves; sprinkle over lamb. Yield: 9 servings (serving size: 1 chop, ⅔ cup polenta, ½ cup vegetable mixture, and 1 tablespoon gremolata).

CALORIES 420 (28% from fat); FAT 13.2g (sat 5.7g, mono 5.2g, poly 0.8g); PROTEIN 34g; CARB 40.4g; FIBER 4.9g; CHOL 88mg; IRON 3.3mg; SODIUM 975mg; CALC 264mg

lamb cuts Here are the cuts of fresh lamb that you'll see most often at the supermarket meat counter.

Ground: has a more delicate flavor than other ground meats, but can be used in most recipes that call for ground beef. A 3-ounce portion of cooked ground lamb has 1 gram of fat more than the same amount of ground chuck.

Lamb stew meat: cubes of meat that are ideal for cooking slowly in liquid.

Loin chops: a very tender cut that is good for grilling, broiling, and pan-roasting. One 4-ounce chop yields about 1½ to 2 ounces of cooked meat, so in *Cooking Light* recipes, one serving is 2 (4-ounce) chops.

Boneless leg of lamb: this cut is most commonly roasted or grilled whole. You may also see boneless leg of lamb cut into cubes for grilling on skewers, or sliced into steaks.

Boneless loin: a tender and flavorful cut that is good for grilling, oven-broiling, and roasting. With only 8 grams of fat per 3-ounce cooked portion, this is one of the leaner cuts of lamb available.

Shank: the front leg of lamb is very flavorful, but full of connective tissue and very tough. Shanks require a long, slow-cooking method such as braising.

Boneless shoulder: a tender, affordable cut, this type of roast is ideal for braising and grilling. You may also see chops cut from the shoulder section.

Rack of lamb (rib roast): contains rib bones, backbone, and thick, meaty rib-eye muscle. It has an outside covering of fat, which is usually removed. This elegant cut can be purchased as a "crown" or a French rack. A crown is made by curving around two rib halves, 8 ribs each (racks), and tying them to resemble a crown. In a French rack, 1½ inches of meat is removed from the bone ends of a rib roast or rib chops. The rack can be cut into individual (4-ounce) rib chops.

Remove the lamb from the oven or grill at a slightly lower degree of doneness than you prefer. The temperature will rise about 5 to 10 degrees upon standing.

Lamb Shanks on Cannellini Beans

Soak and cook the beans while the lamb simmers so they'll be ready at the same time.

Prep: 35 minutes • Cook: 2 hours, 31 minutes
Other: 1 hour

  6 (¾-pound) lamb shanks, trimmed
  ½ teaspoon salt
  ¼ teaspoon pepper
  2 cups finely chopped carrot
  1 cup finely chopped onion
  1 cup finely chopped celery
  1 cup dry red wine
  ½ cup beef broth
1½ teaspoons dried rosemary
  2 (14.5-ounce) cans diced tomatoes, undrained
  2 bay leaves
  1 cup dried cannellini beans
  4 bacon slices
  4 garlic cloves, sliced
     Rosemary sprigs (optional)

1. Sprinkle lamb with salt and pepper. Heat a large nonstick skillet over medium-high heat. Add lamb; cook 12 minutes, browning on all sides. Remove from pan. Add carrot, onion, and celery to pan; sauté 3 minutes. Add wine. Bring to a boil; cook 5 minutes. Stir in broth, dried rosemary, tomatoes, and bay leaves. Return lamb to pan (pan will be very full). Cover, reduce heat, and simmer 2 hours or until lamb is very tender, turning lamb once. Remove lamb from pan; bring liquid to a boil, and cook 5 minutes. Discard bay leaves.

2. While lamb cooks, sort and wash beans; place in a Dutch oven. Cover with water to 2 inches above beans; bring to a boil, and cook 2 minutes. Remove from heat; cover and let stand 1 hour. Drain; place in Dutch oven. Cover with water to 2 inches above beans; bring to a boil. Reduce heat, and simmer 1 hour or until tender. Drain.

3. Cook bacon in Dutch oven over medium-high heat until crisp. Remove bacon from pan, reserving 2 teaspoons drippings in pan. Crumble bacon. Heat drippings over medium-high heat. Add garlic, and sauté 2 minutes or until golden. Stir in beans and bacon; remove from heat.

4. Place beans on each of 6 plates; arrange lamb over beans. Spoon sauce over lamb. Garnish with rosemary sprigs, if desired. Yield: 6 servings (serving size: 1 shank, ⅔ cup beans, and 1⅓ cups sauce).

CALORIES 506 (26% from fat); FAT 14.5g (sat 5.1g, mono 5.9g, poly 1.7g); PROTEIN 60.2g; CARB 39.2g; FIBER 6.3g; CHOL 156mg; IRON 8.3mg; SODIUM 791mg; CALC 130mg

Test Kitchen Tip: We loved the use of dried beans, but for a quicker version, substitute drained canned beans. You can use cannellini or any other white bean. Just stir them in along with the bacon.

Lamb Shanks Hestia with Cucumber Raita

This earthy meal of braised lamb shanks in a richly flavored sauce is named for Hestia, the Greek goddess of the hearth. Since the *raita* needs to chill, make it first.

Prep: 23 minutes
Cook: 2 hours, 12 minutes

Cucumber Raita (page 465)
4   lamb shanks (about 1 1/4 pounds each)
Cooking spray
1 1/2   cups chopped onion
6   garlic cloves, minced
1   cup dry Marsala or Madeira
1   cup less-sodium beef broth
1   cup tomato sauce
1   teaspoon dried rosemary
1/4   teaspoon salt
1/4   teaspoon pepper
1   (3-inch) cinnamon stick
1   cup golden raisins
Mint sprigs (optional)

1. Prepare Cucumber Raita.
2. Preheat oven to 350°.
3. Rinse lamb with cold water; pat dry.
4. Heat a large Dutch oven over medium-high heat. Coat pan with cooking spray. Add 2 lamb shanks; cook 10 minutes, browning on all sides. Remove from pan. Repeat procedure with remaining lamb; remove from pan.
5. Add onion and garlic to pan; sauté 2 minutes. Add wine; cook 2 minutes, stirring frequently. Add broth, tomato sauce, rosemary, salt, pepper, and cinnamon stick.
6. Return lamb to pan; bring mixture to a simmer. Cover pan and bake at 350° for 1 hour.
7. Remove lamb mixture from oven; stir in raisins. Cover and bake an additional 45 minutes or until lamb is tender. Remove cinnamon stick; discard. Serve lamb with pan sauce and Cucumber Raita. Garnish with mint sprigs, if desired. Yield: 10 servings (serving size: 3 ounces lamb, about 1/3 cup sauce, and 2 tablespoons raita).

(Totals include Cucumber Raita) CALORIES 282 (25% from fat); FAT 7.9g (sat 2.9g, mono 3.3g, poly 0.6g); PROTEIN 33.6g; CARB 18.9g; FIBER 1.7g; CHOL 95mg; IRON 3.1mg; SODIUM 336mg; CALC 81mg

Curried Lamb Kebabs with Cucumber Raita

This Indian-style recipe features lamb kebabs and, like the Lamb Shanks Hestia (at left), also calls for the cucumber-based Indian salad, *raita*.

Prep: 18 minutes • **Cook: 17 minutes**

1   cup uncooked couscous
Cucumber Raita (page 465)
Kebabs:
1   pound boneless leg of lamb, trimmed and cut into 1-inch pieces
1   tablespoon curry powder
2   teaspoons olive oil, divided
1   teaspoon brown sugar
1/2   teaspoon salt
1/2   teaspoon ground red pepper
1   cup (1/2-inch) pieces yellow bell pepper
16   large cherry tomatoes
Cooking spray

1. Prepare couscous according to package directions, omitting salt and fat. Set aside.
2. While couscous stands, prepare raita.
3. Prepare broiler or grill.
4. To prepare kebabs, combine lamb, curry, 1 teaspoon oil, sugar, 1/2 teaspoon salt, and red pepper in a medium bowl; toss well. Combine 1 teaspoon oil, bell pepper, and tomatoes in a bowl; toss well. Thread lamb, bell pepper, and tomatoes alternately onto 4 (10-inch) skewers.
5. Place kebabs on broiler pan or grill rack coated with cooking spray; cook 7 minutes on each side or until done. Serve kebabs with raita and couscous. Yield: 4 servings (serving size: 1 lamb kebab, 1/4 cup raita, and 3/4 cup couscous)

(Totals include Cucumber Raita) CALORIES 381 (33% from fat); FAT 14g (sat 4.9g, mono 5.5g, poly 1.2g); PROTEIN 48.3g; CARB 13.7g; FIBER 0.4g; CHOL 150mg; IRON 4.8mg; SODIUM 405mg; CALC 43mg

Test Kitchen Tip: It's important to watch the cooking time and temperature for lamb carefully or the meat will be overcooked and tough. For the best flavor and tenderness, cook lamb only until it's pink: medium-rare (145°) or medium (160°).

menu

serves 4

Curried Lamb Kebabs with Cucumber Raita

Cauliflower and Potato Sabzi with Spices (page 518)

Naan (page 110)

Roast Lamb with Rosemary and Garlic

Elegant and simple, this lamb is ideal for a holiday meal. The roast cooks with just a simple rub of rosemary and garlic; coarse salt goes on the lamb the second it emerges from the oven.

Prep: 6 minutes • Cook: 1 hour, 15 minutes Other: 10 minutes

Roast:

- 1 (3-pound) rolled boneless leg of lamb, trimmed
- 1 tablespoon chopped fresh rosemary
- 3 garlic cloves, minced
- 1 teaspoon kosher or sea salt
- Rosemary sprigs (optional)
- Roasted garlic cloves (optional)

1. Preheat oven to 450°.

2. Secure roast at 1-inch intervals with twine. Rub surface of roast with rosemary and garlic. Place roast on rack of a broiler pan or roasting pan; insert a meat thermometer into thickest portion of roast. Bake at 450° for 1 hour and 15 minutes or until thermometer registers 145° (medium-rare) to 160° (medium).

3. Sprinkle roast with salt. Place roast on a cutting board; cover loosely with foil. Let stand 10 minutes (temperature of roast will increase 5° upon standing). Remove twine before slicing. Garnish with rosemary sprigs and roasted garlic cloves, if desired. Yield: 8 servings (serving size: 3 ounces).

CALORIES 165 (36% from fat); FAT 6.6g (sat 2.4g, mono 2.9g, poly 0.4g); PROTEIN 24.2g; CARB 0.5g; FIBER 0g; CHOL 76mg; IRON 1.9mg; SODIUM 293mg; CALC 12mg

Roast Lamb with Rosemary and Garlic

Pistachio-Encrusted Rack of Lamb

Serve this striking yet simple entrée at your next dinner party, and you'll win applause from your guests. Prepare the mustard mixture and breadcrumb mixture (minus the lemon juice) ahead; just remember to add the juice before patting the pistachio crust onto the lamb.

Prep: 25 minutes • Cook: 39 minutes Other: 10 minutes

- 3 (1-ounce) slices day-old white bread
- 1/3 cup finely chopped pistachios
- 1 1/4 teaspoons grated lemon rind
- 2 1/2 tablespoons chopped fresh parsley
- 1/4 cup lemon juice
- 3/4 teaspoon salt, divided
- 1/4 cup finely chopped fresh chives
- 1/4 cup finely chopped fresh mint
- 2 1/2 tablespoons Dijon mustard
- 2 garlic cloves, minced
- 2 (1 1/2-pound) French-cut racks of lamb (8 ribs each), trimmed
- Cooking spray

1. Preheat oven to 425°.

2. Place bread in a food processor; pulse 10 times or until coarse crumbs form to measure about 1 1/4 cups.

3. Combine breadcrumbs, nuts, rind, parsley, juice, and 1/2 teaspoon salt in a small bowl.

4. Combine chives, mint, mustard, and garlic in a small bowl.

5. Sprinkle lamb with 1/4 teaspoon salt. Heat a large nonstick skillet over medium-high heat. Coat pan with cooking spray. Add lamb; cook 2 minutes on each side or until browned. Spread half of mustard mixture over meaty portion of each lamb rack. Carefully pat half of breadcrumb mixture into mustard mixture on each lamb rack.

6. Place lamb on a broiler pan coated with cooking spray. Bake at 425° for 35 minutes or until meat thermometer registers 140° (medium-rare) to 155° (medium). Place lamb on a platter; cover with foil. Let stand 10 minutes before serving (temperature of lamb will increase 5° upon standing). Slice each rack into 4 pieces (2 ribs per piece). Yield: 8 servings (serving size: 1 piece, 2 ribs).

CALORIES 206 (47% from fat); FAT 10.8g (sat 3.1g, mono 4.6g, poly 1.5g); PROTEIN 18.5g; CARB 8.5g; FIBER 0.9g; CHOL 52mg; IRON 2.1mg; SODIUM 472mg; CALC 37mg

Pork
From chops and tenderloins to whole hams, using the right cooking method guarantees flavorful, tender results every time.

Barbecued Pork Chops

Serve these saucy chops with sautéed apples and rolls for a satisfying, homestyle supper.

Prep: 13 minutes • Cook: 12 minutes

Sauce:
- ¼ cup packed brown sugar
- ¼ cup ketchup
- 1 tablespoon Worcestershire sauce
- 1 tablespoon low-sodium soy sauce

Remaining ingredients:
- 6 (6-ounce) bone-in center-cut pork chops (about ½ inch thick)
- 1 teaspoon dried thyme
- 1 teaspoon garlic salt
- ¼ teaspoon ground red pepper
- Cooking spray

1. Prepare grill or broiler.

2. To prepare sauce, combine first 4 ingredients in a small bowl. Place ¼ cup sauce in a small bowl, and set aside.

3. Trim fat from pork. Combine thyme, garlic salt, and pepper; sprinkle over pork. Place pork on grill rack or broiler pan coated with cooking spray; cook 6 minutes on each side, basting with remaining sauce. Serve pork chops with reserved ¼ cup sauce. Yield: 6 servings (serving size: 1 pork chop and 2 teaspoons sauce).

CALORIES 244 (42% from fat); FAT 11.3g (sat 3.9g, mono 5g, poly 1.4g); PROTEIN 24.6g; CARB 9.9g; FIBER 0.2g; CHOL 77mg; IRON 1.5mg; SODIUM 649mg; CALC 22mg

Peach-Glazed Barbecue Pork Chops and Peaches

Summer—when peaches are at their peak—is the best time
to make this fruited pork dish. Cooking time for the peaches will vary
depending on their ripeness. The glaze also works well on chicken.

Prep: 25 minutes • Cook: 43 minutes • Other: 35 minutes to 4 hours

3 cups chopped peeled peaches (about
   1½ pounds)

1 cup dry white wine

¼ cup sugar

1 teaspoon salt, divided

¼ teaspoon black pepper, divided

2 tablespoons white wine vinegar

2 tablespoons molasses

1 teaspoon chili powder

½ teaspoon paprika

¼ teaspoon ground red pepper

6 (6-ounce) bone-in center-cut pork
   chops (about ½ inch thick), trimmed

6 peaches, halved and pitted

Cooking spray

1. Combine first 3 ingredients in a small saucepan; bring to a boil. Cover, reduce heat, and simmer 25 minutes. Uncover and simmer 5 minutes.

2. Place peach mixture in a food processor; process until smooth. Add ¾ teaspoon salt, ⅛ teaspoon black pepper, vinegar, and next 4 ingredients; pulse to combine. Let stand 5 minutes.

3. Place half of peach mixture in a large, heavy-duty zip-top plastic bag; reserve other half for basting. Add pork chops to bag; seal bag, and refrigerate 30 minutes to 4 hours.

4. Prepare grill.

5. Remove pork from bag; discard marinade. Sprinkle pork with ¼ teaspoon salt and ⅛ teaspoon black pepper. Place pork and peach halves on grill rack coated with cooking spray, and grill 10 minutes or until pork is done and peaches are tender, turning once. Baste pork and peach halves with reserved peach mixture every 2 minutes during first 6 minutes of cooking. Yield: 6 servings (serving size: 1 pork chop and 2 peach halves).

CALORIES 301 (23% from fat); FAT 7.6g (sat 2.6g, mono 3.4g, poly 0.9g); PROTEIN 26.1g; CARB 33.1g; FIBER 3.5g; CHOL 62mg; IRON 1.7mg; SODIUM 449mg; CALC 34mg

Pork-and-Pear Sauté with Lemon-Vodka Sauce

Tender and lean, these boneless chops are done in minutes. Be careful not to over-cook the meat or it will be tough.

Prep: 10 minutes • Cook: 13 minutes

- 2 teaspoons olive oil, divided
- 2 (4-ounce) boneless center-cut loin pork chops (about ¾ inch thick)
- ½ teaspoon salt, divided
- ½ teaspoon cracked black pepper, divided
- 2 peeled Anjou pears, cored and halved (about 1 pound)
- ¼ cup vodka or dry white wine
- 2 teaspoons grated lemon rind
- 1 tablespoon fresh lemon juice
- 1 tablespoon chopped fresh chives

1. Heat 1 teaspoon olive oil in a 10-inch skillet over medium heat. Sprinkle pork chops with ¼ teaspoon salt and ¼ tea-spoon pepper. Add pork chops to pan; sauté 3 minutes on each side or until pork is done. Remove pork chops from pan, and keep warm.
2. Heat 1 teaspoon oil in pan over medi-um heat. Place pear in pan, cut sides down. Sauté 2 minutes on each side or until golden. Remove pear from pan, and keep warm. Add vodka to pan, scraping pan to loosen browned bits. Stir in ¼ tea-spoon salt, ¼ teaspoon pepper, rind, juice, and chives, and cook 1 minute. Yield: 2 servings (serving size: 1 pork chop, 2 pear halves, and 1 tablespoon sauce).

CALORIES 338 (36% from fat); FAT 13.3g (sat 3.2g, mono 5.5g, poly 1.2g); PROTEIN 25.9g; CARB 30.5g; FIBER 4.9g; CHOL 71mg; IRON 1.6mg; SODIUM 661mg; CALC 34mg

Pork-and-Pear Sauté with Lemon-Vodka Sauce

Ancho Pork and Peppers

Ancho chile powder transforms ordinary pork chops into a Mexican-inspired meal.

Prep: 15 minutes • Cook: 14 minutes

- 2 teaspoons ancho chile powder
- 1 teaspoon ground cumin
- 1 teaspoon salt, divided
- 4 (4-ounce) boneless center-cut loin pork chops (about ½ inch thick)
- Cooking spray
- 1 teaspoon olive oil
- 3 cups vertically sliced onion
- 1 red bell pepper, cut into strips
- 1 green bell pepper, cut into strips
- 2 garlic cloves, minced
- 2 tablespoons fresh lime juice

1. Combine chile powder, cumin, and ½ teaspoon salt in a small bowl. Sprinkle both sides of pork with chile powder mixture. Heat a large nonstick skillet over medium-high heat. Coat pan with cooking spray. Add pork; cook 4 minutes on each side or until done. Remove from pan; keep warm.
2. Heat oil in pan over medium-high heat. Add onion, peppers, and ½ teaspoon salt; sauté 4 minutes. Add garlic; sauté 1 minute. Remove from heat. Stir in juice. Yield: 4 servings (serving size: 1 pork chop and about ¾ cup pepper mixture).

CALORIES 248 (32% from fat); FAT 8.9g (sat 2.8g, mono 4.1g, poly 0.8g); PROTEIN 27.7g; CARB 14.1g; FIBER 3.3g; CHOL 73mg; IRON 1.9mg; SODIUM 675mg; CALC 57mg

---

menu

serves 4

Ancho Pork and Peppers

Spanish rice*

Green beans sautéed with garlic

*Sauté 1 cup chopped onion and 2 minced garlic cloves in 1 tablespoon butter; stir in 1 cup rice and 1½ teaspoons salt. Add 1 (14.5-ounce) can undrained diced tomatoes and green chiles and 1 cup fat-free, less-sodium chicken broth. Bring mixture to a boil; cover, reduce heat, and simmer 20 minutes or until done.

Chipotle-Marinated Pork Chops with Chimichurri Sauce

Chimichurri, an Argentine condiment, is a thick herb sauce that's similar to pesto. The sauce in this recipe is enhanced with shredded carrot and minced onion.

Prep: 15 minutes • Cook: 10 minutes
Other: 2 hours

- ¾ cup fat-free, less-sodium chicken broth
- 1 drained canned chipotle chile in adobo sauce
- 4 (6-ounce) center-cut pork chops
- 1 cup fresh flat-leaf parsley leaves
- ¼ cup fat-free, less-sodium chicken broth
- 2 tablespoons extravirgin olive oil
- 2 tablespoons white wine vinegar
- ½ teaspoon dried oregano
- ¼ teaspoon salt
- ⅛ teaspoon freshly ground black pepper
- 2 garlic cloves
- ½ cup shredded carrot
- ½ cup minced fresh onion
  Cooking spray

1. Place ¾ cup chicken broth and chipotle chile in a blender; process until smooth. Combine chile mixture and pork chops in a large zip-top plastic bag. Seal and marinate in refrigerator 2 hours. Remove chops from bag; discard marinade.
2. Prepare grill.
3. Place parsley and next 7 ingredients in a blender; process until smooth. Pour into a bowl; stir in carrot and onion.
4. Place chops on grill rack coated with cooking spray; cook 5 minutes on each side or until done. Serve with chimichurri sauce. Yield: 4 servings (serving size: 1 pork chop and ¼ cup sauce).

CALORIES 311 (56% from fat); FAT 19.2g (sat 5.1g, mono 10.5g, poly 2.2g); PROTEIN 27.6g; CARB 5.4g; FIBER 1.6g; CHOL 84mg; IRON 2.2mg; SODIUM 321mg; CALC 42mg

Vanilla-Glazed Pork Chops with Cipollini Onions

These pork chops benefit from the sweet surprise of vanilla. Don't substitute vanilla extract for the vanilla bean; the flavor won't be the same.

Prep: 11 minutes • Cook: 31 minutes

- 4 (4-ounce) boneless center-cut loin pork chops (about ½ inch thick)
- ½ teaspoon salt
- ½ teaspoon pepper
- 1 teaspoon canola oil
  Cooking spray
- 12 cipollini onions or small boiling onions, peeled (about ¾ pound)
- 1 (3-inch) piece vanilla bean, split lengthwise
- ¾ cup Madeira wine
- 1 tablespoon brown sugar
- 2 tablespoons balsamic vinegar
- 1 teaspoon cornstarch

1. Sprinkle chops with salt and pepper. Heat oil in a large nonstick skillet coated with cooking spray over medium-high heat until hot. Add chops and onions; cook 4 minutes on each side or until lightly browned. Scrape seeds from vanilla bean; add seeds, bean, and wine to pan, scraping pan to loosen browned bits. Cover, reduce heat, and simmer 20 minutes or until pork and onions are tender. Remove pork and onions from pan with a slotted spoon; keep warm.
2. Combine brown sugar, balsamic vinegar, and cornstarch in a small bowl. Add to wine mixture in pan, and bring mixture to a boil. Cook 1 minute, stirring constantly. Discard vanilla bean. Serve vanilla sauce with pork chops and onions. Yield: 4 servings (serving size: 1 pork chop, 3 onions, and about 2 tablespoons sauce).

CALORIES 222 (31% from fat); FAT 7.6g (sat 2.4g, mono 3.6g, poly 0.8g); PROTEIN 24.7g; CARB 12.4g; FIBER 1.2g; CHOL 65mg; IRON 1.1mg; SODIUM 352mg; CALC 48mg

Vanilla-Glazed Pork Chops with Cipollini Onions

Galician Pork and Pepper Pie

A large, two-crusted, savory pie from Galicia, this Spanish empanada is typically filled with fish or meat, red or green bell peppers, and lots of onion. Substitute pizza dough if you're pressed for time, though the pastry crust is easy to make. Serve the empanada at room temperature.

Prep: 40 minutes • Cook: 1 hour, 5 minutes
Other: 2 hours, 30 minutes

Pork:
- 2 tablespoons minced fresh parsley
- 1 tablespoon Spanish smoked paprika or hot paprika
- 1 tablespoon extravirgin olive oil
- 1 teaspoon dried oregano
- 3 garlic cloves, minced
- 1 (1-pound) pork tenderloin, trimmed and cut into ½-inch-wide strips

Dough:
- 2¾ cups all-purpose flour
- 1 tablespoon baking powder
- 1½ teaspoons salt
- ½ cup water
- ¼ cup olive oil
- 1 large egg, lightly beaten

Filling:
- Cooking spray
- ¼ teaspoon salt
- 2 cups thinly sliced sweet onion
- 2 cups red bell pepper strips
- 1 cup chopped tomato
- ¼ cup chopped Spanish serrano ham or prosciutto (about 1½ ounces)
- 2 tablespoons dry white wine or water
- Dash of crumbled saffron threads

Remaining ingredient:
- 1 large egg, lightly beaten

1. To prepare pork, combine first 5 ingredients in a large zip-top plastic bag; add pork to bag. Seal and marinate in refrigerator 2 hours, turning bag occasionally.

2. To prepare dough, lightly spoon flour into dry measuring cups; level with a knife. Combine flour, baking powder, and 1½ teaspoons salt in a large bowl, stirring with a whisk. Combine water, oil, and egg in a medium bowl. Gradually add oil mixture to flour mixture, stirring just until moist. Turn dough out onto a lightly floured surface; knead lightly until smooth. Divide dough in half. Cover with plastic; let rest 30 minutes.

3. To prepare filling, heat a large nonstick skillet over medium heat. Coat pan with cooking spray. Add pork mixture; sprinkle with ¼ teaspoon salt. Cook 5 minutes or until pork loses its pink color. Add onion and bell pepper; cook 5 minutes. Cover, reduce heat, and simmer 20 minutes or until vegetables are tender. Stir in tomato, ham, wine, and saffron; cook 5 minutes.

4. Preheat oven to 350°.

5. Working with one portion of dough at a time (cover remaining dough to keep from drying), roll portion into a 13-inch circle on a floured surface. Place one circle on a large baking sheet coated with cooking spray. Spoon filling onto circle using a slotted spoon, leaving a 1-inch border around edge. Place remaining circle over filling. Pinch edges to seal. Cut several slits in top of dough to allow steam to escape. Brush with egg. Bake at 350° for 30 minutes or until golden brown; cool. Cut into wedges. Yield: 8 servings (serving size: 1 wedge).

CALORIES 366 (33% from fat); FAT 13.5g (sat 2.7g, mono 8g, poly 1.5g); PROTEIN 21g; CARB 39.5g; FIBER 3g; CHOL 96mg; IRON 3.7mg; SODIUM 814mg; CALC 134mg

how to prepare pork tenderloin

To prepare pork tenderloin, you'll need to remove the silver skin, which is the thin, shiny membrane that runs along the surface of the meat. Leaving it on can cause the tenderloin to toughen and lose its shape during cooking.

1. Stretching the membrane with one hand so it's tight, use your other hand to slip the tip of the knife underneath the silvery skin.

2. Slowly slice back and forth, angling the sharp edge of the blade up, rather than down, through the meat. Continue until all the silver skin is removed, then discard.

Spicy Korean Pork Barbecue

Sambal oelek is a chile sauce that's neither sweetened nor seasoned with garlic, so the pure taste and fiery heat of the chiles really come through. In this recipe, the caramel notes of brown sugar balance the heat of sambal oelek and crushed red pepper.

**Prep: 15 minutes • Cook: 5 minutes
Other: 2 hours, 30 minutes**

    1   (1-pound) pork tenderloin, trimmed
    2   tablespoons brown sugar
    2   tablespoons low-sodium soy sauce
 1½   tablespoons sambal oelek or Thai
        chile paste
    1   teaspoon minced peeled fresh ginger
    1   teaspoon dark sesame oil
   ½   teaspoon crushed red pepper
    3   garlic cloves, minced
        Cooking spray

1. Wrap pork in plastic wrap; freeze 1½ hours or until firm. Remove plastic wrap; cut pork diagonally across grain into ¹⁄₁₆-inch-thick slices.
2. Combine pork, sugar, and next 6 ingredients in a large zip-top plastic bag. Seal and marinate in refrigerator 1 hour, turning bag occasionally.
3. Prepare grill.
4. Place a wire grilling basket on grill rack. Remove pork from bag; discard marinade. Place pork on grilling basket coated with cooking spray; grill 5 minutes or until desired degree of doneness, turning frequently. Yield: 4 servings (serving size: 3 ounces).

CALORIES 205 (29% from fat); FAT 6.6g (sat 2.1g, mono 2.7g, poly 1g); PROTEIN 26.5g; CARB 8.9g; FIBER 0.3g; CHOL 80mg; IRON 1.6mg; SODIUM 471mg; CALC 16mg

Pork Medallions in Caribbean Nut Sauce

Take tenderloin to the tropics by topping it with this island-inspired sauce of coconut milk, ginger, curry, and cumin. The peanuts add a delightful crunch to the creamy sauce. Start the rice before you cook the pork.

Prep: 25 minutes • Cook: 35 minutes

    6   garlic cloves, peeled
    4   teaspoons chopped peeled fresh
        ginger
    2   teaspoons cumin seeds
   ¼   teaspoon curry powder
   ¼   teaspoon crushed red pepper
   ¼   cup unsalted, dry-roasted peanuts
    1   tablespoon hot water
    1   (1-pound) pork tenderloin, trimmed
        Cooking spray
    2   tablespoons low-sodium soy sauce
    6   tablespoons water, divided
    2   cups thinly sliced red onion
    3   tablespoons light coconut milk
    1   tablespoon brown sugar
   ½   teaspoon salt
   ⅛   teaspoon black pepper
    4   cups hot cooked long-grain rice

1. Place garlic cloves in a food processor, and process until minced. Add ginger, cumin, curry, and red pepper, and process until blended. Add peanuts and hot water, and pulse until well blended, scraping sides of bowl occasionally.
2. Cut pork crosswise into 1-inch slices. Place each piece between 2 sheets of heavy-duty plastic wrap; flatten each piece to ½-inch thickness using a meat mallet or rolling pin. Coat pork with cooking spray. Heat a large nonstick skillet over medium-high heat. Add pork; cook 2 minutes on each side or until browned. Place pork in a shallow bowl. Add soy sauce and 2 tablespoons water to pan, scraping pan to loosen browned bits. Add soy sauce mixture to pork; keep warm.
3. Add onion to pan; sauté 3 minutes. Add ¼ cup peanut mixture; cook 4 minutes. Stir in ¼ cup water, coconut milk, sugar, salt, and black pepper. Return pork mixture to pan; bring to a boil. Reduce heat; simmer 1 minute. Combine remaining peanut mixture with rice. Serve pork and sauce with rice. Yield: 4 servings (serving size: 3 ounces pork, ½ cup sauce, and 1 cup rice).

CALORIES 460 (16% from fat); FAT 8.9g (sat 2.1g, mono 3.9g, poly 2.1g); PROTEIN 31.5g; CARB 61.2g; FIBER 3.1g; CHOL 74mg; IRON 4.5mg; SODIUM 554mg; CALC 69mg

Test Kitchen Tip: Transfer the remaining coconut milk to an airtight container, and store it in the refrigerator for three to four days.

menu

serves 4

Pork Medallions in
Caribbean Nut Sauce

Sugar snap peas with basil*

Pineapple Sorbet (page 189)

*Combine 1 pound sugar snap peas, ¼ cup orange juice, 1 tablespoon butter, and 2 tablespoons finely chopped fresh basil in a microwave-safe dish, and stir gently. Cover with heavy-duty plastic wrap and vent. Microwave at HIGH 2 to 3 minutes or until peas are crisp-tender, stirring after 1 minute.

Hoisin and Bourbon-Glazed Pork Tenderloin

The basting liquid in this recipe has a range of flavors—sweet, sour, salty, woody, and spicy. Soaking wood chips in water prevents flare-ups on the grill. Butterflying the tenderloin exposes more surface area, which allows the pork to absorb the smoky flavor, creates a nice caramelized exterior, and cooks faster. Serve with Three-Fruit Salsa (page 39).

Prep: 15 minutes • Cook: 15 minutes • Other: 35 minutes

1   cup hickory wood chips
⅓   cup hoisin sauce
2   tablespoons seasoned rice vinegar
2   tablespoons bourbon
2   tablespoons maple syrup
1½ teaspoons grated peeled fresh ginger
1½ teaspoons fresh lime juice
½   teaspoon chile paste with garlic
1   garlic clove, minced
2   (1-pound) pork tenderloins, trimmed
½   teaspoon salt
½   teaspoon freshly ground black pepper
Cooking spray
Mint sprigs (optional)

1. Soak wood chips in water 30 minutes; drain well.

2. Prepare grill.

3. Combine hoisin sauce and next 7 ingredients in a small bowl; stir with a whisk.

4. Slice pork lengthwise, cutting to, but not through, other side. Open halves, laying pork flat. Sprinkle pork with salt and pepper. Add wood chips to grill. Place pork on grill rack coated with cooking spray; cook 5 minutes. Turn and baste pork with hoisin mixture; cook 5 minutes. Turn and baste pork with hoisin mixture; cook 5 minutes or until pork reaches 155° or desired degree of doneness. Let stand 5 minutes; cut pork into ½-inch slices. Serve with salsa and garnish with mint, if desired. Yield: 8 servings (serving size: 3 ounces).

CALORIES 209 (25% from fat); FAT 5.8g (sat 2g, mono 2.3g, poly 0.7g); PROTEIN 26.3g; CARB 9.2g; FIBER 0.4g; CHOL 80mg; IRON 1.4mg; SODIUM 452mg; CALC 13mg

Pork Tenderloin with Maple Pan Juices

Maple syrup contributes a unique depth of flavor to this pork dish. Use real maple syrup instead of maple-flavored pancake syrup for the best results.

Prep: 12 minutes • Cook: 38 minutes
Other: 2 hours

 ⅓ cup diced onion
 ¼ cup fresh orange juice, divided
 ¼ cup maple syrup, divided
 2 tablespoons sake (rice wine)
 2 tablespoons low-sodium soy sauce
 ⅛ teaspoon pepper
 2 garlic cloves, minced
 1 (1-pound) pork tenderloin, trimmed
Cooking spray
 ⅓ cup fat-free, less-sodium chicken
     broth

1. Combine onion, 2 tablespoons juice, 2 tablespoons syrup, sake, soy sauce, pepper, and garlic in a large zip-top plastic bag. Add pork to syrup mixture; seal and marinate in refrigerator 2 hours.
2. Preheat oven to 400°.
3. Heat a 9-inch heavy, ovenproof skillet over medium-high heat. Coat pan with cooking spray. Remove pork from bag, reserving marinade. Add pork to pan; cook 5 minutes, browning on all sides. Insert meat thermometer into thickest part of pork. Place pan in oven; bake at 400° for 25 minutes or until meat thermometer registers 155° or desired degree of doneness. Remove pork from pan. Set aside, and keep warm.
4. Combine 2 tablespoons juice, 2 tablespoons syrup, reserved marinade, and broth in a small bowl. Add syrup mixture to pan, and place over medium-high heat, scraping pan to loosen browned bits. Bring to a boil; reduce heat, and simmer 5 minutes or until slightly thick. Serve sauce with pork. Yield: 4 servings (serving size: 3 ounces pork and 2 tablespoons sauce).

CALORIES 204 (13% from fat); FAT 3g (sat 1g, mono 1.3g, poly 0.4g); PROTEIN 24.4g; CARB 16.9g; FIBER 0.3g; CHOL 74mg; IRON 1.8mg; SODIUM 293mg; CALC 29mg

Pecan-Crusted Pork with Red Onion Marmalade and Roasted Sweet Potatoes

In this holiday-inspired one-dish meal, the pecan-coated pork is topped with onion marmalade, and served with sweet potatoes.

Prep: 30 minutes • Cook: 1 hour, 20 minutes

Roasted Sweet Potatoes:
 2 pounds peeled sweet potatoes, cut
     into ½-inch-thick slices
Cooking spray
 ¼ cup packed brown sugar, divided
 1 bacon slice, cut into 1-inch pieces
Red Onion Marmalade:
 1 teaspoon canola oil
 1 medium red onion, sliced and
     separated into rings (about 1½ cups)
 ¼ cup water
 ¼ cup balsamic vinegar
 1 tablespoon grated peeled fresh ginger
Pork:
 1 (1-pound) pork tenderloin, trimmed
 ½ cup all-purpose flour, divided
 ⅓ cup ground pecans
 ½ teaspoon cracked black pepper
 2 large egg whites, lightly beaten
 1 tablespoon butter
 4 teaspoons chopped pecans, toasted

1. Preheat oven to 400°.
2. To prepare potatoes, arrange potato slices in a 13 x 9–inch baking dish coated with cooking spray. Sprinkle potato with 2 tablespoons sugar; arrange bacon on top. Bake at 400° for 30 minutes. Turn potatoes over; bake an additional 30 minutes or until tender. Keep warm.
3. To prepare marmalade, heat oil in a large nonstick skillet over medium-high heat. Add onion and 2 tablespoons sugar; cook 6 minutes or until onion is tender and lightly browned, stirring frequently. Stir in water, vinegar, and ginger; bring to a boil. Cook 3 minutes, and remove from heat.
4. To prepare pork, cut pork crosswise into 8 pieces. Place each piece between 2 sheets of heavy-duty plastic wrap, and flatten to ½-inch thickness using a meat mallet or rolling pin.
5. Lightly spoon flour into a dry measuring cup. Place ¼ cup flour in a shallow dish. Combine ¼ cup flour, ground pecans, and pepper in a separate shallow dish. Dredge pork in flour, shaking off excess. Dip pork in egg whites; dredge in pecan mixture, coating both sides.
6. Melt butter in pan coated with cooking spray over medium-high heat. Arrange pork in pan in a single layer. Cook 3 minutes on each side. Top with onion mixture; sprinkle with pecans. Serve with sweet potatoes. Yield: 4 servings (serving size: 2 cutlets, ¼ cup onion marmalade, and ¾ cup sweet potatoes).

CALORIES 685 (30% from fat); FAT 23.2g (sat 5.4g, mono 11.4g, poly 4.9g); PROTEIN 33.2g; CARB 87.3g; FIBER 9.1g; CHOL 86mg; IRON 4.5mg; SODIUM 190mg; CALC 89mg

Test Kitchen Tip: Arrange the sweet potato slices in a single layer in the baking dish so they will cook evenly. If they're piled up in the dish, the slices on the bottom will steam instead of roast.

Pork Tenderloin Studded with Rosemary and Garlic

Think it takes all day to cook a roast? With a smaller cut, such as a tenderloin, and intense heat, mere minutes are all you need.

Prep: 10 minutes • Cook: 20 minutes
Other: 5 minutes

- 2 tablespoons finely chopped fresh rosemary
- 4 garlic cloves, minced
- 1 (1-pound) pork tenderloin, trimmed
- ½ teaspoon salt
- ¼ teaspoon pepper
- Cooking spray

1. Preheat oven to 475°.

2. Combine rosemary and garlic. Make several ½-inch-deep slits in pork; place half of rosemary mixture in slits. Rub pork with remaining rosemary mixture; sprinkle with salt and pepper. Place pork on a jelly-roll pan coated with cooking spray. Insert a meat thermometer into thickest portion of pork.

3. Bake at 475° for 20 minutes or until thermometer registers 155° or desired degree of doneness. Let stand 5 minutes, and cut into ¼-inch-thick slices. Yield: 4 servings (serving size: 3 ounces).

CALORIES 147 (26% from fat); FAT 4.2g (sat 1.4g, mono 1.6g, poly 0.4g); PROTEIN 24.2g; CARB 1.5g; FIBER 0.1g; CHOL 67mg; IRON 1.6mg; SODIUM 342mg; CALC 23mg

Test Kitchen Tip: Strip rosemary leaves by running your fingertips along the stem in the opposite direction from which the leaves grow.

menu

serves 4

Pork Tenderloin Studded with Rosemary and Garlic

Boiled red potatoes

Caramelized Carrots*

*Combine 1 pound baby carrots, 1 tablespoon low-sodium soy sauce, 2 teaspoons brown sugar, 2 teaspoons olive oil, ¼ teaspoon salt, and ¼ teaspoon black pepper. Arrange in a single layer on a baking sheet coated with cooking spray; place in oven on rack below pork. Bake at 475° for 15 minutes or until tender, turning once.

Pork Medallions with Port Wine-Dried Cherry Pan Sauce

Here, a pork tenderloin is cut into 16 medallions, an ideal shape and size for sautéing. Butter, whisked into the red wine mixture at the end, creates a velvety sauce. Serve with plain or garlic-flavored couscous.

Prep: 11 minutes • Cook: 16 minutes

> 1 cup ruby port or other sweet red wine
> 1/3 cup dried sweet cherries
> 4 teaspoons seedless raspberry jam
> 1 teaspoon Dijon mustard
> 1 tablespoon canola oil
> 1 1/2 pounds pork tenderloin, trimmed
> 1/2 teaspoon salt
> 1/4 teaspoon freshly ground black pepper
> 1 tablespoon butter
> Parsley sprigs (optional)

1. Combine first 4 ingredients.
2. Heat oil in a large nonstick skillet over low heat 2 minutes. Cut pork crosswise into 16 pieces. Sprinkle evenly with salt and pepper.
3. Place pork in pan; cook 4 minutes on each side or until golden brown. Remove pork from pan. Stir in wine mixture, scraping to loosen browned bits. Increase heat to high; bring to a boil. Cook until reduced to 1/2 cup (about 3 minutes). Remove from heat. Stir in butter with a whisk. Serve sauce over pork. Garnish with parsley, if desired. Yield: 4 servings (serving size: 4 pieces pork and 2 tablespoons sauce).

CALORIES 353 (40% from fat); FAT 15.6g (sat 5.2g, mono 6.9g, poly 2.1g); PROTEIN 35.4g; CARB 15.2g; FIBER 1.4g; CHOL 120mg; IRON 2.4mg; SODIUM 419mg; CALC 26mg

---

Pan-Roasted Pork Loin with Leeks

This seasoned pork loin received our Test Kitchens' highest rating. The combination of buttered leeks and roasted pork is superb.

Prep: 15 minutes • Cook: 2 hours, 17 minutes

> 4 large leeks (about 2 1/4 pounds)
> 1/2 cup water
> 1 tablespoon butter, divided
> 1/2 teaspoon salt, divided
> 1/2 teaspoon pepper, divided
> 1 (2-pound) boneless pork loin, trimmed
> 1/2 cup dry white wine

1. Remove roots and tough upper leaves from leeks. Cut each leek in half lengthwise. Cut each half crosswise into 1/2-inch-thick slices (about 6 cups). Soak in cold water to loosen dirt; rinse and drain.
2. Place sliced leek, 1/2 cup water, 1 teaspoon butter, 1/4 teaspoon salt, and 1/4 teaspoon pepper in a Dutch oven or deep sauté pan, and place over medium-high heat. Cook 10 minutes or until leeks have wilted. Pour leeks into a bowl.
3. Heat 2 teaspoons butter in pan over medium-high heat. Add pork; cook 5 minutes, browning on all sides. Add 1/4 teaspoon salt, 1/4 teaspoon pepper, and wine; cook 15 seconds, scraping pan to loosen browned bits. Return sliced leek to pan.
4. Cover, reduce heat, and simmer 2 hours or until pork is tender. Remove pork from pan; increase heat to reduce leek sauce if it's too watery. Cut pork into 1/4-inch-thick slices; serve with leek mixture. Yield: 6 servings (serving size: about 3 ounces pork and 2 1/2 tablespoons leek mixture).

CALORIES 246 (39% from fat); FAT 10.7g (sat 4.2g, mono 4.4g, poly 1.1g); PROTEIN 24.8g; CARB 12.1g; FIBER 1g; CHOL 73mg; IRON 2.8mg; SODIUM 306mg; CALC 60mg

Pork Loin with Dried-Plum Stuffing

Stuffed pork loin is a smart choice for entertaining because you can prepare it up to a day ahead.

Prep: 40 minutes • Cook: 49 minutes
Other: 10 minutes

Stuffing:

Cooking spray
1⅓ cups finely chopped red onion
½ cup finely chopped celery
2 garlic cloves, minced
1 cup finely chopped dried plums
⅓ cup finely chopped pecans
1 tablespoon grated orange rind
¼ cup fresh orange juice (about
 1 medium orange)
2 tablespoons minced fresh parsley
1 tablespoon chopped fresh thyme
1 tablespoon chopped fresh rosemary
½ teaspoon salt
¼ teaspoon freshly ground black pepper

Pork:

1 (2-pound) boneless pork loin,
 trimmed
¼ teaspoon salt
¼ teaspoon freshly ground black pepper

Sauce:

1 tablespoon all-purpose flour
1½ cups fat-free, less-sodium chicken
 broth, divided
¼ cup port or other sweet red wine
1 tablespoon Dijon mustard
¼ teaspoon salt
⅛ teaspoon freshly ground black pepper
Flat-leaf parsley sprigs (optional)

1. Preheat oven to 425°.
2. To prepare stuffing, heat a large nonstick skillet over medium heat. Coat pan with cooking spray. Add onion, celery, and garlic; cook 7 minutes or until tender,

stirring frequently. Remove from heat. Stir in dried plums and next 8 ingredients; set aside.
3. To prepare pork, slice pork lengthwise, cutting to, but not through, other side. Open halves, laying pork flat. Place plastic wrap over pork; pound to ½-inch thickness using a meat mallet or rolling pin. Remove plastic wrap; discard.
4. Spread stuffing over pork, leaving a 1-inch border. Roll up tightly; secure at 1½-inch intervals with twine. Rub pork with ¼ teaspoon salt and ¼ teaspoon pepper. Place pork on a rack in a broiler pan coated with cooking spray. Bake at 425° for 40 minutes or until a meat thermometer inserted in center of pork registers 155°,

turning pork after 20 minutes. Place pork on a cutting board; let stand 10 minutes. Cut into thin slices.
5. To prepare sauce, whisk together flour and ¼ cup broth. Place roasting pan over medium heat. Add port, stirring to loosen browned bits. Whisk in flour mixture, mustard, and 1¼ cups broth. Cook 2 minutes or until slightly thick, stirring frequently with a whisk. Stir in ¼ teaspoon salt and ⅛ teaspoon pepper. Serve with pork. Garnish with parsley, if desired. Yield: 8 servings (serving size: 3 ounces pork and 3 tablespoons sauce).

CALORIES 260 (27% from fat); FAT 7.8g (sat 1.7g, mono 3.9g, poly 1.6g); PROTEIN 26.2g; CARB 20.1g; FIBER 2.9g; CHOL 74mg; IRON 2.5mg; SODIUM 489mg; CALC 39mg

Maple and Calvados-Glazed Pork Crown Roast with Apple-Chestnut Puree

A spectacular-looking crown roast is an impressive holiday menu offering. If you can't find Calvados, use a combination of three parts brandy to one part apple cider.

**Prep: 30 minutes • Cook: 2 hours, 42 minutes
Other: 20 minutes**

Roast:

½ cup Calvados (apple brandy)
¼ cup maple syrup
1 sage sprig
1 (16-rib) crown roast of pork (about 10¼ pounds), trimmed
Cooking spray
1½ teaspoons salt
1 teaspoon freshly ground black pepper

Puree:

4 cups chopped peeled Granny Smith apple (about 1½ pounds)
1 cup bottled chestnuts
½ cup Calvados
⅓ cup packed brown sugar
2 tablespoons maple syrup
2 tablespoons half-and-half
2 tablespoons Calvados
½ teaspoon salt
1 teaspoon finely chopped fresh sage
Fresh sage leaves (optional)
Fresh rosemary sprigs (optional)

1. Preheat oven to 450°.
2. To prepare roast, combine ½ cup Calvados, ¼ cup syrup, and sage sprig in a small saucepan; bring to a boil over medium-high heat. Reduce heat; simmer 5 minutes or until slightly thick. Remove from heat; discard sage sprig.
3. Lightly coat roast with cooking spray; rub 1½ teaspoons salt and pepper over roast. Place roast on a broiler pan coated with cooking spray. Brush one-fourth of glaze over roast. Bake at 450° for 25 minutes or until browned.
4. Reduce oven temperature to 300° (do not remove roast from oven); bake at 300° for 1 hour and 45 minutes, brushing with glaze every 30 minutes. (Cover bones with foil if they start to become too brown.)
5. Increase oven temperature to 400° (do not remove roast from oven); cook an additional 25 minutes or until a meat thermometer inserted in meaty part of roast registers 150°. Remove roast from oven; let stand 20 minutes before carving.
6. To prepare puree, while roast bakes, combine apple, chestnuts, ½ cup Calvados, sugar, and 2 tablespoons syrup in a medium saucepan; bring to a boil. Reduce heat, and simmer 15 minutes or until apple is tender. Place mixture in a food processor; add half-and-half, 2 tablespoons Calvados, ½ teaspoon salt, and chopped sage. Process 1 minute or until smooth.
7. Slice roast vertically between each rib bone. Serve pork with puree. Garnish with sage and rosemary, if desired. Yield: 16 servings (serving size: 1 pork rib chop and about 2½ tablespoons puree).

CALORIES 374 (29% from fat); FAT 11.9g (sat 4.4g, mono 5.3g, poly 0.9g); PROTEIN 43.8g; CARB 16.2g; FIBER 0.9g; CHOL 119mg; IRON 1.5mg; SODIUM 385mg; CALC 58mg

WINE NOTE: A dish with flavors as complex as this deserves an equally complex wine. With its earthy character, pinot noir is a great foil to maple and chestnut flavors. Plus, compared to other reds, pinot noir has good underlying acidity to balance the richness of roast pork.

Vietnamese Caramelized Pork with Pickled Bean Sprouts

When you cook in a clay pot, the meat becomes unbelievably tender. If you don't have a clay pot, prepare this recipe in a covered roasting pan or Dutch oven. Cook the rice while the pork bakes.

**Prep: 10 minutes • Cook: 1 hour, 42 minutes
Other: 1 hour, 40 minutes**

Pickled Bean Sprouts:
4   cups warm water
⅓   cup white vinegar
¾   teaspoon salt
1   pound fresh bean sprouts
½   cup (1½-inch) julienne-cut green onions
¼   cup chopped fresh cilantro
1   teaspoon dark sesame oil

Pork:
⅓   cup sugar
3   tablespoons fish sauce
2   cups thinly sliced shallots
¼   teaspoon pepper
1   (2-pound) boneless pork loin roast, trimmed and cut into ½-inch slices
½   cup fat-free, less-sodium chicken broth
5   (⅛-inch) slices peeled fresh ginger
2   garlic cloves, sliced
6   cups hot cooked long-grain rice

1. To prepare sprouts, combine first 3 ingredients. Add sprouts and onions; toss well. Cover and refrigerate 90 minutes. Drain well. Toss with cilantro and oil.
2. Immerse top and bottom of a 3-quart clay cooking pot in water 10 minutes. Empty and drain well.
3. To prepare pork, place sugar in a small, heavy saucepan over medium heat; cook until sugar dissolves, stirring frequently.

Cook until golden and foamy (about 5 minutes). Remove from heat; carefully stir in fish sauce (mixture will splatter). Stir in shallots and pepper. Place over low heat; cook 5 minutes or until shallots are soft.
4. Pour into a large bowl. Add pork, broth, ginger, and garlic; toss. Place in clay pot. Place clay pot in cold oven, and set to 450°. Bake for 1 hour. Remove clay pot from oven; remove top. Stir pork mixture. Cover, return to oven, and bake 30 minutes. Place pork on a serving platter; drizzle caramel sauce over pork. Serve with sprouts and rice. Yield: 6 servings (serving size: 3 ounces pork, about 1½ tablespoons sauce, 1 cup pickled sprouts, and 1 cup rice).

CALORIES 569 (19% from fat); FAT 11.9g (sat 3.9g, mono 5.2g, poly 1.6g); PROTEIN 38.1g; CARB 76.6g; FIBER 2.6g; CHOL 85mg; IRON 4.7mg; SODIUM 944mg; CALC 73mg

Ham with Champagne and Vanilla Glaze

Champagne and vanilla bean seeds flavor the pan drippings, which are then used to create a simple sauce.

**Prep: 8 minutes • Cook: 1 hour, 53 minutes
Other: 25 minutes**

1   (11-pound) 33%-less-sodium smoked, fully cooked, bone-in ham
24   whole cloves
      Cooking spray
1½   cups Champagne or sparkling wine, divided
1   (2-inch) piece vanilla bean, split lengthwise
1   cup apple jelly

1. Preheat oven to 350°.
2. Trim fat and rind from ham. Score outside of ham in a diamond pattern, and stud with cloves. Place ham, bone end up, in a

roasting pan coated with cooking spray. Pour 1 cup Champagne over ham. Bake at 350° for 45 minutes.
3. Scrape seeds from vanilla bean into a small saucepan. Add vanilla bean and remaining ½ cup Champagne to pan. Bring to a boil; cook 2 minutes. Stir in apple jelly; cook 3 minutes or until jelly dissolves, stirring constantly. Remove from heat. Discard vanilla bean. Pour half of Champagne mixture over ham. Bake 30 minutes; pour remaining Champagne mixture over ham. Bake an additional 30 minutes or until ham is thoroughly heated. Place ham on a platter; cover loosely with foil. Let stand 15 minutes. Do not discard pan drippings.
4. Place a zip-top plastic bag inside a 2-cup glass measure. Pour pan drippings into bag; let stand 10 minutes (fat will rise to top). Seal bag; carefully snip off 1 bottom corner of bag. Drain drippings into measure, stopping before fat layer reaches opening; discard fat. Serve sauce with ham. Yield: 30 servings (serving size: 3 ounces ham and about 1½ teaspoons sauce).

CALORIES 154 (28% from fat); FAT 4.7g (sat 1.5g, mono 2.2g, poly 0.5g); PROTEIN 17.8g; CARB 8.4g; FIBER 0g; CHOL 45mg; IRON 1.3mg; SODIUM 830mg; CALC 8mg

WINE NOTE: Pairing ham with wine takes some care. But this recipe, oriented as it is to vanilla and apple flavors, takes the ham in a chardonnay direction. And, like this ham dish, chardonnay has vanilla and apple flavors, and its light sweetness mirrors that of the ham. Opt for a chardonnay that's not too oaky. Try the Gloria Ferrer from the Carneros region of California or the McPherson chardonnay from South Eastern Australia.

Slow Cooker
Red Beans and
Rice

Slow Cooker Red Beans and Rice

Beans in a slow cooker—the ultimate in thriftiness and convenience. The long, slow cooking time melds the separate ingredients into one satisfying dish. You can also cook it on LOW for 8 hours. Prepare the rice the last 20 minutes of cooking time for the bean mixture.

Prep: 12 minutes • Cook: 5 hours

 3 cups water
 1 cup dried red kidney beans
 1 cup chopped onion
 1 cup chopped green bell pepper
 ¾ cup chopped celery
 1 teaspoon dried thyme
 1 teaspoon paprika
 ¾ teaspoon ground red pepper
 ½ teaspoon black pepper
 ½ (14-ounce) package turkey, pork, and beef smoked sausage, sliced
 1 bay leaf
 5 garlic cloves, minced
 ½ teaspoon salt
 3 cups hot cooked long-grain rice
 ¼ cup chopped green onions

1. Place first 12 ingredients in a 2-quart electric slow cooker. Cover with lid; cook on HIGH 5 hours.

2. Discard bay leaf; stir in salt. Serve over rice; sprinkle with green onions. Yield: 4 servings (serving size: 1 cup bean mixture, ¾ cup rice, and 1 tablespoon green onions).

CALORIES 413 (5% from fat); FAT 2.5g (sat 0.7g, mono 0.2g, poly 0.5g); PROTEIN 21.1g; CARB 76.3g; FIBER 10.1g; CHOL 18mg; IRON 6mg; SODIUM 749mg; CALC 102mg

Test Kitchen Tip: A new product that simplifies slow cooker cleanup is a clear, heavy-duty plastic liner made to fit 3- to 6½-quart oval and round electric slow cookers. Fit the plastic liner inside the slow cooker before adding the ingredients. When you're finished cooking and serving, discard the liner—and the mess. Look for the liners in the section of the supermarket where you find aluminum foil and plastic wrap.

Goat Cheese, Artichoke, and Smoked Ham Strata

Serve this strata for your next brunch or casual supper. Although sourdough bread has a nice, subtle tanginess, French bread works, too. To make the strata ahead, assemble, cover, and refrigerate it overnight. Let it stand at room temperature while the oven preheats. Bake as directed.

Prep: 25 minutes • Cook: 40 minutes
Other: 25 minutes

 3¼ cups 1% low-fat milk, divided
 1 (8-ounce) carton egg substitute
 1 (4-ounce) package goat cheese
 ¾ teaspoon freshly ground black pepper
 ½ teaspoon chopped fresh thyme
 ⅛ teaspoon ground nutmeg
 2 garlic cloves, minced
 10 (1½-ounce) slices sourdough bread, cut into ½-inch cubes
Cooking spray
 ½ cup (2 ounces) grated fresh Parmesan cheese
 8 ounces 33%-less-sodium smoked ham, coarsely chopped
 2 (14-ounce) cans artichoke hearts, drained, rinsed, and coarsely chopped
 ½ cup (2 ounces) shredded fontina cheese

1. Preheat oven to 350°.

2. Place 1 cup milk, egg substitute, and goat cheese in a blender; process until smooth. Combine goat cheese mixture, remaining 2¼ cups milk, black pepper, thyme, nutmeg, and garlic in a large bowl, stirring with a whisk. Add bread cubes; stir gently to combine. Let stand 10 minutes.

3. Place half of bread mixture in a 13 x 9–inch baking dish coated with cooking spray. Arrange Parmesan cheese, ham, and artichoke hearts evenly over bread mixture.

Top with remaining bread mixture, and sprinkle evenly with fontina cheese.

4. Bake strata at 350° for 40 minutes or until edges are bubbly. Let stand 15 minutes. Yield: 8 servings (serving size: about 1½ cups).

CALORIES 379 (29% from fat); FAT 12.4g (sat 6.9g, mono 3.8g, poly 0.8g); PROTEIN 25.2g; CARB 40.2g; FIBER 2.7g; CHOL 43mg; IRON 3.8mg; SODIUM 1107mg; CALC 331mg

Warm Ham with Shallots and Vinegar

This quick and easy dish is best when prepared just before you serve it. If you need a head start, mince the shallots and cut the ham the day before. Serve this entrée at a breakfast or brunch with a quiche or breakfast casserole and a fruit compote.

Prep: 7 minutes • Cook: 8 minutes

    1   tablespoon olive oil
    ⅓   cup minced shallots
    ⅓   cup red wine vinegar
    2   tablespoons water
    4   (4-ounce) slices smoked ham (about
        ¼ inch thick), cut into thin strips
    2   tablespoons chopped fresh parsley

1. Heat oil in a 9-inch cast-iron or heavy skillet over medium heat. Add shallots; sauté 2 minutes. Add vinegar and water; cook until reduced by half (about 1 minute). Add ham; cook 4 minutes or until thoroughly heated, stirring occasionally. Remove ham from pan; sprinkle with parsley. Yield: 8 servings (serving size: 2 ounces).

CALORIES 95 (43% from fat); FAT 4.5g (sat 1.2g, mono 2.6g, poly 0.4g); PROTEIN 11.2g; CARB 2.1g; FIBER 0.1g; CHOL 26mg; IRON 0.5mg; SODIUM 811mg; CALC 8mg

Ham with Cranberry and Bourbon Glaze

The sweet cranberry glaze gets its kick from bourbon and a bit of horseradish.

Prep: 13 minutes • Cook: 1 hour, 53 minutes
Other: 25 minutes

    1   (10-pound) 33%-less-sodium
        smoked, fully cooked, bone-in ham
    Cooking spray
    ¾   cup packed brown sugar
    ¾   cup canned whole-berry cranberry
        sauce
    ¼   cup bourbon
    1   tablespoon prepared horseradish
    1   bay leaf

1. Preheat oven to 325°.

2. Trim fat and rind from ham. Score outside of ham in a diamond pattern. Place ham, bone end up, on a roasting pan coated with cooking spray. Bake at 325° for 1½ hours.

3. Combine sugar and remaining 4 ingredients in a small saucepan. Bring to a boil. Reduce heat; simmer 5 minutes. Remove from heat; discard bay leaf.

4. Increase oven temperature to 400° (do not remove ham from oven). Brush cranberry mixture over ham. Bake at 400° for 15 minutes. Place ham on a platter, and cover with foil. Let stand 15 minutes. Do not discard drippings.

5. Place a zip-top plastic bag inside a 2-cup glass measure or bowl. Pour drippings into bag, and let stand 10 minutes (fat will rise to top). Seal bag, and carefully snip off 1 bottom corner of the bag. Drain drippings into a bowl, stopping before fat layer reaches the opening; discard fat. Serve sauce with ham. Yield: 25 servings (serving size: 3 ounces ham and about 2 teaspoons sauce).

CALORIES 146 (26% from fat); FAT 4.2g (sat 1.4g, mono 2g, poly 0.4g); PROTEIN 15.9g; CARB 9.7g; FIBER 0.1g; CHOL 40mg; IRON 1.2mg; SODIUM 741mg; CALC 11mg

WINE NOTE: The tartness of the cranberries, the sweetness of the bourbon, and the pungency of the horseradish call for an equally bold and very fruity wine. Gewürztraminers from Alsace, France, fit the bill.

how to de-fat the drippings

1. Place a zip-top plastic bag in a large measuring cup or bowl, fold back opening of bag, and pour the drippings into it.

2. Once the fat rises to the top, snip off a bottom corner of the bag, and drain the defatted liquid.

Venison Lean cuts of venison offer rich flavor with very little fat.

Venison Kebabs

Sweet-hot chutney complements the hearty flavor of the lean venison. If you want to grill instead of broil, grill 8 to 10 minutes over medium-hot coals.

Prep: 15 minutes • Cook: 8 minutes

- 1 pound lean venison, cut into 1½-inch cubes
- 1 red onion, cut into 1-inch pieces
- 1 red bell pepper, cut into 1-inch pieces
- 1 green bell pepper, cut into 1-inch pieces
- ½ cup mango or other fruit chutney
- ⅓ cup honey mustard
- 1 tablespoon water
- 1 teaspoon minced garlic
Cooking spray

1. Preheat broiler.
2. Thread venison, onion pieces, and pepper pieces alternately onto 4 (15-inch) metal skewers. Combine chutney and next 3 ingredients in a small bowl; stir well. Brush mixture evenly on kebabs.
3. Coat rack of a broiler pan with cooking spray. Place kebabs on rack in a broiler pan coated with cooking spray; broil 8 to 10 minutes or until desired degree of doneness, turning occasionally. Yield: 4 servings (serving size: 1 kebab).

CALORIES 320 (19% from fat); FAT 6.6g (sat 1.6g, mono 2g, poly 2.5g); PROTEIN 27.1g; CARB 37.6g; FIBER 1g; CHOL 96mg; IRON 4.7mg; SODIUM 614mg; CALC 22mg

Grilled Venison Steaks

A cranberry-orange topping adds color and sweetness to the steaks.

Prep: 8 minutes • Cook: 10 minutes
Other: 4 hours

- 4 (4-ounce) lean, boneless venison loin steaks (1 inch thick), trimmed
- 1 cup cranberry-orange crushed fruit, divided
- ½ cup dry red wine
- 2 tablespoons Dijon mustard
- 2 teaspoons minced garlic
- 2 teaspoons dried rosemary, crushed
- ½ teaspoon freshly ground black pepper
Cooking spray

1. Place steaks in a large, heavy-duty zip-top plastic bag. Combine ½ cup cranberry-orange sauce, red wine, and next 4 ingredients; pour over steaks. Seal bag; turn to coat steaks. Marinate in refrigerator 4 to 8 hours, turning bag occasionally.
2. Prepare grill.
3. Remove steaks from marinade, discarding marinade. Place steaks on grill rack coated with cooking spray; grill, covered, 5 minutes on each side or to desired degree of doneness. Serve with remaining ½ cup cranberry-orange sauce. Yield: 4 servings (serving size: 1 steak and 2 tablespoons sauce).

CALORIES 236 (12% from fat); FAT 3.2g (sat 1.1g, mono 0.9g, poly 0.7g); PROTEIN 26.5g; CARB 25g; FIBER 0.2g; CHOL 96mg; IRON 4.2mg; SODIUM 170mg; CALC 23mg

Venison with Mushroom Sauce

Wild rice is a perfect side for this venison.

Prep: 14 minutes • Cook: 40 minutes
Other: 10 minutes

- 2 (1-pound) venison tenderloins
Cooking spray
- ¾ teaspoon salt, divided
- ¼ teaspoon pepper, divided
- 7 ounces fresh shiitake mushrooms
- ¼ cup minced shallots
- ¾ cup port or other sweet red wine
- 1 cup beef broth
- 2¼ teaspoons cornstarch

1. Preheat oven to 425°.
2. Place venison on a rack coated with cooking spray. Sprinkle with ½ teaspoon salt and ⅛ teaspoon pepper; insert a meat thermometer into thickest part of venison. Bake at 425° for 30 minutes or until thermometer reaches 145° (medium-rare) to 160° (medium). Cover; let stand 10 minutes.
3. Remove stems from mushrooms and discard; slice caps. Place a skillet over medium-high heat. Coat pan with cooking spray. Add mushrooms and shallots; sauté 4 minutes. Add ¼ teaspoon salt, ⅛ teaspoon pepper, and port; cook 2 minutes. Combine broth and cornstarch. Add to pan; bring to a boil, and cook 1 minute or until thick, stirring constantly. Serve with venison. Yield: 8 servings (serving size: 3 ounces meat and 3 tablespoons sauce).

CALORIES 156 (17% from fat); FAT 2.9g (sat 1.1g, mono 0.8g, poly 0.6g); PROTEIN 27.7g; CARB 3.3g; FIBER 0.3g; CHOL 95mg; IRON 4.4mg; SODIUM 429mg; CALC 13mg

poultry

Oven-Braised Cornish Hens
with Cider Vinegar and Warm
Vegetable Sauce, page 380

Chicken

Whatever form—chopped, shredded, breasts, thighs, legs, whole hens— versatile chicken is a must in the *Cooking Light* kitchen.

Ratatouille Pizza with Chicken

Ratatouille is a well-loved dish from the Provence region of France that consists of eggplant, tomatoes, onions, bell peppers, and herbs—all simmered in olive oil. The addition of chicken to our ratatouille makes a great-tasting, satisfying pizza.

Prep: 20 minutes • Cook: 32 minutes

 1   teaspoon olive oil
 1   Japanese eggplant, halved lengthwise and cut into ¼-inch-thick slices
 1   red bell pepper, cut into ¼-inch strips
 ½   small red onion, thinly sliced
 1   cup sliced mushrooms
 ¾   teaspoon dried Italian seasoning
 ¼   teaspoon salt
 4   garlic cloves, minced
 1   (10-ounce) Italian cheese-flavored thin pizza crust (such as Boboli)
 1   cup chopped skinless, boneless rotisserie chicken breast (about 6 ounces)
 1   cup (4 ounces) preshredded reduced-fat pizza-blend cheese
 3   plum tomatoes, cut into ¼-inch-thick slices
Cooking spray
 3   tablespoons finely chopped fresh flat-leaf parsley

1. Preheat oven to 375°.
2. Heat a large nonstick skillet over medium-high heat. Add oil to pan. Add eggplant, bell pepper, and onion; sauté 3 minutes or until eggplant begins to soften.

Reduce heat to medium. Add mushrooms; cook 3 minutes, stirring frequently. Add Italian seasoning, salt, and garlic; cook 1 minute, stirring mixture constantly. Remove from heat.
3. Place crust on a baking sheet. Spread vegetable mixture evenly over crust, leaving a ½-inch border. Arrange chicken over vegetable mixture; sprinkle evenly

with cheese. Arrange tomato slices over cheese, and lightly coat with cooking spray. Bake at 375° for 25 minutes or until cheese is bubbly and tomatoes are softened. Sprinkle with parsley. Cut into wedges. Yield: 6 servings (serving size: 1 wedge).

CALORIES 249 (30% from fat); FAT 8.3g (sat 3.9g, mono 2g, poly 0.8g); PROTEIN 18.1g; CARB 26.3g; FIBER 1.8g; CHOL 33mg; IRON 2mg; SODIUM 409mg; CALC 273mg

Malaysian Chicken Pizza

Inspired by her travels in Malaysia, one of our food editors created a pizza recipe using the flavors and spices she encountered there. An exotic peanut-ginger sauce tops an Italian pizza crust.

Prep: 30 minutes • Cook: 24 minutes
Other: 2 hours, 50 minutes

Pizza Dough (page 111)
¾   cup rice vinegar
¼   cup packed brown sugar
¼   cup low-sodium soy sauce
3   tablespoons water
1   tablespoon minced peeled fresh
      ginger
2   tablespoons chunky peanut butter
½   to ¾ teaspoon crushed red pepper
4   garlic cloves, minced
Cooking spray
½   pound skinless, boneless chicken
      breast, cut into bite-sized pieces
½   cup (2 ounces) shredded reduced-fat
      Swiss cheese
¼   cup (1 ounce) shredded part-skim
      mozzarella cheese
¼   cup chopped green onions

1. Prepare Pizza Dough.
2. Preheat oven to 500°.
3. Combine rice vinegar and next 7 ingredients in a bowl; stir well with a whisk.
4. Heat a nonstick skillet over medium heat. Coat pan with cooking spray. Add chicken, and sauté 2 minutes. Remove from pan.
5. Pour rice vinegar mixture into pan, and bring to a boil over medium-high heat. Cook mixture 6 minutes or until slightly thickened. Return chicken to pan; cook 1 minute or until chicken is done. (Mixture will be consistency of thick syrup.)

6. Sprinkle cheeses over prepared crust, leaving a ½-inch border, and top with chicken mixture. Bake at 500° for 12 minutes on bottom rack in oven. Sprinkle with green onions. Place pizza on a cutting board; let stand 5 minutes. Yield: 6 servings (serving size: 1 wedge).

(Totals include Pizza Dough) CALORIES 296 (22% from fat); FAT 7.2g (sat 2.2g, mono 2.9g, poly 1.1g); PROTEIN 19.7g; CARB 38.8g; FIBER 2g; CHOL 25mg; IRON 2.7mg; SODIUM 678mg; CALC 151mg

Precooked Chicken

If your recipe calls for chopped cooked chicken, you can cook your own or use rotisserie chicken, packaged cooked chicken, or frozen cooked chicken. Here are some substitution amounts that will be useful.

Type	Cup Measures
1 pound uncooked skinless, boneless chicken	3 cups chopped cooked chicken
1 (5.5-ounce) skinless, boneless chicken breast half	1 cup chopped cooked chicken
1 (2-pound) uncooked chicken	2¼ cups chopped cooked chicken
1 (2-pound) rotisserie chicken	3 to 3½ cups chopped chicken
1 (6-ounce) package grilled chicken strips	1⅓ cups chopped cooked chicken
1 (9-ounce) package frozen chopped cooked chicken	1⅔ cups chopped cooked chicken

BBQ Chicken Pizza

We love the contrast provided by sweet tomato chutney, savory chicken, and sharp Cheddar cheese.

Prep: 14 minutes • Cook: 12 minutes

1   (10-ounce) Italian cheese-flavored
      thin pizza crust (such as Boboli)
¾   cup tomato chutney
2   cups chopped roasted skinless,
      boneless chicken breast (about 2
      breasts)
⅔   cup chopped plum tomato
¾   cup (3 ounces) shredded extrasharp
      white Cheddar cheese
⅓   cup chopped green onions

1. Preheat oven to 450°.
2. Place crust on a baking sheet. Bake at 450° for 3 minutes. Remove from oven; spread chutney over crust, leaving a ½-inch border. Top with chicken. Sprinkle tomato, cheese, and onions over chicken. Bake at 450° for 9 minutes or until cheese melts. Cut pizza into 6 wedges. Yield: 6 servings (serving size: 1 wedge).

CALORIES 300 (26% from fat); FAT 8.5g (sat 3.9g, mono 2.9g, poly 1g); PROTEIN 21.3g; CARB 35.2g; FIBER 1.2g; CHOL 48mg; IRON 1.7mg; SODIUM 622mg; CALC 247mg

Test Kitchen Tip: Look for tomato chutney in the condiment section of the supermarket, or use our recipe on page 463.

Chicken Nuggets with Mustard Dipping Sauce

Most children adore chicken nuggets. This healthful makeover begins with a soak in buttermilk to tenderize the lean meat and make it juicy.

Prep: 17 minutes • Cook: 15 minutes
Other: 30 minutes

Chicken:

½ cup low-fat buttermilk
1½ pounds skinless, boneless chicken breast, cut into 40 pieces
3¾ cups cornflakes
1 teaspoon paprika
½ teaspoon sugar
¼ teaspoon salt
Cooking spray

Mustard Dipping Sauce:

½ cup prepared mustard
¼ cup honey
½ teaspoon grated peeled fresh ginger

1. To prepare chicken, combine buttermilk and chicken. Marinate in refrigerator 30 minutes; drain.
2. Preheat oven to 375°.
3. Place cornflakes, paprika, sugar, and salt in a food processor; process until cornflakes are finely chopped. Combine chicken and cornflake mixture, tossing well to coat. Place chicken on a baking sheet coated with cooking spray. Bake at 375° for 15 minutes or until done.
4. To prepare sauce, combine mustard, honey, and ginger. Serve with chicken. Yield: 8 servings (serving size: 5 nuggets and 1½ tablespoons sauce).

CALORIES 190 (9% from fat); FAT 1.8g (sat 0.4g, mono 0.6g, poly 0.4g); PROTEIN 21.8g; CARB 21.3g; FIBER 0.8g; CHOL 50mg; IRON 1.3mg; SODIUM 425mg; CALC 40mg

Green Chile-Chicken Casserole

Green Chile-Chicken Casserole

Just about every New Mexican home has a unique version of this recipe. This one features the convenience of canned cream of chicken soup and precooked chicken. Leftover turkey works, too.

Prep: 25 minutes • Cook: 35 minutes

1⅓ cups fat-free, less-sodium chicken broth
1 cup canned chopped green chiles, drained
1 cup chopped onion
1 cup fat-free sour cream
¾ teaspoon salt
½ teaspoon ground cumin
½ teaspoon freshly ground black pepper
2 (10½-ounce) cans condensed 98%-fat-free cream of chicken soup, undiluted (such as Campbell's)
1 garlic clove, minced
Cooking spray
24 (6-inch) corn tortillas
4 cups shredded cooked chicken breast (about 1½ pounds)
2 cups (8 ounces) finely shredded sharp Cheddar cheese

1. Preheat oven to 350°.
2. Combine first 9 ingredients in a large saucepan, stirring with a whisk. Bring to a boil, stirring constantly. Remove from heat.
3. Spread 1 cup soup mixture in a 13 x 9–inch baking dish coated with cooking spray. Arrange 6 tortillas over soup mixture, and top with 1 cup chicken and ½ cup cheese. Repeat layers 3 times, ending with cheese. Spread remaining soup mixture over cheese. Bake at 350° for 30 minutes or until bubbly. Yield: 12 servings (serving size: about ¾ cup).

CALORIES 335 (29% from fat); FAT 10.8g (sat 5.9g, mono 2.7g, poly 1.2g); PROTEIN 23.9g; CARB 34.3g; FIBER 3.2g; CHOL 66mg; IRON 1.5mg; SODIUM 693mg; CALC 270mg

Test Kitchen Tip: If you assemble the casserole the day before, cover it with cooking spray-coated foil. When ready to serve, bake 1 hour; then uncover and bake an additional 30 minutes or until the cheese is bubbly and begins to brown.

Green Chile and Chicken Enchiladas

Instead of being rolled like most enchiladas, these end up as two-layered tortilla stacks, which are then cut in half to serve four. This is a distinctive New Mexican tradition.

Prep: 39 minutes • Cook: 54 minutes
Other: 15 minutes

½ teaspoon canola oil
1 cup chopped onion
2 garlic cloves, minced
1 cup shredded cooked chicken breast (about 6 ounces)
¼ teaspoon salt
¼ teaspoon pepper
2 cups Green Chile Sauce (page 454)
Cooking spray
6 (6-inch) corn tortillas
¼ cup (1 ounce) crumbled feta cheese

1. Preheat oven to 350°.
2. Heat oil in a nonstick skillet over medium-high heat. Add onion; sauté 4 minutes or until tender. Add garlic; sauté 1 minute. Combine onion mixture, chicken, salt, and pepper.
3. Spread ¼ cup Green Chile Sauce in an 11 x 7–inch baking dish coated with cooking spray. Arrange 2 tortillas over sauce; top evenly with half of chicken mixture and ½ cup Green Chile Sauce. Repeat layers, ending with tortillas. Spread remaining sauce over tortillas. Sprinkle with cheese.
4. Bake at 350° for 20 minutes or until thoroughly heated. Cut each tortilla stack in half. Yield: 4 servings (serving size: ½ tortilla stack).

CALORIES 227 (21% from fat); FAT 5.3g (sat 1.8g, mono 1.3g, poly 1.4g); PROTEIN 18.4g; CARB 27.6g; FIBER 4.7g; CHOL 42mg; IRON 1.7mg; SODIUM 543mg; CALC 131mg

Curried-Chicken Potpie

Not your grandma's chicken potpie, this one combines the highlights of Indian food with a legendary Carolina chicken casserole called Country Captain.

Prep: 30 minutes • Cook: 45 minutes
Other: 25 minutes

Crust:
1 cup all-purpose flour, divided
3 tablespoons ice water
1 tablespoon cider vinegar
¼ teaspoon salt
¼ cup vegetable shortening
Filling:
1 teaspoon olive oil
2 tablespoons curry powder
2 cups diced peeled baking potato (about 12 ounces)
¾ cup chopped onion
¾ cup chopped red bell pepper
2 garlic cloves, minced
1½ pounds skinless, boneless chicken breast, cut into bite-sized pieces
1½ cups fat-free, less-sodium chicken broth
1 cup sliced fresh mushrooms
¾ cup frozen green peas, thawed
½ cup golden raisins
1 teaspoon salt
½ teaspoon black pepper
2 tablespoons cornstarch
1 tablespoon water
½ cup (4 ounces) ⅓-less-fat cream cheese
Cooking spray

1. To prepare crust, lightly spoon flour into a dry measuring cup, and level with a knife. Combine ¼ cup flour, ice water, and vinegar in a small bowl, and stir with a whisk until well blended to create a slurry. Set aside. Combine ¾ cup flour and

¼ teaspoon salt in a large bowl, and cut in shortening with a pastry blender or 2 knives until mixture resembles coarse meal. Add slurry to flour mixture, and toss with a fork until moist. Press mixture gently into a 4-inch circle on heavy-duty plastic wrap; cover with additional plastic wrap. Chill 15 minutes.
2. Preheat oven to 400°.
3. To prepare filling, heat oil in a large nonstick skillet over medium-high heat. Add curry; cook 2 minutes. Add potato, onion, bell pepper, garlic, and chicken; stir-fry 3 minutes. Add broth and next 5 ingredients; bring to a boil. Cover, reduce heat, and simmer 5 minutes or until chicken is done. Combine cornstarch and 1 tablespoon water in a small bowl. Stir cornstarch mixture and cream cheese into chicken mixture; cook 1 minute or until cream cheese is melted.
4. Spoon filling into a round 2-quart casserole coated with cooking spray. Roll crust into an 11-inch circle, and place over mixture. Cut 6 slits in top of dough to allow steam to escape. Bake at 400° for 30 minutes or until golden brown and bubbly around edges. Let stand 10 minutes. Yield: 6 servings (serving size: about 1⅓ cups).

CALORIES 454 (29% from fat); FAT 14.5g (sat 5.2g, mono 4.7g, poly 2.9g); PROTEIN 34.1g; CARB 46.1g; FIBER 4.1g; CHOL 80mg; IRON 3.6mg; SODIUM 786mg; CALC 62mg

Test Kitchen Tip: You can also make this in an 11 x 7–inch baking dish. When you prepare the crust, press the dough into a 6 x 4–inch rectangle, and chill. Roll the dough into an 11 x 7–inch rectangle, and place over the filling.

Chicken Potpies

Because the piecrust topping cooks on a baking sheet and is then placed over the filling, you don't need to use ovenproof bowls for the pies. Use a bowl or ramekin as a guide for cutting the dough.

Prep: 15 minutes • Cook: 26 minutes

½   (15-ounce) package refrigerated pie
    dough (such as Pillsbury)
Cooking spray
⅛   teaspoon salt
2   tablespoons all-purpose flour
1   teaspoon dried rubbed sage
¼   teaspoon salt
¼   teaspoon pepper
½   pound chicken breast tenders, cut
    into bite-sized pieces
1¼   cups water
1½   cups frozen mixed vegetables
1   cup mushrooms, quartered
1   (10½-ounce) can condensed
    reduced-fat, reduced-sodium cream
    of chicken soup

1. Preheat oven to 425°.
2. Cut 3 (4-inch) circles out of dough; discard remaining dough. Place dough circles on a baking sheet coated with cooking spray. Lightly coat dough circles with cooking spray; sprinkle evenly with ⅛ teaspoon salt. Pierce top of dough with a fork. Bake at 425° for 8 minutes or until golden.
3. Combine flour, sage, ¼ teaspoon salt, and pepper in a zip-top plastic bag; add chicken. Seal bag, and toss to coat. Heat a large nonstick skillet over medium-high heat. Coat pan with cooking spray. Add chicken mixture; cook 5 minutes, browning on all sides. Stir in water, scraping pan to loosen browned bits. Stir in vegetables, mushrooms, and soup; bring to a boil. Reduce heat, and cook 10 minutes. Spoon 1 cup chicken mixture into each of 3 (1-cup) ramekins or bowls; top each serving with 1 piecrust. Yield: 3 servings (serving size: 1 pie).

CALORIES 374 (27% from fat); FAT 11.4g (sat 4.8g, mono 4.2g, poly 1.2g); PROTEIN 24.1g; CARB 42.6g; FIBER 4.6g; CHOL 58mg; IRON 1.9mg; SODIUM 882mg; CALC 38mg

Mediterranean Chicken and Vegetable Kebabs

Serve these kebabs over couscous tossed with a bit of salt, cherry tomatoes, and chopped fresh mint.

Prep: 25 minutes • Cook: 14 minutes
Other: 20 minutes

¼   cup fresh lemon juice
2   tablespoons chopped fresh or
    2 teaspoons dried oregano
2   tablespoons olive oil
2   pounds skinless, boneless chicken
    breast, cut into 24 strips
18   (½-inch-thick) slices zucchini
1   fennel bulb, cut into 12 wedges
12   garlic cloves, peeled
½   teaspoon salt
¼   teaspoon pepper
Cooking spray

1. Combine first 6 ingredients in a zip-top plastic bag; seal and shake well. Marinate in refrigerator 20 minutes. Remove chicken and vegetables from bag; discard marinade.
2. Prepare grill.
3. Cook garlic cloves in boiling water to cover 3 minutes; drain and cool.
4. Thread 4 chicken strips, 3 zucchini slices, 2 fennel wedges, and 2 garlic cloves alternately onto each of 6 (12-inch) skewers. Sprinkle with salt and pepper. Place kebabs on grill rack coated with cooking spray. Grill, turning once, 8 minutes or until chicken is done. Yield: 6 servings (serving size: 1 kebab).

CALORIES 238 (25% from fat); FAT 6.6g (sat 1.1g, mono 3.8g, poly 0.9g); PROTEIN 36.3g; CARB 7.4g; FIBER 2g; CHOL 88mg; IRON 1.9mg; SODIUM 317mg; CALC 67mg

Chicken Potpies

Fragrant Chicken in Creamy Almond Sauce

Capture the essence of Indian cooking with spices such as cinnamon, curry, and turmeric.

Prep: 20 minutes • Cook: 58 minutes

1	tablespoon olive oil
6	(3-inch) cinnamon sticks
5	bay leaves
1½	cups finely chopped onion
6	garlic cloves, minced
2	teaspoons curry powder
½	teaspoon salt
½	teaspoon ground turmeric
¼	teaspoon ground cardamom
2½	pounds skinless, boneless chicken breast, cut into 1-inch pieces
1	cup fat-free, less-sodium chicken broth
¼	cup fat-free sour cream
1	teaspoon all-purpose flour
½	teaspoon sugar
¼	cup slivered almonds, toasted and ground
⅓	cup chopped red bell pepper
2	tablespoons slivered almonds, toasted

1. Heat oil in a large nonstick skillet over medium heat. Add 6 cinnamon sticks and bay leaves. Cook 2 minutes or until fragrant. Add onion and garlic; sauté 5 minutes. Add curry powder, salt, turmeric, and cardamom. Add chicken and broth; bring to a boil. Cover, reduce heat, and simmer 35 minutes.

2. Remove chicken from pan with a slotted spoon. Cook liquid remaining in pan over low heat 5 minutes. Combine sour cream, flour, and sugar in a small bowl; stir in ½ cup hot liquid. Add sour cream mixture to pan, stirring until smooth. Return chicken to pan; stir in ground almonds. Cook 5 minutes or until thick, stirring frequently. Sprinkle with bell pepper. Remove and discard cinnamon sticks and bay leaves. Sprinkle with slivered almonds. Yield: 6 servings (serving size: about 1 cup chicken mixture and 1 teaspoon almonds).

CALORIES 304 (23% from fat); FAT 7.9g (sat 1.3g, mono 4.2g, poly 1.3g); PROTEIN 46.9g; CARB 8.7g; FIBER 2.1g; CHOL 110mg; IRON 2.4mg; SODIUM 410mg; CALC 60mg

Spicy Cumin-Crusted Chicken with Orange-Chipotle Sauce

To avoid charring the chicken, slather on the sauce during the last half of the cooking time.

Prep: 30 minutes • Cook: 1 hour, 4 minutes

⅓	cup cumin seeds
½	teaspoon kosher salt
¼	teaspoon pepper
4	(6-ounce) skinless, boneless chicken breast halves
	Cooking spray
	Orange-Chipotle Sauce (page 454)

1. Prepare grill.
2. Combine first 3 ingredients in a small bowl. Rub both sides of chicken with spice mixture. Place chicken on grill rack coated with cooking spray; cover and grill 6 minutes.
3. Uncover chicken, and brush with ½ cup Orange-Chipotle Sauce; cook 6 minutes or until done, turning once. Serve with remaining sauce. Yield: 4 servings (serving size: 1 chicken breast half and about ⅓ cup sauce).

(Totals include Orange-Chipotle Sauce) CALORIES 531 (21% from fat); FAT 12.2g (sat 1.7g, mono 6.8g, poly 1.6g); PROTEIN 43.1g; CARB 62.3g; FIBER 3.4g; CHOL 99mg; IRON 8.9mg; SODIUM 912mg; CALC 188mg

Chicken, Eggplant, and Tomato Curry

Curry is the star ingredient in this saucy, one-skillet meal.

Prep: 15 minutes • Cook: 1 hour, 28 minutes

1	tablespoon curry powder
1	teaspoon salt
1	teaspoon paprika
8	(6-ounce) skinless, boneless chicken breast halves
3	teaspoons olive oil
5	cups coarsely chopped eggplant (about 1 pound)
1⅔	cups thinly sliced onion
1½	cups (¼-inch-thick) slices green bell pepper
¾	cup tomato juice
1	teaspoon crushed red pepper
1	garlic clove, minced
4	cups hot cooked basmati rice

1. Combine curry powder, salt, and paprika in a shallow dish. Dredge chicken in curry mixture.
2. Heat 1½ teaspoons oil in a large nonstick skillet over medium heat. Add half of chicken; cook 5 minutes on each side or until browned. Remove chicken from pan. Repeat procedure with 1½ teaspoons oil and remaining chicken.
3. Add eggplant, onion, and bell pepper to pan; cook 3 minutes or until vegetables are crisp-tender, stirring frequently. Return chicken to pan. Add tomato juice, red pepper, and garlic; bring to a boil. Cover, reduce heat, and simmer 35 minutes or until chicken is done. Serve with rice. Yield: 8 servings (serving size: 1 chicken breast half, about ⅓ cup vegetables, and ½ cup rice).

CALORIES 363 (11% from fat); FAT 4.5g (sat 0.9g, mono 1.9g, poly 0.9g); PROTEIN 43.3g; CARB 35.9g; FIBER 4.4g; CHOL 99mg; IRON 3mg; SODIUM 452mg; CALC 57mg

Chicken with Black Bean Salsa

Serve this zesty chicken and bean dish as is, or wrap it up in a warm flour tortilla.

Prep: 11 minutes • Cook: 13 minutes

Black Bean Salsa:
- ½ cup canned black beans, rinsed and drained
- ¼ cup fresh corn kernels
- 1 tablespoon chopped red onion
- 1 teaspoon chopped seeded jalapeño pepper
- 1 teaspoon fresh lime juice
- 1 teaspoon extravirgin olive oil
- ⅛ teaspoon salt
- ⅛ teaspoon ground coriander
- 4 grape or cherry tomatoes, quartered

Chicken:
- 1 teaspoon butter
- Cooking spray
- 1 (6-ounce) skinless, boneless chicken breast half
- Dash of salt
- Dash of freshly ground black pepper
- Lime slice (optional)

1. To prepare salsa, combine first 9 ingredients, tossing well to combine.

2. To prepare chicken, heat butter in a small nonstick skillet coated with cooking spray over medium-high heat. Sprinkle chicken with dash of salt and black pepper. Add chicken to pan; cook 6 minutes on each side or until done. Serve with salsa and lime slice, if desired. Yield: 1 serving (serving size: 1 chicken breast half and ¾ cup salsa).

CALORIES 425 (26% from fat); FAT 12.2g (sat 3.7g, mono 5.1g, poly 2.3g); PROTEIN 48.4g; CARB 29.1g; FIBER 9.2g; CHOL 109mg; IRON 4.6mg; SODIUM 867mg; CALC 69mg

Grilled Chicken with Grape Chutney

Beautiful red and green grapes retain their shape in the thickened syrup. The chutney is also good with pork or beef.

Prep: 15 minutes • Cook: 43 minutes

- ½ cup chopped onion
- ½ cup red wine vinegar
- ½ cup dry red wine
- ¼ cup chopped dried figs
- 2 tablespoons sugar
- 2 teaspoons hot paprika
- 1 teaspoon grated peeled fresh ginger
- 1 (3-inch) cinnamon stick
- 1 cup seedless green grapes, halved
- 1 cup seedless red grapes, halved
- 4 (6-ounce) skinless, boneless chicken breast halves
- 2 teaspoons canola oil
- ½ teaspoon salt
- ¼ teaspoon freshly ground black pepper

1. Prepare grill.

2. Combine first 8 ingredients in a medium saucepan over medium-high heat. Bring to a boil; cook 10 minutes. Stir in grapes; reduce heat, and simmer 20 minutes. Remove cinnamon stick.

3. Coat chicken with oil; sprinkle with salt and pepper. Place chicken on grill rack. Grill 5 minutes on each side or until done. Serve with chutney. Yield: 4 servings (serving size: 1 chicken breast half and ¼ cup chutney).

CALORIES 343 (13% from fat); FAT 4.9g (sat 0.8g, mono 1.9g, poly 1.4g); PROTEIN 40.7g; CARB 34.9g; FIBER 2.7g; CHOL 99mg; IRON 2.5mg; SODIUM 409mg; CALC 59mg

Chicken Marsala

Because the sauce cooks in the microwave, this is a perfect option for last-minute dinner guests.

Prep: 9 minutes • Cook: 20 minutes

- ½ cup dry Marsala
- 1 teaspoon cornstarch
- ½ teaspoon dried tarragon
- ⅛ teaspoon salt
- ¼ cup Italian-seasoned breadcrumbs
- 2 tablespoons grated Parmesan cheese
- ⅛ teaspoon garlic powder
- 4 (6-ounce) skinless, boneless chicken breast halves
- 2 teaspoons olive oil
- 2 cups hot cooked angel hair (about 4 ounces uncooked pasta)

1. Combine first 4 ingredients in a 1-cup glass measure, stirring with a whisk until blended.

2. Combine breadcrumbs, cheese, and garlic powder in a shallow dish; stir well with a whisk. Dredge chicken in breadcrumb mixture.

3. Heat oil in a large nonstick skillet over medium-high heat. Add chicken; cook 4 minutes on each side or until done.

4. Microwave wine mixture at HIGH 30 seconds or until slightly thick, stirring once. Arrange chicken over pasta; top with sauce. Yield: 4 servings (serving size: 1 chicken breast half, ½ cup pasta, and about 2 tablespoons sauce).

CALORIES 361 (16% from fat); FAT 6.4g (sat 1.8g, mono 2.3g, poly 1.1g); PROTEIN 45.6g; CARB 27.5g; FIBER 1.1g; CHOL 102mg; IRON 2.9mg; SODIUM 383mg; CALC 87mg

Chicken Français

A light Parmesan-herb coating and a citrusy butter-wine sauce elevate plain chicken breasts to made-for-company elegance.

Prep: 20 minutes • Cook: 23 minutes

¾ cup egg substitute
¼ cup (1 ounce) grated fresh Parmesan cheese
¼ cup chopped fresh parsley
¼ cup dry white wine
2 tablespoons fresh lemon juice
¼ teaspoon salt
⅛ teaspoon hot pepper sauce
3 garlic cloves, minced
8 (6-ounce) skinless, boneless chicken breast halves
¼ cup all-purpose flour
1 tablespoon olive oil
Cooking spray
2 tablespoons butter
¼ cup dry white wine
3 tablespoons fresh lemon juice

1. Combine first 8 ingredients in a dish.
2. Place each chicken breast half between 2 sheets of plastic wrap, and pound to ¼-inch thickness using a meat mallet or rolling pin. Discard plastic wrap. Dredge chicken in flour, and dip in egg substitute mixture.
3. Heat 1½ teaspoons oil in a large non-stick skillet coated with cooking spray over medium heat. Add 4 chicken breast halves; cook 4 minutes on each side or until done. Remove from pan, and keep warm. Wipe drippings from pan with a paper towel. Repeat procedure with 1½ teaspoons olive oil and remaining chicken breast halves.
4. Melt butter in pan; add ¼ cup wine and 3 tablespoons lemon juice. Bring to a boil; cook 10 seconds. Serve immediately over chicken. Yield: 8 servings (serving size: 1 chicken breast half and 2 teaspoons sauce).

CALORIES 266 (33% from fat); FAT 9.4g (sat 3.7g, mono 3.4g, poly 1.2g); PROTEIN 38.3g; CARB 5.0g; FIBER 0.3g; CHOL 104mg; IRON 2mg; SODIUM 280mg; CALC 69mg

Chicken with Eggplant-Pepper Sauce

Use your microwave and food processor to get dinner on the table in a hurry.

Prep: 13 minutes • Cook: 21 minutes

1 medium eggplant (about ½ pound)
2 medium red bell peppers (about 1 pound)
¾ teaspoon salt, divided
¼ teaspoon ground ginger
¼ teaspoon garlic powder
¼ teaspoon ground red pepper, divided
4 (6-ounce) skinless, boneless chicken breast halves
2 teaspoons olive oil, divided
1 teaspoon paprika
4 teaspoons lemon juice

1. Slice eggplant in half lengthwise, and pierce skin with a fork. Cut tops off bell peppers; discard tops, seeds, and membranes. Place eggplant and bell peppers on a microwave-safe plate. Microwave at HIGH 8 minutes or until tender.
2. While eggplant and bell peppers cook, combine ¼ teaspoon salt, ginger, garlic powder, and ⅛ teaspoon red pepper; sprinkle chicken with ginger mixture. Heat 1 teaspoon olive oil in a large non-stick skillet over medium-high heat. Add chicken, and cook 6 minutes on each side or until chicken is done.
3. Place eggplant and bell peppers in a blender or food processor. Add ½ teaspoon salt, ⅛ teaspoon red pepper, 1 teaspoon oil, paprika, and juice; process until smooth. Serve chicken with sauce. Yield: 4 servings (serving size: 1 chicken breast half and about ⅓ cup sauce).

CALORIES 260 (17% from fat); FAT 4.9g (sat 0.9g, mono 2.2g, poly 0.8g); PROTEIN 42g; CARB 12.3g; FIBER 2.2g; CHOL 99mg; IRON 2.2mg; SODIUM 548mg; CALC 41mg

All-Time Favorite

Gruyère, Arugula, and Prosciutto-Stuffed Chicken Breasts with Caramelized Shallot Sauce

Stuff the chicken a day ahead and refrigerate it; it will be easier to sauté. See our technique for stuffing the chicken breasts on the right.

Prep: 30 minutes • Cook: 45 minutes

Chicken:

  6   (6-ounce) skinless, boneless chicken breast halves
  6   (½-ounce) slices prosciutto
  6   (½-ounce) slices Gruyère cheese
1½   cups trimmed arugula
  ½   teaspoon salt
  ½   teaspoon pepper
  3   tablespoons all-purpose flour
  1   tablespoon olive oil

Caramelized Shallot Sauce:

  1   cup thinly sliced shallots
  2   teaspoons tomato paste
  2   cups dry white wine
2¼   cups fat-free, less-sodium chicken broth
1½   teaspoons water
  1   teaspoon cornstarch

1. Preheat oven to 350°.
2. To prepare chicken, place each breast half between 2 sheets of heavy-duty plastic wrap; pound to ¼-inch thickness using a meat mallet or rolling pin. Discard plastic wrap. Top each half with 1 slice prosciutto, 1 slice cheese, and ¼ cup arugula, leaving a ¼-inch border around edges. Fold in half, pinching edges together to seal; sprinkle with salt and pepper. (Chicken can be prepared up to a day ahead, and refrigerated.)
3. Dredge chicken in flour, shaking off excess. Heat oil in a large nonstick skillet over medium-high heat. Add chicken; cook 5 minutes on each side. Place chicken in a shallow baking pan; bake at 350° for 5 minutes or until done. Keep warm.
4. To prepare sauce, add shallots to skillet; sauté 4 minutes over medium-high heat or until browned. Add tomato paste; cook 1 minute, stirring constantly. Stir in wine; bring to a boil over medium-high heat. Cook until reduced to 1 cup (about 6 minutes). Add broth; bring to a boil. Cook until reduced by half (about 8 minutes).
5. Combine water and cornstarch in a small bowl; stir with a fork until smooth. Add cornstarch mixture to sauce; bring to a boil. Cook 1 minute, stirring constantly. Yield: 6 servings (serving size: 1 chicken breast half and about ¼ cup sauce).

CALORIES 339 (27% from fat); FAT 10.3g (sat 4g, mono 4.2g, poly 1.2g); PROTEIN 49.2g; CARB 10.1g; FIBER 0.5g; CHOL 123mg; IRON 2.4mg; SODIUM 809mg; CALC 189mg

1. Pound the chicken between two sheets of plastic wrap to keep the work surface clean.

2. Leave a ¼-inch border around edges so filling won't spill out during cooking.

3. Fold the chicken breast in half. Press the edges together to seal.

Instead of pounding the chicken breasts, you can use individually packaged 6-ounce skinless, boneless breast halves that are about ¼ inch thick.

Chicken with Fruit and Olives

Chicken soaks in a vinegar-oil-garlic mixture before it's cooked, then it chills
in the cooking juices, making the meat very tender.

Prep: 20 minutes • Cook: 35 minutes • Other: 8 hours, 45 minutes

¼   cup red wine vinegar
3   tablespoons extravirgin olive oil
½   teaspoon salt
¼   teaspoon freshly ground black
    pepper
4   garlic cloves, minced
½   cup pitted prunes, chopped
½   cup dried apricots, chopped
½   cup pitted green olives, halved
6   (8-ounce) bone-in chicken breast
    halves, skinned
1   cup dry white wine
½   cup finely chopped fresh flat-leaf
    parsley

1. Combine first 5 ingredients in a 13 x
9–inch baking dish, stirring with a whisk.
Add prunes, apricots, and olives; toss well
to coat. Add chicken; turn to coat. Cover
and chill at least 6 hours or overnight.
2. Preheat oven to 450°.
3. Pour wine around, but not over, chick-
en; let stand 15 minutes. Bake at 450° for
35 minutes or until chicken is done; let
stand 15 minutes. Sprinkle with parsley.
Cover and refrigerate at least 2 hours or

overnight. Remove chicken from bones;
discard bones. Return chicken to fruit mixture; let stand 15 minutes. Serve with a
slotted spoon. Yield: 6 servings (serving
size: 1 chicken breast half and about ¼
cup fruit mixture).

CALORIES 328 (26% from fat); FAT 9.6g (sat 1.7g, mono 5.4g,
poly 1.7g); PROTEIN 38.2g; CARB 19g; FIBER 2.4g; CHOL 102mg;
IRON 2.7mg; SODIUM 393mg; CALC 42mg

Senegalese Lemon Chicken

In the West African country of Senegal, this chicken stew is called *yassa*. Serve the chicken on top of the rice in a large deep pan. You'll be seduced by the flavors of the lemon and chiles.

Prep: 25 minutes • Cook: 1 hour, 50 minutes • Other: 3 hours

6 cups sliced onion (about 3 pounds)
⅓ cup fresh lemon juice
1 teaspoon salt
½ teaspoon black pepper
1 jalapeño pepper, seeded and minced
4 (8-ounce) bone-in chicken breast halves, skinned
Cooking spray
1½ tablespoons peanut oil
2 cups thinly sliced carrot
1½ cups fat-free, less-sodium chicken broth
½ cup pimiento-stuffed olives
½ cup water
1 tablespoon Dijon mustard
1 Scotch bonnet pepper, pierced with a fork
4 cups hot cooked long-grain rice

1. Combine first 5 ingredients; divide evenly between 2 (1-gallon) heavy-duty zip-top plastic bags. Divide chicken evenly between bags; seal bags. Toss each bag well to coat. Refrigerate 3 hours, turning bags occasionally.

2. Preheat broiler.

3. Remove chicken from bags, reserving marinade. Place chicken on broiler pan coated with cooking spray; broil 6 minutes on each side or until lightly browned.

4. Strain marinade through a colander over a bowl, reserving marinade and onion. Heat oil in a Dutch oven over medium-high heat. Add onion to pan; sauté 5 minutes. Add reserved marinade; bring to a boil. Cook 1 minute; add chicken, carrot, and next 5 ingredients. Bring to a boil; cover, reduce heat, and simmer 1 hour or until chicken is done. Discard Scotch bonnet pepper. Serve over rice. Yield: 8 servings (serving size: about 4 ounces chicken, ⅔ cup stew, and ½ cup rice).

CALORIES 422 (29% from fat); FAT 13.6g (sat 3g, mono 5.5g, poly 3.6g); PROTEIN 32.7g; CARB 40.4g; FIBER 3.6g; CHOL 99mg; IRON 3mg; SODIUM 704mg; CALC 48mg

Mediterranean Grilled Chicken

Serve with skewers of eggplant, tomatoes, onions, bell peppers, and zucchini—the key ingredients of Provence's ratatouille. To prepare the skewers, brush the vegetables with olive oil, sprinkle with salt, and grill for six minutes, turning once. If you don't need six servings, save two cooked chicken breast halves to use in Chicken-Arugula Focaccia Sandwiches (page 431). Store cooked chicken in refrigerator up to two days.

**Prep: 22 minutes • Cook: 25 minutes
Other: 4 hours**

6 (8-ounce) bone-in chicken breast halves
3 tablespoons Rosemary-Garlic Rub (recipe at right)
6 rosemary sprigs
6 thyme sprigs
½ teaspoon freshly ground black pepper
Cooking spray

1. Loosen skin from chicken by inserting fingers, gently pushing between skin and meat. Rub Rosemary-Garlic Rub evenly over breast meat. Place 1 rosemary sprig and 1 thyme sprig between skin and meat of each breast half. Gently press skin to secure. Cover and refrigerate 4 hours.

2. Prepare grill.

3. Sprinkle chicken with pepper. Place chicken, skin sides down, on grill rack coated with cooking spray. Grill 25 minutes or until done, turning occasionally. Discard skin before serving. Yield: 6 servings (serving size: 1 chicken breast half).

(Totals include Rosemary-Garlic Rub) CALORIES 167 (10% from fat); FAT 1.9g (sat 0.5g, mono 0.5g, poly 0.4g); PROTEIN 34.3g; CARB 1g; FIBER 0.1g; CHOL 86mg; IRON 1.2mg; SODIUM 151mg; CALC 28mg

Rosemary-Garlic Rub

2 tablespoons chopped fresh rosemary
2 tablespoons plain fat-free yogurt
½ teaspoon grated lemon rind
1 tablespoon fresh lemon juice
1 teaspoon minced fresh thyme
¼ teaspoon salt
3 garlic cloves, crushed

1. Combine all ingredients. Store in refrigerator up to three days. Yield: ¼ cup (serving size: about 1 teaspoon).

CALORIES 3 (0% from fat); FAT 0g (sat 0g, mon 0g, poly 0g); PROTEIN 0.2g; CARB 0.6g; FIBER 0.1g; CHOL 0mg; IRON 0mg; SODIUM 41mg; CALC 8mg

WINE NOTE: Pair this dish with a dry rosé to emphasize the herbal flavors of Provence. Although the United States imports many dry rosés from the South of France, none is widely distributed. Just ask your wine clerk to recommend a good producer from Tavel, Provence's famous rosé village.

menu

serves 6

Mediterranean Grilled Chicken

Garlicky Vegetable Pasta Salad
(page 417)

French bread

Melon slices

Jerk Chicken

This Jamaican-style chicken starts out with bottled jerk sauce, which helps keep preparation simple.

Prep: 15 minutes • Cook: 20 minutes
Other: 8 hours

1 cup vertically sliced onion
¼ cup fresh lemon juice
¼ cup bottled jerk sauce
¼ teaspoon salt
¼ teaspoon pepper
3 garlic cloves, chopped
4 bone-in chicken breast halves, skinned (about 1½ pounds)
4 chicken thighs (about 1 pound), skinned
½ cup light beer
¼ cup bottled jerk sauce
3 tablespoons ketchup
1 tablespoon hot sauce
Cooking spray
Julienne-cut green onions (optional)

1. Combine first 6 ingredients in a large zip-top plastic bag. Add chicken to bag; seal. Marinate in refrigerator 8 hours or overnight, turning occasionally. Remove chicken from bag; discard marinade.
2. Prepare grill.
3. Combine beer, ¼ cup jerk sauce, ketchup, and hot sauce.
4. Place chicken on grill rack coated with cooking spray; grill 20 minutes or until done, turning and basting frequently with beer mixture. Garnish chicken with green onions, if desired. Yield: 6 servings (serving size: 1 breast half or 2 thighs).

CALORIES 245 (20% from fat); FAT 5.4g (sat 1.1g, mono 1.3g, poly 1.1g); PROTEIN 42.4g; CARB 6g; FIBER 1.3g; CHOL 129mg; IRON 1.9mg; SODIUM 589mg; CALC 26mg

Thai Grilled Chicken

Highly aromatic and flavorful, the cilantro, coriander, and soy sauce give this chicken a touch of Thai.

Prep: 25 minutes • Cook: 17 minutes
Other: 3 hours

2 tablespoons white peppercorns
1 tablespoon coriander seeds
1 cup minced fresh cilantro stems (optional)
3 tablespoons low-sodium soy sauce
2 tablespoons canola oil
1 teaspoon kosher or sea salt
10 garlic cloves, minced
2 bone-in chicken breast halves (about 1½ pounds)
2 chicken leg quarters (about 1½ pounds)
Cooking spray

1. Place peppercorns and coriander seeds in a large skillet over medium-high heat; cook 1 minute or until toasted. Place peppercorns and coriander seeds in a spice or coffee grinder; process until finely ground.
2. Combine pepper mixture, cilantro (if desired), and next 4 ingredients. Loosen skin from chicken breasts and thighs by inserting fingers, gently pushing between skin and meat. Rub seasoning mixture under loosened chicken skin. Place chicken in a large zip-top plastic bag. Seal and marinate in refrigerator 3 to 8 hours.
3. Prepare grill.
4. Remove chicken from bag; discard marinade. Place chicken on grill rack coated with cooking spray; grill 8 minutes on each side or until chicken is done. Discard skin. Yield: 4 servings (serving size: 1 chicken piece).

CALORIES 316 (33% from fat); FAT 11.5g (sat 2.4g, mono 4.8g, poly 2.9g); PROTEIN 47g; CARB 3.4g; FIBER 0.7g; CHOL 136mg; IRON 2.2mg; SODIUM 342mg; CALC 37mg

Classic Makeover: Fried Chicken

The fried chicken we grew up eating is high in fat for two main reasons: the skin on the chicken and the frying oil. By oven-frying the chicken and removing the skin, we've reduced the fat by an amazing 92 percent. But the fat is what gives fried chicken its flavor and crispiness, right? Not necessarily. We've added salt-free Cajun seasoning to the dredging mixture, giving the chicken a punch without adding a lot of salt. Also, instead of a flour coating, we've coated the chicken with panko (Japanese breadcrumbs) to give it the desired crispiness. Panko are coarser than regular breadcrumbs, and that results in a crunchier coating. Just like many traditional fried chicken recipes, we've dipped ours in buttermilk, but we used low-fat buttermilk instead of the full-fat version. In addition to coating the baking sheet with cooking spray, we lightly coated the dredged chicken with cooking spray, which helps the coating get golden brown.

Before	After
• 683 calories	• 206 calories
• 38g fat	• 3.7g fat
• percentage of calories from fat 51%	• percentage of calories from fat 16%
• 950mg sodium	• 439mg sodium

Cajun Oven-Fried Chicken

Panko, fresh crunchy Japanese bread-crumbs, can be found at Asian markets. They produce the crispiest oven-fried chicken, so it's worth the shopping trip.

Prep: 14 minutes • Cook: 40 minutes

⅓ cup low-fat buttermilk
1 tablespoon salt-free Cajun seasoning
½ teaspoon salt
1 cup panko (Japanese breadcrumbs)
2 bone-in chicken breast halves (about 1½ pounds), skinned
2 chicken drumsticks (about ¾ pound), skinned
2 chicken thighs (about ¾ pound), skinned
Cooking spray

1. Preheat oven to 400°.

2. Combine first 3 ingredients in a shallow dish. Place panko in a shallow dish. Dip chicken, one piece at a time, into butter-milk mixture; dredge in panko.

3. Place chicken on a baking sheet coated with cooking spray. Lightly coat chicken with cooking spray. Bake at 400° for 40 to 45 minutes or until done, turning after 20 minutes. Yield: 4 servings (serving size: 1 breast half or 1 thigh and 1 drumstick).

CALORIES 206 (16% from fat); FAT 3.7g (sat 1g, mono 1g, poly 0.8g); PROTEIN 31.7g; CARB 9g; FIBER 0.3g; CHOL 95mg; IRON 1.2mg; SODIUM 439mg; CALC 39mg

Test Kitchen Tip: Lightly coating the breadcrumb-dredged chicken with cooking spray helps to create a nicely browned crust.

Hoisin Barbecued Chicken

Hoisin sauce, rice wine, and soy sauce give the barbecue sauce an Asian twist. Marinating the chicken overnight is the key to great flavor.

Prep: 20 minutes • Cook: 57 minutes
Other: 8 hours

Barbecue sauce:
⅔ cup hoisin sauce
3 tablespoons rice wine or sake
3 tablespoons low-sodium soy sauce
3 tablespoons ketchup
2 tablespoons brown sugar
1 tablespoon minced garlic

Remaining ingredients:
8 chicken drumsticks, skinned and trimmed (about 2 pounds)
8 chicken thighs, skinned and trimmed (about 2 pounds)
Cooking spray

1. To prepare barbecue sauce, combine first 6 ingredients in a medium bowl. Place ¾ cup sauce in a large bowl; cover and chill remaining barbecue sauce.
2. Add chicken to barbecue sauce in large bowl; toss to coat. Cover and marinate chicken in refrigerator 8 hours or overnight.
3. Preheat oven to 375°.
4. Remove chicken from bowl; reserve marinade. Place chicken on a broiler pan coated with cooking spray. Bake at 375° for 30 minutes. Turn chicken and baste with reserved marinade. Bake an additional 20 minutes or until done. Discard marinade.
5. Bring remaining ¾ cup barbecue sauce to a boil in a small saucepan; reduce heat, and cook until slightly thick and reduced to about ½ cup (about 5 minutes). Drizzle chicken with sauce. Yield: 8 servings

(serving size: 1 drumstick, 1 thigh, and about 1 tablespoon sauce).

CALORIES 241 (23% from fat); FAT 6.1g (sat 1.5g, mono 1.9g, poly 1.8g); PROTEIN 26.6g; CARB 17.8g; FIBER 0.7g; CHOL 97mg; IRON 1.7mg; SODIUM 727mg; CALC 26mg

Arroz con Pollo

A Cuban specialty, *arroz con pollo* (chicken with rice) features a colorful blend of ingredients. With annatto seeds forming the base, Bijol powder serves mostly as a colorant. You can combine equal parts ground cumin and turmeric to use as a substitute for Bijol seasoning.

Prep: 25 minutes • Cook: 50 minutes
Other: 1 hour, 10 minutes

Chicken:
¼ cup fresh lemon juice
1 teaspoon salt
1 teaspoon dried oregano
⅛ teaspoon Bijol seasoning
6 chicken drumsticks (about 1½ pounds), skinned
6 chicken thighs (about 2 pounds), skinned
4 garlic cloves, minced

Rice:
2 cups uncooked Valencia or other short-grain rice
2 teaspoons olive oil, divided
2½ cups fat-free, less-sodium chicken broth
3 tablespoons commercial sofrito (such as Goya)
½ teaspoon Bijol seasoning
½ teaspoon saffron threads (optional)
½ cup frozen petite green peas, thawed
1 (7-ounce) jar sliced pimiento, drained

1. To prepare chicken, combine first 7 ingredients in a large zip-top plastic bag; seal and marinate in refrigerator 1 hour,

turning bag occasionally. Remove chicken from bag, reserving marinade.
2. To prepare rice, place rice in a colander in a large bowl, and rinse with cold water until water runs clear. Drain well.
3. Heat 1 teaspoon oil in a large Dutch oven over medium-high heat. Add drumsticks, and cook 5 minutes on each side or until browned. Remove from pan; keep warm. Repeat procedure with 1 teaspoon oil and thighs.
4. Add reserved marinade, rice, chicken, chicken broth, sofrito, ½ teaspoon Bijol, and saffron threads, if desired, to pan. Bring to a boil. Cover, reduce heat, and simmer 25 minutes. Stir in peas and pimiento; let stand, covered, 10 minutes. Yield: 6 servings (serving size: 1 drumstick, 1 thigh, and about ⅔ cup rice mixture).

CALORIES 472 (17% from fat); FAT 8.7g (sat 2.1g, mono 3.5g, poly 1.8g); PROTEIN 37.1g; CARB 57.8g; FIBER 3.1g; CHOL 122mg; IRON 5.2mg; SODIUM 773mg; CALC 32mg

---

menu

serves 6

Arroz con Pollo

Black beans

Green salad with avocado and tomatoes*

Angela's Flan (page 169)

*Combine 4 cups chopped romaine lettuce, 1 cup halved cherry tomatoes, ½ cup sliced red onion, and 1 sliced avocado. Combine 2 tablespoons fresh lime juice, 2 teaspoons olive oil, 1 teaspoon minced garlic, ¼ teaspoon salt, and ¼ teaspoon pepper, stirring well. Drizzle dressing over salad; toss.

Easy Greek Chicken Casserole

A meal prepared and cooked in only one pot saves you space and cleanup time. You can decrease the sodium by using less anchovy paste or by replacing it with the olives.

Prep: 20 minutes • Cook: 58 minutes

 1 tablespoon olive oil
 2 cups chopped onion (about 1 large)
 2 tablespoons dried thyme
 1 to 2 teaspoons pepper
10 garlic cloves, minced
 6 cups (½-inch) cubed red potato (about 2 pounds)
 2 cups (1-inch) cut green beans (about ½ pound)
¼ cup water
 2 tablespoons anchovy paste or finely chopped olives
 2 (14.5-ounce) cans no-salt-added diced tomatoes, undrained
 8 skinless, boneless chicken thighs (about 1 pound)
½ cup (2 ounces) crumbled feta cheese

1. Preheat oven to 375°.

2. Heat oil in a large ovenproof Dutch oven over medium heat. Add onion; sauté 3 minutes. Add thyme, pepper, and garlic; sauté 1 minute. Increase heat to medium-high. Add potato; sauté 8 minutes or until potato begins to brown. Stir in beans, water, anchovy paste, and tomatoes. Remove mixture from heat. Nestle chicken thighs into potato mixture. Top with feta. Cover and bake at 375° for 45 minutes. Yield: 4 servings (serving size: 2 thighs and 2 cups potato mixture).

CALORIES 488 (23% from fat); FAT 12.6g (sat 4.2g, mono 4.9g, poly 2.1g); PROTEIN 34.5g; CARB 62g; FIBER 7.3g; CHOL 134mg; IRON 7.8mg; SODIUM 775mg; CALC 250mg

Tandoori Chicken with Curried Potatoes

Authentic tandoori dishes cook in a rounded-top tandoor oven made of brick and clay. This Indian-style recipe bakes in a clay pot. If you don't have a clay pot cooker, you can cook it, covered, in a roasting pan at 450° for 1 hour.

Prep: 25 minutes • Cook: 1 hour, 3 minutes
Other: 24 hours, 20 minutes

 1 teaspoon canola oil
 1 tablespoon curry powder
 1 tablespoon paprika, divided
 1 teaspoon salt, divided
¾ cup plain low-fat yogurt
 2 tablespoons fresh lemon juice
 1 tablespoon chopped peeled fresh ginger
 1 medium onion, quartered
 1 large garlic clove, peeled
 8 chicken thighs (about 2¼ pounds), skinned
 3 peeled baking potatoes, cut into ¼-inch-thick slices
 1 cup sliced peeled Granny Smith apple (about 8 ounces)
 2 tablespoons chopped fresh cilantro
 2 tablespoons sliced almonds, toasted
 2 tablespoons golden raisins

1. Heat oil in a nonstick skillet over medium heat. Add curry powder; cook 1 minute. Place curry mixture, 1½ teaspoons paprika, ½ teaspoon salt, yogurt, and next 4 ingredients in a food processor; process until smooth. Place in a large zip-top plastic bag. Add chicken; seal and marinate in refrigerator 24 hours.

2. Remove chicken from bag, reserving marinade. Place marinade in a large bowl; add ½ teaspoon salt, potatoes, and apple, tossing well to coat.

3. Immerse top and bottom of a 3-quart clay pot in water 10 minutes. Empty pot, and drain well. Arrange potato mixture in a single layer; top with chicken thighs, and sprinkle with 1½ teaspoons paprika.
4. Place clay pot in cold oven, and set to 450°. Bake chicken 1 hour. Carefully remove clay pot from oven; let stand 10 minutes before serving. Serve with cilantro, almonds, and raisins. Yield: 4 servings (serving size: 2 chicken thighs, 1 cup potatoes, 1½ teaspoons cilantro, 1½ teaspoons almonds, and 1½ teaspoons raisins).

CALORIES 451 (33% from fat); FAT 16.5g (sat 4.3g, mono 66.7g, poly 3.8g); PROTEIN 35.7g; CARB 41g; FIBER 4.6g; CHOL 111mg; IRON 2.9mg; SODIUM 722mg; CALC 135mg

clay pot cooking
Cooking chicken in a clay pot can result in some of the most tender, tasty chicken you've ever eaten. The technique is perfect for cooking poultry because the high heat forces moisture inward, cooking the interior of the meat. The moisture is then trapped as the clay lid reflects sufficient heat to cook the meat's surface.

Because clay-pot cookers come in a variety of sizes and types, labeling can vary greatly among brands. Look for cookers labeled "for three to six people" or "4- to 6-pound capacity." These are best suited for all-purpose applications and work perfectly with the recipes in this cookbook. In testing, we used both Romertopf and SchlemmerTopf bakers, as well as handmade specialty varieties. Clay pots are available in cookware shops or at Internet kitchen-supply sources.

Chicken Thighs with Thyme and Lemon
For a healthier alternative to fried chicken, try this grilled dish at your next family reunion.

Prep: 20 minutes • Cook: 10 minutes
Other: 2 hours

- 2½ tablespoons honey
- ½ teaspoon grated lemon rind
- 1½ cups fresh lemon juice (about 6 lemons)
- ¼ cup chopped fresh or 1 tablespoon dried thyme
- 1 tablespoon olive oil
- 16 skinless, boneless chicken thighs (about 3 pounds)
- ½ teaspoon salt
- ¼ teaspoon pepper
- Cooking spray

1. Place first 5 ingredients in a large zip-top plastic bag. Add chicken; seal bag. Chill 2 hours, turning occasionally.
2. Prepare grill or preheat broiler.
3. Remove chicken from bag; discard marinade. Sprinkle chicken with salt and pepper. Place chicken on grill rack or broiler pan coated with cooking spray;

menu
serves 8
Chicken Thighs with Thyme and Lemon
Lemony Orzo Salad (page 417)
Grilled corn
Whole wheat rolls
Lattice-Topped Blueberry Pie (page 213)

cook 5 minutes on each side or until done. Yield: 8 servings (serving size: 2 thighs).

CALORIES 212 (30% from fat); FAT 7.1g (sat 1.6g, mono 2.9g, poly 1.5g); PROTEIN 27.4g; CARB 9.8g; FIBER 0.4g; CHOL 115mg; IRON 1.7mg; SODIUM 266mg; CALC 23mg

Spiced Chicken Thighs
Basmati rice pairs particularly well with garam masala and complements the saucy chicken.

Prep: 14 minutes • Cook: 35 minutes

- ¾ teaspoon olive oil
- Cooking spray
- 1 cup vertically sliced onion
- 2 teaspoons garam masala
- ½ teaspoon salt
- ¼ teaspoon curry powder
- 8 chicken thighs (about 2¼ pounds), skinned
- ¼ cup dry red wine
- 2 tablespoons red wine vinegar
- 1 cup fat-free, less-sodium chicken broth
- 3 tablespoons chopped fresh parsley

1. Heat oil in a large nonstick skillet over medium-high heat. Coat pan with cooking spray. Add onion, and sauté 3 minutes. Remove from pan.
2. Combine garam masala, salt, and curry powder; sprinkle evenly over chicken. Add chicken to pan; cook over medium-high heat 4 minutes on each side. Add wine and vinegar; cook 30 seconds, scraping pan to loosen browned bits. Add onion and broth; bring to a boil. Cover, reduce heat, and simmer 20 minutes. Stir in parsley. Yield: 4 servings (serving size: 2 thighs and about ⅓ cup sauce).

CALORIES 203 (30% from fat); FAT 6.7g (sat 1.6g, mono 2.4g, poly 1.5g); PROTEIN 29.9g; CARB 3.9g; FIBER 1.1g; CHOL 121mg; IRON 2.1mg; SODIUM 536mg; CALC 35mg

Moroccan Chicken Thighs

Figs, olives, spices, and a touch of honey give this chicken its Moroccan character. Serve it over a bed of couscous.

Prep: 12 minutes • Cook: 14 minutes

  2 teaspoons olive oil
1½ pounds skinless, boneless chicken thighs, trimmed and cut into bite-sized pieces
  ½ cup chopped fresh cilantro
  ½ cup quartered dried Calimyrna figs
  ¼ cup chopped green olives
  3 tablespoons sweet Marsala or Madeira
  2 tablespoons honey
  1 tablespoon bottled minced garlic
  2 tablespoons balsamic vinegar
  ½ teaspoon ground coriander
  ½ teaspoon ground cumin
  ¼ teaspoon ground cardamom
Cilantro sprigs (optional)

1. Heat oil in a large nonstick skillet over medium-high heat. Add chicken; cook 5 minutes or until browned, stirring frequently. Stir in chopped cilantro and next 9 ingredients; reduce heat to medium, and cook 8 minutes, stirring occasionally. Garnish with cilantro sprigs, if desired. Yield: 4 servings (serving size: ¾ cup).

CALORIES 389 (39% from fat); FAT 16.7g (sat 4g, mono 7.2g, poly 3.3g); PROTEIN 31.6g; CARB 27.6g; FIBER 3g; CHOL 112mg; IRON 2.7mg; SODIUM 183mg; CALC 72mg

portion sizes In *Cooking Light* recipes, one serving of chicken thighs is about 6 ounces uncooked meat (4 ounces cooked). The size of thighs can vary, but usually one serving is 2 (4-ounce) bone-in thighs or 2 (3-ounce) skinless, boneless thighs.

Chicken with Pancetta and Figs

Pancetta—Italian unsmoked bacon found in the deli of many supermarkets—adds saltiness. If you can't find it, substitute lean cooked bacon. If fresh figs are available, stir them in just before serving, omitting the dried figs. Serve over basmati rice in rimmed soup bowls.

Prep: 17 minutes • Cook: 33 minutes

  ¾ teaspoon olive oil
Cooking spray
  1 cup vertically sliced onion
  1 ounce pancetta, finely chopped
  2 teaspoons garam masala
  1 teaspoon brown sugar
  ½ teaspoon salt
  ¼ teaspoon freshly ground black pepper
  8 chicken thighs (about 2¼ pounds), skinned
  ¼ cup tawny port
  2 tablespoons red wine vinegar
  1 cup fat-free, less-sodium chicken broth
 12 dried Calimyrna figs, quartered
  3 tablespoons chopped fresh parsley
  1 tablespoon chopped fresh thyme
Thyme sprigs (optional)

1. Heat oil in a large nonstick skillet coated with cooking spray over medium-high heat. Add onion and pancetta; sauté 3 minutes. Remove from pan.
2. Combine garam masala, sugar, salt, and pepper; sprinkle evenly over chicken. Add chicken to pan; cook over medium-high heat 4 minutes on each side or until browned. Add port and vinegar; cook 30 seconds, scraping pan to loosen browned bits. Add onion mixture and broth; bring to a boil. Cover, reduce heat, and simmer 10 minutes. Add figs; cover and simmer 8 minutes or until chicken is done. Stir in parsley and chopped thyme. Garnish with thyme sprigs, if desired. Yield: 4 servings (serving size: 2 thighs and about ⅔ cup sauce).

CALORIES 392 (26% from fat); FAT 11.5g (sat 3.2g, mono 4.4g, poly 2.3g); PROTEIN 32.3g; CARB 42.3g; FIBER 8g; CHOL 125mg; IRON 3.5mg; SODIUM 594mg; CALC 125mg

Chicken with Olives and Lemon

Known in Morocco as *tajine msir zeetoon*, this stewlike dish is best served over couscous or basmati rice to capture all the sauce.

Prep: 20 minutes • Cook: 1 hour

- ½ cup chopped fresh cilantro
- 1 tablespoon ground cumin
- 2 teaspoons paprika
- 1 teaspoon ground ginger
- 1 teaspoon ground turmeric
- 1 teaspoon ground red pepper
- ¼ teaspoon salt
- 4 garlic cloves, minced
- 8 chicken thighs (about 2¼ pounds), skinned
- Cooking spray
- ½ cup all-purpose flour
- ¼ cup fresh lemon juice
- 1 (14-ounce) can fat-free, less-sodium chicken broth
- 24 pimiento-stuffed olives, chopped
- 8 lemon wedges

1. Preheat oven to 325°.
2. Combine first 8 ingredients in a large bowl; stir well. Add chicken; toss to coat. Arrange in a single layer in a 13 x 9–inch baking dish coated with cooking spray.
3. Lightly spoon flour into a dry measuring cup; level with a knife. Combine flour, juice, and broth, stirring with a whisk until smooth. Sprinkle flour mixture over chicken, tossing to coat. Top chicken with olives and lemon. Bake at 325° for 1 hour or until a thermometer registers 180°. Yield: 4 servings (serving size: 2 thighs and about ⅓ cup sauce).

CALORIES 287 (29% from fat); FAT 9.1g (sat 1.9g, mono 3.7g, poly 1.9g); PROTEIN 32.7g; CARB 18.3g; FIBER 2.1g; CHOL 121mg; IRON 3.8mg; SODIUM 1034mg; CALC 56mg

Dry-Rub Chicken with Honey Barbecue Sauce

Offer this succulent chicken with an irresistible sweet-and-sour barbecue sauce at your next backyard cookout.

Prep: 30 minutes • Cook: 1 hour, 48 minutes
Other: 5 minutes

Chicken:
- 1 (3-pound) whole chicken
- 1 tablespoon paprika
- 2 teaspoons lemon pepper
- ½ teaspoon garlic powder
- ¼ teaspoon black pepper
- ⅛ teaspoon seasoned salt
- Cooking spray

Honey Barbecue Sauce:
- ½ cup ketchup
- ¼ cup fresh lemon juice
- 2 tablespoons cider vinegar
- 2 tablespoons honey
- ½ teaspoon garlic powder
- ¼ teaspoon black pepper

1. To prepare chicken, remove and discard giblets and neck from chicken. Rinse chicken with cold water; pat dry. Trim excess fat. Place chicken, breast side down, on a cutting surface. Cut chicken in half lengthwise along backbone (do not cut through breastbone). Turn chicken over. Starting at neck cavity, loosen skin from breast and drumsticks by inserting fingers, gently pushing between skin and meat.
2. Combine paprika and next 4 ingredients. Rub paprika mixture under loosened skin, and rub over breast and drumsticks. Gently press skin to secure. Cut a 1-inch slit in skin at bottom of each breast half; insert tips of drumsticks into slits.
3. To prepare grill for indirect grilling, place a disposable aluminum foil pan in grill; pour water into pan. Arrange charcoal around pan; heat to medium. Coat grill rack with cooking spray; place rack on grill. Place chicken, breast side down, on grill rack over foil pan. Cover and grill 1½ hours or until a thermometer registers 180°. Remove chicken from grill; place on a clean cutting surface. Cover with foil, and let stand 5 minutes.
4. To prepare sauce, combine ketchup and remaining 5 ingredients in a small saucepan. Bring sauce to a simmer over medium-low heat; cook 15 minutes, stirring frequently. Remove skin from chicken, and brush chicken with ⅓ cup sauce. Serve remaining sauce with chicken. Yield: 4 servings (serving size: about 4 ounces chicken and about 4 teaspoons sauce).

CALORIES 265 (26% from fat); FAT 7.8g (sat 2.1g, mono 2.9g, poly 1.9g); PROTEIN 29.3g; CARB 20.3g; FIBER 1g; CHOL 85mg; IRON 2.2mg; SODIUM 650mg; CALC 27mg

how to cut a chicken in half

1. Use kitchen shears instead of a knife to cut down the backbone of the chicken.

2. Once the chicken is cut, it will open up and lie flat for even cooking.

Coq au Vin

You'll need to start preparing this classic recipe a day ahead. We've made bouquet garni in leek leaves, but you can do it in cheesecloth, if you prefer.

Prep: 35 minutes • Cook: 3 hours, 26 minutes
Other: 8 hours

Bouquet garni:
- 2 large leeks
- 12 thyme sprigs
- 12 parsley stems
- 4 bay leaves

Chicken:
- 1 (3-pound) roasting chicken
- ½ teaspoon kosher or sea salt, divided
- ¾ teaspoon pepper, divided
- 3 tablespoons unsalted butter, divided
- 1 bacon slice, cut into 1-inch pieces
- ½ cup Calvados (apple brandy) or brandy
- 4 cups fat-free, less-sodium chicken broth, divided
- 1 (750-milliliter) bottle hearty dry red wine (Burgundy or pinot noir)
- 2 garlic cloves, halved
- 3 (8-ounce) packages mushrooms, stemmed
- 3 tablespoons all-purpose flour

1. To make bouquet garni, remove and reserve 8 leek leaves; remove white portion of leek leaves (reserve remaining leaves for another use). Flatten leaves. Place 3 thyme sprigs, 3 parsley sprigs, and 1 bay leaf lengthwise in each of 4 leek leaves. Top each filled leaf with one of remaining leek leaves. Tie leaves with string at 2-inch intervals.

2. To prepare chicken, remove giblets and neck from chicken; discard neck. Rinse chicken with cold water; pat dry. Trim excess fat. Remove skin; cut chicken into quarters. Mince giblets; set aside. Sprinkle chicken pieces with ¼ teaspoon salt and ½ teaspoon pepper. Heat 1 tablespoon butter in a large Dutch oven over medium heat. Add chicken to pan; cook 10 minutes, browning on all sides. Remove from pan. Add bacon; cook until crisp. Return chicken to pan. Add bouquet garni, giblets, Calvados, 2 cups broth, wine, and garlic; bring to a boil. Cover, reduce heat, and simmer 1½ hours.

3. Remove chicken from wine mixture; cover and refrigerate. Cover and chill wine mixture 8 to 24 hours. Discard bouquet garni. Skim solidified fat from surface of wine mixture; discard.

4. Combine mushrooms and 2 cups broth in a large nonstick skillet; bring to a boil. Partially cover, reduce heat, and simmer 30 minutes. Uncover and cook 10 minutes or until liquid almost evaporates. Sprinkle with ¼ teaspoon salt and ¼ teaspoon pepper. Remove from pan.

5. Add wine mixture to pan; bring to a boil. Reduce heat, and simmer 20 minutes. Combine 2 tablespoons butter and flour in a small bowl; work into a paste with your fingers or a fork. Add ¼ cup wine mixture, stirring with a whisk until well blended. Add butter mixture to wine mixture in pan; bring to a boil. Reduce heat, and simmer 10 minutes. Add chicken and mushrooms to pan. Bring to a boil; reduce heat, and simmer 10 minutes or until thoroughly heated. Yield: 4 servings (serving size: 4 ounces chicken and 1 cup broth mixture).

CALORIES 433 (30% from fat); FAT 14.5g (sat 6.9g, mono 4g, poly 1.8g); PROTEIN 45.2g; CARB 14.3; FIBER 2.3g; CHOL 137mg; IRON 3.8mg; SODIUM 995mg; CALC 44mg

WINE NOTE: The quintessential French comfort food, Coq au Vin is traditionally served with a red Burgundy. An exemplary choice would be a sublime, earthy wine like Domaine de l'Arlot Nuits-St.-Georges Clos des Fôrets Premier Cru. But a more hearty Rhône wine such as Domaine Santa Duc Côtes-du-Rhône would be nearly as good.

how to make coq au vin

1. Brown the chicken in butter to develop rich, caramelized flavors.

2. Add the liquor, giblets, bouquet garni, broth, wine, and garlic. Simmer 1½ hours. Refrigerate the chicken and wine mixture separately overnight.

3. Work softened butter and flour together until a paste forms. Then stir into the wine mixture to thicken it.

Brined Chicken with Lemon

Soaking the chicken in a salt solution (brining) overnight allows for uniform salting and produces a very moist chicken.

Prep: 20 minutes • Cook: 1 hour, 10 minutes
Other: 8 hours

    4   quarts water
    ⅔   cup kosher salt
    1   (5-pound) roasting chicken
    4   (⅛-inch-thick) slices lemon
    ¼   teaspoon pepper
    4   lemon wedges
    4   flat-leaf parsley sprigs
    2   garlic cloves, cut in half
    1   shallot, peeled and quartered
    Cooking spray

1. Combine 4 quarts water and salt in a Dutch oven, stirring until salt dissolves. Remove and discard giblets and neck from chicken. Rinse chicken with cold water; pat dry. Trim excess fat. Add chicken to salt mixture; cover and refrigerate 8 hours.
2. Preheat oven to 400°.
3. Remove chicken from brine; discard brine. Pat chicken dry with paper towels. Starting at neck cavity, loosen skin from breast and drumsticks by inserting fingers, gently pushing between skin and meat. Place lemon slices under loosened skin. Sprinkle cavity with pepper; place lemon wedges, parsley, garlic, and shallot into cavity. Lift wing tips up and over back; tuck under chicken. Place chicken, breast side up, on rack of a broiler pan coated with cooking spray. Bake at 400° for 1 hour and 10 minutes or until thermometer registers 180°. Discard skin. Yield: 6 servings (serving size: 4 ounces).

CALORIES 215 (22% from fat); FAT 5.2g (sat 1.3g, mono 1.6g, poly 1.3g); PROTEIN 39.2g; CARB 0.4g; FIBER 0g; CHOL 125mg; IRON 2mg; SODIUM 458mg; CALC 20mg

Cider-Roasted Chicken and Spicy Sweet Potato Wedges, page 531

Cider-Roasted Chicken

Basting the chicken with reduced apple cider adds a hint of sweetness and makes it incredibly juicy. Use tongs to carefully remove the skin.

Prep: 20 minutes • Cook: 2 hours, 5 minutes
Other: 8 hours, 10 minutes

    3   quarts water
    1   quart apple cider
    ¼   cup kosher salt
    1   tablespoon black peppercorns
    1   bay leaf
    1   (6-pound) roasting chicken
    2   cups apple cider
    1   large onion, peeled and halved
    4   flat-leaf parsley sprigs
    4   garlic cloves, peeled
    Cooking spray

1. Combine first 5 ingredients in a saucepan; bring to a boil, stirring until salt dissolves. Remove from heat; cool completely. Remove and discard giblets and neck from chicken. Rinse chicken with cold water; pat dry. Trim excess fat. Pour brine into a 2-gallon zip-top plastic bag. Add chicken; seal. Refrigerate 8 hours or overnight, turning bag occasionally.
2. Preheat oven to 400°.

3. Bring 2 cups cider to a boil in a small saucepan over medium-high heat. Cook until cider is thickened and reduced to ¼ cup (about 15 minutes). Set aside.
4. Remove chicken from bag; discard brine. Pat chicken dry with paper towels. Place onion halves, parsley, and garlic in cavity. Lift wing tips up and over back; tuck under chicken. Tie legs. Place chicken, breast side up, on rack of a broiler pan coated with cooking spray. Bake at 400° for 1½ hours or until thermometer registers 175°. Remove from oven (do not turn oven off). Carefully remove and discard skin. Baste chicken with half of reduced cider; return to 400° oven for 10 minutes. Remove from oven; baste with remaining cider reduction. Transfer chicken to a platter.
5. Place a zip-top plastic bag inside a 2-cup glass measure. Pour drippings into bag; let stand 10 minutes (fat will rise to top). Seal bag; carefully snip off 1 bottom corner of bag. Drain drippings into a small bowl, stopping before fat layer reaches opening; discard fat. Serve jus over chicken. Yield: 8 servings (serving size: about 4 ounces chicken and about 1 tablespoon jus).

CALORIES 224 (29% from fat); FAT 7.1g (sat 2g, mono 2.7g, poly 1.7g); PROTEIN 26.9g; CARB 11.3g; FIBER 0.4g; CHOL 80mg; IRON 1.4mg; SODIUM 452mg; CALC 26mg

Roasted Chicken with Lemon Curd

Chicken and lemon are natural culinary partners, and in this recipe, the Lemon Curd acts as a tangy glaze.

Prep: 26 minutes • Cook: 1 hour, 46 minutes
Other: 10 minutes

  1   (3-pound) roasting chicken
  1   tablespoon chopped fresh rosemary
  2   teaspoons chopped fresh thyme
  ½   teaspoon salt
  ¼   teaspoon freshly ground black pepper
  4   garlic cloves, crushed
Cooking spray
  ½   cup Lemon Curd (page 460)
  2   large lemons, halved

1. Preheat oven to 450°.
2. Remove and discard giblets and neck from chicken. Rinse chicken with cold water; pat dry. Trim excess fat. Starting at neck cavity, loosen skin from breast and drumsticks by inserting fingers, gently pushing between skin and meat.
3. Combine rosemary and next 4 ingredients. Rub under loosened skin, and rub over breast and drumsticks. Lift wing tips up and over back; tuck under chicken.
4. Place chicken, breast side up, on a broiler pan coated with cooking spray. Pierce skin several times with a meat fork. Insert a meat thermometer into meaty part of thigh, making sure not to touch bone; brush chicken with Lemon Curd. Arrange lemons around chicken. Bake at 450° for 30 minutes. Reduce oven temperature to 350° (do not remove chicken from oven), and bake an additional 1 hour or until thermometer registers 180°. (Cover chicken loosely with foil if it gets too brown.) Remove chicken from oven. Cover loosely with foil, and let stand 10 minutes. Discard skin. Serve with lemon halves. Yield: 4 servings (serving size: 4 ounces chicken and 1 lemon half).

(Totals include Lemon Curd) CALORIES 304 (24% from fat); FAT 7.9g (sat 2.9g, mono 2.4g, poly 1.4g); PROTEIN 36.8g; CARB 21.1g; FIBER 1g; CHOL 159mg; IRON 2.2mg; SODIUM 459mg; CALC 53mg

Oven-Braised Cornish Hens with Cider Vinegar and Warm Vegetable Sauce
(pictured on page 359)

Warm crusty bread is all you need to round out this one-dish meal. Use it to soak up the last drops of the zippy broth.

Prep: 25 minutes • Cook: 58 minutes

  2   (1½-pound) Cornish hens
  3   tablespoons all-purpose flour
  ½   teaspoon salt
  ¼   teaspoon freshly ground black pepper
  1½ teaspoons butter
  1   teaspoon olive oil
  2   cups (1-inch) slices leek (about 2 large)
  ½   pound cremini mushrooms, halved
  2   garlic cloves, minced
  3   cups fat-free, less-sodium chicken broth
  1   cup cider vinegar
  3   plum tomatoes, quartered
  1   Granny Smith apple, peeled and cut into ½-inch slices
  ½   pound small red potatoes, quartered
  2   tablespoons chopped fresh parsley

1. Preheat oven to 350°.
2. Rinse hens with cold water; pat dry. Remove skin; trim excess fat. Split hens in half lengthwise. Combine flour, salt, and pepper in a shallow dish; dredge hens in flour mixture. Melt butter in a large Dutch oven over medium-high heat. Add oil and hens, and cook 4 minutes on each side or until browned. Remove from pan.
3. Add leek, mushrooms, and garlic to pan; sauté 5 minutes. Add broth and vinegar, stirring to loosen browned bits. Return hens to pan; add tomatoes, apple, and potatoes. Bring mixture to a simmer. Cover and bake at 350° for 30 minutes or until hens are done. Place hens on a serving platter, and keep warm. Remove vegetable mixture from pan with a slotted spoon; place in a serving bowl. Reserve 2 cups cooking liquid in pan; discard remaining liquid. Bring reserved cooking liquid to a boil; cook 8 minutes or until reduced to 1 cup, stirring occasionally. Pour over vegetable mixture. Sprinkle with parsley. Serve with hens. Yield: 4 servings (serving size: 1 hen half and 1 cup vegetable mixture).

CALORIES 327 (22% from fat); FAT 7.9g (sat 2.4g, mono 2.8g, poly 1.6g); PROTEIN 34.1g; CARB 30.6g; FIBER 3.4g; CHOL 137mg; IRON 3.4mg; SODIUM 491mg; CALC 75mg

fresh whole chickens

Chickens are categorized by their age and weight.

- Broiler-fryers weigh 3 to 4 pounds. They don't have as much meat as roasters and are best used for recipes that call for cut-up fryers, or to make chicken stock.
- Roasters weigh 4 to 7 pounds and are good to use when you want to roast or bake a whole chicken.
- Cornish hens are also known as Rock Cornish hens or Cornish Game hens and are miniature chickens, 4 to 6 weeks old, and weighing up to 2½ pounds. Because of the small amount of meat to bone, each hen is just enough for one or two servings.

Game Hens with Pesto Rub and Roasted Potatoes

Golden roasted potatoes are a great match for the basil-and-Parmesan-scented hens. Use kitchen shears or a sharp knife to split the hens.

Prep: 40 minutes • Cook: 51 minutes
Other: 20 minutes

4 cups loosely packed fresh basil leaves
⅓ cup (about 1½ ounces) grated fresh Parmesan cheese
1 tablespoon water
1 tablespoon olive oil
¼ teaspoon salt
⅛ teaspoon pepper
2 garlic cloves, chopped
4 (1½-pound) Cornish hens
Cooking spray
7 cups small red potatoes, quartered (about 2 pounds)
1 tablespoon olive oil
½ teaspoon salt
¼ teaspoon pepper
1 cup fat-free, less-sodium chicken broth
1 tablespoon water
1 teaspoon cornstarch
Basil sprigs (optional)

1. Preheat oven to 375°.
2. Place first 7 ingredients in a food processor; process until smooth.
3. Remove and discard giblets and necks from hens. Rinse hens with cold water; pat dry. Starting at neck cavity, loosen skin from breast and drumsticks by inserting fingers, gently pushing between skin and meat. Rub pesto under loosened skin. Gently press skin to secure. Lift wing tips up and over back; tuck under hens.
4. Place hens on a broiler pan coated with cooking spray. Insert a meat thermometer into meaty part of a thigh, making sure not to touch bone.
5. Combine potatoes and next 3 ingredients, tossing well to coat. Arrange potatoes around hens; bake at 375° for 45 minutes or until thermometer registers 180° and potatoes are tender.
6. Remove hens and potatoes from pan, and cover loosely with foil. Let stand 10 minutes. Discard skin from hens. Cut hens in half, and cover loosely with foil.
7. Place a zip-top plastic bag inside a 2-cup glass measure. Pour pan drippings into zip-top plastic bag; let stand 10 minutes (fat will rise to top). Seal bag, and carefully snip off 1 bottom corner. Drain pan drippings into pan, stopping before fat layer reaches opening; discard fat.
8. Place pan over medium-high heat. Stir in broth, scraping pan to loosen browned bits. Combine 1 tablespoon water and cornstarch, stirring well with a whisk. Add to pan. Bring to a boil; cook until reduced to ½ cup (about 3 minutes). Serve sauce with hens and potatoes. Garnish with basil sprigs, if desired. Yield: 8 servings (serving size: 1 hen half, about ¾ cup potatoes, and 1 tablespoon sauce).

CALORIES 306 (28% from fat); FAT 9.5g (sat 2.3g, mono 4.4g, poly 1.7g); PROTEIN 33.7g; CARB 19.8g; FIBER 2.8g; CHOL 136mg; IRON 2.7mg; SODIUM 454mg; CALC 100mg

how to skim fat from drippings

Place a zip-top plastic bag inside a 2-cup glass measure. Pour pan drippings into bag; let stand 10 minutes (the fat will rise to the top). Seal bag; carefully snip off 1 bottom corner. Drain drippings into measuring cup or pan, stopping before fat layer reaches opening; discard fat.

Orange-Ginger Glazed Cornish Hens

Line your pan with foil for mess-free cleanup. Don't worry if the glaze burns on the foil; it won't burn on the hens.

Prep: 15 minutes • Cook: 29 minutes

¾ cup fresh orange juice (about 3 oranges)

2 tablespoons minced peeled fresh ginger

2 tablespoons honey

1 tablespoon low-sodium soy sauce

1 tablespoon water

2 teaspoons cornstarch

2 (1½-pound) Cornish hens, skinned and halved

Cooking spray

½ teaspoon salt

½ teaspoon ground ginger

1. Preheat oven to 475°.

2. Combine first 4 ingredients in a small saucepan; bring to a boil. Combine water and cornstarch in a small bowl, stirring with a whisk. Add to juice mixture in pan, stirring with a whisk. Cook 2 minutes or until thick and glossy, stirring constantly.

3. Place hen halves, meaty sides up, on a foil-lined jelly-roll pan coated with cooking spray; sprinkle hen halves with salt and ground ginger. Spoon juice mixture evenly over hen halves.

4. Insert a meat thermometer into meaty part of a thigh, making sure not to touch bone. Bake at 475° for 25 minutes or until thermometer registers 180°. Yield: 4 servings (serving size: 1 hen half).

CALORIES 188 (18% from fat); FAT 3.8g (sat 1g, mono 1.2g, poly 0.9g); PROTEIN 22.5g; CARB 15.6g; FIBER 0.3g; CHOL 99mg; IRON 1mg; SODIUM 487mg; CALC 19mg

menu

serves 4

Orange-Ginger Glazed Cornish Hens

Oven-Roasted Green Beans
(page 515)

Rice pilaf with walnuts*

Espresso Crème Brûlée (page 170)

*Melt 1 teaspoon butter in a small saucepan over medium heat. Add ¼ cup chopped onion; sauté 3 minutes. Stir in 2½ cups water, ¾ cup long-grain and wild rice blend, and ¼ teaspoon salt; bring to a boil. Cover, reduce heat, and simmer 40 minutes or until liquid is absorbed. Remove from heat; stir in 2 tablespoons finely chopped toasted walnuts.

Duck & Quail

Domestic or wild, these birds offer rich flavor and can be prepared in a variety of ways.

Rosemary-Rubbed Duck Breast with Caramelized Apricots

Serve this fruited duck entrée with couscous or brown rice. If you're not
a duck fan, you can also make the recipe with chicken breasts.

Prep: 15 minutes • Cook: 19 minutes • Other: 2 hours, 10 minutes

3 tablespoons chopped fresh rosemary
2 tablespoons brown sugar
1 tablespoon freshly ground black pepper
2 teaspoons salt
2 (12-ounce) duck breasts, skinned and halved
1 tablespoon olive oil
½ cup granulated sugar
½ cup Champagne vinegar or white wine vinegar
5 apricots, quartered
Rosemary sprigs (optional)

1. Combine first 4 ingredients. Rub rosemary mixture over duck. Cover and chill 2 hours. Rinse duck with cold water; pat dry.

2. Heat oil in a large nonstick skillet over medium-high heat. Add duck, and cook 5 minutes on each side or until done. Remove from pan; let stand 10 minutes.

3. Combine granulated sugar and vinegar in a small saucepan, and bring to a boil. Cook until thick and amber-colored (about 5 minutes). Add apricots; reduce heat, and cook 1 minute or until apricots begin to soften. Cut duck diagonally across grain into slices. Serve with caramelized apricots. Garnish with rosemary sprigs, if desired. Yield: 4 servings (serving size: 3 ounces duck, 5 apricot quarters, and 3 tablespoons sauce).

CALORIES 374 (26% from fat); FAT 10.9g (sat 2.8g, mono 4.6g, poly 1.3g); PROTEIN 34.5g; CARB 33.2g; FIBER 1.5g; CHOL 0mg; IRON 8.4mg; SODIUM 688mg; CALC 23mg

Seared Orange Duck Breast

Be careful not to overcook duck breast. If you cook it past medium-rare, you lose flavor and compromise the texture. If your supermarket doesn't carry fresh duck breast, look for it in the freezer section.

Prep: 20 minutes • Cook: 28 minutes
Other: 30 minutes

- 3 (12-ounce) duck breasts, skinned and halved
- 1½ tablespoons grated orange rind
- 1 teaspoon salt
- ¼ teaspoon pepper
- 4 garlic cloves, crushed
- ½ cup fresh orange juice (about 2 oranges)
- ¼ cup sake (rice wine)
- 1½ tablespoons low-sodium soy sauce
- 1 tablespoon honey
- 1 tablespoon canola oil

1. Combine duck, orange rind, salt, pepper, and garlic in a medium bowl. Cover and refrigerate 30 minutes.
2. Preheat oven to 400°.
3. Combine juice, sake, soy sauce, and honey in a small saucepan; bring to a boil. Reduce heat to medium-low, and simmer until mixture is reduced to ⅔ cup (about 10 minutes).
4. Heat canola oil in a large ovenproof skillet over medium-high heat. Add duck; sauté 5 minutes. Turn duck over; drizzle with 3 tablespoons juice mixture. Bake at 400° for 10 minutes. Remove duck from pan; cut duck into ¼-inch-thick slices. Serve with orange sauce. Yield: 6 servings (serving size: 3 ounces duck and about 2 tablespoons sauce).

CALORIES 167 (34% from fat); FAT 6.3g (sat 1.4g, mono 2.5g, poly 1.2g); PROTEIN 18.8g; CARB 6.7g; FIBER 0.3g; CHOL 71mg; IRON 4.4mg; SODIUM 580mg; CALC 13mg

WINE NOTE: Try pairing this recipe with Saintsbury Pinot Noir 1998 (Carneros). It's an earthy wine with hints of mandarin orange.

Sautéed Duck Breast with Cherry-Pistachio Salsa

If you want something other than turkey for your holiday meal, duck breasts cook more quickly than turkey. You can easily adjust this recipe for the number of guests.

Prep: 20 minutes • Cook: 15 minutes
Other: 30 minutes

Cherry-Pistachio Salsa:
- 1½ cups dried sweet or tart cherries (about 8 ounces)
- 1½ cups boiling water
- 1 dried chipotle chile
- ½ cup shelled dry-roasted pistachios, coarsely chopped
- ⅓ cup finely chopped red onion
- ¼ cup chopped fresh cilantro
- 2 tablespoons fresh lime juice
- 1 teaspoon chili powder
- 1 teaspoon honey
- 1 jalapeño pepper, seeded and finely chopped
- 1¼ teaspoons salt, divided

Duck:
- 1 teaspoon black pepper
- 8 (6-ounce) boneless duck breast halves, skinned
- 1 teaspoon canola oil
- Cooking spray

1. To prepare salsa, combine first 3 ingredients in a large bowl; let stand 30 minutes. Drain well; discard chile. Combine cherries, pistachios, and next 6 ingredients. Stir in ¼ teaspoon salt.
2. To prepare duck, sprinkle 1 teaspoon salt and pepper over duck. Heat oil in a large nonstick skillet coated with cooking spray over medium-high heat. Add duck; sauté 6 minutes on each side or until desired degree of doneness. Serve with salsa. Yield: 8 servings (serving size: 1 duck breast half and about ⅓ cup salsa).

CALORIES 354 (29% from fat); FAT 11.4g (sat 2.7g, mono 4.3g, poly 2.3g); PROTEIN 37.1g; CARB 23.1g; FIBER 3.3g; CHOL 131mg; IRON 8.4mg; SODIUM 469mg; CALC 32mg

duck Duck breast, without the skin, has 30 percent less fat than skinless chicken breast. The most widely sold domestic duck in the U.S. is the White Pekin. A Pekin duck usually weighs between 3 to 6 pounds, a large proportion of the weight being fat in the skin. This duck is heavily boned and yields proportionally less meat per pound than some other varieties.

Ducks are available fresh on a limited basis from late spring through late winter, but 90 percent of the supply is sold frozen. Store frozen duck in the freezer in its original wrapping for up to three months. (Some frozen duck packages contain an expiration date.)

Quail with Grapes and Grappa

Use red and green grapes for an attractive presentation. Serve with green beans and wild rice tossed with toasted hazelnuts.

Prep: 25 minutes • Cook: 36 minutes

1½ cups seedless green grapes, divided
 8 (4-ounce) quail, skinned
 ½ teaspoon salt
 ½ teaspoon pepper
 8 (1-inch) rosemary sprigs
 8 (1-inch) thyme sprigs
 2 teaspoons olive oil
1¼ cups fat-free, less-sodium chicken broth, divided
 ¼ cup finely chopped prosciutto (about 1 ounce)
 3 tablespoons grappa (Italian brandy) or cognac
1½ tablespoons minced shallots
 Rosemary sprigs (optional)

1. Cut ½ cup grapes in half lengthwise.
2. Sprinkle quail with salt and pepper. Place 1 (1-inch) rosemary sprig and 1 (1-inch) thyme sprig into cavity of each quail.
3. Heat oil in a large nonstick skillet over medium-high heat. Add quail, and cook 3 minutes on each side or until browned. Arrange quail, breast sides up, in pan; add ½ cup broth. Partially cover, reduce heat to medium-low, and cook 25 minutes or until done. Place quail on a platter; cover loosely with foil.
4. Add ¼ cup broth, prosciutto, grappa, and shallots to pan; cook over medium-high heat 1½ minutes or until shallots are tender, scraping pan to loosen browned bits. Stir in ½ cup broth and whole and halved grapes; cook 2 minutes or until grapes are thoroughly heated. Pour grape mixture over quail; garnish with rosemary sprigs, if desired. Yield: 4 servings (serving size: 2 quail and about ⅓ cup sauce).

CALORIES 355 (29% from fat); FAT 11.6g (sat 3.1g, mono 4.4g, poly 2.6g); PROTEIN 43.1g; CARB 11.8g; FIBER 0.7g; CHOL 133mg; IRON 8.7mg; SODIUM 636mg; CALC 34mg

Test Kitchen Tip: Grappa is an Italian liquor distilled from grape pressings left over after winemaking; cognac is a good substitute. If you prefer a nonalcoholic substitution, use an additional 3 tablespoons of chicken broth.

Turkey No longer simply a holiday offering, turkey takes its place at the weeknight dinner table.

Cheesy Brunch Casserole

Because herb-seasoned stuffing mix is the base of this casserole, you have to add only a touch of seasoning. If you'd prefer a bit of heat, substitute hot turkey Italian sausage.

**Prep: 14 minutes • Cook: 50 minutes
Other: 5 minutes**

1 pound turkey Italian sausage
5 cups herb-seasoned stuffing mix (such as Pepperidge Farm)
Cooking spray
½ cup fat-free, less-sodium chicken broth
2 tablespoons butter, melted
1½ cups (6 ounces) shredded reduced-fat extrasharp Cheddar cheese
2 cups 2% reduced-fat milk
½ teaspoon onion powder
½ teaspoon freshly ground black pepper
2 (8-ounce) cartons egg substitute

1. Preheat oven to 325°.
2. Remove casings from sausage. Cook sausage in a large nonstick skillet over medium-high heat until browned, stirring to crumble. Drain. Place sausage in a large bowl; add stuffing mix, tossing to combine.
3. Place stuffing mixture in a 13 x 9–inch baking dish coated with cooking spray. Drizzle stuffing mixture with broth and butter; sprinkle with cheese. Combine milk and next 3 ingredients, stirring with a whisk; pour milk mixture over stuffing mixture.
4. Bake at 325° for 40 minutes or until set. Let casserole stand 5 minutes before serving. Yield: 9 servings (serving size: about 1½ cups).

CALORIES 298 (29% from fat); FAT 9.6g (sat 4g, mono 3.6g, poly 1.3g); PROTEIN 19.8g; CARB 31.5g; FIBER 2.9g; CHOL 50mg; IRON 2.8mg; SODIUM 986mg; CALC 284mg

La Bamba Casserole

Serve this easy weeknight favorite with Corn Bread Muffins (page 76) and a tossed green salad.

**Prep: 15 minutes • Cook: 40 minutes
Other: 5 minutes**

1 (4-ounce) can whole green chiles, drained
Cooking spray
1 pound ground turkey breast
1 cup chopped onion
2 teaspoons chili powder
½ teaspoon ground cumin
¼ teaspoon salt
2 garlic cloves, minced
1 (10-ounce) can diced tomatoes and green chiles, undrained
2 cups frozen whole-kernel corn, thawed
1 (16-ounce) can fat-free refried beans
1½ cups (6 ounces) shredded Cheddar cheese
1 cup chopped tomato
½ cup chopped green onions

1. Preheat oven to 375°.
2. Cut chiles in half lengthwise. Arrange chiles in a single layer in an 8-inch square baking dish coated with cooking spray.
3. Heat a large nonstick skillet over medium-high heat. Coat pan with cooking spray. Add turkey and next 5 ingredients; sauté 5 minutes, stirring to crumble. Add diced tomatoes; cook 5 minutes or until liquid evaporates.
4. Spoon turkey mixture over chiles. Top with corn. Carefully spread beans over corn. Sprinkle cheese over beans. Bake at 375° for 30 minutes. Let stand 5 minutes; top with chopped tomato and green onions. Yield: 6 servings (serving size: 1⅓ cups).

CALORIES 344 (28% from fat); FAT 10.7g (sat 6.3g, mono 2.9g, poly 0.8g); PROTEIN 32.2g; CARB 30.7g; FIBER 7.4g; CHOL 77mg; IRON 3.2mg; SODIUM 902mg; CALC 269mg

ground turkey You'll see several types of ground turkey in the supermarket, so read the label to be sure you get what you want. The leanest (about 3 percent fat) is white meat only, with no skin. It's labeled "ground turkey breast." Regular "ground turkey" is made from white and dark meat with some skin, and is about 10 percent fat (similar to ground round). Frozen ground turkey is usually all dark meat with skin, and is 15 percent fat, similar to ground sirloin.

Chiles Rellenos Casserole

Chiles rellenos are cheese-stuffed peppers covered in a batter and fried. In this casserole, the chiles are topped with cheese and a ground turkey mixture instead of being stuffed. A batter is poured over the chiles, and they're baked rather than being fried.

Prep: 20 minutes • Cook: 1 hour, 15 minutes • Other: 5 minutes

½ pound ground turkey
1 cup chopped onion
1¾ teaspoons ground cumin
1½ teaspoons dried oregano
½ teaspoon garlic powder
¼ teaspoon salt
¼ teaspoon pepper
1 (16-ounce) can fat-free refried beans
2 (4-ounce) cans whole green chiles, drained and cut lengthwise into quarters
1 cup (4 ounces) shredded colby-Jack cheese
1 cup frozen whole-kernel corn, thawed and drained
⅓ cup all-purpose flour
¼ teaspoon salt
1⅓ cups fat-free milk
⅛ teaspoon hot sauce
2 large eggs, lightly beaten
2 large egg whites, lightly beaten
Red onion slices (optional)
Chopped cilantro (optional)

1. Preheat oven to 350°.

2. Cook turkey and chopped onion in a nonstick skillet over medium-high heat until browned, stirring to crumble. Remove from heat; add cumin and next 5 ingredients. Stir until well combined. Set aside.

3. Arrange half of green chiles in an 11 x 7–inch baking dish, and top with ½ cup cheese. Spoon mounds of turkey mixture onto cheese, and spread gently, leaving a ¼-inch border around edge of dish. Top with corn. Arrange remaining green chiles over corn; top with ½ cup cheese.

4. Combine flour and salt in a bowl; gradually add milk, hot sauce, eggs, and egg whites, stirring with a whisk until blended. Pour over casserole. Bake at 350° for 1 hour and 5 minutes or until set; let stand 5 minutes. Garnish with onion slices and cilantro, if desired. Yield: 6 servings (serving size: about 1⅓ cups).

CALORIES 335 (24% from fat); FAT 9g (sat 4.5g, mono 2.7g, poly 1.6g); PROTEIN 26.9g; CARB 37.7g; FIBER 5.5g; CHOL 112mg; IRON 3.8mg; SODIUM 825mg; CALC 280mg

Test Kitchen Tip: Two (4.5-ounce) cans chopped green chiles can be substituted for whole chiles, if desired.

Skinny Turkey-Spinach Meat Loaf

Ground beef and ground turkey breast combine with spinach to yield a moist meat loaf.

Prep: 15 minutes • Cook: 50 minutes
Other: 10 minutes

Skinny Turkey-Spinach Meat Loaf

Cooking spray
1 cup finely chopped onion
3 garlic cloves, minced
1 cup dry breadcrumbs
½ cup fat-free milk
1 tablespoon Worcestershire sauce
1 teaspoon salt
½ teaspoon freshly ground black pepper
4 large egg whites
1½ pounds ground turkey breast
½ pound extralean ground beef
2 (10-ounce) packages frozen leaf spinach, thawed, drained, and squeezed dry
½ cup ketchup

1. Preheat oven to 350°.
2. Heat a large nonstick skillet over medium-high heat. Coat pan with cooking spray. Add onion, and sauté 4 minutes. Add garlic, and sauté 30 seconds. Remove from heat. Combine onion mixture, breadcrumbs, and next 8 ingredients; stir well.
3. Shape meat mixture into a 12 x 5–inch loaf on a broiler pan coated with cooking spray. Brush ketchup over top of loaf. Bake at 350° for 45 minutes or until a thermometer registers 160°; let stand 10 minutes before slicing. Yield: 8 servings (serving size: 1 slice).

CALORIES 292 (30% from fat); FAT 9.6g (sat 2.9g, mono 3.7g, poly 1.8g); PROTEIN 31g; CARB 20.2g; FIBER 3.1g; CHOL 66mg; IRON 4.2mg; SODIUM 765mg; CALC 154mg

Collard Greens with Lima Beans and Smoked Turkey

Make this one-dish meal up to three days ahead and refrigerate. Enjoy it with a piece of corn bread so you can sop up the juice.

Prep: 20 minutes
Cook: 2 hours, 53 minutes

1½ cups dried baby lima beans
1 tablespoon olive oil
2 cups vertically sliced red onion
3 cups fat-free, less-sodium chicken broth
1 cup diced smoked turkey breast (about 6 ounces)
½ teaspoon dried thyme
¼ teaspoon crushed red pepper
3 garlic cloves, minced
1 bay leaf
8 cups sliced collard greens (about ½ pound)
2 tablespoons red wine vinegar
1 (14.5-ounce) can diced tomatoes, undrained
¼ teaspoon salt
¼ teaspoon black pepper
Thyme sprigs (optional)

1. Sort and wash beans; place in an ovenproof Dutch oven. Cover with water to 2 inches above beans; bring to a boil, and cook 20 minutes. Remove from heat; drain.
2. Preheat oven to 375°.
3. Heat oil in pan over medium-low heat. Add onion; sauté 10 minutes. Add beans, broth, and next 5 ingredients; bring to a boil. Cover and bake at 375° for 1 hour and 15 minutes. Stir in sliced collards, vinegar, and tomatoes. Cover and bake an additional 1 hour or until beans are tender, stirring occasionally. Stir in salt and pepper. Discard bay leaf. Garnish with thyme sprigs, if desired. Yield: 7 servings (serving size: 1 cup).

CALORIES 230 (13% from fat); FAT 3.3g (sat 0.7g, mono 1.7g, poly 0.7g); PROTEIN 17.4g; CARB 34.5g; FIBER 18.3g; CHOL 14mg; IRON 3.5mg; SODIUM 604mg; CALC 216mg

Test Kitchen Tip: Because most corn bread recipes have baking temperatures higher than 375°, bake the corn bread while the beans are cooking on the stovetop. Keep it warm until time to serve. (See page 76 for corn bread recipes.)

Turkey Jambalaya

Andouille sausage adds a kick to this turkey variation on the Cajun classic
from Louisiana. The rice and shredded turkey absorb a mixture of tomatoes
and spices for a high-flavor transformation for leftover turkey.

Prep: 13 minutes • Cook: 32 minutes

1 tablespoon olive oil
1½ cups chopped onion
1 teaspoon bottled minced garlic
1 cup chopped green bell pepper
1 cup chopped red bell pepper
2½ teaspoons paprika
½ teaspoon salt
½ teaspoon dried oregano
½ teaspoon ground red pepper
½ teaspoon black pepper
1 cup uncooked long-grain rice
2 cups fat-free, less-sodium chicken broth
1 (14.5-ounce) can diced tomatoes, undrained
2 cups shredded cooked turkey
6 ounces andouille sausage, chopped
2 tablespoons sliced green onions

1. Heat oil in a large Dutch oven over medium-high heat. Add chopped onion and garlic; sauté 6 minutes or until lightly browned. Stir in bell peppers and next 5 ingredients; sauté 1 minute. Add rice; sauté 1 minute. Stir in broth and tomatoes; bring to a boil. Cover, reduce heat, and simmer 15 minutes. Add turkey and sausage; cover and cook 5 minutes. Sprinkle with green onions. Yield: 8 servings (serving size: 1 cup).

CALORIES 249 (27% from fat); FAT 7.6g (sat 2.4g, mono 3.4g, poly 1.3g); PROTEIN 17.3g; CARB 27.4g; FIBER 2.7g; CHOL 42mg; IRON 2.7mg; SODIUM 523mg; CALC 37mg

Smokey Turkey Almond Mole

A mole is a rich, dark, reddish brown sauce usually served with poultry. There are many versions of this Mexican sauce, but it's generally a smooth blend of cooked onion, garlic, and several varieties of chiles. Instead of bittersweet chocolate that's usually added to a mole, we substituted ground almonds. If you like your mole really hot, use a whole chipotle chile.

Prep: 20 minutes • Cook: 25 minutes

½ cup roasted almonds
½ teaspoon canola oil
2 dried Anaheim chiles, stemmed, seeded, and chopped
1 cup chopped onion
1 garlic clove, crushed
1 (7-ounce) can chipotle chiles in adobo sauce
1½ cups fire-roasted crushed tomatoes (such as Muir Glen)
1 tablespoon sugar
½ teaspoon ground cumin
¼ teaspoon salt
⅛ teaspoon ground cloves
2 (6-inch) corn tortillas, torn into small pieces
1 (14-ounce) can vegetable broth
1 tablespoon white wine vinegar
3 cups chopped cooked turkey breast
Cilantro sprigs (optional)

1. Place roasted almonds in a food processor; process until smooth (about 2½ minutes), scraping sides of bowl once. Set almonds aside.
2. Heat oil in a large nonstick skillet over medium-high heat. Add Anaheim chiles; sauté 1 minute or until softened. Add onion and garlic; sauté 4 minutes or until onion is lightly browned.

3. Remove 1 chipotle chile from can, and cut chile in half. Add 1 chile half to onion mixture. Reserve remaining chile half, chiles, and adobo sauce for another use. Add tomatoes and next 6 ingredients to onion mixture; bring to a boil. Reduce heat; simmer 15 minutes, stirring occasionally.
4. Spoon mixture into food processor; process until smooth. Return mixture to pan; stir in almond butter and vinegar. Cook 1 minute. Stir in turkey. Garnish with cilantro, if desired. Yield: 4 servings (serving size: 1 cup).

CALORIES 366 (30% from fat); FAT 12.1g (sat 1.1g, mono 6.4g, poly 3.1g); PROTEIN 40.7g; CARB 25.9g; FIBER 6.2g; CHOL 94mg; IRON 4.2mg; SODIUM 737mg; CALC 117mg

Test Kitchen Tip: This recipe freezes well, so make a double batch, and save half for later.

menu
serves 4

Smoked Turkey Almond Mole

Green rice*

Shredded lettuce salad

*Bring 2 cups fat-free, less-sodium chicken broth to a boil in a medium saucepan; stir in 1 cup long-grain white rice. Cover and cook 20 minutes or until liquid is absorbed and rice is tender. Stir in 2 tablespoons butter and ½ teaspoon salt. Combine ¾ cup chopped fresh cilantro, ¾ cup sliced green onions, and 2 tablespoons fresh lime juice. Add to rice; stir well.

Turkey Scaloppine with Porcini and Marsala

Scaloppine is a very lean, thin cut and will dry out if cooked over high heat. Brown the turkey over medium heat to keep it juicy. The cutlets are browned first and added back at the end to finish cooking. Serve with mashed potatoes, rice, or pasta.

Prep: 14 minutes • Cook: 24 minutes
Other: 20 minutes

1 cup fat-free, less-sodium chicken broth
⅓ cup dry Marsala
1 ounce dried porcini mushrooms
1 tablespoon olive oil, divided
4 (½-inch-thick) turkey breast cutlets (about 1½ pounds)
½ teaspoon salt
¼ teaspoon freshly ground black pepper
3 cups sliced cremini mushrooms (about 8 ounces)
2 tablespoons finely chopped shallots
1 tablespoon all-purpose flour

1. Bring first 3 ingredients to a boil in a small saucepan. Cover; remove from heat. Let stand 20 minutes or until mushrooms are tender. Drain mushrooms in a fine sieve over a bowl, reserving soaking liquid. Coarsely chop porcini mushrooms.
2. Heat 1 teaspoon oil in a nonstick skillet over medium heat. Sprinkle turkey with salt and pepper. Add turkey to pan; cook 2 minutes on each side or just until browned. Remove turkey from pan.
3. Heat 2 teaspoons olive oil in pan over medium-high heat. Add cremini mushrooms; sauté 5 minutes. Add porcini mushrooms and shallots, and sauté 2 minutes. Sprinkle with flour, stirring to coat. Stir in reserved soaking liquid; bring to a boil. Return turkey to pan. Reduce heat to

medium-low. Cover and cook 5 minutes or until turkey is done and sauce is slightly thick. Yield: 4 servings (serving size: 1 turkey cutlet and about ¼ cup sauce).

CALORIES 263 (15% from fat); FAT 4.5g (sat 0.5g, mono 2.6g, poly 0.5g); PROTEIN 46.7g; CARB 8.8g; FIBER 1.6g; CHOL 68mg; IRON 4.1mg; SODIUM 592mg; CALC 16mg

Jerk Turkey Cutlets with Cranberry-Habanero Salsa

Here's a quicker, spicy alternative to the Thanksgiving bird that's ideal for a small, four-person gathering. Don't let the ingredient list intimidate you—many of the items are already in your pantry.

Prep: 30 minutes • Cook: 9 minutes
Other: 4 hours

Marinade:
- ½ cup (2-inch) sliced green onions
- 2 tablespoons ground allspice
- 2 tablespoons fresh thyme
- 2 tablespoons fresh lime juice
- 2 tablespoons canola oil
- 1 tablespoon soy sauce
- 1 tablespoon honey
- 1½ teaspoons grated peeled fresh ginger
- 1½ teaspoons black pepper
- ¾ teaspoon salt
- ¾ teaspoon Worcestershire sauce
- ½ teaspoon ground nutmeg
- ½ teaspoon ground cinnamon
- ½ teaspoon hot pepper sauce
- ¼ teaspoon ground cloves
- 2 garlic cloves, minced
- 1 habanero pepper, seeded and chopped (optional)

Turkey:
- 12 (3-ounce) turkey cutlets
- 1½ teaspoons Jamaican jerk seasoning
- 1 tablespoon canola oil
- Cranberry-Habanero Salsa (page 456)

1. To prepare marinade, place first 16 ingredients and habanero pepper, if desired, in a blender or food processor, and process until mixture forms a paste; divide mixture in half, reserving ¼ cup for another use.

2. To prepare turkey, combine ¼ cup marinade, turkey cutlets, and jerk seasoning in a large zip-top plastic bag; seal, and toss well to coat. Marinate in refrigerator 4 hours or overnight, turning bag occasionally.

3. Remove cutlets from bag, and discard marinade. Heat 1 teaspoon oil in a non-stick skillet over medium-high heat. Add 4 cutlets, and sauté 1 minute on each side or until done. Repeat procedure with remaining oil and cutlets. Serve with Cranberry-Habanero Salsa. Yield: 4 servings (serving size: 3 cutlets and ¼ cup salsa).

(Totals include Cranberry-Habanero Salsa) CALORIES 431 (8% from fat); FAT 3.8g (sat 0.8g, mono 1.4g, poly 1.1g); PROTEIN 77.2g; CARB 18.3g; FIBER 2.7g; CHOL 212mg; IRON 4.3mg; SODIUM 512mg; CALC 53mg

Turkey Breast with Spinach-Feta Stuffing

Don't pound the turkey breast meat too hard; it's delicate and can tear. After spreading the spinach mixture and rolling the turkey, secure it with twine.

Prep: 35 minutes • Cook: 1 hour, 1 minute

- 4 tablespoons water, divided
- 1 (6-ounce) package prewashed baby spinach
- 1 tablespoon olive oil, divided
- ¼ cup finely chopped shallots, divided
- 1 garlic clove, minced
- ½ cup (2 ounces) crumbled feta cheese
- 1 tablespoon dry breadcrumbs
- ½ teaspoon dried oregano
- ¾ teaspoon salt, divided
- ⅛ teaspoon freshly ground black pepper
- 1 large egg white, lightly beaten
- 1 (1¾-pound) boneless turkey breast half
- ¼ teaspoon freshly ground black pepper
- ½ cup dry white wine
- ¾ cup fat-free, less-sodium chicken broth
- 1½ teaspoons cornstarch
- 1 tablespoon butter

1. Heat a large saucepan over medium-high heat. Add 1 tablespoon water and spinach; cover and cook 5 minutes or until spinach wilts, stirring occasionally. Place spinach mixture in a colander, pressing until barely moist.

2. Heat 1 teaspoon oil in a small saucepan over medium-high heat. Add 2 tablespoons chopped shallots, 2 tablespoons water, and garlic; cover and cook 3 minutes or until liquid evaporates. Spoon shallot mixture into a medium bowl. Add spinach, feta, breadcrumbs, oregano, ¼ teaspoon salt, ⅛ teaspoon pepper, and egg white.

3. Cut horizontally through center of turkey breast, cutting to, but not through, other side using a sharp knife; open flat as you would a book. Place breast between two sheets of plastic wrap; pound to an even ½-inch thickness using a meat mallet or rolling pin. Discard plastic wrap. Spread spinach mixture over turkey, leaving a 1-inch border. Roll up breast, jelly-roll fashion, starting with one short side. Secure at 2-inch intervals with twine. Rub ½ teaspoon salt and ¼ teaspoon pepper over turkey.

4. Preheat oven to 325°.

5. Heat 2 teaspoons oil in a large Dutch oven over medium-high heat. Add turkey, and cook 5 minutes, browning on all sides. Remove turkey from pan. Add 2 tablespoons shallots to pan, and sauté 30 seconds. Stir in wine, scraping pan to loosen browned bits. Add turkey and broth to pan; bring to a boil. Cover and bake at 325° for 40 minutes or until a thermometer inserted in thickest portion of turkey registers 170°. Remove turkey from pan, and keep warm.

6. Place pan on stovetop over high heat. Combine cornstarch and 1 tablespoon water, stirring with a whisk. Add cornstarch mixture to pan; bring to a boil. Cook 1 minute or until slightly thick, stirring constantly. Remove from heat. Add butter, stirring with a whisk. Remove twine from turkey. Cut turkey into slices. Serve sauce with turkey. Yield: 6 servings (serving size: 1 turkey slice and 2 tablespoons sauce).

CALORIES 242 (29% from fat); FAT 7.7g (sat 3.6g, mono 2.9g, poly 0.6g); PROTEIN 35.3g; CARB 6.8g; FIBER 1.5g; CHOL 103mg; IRON 2.9mg; SODIUM 634mg; CALC 105mg

how to stuff a turkey breast

1. Slice through the thickest part of the breast, leaving it attached at one side.

2. When spreading the filling over the flattened breast, leave a 1-inch border so the filling doesn't fall out.

3. Secure the breast with twine to hold it together.

Roast Turkey with Sausage Gravy

Salting the turkey and refrigerating it 24 hours lets the seasoning spread throughout the meat and keeps moisture in. You get the benefits of brining, but it takes up less space in the refrigerator.

Prep: 30 minutes • Cook: 4 hours
Other: 24 hours, 40 minutes

- 1 (12-pound) fresh or frozen turkey, thawed
- 4½ teaspoons salt, divided
- 2 cups chopped onion
- 1 cup chopped celery
- 8 rosemary sprigs
- 12 thyme sprigs
- 12 sage sprigs
- ¾ teaspoon pepper, divided
- Cooking spray
- 5 cups fat-free, less-sodium chicken broth, divided
- 2 (3.5-ounce) links sweet Italian turkey sausage, casings removed
- ⅓ cup all-purpose flour
- 2 tablespoons cornstarch
- 1 tablespoon water

1. Remove giblets, neck, and heart from turkey, and reserve for Turkey Stock (recipe on page 472). Rinse turkey with cold water; pat dry. Trim excess fat. Sprinkle 4 teaspoons salt over turkey and in body cavity; refrigerate, uncovered, 24 hours.

2. Preheat oven to 325°.

3. Rinse turkey with cold water; pat dry. Stuff body cavity with onion, celery, herbs, and ¼ teaspoon pepper. Lift wing tips up and over back; tuck under turkey. Tie legs together with twine. Place turkey, breast side up, on a rack in a roasting pan coated with cooking spray. Insert a meat thermometer into meaty part of thigh, making sure not to touch bone. Sprinkle turkey with ½ teaspoon salt and ½ teaspoon pepper. Cover breast with foil. Bake at 325° for 2 hours, basting turkey with ⅓ cup broth every 30 minutes. Remove foil; bake an additional 1 hour and 45 minutes or until thermometer registers 180°, basting turkey with remaining ⅔ cup broth every 30 minutes. Remove turkey from oven. Place on a platter, reserving pan drippings. Cover turkey loosely with foil, and let stand 30 minutes before carving. Discard skin.

4. Cook sausage in a large nonstick skillet over medium-high heat until browned, stirring to crumble. Drain and set aside.

5. Place a zip-top plastic bag in a 2-cup measure. Pour reserved drippings into bag; let stand 10 minutes (fat will rise to the top). Seal bag, and snip off 1 bottom corner. Drain into a medium saucepan; stop before fat reaches opening. Reserve 1 tablespoon fat; discard remaining fat. Cook reserved fat and flour in roasting pan over medium heat 1 minute; stir constantly with a whisk. Add drippings, 3 cups broth, and sausage. Combine cornstarch and water; add to pan. Bring to a boil. Cook 2 minutes or until thick; stir constantly. Yield: 12 servings (serving size: 6 ounces turkey and ⅓ cup gravy).

CALORIES 353 (28% from fat); FAT 11.1g (sat 3.6g, mono 2.8g, poly 3.1g); PROTEIN 54.5g; CARB 4.8g; FIBER 0.2g; CHOL 144mg; IRON 3.2mg; SODIUM 603mg; CALC 45mg

Lemon-Sage Turkey with Wild-Mushroom Gravy

Let this herbed turkey take center stage at your Thanksgiving feast. After you've roasted the bird, reserve the drippings from the bottom of the pan to use for making the memorably rich mushroom gravy.

Prep: 40 minutes • Cook: 3 hours, 47 minutes
Other: 25 minutes

    3 tablespoons grated lemon rind
    ¼ cup fresh lemon juice
    3 tablespoons dried thyme
    2 tablespoons dried rubbed sage
    1 tablespoon cracked black pepper
    1 teaspoon salt
    1 (12-pound) fresh or frozen turkey,
       thawed
    1 (32-ounce) container fat-free,
       less-sodium chicken broth, divided
    Cooking spray
    Wild-Mushroom Gravy

1. Combine first 6 ingredients; set aside.
2. Remove and discard giblets from turkey, reserving neck for gravy. Rinse turkey with cold water; pat dry. Trim excess fat. Starting at neck cavity, loosen skin from breast and drumsticks by inserting fingers, gently pushing between skin and meat. Lift wing tips up and over back; tuck under turkey. Rub spice mixture under loosened skin and rub into body cavity.
3. Preheat oven to 350°.
4. Pour 2 cups broth into a shallow roasting pan. Place turkey, breast side up, on a rack coated with cooking spray. Place rack in roasting pan. Insert meat thermometer into meaty part of thigh, making sure not to touch bone. Bake at 350° for 1½ hours. Carefully pour remaining 2 cups broth into pan. Bake an additional 1½ hours or until thermometer registers 180°. Remove

turkey from oven; reserve pan drippings to make gravy. Cover turkey loosely with foil; let stand 15 to 20 minutes. Discard skin. Serve with Wild-Mushroom Gravy. Yield: 12 servings (serving size: 6 ounces turkey and ¼ cup gravy).

(Totals include Wild-Mushroom Gravy) CALORIES 308 (20% from fat); FAT 6.7g (sat 2.1g, mono 1.9g, poly 1.8g); PROTEIN 53.4g; CARB 5.8g; FIBER 0.7g; CHOL 147mg; IRON 4.9mg; SODIUM 460mg; CALC 62mg

Wild-Mushroom Gravy

    Pan drippings
    2 cups water
    ¾ cup thinly sliced shallots
    ½ cup thinly sliced carrot
    1 turkey neck
    1 cup sliced button mushrooms
    1 cup thinly sliced shiitake mushroom
       caps (about 3½ ounces)
    5 tablespoons all-purpose flour
    1 teaspoon red currant jelly
    ¼ teaspoon pepper

1. Place a large zip-top plastic bag inside a 4-cup measure. Pour drippings from turkey roasting pan into bag; let stand 10 minutes (fat will rise to top). Seal bag; carefully snip off 1 bottom corner of bag. Drain drippings to measure 2 cups, stopping before fat layer reaches opening. Reserve 2 tablespoons fat in bag; set aside.
2. Combine water, shallots, carrot, and turkey neck in a medium saucepan; bring to a boil. Cover, reduce heat, and simmer 30 minutes. Strain cooking liquid though a sieve over a bowl, reserving ¾ cup cooking liquid. Discard solids, reserving turkey neck. Remove meat from neck, and chop. Add meat and reserved ¾ cup cooking liquid to defatted 2 cups drippings in 4-cup measure.
3. Heat reserved 2 tablespoons fat in a saucepan over medium heat. Add mushrooms; sauté 2 minutes. Add flour; cook 1 minute. Gradually add cooking liquid mixture; cook 10 minutes or until slightly thick, stirring occasionally. Remove from heat; stir in jelly and pepper. Yield: 3 cups (serving size: ¼ cup).

CALORIES 43 (52% from fat); FAT 2.5g (sat 0.7g, mono 1g, poly 0.6g); PROTEIN 1.6g; CARB 3.5g; FIBER 0.3g; CHOL 5mg; IRON 0.4mg; SODIUM 4mg; CALC 3mg

Honey and Thyme-Brined Turkey Breast

Briefly boiling the thyme and black pepper extracts their flavors that infuse the brine. If the turkey starts to brown too fast, shield it with aluminum foil.

Prep: 20 minutes • Cook: 1 hour, 3 minutes Other: 24 hours, 15 minutes

- 7 cups water, divided
- 3 tablespoons freshly ground black pepper, divided
- 6 thyme sprigs
- ½ cup kosher salt
- ½ cup honey
- ¼ cup packed brown sugar
- 2 cups ice cubes
- 1 (6-pound) whole bone-in turkey breast, skinned
- 2 tablespoons olive oil
- 1 tablespoon chopped fresh thyme
- Cooking spray
- Thyme sprigs (optional)

1. Combine 1 cup water, 2 tablespoons pepper, and 6 thyme sprigs in a small saucepan. Bring to a boil, and remove from heat. Pour into a large bowl; cool to room temperature. Add 6 cups water, salt, honey, and sugar, stirring until salt and sugar dissolve. Pour salt mixture into a 2-gallon zip-top plastic bag. Add ice and turkey; seal. Refrigerate 24 hours, turning bag occasionally. Remove turkey from bag; discard brine. Pat turkey dry with paper towels.

2. Rub turkey with oil. Combine 1 tablespoon pepper and chopped thyme; rub over turkey.

3. Preheat oven to 400°.

4. Place turkey on a roasting pan coated with cooking spray. Bake at 400° for 1 hour or until thermometer inserted into thickest portion of breast registers 180°. Place turkey on a platter. Cover with foil, and let stand 15 minutes. Garnish with thyme sprigs, if desired. Yield: 12 servings (serving size: about 4 ounces).

CALORIES 207 (26% from fat); FAT 5.9g (sat 1.5g, mono 2.3g, poly 1.2g); PROTEIN 34g; CARB 2.5g; FIBER 0.2g; CHOL 78mg; IRON 1.8mg; SODIUM 359 mg; CALC 29mg

---

menu
serves 12

Spinach and orange salad*

Honey and Thyme-Brined Turkey Breast

Steamed green beans

Potato Gratin with Goat Cheese and Garlic (page 529)

Fruited Port-Cranberry Salad (page 399)

Buttered Sweet Potato Knot Rolls (page 105)

German Chocolate Cheesecake (page 136)

*Combine 5 cups packaged baby spinach, 1 cup drained mandarin oranges in light syrup, and ¼ cup slivered red onion. Combine 2 tablespoons balsamic vinegar, 1 tablespoon honey, 2 teaspoons Dijon mustard, 1 teaspoon olive oil, ⅛ teaspoon salt, and ⅛ teaspoon black pepper, stirring with a whisk. Drizzle vinaigrette over salad; toss gently to coat.

---

brining basics

Keep it cold. All brining should be done at refrigerator temperature—45°F or lower—to limit bacterial growth. In the Honey and Thyme-Brined Turkey Breast recipe, a portion of the brining water is added in the form of ice. This ensures that the brine is a safe temperature from the moment the meat is added to the liquid.

Pass the salt. We like to use Diamond Crystal brand kosher salt because the flakes are larger and lighter than those of table salt or other brands of kosher salt, and easier to dissolve. (If you're using table salt, use half the amount called for in the recipe.) The proportion of salt to water allows the brining process to be slow and controlled. Saltier brines take less time but are much more difficult to control and can begin to pull moisture from the meat.

Make room. Prepare the brine in a large bowl so you have plenty of space to stir the salt (and sugar) so it dissolves completely. Once the salt is dissolved, add any other flavorings, then transfer the brine to a container large enough to allow the meat to be completely submerged. Large zip-top plastic bags work well.

Time it. The size and type of meat determine the brining time. Large pieces, like a turkey, should soak overnight. Stick with the time specified in the recipe so you won't overbrine, which will cause the meat to become too salty or dry.

Brined Maple Turkey with Cream Gravy

Brining makes for a juicier, more flavorful turkey. Kosher salt works well for the brine because it dissolves more easily than table salt. (See page 395.) If you have the time and refrigerator space, the brining procedure is worthwhile. If not, the turkey will still be quite good.

Prep: 50 minutes
Cook: 2 hours, 37 minutes
Other: 24 hours, 20 minutes

Brine:

    8   quarts water
    ¾   cup kosher salt
    ¾   cup maple syrup
    3   tablespoons black peppercorns
    8   garlic cloves, crushed
    1   lemon, thinly sliced

Turkey:

    1   (12-pound) fresh or frozen turkey,
        thawed
    1   cup cola
    ½   cup maple syrup
    2   tablespoons minced fresh thyme
    1   tablespoon dried rubbed sage
    1   tablespoon poultry seasoning
    ½   teaspoon black pepper
    4   garlic cloves, chopped
    2   onions, quartered
        Cooking spray

Cream Gravy:

    1   (14-ounce) can fat-free, less-sodium
        chicken broth
    1   cup whole milk
    2   tablespoons cornstarch
    ¼   teaspoon salt
    ¼   teaspoon black pepper

1. To prepare brine, combine first 6 ingredients in a stockpot; stir until salt dissolves.

2. To prepare turkey, remove and reserve giblets and neck from turkey. Rinse turkey with cold water; pat dry. Trim excess fat. Add turkey to pot, turning to coat. Cover and refrigerate 24 hours, turning occasionally.

3. Preheat oven to 375°.

4. Bring cola and ½ cup syrup to a boil in a small saucepan; cook 1 minute.

5. Combine thyme, sage, seasoning, and ½ teaspoon pepper. Remove turkey from brine; pat dry. Starting at neck cavity, loosen skin from breast and drumsticks by inserting fingers, gently pushing between skin and meat. Rub thyme mixture under loosened skin; sprinkle inside body cavity. Place chopped garlic and onions in body cavity. Tie ends of legs together with twine. Lift wing tips up and over back; tuck under turkey.

6. Place turkey on a broiler pan coated with cooking spray. Insert a meat thermometer into meaty part of a thigh, making sure not to touch bone. Bake at 375° for 45 minutes. Pour cola mixture over turkey; cover with foil. Bake an additional 1 hour and 45 minutes or until thermometer registers 180°. Remove turkey from pan, reserving drippings for gravy. Place turkey on a platter. Cover loosely with foil; let stand 10 minutes. Remove twine. Discard skin.

7. To prepare gravy, while turkey bakes, combine reserved giblet and neck and broth in a saucepan; bring to a boil. Cover, reduce heat, and simmer 45 minutes. Strain mixture through a colander into a bowl, discarding solids.

8. Place a zip-top plastic bag inside a 2-cup glass measure. Pour pan drippings into bag; let stand 10 minutes (fat will rise to top). Seal bag; carefully snip off 1 bottom corner of bag. Drain drippings into broiler pan, stopping before fat layer reaches opening; discard fat. Add broth mixture. Place broiler pan on stovetop over medium heat, scraping pan to loosen browned bits. Combine milk and cornstarch in a small bowl, stirring well with a whisk; add to pan. Bring to a boil; cook 1 minute, stirring constantly.

9. Strain gravy through a sieve into a bowl; discard solids. Stir in ¼ teaspoon salt and ¼ teaspoon pepper. Yield: 12 servings (serving size: 6 ounces turkey and about ¼ cup gravy).

CALORIES 375 (25% from fat); FAT 10.5g (sat 3.6g, mono 2.5g, poly 2.8g); PROTEIN 51.7g; CARB 15.7g; FIBER 0.2g; CHOL 140mg; IRON 3.6mg; SODIUM 809mg; CALC 91mg

WINE NOTE: The sweet and savory flavors of this turkey call for a soft, rich zinfandel with a lot of berry flavors.

thawing a turkey You can thaw a turkey safely a number of ways.

- The best method is to set the bird in a shallow pan in the refrigerator for 24 hours per 5 pounds of turkey. This process will take several days, so plan accordingly and make room in the refrigerator.

- If you lack refrigerator space, submerge the unwrapped turkey in a sink filled with cold water for about an hour per pound, changing the water every 30 minutes.

- In any case, the turkey is fully thawed when a meat thermometer inserted into a thick part of the turkey registers 40°. Store thawed turkey in the refrigerator until ready to cook.

salads & dressings

Farm Stand Potato
Salad, page 412

Fruit Salads Featuring the natural sweetness of fresh fruit, some of these salads could stand in for dessert.

Poppy Seed Fruit Salad

We stretched a high-calorie poppy seed dressing a bit—and added flavor—by stirring in fruit-flavored yogurt.

Prep: 13 minutes

- 3 tablespoons orange-mango fat-free yogurt (such as Dannon)
- 3 tablespoons poppy seed salad dressing
- 2 cups halved strawberries
- 2 cups cubed pineapple
- 1 cup honeydew melon balls
- 1 cup cantaloupe balls
- 12 Boston lettuce leaves

1. Combine yogurt and salad dressing; stir well with a whisk. Combine strawberries, pineapple, and melon balls in a large bowl, tossing gently. Line 6 plates with lettuce leaves; top with fruit mixture. Drizzle each salad with dressing. Serve immediately. Yield: 6 servings (serving size: 2 lettuce leaves, 1 cup fruit mixture, and 1 tablespoon dressing).

CALORIES 106 (31% from fat); FAT 3.6g (sat 0.4g, mono 0.1g, poly 0.3g); PROTEIN 1.5g; CARB 18.5g; FIBER 3g; CHOL 3mg; IRON 1mg; SODIUM 62mg; CALC 25mg

Spicy-Sweet Melon Salad

The longer this salad sits, the spicier it gets.

Prep: 8 minutes • Cook: 2 minutes
Other: 4 hours

- ½ cup sugar
- ½ cup water
- ½ small jalapeño pepper, thinly sliced
- 2 cups cubed peeled honeydew melon
- 2 cups cubed peeled cantaloupe

1. Combine sugar and water in a small saucepan; bring to a boil, stirring until sugar dissolves. Remove from heat; add pepper. Chill.

2. Combine sugar mixture, honeydew, and cantaloupe in a large bowl. Cover and chill 4 hours or overnight. Serve with a slotted spoon. Yield: 6 servings (serving size: ⅔ cup).

CALORIES 104 (2% from fat); FAT 0.2g (sat 0.1g, mono 0g, poly 0.1g); PROTEIN 0.8g; CARB 26.5g; FIBER 0.8g; CHOL 0mg; IRON 0.2mg; SODIUM 11mg; CALC 10mg

Strawberry-Kiwi Salad with Basil

The creamy sauce on this salad is irresistible. If you want to turn the salad into dessert, serve it with angel-food cake "dunkers."

Prep: 9 minutes • Other: 1 hour

- ¼ cup half-and-half
- 2 tablespoons white balsamic vinegar
- 1 tablespoon sugar
- ¼ teaspoon salt
- 3 peeled kiwifruit, each cut into 6 wedges
- 2 cups quartered strawberries
- 2 tablespoons finely chopped fresh basil

1. Combine first 4 ingredients in a bowl. Add kiwifruit and strawberries; toss well. Cover and chill 1 hour. Stir in basil just before serving. Yield: 4 servings (serving size: ¾ cup).

CALORIES 90 (23% from fat); FAT 2.3g (sat 1.1g, mono 0.6g, poly 0.4g); PROTEIN 1.6g; CARB 17.8g; FIBER 3.8g; CHOL 6mg; IRON 0.7mg; SODIUM 157mg; CALC 46mg

Poppy Seed Fruit Salad

Three Kings Salad

The colorful trio of beets, oranges, and red onion represents the three wise men from the nativity story. You can section the oranges, cut the beets and onions, and make the vinaigrette ahead (store them in separate containers so the colors don't bleed). Assemble up to one hour before serving.

Prep: 17 minutes

- 4   navel oranges
- 1   (15-ounce) can whole beets, drained
- 3   tablespoons balsamic vinegar
- 2   tablespoons walnut oil or olive oil
- ½   teaspoon salt
- ½   teaspoon pepper
- ¾   cup slivered red onion

1. Peel and section oranges over a bowl; squeeze membranes to extract juice. Set sections aside; reserve 1½ tablespoons juice. Discard membranes.
2. Cut beets into wedges. Set aside. Combine reserved 1½ tablespoons juice, vinegar, oil, salt, and pepper in a medium bowl; stir well with a whisk.
3. Place beet wedges and orange sections on each of 6 salad plates. Top each serving with onion. Drizzle with vinaigrette. Yield: 6 servings (serving size: ⅙ of oranges and beets, 2 tablespoons onion, and 1 tablespoon vinaigrette).

CALORIES 116 (37% from fat); FAT 4.8g (sat 0.4g, mono 3.2g, poly 0.9g); PROTEIN 1.7g; CARB 18.6g; FIBER 4.8g; CHOL 0mg; IRON 0.7mg; SODIUM 363mg; CALC 53mg

Sparkling White-Sangría Salad

To many families, it isn't a holiday dinner without a gelatin salad. This rendition uses riesling, but for a nonalcoholic version, substitute sparkling white grape juice. Make up to a day ahead and refrigerate. To make the salad easier to unmold, dip the covered mold into a bowl of warm water for five seconds.

Prep: 11 minutes • Cook: 3 minutes
Other: 4 hours, 25 minutes

- 2   envelopes unflavored gelatin
- 1½ cups sweet riesling or other sweet white wine, divided
- 1½ cups white grape juice
- ¼   cup sugar
- 1½ cups orange sections
- 1   cup seedless green grapes, halved
- ¾   cup fresh raspberries
- Cooking spray

1. Sprinkle gelatin over ½ cup wine, and let stand 5 minutes.
2. Combine 1 cup wine, juice, and sugar in a medium saucepan; bring to a boil over medium-high heat. Remove from heat; add gelatin mixture, stirring until gelatin dissolves. Place pan in a large ice-filled bowl; let stand 20 minutes or until thick but not set, stirring occasionally. Whisk gelatin mixture to form small bubbles; fold in orange sections, grapes, and raspberries. Spoon gelatin mixture into a 5-cup decorative mold coated with cooking spray. Cover and chill at least 4 hours. To unmold, place a plate upside down on top of mold; invert mold onto plate. Yield: 12 servings (serving size: 1 slice).

CALORIES 82 (2% from fat); FAT 0.2g (sat 0.1g, mono 0g, poly 0.1g); PROTEIN 1.5g; CARB 14.7g; FIBER 1.2g; CHOL 0mg; IRON 0.3mg; SODIUM 6mg; CALC 20mg

Fruited Port-Cranberry Salad

Not your ordinary congealed salad, this one gets its deep red color from the cranberry sauce and raspberries and its rich sweetness from the port.

Prep: 13 minutes
Other: 4 hours, 30 minutes

- 1   envelope unflavored gelatin
- ½   cup port or other sweet red wine
- 2   (3-ounce) packages cranberry-flavored gelatin
- ¼   teaspoon ground ginger
- ¼   teaspoon ground allspice
- 2   cups boiling water
- 1   (16-ounce) can whole-berry cranberry sauce
- ½   cup ice water
- 1½ cups finely chopped Granny Smith apple (about 1 large apple)
- 1   (14-ounce) package frozen unsweetened raspberries, thawed
- 1   (8¼-ounce) can crushed pineapple in juice, drained

1. Sprinkle unflavored gelatin over port; set aside. Combine cranberry gelatin, ginger, and allspice in a large bowl; stir well. Stir in boiling water and port mixture. Add cranberry sauce and ice water; stir well. Chill 30 minutes.
2. Combine apple, raspberries, and pineapple; stir into gelatin mixture. Pour into an 8-cup gelatin mold; chill 4 hours or until set. To unmold, dip mold into hot water 5 seconds; invert onto a serving platter. Yield: 12 servings (serving size: 1 slice).

CALORIES 178 (1% from fat); FAT 0.2g (sat 0g, mono 0g, poly 0.1g); PROTEIN 2.3g; CARB 41.3g; FIBER 2g; CHOL 0mg; IRON 0.4mg; SODIUM 63mg; CALC 10mg

Green salads

There's no need to rely on the same ol' mound of lettuce. Explore the possibilities of arugula, bibb, gourmet greens, romaine, and spinach.

Mesclun and Romaine Salad with Warm Parmesan Toasts

Dress up a typical salad by using more refined greens, adding fresh herbs, and tossing it with high-quality olive oil and vinegar. Top the salad with warm slices of cheese-topped baguette. You can substitute chopped red onions for the shallots.

Prep: 14 minutes • Cook: 2 minutes • Other: 5 minutes

Warm Parmesan Toasts:

8   (½-ounce) slices French bread baguette
¼   cup (1 ounce) grated fresh Parmesan cheese

Vinaigrette:

2   tablespoons minced shallots
1   tablespoon sherry vinegar
2   teaspoons extravirgin olive oil
¼   teaspoon salt
¼   teaspoon Dijon mustard
⅛   teaspoon freshly ground black pepper

Salad:

3   cups gourmet salad greens
3   cups torn romaine lettuce
¼   cup thinly vertically sliced red onion
3   tablespoons chopped fresh parsley
3   tablespoons chopped fresh basil
1   pint cherry tomatoes, halved

1. Preheat broiler.

2. To prepare toasts, arrange bread slices on a baking sheet. Broil 1 minute or until lightly browned. Turn bread over; sprinkle each slice with 1½ teaspoons cheese. Broil 1 minute or until cheese begins to melt.

3. To prepare vinaigrette, combine shallots and vinegar; let stand 5 minutes. Add oil, salt, mustard, and pepper; stir well with a whisk.

4. To prepare salad, place salad greens and remaining ingredients in a large bowl; toss gently to combine. Drizzle vinaigrette over salad, and toss gently to coat. Serve with toasts. Yield: 4 servings (serving size: 2 cups salad and 2 toasts).

CALORIES 165 (30% from fat); FAT 5.5g (sat 1.7g, mono 2.6g, poly 0.7g); PROTEIN 7.4g; CARB 23; FIBER 3.6g; CHOL 4.8mg; IRON 2.5mg; SODIUM 465mg; CALC 159mg

Romaine Lettuce with Red Pepper and Olives

The Mediterranean ingredients in this salad pair well with pasta and marinara sauce.

Prep: 9 minutes

- 4 cups (1-inch) chopped romaine lettuce
- ⅓ cup (¼-inch) diced red bell pepper
- ¼ cup (¼-inch) diced red onion
- ¼ cup (1 ounce) crumbled feta cheese
- 2 tablespoons coarsely chopped pitted kalamata olives
- ¼ teaspoon dried oregano
- ¼ cup fat-free Italian dressing

1. Combine first 6 ingredients in a large bowl. Add dressing; toss well. Yield: 4 servings (serving size: 1 cup).

CALORIES 55 (46% from fat); FAT 2.8g (sat 1.3g, mono 1.1g, poly 0.2g); PROTEIN 2.4g; CARB 5.4g; FIBER 1.6g; CHOL 7mg; IRON 0.9mg; SODIUM 360mg; CALC 68mg

Simple Green Salad with Vinaigrette

Toss any lettuce or field greens you have on hand with this easy dressing.

Prep: 8 minutes • Other: 5 minutes

- 2 tablespoons minced red onion
- 1½ tablespoons red wine vinegar
- 2 teaspoons olive oil
- ¼ teaspoon salt
- ¼ teaspoon freshly ground black pepper
- ¼ teaspoon Dijon mustard
- 6 cups torn curly leaf lettuce
- ¼ cup thinly vertically sliced red onion
- 1 pint cherry tomatoes, halved

1. Combine minced onion and vinegar in a small bowl; let stand 5 minutes. Add olive oil, salt, pepper, and Dijon mustard; stir well with a whisk.

2. Place lettuce, sliced onion, and tomatoes in a large bowl; toss gently to combine. Drizzle vinaigrette over salad; toss gently to coat. Yield: 4 servings (serving size: 2 cups).

CALORIES 49 (44% from fat); FAT 2.4g (sat 0.3g, mono 1.7g, poly 0.3g); PROTEIN 1.5g; CARB 7.2g; FIBER 2.7g; CHOL 0mg; IRON 0.3mg; SODIUM 189mg; CALC 46mg

Hearts of Romaine Salad with Creamy Soy Dressing

Silken tofu gives this dressing its smooth texture and is a great substitute for the raw eggs that are often used in Caesar salads. Leftover dressing will keep in the refrigerator up to one week.

Prep: 14 minutes

- 2 tablespoons fresh lemon juice
- 2 tablespoons water
- 1 teaspoon Dijon mustard
- ¼ teaspoon sea salt
- 2 ounces firm silken tofu
- 1 garlic clove, minced
- 2 teaspoons extravirgin olive oil
- 1 tablespoon chopped fresh parsley
- 12 cups torn romaine lettuce (about 2 hearts)
- 3 tablespoons grated fresh Parmesan cheese

1. Place first 6 ingredients in a food processor; process until smooth. With processor on, slowly pour oil through food chute; process until well blended. Pour tofu mixture into a small bowl; stir in parsley.

2. Combine lettuce and tofu mixture in a large bowl; toss to combine. Top with Parmesan cheese. Yield: 8 servings (serving size: 1½ cups salad and 1 teaspoon cheese).

CALORIES 40 (52% from fat); FAT 2.3g (sat 0.7g, mono 1.1g, poly 0.3g); PROTEIN 2.8g; CARB 2.7g; FIBER 1.5g; CHOL 2mg; IRON 1.1mg; SODIUM 139mg; CALC 67mg

Creamy Caesar Salad with Spicy Croutons

Here's our lightened version of a classic Caesar salad. We've omitted the raw egg and added Cajun spice to the croutons.

Prep: 20 minutes • Cook: 16 minutes
Other: 1 hour

- 1 garlic clove, halved
- ½ cup fat-free mayonnaise
- 2 tablespoons red wine vinegar
- 2 teaspoons Dijon mustard
- 2 teaspoons white wine Worcestershire sauce
- 1 teaspoon anchovy paste
- ¼ teaspoon pepper
- 2 teaspoons olive oil
- ¾ teaspoon Cajun seasoning
- 1 garlic clove, minced
- 2 cups (¾-inch) sourdough bread cubes
- 18 cups torn romaine lettuce
- ⅓ cup (1½ ounces) grated fresh Parmesan cheese

1. Drop garlic halves through opening in blender lid with blender on; process until minced. Add mayonnaise and next 5 ingredients; process until well blended. Cover and chill at least 1 hour.

2. Preheat oven to 400°.

3. Combine oil, Cajun seasoning, and minced garlic in a medium microwave-safe bowl. Microwave at HIGH 20 seconds. Add bread cubes; toss gently to coat. Spread bread cubes in a single layer on a baking sheet; bake at 400° for 15 minutes.

4. Place lettuce in a large bowl. Add dressing; toss gently to coat. Sprinkle with cheese, and top with croutons. Yield: 6 servings (serving size: 2 cups).

CALORIES 137 (27% from fat); FAT 4.1g (sat 1.3g, mono 1.6g, poly 0.4g); PROTEIN 7.7g; CARB 18.2g; FIBER 4.1g; CHOL 4mg; IRON 3mg; SODIUM 836mg; CALC 176mg

Bitter Greens with Tarragon Vinaigrette and Pine Nuts

Look for loose bitter greens in the produce section of your supermarket, or create your own mix with watercress, endive, arugula, radicchio, and mesclun. Just about any nut will work nicely.

Prep: 10 minutes

  2 tablespoons white wine vinegar
  2 tablespoons plain fat-free yogurt
  1 tablespoon chopped fresh or
     1 teaspoon dried tarragon
  2 teaspoons Dijon mustard
  2 teaspoons honey
  1 teaspoon olive oil
  ⅛ teaspoon salt
  ⅛ teaspoon pepper
  5 cups mixed bitter greens
  1 tablespoon pine nuts, toasted

1. Combine first 8 ingredients in a small bowl; stir well with a whisk. Place greens and pine nuts in a large bowl, and drizzle with vinaigrette. Yield: 2 servings (serving size: 2 cups).

CALORIES 74 (36% from fat); FAT 3g (sat 0.4g, mono 1g, poly 1.1g); PROTEIN 4g; CARB 9.2g; FIBER 2.2g; CHOL 0mg; IRON 0.8mg; SODIUM 337mg; CALC 136mg

storing greens Store salad greens unwashed in plastic bags. (If you wash them before storing, moisture will collect on the leaves and cause them to wilt or discolor before you're ready to use them.) Tender-leaved lettuces will keep for about four days in the crisper compartment of the refrigerator; firm lettuces such as iceberg and romaine will keep for up to 10 days.

Orange and Arugula Salad

The honey in the vinaigrette balances the salad's citrusy flavors.

Prep: 15 minutes

  3 tablespoons fresh lemon juice
  1 tablespoon olive oil
  ¾ teaspoon honey
  2 garlic cloves, crushed
  6 navel oranges
  3 cups trimmed arugula
  6 tablespoons (1½ ounces) crumbled
     feta cheese

1. Combine first 4 ingredients in a small bowl, stirring with a whisk.
2. Peel oranges, and cut each crosswise into 6 slices. Arrange arugula on plates; arrange orange slices on top of arugula. Sprinkle with feta, and drizzle with dressing. Yield: 6 servings (serving size: ½ cup arugula, 6 orange slices, 1 tablespoon feta, and 1 tablespoon dressing).

CALORIES 118 (34% from fat); FAT 4.4g (sat 1.7g, mono 2.1g, poly 0.3g); PROTEIN 3.1g; CARB 18.8g; FIBER 3.6g; CHOL 8mg; IRON 0.4mg; SODIUM 109mg; CALC 121mg

Fig and Arugula Salad with Parmesan

Sweet figs, sharp cheese, and peppery arugula offer extraordinary flavor.

Prep: 12 minutes • Other: 20 minutes

  2 tablespoons minced shallots
1½ tablespoons balsamic vinegar
  1 tablespoon extravirgin olive oil
  ¼ teaspoon salt
16 fresh figs, each cut in half lengthwise
  6 cups trimmed arugula (about 6 ounces)
  ¼ teaspoon freshly ground black pepper
  ¼ cup (1 ounce) shaved fresh Parmesan cheese

1. Combine first 4 ingredients in a large bowl; stir well with a whisk. Add figs; cover and let stand 20 minutes. Add arugula and pepper; toss well. Top with cheese. Serve immediately. Yield: 4 servings (serving size: 1½ cups).

CALORIES 156 (33% from fat); FAT 5.8g (sat 1.7g, mono 3.1g, poly 0.5g); PROTEIN 4.6g; CARB 25.1g; FIBER 4.9g; CHOL 5mg; IRON 1.1mg; SODIUM 273mg; CALC 194mg

Broccoli, Orange, and Watercress Salad

To get a head start, steam the broccoli ahead; cover and chill. Section the oranges ahead, too.

Prep: 15 minutes • Cook: 5 minutes

Dressing:
  ¼ cup cider vinegar
  2 tablespoons rice vinegar
  1 tablespoon olive oil
  2 teaspoons sugar
  1 teaspoon honey mustard
  ¼ teaspoon salt
  ⅛ teaspoon coarsely ground black pepper
Salad:
  4 cups thinly sliced iceberg lettuce
  3 cups small broccoli florets, steamed
  3 cups trimmed watercress
  2 cups orange sections (about 4 oranges)

1. To prepare dressing, combine first 7 ingredients in a jar. Cover tightly; shake vigorously.
2. To prepare salad, combine lettuce and remaining ingredients in a large bowl. Add dressing; toss well to coat. Yield: 6 servings (serving size: 1½ cups).

CALORIES 88 (28% from fat); FAT 2.8g (sat 0.4g, mono 1.8g, poly 0.5g); PROTEIN 3.7g; CARB 15g; FIBER 4.3g; CHOL 0mg; IRON 1.1mg; SODIUM 130mg; CALC 88mg

Watercress-Bibb Salad with Apples and Blue Cheese

You can prepare the dressing up to three days ahead, refrigerate it in a jar, and shake it well before tossing with the salad.

Prep: 12 minutes • Other: 2 hours

Dressing:

- 1 tablespoon finely chopped shallots
- 3 tablespoons apple juice
- 1 tablespoon cider vinegar
- 2 teaspoons Dijon mustard
- 1 teaspoon canola oil
- ¼ teaspoon salt
- ¼ teaspoon freshly ground black pepper

Salad:

- 7 cups torn Bibb lettuce
- 2½ cups trimmed watercress
- 2 cups thinly sliced Granny Smith apple (about ½ pound)
- ¼ cup (1 ounce) crumbled blue cheese

1. To prepare dressing, combine first 7 ingredients in a jar. Cover tightly; shake vigorously. Refrigerate at least 2 hours.
2. To prepare salad, combine lettuce and remaining ingredients in a bowl. Add dressing; toss well. Yield: 6 servings (serving size: about 1½ cups).

CALORIES 56 (37% from fat); FAT 2.3g (sat 1g, mono 0.8g, poly 0.4g); PROTEIN 2.4g; CARB 7.8g; FIBER 1.5g; CHOL 4mg; IRON 1mg; SODIUM 196mg; CALC 68mg

Test Kitchen Tip: If you can't find watercress, you can substitute arugula.

Beet, Jícama, and Watercress Salad

Ruby red beets, white jícama, emerald watercress, and sunny tangerines make a stunning salad. Since the vinaigrette for the jícama and tangerines needs to stand 30 minutes, prepare it while the beets cool. If you can't find tangerines, use small orange sections instead.

Prep: 30 minutes • Cook: 45 minutes • Other: 30 minutes

- 2½ pounds beets, with tops
- 5 teaspoons white balsamic vinegar, divided
- 1 teaspoon extravirgin olive oil
- ½ teaspoon freshly ground black pepper, divided
- ¼ teaspoon salt, divided
- ⅓ cup thinly sliced red onion
- ¼ cup fresh orange juice
- 2½ cups (½-inch) diced peeled jícama
- ⅓ cup tangerine sections
- 2 cups trimmed watercress

1. Preheat oven to 425°.
2. Leave root and 1 inch stem on beets; scrub with a brush. Wrap each beet in foil. Place on a baking sheet. Bake at 425° for 45 minutes or until tender. Cool. Trim off roots and stems; rub off skin. Cut beets into ½-inch slices. Cut each slice into quarters.

Combine beets, 1 teaspoon vinegar, oil, ¼ teaspoon pepper, and ⅛ teaspoon salt.
3. Combine 4 teaspoons vinegar, ¼ teaspoon pepper, ⅛ teaspoon salt, onion, and juice; let stand 30 minutes. Stir in jícama and tangerine.
4. Arrange watercress on salad plates. Mound beet mixture in center of each serving. Arrange jícama mixture around beets. Serve immediately. Yield: 4 servings (serving size: ½ cup watercress, ¾ cup beet mixture, and ¾ cup jícama mixture).

CALORIES 147 (10% from fat); FAT 1.7g (sat 0.3g, mono 1g, poly 0.3g); PROTEIN 4.4g; CARB 30.9g; FIBER 10.2g; CHOL 0mg; IRON 2.2mg; SODIUM 306mg; CALC 70mg

Test Kitchen Tip: Instead of tossing all the ingredients, arrange the various components so that the beets won't turn the lighter-colored ingredients pink.

guide to salad greens

Arugula: This peppery, pungent, leafy green is often found in mesclun salad mixes, where it behaves like a cross between lettuce and herb.

Curly Endive: This lettucelike salad green has an off-white, compact center and loose, lacy, green-rimmed outer leaves that curl at the tips. It has a prickly texture and a slightly bitter taste.

Escarole: Escarole has broad bright green leaves that grow in loose heads. It's a variety of endive but isn't as bitter as Belgian endive or chicory.

Mesclun: This term applies to a mixture of salad greens such as arugula, dandelion, frisée, oak leaf, radicchio, and sorrel. It's often packaged as "gourmet salad greens."

Radicchio: This bitter-flavored member of the chicory family has burgundy-red leaves with white ribs. Most often used in salads, radicchio can also be grilled or roasted. Escarole, another member of the chicory family, is a good substitute.

Spinach: Spinach has dark green leaves that may be curled or smooth, depending on the variety. Choose leaves that are crisp and dark green with a fresh fragrance. Spinach is usually very gritty and must be thoroughly washed.

Watercress: This member of the mustard family has small, crisp, dark leaves with a sharp, peppery flavor. It's best eaten raw. A good substitute is another pungent-flavored green, such as arugula. If you don't care for the sharp flavor, you can use spinach.

Grapefruit, Beet, and Blue Cheese Salad

You can substitute regular brown balsamic vinegar for the white, but the salad won't be as attractive because the dark vinegar discolors the grapefruit and the cheese.

Prep: 20 minutes • Cook: 38 minutes

- ¾ pound beets (about 2 medium)
- 3 pink grapefruit
- ¼ cup (1 ounce) crumbled blue cheese
- 2 tablespoons white balsamic vinegar
- 2 teaspoons olive oil
- 2 teaspoons Dijon mustard
- ⅛ teaspoon salt
- ⅛ teaspoon freshly ground black pepper
- 6 cups torn romaine lettuce

1. Leave root and 1 inch of stem on the beets; scrub with a brush. Place in a medium saucepan; cover with water. Bring to a boil; cover, reduce heat, and simmer 35 minutes or until tender. Drain and rinse with cold water. Drain; cool. Trim off beet roots; rub off skins. Cut beets into ½-inch cubes.
2. Peel and section grapefruit over a bowl, and squeeze membranes to extract juice. Set 1½ cups sections aside, and reserve 2 tablespoons juice. Discard membranes.
3. Place cheese in a small bowl; mash with a fork until smooth. Add reserved grapefruit juice, vinegar, and next 4 ingredients; stir well with a whisk.
4. Pour dressing over lettuce, tossing gently to coat. Top with beets and grapefruit sections. Yield: 6 servings (serving size: 1 cup lettuce, ¼ cup beets, and ¼ cup grapefruit sections).

CALORIES 106 (28% from fat); FAT 3.3g (sat 1.1g, mono 1.6g, poly 0.3g); PROTEIN 3.6g; CARB 17.4g; FIBER 2.8g; CHOL 4mg; IRON 1.3mg; SODIUM 191mg; CALC 70mg

Baby Spinach Salad with Candied Hazelnuts

Nut oils add a distinctive flavor to vinaigrettes. Try this salad with other oil and nut varieties, such as walnuts or almonds.

Prep: 15 minutes • Cook: 6 minutes

- ¼ cup chopped hazelnuts
- 1½ tablespoons light brown sugar
- 1½ teaspoons egg white
- ⅛ teaspoon salt
  Cooking spray
- 2 teaspoons fresh orange juice
- 1½ teaspoons toasted hazelnut oil
- ½ teaspoon Dijon mustard
- ¼ teaspoon salt
- ¼ teaspoon freshly ground black pepper
- 1 (7-ounce) package fresh baby spinach (about 8 cups)
- 1 cup orange sections (about 4 oranges)

1. Preheat oven to 350°.
2. Combine first 4 ingredients, tossing well to coat. Place hazelnut mixture on a nonstick baking sheet coated with cooking spray; bake at 350° for 6 minutes or until lightly browned. Remove from oven; cool.
3. Combine juice and next 4 ingredients, stirring well with a whisk. Place spinach in a large bowl; drizzle with juice mixture. Toss gently to coat. Place spinach mixture on plates; top with orange sections and hazelnut mixture. Yield: 4 servings (serving size: 1¾ cups spinach mixture, ¼ cup orange sections, and 1 tablespoon hazelnut mixture).

CALORIES 117 (49% from fat); FAT 6.4g (sat 0.5g, mono 4.7g, poly 0.9g); PROTEIN 3.5g; CARB 14.1g; FIBER 3.4g; CHOL 0mg; IRON 2.2mg; SODIUM 286mg; CALC 92mg

Slaws

Based on the Dutch word *koosla* or "cold cabbage," coleslaw is a mixture of shredded cabbage, vinaigrette or dressing, and any number of other chopped ingredients.

Simple Slaw

Prepare and refrigerate this side several hours before serving, if you like. For more color in the dish, toss in red bell pepper strips.

Prep: 10 minutes

- ½ cup fat-free buttermilk
- ⅓ cup low-fat mayonnaise
- ½ teaspoon celery salt
- ½ teaspoon freshly ground black pepper
- 12 cups thinly sliced green cabbage
- ½ cup finely chopped green onions

1. Combine first 4 ingredients, stirring with a whisk. Place cabbage and onions in a large bowl. Spoon buttermilk mixture over cabbage; toss to coat. Yield: 8 servings (serving size: about 1 cup).

CALORIES 52 (17% from fat); FAT 1g (sat 0.1g, mono 0.2g, poly 0.5g); PROTEIN 2.1g; CARB 9.8g; FIBER 2.7g; CHOL 0mg; IRON 0.7mg; SODIUM 221mg; CALC 70mg

Thai Cabbage Slaw

To make a more memorable slaw, we've added some Thai ingredients—lime juice, fish sauce, chile paste, cilantro, and peanut butter—to the cabbage.

Prep: 15 minutes • Other: 1 hour

- 3 tablespoons fresh lime juice
- 3 tablespoons rice vinegar
- 2 tablespoons fish sauce
- 1 tablespoon water
- 1 tablespoon creamy peanut butter
- 1 teaspoon chile paste with garlic
- 1 garlic clove, minced
- 6 cups shredded napa (Chinese) cabbage
- 2 cups shredded red cabbage
- 1 cup red bell pepper strips
- 1 cup shredded carrot
- 2 tablespoons chopped dry-roasted peanuts
- 1 tablespoon chopped fresh cilantro
- 1 tablespoon chopped fresh mint

1. Combine first 7 ingredients in a large bowl, stirring with a whisk until blended. Add cabbages, bell pepper, and carrot, and toss gently to coat. Cover and marinate in refrigerator 1 hour. Stir in peanuts, cilantro, and mint just before serving. Yield: 8 servings (serving size: ¾ cup).

CALORIES 66 (34% from fat); FAT 2.5g (sat 0.4g, mono 1.1g, poly 0.8g); PROTEIN 2.9g; CARB 10g; FIBER 3.2g; CHOL 0mg; IRON 0.9mg; SODIUM 540mg; CALC 55mg

Sweet-and-Sour Slaw

Try varying the slaw by adding slices of Granny Smith or Pink Lady apples to give it a slightly sweet-tart flavor and a crunchy bite.

Prep: 5 minutes

- 1 tablespoon sugar
- 3 tablespoons cider vinegar
- 2 teaspoons canola oil
- ¼ teaspoon salt
- 4½ cups packaged cabbage-and-carrot coleslaw (about 8 ounces)
- ¼ cup chopped green onions

1. Combine first 4 ingredients in a large bowl, stirring with a whisk until sugar dissolves. Add coleslaw and onions to vinegar mixture; toss to combine. Serve chilled or at room temperature. Yield: 4 servings (serving size: 1 cup).

CALORIES 59 (38% from fat); FAT 2.5g (sat 0.2g, mono 1.4g, poly 0.8g); PROTEIN 1.1g; CARB 9.5g; FIBER 2.2g; CHOL 0mg; IRON 0.5mg; SODIUM 172mg; CALC 43mg

Thai Cabbage Slaw

Garden Slaw with Tarragon

The tarragon adds a bit of subtle aniselike flavor to this veggie-packed slaw.

**Prep: 15 minutes • Cook: 5 minutes
Other: 30 minutes**

Dressing:
- ¼ cup low-fat buttermilk
- 3 tablespoons light mayonnaise
- 1 tablespoon fresh lemon juice
- 2 teaspoons sugar
- ¼ teaspoon salt
- ¼ teaspoon coarsely ground black pepper

Salad:
- 3 cups sliced Savoy cabbage
- 1 cup (1-inch) diagonally cut wax beans, steamed
- ½ cup snow peas, trimmed and cut lengthwise into thin strips
- ½ cup red bell pepper strips
- ⅓ cup shredded carrot
- ¼ cup vertically sliced red onion
- 1 tablespoon chopped fresh tarragon

1. To prepare dressing, combine first 6 ingredients, stirring with a whisk.
2. To prepare salad, combine cabbage and remaining ingredients in a bowl. Add dressing mixture; toss. Chill 30 minutes. Yield: 6 servings (serving size: ¾ cup).

CALORIES 62 (39% from fat); FAT 2.7g (sat 0.5g, mono 0.7g, poly 1.3g); PROTEIN 1.9g; CARB 8.6g; FIBER 2.4g; CHOL 3mg; IRON 0.6mg; SODIUM 183mg; CALC 39mg

Savoy cabbage The crinkled leaves of this cabbage are mild, so it's a good choice for salads. Because of its tightly wrapped leaves that lock out oxygen, you can store Savoy (and other cabbages) in the refrigerator for up to three months.

Napa Cabbage and Snow Pea Slaw

This salad tastes best after chilling in the refrigerator for about 30 minutes.

Prep: 15 minutes • Other: 30 minutes

Dressing:
- 2 tablespoons sugar
- 2 tablespoons fresh lime juice
- 1 tablespoon fish sauce
- 1 teaspoon dark sesame oil
- ½ teaspoon grated peeled fresh ginger
- Dash of ground red pepper

Slaw:
- 4 cups (¼-inch) sliced napa (Chinese) cabbage
- ½ cup snow peas, trimmed and cut lengthwise into (⅛-inch) thin strips
- ½ cup fresh bean sprouts
- ½ cup (⅛-inch) julienne-cut peeled jícama
- ¼ cup (⅛-inch) julienne-cut red bell pepper
- 2 tablespoons thinly sliced green onions
- 2 tablespoons finely chopped fresh cilantro

1. To prepare dressing, combine first 6 ingredients, stirring with a whisk.
2. To prepare slaw, combine cabbage and remaining ingredients in a large bowl. Add dressing, and toss well to coat. Chill 30 minutes. Yield: 4 servings (serving size: 1 cup).

CALORIES 65 (19% from fat); FAT 1.4g (sat 0.2g, mono 0.5g, poly 0.6g); PROTEIN 2.2g; CARB 12.3g; FIBER 2.3g; CHOL 0mg; IRON 1.1mg; SODIUM 396mg; CALC 86mg

Vegetable Salads Use garden-fresh veggies, canned beans, and potatoes to create inspired and flavorful side-dish salads.

Spicy Cucumber Salad

Serve these sweet-hot cucumbers with any of your favorite Asian-style entrées.

Prep: 10 minutes

2 cups thinly sliced seeded peeled cucumber
1 cup julienne-cut red bell pepper
¼ cup thinly sliced red onion
1 tablespoon sugar
2 tablespoons fresh lime juice
1 tablespoon fish sauce
½ teaspoon crushed red pepper

1. Combine first 3 ingredients in a bowl. Combine sugar and next 3 ingredients, stirring well with a whisk.
2. Pour dressing mixture over cucumber mixture; toss to combine. Yield: 6 servings (serving size: ½ cup).

CALORIES 22 (6% from fat); FAT 0.1g (sat 0g, mono 0g, poly 0g); PROTEIN 0.6g; CARB 5g; FIBER 0.4g; CHOL 0mg; IRON 0.2mg; SODIUM 233mg; CALC 10mg

Test Kitchen Tip: Store unwashed cucumbers unwrapped in the crisper bin of the refrigerator. Keep them away from apples and citrus fruits because these fruits produce ethylene gas that can decay cucumbers.

Roasted Beet Salad with Raspberry Vinaigrette

Roasting enhances the natural sweetness of beets, and the tangy honeyed vinaigrette complements them.

Prep: 20 minutes • Cook: 45 minutes

8 beets (about 2½ pounds)
½ cup coarsely chopped red onion
½ cup coarsely chopped celery
2 tablespoons raspberry vinegar
1 tablespoon honey
2½ teaspoons extravirgin olive oil
¼ teaspoon salt
⅛ teaspoon freshly ground black pepper

1. Preheat oven to 425°.
2. Leave root and 1 inch of stem on the beets; scrub with a brush. Place beets on a foil-lined baking sheet. Bake at 425° for 45 minutes or until tender; cool. Trim off beet roots, and rub off skins. Coarsely chop beets. Combine beets, onion, and celery in a large bowl.
3. Combine vinegar and remaining ingredients. Pour over beet mixture; toss gently to coat. Serve at room temperature or chilled. Yield: 6 servings (serving size: ⅔ cup).

CALORIES 82 (23% from fat); FAT 2.1g (sat 0.3g, mono 1.4g, poly 0.2g); PROTEIN 2g; CARB 15.1g; FIBER 3.5g; CHOL 0mg; IRON 1mg; SODIUM 194mg; CALC 25mg

Radish and Carrot Salad

This salad serves as a cool break from spicier foods. You'll almost always see some rendition of this dish at a Korean meal. It's traditionally made with *moo* (sweet Korean radish), but daikon radish is more readily available and makes a fine substitute. Salting the daikon helps extract some of its bitterness.

Prep: 10 minutes • Other: 30 minutes

2 cups (3-inch) julienne-cut peeled daikon radish
1 teaspoon kosher salt
1 cup (3-inch) julienne-cut carrot
1 tablespoon rice vinegar
2 teaspoons sugar
1 teaspoon mirin (sweet rice wine)

1. Combine daikon and salt, tossing well to coat. Let stand at room temperature 30 minutes. Rinse with cold water; drain. Combine daikon and carrot.
2. Combine vinegar, sugar, and mirin, stirring until sugar dissolves. Drizzle over daikon mixture; toss to combine. Cover and chill. Yield: 10 servings (serving size: ¼ cup).

CALORIES 13 (0% from fat); FAT 0g (sat 0g, mono 0g, poly 0g); PROTEIN 0.2g; CARB 3g; FIBER 0.7g; CHOL 0mg; IRON 0.1mg; SODIUM 55mg; CALC 8mg

Green Bean and Cherry Tomato Salad

Fresh green beans and cherry tomatoes need little more than a simple vinaigrette.

Prep: 20 minutes • Cook: 7 minutes
Other: 10 minutes

1¼ pounds green beans, trimmed
1¼ pounds cherry tomatoes, quartered
  1 teaspoon chopped fresh oregano
  1 tablespoon minced shallots
  2 tablespoons red wine vinegar
2½ teaspoons extravirgin olive oil
  ½ teaspoon salt
  ¼ teaspoon freshly ground black pepper

1. Cook beans in boiling water 7 minutes or until tender. Drain. Place green beans, tomatoes, and oregano in a large bowl; toss gently to combine.
2. Combine shallots and vinegar, stirring with a whisk. Let vinegar mixture stand 10 minutes. Add oil, salt, and pepper to vinegar mixture, stirring with a whisk until well blended. Pour vinaigrette over bean mixture; toss well. Yield: 8 servings (serving size: 1 cup).

CALORIES 51 (30% from fat); FAT 1.7g (sat 0.2g, mono 1.1g, poly 0.3g); PROTEIN 1.9g; CARB 8.7g; FIBER 3.2g; CHOL 0mg; IRON 1.1mg; SODIUM 158mg; CALC 32mg

Green Bean and Cherry Tomato Salad

Green Bean, Corn, and Roasted Poblano Chile Salad

Add some south-of-the-border flavor to your summer produce by combining corn, green beans, and tomatoes with a chopped chile and a cumin vinaigrette.

Prep: 25 minutes • Cook: 18 minutes
Other: 15 minutes

  1 poblano chile
  2 cups (1-inch) diagonally sliced green beans (about ½ pound)
  2 cups fresh corn kernels (about 2 ears)
  2 cups chopped spinach
  1 cup cherry tomatoes, halved
  ⅓ cup Cumin-Lime Vinaigrette (page 427)
  3 tablespoons thinly sliced green onions
  2 tablespoons finely chopped fresh cilantro
Freshly ground black pepper (optional)

1. Preheat broiler.
2. Place chile on a foil-lined baking sheet; broil 10 minutes or until blackened, turning occasionally. Place in a zip-top plastic bag; seal. Let stand 15 minutes. Peel and cut in half lengthwise. Discard seeds and membranes; chop.
3. Steam green beans, covered, 5 minutes or until crisp-tender; drain. Rinse with cold water; drain well.
4. Combine chopped chile, beans, corn, chopped spinach, tomatoes, Cumin-Lime Vinaigrette, green onions, and fresh cilantro, tossing gently to coat. Sprinkle with black pepper, if desired. Yield: 6 servings (serving size: 1 cup).

(Totals include Cumin-Lime Vinaigrette) CALORIES 78 (18% from fat); FAT 1.6g (sat 0.2g, mono 0.7g, poly 0.4g); PROTEIN 3.1g; CARB 15.8g; FIBER 3.4g; CHOL 0mg; IRON 1.1mg; SODIUM 106mg; CALC 26mg

Lemon-Basil Bean Bowl

Lima beans go upscale in this main-dish salad. Paired with green beans, tomatoes, and bacon, and then dressed with a lemon-basil vinaigrette, the end result is so spectacular our Test Kitchens gave it our highest rating.

Prep: 20 minutes • Cook: 36 minutes

⅓ cup chopped fresh basil
1 teaspoon grated lemon rind
2 tablespoons fresh lemon juice
1 tablespoon olive oil
2½ teaspoons Dijon mustard
½ teaspoon sugar
¼ teaspoon salt
¼ teaspoon freshly ground black pepper
1 garlic clove, minced
4 cups (1-inch) cut green beans (about 1 pound)
1½ cups chopped plum tomato
1 (10-ounce) package frozen baby lima beans, cooked and drained
4 reduced-fat bacon slices, cooked and crumbled (drained)

1. Combine first 9 ingredients in a bowl; stir with a whisk.

2. Steam green beans, covered, 8 minutes or until tender. Combine green beans, tomato, and lima beans in a large bowl. Pour basil mixture over bean mixture, and toss well. Sprinkle with bacon. Yield: 6 servings (serving size: 1 cup).

CALORIES 133 (25% from fat); FAT 3.7g (sat 0.7g, mono 2.1g, poly 1g); PROTEIN 7.1g; CARB 19.4g; FIBER 3g; CHOL 3mg; IRON 2.4mg; SODIUM 334mg; CALC 53mg

Tomato, Basil, and Fresh Mozzarella Salad

In this popular salad, infused vegetable broth provides the base for a basil sauce that can stand in for the pesto or vinaigrette. Blanching the basil leaves briefly in water brightens the color and intensifies the flavor. Dress the salad just before serving to preserve the brilliant colors of the tomatoes.

Prep: 15 minutes • Cook: 3 minutes • Other: 2 hours

Basil sauce:
1 cup loosely packed fresh basil leaves
⅓ cup vegetable broth
¼ cup balsamic vinegar
1 teaspoon sea salt

Salad:
12 (¼-inch-thick) slices yellow tomato (1½ pounds)
12 (¼-inch-thick) slices red tomato (1½ pounds)
½ cup (2 ounces) shredded fresh mozzarella cheese
1 teaspoon freshly ground black pepper
½ cup thinly sliced fresh basil

1. To prepare basil sauce, cook 1 cup basil leaves in boiling water 15 seconds; drain.

Plunge basil into ice water; drain and pat dry. Place basil and broth in a blender; process until smooth. Let mixture stand at room temperature 2 hours. Strain through a fine sieve into a bowl; discard solids. Add vinegar and salt, stirring with a whisk.

2. To prepare salad, arrange yellow and red tomato slices alternately in a large serving dish. Drizzle with basil sauce; sprinkle with cheese and pepper. Top with ½ cup sliced basil. Serve immediately. Yield: 8 servings (serving size: 3 tomato slices, about 1 tablespoon basil sauce, and 1 tablespoon cheese).

CALORIES 60 (32% from fat); FAT 2.1g (sat 1.1g, mono 0.6g, poly 0.3g); PROTEIN 3.2g; CARB 8.4g; FIBER 2g; CHOL 6mg; IRON 1.2mg; SODIUM 369mg; CALC 70mg

Tomato and Cucumber Salad with Feta

The Dijon Vinaigrette (page 427) is also good in this salad.

Prep: 12 minutes • Cook: 3 minutes

　2　cups (½-inch) diced tomato (about 1 pound)
　1　cup (¼-inch) diced English cucumber
　¼　cup (1 ounce) crumbled feta cheese
　1　tablespoon finely chopped fresh mint
　¼　cup Versatile Vinaigrette (page 427)

1. Combine first 4 ingredients in a large bowl. Add vinaigrette, and toss gently to coat. Yield: 4 servings (serving size: ¾ cup).

(Totals include Versatile Vinaigrette) CALORIES 54 (47% from fat); FAT 2.8g (sat 1.2g, mono 1g, poly 0.3g); PROTEIN 2.1g; CARB 6.4g; FIBER 1.3g; CHOL 6mg; IRON 0.6mg; SODIUM 188mg; CALC 46mg

Gazpacho Salad with Tomato Vinaigrette

You can also serve this refreshing salad like a salsa with chips.

Prep: 15 minutes

　2　cups (½-inch) diced tomato (about 1 pound)
1½　cups (½-inch) diced cucumber
　½　cup (¼-inch) diced green bell pepper
　2　tablespoons minced shallots
　2　tablespoons chopped fresh basil
Tomato Vinaigrette (page 428)

1. Combine tomato, cucumber, bell pepper, shallots, and basil in a large bowl. Add vinaigrette; toss gently to coat. Yield: 5 servings (serving size: ¾ cup).

(Totals include Tomato Vinaigrette) CALORIES 57 (49% from fat); FAT 3.1g (sat 0.4g, mono 2g, poly 0.4g); PROTEIN 1.3g; CARB 7.7g; FIBER 2g; CHOL 0mg; IRON 0.7mg; SODIUM 171mg; CALC 20mg

Garden Salad with Citrus Vinaigrette

This salad holds well, so it's a fine side to take to a cookout or to pack with a lunch.

Prep: 20 minutes

1½　cups (1 x ¼–inch) julienne-cut zucchini
1½　cups (1 x ¼–inch) julienne-cut yellow squash
　1　cup fresh corn kernels (about 2 ears)
　2　tablespoons finely chopped red onion
　1　tablespoon finely chopped fresh flat-leaf parsley
　1　tablespoon finely chopped fresh basil
Citrus Vinaigrette (page 427)

1. Combine zucchini and next 5 ingredients in a large bowl. Add vinaigrette; toss well. Cover and chill. Yield: 4 servings (serving size: 1 cup).

(Totals include Citrus Vinaigrette) CALORIES 101 (30% from fat); FAT 3.4g (sat 0.5g, mono 2.2g,poly 0.5g); PROTEIN 2.6g; CARB 17.4g; FIBER 3.6g; CHOL 0mg; IRON 0.8mg; SODIUM 154mg; CALC 30mg

White Bean, Tomato, and Green Bean Salad

Fresh dill adds zestiness to this salad without overpowering it.

Prep: 20 minutes • Cook: 8 minutes
Other: 1 hour

Dressing:
　1　tablespoon fresh lemon juice
　1　tablespoon balsamic vinegar
　1　tablespoon extravirgin olive oil
　¼　teaspoon sugar
　¼　teaspoon salt
　¼　teaspoon freshly ground black pepper
　1　garlic clove, minced
Salad:
　5　cups (1-inch) cut green beans (about 1 pound)
　1　cup finely chopped tomato
　1　tablespoon chopped fresh dill
　1　(15-ounce) can navy beans, rinsed and drained
　½　cup (2 ounces) feta cheese, crumbled

1. To prepare dressing, combine first 7 ingredients, stirring with a whisk.
2. To prepare salad, place green beans in a large saucepan of boiling water; cook 5 minutes. Drain and plunge beans in ice water; drain. Place beans in a large bowl. Add tomato, dill, and navy beans; toss to combine. Drizzle with dressing; toss gently to coat. Sprinkle with cheese. Cover and chill at least 1 hour. Yield: 4 servings (serving size: 1½ cups).

CALORIES 214 (30% from fat); FAT 7.1g (sat 2.7g, mono 3.2g, poly 0.7g); PROTEIN 11g; CARB 29.6g; FIBER 8.7g; CHOL 13mg; IRON 3.1mg; SODIUM 698mg; CALC 158mg

Test Kitchen Tip: You can use cannellini beans or Great Northern beans in place of the navy beans.

Gazpacho Salad with Tomato Vinaigrette

Arugula, White Bean, and Roasted Red Pepper Salad

It's common in many Italian-style salads to combine beans and greens and toss them with a sweet balsamic vinaigrette.

Prep: 10 minutes

Salad:

   3 cups torn arugula leaves
  ½ cup chopped bottled roasted red bell peppers
  ⅓ cup vertically sliced red onion
  1 (16-ounce) can navy beans, rinsed and drained

Dressing:

1½ tablespoons balsamic vinegar
  1 tablespoon olive oil
  1 teaspoon honey
  ¼ teaspoon salt
  ¼ teaspoon pepper
  1 garlic clove, minced

1. To prepare salad, combine first 4 ingredients in a large bowl.

2. To prepare dressing, combine vinegar and remaining ingredients in a small bowl, stirring with a whisk until blended. Pour over salad, tossing to coat. Yield: 4 servings (serving size: 1 cup).

CALORIES 164 (29% from fat); FAT 5.3g (sat 0.7g, mono 2.9g, poly 1.2g); PROTEIN 7.1g; CARB 23.6g; FIBER 2.9g; CHOL 0mg; IRON 2.3mg; SODIUM 500mg; CALC 80mg

Test Kitchen Tip: If you want to roast your own peppers instead of using bottled, see the directions on pages 32 and 450.

Zesty Black Bean and Corn Salad

This salad is good on its own or as a filling in a southwestern wrap. If you make it a day ahead, the flavors will have more time to blend.

Prep: 20 minutes • Cook: 10 minutes

  2 teaspoons canola oil
Cooking spray
  2 garlic cloves, minced
2½ cups fresh corn kernels (about 4 large ears)
  ¼ cup fresh lime juice (about 2 limes)
  1 tablespoon extravirgin olive oil
  2 tablespoons red wine vinegar
  ¾ teaspoon ground cumin
  ¼ teaspoon salt
  1 cup halved grape tomatoes
  1 cup chopped red bell pepper
  ¾ cup chopped red onion
  2 tablespoons chopped fresh cilantro
  2 tablespoons minced seeded jalapeño pepper
  1 tablespoon chopped fresh oregano
  1 (19-ounce) can black beans, rinsed and drained

1. Heat canola oil in a large nonstick skillet coated with cooking spray over medium-high heat. Add garlic; sauté 30 seconds. Add corn; sauté 8 minutes or until browned. Remove from pan; let cool completely.

2. Combine juice and next 4 ingredients, stirring with a whisk. Combine corn mixture, tomatoes, and remaining ingredients. Drizzle juice mixture over corn mixture, and toss gently to coat. Yield: 6 servings (serving size: 1 cup).

CALORIES 164 (26% from fat); FAT 4.8g (sat 0.6g, mono 3g, poly 1.1g); PROTEIN 6.5g; CARB 30.3g; FIBER 7.3g; CHOL 0mg; IRON 2.1mg; SODIUM 359mg; CALC 46mg

Triple Bean Salad

This make-ahead salad can be served as a side dish or over a bed of lettuce as a light lunch.

Prep: 9 minutes

  ½ cup chopped green onions
  ½ cup chopped green bell pepper
  ½ cup chopped red bell pepper
  1 (15.5-ounce) can chickpeas (garbanzo beans), rinsed and drained
  1 (15.5-ounce) can kidney beans, rinsed and drained
  1 (15.5-ounce) can black beans, rinsed and drained
  3 tablespoons red wine vinegar
  2 tablespoons olive oil
  1 teaspoon freshly ground black pepper
  1 teaspoon lemon juice
  ½ teaspoon salt

1. Combine first 6 ingredients in a large bowl. Combine vinegar, oil, pepper, juice, and salt, stirring with a whisk; pour over bean mixture, stirring to coat. Cover and chill. Yield: 12 servings (serving size: ½ cup).

CALORIES 128 (30% from fat); FAT 4.2g (sat 0.3g, mono 1.7g, poly 0.2g); PROTEIN 5.8g; CARB 20.8g; FIBER 6.3g; CHOL 0mg; IRON 1.6mg; SODIUM 321mg; CALC 34mg

Test Kitchen Tip: Not only does rinsing and draining canned beans get rid of the starchy bean liquid, it also reduces the sodium of regular canned beans by 40 percent.

Potato Salad 101

An all-American necessity at summer get-togethers and reunions, this creamy, old-fashioned potato salad features pickle relish, eggs, and mustard.

Prep: 15 minutes • Cook: 33 minutes
Other: 1 hour

    2   pounds small all-purpose white or
        red potatoes
    3   tablespoons white vinegar
    1   tablespoon canola oil
    ½   cup chopped celery
    ½   cup finely chopped red onion
    2   tablespoons sweet pickle relish,
        drained
    3   hard-cooked large eggs, chopped
    ¾   cup low-fat mayonnaise
    2   tablespoons prepared mustard
    ½   teaspoon salt
    ¼   teaspoon freshly ground black pepper

1. Place potatoes in a saucepan, and cover with water. Bring to a boil. Reduce heat; simmer 10 minutes or until tender. Drain. Cool and peel. Cut potatoes into ½-inch cubes. Place potatoes in a large bowl; sprinkle with vinegar and oil. Add celery, onion, pickle relish, and eggs; toss gently.
2. Combine mayonnaise, mustard, salt, and pepper. Spoon mayonnaise mixture over potato mixture; toss gently to coat. Cover and chill 1 to 24 hours. Yield: 7 servings (serving size: about 1 cup).

CALORIES 215 (26% from fat); FAT 6.1g (sat 1.1g, mono 2.5g, poly 2g); PROTEIN 4.9g; CARB 35.9g; FIBER 1.9g; CHOL 91mg; IRON 0.9mg; SODIUM 536mg; CALC 26mg

Farm Stand Potato Salad
(pictured on page 397)

Summer's bounty from the local farm stand inspired this salad, made with fingerling potatoes, crisp sugar snap peas, crunchy broccoli, and a colorful confetti of bell peppers.

Prep: 15 minutes • Cook: 16 minutes

Dressing:
    3   tablespoons fresh lemon juice
    2   tablespoons olive oil
    1   tablespoon country-style Dijon
        mustard
    1   teaspoon minced fresh or
        ¼ teaspoon dried thyme
    ½   teaspoon salt
    ½   teaspoon celery seeds
Salad:
    1¾ pounds fingerling potatoes
    1   cup sugar snap peas, trimmed
    1   cup broccoli florets
    ¼   cup diced red bell pepper
    ¼   cup diced green bell pepper
    ¼   cup diced yellow bell pepper
    ¼   cup chopped green onions

1. To prepare dressing, combine first 6 ingredients, stirring with a whisk.
2. To prepare salad, place potatoes in a saucepan, and cover with water. Bring to a boil. Reduce heat, and simmer 10 minutes or until tender. Remove potatoes from pan with a slotted spoon. Add peas and broccoli florets to pan. Cook 1 minute; drain.
3. Cut potatoes into ¼-inch-thick slices. Combine potatoes, peas, broccoli, bell peppers, and green onions in a large bowl. Add dressing; toss well. Yield: 8 servings (serving size: 1 cup).

CALORIES 120 (29% from fat); FAT 3.8g (sat 0.5g, mono 2.6g, poly 0.4g); PROTEIN 3.1g; CARB 19.8g; FIBER 2.6g; CHOL 0mg; IRON 1.9mg; SODIUM 204mg; CALC 29mg

Hot German Potato Salad

This much-loved potato salad gets its unique flavor from bacon and a piquant vinaigrette.

Prep: 15 minutes • Cook: 30 minutes

    2   pounds small red potatoes
    6   tablespoons white wine vinegar,
        divided
    Cooking spray
    ½   cup finely chopped red onion
    4   ounces turkey kielbasa, diced
    ½   cup fat-free, less-sodium chicken
        broth
    3   bacon slices, cooked and crumbled
    1   teaspoon caraway seeds
    ½   teaspoon salt
    ¼   teaspoon freshly ground black
        pepper
    ½   cup minced fresh parsley

1. Place potatoes in a saucepan, and cover with water. Bring to a boil. Reduce heat, and simmer 10 minutes or until tender. Drain; cool slightly. Cut potatoes in half lengthwise; cut halves crosswise into ¼-inch-thick slices. Place potatoes in a large bowl; sprinkle with 2 tablespoons vinegar.
2. Heat a large nonstick skillet over medium heat. Coat pan with cooking spray. Add onion and kielbasa to pan; cook 3 minutes or until onion is tender. Add ¼ cup vinegar, broth, and bacon. Bring to a boil; cook 1 minute. Stir in caraway seeds, salt, and pepper.
3. Pour vinegar mixture over potato slices; toss gently. Sprinkle with parsley. Serve immediately. Yield: 6 servings (serving size: 1 cup).

CALORIES 195 (30% from fat); FAT 6.4g (sat 2.2g, mono 2.9g, poly 1.1g); PROTEIN 8.6g; CARB 27g; FIBER 2.1g; CHOL 20mg; IRON 1.2mg; SODIUM 559mg; CALC 21mg

Grain & Bread Salads

Salads don't all have to be green: The star ingredients of these hearty dishes are bulgur, rice, and bread.

Lemon Garbanzo Salad with Feta

Bulgur can be quickly hydrated in boiling water. (See page 414 for more information on bulgur.) Combine it with canned beans and feta cheese for a nutritious vegetarian salad. This makes one main-dish serving, but can be doubled easily; it's even better the next day.

Prep: 14 minutes • Other: 15 minutes

½	cup boiling water
⅓	cup uncooked bulgur
1½	tablespoons fresh lemon juice, divided
⅓	cup canned chickpeas (garbanzo beans), rinsed and drained
2	tablespoons chopped peeled cucumber
2	tablespoons chopped celery
2	tablespoons diced red onion
1½	tablespoons crumbled feta cheese
1½	teaspoons chopped fresh or
¼	teaspoon dried dill
2	teaspoons extravirgin olive oil
⅛	teaspoon salt
⅛	teaspoon freshly ground black pepper

1. Combine ½ cup boiling water, bulgur, and 1 tablespoon lemon juice in a medium bowl. Let mixture stand 15 minutes. Add chickpeas, cucumber, celery, diced red onion, feta cheese, and dill; toss gently to combine.

2. Combine 1½ teaspoons lemon juice, olive oil, salt, and pepper, stirring with a whisk. Drizzle over bulgur mixture, and toss gently to coat. Cover and chill. Yield: 1 serving (serving size: 1½ cups).

CALORIES 390 (31% from fat); FAT 13.6g (sat 3.5g, mono 7.6g, poly 1.5g); PROTEIN 12.3g; CARB 58.9g; FIBER 13g; CHOL 13mg; IRON 2.6mg; SODIUM 713mg; CALC 129mg

Tabbouleh

The amount of bulgur used in this Lebanese salad varies according to family tradition. We've included less here to allow the flavors of the tomato and parsley to come through.

Prep: 14 minutes • Other: 30 minutes

    4   cups diced tomato
    ⅔   cup chopped fresh flat-leaf parsley
    ⅓   cup thinly sliced green onions
    ¼   cup uncooked bulgur
    ¼   cup chopped fresh mint
    2½ teaspoons extravirgin olive oil
    2   tablespoons fresh lemon juice
    ½   teaspoon kosher salt
    ½   teaspoon ground allspice
    ¼   teaspoon ground cinnamon
    ¼   teaspoon freshly ground black pepper
    5   large iceberg lettuce leaves

1. Combine first 5 ingredients in a large bowl. Cover and let stand 30 minutes. Stir in oil and next 5 ingredients; toss well. Serve on lettuce leaves. Yield: 5 servings (serving size: 1 cup salad and 1 lettuce leaf).

CALORIES 83 (31% from fat); FAT 2.9g (sat 0.4g,mono 1.8g, poly 0.5g); PROTEIN 2.6g; CARB 14g; FIBER 3.6g; CHOL 0mg; IRON 1.6mg; SODIUM 255mg; CALC 31mg

bulgur This grain comes from wheat berries that have been steamed, dried, and then cracked. Because bulgur is essentially precooked, it's quick to prepare. It comes in three types of grinds—coarse, medium, and fine. In most recipes, the bulgur needs only to be soaked to become tender, but it can be cooked pilaf-style.

Sushi-Rice Salad

Pair this Asian-style salad with seared tuna or soy-glazed salmon.

Prep: 15 minutes • Cook: 24 minutes

Rice:

    2   cups uncooked sushi rice
    2   cups water
    1   teaspoon kosher salt

Dressing:

    ½   cup rice vinegar
    1   tablespoon canola oil
    1   tablespoon dark sesame oil
    1   tablespoon low-sodium soy sauce
    1   teaspoon grated peeled fresh ginger
    1   garlic clove, minced
    ¼   to ¾ teaspoon prepared wasabi or
        Japanese horseradish (optional)

Remaining ingredients:

    1   cup (2-inch) julienne-cut peeled
        English cucumber
    ¼   cup minced red onion
    1   tablespoon sesame seeds, toasted
    1   sheet nori (seaweed), cut into 2-inch
        julienne strips

1. To prepare rice, rinse rice thoroughly in a sieve. Drain well. Bring 2 cups water to a boil in a medium saucepan; add rice and salt. Cover, reduce heat, and simmer 20 minutes or until liquid is absorbed. Remove from heat; uncover and cool to room temperature.

2. To prepare dressing, combine vinegar and next 5 ingredients in a small bowl. Add wasabi, if desired. Combine cooled rice, dressing, cucumber, onion, and sesame seeds in a large bowl. Sprinkle evenly with nori. Yield: 7 servings (serving size: 1 cup).

CALORIES 273 (16% from fat); FAT 4.9g (sat 0.5g, mono 2.1g, poly 1.5g); PROTEIN 4.6g; CARB 50.7g; FIBER 0.8g; CHOL 0mg; IRON 4.5mg; SODIUM 347mg; CALC 11mg

Wild Rice-Sweet Potato Salad with Pears

This innovative match-up of unexpected ingredients is terrific with ham or pork.

Prep: 20 minutes • Cook: 1 hour, 12 minutes

Salad:

    2   cups water
    1   cup uncooked wild rice
    1   cup diced peeled sweet potato
    1⅓ cups peeled Bartlett pear, cored and
        diced (about 2 pears)
    ½   teaspoon fresh lemon juice
    1   cup diced yellow bell pepper
    ¼   cup sliced green onions
    1   tablespoon toasted sesame seeds
    1   teaspoon salt

Vinaigrette:

    3   tablespoons cider vinegar
    3   tablespoons apple cider
    2   tablespoons dark sesame oil
    1   tablespoon thawed orange juice
        concentrate
    ½   teaspoon dried rubbed sage
    1   garlic clove, minced

1. To prepare salad, bring 2 cups water to a boil in a saucepan. Add rice; cover, reduce heat, and simmer 1 hour or until tender.

2. Cook diced sweet potato in boiling water 5 minutes or until tender. Drain and rinse with cold water; drain well.

3. Combine pear and lemon juice in a large bowl, and toss to coat. Add cooked wild rice, sweet potato, bell pepper, green onions, sesame seeds, and salt; toss well.

4. To prepare vinaigrette, combine vinegar and remaining ingredients; stir well with a whisk. Pour over rice mixture, tossing to coat. Yield: 8 servings (serving size: ½ cup).

CALORIES 153 (26% from fat); FAT 4.4g (sat 0.6g, mono 1.6g, poly 1.9g); PROTEIN 3.7g; CARB 26.2g; FIBER 2.5g; CHOL 0mg; IRON 1mg; SODIUM 298mg; CALC 28mg

Fattoosh (Mixed Herb and Toasted Pita Salad)

Instead of using pita bread as a salad accompaniment, this traditional Lebanese salad has pieces of toasted pita tossed in with the greens.

Prep: 20 minutes • Cook: 6 minutes

    2 (6-inch) pitas
    3 tablespoons ground sumac or
       2 tablespoons grated lemon rind
    1 tablespoon extravirgin olive oil
    8 cups thinly sliced romaine lettuce
    2 cups chopped tomato
1 ½ cups chopped fresh parsley
    1 cup thinly sliced green onions
    ½ cup chopped fresh mint
    ½ teaspoon salt
    1 cucumber, quartered lengthwise and
       thinly sliced (about 2 cups)

1. Preheat oven to 400°.
2. Place pitas in a single layer on a baking sheet. Bake at 400° for 6 minutes or until toasted; break into bite-sized pieces.
3. Combine pita, sumac, and oil in a large bowl, tossing well to coat. Add lettuce and remaining ingredients; toss well. Yield: 4 servings (serving size: 2 cups).

CALORIES 169 (24% from fat); FAT 4.6g (sat 0.6g, mono 2.7g, poly 0.8g); PROTEIN 6.8g; CARB 28.1g; FIBER 5.7g; CHOL 0mg; IRON 4.4mg; SODIUM 480mg; CALC 133mg

Test Kitchen Tip: Sumac is a spice that comes from the brick- to dark purple-red berries of a bush that grows wild throughout the Middle East and in parts of Italy. It's sold in either dried-berry form or ground, and has a fruity, astringent flavor. Look for sumac in Middle Eastern markets.

BLT Bread Salad

Here's our salad version of a classic BLT (bacon, lettuce, and tomato) sandwich. It's best to make it while summertime tomatoes are at their juicy peak.

Prep: 15 minutes • Cook: 20 minutes

    6 cups (½-inch) cubed French bread
       or other firm white bread (4 ounces)
       Cooking spray
    ¼ cup white wine vinegar
    2 tablespoons water
    2 tablespoons fat-free mayonnaise
2 ½ teaspoons sugar
    2 teaspoons extravirgin olive oil
    ¼ teaspoon salt
    ¼ teaspoon freshly ground black
       pepper
    ⅛ teaspoon ground red pepper
    3 cups torn curly leaf lettuce
    2 cups chopped seeded tomato
    2 tablespoons thinly sliced green
       onions
    4 bacon slices, cooked and crumbled

1. Preheat oven to 400°.
2. Place bread cubes in a single layer on a jelly-roll pan. Lightly coat bread cubes with cooking spray. Bake at 400° for 10 minutes or until golden, stirring once.
3. Combine vinegar and next 7 ingredients in a large bowl, stirring with a whisk. Add toasted bread cubes, lettuce, and tomato; toss gently to coat. Sprinkle with onions and bacon. Serve immediately. Yield: 6 servings (serving size: about 1⅓ cups).

CALORIES 159 (29% from fat); FAT 5.2g (sat 1.2g, mono 2.4g, poly 1.2g); PROTEIN 5.0g; CARB 23.4g; FIBER 2.1g; CHOL 4mg; IRON 1.7mg; SODIUM 402mg; CALC 48mg

Bread Salad with Tomatoes, Herbs, and Ricotta Salata

With flavor and texture like feta, ricotta salata is a versatile, mild, and slightly sweet cheese. Its flavors blend nicely with the tomatoes and fresh herbs in this version of panzanella (Italian bread salad).

Prep: 20 minutes • Other: 22 minutes

    8 (1-ounce) slices sourdough bread
    ⅓ cup water
    ¼ cup red wine vinegar
    1 teaspoon extravirgin olive oil
    ¼ teaspoon salt
    ¼ teaspoon freshly ground black pepper
    1 cup (4 ounces) crumbled ricotta
       salata
    2 tablespoons chopped fresh basil
    2 tablespoons chopped fresh chives
    1 tablespoon chopped fresh mint
    1 teaspoon chopped fresh oregano
    1 teaspoon chopped fresh thyme
    4 cups cherry tomatoes, halved (about
       2 pints)
    1 cup diced red onion

1. Sprinkle bread with ⅓ cup water; let stand 2 minutes. Carefully squeeze moisture from bread. Tear into 1-inch pieces. Let stand on paper towels 20 minutes.
2. Combine vinegar, oil, salt, and pepper, stirring with a whisk. Combine ricotta and next 5 ingredients in a large bowl. Add bread, tomatoes, and onion to ricotta mixture. Drizzle with vinaigrette; toss gently to coat. Yield: 6 servings (serving size: 1⅔ cups).

CALORIES 193 (29% from fat); FAT 6.3g (sat 3.2g, mono 2g, poly 0.6g); PROTEIN 7.3g; CARB 28.2g; FIBER 2.8g; CHOL 17mg; IRON 1.7mg; SODIUM 548mg; CALC 137mg

Pasta Salads

The great thing about pasta salads is their versatility. Serve them as sides or main dishes, and use whatever pasta you have on hand.

Niçoise-Style Couscous Salad

Combine tuna, olives, and green beans with fluffy, tender couscous for a one-dish meal.

Prep: 20 minutes • Cook: 34 minutes
Other: 5 minutes

1½   cups (2-inch) sliced green beans
¼   teaspoon salt, divided
1   (8-ounce) tuna steak (1 inch thick)
  Cooking spray
1¼   cups water
1   cup uncooked couscous
3   tablespoons fresh lemon juice
1   tablespoon extravirgin olive oil
1½   teaspoons anchovy paste
¼   teaspoon pepper
2   garlic cloves, crushed
1   cup chopped tomato
⅓   cup coarsely chopped pitted
    kalamata olives
¼   cup chopped red onion
¼   cup chopped fresh parsley
1   hard-cooked large egg, cut into
    4 wedges

1. Steam sliced green beans, covered, 7 minutes.
2. Sprinkle ⅛ teaspoon salt over tuna. Place a medium nonstick skillet over medium-high heat. Coat pan with cooking spray. Add tuna; cook 3 minutes on each side or until tuna is medium-rare or desired degree of doneness. Break tuna into chunks.
3. Bring 1¼ cups water to a boil in a medium saucepan; gradually stir in couscous. Remove from heat; cover and let stand 5 minutes. Fluff with a fork; cool.
4. Combine ⅛ teaspoon salt, lemon juice, oil, anchovy paste, pepper, and garlic in a large bowl; stir well with a whisk. Add beans, tuna, couscous, tomato, olives, onion, and parsley; toss gently. Top with egg wedges. Yield: 4 servings (serving size: 1½ cups salad and 1 egg wedge).

CALORIES 310 (28% from fat); FAT 9.7g (sat 1.8g, mono 4.7g, poly 1.7g); PROTEIN 21.6g; CARB 35.4g; FIBER 3.6g; CHOL 75mg; IRON 2.8mg; SODIUM 552mg; CALC 46mg

Vegetable Couscous Salad

Since there's nothing to wilt or water out, this is a salad that travels well. Pack it in a zip-top plastic bag, and store in a cooler.

Prep: 15 minutes • Cook: 3 minutes
Other: 5 minutes

Dressing:
⅓   cup water
¼   cup sherry or balsamic vinegar
1   tablespoon olive oil
1   (.6-ounce) envelope Italian dressing
    mix (such as Good Seasons)
Salad:
1½   cups water
1   cup uncooked couscous
2   cups chopped red bell pepper
2   cups chopped tomato
½   cup (2 ounces) crumbled feta cheese
½   cup finely chopped green onions
¼   cup chopped pitted kalamata olives
¼   cup chopped fresh parsley

1. To prepare dressing, combine first 4 ingredients in a jar. Cover tightly, and shake vigorously.
2. To prepare salad, bring 1½ cups water to a boil in a medium saucepan; gradually stir in couscous. Remove from heat. Cover and let stand 5 minutes. Fluff with a fork. Combine couscous, bell pepper, and remaining ingredients in a large bowl. Add dressing mixture. Toss couscous mixture gently to coat. Yield: 8 servings (serving size: 1 cup).

CALORIES 169 (30% from fat); FAT 5.6g (sat 1.6g, mono 3.1g, poly 0.6g); PROTEIN 4.7g; CARB 25.1g; FIBER 2.7g; CHOL 6mg; IRON 0.9mg; SODIUM 446mg; CALC 53mg

Vegetable Couscous Salad

Garlicky Vegetable Pasta Salad

The flavors of this robust pasta salad work well for a picnic or alfresco lunch. Toss the vegetables with the pasta when they're hot off the grill or after they've chilled. The vinaigrette that flavors the vegetables also dresses the pasta salad.

**Prep: 29 minutes • Cook: 36 minutes
Other: 15 minutes**

   1   large red bell pepper, halved and
        seeded
   1   red onion, peeled and cut into
        6 wedges
        Cooking spray
   ½   teaspoon olive oil
   2   (4-inch) portobello mushroom caps
   ½   pound asparagus
   ¼   cup plus 1½ tablespoons Chile-Garlic
        Vinaigrette (page 427), divided
   4   cups cooked fusilli (about 8 ounces
        uncooked short twisted spaghetti)
   ¾   cup (3 ounces) crumbled feta cheese
   ½   cup chopped fresh basil
   3   tablespoons chopped pitted
        kalamata olives

1. Prepare grill.
2. Coat bell pepper and onion with cooking spray. Place on grill rack coated with cooking spray; grill 15 minutes or until pepper is blackened, turning occasionally. Place pepper in a zip-top plastic bag; seal. Let stand 15 minutes.
3. Chop onion into 1-inch pieces; place in a large bowl. Peel and slice pepper into ½-inch strips; add to onions.
4. Combine oil, mushroom caps, and asparagus in a large bowl; toss well to coat. Place mushroom caps and asparagus on grill rack; grill 3 minutes on each side or until tender.
5. Chop mushrooms into 1-inch pieces; add to onion mixture. Slice asparagus diagonally into 1½-inch pieces; add to onion mixture. Drizzle 1½ tablespoons Chile-Garlic Vinaigrette over mixture; toss to coat.
6. Combine grilled vegetables, pasta, feta, basil, and ¼ cup Chile-Garlic Vinaigrette in a large bowl, tossing gently. Yield: 4 servings (serving size: 1¾ cups).

(Totals include Chile-Garlic Vinaigrette) CALORIES 405 (28% from fat); FAT 12.5g (sat 4.2g, mono 6.2g, poly 1.3g); PROTEIN 15.2g; CARB 60.1g; FIBER 6.8g; CHOL 20mg; IRON 4.7mg; SODIUM 854mg; CALC 190mg

Tortellini Pepperoncini Salad

Taking its cue from rustic Italian fare, this hearty salad showcases cheese-filled pasta, spinach, beans, pepperoncini, and Parmesan cheese.

Prep: 13 minutes • Cook: 13 minutes

   1   (9-ounce) package fresh cheese
        tortellini
   2   cups halved cherry tomatoes
   2   cups fresh spinach leaves, coarsely
        chopped
   ½   cup chopped pepperoncini peppers
   6   tablespoons (1½ ounces) shredded
        fresh Parmesan cheese
   ¼   cup capers
   ¼   cup chopped fresh basil
   1   (16-ounce) can navy beans, rinsed
        and drained
   2   tablespoons fresh lemon juice
   1½ tablespoons extravirgin olive oil

1. Cook pasta according to package directions, omitting salt and fat.
2. While pasta cooks, combine tomatoes, spinach, peppers, cheese, capers, basil, and beans in a large bowl. Drain pasta; rinse with cold water. Add pasta, lemon juice, and oil to tomato mixture; toss gently. Serve immediately. Yield: 7 servings (serving size: 1 cup).

CALORIES 208 (30% from fat); FAT 7g (sat 2.3g, mono 2.8g, poly 0.6g); PROTEIN 10.8g; CARB 26.7g; FIBER 4.8g; CHOL 9mg; IRON 2.4mg; SODIUM 955mg; CALC 112mg

Lemony Orzo Salad

Lemon, mint, feta, and kalamata olives add Mediterranean style to this pasta salad.

Prep: 14 minutes • Cook: 15 minutes

   1   cup uncooked orzo (rice-shaped
        pasta)
   1⅓ cups diced zucchini
   ⅓   cup diced red onion
   ⅓   cup minced fresh parsley
   3   tablespoons fresh lemon juice
   1   tablespoon minced fresh or
        1 teaspoon dried basil
   1   tablespoon olive oil
   2   teaspoons minced fresh mint
   ½   teaspoon salt
   ¼   teaspoon pepper
   1   cup diced tomato
   ⅓   cup (1½ ounces) crumbled feta
        cheese
   2   tablespoons chopped pitted kalamata
        olives

1. Cook orzo according to package directions, omitting salt and fat. Drain well. Combine orzo, zucchini, and onion in a large bowl; toss well. Combine parsley and next 6 ingredients; stir well with a whisk. Stir into orzo mixture; add tomato, cheese, and olives, tossing gently to coat. Yield: 6 servings (serving size: ¾ cup).

CALORIES 199 (22% from fat); FAT 4.8g (sat 1.5g, mono 2.3g, poly 0.6g); PROTEIN 6.7g; CARB 32.7g; FIBER 1.8g; CHOL 6mg; IRON 2.1mg; SODIUM 307mg; CALC 58mg

Confetti Pasta Salad with Chicken

Draining plain yogurt on paper towels for just five minutes gives it a thick consistency that's almost like sour cream. Cook the pasta while the chicken is simmering.

Prep: 20 minutes • Cook: 26 minutes • Other: 5 minutes

½ cup water

¼ cup dry white wine

3 (6-ounce) skinless, boneless chicken breast halves

1 large garlic clove, sliced

1½ cups plain low-fat yogurt

¼ cup light mayonnaise

2½ tablespoons fresh lemon juice

1 tablespoon cider vinegar

2 teaspoons spicy brown mustard

¾ teaspoon salt

½ teaspoon dried oregano

¼ teaspoon garlic powder

¼ teaspoon black pepper

4 cups cooked tubetti or ditalini (about 1⅓ cups uncooked short tube-shaped pasta)

½ cup chopped celery

½ cup finely chopped red bell pepper

½ cup finely chopped green bell pepper

½ cup finely chopped carrot

¼ cup chopped fresh parsley

1. Combine first 4 ingredients in a saucepan; bring to a simmer. Cover and simmer 15 minutes or until chicken is done. Remove chicken pieces from broth; cool and coarsely chop. Bring broth to a boil over high heat; cook until reduced to ¼ cup (about 5 minutes). Cool.

2. Spoon yogurt onto several layers of heavy-duty paper towels, and spread to ½-inch thickness. Cover with additional paper towels, and let stand 5 minutes. Scrape into a bowl using a rubber spatula.

3. Combine reduced broth, yogurt, mayonnaise, and next 7 ingredients in a large bowl. Stir in chicken, pasta, and remaining ingredients. Cover and chill thoroughly. Yield: 8 servings (serving size: 1 cup).

CALORIES 209 (17% from fat); FAT 3.9g (sat 1.1g, mono 1g, poly 1.4g); PROTEIN 16g; CARB 25.7g; FIBER 1.9g; CHOL 30mg; IRON 1.8mg; SODIUM 359mg; CALC 106mg

Glass-Noodle Salad with Chicken and Shrimp

Also called bean threads, translucent cellophane noodles are made from the starch of mung beans, potatoes, or green peas. Because the noodles absorb the flavors of the foods they're combined with, this salad brims with distinctive Thai style.

Prep: 30 minutes • Cook: 37 minutes

Dressing:

½ cup sugar

¼ cup Thai fish sauce

3 tablespoons light brown sugar

2 tablespoons cider vinegar

½ cup fresh lime juice

1 tablespoon minced fresh cilantro stems

2 teaspoons minced serrano chile

1 garlic clove, minced

Salad:

2 ounces uncooked bean threads (cellophane noodles)

2 cups chopped cooked and peeled shrimp (about ½ pound)

6 ounces cooked chicken breast, cut into ¼-inch strips

2 cups torn romaine lettuce

1 cup chopped tomato

½ cup thinly sliced onion

⅓ cup thinly sliced celery

2 tablespoons chopped, dry-roasted peanuts

2 tablespoons minced fresh cilantro stems

4 teaspoons minced serrano chile

1. To prepare dressing, combine first 4 ingredients in a small saucepan. Bring to a boil, and cook 2 minutes or until sugar dissolves. Cool; stir in lime juice, 1 tablespoon cilantro, 2 teaspoons chile, and garlic.

2. To prepare salad, cook noodles in boiling water 1½ minutes; drain. Rinse under cold water. Drain. Coarsely chop noodles. Combine noodles, shrimp, and next 5 ingredients in a large bowl. Drizzle dressing over salad; toss gently to coat. Sprinkle with peanuts, 2 tablespoons cilantro, and 4 teaspoons chile. Yield: 5 servings (serving size: 1 cup).

CALORIES 249 (13% from fat); FAT 3.6g (sat 0.7g, mono 1.4g, poly 1.1g); PROTEIN 21.1g; CARB 34.5g; FIBER 1.6g; CHOL 113mg; IRON 2.7mg; SODIUM 1250mg; CALC 60mg

Greek Pasta Salad

For a pasta salad that's decidedly Greek, stir in shrimp, rosemary, cucumbers, kalamata olives, and feta.

Prep: 25 minutes • Cook: 23 minutes
Other: 1 hour

    6 cups water
    1 pound large shrimp
    ½ cup low-fat Caesar dressing
    2 teaspoons sun-dried tomato sprinkles
    ¾ teaspoon dried rosemary, crushed
    5 cups cooked penne (10 ounces uncooked tube-shaped pasta)
    ¾ cup thinly sliced cucumber
    ⅓ cup chopped fresh basil
    ¼ cup chopped pitted kalamata olives
    ¼ cup sliced red onion, separated into rings
    1 (7-ounce) bottle roasted red bell peppers, drained and cut into strips
    ¾ cup (3 ounces) crumbled feta cheese
    ¼ teaspoon freshly ground black pepper

1. Bring 6 cups water to a boil in a large saucepan. Add shrimp; cook 3 minutes or until done. Drain and rinse with cold water. Peel and chill shrimp.
2. Combine shrimp, dressing, tomato sprinkles, and rosemary in a large bowl. Add

pasta and next 5 ingredients; toss gently to coat. Cover; chill 1 hour. Sprinkle with cheese and black pepper. Yield: 6 servings (serving size: 1½ cups).

CALORIES 344 (27% from fat); FAT 10.2g (sat 3.2g, mono 3.3g, poly 2.9g); PROTEIN 20.7g; CARB 40g; FIBER 1.9g; CHOL 106mg; IRON 3.7mg; SODIUM 552mg; CALC 125mg

Mediterranean Shrimp-and-Pasta Salad

Fresh herbs are crucial to the flavor of this pasta salad.

Prep: 35 minutes • Cook: 28 minutes

Vinaigrette:

    ¼ cup extravirgin olive oil
    ¼ cup fresh lemon juice
    2 tablespoons sherry vinegar
    1 teaspoon Dijon mustard
    ¾ teaspoon kosher salt
    ½ teaspoon freshly ground black pepper

Salad:

    6   cups water
    2   bay leaves
    1   pound medium shrimp, peeled and deveined
    ¼   teaspoon kosher salt
    ¼   teaspoon freshly ground black pepper
    6⅔ cups cooked cavatappi (4 cups uncooked short twisted pasta)
    1   cup trimmed arugula
    1   zucchini, halved lengthwise and thinly sliced (about 1 cup)
    1   cup yellow bell pepper strips
    ¾   cup (3 ounces) crumbled feta cheese
    ½   cup vertically sliced red onion
    3   tablespoons chopped fresh parsley
    3   tablespoons chopped fresh basil
    1   tablespoon chopped fresh oregano

1. To prepare vinaigrette, combine first 6 ingredients in a small bowl; stir with a whisk. Set aside.
2. To prepare salad, combine water and bay leaves in a large saucepan; bring to a boil. Add shrimp; cook 3 minutes or until done. Drain and rinse with cold water. Discard bay leaves. Sprinkle shrimp with ¼ teaspoon salt and ¼ teaspoon black pepper. Cover and chill.
3. Combine shrimp, pasta, arugula, and remaining ingredients in a large bowl. Drizzle vinaigrette over salad, and toss gently to coat. Yield: 5 servings (serving size: 2 cups).

CALORIES 577 (28% from fat); FAT 17.8g (sat 5g, mono 4.4g, poly 6.6g); PROTEIN 32.5g; CARB 69.4g; FIBER 3g; CHOL 153mg; IRON 6.4mg; SODIUM 688mg; CALC 178mg

how to devein shrimp

To devein shrimp, remove the dark vein using a sharp knife or deveining tool.

Seafood & Meat Salads
Create satisfying main-dish salads by combining salmon, shrimp, chicken, and beef with a variety of fresh vegetables and fruits.

Warm Salmon Salad à la Provençal

Capers and olives—two signature ingredients in Provençal-style cuisine—are featured in this distinctive heart-healthy salad.

Prep: 20 minutes • Cook: 13 minutes

1   (¾-pound) salmon fillet
⅛   teaspoon salt
⅛   teaspoon freshly ground black
      pepper
      Cooking spray
¼   cup fresh lemon juice
3   tablespoons reduced-fat Caesar
      dressing
10   cups gourmet salad greens
½   cup finely chopped red onion
4   teaspoons capers
4   (1½-ounce) slices French bread,
      toasted
¼   cup finely chopped black olives

1. Preheat broiler.
2. Sprinkle fish with salt and pepper. Place fish, skin side down, on a broiler pan coated with cooking spray; broil 12 minutes or until fish flakes easily when tested with a fork. Remove skin from fish; discard skin. Break fish into chunks.
3. Place salad greens in a large bowl. Drizzle juice and Caesar dressing over greens, tossing to coat. Add onion and capers; toss gently to combine. Place salad on plates. Divide salmon among salads. Top each bread slice with 1 tablespoon olives, spreading with a knife. Cut each slice in half. Serve immediately.

Yield: 4 servings (serving size: 1½ cups greens, about 2 ounces salmon, and 2 bread pieces).

CALORIES 335 (32% from fat); FAT 11.8g (sat 2.4g, mono 4.1g, poly 2.2g); PROTEIN 25.1g; CARB 32.7g; FIBER 5g; CHOL 47mg; IRON 3.6mg; SODIUM 727mg; CALC 133mg

Grilled-Salmon Salad

Tangy cucumber dressing tops savory grilled salmon and sweet mango in this sophisticated salad.

Prep: 20 minutes • Cook: 10 minutes

¾   cup chopped seeded peeled cucumber
3   tablespoons plain low-fat yogurt
2   tablespoons lemon juice
1½   teaspoons chopped fresh parsley
1½   teaspoons chopped fresh chives
1¼   teaspoons grated lemon rind
¼   teaspoon pepper
1   garlic clove, sliced
4   (6-ounce) salmon fillets (about 1
      inch thick)
1   teaspoon pepper
½   teaspoon salt
      Cooking spray
4   cups gourmet salad greens
¾   cup basil leaves
½   cup cubed peeled ripe mango

1. Prepare grill.
2. Place first 8 ingredients in a blender or food processor; process until almost smooth.
3. Sprinkle fish with 1 teaspoon pepper and salt. Place fish, skin sides up, on a grill rack coated with cooking spray; grill 5 minutes on each side or until fish flakes easily when tested with a fork. Remove skin from fillets; discard skin. Break fish into chunks.
4. Place greens and basil in a large bowl; add ¼ cup cucumber dressing, tossing well. Arrange salad on plates. Place salmon on salads; top with cucumber dressing and mango. Yield: 4 servings (serving size: 1 cup greens, 6 ounces salmon, 2 tablespoons dressing, and 2 tablespoons mango).

CALORIES 317 (41% from fat); FAT 14.6g (sat 2.6g, mono 6.9g, poly 3.3g); PROTEIN 37g; CARB 8.1g; FIBER 2g; CHOL 112mg; IRON 1.9mg; SODIUM 392mg; CALC 75mg

menu
serves 4

Grilled Salmon Salad

Herb and Parmesan Breadsticks*

Raspberry sorbet

*Unroll 1 (11-ounce) can refrigerated breadstick dough; separate into 12 pieces. Combine 3 tablespoons grated Parmesan cheese and 2 teaspoons herbes de Provence on a plate. Coat each piece of dough lightly with cheese mixture. Twist each piece several times, forming a spiral; place on an ungreased baking sheet, pressing down lightly on both ends. Bake at 375° for 13 minutes.

Grilled Tuna Niçoise

Our version of classic *salade niçoise* contains the basic ingredients (olives, tomato, tuna, onion, potato, and green beans), but no anchovies or hard-cooked eggs.

Prep: 30 minutes • Cook: 19 minutes

  4 cups cubed red potato
  ½ pound green beans, trimmed
  1 (8-ounce) tuna steak (¾ inch thick)
Cooking spray
  ½ cup vertically sliced red onion
  ½ cup chopped fresh parsley
  1 tablespoon chopped fresh or
     1 teaspoon dried tarragon
  ½ cup fat-free, less-sodium chicken
     broth
  3 tablespoons white wine vinegar
  1 tablespoon extravirgin olive oil
  1 tablespoon Dijon mustard
  ¼ teaspoon salt
  ¼ teaspoon freshly ground black pepper
  8 cups gourmet salad greens
  ½ cup cherry tomatoes, halved
  ½ cup yellow teardrop tomatoes, halved
  ¼ cup niçoise olives

1. Cook potato in boiling water 6 minutes or until tender; remove with a slotted spoon. Add green beans to boiling water, and cook 3 minutes or until crisp-tender. Drain.
2. Prepare grill or broiler.
3. Place fish on a grill rack or broiler pan coated with cooking spray; grill 3 minutes on each side or until desired degree of doneness. Cut fish into 1-inch chunks.
4. Combine potato, fish, onion, parsley, and tarragon in a large bowl. Combine broth and next 5 ingredients; stir well with a whisk. Pour ½ cup broth mixture over potato mixture, and toss well.
5. Place beans, greens, and tomatoes on plates. Top with potato mixture and olives. Drizzle remaining broth mixture over salads. Yield: 4 servings (serving size: 2 ounces beans, 2 cups greens, ¼ cup tomato, 1½ cups potato mixture, 1 tablespoon olives, and 1 tablespoon broth mixture).

CALORIES 299 (26% from fat); FAT 8.6g (sat 1.6g, mono 4.8g, poly 1.8g); PROTEIN 19.8g; CARB 37.2g; FIBER 6.9g; CHOL 21mg; IRON 4.7mg; SODIUM 458mg; CALC 104mg

Shrimp Salad with Mango and Avocado

Fanning the mango and avocado slices around the shrimp salad makes an impressive presentation.

Prep: 40 minutes • Cook: 7 minutes

  4 quarts water
2¼ pounds large shrimp, peeled and
     deveined
  ½ cup thinly sliced red onion
  3 tablespoons chopped fresh cilantro
  2 teaspoons grated lime rind
  2 tablespoons fresh lime juice
  1 tablespoon extravirgin olive oil
  ½ teaspoon salt
  ¼ teaspoon freshly ground black pepper
  1 jalapeño pepper, seeded and minced
  2 peeled ripe mangoes, each cut into
     6 wedges
  1 peeled avocado, seeded and cut into
     12 wedges
  6 cilantro sprigs (optional)

1. Bring water to a boil in a large Dutch oven. Add shrimp; cook 2 minutes or until done. Drain and rinse with cold water. Chill.
2. Combine onion and next 7 ingredients in a large bowl. Add shrimp; toss to coat.
3. Spoon shrimp mixture into center of salad plates. Arrange mango slices and avocado slices spokelike around each serving. Garnish with cilantro sprigs, if desired. Yield: 6 servings (serving size: ¾ cup shrimp mixture, 2 mango slices, and 2 avocado slices).

CALORIES 257 (29% from fat); FAT 8.3g (sat 1.6g, mono 4.6g, poly 1.5g); PROTEIN 23.3g; CARB 24.4g; FIBER 2.6g; CHOL 202mg; IRON 3.9mg; SODIUM 431mg; CALC 64mg

Grilled Tuna Niçoise

Edamame and Bean Salad with Shrimp and Fresh Salsa

To save time, cook the edamame in the microwave, and purchase everything else already cooked.

Prep: 11 minutes • Cook: 8 minutes

½ cup frozen shelled edamame
1 cup chopped cooked small shrimp (about 6 ounces)
1 cup canned cannellini beans, rinsed and drained
1 cup halved cherry tomatoes
2 tablespoons chopped red onion
2 teaspoons minced jalapeño pepper
2 tablespoons chopped fresh cilantro
1 tablespoon fresh lime juice
1 tablespoon extravirgin olive oil
¼ teaspoon salt

1. Cook edamame according to package directions. Drain and rinse with cold water; drain.

2. Combine edamame, shrimp, cannellini beans, cherry tomatoes, onion, and jalapeño pepper. Combine cilantro and remaining 3 ingredients, stirring with a whisk. Drizzle over edamame mixture, and toss gently to combine. Cover and chill. Yield: 2 servings (serving size: 1⅓ cups).

CALORIES 314 (29% from fat); FAT 10.1g (sat 1g, mono 5g, poly 1.2g); PROTEIN 28.1g; CARB 28g; FIBER 8.2g; CHOL 167mg; IRON 5.8mg; SODIUM 803mg; CALC 94mg

Test Kitchen Tip: Look for frozen edamame in the frozen vegetable section or the frozen organic foods section of the supermarket.

menu

serves 2

Edamame and Bean Salad with Shrimp and Fresh Salsa

Toasted pita chips*

Meyer-Lemon Sorbet (page 189)

*Cut 2 whole wheat pitas into 8 wedges each. Coat with cooking spray and sprinkle evenly with ¼ teaspoon garlic powder, ¼ teaspoon onion powder, ⅛ teaspoon ground red pepper, and ¼ teaspoon salt. Bake at 450° for 4 minutes or until crisp.

Thai Beef Salad

The salad gets its heat from 2 tablespoons of chile paste. If you prefer milder food, use half that amount.

Prep: 35 minutes • Cook: 17 minutes
Other: 15 minutes

½ cup fresh lime juice
¼ cup chopped fresh cilantro
2 tablespoons brown sugar
2 tablespoons Thai fish sauce
2 tablespoons chile paste with garlic
2 garlic cloves, minced
1 (1½-pound) flank steak, trimmed
Cooking spray
1½ cups vertically sliced red onion
4 plum tomatoes, each cut into 6 wedges
6 cups torn romaine lettuce
1¼ cups thinly sliced English cucumber
2 tablespoons chopped fresh mint

1. Prepare grill or broiler.
2. Combine first 6 ingredients, stirring until sugar dissolves; set half of lime mixture aside. Combine other half of lime mixture and steak in a large zip-top plastic bag; seal. Marinate in refrigerator 10 minutes, turning once. Remove steak from bag; discard marinade.
3. Place steak on grill rack or broiler pan coated with cooking spray; grill 6 minutes on each side or until desired degree of doneness. Let stand 5 minutes. Cut steak diagonally across grain into thin slices.
4. Heat a large nonstick skillet over medium-high heat. Coat pan with cooking spray. Add onion; sauté 3 minutes. Add tomatoes; sauté 2 minutes. Place onion mixture, lettuce, cucumber, and mint in a large bowl; toss gently to combine. Place salad on plates. Top with steak; drizzle each serving with reserved lime mixture. Yield: 6 servings (serving size: about 1½ cups salad mixture, 3 ounces steak, and 1 tablespoon lime mixture).

CALORIES 219 (35% from fat); FAT 8.6g (sat 3.6g, mono 3.3g, poly 0.5g); PROTEIN 24.1g; CARB 12.3g; FIBER 2.2g; CHOL 54mg; IRON 3.1mg; SODIUM 456mg; CALC 44mg

Grilled Onion, Beef, and Sweet Potato Salad

This warm, main-course salad is best served with bread to mop up the delicious dressing. Grill the onion slices on skewers or in a grill basket so they won't fall apart when turned.

Prep: 35 minutes • Cook: 28 minutes
Other: 5 minutes

Salad:
1 teaspoon coriander seeds, crushed
1⅛ teaspoons freshly ground black pepper, divided
1 teaspoon chopped fresh thyme
¼ teaspoon salt, divided
1 (1-pound) flank steak, trimmed
2 large white onions, cut into ½-inch-thick slices
Cooking spray
2 large sweet potatoes, peeled and cut horizontally into ½-inch-thick slices (about 1 pound)

Dressing:
⅓ cup fresh orange juice
¼ cup finely chopped shallots
1 tablespoon chopped fresh parsley
1 tablespoon extravirgin olive oil
2 teaspoons low-sodium soy sauce
1 teaspoon stone-ground mustard
¼ teaspoon salt

Remaining ingredient:
4 cups trimmed arugula or baby spinach

1. To prepare salad, combine coriander, 1 teaspoon pepper, thyme, and ⅛ teaspoon salt; rub over both sides of steak.
2. Prepare grill.
3. Sprinkle onion slices with ⅛ teaspoon pepper and ⅛ teaspoon salt; spray with cooking spray. Thread onion slices onto skewers, or arrange in grilling basket. Place skewers or grilling basket on a grill rack coated with cooking spray; grill onions 5 minutes on each side or until tender. Remove onions from skewers or basket; place in a large bowl.
4. Lightly coat sweet potato with cooking spray. Place on grill rack coated with cooking spray; grill 5 minutes on each side or until lightly browned. Cool slightly; slice potatoes into ¼-inch strips. Add to onion; toss to combine.
5. To prepare dressing, combine orange juice and next 6 ingredients, stirring with a whisk.
6. Place steak on grill rack coated with cooking spray; grill 4 minutes on each side or until desired degree of doneness. Place steak on a cutting board; let stand 5 minutes. Cut steak diagonally across grain into thin slices.
7. Place arugula in a large bowl; drizzle with ¼ cup dressing, tossing gently to coat. Place arugula mixture on plates; top with onion mixture. Arrange steak over onion mixture; drizzle each serving with dressing. Serve immediately. Yield: 4 servings (serving size: 1 cup arugula, 1 cup onion mixture, 3 ounces steak, and 1 tablespoon dressing).

CALORIES 390 (30% from fat); FAT 13.1g (sat 4.4g, mono 6.1g, poly 0.9g); PROTEIN 28.3g; CARB 40.4g; FIBER 6.6g; CHOL 59mg; IRON 3.9mg; SODIUM 498mg; CALC 107mg

Test Kitchen Tip: If the sweet potatoes aren't tender by the time they've browned on the grill, microwave them at HIGH for 20-second intervals until done.

Chicken and Strawberries over Mixed Greens

Celebrate the arrival of juicy springtime strawberries: Combine them with chicken and serve over tender salad greens.

Prep: 14 minutes • Cook: 21 minutes
Other: 1 hour

  2 cups chopped roasted skinless, boneless chicken breast (about 2 breast halves)
  2 cups quartered small strawberries (about 1 pint)
  ⅓ cup finely chopped celery
  ⅓ cup finely chopped red onion
  2 tablespoons golden raisins
  1 tablespoon sesame seeds, toasted
  1 tablespoon chopped fresh or
  1 teaspoon dried tarragon
  1 tablespoon extravirgin olive oil
  1 tablespoon balsamic vinegar
  ½ teaspoon paprika
  ⅛ teaspoon salt
  ⅛ teaspoon pepper
  4 cups gourmet salad greens

1. Combine first 5 ingredients in a large bowl. Combine sesame seeds and next 6 ingredients in a small bowl, stirring well with a whisk. Pour over chicken mixture; toss well to coat. Cover and chill 1 hour. Serve over salad greens. Yield: 4 servings (serving size: 1¼ cups chicken mixture and 1 cup greens).

CALORIES 164 (35% from fat); FAT 6.3g (sat 1.2g, mono 3.4g, poly 1.3g); PROTEIN 15.3g; CARB 13.3g; FIBER 3.5g; CHOL 35mg; IRON 1.7mg; SODIUM 376mg; CALC 78mg

Curried Chicken Salad

Take brown-bag lunch fare up a notch with this spicy, fruited chicken salad. Enjoy it with whole-grain crackers or bread. If you don't have time to cook chicken, pick up a rotisserie chicken at the supermarket.

Prep: 12 minutes • Cook: 21 minutes

  1½ cups chopped cooked chicken breast (about 8 ounces)
  ½ cup halved seedless red grapes
  ½ cup diced peeled apple
  2 tablespoons diced pineapple
  1 tablespoon dried currants
  3 tablespoons low-fat mayonnaise
  1 teaspoon honey
  ½ teaspoon curry powder
  ½ teaspoon fresh lemon juice
  ⅛ teaspoon salt
  ⅛ teaspoon freshly ground black pepper
  1 tablespoon sliced almonds, toasted

1. Combine first 5 ingredients in a large bowl. Combine mayonnaise and next 5 ingredients, stirring with a whisk. Pour mayonnaise mixture over chicken mixture; toss gently to coat. Sprinkle with almonds. Cover and chill. Yield: 2 servings (serving size: 1¼ cups).

CALORIES 303 (21% from fat); FAT 7.2g (sat 1.3g, mono 2.3g, poly 1.3g); PROTEIN 33.8g; CARB 25.7g; FIBER 1.9g; CHOL 89mg; IRON 1.7mg; SODIUM 435mg; CALC 37mg

Test Kitchen Tip: We used currants in this salad because they're smaller than raisins and can disperse more widely throughout the chicken mixture. But if you have raisins on hand, use those instead.

Chicken Caesar Salad

Using a precooked rotisserie chicken makes this salad extra easy and fast, although any leftover cooked chicken will work.

Prep: 20 minutes

Salad:
  1 (2-pound) whole roasted chicken, skinned
  11 cups torn romaine lettuce (about 1¼ pounds)
  1 cup red bell pepper strips
Vinaigrette:
  3 tablespoons olive oil
  1½ tablespoons fresh lemon juice
  2 teaspoons Worcestershire sauce
  2 teaspoons Dijon mustard
  ¼ teaspoon sugar
  ¼ teaspoon salt
  ¼ teaspoon black pepper
  1 garlic clove, crushed
  1½ cups plain croutons
  ½ cup (2 ounces) grated fresh Parmesan cheese

1. To prepare salad, remove chicken from bones; shred with 2 forks to measure 3 cups meat. Combine chicken, lettuce, and bell pepper in a large bowl.
2. To prepare vinaigrette, combine oil and next 7 ingredients in a bowl, stirring well with a whisk. Pour over salad; toss well. Sprinkle with croutons and cheese; toss gently to combine. Yield: 6 servings (serving size: 2 cups).

CALORIES 306 (47% from fat); FAT 16g (sat 4.3g, mono 8.2g, poly 2.2g); PROTEIN 29.4g; CARB 10.3g; FIBER 2.4g; CHOL 78mg; IRON 2.8mg; SODIUM 445mg; CALC 171mg

Test Kitchen Tip: To make this a super-quick salad, use a reduced-fat Caesar dressing instead of making the vinaigrette.

Classic Makeover: Fried Chicken Salad

It's a myth that just because a dish is a salad that it's low in fat and calories. That's definitely not the case with the popular fried chicken salad. Most of the fat and calories in a traditional fried chicken salad are from the fried chicken. By switching from store-bought breaded fried chicken to chicken tenders, and sautéing them in a light breading with a very small amount of olive oil, we were able to reduce the fat in the chicken from about 16 grams to 5 grams.

Another source of calories and fat is the dressing. By switching from regular blue cheese dressing to fat-free honey mustard, and sprinkling with just a bit of crumbled blue cheese, we were able to save 12 fat grams.

We also added canned beets to our salad for additional flavor, color, and texture, and very few calories. We loved the way the sweetness of the beets complemented the savory chicken and tender greens.

Before	After
• 506 calories	• 287 calories
• 37.2g fat	• 7.4g fat
• percentage of calories from fat 66%	• percentage of calories from fat 27%
• 965mg sodium	• 710mg sodium

Fried Chicken Salad

This popular restaurant salad features baby beets for added flavor and color.

Prep: 20 minutes • Cook: 7 minutes
Other: 30 minutes

- ¼ cup all-purpose flour
- ¼ cup dry breadcrumbs
- 1 teaspoon garlic powder
- 1 teaspoon dried thyme
- ½ teaspoon salt
- ½ teaspoon pepper
- ¾ pound skinless, boneless chicken breast, cut into thin strips
- ½ cup low-fat buttermilk
- 1 tablespoon olive oil
- Cooking spray
- 4 cups thickly sliced romaine lettuce, cut across rib
- 1 (15-ounce) can cut baby beets, drained
- ½ cup fat-free honey-Dijon mustard salad dressing
- ½ cup (2 ounces) crumbled blue cheese

1. Combine first 6 ingredients in a shallow dish, and set aside. Combine chicken and buttermilk in a zip-top plastic bag; seal and marinate in refrigerator 30 minutes.

2. Remove chicken, and discard marinade. Heat oil in a nonstick skillet coated with cooking spray over medium heat. Dredge a few chicken strips at a time in breadcrumb mixture, tossing to coat. Add chicken to pan, and cook 3 minutes on each side or until done.

3. Arrange lettuce on salad plates, and top with chicken and beets. Top with dressing and cheese. Yield: 4 servings (serving size: 1 cup lettuce, 3 ounces chicken, about ⅓ cup beets, 2 tablespoons dressing, and 2 tablespoons cheese).

CALORIES 287 (27% from fat); FAT 7.4g (sat 2.2g, mono 3.4g, poly 0.8g); PROTEIN 25.8g; CARB 28.3g; FIBER 2g; CHOL 60mg; IRON 2.9mg; SODIUM 710mg; CALC 116mg

Chicken Taco Salad

Taco salad was made for the crunch and texture of iceberg lettuce, but you can also use romaine or Bibb.

**Prep: 15 minutes • Cook: 5 minutes
Other: 1 hour**

- ¾ cup bottled salsa
- 3 tablespoons white wine vinegar
- 1 teaspoon sugar
- ½ teaspoon ground cumin
- ¼ teaspoon dried thyme
- ¼ teaspoon bottled minced garlic
- Dash of ground red pepper
- ½ pound skinless, boneless chicken breast, cut into 1-inch strips
- 1 cup halved cherry tomatoes (about 12 tomatoes)
- 1 cup canned kidney beans, rinsed and drained
- ¼ cup minced fresh cilantro
- 1 tablespoon olive oil
- Cooking spray
- 4 cups coarsely chopped iceberg lettuce
- 1 cup (4 ounces) shredded reduced-fat Cheddar cheese
- 32 baked tortilla chips

1. Combine first 7 ingredients in a bowl. Combine ½ cup salsa mixture and chicken in a zip-top plastic bag; seal and marinate in refrigerator 30 minutes. Add tomatoes, beans, cilantro, and oil to remaining salsa mixture; cover and marinate in refrigerator 30 minutes.

2. Heat a medium nonstick skillet over medium-high heat. Coat pan with cooking spray. Add chicken mixture; sauté 5 minutes or until chicken is done.

3. Place lettuce on plates; top with bean mixture and chicken mixture. Sprinkle with cheese. Serve with baked tortilla chips. Yield: 4 servings (serving size: 1 cup lettuce, ½ cup bean mixture, ¼ of chicken mixture, ¼ cup cheese, and 8 tortilla chips).

CALORIES 391 (25% from fat); FAT 11g (sat 3.9g, mono 2.8g, poly 1g); PROTEIN 30.4g; CARB 43.8g; FIBER 6g; CHOL 51mg; IRON 4mg; SODIUM 767mg; CALC 320mg

Curry Turkey Salad

Avoid the predictable with a creative take on leftover turkey. This flavorful salad is chock-full of grapes, cashews, and turkey, and it's dressed with a creamy honey-lime sauce.

Prep: 11 minutes

- 2 tablespoons reduced-fat sour cream
- 2 tablespoons plain yogurt
- 1 tablespoon fresh lime juice
- 1 tablespoon honey
- 1 teaspoon curry powder
- ¼ teaspoon salt
- ¼ teaspoon freshly ground black pepper
- 2 cups chopped cooked turkey
- 1 cup seedless red grapes, halved
- ½ cup diced celery
- ¼ cup chopped red onion
- 2 tablespoons cashew pieces
- 20 mini pita rounds (about 5 ounces)

1. Combine first 7 ingredients in a large bowl. Add turkey, grapes, celery, onion, and cashews; stir gently to combine. Serve with pitas. Yield: 4 servings (serving size: about 1 cup salad and 5 pitas).

CALORIES 309 (21% from fat); FAT 7.3g (sat 2.4g, mono 2.2g, poly 1.7g); PROTEIN 25.5g; CARB 35.3g; FIBER 2g; CHOL 57mg; IRON 2.8mg; SODIUM 419mg; CALC 83mg

Test Kitchen Tip: If you can't find mini pita rounds, use five regular pitas and cut each one into four wedges.

Asian Turkey Salad

This fresh, bright salad takes leftover roasted turkey on a trip to the East. And the day after a big Thanksgiving meal, you'll welcome its lightness.

Prep: 20 minutes

Dressing:
- ¼ cup rice vinegar
- ¼ cup vegetable broth
- 1 tablespoon low-sodium soy sauce
- 2 teaspoons bottled ground fresh ginger (such as Spice World)
- 2 teaspoons lime juice
- 1 teaspoon bottled minced garlic
- 1 teaspoon peanut oil
- 1 teaspoon sesame oil
- ½ teaspoon salt
- ½ teaspoon sugar
- 1 serrano chile

Salad:
- 4 cups thinly sliced napa (Chinese) cabbage
- 3 cups shredded cooked turkey
- 1 cup red bell pepper strips (about 1 small pepper)
- ½ cup thinly sliced red onion
- ½ cup chopped fresh cilantro
- ¼ cup sliced green onions
- 1 tablespoon dry-roasted peanuts, chopped

1. To prepare salad dressing, place first 11 ingredients in a blender, and process until smooth.

2. To prepare salad, combine cabbage and remaining ingredients in a large bowl, and pour dressing over salad, tossing to coat. Yield: 4 servings (serving size: 1¾ cups).

CALORIES 250 (30% from fat); FAT 8.3g (sat 2.2g, mono 2.3g, poly 2.6g); PROTEIN 33.2g; CARB 10.3g; FIBER 3.4g; CHOL 80mg; IRON 2.8mg; SODIUM 592mg; CALC 80mg

Salad Dressings
From zesty vinaigrettes to thick and creamy blue cheese dressing, these recipes are guaranteed to put your salads on the best-dressed list.

Versatile Vinaigrette

Cornstarch, commonly used as a thickening agent, gives this red wine vinaigrette body so it can better coat a salad. Store remaining vinaigrette in the refrigerator up to one week. Use this vinaigrette in Tomato and Cucumber Salad with Feta (page 410).

Prep: 5 minutes • Cook: 3 minutes

- 1　cup vegetable broth
- 2　teaspoons cornstarch
- 2　tablespoons red wine vinegar
- 1　tablespoon extravirgin olive oil
- 1　teaspoon sugar
- ¼　teaspoon salt
- ⅛　teaspoon freshly ground black pepper

1. Combine broth and cornstarch in a small saucepan, stirring with a whisk. Bring broth mixture to a boil over medium heat; cook 1 minute, stirring constantly. Remove from heat, and stir in remaining ingredients. Cover and chill. Stir before using. Yield: 1 cup (serving size: 2 tablespoons).

CALORIES 21 (77% from fat); FAT 1.8g (sat 0.2g, mono 1.2g, poly 0.2g); PROTEIN 0.3g; CARB 1.3g; FIBER 0g; CHOL 0mg; IRON 0.1mg; SODIUM 199mg; CALC 0mg

Variations

Dijon Vinaigrette: Add 2 teaspoons Dijon mustard to broth mixture with red wine vinegar and remaining ingredients.

Roasted Garlic Vinaigrette: Add 2 teaspoons bottled minced roasted garlic to broth mixture with red wine vinegar and remaining ingredients.

Cumin-Lime Vinaigrette: Omit vinegar. Add 3 tablespoons fresh lime juice and ¼ teaspoon ground cumin to broth mixture with oil and remaining ingredients.

Chile-Garlic Vinaigrette

Use this light vinaigrette to dress Garlicky Vegetable Pasta Salad (page 417) or grilled vegetables.

Prep: 9 minutes

- 1　tablespoon chopped serrano chile
- ¾　teaspoon salt
- 6　garlic cloves, crushed
- 3　tablespoons red wine vinegar
- 2　tablespoons water
- 2　tablespoons fresh lemon juice
- 1½　tablespoons extravirgin olive oil
- 1½　tablespoons anchovy paste

1. Combine first 3 ingredients in a mortar; mash to a paste with a pestle. Combine garlic paste mixture, vinegar, and remaining ingredients in a small bowl, stirring with a whisk. Yield: ¾ cup (serving size: 1 tablespoon).

CALORIES 21 (73% from fat); FAT 1.7g (sat 0.2g, mono 1.2g, poly 0.2g); PROTEIN 0.3g; CARB 1.1g; FIBER 0.1g; CHOL 1mg; IRON 0.7mg; SODIUM 266mg; CALC 8mg

Test Kitchen Tip: To get more juice from a lemon, put it in the microwave on HIGH for about 30 seconds before squeezing.

Citrus Vinaigrette

Orange and lime juices add the citrus flavor; honey provides a touch of sweetness. Use in Garden Salad with Citrus Vinaigrette (page 410).

Prep: 2 minutes

- 3　tablespoons fresh orange juice
- 1½　tablespoons fresh lime juice
- 2½　teaspoons extravirgin olive oil
- 2　teaspoons honey
- 1　teaspoon red wine vinegar
- ¼　teaspoon salt
- ⅛　teaspoon freshly ground black pepper

1. Combine all ingredients, stirring with a whisk. Yield: ¼ cup (serving size: 1 tablespoon).

CALORIES 43 (63% from fat); FAT 3g (sat 0.4g, mono 2.1g, poly 0.4g); PROTEIN 0.1g; CARB 4.7g; FIBER 0.1g; CHOL 0mg; IRON 0.1mg; SODIUM 148mg; CALC 3mg

Test Kitchen Tip: For juicing oranges, we prefer to use a handheld juicer that resembles a shallow bowl with a fluted, inverted cone in the center. Cut the orange in half, and place the cut half over the cone, pressing down and turning to extract the juice. One medium orange will give you about ½ cup juice.

Tomato Vinaigrette

Use this piquant dressing in Gazpacho Salad with Tomato Vinaigrette (page 410).

Prep: 1 minute

  3 tablespoons tomato juice
  2 tablespoons red wine vinegar
  1 tablespoon extravirgin olive oil
  1 teaspoon Worcestershire sauce
  ¼ teaspoon salt
  ¼ to ½ teaspoon hot sauce
  ⅛ teaspoon freshly ground black pepper

1. Combine all ingredients, stirring well with a whisk. Yield: ⅓ cup (serving size: 1 tablespoon).

CALORIES 27 (93% from fat); FAT 2.8g (sat 0.4g, mono 2g, poly 0.4g); PROTEIN 0.1g; CARB 0.6g; FIBER 0.1g; CHOL 0mg; IRON 0.1mg; SODIUM 155mg; CALC 2mg

Balsamic Vinaigrette

This intensely flavorful and versatile vinaigrette will keep in the refrigerator for up to one week.

Prep: 6 minutes

  ½ cup basil leaves
  ⅓ cup balsamic or sherry vinegar
  ⅓ cup finely chopped shallots
  ¼ cup water
  2 tablespoons honey
  1 tablespoon olive oil
  ¼ teaspoon freshly ground black pepper

1. Place all ingredients in a blender; process until smooth. Yield: 1 cup (serving size: 2 tablespoons).

CALORIES 37 (41% from fat); FAT 1.7g (sat 0.2g, mono 1.3g, poly 0.2g); PROTEIN 0.3g; CARB 5.8g; FIBER 0.1g; CHOL 0mg; IRON 0.2mg; SODIUM 1mg; CALC 7mg

Raspberry Dressing

Drizzle this tangy dressing over mixed greens or a fresh fruit salad. You can store this dressing in the refrigerator up to one week.

Prep: 5 minutes

  ⅓ cup honey
  ¼ cup raspberry or red wine vinegar
  ¼ cup plain fat-free yogurt
  1 tablespoon Dijon mustard
  2 teaspoons olive oil
  ¼ teaspoon salt
  ¼ teaspoon pepper

1. Combine all ingredients; stir with a whisk. Yield: ¾ cup (serving size: 3 tablespoons).

CALORIES 120 (20% from fat); FAT 2.6g (sat 0.3g, mono 1.8g, poly 0.3g); PROTEIN 1.2g; CARB 25.1g; FIBER 0.1g; CHOL 0mg; IRON 0.4mg; SODIUM 257mg; CALC 39mg

Shallot and Grapefruit Dressing

Drizzle this zesty dressing over mixed gourmet greens topped with goat cheese and roasted corn. You can squeeze your own grapefruit juice, or look for fresh grapefruit juice in the produce section of the grocery store.

Prep: 12 minutes • Cook: 15 minutes

  1 teaspoon olive oil
  ½ cup chopped shallots
  2 cups fresh grapefruit juice (about 3 grapefruits)
  2 tablespoons chopped fresh cilantro
  2 teaspoons sugar
  ¼ teaspoon freshly ground black pepper
  2 tablespoons olive oil

1. Heat 1 teaspoon oil in a large nonstick skillet over medium heat. Add shallots;

cook 5 minutes or until golden brown. Stir in juice. Bring to a boil over medium-high heat, and cook until reduced to 1 cup (about 6 minutes). Remove from heat; cool.

2. Place grapefruit juice mixture, cilantro, sugar, and pepper in a blender; process until smooth. With blender on, slowly add 2 tablespoons oil; process until smooth. Yield: 1 cup (serving size: 1 tablespoon).

CALORIES 35 (51% from fat); FAT 2g (sat 0.3g, mono 1.5g, poly 0.2g); PROTEIN 0.3g; CARB 4.2g; FIBER 0.1g; CHOL 0mg; IRON 0.1mg; SODIUM 1mg; CALC 4mg

Blue Cheese Salad Dressing

Use this as an all-purpose dressing or dip. Try adding chopped anchovies to a portion of the dressing and pouring it over celery stalks. Or add chopped green onions, and pour it over baked potatoes. Low-fat mayonnaise and fat-free sour cream dramatically reduce the calories and fat, and allow a generous amount of blue cheese.

Prep: 6 minutes • Other: 3 hours

  1 cup low-fat mayonnaise
  2 tablespoons cider vinegar
  1 tablespoon canola oil
  ½ teaspoon dried oregano
  ¼ teaspoon salt
  ¼ teaspoon freshly ground black pepper
  1 (8-ounce) carton fat-free sour cream
  1 garlic clove, crushed
  ½ cup (2 ounces) crumbled blue cheese

1. Combine first 8 ingredients, stirring with a whisk. Stir in cheese. Cover and refrigerate at least 3 hours. Yield: 2½ cups (serving size: 1 tablespoon).

CALORIES 23 (47% from fat); FAT 1.2g (sat 0.3g, mono 0.3g, poly 0.1g); PROTEIN 0.5g; CARB 2.6g; FIBER 0g; CHOL 2mg; IRON 0mg; SODIUM 99mg; CALC 15mg

sandwiches

Open-Faced Turkey
Sandwiches with Apple
and Havarti, page 440

Cold Sandwiches
When you need portable fare for a picnic or a wholesome brown-bag lunch, these sandwiches are sure to satisfy.

Roasted Red Pepper Spread Sandwiches

If you like pimiento cheese, you'll enjoy this recipe. Keep the sandwiches well chilled so the cream cheese spread will remain firm. Sturdy, whole-grain bread works best.

Prep: 11 minutes • Other: 5 minutes

- ½ cup finely chopped seeded cucumber
- 1 (7-ounce) bottle roasted red bell peppers, drained and finely chopped
- ¾ cup (6 ounces) ⅓-less-fat cream cheese, softened
- ⅓ cup (about 3 ounces) block-style fat-free cream cheese, softened
- 3 tablespoons minced red onion
- ¼ teaspoon salt
- 1 garlic clove, minced
- 8 (1½-ounce) slices whole-grain bread
- 8 romaine lettuce leaves

1. Spread chopped cucumber and roasted red bell peppers onto several layers of heavy-duty paper towels; let stand 5 minutes to drain excess moisture.

2. Scrape into a medium bowl using a rubber spatula. Add cheeses, onion, salt, and garlic; stir with a fork until well blended. Spread about ½ cup cheese mixture over each of 4 bread slices; top each serving with 2 lettuce leaves and 1 bread slice. Yield: 4 servings (serving size: 1 sandwich).

CALORIES 356 (30% from fat); FAT 11.9g (sat 6.4g, mono 2.9g, poly 0.4g); PROTEIN 14.9g; CARB 43.6g; FIBER 4.1g; CHOL 36mg; IRON 2.9mg; SODIUM 875mg; CALC 173mg

Test Kitchen Tip: We used a combination of fat-free and ⅓-less-fat cream cheese (instead of all fat-free) in order to get a creamier mixture.

Salad Niçoise in Pita Pockets

Fresh green beans give this tuna sandwich, inspired by the classic French salad, a distinct crunch.

Prep: 20 minutes • Cook: 1½ minutes

- 1 cup (1-inch) cut fresh green beans (about 4 ounces)
- 1 tablespoon water
- ¼ cup niçoise olives, pitted and chopped (about 18 olives)
- 1 tablespoon capers
- 1 (12-ounce) can solid white tuna in water, drained
- 1 tablespoon extravirgin olive oil
- 1 tablespoon fresh lemon juice
- ½ teaspoon salt
- 2 (6-inch) whole wheat pita rounds, cut in half
- 4 curly leaf lettuce leaves

1. Combine beans and water in a small microwave-safe bowl; cover with plastic wrap. Microwave at HIGH 1½ minutes or until beans are crisp-tender; drain. Rinse with cold water. Drain well; cool.

2. Combine beans, olives, capers, and tuna. Combine oil, juice, and salt, stirring with a whisk. Pour oil mixture over tuna mixture; toss gently to coat.

3. Line each pita half with 1 lettuce leaf; spoon about ½ cup tuna mixture into each lettuce-lined pita half. Yield: 4 servings (serving size: 1 pita half).

CALORIES 253 (30% from fat); FAT 8.3g (sat 1.5g, mono 4.4g, poly 1.7g); PROTEIN 24.1g; CARB 21.6g; FIBER 4.2g; CHOL 30mg; IRON 2.6mg; SODIUM 702mg; CALC 48mg

Roasted Red Pepper Spread Sandwiches

Chicken-Arugula Focaccia Sandwiches

Chicken-Arugula Focaccia Sandwiches

Transform extra Mediterranean Grilled Chicken (page 370) into a focaccia sandwich by adding arugula, olives, onions, and a zesty yogurt sauce.

Prep: 16 minutes • Cook: 1 minute

¼ cup plain fat-free yogurt
1½ teaspoons chopped fresh rosemary
⅛ teaspoon grated lemon rind
¾ teaspoon fresh lemon juice
¼ teaspoon minced fresh thyme
Dash of salt
1 small garlic clove, crushed
2 Mediterranean Grilled Chicken breast halves (page 370)
1 teaspoon lemon juice
1 teaspoon extravirgin olive oil
⅛ teaspoon salt
⅛ teaspoon pepper
3 cups trimmed arugula
1 (8.8-ounce) loaf rosemary focaccia (such as Alessi), cut in half horizontally and toasted
½ cup thinly sliced red onion
¼ cup chopped pitted kalamata olives

1. Combine first 7 ingredients.
2. Remove Mediterranean Grilled Chicken from bones; thinly slice. Combine juice, oil, salt, and pepper; drizzle over arugula, tossing to coat.
3. Spread yogurt mixture over cut sides of bread. Arrange arugula, sliced chicken, onion, and olives over bottom half of loaf; cover with top half of loaf. Cut into 4 wedges. Yield: 4 servings (serving size: 1 wedge).

(Totals include Mediterranean Grilled Chicken) CALORIES 328 (27% from fat); FAT 9.7g (sat 2.1g, mono 5.3g, poly 2g); PROTEIN 23.5g; CARB 36.5g; FIBER 1.9g; CHOL 43mg; IRON 2.6mg; SODIUM 702mg; CALC 88mg

kalamata olives These Greek black olives are plump and juicy with a powerful flavor, bright acidity, and high salt content. Like other olives, kalamatas can be stored in the refrigerator up to one year if they are purchased packed in water, brine, or oil.

Cashew Chicken Salad Sandwiches

This chicken salad features the crunch of celery and cashews and the sweet-hot spice of curry powder.

Prep: 9 minutes

¼ cup fat-free sour cream
1 tablespoon light mayonnaise
¼ teaspoon curry powder
2 cups chopped roasted skinless, boneless chicken breast (about 2 breasts)
⅓ cup chopped celery
2 tablespoons chopped dry-roasted cashews
1 tablespoon finely chopped green onions
2 (2-ounce) whole wheat hamburger buns

1. Combine first 3 ingredients in a large bowl, stirring until well blended. Add chicken, celery, cashews, and green onions; stir well. Serve chicken salad on buns. Yield: 2 servings (serving size: ⅔ cup chicken salad and 1 bun).

CALORIES 353 (26% from fat); FAT 10.3g (sat 2.6g, mono 1.5g, poly 1.8g); PROTEIN 31.6g; CARB 35.8g; FIBER 4.8g; CHOL 69mg; IRON 1.8mg; SODIUM 925mg; CALC 115mg

Test Kitchen Tip: A freshly prepared or prepackaged rotisserie chicken from the grocery is a time-saving ingredient for quick and easy sandwiches. A 2-pound rotisserie chicken yields about 3 cups chopped chicken. Or look for a package of roasted breasts. You'll need two breasts to get 2 cups chopped chicken.

Sunchoke-Chicken Salad Wraps

These wraps highlight the crunchy texture of raw sunchokes, which, along with the pecans, add a nutty flavor.

Prep: 20 minutes

- ¼ cup chopped pecans, toasted
- 5 ounces Jerusalem artichokes (sunchokes), peeled and chopped (about 1 cup)
- ½ cup (4 ounces) block-style fat-free cream cheese, softened
- 1 tablespoon fresh lemon juice
- 3 tablespoons light mayonnaise
- ¼ teaspoon salt
- ⅛ teaspoon ground red pepper
- 2 cups shredded skinless, boneless rotisserie chicken breast
- 6 (8-inch) fat-free flour tortillas
- 12 (⅛-inch-thick) slices tomato
- 3 cups shredded leaf lettuce

1. Place pecans and artichokes in a food processor; pulse 5 times or until finely chopped.

2. Combine cream cheese and next 4 ingredients in a large bowl; stir until smooth. Stir in artichoke mixture and shredded chicken. Spread ⅓ cup artichoke mixture over each tortilla; top with 2 tomato slices and ½ cup lettuce. Roll up. Yield: 6 servings (serving size: 1 wrap).

CALORIES 298 (24% from fat); FAT 8g (sat 1.3g, mono 4.1g, poly 1.5g); PROTEIN 20.6g; CARB 25.4g; FIBER 3.7g; CHOL 46mg; IRON 1.7mg; SODIUM 512mg; CALC 87mg

Test Kitchen Tip: Vary this recipe by using flavored tortillas (spinach or tomato-basil). The flavored tortillas (sometimes labeled "wraps") have 4 to 5 grams of fat per tortilla, depending on the brand.

Smoky Bacon and Blue Cheese Chicken Salad Pitas

You only need a small amount of bacon and blue cheese to pump up the flavor in these chicken salad pitas. The chicken salad is fabulous—in or out of a pita half.

Prep: 13 minutes • Cook: 30 minutes

- ¾ cup plain fat-free yogurt
- ¼ cup (1 ounce) crumbled blue cheese
- 2 tablespoons light mayonnaise
- ½ teaspoon freshly ground black pepper
- 3 cups shredded romaine lettuce
- 1½ cups shredded cooked chicken (about 6 ounces)
- 4 bacon slices, cooked and crumbled
- 2 medium tomatoes, seeded and chopped
- 4 (6-inch) whole wheat pitas, cut in half

1. Combine first 4 ingredients, stirring well. Combine lettuce, chicken, bacon, and tomatoes in a medium bowl, stirring well. Drizzle yogurt mixture over chicken mixture; toss gently to coat. Spoon ½ cup chicken salad into each pita half. Serve immediately. Yield: 4 servings (serving size: 2 pita halves).

CALORIES 375 (29% from fat); FAT 12.1g (sat 3.7g, mono 3.6g, poly 3.1g); PROTEIN 26.1g; CARB 43.8g; FIBER 6.3g; CHOL 55mg; IRON 3.5mg; SODIUM 696mg; CALC 130mg

how to shred chicken

Cut cooked chicken breast halves into large pieces, then pull apart into shreds using two forks.

Guacamole and Turkey Sandwiches

If you like hot foods, add minced jalapeño peppers to the avocado mixture.

Prep: 15 minutes

- ½ cup coarsely mashed avocado
- 1 tablespoon fresh lime juice
- 8 (1-ounce) slices whole-grain bread
- 4 plum tomatoes, each cut into 4 slices
- ¼ teaspoon salt
- ⅛ teaspoon ground red pepper
- ⅔ cup alfalfa sprouts
- ½ cup thinly sliced red onion
- ¼ cup chopped fresh cilantro
- 8 ounces thinly sliced deli turkey

1. Combine avocado and lime juice. Spread 2 tablespoons avocado mixture on each of 4 bread slices. Arrange tomato slices over avocado mixture; sprinkle evenly with salt and pepper. Divide sprouts, onion, cilantro, and turkey evenly over tomato slices. Top with remaining bread slices. Yield: 4 servings (serving size: 1 sandwich).

CALORIES 205 (22% from fat); FAT 5g (sat 1g, mono 2.2g, poly 0.7g); PROTEIN 14g; CARB 31.4g; FIBER 10.4g; CHOL 23mg; IRON 3.1mg; SODIUM 954mg; CALC 188mg

how to remove avocado flesh

After you've removed the pit (see page 54), use the knife's tip to pierce the flesh in horizontal and vertical rows. Don't cut through the skin. Remove the meat gently with a spoon.

Muffuletta

The muffuletta (which originated in New Orleans) is stuffed with thinly sliced salami, provolone cheese, and the essential "olive salad"—a relish-like mixture of olives and a tangy seasoning. Our version, featuring half the meat and cheese that normally grace this specialty, includes marinated grilled vegetables.

Prep: 20 minutes • Cook: 10 minutes • Other: 26 hours

Grilled vegetables:
- ¼ cup reduced-fat Italian dressing
- 8 (½-inch-thick) slices eggplant (about 1 pound)
- 2 (½-inch-thick) slices Vidalia or other sweet onion
- 1 medium yellow squash, thinly sliced
- 1 medium red bell pepper, cut into 4 wedges
- Cooking spray

Olive salad:
- 1 cup chopped tomato or quartered cherry tomatoes
- ⅓ cup chopped pepperoncini peppers
- ¼ cup sliced pimiento-stuffed olives
- 2 tablespoons pepperoncini juice
- ½ teaspoon dried thyme
- ½ teaspoon cracked black pepper

Remaining ingredients:
- 1 (16-ounce) loaf French bread, cut in half horizontally
- 2 ounces thinly sliced provolone cheese
- 2 ounces thinly sliced reduced-fat hard salami (such as Franklin)

1. To prepare grilled vegetables, combine first 5 ingredients in a zip-top plastic bag; seal and marinate in refrigerator 2 hours, turning bag occasionally.

2. Prepare grill.

3. Remove vegetables from plastic bag; discard marinade. Place vegetables on grill rack coated with cooking spray. Grill 5 minutes on each side or until vegetables are tender.

4. To prepare olive salad, combine tomato and next 5 ingredients.

5. Hollow out bottom half of loaf, leaving a 1-inch-thick shell; reserve torn bread for another use. Arrange cheese in bottom half of loaf. Top with salami, grilled vegetables, olive salad, and top half of loaf. Wrap loaf with plastic wrap; refrigerate up to 24 hours. Cut into 4 pieces just before serving. Yield: 4 servings (serving size: 1 piece).

CALORIES 384 (28% from fat); FAT 11.9g (sat 4.3g, mono 3.4g, poly 1.9g); PROTEIN 16.3g; CARB 55.1g; FIBER 7.9g; CHOL 23mg; IRON 3.4mg; SODIUM 1313mg; CALC 204mg

Hot Sandwiches

Whether it's a burger on the grill, a patty melt in the skillet, or sizzling steak in a wrap, something magical happens when you cook a sandwich.

Grilled Goat Cheese Sandwiches with Fig and Honey

These sweet and savory sandwiches are equally good for breakfast or dinner. Mixing honey with the goat cheese makes it easier to spread over the cinnamon-raisin bread.

Prep: 10 minutes • Cook: 12 minutes

> 2 teaspoons honey
> ¼ teaspoon grated lemon rind
> 1 (4-ounce) package goat cheese
> 8 (1-ounce) slices cinnamon-raisin bread
> 2 tablespoons fig preserves
> 2 teaspoons thinly sliced fresh basil
> Cooking spray
> 1 teaspoon powdered sugar

1. Combine first 3 ingredients, stirring until well blended. Spread 1 tablespoon goat cheese mixture on each of 4 cinnamon-raisin bread slices; top each slice with 1½ teaspoons preserves and ½ teaspoon basil. Top with remaining bread slices. Lightly coat outside of bread with cooking spray.

2. Heat a large nonstick skillet over medium heat. Add 2 sandwiches to pan. Place a cast-iron or heavy skillet on top of sandwiches; press sandwiches gently to flatten. Cook 3 minutes on each side or until bread is lightly toasted (leave cast-iron skillet on sandwiches while they cook). Remove from pan, and repeat procedure with remaining sandwiches. Sprinkle with sugar. Yield: 4 servings (serving size: 1 sandwich).

CALORIES 243 (31% from fat); FAT 8.5g (sat 4.8g, mono 2.7g, poly 0.5g); PROTEIN 9.8g; CARB 33.1g; FIBER 2.5g; CHOL 13mg; IRON 2.2mg; SODIUM 326mg; CALC 78mg

Grilled Eggplant-and-Green-Tomato Sandwiches

Grilling the tomatoes softens their texture a bit but doesn't take away their tang.

Prep: 20 minutes • Cook: 14 minutes
Other: 20 minutes

> 1 large eggplant (about 1¼ pounds), cut crosswise into 8 slices
> ¼ teaspoon salt
> ½ cup low-fat mayonnaise
> 5 tablespoons fat-free milk
> 2 tablespoons Dijon mustard
> 2 teaspoons chopped fresh or ½ teaspoon dried rosemary
> 1 teaspoon fresh lemon juice
> 2 garlic cloves, minced
> 2 cups trimmed arugula
> Cooking spray
> 2 green tomatoes, each cut into 4 slices
> 8 (1-ounce) slices sourdough bread
> ¼ cup (1 ounce) crumbled goat cheese

1. Prepare grill.

2. Sprinkle eggplant slices with salt. Place slices on paper towels; let stand 20 minutes. Pat dry with paper towels.

3. Combine mayonnaise and next 5 ingredients in a bowl. Remove ¼ cup mayonnaise mixture; set aside. Add arugula to mayonnaise mixture in bowl; toss.

4. Coat both sides of eggplant slices with cooking spray. Place on grill rack; grill 5 minutes on each side. Transfer to a plate. Coat both sides of tomato slices with cooking spray. Place tomato and bread on grill rack; grill 2 minutes on each side.

Grilled Goat Cheese Sandwiches with Fig and Honey

5. Top each bread slice with ⅓ cup arugula mixture, 2 eggplant slices, 2 tomato slices, 1 tablespoon cheese, and 1 tablespoon reserved mayonnaise mixture. Top with remaining bread slices. Yield: 4 servings (serving size: 1 sandwich).

CALORIES 295 (21% from fat); FAT 6.8g (sat 1.9g, mono 1.7g, poly 2g); PROTEIN 8.8g; CARB 50.6g; FIBER 5.8g; CHOL 7mg; IRON 2.2mg; SODIUM 926mg; CALC 145mg

Roasted Pepper, Tomato, and Feta Sandwich

The smooth pesto and mayonnaise spread makes this sandwich extraspecial.

Prep: 20 minutes • Cook: 15 minutes
Other: 15 minutes

    1   yellow bell pepper
    1   (8-ounce) loaf French bread
  Pesto Mayonnaise (page 452)
    ½   cup (2 ounces) crumbled feta cheese
    8   (¼-inch-thick) slices tomato
    4   (⅛-inch-thick) slices red onion,
        separated into rings

1. Preheat broiler.
2. Cut bell pepper in half lengthwise; discard seeds and membranes. Place pepper halves, skin sides up, on a foil-lined baking sheet; flatten with hand. Broil 15 minutes or until blackened. Place in a zip-top plastic bag; seal. Let stand 15 minutes. Peel and cut each piece in half.
3. Cut loaf in half lengthwise. Spread Pesto Mayonnaise over bottom half of loaf; sprinkle with feta. Arrange pepper, tomato, and onion over bottom half of loaf; top with remaining half. Cut into 4 pieces. Yield: 4 servings (serving size: 1 piece).

(Totals include Pesto Mayonnaise) CALORIES 256 (28% from fat); FAT 8.1g (sat 3.2g, mono 3.0g, poly 1.3g); PROTEIN 8.8g; CARB 37.3g; FIBER 3.2g; CHOL 14mg; IRON 2.2mg; SODIUM 713mg; CALC 157mg

Lentil Burgers with Tzatziki

Tzatziki, a garlicky Greek yogurt sauce, makes a healthful and tasty alternative to mayonnaise for these meatless burgers.

Prep: 25 minutes • Cook: 49 minutes
Other: 5 minutes

Tzatziki:
    1   cup grated peeled English cucumber
  1½   cups plain low-fat yogurt
    ½   teaspoon salt
    2   garlic cloves, crushed
    ¼   cup chopped green onions
    1   teaspoon extravirgin olive oil
Burgers:
    2   teaspoons olive oil
    1   cup chopped onion
    ¾   teaspoon dried oregano
    ⅛   teaspoon crushed red pepper
    2   garlic cloves, minced
  1½   cups fat-free, less-sodium chicken
        broth
    ⅔   cup dried lentils
    ¼   cup sun-dried tomato sprinkles
    ⅔   cup (2½ ounces) crumbled feta cheese
    ½   cup grated carrot
    ⅓   cup Italian-seasoned breadcrumbs
    ⅓   cup toasted wheat germ
    3   tablespoons chopped pitted kalamata
        olives
    ¼   cup chopped fresh flat-leaf parsley
    ¼   teaspoon freshly ground black pepper
  Cooking spray
    8   (1½-ounce) whole wheat hamburger
        buns, toasted
   16   arugula leaves
    2   tomatoes, cut into ¼-inch-thick
        slices (about ¾ pound)

1. To prepare tzatziki, place cucumber on paper towels, and squeeze until barely moist. Place in a medium bowl. Spoon yogurt onto several layers of heavy-duty paper towels; spread to ½-inch thickness. Cover with additional paper towels, and let stand 5 minutes. Scrape into bowl using a rubber spatula. Add salt, crushed garlic, green onions, and 1 teaspoon olive oil; chill.
2. To prepare burgers, heat 2 teaspoons oil in a medium saucepan over medium-high heat. Add onion; sauté 2 minutes or until tender. Stir in oregano, red pepper, and minced garlic; cook 30 seconds, stirring constantly. Stir in broth, lentils, and sun-dried tomatoes; bring to a boil. Cover, reduce heat, and simmer 35 minutes or until lentils are tender; drain. Cool.
3. Place lentil mixture, cheese, and next 6 ingredients in a food processor; pulse until coarsely ground. Divide lentil mixture into 8 equal portions, shaping each into a ½-inch-thick patty.
4. Heat a large nonstick skillet over medium-high heat. Coat pan with cooking spray. Add patties, and cook 3 minutes. Turn patties over; reduce heat to medium, and cook 3 minutes. Spread 1 tablespoon tzatziki evenly on each bun top and bottom. Arrange arugula, patties, and tomato slices evenly over bottom halves of buns; top with remaining bun halves. Yield: 8 servings (serving size: 1 burger).

CALORIES 328 (27% from fat); FAT 9.8g (sat 3g, mono 4.5g, poly 1.4g); PROTEIN 15.8g; CARB 46.7g; FIBER 9.2g; CHOL 11mg; IRON 4.5mg; SODIUM 891mg; CALC 250mg

Test Kitchen Tip: English cucumbers are a variety with naturally fewer seeds. You can find them in most major supermarkets (usually individually wrapped), but they're more expensive than regular cucumbers. If you don't mind a few extra seeds, or want to seed the cucumber, you can use the regular variety in this sandwich.

Falafel-Stuffed Pitas

The patties will seem small when you're forming them, but they fit perfectly in the pita halves. Look for tahini near the peanut butter and other nut butters.

Prep: 20 minutes • Cook: 11 minutes

Falafel:
- ¼ cup dry breadcrumbs
- ¼ cup chopped cilantro
- 1½ teaspoons ground cumin
- ½ teaspoon salt
- ¼ teaspoon ground red pepper
- 2 garlic cloves, crushed
- 1 large egg
- 1 (15-ounce) can chickpeas (garbanzo beans), rinsed and drained
- 1 tablespoon olive oil

Sauce:
- ½ cup plain low-fat yogurt
- 2 tablespoons fresh lemon juice
- 2 tablespoons tahini (sesame-seed paste)
- 1 garlic clove, minced

Remaining ingredients:
- 4 (6-inch) whole wheat pitas, cut in half
- 8 curly leaf lettuce leaves
- 16 (¼-inch-thick) slices tomato

1. To prepare falafel, place first 8 ingredients in a food processor; process mixture until smooth. Divide mixture into 16 equal portions, and shape each portion into a ¼-inch-thick patty. Heat olive oil in a large nonstick skillet over medium-high heat. Add patties, and cook 5 minutes on each side or until patties are browned.

2. To prepare sauce, combine yogurt, lemon juice, tahini, and 1 garlic clove, stirring mixture with a whisk. Spread about 1½ tablespoons tahini sauce into each pita half. Fill each pita half with 1 lettuce leaf, 2 tomato slices, and 2 patties. Yield: 4 servings (serving size: 2 stuffed pita halves).

CALORIES 403 (28% from fat); FAT 12.6g (sat 1.9g, mono 5.6g, poly 3.9g); PROTEIN 15g; CARB 59g; FIBER 6.8g; CHOL 56mg; IRON 4.4mg; SODIUM 901mg; CALC 188mg

Test Kitchen Tip: To prevent the falafel mixture from sticking to your hands, dip your hands in water before forming the patties.

Seared Tuna Sandwiches
with Balsamic Onions

Cajun Catfish Wraps with Slaw

Mellow cabbage slaw is a good companion for the crisp catfish.

Prep: 20 minutes • Cook: 14 minutes

Slaw:

3 ½ cups thinly sliced red or green
    cabbage
¼ cup light mayonnaise
1 ½ tablespoons cider vinegar
½ teaspoon sugar

Wraps:

1 tablespoon all-purpose flour
1 tablespoon paprika
1 ½ teaspoons dried thyme
1 ½ teaspoons dried oregano
1 teaspoon garlic powder
1 teaspoon black pepper
½ teaspoon salt
¼ teaspoon ground red pepper
4 (6-ounce) farm-raised catfish fillets
1 tablespoon butter
4 (8-inch) fat-free flour tortillas

1. To prepare slaw, combine first 4 ingredients in a bowl; cover and chill.
2. To prepare wraps, combine flour and next 7 ingredients in a shallow dish. Dredge fillets in flour mixture. Melt butter in a large nonstick skillet over medium-high heat. Add fillets; cook 5 minutes. Turn fillets over; cook 4 minutes or until fish flakes easily when tested with a fork.
3. Heat tortillas according to package directions. Cut each catfish fillet lengthwise into 4 pieces. Arrange 4 fillet pieces on each tortilla; top each serving with about ¾ cup slaw, and roll up. Yield: 4 servings (serving size: 1 wrap).

CALORIES 397 (27% from fat); FAT 11.7g (sat 3.7g, mono 3.9g, poly 2.7g); PROTEIN 35.6g; CARB 36.6g; FIBER 3g; CHOL 106mg; IRON 4.7mg; SODIUM 918mg; CALC 126mg

Test Kitchen Tip: If the tortillas are dry, revive them by wrapping them in damp paper towels and microwaving at HIGH for 10 seconds. This will keep them from cracking when you roll them up.

Seared Tuna Sandwiches with Balsamic Onions

Balsamic vinegar lends the onions a rich, sweet flavor.

Prep: 12 minutes • Cook: 17 minutes

2 teaspoons butter
2 cups vertically sliced onion
1 ½ tablespoons balsamic vinegar
¼ teaspoon dried thyme
1 tablespoon all-purpose flour
½ teaspoon salt
¼ teaspoon garlic powder
¼ teaspoon pepper
4 (6-ounce) tuna steaks (about ½ inch
    thick)
Cooking spray
4 teaspoons Dijon mustard
4 (2-ounce) whole wheat hamburger
    buns
4 curly leaf lettuce leaves
4 (¼-inch-thick) slices tomato

1. Melt butter in a medium skillet over medium-high heat. Add onion; sauté 5 minutes. Stir in vinegar and thyme; cover and cook 5 minutes, stirring occasionally.
2. Combine flour, salt, garlic powder, and pepper in a shallow dish. Dredge fish in flour mixture. Heat a large nonstick skillet over medium-high heat. Coat pan with cooking spray. Add fish; cook 3 minutes on each side or until desired degree of doneness.
3. Spread 1 teaspoon mustard over top half of each bun. Layer 1 lettuce leaf, 1 fish steak, 1 tomato slice, and ¼ cup onion mixture on bottom half of each bun. Top with top halves of buns. Yield: 4 servings (serving size: 1 sandwich).

CALORIES 402 (17% from fat); FAT 7.8g (sat 2.5g, mono 2.8g, poly 1.4g); PROTEIN 46.2g; CARB 35.5g; FIBER 3.8g; CHOL 82mg; IRON 4mg; SODIUM 701mg; CALC 158mg

Shrimp Po'boys with Spicy Ketchup

A New Orleans specialty, this sandwich is often made with deep-fried shrimp. Broiling the garlicky breaded shrimp delivers lots of flavor without the fat.

Prep: 25 minutes • Cook: 4 minutes

- 3 tablespoons dry breadcrumbs
- ¼ teaspoon salt
- ¼ teaspoon pepper
- 1 garlic clove, minced
- 1 tablespoon olive oil
- ¾ pound large peeled and deveined shrimp
- ¼ cup ketchup
- 1½ teaspoons fresh lemon juice
- ½ teaspoon Worcestershire sauce
- ¼ teaspoon chili powder
- ¼ teaspoon hot sauce
- 2 (10-inch) submarine rolls, split
- 2 cups torn curly leaf lettuce
- ½ cup thinly sliced red onion

1. Prepare broiler.
2. Line a baking sheet with heavy-duty aluminum foil. Combine breadcrumbs, salt, pepper, and garlic in a medium bowl, stirring with a fork. Combine oil and shrimp; toss well. Place half of the shrimp in breadcrumb mixture; toss well to coat. Place breaded shrimp in a single layer on prepared baking sheet. Repeat procedure with remaining shrimp and breadcrumb mixture. Broil 4 minutes or until shrimp are done.
3. Combine ketchup, juice, Worcestershire, chili powder, and hot sauce in a small bowl, stirring with a whisk.
4. Spread 2 tablespoons ketchup mixture over cut sides of each roll half. Place 1 cup lettuce over bottom half of each roll; top with ¼ cup onion. Arrange 1 cup shrimp on each roll half; top each with remaining

Shrimp Po'boys with Spicy Ketchup

roll half. Cut sandwiches in half. Yield: 4 servings (serving size: 1 sandwich half).

CALORIES 401 (20% from fat); FAT 9.1g (sat 1.7g, mono 4.6g, poly 1.7g); PROTEIN 30g; CARB 48.9g; FIBER 3g; CHOL 172mg; IRON 5.3mg; SODIUM 864mg; CALC 183mg

Chicken Burgers with Peanut Sauce

Here's an Asian-style burger made spicy with Thai chile paste and rounded out with a sweet, creamy Thai-style peanut sauce.

Prep: 20 minutes • Cook: 9 minutes

Peanut Sauce:
- 2 tablespoons peanut butter
- 2 teaspoons low-sodium soy sauce
- 1½ teaspoons dark sesame oil
- 1 teaspoon water
- 1 teaspoon rice vinegar
- 1 garlic clove, minced

Burgers:
- ½ cup finely chopped green onions
- 1 tablespoon chile paste with garlic
- 2 teaspoons grated peeled fresh ginger
- 2 teaspoons low-sodium soy sauce
- ¼ teaspoon salt
- 1 pound skinless, boneless chicken breast, chopped
- Cooking spray
- 4 (2-ounce) sandwich rolls with sesame seeds
- 1 cup onion sprouts or alfalfa sprouts

1. To prepare sauce, combine first 6 ingredients, stirring with a whisk until smooth.
2. Prepare grill.
3. To prepare burgers, place onions and next 5 ingredients in a food processor; process until coarsely ground. Divide mixture into 4 equal portions, shaping each into a ½-inch-thick patty.
4. Place patties on grill rack coated with cooking spray; grill 4 minutes on each side or until done. Place rolls, cut sides down, on grill rack; grill 1 minute or until toasted. Place 1 patty on bottom half of each roll; top each serving with ¼ cup sprouts, about 1 tablespoon sauce, and top half of roll. Yield: 4 servings (serving size: 1 burger).

CALORIES 341 (28% from fat); FAT 10.6g (sat 3.2g, mono 3.5g, poly 3.3g); PROTEIN 28.5g; CARB 32.8g; FIBER 2.5g; CHOL 49mg; IRON 2.7mg; SODIUM 769mg; CALC 67mg

Test Kitchen Tip: Onion sprouts, which look similar to alfalfa sprouts, have a pungent bite. You can find them next to the alfalfa sprouts in many supermarkets.

Grilled Chicken and Roasted Red Pepper Sandwiches with Fontina Cheese

Marinating the chicken in a garlic-herb mixture gives this hot sandwich maximum flavor.

Prep: 30 minutes • Cook: 22 minutes
Other: 2 hours

- 1 pound skinless, boneless chicken breast
- 1 tablespoon fresh lemon juice
- 1 tablespoon Dijon mustard
- 2 teaspoons extravirgin olive oil
- ¼ teaspoon dried marjoram
- ¼ teaspoon dried thyme
- 5 garlic cloves, minced and divided

Cooking spray

- 1 cup vertically sliced onion
- 1 teaspoon sugar
- ¾ teaspoon fennel seeds, crushed
- ¼ teaspoon crushed red pepper
- ¼ teaspoon salt
- 1 (7-ounce) bottle roasted red bell peppers, drained and sliced
- 1 tablespoon red wine vinegar
- ⅛ teaspoon freshly ground black pepper
- 1 (12-ounce) loaf rosemary focaccia, cut in half horizontally
- 4 teaspoons low-fat mayonnaise
- 3 ounces fontina cheese, thinly sliced

1. Place chicken between 2 sheets of heavy-duty plastic wrap, and pound to ¾-inch thickness using a meat mallet or rolling pin.

2. Combine juice, mustard, oil, marjoram, thyme, 1 garlic clove, and chicken in a large zip-top plastic bag; seal. Marinate in refrigerator 2 hours, turning occasionally.

3. Heat a large nonstick skillet over medium-high heat. Coat pan with cooking spray. Add remaining 4 garlic cloves, onion, sugar, fennel, crushed red pepper, and salt, and sauté 1 minute. Add roasted bell peppers; cook 5 minutes or until onions are tender, stirring frequently. Stir in vinegar and black pepper.

4. Prepare grill.

5. Remove chicken from bag; discard marinade. Place chicken on grill rack coated with cooking spray; grill 5 minutes on each side or until done. Cool slightly; cut chicken into slices.

6. Spread cut sides of bread evenly with mayonnaise. Arrange cheese on bottom half of bread. Arrange chicken and pepper mixture over cheese. Top with top half of bread; press lightly.

7. Place stuffed loaf on grill rack; grill 3 minutes on each side or until cheese melts. Cut into quarters. Yield: 4 servings (serving size: 1 sandwich quarter).

CALORIES 462 (24% from fat); FAT 12.2g (sat 4.7g, mono 3.7g, poly 1.7g); PROTEIN 39.5g; CARB 51.2g; FIBER 5.6g; CHOL 90mg; IRON 3mg; SODIUM 981mg; CALC 199mg

Chicken Philly Sandwiches

Taking a cue from the classic Philly cheese steak, this recipe replaces beef with chicken but keeps the cheese and onion-bell pepper topping. Pressing the already-warm filling helps the cheese melt and binds the ingredients so they don't fall out as you enjoy the sandwich.

Prep: 20 minutes • Cook: 28 minutes

  2 teaspoons olive oil
  ¾ pound skinless, boneless chicken
     breast, cut into (1-inch-thick) strips
  ⅛ teaspoon salt
  ⅛ teaspoon freshly ground black pepper
  1 cup red bell pepper strips
  1 cup green bell pepper strips
  1 cup vertically sliced onion
  1½ teaspoons white wine vinegar
  ⅛ teaspoon salt
  2 garlic cloves, minced
  ½ teaspoon hot pepper sauce
  4 (3-ounce) submarine rolls
  4 (1-ounce) slices provolone cheese

1. Heat oil in a medium nonstick skillet over medium-high heat. Add chicken to pan; sprinkle with ⅛ teaspoon salt and black pepper. Sauté 5 minutes or until chicken is done. Remove chicken from pan. Add red bell pepper and next 5 ingredients to pan; sauté 6 minutes or until tender. Stir in chicken and pepper sauce; remove from heat.
2. Slice each roll in half horizontally, cutting to, but not through, other side. Place 1 cheese slice and 1 cup chicken mixture on bottom half of each roll, and gently press roll halves together.
3. Heat a large nonstick skillet over medium heat; add 2 sandwiches. Place a cast-iron or heavy skillet on top of sandwiches; press gently to flatten. Cook 4 minutes on each side or until cheese melts and bread is toasted (leave skillet on sandwiches while they cook). Repeat with remaining sandwiches. Yield: 4 servings (serving size: 1 sandwich).

CALORIES 490 (28% from fat); FAT 15.4g (sat 6.5g, mono 6.2g, poly 1.5g); PROTEIN 35.2g; CARB 51.3g; FIBER 4.2g; CHOL 69mg; IRON 3.9mg; SODIUM 945mg; CALC 359mg

Smoked Turkey, Brie, Green Apple, and Watercress Sandwiches

Buttery Brie, tart green apple, and tender watercress add a touch of sophistication to a humble turkey sandwich.

Prep: 12 minutes • Cook: 5 minutes

  1½ tablespoons honey
  1½ tablespoons mustard
  1 (8-ounce) French bread baguette
  6 ounces thinly sliced smoked turkey
     breast
  ¼ pound Brie cheese, thinly sliced
  1 cup trimmed watercress
  1 cup thinly sliced peeled Granny
     Smith apple
  ⅛ teaspoon freshly ground black pepper

1. Preheat oven to 350°.
2. Combine honey and mustard in a small bowl. Cut bread in half lengthwise; place on a baking sheet. Spread honey mixture on bottom half of loaf; top with turkey and cheese. Bake at 350° for 5 minutes or until cheese begins to melt.
3. Arrange watercress and apple slices on melted cheese; sprinkle with pepper. Cover with top half of loaf, and cut into 4 pieces. Yield: 4 servings (serving size: 1 piece).

CALORIES 337 (29% from fat); FAT 10.7g (sat 5.3g, mono 3.1g, poly 0.7g); PROTEIN 19.4g; CARB 40.8g; FIBER 2.5g; CHOL 45mg; IRON 3.5mg; SODIUM 926mg; CALC 114mg

Open-Faced Turkey Sandwiches with Apple and Havarti
(pictured on page 429)

The flavors of fall meet in this sandwich. Havarti cheese provides a pleasing contrast to the apples and arugula. Substitute fontina or mild Muenster for the Havarti, if you prefer.

Prep: 12 minutes • Cook: 4 minutes

  4 (2-ounce) slices country or peasant
     bread
  4 teaspoons light mayonnaise
  4 teaspoons Dijon mustard
  1 cup trimmed arugula
 16 (⅛-inch-thick) slices red onion
  8 ounces thinly sliced deli turkey
  2 Pink Lady or Cameo apples, each
     cored and cut crosswise into 8
     (¼-inch-thick) slices
  ½ cup (2 ounces) grated Havarti cheese
     Coarsely ground black pepper (optional)

1. Preheat broiler with oven rack in middle position.
2. Spread each bread slice with 1 teaspoon mayonnaise and 1 teaspoon mustard. Layer each slice with ¼ cup arugula, 4 onion slices, 2 ounces turkey, 4 apple slices, and 2 tablespoons cheese.
3. Place sandwiches on a baking sheet; broil 4 minutes or until cheese is bubbly. Remove from heat; sprinkle with pepper, if desired. Serve immediately. Yield: 4 servings (serving size: 1 sandwich).

CALORIES 381 (22% from fat); FAT 9.4g (sat 3.8g, mono 0.2g, poly 0.2g); PROTEIN 23.3g; CARB 46.4g; FIBER 5.6g; CHOL 38mg; IRON 2.9mg; SODIUM 948mg; CALC 167mg

Classic Makeover: Hot Browns

Hot Browns are open-faced sandwiches that were created by the chef at the Brown Hotel in Louisville, Kentucky. Typically, these sandwiches are topped with turkey, tomato, bacon, and a rich cheese sauce. Our version of Hot Browns has about 300 fewer calories than the traditional recipe because we made the sauce with 2% milk instead of half-and-half and reduced the amount of bacon. Because we replaced the high-fat cream with 2% milk, we were able to keep the original amount of cheese. We used reduced-fat extrasharp Cheddar and were pleased with the sharp cheese flavor. Since we cut the amount of bacon, we crumbled the slices so they'd distribute better.

Before	After
• 739 calories	• 440 calories
• 44.7g fat	• 14.9g fat
• percentage of calories from fat 54%	• percentage of calories from fat 30%

Hot Browns

You can use leftover chicken in place of the turkey. Broiling the sandwiches browns and melts the Parmesan cheese that tops them.

Prep: 15 minutes • Cook: 23 minutes

1½ tablespoons butter
2 tablespoons all-purpose flour
¼ teaspoon salt
⅛ teaspoon paprika
⅛ teaspoon pepper
1 cup 2% reduced-fat milk
½ cup (2 ounces) shredded reduced-fat extrasharp Cheddar cheese
½ teaspoon Worcestershire sauce
⅛ teaspoon dry mustard
12 (1-ounce) slices white bread, toasted
3 cups shredded cooked turkey
12 (¼-inch-thick) slices tomato
5 bacon slices, cooked and crumbled
¼ cup (1 ounce) grated fresh Parmesan cheese

1. Preheat broiler.
2. Melt butter in a saucepan over medium heat; stir in flour, salt, paprika, and pepper. Cook mixture 30 seconds, stirring constantly. Gradually add milk, stirring with a whisk. Cook 3 minutes or until thick, stirring constantly. Remove from heat. Add cheese, Worcestershire, and mustard; stir with a whisk until smooth. Keep warm.
3. Arrange toast on a large baking sheet. Arrange turkey evenly over toast. Drizzle sauce evenly over turkey; top each with 1 tomato slice. Sprinkle evenly with bacon and Parmesan. Broil 7 minutes or until thoroughly heated and lightly browned. Serve immediately. Yield: 6 servings (serving size: 2 open-faced sandwiches).

CALORIES 440 (30% from fat); FAT 14.9g (sat 6.2g, mono 4.0g, poly 1.6g); PROTEIN 34.6g; CARB 44.3g; FIBER 4.5g; CHOL 79mg; IRON 3.2mg; SODIUM 815mg; CALC 255mg

Turkey and Oat Burgers

Think of this burger as a "mini-meat loaf on a bun." We've used turkey, not ground beef, and added chili powder for a flavor boost. The patties might seem a little wet, but they bind together nicely once they begin to cook. Because they're delicate, a grill pan works best.

Prep: 12 minutes • Cook: 13 minutes

    1   cup regular oats
    1   cup finely chopped Vidalia onion
    1   tablespoon chili powder
 1¼   teaspoons salt
    2   large egg whites, lightly beaten
    1   (14.5-ounce) can no-salt-added
        tomatoes, drained and chopped
 1½   pounds ground turkey
      Cooking spray
    6   (2-ounce) onion sandwich buns,
        toasted
    6   curly leaf lettuce leaves
    6   (¼-inch-thick) slices tomato

1. Combine first 7 ingredients. Divide mixture into 6 equal portions, shaping each into a ½-inch-thick patty.
2. Heat a grill pan over medium-high heat. Coat pan with cooking spray. Add patties; cook 6 minutes on each side or until done. Place 1 patty on bottom half of each bun; top each with 1 lettuce leaf, 1 tomato slice, and top half of bun. Yield: 6 servings (serving size: 1 burger).

CALORIES 394 (30% from fat); FAT 13.2g (sat 4.7g, mono 4.1g, poly 4.2g); PROTEIN 26.1g; CARB 43.6g; FIBER 4.5g; CHOL 73mg; IRON 4.1mg; SODIUM 946mg; CALC 97mg

Test Kitchen Tip: We recommend using ground turkey (with a mixture of white and dark meat) instead of ground turkey breast, which is white meat only.

Pressed Cubano with Bacon

Garlic oil gives these sandwiches a crisp, flavorful crust. Hawaiian rolls provide a slightly sweet contrast to the salty ham, pickles, and mustard.

Prep: 12 minutes • Cook: 23 minutes

    1   teaspoon extravirgin olive oil
    1   garlic clove, minced
    4   (3-ounce) Hawaiian rolls, sliced in
        half horizontally
    2   tablespoons yellow mustard
    8   (½-ounce) slices reduced-fat Swiss
        cheese, divided
    4   bacon slices, cooked and halved
  12   dill pickle slices
    2   teaspoons minced fresh cilantro
    6   ounces thinly sliced 33%-less-sodium
        ham
    2   ounces thinly sliced deli roasted
        turkey breast

1. Combine oil and garlic.
2. Spread cut sides of rolls evenly with mustard. Place 1 cheese slice, 2 bacon halves, 3 pickle slices, and ½ teaspoon cilantro on bottom half of each roll. Divide ham and turkey evenly among bottom halves of rolls; top each serving with 1 cheese slice and top half of roll. Brush garlic oil evenly over outside of rolls.
3. Heat a large nonstick skillet over medium heat. Add 2 sandwiches to pan. Place a cast-iron or heavy skillet on top of sandwiches, and press gently to flatten. Cook 3 minutes on each side or until cheese melts and bread is toasted (leave cast-iron skillet on sandwiches while they cook). Repeat with remaining sandwiches. Yield: 4 servings (serving size: 1 sandwich).

CALORIES 432 (30% from fat); FAT 14.5g (sat 6.3g, mono 4.1g, poly 1.2g); PROTEIN 27.1g; CARB 47.6g; FIBER 2.8g; CHOL 49mg; IRON 3.1mg; SODIUM 1053mg; CALC 292mg

Monte Cristo Sandwiches

A Monte Cristo sandwich features slices of ham, chicken or turkey, and Swiss cheese. The sandwich is dipped into beaten egg and cooked on a griddle or in a skillet until golden brown. The traditional toppings are jam and a sprinkling of powdered sugar.

Prep: 10 minutes • Cook: 12 minutes

    3   tablespoons honey mustard
    8   (1-ounce) slices white bread
    4   (1-ounce) slices Swiss cheese
   ¼   pound thinly sliced smoked ham
   ⅓   cup fat-free milk
    2   large egg whites, lightly beaten
      Cooking spray
    2   teaspoons powdered sugar
   ¼   cup seedless raspberry jam

1. Spread about 1 teaspoon mustard over each bread slice. Place 1 cheese slice on each of 4 bread slices. Divide ham evenly over cheese. Cover with remaining 4 bread slices, mustard sides down. Combine milk and egg whites in a shallow dish. Dip both sides of each sandwich into milk mixture.
2. Heat a large nonstick skillet over medium heat. Coat pan with cooking spray. Place 2 sandwiches in pan, and cook 3 minutes on each side or until lightly browned. Repeat with remaining 2 sandwiches. Sprinkle each sandwich with ½ teaspoon sugar; top each with 1 tablespoon jam. Yield: 4 servings (serving size: 1 sandwich).

CALORIES 387 (27% from fat); FAT 11.5g (sat 6g, mono 3.7g, poly 0.9g); PROTEIN 20.7g; CARB 49.1g; FIBER 1.6g; CHOL 40mg; IRON 2.1mg; SODIUM 840mg; CALC 366mg

Grilled Ham and Cheese with Tomato

A creamy spread of sour cream, Dijon mustard, and Parmesan cheese adds lots of depth to this modified ham-and-cheese sandwich. The ingredients needn't be exotic to yield delicious results. Simplicity is key.

Prep: 12 minutes • Cook: 12 minutes

- 2 tablespoons Dijon mustard
- 2 tablespoons reduced-fat sour cream
- 1 tablespoon grated fresh Parmesan cheese
- 8 (1½-ounce) slices hearty white bread
- 16 (½-ounce) slices 33%-less-sodium ham
- 8 (⅛-inch-thick) slices tomato (about 1 medium)
- 8 (½-ounce) slices reduced-fat Swiss cheese
- 2 teaspoons chopped fresh chives
  Cooking spray

1. Combine mustard, sour cream, and Parmesan cheese in a small bowl.

2. Spread 2 teaspoons mustard mixture over each bread slice. Top each of 4 bread slices with 4 ham slices, 2 tomato slices, 2 cheese slices, and ½ teaspoon fresh chives. Top with remaining bread slices. Lightly coat outside of bread with cooking spray.

3. Heat a large nonstick skillet over medium heat. Add 2 sandwiches to pan. Place a cast-iron or heavy skillet on top of sandwiches; press gently to flatten. Cook 3 minutes on each side or until cheese melts and bread is toasted (leave cast-iron skillet on sandwiches while they cook). Repeat with remaining sandwiches. Yield: 4 servings (serving size: 1 sandwich).

CALORIES 407 (30% from fat); FAT 13.5g (sat 5.9g, mono 3.7g, poly 0.8g); PROTEIN 28.2g; CARB 47.5g; FIBER 5g; CHOL 54mg; IRON 2.9mg; SODIUM 1229mg; CALC 337mg

Chipotle Pulled-Pork Barbecue Sandwiches

Chipotle Pulled-Pork Barbecue Sandwiches

Sweet-and-sour pickles are a tasty foil to the smoky barbecue sauce in this updated Southern-style sandwich. Serve with Sweet-and-Sour Slaw (page 405).

Prep: 20 minutes • Cook: 1 hour, 17 minutes

- 1 (7-ounce) can chipotle chiles in adobo sauce
- ¼ cup barbecue sauce
- 1 teaspoon garlic powder
- 1½ teaspoons ground cumin
- 1 (1-pound) pork tenderloin, trimmed and cut into ½-inch cubes
- 1 (14.5-ounce) can diced tomatoes, undrained
- 1 tablespoon olive oil
- 3 cups thinly sliced onion
- 2 teaspoons chopped fresh thyme
- 1 teaspoon sugar
- 6 (½-ounce) slices provolone cheese
- 12 sandwich-cut bread-and-butter pickles
- 6 (2½-ounce) Kaiser rolls

1. Remove 1 chile from can; reserve remaining chiles and sauce for another use. Finely chop chile.

2. Place chopped chile, barbecue sauce, and next 4 ingredients in a medium saucepan; bring to a boil over medium-high heat. Cover, reduce heat, and simmer 45 minutes, stirring occasionally. Uncover and cook 10 minutes or until sauce thickens and pork is very tender. Remove from heat. Remove pork from sauce; shred pork. Return pork to sauce.

3. Heat oil in a large nonstick skillet over medium-high heat. Add onion, thyme, and sugar; cook 10 minutes or until golden, stirring occasionally.

4. Heat a large nonstick skillet over medium heat. Place 1 cheese slice, ½ cup pork mixture, about 2 tablespoons onions, and 2 pickle slices on bottom half of each roll. Cover with top halves of rolls. Add 3 sandwiches to pan. Place a cast-iron or heavy skillet on top of sandwiches, and press gently to flatten. Cook 2 minutes on each side or until cheese melts and bread is toasted (leave cast-iron skillet on sandwiches while they cook). Repeat procedure with remaining sandwiches. Yield: 6 servings (serving size: 1 sandwich).

CALORIES 431 (26% from fat); FAT 12.4g (sat 3.9g, mono 3.7g, poly 1.8g); PROTEIN 28.3g; CARB 51.4g; FIBER 4.7g; CHOL 59mg; IRON 4.1mg; SODIUM 910mg; CALC 207mg

Shawarma (Lamb Pitas)

Often sold by street vendors, this Lebanese favorite starts with lamb that's marinated overnight, threaded onto a long skewer, and placed in front of a vertical grill. The meat rotates and cooks, allowing the shawarma seller to slice it and make sandwiches. Although the lamb in our rendition is baked rather than skewered and grilled, it's very close to the real thing. Prepare the dip and chill it while the lamb is marinating.

Prep: 35 minutes • Cook: 1 hour
Other: 2 hours, 15 minutes

Yogurt-Tahini Dip
2 cups thinly sliced onion
⅓ cup fresh lemon juice
½ teaspoon ground cinnamon
½ teaspoon ground allspice
½ teaspoon pepper
¼ teaspoon salt
5 thyme sprigs
1½ pounds boned leg of lamb, trimmed
6 (7-inch) pitas
½ cup red onion slices, separated into rings
¼ cup chopped fresh mint
12 (¼-inch-thick) slices tomato, halved
3 gherkin pickles, thinly sliced lengthwise

1. Prepare Yogurt-Tahini Dip.
2. Combine 2 cups onion and next 6 ingredients in a large zip-top plastic bag. Add lamb to bag; seal. Marinate in refrigerator 2 hours, turning occasionally. Remove lamb from bag; discard marinade.
3. Preheat oven to 350°.
4. Place lamb on a broiler pan; insert meat thermometer into thickest portion of lamb. Bake at 350° for 1 hour or until thermometer registers 145° (medium-rare) to 160° (medium). Remove from oven, and let stand 15 minutes. Slice lamb lengthwise into thin strips.
5. Spread each pita with about 2½ tablespoons Yogurt-Tahini Dip. Divide lamb, red onion, mint, tomato, and pickles evenly among each pita; roll up. Serve immediately. Yield: 6 servings (serving size: 1 pita roll).

(Totals include Yogurt-Tahini Dip) CALORIES 397 (24% from fat); FAT 10.7g (sat 2.9g, mono 3.8g, poly 2.5g); PROTEIN 32.8g; CARB 42.1g; FIBER 3.3g; CHOL 75mg; IRON 4.9mg; SODIUM 1117mg; CALC 183mg

Yogurt-Tahini Dip

1 cup plain low-fat yogurt
3 tablespoons tahini (sesame-seed paste)
2 tablespoons fresh lemon juice
1 tablespoon chopped fresh flat-leaf parsley
½ teaspoon salt
1 garlic clove, crushed

1. Combine all ingredients in a large bowl; cover and refrigerate 30 minutes. Yield: 1 cup (serving size: 1 tablespoon).

CALORIES 27 (60% from fat); FAT 1.8g (sat 0.4g, mono 0.6g, poly 0.6g); PROTEIN 1.3g; CARB 1.9g; FIBER 0.3g; CHOL 1mg; IRON 0.3mg; SODIUM 87mg; CALC 41mg

Test Kitchen Tip: If you're lucky enough to live near a Middle Eastern market that sells fresh pitas, use those in this recipe. Fresh pitas are softer and more pliable than the packaged ones in the supermarket. If your pitas aren't fresh, you can soften them by wrapping them in a damp paper towel and heating them in the microwave at MEDIUM for no longer than 10 to 15 seconds.

Thai Beef Salad Wraps

This wrap has all the bright, fresh flavors and crunchy textures of a summer roll.

Prep: 25 minutes • Cook: 10 minutes
Other: 5 minutes

1 (1-pound) flank steak, trimmed
¼ teaspoon salt
¼ teaspoon black pepper
Cooking spray
1 cup cubed peeled cucumber
½ cup grape or cherry tomato halves
¼ cup thinly sliced shallots
1 tablespoon chopped fresh mint
1 tablespoon chopped fresh basil
1 tablespoon chopped fresh cilantro
2 tablespoons brown sugar
3 tablespoons low-sodium soy sauce
2 tablespoons fresh lime juice
½ teaspoon crushed red pepper
6 (10-inch) flour tortillas
12 Bibb lettuce leaves

1. Prepare grill.
2. Sprinkle steak with salt and black pepper. Place steak on grill rack coated with cooking spray, and grill 4 minutes on each side or until desired degree of doneness. Let rest 5 minutes.
3. Cut steak diagonally across grain into thin slices. Combine sliced steak, cucumber, and next 5 ingredients in a large bowl. Combine sugar, soy sauce, juice, and red pepper. Drizzle over steak mixture; toss well to coat.
4. Warm tortillas according to package directions. Arrange 2 lettuce leaves on each tortilla. Spoon ⅔ cup steak mixture down center of each tortilla; roll up. Yield: 6 servings (serving size: 1 wrap).

CALORIES 399 (28% from fat); FAT 12.4g (sat 4.3g, mono 5.6g, poly 1.1g); PROTEIN 22.4g; CARB 48.5g; FIBER 3.1g; CHOL 39mg; IRON 4.4mg; SODIUM 760mg; CALC 113mg

Grilled Sourdough Cheddar Melts

Also known as a patty melt, this grilled sandwich features ground meat and cheese nestled between slices of bread. We used prewrapped slices of processed Cheddar cheese because they melt better.

Prep: 10 minutes • Cook: 41 minutes

2 teaspoons butter, divided
Cooking spray
2 cups coarsely chopped onion
1 pound ground round
¼ teaspoon freshly ground black pepper
⅛ teaspoon salt
4 (¾-ounce) slices 2% reduced-fat processed sharp Cheddar cheese
8 (1½-ounce) slices sourdough or white bread

1. Melt 1 teaspoon butter in a large non-stick skillet coated with cooking spray over medium-high heat. Add onion, and sauté 4 minutes or until golden brown. Reduce heat; cook 10 minutes or until tender, stirring occasionally. Set aside.
2. Preheat broiler.
3. Combine beef, pepper, and salt in a medium bowl. Divide beef mixture into 4 equal portions, shaping each into a ¼-inch-thick oval patty. Place patties on a broiler pan coated with cooking spray; broil 4 minutes on each side or until done.
4. Place 1 cheese slice over each of 4 bread slices; top each slice with 1 patty and 3 tablespoons onion mixture. Cover with remaining bread slices. Melt ½ tea-spoon butter in pan coated with cooking spray over medium heat; add 2 sandwiches to pan. Cook 4 minutes on each side or until browned and cheese melts. Repeat procedure with ½ teaspoon butter and remaining sandwiches. Yield: 4 servings (serving size: 1 sandwich).

CALORIES 462 (22% from fat); FAT 11.5g (sat 5.3g, mono 3.1g, poly 0.9g); PROTEIN 38.5g; CARB 49.3g; FIBER 3g; CHOL 80mg; IRON 5.2mg; SODIUM 909mg; CALC 357mg

Sloppy Joes

Kids and adults alike will love these little sweet-savory sandwiches. If you're serving a crowd, keep the meat mixture warm in an electric slow cooker set on LOW. They're an ideal size to accompany a bowl of steaming vegetable soup.

Prep: 11 minutes • Cook: 25 minutes

¾ cup chopped onion
½ cup chopped green bell pepper
¾ pound ground round
2 cups no-salt-added tomato sauce
2 tablespoons tomato paste
1 tablespoon prepared mustard
1 teaspoon chili powder
2 teaspoons Worcestershire sauce
½ teaspoon salt
½ teaspoon sugar
½ teaspoon dried oregano
⅛ teaspoon black pepper
12 (1½-ounce) rolls, split

1. Heat a large nonstick skillet over medium heat. Add first 3 ingredients; cook until beef is browned, stirring to crumble. Stir in tomato sauce and next 8 ingredients; reduce heat to medium-low. Cover and cook 15 minutes, stirring occasionally. Spoon ¼ cup beef mixture over bottom half of each roll. Cover with top halves. Yield: 12 servings (serving size: 1 sandwich).

CALORIES 202 (27% from fat); FAT 6.2g (sat 2g, mono 2.9g, poly 0.7g); PROTEIN 10.2g; CARB 27g; FIBER 2.5g; CHOL 19mg; IRON 2.6mg; SODIUM 392mg; CALC 68mg

Cajun Cool Cheeseburgers

Combine feta and blue cheese with ground round and ground turkey breast—along with Cajun spices—to create a piquant burger with a big cheese taste.

Prep: 15 minutes • Cook: 12 minutes

   3 tablespoons crumbled feta cheese
   3 tablespoons crumbled blue cheese
  ¼ cup dry breadcrumbs
   1 teaspoon Creole seasoning
  ¼ teaspoon paprika
  ¼ teaspoon ground red pepper
  ¾ pound ground round
  ¼ pound ground turkey breast
Cooking spray
   4 (1½-ounce) whole wheat
      hamburger buns
   1 cup shredded iceberg lettuce
  ¾ cup green onion tops, cut into
      2-inch julienne strips

1. Prepare grill.
2. Combine cheeses; set aside.
3. Combine breadcrumbs and next 5 ingredients. Divide mixture into 4 equal portions; shape each into a ½-inch-thick patty.
4. Place patties on grill rack coated with cooking spray; grill 5 minutes on each side. Sprinkle burgers evenly with cheese mixture. Cook 1 to 2 minutes or until burgers are done and cheese melts. Place buns, cut sides down, on grill rack; grill 1 minute or until toasted. Place 1 patty on bottom half of each bun; top each serving with ¼ cup lettuce, 3 tablespoons onions, and top half of bun. Yield: 4 servings (serving size: 1 burger).

CALORIES 463 (33% from fat); FAT 17g (sat 7g, mono 5.6g, poly 2.6g); PROTEIN 33.1g; CARB 43.1g; FIBER 2.1g; CHOL 82mg; IRON 5.2mg; SODIUM 956mg; CALC 194mg

Smothered Burgers

If you find that many sandwiches are too big to eat easily, try these open-faced burgers. There's no reason a burger can't be a knife-and-fork meal.

Prep: 15 minutes • Cook: 29 minutes

Cooking spray
   2 cups vertically sliced onion
   2 teaspoons sugar
  ¾ teaspoon salt, divided
  ½ teaspoon freshly ground black
      pepper, divided
   1 (8-ounce) package presliced
      mushrooms
   2 tablespoons Worcestershire sauce
   1 pound ground round
   4 (1-ounce) slices Texas toast
  ½ cup (2 ounces) shredded Swiss cheese

1. Prepare grill.
2. Heat a medium nonstick skillet over medium heat. Coat pan with cooking spray. Add onion; cover and cook 5 minutes, stirring occasionally. Add sugar, ¼ teaspoon salt, and ¼ teaspoon pepper; cook, uncovered, 5 minutes or until tender, stirring frequently. Remove onion from pan, and keep warm.
3. Heat pan over medium-high heat. Coat pan with cooking spray. Add mushrooms and ¼ teaspoon salt; sauté 5 minutes or until tender.
4. Combine ¼ teaspoon salt, ¼ teaspoon pepper, Worcestershire sauce, and beef. Divide mixture into 4 equal portions, shaping each into a ½-inch-thick patty.
5. Preheat broiler.
6. Place patties on grill rack coated with cooking spray; grill 5 minutes on each side or until done. Place bread on grill rack; grill 1 minute on each side or until toasted.
7. Arrange bread on a baking sheet. Top each bread slice with 1 patty, ¼ cup onion, ¼ cup mushrooms, and 2 tablespoons cheese; broil 2 minutes or until cheese melts. Yield: 4 servings (serving size: 1 open-faced burger).

CALORIES 393 (40% from fat); FAT 17.5g (sat 7.5g, mono 6.7g, poly 1.4g); PROTEIN 31.1g; CARB 27.1g; FIBER 2.5g; CHOL 91mg; IRON 4.4mg; SODIUM 786mg; CALC 204mg

Smothered Burgers

sauces & condiments

Warm Chocolate
Sauce, page 457

Savory Sauces
Cream sauces, tomato sauces, pestos, and gravies harmonize in a recipe and add unity to the finished dish.

Alfredo Sauce

Alfredo sauce is best known in the traditional dish Fettuccine Alfredo, where the pasta is coated in a rich sauce of butter, grated Parmesan cheese, and heavy cream. In our lightened version, we use half-and-half instead of whipping cream and decrease the amount of butter and cheese slightly.

Prep: 4 minutes • Cook: 2 minutes

  1   tablespoon butter
1¼ cups half-and-half
 ¾   cup (3 ounces) grated fresh
      Parmesan cheese
 ½   teaspoon salt
 ¼   teaspoon freshly ground black pepper

1. Melt butter in a large skillet over medium heat. Add half-and-half, cheese, salt, and pepper; cook 1 minute, stirring constantly. Yield: 1½ cups (serving size: about ¼ cup).

CALORIES 145 (68% from fat); FAT 11g (sat 6.7g, mono 3.6g, poly 0.2g); PROTEIN 7.2g; CARB 2.3g; FIBER 0g; CHOL 42mg; IRON 0.2mg; SODIUM 452mg; CALC 225mg

Test Kitchen Tip: To get the best-tasting Alfredo sauce, use fresh Parmesan cheese and freshly ground pepper. This sauce is usually tossed with fettuccine. For this amount of sauce, you'll need to cook 1 pound of uncooked pasta to get 8 cups cooked pasta.

Classic Cheese Sauce

To make this creamy sauce, start by steeping peppercorns and a bay leaf in milk, much like in the Béchamel Sauce on page 449.

**Prep: 7 minutes • Cook: 11 minutes
Other: 5 minutes**

1⅓ cups 1% low-fat milk
  3   whole black peppercorns
  1   bay leaf
  3   tablespoons all-purpose flour
  1   cup (4 ounces) finely shredded
      extrasharp Cheddar cheese

1. Combine first 3 ingredients in a saucepan; cook over low heat 5 minutes. Remove from heat; cool 5 minutes. Strain mixture through a sieve into a bowl; discard solids.
2. Place flour in pan; gradually add ¼ cup milk, stirring with a whisk until blended. Cook over low heat 1 minute, stirring constantly. Add remaining milk; cook until thick (about 5 minutes), stirring constantly. Remove from heat, and add cheese, stirring until melted. Yield: 1½ cups (serving size: about ¼ cup).

CALORIES 113 (55% from fat); FAT 6.8g (sat 4.3g, mono 1.9g, poly 0.2g); PROTEIN 6.8g; CARB 5.8g; FIBER 0.1g; CHOL 22mg; IRON 0.3mg; SODIUM 144mg; CALC 203mg

Test Kitchen Tip: Don't try to save time by cubing the cheese instead of shredding it. Shredding makes for quick, even melting. Add the cheese after you remove the sauce from the heat so the cheese won't get too hot and curdle.

Béarnaise Sauce

Béarnaise sauce is a classic French sauce made with a reduction of vinegar, wine, tarragon, and shallots, and finished with egg yolks and butter. It's usually served with meat, fish, eggs, and vegetables. In this recipe, the egg yolks and butter are replaced with low-fat sour cream.

Prep: 7 minutes • Cook: 4 minutes

 ½   cup thinly sliced shallots (about
      2 ounces)
  3   tablespoons dry white wine
  2   tablespoons white wine vinegar
  1   teaspoon dried tarragon
Dash of salt
Dash of pepper
 ⅔   cup low-fat sour cream

1. Combine first 6 ingredients in a small, heavy saucepan; bring to a boil, and cook 1 minute. Strain mixture through a sieve into a bowl; discard solids. Return liquid to saucepan; stir in sour cream. Place over low heat, and cook 1 minute or until warm, stirring frequently. Yield: ¾ cup (serving size: 3 tablespoons).

CALORIES 76 (60% from fat); FAT 5.1g (sat 3g, mono 1.6g, poly 0.2g); PROTEIN 2.4g; CARB 6g; FIBER 0.4g; CHOL 15mg; IRON 1.4mg; SODIUM 21mg; CALC 88mg

Test Kitchen Tip: Be sure to use low-fat sour cream and not fat-free in this recipe because the fat-free tends to curdle when it's heated.

Béchamel Sauce

This light white sauce is one of the most versatile sauces you can have in your recipe collection. It's the secret to our reduced-fat cream soups, bisques, and chowders.

**Prep: 9 minutes • Cook: 11 minutes
Other: 10 minutes**

2½ cups 1% low-fat milk
8 black peppercorns
1 (½-inch-thick) slice onion
1 bay leaf
2 tablespoons butter
¼ cup all-purpose flour
¼ teaspoon salt
⅛ teaspoon ground white pepper
Dash of ground nutmeg

1. Combine first 4 ingredients in a heavy saucepan; cook over low heat to 180° or until tiny bubbles form around edge (do not boil). Remove from heat. Cover; let stand 10 minutes. Strain mixture through a sieve into a bowl; discard solids. Set aside.
2. Melt butter in saucepan over low heat. Lightly spoon flour into a dry measuring cup; level with a knife. Add flour to saucepan, stirring with a whisk until blended. Cook 1 minute, stirring constantly. Gradually add milk; cook over low heat 5 minutes or until thick, stirring constantly. Stir in salt, white pepper, and nutmeg. Yield: 2¼ cups (serving size: ¼ cup).

CALORIES 66 (45% from fat); FAT 3.3g (sat 1.7g, mono 1.3g, poly 0.1g); PROTEIN 2.7g; CARB 6.4g; FIBER 0.2; CHOL 9mg; IRON 0.2mg; SODIUM 120mg; CALC 86mg

Test Kitchen Tip: If the sauce hasn't thickened after 5 minutes, continue to cook it, stirring constantly.

how to make a béchamel sauce (light white sauce)

1. Steep the peppercorns, onion, and bay leaf in the milk over low heat for about 5 minutes. This flavor combination infuses the milk with sweet and nutty tones.

2. Remove the mixture from heat; cool 10 minutes. Strain the milk mixture through a sieve; discard solids.

3. Lightly spoon the flour into a measuring cup, and level with a knife. Too much flour will make the sauce too thick; too little will leave it thin and watery.

4. Carefully whisk the flour into the melted butter, and cook 1 minute, stirring constantly. Watch carefully because an overcooked roux will make the white sauce taste burned.

5. Add milk to the flour gradually, whisking the mixture constantly. If you pour all the milk in at once, you'll get lumps.

6. Heat the sauce over low heat until it's thick, stirring constantly. It should coat a spoon when it's ready.

Marinara Sauce

For a truly Italian combination, serve this easy tomato sauce over spaghetti.

Prep: 15 minutes • Cook: 32 minutes

- 1 tablespoon olive oil
- 1½ tablespoons minced garlic
- 6 cups chopped peeled tomato
- ¾ teaspoon salt
- ½ teaspoon pepper
- ¼ cup chopped fresh basil
- ¼ cup chopped fresh parsley

1. Heat oil in a large saucepan over medium heat. Add garlic; sauté 2 minutes. Add tomato, salt, and pepper; bring to a boil. Reduce heat; simmer 25 minutes, stirring occasionally. Stir in basil and parsley, and cook 1 minute. Yield: 6 cups (serving size: 1 cup).

CALORIES 128 (26% from fat); FAT 4.2g (sat 0.5g, mono 1.9g, poly 0.9g); PROTEIN 4g; CARB 22.2g; FIBER 5.2g; CHOL 0mg; IRON 2.3mg; SODIUM 337mg; CALC 30mg

Tomato Sauce

Here's a basic tomato sauce that features canned tomatoes instead of fresh. We feature it in our Veal Parmesan (page 335).

Prep: 7 minutes • Cook: 25 minutes

- 1 teaspoon olive oil
- 1 cup chopped onion
- 2 garlic cloves, minced
- ½ cup dry white wine
- 2 tablespoons tomato paste
- 2 teaspoons dried basil
- 2 teaspoons dried oregano
- ¼ teaspoon pepper
- 1 (14.5-ounce) can diced tomatoes with basil, garlic, and oregano, undrained
- 1 (8-ounce) can no-salt-added tomato sauce

1. Heat oil in a large nonstick skillet over medium-high heat. Add onion and garlic, and sauté 5 minutes. Stir in wine and remaining ingredients; bring to a boil. Reduce heat; simmer 15 minutes. Yield: 4 cups (serving size: ½ cup).

CALORIES 41 (18% from fat); FAT 0.8g (sat 0.1g, mono 0.4g, poly 0.2g); PROTEIN 1.4g; CARB 8g; FIBER 1.4g; CHOL 0mg; IRON 1.1mg; SODIUM 78mg; CALC 46mg

Romesco Sauce

There are several versions of this pepper-tomato sauce; this one is thick and smooth. A high percentage of its calories comes from fat, but think of it more as a condiment—a little goes a long way. It does wonders for tying together the elements of a vegetable stew and can easily replace mayonnaise on a grilled vegetable sandwich.

Prep: 12 minutes • Cook: 16 minutes
Other: 15 minutes

- 1 large red bell pepper
- ⅓ cup blanched almonds (about 1½ ounces)
- 1 teaspoon paprika
- ½ teaspoon salt
- ¼ teaspoon ground red pepper
- 4 plum tomatoes, quartered and seeded
- 2 (1-inch-thick) slices Italian bread, toasted (about 2 ounces)
- 3 garlic cloves, peeled
- ¼ cup extravirgin olive oil
- 2 tablespoons sherry vinegar or white wine vinegar

1. Preheat broiler.
2. Cut bell pepper in half lengthwise; discard seeds and membranes. Place pepper halves, skin sides up, on a foil-lined baking sheet; flatten with hand. Broil 15 minutes or until blackened.

3. Place in a zip-top plastic bag; seal. Let stand 15 minutes; peel.
4. Place bell pepper, almonds, and next 6 ingredients in a food processor, and process until minced. Add oil and vinegar; process until smooth. Yield: 2 cups (serving size: 1 tablespoon).

CALORIES 35 (67% from fat); FAT 2.6g (sat 0.3g, mono 1.8g, poly 0.4g); PROTEIN 0.7g; CARB 2.4g; FIBER 0.5g; CHOL 0mg; IRON 0.3mg; SODIUM 54mg; CALC 17mg

how to roast bell peppers

Roasting bell peppers is one of the least labor-intensive methods in cooking, and the transformation from plump, crisp bell peppers to smoky, velvety, and sweet is nothing short of magical.

Broil the peppers 15 minutes or until blackened. Place the peppers in a zip-top plastic bag; seal and let stand 15 minutes. This will loosen the skin and make peeling them much easier. Peel and discard skins. (See page 32 for additional techniques for roasting bell peppers.)

Port Wine-Mushroom Sauce

Reminiscent of bordelaise sauce (a French sauce made with wine, brown stock, and bone marrow), this brown sauce comes together in a fraction of the time. It's virtually fat-free—another plus.

Prep: 10 minutes • Cook: 9 minutes

1½   cups sliced shiitake mushroom caps
     (about 3½ ounces)
  1   tablespoon all-purpose flour
⅓   cup port or other sweet red wine
¼   cup minced shallots
  1   tablespoon balsamic vinegar
  1   cup beef broth
  2   teaspoons Worcestershire sauce
  1   teaspoon tomato paste
⅛   teaspoon dried rosemary
½   teaspoon Dijon mustard

1. Combine mushrooms and flour in a bowl; toss well.
2. Combine wine, shallots, and vinegar in a medium skillet. Bring to a boil; cook until thick (about 3 minutes). Reduce heat to medium. Add broth, Worcestershire, tomato paste, and rosemary; cook 1 minute. Add mushroom mixture; cook 3 minutes, stirring constantly. Stir in mustard. Yield: 1 cup (serving size: ¼ cup).

CALORIES 69 (3% from fat); FAT 0.2g (sat 0g, mono 0g, poly 0.1g); PROTEIN 3.8g; CARB 8.4g; FIBER 0.5g; CHOL 0mg; IRON 1mg; SODIUM 367mg; CALC 14mg

White Barbecue Sauce

A peppery white sauce is a unique alternative to a tomato-based barbecue sauce. Spoon the sauce over grilled chicken breasts, pork tenderloin, or pork chops after grilling.

Prep: 4 minutes

½   cup light mayonnaise
⅓   cup white vinegar
  1   tablespoon coarsely ground black
     pepper
½   teaspoon ground red pepper
1½   teaspoons fresh lemon juice
   Dash of salt

1. Combine all ingredients, stirring well with a whisk. Yield: 1 cup (serving size: 2 tablespoons).

CALORIES 53 (87% from fat); FAT 5.1g (sat 1g, mono 0g, poly 0g); PROTEIN 0.1g; CARB 1.7g; FIBER 0.3g; CHOL 5mg; IRON 0.3mg; SODIUM 139mg; CALC 4mg

Test Kitchen Tip: We don't recommend using fat-free mayonnaise in this recipe; the sauce will be too gloppy.

Blueberry-Balsamic Barbecue Sauce

Try this sweet, tangy sauce the next time you grill chicken, pork, or tuna. Brush on some of it right at the end of cooking, and pass the rest at the table. If fresh blueberries aren't available, 2 cups of thawed frozen blueberries will do.

Prep: 6 minutes • Cook: 18 minutes

  2   cups fresh blueberries
¼   cup balsamic vinegar
  3   tablespoons sugar
  3   tablespoons ketchup
½   teaspoon garlic powder
¼   teaspoon salt

1. Place all ingredients in a saucepan. Bring to a boil; reduce heat, and simmer 15 minutes or until slightly thick. Remove from heat; cool. Place blueberry mixture in a blender; process until smooth. Yield: 1½ cups (serving size: about ¼ cup).

CALORIES 67 (3% from fat); FAT 0.2g (sat 0g, mono 0g, poly 0.1g); PROTEIN 0.5g; CARB 16.9g; FIBER 1.4g; CHOL 0mg; IRON 0.2mg; SODIUM 194mg; CALC 8mg

how to make port wine-mushroom sauce

1. Combine the wine, shallots, and vinegar in a medium skillet. Bring to a boil; reduce liquid by cooking about 3 minutes until thick and syrupy.

2. Lower heat to medium. Add the broth, Worcestershire sauce, tomato paste, and rosemary; cook 1 minute. Add the mushroom mixture; cook 3 minutes, stirring constantly. Stir in the mustard.

Classic Pesto

Classic Pesto

When you have a bumper crop of basil, make extra batches of pesto so you'll have enough to last all winter. Simple dishes take on an easy sophistication as you swirl the bold sauce into penne pasta or use it to spruce up pizza, chili, or omelets.

Prep: 9 minutes

- 2 tablespoons coarsely chopped walnuts or pine nuts
- 2 garlic cloves, peeled
- 3 tablespoons extravirgin olive oil
- 4 cups basil leaves (about 4 ounces)
- ½ cup (2 ounces) grated fresh Parmesan cheese
- ¼ teaspoon salt

1. With food processor on, drop nuts and garlic through food chute; process until minced. Add oil; pulse 3 times. Add basil, cheese, and salt; process until finely minced, scraping sides of bowl once. Yield: ¾ cup (serving size: 1 tablespoon).

CALORIES 58 (82% from fat); FAT 5.3g (sat 1.3g, mono 3g, poly 0.8g); PROTEIN 2.1g; CARB 0.9g; FIBER 0.6g; CHOL 3mg; IRON 0.5mg; SODIUM 125mg; CALC 72mg

Pesto Mayonnaise

Combine 2 tablespoons light mayonnaise, 2 tablespoons Classic Pesto, ⅛ teaspoon salt, and ⅛ teaspoon black pepper in a small bowl. Yield: ¼ cup (serving size: 1 tablespoon). Store in an airtight container in the refrigerator up to five days.

CALORIES 42 (69% from fat); FAT 3.2g (sat 0.7g, mono 1.6g, poly 0.7g); PROTEIN 1.1g; CARB 2.5g; FIBER 0.3g; CHOL 2mg; IRON 0.3mg; SODIUM 206mg; CALC 36mg

freezing pesto Thanks to olive oil, pesto retains its bright color when frozen. Just drop a tablespoon of pesto into each section of an ice tray, and freeze. Remove the frozen cubes, and transfer them to a heavy-duty zip-top plastic bag. Or skip the ice tray, and spoon the pesto directly into a plastic bag or container to freeze. Let the pesto thaw for a few hours before you use it. Pesto will keep in the freezer up to three months and in the refrigerator up to five days.

Salmoriglio Sauce

Salmoriglio (sahl-more-REE-lyee-o) is a pungent Italian sauce of olive oil, lemon, garlic, and oregano. Pass it around the table for drizzling over fish. (Try it with Baked Flounder with Fresh Lemon Pepper on page 237.) Freshness is key for this vibrant sauce, so make it as close to serving time as possible.

Prep: 7 minutes

- 2 tablespoons fresh lemon juice
- 2 tablespoons extravirgin olive oil
- 1½ teaspoons chopped fresh or ½ teaspoon dried oregano
- 1 teaspoon kosher salt
- 1 teaspoon grated lemon rind
- 2 garlic cloves, minced

Dash of freshly ground black pepper

1. Combine all ingredients, stirring well with a whisk. Yield: ¼ cup (serving size: 2 teaspoons).

CALORIES 44 (92% from fat); FAT 4.5g (sat 0.6g, mono 3.3g, poly 0.4g); PROTEIN 0.1g; CARB 1.1g; FIBER 0.1g; CHOL 0mg; IRON 0.2mg; SODIUM 320mg; CALC 9mg

Pebre

This fresh herb sauce is a staple on Chilean tables. It pairs well with grilled meats and is delicious stirred into pasta or rice. For a variation, see Grilled Beef Tenderloin with Chilean Cilantro Sauce on page 330.

Prep: 12 minutes • Other: 1 hour

- 2 cups fresh parsley leaves (about 1 bunch)
- 2 cups fresh cilantro leaves (about 1 bunch)
- ¾ cup chopped onion
- ¼ cup water
- 1 tablespoon fresh lemon juice
- 1 teaspoon hot pepper sauce or crushed red pepper
- ¾ teaspoon salt
- ¼ teaspoon pepper
- 2 garlic cloves, minced
- 1½ tablespoons extravirgin olive oil

1. Place first 9 ingredients in a food processor; pulse until minced, scraping sides occasionally. Place herb mixture in a bowl; cover and refrigerate 1 hour. Stir in oil before serving. Yield: 1 cup (serving size: 2 tablespoons).

CALORIES 37 (66% from fat); FAT 2.7g (sat 0.4g, mono 1.9g, poly 0.2g); PROTEIN 0.8g; CARB 3g; FIBER 0.9g; CHOL 0mg; IRON 1.1mg; SODIUM 240mg; CALC 28mg

Easy Savory Gravy

Thickened with a roux, a cooked flour-fat mixture that adds richness, this gravy doesn't rely on pan drippings from turkey or meat. Soy sauce lends it a hearty flavor that enhances mashed potatoes, turkey, chicken, or pork.

Prep: 4 minutes • Cook: 21 minutes

  2 tablespoons olive oil
  6 tablespoons all-purpose flour
  2 (14-ounce) cans vegetable broth
  ¼ cup low-sodium soy sauce
  ½ teaspoon freshly ground black pepper

1. Heat oil in a saucepan over medium heat. Add flour; cook 5 minutes or until lightly browned and fragrant, stirring constantly with a whisk. (If flour browns too quickly, remove pan from heat; stir constantly until it cools.)
2. Gradually add broth to pan, stirring constantly with a whisk. Stir in soy sauce and pepper; cook until thick (about 15 minutes), stirring frequently. Yield: 3 cups (serving size: about ¼ cup).

CALORIES 42 (54% from fat); FAT 2.5g (sat 0.3g, mono 1.7g, poly 0.2g); PROTEIN 1.3g; CARB 4.1g; FIBER 0.1g; CHOL 0mg; IRON 0.2mg; SODIUM 493mg; CALC 0mg

Test Kitchen Tip: The key to a smooth, creamy gravy is to stir, stir, stir.

Classic Giblet Gravy

You'll need turkey drippings for this gravy, so make it to serve with any of our roasted turkey recipes (pages 393 - 396). It takes about 1½ hours to make the stock, so you'll need to start the stock about two hours before the turkey is done. That way, they'll be finished at the same time.

Prep: 11 minutes • Cook: 1 hour, 54 minutes

  4 cups water
  ½ cup parsley sprigs
  1 teaspoon black peppercorns
  2 medium carrots, each cut into 3 pieces
  1 large onion, cut into 8 wedges
  1 bay leaf
  1 (14-ounce) can fat-free, less-sodium chicken broth
     Reserved turkey neck and giblets (from a 12-pound fresh or frozen thawed turkey)
  ¾ cup dry white wine
  3 tablespoons all-purpose flour
  3 tablespoons reserved turkey drippings
  ¼ teaspoon salt
  ¼ teaspoon freshly ground black pepper

1. Combine first 8 ingredients in a large saucepan. Bring to a boil. Reduce heat, and simmer over medium-low heat until reduced to 2½ cups (about 1½ hours). Strain stock through a sieve into a bowl; discard solids.
2. Bring wine to a boil in pan until reduced to ½ cup (about 3 minutes). Combine flour and turkey drippings in a bowl, stirring with a whisk until smooth. Add to pan; cook over medium heat 1 minute, stirring constantly. Stir in strained stock, salt, and ground black pepper; cook

over medium heat 15 minutes, stirring occasionally. Yield: 2½ cups (serving size: about 3 tablespoons).

CALORIES 20 (45% from fat); FAT 1g (sat 0.3g, mono 0.4g, poly 0.2g); PROTEIN 0.7g; CARB 1.9g; FIBER 0.1g; CHOL 1mg; IRON 0.2mg; SODIUM 118mg; CALC 2mg

how to make giblet gravy

1. Combine the flour and reserved turkey drippings to keep the flour from clumping when you add it to the wine.

2. Whisk the flour-wine mixture constantly as it begins to cook to ensure a smooth gravy with no lumps.

Green Chile Sauce

Green Chile Sauce

Tangy tomatillos and roasted chiles are the stars of this piquant sauce. If you're unable to find fresh tomatillos, omit the ½ teaspoon salt and use 1 (11-ounce) can tomatillos, rinsed and drained, plus 2 tablespoons lime juice. Serve with baked tortilla chips.

Prep: 25 minutes • Cook: 28 minutes
Other: 15 minutes

  7   large tomatillos (about 12 ounces)
  1   cup fat-free, less-sodium chicken broth
  ⅓   cup chopped fresh cilantro
  ⅓   cup chopped Roasted Anaheim Chiles (page 465)
  ¼   cup chopped onion
  ½   teaspoon salt
  ¼   teaspoon black pepper
  2   garlic cloves, chopped

1. Discard husks and stems of tomatillos. Cook tomatillos in boiling water 10 minutes or until tender. Drain.
2. Place tomatillos, broth, and remaining ingredients in a blender; process until mixture is smooth. Yield: 3 cups (serving size: ¼ cup).

(Totals include Roasted Anaheim Chiles) CALORIES 18 (20% from fat); FAT 0.4g (sat 0.1g, mono 0.1g, poly 0.2g); PROTEIN 0.9g; CARB 3.2g; FIBER 1.1g; CHOL 0mg; IRON 0.3mg; SODIUM 138mg; CALC 6mg

New Mexican Red Chile Sauce

New Mexico chile powder gives this sauce an authentic spicy, slightly bitter flavor. You can get similar results by substituting 7 tablespoons top-quality sweet paprika mixed with 1 tablespoon ground red pepper. Don't use commercial chili powder in its place, though. Serve with meat, vegetables, or as enchilada sauce.

Prep: 7 minutes • Cook: 19 minutes

  ½   teaspoon canola oil
  ½   cup finely chopped onion
  ½   cup New Mexico chile powder
  1   garlic clove, minced
  1   cup canned crushed tomatoes
  3   tablespoons honey
  1   teaspoon ground cumin
  ¼   teaspoon pepper
  1   (14-ounce) can vegetable broth

1. Heat oil in a large saucepan over medium-high heat. Add onion; sauté 4 minutes. Add chile powder and garlic; sauté 1 minute. Stir in tomatoes and remaining ingredients. Bring to a boil; reduce heat, and simmer 10 minutes. Yield: 3 cups (serving size: ¼ cup).

CALORIES 50 (20% from fat); FAT 1.1g (sat 0g, mono 0.1g, poly 0.1g); PROTEIN 1.1g; CARB 9.5g; FIBER 1.2g; CHOL 0mg; IRON 1mg; SODIUM 266mg; CALC 27mg

New Mexico chile powder

This chile powder is different from commercial chili powder (a powdered seasoning mixture of chiles, garlic, oregano, cumin, and coriander) because it's made from pure dried New Mexican chiles.

Orange-Chipotle Sauce

This smoky, citrus-infused sauce is a tasty alternative to a traditional barbecue sauce. It's equally good on both chicken and pork. In fact, it's part of the Spicy Cumin-Crusted Chicken with Orange-Chipotle Sauce recipe on page 365.

Prep: 20 minutes • Cook: 52 minutes

  2   tablespoons olive oil
  1   cup chopped onion
  1   cup chopped tomato
  2   tablespoons minced garlic (about 6 cloves)
  2   tablespoons chopped drained canned chipotle chile in adobo sauce
  2   cups fresh orange juice (about 4 oranges)
  1   cup white vinegar
  ½   cup ketchup
  ¼   cup packed brown sugar
  ¼   cup molasses
  ¼   teaspoon kosher salt
  ¼   teaspoon black pepper
  ¼   cup fresh lime juice
  ½   cup chopped fresh cilantro

1. Heat oil in a large nonstick skillet over medium-high heat. Add onion; sauté 10 minutes or until browned. Add tomato, garlic, and chile; cook 3 minutes. Add orange juice and vinegar; bring to a boil. Reduce heat; simmer until reduced to 1⅓ cups (about 30 minutes). Stir in ketchup, sugar, molasses, salt, and pepper; cook 5 minutes. Place mixture in a food processor; process until smooth. Stir in lime juice and cilantro. Yield: 2 cups (serving size: 1 tablespoon).

CALORIES 36 (23% from fat); FAT 0.9g (sat 0.1g, mono 0.6g, poly 0.1g); PROTEIN 0.4g; CARB 7.2g; FIBER 0.3g; CHOL 0mg; IRON 0.3mg; SODIUM 71mg; CALC 13mg

Salsas It's the Spanish word for "sauce," and it's not just for serving with chips. Perk up fish, chicken, beef, or pork with these fresh, lively salsas.

Hearty Fresh Tomato Salsa

Adjust the amount of jalapeños and chipotles to match your tolerance to "heat."

Prep: 25 minutes • Other: 30 minutes

- 4 pounds tomatoes, peeled, seeded, and chopped (about 6 cups)
- ½ teaspoon salt
- 1 cup fresh corn kernels (about 2 ears)
- 1 cup minced fresh cilantro
- ¼ cup finely chopped Vidalia or other sweet onion
- ¼ cup finely chopped red onion
- 3 tablespoons fresh lime juice
- 2 teaspoons sugar
- ¼ teaspoon freshly ground black pepper
- 3 jalapeño peppers, seeded and chopped
- 2 garlic cloves, minced
- 1 (15-ounce) can black beans, rinsed and drained
- 1 (7-ounce) can chipotle chiles in adobo sauce

1. Place tomatoes in a colander; sprinkle with salt. Toss gently; drain 30 minutes.
2. Combine tomatoes, corn, and next 9 ingredients in a large bowl. Remove 1 chipotle chile from can; finely chop. Add chile and 8 teaspoons adobo sauce to corn mixture, stirring to combine. (Reserve remaining chiles and adobo sauce for another use.) Yield: 8 cups (serving size: ½ cup).

CALORIES 86 (12% from fat); FAT 1.1g (sat 0.1g, mono 0.1g, poly 0.3g); PROTEIN 4g; CARB 17.1g; FIBER 4.1g; CHOL 0mg; IRON 1.3mg; SODIUM 253mg; CALC 25mg

Tomatillo Salsa

Although available canned, fresh tomatillos taste better in this salsa. Serve it with baked tortilla chips, or spoon it over burritos, quesadillas, or tacos.

Prep: 20 minutes • Cook: 17 minutes

- 1 teaspoon cumin seeds
- 2 jalapeño peppers
- 1 pound tomatillos, husks and stems removed
- 2 tablespoons chopped Vidalia or other sweet onion
- ¼ cup chopped fresh cilantro
- 1 tablespoon fresh lime juice
- ¾ teaspoon sea salt

1. Place cumin seeds in a cast-iron skillet over medium heat; cook 2 minutes or until toasted. Transfer to a spice or coffee grinder; process until finely ground.
2. Cut ¼ inch off stem ends of peppers; discard stem ends. Using tip of a paring knife, carefully remove and discard membranes and seeds, leaving peppers intact.
3. Heat skillet over medium heat. Add peppers and tomatillos. Cook 15 minutes, turning frequently (peppers and tomatillos will become speckled with black marks).
4. Place pepper mixture in a food processor, and puree until smooth. Add onion, and pulse 5 times or until blended. Pour pepper mixture into a medium bowl. Stir in cumin, cilantro, lime juice, and salt. Yield: 2 cups (serving size: ¼ cup).

CALORIES 22 (29% from fat); FAT 0.7g (sat 0.1g, mono 0.1g, poly 0.3g); PROTEIN 0.7g; CARB 4g; FIBER 1.3g; CHOL 0mg; IRON 0.6mg; SODIUM 217mg; CALC 8mg

Tomatillo Salsa

Fresh Tomato Relish

Cucumbers and mint enhance this easy relish.

Prep: 11 minutes

- 2 cups chopped tomato
- 1 cup chopped yellow tomato
- ½ cup chopped seeded peeled cucumber
- ½ cup finely chopped green bell pepper
- ½ cup finely chopped red onion
- 3 tablespoons chopped fresh basil
- 2 tablespoons fresh lime juice
- 1½ teaspoons chopped fresh mint
- ½ teaspoon salt
- ½ teaspoon sugar
- ½ teaspoon crushed red pepper

1. Combine all ingredients; toss. Yield: 4 cups (serving size: ⅔ cup).

CALORIES 33 (11% from fat); FAT 0.4g (sat 0.1g, mono 0.1g, poly 0.2g); PROTEIN 1.2g; CARB 7.5g; FIBER 1.8g; CHOL 0mg; IRON 0.8mg; SODIUM 205mg; CALC 16mg

Avocado Salsa

Top Black Bean Tacos (page 293) with this chunky salsa, or serve it with tortilla chips.

Prep: 8 minutes

- 1 cup finely chopped tomato
- ½ cup chopped fresh cilantro
- ½ cup chopped peeled avocado
- 2 tablespoons chopped red onion
- 3 tablespoons fresh lime juice
- ¼ teaspoon sea salt
- 1 garlic clove, minced
- 1 jalapeño pepper, seeded and minced

1. Combine all ingredients; mash with a fork. Yield: 2 cups (serving size: ¼ cup).

CALORIES 24 (56% from fat); FAT 1.5g (sat 0.2g, mono 0.9g, poly 0.2g); PROTEIN 0.5g; CARB 2.7g; FIBER 0.9; CHOL 0mg; IRON 0.2mg; SODIUM 75mg; CALC 5mg

Cranberry-Habanero Salsa

Serve this holiday-inspired salsa with Jerk Turkey Cutlets with Cranberry-Habanero Salsa (page 391) or with chicken.

Prep: 11 minutes

- 1½ cups fresh or frozen cranberries
- 3 tablespoons thinly sliced green onions
- 2 tablespoons fresh orange juice
- 2 tablespoons honey
- 1 tablespoon water
- 1 tablespoon chopped green bell pepper
- 1 tablespoon chopped fresh cilantro
- 1 teaspoon sugar
- ⅛ teaspoon salt
- ½ habanero pepper, seeded and minced
- Dash of black pepper

1. Place cranberries in a food processor; pulse 3 times. Combine cranberries, onions, and remaining ingredients. Cover; refrigerate. Yield: 1 cup (serving size: ¼ cup).

CALORIES 60 (2% from fat); FAT 0.1g (sat 0g, mono 0g, poly 0g); PROTEIN 0.4g; CARB 15.8g; FIBER 0.7g; CHOL 0mg; IRON 0.3mg; SODIUM 76mg; CALC 9mg

Papaya and Mango Salsa

Jazz up grilled fish or chicken with this tropical fruit salsa, or use it as a topping for an island-style burger.

Prep: 12 minutes

- 2 cups shredded peeled firm papaya
- 2 cups chopped peeled mango
- 1 cup finely chopped red onion
- ¼ cup chopped fresh cilantro
- ¼ cup chopped fresh mint
- 1½ tablespoons fresh lemon juice
- 1 tablespoon finely chopped seeded jalapeño pepper
- ⅛ teaspoon salt
- Dash of sugar

1. Combine all ingredients in a large bowl; toss gently to coat. Yield: 4 cups (serving size: ½ cup).

CALORIES 51 (5% from fat); FAT 0.3g (sat 0.1g, mono 0.1g, poly 0.1g); PROTEIN 0.8g; CARB 12.8g; FIBER 2g; CHOL 0mg; IRON 0.5mg; SODIUM 40mg; CALC 23mg

Fresh Pineapple Salsa

Black pepper brings out the sweetness of the pineapple. Serve this salsa with shrimp, pork, or chicken.

Prep: 9 minutes • Other: 1 hour

- 1 cup chopped fresh pineapple
- ½ cup chopped peeled kiwifruit
- 2 tablespoons chopped jalapeño pepper
- 2 tablespoons finely chopped red onion
- 2 tablespoons chopped fresh cilantro
- 1 tablespoon seasoned rice vinegar
- ½ teaspoon sugar
- ½ teaspoon grated lime rind
- ¼ teaspoon freshly ground black pepper
- ⅛ teaspoon ground cardamom
- Dash of salt

1. Combine all ingredients, tossing gently. Let stand 1 hour. Yield: 1½ cups (serving size: ¼ cup).

CALORIES 28 (6% from fat); FAT 0.2g (sat 0g, mono 0g, poly 0.1g); PROTEIN 0.4g; CARB 6.8g; FIBER 1g; CHOL 0mg; IRON 0.2mg; SODIUM 77mg; CALC 8mg

Test Kitchen Tip: Instead of buying a whole fresh pineapple, you can get a container of fresh slices in the produce department of the supermarket.

Dessert Sauces
Let your dessert imagination soar as you master three different chocolate sauces, a classic custard sauce, and refreshing fruit sauces.

Rich Chocolate Sauce

Pair this thick chocolate sauce with cake, frozen yogurt, or fresh fruit.

Prep: 7 minutes • Cook: 6 minutes
Other: 10 minutes

- ½ cup sugar
- ½ cup unsweetened cocoa
- 1 cup fat-free milk
- 1 tablespoon butter
- 1½ ounces semisweet chocolate, chopped
- ½ teaspoon vanilla extract

1. Combine sugar and cocoa in a small saucepan; stir in milk and butter. Bring to a boil over medium heat, stirring constantly. Cook 3 minutes, stirring constantly. Remove from heat; stir in chocolate and vanilla, stirring until chocolate melts. Serve warm or let stand 10 minutes to thicken. Yield: 1½ cups (serving size: 2 tablespoons).

CALORIES 73 (36% from fat); FAT 2.9g (sat 1.7g, mono 1g, poly 0.1g); PROTEIN 1.7g; CARB 12.9g; FIBER 1.3g; CHOL 3mg; IRON 0.7mg; SODIUM 21mg; CALC 32mg

Warm Chocolate Sauce
(pictured on page 447)

The consistency of this ultrachocolaty sauce falls somewhere between hot fudge sauce and chocolate syrup. Drizzle it over low-fat ice cream, frozen yogurt, or, if you're really feeling decadent, Chocolate Bundt Cake (page 127).

Prep: 7 minutes • Cook: 6 minutes

- ⅔ cup 2% reduced-fat milk
- ½ cup dark corn syrup
- ¼ cup sugar
- ¼ cup unsweetened cocoa
- Dash of salt
- 2½ ounces semisweet baking chocolate, chopped
- 1½ tablespoons butter
- 1 teaspoon vanilla extract

1. Combine first 5 ingredients in a saucepan over medium-high heat, stirring with a whisk. Bring to a boil. Reduce heat to medium; cook 3 minutes, stirring frequently. Remove from heat. Add chopped chocolate, butter, and vanilla; stir until chocolate melts. Yield: 1¾ cups (serving size: 2 tablespoons).

CALORIES 99 (29% from fat); FAT 3.2g (sat 1.9g, mono 1.1g, poly 0.1g); PROTEIN 1g; CARB 19g; FIBER 1g; CHOL 2mg; IRON 0.5mg; SODIUM 40mg; CALC 21mg

Bittersweet Chocolate Sauce

Light corn syrup gives this intense chocolate sauce a silky-smooth texture. Because corn syrup is about half as sweet as granulated sugar, it's necessary to add a little of the latter to prevent the sauce from becoming too bitter. Although thin when taken off the stove, the sauce thickens as it chills. Store it in an airtight container in the refrigerator up to two weeks.

Prep: 6 minutes • Cook: 9 minutes

- 1 cup light-colored corn syrup
- ¾ cup Dutch process cocoa
- ½ cup water
- ¼ cup sugar
- ¼ cup evaporated fat-free milk
- ⅛ teaspoon salt
- 2 teaspoons vanilla extract

1. Combine first 6 ingredients in a small saucepan, stirring with a whisk until blended. Bring to a simmer over medium heat. Reduce heat; simmer 6 minutes, stirring occasionally. Remove from heat; stir in vanilla. Cover and chill. Yield: 2¼ cups (serving size: 2 tablespoons).

CALORIES 74 (6% from fat); FAT 0.5g (sat 0.3g, mono 0.2g, poly 0g); PROTEIN 0.9g; CARB 19.2g; FIBER 1.1g; CHOL 0mg; IRON 0.6mg; SODIUM 43mg; CALC 15mg

Classic Makeover: Crème Anglaise

Crème Anglaise, or custard sauce, goes by all kinds of names: stirred custard, boiled custard, and soft custard. Whatever it's called, it's a decadently rich liquid custard that's used for ice creams and Bavarian creams, and for spooning over fruits and desserts. A traditional Crème Anglaise is made with whole milk, cream, sugar, and whole eggs or egg yolks, so it's high in both calories and fat.

The creamiest custards are thickened with just egg yolks, which contribute fat. When lightening a custard sauce recipe, it's tempting to use cornstarch or flour to add body while reducing the fat. We decided to keep the egg yolks, but switch to low-fat milk because the yolks are what make the sauce luscious and smooth.

We also reduced the amount of sugar by half, but kept the depth of flavor by using a vanilla bean instead of extract.

Before	After
• 179 calories	• 97 calories
• 9.1g fat	• 3.6g fat
• percentage of calories from fat 46%	• percentage of calories from fat 33%

Custard Sauce (Crème Anglaise)

Because this is such an uncomplicated sauce, quality ingredients are key. We've opted for a vanilla bean, which can be found in your supermarket's spice section. You can substitute 2 teaspoons vanilla extract for the bean, but the flavor will suffer.

Prep: 8 minutes • Cook: 12 minutes

1¾ cups 1% low-fat milk
1 (3-inch) piece vanilla bean, split lengthwise
⅓ cup sugar
4 large egg yolks

1. Pour milk into a medium saucepan. Scrape seeds from vanilla bean; add seeds and bean to milk. Cook over medium heat 6 minutes (do not boil); discard bean. Remove from heat.

2. Combine sugar and yolks in a small bowl, stirring with a whisk until blended. Gradually add milk mixture to bowl, stirring constantly with a whisk. Return mixture to pan. Cook over medium heat 6 minutes or until mixture thinly coats back of a spoon, stirring constantly with a whisk. Immediately pour mixture into a bowl. Cover and chill (mixture will thicken as it cools). Yield: 1¾ cups (serving size: ¼ cup).

CALORIES 97 (33% from fat); FAT 3.6g (sat 1.3g, mono 1.3g, poly 0.4g); PROTEIN 3.6g; CARB 12.6g; FIBER 0g; CHOL 127mg; IRON 0.4mg; SODIUM 35mg; CALC 88mg

Test Kitchen Tip: Store Crème Anglaise in the refrigerator for up to three days.

how to make custard sauce (crème anglaise)

1. Scrape the seeds from the vanilla bean; add the seeds and bean to the milk. Cook the milk mixture 6 minutes to bring out the bean's full flavor. If you don't get all of the seeds out when you scrape the bean, they'll be released as the bean steeps.

2. Gradually pour the hot milk mixture into the egg yolk mixture in the bowl, stirring constantly with a whisk. By doing this, you eliminate the risk of cooking the egg mixture too quickly, which could result in scrambled eggs.

3. Cook over medium heat until the sauce thickens and coats the back of a spoon. Don't get impatient and turn the heat too high; the eggs could curdle.

4. Immediately pour the finished sauce into a bowl. Curdling is possible as long as the sauce stays in the hot pan.

Very Butterscotch Sauce

Ice cream, frozen yogurt, or sliced apples are pleasing partners for butterscotch sauce. Store in the refrigerator for up to two weeks.

Prep: 5 minutes • Cook: 12 minutes

2½ tablespoons butter
1 cup packed dark brown sugar
¼ cup evaporated low-fat milk
2 tablespoons light-colored corn syrup
½ cup water
1 tablespoon cornstarch

1. Melt butter in a small, heavy saucepan over medium-high heat; stir in sugar, milk, and syrup. Bring to a boil; reduce heat to medium, and cook 5 minutes, stirring frequently. Combine water and cornstarch; stir into milk mixture. Bring to a boil; cook 1 minute, stirring constantly. Remove from heat, and cool to room temperature. Yield: 1½ cups (serving size: 2 tablespoons).

CALORIES 107 (21% from fat); FAT 2.5g (sat 1.5g, mono 0.7g, poly 0.1g); PROTEIN 0.4g; CARB 21.5g; FIBER 0g; CHOL 7mg; IRON 0.4mg; SODIUM 42mg; CALC 30mg

Test Kitchen Tip: We recommend using a saucepan with a heavy bottom when making sauces. A heavy saucepan moderates temperature well and distributes the heat evenly.

Never stop stirring a custard sauce that calls for constant stirring—it can cause the custard to overheat. Stir in either a figure-eight pattern, a zig-zag motion, or a circular motion—just keep the mixture moving away from the bottom of the pan.

Blueberry Sauce

We've included this summertime sauce in the recipe for Frozen Lemonade Pie with Blueberry Sauce (page 210). Drizzle it on top of low-fat ice cream, sorbet, pound cake, or cheesecake.

Prep: 4 minutes • Cook: 5 minutes

¾ cup water
¼ cup sugar
2¼ teaspoons cornstarch
1½ cups blueberries

1. Combine first 3 ingredients in a small heavy saucepan; stir with a whisk. Bring to a boil; cook, stirring constantly, 1 minute or until thick. Add blueberries; cook 2 minutes or until bubbly. Yield: 1½ cups (serving size: 3 tablespoons).

CALORIES 38 (2% from fat); FAT 0.1g (sat 0g, mono 0.1g, poly 0g); PROTEIN 0.2g; CARB 9.6g; FIBER 1.1g; CHOL 0mg; IRON 0mg; SODIUM 2mg; CALC 2mg

Pineapple Sauce

Fresh pineapple is the star of this no-cook sauce. Serve it over low-fat ice cream or frozen yogurt.

Prep: 7 minutes

3 cups coarsely chopped pineapple
2 tablespoons brown sugar
¼ teaspoon vanilla extract

1. Place all ingredients in a food processor, and pulse 10 times or until finely chopped. Cover and chill. Yield: 1¾ cups (serving size: 2 tablespoons).

CALORIES 24 (4% from fat); FAT 0.1g (sat 0g, mono 0g, poly 0.1g); PROTEIN 0.1g; CARB 6g; FIBER 0.4g; CHOL 0mg; IRON 0.2mg; SODIUM 1mg; CALC 4mg

Strawberry-Rum Sauce

Serve with the Frozen Strawberry Daiquiri Pie on page 211. It's also yummy with low-fat ice cream or angel food cake.

Prep: 7 minutes • Other: 20 minutes

2½ cups quartered strawberries
2 tablespoons sugar
2 tablespoons white rum
1 teaspoon grated lime rind

1. Combine first 3 ingredients in a small bowl; stir gently. Let stand 20 minutes.
2. Place half of strawberry mixture and lime rind in a blender; cover and process until smooth. Add to remaining strawberry mixture; stir well. Cover and chill. Yield: 1½ cups (serving size: 3 tablespoons).

CALORIES 37 (5% from fat); FAT 0.2g (sat 0g, mono 0g, poly 0.1g); PROTEIN 0.3g; CARB 6.4g; FIBER 1.2g; CHOL 0mg; IRON 0.2mg; SODIUM 1mg; CALC 7mg

Fresh Strawberry Sauce

Boiling mashed strawberries in water creates the flavorful, juicy base for the sauce. Lemon juice lends bright acidity; balsamic vinegar is a more mellow choice. Spoon over ice cream sundaes or angel food cake.

Prep: 12 minutes • Cook: 13 minutes

1 cup ripe strawberries
⅓ cup water
⅓ cup sugar
1½ teaspoons cornstarch
1½ teaspoons fresh lemon juice or balsamic vinegar
2 cups finely chopped strawberries

1. Mash 1 cup strawberries. Combine mashed strawberries and water in a small saucepan; bring to a boil. Cook 5 minutes, stirring occasionally. Press through a sieve

into a bowl; reserve ½ cup strawberry liquid (add enough water to measure ½ cup, if necessary). Discard pulp.
2. Combine sugar and cornstarch in pan. Add strawberry liquid; stir well. Bring to a boil; cook 1 minute, stirring constantly. Reduce heat; cook 2 minutes. Remove from heat; stir in lemon juice. Cool slightly. Stir in chopped strawberries. Yield: 2 cups (serving size: 2 tablespoons).

CALORIES 25 (4% from fat); FAT 0.1g (sat 0g, mono 0g, poly 0.1g); PROTEIN 0.2g; CARB 6.2g; FIBER 0.6g; CHOL 0mg; IRON 0.1mg; SODIUM 0mg; CALC 4mg

Lemon Curd

For a lime-curd variation, substitute lime rind and juice for the lemon rind and juice. Store in the refrigerator up to one week.

Prep: 10 minutes • Cook: 8 minutes

¾ cup sugar
1 tablespoon grated lemon rind
2 large eggs
⅔ cup fresh lemon juice (about 3 large lemons)
2 tablespoons butter

1. Combine first 3 ingredients in a saucepan over medium heat, stirring with a whisk. Cook until sugar dissolves and mixture is light in color (about 3 minutes). Stir in lemon juice and butter; cook 5 minutes or until mixture thinly coats back of a spoon, stirring constantly with a whisk. Cool. Cover and chill (mixture will thicken as it cools). Yield: 1⅓ cups (serving size: 1 tablespoon).

CALORIES 47 (31% from fat); FAT 1.6g (sat 0.8g, mono 0.5g, poly 0.1g); PROTEIN 0.7g; CARB 7.9g; FIBER 0g; CHOL 24mg; IRON 0.1mg; SODIUM 18mg; CALC 4mg

Condiments
Fruit butters, relishes, chutneys, and chiles take light recipes from ordinary to spectacular.

Overnight Apple Butter

A mixture of apple varieties, rather than just one type, will produce apple butter with rich, complex flavor. Good choices include Esopus Spitzenburg, Granny Smith, Jonathan, Northern Spy, Rome, Stayman, Winesap, and York. Enjoy the apple butter over toast or English muffins, or serve it with pork chops or chicken.

Prep: 20 minutes
Cook: 11 hours, 30 minutes

- 1 cup packed brown sugar
- ½ cup honey
- ¼ cup apple cider
- 1 tablespoon ground cinnamon
- ¼ teaspoon ground cloves
- ⅛ teaspoon ground mace
- 10 apples, peeled, cored, and cut into large chunks (about 2½ pounds)

1. Place all ingredients in a 5-quart electric slow cooker; stir. Cover and cook on LOW 10 hours or until apples are very tender.

2. Place a large fine-mesh sieve over a bowl; spoon one-third of apple mixture into sieve. Press mixture through sieve using back of a spoon or ladle. Discard pulp. Repeat procedure with remaining apple mixture. Return apple mixture to slow cooker. Cook, uncovered, on HIGH 1½ hours or until mixture is thick, stirring occasionally. Spoon into a bowl; cover and chill up to 1 week. Yield: 4 cups (serving size: ¼ cup).

CALORIES 132 (0% from fat); FAT 0g (sat 0g, mono 0g, poly 0g); PROTEIN 0.1g; CARB 35.3g; FIBER 3.1g; CHOL 0mg; IRON 0.7mg; SODIUM 6mg; CALC 18mg

Variation

Stovetop Apple Butter: Combine all ingredients in a Dutch oven. Cover and cook over medium-low heat 1 hour or until apples are very tender, stirring occasionally. Strain through a sieve as recipe instructs in Step 2. Return mixture to pan. Cook, uncovered, over medium-low heat 15 minutes or until thick, stirring frequently.

Cranberry Sauce with Apple Cider

Apple cider stands in for water to add dimension to this cranberry sauce. It's great with pork or turkey.

Prep: 3 minutes • Cook: 15 minutes

- 1 cup sugar
- 1 cup apple cider or apple juice
- 1 (12-ounce) package fresh cranberries

1. Combine all ingredients in a saucepan; bring to a boil over medium-high heat. Reduce heat; simmer 10 minutes or until cranberries pop, stirring occasionally. Chill. Yield: 2 cups (serving size: ¼ cup).

CALORIES 135 (0% from fat); FAT 0g (sat. 0g, mono 0g, poly 0g); PROTEIN 0.3g; CARB 35g; FIBER 1.8g; CHOL 0mg; IRON 0.1mg; SODIUM 1mg; CALC 3mg

Cranberry-Apple Relish

Serve this relish instead of cranberry sauce at your holiday meal.

Prep: 6 minutes • Cook: 20 minutes

- 1½ cups chopped peeled Granny Smith apple (about ½ pound)
- 1 cup packed brown sugar
- ½ cup white grape juice
- 1 teaspoon ground ginger
- 1 teaspoon ground cinnamon
- 1 (12-ounce) package fresh cranberries

1. Combine all ingredients in a medium saucepan. Bring to a boil; reduce heat, and simmer until thick (about 15 minutes), stirring occasionally. Cool completely. Yield: 3 cups (serving size: 3 tablespoons).

CALORIES 75 (1% from fat); FAT 0.1g (sat 0g, mono 0g, poly 0.1g); PROTEIN 0.2g; CARB 19.3g; FIBER 1.2g; CHOL 0mg; IRON 0.5mg; SODIUM 6mg; CALC 16mg

Cranberry, Pear, and Ginger Relish

Start with this basic relish and improvise as you wish: Substitute other dried fruits, such as finely diced dried apple, pear, or apricot.

Prep: 7 minutes • Cook: 15 minutes

- 3 cups fresh cranberries
- 2 cups finely chopped peeled Anjou pear (about 3 pears)
- 1⅓ cups orange juice
- 1¼ cups dried cranberries
- ⅔ cup packed brown sugar
- 3 tablespoons dried currants or raisins
- 3 tablespoons minced crystallized ginger
- ⅛ teaspoon ground cardamom

1. Combine all ingredients in a large saucepan; bring to a boil. Reduce heat, and simmer 10 minutes, stirring occasionally. Chill. Yield: 5 cups (serving size: ⅓ cup).

CALORIES 123 (1% from fat); FAT 0.2g (sat 0g, mono 0.1g, poly 0.1g); PROTEIN 0.4g; CARB 30.8g; FIBER 2.3g; CHOL 0mg; IRON 1.6mg; SODIUM 8mg; CALC 29mg

Cranberry-Kumquat-Date Relish

Tart kumquats contribute a distinct citrus note to cranberry relish. Fresh kumquats are in season from November through March.

Prep: 7 minutes • Other: 1 hour

- 1 (12-ounce) package fresh cranberries
- 1 cup kumquats, quartered
- ¾ cup sugar
- ½ cup chopped pitted dates

1. Place first 3 ingredients in a food processor, and pulse 10 times or until fruit is coarsely chopped. Add dates, and pulse

5 times or until blended. Cover and let stand at room temperature 1 hour. Yield: 2½ cups (serving size: ¼ cup).

CALORIES 111 (1% from fat); FAT 0.1g (sat 0g, mono 0g, poly 0.1g); PROTEIN 0.5g; CARB 29g; FIBER 3.4g; CHOL 0mg; IRON 0.3mg; SODIUM 2mg; CALC 14mg

Quick Preserved Lemons

Preserved lemons, a popular Moroccan condiment, typically takes four to six weeks to make in order to acquire the right consistency and flavor. However, this quick method bypasses the lengthy preservation time and is an ideal substitute for the original. The lemon rind can accent a variety of dishes, from seafood to vegetable stir-fries. Mash the pulp and stir it into a sauce or a stew, or use it to baste chicken or lamb.

Prep: 4 minutes • Cook: 32 minutes

- 1 cup water
- 2 tablespoons kosher salt
- 2 lemons, washed and quartered

1. Combine water and salt in a small saucepan; bring to a boil. Add lemons; cook 30 minutes or until liquid is reduced to ½ cup and lemon rind is tender. Remove from heat; cool to room temperature. Yield: ½ cup (serving size: 1 teaspoon).

CALORIES 2 (0% from fat); FAT 0g (sat 0g, mono 0g, poly 0g); PROTEIN 0.1g; CARB 1g; FIBER 0.4g; CHOL 0mg; IRON 0.1mg; SODIUM 235mg; CALC 6mg

Test Kitchen Tip: The preserved lemons can be made several days ahead and stored in the refrigerator up to one week. To distribute the flavor, chop before adding to a dish.

Date Chutney

This jalapeño-accented chutney is excellent as a topping for Brown-and-Wild Rice Pilaf (page 267) or with roasted pork or chicken. Keep in the refrigerator up to two days.

Prep: 13 minutes

> 1 cup chopped pitted dates (about 16 dates)
> ½ cup fresh lemon juice (about 3 lemons)
> ¼ cup water
> 2 tablespoons chopped fresh cilantro
> 1 tablespoon chopped seeded jalapeño pepper
> ½ teaspoon salt

1. Place all ingredients in a blender or food processor; process until thick and smooth. Yield: 1 cup (serving size: 1 tablespoon).

CALORIES 326 (28% from fat); FAT 10.3g (sat 1.2g, mono 6.1g, poly 2.1g); PROTEIN 12g; CARB 50.1g; FIBER 5.5g; CHOL 0mg; IRON 3.3mg; SODIUM 688mg; CALC 74mg

Tomato Chutney

Slightly thicker and sweeter than tomato sauce, warm or chilled tomato chutney makes a spicy accompaniment for fish, chicken, or rice.

Prep: 11 minutes • Cook: 25 minutes

> 2 teaspoons canola oil
> 1 tablespoon minced peeled fresh ginger
> 3 garlic cloves, minced
> 5 cups chopped seeded tomato (about 2 pounds)
> 2 tablespoons sugar
> 1 teaspoon ground cumin
> ½ teaspoon salt
> ¼ teaspoon ground turmeric

1. Heat oil in a large nonstick skillet over medium heat. Add ginger and garlic; sauté

Tomato Chutney

1 minute. Add tomato and remaining ingredients; bring to a boil. Cover and cook 5 minutes, stirring occasionally. Uncover and cook 15 minutes, stirring frequently. Yield: 1½ cups (serving size: 2 tablespoons).

CALORIES 32 (28% from fat); FAT 1g (sat 0.1g, mono 0.5g, poly 0.3g); PROTEIN 0.8g; CARB 6g; FIBER 0.8g; CHOL 0mg; IRON 0.4mg; SODIUM 104mg; CALC 6mg

Tomato-Garlic Chutney

Of all the cooked chutneys in India, tomato chutneys are, by far, the most popular. This rendition includes loads of garlic and mustard seeds.

Prep: 7 minutes • Cook: 10 minutes

> 1 tablespoon canola oil
> 1 teaspoon mustard seeds, crushed
> 8 garlic cloves, sliced
> 2 cups chopped seeded plum tomato
> 1½ teaspoons curry powder
> ½ teaspoon salt

1. Heat oil in a large nonstick skillet over medium-high heat. Add mustard seeds and garlic; cover pan immediately, and cook 10 seconds, shaking pan constantly (mustard seeds will pop once they hit the hot pan, causing oil to spatter). Stir in chopped plum tomato, curry powder, and salt; cook 2 minutes. Reduce heat to medium; cook 6 minutes, stirring occasionally. Yield: 2 cups (serving size: ¼ cup).

CALORIES 32 (56% from fat); FAT 2g (sat 0.3g, mono 0.5g, poly 1g); PROTEIN 0.7g; CARB 3.4g; FIBER 0.7g; CHOL 0mg; IRON 0.4mg; SODIUM 151mg; CALC 12mg

Test Kitchen Tip: Be careful not to overcook the mustard seeds, as they'll burn and turn bitter. Look for mustard seeds in the spice section of the supermarket.

Sweet Pepper and Onion Relish with Pine Nuts

Spread goat cheese on sourdough bread, then slather with the relish. It's also tasty on ham sandwiches or grilled chicken.

Prep: 15 minutes • Cook: 27 minutes

  1   teaspoon olive oil
Cooking spray
  8   cups vertically sliced Vidalia or other sweet onion (about 1¾ pounds)
1½ cups red bell pepper strips
 ¾ teaspoon dried thyme
  2   tablespoons pine nuts, toasted
1½ tablespoons rice vinegar
  1   tablespoon honey
 ¼ teaspoon salt
 ⅛ teaspoon coarsely ground black pepper

1. Heat oil in a large nonstick skillet coated with cooking spray over medium heat. Add onion, bell pepper, and thyme; cook 25 minutes or until golden brown, stirring frequently. Remove from heat. Add pine nuts and remaining ingredients, and stir well. Serve at room temperature. Yield: 2 cups (serving size: ¼ cup).

CALORIES 74 (23% from fat); FAT 1.9g (sat 0.3g, mono 0.9g, poly 0.6g); PROTEIN 2g; CARB 13.6g; FIBER 2.6g; CHOL 0mg; IRON 0.6mg; SODIUM 78mg; CALC 27mg

Vidalia onions Grown only in a small corner of Georgia, these onions are famous for their subtle sweetness. They are juicy, mild, and very sweet due to the area's unique combination of soils and climate. Vidalias shine in recipes that let them steal the show—in relishes, baked whole, or caramelized.

Sweet Pepper and Onion Relish with Pine Nuts

Red Onion Marmalade

We recommend this as a spread on rosemary focaccia or as a topping for pork tenderloin. Store in the refrigerator up to one week.

Prep: 15 minutes • Cook: 43 minutes

  2   tablespoons olive oil
  8   cups thinly sliced red onion (about 2 pounds)
  1   teaspoon fresh thyme leaves
  1   bay leaf
 ¾ teaspoon fine sea salt
  3   garlic cloves, minced
  1   cup cabernet sauvignon or other dry red wine
 ¼ cup packed brown sugar
  2   tablespoons balsamic vinegar
 ¼ teaspoon freshly ground black pepper

1. Heat oil in a large nonstick skillet over medium heat. Add onion, thyme, and bay leaf. Cover and cook 25 minutes, stirring occasionally.
2. Stir in salt and garlic; cook, uncovered, 2 minutes, stirring frequently. Stir in wine, brown sugar, and vinegar; bring to a boil. Reduce heat; simmer 12 minutes or until liquid almost evaporates and becomes syrupy.

3. Remove from heat; stir in pepper. Cool to room temperature. Discard bay leaf. Yield: 3 cups (serving size: ¼ cup).

CALORIES 77 (28% from fat); FAT 2.4g (sat 0.3g, mono 1.7g, poly 0.2g); PROTEIN 1g; CARB 10.5g; FIBER 1.4g; CHOL 0mg; IRON 0.4mg; SODIUM 149mg; CALC 22mg

Corn Chow-Chow

This mustard-laced relish gets better the longer it sits. It pairs well with peas, such as our Basic Pot of Peas (page 524), black-eyed peas, crowder peas, or beans. Cane syrup is golden, thick, and very sweet; use dark corn syrup in its place if you can't find it.

Prep: 8 minutes • Cook: 8 minutes
Other: 30 minutes

  1   cup water
  2   cups frozen whole-kernel corn
  1   tablespoon whole-grain Dijon mustard
  1   tablespoon cane syrup
  2   teaspoons cider vinegar
 ½ teaspoon celery salt
 ⅓ cup finely chopped onion
 ¼ cup finely chopped red bell pepper

1. Bring water to a boil in a small saucepan. Add corn; cover, reduce heat, and simmer 5 minutes. Drain.

2. Combine mustard, syrup, vinegar, and celery salt in a medium bowl, stirring with a whisk. Add onion and bell pepper, stirring to coat. Stir in corn. Let stand at least 30 minutes before serving. Yield: 2 cups (serving size: ¼ cup).

CALORIES 46 (8% from fat); FAT 0.4g (sat 0.1g, mono 0.1g, poly 0.1g); PROTEIN 1.4g; CARB 11g; FIBER 1.2g; CHOL 0mg; IRON 0.3mg; SODIUM 145mg; CALC 7mg

Cucumber Raita

Pressing the shredded cucumber removes excess water so the sauce isn't diluted. Use this fresh condiment as part of Lamb Shanks Hestia and Curried Lamb Kebabs with Raita (page 341).

Prep: 7 minutes

¾ cup shredded peeled cucumber
1 cup plain low-fat yogurt
1 tablespoon chopped fresh mint
⅛ teaspoon salt
⅛ teaspoon white pepper

1. Place cucumber in a colander, pressing until barely moist. Combine cucumber, yogurt, and remaining ingredients. Cover and chill. Yield: 1¼ cups (serving size: 2 tablespoons).

CALORIES 19 (19% from fat); FAT 0.4g (sat 0.3g, mono 0.1g, poly 0g); PROTEIN 1.5g; CARB 2.4g; FIBER 0.2g; CHOL 1mg; IRON 0.1mg; SODIUM 47mg; CALC 49mg

Roasted Anaheim Chiles

Roasted chiles are ideal for making ahead and are easy to store. They'll keep for up to two weeks in the refrigerator and three months in the freezer. These mellow-flavored chiles add zest to Granny Smith-Green Chile Salsa (page 39) and Green Chile Sauce (page 454).

Prep: 12 minutes • Cook: 15 minutes
Other: 15 minutes

5 Anaheim chiles (about 10 ounces)

1. Preheat broiler.
2. Cut chiles in half lengthwise; discard seeds and membranes. Place chile halves, skin sides up, on a foil-lined baking sheet; flatten with hand. Broil 15 minutes or until blackened.
3. Place in a zip-top plastic bag; seal. Let stand 15 minutes. Peel and chop. Cover and refrigerate. Yield: 1 cup (serving size: ¼ cup).

CALORIES 19 (5% from fat); FAT 0.1g (sat 0g, mono 0g, poly 0.1g); PROTEIN 0.6g; CARB 4.6g; FIBER 1.3g; CHOL 0mg; IRON 0.3mg; SODIUM 1mg; CALC 6mg

Test Kitchen Tip: Don't worry if you can't get every shred of peel off the chile peppers; a little peel adds interesting texture.

Oven-Dried Tomatoes

Cooking tomatoes for a long time at a low temperature dehydrates them and concentrates their flavor. These tomatoes are plumper and softer than commercial sun-dried tomatoes, with a delicate richness. They'll keep for one week, covered, in the refrigerator, or up to one month in the freezer in an airtight container.

Prep: 10 minutes
Cook: 3 hours, 30 minutes • Other: 1 hour

1½ pounds (about 10) plum tomatoes, cored and cut in half lengthwise
1 teaspoon kosher salt

1. Sprinkle cut sides of tomato halves with kosher salt. Place tomato halves, cut sides down, on paper towels. Let stand 1 hour.
2. Preheat oven to 300°.
3. Arrange tomato halves, cut sides up, in a single layer on a baking sheet. Bake at 300° for 3½ to 4 hours or until edges of tomatoes curl (tomatoes will feel dry to the touch). Yield: 1 cup (serving size: ¼ cup).

CALORIES 36 (15% from fat); FAT 0.6g (sat 0.1g, mono 0.1g, poly 0.2g); PROTEIN 1.5g; CARB 7.9g; FIBER 1.9g; CHOL 0mg; IRON 0.8mg; SODIUM 251mg; CALC 9mg

Oven-Dried Tomatoes

Syrups & Oils Drizzle sweet fruit syrup over pancakes or dip French bread in an herbed oil for a memorable flavor experience.

Golden Vanilla Syrup

For a gift idea, pour the syrup into a decorative glass container and attach your favorite pancake recipe. This syrup is also fantastic poured over ice cream or pound cake. Store in the refrigerator up to one month.

Prep: 9 minutes • Cook: 8 minutes

 1 vanilla bean, split lengthwise
 2 cups granulated sugar
1½ cups water
 ⅓ cup fresh lemon juice, strained
 1 tablespoon light brown sugar

1. Scrape seeds from vanilla bean; place seeds and bean in a small bowl.
2. Combine granulated sugar and remaining ingredients in a medium saucepan. Bring to a boil over medium-high heat, stirring until sugars dissolve. Reduce heat; simmer 5 minutes. Remove from heat. Add vanilla bean and seeds, stirring gently. Cool syrup to room temperature.
3. Pour syrup into a glass container. Cover and chill. Yield: 2¼ cups (serving size: 2 tablespoons).

CALORIES 89 (0% from fat); FAT 0g (sat 0g, mono 0g, poly 0g); PROTEIN 0g; CARB 23.1g; FIBER 0g; CHOL 0mg; IRON 0mg; SODIUM 1mg; CALC 1mg

Test Kitchen Tip: Vanilla beans freeze well; just put them in the microwave for 15 to 30 seconds to plump and thaw.

Cran-Grape Syrup

Stir this syrup into iced tea or lemonade, or use it as a glaze for chicken and pork. It's delicious served over pancakes, waffles, or ice cream, too. Store in the refrigerator up to one week.

Prep: 3 minutes • Cook: 48 minutes
Other: 8 hours

 4 cups cranberry-grape juice drink
 2 tablespoons honey

1. Bring juice to a boil in a medium saucepan. Reduce heat; simmer until thick and reduced to ¾ cup (about 45 minutes to 1 hour). Remove from heat; stir in honey. Cover and chill 8 hours (syrup will thicken as it cools). Yield: ¾ cup (serving size: 1 tablespoon).

CALORIES 56 (2% from fat); FAT 0.1g (sat 0g, mono 0g, poly 0g); PROTEIN 0.2g; CARB 14.3g; FIBER 0.1g; CHOL 0mg; IRON 0mg; SODIUM 3mg; CALC 7mg

Cran-Grape
Syrup

Maple-Blueberry Syrup

Add a splash of New England fall to your pancakes with this blueberry-enhanced maple syrup. Store in the refrigerator up to two weeks.

Prep: 5 minutes • Cook: 5 minutes

  2 cups maple syrup
  1 (12-ounce) bag frozen blueberries
  1 tablespoon fresh lemon juice

1. Combine syrup and blueberries in a medium saucepan. Bring to a boil over medium-high heat, stirring occasionally. Remove from heat; stir in lemon juice. Serve warm, or cover and chill until ready to serve. Yield: 3 cups (serving size: about 3 tablespoons).

CALORIES 116 (2% from fat); FAT 0.2g (sat 0g, mono 0g, poly 0.1g); PROTEIN 0.1g; CARB 29.6g; FIBER 0.6g; CHOL 0mg; IRON 0.5mg; SODIUM 4mg; CALC 29mg

Pomegranate Syrup

This is a sweet-tart syrup similar in consistency to maple syrup. Brush it on chicken, lamb, or pork, or drizzle over pancakes or ice cream. Store in the refrigerator up to two weeks.

Prep: 20 minutes • Cook: 31 minutes

  2 cups Pomegranate Juice
1¼ cups sugar
  1 (2 x 1-inch) strip orange rind

1. Combine all ingredients in a medium nonreactive saucepan. Bring to a boil; reduce heat to medium, and cook mixture until reduced to 1½ cups (about 15 minutes). Discard rind. Yield: 1½ cups (serving size: 2 tablespoons).

(Totals include Pomegranate Juice) CALORIES 98 (1% from fat); FAT 0.1g (sat 0g, mono 0g, poly 0g); PROTEIN 0.2g; CARB 25.2g; FIBER 0.1g; CHOL 0mg; IRON 0.1mg; SODIUM 1mg; CALC 1mg

Pomegranate Juice

  3 cups pomegranate seeds
  2 cups water

1. Place seeds in a heavy-duty zip-top plastic bag; seal, pressing as much air as possible out of bag. Gently mash seeds with a rolling pin or bottom of a bottle. Place mashed seeds, juice, and water in a medium nonreactive saucepan, and bring to a boil. Cook 10 minutes. Strain mixture through a sieve into a bowl; discard solids. Yield: 2 cups (serving size: ½ cup).

CALORIES 52 (3% from fat); FAT 0.2g (sat 0g, mono 0g, poly 0.1g); PROTEIN 0.7g; CARB 13.1g; FIBER 0.2g; CHOL 0mg; IRON 0.2mg; SODIUM 2mg; CALC 2mg

Test Kitchen Tip: Use a nonreactive saucepan, such as one with a nonstick coating. Aluminum will react with the acid in the seeds, giving the juice a slightly metallic or "off" taste.

how to seed a pomegranate

Pomegranates have a tendency to stain anything they touch. Use this method to keep the pomegranate and its seeds underwater, and wear an apron.

1. Place the pomegranate in a bowl of water large enough to fit both the fruit and your hands without spilling over.
2. Under the water, use a medium-sized knife to slice off the crown and opposite end of the pomegranate so the seeds are just visible (don't slice too deeply), then

score the pomegranate lengthwise into 1½-inch-wide wedges.
3. With your thumbs, pry the pomegranate apart beneath the water and turn each section inside out (A). Separate the seeds from the inner white membrane. Take care not to burst the individual juice sacs (B).

The membrane will float to the top while the seeds sink to the bottom.
4. With a slotted spoon, skim off the floating membrane (C). Sort through the seeds beneath the water, discarding any stray pieces of membrane.
5. Drain the seeds in a fine mesh strainer.

Sage, Bay, and Garlic Dipping Oil

Bay and sage permeate this garlicky oil, infusing it with wonderful earthy, woodsy flavors.

Prep: 5 minutes • Cook: 24 minutes

½   cup extravirgin olive oil
2   garlic cloves, crushed
2   fresh sage leaves
1   bay leaf

1. Combine all ingredients in a small, heavy saucepan. Cook over medium-low heat until thermometer registers 180°. Reduce heat to low, and cook 20 minutes (do not allow temperature to rise above 200°). Cool to room temperature. Strain oil mixture through a sieve into a bowl, and discard solids. Yield: ½ cup (serving size: 2 teaspoons).

CALORIES 80 (100% from fat); FAT 9g (sat 1.2g, mono 6.6g, poly 0.8g); PROTEIN 0g; CARB 0g; FIBER 0g; CHOL 0mg; IRON 0mg; SODIUM 0mg; CALC 0mg

Basil Dipping Oil

In addition to serving this oil with bread, let it replace plain olive oil in herbed vinaigrettes.

Prep: 7 minutes • Cook: 24 minutes

2   cups chopped fresh basil leaves
    (about 2 [¾-ounce] packages)
½   cup extravirgin olive oil

1. Combine basil and oil in a small, heavy saucepan. Cook over medium-low heat until thermometer registers 180°. Reduce heat to low; cook 20 minutes (do not allow temperature to rise above 200°). Cool to room temperature. Strain oil mixture

through a sieve into a bowl; discard solids. Yield: ½ cup (serving size: 2 teaspoons).

CALORIES 80 (100% from fat); FAT 9g (sat 1.2g, mono 6.6g, poly 0.8g); PROTEIN 0g; CARB 0g; FIBER 0g; CHOL 0mg; IRON 0mg; SODIUM 0mg; CALC 0mg

Three-Pepper Dipping Oil

Enliven plain bread by serving it with this peppery oil.

Prep: 6 minutes • Cook: 24 minutes

½   cup extravirgin olive oil
1   pepperoncini pepper, halved
    lengthwise
1   whole dried hot red chile, crushed
2   whole black peppercorns

1. Combine all ingredients in a small, heavy saucepan. Cook over medium-low heat until thermometer registers 180°. Reduce heat to low, and cook 20 minutes (do not allow temperature to rise above 200°). Cool to room temperature. Strain oil mixture through a sieve into a bowl, and discard solids. Yield: ½ cup (serving size: 2 teaspoons).

CALORIES 80 (100% from fat); FAT 9g (sat 1.2g, mono 6.6g, poly 0.8g); PROTEIN 0g; CARB 0g; FIBER 0g; CHOL 0mg; IRON 0mg; SODIUM 0mg; CALC 0mg

Spicy Thyme and Garlic Oil

Crushed red pepper adds a "bite" to this herbed dipping oil. Serve it with a fresh French baguette. Be careful not to let the oil temperature rise above 200°; too much heat could ruin the flavor. Store it in the refrigerator in a glass container up to one week.

Prep: 6 minutes • Cook: 25 minutes

1   cup extravirgin olive oil
½   teaspoon crushed red pepper
4   garlic cloves, halved
2   bay leaves, crumbled
1   (4-inch) thyme sprig

1. Combine all ingredients in a small, heavy saucepan. Cook over medium-low heat until thermometer registers 180°. Reduce heat to low; cook 20 minutes (do not allow temperature to rise above 200°). Cool to room temperature.
2. Strain oil mixture through a sieve into a bowl; discard solids. Store in refrigerator. Yield: 1 cup (serving size: 1 tablespoon).

CALORIES 119 (100% from fat); FAT 13.5g (sat 1.8g, mono 10g, poly 1.1g); PROTEIN 0g; CARB 0g; FIBER 0g; CHOL 0mg; IRON 0.1mg; SODIUM 0mg; CALC 0mg

dipping oils Cooking the oil gently infuses it with flavor. If the temperature rises above 200°, though, the oil may develop a bitter flavor, so watch the thermometer closely. To serve dipping oils, pour them into small, wide bowls to facilitate dipping, and garnish each oil with its seasonings. Refrigerate oils up to one week in glass containers. Toss leftover oil with pasta, or use it in salad dressing.

soups & stews

Spring Seafood
Stew, page 508

Stocks   Homemade stocks create an ideal base of flavor for soups and stews as well as for a variety of other recipes.

Beef Stock

Beef stock—made from beef and veal bones—is the basis of many classic European sauces. It makes quick, deeply flavored pan sauces.

Prep: 15 minutes • Cook: 5 hours, 50 minutes
Other: 8 hours

3½ pounds meaty beef bones (such as oxtail)
  3 cups coarsely chopped celery
1½ cups coarsely chopped carrot (about ¾ pound)
  2 tablespoons tomato paste
  3 medium onions, peeled and halved
 20 cups water

1. Preheat oven to 400°.
2. Arrange bones in an even layer in a shallow roasting pan. Bake at 400° for 45 minutes or until browned.
3. Transfer bones to an 8-quart stockpot. Add celery, carrot, tomato paste, and onions to pot; stir well to combine. Pour water over mixture; bring mixture to a simmer. Reduce heat, and simmer 5 hours, skimming surface occasionally.
4. Strain stock through a fine sieve into a large bowl; discard solids. Cool stock to room temperature. Cover and chill stock 8 to 24 hours. Skim solidified fat from surface of broth, and discard. Yield: 10 cups (serving size: 1 cup).

CALORIES 8 (31% from fat); FAT 0.3g (sat 0.1g, mono 0.1g, poly 0g); PROTEIN 0.7g; CARB 0.7g; FIBER 0.1g; CHOL 2mg; IRON 0.1mg; SODIUM 9mg; CALC 4mg

Brown Chicken Stock

Make sure your pan is large enough to roast the chicken and all the vegetables. If the pan is too small, the chicken won't brown properly.

Prep: 14 minutes • Cook: 3 hours, 20 minutes
Other: 8 hours

¼ pound fennel stalks, cut into 2-inch pieces
  3 carrots, cut into 2-inch pieces
  1 celery stalk, cut into 2-inch pieces
  1 onion, unpeeled and quartered
  6 pounds chicken pieces
½ teaspoon black peppercorns
  6 parsley sprigs
  5 thyme sprigs
  2 bay leaves
 16 cups cold water, divided

1. Preheat oven to 400°.
2. Arrange first 4 ingredients in bottom of a broiler or roasting pan, and top with chicken pieces. Bake at 400° for 1½ hours, turning chicken once every 30 minutes (chicken and vegetables should be very brown).
3. Place peppercorns, parsley, thyme, and bay leaves in an 8-quart stockpot. Remove vegetables and chicken from broiler pan, and place in stockpot. Carefully discard drippings from broiler pan, leaving browned bits. Place broiler pan on stovetop; add 4 cups water. Bring to a boil over medium-high heat. Reduce heat; simmer 10 minutes, scraping bottom to loosen browned bits.

4. Pour contents of broiler pan into stockpot. Add 12 cups water, and bring to a boil over medium-high heat. Reduce heat, and simmer 1½ hours.
5. Strain stock through a fine sieve into a large bowl. Reserve chicken for another use; discard remaining solids. Cover and chill stock 8 hours. Skim solidified fat from surface of broth, and discard fat. Yield: 10 cups (serving size: 1 cup).

CALORIES 31 (32% from fat); FAT 1.1g (sat 0.3g, mono 0.4g, poly 0.2g); PROTEIN 4.7g; CARB 0.4g; FIBER 0.1g; CHOL 15mg; IRON 0.3mg; SODIUM 19mg; CALC 4mg

how to make brown stock

1. Roast the vegetables and chicken until browned to create a deep, rich caramelized flavor.

2. The browned bits from the pan add even more flavor. Deglaze the pan by adding water and scraping up the bits.

White Chicken Stock

White stock has a light, clean flavor that provides a nice backdrop for more delicate ingredients. It's good in any recipes that call for canned fat-free, less-sodium chicken broth. Any variety of chicken pieces will work.

Prep: 11 minutes • Cook: 3 hours, 10 minutes
Other: 8 hours

- ½ teaspoon black peppercorns
- 10 parsley sprigs
- 8 thyme sprigs
- 3 celery stalks, cut into 2-inch pieces
- 3 bay leaves
- 2 onions, peeled and quartered
- 2 carrots, cut into 2-inch pieces
- 2 garlic cloves, crushed
- 16 cups cold water
- 1 (6-pound) roasting chicken or 6 pounds chicken pieces

1. Place first 8 ingredients in an 8-quart stockpot; add water and chicken. Bring mixture to a boil over medium heat. Reduce heat, and simmer, uncovered, 3 hours.

2. Strain stock through a fine sieve into a large bowl. Reserve chicken for another use; discard remaining solids. Cover and chill stock 8 hours. Skim solidified fat from surface of broth, and discard. Yield: 10 cups (serving size: 1 cup).

CALORIES 28 (26% from fat); FAT 0.8g (sat 0.2g, mono 0.3g, poly 0.2g); PROTEIN 4.7g; CARB 0.4g; FIBER 0.1g; CHOL 15mg; IRON 0.3mg; SODIUM 18mg; CALC 4mg

how to make white stock

1. Peel and quarter the onions. Rinse, peel, and trim the carrots and celery. This results in a less cloudy stock and infuses the stock with flavor.

2. Add only enough cold water to barely cover the ingredients in the pot. Too much water will dilute the flavor.

3. Simmer the ingredients for 3 hours. Remove and discard the gray foam that rises to the surface.

4. Place a fine sieve over a large bowl or pot in the sink. Strain the stock in batches, transferring it from the pot to the sieve with a ladle until the stockpot is light enough to lift.

5. Skim the fat from the stock after the stock has chilled for 8 hours or overnight.

6. If you don't have time to chill the stock overnight, pour it into a zip-top plastic bag; let stand 10 minutes (the fat will rise to the top). Seal bag; carefully snip off one bottom corner. Drain the stock into a container, stopping before fat layer reaches opening. Discard fat.

If you're not using the stock immediately,
place it in an airtight container and store in the refrigerator
up to three days or in the freezer up to three months.

Turkey Stock

Refrigerate this stock in an airtight container for up to three weeks, or freeze up to three months.

Prep: 12 minutes • Cook: 2 hours, 13 minutes
Other: 8 hours

 2 teaspoons canola oil
Turkey heart, neck, and gizzard from
    1 (12-pound) turkey
 ½ cup chopped onion
 ½ cup chopped carrot
 ½ cup chopped celery
 8 cups cold water
 2 (14-ounce) cans fat-free, less-sodium
    chicken broth
 ½ teaspoon dried thyme
 ¼ teaspoon black peppercorns
 3 parsley sprigs
 1 bay leaf

1. Heat oil in a stockpot over medium-high heat. Add heart, neck, and gizzard; sauté 5 minutes. Add onion, carrot, and celery; sauté 4 minutes. Add water and broth; bring to a boil. Add thyme, peppercorns, parsley, and bay leaf. Reduce heat; simmer 2 hours. Strain through a sieve over a bowl; discard solids. Cool to room temperature. Cover and chill 8 hours. Skim solidified fat from surface. Yield: 7 cups (serving size: 1 cup).

CALORIES 31 (55% from fat); FAT 1.9g (sat 0.3g, mono 0.5g, poly 0.9g); PROTEIN 2.4g; CARB 0.9g; FIBER 0.2g; CHOL 3mg; IRON 0.3mg; SODIUM 228mg; CALC 10mg

Rich Porcini Stock

Prepare this mushroom stock to use in Wild Mushroom Barley "Risotto" with Sage (page 262) or in recipes as a meatless alternative to beef stock.

Prep: 10 minutes • Cook: 1 hour, 5 minutes
Other: 20 minutes

 1 cup dried porcini mushrooms (about
    2 ounces)
 5 cups warm water, divided
1½ cups coarsely chopped red onion
 1 cup dry red wine
 ½ cup coarsely chopped celery
 ½ cup chopped shallots
 ⅓ cup chopped carrot
 1 whole garlic head, halved
 2 thyme sprigs
 1 flat-leaf parsley sprig
 1 sage sprig

1. Combine mushrooms and 2 cups water in a bowl; cover and let stand 20 minutes. Drain mushrooms in a colander over a bowl, reserving liquid. Rinse mushrooms. Place in a 3-quart saucepan; strain reserved liquid into pan. Add 3 cups water, red onion, and remaining ingredients.
2. Bring mushroom mixture to a boil over medium heat; reduce heat, and simmer, partially covered, 1 hour. Strain. Yield: 4 cups (serving size: 1 cup).

CALORIES 53 (2% from fat); FAT 0.1g (sat 0g, mono 0.1g, poly 0g); PROTEIN 0.8g; CARB 3g; FIBER 0.4g; CHOL 0mg; IRON 0.6mg; SODIUM 6mg; CALC 10mg

Vegetable Stock

This all-purpose vegetable stock has woodsy undertones from the mushrooms and subtle sweetness from the parsnip. It will fill in for canned vegetable broth in any recipe.

Prep: 10 minutes • Cook: 1 hour, 10 minutes

12 cups water
 1 (8-ounce) package presliced
    mushrooms
 1 cup chopped onion
 ¾ cup chopped carrot
 ½ cup coarsely chopped celery
 ½ cup chopped parsnip
 2 bay leaves
 2 thyme sprigs
 1 whole garlic head, halved

1. Combine all ingredients in a Dutch oven; bring to a boil. Reduce heat, and simmer until reduced to 6 cups (about 1 hour). Strain stock through a sieve into a large bowl; discard solids. Yield: 6 cups (serving size: 1 cup).

CALORIES 8 (11% from fat); FAT 0.1g (sat 0g, mono 0g, poly 0.1g); PROTEIN 0.3g; CARB 1.7g; FIBER 0.3g; CHOL 0mg; IRON 0.1mg; SODIUM 2mg; CALC 7mg

Fruit Soups

Naturally low in fat and calories, fruit soups make an excellent appetizer, light lunch, or dessert.

Cool Summer-Berry Soup

Instead of using white wine, you can substitute white grape juice. Because the grape juice is much sweeter than the wine, omit the ¼ cup sugar.

Prep: 5 minutes • Cook: 5 minutes
Other: 3 hours

Soup:
- 2 cups fresh raspberries
- 2 cups halved fresh strawberries
- ½ cup cranberry-raspberry juice drink
- ½ cup dry white wine
- ¼ cup sugar
- ⅛ teaspoon ground cinnamon
- 1 (8-ounce) carton strawberry low-fat yogurt

Garnish:
- 1 cup fresh blueberries
- 2 teaspoons sugar
- 2 teaspoons cranberry-raspberry juice drink

1. To prepare soup, place first 3 ingredients in a blender, and process until smooth. Strain raspberry mixture through a sieve into a medium saucepan. Stir in wine, ¼ cup sugar, and cinnamon. Bring to a boil over medium heat; cook 2 minutes. Remove from heat. Place soup in a large bowl; cover and chill 3 hours. Stir in strawberry yogurt.

2. To prepare garnish, place blueberries and remaining ingredients in a blender; process until smooth. Strain blueberry mixture through a sieve.

3. Ladle soup into bowls. Top with garnish. Yield: 4 servings (serving size: 1 cup soup and 1 tablespoon garnish).

CALORIES 208 (6% from fat); FAT 1.4g (sat 0.5g, mono 0.3g, poly 0.4g); PROTEIN 3.6g; CARB 48.4g; FIBER 7g; CHOL 2mg; IRON 0.9mg; SODIUM 37mg; CALC 109mg

Strawberry-Champagne Soup

Try serving this simple soup with an herb cheese (such as Boursin) and crackers.

Prep: 8 minutes • Other: 2 hours

       5   cups quartered strawberries
     ¼   cup sugar
     ⅛   teaspoon salt
       1   cup Champagne
Cracked black pepper (optional)

1. Place strawberries in a medium bowl. Sprinkle with sugar and salt; toss well. Place strawberry mixture in a blender or food processor, and process until smooth. Cover mixture, and chill 2 hours.
2. Stir in Champagne. Serve soup immediately. Sprinkle with black pepper, if desired. Yield: 4 servings (serving size: 1 cup).

CALORIES 161 (4% from fat); FAT 0.8g (sat 0.1g, mono 0.1g, poly 0.4g); PROTEIN 1.6g; CARB 29.1g; FIBER 5.2g; CHOL 0mg; IRON 1.2mg; SODIUM 78mg; CALC 34mg

Chilled Cherry Soup

This dessert soup is perfect for a summer meal. You can substitute white grape juice for the wine.

Prep: 15 minutes

       4   cups pitted sweet cherries
       2   tablespoons sugar
       1   teaspoon grated lemon rind
     ¼   teaspoon ground ginger
     ⅛   teaspoon ground allspice
     ⅓   cup sweet riesling or other slightly
              sweet white wine
       2   tablespoons low-fat sour cream
       2   tablespoons fresh lemon juice
       1   (8-ounce) carton vanilla low-fat yogurt

1. Place first 5 ingredients in a blender or food processor, and process until cherries

are finely chopped. Add wine, sour cream, and lemon juice; process until smooth. Add yogurt, and pulse 3 or 4 times or until blended. Pour into a bowl, and cover surface of soup with plastic wrap. Chill thoroughly. Yield: 7 servings (serving size: ½ cup).

CALORIES 116 (13% from fat); FAT 1.7g (sat 0.8g, mono 0.5g, poly 0.3g); PROTEIN 2.8g; CARB 22.6g; FIBER 1.9g; CHOL 3mg; IRON 0.4mg; SODIUM 24mg; CALC 74mg

Tropical Fruit Soup with Pineapple Salsa

If you don't have papaya, try mango, or just use pineapple for the salsa.

Prep: 10 minutes

Pineapple Salsa:
     ½   cup diced peeled pineapple
     ½   cup diced peeled papaya
       2   tablespoons dark rum or 1 teaspoon
              rum extract
       2   teaspoons sugar
Soup:
       3   cups vanilla low-fat yogurt
       1   cup passion fruit nectar
     ⅓   cup pineapple juice
     ¼   teaspoon coconut extract
     ⅛   teaspoon salt
     ¼   cup flaked sweetened coconut, toasted

1. To prepare salsa, combine first 4 ingredients in a small bowl; set aside.
2. To prepare soup, combine yogurt and next 4 ingredients in a medium bowl, and stir well with a whisk. Cover and chill.
3. Ladle soup into bowls; top with salsa. Sprinkle with toasted coconut. Yield: 4 servings (serving size: 1 cup soup, ¼ cup salsa, and 1 tablespoon coconut).

CALORIES 264 (15% from fat); FAT 4.3g (sat 3.2g, mono 0.7g, poly 0.1g); PROTEIN 8.8g; CARB 43.3g; FIBER 0.9g; CHOL 9mg; IRON 0.4mg; SODIUM 204mg; CALC 301mg

Vanilla-Roasted Peach Soup with Cardamom Cream

Roasting the peaches brings out their natural sweetness and makes them soft and easy to peel. But if you want to bypass that step, puree very ripe peeled peaches and the honey.

Prep: 20 minutes • Cook: 25 minutes Other: 2 hours

       3   peaches, halved and pitted (about
              2 pounds)
       2   tablespoons sugar
       1   (4-inch) piece vanilla bean, split
              lengthwise
     1½   tablespoons honey
     1½   cups orange juice
     ⅛   teaspoon salt
     ⅛   teaspoon vanilla extract
     ¼   cup low-fat sour cream
     ⅛   teaspoon ground cardamom

1. Preheat oven to 350°.
2. Combine peach halves and sugar in a large bowl. Scrape seeds from vanilla bean, and add seeds to bowl; discard bean. Toss peach mixture well. Place peach halves, cut sides down, on a baking sheet lined with parchment paper. Bake at 350° for 25 minutes or until tender; cool. Peel and discard skins. Place peach halves and honey in a blender or food processor, and process until smooth. Add orange juice, salt, and vanilla extract; process until well blended. Pour into a bowl; cover and chill 2 hours.
3. Combine sour cream and cardamom. Ladle soup into bowls; top with cardamom cream. Yield: 4 servings (serving size: 1 cup soup and 1 tablespoon cardamom cream).

CALORIES 143 (12% from fat); FAT 1.9g (sat 1.1g, mono 0.6g, poly 0.1g); PROTEIN 1.6g; CARB 31.7g; FIBER 1.7g; CHOL 6mg; IRON 0.2mg; SODIUM 81mg; CALC 29mg

Cream Soups, Bisques & Chowders

Reduced-fat milk, a touch of cream, and pureed fruits and vegetables contribute rich smoothness without excess fat to these velvety soups.

Cream of Asparagus Soup

For a vegetarian dish, vegetable broth can replace the chicken broth. Garnish with thin asparagus spears for a graceful presentation.

Prep: 13 minutes • Cook: 21 minutes

- 3 cups (½-inch) sliced asparagus (about 1 pound)
- 2 cups fat-free, less-sodium chicken broth
- ¾ teaspoon fresh thyme, divided
- 1 bay leaf
- 1 garlic clove, crushed
- 1 tablespoon all-purpose flour
- 2 cups 1% low-fat milk
- Dash of ground nutmeg
- 2 teaspoons butter
- ¾ teaspoon salt
- ¼ teaspoon grated lemon rind

1. Combine asparagus, broth, ½ teaspoon thyme, bay leaf, and garlic in a large saucepan over medium-high heat; bring to a boil. Reduce heat, cover, and simmer 10 minutes. Discard bay leaf. Place asparagus mixture in a blender; process until smooth. **2.** Place flour in pan. Gradually add milk, stirring with a whisk until blended. Stir in pureed asparagus and ground nutmeg. Bring to a boil. Reduce heat; simmer 5 minutes, stirring constantly. Remove from heat, and stir in ¼ teaspoon thyme, butter, salt, and lemon rind. Yield: 4 servings (serving size: 1¼ cups).

CALORIES 117 (27% from fat); FAT 3.5g (sat 2g, mono 0.8g, poly 0.2g); PROTEIN 8.9g; CARB 14g; FIBER 2.5g; CHOL 13mg; IRON 1.1mg; SODIUM 748mg; CALC 163mg

Variations

Cream of Carrot Soup: Substitute 2 cups baby carrots for asparagus. Omit bay leaf. Yield: 4 servings (serving size: 1 cup).

CALORIES 112 (28% from fat); FAT 3.5g (sat 2g, mono 0.8g, poly 0.2g); PROTEIN 6.7g; CARB 13.4g; FIBER 1.1g; CHOL 13mg; IRON 0.6mg; SODIUM 765mg; CALC 152mg

Cream of Leek Soup: Substitute 3 cups sliced leek for asparagus. Substitute ¾ teaspoon fresh rosemary for thyme. Omit bay leaf. Yield: 4 servings (serving size: 1 cup).

CALORIES 131 (23% from fat); FAT 3.4g (sat 2g, mono 0.8g, poly 0.2g); PROTEIN 7.3g; CARB 18.3g; FIBER 1.3g; CHOL 13mg; IRON 1.5mg; SODIUM 759mg; CALC 178mg

Broccoli and Cheese Soup

Processed cheese melts beautifully, giving this soup a smooth texture and mild flavor.

Prep: 10 minutes • Cook: 26 minutes

Cooking spray
1 cup chopped onion
2 garlic cloves, minced
3 cups fat-free, less-sodium chicken broth
1 (16-ounce) package broccoli florets
⅓ cup all-purpose flour
2½ cups 2% reduced-fat milk
¼ teaspoon pepper
8 ounces light processed cheese, cubed (such as Velveeta Light)

1. Heat a large nonstick saucepan over medium-high heat. Coat pan with cooking spray. Add onion and garlic; sauté 3 minutes or until tender. Add broth and broccoli. Bring broccoli mixture to a boil over medium-high heat. Reduce heat to medium; cook 10 minutes.

2. Lightly spoon flour into a dry measuring cup; level with a knife. Combine flour and milk, stirring with a whisk until well blended. Add milk mixture to broccoli mixture. Cook 5 minutes or until slightly thick, stirring constantly. Stir in pepper. Remove from heat; add cheese, stirring until cheese melts.

3. Place one-third of soup in a blender or food processor, and process until smooth. Return pureed soup mixture to pan. Cook soup over low heat 5 minutes or until thoroughly heated. Yield: 6 servings (serving size: 1⅓ cups).

CALORIES 203 (28% from fat); FAT 6.3g (sat 4g, mono 1.8g, poly 0.4g); PROTEIN 15.6g; CARB 21.7g; FIBER 2.9g; CHOL 24mg; IRON 1.2mg; SODIUM 897mg; CALC 385mg

Yellow Pepper Soup with Cilantro Puree

Yellow Pepper Soup with Cilantro Puree

Peas add body and sweetness to the puree. You can substitute sour cream for the crème fraîche.

Prep: 30 minutes • Cook: 29 minutes
Other: 2 hours

Soup:
1 teaspoon butter
1½ cups chopped onion
1 cup chopped fennel bulb
1 teaspoon curry powder
1 teaspoon grated peeled fresh ginger
2 garlic cloves, chopped
⅓ cup dry white wine
3¼ cups chopped yellow bell pepper
3 cups fat-free, less-sodium chicken broth
1½ cups chopped peeled Granny Smith apple (about ½ pound)
1 cup cubed peeled red potato
¼ teaspoon salt
2 tablespoons fresh lemon juice
Puree:
⅓ cup frozen green peas, thawed
⅓ cup fresh cilantro leaves
3 tablespoons fat-free, less-sodium chicken broth
1 tablespoon mirin (sweet rice wine)
1 teaspoon canola oil
Dash of salt
2 tablespoons crème fraîche

1. To prepare soup, melt butter in a Dutch oven over medium-high heat. Add onion and fennel, and sauté 3 minutes. Add curry, ginger, and garlic; sauté 1 minute. Stir in white wine; cook 1 minute. Add bell pepper and next 4 ingredients; bring to a boil. Reduce heat; simmer 20 minutes. Cool.

2. Place half of soup in a blender; process until smooth. Pour into a bowl. Repeat with remaining soup. Chill at least 2 hours. Stir in juice.

3. To prepare puree, place peas and next 5 ingredients in a blender; process until smooth.

4. Ladle soup into bowls. Add 3 dollops of puree on top of each serving. Using tip of a knife, swirl each dollop into a "V" shape. Dollop crème fraîche in center of each serving. Yield: 6 servings (serving size: ¾ cup soup, 3 teaspoons puree, and 1 teaspoon crème fraîche).

CALORIES 134 (24% from fat); FAT 3.5g (sat 1.6g, mono 0.7g, poly 0.4g); PROTEIN 4.3g; CARB 22.8g; FIBER 3.3g; CHOL 6mg; IRON 1mg; SODIUM 445mg; CALC 36mg

Cream of Mushroom Soup with Sherry

We don't recommend substituting cooking sherry for the dry sherry because it tastes a bit salty and doesn't provide the rich depth of flavor that sherry offers.

Prep: 25 minutes • Cook: 48 minutes
Other: 5 minutes

    2   teaspoons olive oil
    2   cups chopped onion
    1   cup thinly sliced carrot
    ⅔   cup chopped celery
    8   cups sliced button mushrooms
        (about 1½ pounds)
    4   cups sliced shiitake mushroom caps
        (about 7 ounces)
    2   garlic cloves, minced
    4   (14-ounce) cans fat-free, less-sodium
        chicken broth
    1   cup water
    1   teaspoon dried rubbed sage
    ¼   teaspoon salt
    ¼   teaspoon pepper
    6   tablespoons half-and-half
    ¼   cup dry sherry
    ¼   cup chopped fresh parsley

1. Heat oil in a Dutch oven over medium-high heat. Add onion, carrot, and celery; sauté 6 minutes or until tender. Reduce heat to medium; add mushrooms and garlic. Cook 7 minutes or until mushrooms are tender, stirring frequently. Add broth, water, sage, salt, and pepper; bring to a simmer. Cover and simmer 25 minutes. Remove from heat; cool 5 minutes.
2. Place half of mushroom mixture in a blender; process until smooth. Pour pureed soup into a large bowl. Repeat procedure with remaining mushroom mixture. Return soup to pan. Stir in half-and-half and sherry; cook soup over low heat 5 minutes or until thoroughly heated, stirring frequently. Ladle into bowls, and sprinkle evenly with parsley. Yield: 12 servings (serving size: 1 cup).

CALORIES 71 (24% from fat); FAT 1.9g (sat 0.7g, mono 0.8g, poly 0.2g); PROTEIN 4.7g; CARB 8.4g; FIBER 1.9g; CHOL 3mg; IRON 1.2mg; SODIUM 321mg; CALC 26mg

---

All-Time Favorite
Vichyssoise

Formally known as *crème vichyssoise glacée*, this cold potato-and-leek soup was created by Louis Diat, a chef at the Ritz-Carlton Hotel in New York City. The name, translated literally, means "coming from Vichy," a French city near Diat's childhood home.

Prep: 13 minutes • Cook: 29 minutes

    1   tablespoon canola oil
    3   cups diced leek (about 3 large)
    3   cups diced peeled baking potato
        (about 1¼ pounds)
    2   cups fat-free, less-sodium chicken
        broth
    ⅔   cup half-and-half
    ¼   teaspoon salt
    ⅛   teaspoon pepper
    1   tablespoon minced fresh chives

1. Heat canola oil in a large saucepan over medium-low heat. Add diced leek; cover and cook 10 minutes or until soft. Stir in diced potato and chicken broth; bring to a boil. Cover potato mixture, reduce heat, and simmer 15 minutes or until potato is tender.
2. Place potato mixture in a blender or food processor, and process until smooth. Place potato mixture in a large bowl, and cool to room temperature. Stir in half-and-half, salt, and pepper. Cover and chill. Ladle into bowls, and sprinkle evenly with minced chives. Yield: 5 servings (serving size: 1 cup).

CALORIES 221 (27% from fat); FAT 6.7g (sat 2.5g, mono 2.7g, poly 1.1g); PROTEIN 5.3g; CARB 35.1g; FIBER 2.5g; CHOL 12mg; IRON 1.7mg; SODIUM 340mg; CALC 77mg

---

how to clean leeks

Dirt is sometimes trapped between the layers of leeks. To clean, cut the root end, then slit the leek lengthwise. Fan the layers out, and rinse under cold water.

half-and-half Cream generally comes in two forms: whipping cream and half-and-half. Whipping cream must contain at least 35 percent milk fat. Half-and-half, also called light cream, is a mixture of equal parts milk and cream and must contain at least 10½ percent milk fat. Half-and-half is more delicate than whipping cream and curdles easier. Half-and-half can't be whipped.

Apple Bisque with Chestnuts

This unique recipe pairs the homey sweetness of apples with the rich flavor of chestnuts. Choose at least two varieties of all-purpose cooking apples for the best flavor—try a combination of Cortland, Gravenstein, Stayman, Winesap, Granny Smith, McIntosh, Grimes Golden, or York.

Prep: 20 minutes • Cook: 56 minutes
Other: 5 minutes

1 tablespoon butter
2 teaspoons extravirgin olive oil
3 cups chopped onion
1 teaspoon finely chopped fresh thyme
1 (14-ounce) can fat-free,
   less-sodium chicken broth
2 cooking apples, peeled, cored, and
   chopped (about 3 cups)
2 cups water
1 cup coarsely chopped bottled
   chestnuts
¼ cup cream sherry
¾ teaspoon salt
¼ teaspoon freshly ground black pepper
Thyme leaves (optional)

1. Heat butter and oil in a large Dutch oven over medium heat. Add onion and chopped thyme; cook 10 minutes or until onion is tender, stirring frequently. Stir in broth and apple; cover and cook 30 minutes, stirring occasionally.
2. Add water and next 4 ingredients. Reduce heat to medium-low; simmer, uncovered, 10 minutes, stirring occasionally. Remove from heat; cool 5 minutes.
3. Place half of apple mixture in a blender; process until smooth. Pour pureed bisque into a large bowl. Repeat procedure with remaining apple mixture. Return bisque to pan; cook over low heat 5 minutes or just until heated. Ladle soup into bowls. Garnish with thyme leaves, if desired. Yield: 6 servings (serving size: about ¾ cup).

CALORIES 131 (25% from fat); FAT 3.7g (sat 1.4g, mono 1.7g, poly 0.3g); PROTEIN 2.5g; CARB 21.7g; FIBER 3.6g; CHOL 5mg; IRON 0.3mg; SODIUM 437mg; CALC 21mg

Thai Shrimp Bisque

A bisque is a thickened soup that often contains or is made from seafood. We've combined Thai seasonings with a French shrimp bisque for a creamy main-dish soup.

Prep: 30 minutes • Cook: 36 minutes
Other: 30 minutes

1½ pounds medium shrimp
Marinade:
1½ tablespoons grated lime rind
⅓ cup fresh lime juice
1½ tablespoons ground coriander
1 tablespoon minced fresh cilantro
1 tablespoon minced peeled fresh
   ginger
1½ teaspoons sugar
¼ teaspoon ground red pepper
2 garlic cloves, crushed
Shrimp Stock:
2 cups water
¼ cup dry white wine
1 tablespoon tomato paste
Soup:
1 teaspoon olive oil
½ cup chopped onion
⅓ cup chopped celery
1 (14-ounce) can light coconut milk
1 tablespoon tomato paste
¼ cup all-purpose flour
1 cup 2% reduced-fat milk
1 tablespoon grated lime rind
1 tablespoon minced fresh cilantro
½ teaspoon salt

1. Peel shrimp, reserving shells.
2. To prepare marinade, combine lime rind and next 7 ingredients in a large zip-top plastic bag. Add shrimp to bag; seal and marinate in refrigerator 30 minutes.
3. To prepare shrimp stock, combine reserved shrimp shells, water, wine, and 1 tablespoon tomato paste in a large Dutch oven. Bring mixture to a boil. Reduce heat; simmer until liquid is reduced to 1 cup (about 10 minutes). Strain mixture through a sieve over a bowl, and discard solids.
4. To prepare soup, heat olive oil in a large Dutch oven over medium heat. Add onion and celery, and sauté 8 minutes or until browned. Add 1 cup shrimp stock, coconut milk, and 1 tablespoon tomato paste, scraping pan to loosen browned bits. Bring to a boil. Lightly spoon flour into a dry measuring cup, and level with a knife. Combine flour and reduced-fat milk in a small bowl, stirring with a whisk. Add to pan; reduce heat, and simmer until thick (about 5 minutes). Add shrimp and marinade, and cook 5 minutes. Stir in 1 tablespoon lime rind, 1 tablespoon cilantro, and salt. Yield: 4 servings (serving size: 1½ cups).

CALORIES 201 (30% from fat); FAT 6.7g (sat 3.2g, mono 1.7g, poly 1.2g); PROTEIN 19.9g; CARB 15.2g; FIBER 0.9g; CHOL 133mg; IRON 3.3mg; SODIUM 380mg; CALC 117mg

Test Kitchen Tip: To get ⅓ cup of fresh lime juice you'll need four medium limes. Use three of those limes to get 1½ tablespoons of rind.

Oyster-Crab Bisque

Be careful not to overcook the oysters when you first add them to the broth mixture or they'll be tough and rubbery. Three minutes is plenty of time.

Prep: 20 minutes • Cook: 13 minutes

3 (12-ounce) containers standard oysters, undrained
Cooking spray
1 cup chopped onion
½ cup chopped celery
½ cup chopped green bell pepper
2 garlic cloves, minced
½ cup all-purpose flour
1 (14-ounce) can fat-free, less-sodium chicken broth
½ teaspoon dried thyme
1 bay leaf
½ cup sliced green onions
1 (12-ounce) can evaporated fat-free milk
1 pound lump crabmeat, shell pieces removed
¼ teaspoon salt
¼ teaspoon black pepper

1. Drain oysters in a colander over a bowl, reserving 1 cup oyster liquid.
2. Heat a large Dutch oven over medium-high heat. Coat pan with cooking spray. Add chopped onion, celery, bell pepper, and garlic; sauté 5 minutes. Lightly spoon flour into a dry measuring cup; level with a knife. Add flour to onion mixture; cook 1 minute, stirring constantly. Gradually add reserved oyster liquid and broth, stirring with a whisk until blended. Stir in thyme and bay leaf, and bring to a boil. Add oysters, green onions, and milk; cook 3 minutes or until edges of oysters curl. Gently stir in crabmeat, salt, and black pepper; cook 1 minute or until thoroughly heated. Discard bay leaf. Yield: 7 servings (serving size: about 1½ cups).

CALORIES 263 (18% from fat); FAT 5.3g (sat 1.2g, mono 0.7g, poly 1.8g); PROTEIN 29.5g; CARB 22.2g; FIBER 1.2g; CHOL 147mg; IRON 11.4mg; SODIUM 631mg; CALC 293mg

Curried Squash-and-Pear Bisque

Celebrate the harvest with a savory-sweet soup featuring peak seasonal produce.

Prep: 25 minutes • Cook: 1 hour, 42 minutes

1 butternut squash (about 2¾ pounds)
1 tablespoon butter
2 cups chopped peeled Bartlett pear
1½ cups thinly sliced onion
2⅓ cups water
1 cup pear nectar
2 (14-ounce) cans vegetable broth
2½ teaspoons curry powder
½ teaspoon salt
⅛ teaspoon pepper
½ cup half-and-half
1 small Bartlett pear, cored and thinly sliced

1. Preheat oven to 375°.
2. Cut squash in half lengthwise; discard seeds and membrane. Place halves, cut sides down, on a baking sheet; bake at 375° for 45 minutes or until tender. Cool. Peel squash; mash pulp. Set aside 3½ cups pulp. Reserve remaining pulp for another use.
3. Melt butter in a Dutch oven over medium-high heat. Add chopped pear and onion; sauté 10 minutes. Add squash pulp, water, and next 5 ingredients. Bring to a boil; partially cover, reduce heat, and simmer 40 minutes. Place one-third of squash mixture in a blender; process until smooth. Pour mixture into a large bowl; repeat with remaining squash mixture. Return mixture to pan; stir in half-and-half. Cook over low heat 3 minutes. Ladle into bowls, and top evenly with pear slices. Yield: 8 servings (serving size: 1¼ cups).

CALORIES 149 (25% from fat); FAT 4.2g (sat 2g, mono 1g, poly 0.2g); PROTEIN 1.9g; CARB 29.4g; FIBER 3.7g; CHOL 10mg; IRON 1mg; SODIUM 622mg; CALC 70mg

Chile-Cheese Chowder

For a vegetarian soup, substitute 1 tablespoon canola oil for the bacon drippings and vegetable broth for the chicken broth.

Prep: 25 minutes • Cook: 1 hour

 2 bacon slices
 1 cup chopped carrot
 1 cup chopped seeded poblano chiles
    (about 3 large)
 1 cup chopped onion
 2 tablespoons minced seeded jalapeño
    pepper
 ½ teaspoon ground cumin
 3 garlic cloves, minced
 2 (16-ounce) cans fat-free,
    less-sodium chicken broth
 5 cups diced peeled baking potato
    (about 1½ pounds)
 ½ teaspoon salt
 ⅓ cup all-purpose flour
 2½ cups 1% low-fat milk
 ¾ cup (3 ounces) shredded Monterey
    Jack cheese with jalapeño peppers
 ½ cup (2 ounces) shredded reduced-fat
    sharp Cheddar cheese
 ⅔ cup sliced green onions

how to make chowder

1. Cook bacon in a Dutch oven over medium-high heat until crisp. Remove bacon from pan, reserving 1 tablespoon drippings in pan. Crumble bacon; set aside.
2. Add carrot and next 5 ingredients to drippings in pan; sauté 10 minutes or until browned. Stir in broth, scraping pan to loosen browned bits. Add potato and salt. Bring to a boil; cover, reduce heat, and simmer 25 minutes or until potato is tender.
3. Lightly spoon flour into a dry measuring cup; level with a knife. Place flour in a bowl; gradually add milk, stirring with a whisk until well blended to form a slurry. Stir into vegetable mixture. Cook over medium heat until thick (about 12 minutes), stirring frequently. Remove from heat. Add cheeses, stirring until cheeses melt. Ladle soup into bowls; top with green onions and crumbled bacon. Yield: 10 servings (serving size: 1 cup soup, about 1 tablespoon green onions, and about 1 teaspoon bacon).

CALORIES 198 (30% from fat); FAT 6.7g (sat 3.9g, mono 2g, poly 0.4g); PROTEIN 9.7g; CARB 25.1g; FIBER 2.5g; CHOL 18mg; IRON 1.4mg; SODIUM 442mg; CALC 202mg

Curried Chicken Corn Chowder

Curry creates a distinctive balance for sugary summertime corn, jalapeño, and cilantro.

Prep: 20 minutes • Cook: 55 minutes

 1 tablespoon butter
 2 cups chopped onion
 2 tablespoons chopped seeded
    jalapeño pepper
 2 teaspoons curry powder
 6 cups fat-free, less-sodium chicken
    broth
 5 cups fresh corn kernels (about 7 ears)
 ½ cup all-purpose flour
 ½ cup 2% reduced-fat milk
 2 cups shredded cooked chicken
    breast (about 1 pound)
 ⅓ cup chopped fresh cilantro
 ¾ teaspoon salt
 ½ teaspoon black pepper

1. Melt butter in a Dutch oven over medium heat. Add onion and jalapeño, and cook 10 minutes, stirring frequently. Add curry, and cook 30 seconds, stirring constantly. Add broth and corn, and bring to a boil, stirring occasionally. Reduce heat; simmer 15 minutes.
2. Lightly spoon flour into a dry measuring cup, and level with a knife. Place flour in a small bowl; gradually add milk, stirring with a whisk until well blended to form a slurry. Stir slurry into corn mixture, and bring to a boil. Cook 3 minutes or until mixture thickens, stirring frequently. Stir in chicken, cilantro, salt, and black pepper. Cook until thoroughly heated. Yield: 6 servings (serving size: 1⅔ cups).

CALORIES 293 (18% from fat); FAT 5.7g (sat 2g, mono 1.2g, poly 0.5g); PROTEIN 24g; CARB 40.4g; FIBER 2.3g; CHOL 46mg; IRON 2mg; SODIUM 945mg; CALC 53mg

1. Traditional creamy soups are thickened with cream or a *roux* (a mixture of cooked butter and flour), but we've used a slurry to reduce fat. To make a slurry, gradually whisk milk into flour until smooth.

2. Slowly add slurry to soup, bring to a boil, and cook until thick—at least 10 to 15 minutes, or the results may taste of uncooked flour and be too thin.

Chunky Southwestern Clam Chowder

Typically, New England-style chowders are simply cream, fish, and butter. In our southwestern-style version, we omitted butter and substituted half-and-half for the whipping cream, cutting the fat and calories while maintaining the rich creamy texture and flavor.

Prep: 25 minutes • Cook: 1 hour, 5 minutes Other: 5 minutes

- 2   red bell peppers (about ¾ pound)
- 1   jalapeño pepper
- 1   (10-ounce) can whole clams, undrained
- 1   bacon slice
- 1½ cups chopped onion
- 1½ tablespoons all-purpose flour
- 4   cups (½-inch) cubed peeled baking potato (about 2 pounds)
- 2   cups fresh corn kernels (about 4 ears)
- 1   cup chardonnay or other dry white wine
- 2   (8-ounce) bottles clam juice
- ¾   cup half-and-half
- ½   cup chopped green onions
- 1   tablespoon chopped fresh basil
- ¼   teaspoon freshly ground black pepper

1. Preheat broiler.

2. Cut bell peppers in half lengthwise; discard seeds and membranes. Place bell pepper halves, skin sides up, and jalapeño pepper on a foil-lined baking sheet; flatten bell peppers with hand. Broil 10 minutes or until blackened. Place peppers in a zip-top plastic bag; seal. Let stand 5 minutes.

3. Discard seeds and membranes from jalapeño pepper. Peel and chop bell peppers and jalapeño pepper; set aside. Drain clams in a colander over a bowl, reserving liquid.

4. Cook bacon in a Dutch oven over medium heat until crisp. Remove bacon from pan, reserving drippings in pan. Crumble bacon; set aside.

5. Add 1½ cups onion to pan; sauté 10 minutes. Add flour; cook 2 minutes, stirring constantly. Stir in reserved clam liquid, potato, corn, wine, and clam juice; bring to a boil. Partially cover, reduce heat, and simmer 25 minutes or until potato is tender. Stir in roasted peppers, clams, half-and-half, green onions, basil, and black pepper. Cook 5 minutes or until thoroughly heated. Sprinkle with crumbled bacon. Yield: 6 servings (serving size: 1½ cups).

CALORIES 241 (25% from fat); FAT 6.6g (sat 3.1g, mono 2.2g, poly 0.8g); PROTEIN 6.4g; CARB 37.8g; FIBER 4.7g; CHOL 37mg; IRON 3.2mg; SODIUM 339mg; CALC 154mg

Test Kitchen Tip: When cutting the corn kernels off the cob, stand the cob in the center opening of a Bundt pan, and cut the kernels off into the pan.

---

menu

serves 6

Chunky Southwestern Clam Chowder

Citrus and romaine salad*

Low-fat chocolate ice cream

*Combine 6 cups torn romaine lettuce, 1½ cups fresh orange sections, and ¾ cup sliced red onion in a bowl. Combine ⅓ cup red wine vinegar, 1 tablespoon olive oil, and 1 table-spoon honey in a bowl; stir with a whisk. Drizzle over salad; toss gently.

Shrimp-and-Corn Chowder

It takes just a small amount of cream to make this soup velvety. Serve with crusty sourdough bread.

Prep: 20 minutes • Cook: 20 minutes

- 1   bunch green onions
- 3   cups diced red potato
- 3   cups fat-free, less-sodium chicken broth
- 1   (16-ounce) package frozen white shoepeg corn, thawed
- ½   pound shrimp, peeled, deveined, and cut into ½-inch pieces
- ¼   cup heavy cream
- 1   tablespoon fresh lemon juice
- Freshly ground black pepper (optional)

1. Remove green tops from onions; chop and set aside. Chop white portion of onions; set aside.

2. Combine potato and chicken broth in a medium saucepan; bring mixture to a boil. Cook 5 minutes; add corn and white portion of onions. Reduce heat, and simmer 8 minutes. Place 2 cups potato mixture in a blender, and process until smooth. Return to pan, and stir in shrimp. Cook 3 minutes or until shrimp are done; stir in onion tops, cream, and lemon juice. Ladle soup into bowls. Sprinkle with freshly ground pepper, if desired. Yield: 4 servings (serving size: 1½ cups).

CALORIES 259 (24% from fat); FAT 7g (sat 4g, mono 2g, poly 1g); PROTEIN 18g; CARB 29g; FIBER 6g; CHOL 107mg; IRON 2mg; SODIUM 503mg; CALC 42mg

Test Kitchen Tip: Adding the cream to the soup after it's cooked helps prevent the cream from breaking down and curdling. Just a small amount of cream adds a velvety texture to the chowder.

Vegetable & Bean Soups   Chilled garden-fresh soups, thick potato soups, and hearty bowls of beans and greens make the most of seasonal produce.

Yellow Tomato Gazpacho

A few ripe tomatoes and bell peppers, be they yellow, orange, or red, are the keys to this marvelous Mediterranean soup. The soup itself requires no cooking—only the croutons that are used as a garnish.

Prep: 25 minutes   •   Cook: 10 minutes

Gazpacho:

1½   cups chopped seeded peeled cucumber

1   cup chopped Vidalia or other sweet onion

1   cup coarsely chopped yellow bell pepper

6   tablespoons white wine vinegar

1   tablespoon extravirgin olive oil

½   teaspoon salt

¼   teaspoon freshly ground black pepper

2   pounds chopped seeded peeled yellow tomatoes (about 6 large)

1   garlic clove, minced

Garnish:

2   (1-ounce) slices French bread, torn into ½-inch pieces

1   teaspoon extravirgin olive oil

1   cup quartered grape or cherry tomatoes

½   cup chopped seeded peeled cucumber

1. To prepare gazpacho, combine first 9 ingredients. Place one-third of vegetable mixture in a food processor; process until smooth. Pour pureed mixture into a large

bowl. Repeat procedure with remaining vegetable mixture. Cover and chill.

2. Preheat oven to 375°.

3. To prepare garnish, place bread in a small bowl; drizzle with 1 teaspoon oil, tossing gently to coat. Spread bread mixture in a single layer on a baking sheet. Bake at 375° for 10 minutes or until golden brown, stirring occasionally. Cool to

room temperature. Ladle soup into bowls; top with croutons, quartered tomatoes, and cucumber. Yield: 8 servings (serving size: ¾ cup gazpacho, a few croutons, 2 tablespoons quartered tomatoes, and 1 tablespoon cucumber).

CALORIES 89 (31% from fat); FAT 3.1g (sat 0.5g, mono 2g, poly 0.5g); PROTEIN 2.4g; CARB 13.8g; FIBER 2.6g; CHOL 0mg; IRON 1mg; SODIUM 203mg; CALC 24mg

Cold Cucumber Soup with Cherry Tomato Confetti

Gazpacho Andaluz

Gazpacho, a traditional Spanish chilled soup, is an excellent start to a meal.

Prep: 12 minutes

1½ pounds ripe tomatoes, each cut into quarters
1 cup coarsely chopped peeled cucumber
½ cup coarsely chopped Vidalia or other sweet onion
½ cup coarsely chopped red bell pepper
½ cup coarsely chopped green bell pepper
3 tablespoons sherry vinegar
2 tablespoons extravirgin olive oil
½ teaspoon salt
¼ teaspoon sugar
¼ teaspoon ground cumin
5 garlic cloves, coarsely chopped

1. Place all ingredients in a food processor; process until smooth. Press tomato mixture through a sieve over a bowl, pressing solids through with back of a spoon; discard any remaining solids. Cover and chill. Yield: 6 servings (serving size: ½ cup).

CALORIES 80 (51% from fat); FAT 5g (sat 0.7g, mono 3.4g, poly 0.6g); PROTEIN 1.5g; CARB 9g; FIBER 2g; CHOL 0mg; IRON 0.8mg; SODIUM 207mg; CALC 18mg

Cold Cucumber Soup with Cherry Tomato Confetti

Cherry tomatoes float atop tangy cucumber soup for a refreshing lunch or light supper.

Prep: 15 minutes

½ cup chopped fresh cilantro
¼ cup chopped onion
¼ cup fresh lime juice
¼ cup fat-free buttermilk
¼ cup reduced-fat sour cream
½ teaspoon salt
½ teaspoon freshly ground black pepper
5 cucumbers (about 2½ pounds), peeled, halved lengthwise, seeded, and coarsely chopped
1 jalapeño pepper, halved and seeded
1 cup cherry tomatoes, halved

1. Place first 9 ingredients in a food processor; process until smooth.
2. Ladle soup into bowls. Top with tomatoes. Yield: 4 servings (serving size: 1 cup soup and ¼ cup tomatoes).

CALORIES 74 (29% from fat); FAT 2.4g (sat 1.3g, mono 0g, poly 0.2g); PROTEIN 3.2g; CARB 11.9g; FIBER 2.5g; CHOL 8mg; IRON 0.7mg; SODIUM 620mg; CALC 85mg

Tomato-Basil Soup

The perfect pairing—tomato and basil—team up in a soup that's just right for a Mediterranean-style lunch.

Prep: 12 minutes • Cook: 38 minutes

4 cups chopped seeded peeled tomato (about 4 large)
4 cups low-sodium tomato juice
⅓ cup fresh basil leaves
1 cup 1% low-fat milk
¼ teaspoon salt
¼ teaspoon cracked black pepper
½ cup (4 ounces) ⅓-less-fat cream cheese, softened
Basil leaves, thinly sliced (optional)
8 (½-inch-thick) slices diagonally cut French bread baguette

1. Bring tomato and juice to a boil in a large saucepan. Reduce heat; simmer, uncovered, 30 minutes.
2. Place tomato mixture and ⅓ cup basil in a blender or food processor; process until smooth. Return pureed mixture to pan; stir in milk, salt, and pepper. Add cream cheese, stirring well with a whisk, and cook over medium heat until thick (about 5 minutes). Ladle soup into bowls; garnish with sliced basil, if desired. Serve with bread. Yield: 8 servings (serving size: 1 cup soup and 1 bread slice).

CALORIES 133 (30% from fat); FAT 4.4g (sat 2.4g, mono 1.3g, poly 0.4g); PROTEIN 5.4g; CARB 18.7g; FIBER 1.9g; CHOL 12mg; IRON 1.5mg; SODIUM 310mg; CALC 77mg

Test Kitchen Tip: Refrigerate any remaining soup in an airtight container up to one week.

Onion Soup Gratinée

Canned beef broth and aromatic celery, carrots, and mushrooms create the stock for this classic French onion soup.

Prep: 20 minutes • Cook: 1 hour, 24 minutes

Cooking spray
2   cups coarsely chopped celery
½   cup chopped carrot
1   (8-ounce) package sliced mushrooms
1   cup dry red wine
4   cups less-sodium beef broth
4   cups water
3   parsley sprigs
2   thyme sprigs
7   cups thinly sliced yellow onion
    (about 3 large)
½   teaspoon salt
3   tablespoons dry red wine
¼   teaspoon freshly ground black pepper
8   (½-ounce) slices French bread
    baguette
¾   cup (3 ounces) shredded Gruyère
    cheese

1. Heat a large Dutch oven over medium-high heat; coat pan with cooking spray. Add celery, carrot, and mushrooms; sauté 5 minutes or until lightly browned. Remove from heat; slowly stir in 1 cup wine, scraping pan to loosen browned bits. Add broth, water, parsley, and 2 thyme sprigs. Bring to a simmer over medium heat; cook 30 minutes. Strain broth mixture through a sieve into a bowl; discard solids.
2. Heat pan over medium heat; coat pan with cooking spray. Add onion and salt; cook 20 minutes or until golden brown, stirring frequently. Stir in strained broth; bring to a boil. Reduce heat, and simmer 20 minutes or until onions are very tender. Remove from heat; stir in 3 tablespoons wine and pepper.

3. Preheat broiler.
4. Ladle soup into ovenproof bowls. Place bowls on a jelly-roll pan. Top with bread slices and cheese. Broil 1 minute or until cheese begins to brown. Serve immediately. Yield: 8 servings (serving size: ¾ cup soup, 1 bread slice, and 1½ tablespoons cheese).

CALORIES 146 (29% from fat); FAT 4.7g (sat 2.3g, mono 1.6g, poly 0.5g); PROTEIN 7.8g; CARB 18.6g; FIBER 1.9g; CHOL 12mg; IRON 1mg; SODIUM 311mg; CALC 148mg

Roasted Garlic and Shallot Potato Soup with Cheesy Croutons

Roasted garlic contributes subtle sweetness and blue cheese adds a bit of sharpness.

Prep: 40 minutes • Cook: 1 hour, 45 minutes

Soup:
5   whole garlic heads, unpeeled
3½ tablespoons olive oil, divided
1¼ teaspoons salt, divided
1   teaspoon freshly ground black
    pepper, divided
10 shallots, unpeeled (about ¾ pound)
2   cups coarsely chopped onion
1   cup dry white wine
3   cups fat-free, less-sodium chicken
    broth
2   cups (½-inch) cubed peeled baking
    potato (about ¾ pound)
1   teaspoon chopped fresh thyme
1   cup 2% reduced-fat milk
Cheesy Croutons:
16 (½-inch-thick) slices French bread
    baguette
Cooking spray
¾   cup (3 ounces) crumbled blue cheese
2   tablespoons grated fresh Parmesan
    cheese

1. Preheat oven to 400°.
2. To prepare soup, remove white papery skins from garlic heads (do not peel or separate cloves); cut off tops, leaving root ends intact. Place garlic in a shallow roasting pan. Drizzle 1 tablespoon oil over garlic; sprinkle with ¼ teaspoon salt and ¼ teaspoon pepper. Cover with foil. Bake at 400° for 20 minutes. Add shallots to pan. Drizzle 1 tablespoon oil over shallots; sprinkle with ¼ teaspoon salt and ¼ teaspoon pepper. Cover and bake at 400° for 25 minutes or until tender and browned. Cool. Squeeze garlic to extract pulp; peel shallots. Discard skins. Set garlic pulp and shallots aside.
3. Heat 1½ tablespoons oil in a Dutch oven over medium heat; add onion. Cover and cook 15 minutes or until lightly browned, stirring occasionally. Add garlic pulp, peeled shallots, and wine. Reduce heat; simmer, uncovered, 5 minutes.
4. Stir in broth, potato, and thyme; bring to a boil. Cover, reduce heat, and simmer 20 minutes. Cool slightly. Place half of potato mixture in a blender; process until smooth. Pour mixture into a large bowl. Repeat with remaining potato mixture.
5. Return pureed mixture to pan; stir in milk, ¾ teaspoon salt, and ½ teaspoon pepper. Cook over medium heat 5 minutes or until thoroughly heated.
6. Preheat oven to 400°.
7. To prepare croutons, place bread slices in a single layer on a large baking sheet. Coat tops of bread with cooking spray. Bake at 400° for 8 minutes or until lightly browned. Sprinkle cheeses evenly over bread slices. Bake 3 minutes or until cheese melts. Serve with soup. Yield: 8 servings (serving size: 1 cup soup and 2 croutons).

CALORIES 290 (30% from fat); FAT 9.6g (sat 3.5g, mono 4.7g, poly 0.8g); PROTEIN 11.1g; CARB 41g; FIBER 3.3g; CHOL 12mg; IRON 2mg; SODIUM 806mg; CALC 202mg

Baked Potato Soup

All the flavors of a loaded baked potato come together in this thick soup that's guaranteed to offer comfort on a cold winter's night.

Prep: 15 minutes • Cook: 1 hour, 28 minutes

   4 baking potatoes (about 2½ pounds)
   ⅔ cup all-purpose flour
   6 cups 2% reduced-fat milk
   1 cup (4 ounces) shredded reduced-fat extrasharp Cheddar cheese, divided
   1 teaspoon salt
   ½ teaspoon pepper
   1 cup reduced-fat sour cream
   ¾ cup chopped green onions, divided
   6 bacon slices, cooked and crumbled

1. Preheat oven to 400°.
2. Pierce potatoes with a fork; bake at 400° for 1 hour or until tender. Cool. Peel potatoes; coarsely mash. Discard skins.
3. Lightly spoon flour into dry measuring cups; level with a knife. Place flour in a large Dutch oven; gradually add milk, stirring with a whisk until blended. Cook over medium heat until thick and bubbly (about 8 minutes). Add mashed potatoes, ¾ cup cheese, salt, and pepper, stirring until cheese melts. Remove from heat.
4. Stir in sour cream and ½ cup onions. Cook over low heat 10 minutes or until thoroughly heated (do not boil). Ladle into bowls, and sprinkle with cheese, onions, and bacon. Yield: 8 servings (serving size: about 1½ cups soup, 1½ teaspoons cheese, 1½ teaspoons onions, and about 1 tablespoon bacon).

CALORIES 329 (30% from fat); FAT 10.8g (sat 5.9g, mono 3.5g, poly 0.7g); PROTEIN 13.6g; CARB 44.5g; FIBER 2.8g; CHOL 38mg; IRON 1.1mg; SODIUM 587mg; CALC 407mg

Potato-Kale Soup with Gruyère

Dark green, earthy kale contrasts with the mild yellow potatoes, but you can use fresh spinach in place of kale.

Prep: 20 minutes • Cook: 40 minutes

   2 tablespoons butter
   1½ cups finely chopped onion
   1 garlic clove, minced
   7 cups fat-free, less-sodium chicken broth
   4 cups coarsely chopped peeled Yukon gold potato (about 1½ pounds)
   ¼ teaspoon salt
   1 bay leaf
   6 cups chopped fresh kale (about ¾ pound)
   1 teaspoon dried basil
   9 tablespoons (about 2 ounces) shredded Gruyère cheese

1. Melt butter in a large saucepan over medium heat. Add onion; cook 8 minutes or until tender, stirring frequently. Add garlic; cook 30 seconds, stirring constantly. Stir in broth, potato, salt, and bay leaf; bring to a boil. Cover, reduce heat, and simmer 15 minutes or until potato is tender.
2. Stir in kale and basil. Cover and simmer 10 minutes or until kale is tender. Discard bay leaf. Partially mash potatoes with a potato masher until thick and chunky. Ladle soup into bowls. Top with cheese. Yield: 6 servings (serving size: 1⅔ cups soup and 1½ tablespoons cheese).

CALORIES 239 (29% from fat); FAT 7.8g (sat 4.4g, mono 2.2g, poly 0.6g); PROTEIN 11.7g; CARB 32g; FIBER 3.9g; CHOL 21mg; IRON 2.2mg; SODIUM 733mg; CALC 215mg

Curried Butternut Soup

You can make this savory-sweet autumn soup with any kind of winter squash, or even sweet potatoes.

Prep: 20 minutes • Cook: 1 hour, 27 minutes

  8 cups cubed peeled butternut squash (about 2 pounds)
  Cooking spray
  1 tablespoon butter
  2 cups chopped peeled Granny Smith apple (about ¾ pound)
1½ cups finely chopped onion
  ½ cup thinly sliced celery
  1 bay leaf
  2 teaspoons curry powder
  1 garlic clove, minced
  3 (14-ounce) cans fat-free, less-sodium chicken broth
  ⅛ teaspoon salt
  ½ cup (2 ounces) grated extrasharp white Cheddar cheese

1. Preheat oven to 400°.
2. Arrange squash in a single layer on a foil-lined baking sheet coated with cooking spray. Bake at 400° for 45 minutes or until tender.
3. Melt butter in a Dutch oven over medium-high heat. Add apple, onion, celery, and bay leaf; sauté 10 minutes. Stir in curry powder and garlic; sauté 1 minute. Add squash, broth, and salt; stir well.
4. Reduce heat to medium-low; simmer, uncovered, 30 minutes. Discard bay leaf. Partially mash mixture with a potato masher until thick and chunky; stir well with a spoon. Ladle soup into bowls, and top with cheese. Yield: 4 servings (serving size: 1½ cups soup and 2 tablespoons cheese).

CALORIES 270 (27% from fat); FAT 8.2g (sat 4.5g, mono 2.3g, poly 0.5g); PROTEIN 10.4g; CARB 42.7g; FIBER 9.8g; CHOL 23mg; IRON 1.9mg; SODIUM 783mg; CALC 221mg

Roasted Tomato-and-Red Pepper Soup

Roasting tomatoes and bell peppers concentrates their natural sugars and brings out a mellow sweetness.

Prep: 25 minutes • Cook: 26 minutes
Other: 10 minutes

1½ pounds red bell peppers
  2 pounds tomatoes, halved and seeded
  2 tablespoons olive oil
  1 cup chopped onion
  4 garlic cloves, minced
1½ cups tomato juice
  1 tablespoon chopped fresh or 1 teaspoon dried marjoram
  ½ teaspoon salt
1¼ teaspoons black pepper

1. Preheat broiler.
2. Cut bell peppers in half lengthwise; discard seeds and membranes. Place bell peppers and tomatoes, skin sides up, on a foil-lined baking sheet; flatten peppers with hand. Broil 15 minutes or until vegetables are blackened. Place peppers in a zip-top plastic bag; seal and let stand 10 minutes. Peel peppers and tomatoes; chop. Place half of chopped peppers and half of chopped tomatoes in a blender; process until smooth. Set aside.
3. Heat oil in a saucepan over medium-low heat. Add onion and garlic; cover and cook 5 minutes. Add pureed vegetables, remaining chopped bell peppers and tomatoes, tomato juice, chopped marjoram, salt, and black pepper; cook over medium heat 5 minutes or until thoroughly heated. Yield: 5 servings (serving size: 1 cup).

CALORIES 126 (25% from fat); FAT 4g (sat 0.6g, mono 2.1g, poly 0g); PROTEIN 3.9g; CARB 22.7g; FIBER 5.6g; CHOL 0mg; IRON 3.4mg; SODIUM 521mg; CALC 42mg

Miso Soup

Bonito is a type of strong-flavored tuna that is often dried and used as the base for soups. Look for it in the Asian section of the supermarket. The stock adds a distinctive depth of flavor to this soy-based soup. A small bowl of miso soup is a great starter for an Asian-style meal.

Prep: 6 minutes • Cook: 8 minutes

  6 cups water
  1 tablespoon bonito-flavored soup stock or other fish stock
  ¼ cup white miso (soybean paste)
  ½ cup cubed firm tofu (about 3 ounces)
  ⅓ cup sliced green onions

1. Combine water and soup stock in a large saucepan; bring to a boil. Add miso, and cook 3 minutes or until miso is blended, stirring constantly. Ladle soup into bowls, and sprinkle with tofu and green onions. Yield: 6 servings (serving size: about 1 cup soup, about 1½ tablespoons tofu, and about 1 tablespoon green onions).

CALORIES 61 (37% from fat); FAT 2.5g (sat 0.4g, mono 0.6g, poly 1.4g); PROTEIN 4.7g; CARB 5.1g; FIBER 1.3g; CHOL 0mg; IRON 2.5mg; SODIUM 712mg; CALC 151mg

miso Made from a blend of soy and grain or with soy alone, miso resembles peanut butter. It ranges in color from light to dark and in taste from mildly sweet to very salty. It's often added to sauces and soups to contribute flavor and to slightly thicken. Store miso in a glass jar in the refrigerator; it will keep indefinitely.

Tofu Vegetable Hot Pot

Tame this fiery soup by seeding the chile. If you love heat, try using two chiles. Start cooking the rice before you sauté the shallots and spices so it will be ready at the same time as the soup.

Prep: 20 minutes • Cook: 42 minutes

    1   teaspoon canola oil
    Cooking spray
    1   cup thinly sliced shallots
    1   tablespoon matchstick-cut peeled
        fresh ginger
    1   teaspoon ground turmeric
    1   jalapeño or serrano chile,
        thinly sliced
    1   garlic clove, minced
 1 ½   cups shredded green cabbage
    1   cup sliced shiitake mushroom caps
        (about 3 ounces)
    ½   cup (¼-inch-thick) diagonally cut
        carrot
    1   cup water
    ¼   cup low-sodium soy sauce
    ½   teaspoon sea salt
    1   (14-ounce) can light coconut milk
    1   pound water-packed firm tofu,
        drained and cut into 1-inch cubes
    2   tomatoes, cut into 1-inch-thick
        wedges
    ½   cup torn fresh basil leaves
    ¼   cup (1-inch) sliced green onions
    2   cups hot cooked jasmine rice
    4   lime wedges

1. Heat oil in a large nonstick saucepan coated with cooking spray over medium-high heat. Add shallots; sauté 2 minutes. Reduce heat to medium. Add ginger, turmeric, chile, and garlic; cook 1 minute, stirring constantly. Add cabbage, mushroom, and carrot; cook 2 minutes, stirring occasionally.

2. Stir in water, soy sauce, salt, and coconut milk; bring to a boil. Add tofu. Reduce heat; simmer 5 minutes. Add tomato; simmer 3 minutes. Stir in basil and onions. Serve over rice with lime wedges. Yield: 4 servings (serving size: 2 cups soup, ½ cup rice, and 1 lime wedge).

CALORIES 409 (30% from fat); FAT 13.9g (sat 5.8g, mono 0.8g, poly 0.6g); PROTEIN 22.7g; CARB 57.9g; FIBER 4.5g; CHOL 0mg; IRON 6.6mg; SODIUM 881mg; CALC 178mg

how to seed a chile pepper

Wearing protective gloves, slice the pepper in half lengthwise. Using a paring knife, cut out and discard the seeds and membranes.

White-Bean Soup with Peppers and Bacon

The addition of bacon, bell pepper, and carrot transforms a basic bean soup.

Prep: 25 minutes • Cook: 1 hour, 33 minutes
Other: 1 hour

1½ cups dried navy beans
 5 bacon slices
 2 cups chopped red bell pepper
 2 cups chopped onion
 1 cup chopped carrot
 1 teaspoon sugar
 1 teaspoon onion powder
 1 teaspoon garlic powder
 ¼ teaspoon black pepper
 ⅛ teaspoon ground red pepper
 4 garlic cloves, minced
 3 (14-ounce) cans fat-free, less-sodium chicken broth
 ½ cup chopped fresh parsley

1. Sort and wash beans; place in a large Dutch oven. Cover with water to 2 inches above beans; bring to a boil, and cook 2 minutes. Remove from heat; cover and let stand 1 hour. Drain beans.

2. Cook bacon in pan over medium heat until crisp. Remove bacon from pan, reserving drippings in pan; crumble bacon, and set aside. Add bell pepper and next 8 ingredients to drippings in pan; sauté 10 minutes. Stir in broth, scraping pan to loosen browned bits. Add beans. Bring to a boil; cover, reduce heat, and simmer 1 hour.

3. Place 3 cups bean mixture in a blender; process until smooth. Return pureed mixture to pan; simmer 5 minutes. Stir in bacon and parsley. Yield: 8 servings (serving size: 1 cup).

CALORIES 267 (30% from fat); FAT 9g (sat 3.2g, mono 3.8g, poly 1.3g); PROTEIN 13.6g; CARB 33.8g; FIBER 5.9g; CHOL 9mg; IRON 3.6mg; SODIUM 479mg; CALC 87mg

Butternut Squash-White Bean Soup

Cream adds a silky finish to the soup, while crumbled bacon and toasted pumpkinseeds lend crunch.

Prep: 20 minutes • Cook: 27 minutes

 3 bacon slices
 1 cup chopped onion
 ⅔ cup chopped celery
 3 garlic cloves, minced
 4 cups (¾-inch) cubed peeled butternut squash (about 1½ pounds)
 ¼ cup dry white wine
 4 cups fat-free, less-sodium chicken broth
 1 teaspoon ground cumin
 ¼ teaspoon ground red pepper
 ⅛ teaspoon ground cinnamon
 ⅛ teaspoon ground cloves
 ¼ cup whipping cream
 1 tablespoon chopped fresh oregano
 1 teaspoon salt
 ¼ teaspoon freshly ground black pepper
 2 (15-ounce) cans Great Northern beans, rinsed and drained
 3 tablespoons unsalted pumpkinseed kernels, toasted

1. Cook bacon in a Dutch oven over medium heat until crisp. Remove bacon from pan, reserving 2 teaspoons drippings in pan; crumble bacon, and set aside.

2. Add onion, celery, and garlic to pan; cook 3 minutes or until tender, stirring occasionally. Add squash; cook 3 minutes, stirring occasionally. Add wine; cook until almost all liquid evaporates. Stir in broth, cumin, red pepper, cinnamon, and cloves; bring to a boil. Reduce heat; simmer 5 minutes or until squash is tender. Stir in cream, oregano, salt, black pepper, and beans; bring to a boil. Remove from heat. Ladle soup into bowls. Sprinkle each serving evenly with crumbled bacon and pumpkinseeds. Yield: 6 servings (serving size: 1½ cups).

CALORIES 324 (30% from fat); FAT 10.7g (sat 4.3g, mono 3.4g, poly 2.1g); PROTEIN 17.7g; CARB 42.2g; FIBER 9.2g; CHOL 18mg; IRON 4.1mg; SODIUM 774mg; CALC 129mg

Pressure Cooker Bean and Pasta Soup

Instead of soaking beans overnight, use a pressure cooker and they'll be ready for the soup in about five minutes. And instead of simmering on the stovetop for hours, the soup will achieve maximum flavor in the pressure cooker in only 40 minutes.

Prep: 25 minutes • Cook: 1 hour, 5 minutes

  2 cups dried cannellini beans or other white beans
  4 quarts water, divided
  2 tablespoons olive oil
  2 cups cubed peeled baking potato
1½ cups chopped onion
1½ tablespoons minced fresh or 1 teaspoon dried crushed rosemary
  2 garlic cloves, chopped
  ½ teaspoon freshly ground black pepper
  1 (3-inch) piece Parmigiano-Reggiano cheese rind
  2 cups uncooked whole wheat seashell pasta
2½ teaspoons sea salt
  1 (14.5-ounce) can diced tomatoes, undrained
  ½ cup (2 ounces) grated Parmigiano-Reggiano cheese
  2 tablespoons balsamic vinegar
  4 teaspoons extravirgin olive oil

1. Sort and wash beans. Combine beans and 2 quarts water in a 6-quart pressure cooker. Close lid securely; bring to high pressure over high heat. Adjust heat to medium or level needed to maintain high pressure; cook 3 minutes. Remove from heat; place pressure cooker under cold running water. Remove lid. Drain beans. Place beans in a bowl; wipe pan dry with paper towels.

2. Heat 2 tablespoons oil in pan over medium-high heat. Add potato, onion, rosemary, and garlic; sauté 3 minutes. Add beans, 2 quarts water, pepper, and cheese rind to pan. Close lid securely; bring to high pressure over high heat. Adjust heat to medium or level needed to maintain high pressure; cook 40 minutes. Remove from heat; place pressure cooker under cold running water. Remove lid. Remove and discard cheese rind.

3. Cook pasta according to package directions, omitting salt and fat. Add pasta, salt, and tomatoes to soup. Ladle soup into bowls; top with grated cheese, vinegar, and extravirgin olive oil. Yield: 8 servings (serving size: 1¼ cups soup, 1 tablespoon grated cheese, ¾ teaspoon vinegar, and ½ teaspoon extravirgin olive oil).

CALORIES 372 (21% from fat); FAT 8.5g (sat 2.2g, mono 4.8g, poly 0.9g); PROTEIN 17.7g; CARB 59.4g; FIBER 13.3g; CHOL 5mg; IRON 4mg; SODIUM 910mg; CALC 198mg

---

Test Kitchen Tip: A piece of Parmigiano-Reggiano rind adds flavor and richness to this broth.

---

pressure cookers Pressure cookers save you time by cooking foods at above-boiling-point temperatures, usually from 212° to 250°. Both the traditional jiggle-top cookers and the spring-valve cookers are safe, but they vary in design, operation, and cost. The models with a spring-release valve are more expensive but are quieter and quicker to decompress. Both types cook just the same inside where superheated steam seals in nutrients.

Mexican Ham and Bean Soup

Chipotle chile, cumin, and Manchego cheese contribute authentic Mexican flavor.

Prep: 20 minutes • Cook: 2 hours, 12 minutes
Other: 1 hour

  1 pound dried pinto beans
  8 cups fat-free, less-sodium chicken broth
  2 cups chopped onion
  2 cups water
  8 ounces cubed smoked ham steak
  1 tablespoon chili powder
  2 teaspoons ground cumin
  2 teaspoons dried oregano
  3 bay leaves
  3 garlic cloves, crushed
  1 (14.5-ounce) can diced tomatoes, undrained
  1 chipotle chile
  ½ cup (2 ounces) shredded Manchego cheese or Monterey Jack cheese
  ½ cup minced fresh cilantro

1. Sort and wash beans; place in a Dutch oven. Cover with water to 2 inches above beans; bring to a boil. Cook 2 minutes; remove from heat. Cover and let stand 1 hour. Drain.

2. Combine beans, broth, and next 8 ingredients in a Dutch oven; bring to a boil. Partially cover; reduce heat to medium-low. Simmer 1½ hours or until beans are tender.

3. Stir in tomatoes and chile; simmer 30 minutes. Discard bay leaves and chile. Ladle soup into bowls. Top with cheese; sprinkle with cilantro. Yield: 8 servings (serving size: 1½ cups soup, 1 tablespoon cheese, and 1 tablespoon cilantro).

CALORIES 303 (12% from fat); FAT 4.2g (sat 1.8g, mono 1.3g, poly 0.5g); PROTEIN 20.3g; CARB 46.8g; FIBER 16.1g; CHOL 22mg; IRON 4.3mg; SODIUM 958mg; CALC 153mg

Black Bean Soup

Packed with nutrients and fiber, black beans are also an economical source of protein. This recipe employs the overnight soak method for the dried beans, so you'll need to start a day ahead. Or, use the quick-soak method: Place the beans in a Dutch oven; cover with water to 2 inches above the beans. Bring to a boil, and cook 2 minutes. Remove from heat; cover and let stand 1 hour. Drain.

Prep: 25 minutes • Cook: 1 hour, 55 minutes
Other: 8 hours, 5 minutes

    1   pound dried black beans
    2   bacon slices, chopped
    1   cup chopped onion
    ¾   cup chopped carrot
    ¾   cup chopped celery
    2   garlic cloves, minced
    1   jalapeño pepper, seeded and minced
    4   (14-ounce) cans fat-free, less-sodium chicken broth
    1   (28-ounce) can crushed tomatoes, undrained
    ⅓   cup minced fresh cilantro
    2   tablespoons fresh lime juice
    1   teaspoon salt
    ½   teaspoon freshly ground black pepper
    ¾   cup reduced-fat sour cream

1. Sort and wash beans; place in a large bowl. Cover with water to 2 inches above beans; cover and let stand 8 hours or overnight. Drain and rinse beans.
2. Cook bacon in a large Dutch oven over medium-high heat until crisp. Remove bacon from pan, reserving drippings in pan. Add onion, carrot, and celery to pan; sauté 10 minutes or until tender. Add garlic and jalapeño; sauté 2 minutes. Add beans, bacon, broth, and tomatoes; bring to a boil. Cover, reduce heat, and simmer 1½ hours or until beans are tender. Place 4 cups soup in a blender or food processor; let stand 5 minutes. Process until smooth; return pureed soup to pan. Stir in cilantro, lime juice, salt, and pepper. Ladle soup into bowls. Serve with sour cream. Yield: 12 servings (serving size: 1 cup soup and 1 tablespoon sour cream).

CALORIES 215 (20% from fat); FAT 4.8g (sat 2.1g, mono 1.6g, poly 0.7g); PROTEIN 12g; CARB 32.5g; FIBER 7.7g; CHOL 8mg; IRON 3mg; SODIUM 570mg; CALC 95mg

Chipotle-Black Bean Soup

The chipotle chile gives this soup a smokiness that makes it different from other black bean soups.

Prep: 20 minutes • Cook: 3 hours, 30 minutes
Other: 1 hour, 15 minutes

Soup:
    1   cup dried black beans (about 6 ounces)
    ½   cup boiling water
    1   dried chipotle chile
    1   teaspoon olive oil
    ¼   cup chopped onion
    1   garlic clove, minced
    2   cups water
    ¼   teaspoon dried oregano
    ⅛   teaspoon ground cumin
    2   cups fat-free, less-sodium chicken broth
    ¼   teaspoon ground red pepper
    1   (14.5-ounce) can diced tomatoes and green chiles, undrained

Toppings:
    2   (6-inch) corn tortillas, cut into ¼-inch strips
    Cooking spray
    ½   cup plain fat-free yogurt
    ¼   cup (1 ounce) finely shredded reduced-fat sharp Cheddar cheese

1. To prepare soup, sort and wash beans; place in a large Dutch oven. Cover with water to 2 inches above beans; bring to a boil, and cook 2 minutes. Remove from heat; cover and let stand 1 hour. Drain.
2. Combine boiling water and chipotle chile in a bowl; let stand 15 minutes or until soft. Drain, seed, and chop.
3. Heat oil in a large Dutch oven over medium-high heat. Add onion; sauté 2 minutes. Add garlic; sauté 1 minute. Add beans, chipotle chile, 2 cups water, oregano, cumin, and broth; bring to a boil. Cover, reduce heat, and simmer 3 hours or until beans are soft. Place 1 cup soup in a blender; process until smooth. Return to pan. Stir in pepper and tomatoes; cook until thoroughly heated.
4. Preheat oven to 350°.
5. To prepare toppings, place tortilla strips in a single layer on a baking sheet. Lightly coat tortilla strips with cooking spray. Bake at 350° for 12 minutes or until toasted.
6. Ladle soup into bowls; top with tortilla strips, yogurt, and cheese. Yield: 4 servings (serving size: 1¼ cups soup, ¼ cup tortilla strips, 2 tablespoons yogurt, and 1 tablespoon cheese).

CALORIES 276 (12% from fat); FAT 3.7g (sat 1.2g, mono 1.4g, poly 0.7g); PROTEIN 15.8g; CARB 42.7g; FIBER 7.9g; CHOL 5mg; IRON 3.4mg; SODIUM 769mg; CALC 222mg

Test Kitchen Tip: If you want to use canned black beans in this soup, use two (15-ounce) cans black beans, rinsed and drained, and omit the first step of soaking the beans.

Chili
Our collection of vegetarian, chicken, venison, and beef chili recipes will please both traditional and adventurous chili fans.

Quick Vegetarian Chili with Avocado Salsa

This chili's flavor, considering its humble ingredients and quick prep time, is outstanding. We rated it a 3, our highest Test Kitchens rating. And because of the canola oil and the avocado, it's a source of heart-healthy fats.

Prep: 25 minutes • Cook: 28 minutes

- 2 teaspoons canola oil
- 1 cup chopped onion
- 1 cup chopped red bell pepper
- 2 teaspoons chili powder
- 1 teaspoon ground cumin
- 1 teaspoon dried oregano
- 3 garlic cloves, minced
- 1 (4.5-ounce) can chopped green chiles, undrained
- ⅔ cup uncooked quick-cooking barley
- ¼ cup water
- 1 (15-ounce) can black beans, rinsed and drained
- 1 (14.5-ounce) can no-salt-added diced tomatoes, undrained
- 1 (14-ounce) can vegetable broth
- 3 tablespoons chopped fresh cilantro
- 6 tablespoons reduced-fat sour cream
- 6 lime wedges

Avocado Salsa (page 456)
Baked tortilla chips (optional)

1. Heat oil in a Dutch oven over medium-high heat. Add onion and bell pepper; sauté 3 minutes. Add chili powder and next 4 ingredients; cook 1 minute. Stir in barley and next 4 ingredients; bring to a boil. Cover, reduce heat, and simmer 20 minutes or until barley is tender. Stir in cilantro. Top with sour cream, lime wedges, and Avocado Salsa. Serve with baked tortilla chips, if desired. Yield: 6 servings (serving size: 1 cup chili, 1 tablespoon sour cream, 1 lime wedge, and about 2 tablespoons Avocado Salsa).

(Totals include Avocado Salsa) CALORIES 205 (22% from fat); FAT 4.9g (sat 1.5g, mono 2g, poly 1g); PROTEIN 7.2g; CARB 34.9g; FIBER 10g; CHOL 6mg; IRON 2.5mg; SODIUM 667mg; CALC 98mg

Twenty-Minute Chili

There's no need for long simmering with this quick-and-easy chili. It's full of flavor after only 10 minutes. Spooned over rice, it makes a satisfying one-dish meal.

Prep: 11 minutes • Cook: 17 minutes

- 1 (3½-ounce) bag boil-in-bag long-grain rice
- 1 tablespoon canola oil
- 1 cup chopped onion
- ¾ cup chopped green bell pepper
- ½ pound ground turkey breast
- 1 tablespoon chili powder
- 1 teaspoon Worcestershire sauce
- ½ teaspoon ground cumin
- ½ teaspoon dried oregano
- ¼ teaspoon salt
- ¼ teaspoon black pepper
- 1 (15-ounce) can kidney beans, rinsed and drained
- 1 (14.5-ounce) can Mexican-style stewed tomatoes with jalapeño peppers and spices, undrained
- 1 (5.5-ounce) can tomato juice
- ¼ cup (1 ounce) preshredded reduced-fat Cheddar cheese

1. Cook rice according to package directions, omitting salt and fat.

2. While rice cooks, heat oil in a large nonstick skillet over medium-high heat. Add onion, bell pepper, and turkey, and cook 3 minutes or until done, stirring to crumble. Stir in chili powder and next 8 ingredients; bring to a boil. Cover, reduce heat, and simmer 10 minutes. Place rice in bowls, and spoon chili over rice. Sprinkle with cheese. Yield: 4 servings (serving size: ½ cup rice, 1¼ cups chili, and 1 tablespoon cheese).

CALORIES 380 (26% from fat); FAT 10.5g (sat 2.6g, mono 3.9g, poly 2.4g); PROTEIN 21.4g; CARB 51g; FIBER 11.2g; CHOL 50mg; IRON 4mg; SODIUM 739mg; CALC 125mg

White Chicken Chili

Once you make the switch from red to white, this chicken chili just might become your standard.

Prep: 20 minutes • Cook: 42 minutes

Cooking spray
- 2 pounds skinless, boneless chicken breast, cut into bite-sized pieces
- 2 cups finely chopped onion
- 2 garlic cloves, minced
- 2 teaspoons ground cumin
- ½ teaspoon dried oregano
- 1 teaspoon ground coriander
- 2 (4.5-ounce) cans chopped green chiles, undrained
- 1 cup water
- 2 (15.5-ounce) cans cannellini beans, rinsed and drained (such as Goya)
- 1 (14-ounce) can fat-free, less-sodium chicken broth
- ½ teaspoon hot pepper sauce
- 1 cup (4 ounces) shredded Monterey Jack cheese
- ½ cup chopped fresh cilantro
- ½ cup chopped green onions

1. Heat a large nonstick skillet over medium-high heat. Coat pan with cooking spray. Add chicken to pan; cook 10 minutes or until chicken is browned, stirring frequently.

2. Heat a large Dutch oven over medium-high heat. Coat pan with cooking spray. Add onion to pan; sauté 6 minutes or until tender. Add garlic; sauté 2 minutes. Stir in cumin, oregano, and coriander; sauté 1 minute. Stir in chiles; reduce heat to low, partially cover, and cook 10 minutes. Add chicken, 1 cup water, beans, and broth; bring to a simmer. Cover and simmer 10 minutes. Stir in hot sauce. Ladle into bowls; sprinkle with cheese, cilantro, and green onions. Yield: 8 servings (serving size: 1 cup chili, 2 tablespoons cheese, 1 tablespoon cilantro, and 1 tablespoon onions).

CALORIES 233 (23% from fat); FAT 5.9g (sat 3.1g, mono 1.6g, poly 0.5g); PROTEIN 32.7g; CARB 11.7g; FIBER 3.4g; CHOL 78mg; IRON 3.2mg; SODIUM 694mg; CALC 180mg

Test Kitchen Tip: You can leave out the hot sauce if you prefer a less spicy dish. And you can use turkey instead of chicken.

All-American Chili

The key to this chili's exceptional flavor is the hot sausage and the jalapeño.

Prep: 20 minutes • Cook: 1 hour, 42 minutes

- 6 ounces hot turkey Italian sausage
- 2 cups chopped onion
- 1 cup chopped green bell pepper
- 8 garlic cloves, minced
- 1 pound ground sirloin
- 1 jalapeño pepper, chopped
- 3 tablespoons tomato paste
- 2 tablespoons chili powder
- 2 tablespoons brown sugar
- 1 tablespoon ground cumin
- 1 teaspoon dried oregano
- ½ teaspoon freshly ground black pepper
- 2 bay leaves
- 1¼ cups merlot or other fruity red wine
- 2 (28-ounce) cans whole tomatoes, undrained and coarsely chopped
- 2 (15-ounce) cans kidney beans, rinsed and drained
- ½ cup (2 ounces) shredded reduced-fat sharp Cheddar cheese

1. Heat a large Dutch oven over medium-high heat. Remove casings from sausage. Add sausage, onion, and next 4 ingredients to pan; cook 8 minutes or until sausage and beef are browned, stirring to crumble.
2. Add tomato paste and next 6 ingredients, and cook 1 minute, stirring constantly. Stir in wine, tomatoes, and kidney beans; bring to a boil. Cover, reduce heat, and simmer 1 hour, stirring occasionally.
3. Uncover and cook 30 minutes, stirring occasionally. Discard bay leaves. Sprinkle with cheese. Yield: 8 servings (serving size: 1¼ cups chili and 1 tablespoon cheese).

CALORIES 375 (29% from fat); FAT 12g (sat 4.6g, mono 4.1g, poly 1.1g); PROTEIN 28.9g; CARB 33.7g; FIBER 8.2g; CHOL 59mg; IRON 5mg; SODIUM 895mg; CALC 165mg

Real Texas Chili

In the Lone Star state, purists insist that chili has no beans.

Prep: 25 minutes • Cook: 2 hours, 55 minutes

- Cooking spray
- 2 pounds beef stew meat
- ½ teaspoon kosher salt
- ½ teaspoon cracked black pepper
- 3 cups chopped onion
- 1 tablespoon cumin seeds
- 3 tablespoons chopped jalapeño pepper
- 6 garlic cloves, minced
- 1 cup dry red wine
- ¼ cup white vinegar
- 2 tablespoons chili powder
- 2 tablespoons dried oregano
- 1 (14-ounce) can less-sodium beef broth
- 1 (12-ounce) can beer
- ½ cup chopped fresh cilantro
- ½ cup chopped onion
- ½ cup fat-free sour cream

1. Heat a Dutch oven over medium-high heat. Coat pan with cooking spray. Sprinkle beef with salt and pepper. Place half of beef in pan; cook 8 minutes. Remove from pan. Repeat with remaining beef.
2. Add 3 cups onion to pan; sauté 5 minutes. Add cumin, jalapeño, and garlic; sauté 1 minute. Add wine, scraping pan to loosen browned bits. Return beef to pan. Stir in vinegar and next 4 ingredients; bring to a boil. Cover, reduce heat, and simmer 1½ hours, stirring occasionally. Uncover and simmer 1 hour, stirring occasionally. Stir in cilantro. Ladle into bowls, and top with onion and sour cream. Yield: 8 servings (serving size: 1 cup chili, 1 tablespoon onion, and 1 tablespoon sour cream).

CALORIES 268 (30% from fat); FAT 9g (sat 3.3g, mono 3.7g, poly 0.6g); PROTEIN 25.1g; CARB 13.8g; FIBER 2.7g; CHOL 72mg; IRON 4.3mg; SODIUM 218mg; CALC 85mg

Venison Chili

If you don't have venison, use ground sirloin.

Prep: 15 minutes • Cook: 1 hour, 1 minute

- Cooking spray
- 1 pound ground venison
- 1 cup chopped sweet onion
- 1 cup chopped green bell pepper
- 4 garlic cloves, minced
- 1 jalapeño pepper, seeded and chopped
- 2 tablespoons chili powder
- ½ teaspoon ground cumin
- ½ teaspoon ground red pepper
- ½ teaspoon freshly ground black pepper
- 1 (14.5-ounce) can diced tomatoes, undrained
- 1 (14-ounce) can fat-free, less-sodium chicken broth
- 1 tablespoon tomato paste
- 1 (15-ounce) can red kidney beans, rinsed and drained

1. Heat a small Dutch oven over medium-high heat. Coat pan with cooking spray. Add venison; cook 3 minutes or until browned, stirring to crumble. Remove from pan with a slotted spoon. Cover; keep warm.
2. Reduce heat to medium. Add onion, bell pepper, garlic, and jalapeño to pan; sauté 10 minutes. Stir in chili powder and next 4 ingredients. Stir in venison, tomatoes, broth, and tomato paste; bring to a boil. Cover, reduce heat, and simmer 30 minutes. Add beans; cook, uncovered, 15 minutes. Yield: 4 servings (serving size: 1½ cups).

CALORIES 319 (12% from fat); FAT 4.1g (sat 1.2g, mono 0.9g, poly 1g); PROTEIN 35.8g; CARB 35.8g; FIBER 12.5g; CHOL 96mg; IRON 6.6mg; SODIUM 646mg; CALC 87mg

Seafood, Poultry & Meat Soups
Warm and comforting, each of these hearty soups is basically a meal in a bowl.

Sour and Spicy Shrimp Soup

The base of this Thai-inspired recipe is the flavorful broth, made by combining canned chicken broth, shrimp shells, chiles, and seasonings. After the mixture cooks for 30 minutes, it's strained, and the seasonings are discarded.

Prep: 30 minutes • Cook: 39 minutes

1½   pounds medium shrimp
2   tablespoons canola oil
6   dried japones or arbol chiles
3   (14-ounce) cans fat-free, less-sodium chicken broth
10   thinly sliced peeled fresh galangal pieces or 7 slices peeled fresh ginger, lightly crushed
6   kaffir lime leaves or 2½ teaspoons grated lime rind
4   bird chiles or serrano chiles, lightly crushed
4   cilantro stems, lightly crushed
2   stalks chopped peeled fresh lemongrass, lightly crushed
2   large shallots, peeled and halved
3   tablespoons Thai fish sauce
3   tablespoons fresh lime juice
½   cup cilantro leaves

1. Peel shrimp, reserving 6 shells; set shrimp aside. Heat oil in a large Dutch oven over medium-high heat. Add japones chiles and shrimp shells; sauté 3 minutes or until chiles are blackened. Add broth, and bring to a boil. Add galangal and next 5 ingredients. Cover, reduce heat to medium-low, and simmer 30 minutes.

2. Strain soup through a sieve over a bowl; discard solids. Return soup to pan. Increase heat to medium-high. Add shrimp and fish sauce; cook 2 minutes or until shrimp are done. Remove from heat; stir in lime juice. Sprinkle with cilantro leaves. Serve immediately. Yield: 7 servings (serving size: 1 cup).

CALORIES 135 (35% from fat); FAT 5.2g (sat 1g, mono 1.4g, poly 2.4g); PROTEIN 17.9g; CARB 6.6g; FIBER 0.2g; CHOL 111mg; IRON 2.1mg; SODIUM 1118mg; CALC 48mg

how to crush lemongrass

1. Look for stalks that have thick, firm, heavy bulbs and tightly bound green leaves. You should smell a citrus scent when you press your fingernail into the bulb. Remove the outer woody leaves to expose the white inner core.

2. Thinly chop or slice the core. Crush the slices with the back of a knife to release the aroma and oils.

Seafood Soup

A specialty of the Veracruz coast, this soup is similar to bouillabaisse. Seafood soup—in one variation or another, depending on the catch of the day—is found all across Mexico.

Prep: 45 minutes • Cook: 44 minutes
Other: 15 minutes

3   poblano chiles
1½   teaspoons aniseed
1½   teaspoons cumin seeds
2   tablespoons canola oil
1½   cups finely chopped onion
4   garlic cloves, minced
2   tablespoons sugar
½   teaspoon salt
4   (8-ounce) bottles clam juice
2   jalapeño peppers, seeded and finely chopped
1   (28-ounce) can fire-roasted crushed tomatoes, undrained (such as Muir Glen)
¼   cup fresh lime juice
2   (6-ounce) tilapia fillets, cut into 2-inch pieces
1   pound medium shrimp, peeled and deveined
1   pound mussels, scrubbed and debearded
¾   cup minced fresh cilantro
8   lime slices

1. Preheat broiler.
2. Cut chiles in half; discard seeds and membranes. Place halves, skin sides up, on a foil-lined baking sheet; flatten with

hand. Broil 5 minutes or until blackened. Place in a heavy-duty zip-top plastic bag, and seal. Let stand 15 minutes. Peel chiles; discard skins. Finely chop chiles.

3. Cook aniseed and cumin seeds in a saucepan over medium heat 1 minute or until toasted and fragrant. Place in a spice or coffee grinder, and process until finely ground.

4. Heat oil in a Dutch oven over medium heat. Add onion and garlic; cook 15 minutes, stirring occasionally. Add toasted ground spices; cook 1 minute. Add sugar and next 4 ingredients; bring to a simmer. Cook 10 minutes, stirring occasionally. Add chopped poblano chiles, lime juice, tilapia, shrimp, and mussels; bring to a simmer. Cook 5 minutes or until shrimp are done and mussels open; discard any unopened shells. Stir in cilantro; serve with lime slices. Yield: 8 servings (serving size: 1¾ cups).

CALORIES 253 (24% from fat); FAT 6.8g (sat 1.2g, mono 2.6g, poly 2g); PROTEIN 29.5g; CARB 19.8g; FIBER 3.4g; CHOL 126mg; IRON 6.1mg; SODIUM 806mg; CALC 124mg

---

menu

serves 8

Green salad with cumin-lime dressing*

Seafood Soup

Sourdough bread

*Combine 2 tablespoons fresh lime juice, 1 tablespoon olive oil, 1 tablespoon honey, ¼ teaspoon salt, ¼ teaspoon pepper, and ⅛ teaspoon ground cumin in a large bowl; stir. Add 10 cups gourmet salad greens; toss.

Shrimp and Crab Gumbo

To make this recipe quicker, we've called for peeled and deveined shrimp, which you can get in the seafood department of the grocery store. If you want to peel your own, you'll need to buy 1⅓ pounds of unpeeled shrimp. Cook the rice while the gumbo is simmering.

Prep: 15 minutes • Cook: 45 minutes

⅓ cup all-purpose flour
3 bacon slices, diced
2 cups finely chopped onion
1½ cups finely chopped green bell pepper (about 1 large)
4 celery stalks, thinly sliced
4 garlic cloves, minced
1 cup water
2 (14-ounce) cans fat-free, less-sodium chicken broth, divided
2 teaspoons salt-free Cajun seasoning
½ teaspoon salt
¼ teaspoon crushed red pepper
1 (16-ounce) bag frozen cut okra, thawed
1 pound peeled and deveined medium shrimp
2 (6-ounce) cans lump crabmeat (such as Chicken of the Sea), drained
3 cups hot cooked long-grain white rice
Hot pepper sauce (optional)

1. Lightly spoon flour into a dry measuring cup; level with a knife. Place flour in a small cast-iron skillet; cook over medium heat 10 to 15 minutes or until flour is brown, stirring constantly with a whisk. Remove from heat.

2. Cook bacon in a Dutch oven over medium-high heat 3 minutes. Add onion, bell pepper, celery, and garlic; sauté 10 minutes or until vegetables are tender and lightly browned. Add 1 cup water, and cook 1 minute, stirring constantly.

3. Combine toasted flour and 1 can chicken broth in a medium bowl, stirring well with a whisk. Gradually pour broth mixture into pan. Stir in 1 can chicken broth, Cajun seasoning, salt, crushed red pepper, and okra; bring to a boil. Cover, reduce heat, and simmer 15 minutes.

4. Add shrimp; cook 3 minutes or until shrimp are done. Gently stir in crabmeat. Remove from heat; serve gumbo over rice. Serve with hot pepper sauce, if desired. Yield: 6 servings (serving size: ½ cup rice and 1¼ cups gumbo).

CALORIES 464 (28% from fat); FAT 9g (sat 2.9g, mono 3.4g, poly 1.7g); PROTEIN 33.8g; CARB 60.2g; FIBER 5.4g; CHOL 160mg; IRON 5.5mg; SODIUM 955mg; CALC 192mg

Classic Makeover: Crab Soup

The original recipe—inspired by a rich crab soup from a restaurant in Savannah, Georgia—had a cup of butter and 2 cups of whipping cream. Some of the rich creaminess came from a classic butter-flour roux; we substituted flour browned in a skillet and saved more than 200 calories per serving. To maintain authenticity, we had to keep the soup's velvety texture, but without using 2 cups of whipping cream. Instead, we sautéed carrots and blended them with the other vegetables to add body as well as a subtle flavor that was compatible with the crab. We finished the soup with whole milk and a small amount of half-and-half. The lightened version is as creamy and filling as the original, and getting rid of the excess butter allows the succulent flavor of the crab to come through.

Before	After
• 543 calories	• 151 calories
• 41g fat	• 5g fat
• percentage of calories from fat 68%	• percentage of calories from fat 30%

Savannah-Style Crab Soup

This soup, like a gumbo, begins with a *roux*—a mixture of flour browned in fat—that gives the soup its rich flavor. For our lightened roux, you just brown the flour in a cast-iron skillet. If the flour starts to brown too quickly, remove the skillet from the heat, and stir the flour constantly until it cools.

Prep: 20 minutes • Cook: 40 minutes

½ cup all-purpose flour
 1 tablespoon butter
Cooking spray
 2 cups chopped carrot
 1 cup chopped celery
 1 cup chopped onion
¼ cup chopped red bell pepper
¼ cup chopped green bell pepper
 1 garlic clove, minced
 1 tablespoon Old Bay seasoning
¼ teaspoon salt
¼ teaspoon black pepper
¼ teaspoon dried thyme
 1 bay leaf
 4 cups clam juice
1½ cups whole milk
½ cup half-and-half
 1 pound lump crabmeat, shell pieces removed
⅓ cup dry sherry

1. Lightly spoon flour into a dry measuring cup; level with a knife. Place flour in a 9-inch cast-iron skillet; cook over medium heat 10 to 15 minutes or until brown, stirring constantly with a whisk. Remove browned flour from heat.
2. Melt butter in a Dutch oven coated with cooking spray over medium-high heat. Add carrot and next 5 ingredients, and sauté 5 minutes or until vegetables are tender. Add Old Bay seasoning, salt, black

pepper, dried thyme, and bay leaf; cook 1 minute. Sprinkle browned flour over vegetable mixture, and cook 1 minute, stirring frequently. Stir in clam juice, and bring to a boil. Reduce heat, and simmer 10 minutes or until slightly thick, stirring frequently.

3. Stir in milk and half-and-half; cook 4 minutes. Stir in crabmeat and sherry; cook 5 minutes or until soup is thoroughly heated. Discard bay leaf. Yield: 9 servings (serving size: 1 cup).

CALORIES 151 (30% from fat); FAT 5g (sat 2.6g, mono 1.4g, poly 0.4g); PROTEIN 13g; CARB 13.3g; FIBER 1.8g; CHOL 46mg; IRON 2.2mg; SODIUM 835mg; CALC 112mg

---

cast-iron skillets Because a
well-seasoned cast-iron skillet requires little or no oil for cooking, it's ideal for light recipes. It can rust if neglected, but if you take care of it using the following tips, a cast-iron skillet can last for generations.

- Remove acidic foods, such as tomatoes, from the skillet as soon as the dish has finished cooking.
- Scrub the skillet under hot water as soon as the food is removed, then place on a warm burner for a few minutes to dry. After drying, dribble some vegetable oil in the skillet and rub the oil all over the inside of the skillet with a paper towel. Let cool.
- Never put a cast-iron skillet in the dishwasher because it's not good for the cast iron to be left in a moist environment.

Sausage and Chicken Gumbo

There are many variations of this Creole specialty, but they typically begin with a roux (flour browned in fat) and are often thickened with okra. This quick-and-easy recipe takes only 27 minutes from start to finish.

Prep: 12 minutes • Cook: 15 minutes

1 (3½-ounce) bag boil-in-bag rice
2 tablespoons all-purpose flour
1 tablespoon canola oil
1 cup frozen chopped onion
1 cup frozen chopped green bell pepper
1 cup frozen cut okra
1 cup chopped celery
1 teaspoon bottled minced garlic
½ teaspoon dried thyme
¼ teaspoon ground red pepper
2 cups chopped roasted skinless, boneless chicken breast (about 2 breasts)
8 ounces turkey kielbasa, cut into 1-inch pieces
1 (14.5-ounce) can diced tomatoes with peppers and onion
1 (14-ounce) can fat-free, less-sodium chicken broth

1. Cook rice according to package directions, omitting salt and fat.
2. While rice cooks, combine flour and oil in a Dutch oven; sauté over medium-high heat 3 minutes. Add onion and next 6 ingredients; cook 3 minutes or until tender, stirring frequently.
3. Stir in chicken, kielbasa, tomatoes, and broth; cook 6 minutes or until heated. Serve over rice. Yield: 4 servings (serving size: ½ cup rice and 1½ cups gumbo).

CALORIES 387 (22% from fat); FAT 9.4g (sat 2.5g, mono 3g, poly 1.7g); PROTEIN 35.8g; CARB 39.5g; FIBER 3.8g; CHOL 74mg; IRON 3.2mg; SODIUM 1048mg; CALC 147mg

---

Chicken and Wild Rice Soup

Because wild rice is a natural match for smoked foods, the broth is infused with a little bacon to add a smoky flavor. Canned fat-free, less-sodium chicken broth can be used instead of Brown Chicken Stock, but the flavor will not be as rich.

Prep: 12 minutes • Cook: 1 hour, 38 minutes

6 cups water
2 cups uncooked wild rice
3 thick-cut bacon slices, chopped (about 3 ounces)
5 cups thinly sliced red onion (about 1 large)
¼ cup port or other sweet red wine
6 cups Brown Chicken Stock (page 470)
3 cups shredded roasted chicken breast (about 1 pound)
2 tablespoons red wine vinegar
½ teaspoon salt
½ teaspoon pepper

1. Bring 6 cups water to a boil in a medium saucepan, and stir in wild rice. Reduce heat; simmer, partially covered, 35 minutes or until rice is tender. Drain and set aside.
2. Place bacon in an 8-quart stockpot over medium heat. Cook 10 minutes or until bacon begins to crisp, stirring frequently. Add onion; increase heat to medium-high. Cook 10 minutes or until golden brown, stirring frequently. Add port, and simmer 8 minutes or until port evaporates. Add stock; simmer 5 minutes. Stir in rice, chicken, and remaining ingredients, and simmer 5 minutes or until thoroughly heated. Yield: 8 servings (serving size: 1¼ cups).

(Totals include Brown Chicken Stock) CALORIES 345 (24% from fat); FAT 9.3g (sat 3.1g, mono 3.8g, poly 1.6g); PROTEIN 27.5g; CARB 37g; FIBER 3.9g; CHOL 63mg; IRON 1.8mg; SODIUM 283mg; CALC 36mg

Tortilla Soup

It takes only 20 minutes to make home-made chicken stock in a pressure cooker.

**Prep: 35 minutes • Cook: 30 minutes
Other: 5 minutes**

8 (6-inch) corn tortillas

Quick Homemade Chicken Stock:

2 cups thinly sliced onion
¾ teaspoon salt
½ teaspoon coarsely ground black
     pepper
Dash of ground allspice
3 pounds chicken pieces, skinned
3 (14-ounce) cans fat-free, less-sodium
     chicken broth
2 garlic cloves, crushed
1 carrot, cut into 3 pieces
1 celery stalk, cut in half crosswise
1 bay leaf

Remaining ingredients:

¼ cup ground red chiles
1 tablespoon dried oregano
1 tablespoon ground cumin
1 cup diced peeled avocado
½ cup fat-free sour cream
2 tablespoons chopped fresh cilantro

1. Preheat oven to 350°.
2. Cut each tortilla in half; cut halves into ¼-inch strips. Arrange strips in a single layer on a baking sheet. Bake at 350° for 6 minutes, stirring after 3 minutes.
3. To prepare stock, combine onion and next 9 ingredients in a 6-quart pressure cooker. Close lid securely; bring to high pressure over high heat. Adjust heat to medium or level needed to maintain high pressure; cook 20 minutes. Remove from heat; place cooker under cold running water. Remove lid. Remove chicken from broth; cool slightly. Remove chicken

from bones; cut meat into bite-sized pieces. Discard bones.
4. Strain stock through a sieve into a bowl, and discard solids. Return stock to cooker; stir in ground chiles, oregano, cumin, and chicken; let stand 5 minutes.
5. Place tortilla strips in bowls; ladle soup into bowls. Top with avocado, sour cream, and cilantro. Yield: 8 servings (serving size: about 24 tortilla strips, 1⅓ cups soup, 2 tablespoons avocado, 1 tablespoon sour cream, and ¾ teaspoon cilantro).

CALORIES 226 (27% from fat); FAT 6.7g (sat 1.3g, mono 2.7g, poly 1.3g); PROTEIN 22.5g; CARB 20.1g; FIBER 3.6g; CHOL 59mg; IRON 2.9mg; SODIUM 630mg; CALC 105mg

Chicken Noodle Soup with Fresh Tarragon

Tarragon, with its licorice-like flavor, elevates this simple soup. Fresh marjoram, parsley, chives, or basil can stand in for tarragon. If you use canned broth, omit the salt.

Prep: 7 minutes • Cook: 37 minutes

⅓ pound uncooked vermicelli,
     broken into 2-inch pieces
8 cups Brown Chicken Stock (page 470)
     or canned fat-free, less-sodium
     chicken broth
1¼ teaspoons salt
½ teaspoon pepper
3 cups shredded cooked chicken
     breast (about 1 pound)
2 tablespoons fresh whole tarragon
     leaves

1. Cook pasta according to package directions, omitting salt and fat.
2. Place stock, salt, and pepper in a large stockpot; bring to a simmer. Add chicken

and tarragon; cook 2 minutes or until thoroughly heated. Add pasta. Yield: 4 servings (serving size: 2 cups).

(Totals include Brown Chicken Stock) CALORIES 373 (16% from fat); FAT 6.8g (sat 1.8g, mono 2.2g, poly 1.8g); PROTEIN 47.1g; CARB 28.6g; FIBER 1.6g; CHOL 119mg; IRON 2.8mg; SODIUM 851mg; CALC 38mg

Chicken-Ginseng Soup

The Chinese believe cold drinks are harmful to the digestive system, so soup is served not as a first course, but along with the meal in place of a cold beverage. Because it's more readily available than fresh ginseng, we tested the recipe with ginseng tea.

Prep: 20 minutes • Cook: 33 minutes

2 tablespoons canola oil
2 cups chopped onion
2 tablespoons diced peeled fresh
     ginger
6 garlic cloves, minced
1 pound skinless, boneless chicken
     breast, cut into 1-inch pieces
3 cups water
3 (14-ounce) cans fat-free,
     less-sodium chicken broth
3 cups fresh or frozen yellow corn
4 ginseng teabags or 2 sliced ginseng
     roots
¼ teaspoon salt
⅛ teaspoon white pepper

1. Heat oil in a Dutch oven over medium-high heat. Add onion, ginger, and garlic; sauté 2 minutes. Add chicken; sauté 4 minutes. Add 3 cups water and chicken broth; bring to a boil. Stir in corn and ginseng teabags; bring to a boil. Reduce heat; simmer 20 minutes. Remove and discard

teabags. Sprinkle with salt and pepper.
Yield: 8 servings (serving size: 1½ cups).

CALORIES 166 (29% from fat); FAT 5.3g (sat 0.7g, mono 2.7g,
poly 1.5g); PROTEIN 15.7g; CARB 15.7g; FIBER 1.8g; CHOL 31mg;
IRON 0.8mg; SODIUM 531mg; CALC 16mg

Rice Cake Soup

Store the rice cakes in an airtight container if
you're not serving immediately. If you're using
vacuum-packed rice cakes, don't presoak
them; cook for 10 minutes instead of 5.

Prep: 20 minutes • Cook: 32 minutes
Other: 10 minutes

1	nori (seaweed) sheet
1½	teaspoons dark sesame oil, divided
2	teaspoons canola oil
1	tablespoon minced peeled fresh ginger
4	garlic cloves, minced
1	pound skinless, boneless chicken breast, cut into bite-sized pieces
1	cup water
2	teaspoons low-sodium soy sauce
2	(14-ounce) cans fat-free, less-sodium chicken broth
2½	cups frozen sliced rice cakes (rice ovaletts)
1	large egg, lightly beaten
¼	cup thinly sliced green onions
2½	teaspoons sesame seeds, toasted

1. Preheat broiler.
2. Rub 1 side of nori with ½ teaspoon
sesame oil; broil, oiled side up, 30 seconds.
Turn nori; broil 30 seconds or until
browned (or a dark green color). Crumble
nori; set aside.
3. Heat canola oil in a large Dutch
oven over medium-high heat. Add ginger

and garlic, and stir-fry 30 seconds. Add
chicken, and stir-fry 4 minutes. Add 1 cup
water, soy sauce, and broth, and bring to
a boil. Cover, reduce heat, and simmer
15 minutes.
4. Soak rice cake slices in cold water to
cover 10 minutes; drain. Add to broth
mixture. Increase heat to medium; cook,
uncovered, 5 minutes or until rice cake
slices are tender.
5. Reduce heat to low. Slowly drizzle egg
into soup, stirring constantly. Cook 1
minute, stirring constantly. Stir in onions
and 1 teaspoon sesame oil. Ladle into
bowls, and sprinkle with nori and sesame
seeds. Yield: 5 servings (serving size: about

1½ cups soup, about 1 tablespoon nori,
and ½ teaspoon sesame seeds).

CALORIES 308 (19% from fat); FAT 6.6g (sat 1g, mono 2.4g,
poly 1.6g); PROTEIN 27.8g; CARB 32.4g; FIBER 1.3g; CHOL 95mg;
IRON 2.2mg; SODIUM 458mg; CALC 25mg

rice cakes You'll find sliced rice
cakes either in the freezer case or
vacuum-packed on the shelves of your
local Asian market. (They're sometimes
labeled "rice ovaletts.") Sliced rice
cakes are about the size and shape of
sliced water chestnuts. When thawed
and tossed into soup, they become
soft but retain a pleasant resilience.

Wonton Soup

Wonton Soup

To add a little spice, sprinkle with crushed red pepper. If you use canned chicken broth instead of White Chicken Stock, omit the salt.

Prep: 30 minutes • Cook: 27 minutes
Other: 20 minutes

    4   cups spinach leaves
    ¾   cup cooked dark-meat chicken
        (about ½ pound skinless, boneless
        thighs)
    1   tablespoon low-sodium soy sauce
    ¾   teaspoon pepper
    ¾   teaspoon chopped peeled fresh ginger
    ¾   teaspoon dark sesame oil
    2   garlic cloves, chopped
    1   teaspoon salt, divided
   36   wonton wrappers
    1   large egg white, lightly beaten
    2   teaspoons cornstarch
    8   cups White Chicken Stock (page 471)
        or fat-free, less-sodium chicken broth
   Crushed red pepper (optional)

1. Place first 7 ingredients in a food processor; add ½ teaspoon salt. Pulse until coarsely chopped.

2. Working with 1 wonton wrapper at a time (cover remaining wrappers with a damp towel to prevent drying), spoon about 1 teaspoon chicken mixture into center of wrapper. Moisten edges of wrapper with egg white; bring 2 opposite corners to center, pinching points to seal. Bring remaining 2 corners to center, pinching points to seal. Pinch 4 edges together to seal. Place wonton on a baking sheet sprinkled with cornstarch. Refrigerate wontons 20 minutes.
3. Bring stock to a simmer over medium heat; add ½ teaspoon salt. Add wontons; cook 4 minutes or until wontons float to top, stirring gently. Sprinkle with crushed red pepper, if desired. Yield: 6 servings (serving size: 1⅓ cups broth and 6 wontons).

(Totals include White Chicken Stock) CALORIES 253 (18% from fat); FAT 5g (sat 1.2g, mono 1.6g, poly 1.4g); PROTEIN 18g; CARB 32.7g; FIBER 1.8g; CHOL 76mg; IRON 3.2mg; SODIUM 852mg; CALC 58mg

Test Kitchen Tip: To freeze wontons, place them uncooked on a baking sheet. Freeze, then store in a zip-top plastic bag up to two weeks. Add them, still frozen, to the simmering broth.

Coconut Soup with Chicken

Like many Thai dishes, this soup rewards you at the first spoonful with its sensual and aromatic ingredients.

Prep: 20 minutes • Cook: 57 minutes
Other: 15 minutes

    4   cups water
    1   (14-ounce) can coconut milk
    ½   cup sliced peeled fresh lemongrass,
        slightly crushed
   15   pieces thinly sliced peeled fresh
        ginger, slightly crushed
    4   serrano chiles, slightly crushed
    5   kaffir lime leaves, slightly torn, or
        1½ teaspoons grated lime rind
   1¾   pounds chicken breast quarters,
        skinned
    ¾   pound chicken thigh quarters,
        skinned
    ¼   cup Thai fish sauce
    3   tablespoons fresh lime juice
    6   tablespoons chopped fresh cilantro

1. Combine water and coconut milk in a Dutch oven; bring to a boil over medium heat. Stir in lemongrass, ginger, chiles, and lime leaves; bring to a boil. Add chicken; cover, reduce heat, and simmer 50 minutes or until chicken is done.
2. Remove chicken from broth. Place chicken in a bowl; chill 15 minutes. Strain broth through a colander into a bowl; discard solids. Return broth to pan.
3. Remove chicken from bones; cut meat into bite-sized pieces. Discard bones. Return chicken to pan. Stir in fish sauce; cook 1 minute over medium heat. Stir in lime juice. Sprinkle with cilantro. Yield: 6 servings (serving size: 1 cup).

CALORIES 298 (51% from fat); FAT 17g (sat 13.3g, mono 1.4g, poly 0.9g); PROTEIN 33.3g; CARB 3.2g; FIBER 0.2g; CHOL 93mg; IRON 3.7mg; SODIUM 1038mg; CALC 38mg

Spicy Mulligatawny

The name of this highly seasoned Indian soup means "pepper water." It gets quite a kick from the combination of curry powder, ground ginger, and crushed red pepper, but you can halve those ingredients if you don't like spicy foods.

Prep: 15 minutes • Cook: 24 minutes

1	tablespoon canola oil, divided
½	pound skinless, boneless chicken breast, cut into bite-sized pieces
1	cup chopped peeled Gala or Braeburn apple
¾	cup chopped onion
½	cup chopped carrot
½	cup chopped celery
½	cup chopped green bell pepper
2	tablespoons all-purpose flour
1	tablespoon curry powder
1	teaspoon ground ginger
½	teaspoon crushed red pepper
¼	teaspoon salt
2	(14-ounce) cans fat-free, less-sodium chicken broth
⅓	cup mango chutney
¼	cup tomato paste
	Chopped fresh parsley (optional)

1. Heat 1 teaspoon oil in a Dutch oven over medium-high heat. Add chicken; sauté 3 minutes. Remove from pan; set aside.

2. Heat 2 teaspoons oil in pan. Add apple and next 4 ingredients; sauté 5 minutes. Stir in flour and next 4 ingredients; cook 1 minute. Stir in broth, chutney, and tomato paste; bring to a boil.

3. Reduce heat; simmer 8 minutes. Return chicken to pan; cook 2 minutes or until mixture is thoroughly heated. Sprinkle with parsley, if desired. Yield: 4 servings (serving size: 1¼ cups).

CALORIES 242 (20% from fat); FAT 5.4g (sat 0.7g, mono 2.6g, poly 1.5g); PROTEIN 16.6g; CARB 33g; FIBER 3.3g; CHOL 31mg; IRON 2mg; SODIUM 1238mg; CALC 41mg

Test Kitchen Tip: Slightly frozen chicken cuts quickly and easily. Place raw chicken in the freezer 20 minutes before cutting it into bite-sized pieces.

Spring Posole

This hearty soup has its roots in Mexico's Pacific Coast region; it's often served at Christmastime. Our spring version contains spinach plus the traditional garnishes.

Prep: 30 minutes • Cook: 32 minutes

2	teaspoons olive oil
1	cup chopped onion
2	teaspoons ground cumin
1½	teaspoons ground coriander
¼	teaspoon salt
1	chipotle chile, canned in adobo sauce, drained and minced
2½	cups diced plum tomato
3	garlic cloves, minced
2	(15.5-ounce) cans golden hominy, rinsed and drained
1	(32-ounce) carton fat-free, less-sodium chicken broth
1	(1-pound) pork tenderloin, trimmed
6	cups chopped spinach
1	cup cilantro sprigs
1½	cups thinly sliced romaine lettuce
¾	cup thinly sliced radishes
¾	cup (3 ounces) shredded Manchego cheese or Monterey Jack cheese
¼	cup thinly sliced green onions

1. Heat olive oil in a Dutch oven over medium heat. Add onion and next 4 ingredients; cook 4 minutes, stirring frequently. Stir in tomato, garlic, hominy, and broth. Reduce heat, and simmer 20 minutes.

2. Cut pork into bite-sized pieces. Add pork, spinach, and cilantro to pan. Cook 7 minutes or until pork is done. Ladle soup into bowls; top evenly with lettuce, radishes, cheese, and green onions. Yield: 6 servings (serving size: 1½ cups).

CALORIES 287 (28% from fat); FAT 9g (sat 3.7g, mono 3.5g, poly 0.9g); PROTEIN 26g; CARB 25.9g; FIBER 6.8g; CHOL 60mg; IRON 5mg; SODIUM 814mg; CALC 223mg

Meatball Soup

Meatballs are not just a part of Italian cuisine. In Mexico, *albóndigas* (meatballs) are sometimes made with rice used as the binding agent, as they are in this vegetable-packed soup.

Prep: 25 minutes • Cook: 48 minutes

  2 teaspoons coriander seeds
1½ teaspoons cumin seeds
  4 whole cloves
  1 (3-inch) cinnamon stick, broken
 ½ cup uncooked long-grain white rice
  2 tablespoons grated fresh onion
 ½ teaspoon salt
  1 pound ground round
  1 large egg white, lightly beaten
  1 garlic clove, minced
Cooking spray
  3 cups chopped green cabbage
  2 cups chopped onion
  1 cup sliced carrot
 ½ cup chopped celery
  1 tablespoon chili powder
1½ tablespoons drained chopped chipotle chile in adobo sauce
 ¼ teaspoon salt
  2 (14-ounce) cans fat-free, less-sodium chicken broth
  1 (14.5-ounce) can fire-roasted whole tomatoes, undrained and chopped (such as Muir Glen)
1½ cups cubed peeled baking potato

1. Cook coriander seeds and cumin seeds in a large Dutch oven over medium heat 1 minute or until toasted and fragrant. Place toasted spices, cloves, and cinnamon in a spice or coffee grinder; process until finely ground.

2. Combine 2 teaspoons cinnamon mixture, rice, and next 5 ingredients in a large bowl; set remaining cinnamon mixture aside. Shape beef mixture into 24 (1-inch) meatballs.

3. Heat pan over medium heat. Coat pan with cooking spray. Add cabbage, chopped onion, carrot, and celery to pan; cook 8 minutes, stirring frequently. Add remaining cinnamon mixture, chili powder, and chipotle; cook 1 minute, stirring constantly. Stir in ¼ teaspoon salt, broth, and tomatoes; bring to a boil. Reduce heat to simmer. Add meatballs; cover and cook 15 minutes. Add potato; cook, uncovered, over medium heat 20 minutes or until potato is tender. Yield: 6 servings (serving size: 1⅔ cups).

CALORIES 330 (34% from fat); FAT 12.4g (sat 4.6g, mono 5.2g, poly 0.6g); PROTEIN 20.6g; CARB 34.5g; FIBER 4.9g; CHOL 51mg; IRON 4mg; SODIUM 780mg; CALC 97mg

French Onion Soup with Beef and Barley

Nutty-tasting barley and tender sirloin steak elevate French onion soup to a one-dish meal.

Prep: 25 minutes • Cook: 1 hour, 18 minutes
Other: 30 minutes

  1   cup boiling water
½   ounce dried shiitake mushrooms
  1   tablespoon dark sesame oil, divided
  2   medium onions, each cut into
         8 wedges (about 4 cups)
½   cup chopped shallots or onion
  2   teaspoons chopped peeled fresh
         ginger
  4   garlic cloves, minced
  3   cups sliced button mushrooms
  1   teaspoon brown sugar
  1   (12-ounce) lean boneless sirloin
         steak, cut into 2-inch strips
  4   cups water
⅔   cup uncooked pearl barley
¼   cup dry sherry
  3   tablespoons low-sodium soy sauce
  1   (10½-ounce) can beef consommé
 12   (¼-inch-thick) slices diagonally cut
         French bread baguette
¾   cup (3 ounces) shredded Gruyère or
         Swiss cheese

1. Combine boiling water and shiitakes in a bowl. Cover; let stand 30 minutes. Drain shiitakes in a colander over a bowl, reserving liquid. Slice shiitakes, discarding stems.
2. Heat 2 teaspoons oil in a large Dutch oven over medium-high heat. Add onion, shallots, ginger, and garlic; sauté 10 minutes or until lightly browned. Add shiitakes, button mushrooms, sugar, and beef. Sauté 10 minutes, scraping pan to loosen browned bits. Add reserved mushroom liquid, 4 cups water, and next 4 ingredients; bring to a boil. Cover, reduce heat, and simmer 50 minutes or until barley is tender. Stir in 1 teaspoon sesame oil.
3. Preheat broiler.
4. Ladle soup into ovenproof soup bowls; top with bread slices and cheese. Broil 1 minute or until cheese melts. Serve immediately. Yield: 6 servings (serving size: 1½ cups soup, 2 bread slices, and 2 tablespoons cheese).

CALORIES 351 (27% from fat); FAT 10.7g (sat 4.3g, mono 3.8g, poly 1.7g); PROTEIN 24.6g; CARB 40g; FIBER 6.2g; CHOL 50mg; IRON 3.7mg; SODIUM 676mg; CALC 196mg

Beef and Vegetable Soup

In this authentic Mexican soup, the distinctive flavor comes from achiote paste. When handling the paste, wear gloves to avoid staining your hands.

Prep: 30 minutes • Cook: 1 hour, 21 minutes

  2   tablespoons achiote paste
  2   teaspoons chili powder
1½   teaspoons salt
  1   teaspoon ground cumin
  1   teaspoon olive oil
¼   teaspoon ground red pepper
  4   garlic cloves, minced
  2   pounds boneless sirloin steak,
         trimmed and cut into 1-inch
         pieces
  1   tablespoon olive oil
  4   cups chopped onion
  2   (14-ounce) cans fat-free,
         less-sodium chicken broth
  1   (14.5-ounce) can fire-roasted diced
         tomatoes with green chiles,
         undrained (such as Muir Glen)
  4   cups cubed peeled baking potato
  3   cups cubed peeled chayote squash
  2   cups (½-inch-thick) slices carrot
  1   tablespoon white wine vinegar

1. Combine first 7 ingredients, stirring with a fork until mixture resembles coarse meal; sprinkle 1½ tablespoons achiote mixture evenly over beef, tossing to coat. Set remaining achiote mixture aside.
2. Heat oil in a Dutch oven over medium-high heat. Add beef mixture; cook 2 minutes, browning on all sides. Remove beef from pan. Add onion to pan; sauté 3 minutes. Add remaining achiote mixture; cook 2 minutes, stirring frequently. Return beef mixture to pan. Stir in broth and tomatoes; bring to a boil. Cover, reduce heat, and simmer 35 minutes. Add potato, chayote, and carrot; cover and simmer 35 minutes or until potato is tender. Remove from heat. Stir in vinegar. Yield: 10 servings (serving size: 1½ cups).

CALORIES 243 (25% from fat); FAT 6.8g (sat 2.1g, mono 3.3g, poly 0.5g); PROTEIN 21.1g; CARB 24.9g; FIBER 4.1g; CHOL 50mg; IRON 2.9mg; SODIUM 607mg; CALC 51mg

Mexican kitchen Look for these Mexican ingredients in your local supermarket or a Latin market.

Achiote paste: often used in Yucatan and Oaxacan cuisine; made from grinding earthy-flavored, red-colored annatto seeds into a paste.

Chayote: gourdlike squash that looks like a large green pear. It's also known as a mirliton in Louisiana.

Cumin: an aromatic spice with a pungent, nutty flavor used widely in Mexican cuisine. It's typically ground, but you can also buy cumin seeds to toast and grind.

Beef-Barley Pho

Beef and barley soup is a staple American comfort food; *pho*—beef and rice noodle soup—is the Vietnamese equivalent. Barley lends an interesting twist, as well as heartiness, to this anise-flavored soup.

Prep: 25 minutes • Cook: 1 hour, 26 minutes

  2 cups sliced onion
  4 (⅛-inch) slices unpeeled fresh ginger
  5 cups less-sodium beef broth
  2 tablespoons sugar
  2 tablespoons fish sauce
  5 star anise
  3 whole cloves
  4 cups water
  ½ cup uncooked pearl barley
Cooking spray
  3 (4-ounce) beef tenderloin steaks, trimmed
  1 cup fresh bean sprouts
  ½ cup vertically sliced onion
  ½ cup chopped green onions
 12 fresh basil leaves
  4 lime wedges
Chopped seeded serrano chiles (optional)

1. Combine 2 cups onion and ginger in a heavy skillet over high heat. Cook 4 minutes or until charred, stirring frequently. Remove from heat. Combine onion mixture, broth, and next 4 ingredients in a large saucepan. Bring to a boil; cover, reduce heat, and simmer 30 minutes. Strain broth mixture through a sieve over a large bowl, reserving liquid; discard solids. Return broth to pan; set aside.

2. Bring 4 cups water to a boil in a large saucepan. Add barley. Cover, reduce heat, and simmer 35 minutes or until done. Drain.

3. Heat a large nonstick skillet over medium-high heat. Coat pan with cooking spray. Add steaks; cook 4 minutes on each side or until desired degree of doneness. Remove from pan; cut steaks diagonally across grain into thin slices.

4. Bring broth to a boil. Spoon barley into bowls, and ladle boiling broth over barley in each bowl. Top with beef, bean sprouts, sliced onion, green onions, and basil. Serve with lime wedges and chiles, if desired. Yield: 4 servings (serving size: ½ cup barley, ⅔ cup boiling broth, about 3 ounces beef, ¼ cup sprouts, 2 tablespoons sliced onion, 2 tablespoons green onions, 3 basil leaves, and 1 lime wedge).

CALORIES 315 (23% from fat); FAT 8.2g (sat 2.9g, mono 3.2g, poly 0.8g); PROTEIN 28g; CARB 31.2g; FIBER 5.2g; CHOL 54mg; IRON 3.9mg; SODIUM 787mg; CALC 32mg

Test Kitchen Tip: Charring the onion and ginger in a dry skillet gives the broth a deep flavor.

> *menu*
> *serves 4*
>
> *Beef-Barley Pho*
> *Sweet-and-Sour Slaw (page 405)*
> *Green Tea Granita (page 188)*

Stews

What separates a soup from a stew? The long simmering time in a tightly covered pot with a small amount of liquid. The result is flavorful vegetables, fall-apart tender meat, and a delicious melding of flavors.

Summer Vegetable Stew with Basil Puree

Chunks of garden-fresh veggies are simmered together for exceptional flavor, then topped with a pesto-like basil puree.

Prep: 30 minutes • Cook: 57 minutes

Basil Puree:

  1 cup basil leaves
  1 garlic clove
  3 tablespoons water
  2 tablespoons olive oil
 ⅛ teaspoon salt

Vegetables:

  1 tablespoon olive oil
  2 bay leaves
  1 onion, cut into ¼-inch-thick wedges
  6 garlic cloves, halved
  2 thyme sprigs
1½ cups (2-inch-thick) sliced carrot
  1 pound small red potatoes, halved
 ½ teaspoon salt
 ½ teaspoon black pepper
  3 cups (1-inch) cubed yellow squash (about ¾ pound)
  1 cup yellow bell pepper strips
 ½ pound green beans, trimmed and cut into 3-inch pieces
  2 tomatoes, peeled and cut into 1-inch pieces
  2 tablespoons (½ ounce) grated fresh Parmesan cheese

1. To prepare basil puree, place basil and 1 garlic clove in a blender; process until smooth. Add 3 tablespoons water, 2 tablespoons oil, and ⅛ teaspoon salt; process until blended. Set aside.

2. To prepare vegetables, heat 1 tablespoon oil in a large Dutch oven over low heat. Add bay leaves; cook 1 minute. Add onion, 6 garlic cloves, and thyme; cover and cook 10 minutes. Add carrot, potatoes, ½ teaspoon salt, and black pepper; cover and cook 20 minutes. Add squash, yellow bell pepper, and green beans; cover and cook 15 minutes. Add tomatoes; cover and cook 10 minutes. Discard bay leaves and thyme. Ladle stew into bowls; drizzle with basil puree, and sprinkle with Parmesan. Yield: 5 servings (serving size: 2 cups stew, about 1 tablespoon basil puree, and about 1 teaspoon cheese).

CALORIES 240 (36% from fat); FAT 9.7g (sat 1.7g, mono 6.3g, poly 1.1g); PROTEIN 6.8g; CARB 35.4g; FIBER 7.5g; CHOL 2mg; IRON 3.3mg; SODIUM 373mg; CALC 123mg

Roasted-Root Vegetable Stew

Root vegetables—carrots, beets, turnips, parsnips, and shallots—add an earthy flavor to this hearty meatless stew. Use large shallots; they're easier to peel.

Prep: 25 minutes • Cook: 1 hour, 6 minutes

  2 cups (1-inch-thick) slices carrot
  2 cups (1-inch) cubed peeled beets
  1 cup (1-inch) cubed peeled turnips
  ¾ cup (1-inch-thick) slices parsnip
 12 large shallots, peeled (about 8 ounces)
  8 large garlic cloves, peeled
  1 tablespoon olive oil
  2 tablespoons all-purpose flour
  2 teaspoons minced peeled fresh ginger
1½ teaspoons chopped fresh sage
  3 cups Vegetable Stock (page 472), vegetable broth, or water
  ¾ teaspoon salt
  ½ teaspoon pepper
  2 tablespoons chopped fresh flat-leaf parsley
  4 teaspoons crème fraîche or light sour cream

1. Preheat oven to 450°.
2. Combine first 7 ingredients in a shallow roasting pan. Bake at 450° for 30 minutes.
3. Place vegetable mixture in a Dutch oven over medium heat. Add flour, ginger, and sage; cook 3 minutes. Add Vegetable Stock, and bring to a boil. Cover, reduce heat, and simmer 30 minutes. Stir in salt and pepper. Ladle stew into bowls. Sprinkle with parsley, and top with crème fraîche. Yield: 4 servings (serving size: about 1⅓ cups stew, 1½ teaspoons parsley, and 1 teaspoon crème fraîche).

(Totals include Vegetable Stock) CALORIES 189 (24% from fat); FAT 5.1g (sat 1.4g, mono 2.9g, poly 0.5g); PROTEIN 4.7g; CARB 33.7g; FIBER 6.9g; CHOL 3mg; IRON 2.2mg; SODIUM 540mg; CALC 88mg

Lentil Stew with Ham and Greens

Lentil Stew with Ham and Greens

Lentils generally cook in 30 minutes or less and don't require the soaking time necessary for dried beans. Serve this one-dish meal with a rustic bread.

Prep: 15 minutes • Cook: 57 minutes

1½ tablespoons olive oil
  1 cup chopped onion
  3 garlic cloves, minced
  5 cups fat-free, less-sodium chicken broth
  1 cup dried lentils
  ½ cup chopped carrot
  2 bay leaves
  3 cups chopped Swiss chard, collard greens, or spinach
1½ cups chopped baking potato
  1 cup chopped smoked ham
  1 (14.5-ounce) can diced tomatoes, drained
  1 teaspoon dried basil
  ½ teaspoon dried thyme
  ½ teaspoon black pepper
  3 tablespoons chopped fresh parsley

1. Heat oil in a Dutch oven over medium-high heat. Add onion and garlic; sauté 5 minutes. Add broth, lentils, carrot, and bay leaves; bring to a boil. Partially cover, reduce heat, and simmer 20 minutes. Add Swiss chard, potato, and ham; bring to a boil. Reduce heat; simmer 15 minutes or until potato is tender. Stir in tomatoes, basil, thyme, and pepper; simmer 10 minutes. Discard bay leaves. Sprinkle with parsley. Yield: 5 servings (serving size: about 1½ cups).

CALORIES 320 (24% from fat); FAT 8.6g (sat 2g, mono 5g, poly 1.1g); PROTEIN 20.4g; CARB 41.7g; FIBER 15.1g; CHOL 12mg; IRON 5.6mg; SODIUM 943mg; CALC 84mg

WINE NOTE: Riesling's tingling acidity is a terrific counterpoint to the sweetness and smokiness of the ham and the earthiness of the lentils. A riesling from Alsace, France, (try Trimbach or Hugel) would be lovely. Closer to home is Trefethen's Dry Riesling from the Napa Valley.

Bouillabaisse

The traditional seafood stew of Provence, bouillabaisse is typically made with tomatoes, onions, wine, olive oil, garlic, herbs, fish, and shellfish. Soak up the delicious broth with a slice of crusty French bread.

Prep: 45 minutes • Cook: 1 hour, 20 minutes

8	cups water
3	(1¼-pound) whole lobsters
1	tablespoon olive oil
2	cups chopped onion
2	cups coarsely chopped celery
1½	cups coarsely chopped carrot
4	garlic cloves, minced
4	cups coarsely chopped tomato (about 1½ pounds)
½	teaspoon salt
½	teaspoon saffron threads, crushed
½	teaspoon dried thyme
¼	teaspoon pepper
2	bay leaves
1	pound skinned halibut fillets or other lean white fish fillets, cut into 2-inch pieces
22	small clams, scrubbed (about 1¾ pounds)
30	small mussels, scrubbed and debearded (about 1½ pounds)
½	pound medium shrimp, peeled and deveined

1. Bring 8 cups water to a boil in an 8-quart stockpot. Plunge lobsters headfirst into water. Return to a boil; cover, reduce heat, and simmer 12 minutes. Remove lobsters from water (do not drain); cool. Remove meat from cooked lobster tails; cut into 1-inch pieces, reserving shells. Cover and refrigerate pieces and claws.

2. Return reserved shells to water; bring to a boil. Reduce heat, and simmer 5 minutes. Drain through a colander over a large bowl, reserving broth; discard shells. Wipe pan dry with a paper towel.

3. Heat oil in pan over medium-high heat. Add onion, celery, carrot, and garlic; sauté 5 minutes. Add reserved broth, tomato, and next 5 ingredients; bring to a boil. Reduce heat, and simmer 15 minutes; discard bay leaves. Bring to a boil; add fish, reduce heat, and simmer 4 minutes. Add clams; cook 1 minute. Add mussels; cook 2 minutes. Add shrimp; cook 3 minutes. Bring to a boil. Add reserved lobster meat; cook until thoroughly heated. Discard unopened shells. Yield: 6 servings (serving size: about 3 cups).

CALORIES 332 (19% from fat); FAT 7.1g (sat 1g, mono 2.6g, poly 1.7g); PROTEIN 48.2g; CARB 18.5g; FIBER 4.1g; CHOL 146mg; IRON 8.1mg; SODIUM 701mg; CALC 162mg

Test Kitchen Tip: While 8 cups of water doesn't seem like much, it's enough to steam the lobsters. If clams are unavailable, substitute an equal weight of mussels.

Spring Seafood Stew
(pictured on page 469)

Poaching is an excellent way to cook seafood, since the cooking liquid makes a tasty base for sauce. This recipe features a French technique called *monter au beurre* (to mount with butter), whereby chilled butter is whisked into the cooking liquid at the last minute to ensure a satiny sauce.

Prep: 30 minutes • Cook: 21 minutes

1	teaspoon olive oil

Cooking spray

1	cup thinly sliced leek (about 1 large)
3	garlic cloves, minced
1	cup dry white wine
1	(14-ounce) can fat-free, less-sodium chicken broth
¾	pound medium shrimp, peeled and deveined
¾	pound large sea scallops, cut in half horizontally
2	tablespoons chilled butter, cut into small pieces
1½	cups chopped plum tomato
1	tablespoon minced fresh tarragon
1	teaspoon grated lemon rind
½	teaspoon salt
½	teaspoon black pepper
¼	teaspoon ground red pepper

1. Heat oil in a large Dutch oven coated with cooking spray over medium heat. Add leek and garlic; cook 4 minutes or until tender, stirring occasionally. Add wine and broth; bring to a simmer. Stir in shrimp and scallops; bring to a boil. Reduce heat; simmer 3 minutes or until shrimp and scallops are done.
2. Remove shrimp and scallops from pan with a slotted spoon; keep warm. Bring broth mixture to a boil; cook 4 minutes. Reduce heat to low. Add butter, stirring constantly with a whisk. Stir in tomato and remaining ingredients.
3. Place shrimp and scallops in bowls; add broth. Yield: 4 servings (serving size: 3 ounces shrimp, 3 ounces scallops, and ¾ cup broth).

CALORIES 287 (29% from fat); FAT 9.3g (sat 4.1g, mono 2.8g, poly 1.2g); PROTEIN 34g; CARB 10.8g; FIBER 1.3g; CHOL 173mg; IRON 3.3mg; SODIUM 817mg; CALC 93mg

Pork Stew with Pumpkin

Use butternut or acorn squash when pumpkin is out of season. Cook the noodles during the last 15 minutes of simmering time for the pork-pumpkin mixture.

Prep: 20 minutes • Cook: 1 hour, 43 minutes

1	tablespoon olive oil
1½	pounds boneless pork loin, trimmed and cut into ½-inch pieces
1	cup finely chopped onion
1	cup finely chopped red bell pepper
¾	cup finely chopped celery
2	teaspoons dried rubbed sage
1	teaspoon salt
½	teaspoon freshly ground black pepper
1	(28-ounce) can diced tomatoes, undrained
1	(14-ounce) can fat-free, less-sodium chicken broth
4	cups (½-inch) cubed peeled fresh pumpkin
1	(10-ounce) package frozen whole-kernel corn
2	teaspoons grated orange rind
4½	cups hot cooked egg noodles (about 3 cups uncooked)
6	tablespoons chopped fresh flat-leaf parsley

1. Heat oil in a large Dutch oven over high heat. Add pork; cook 4 minutes or until browned, stirring occasionally. Add onion, bell pepper, and celery; cook 2 minutes, stirring occasionally. Stir in sage, salt, black pepper, tomatoes, and broth; bring to a boil. Cover, reduce heat, and simmer 30 minutes. Stir in pumpkin and corn; bring to a boil. Cover, reduce heat, and simmer 1 hour or until pumpkin is tender. Stir in rind. Serve over noodles; sprinkle with parsley. Yield: 6 servings (serving size: ¾ cup noodles, 2 cups stew, and 1 tablespoon parsley).

CALORIES 463 (23% from fat); FAT 11.8g (sat 3.4g, mono 5.3g, poly 1.7g); PROTEIN 35.4g; CARB 56.2g; FIBER 5.7g; CHOL 108mg; IRON 5mg; SODIUM 715mg; CALC 122mg

Lamb Stew with Hazelnut Butter and Dates

Ground hazelnuts flavor and thicken this stew. Serve over couscous or rice.

Prep: 25 minutes • Cook: 1 hour, 56 minutes

⅔	cup coarsely chopped hazelnuts, toasted

Cooking spray

1½	pounds lean lamb stew meat, cubed
2½	cups chopped onion
¾	teaspoon salt
¼	teaspoon ground cinnamon
¼	teaspoon ground allspice
¼	teaspoon crushed red pepper
3	garlic cloves, crushed
2	(14-ounce) cans fat-free, less-sodium chicken broth
2½	cups (½-inch) cubed peeled turnips (about 1 pound)
2½	cups small red potatoes, halved (about 1 pound)
1½	cups baby carrots, peeled
½	cup whole pitted dates, chopped
2	cups water
1½	cups frozen green peas

1. Place hazelnuts in a food processor; process until smooth (about 2½ minutes), scraping sides of bowl once.

2. Heat a large Dutch oven over high heat. Coat pan with cooking spray. Add lamb; cook 5 minutes, browning on all sides. Reduce heat to medium-high. Add onion and next 5 ingredients; sauté 7 minutes or until onion is lightly browned.

3. Add hazelnut butter and broth to pan; stir well, scraping pan to loosen browned bits. Stir in turnips, potatoes, carrots, dates, and 2 cups water; bring to a boil.

4. Reduce heat to medium. Cover and simmer 15 minutes. Uncover and simmer 1 hour and 20 minutes, or until lamb is tender and sauce has thickened. Stir in peas; simmer 5 minutes. Yield: 8 servings (serving size: about 1 cup).

CALORIES 361 (29% from fat); FAT 11.8g (sat 2.5g, mono 6.7g, poly 1.4g); PROTEIN 28.4g; CARB 36.7g; FIBER 608g; CHOL 69mg; IRON 3.8mg; SODIUM 518mg; CALC 65mg

Test Kitchen Tip: To toast hazelnuts, place them in a single layer on an ungreased baking sheet and bake at 350° for 10 to 15 minutes or until the skins crack and the nut meats turn a light golden color. Remove the skins before chopping and adding to the recipe.

menu

serves 8

Lamb Stew with Hazelnut Butter and Dates

Whole wheat couscous

Iced Mint Tea (page 63)

Beef Stew

Serve this Mediterranean-inspired stew over Basic Mashed Potatoes (page 527).

Prep: 20 minutes • Cook: 1 hour, 44 minutes

1½ teaspoons olive oil
1½ pounds beef stew meat, cut into 1-inch pieces
3½ cups halved mushrooms (about 8 ounces)
 2 cups diagonally cut carrot
1½ cups coarsely chopped onion
1½ cups sliced celery
 2 garlic cloves, minced
1½ cups water
 1 cup cabernet sauvignon or other dry red wine
 ½ teaspoon dried thyme
1¼ teaspoons kosher salt
 ¼ teaspoon coarsely ground black pepper
 2 (14.5-ounce) cans no-salt-added stewed tomatoes, undrained
 2 bay leaves
 1 (2¼-ounce) can sliced ripe olives, drained
 2 tablespoons red wine vinegar
 ¼ cup chopped fresh flat-leaf parsley

1. Heat oil in a large Dutch oven over medium-high heat. Add beef; cook 5 minutes, browning on all sides. Remove from pan. Add mushrooms and next 4 ingredients to pan; cook 5 minutes, stirring occasionally. Return beef to pan. Stir in 1½ cups water and next 6 ingredients; bring to a boil. Cover, reduce heat, and simmer 1 hour.

2. Stir in olives, and cook 30 minutes or until beef is tender. Discard bay leaves. Stir in vinegar. Sprinkle with parsley. Yield: 6 servings (serving size: 1⅓ cups).

CALORIES 288 (32% from fat); FAT 10.3g (sat 3.3g, mono 5g, poly 0.6g); PROTEIN 25.2g; CARB 20.1g; FIBER 5.7g; CHOL 71mg; IRON 5.5mg; SODIUM 584mg; CALC 100mg

Test Kitchen Tip: While the wine you cook with doesn't have to be expensive, it needs to be of good quality because it will contribute its flavors to the final dish.

Beef Daube Provençal

Savor a favorite French dish of braised beef, red wine, and vegetable stew. Start cooking the noodles when the meat is almost done.

Prep: 20 minutes • Cook: 2 hours, 47 minutes

- 2 teaspoons olive oil
- 12 garlic cloves, crushed
- 1 (2-pound) boneless chuck roast, trimmed and cut into 2-inch cubes
- 1½ teaspoons salt, divided
- ½ teaspoon freshly ground black pepper, divided
- 1 cup dry red wine
- 2 cups chopped carrot
- 1½ cups chopped onion
- ½ cup less-sodium beef broth
- 1 tablespoon tomato paste
- 1 teaspoon chopped fresh rosemary
- 1 teaspoon chopped fresh thyme
- Dash of ground cloves
- 1 (14.5-ounce) can diced tomatoes
- 1 bay leaf
- 3 cups hot cooked medium egg noodles (about 4 cups uncooked noodles)

1. Preheat oven to 300°.
2. Heat oil in a Dutch oven over low heat. Add garlic; cook 5 minutes or until garlic is fragrant, stirring occasionally. Remove garlic with a slotted spoon, and set aside. Increase heat to medium-high. Add beef to pan; sprinkle with ½ teaspoon salt and ¼ teaspoon pepper. Cook 5 minutes, browning on all sides. Remove beef from pan. Add wine to pan; bring to a boil, scraping pan to loosen browned bits. Add garlic, beef, 1 teaspoon salt, ¼ teaspoon pepper, carrot, and next 8 ingredients, and bring to a boil.
3. Cover; bake at 300° for 2½ hours or until beef is tender. Discard bay leaf.

Serve over noodles. Yield: 6 servings (serving size: ½ cup noodles and about ¾ cup stew).

CALORIES 367 (31% from fat); FAT 12.8g (sat 4.3g, mono 5.8g, poly 0.9g); PROTEIN 29.1g; CARB 33.4g; FIBER 3.9g; CHOL 105mg; IRON 4.3mg; SODIUM 776mg; CALC 76mg

Veal-and-Artichoke Stew with Avgolemono

Meat cooked with artichokes takes on a sweet note that contrasts with the lemon juice. This dish is usually served on its own, but it's equally delicious with rice, orzo, or egg noodles mixed into the sauce.

Prep: 55 minutes • Cook: 1 hour, 36 minutes

Stew:
- 4 cups water, divided
- ⅔ cup fresh lemon juice (about 4 lemons), divided
- 8 medium artichokes (about 10 ounces each)
- 4 lemons, cut in half
- 2½ pounds veal round, trimmed and cut into 2-inch cubes
- 1½ cups coarsely chopped onion
- ¾ cup dry white wine
- 2 (14-ounce) cans fat-free, less-sodium chicken broth, divided
- ½ cup chopped fresh dill
- ½ teaspoon sea salt
- ½ teaspoon freshly ground black pepper

Avgolemono:
- 1 large egg
- 5 tablespoons water, divided
- 2 tablespoons fresh lemon juice
- 1½ teaspoons cornstarch

Remaining Ingredients:
- ¼ cup chopped fresh dill
- Lemon wedges (optional)

1. To prepare stew, combine 3 cups water and ⅓ cup lemon juice in a large bowl. Working with 1 artichoke at a time, cut off stem to within 1 inch of base; peel stem. Remove bottom leaves and tough outer leaves, and trim about 2 inches from top of artichoke. Cut artichoke in half vertically. Remove fuzzy thistle from bottom with a spoon. Trim any remaining leaves and dark green layer from base. Rub edges with a lemon half, and place artichoke halves in lemon water.
2. Heat a Dutch oven over medium-high heat. Add veal to pan; cook 5 minutes, browning on all sides. Add onion, and cook 5 minutes. Add wine and 1 can of broth; bring to a boil. Cover, reduce heat, and simmer 45 minutes.
3. Drain artichoke halves. Add artichoke halves, 1 cup water, ⅓ cup lemon juice, 1 can broth, ½ cup dill, salt, and pepper to pan; cover and simmer 30 minutes or until artichokes are tender. Remove veal and artichoke halves with a slotted spoon. Keep warm.
4. To prepare avgolemono, combine egg, 3 tablespoons water, and 2 tablespoons lemon juice in a medium bowl. Combine 2 tablespoons water and cornstarch in a small bowl; add to egg mixture. Add egg mixture to juices in pan. Bring to a boil, and cook 5 minutes, stirring constantly with a whisk. Serve over veal and artichokes; sprinkle with dill. Garnish with lemon wedges, if desired. Yield: 8 servings (serving size: 4 ounces meat, 2 artichoke halves, ¼ cup sauce, and 1½ teaspoons dill).

CALORIES 290 (14% from fat); FAT 4.6g (sat 1.7g, mono 1.7g, poly 0.4g); PROTEIN 38.2g; CARB 29.5g; FIBER 11.3g; CHOL 132mg; IRON 3.9mg; SODIUM 751mg; CALC 101mg

fruit &
vegetable
side dishes

Roasted Potatoes with Tangy
Watercress Sauce, page 527

Fruit Side Dishes

A fruit dish, such as a compote or applesauce, is a welcome addition to any entrée.

Cinnamon Stewed Apples

A terrific companion for ham or pork, these fragrant apples can be doubled easily, and will keep in the refrigerator for about a week. The sauce is somewhat thin just after cooking, but it will thicken upon standing.

Prep: 10 minutes • Cook: 45 minutes
Other: 5 minutes

 6   cups chopped peeled Granny Smith
     apple (about 2 pounds)
 ½   cup packed brown sugar
 ¼   cup apple juice
 1   teaspoon ground cinnamon
 ⅛   teaspoon ground nutmeg
 ⅛   teaspoon salt

1. Combine all ingredients in a large, heavy saucepan. Cover and cook over medium-low heat 45 minutes or until apple is tender, stirring occasionally. Let stand 5 minutes. Yield: 8 servings (serving size: ¼ cup).

CALORIES 121 (3% from fat); FAT 0.4g (sat 0.1g, mono 0g, poly 0.1g); PROTEIN 0.2g; CARB 31.3g; FIBER 2.3g; CHOL 0mg; IRON 0.4mg; SODIUM 42mg; CALC 19mg

Rustic Applesauce

A combination of sweet Braeburns and tart Granny Smiths gives this applesauce a pleasant balance. Mashing the apples creates a chunky sauce; for a smoother texture, process part or all of the apple mixture in a food processor or blender. Crème fraîche lends a silky finish; substitute full-fat sour cream if your market doesn't carry crème fraîche.

Prep: 15 minutes • Cook: 25 minutes

 4   cups cubed peeled Braeburn or Pink
     Lady apple
 4   cups cubed peeled Granny Smith
     apple
 ½   cup packed brown sugar
 2   teaspoons grated lemon rind
 3   tablespoons fresh lemon juice
 1   teaspoon ground cinnamon
 1   teaspoon vanilla extract
Dash of salt
 2   tablespoons crème fraîche

1. Combine first 8 ingredients in a Dutch oven over medium heat. Cook 25 minutes or until apples are tender, stirring occasionally.
2. Remove from heat; mash to desired consistency with a fork or potato masher. Stir in crème fraîche. Serve warm or chilled. Yield: 7 servings (serving size: about ½ cup).

CALORIES 140 (12% from fat); FAT 1.8g (sat 1g, mono 0.5g, poly 0.2g); PROTEIN 0.3g; CARB 32.5g; FIBER 2.3g; CHOL 3mg; IRON 0.5mg; SODIUM 30mg; CALC 31mg

Spiced Winter Fruit

This dish will hold up to three days if refrigerated in an airtight container. To serve, reheat over low heat. Topped with low-fat vanilla ice cream, it also makes an elegant holiday dessert.

Prep: 13 minutes • Cook: 19 minutes

 1   cup packed light brown sugar
 1   teaspoon ground ginger
 1   teaspoon ground cinnamon
 ½   teaspoon ground nutmeg
 2   tablespoons butter
 2   quinces, each cut into 8 wedges
      (about ¾ pound)
 3   cups sliced peeled Bartlett or Anjou
      pear (about 1½ pounds)
 2½   cups sliced peeled Granny Smith
      apple (about 1½ pounds)
 ¼   teaspoon freshly ground black pepper
 Cinnamon sticks (optional)

1. Combine first 4 ingredients in a small bowl; set aside.
2. Melt butter in a large nonstick skillet over medium heat. Add quince; cover and cook 6 minutes, stirring occasionally. Add sugar mixture, pear, and apple; cover and cook 12 minutes, stirring occasionally. Stir in pepper; garnish with cinnamon sticks, if desired. Yield: 8 servings (serving size: ¾ cup).

CALORIES 219 (15% from fat); FAT 3.6g (sat 1.9g, mono 0.9g, poly 0.3g); PROTEIN 0.7g; CARB 50.1g; FIBER 4.5g; CHOL 8mg; IRON 1.1mg; SODIUM 38mg; CALC 38mg

Mixed Fruit Compote

Serve this brandied compote with pork or turkey, or as an accompaniment to a brunch casserole. If you don't want to use brandy, add 3 more tablespoons of orange juice.

Prep: 12 minutes • Cook: 25 minutes

  ½ teaspoon grated orange rind
  2 cups fresh orange juice (about 6 oranges)
  3 tablespoons brandy
  ¼ teaspoon whole cloves
  2 (7-ounce) packages dried mixed fruit
  2 (3-inch) cinnamon sticks
  1 lemon, quartered

1. Place all ingredients in a medium saucepan; bring to a boil. Reduce heat, cover, and simmer 20 minutes. Cool. Discard cloves, cinnamon, and lemon. Yield: 8 servings (serving size: ½ cup).

CALORIES 160 (2% from fat); FAT 0.4g (sat 0g, mono 0.1g, poly 0.1g); PROTEIN 1.7g; CARB 38.3g; FIBER 4g; CHOL 0mg; IRON 1.5mg; SODIUM 10mg; CALC 28mg

Test Kitchen Tip: Store the compote in the refrigerator up to one week.

menu
serves 8

Bloody Marys (page 69)

Mixed Fruit Compote

Cheesy Brunch Casserole (page 386)

Sour Cream Coffee Cake (page 86)

Tropical Fruit Ambrosia with Rum

Whether ambrosia is a side dish or a dessert is a subject for debate. Either way, your guests will enjoy this tropical version.

Prep: 15 minutes • Cook: 4 minutes

  ¼ cup sugar
  ¼ cup water
  2 tablespoons white rum
  2 tablespoons fresh lime juice
  2 cups cubed peeled ripe mango (about 2 mangoes)
  2 cups cubed peeled kiwifruit (about 6 kiwifruit)
  2 tablespoons flaked sweetened coconut, toasted

1. Combine sugar and water in a small saucepan. Bring to a boil, and cook 1 minute or until sugar dissolves. Remove from heat; stir in rum and lime juice. Cool completely.

2. Combine mango and kiwifruit; add rum syrup, tossing gently. Sprinkle with coconut. Yield: 4 servings (serving size: 1 cup fruit and 1½ teaspoons coconut).

CALORIES 185 (7% from fat); FAT 1.4g (sat 0.7g, mono 0.2g, poly 0.3g); PROTEIN 1.4g; CARB 41.3g; FIBER 4.6g; CHOL 0mg; IRON 0.6mg; SODIUM 14mg; CALC 33mg

Test Kitchen Tip: Although the rum certainly adds distinct flavor to the fruit, the ambrosia is still good without it.

Vegetable Side Dishes
An ear of corn, a pot of peas, a side of fries— what's a meal without the contribution of garden-fresh vegetables and potatoes?

Roasted Asparagus with Balsamic Browned Butter

Browning the butter takes a watchful eye, yet it's the browned butter that makes this dish sing. Our Test Kitchens staff unanimously agreed that this tops any asparagus recipe we've ever done.

Prep: 7 minutes • Cook: 16 minutes

40 asparagus spears, trimmed (about 2 pounds)
Cooking spray
¼ teaspoon kosher salt
⅛ teaspoon pepper
2 tablespoons butter
2 teaspoons low-sodium soy sauce
1 teaspoon balsamic vinegar

1. Preheat oven to 400°.
2. Arrange asparagus in a single layer on a baking sheet; coat with cooking spray. Sprinkle with salt and pepper. Bake at 400° for 12 minutes or until tender.
3. Melt butter in a small skillet over medium heat; cook 3 minutes or until lightly browned, shaking pan occasionally. Remove from heat; stir in soy sauce and vinegar. Drizzle over asparagus, tossing well to coat. Serve immediately. Yield: 8 servings (serving size: 5 spears).

CALORIES 45 (60% from fat); FAT 3g (sat 1.8g, mono 0.9g, poly 0.2g); PROTEIN 1.9g; CARB 3.9g; FIBER 1.7g; CHOL 8mg; IRON 0.7mg; SODIUM 134mg; CALC 18mg

Green Beans and Sautéed Onions with Bacon

This flavorful side is an ideal partner for turkey or ham. The bacon and the onions create a pleasing balance of salty and sweet.

Prep: 15 minutes • Cook: 20 minutes

1 pound green beans, trimmed and halved crosswise
4 bacon slices
1 (16-ounce) bottle cocktail onions, drained
2 teaspoons sugar
½ teaspoon dried thyme
1½ tablespoons cider vinegar
¾ teaspoon salt
¼ teaspoon pepper

1. Place beans in a saucepan of boiling water; cook 4 minutes or until crisp-tender. Rinse with cold water; drain and pat dry.
2. Cook bacon in a large nonstick skillet over medium-high heat until crisp. Remove bacon from pan, reserving 2 tablespoons drippings in pan; crumble bacon, and set aside. Add onions to drippings in pan; cook 3 minutes, stirring occasionally. Add sugar and thyme; cook 3 minutes or until onions are golden brown, stirring occasionally. Add beans; cook 2 minutes. Add vinegar, salt, and pepper; toss. Stir in bacon just before serving. Yield: 8 servings (serving size: ½ cup).

CALORIES 59 (46% from fat); FAT 3g (sat 1.1g, mono 1.4g, poly 0.4g); PROTEIN 2.2g; CARB 6.5g; FIBER 1.2g; CHOL 4mg; IRON 0.8mg; SODIUM 621mg; CALC 24mg

Green Beans with Toasted Almond Gremolata

A garnish of garlic, lemon rind, and parsley is called gremolata; we've added nuts for crunch. It typically accompanies the veal dish *osso buco*, but it also can enhance steamed vegetables.

Prep: 14 minutes • Cook: 8 minutes

1 pound green beans, trimmed
2 tablespoons chopped fresh flat-leaf parsley
1 tablespoon sliced almonds, toasted
¼ teaspoon grated lemon rind
1½ teaspoons fresh lemon juice
1 teaspoon olive oil
¼ teaspoon salt
⅛ teaspoon freshly ground black pepper
1 garlic clove, minced

1. Steam beans, covered, 7 minutes or until crisp-tender. Drain and return to pan. Add parsley and remaining ingredients; toss gently to combine. Yield: 4 servings (serving size: 1 cup).

CALORIES 59 (35% from fat); FAT 2.3g (sat 0.2g, mono 1.5g, poly 0.4g); PROTEIN 2.6g; CARB 9.1g; FIBER 1.6g; CHOL 0mg; IRON 1.4mg; SODIUM 155mg; CALC 52mg

Green Beans with Crushed Walnuts

This easy dish relies on freshly ground nutmeg. Look for whole nutmeg in the spice aisle; store it in the freezer up to one year.

Prep: 13 minutes • Cook: 11 minutes

1¼ pounds green beans, trimmed
2 teaspoons butter
2 tablespoons finely crushed walnuts
½ teaspoon salt
¼ teaspoon freshly grated whole nutmeg

1. Place beans in a large saucepan of boiling water; cook 5 minutes. Drain.
2. Heat butter in a large nonstick skillet over medium-high heat. Add walnuts; sauté 1 minute, stirring constantly. Add beans, salt, and nutmeg; cook 1 minute. Yield: 6 servings (serving size: ⅔ cup).

CALORIES 52 (52% from fat); FAT 3g (sat 1g, mono 0.6g, poly 1.3g); PROTEIN 1.8g; CARB 5.8g; FIBER 2.8g; CHOL 3mg; IRON 0.9mg; SODIUM 213mg; CALC 31mg

how to grate nutmeg

The flavor of freshly grated nutmeg goes a long way. Grating is quick and easy—simply rub whole nutmeg across the grater's surface; the taste of commercially ground and packaged nutmeg doesn't compare.

Chive Green Beans

Leave green beans whole for a restaurant-style look.

Prep: 12 minutes • Cook: 5 minutes

1 pound green beans, trimmed
1 tablespoon chopped fresh chives
1 tablespoon chopped fresh parsley
2 teaspoons butter
½ teaspoon stone-ground mustard
¼ teaspoon salt
⅛ teaspoon pepper

1. Steam green beans, covered, 5 minutes or until crisp-tender. Remove from pan; toss with chives and remaining ingredients. Yield: 4 servings (serving size: ¾ cup).

CALORIES 53 (32% from fat); FAT 1.9g (sat 1.2g, mono 0.6g, poly 0.1g); PROTEIN 1.5g; CARB 7.1g; FIBER 4.2g; CHOL 5mg; IRON 0.6mg; SODIUM 175mg; CALC 58mg

Oven-Roasted Green Beans

Roasting brings out so much more flavor from the beans than steaming. Make this your "go-to" recipe when you need a quick side dish.

Prep: 12 minutes • Cook: 10 minutes

1 pound green beans, trimmed
2 teaspoons olive oil
½ teaspoon salt
⅛ teaspoon coarsely ground black pepper
Cooking spray
2 teaspoons fresh lemon juice

1. Preheat oven to 475°.
2. Combine beans and next 3 ingredients in a large bowl, tossing well to coat. Arrange in a single layer on a baking sheet coated with cooking spray. Bake at 475° for 10 minutes or until tender, turning once.

3. Remove pan from oven; add lemon juice to beans, and toss. Yield: 4 servings (serving size: about ¾ cup).

CALORIES 56 (39% from fat); FAT 2.4g (sat 0.3g, mono 1.7g, poly 0.3g); PROTEIN 2.1g; CARB 8.4g; FIBER 3.9g; CHOL 0mg; IRON 1.2mg; SODIUM 302mg; CALC 42mg

Shredded Brussels Sprouts with Bacon and Hazelnuts

Use a food processor's thin slicing blade attachment to prepare the Brussels sprouts.

Prep: 10 minutes • Cook: 11 minutes

½ cup chopped bacon (about 3 slices)
½ cup fat-free, less-sodium chicken broth
13 cups thinly sliced Brussels sprouts (about 2 pounds)
1 teaspoon salt
½ teaspoon freshly ground black pepper
3 tablespoons chopped hazelnuts, toasted

1. Cook bacon in a large Dutch oven over medium-high heat 4 minutes or until crisp.
2. Remove bacon from pan, reserving 1½ teaspoons bacon drippings in pan; set bacon aside. Add broth to pan; bring to a simmer. Add Brussels sprouts; cook 4 minutes or until Brussels sprouts are crisp-tender, stirring frequently. Sprinkle with salt and pepper, tossing gently to combine. Sprinkle evenly with bacon and hazelnuts. Serve immediately. Yield: 12 servings (serving size: ¾ cup).

CALORIES 59 (41% from fat); FAT 2.7g (sat 0.7g, mono 1.5g, poly 0.4g); PROTEIN 3.4g; CARB 7.2g; FIBER 3.1g; CHOL 2mg; IRON 1.2mg; SODIUM 262mg; CALC 35mg

Brussels Sprouts with Pecans

The sprouts take just a brief turn in the pan—slicing them cuts down on their cooking time. Butter and sugar mellow their bite.

Prep: 15 minutes • Cook: 13 minutes

   2   teaspoons butter
   1   cup chopped onion
   4   garlic cloves, thinly sliced
   8   cups halved and thinly sliced
        Brussels sprouts (about 1½ pounds)
 ½   cup fat-free, less-sodium chicken
        broth
1½   tablespoons sugar
 ½   teaspoon salt
2½   tablespoons coarsely chopped
        pecans, toasted

1. Melt butter in a large nonstick skillet over medium-high heat. Add onion and garlic; sauté 4 minutes or until lightly browned. Stir in Brussels sprouts, and sauté 2 minutes. Add broth and sugar; cook 5 minutes or until liquid almost evaporates, stirring frequently. Stir in salt. Sprinkle with pecans. Yield: 8 servings (serving size: about ⅔ cup).

CALORIES 82 (33% from fat); FAT 3g (sat 0.8g, mono 1.3g, poly 0.7g); PROTEIN 3.6g; CARB 12.6g; FIBER 3.9g; CHOL 3mg; IRON 1.3mg; SODIUM 207mg; CALC 45mg

Test Kitchen Tip: To toast pecans, place them in a dry skillet and cook them over medium heat, stirring frequently, for about 1 minute. Or, place them in a shallow microwave-safe dish, and microwave at HIGH 1 minute, stirring after 30 seconds.

Cabbage with Green Onions and Caraway

Cabbage and caraway seeds are always a good combo. Serve this savory dish with corned beef or pork chops.

Prep: 10 minutes • Cook: 12 minutes

   6   cups thinly sliced green cabbage
        (about 1½ pounds)
   1   cup finely chopped peeled cucumber
 ½   cup thinly sliced green onions
   2   tablespoons water
 ½   teaspoon caraway seeds
 ¼   teaspoon salt
 ⅛   teaspoon pepper
 ¼   cup dry vermouth or dry white wine

1. Heat a large nonstick skillet over medium heat. Add first 7 ingredients. Cover; cook 10 minutes or until cabbage wilts, stirring occasionally. Add vermouth; cook 2 minutes. Yield: 4 servings (serving size: 1 cup).

CALORIES 40 (7% from fat); FAT 0.3g (sat 0.1g, mono 0g, poly 0.2g); PROTEIN 2.1g; CARB 5g; FIBER 1.6g; CHOL 0mg; IRON 1.2mg; SODIUM 220mg; CALC 127mg

Cabbage Gremolata

Parsley, lemon rind, and garlic give this side dish a fresh, citrusy kick.

Prep: 11 minutes • Cook: 14 minutes

   2   teaspoons butter
   1   tablespoon minced shallots
   1   garlic clove, minced
   6   cups thinly sliced green cabbage
        (about 1½ pounds)
   2   tablespoons fresh lemon juice
   2   tablespoons chopped fresh parsley
   2   teaspoons grated lemon rind
 ¼   teaspoon salt
 ⅛   teaspoon pepper

1. Melt butter in a large nonstick skillet over medium-high heat. Add shallots and garlic; cook 3 minutes or until tender, stirring frequently. Add cabbage and juice. Cover and cook over medium heat 10 minutes, stirring occasionally.
2. Remove from heat; stir in parsley and remaining ingredients. Serve immediately. Yield: 4 servings (serving size: ¾ cup).

CALORIES 63 (33% from fat); FAT 2.3g (sat 1.2g, mono 0.6g, poly 0.2g); PROTEIN 2.3g; CARB 10.8g; FIBER 4.2g; CHOL 5mg; IRON 1.1mg; SODIUM 198mg; CALC 88mg

Carrot Coins with Maple-Balsamic Browned Butter

For the best flavor, start with whole carrots. The peeling and slicing take less than five minutes.

Prep: 10 minutes • Cook: 20 minutes

3¼   cups (¼-inch-thick) slices peeled
        carrots (about 1 pound)
   1   tablespoon butter
   1   tablespoon maple syrup
   1   teaspoon balsamic vinegar
 ⅛   teaspoon salt
 ⅛   teaspoon freshly ground black pepper
   1   teaspoon chopped fresh parsley

1. Steam carrots, covered, 15 minutes or until tender.
2. Melt butter in a medium nonstick skillet over medium heat. Cook butter 3 minutes or until lightly browned, stirring occasionally. Stir in syrup, vinegar, salt, and pepper. Add carrots; cook 1 minute or until thoroughly heated, stirring to coat. Stir in parsley. Yield: 4 servings (serving size: about ⅔ cup).

CALORIES 86 (32% from fat); FAT 3.1g (sat 1.8g, mono 0.8g, poly 0.2g); PROTEIN 1.1g; CARB 14.5g; FIBER 3.4g; CHOL 8mg; IRON 0.5mg; SODIUM 173mg; CALC 43mg

Roasted Root Vegetables

Balsamic vinegar adds a subtle sweetness to these hearty vegetables.

Prep: 15 minutes • Cook: 1 hour

- 3½ cups coarsely chopped carrot (about 1½ pounds)
- 3 cups coarsely chopped parsnip (about 1 pound)
- 1¾ cups coarsely chopped peeled turnip (about ½ pound)
- 2 tablespoons olive oil
- 1 teaspoon brown sugar
- ½ teaspoon sea salt
- 2 red onions, each cut into 8 wedges
- 2 tablespoons chopped fresh parsley
- 1 tablespoon balsamic vinegar
- ¼ teaspoon freshly ground black pepper

1. Preheat oven to 450°.
2. Combine first 7 ingredients in a shallow roasting pan; toss well. Bake at 450° for 1 hour, stirring after 30 minutes. Add parsley, vinegar, and pepper, tossing to coat. Yield: 6 servings (serving size: about 1 cup).

CALORIES 175 (26% from fat); FAT 5.1g (sat 0.7g, mono 3.4g, poly 0.6g); PROTEIN 2.9g; CARB 31.9g; FIBER 6.7g; CHOL 0mg; IRON 1.3mg; SODIUM 267mg; CALC 80mg

Test Kitchen Tip: Spread the vegetables out evenly in the pan instead of piling them up in order to get them completely roasted.

quick veggie sides

Grilled Asparagus: Combine 1 pound trimmed asparagus, 3 tablespoons balsamic vinegar, 2 tablespoons fresh lemon juice, 1 tablespoon olive oil, 1 tablespoon low-sodium soy sauce, and ⅛ teaspoon pepper in a large zip-top plastic bag; seal and marinate 30 minutes. Remove asparagus from bag; discard marinade. Place asparagus on grill rack coated with cooking spray; grill 5 minutes on each side. Yield: 4 servings.

Chipotle Refried Beans: Combine 1 (16-ounce) can fat-free refried beans, 2 tablespoons chipotle salsa, and 2 tablespoons chopped fresh cilantro. Microwave at HIGH 1½ minutes or until thoroughly heated. Yield: 4 servings.

Garlic Broccoli: Heat 1 teaspoon sesame oil in a large skillet over medium-high heat; stir in 4 cups broccoli florets and 2 minced garlic cloves. Sauté 4 minutes. Stir in ¼ cup chicken broth and 1 teaspoon low-sodium soy sauce; reduce heat. Cover and cook 4 minutes or until broccoli is tender. Yield: 4 servings.

Italian Broccoli: Steam 1 pound broccoli spears, covered, 5 minutes or until crisp-tender. Toss with 3 tablespoons fat-free Italian dressing; sprinkle with 2 tablespoons grated Parmesan cheese. Yield: 4 servings.

Browned Brussels Sprouts: Heat 1 tablespoon olive oil in a large skillet over medium heat. Add 1½ pounds trimmed, halved Brussels sprouts; ¼ teaspoon salt; and 3 minced garlic cloves; cook 15 minutes or until lightly browned, stirring occasionally. Stir in 2 teaspoons balsamic vinegar; cook 1 minute. Yield: 4 servings.

Roasted Brussels Sprouts: Combine 4 cups trimmed, halved Brussels sprouts; 2 teaspoons melted butter; ½ teaspoon salt; and ¼ teaspoon pepper on a jelly-roll pan coated with cooking spray. Bake at 425° for 25 minutes. Yield: 4 servings.

Glazed Carrots: Melt 2 teaspoons butter in a large skillet over medium heat; stir in 2 tablespoons honey. Add 2 cups (¼-inch) diagonally sliced carrots, ⅛ teaspoon salt, and ⅛ teaspoon pepper. Cover and cook 10 minutes. Yield: 4 servings.

Stewed Okra: Combine 4 cups frozen cut okra; 1 (14.5-ounce) can stewed tomatoes, undrained; ½ teaspoon sugar; and ¼ teaspoon crushed red pepper in a saucepan. Bring to a boil; cover, reduce heat, and simmer 10 minutes. Yield: 8 servings.

Baked Sweet Potatoes: Pierce 4 small sweet potatoes with a fork. Microwave at HIGH 10 minutes or until done, rearranging potatoes after 5 minutes. Combine 2 tablespoons each softened butter and brown sugar. Top each potato with 2 teaspoons butter mixture. Yield: 4 servings.

Wilted Spinach with Pine Nuts: Melt 1 teaspoon butter in a large skillet over medium-high heat. Add 1 (10-ounce) package fresh spinach, trimmed, and 1 minced garlic clove; sauté 2 minutes. Stir in 3 tablespoons raisins, 1 tablespoon pine nuts, and ¼ teaspoon salt. Yield: 4 servings.

Garlicky Zucchini: Heat 1 teaspoon olive oil in a nonstick skillet over medium-high heat. Add 4 cups sliced zucchini; 3 garlic cloves, minced; ¼ teaspoon salt; and ¼ teaspoon black pepper. Sauté 4 minutes or until tender. Sprinkle with 2 tablespoons grated Parmesan cheese. Yield: 4 servings.

Cauliflower and Potato Sabzi with Spices

Stir-fried vegetables with spices, *sabzi* is a popular northern Indian dish that can be made with one or more vegetables. It's often cooked with cumin, ginger, cilantro, and garam masala. Increase the amount of ground red pepper for a hotter dish.

Prep: 20 minutes • Cook: 27 minutes

- 1 head cauliflower (about 1½ pounds)
- 2 tablespoons canola oil, divided
- 2 baking potatoes, peeled, halved lengthwise, and sliced (about 1¾ pounds)
- 2 teaspoons cumin seeds
- 4 garlic cloves, minced
- ⅓ cup water
- ⅓ cup tomato puree
- 3 tablespoons chopped peeled fresh ginger
- 1½ teaspoons salt
- ¾ teaspoon ground turmeric
- ½ teaspoon ground red pepper
- ⅓ cup chopped fresh cilantro
- 1 teaspoon garam masala

1. Separate cauliflower into florets to measure 4 cups, reserving stems. Cut stems into thin slices to measure 1 cup. Heat 1½ tablespoons oil in a Dutch oven over medium-high heat. Add potato, cumin seeds, and garlic; stir-fry 6 minutes or until potato is crisp-tender. Stir in water and next 5 ingredients. Add cauliflower florets and stems, stirring well; cover, reduce heat, and simmer 20 minutes or until vegetables are tender. Uncover, and drizzle with 1½ teaspoons oil, cilantro, and garam masala, tossing well. Yield: 6 servings (serving size: 1 cup).

CALORIES 200 (23% from fat); FAT 5.2g (sat 0.4g, mono 2.9g, poly 1.5g); PROTEIN 4.9g; CARB 36.2g; FIBER 4.8g; CHOL 0mg; IRON 1.8mg; SODIUM 676mg; CALC 43mg

Grilled Corn with Lime Butter

You can make the lime butter up to two days ahead; just be sure to keep it chilled. Melt the butter before brushing it over the grilled corn.

Prep: 15 minutes • Cook: 11 minutes

- 1½ tablespoons butter, melted
- ¼ teaspoon grated lime rind
- 1½ tablespoons fresh lime juice
- ¼ teaspoon salt
- ¼ teaspoon ground red pepper
- 8 ears shucked corn
- Cooking spray

1. Prepare grill or preheat broiler.
2. Combine first 5 ingredients in a bowl.
3. Place corn on grill rack or broiler pan coated with cooking spray. Cook 10 minutes, turning frequently. Remove from heat; brush corn with butter mixture. Yield: 8 servings (serving size: 1 ear).

CALORIES 103 (28% from fat); FAT 3.2g (sat 1.5g, mono 0.9g, poly 0.6g); PROTEIN 2.6g; CARB 19.6g; FIBER 2.2g; CHOL 6mg; IRON 0.5mg; SODIUM 108mg; CALC 3mg

Grilled Corn with Creamy Chipotle Sauce

Instead of butter, try this smoky, spicy sauce on grilled corn. Though the corn needs to be grilled at the last minute, the sauce can be prepared one day ahead.

Prep: 15 minutes • Cook: 10 minutes

- ¼ teaspoon salt
- 1 drained canned chipotle chile, seeded
- 1 garlic clove
- ½ cup 2% reduced-fat cottage cheese
- 2 tablespoons light mayonnaise
- 2 tablespoons plain fat-free yogurt
- 6 ears shucked corn
- Cooking spray

1. Prepare grill.
2. Place first 3 ingredients in a food processor; process until minced. Add cottage cheese; process until smooth, scraping sides of bowl occasionally. Add mayonnaise and yogurt; process until blended. Spoon sauce into a bowl; cover and chill.
3. Place corn on grill rack coated with cooking spray. Grill 10 minutes, turning frequently. Serve corn with sauce. Yield: 6 servings (serving size: 1 ear and 2 tablespoons sauce).

CALORIES 116 (25% from fat); FAT 3.2g (sat 0.7g, mono 0.7g, poly 1.5g); PROTEIN 5.7g; CARB 19g; FIBER 2.5g; CHOL 3mg; IRON 0.5mg; SODIUM 245mg; CALC 23mg

Japanese Eggplant with Onion-Ginger Sauce

Small Japanese eggplants are cut into "sticks" and barely steamed for a crisp-tender side dish that's good with fish.

Prep: 12 minutes • Cook: 2 minutes

- 12 ounces Japanese eggplant, cut into 3 x ½–inch sticks (about 5 cups)
- ⅓ cup minced green onions
- 2 tablespoons low-sodium soy sauce
- 2 tablespoons rice vinegar
- 1 teaspoon grated peeled fresh ginger
- 1 teaspoon extravirgin olive oil
- 1 teaspoon chile paste with garlic

1. Steam eggplant, covered, 2 minutes or until crisp-tender.
2. Combine onions and next 5 ingredients in a bowl; stir. Drizzle sauce over eggplant. Yield: 4 servings (serving size: 1 cup eggplant sticks and 1 tablespoon sauce).

CALORIES 45 (26% from fat); FAT 1.3g (sat 0.2g, mono 0.9g, poly 0.2g); PROTEIN 1.5g; CARB 8g; FIBER 3.1g; CHOL 0mg; IRON 0.5mg; SODIUM 291mg; CALC 11mg

Eggplant and Tomato Gratin

Removing strips of eggplant peel makes for a pretty presentation, but you can remove all the peel if you'd rather.

**Prep: 30 minutes • Cook: 1 hour, 13 minutes
Other: 10 minutes**

- 3 pounds chopped seeded peeled tomato
- 1 teaspoon olive oil
- ¼ cup finely chopped celery
- 3 tablespoons finely chopped onion
- 3 tablespoons finely chopped carrot
- ¾ teaspoon sea salt, divided
- 1 bay leaf
- 1 thyme sprig
- 1 basil sprig
- 2½ pounds eggplant
- Cooking spray
- ¼ teaspoon freshly ground black pepper
- 3 tablespoons thinly sliced fresh basil
- ½ cup (2 ounces) grated fresh Parmesan cheese

1. Cook tomato in a medium saucepan over medium heat 20 minutes or until tender, stirring frequently. Place tomato in a food processor, and pulse 5 times or until pureed. Heat oil in pan over medium-high heat. Add celery, onion, and carrot; sauté 2 minutes. Add pureed tomato, ½ teaspoon salt, bay leaf, thyme sprig, and basil sprig. Reduce heat to medium-low; cook 10 minutes or until slightly thick. Discard bay leaf, thyme sprig, and basil sprig.
2. Preheat broiler.
3. Cut off both ends of eggplant; peel eggplant, leaving narrow strips of peel attached. Cut eggplant into ½-inch-thick slices. Place on a jelly-roll pan coated with cooking spray. Coat slices with cooking spray; sprinkle with ¼ teaspoon salt and pepper. Broil slices 5 minutes on each side.
4. Reduce oven temperature to 375°.
5. Spread ¾ cup tomato sauce in bottom of a shallow 2-quart baking dish coated with cooking spray. Arrange ⅓ of eggplant slices in dish, overlapping slices if necessary. Sprinkle with 1 tablespoon sliced basil, and top with ¾ cup tomato sauce. Repeat layers twice with eggplant, basil, and sauce. Sprinkle with cheese. Cover and bake at 375° for 15 minutes. Uncover and bake an additional 15 minutes or until eggplant is tender and cheese is lightly browned. Remove from oven; let stand 10 minutes. Yield: 6 servings (serving size: about 1⅓ cups).

CALORIES 122 (29% from fat); FAT 3.9g (sat 1.8g, mono 1.4g, poly 0.4g); PROTEIN 6.5g; CARB 18.2g; FIBER 6.3g; CHOL 6mg; IRON 1.2mg; SODIUM 461mg; CALC 138mg

Test Kitchen Tip: Salting eggplant helps decrease bitterness, but fresh seasonal eggplant from the farmers' market doesn't need to be salted because it's usually not bitter. If you're unsure about freshness, place the eggplant slices on paper towels, lightly sprinkle with salt, let stand 30 minutes, then blot dry with paper towels.

Spicy Swiss Chard with Lemon

Although 16 cups seems like a large amount of chard, it will cook down. Three basic ingredients—crushed red pepper, garlic, and fresh lemon juice—round out the flavor.

Prep: 15 minutes • Cook: 9 minutes

- 2 teaspoons olive oil
- 16 cups trimmed Swiss chard (about 2 pounds)
- ¼ to ½ teaspoon crushed red pepper
- 3 garlic cloves, minced
- 1 tablespoon fresh lemon juice
- ⅛ teaspoon salt

1. Heat oil in a large Dutch oven over medium-high heat. Add chard; sauté 1 minute or until slightly wilted. Stir in pepper and garlic. Cover and cook 4 minutes or until tender, stirring occasionally. Uncover and cook 3 minutes or until liquid evaporates. Stir in juice and salt. Yield: 6 servings (serving size: ½ cup).

CALORIES 43 (38% from fat); FAT 1.8g (sat 0.3g, mono 1.2g, poly 0.2g); PROTEIN 2.6g; CARB 6g; FIBER 2.3g; CHOL 0mg; IRON 2.6mg; SODIUM 345mg; CALC 74mg

Braised Kale with Bacon and Cider

This dish is a suitable side for roast chicken or pork. Also, consider using kale as a stand-in for spinach in other dishes.

Prep: 12 minutes • Cook: 30 minutes

- 2 bacon slices
- 1¼ cups thinly sliced onion
- 1 (1-pound) bag chopped kale
- ⅓ cup apple cider
- 1 tablespoon apple cider vinegar
- 1½ cups diced peeled Granny Smith apple (about 10 ounces)
- ½ teaspoon salt
- ¼ teaspoon freshly ground black pepper

1. Cook bacon in a Dutch oven over medium-high heat until crisp. Remove bacon from pan, reserving 1 teaspoon drippings in pan. Crumble bacon; set aside.
2. Increase heat to medium-high. Add onion to drippings in pan; cook 5 minutes or until tender, stirring occasionally. Add kale, and cook 5 minutes or until wilted, stirring frequently. Add cider and vinegar; cover and cook 10 minutes, stirring occasionally. Add apple, salt, and pepper; cook 5 minutes or until apple is tender, stirring occasionally. Sprinkle with bacon. Yield: 6 servings (serving size: ⅔ cup).

CALORIES 75 (28% from fat); FAT 2.3g (sat 0.8g, mono 0.9g, poly 0.4g); PROTEIN 2.5g; CARB 12.7g; FIBER 2.1g; CHOL 3mg; IRON 1mg; SODIUM 255mg; CALC 71mg

Kale with Lemon-Balsamic Butter

If you like your food spicy, add a dash of crushed red pepper.

Prep: 25 minutes • Cook: 15 minutes

- 4 (1-pound) bunches kale
- 4 quarts water
- 3 tablespoons butter
- ½ cup raisins
- 3 tablespoons fresh lemon juice
- 3 tablespoons balsamic vinegar
- ¾ teaspoon fine sea salt
- ¼ teaspoon freshly ground black pepper

1. Remove stems and center ribs from kale. Wash and pat dry. Coarsely chop to measure 24 cups. Bring water to a boil in an 8-quart stockpot. Add kale; cover and cook 3 minutes. Drain well, and place kale in a bowl.
2. Melt butter in a small skillet over medium-high heat; cook 3 minutes or until lightly browned. Stir in raisins, juice, and vinegar; cook 30 seconds, stirring constantly with a whisk. Pour butter mixture over kale. Sprinkle with salt and pepper; toss well to coat. Yield: 10 servings (serving size: about 1 cup).

CALORIES 151 (28% from fat); FAT 4.7g (sat 2.3g, mono 1.1g, poly 0.7g); PROTEIN 6.3g; CARB 25.5g; FIBER 4.9g; CHOL 9mg; IRON 3.4mg; SODIUM 289mg; CALC 252mg

Braised Kale with Bacon and Cider

Turnip Greens

In the South, it's common to cook greens for about two hours until they're extremely tender. To preserve their texture, we cooked these greens less than most Southerners do.

Prep: 10 minutes • Cook: 33 minutes

 1 pound trimmed turnip greens
 2 cups water
 1 teaspoon sugar
 1 (4-ounce) piece salt pork, cubed
 1 dried hot red chile
 ¼ teaspoon salt

1. Wash greens; pat dry. Coarsely chop.
2. Combine 2 cups water, sugar, pork, and chile in a Dutch oven. Bring to a boil; cover, reduce heat, and simmer 20 minutes. Discard chile. Stir in chopped greens and salt; cover and cook over medium heat 10 minutes or until tender, stirring occasionally. Discard pork. Yield: 6 servings (serving size: ½ cup).

CALORIES 53 (68% from fat); FAT 4g (sat 1.4g, mono 1.8g, poly 0.5g); PROTEIN 1.1g; CARB 3.8g; FIBER 1.7g; CHOL 4mg; IRON 0.6mg; SODIUM 189mg; CALC 105mg

Seasoned Spinach

Steam the raw spinach in two batches, since there is so much of it. Combine the cool ingredients with your hands.

Prep: 8 minutes • Cook: 11 minutes

 2 (10-ounce) packages fresh spinach, divided
 ¼ cup finely chopped green onions
 2 teaspoons low-sodium soy sauce
 1 teaspoon sesame seeds, toasted
 ½ teaspoon dark sesame oil
 ¼ teaspoon kosher salt
 2 garlic cloves, minced

1. Steam half of spinach, covered, 5 minutes or until spinach wilts; place steamed spinach in a colander. Repeat procedure with remaining spinach. Cool slightly, and squeeze dry.
2. Place spinach in a bowl. Add onions and remaining ingredients; toss mixture well to combine. Serve chilled or at room temperature. Yield: 6 servings (serving size: about ¼ cup).

CALORIES 31 (26% from fat); FAT 0.9g (sat 0.1g, mono 0.3g, poly 0.4g); PROTEIN 2.9g; CARB 4.2g; FIBER 2.8g; CHOL 0mg; IRON 2.7mg; SODIUM 214mg; CALC 96mg

Spinach and Gruyère Soufflé

Gruyère, which has a nutty, slightly sweet flavor, is an aged Swiss cheese that's most often made in France.

Prep: 25 minutes • Cook: 35 minutes
Other: 5 minutes

 Cooking spray
 3 tablespoons dry breadcrumbs, divided
 ¼ cup finely chopped onion
 2 tablespoons all-purpose flour
 ¼ teaspoon salt
 ¼ teaspoon freshly ground black pepper
 ⅛ teaspoon ground red pepper
 Dash of ground nutmeg
 1 cup fat-free milk, divided
 1 large egg yolk, lightly beaten
 6 tablespoons (1½ ounces) finely grated Gruyère or Swiss cheese
 1 (10-ounce) package frozen chopped spinach, thawed, drained, and squeezed dry
 6 large egg whites, lightly beaten
 ¼ teaspoon cream of tartar

1. Preheat oven to 400°.
2. Coat a 1-quart soufflé dish with cooking spray; sprinkle with 1 tablespoon breadcrumbs.
3. Heat a medium saucepan over medium-high heat. Coat pan with cooking spray. Add onion; sauté 2 minutes or until tender. Remove from heat. Add flour, salt, peppers, and nutmeg, stirring well. Gradually add ½ cup milk, stirring with a whisk until well blended. Stir in remaining ½ cup milk. Cook over medium heat 2 minutes or until thick and bubbly, stirring constantly with a whisk. Remove from heat.
4. Place egg yolk in a bowl. Gradually add milk mixture to egg yolk, stirring constantly with a whisk. Return mixture to pan. Cook 1 minute or until thick. Remove from heat; stir in cheese and spinach. Cool 5 minutes.
5. Place egg whites and cream of tartar in a large bowl; beat with a mixer at high speed until stiff peaks form. Gently stir one-fourth of egg white mixture into spinach mixture; gently fold in remaining egg white mixture and 2 tablespoons breadcrumbs. Spoon into prepared dish. Bake at 400° for 30 minutes or until soufflé is puffy and set. Serve immediately. Yield: 6 servings (serving size: about ⅔ cup).

CALORIES 109 (29% from fat); FAT 3.5g (sat 1.6g, mono 1.1g, poly 0.3g); PROTEIN 9.8g; CARB 9.6g; FIBER 1.8g; CHOL 44mg; IRON 1.4mg; SODIUM 261mg; CALC 187mg

Test Kitchen Tip: See page 147 for tips on separating eggs. See page 180 for tips on beating egg whites for a soufflé.

Stewed Okra and Tomatoes

For a gumbo-style dish (without the seafood or meat), serve this saucy vegetable combo over rice.

Prep: 7 minutes • Cook: 26 minutes

- 1 teaspoon canola oil
- ½ cup chopped onion
- 4 cups okra pods, trimmed (about 1 pound)
- ½ cup water
- ½ teaspoon sugar
- ½ teaspoon salt
- ¼ teaspoon pepper
- 1 (14.5-ounce) can no-salt-added diced tomatoes, undrained

1. Heat oil in a medium saucepan over medium heat. Add onion; sauté 2 minutes. Add okra and remaining ingredients; bring to a boil. Cover, reduce heat, and simmer 20 minutes. Yield: 4 servings (serving size: 1 cup).

CALORIES 72 (18% from fat); FAT 1.4g (sat 0.1g, mono 0.7g, poly 0.4g); PROTEIN 3.2g; CARB 3.2g; FIBER 4.6g; CHOL 0mg; IRON 1.5mg; SODIUM 313mg; CALC 117mg

Test Kitchen Tip: When you're buying fresh okra, look for firm, brightly colored pods. Select pods that are less than 4 inches long because the larger ones may be tough and fibrous.

Beer-Battered Onion Rings

If you don't have an open can of beer in your refrigerator, flatten the suds you need for this batter by measuring ½ cup beer in a small bowl, and stirring with a fork. You'll have about ⅓ cup flat beer.

Prep: 15 minutes • Cook: 25 minutes

- 2 large onions, peeled
- ⅔ cup all-purpose flour
- ½ teaspoon salt
- ¼ teaspoon paprika
- ¼ teaspoon freshly ground black pepper
- ⅓ cup flat beer
- 1 large egg white, lightly beaten
- 1½ tablespoons canola oil, divided
  Cooking spray
- ¼ cup ketchup

1. Preheat oven to 400°.
2. Cut onions crosswise into ¾-inch-thick slices, and separate into rings. Use 16 largest rings; reserve remaining onion for another use. Lightly spoon flour into dry measuring cups; level with a knife. Combine flour, salt, paprika, and pepper in a medium bowl. Stir in beer and egg white (batter will be thick). Heat 1½ teaspoons oil in a large nonstick skillet over medium-high heat. Dip 5 onion rings in batter, letting excess drip off. Add onion rings to pan; cook 2 minutes on each side or until golden. Place onion rings on a jelly-roll pan. Repeat procedure of dipping onion rings in batter and cooking in remaining oil, ending with 6 rings. Coat onion rings with cooking spray. Bake at 400° for 10 minutes or until crisp. Serve rings with ketchup. Yield: 4 servings (serving size: 4 onion rings and 1 tablespoon ketchup).

CALORIES 209 (25% from fat); FAT 5.8g (sat 0.5g, mono 3.2g, poly 1.7g); PROTEIN 5.1g; CARB 34.1g; FIBER 3.7g; CHOL 0mg; IRON 1.5mg; SODIUM 490mg; CALC 39mg

how to make onion rings

1. Dip onion rings in batter, letting excess batter drip off.

2. Add onion rings to hot oil in pan; cook 2 minutes on each side or until golden.

3. Place onion rings on a jelly-roll pan; coat onion with cooking spray, and bake according to recipe.

Baked Onions with Feta

Check the ingredient label when purchasing feta and look for feta packed in water; it has a more pronounced flavor and tastes fresher.

Prep: 14 minutes • Cook: 1 hour, 31 minutes

4 Vidalia or other sweet onions
Olive oil-flavored cooking spray
½ cup fat-free, less-sodium chicken broth
½ cup (2 ounces) crumbled feta cheese
¼ cup dry breadcrumbs
½ teaspoon chopped fresh or
    ⅛ teaspoon dried thyme
Dash of pepper

1. Preheat oven to 450°.
2. Peel onions, leaving root ends intact. Trim top third of each onion; reserve for another use. Arrange onions, cut sides down, in an 8-inch square baking pan coated with cooking spray; add chicken broth. Cover pan with foil; bake at 450° for 30 minutes. Uncover and bake an additional 30 minutes. Carefully turn onions over with a spatula; bake an additional 30 minutes or until onions are soft and liquid has almost evaporated. Remove from oven.
3. Preheat broiler.
4. Combine feta, breadcrumbs, thyme, and pepper; stir with a fork until well blended. Gently pat cheese mixture evenly onto cut sides of onions. Broil onions until cheese mixture begins to brown (about 1 minute). Yield: 4 servings (serving size: 1 onion).

CALORIES 106 (26% from fat); FAT 3.1g (sat 2.5g, mono 0.2g, poly 0.1g); PROTEIN 4.5g; CARB 15.9g; FIBER 3.1g; CHOL 10mg; IRON 0.5mg; SODIUM 306mg; CALC 64mg

Roasted Cipollini Onions

Cipollini (chihp-oh-LEE-nee) are sometimes called wild onions. If you can't find them in the supermarket or at an Italian market, substitute pearl onions. Briefly blanching the onions makes them easy to peel. The cooking liquid takes on a beautiful yellow hue from the peel, so save it to add to rice or soup.

Prep: 15 minutes • Cook: 42 minutes

2 quarts water
4 pounds cipollini onions
4 rosemary sprigs
1 cup dry red wine
½ cup low-sodium soy sauce
⅓ cup balsamic vinegar
2 tablespoons olive oil
2 tablespoons honey
Rosemary sprigs (optional)

1. Preheat oven to 475°.
2. Bring water to a boil in a stockpot. Add onions, and cook 30 seconds. Drain; cool. Peel onions; arrange in a single layer on a jelly-roll pan. Top with 4 rosemary sprigs.
3. Combine wine and next 4 ingredients, stirring with a whisk. Pour wine mixture over onions. Bake at 475° for 30 minutes, turning twice.
4. Remove onions from pan with a slotted spoon. Carefully pour cooking liquid into a small saucepan; bring to a boil. Reduce heat; simmer 3 minutes or until mixture is the consistency of a thin syrup. Pour over onions; toss well to coat. Garnish with rosemary sprigs, if desired. Yield: 10 servings (serving size: about ⅓ cup).

CALORIES 187 (15% from fat); FAT 3.1g (sat 0.4g, mono 2g, poly 0.2g); PROTEIN 3.3g; CARB 32.5g; FIBER 1.2g; CHOL 0mg; IRON 1mg; SODIUM 522mg; CALC 54mg

Black-Eyed Peas with Greens

For a more peppery bite, substitute turnip or mustard greens for the Swiss chard.

Prep: 20 minutes • Cook: 42 minutes

- 4 cups vegetable broth
- 3 cups water
- 2 cups fresh black-eyed peas
- 2 tablespoons butter
- 2 cups finely chopped red onion
- 6 cups coarsely chopped Swiss chard (about 1 pound)
- 1/2 teaspoon pepper
- 1 tablespoon hot pepper vinegar (such as Crystal)

1. Combine first 3 ingredients in a Dutch oven; bring to a boil. Reduce heat; simmer, partially covered, 30 minutes or until tender. Remove from heat.
2. Heat butter in a large skillet over medium-high heat. Add onion; sauté 5 minutes. Add Swiss chard and pepper. Sauté 3 minutes or until wilted; stir in vinegar. Add onion mixture to peas; stir. Yield: 9 servings (serving size: 1 cup).

CALORIES 185 (18% from fat); FAT 3.6g (sat 1.7g, mono 0.8g, poly 0.4g); PROTEIN 11g; CARB 30g; FIBER 5.4g; CHOL 7mg; IRON 4.1mg; SODIUM 586mg; CALC 75mg

Test Kitchen Tip: Buy fresh black-eyed peas when they're available and freeze them for later use. To freeze, shell them first; then blanch briefly in boiling salty water to preserve their color and maintain their shape. Drain, cool, and freeze in an airtight container.

Basic Pot of Peas

Basic Pot of Peas

Use this recipe for any variety of fresh field peas. Top with a spoonful of pepper relish, and serve with corn bread.

Prep: 20 minutes • Cook: 36 minutes

- 2 teaspoons olive oil
- 1/2 cup chopped onion
- 2 garlic cloves, minced
- 3 cups fresh pink-eyed peas
- 3 cups water
- 3 bacon slices
- 1/2 teaspoon salt
- 1/2 teaspoon pepper

1. Heat oil in a large saucepan over medium-high heat. Add onion and garlic; sauté 2 minutes. Add peas, water, and bacon; bring to a boil. Reduce heat; simmer, partially covered, 30 minutes or until tender. Discard bacon. Stir in salt and pepper. Yield: 6 servings (serving size: 1/2 cup).

CALORIES 167 (28% from fat); FAT 5.3g (sat 1.6g, mono 2.8g, poly 0.6g); PROTEIN 4.1g; CARB 26.1g; FIBER 6.3g; CHOL 3mg; IRON 1.4mg; SODIUM 588mg; CALC 157mg

more pleasin' peas

Sautéed Sugar Snap Peas: Cook 1 pound sugar snap peas in boiling water 1 minute; drain. Melt 1 tablespoon butter in a skillet over medium-high heat. Add 2 teaspoons minced garlic; sauté 1 minute. Add peas and 1/4 teaspoon salt; sauté 2 minutes. Yield: 4 servings.

Sesame-Scented Snow Peas and Carrots: Cook 1 1/2 cups snow peas and 1/2 cup sliced carrot in boiling water 30 seconds; drain. Toss with 2 teaspoons low-sodium soy sauce, 1 teaspoon sesame oil, 1 teaspoon rice vinegar, and 1/2 teaspoon sugar. Yield: 4 servings.

Herbed Green Peas: Heat 2 teaspoons butter in a skillet coated with cooking spray over medium-high heat. Add 2 cups frozen green peas, thawed, and 1/4 cup chopped green onions; sauté 5 minutes. Stir in 1/4 teaspoon salt, 1/8 teaspoon pepper, and 1/8 teaspoon dried thyme. Yield: 4 servings.

Lady Peas with Artichoke Hearts

Don't substitute canned artichokes—fresh are needed for both the texture and flavor.

Prep: 1 hour, 15 minutes
Cook: 1 hour, 10 minutes

Artichoke Hearts:

- 2 cups water
- 6 tablespoons fresh lemon juice, divided
- 12 artichokes
- 4 cups fat-free, less-sodium chicken broth
- ¼ teaspoon salt

Peas:

- 4 cups water
- 2 cups fat-free, less-sodium chicken broth
- 4½ cups fresh lady peas
- 2 teaspoons olive oil
- 1 cup sliced shallots
- 2 garlic cloves, minced
- ¾ teaspoon salt
- ¼ teaspoon pepper
- 3 tablespoons fresh lemon juice
- 1 tablespoon chopped fresh parsley

1. To prepare artichokes, combine 2 cups water and 3 tablespoons lemon juice. Cut off stem of each artichoke to within 1 inch of base; peel stem. Remove bottom leaves and tough outer leaves, leaving tender heart and bottom. Remove fuzzy thistle from bottom with a spoon. Cut each artichoke into quarters lengthwise. Place in lemon water, and drain.

2. Combine 4 cups broth, ¼ teaspoon salt, and 3 tablespoons lemon juice in a medium saucepan; bring to a boil. Add artichoke quarters; cook 20 minutes or until tender. Drain through a fine sieve over a bowl, reserving artichokes and ½ cup cooking liquid. Cover and set aside.

3. To prepare peas, combine 4 cups water, 2 cups broth, and peas in a medium saucepan; bring to a boil over medium-high heat. Reduce heat; simmer, partially covered, 30 minutes or until peas are tender. Drain.

4. Heat oil in a nonstick skillet over medium-high heat. Add shallots; sauté 3 minutes. Add garlic; sauté 1 minute. Add reserved cooking liquid, artichokes, peas, ¾ teaspoon salt, and pepper. Bring to a boil, and cook 1 minute. Stir in 3 tablespoons lemon juice and parsley. Yield: 8 servings (serving size: about ¾ cup).

CALORIES 198 (9% from fat); FAT 1.9g (sat 0.4g, mono 0.9g, poly 0.4g); PROTEIN 9.7g; CARB 41g; FIBER 10.6g; CHOL 0mg; IRON 3.7mg; SODIUM 493mg; CALC 200mg

---

field peas Most field peas are interchangeable in recipes. Although different in color, shape, and size, they're all high in protein and fiber and are virtually fat free.

- Pink-eyed peas and black-eyed peas are both members of the field pea family, but they're different varieties that are distinguishable by a slight color variation. And although their flavors are almost indistinguishable, the black-eyed pea has an earthy flavor, while the pink-eyed variety has subtle sweetness.
- Lady peas—sometimes called cream peas—are tiny and oblong with a mild flavor and creamy texture.
- Silver knuckle-hull and purple-hull peas aren't varieties; the descriptions are of the pod in which the peas grow.

Grilled Vegetable Antipasto

Grilling the zucchini and the eggplant makes them more absorbent, which allows them to soak up the flavorful vinaigrette.

Prep: 20 minutes • Cook: 25 minutes
Other: 2 hours, 25 minutes

- 2 red bell peppers
- 2 zucchini (about 1 pound), each cut in half lengthwise
- 2 Japanese eggplant (about 8 ounces), each cut in half lengthwise
- ¼ cup chopped fresh parsley
- ¼ cup balsamic vinegar
- 1 tablespoon extravirgin olive oil
- ¼ teaspoon salt
- 6 garlic cloves, peeled and crushed

1. Prepare grill.

2. Place peppers on grill rack; grill 15 minutes or until charred, turning occasionally. Place peppers in a zip-top plastic bag; seal and let stand 15 minutes. Peel peppers; discard seeds and membranes. Coarsely chop peppers; place in a large zip-top plastic bag.

3. Place zucchini and eggplant on grill rack; grill 10 minutes, turning occasionally. Remove zucchini and eggplant from grill; let stand 10 minutes. Coarsely chop zucchini and eggplant; add to chopped peppers in a zip-top plastic bag.

4. Combine parsley and next 4 ingredients in a small bowl, stirring with a whisk. Pour parsley mixture over pepper mixture. Seal bag; toss gently to coat. Refrigerate at least 2 hours or overnight. Yield: 4 servings (serving size: 1 cup).

CALORIES 122 (30% from fat); FAT 4g (sat 0.6g, mono 2.5g, poly 0.6g); PROTEIN 3.9g; CARB 21.1g; FIBER 6.7g; CHOL 0mg; IRON 1.7mg; SODIUM 163mg; CALC 52mg

Garlic Fries

A side of fries is a fitting partner to most any burger. Tossing the fries in butter and garlic just before they're served makes them unbelievably rich.

Prep: 20 minutes • Cook: 1 hour, 2 minutes

- 3 pounds peeled baking potato, cut into ¼-inch-thick strips
- 4 teaspoons canola oil
- ¾ teaspoon salt
- Cooking spray
- 2 tablespoons butter
- 8 garlic cloves, minced (about 5 teaspoons)
- 2 tablespoons finely chopped fresh parsley
- 2 tablespoons freshly grated Parmesan cheese

1. Preheat oven to 450°.
2. Combine first 3 ingredients in a large zip-top plastic bag, tossing to coat.
3. Arrange potato strips in a single layer on a baking sheet coated with cooking spray. Bake at 450° for 1 hour or until potato is tender and golden brown, turning after 30 minutes.
4. Place butter and garlic in a large non-stick skillet; cook over low heat 2 minutes, stirring constantly. Add potatoes, parsley, and cheese to pan; toss to coat. Serve immediately. Yield: 6 servings (serving size: about 8 ounces potato).

CALORIES 256 (27% from fat); FAT 7.7g (sat 3g, mono 2.8g, poly 1.1g); PROTEIN 5.9g; CARB 42.3g; FIBER 3.5g; CHOL 12mg; IRON 1.9mg; SODIUM 386mg; CALC 55mg

Oven Fries with Crisp Sage Leaves

Beautiful to look at and delicious to eat, these golden slices of potato are scented and subtly flavored with crisp cooked sage. They're an incredible snack or a perfect savory side to any meal.

Prep: 15 minutes • Cook: 1 hour

- 2 small baking potatoes (about 1 pound)
- 1 tablespoon extravirgin olive oil
- ½ teaspoon kosher salt
- 12 sage leaves

1. Preheat oven to 400°.
2. Cut each potato lengthwise into 6 equal slices. Place potato slices in a large bowl, and drizzle with oil. Sprinkle with salt; toss well to coat. Remove potato slices from bowl. Reserve remaining oil and salt in bowl, and set aside. Arrange potato slices in a single layer on a baking sheet.
3. Bake at 400° for 40 minutes or until golden brown on bottom. Remove potato slices from oven (leave oven at 400°).
4. Add sage leaves to reserved oil mixture in bowl. Gently rub sage leaves along bottom of bowl, coating both sides. Lift 1 potato slice from baking sheet with a thin spatula. Lay 1 sage leaf on baking sheet, and cover with potato slice, browned side down. Repeat with remaining potato slices and sage leaves.
5. Bake at 400° for 10 minutes. Remove from heat. Using a thin spatula, carefully turn potato slices over with leaves on top. Bake an additional 10 minutes or until bottoms begin to brown. Serve immediately. Yield: 3 servings (serving size: 4 potato slices).

CALORIES 205 (21% from fat); FAT 4.7g (sat 0.7g, mono 3.3g, poly 0.4g); PROTEIN 3.5g; CARB 38.2g; FIBER 3.6g; CHOL 0mg; IRON 2.1mg; SODIUM 326mg; CALC 15mg

Test Kitchen Tip: You can double this recipe, and use two baking sheets. For even browning, rotate the baking sheets halfway through the first 40 minutes of baking.

Oven Fries with Crisp Sage Leaves

Roasted Potatoes with Tangy Watercress Sauce
(pictured on page 511)

Mix watercress, basil, and mint into a yogurt base for a fragrant, fresh-tasting sauce you can make up to two days ahead. Serve alongside chicken, beef, or lamb. You can also use the sauce as a dip for vegetables.

Prep: 20 minutes • Cook: 35 minutes

Tangy Watercress Sauce:

1½ cups plain fat-free yogurt
1 cup trimmed watercress
⅓ cup light mayonnaise
¼ cup chopped green onions
3 tablespoons chopped fresh basil
1 tablespoon chopped fresh mint
1 teaspoon balsamic vinegar
¼ teaspoon salt
⅛ teaspoon freshly ground black pepper

Potatoes:

3 pounds small red potatoes, quartered
1½ tablespoons olive oil
1 teaspoon freshly ground black pepper
½ teaspoon salt
Cooking spray

1. Preheat oven to 450°.
2. To prepare sauce, place first 9 ingredients in a food processor or blender; process until smooth, scraping sides. Cover; chill.
3. To prepare potatoes, combine potatoes and next 3 ingredients on a jelly-roll pan or in a shallow roasting pan coated with cooking spray, tossing to coat. Bake at 450° for 35 minutes or until tender, stirring occasionally. Serve with sauce. Yield: 8 servings (serving size: 1 cup potatoes and 2 tablespoons sauce).

CALORIES 210 (26% from fat); FAT 6.1g (sat 0.9g, mono 1.9g, poly 0.3g); PROTEIN 6.6g; CARB 33.2g; FIBER 3.1g; CHOL 4mg; IRON 2.6mg; SODIUM 347mg; CALC 123mg

Basic Mashed Potatoes

Chicken broth and milk make these mashed potatoes rich; sour cream gives them tang.

Prep: 15 minutes • Cook: 22 minutes

3 pounds cubed peeled baking potato
½ cup 2% reduced-fat milk
½ cup fat-free, less-sodium chicken broth
3 tablespoons reduced-fat sour cream
1 teaspoon salt
½ teaspoon pepper
¼ cup butter, softened

1. Place potato in a saucepan, and cover with water. Bring to a boil. Reduce heat; simmer 15 minutes or until tender.
2. Drain and return potato to pan. Add milk and broth; mash to desired consistency. Cook 2 minutes or until thoroughly heated, stirring constantly. Stir in sour cream, salt, and pepper. Top with butter. Yield: 8 servings (serving size: about ¾ cup).

CALORIES 162 (30% from fat); FAT 5.4g (sat 3.4g, mono 1.4g, poly 0.2g); PROTEIN 3.7g; CARB 25.4g; FIBER 2.2g; CHOL 15mg; IRON 1mg; SODIUM 306mg; CALC 32mg

Bacon and Cheddar Mashed Potatoes

Vary the flavors by using Swiss cheese instead of Cheddar and prosciutto instead of bacon.

Prep: 18 minutes • Cook: 26 minutes

2½ pounds cubed peeled baking potato
1 cup (4 ounces) shredded extrasharp Cheddar cheese
1 cup 2% reduced-fat milk
½ cup chopped green onions
2 tablespoons reduced-fat sour cream
½ teaspoon salt
½ teaspoon freshly ground black pepper
4 bacon slices, cooked and crumbled

1. Place potato in a saucepan, and cover with water. Bring to a boil. Reduce heat; simmer 15 minutes or until tender.
2. Drain and return potato to pan. Add cheese and milk; mash to desired consistency. Cook 2 minutes or until thoroughly heated, stirring constantly. Stir in onions and remaining ingredients. Yield: 8 servings (serving size: about ¾ cup).

CALORIES 214 (30% from fat); FAT 7.1g (sat 4.1g, mono 2.1g, poly 0.4g); PROTEIN 8.9g; CARB 29.6g; FIBER 2.6g; CHOL 22mg; IRON 1.4mg; SODIUM 330mg; CALC 157mg

how to mash and whip potatoes

potato masher Potato mashers give you a multitude of texture options. They're your best bet if you like the texture of the skin in your mashed potatoes.

electric mixer Use a hand mixer instead of a food processor to whip potatoes. A food processor is so powerful that it will overmix the potatoes and make them gummy.

Ecuadorean Potato-and-Cheese Patties

These skillet-fried potato patties exemplify the Latin-style of cooking in which simple ingredients are prepared with highly flavorful seasonings to create a vibrant dish.

Prep: 20 minutes • Cook: 28 minutes • Other: 20 minutes

1½ teaspoons kosher salt
2 medium peeled baking potatoes, quartered (about 1¼ pounds)
6 tablespoons (1½ ounces) shredded queso fresco or Monterey Jack cheese
2 tablespoons minced green onions
¼ teaspoon kosher salt
¼ teaspoon freshly ground black pepper
1 tablespoon olive oil
¾ cup diced tomato
½ cup julienne-cut red onion

1. Place 1½ teaspoons salt and potato in a saucepan, and cover with water. Bring to a boil; reduce heat, and simmer 15 minutes or until tender. Drain and mash with a potato masher until smooth. Cool.

2. Add cheese, green onions, ¼ teaspoon salt, and pepper to potato mixture, stirring well. Divide potato mixture into 6 balls (about ½ cup per ball). Flatten balls into ½-inch-thick patties (about 3-inch diameter). Place on a baking sheet; cover and refrigerate 20 minutes or until firm.

3. Heat oil in a large nonstick skillet over medium heat. Place potato-and-cheese patties in pan; cook 5 minutes or until bottoms are browned. Turn patties; cook 3 minutes. Remove patties from pan. Top patties evenly with tomato and red onion. Yield: 6 servings (serving size: 1 patty).

CALORIES 157 (26% from fat); FAT 4.6g (sat 1.8g, mono 1.3g, poly 1.2g); PROTEIN 4.2g; CARB 24.9g; FIBER 2.1g; CHOL 6mg; IRON 0.6mg; SODIUM 279mg; CALC 64mg

Potato Latkes

The potato mixture releases moisture as it sits, so squeeze the latkes before cooking them. Place the cooked patties on paper towels to lightly drain some of the oil. Serve with light sour cream and applesauce.

Prep: 15 minutes • Cook: 22 minutes

4 cups shredded peeled baking potato (about 1½ pounds)
1 cup grated fresh onion (about 2 medium)
¼ cup all-purpose flour
1 teaspoon chopped fresh thyme
1 teaspoon salt
¼ teaspoon freshly ground black pepper
1 large egg, lightly beaten
1 large egg white, lightly beaten
3 tablespoons olive oil

1. Combine potato and onion in a sieve; squeeze moisture from potato mixture, discarding liquid. Lightly spoon flour into a dry measuring cup; level with a knife. Combine potato mixture, flour, and next 5 ingredients in a large bowl. Divide mixture into 12 equal portions; squeeze out any remaining liquid. Shape each portion into a ¼-inch-thick patty.

2. Heat 1½ tablespoons oil in a large nonstick skillet over medium heat. Add 6 patties; cook 5 minutes on each side or until golden. Repeat procedure with remaining 1½ tablespoons oil and patties. Yield: 12 servings (serving size: 1 patty).

CALORIES 81 (31% from fat); FAT 2.8g (sat 0.4g, mono 1.8g, poly 0.3g); PROTEIN 2.6g; CARB 11.2g; FIBER 1.3g; CHOL 18mg; IRON 0.6mg; SODIUM 210mg; CALC 10mg

Classic Makeover: Potato Gratin

With 15.4 grams of fat per serving, this ultrarich gratin—with layers of Yukon gold potatoes smothered in a sauce of goat cheese, whole milk, and whipping cream—wasn't exactly healthy. By substituting half-and-half for the whipping cream, we eliminated 64 grams of fat from the recipe. Allowing 1% milk to stand in for whole milk, slightly reducing the cheese, and spraying our pan with cooking spray instead of buttering it brought the total down by another 23 grams of fat. We added a little flour to the sauce and ended up with the same rich texture of the original—with less than half of the fat.

Before	After
• 239 calories	• 193 calories
• 15.4g fat	• 5.8g fat
• percentage of calories from fat 58%	• percentage of calories from fat 27%

Potato Gratin with Goat Cheese and Garlic

A gratin is any dish that is topped with cheese (and sometimes buttered breadcrumbs), and then baked until brown and crispy. This potato version has layers of sliced potatoes topped with a cheesy white sauce.

Prep: 15 minutes • Cook: 1 hour, 10 minutes

    1   cup half-and-half, divided
    1   tablespoon all-purpose flour
    1   cup (4 ounces) crumbled goat cheese
    1   cup 1% low-fat milk
    1   teaspoon salt
    ¾   teaspoon pepper
    ⅛   teaspoon ground nutmeg
    1   garlic clove, minced
    5   cups thinly sliced peeled Yukon gold
        potato (about 2½ pounds)
    Cooking spray

1. Preheat oven to 400°.
2. Combine 2 tablespoons half-and-half and flour in a large bowl, stirring with a whisk. Add remaining half-and-half, cheese, and next 5 ingredients, stirring with a whisk.
3. Arrange half of potato slices in a single layer in an 11 x 7–inch baking dish coated with cooking spray. Stir milk mixture; immediately pour half of milk mixture over potato slices. Repeat procedure with remaining potato slices and milk mixture. Bake at 400° for 1 hour and 10 minutes or until potato is tender and golden brown. Yield: 9 servings (serving size: ⅔ cup).

CALORIES 193 (27% from fat); FAT 5.8g (sat 3.8g, mono 1.6g, poly 0.1g); PROTEIN 6.4g; CARB 28.4g; FIBER 2.4g; CHOL 20mg; IRON 0.7mg; SODIUM 341mg; CALC 90mg

Potatoes Anna

Aw Maw's Potatoes

Instead of using frozen hash browns for this cheesy potato casserole, we've kept the sodium lower by shredding cooked, chilled potatoes.

Prep: 15 minutes • Cook: 1 hour, 34 minutes

  4 pounds baking potatoes
Cooking spray
  ⅓ cup butter
  3 cups fat-free milk
  1 cup (4 ounces) shredded reduced-fat
     sharp Cheddar cheese, divided
  2 teaspoons salt
  ¼ teaspoon freshly ground black pepper

1. Place potatoes in a Dutch oven, and cover with water. Bring to a boil; reduce heat, and simmer 20 minutes or until tender. Drain. Cover and chill.
2. Preheat oven to 350°.
3. Peel and shred potatoes. Place in a 13 x 9–inch baking dish coated with cooking spray. Melt butter in a large saucepan over medium heat. Stir in milk, ½ cup cheese, salt, and pepper. Cook 8 minutes or until cheese melts, stirring occasionally. Pour over potato, and stir gently. Bake at 350° for 45 minutes.
4. Sprinkle potato mixture with remaining ½ cup cheese. Bake an additional 15 minutes or until cheese melts. Yield: 12 servings (serving size: ⅔ cup).

CALORIES 213 (30% from fat); FAT 7g (sat 4.5g, mono 1.9g, poly 0.3g); PROTEIN 8g; CARB 30.2g; FIBER 2.4g; CHOL 20mg; IRON 1.2mg; SODIUM 541mg; CALC 174mg

Potatoes Anna

This classic yet easy potato dish has a wonderfully sophisticated flavor. And it's hard not to love the completely addictive chips that form the top of the dish.

Prep: 15 minutes • Cook: 47 minutes

  1 teaspoon kosher or sea salt
  ½ teaspoon pepper
2½ tablespoons unsalted butter
  3 pounds peeled baking potato, cut
     into ⅛-inch-thick slices
  1 tablespoon unsalted butter, melted
     and divided
  1 tablespoon chopped fresh flat-leaf
     parsley (optional)

1. Preheat oven to 450°.
2. Combine salt and pepper. Melt 2½ tablespoons butter in a 10-inch cast-iron or ovenproof heavy skillet over medium heat. Arrange a single layer of potato slices, slightly overlapping, in a circular pattern in pan; sprinkle with ¼ teaspoon salt mixture. Drizzle ½ teaspoon melted butter over potato. Repeat layers 5 times, ending with butter. Press firmly to pack. Cover and bake at 450° for 20 minutes.
3. Uncover and bake an additional 25 minutes or until potato is golden. Loosen edges of potato with a spatula. Place a plate upside down on top of pan; invert potato onto plate. Sprinkle with parsley, if desired. Yield: 8 servings (serving size: 1 wedge).

CALORIES 208 (23% from fat); FAT 5.2g (sat 3.2g, mono 1.5g, poly 0.3g); PROTEIN 3.4g; CARB 36.7g; FIBER 2.6g; CHOL 14mg; IRON 0.7mg; SODIUM 353mg; CALC 11mg

how to arrange potato

Press down on the finished layers with the bottom of a clean, heavy pan or your hands. You want the potatoes to be dense and compact so that they hold together.

Vanilla Sweet Potatoes

If your oven space is limited during holiday meal preparation, these microwaved sweet potatoes might save the day.

Prep: 10 minutes • Cook: 17 minutes
Other: 5 minutes

  2 pounds sweet potatoes
 ¾ cup 1% low-fat milk
 ¼ cup packed brown sugar
  2 tablespoons vanilla extract
  2 tablespoons butter, softened

1. Pierce potatoes with a fork; arrange in a circle on paper towels in microwave oven. Microwave at HIGH 10 minutes or until tender, rearranging potatoes after 5 minutes. Wrap in a towel; let stand 5 minutes.
2. Peel and mash potatoes. Combine potato, milk, and remaining ingredients. Place in a 1-quart casserole. Cover; microwave at MEDIUM 7 minutes or until heated. Yield: 6 servings (serving size: ⅔ cup).

CALORIES 241 (17% from fat); FAT 4.6g (sat 2.7g, mono 1.2g, poly 0.4g); PROTEIN 3.5g; CARB 44.6g; FIBER 4.5g; CHOL 12mg; IRON 1mg; SODIUM 77mg; CALC 78mg

Spicy Sweet Potato Wedges

Cooking these potatoes at high heat makes their interior tender just as the sugar-and-spice coating begins to caramelize and brown the outside.

Prep: 10 minutes • Cook: 20 minutes

  6 sweet potatoes (about 2¼ pounds)
Cooking spray
  2 teaspoons sugar
 ½ teaspoon salt
 ¼ teaspoon ground red pepper
 ⅛ teaspoon black pepper

1. Preheat oven to 500°.

2. Peel potatoes; cut each lengthwise into quarters. Place potato in a large bowl; coat with cooking spray. Combine sugar, salt, and peppers, and sprinkle over potato, tossing well to coat. Arrange potato, cut sides down, in a single layer on a baking sheet. Bake at 500° for 10 minutes; turn wedges over. Bake an additional 10 minutes or until tender and beginning to brown. Yield: 8 servings (serving size: 3 wedges).

CALORIES 153 (2% from fat); FAT 0.4g (sat 0.1g, mono 0g, poly 0.2g); PROTEIN 2.4g; CARB 35.5g; FIBER 2.3g; CHOL 0mg; IRON 0.9mg; SODIUM 166mg; CALC 31mg

Brown Sugar-Glazed Sweet Potato Wedges

Make this tasty side dish up to two days ahead, and store, covered, in the refrigerator. Reheat, covered, at 350° for 20 minutes.

Prep: 15 minutes • Cook: 49 minutes

 ¼ cup unsalted butter
 ¾ cup packed dark brown sugar
 ¼ cup water
  1 teaspoon salt
 ½ teaspoon ground nutmeg
 ¼ teaspoon ground ginger
  1 (3-inch) cinnamon stick
  4 pounds sweet potatoes, peeled, cut in half crosswise, and cut into ½-inch wedges
Cooking spray

1. Preheat oven to 400°.
2. Melt butter in a medium saucepan over medium heat. Add sugar and next 5 ingredients; bring to a simmer. Cook 5 minutes, stirring frequently. Discard cinnamon stick.
3. Combine sugar mixture and potato wedges in a large bowl; toss well. Arrange on a large jelly-roll pan coated with cooking spray. Bake at 400° for 40 minutes or

until tender, stirring after 20 minutes. Yield: 12 servings (serving size: ⅔ cup).

CALORIES 182 (19% from fat); FAT 3.9g (sat 2.4g, mono 1.1g, poly 0.2g); PROTEIN 1.7g; CARB 36.1g; FIBER 3g; CHOL 10mg; IRON 0.8mg; SODIUM 211mg; CALC 44mg

Spiced Sweet Potato Casserole

What's a Thanksgiving meal without a sweet potato casserole? Assemble this one in its baking dish; store, covered, in the refrigerator up to one day.

Prep: 15 minutes • Cook: 1 hour, 1 minute
Other: 5 minutes

  3 pounds sweet potatoes
 ⅓ cup packed brown sugar
  2 tablespoons butter
  2 tablespoons orange juice concentrate
1½ teaspoons ground cinnamon
 ½ teaspoon salt
 ½ teaspoon ground nutmeg
  2 large eggs
 ¼ cup chopped pecans

1. Preheat oven to 350°.
2. Pierce potatoes with a fork; arrange in a circle on paper towels in microwave oven. Microwave at HIGH 16 minutes or until tender, rearranging potatoes after 8 minutes. Let stand 5 minutes.
3. Cut each potato in half lengthwise; scoop out pulp into a bowl. Discard skins. Add sugar and next 5 ingredients, and beat with a mixer at low speed until combined. Add eggs; beat until smooth. Spoon into a 1½-quart baking dish; sprinkle with pecans. Bake at 350° for 45 minutes. Yield: 8 servings (serving size: ½ cup).

CALORIES 220 (29% from fat); FAT 7g (sat 2.5g, mono 2.9g, poly 1.1g); PROTEIN 3.8g; CARB 36.8g; FIBER 3.8g; CHOL 61mg; IRON 1.1mg; SODIUM 206mg; CALC 53mg

Meringue and Streusel-Topped Sweet Potatoes

If you don't have a pastry bag, simply fill a zip-top plastic bag with the meringue, and snip a corner with kitchen shears. Instead of a lattice, personalize the meringue design any way you desire. (See pages 147 and 149 for tips on separating and beating egg whites and making meringues.)

Prep: 30 minutes • Cook: 1 hour, 10 minutes

Sweet potato puree:

>   8 cups cubed peeled sweet potato
>   (about 3¼ pounds)
>   1 cup sweetened dried cranberries,
>   coarsely chopped
>   ½ cup half-and-half
>   ⅓ cup maple syrup
>   1 teaspoon salt
>   1 teaspoon vanilla extract
>   ½ teaspoon ground cinnamon
>   ½ teaspoon maple flavoring
>   2 large eggs
>   Cooking spray

Streusel:

>   ⅔ cup chopped pecans
>   ½ cup packed light brown sugar
>   2 tablespoons all-purpose flour
>   2 tablespoons butter, melted
>   ¼ teaspoon ground cinnamon

Meringue:

>   4 large egg whites
>   2⅓ cups granulated sugar

1. Preheat oven to 350°.
2. To prepare sweet potato puree, place sweet potato in a stockpot, and cover with water; bring to a boil. Reduce heat; simmer 20 minutes or until tender. Drain potato; place in a large bowl. Add cranberries and next 7 ingredients; beat with a mixer at high speed 2 minutes or until

smooth. Spoon sweet potato puree into a 13 x 9–inch baking dish coated with cooking spray.
3. To prepare streusel, combine pecans, brown sugar, flour, butter, and ¼ teaspoon cinnamon. Sprinkle streusel evenly over sweet potato puree. Bake at 350° for 30 minutes; remove from oven (do not turn oven off).
4. To prepare meringue, place egg whites in a large bowl; beat with mixer at high speed until soft peaks form using clean, dry beaters. Gradually add granulated sugar, 1 tablespoon at a time, beating until stiff peaks form (about 4 minutes).
5. Spoon meringue into a pastry bag fitted with a star tip. Pipe meringue in a lattice design over streusel. Bake at 350° for 15 minutes or until lightly browned. Yield: 16 servings (serving size: ½ cup).

CALORIES 267 (26% from fat); FAT 7.6g (sat 2.3g, mono 3.1g, poly 1.4g); PROTEIN 4.3g; CARB 46g; FIBER 3.6g; CHOL 73mg; IRON 1.1mg; SODIUM 201mg; CALC 53mg

Oven-Roasted Sweet Potatoes and Onions

All-Time Favorite
Oven-Roasted Sweet Potatoes and Onions

The gently flavored onions and potatoes develop a richer, more complex sweetness as they caramelize. This recipe requires only one dish, and it's pretty much hands-off cooking. Serve it alongside roasted chicken, pork loin, or ham at holiday gatherings.

Prep: 9 minutes • Cook: 35 minutes

>   4 medium peeled sweet potatoes, cut
>   into 2-inch pieces (about 2¼ pounds)
>   2 sweet onions, cut into 1-inch pieces
>   (about 1 pound)
>   2 tablespoons extravirgin olive oil
>   ¾ teaspoon garlic-pepper blend (such
>   as McCormick)
>   ½ teaspoon salt

1. Preheat oven to 425°.
2. Combine all ingredients in a 13 x 9–inch baking dish, tossing to coat.
3. Bake at 425° for 35 minutes or until tender, stirring occasionally. Yield: 6 servings (serving size: 1 cup).

CALORIES 247 (19% from fat); FAT 5.1g (sat 0.7g, mono 3.4g, poly 0.6g); PROTEIN 3.6g; CARB 47.8g; FIBER 6.5g; CHOL 0mg; IRON 1.2mg; SODIUM 255mg; CALC 53mg

Grilled Summer Squash

You can use either all yellow squash or zucchini, but the dish is prettiest with a combination of the two.

Prep: 15 minutes • Cook: 10 minutes
Other: 15 minutes

¼ cup fresh lemon juice
¼ cup plain fat-free yogurt
1 tablespoon olive oil
2 teaspoons chopped fresh rosemary
½ teaspoon freshly ground black pepper
2 garlic cloves, minced
¾ teaspoon salt, divided
3 small yellow squash, halved lengthwise (about 1 pound)
3 small zucchini, halved lengthwise (about 1 pound)
Cooking spray

1. Prepare grill.
2. Combine first 6 ingredients in a 13 x 9–inch baking dish. Stir in ½ teaspoon salt. Make 3 (¼-inch-deep) diagonal cuts across cut side of each squash and zucchini half. Place squash and zucchini halves, cut sides down, in baking dish. Marinate squash and zucchini at room temperature 15 minutes.
3. Remove squash and zucchini from marinade, and discard marinade. Place squash and zucchini on grill rack coated with cooking spray. Grill 5 minutes on each side or until tender. Sprinkle evenly with ¼ teaspoon salt. Yield: 6 servings (serving size: 2 squash halves).

CALORIES 45 (30% from fat); FAT 1.5g (sat 0.2g, mono 0.9g, poly 0.2g); PROTEIN 2.1g; CARB 7.7g; FIBER 2.9g; CHOL 0mg; IRON 0.8mg; SODIUM 202mg; CALC 41mg

Yellow Squash Casserole

Here's our lightened rendition of a favorite.

Prep: 20 minutes • Cook: 46 minutes

8 cups sliced yellow squash
1 tablespoon water
6 ounces hot turkey Italian sausage
½ cup chopped onion
2 garlic cloves, minced
2 (1-ounce) slices day-old white bread
½ cup fat-free sour cream
⅓ cup (1½ ounces) diced provolone cheese
¼ teaspoon salt
¼ teaspoon pepper
1 (10¾-ounce) can condensed reduced-fat, reduced-sodium cream of mushroom soup, undiluted
Cooking spray

1. Preheat oven to 350°.
2. Combine squash and water in a large microwave-safe bowl. Cover with plastic wrap; vent. Microwave at HIGH 6 minutes or until tender. Drain well.
3. Remove casings from sausage. Cook sausage, onion, and garlic in a large skillet over medium-high heat until browned, stirring to crumble. Drain.
4. Place bread in a food processor, and pulse 10 times or until coarse crumbs form to measure 1 cup. Combine squash, sausage mixture, ½ cup breadcrumbs, sour cream, cheese, salt, pepper, and soup. Spoon into a 2-quart casserole coated with cooking spray. Top with remaining ½ cup breadcrumbs. Lightly coat breadcrumbs with cooking spray. Bake at 350° for 30 minutes. Yield: 12 servings (serving size: ⅔ cup).

CALORIES 85 (31% from fat); FAT 2.9g (sat 1.2g, mono 0.5g, poly 0.6g); PROTEIN 4.8g; CARB 10.3g; FIBER 1.8g; CHOL 12mg; IRON 0.7mg; SODIUM 279mg; CALC 91mg

Squash-Rice Casserole

Our version of squash casserole features zucchini instead of yellow squash with the addition of cooked rice. Cook the rice while the zucchini and onion are simmering.

Prep: 15 minutes • Cook: 55 minutes

8 cups sliced zucchini (about 2½ pounds)
1 cup chopped onion
½ cup fat-free, less-sodium chicken broth
2 cups cooked rice
1 cup fat-free sour cream
1 cup (4 ounces) shredded reduced-fat sharp Cheddar cheese
¼ cup (1 ounce) grated fresh Parmesan cheese, divided
¼ cup Italian-seasoned breadcrumbs
1 teaspoon salt
¼ teaspoon pepper
2 large eggs, lightly beaten
Cooking spray

1. Preheat oven to 350°.
2. Combine first 3 ingredients in a Dutch oven; bring to a boil. Cover, reduce heat, and simmer 20 minutes or until tender. Drain; partially mash with a potato masher. Combine zucchini mixture, rice, sour cream, Cheddar cheese, 2 tablespoons Parmesan cheese, breadcrumbs, salt, pepper, and eggs in a bowl; stir. Spoon into a 13 x 9–inch baking dish coated with cooking spray; sprinkle with 2 tablespoons Parmesan cheese. Bake at 350° for 30 minutes or until bubbly.
3. Preheat broiler.
4. Broil 1 minute or until lightly browned. Yield: 8 servings (serving size: 1 cup).

CALORIES 197 (25% from fat); FAT 5.5g (sat 2.7g, mono 1.5g, poly 0.4g); PROTEIN 12.7g; CARB 24g; FIBER 1.4g; CHOL 65mg; IRON 1.5mg; SODIUM 623mg; CALC 209mg

Baked Spaghetti Squash with Tomato Sauce and Olives

Spaghetti squash has flesh so stringy that it resembles spaghetti when you scrape it out. So why not serve it with a tomato sauce?

Prep: 20 minutes • Cook: 1 hour, 30 minutes

  1 spaghetti squash (about 3¼ pounds)
1½ tablespoons olive oil
  1 cup minced fresh onion
  1 teaspoon dried oregano
 ½ teaspoon dried thyme
  2 bay leaves
Dash of crushed red pepper
  3 garlic cloves, minced and divided
  1 cup dry red wine
 ½ cup water
 ⅓ cup coarsely chopped pitted kalamata olives
  1 tablespoon capers
 ¼ teaspoon freshly ground black pepper
 ⅛ teaspoon salt
  1 (28-ounce) can crushed tomatoes, undrained
 ¼ cup (1 ounce) grated fresh Parmesan cheese
 ¼ cup chopped fresh parsley

1. Preheat oven to 375°.
2. Pierce squash with a fork. Place squash on a baking sheet; bake at 375° for 1½ hours or until tender. Cool. Cut squash in half lengthwise; discard seeds. Scrape inside of squash with a fork to remove spaghetti-like strands to measure 6 cups. Keep warm.
3. While squash bakes, heat oil in a large nonstick skillet over medium heat. Add onion, oregano, thyme, bay leaves, and red pepper; sauté 5 minutes. Add 2 minced garlic cloves, wine, and next 6 ingredients;

bring to a boil. Reduce heat; simmer until thick (about 30 minutes). Discard bay leaves.
4. Combine 1 minced garlic clove, Parmesan cheese, and parsley. Place spaghetti squash on plates; top with sauce. Sprinkle cheese mixture over each serving. Yield: 6 servings (serving size: 1 cup squash, ¾ cup sauce, and 1 tablespoon cheese mixture).

CALORIES 128 (28% from fat); FAT 3.9g (sat 1.2g, mono 1.9g, poly 0.6g); PROTEIN 4.8g; CARB 20.4g; FIBER 3.5g; CHOL 3mg; IRON 2.2mg; SODIUM 505mg; CALC 159mg

Maple-Roasted Acorn Squash

Real maple syrup yields the best flavor and brings out the natural sweetness of the squash. The darker the syrup, the better.

Prep: 15 minutes • Cook: 25 minutes

  6 acorn squash (about 1 pound each)
 ⅓ cup maple syrup
  2 tablespoons extravirgin olive oil
  1 teaspoon kosher salt
 ½ teaspoon freshly ground black pepper
Cooking spray

1. Preheat oven to 425°.
2. Cut each squash in half lengthwise. Discard seeds and membranes. Cut each half crosswise into 1-inch-thick slices; peel. Combine syrup, oil, salt, and pepper in a large bowl, stirring well. Add squash; toss to coat.
3. Place squash in a 13 x 9–inch baking dish coated with cooking spray. Bake at 425° for 25 minutes or until tender, stirring every 10 minutes. Yield: 9 servings (serving size: about 1 cup).

CALORIES 170 (20% from fat); FAT 3.7g (sat 0.6g, mono 2.3g, poly 0.6g); PROTEIN 4.4g; CARB 34.6g; FIBER 4.9g; CHOL 0mg; IRON 1.9mg; SODIUM 222mg; CALC 102mg

Butternut Squash and Leek Gratins

As an alternative to a squash casserole, bake vegetables in ramekins. Individual gratins bake more quickly than a large casserole.

Prep: 30 minutes • Cook: 1 hour, 58 minutes
Other: 30 minutes

  1 (2-pound) butternut squash, halved lengthwise and seeded
Cooking spray
  1 teaspoon butter
  4 cups finely chopped leek (about 6 large)
  1 tablespoon sugar
 ¾ teaspoon salt
 ¼ teaspoon freshly ground black pepper
Dash of ground nutmeg
  4 large eggs, lightly beaten
  1 large egg yolk, lightly beaten
 ¼ cup (1 ounce) grated fresh Parmesan cheese

1. Preheat oven to 375°.
2. Place squash halves, cut sides down, on a baking sheet coated with cooking spray. Bake at 375° for 45 minutes or until tender. Cool 30 minutes. Scoop out pulp; mash with a potato masher or fork until smooth.
3. Reduce oven temperature to 325°.
4. Heat a large nonstick skillet over medium heat; coat pan with cooking spray. Melt butter in pan. Add leek; cover and cook 20 minutes or until tender, stirring once. Reduce heat to medium-low; uncover and cook 10 minutes or until lightly browned, stirring occasionally. Cool slightly.
5. Combine sugar and next 5 ingredients in a large bowl, stirring with a whisk. Add squash and leek; stir until well combined.

Divide squash mixture evenly among 6 (6-ounce) ramekins or custard cups coated with cooking spray. Place ramekins in a 13 x 9–inch baking pan; add hot water to pan to a depth of 1 inch. Cover pan with foil; bake at 325° for 25 minutes. Uncover and bake an additional 15 minutes or until a knife inserted in center comes out clean. Remove from oven; place ramekins on a baking sheet. Sprinkle 2 teaspoons cheese over each ramekin.

6. Preheat broiler.

7. Broil gratins 2 minutes or until cheese melts and begins to brown. Yield: 6 servings (serving size: 1 gratin).

CALORIES 186 (31% from fat); FAT 6.4g (sat 2.6g, mono 2.2g, poly 0.8g); PROTEIN 8.6g; CARB 25.9g; FIBER 3.6g; CHOL 181mg; IRON 2.9mg; SODIUM 437mg; CALC 170mg

Bay Leaf and Thyme-Scented Roasted Winter Squash and Garlic

Whole, unpeeled garlic cloves roast along with butternut squash in this aromatic side dish. Give each person a couple of garlic cloves, and let them extract the mellow roasted pulp over the squash.

Prep: 11 minutes • Cook: 45 minutes

10 cups (2-inch) cubed peeled butternut squash (about 3 pounds)
 1 tablespoon olive oil
 ¾ teaspoon salt
 ¼ teaspoon freshly ground black pepper
12 garlic cloves, unpeeled
 8 thyme sprigs
 6 bay leaves
Cooking spray

1. Preheat oven to 450°.

2. Combine first 7 ingredients in a large bowl; toss to coat. Arrange in a single layer on a jelly-roll pan coated with cooking spray. Bake at 450° for 45 minutes or until tender, stirring after 20 minutes. Discard thyme and bay leaves before serving. Yield: 6 servings (serving size: 1 cup).

CALORIES 131 (17% from fat); FAT 2.5g (sat 0.4g, mono 1.7g, poly 0.3g); PROTEIN 2.7g; CARB 28.6g; FIBER 7.9g; CHOL 0mg; IRON 1.7mg; SODIUM 303mg; CALC 120mg

how to peel and cube butternut squash

1. Cut the squash in half and remove its seeds and fibers with a spoon.

2. Peel the squash with a vegetable peeler, cut it into cubes, and proceed with recipe.

Butternut Squash and Leek Gratins

Tomatoes Roasted with Rosemary and Lemon

Proof that simple foods are often best, this colorful multipurpose combination of tomatoes, herbs, and lemon smells almost as good as it tastes. To serve over pasta, cook 12 ounces dried pasta; drain and return pasta to pan. Stir in 3 cups of the roasted tomatoes; cook over low heat until liquid thickens. Serve with grated Parmesan cheese.

Prep: 11 minutes • Cook: 40 minutes

¼	cup chopped fresh flat-leaf parsley
1	tablespoon chopped fresh rosemary
1	tablespoon extravirgin olive oil
2	teaspoons grated lemon rind
½	teaspoon salt
½	teaspoon freshly ground black pepper
4	pounds plum tomatoes, quartered lengthwise
3	garlic cloves, minced

1. Preheat oven to 400°.
2. Place all ingredients in a large bowl; toss well to combine. Place in a 13 x 9–inch baking dish. Bake at 400° for 30 minutes, stirring every 10 minutes. Remove tomato mixture from oven.
3. Preheat broiler.
4. Broil tomato mixture 10 minutes or until tomatoes begin to brown. Remove from oven; stir gently. Yield: 10 servings (serving size: ½ cup).

CALORIES 53 (34% from fat); FAT 2g (sat 0.3g, mono 1.1g, poly 0.4g); PROTEIN 1.7g; CARB 9g; FIBER 2.2g; CHOL 0mg; IRON 1mg; SODIUM 134mg; CALC 15mg

Test Kitchen Tip: You can place chilled tomatoes in heavy-duty zip-top plastic bags, and freeze up to three months.

Fried Green Tomatoes

To lighten this southern diner classic, we pan-fried with a small amount of oil. If your skillet isn't large enough for eight tomato slices, cook them in batches using half of the oil and four slices of tomato per batch.

Prep: 6 minutes • Cook: 7 minutes

8	(½-inch-thick) slices green tomato (about 4 tomatoes)
½	teaspoon salt
¼	teaspoon pepper
½	cup yellow cornmeal
1	tablespoon canola oil

1. Sprinkle 1 side of each tomato slice evenly with salt and pepper. Dredge seasoned sides in cornmeal.
2. Heat oil in a large skillet over medium-high heat. Add tomato slices, coated sides down; cook 3 minutes on each side or until lightly browned. Remove tomato slices from pan, and serve immediately. Yield: 4 servings (serving size: 2 slices).

CALORIES 123 (29% from fat); FAT 3.9g (sat 0.4g, mono 2.2g, poly 1.3g); PROTEIN 3g; CARB 19.8g; FIBER 2.7g; CHOL 0mg; IRON 0.9mg; SODIUM 310mg; CALC 18mg

Tomatoes Roasted with Rosemary and Lemon

Dressings & Stuffings

Whether you consider dressing a sidekick to the turkey or pork, or the main part of the meal, we've got a variety of recipes to meet your needs.

Corn Bread Dressing

Approach the holidays with confidence as you add this corn bread dressing to your menu. Make the corn bread a day or two ahead.

Prep: 23 minutes • **Cook: 1 hour, 43 minutes**
Other: 15 minutes

5	cups Quick Buttermilk Corn Bread, crumbled (page 76)
3	cups (1-inch) cubed, toasted white bread (about 5 [1-ounce] slices)
1	cup crushed saltine crackers (about 20 crackers)
3	cups vegetable broth
2	cups chopped celery
2	cups chopped onion
¼	cup butter
1½	teaspoons dried rubbed sage
¼	teaspoon salt
¼	teaspoon pepper
2	large eggs
1	large egg white

Cooking spray

1. Preheat oven to 375°.
2. Combine first 3 ingredients in a large bowl. Combine broth, celery, onion, and butter in a large saucepan; bring to a boil. Reduce heat, and simmer 10 minutes. Add broth mixture to corn bread mixture, stirring well. Add sage and next 4 ingredients; stir well to combine.
3. Pour mixture into an 11 x 7–inch baking dish coated with cooking spray.

Bake at 375° for 45 minutes; cover and bake an additional 30 minutes or until golden. Yield: 12 servings (serving size: ⅔ cup).

(Totals include Quick Buttermilk Corn Bread) CALORIES 233 (31% from fat); FAT 7.9g (sat 3.1g, mono 3g, poly 1.1g); PROTEIN 6.2g; CARB 33.3g; FIBER 1.7g; CHOL 60mg; IRON 1.7mg; SODIUM 737mg; CALC 90mg

Savory Fruited Stuffing

Bits of dried fruit add a touch of sweetness to this herbed stuffing. Serve it with roasted turkey, Cornish hens, or pork. You can make the stuffing ahead, cover, and refrigerate it up to 24 hours before baking. Let the stuffing come to room temperature before baking.

Prep: 8 minutes • **Cook: 44 minutes**
Other: 2 hours, 10 minutes

3½	cups fat-free, less-sodium chicken broth
1	cup dried mixed-fruit bits
2	tablespoons butter
2	cups finely chopped onion
½	cup thinly sliced celery
1	(14-ounce) package cubed country-style stuffing mix (such as Pepperidge Farm)

1. Combine broth and dried fruit in a small microwave-safe bowl; microwave at HIGH 2 minutes or until hot. Cover and let stand 10 minutes.

2. Melt butter in a large saucepan over medium heat. Add onion and celery; cook 8 minutes or until tender, stirring occasionally. Add broth mixture, and bring to a simmer. Remove from heat; stir in stuffing mix, tossing well.
3. Spoon stuffing into a 13 x 9–inch baking dish; cover and refrigerate 2 hours.
4. Preheat oven to 350°.
5. Bake at 350° for 30 minutes. Yield: 10 servings (serving size: 1 cup).

CALORIES 224 (16% from fat); FAT 4g (sat 1.5g, mono 1.8g, poly 0.1g); PROTEIN 7.2g; CARB 41g; FIBER 3.9g; CHOL 6mg; IRON 2mg; SODIUM 597mg; CALC 58mg

dressing or stuffing?

Dressing and stuffing are basically the same thing—a seasoned mixture of some type of breadcrumbs or cubes used to stuff poultry or meat. It can be cooked separately or in the food in which it's stuffed. We don't recommend cooking stuffing in a bird because the stuffing may prevent the inside part of the bird from reaching the safe temperature. If the inside of the bird is not at a safe temperature, the bacteria from the uncooked bird can cross-contaminate the stuffing.

Oyster Dressing

Start the wild rice first, then cook the eggs and prepare the stuffing while the rice cooks.

**Prep: 20 minutes • Cook: 1 hour, 15 minutes
Other: 15 minutes**

1½	cups corn bread stuffing mix
1	(16-ounce) container standard oysters, undrained
4	hard-cooked large eggs
	Cooking spray
½	cup chopped onion
½	cup chopped fresh parsley
½	cup chopped green bell pepper
3	cups cooked wild rice
½	cup fat-free, less-sodium chicken broth
½	cup sliced green onions
½	teaspoon salt
¼	teaspoon black pepper

1. Preheat oven to 350°.
2. Prepare stuffing according to package directions, omitting fat. Set aside.
3. Drain oysters in a colander over a bowl, reserving ⅓ cup oyster liquid.
4. Slice eggs in half lengthwise; discard yolks. Finely chop egg whites.
5. Heat a large nonstick skillet over medium heat. Coat pan with cooking spray. Add chopped onion, parsley, and bell pepper; sauté 3 minutes. Stir in oysters; cook 2 minutes. Stir in prepared stuffing, ⅓ cup oyster liquid, egg whites, wild rice, and remaining ingredients. Spread in an 8-inch square baking dish coated with cooking spray. Bake at 350° for 30 minutes. Yield: 10 servings (serving size: about ¾ cup).

CALORIES 140 (13% from fat); FAT 2g (sat 0.4g, mono 0.3g, poly 0.8g); PROTEIN 8.2g; CARB 22.3g; FIBER 1.8g; CHOL 25mg; IRON 4.1mg; SODIUM 313mg; CALC 43mg

Matzo, Mushroom, and Onion Kugel

This savory dish, also appropriate for a Passover meal, can replace any stuffing served with turkey. The secret to success here is to brown the matzo in the oven first.

**Prep: 20 minutes • Cook: 54 minutes
Other: 15 minutes**

10	(6-inch) matzo crackers
2½	cups fat-free, less-sodium chicken broth
1	cup hot water
¼	cup canola oil
3	cups diced onion
⅔	cup grated carrot
1	teaspoon salt
1	teaspoon paprika
½	teaspoon garlic powder
¼	teaspoon freshly ground black pepper
3	garlic cloves, minced
2	(8-ounce) packages presliced mushrooms
2	tablespoons chopped fresh parsley
4	large egg whites
2	large eggs
	Cooking spray
	Parsley sprigs (optional)

1. Preheat oven to 375°.
2. Place crackers in a single layer on a baking sheet; bake at 375° for 5 minutes or until lightly browned. Break crackers into small pieces, and place in a large bowl. Pour broth and water over matzo, and let stand 10 minutes, stirring occasionally.
3. Heat oil in a large nonstick skillet over medium heat. Add onion; cover and cook 5 minutes, stirring occasionally. Add carrot and next 6 ingredients; cover and cook 5 minutes or until onion is tender. Add mushroom mixture and chopped parsley to matzo mixture, stirring well. Combine egg whites and eggs in a bowl; stir with a whisk. Add egg mixture to matzo mixture; stir well.
4. Press matzo mixture into a 10-inch deep-dish pie plate coated with cooking spray. Bake, covered, at 375° for 20 minutes. Uncover and bake an additional 18 minutes or until lightly browned. Let kugel stand 5 minutes, and cut into wedges. Garnish with parsley sprigs, if desired. Yield: 12 servings (serving size: 1 wedge).

CALORIES 216 (29% from fat); FAT 7g (sat 0.7g, mono 3.5g, poly 1.8g); PROTEIN 7.6g; CARB 30.6g; FIBER 2.1g; CHOL 43mg; IRON 1.4mg; SODIUM 390mg; CALC 28mg

---

passover menu

serves 8

Mixed greens salad with honey-orange dressing*

Roast Lamb with Rosemary and Garlic (page 342)

Matzo, Mushroom, and Onion Kugel

Grilled Asparagus (page 517)

Almond-Apricot Macaroons (page 153)

*Combine 3 tablespoons fresh orange juice, 1 tablespoon honey, 2 teaspoons minced shallots, 2 teaspoons white wine vinegar, ½ teaspoon Dijon mustard, ¼ teaspoon salt, and ¼ teaspoon pepper, stirring with a whisk. Add 4 cups chopped romaine lettuce, 4 cups torn radicchio, and 3 cups baby spinach leaves; toss to coat.

glossary

Here are the definitions of some of the terms and ingredients used throughout this book. You'll find additional definitions in the text boxes and blurbs throughout the recipe chapters. If you can't find a specific term in this glossary, check the index (beginning on page 548) to see if the the term is defined elsewhere in the book.

Aïoli (ay-OH-lee): a garlic-flavored mayonnaise. Usually accompanies fish, meats, and vegetables.

Ancho chile peppers: dried, wrinkled chile peppers that are brick red or mahogany in color. (Fresh ancho peppers are referred to as poblanos.) About 3 inches wide at the stem and 4 inches in length. Have a slightly hot, sweet flavor. For most recipes, soak for 30 minutes in hot water to plump before using. Store dried in airtight containers in freezer for up to one year.

Aniseeds: tiny oval seeds that give a sweet licorice flavor to cookies and other desserts as well as some savory dishes. Can be found with spices in grocery stores. Store in a cool, dark, dry place for up to one year.

Apple butter: a thick preserve made by slowly cooking apples, sugar, spices, and juice or cider. Used as a spread for breads.

Arborio rice: a squat, oval-shaped rice with a delightful taste. The classic rice for risotto. Found with other kinds of rice in large supermarkets. May be labeled Italian risotto.

Baking powder: a leavening agent comprised of baking soda, cream of tartar, and cornstarch, which when combined with a liquid, releases carbon dioxide gas bubbles that cause a dough or batter to rise.

Baking soda: a leavening agent; combined with an acid such as buttermilk, yogurt, or molasses, it produces carbon dioxide gas bubbles that cause a dough or batter to rise.

Balsamic vinegar: made from white Trebbiano grapes. Aromatic and ages to a dark brown. Full-bodied, slightly sweet flavor with a hint of tartness. Use it in small amounts in vinaigrettes and sauces. Available in large supermarkets and gourmet-food markets. Store in a cool, dark place for up to six months.

Barbecue smoke seasoning: a bottled liquid used during cooking to give food a hickory-smoked flavor. May be labeled "liquid smoke" or "liquid barbecue smoke." Found with condiments in grocery stores.

Basmati rice (bas-MAH-tee): a highly aromatic, long-grain rice that has the aroma of popcorn when cooking. Has a nutty flavor and firm texture. Less aromatic varieties are grown in the United States, primarily in the Southwest and California. Available in specialty food stores and large supermarkets.

Bitters: a liquid used to flavor cocktails. Made from the distillation of aromatic herbs, barks, roots, and plants. They generally have a high alcohol content and a bitter or bittersweet flavor.

Blanch: to plunge a food, usually vegetables and fruits, into boiling water briefly, then into cold water to stop the cooking process. Blanching is done to firm the flesh, to loosen the skins, or to heighten and set color and flavor. Often, fresh vegetables are blanched before they're frozen.

Bean threads or cellophane noodles: made from the starch of green mung beans. Have a different texture from traditional noodles. May be labeled as "transparent" or "shining noodles," "pea-stick noodles," or "mung bean sticks." Only require a quick soak to be rehydrated. Commonly used in spring rolls.

Bird chiles: small red or green chiles that are very hot. They're often used in Thai cooking and also known as chiltepín chiles.

Bok choy: a cabbage that has long, pearly-white ribs with dark-green leaves which don't form a head. Also known as "pak choy" or "pak choi." Use in salads and stir-fried dishes. Buy at Chinese markets and large supermarkets. Look for firm ribs and crisp leaves. Store in a plastic bag in refrigerator for up to three days.

Brining: to soak a food in a solution of water and salt in order to pickle, preserve, or add flavor.

Bulgur: wheat kernels that are steamed, dried, and crushed. Has a tender, chewy texture, and works best in salads and pilafs. Main ingredient in tabbouleh.

Capers: dark-green buds of a bush native to the Mediterranean and parts of Asia. Size ranges from the petite (the nonpareil variety) to that of a large pearl. Dried in the sun, and then packed in a vinegar brine. Can be found with pickles, olives, and other condiments in supermarkets. Choose bottles that have clear liquid and little or no sediment. Refrigerate after opening.

Carambola: a deeply ridged, yellow fruit that grows in tropical climates. Sometimes referred to as star fruit because when it's cut in half crosswise, it has a five point star shape. Carambolas don't have to be peeled and can be eaten raw. Flavor ranges from sweet to tart. Vibrant yellow when ripe. Available in large supermarkets with the exotic fruits in the produce section.

Cardamom: a member of the ginger family. Adds an exotic kick to apple pie or spice cookies with its pungent, fresh, spicy-sweet taste. It's native to India and is an essential ingredient in the spice blend, garam masala. It's sold as whole pods, seeds, or ground.

Celery seed: from a wild variety of celery called lovage. Although the flavor resembles that of the familiar garden variety celery, it's under-pinned by an earthier note and a hint of bitter-ness. Whole seeds are the most common form found in the spice section of the supermarket; ground seeds are usually available at specialty stores. Use them sparingly; for such tiny seeds, they have an unexpectedly big flavor.

Chili sauce: a blend of tomatoes, chiles or chili powder, onions, green peppers, vinegar, sugar, and spices that is used as a condi-ment. Similar in appearance to ketchup.

Cilantro: an herb with delicate, lacy green leaves. Resembles flat-leaf parsley in appear-ance but has a pungent flavor. Sometimes called Chinese parsley. (Marketed as coriander when dried.) Used in Latin American and Asian foods. Choose a bunch with unwilted leaves and a good medium-green color. Found year-round in large supermarkets.

Cloves: the unopened flower buds of an ever-green tree. Refreshing fragrance adds a dis-tinctive note to cookies, cakes, muffins, and ham, and is also found in medicines, tooth-paste, mouthwash, and cosmetics. A pinch of ground cloves or a clove or two in a recipe adds a spicy-sweet edge that may be hard to pinpoint but would be missed if left out. Be careful not to use too much because a little goes a long way. You can purchase whole and ground cloves in most supermarkets.

Coriander: dried seeds and a dry spice. Often used in holiday breads and cookies. Flavor sim-ilar to a blend of lemon, sage, and caraway.

Coulis (koo-LEE): a thick puree or sauce. Often made from tomatoes or bell peppers.

Couscous (KOOS-koos): wheat that has been moistened with water, lightly coated with flour, and then rolled into tiny, beadlike pellets. Prepared by steaming or combining with boil-ing liquid and letting it stand until all the liquid is absorbed. Has its origins in the Middle East and North Africa, where it's typically served with stews.

Crème fraîche: a dairy product that has a rich, nutty undertone and a smoother, thicker texture than sour cream. Look for it in gour-met stores. You can use regular sour cream as a substitute, but it won't yield the same subtleties.

Cumin: an aromatic member of the parsley family with a pungent, nutty flavor. Used widely in Indian and Mexican cuisines, as well as Mediterranean and North African dishes. It's typically ground, but you can also find whole seeds ready for toasting in supermarkets or specialty stores.

Deglazing: the process of loosening and dis-solving solidified particles of food left on the surface of a skillet or pan after browning meat. Use a spatula to gently loosen the par-ticles, and stir in a liquid (such as wine or broth). Heat, stirring to dissolve particles.

Dice: to cut food into small ⅛- to ¼-inch cubes.

Dredge: to coat food lightly with flour, corn-meal, or breadcrumbs before cooking.

Edamame: immature soybeans that are picked green and served fresh. They can be served in the shell or shelled like baby lima beans. They're available frozen (in the pod or shelled), and shelled, fully cooked, and pack-aged in a moistureproof bag that you can store in the refrigerator for up to three weeks.

English cucumber: a variety of cucumber with fewer seeds. You can find them in most major supermarkets, but they're more expensive than regular cucumbers. They're also larger and come individually wrapped in plastic.

Fava beans: most often associated with Mediterranean and Middle Eastern dishes. Used in salads, falafel, or soups. The protein-rich beans, which range in color from yellow to green to tan to nearly black, can also be savored on their own, or used in place of limas in recipes. In addition to a pod that must be shelled, the tough outer skin must be removed with a quick blanching.

Fennel: an aromatic plant with pale green, celery-like stems and bright green, feathery foliage. It has a broad, bulbous base that's treated like a vegetable. Both the bulb and the stems can be eaten raw or cooked in a variety of methods.

Fennel seeds: small, oval, brown seeds that come from common fennel. They give foods a mild licorice flavor. Found with dried spices and herbs in grocery stores. Store in a cool, dark, dry place for up to one year.

Feta cheese: cheese made from goat's or sheep's milk that is soft, dry, and crumbly with a tangy taste. Available in jars (packed in brine) and in shrink-wrap packages in the dairy case in supermarkets and ethnic grocery stores.

Fine rice vermicelli: wide, flat Asian noodles. Similar in shape to fettuccine. Can be found labeled as "rice-stick noodles."

Fish sauce: a sauce made from anchovies, water, and salt. Very potent—use sparingly. Common in Asian foods.

Five-spice powder: (Chinese five-spice powder) a fragrant blend of cinnamon, cloves, fennel seed, star anise, and Szechuan peppercorns. The licorice-like anise and fennel meld with the sweet, pungent cloves and cinnamon and are underpinned by the peppercorn's woodsy flavor. Look for it in Asian markets or make your own using equal parts of each spice.

Fold: to incorporate a light mixture, such as beaten egg whites, into a heavier mixture, such as a custard, using a gentle over-and-under motion.

Garam masala: a blend of dry-roasted ground spices used often in Indian cuisines. There are many variations, but most blends include black pepper, cinnamon, cloves, coriander, cumin, cardamom, dried chiles, fennel, mace, nutmeg and other spices.

Groats: any grain—be it oats, wheat, or buckwheat—in its most minimally processed form. In contrast to other forms, in which grains are processed through rolling, steaming, chopping, or flaking, only the hulls are removed from groats, so they retain more nutrients and fiber.

Hoisin sauce: a thick, dark-brown Chinese sauce made from soybeans and chiles. Sugar and salt are added to give the sauce a sweet but biting taste. Available in jars and cans. Can be found in the ethnic-food section of supermarkets and in Asian grocery stores.

Horseradish: a knobby white root with a pungent, spicy flavor used to create a piquant taste. Available fresh in most supermarkets. It can be ground, but the same oils that give horseradish its zing can create strong, stinging fumes, so grind or grate it in a well-ventilated room. Many people opt instead to buy prepared horseradish, which is preground and jarred with vinegar or beet juice.

Hungarian paprika: comes in sweet or hot. Is considered to be the best paprika, but is interchangeable with regular paprika. Found in the spice section of large supermarkets.

Jícama (HEE-ka-ma): a large, light-brown tuberous root with white, juicy, crunchy flesh and a sweet, nutty flavor. It can be eaten either raw or cooked. Look for it in the produce section of large supermarkets and in Mexican markets; choose roots that have thin skin (thick skin means the jícama is old). Will keep for up to five days in the refrigerator.

Kalamata olives: deep-purple olives imported from Greece. Usually packed in oil in bottles. Found with other olives in supermarkets and specialty-food stores. Will keep for several weeks in the refrigerator.

Kosher salt: an additive-free coarse-grained salt used by some Jewish people in the preparation of meat. It's also used by cooks who prefer its texture and flavor, particularly for procedures such as brining.

Lemongrass: an herb with long, reedlike leaves. Use only the bottom 4 inches of the stem. Can be found fresh in the produce section of supermarkets and Asian markets. One teaspoon freshly grated lemon rind can be substituted for 1 teaspoon lemongrass.

Manchego cheese: Spain's most famous cheese. Made from sheep's milk and flavored with herbs. It comes in two varieties: a cured cheese that is aged three to four months and has a semisoft texture, and a more intensely flavored version that is aged longer and has a texture that resembles that of Parmesan cheese.

Masa harina: a corn flour of finer texture than cornmeal. Developed by treating hominy (corn product) with lime again. The wet hominy is freshly ground to make a meal called masa. When masa is dried, it's referred to as masa harina. Can be found along with other flour and cornmeal products in large grocery stores and Mexican-American markets. Store in the refrigerator in air-tight containers for up to six months.

Mesclun: a mixture of salad greens such as arugula, dandelion, frisée, oak leaf, radicchio, and sorrel. It's often packaged as "gourmet salad greens."

Mint: this aromatic herb comprises more than 30 species and hundreds of varieties, although the most familiar are peppermint and spearmint. Milder spearmint is often used in savory dishes, while its bolder cousin, peppermint, is perfect for candy and desserts.

Mirin: (also known as rice wine) a golden liquid used to add a vibrant note of sweetness to Japanese-style dishes. It's similar to sake, another rice wine, but sake is drier and used for both drinking and cooking; mirin is used only as an ingredient in recipes.

Miso: a fermented soybean paste that is the basis of the earthy, salty depth of flavor found in many Japanese dishes. In the U.S., you're most likely to find pungent dark miso, which enhances sturdy broths, and sweet, mild white miso, good for delicate sauces and dressings. Use about 1 tablespoon miso per cup of water, and don't subject it to extremely high temperatures. Stir it in at the end of cooking.

Napa cabbage: a type of cabbage that is usually elongated in shape and similar in appearance to romaine lettuce. It's thin, delicate, and has a mild flavor.

Oyster sauce: a sauce made from oysters, brine, and soy sauce. Used to flavor Asian foods. Bottled and canned versions can be found in Asian grocery stores. Refrigerate after opening; it will keep indefinitely.

Pearl barley: barley with the bran removed. Used in soups and stews. Cooks in 20 to 30 minutes.

Pine nuts (pignolias): Small, oblong, cream-colored nuts gathered from pine trees. Found in the nut section of large supermarkets and in health-food stores. Turn rancid easily, so store in the freezer for up to nine months.

Plantains: (also known as cooking bananas) look like oversized sweet bananas but resemble sweet potatoes in taste and texture. Require cooking before they're eaten. Now widely available in U.S. supermarkets and are often sold green; however, they're equally good and slightly sweeter when yellow or black.

Polenta: a cornmeal mush with Italian origins. Often cooked until firm and cut into squares or other shapes, and then baked, broiled, or fried until golden brown and crisp on the outside, soft and creamy on the inside. Often contains cheese and may be topped with a sauce or flavored with herbs.

Quinoa (KEEN-wah): small, round, cream-colored seeds (although some varieties are black). Becomes soft when cooked, almost resembling caviar in texture. Contains more protein than any other grain.

Radicchio: slightly bitter Italian chicory with firm, deep-red leaves with white ribs. The Verona variety is about the size and shape of Bibb lettuce; the Treviso variety has a long, narrow, tapered head. Can be found in the produce section of large supermarkets and specialty-food stores. Choose a fresh, crisp head with no wilted or bruised leaves. Refrigerate in a plastic bag for up to four days.

Rice paper: an edible, translucent paper similar to phyllo dough in texture. Used to wrap foods to be eaten as is or can be baked. Can be found labeled as "dried pastry flake."

Rice vinegar: made from either fermented rice or rice wine. Mainly used in Asian cooking. Can be found with other vinegars or in the Asian-food section of supermarkets.

Sauté: to cook foods quickly in a small amount of oil in a skillet over direct heat. Also known as stir-frying.

Savoy cabbage: Has crinkled leaves and a mild flavor. Is good as a salad. One of the best cabbages for cooking.

Scaloppine: very thin cuts of meat, most often veal. Usually dredged in flour before cooking.

Sea salt: salt crystals naturally evaporated by the sun and wind, and harvested and sold without processing. They contain the minerals present in sea water. Sea salt is best used as a condiment instead of in cooking. The crystals offer a pleasant crunch and a distinct flavor.

Sherry: a fortified wine made from the town of Jerez in the Andalusia region of southern Spain. Sherries range in color from light to dark and in flavor from dry and light to sweet and full-flavored.

Sherry vinegar: has a sour-sweet flavor and deep notes of oak. (The best ones age in oak barrels.) A good everyday vinegar for use in salad dressings and marinades.

Soba noodles: Japanese noodles made with a combination of buckwheat flour, wheat flour, and water.

Tempeh: made from partially cooked soybeans inoculated with spores of friendly mold in a process that is similar to cheese making. The mold creates threads that bind the soybeans into a flat cake. Tempeh is blanched or frozen to slow fermentation and preserve active enzymes. It has a yeasty flavor and a firm texture.

Turbinado sugar: a honey brown sugar with large crystals. Often sprinkled on sweet breads and desserts. Gives a subtle molasses flavor. Found with other sugar products in large supermarkets and gourmet-food stores. Will keep indefinitely in an airtight container. If not available, substitute raw or granulated sugar.

Udon noodles: thick Japanese noodles that are similar to spaghetti. Available as round or square. Typically made from either wheat or corn flour.

Water bath: a shallow pan of warm water in which containers of food, such as custards, are cooked. The water bath insulates and protects the custards from the heat of the oven so they cook slowly and evenly.

Watercress: a green that's a member of the mustard family. Flat, dark-green leaves that are peppery and pungent. Sold in bunches in the produce section. Used in salads and sandwiches or stirred into soups or pasta dishes before serving.

Wheat berries: whole, unprocessed wheat kernels used in pilafs and casseroles. Makes an excellent crouton alternative for salad toppings. High in protein and fiber. Must be soaked eight hours; then cooked one hour.

Kitchen Companion
This cooking guide gives you the answers to your questions about ingredient substitutions, unfamiliar ingredients, baking pans, and kitchen weights and measures.

Low-Fat Substitutions

Here are a few simple reduced-fat substitutions for high-fat ingredients.

Ingredient	Substitution
Fats and Oils	
Butter	Light butter, reduced-calorie margarine (except for baking)
Margarine	Light butter, reduced-calorie margarine (except for baking)
Mayonnaise	Fat-free, light, or low-fat mayonnaise
Oil	Polyunsaturated or monounsaturated oil in a reduced amount
Salad Dressing	Fat-free or reduced-fat salad dressing or vinaigrette
Shortening	Polyunsaturated or monounsaturated oil in a reduced amount
Meat and Poultry	
Bacon	Reduced-fat bacon; turkey bacon; lean ham; Canadian bacon
Ground Beef	Ground round, extralean ground beef, or ground turkey
Sausage	50%-less-fat pork sausage; turkey sausage
Luncheon Meat	Sliced turkey, chicken, lean roast beef, or lean ham
Tuna Packed in Oil	Tuna packed in water
Egg, whole	2 egg whites or ¼ cup egg substitute
Dairy	
Sour Cream	Fat-free or reduced-fat sour cream; fat-free or low-fat plain yogurt
Cheese, Cheddar, Swiss, Monterey Jack, Mozzarella	Reduced-fat cheeses (or use less of the regular cheese)
Cottage Cheese	Fat-free or 1% low-fat cottage cheese
Cream Cheese	Fat-free or light cream cheese; ⅓-less-fat (Neufchâtel) cheese
Ricotta Cheese	Part-skim ricotta or fat-free ricotta
Whole Milk	Fat-free or skim milk; 1% low-fat milk
Evaporated Milk	Fat-free evaporated milk
Half-and-Half	Fat-free half-and-half or fat-free evaporated milk
Whipped Cream	Fat-free or reduced-calorie frozen whipped topping
Ice Cream	Fat-free or low-fat ice cream or frozen yogurt; sherbet; sorbet
Other	
Soups, canned	Low-fat, reduced-sodium soups
Fudge Sauce	Fat-free chocolate syrup
Nuts	A reduced amount of nuts (one-third to one-half less)
Unsweetened Chocolate, 1 ounce	3 tablespoons unsweetened cocoa and 1 tablespoon butter

Common Ingredient Substitutions

If you're right in the middle of cooking and realize you don't have a particular ingredient, use the substitutions in this list.

Ingredient	Substitution
Baking Products	
Arrowroot, 1 teaspoon	1 tablespoon all-purpose flour or 1½ teaspoons cornstarch
Baking Powder, 1 teaspoon	½ teaspoon cream of tartar and ¼ teaspoon baking soda
Chocolate	
Semisweet, 1 ounce	1 ounce unsweetened chocolate and 1 tablespoon sugar
Unsweetened, 1 ounce	3 tablespoons cocoa and 1 tablespoon butter or margarine
Cocoa, ¼ cup	1 ounce unsweetened chocolate (decrease fat in recipe by ½ tablespoon)
Coconut, fresh, grated, 1½ tablespoons	1 tablespoon flaked coconut
Corn Syrup, light, 1 cup	1 cup sugar and ¼ cup water or 1 cup honey
Cornstarch, 1 tablespoon	2 tablespoons all-purpose flour or granular tapioca
Flour	
All-purpose, 1 tablespoon	1½ teaspoons cornstarch, potato starch, or rice starch
Cake, 1 cup sifted	1 cup minus 2 tablespoons all-purpose flour
Self-rising, 1 cup	1 cup all-purpose flour, 1 teaspoon baking powder, and ½ teaspoon salt
Shortening	
Melted, 1 cup	1 cup vegetable oil (do not use oil if recipe does not call for melted shortening)
Solid, 1 cup	1⅛ cups butter or margarine (decrease salt in recipe by ½ teaspoon)
Sugar	
Brown, firmly packed, 1 cup	1 cup granulated white sugar
Powdered, 1 cup	1 cup sugar and 1 tablespoon cornstarch (processed in food processor)
Honey, ½ cup	½ cup molasses or maple syrup
Eggs	
1 large	2 egg yolks for custards and cream fillings or 2 egg yolks and 1 tablespoon water for cookies
1 large	¼ cup egg substitute
2 large	3 small eggs
1 egg white (2 tablespoons)	2 tablespoons egg substitute
1 egg yolk (1½ tablespoons)	2 tablespoons sifted dry egg yolk powder and 2 teaspoons water or 1½ tablespoons thawed frozen egg yolk
Dairy Products	
Milk	
Buttermilk, low-fat or fat-free, 1 cup	1 tablespoon lemon juice or vinegar and 1 cup low-fat or fat-free milk (let stand 10 minutes)
Fat-free milk, 1 cup	4 to 5 tablespoons fat-free dry milk powder and enough cold water to make 1 cup
Sour Cream, 1 cup	1 cup plain yogurt

Ingredient	Substitution
Fruits and Vegetables	
Lemon, 1 medium	2 to 3 tablespoons juice and 2 teaspoons grated rind
Juice, 1 teaspoon	½ teaspoon vinegar
Peel, dried	2 teaspoons freshly grated lemon rind
Orange, 1 medium	½ cup juice and 2 tablespoons grated rind
Tomatoes, fresh, chopped, 2 cups	1 (16-ounce) can (may need to drain)
Tomato Juice, 1 cup	½ cup tomato sauce and ½ cup water
Tomato Sauce, 2 cups	¾ cup tomato paste and 1 cup water
Miscellaneous	
Broth, beef or chicken, canned, 1 cup	1 bouillon cube dissolved in 1 cup boiling water
Capers, 1 tablespoon	1 tablespoon chopped dill pickles or green olives
Chili Sauce, 1 cup	1 cup tomato sauce, ¼ cup brown sugar, 2 tablespoons vinegar, ¼ teaspoon ground cinnamon, dash of ground cloves, and dash of ground allspice
Chili Paste, 1 teaspoon	¼ teaspoon hot red pepper flakes
Gelatin, flavored, 3-ounce package	1 tablespoon unflavored gelatin and 2 cups fruit juice
Ketchup, 1 cup	1 cup tomato sauce, ½ cup sugar, and 2 tablespoons vinegar (for cooking, not to be used as a condiment)
Tahini (sesame-seed paste), 1 cup	¾ cup creamy peanut butter and ¼ cup sesame oil
Vinegar, cider, 1 teaspoon	2 teaspoons lemon juice mixed with a pinch of sugar
Wasabi, 1 teaspoon	1 teaspoon horseradish or hot dry mustard
Seasonings	
Allspice, ground, 1 teaspoon	½ teaspoon ground cinnamon and ½ teaspoon ground cloves
Apple Pie Spice, 1 teaspoon	½ teaspoon ground cinnamon, ¼ teaspoon ground nutmeg, and ⅛ teaspoon ground cardamom
Bay Leaf, 1 whole	¼ teaspoon crushed bay leaf
Chives, chopped, 1 tablespoon	1 tablespoon chopped green onion tops
Garlic, 1 clove	1 teaspoon bottled minced garlic
Ginger	
Crystallized, 1 tablespoon	⅛ teaspoon ground ginger
Fresh, grated, 1 tablespoon	⅛ teaspoon ground ginger
Herbs, fresh, 1 tablespoon	1 teaspoon dried herbs or ¼ teaspoon ground herbs (except rosemary)
Horseradish, fresh, grated, 1 tablespoon	2 tablespoons prepared horseradish
Lemongrass, 1 stalk, chopped	1 teaspoon grated lemon zest
Mint, fresh, chopped, 3 tablespoons	1 tablespoon dried spearmint or peppermint
Mustard, dried, 1 teaspoon	1 tablespoon prepared mustard
Parsley, fresh, chopped, 1 tablespoon	1 teaspoon dried parsley
Vanilla Bean, 6-inch bean	1 tablespoon vanilla extract

Alcohol Substitutions

Liqueurs, spirits, and wines add special flavors to food that are difficult to replace. Alcohol itself evaporates at 172°, leaving only its flavor behind. However, this chart gives ideas for substitution of alcoholic ingredients, should you choose to change the recipe.

Ingredient	Substitution
Amaretto (2 tablespoons)	¼ to ½ teaspoon almond extract
Grand Marnier or other orange-flavored liqueur (2 tablespoons)	2 tablespoons orange juice concentrate or 2 tablespoons orange juice and ½ teaspoon orange extract
Kahlúa, coffee- or chocolate-flavored liqueur (2 tablespoons)	2 tablespoons strong brewed coffee and 1 teaspoon sugar
Rum or **Brandy** (2 tablespoons)	½ to 1 teaspoon rum or brandy extract for recipes in which liquid amount is not crucial (add water if it is necessary to have a specified amount of liquid)
Sherry or **Bourbon** (2 tablespoons)	1 to 2 teaspoons vanilla extract
Port, Sherry, Rum, Brandy, or fruit-flavored liqueur (¼ cup or more)	equal measure of orange juice or apple juice and 1 teaspoon of corresponding flavored extract or vanilla extract
White Wine (¼ cup or more)	equal measure of white grape juice or apple juice for dessert recipes; equal measure of fat-free, less-sodium chicken broth for savory recipes
Red Wine (¼ cup or more)	equal measure of red grape juice or cranberry juice for dessert recipes; for soups, stews and other savory dishes, sometimes may substitute an equal measure of beef broth

Baking Pan Substitutions

If a recipe calls for a pan you don't have, try substituting one of a similar capacity. You may need to adjust the baking time.

Shape	Dimensions	Capacity	Substitutions
Rectangular	11 x 7–inch	8 cups	8 x 8–inch
	13 x 9–inch	12 to 15 cups	two (9-inch) round or three (8-inch) round
Square	8 x 8–inch	8 cups	11 x 7–inch
	9 x 9–inch	10 cups	9 x 5–inch loaf pan or two (8-inch) round
Round	8 x 1½–inch	5 cups	10 x 6–inch
	8 x 2–inch	6 cups	8½ x 4½–inch loaf pan
	9 x 1½–inch	6 cups	8 x 2-inch round
Tube	10 x 4–inch	16 cups	10-inch ring mold or cake mold
Loaf	8½ x 4½–inch	6 cups	two or three (6 x 3–inch) loaf pans
	9 x 5–inch	8 cups	three or four (6 x 3–inch) loaf pans
Pieplate	9 x 1½–inch	5 cups	No substitution unless tart pans are used
	10 x 1½–inch	6 cups	
Jelly-roll pan	15 x 10–inch	10 cups	Do not substitute baking sheet for jelly-roll pan

Metric Equivalents

The recipes that appear in this cookbook use the standard United States method for measuring liquid and dry or solid ingredients (teaspoons, tablespoons, and cups). The information on this chart is provided to help cooks outside the U.S. successfully use these recipes. All equivalents are approximate.

Metric Equivalents for Different Types of Ingredients

A standard cup measure of a dry or solid ingredient will vary in weight depending on the type of ingredient. A standard cup of liquid is the same volume for any type of liquid. Use the following chart when converting standard cup measures to grams (weight) or milliliters (volume).

Standard Cup	Fine Powder (ex. flour)	Grain (ex. rice)	Granular (ex. sugar)	Liquid Solids (ex. butter)	Liquid (ex. milk)
1	140 g	150 g	190 g	200 g	240 ml
¾	105 g	113 g	143 g	150 g	180 ml
⅔	93 g	100 g	125 g	133 g	160 ml
½	70 g	75 g	95 g	100 g	120 ml
⅓	47 g	50 g	63 g	67 g	80 ml
¼	35 g	38 g	48 g	50 g	60 ml
⅛	18 g	19 g	24 g	25 g	30 ml

Useful Equivalents For Dry Ingredients By Weight

(To convert ounces to grams, multiply the number of ounces by 30.)

1 oz	=	¹⁄₁₆ lb	=	30 g
4 oz	=	¼ lb	=	120 g
8 oz	=	½ lb	=	240 g
12 oz	=	¾ lb	=	360 g
16 oz	=	1 lb	=	480 g

Useful Equivalents For Length

(To convert inches to centimeters, multiply the number of inches by 2.5.)

1 in			=			2.5 cm	
6 in	=	½ ft			=	15 cm	
12 in	=	1 ft			=	30 cm	
36 in	=	3 ft	=	1 yd	=	90 cm	
40 in					=	100 cm	= 1 m

Useful Equivalents For Liquid Ingredients By Volume

¼ tsp						=	1 ml	
½ tsp						=	2 ml	
1 tsp						=	5 ml	
3 tsp	=	1 Tbsp			=	½ fl oz	=	15 ml
		2 Tbsp	=	⅛ cup	=	1 fl oz	=	30 ml
		4 Tbsp	=	¼ cup	=	2 fl oz	=	60 ml
		5⅓ Tbsp	=	⅓ cup	=	3 fl oz	=	80 ml
		8 Tbsp	=	½ cup	=	4 fl oz	=	120 ml
		10⅔ Tbsp	=	⅔ cup	=	5 fl oz	=	160 ml
		12 Tbsp	=	¾ cup	=	6 fl oz	=	180 ml
		16 Tbsp	=	1 cup	=	8 fl oz	=	240 ml
		1 pint	=	2 cups	=	16 fl oz	=	480 ml
		1 quart	=	4 cups	=	32 fl oz	=	960 ml
						33 fl oz	=	1000 ml = 1 l

Useful Equivalents For Cooking/Oven Temperatures

	Fahrenheit	Celsius	Gas Mark
Freeze Water	32° F	0° C	
Room Temperature	68° F	20° C	
Boil Water	212° F	100° C	
Bake	325° F	160° C	3
	350° F	180° C	4
	375° F	190° C	5
	400° F	200° C	6
	425° F	220° C	7
	450° F	230° C	8
Broil			Grill

Handy Kitchen Measurements

1 gallon	=	4 quarts	=	16 cups	=	8 pints						
¼ gallon	=	1 quart	=	4 cups	=	2 pints	=	.94 liter				
⅛ gallon	=	½ quart	=	2 cups	=	1 pint	=	16 fl. oz.				
				1 cup	=	8 fl oz	=	16 Tbsp	=	48 tsp	=	237 ml
				¾ cup	=	6 fl oz	=	12 Tbsp	=	36 tsp	=	177 ml
				⅔ cup	=	5⅓ fl oz	=	10⅔ Tbsp	=	32 tsp	=	158 ml
				½ cup	=	4 fl oz	=	8 Tbsp	=	24 tsp	=	118 ml
				⅓ cup	=	2⅔ fl oz	=	5⅓ Tbsp	=	16 tsp	=	79 ml
				¼ cup	=	2 fl oz	=	4 Tbsp	=	12 tsp	=	59 ml
				⅛ cup	=	1 fl oz	=	2 Tbsp	=	6 tsp	=	30 ml
								1 Tbsp	=	3 tsp	=	15 ml
										1 tsp	=	5 ml

index